S0-BCO-634

REFERENCE ONLY

ST/ESA/STAT/SER.S/38

**Department of Economic
and Social Affairs**
Statistics Division

**Département des affaires
économiques et sociales**
Division de statistique

Statistical Yearbook
2019 edition
Sixty-second issue

Annuaire statistique
2019 édition
Soixante-deuxième édition

United Nations | Nations Unies
New York, 2019

Department of Economic and Social Affairs

The Department of Economic and Social Affairs of the United Nations Secretariat is a vital interface between global policies in the economic, social and environmental spheres and national action. The Department works in three main interlinked areas: (i) it compiles, generates and analyses a wide range of economic, social and environmental data and information on which Member States of the United Nations draw to review common problems and to take stock of policy options; (ii) it facilitates the negotiations of Member States in many intergovernmental bodies on joint courses of action to address ongoing or emerging global challenges; and (iii) it advises interested Governments on the ways and means of translating policy frameworks developed in United Nations conferences and summits into programmes at the country level and, through technical assistance, helps build national capacities.

Note

The designations employed and the presentation of material in this publication do not imply the expression of any opinion whatsoever on the part of the Secretariat of the United Nations concerning the legal status of any country, territory, city or area; or of its authorities, or concerning the delimitation of its frontiers or boundaries.

In general, statistics contained in the present publication cover a period up to 2019 and as available to the United Nations Secretariat as of 31 July 2019. They reflect the country nomenclature currently in use.

The term "country" as used in the text of this publication also refers, as appropriate, to territories or areas.

The designations "developed" and "developing" which appear in some tables are intended for statistical convenience and do not necessarily express a judgement about the stage reached by a particular country or area in the development process.

Symbols of the United Nations documents are composed of capital letters combined with figures.

ST/ESA/STAT/SER.S/38

UNITED NATIONS PUBLICATION
Sales No. B.19.XVII.1.H

ISBN 978-92-1-259132-2
e-ISBN 978-92-1-004618-3
ISSN 0082-8459
eISSN:2412-1436

Copyright © United Nations, 2019
All rights reserved

Département des affaires économiques et sociales

Le Département des affaires économiques et sociales du Secrétariat de l'Organisation des Nations Unies assure le lien essentiel entre les politiques adoptées au plan international dans les domaines économique, social et écologique et les mesures prises au plan national. Il mène ses activités dans trois grands domaines interdépendants : i) il compile, produit et analyse une grand variété de données et d'informations économiques, sociales et écologiques dont les États Membres de l'ONU tirent parti pour examiner les problèmes communs et faire le point sur les possibilités d'action; (ii) il facilite les négociations que les États Membres mènent dans un grand nombre d'organes intergouvernementaux sur les moyens d'action à employer conjointement pour faire face aux problèmes mondiaux existants ou naissants; et (iii) il aide les gouvernements intéressés à traduire les orientations politiques établies lors des conférences et sommets de l'ONU en programmes nationaux et contribue à renforcer les capacités des pays en leur apportant une assistance technique.

Note

Les appellations employées dans la présente publication et la présentation de données qui y figurent n'impliquent, de la part du Secrétariat de l'Organisation des Nations Unies, aucune prise de position quant au statut juridique des pays, territoires, villes ou zones, ou de leurs autorités, ni quant au tracé de leurs frontières ou limites.

En règle générale, les statistiques contenues dans la présente publication couvrent pour la période jusqu'en 2019 et sont celles dont disposait le Secrétariat de l'Organisation des Nations Unies au 31 juillet 2019. Elles reflètent donc la nomenclature de pays en vigueur à l'époque.

Le terme « pays », tel qu'il est utilisé dans la présente publication peut également désigner des territoires ou des zones.

Les appellations « développées » et « en développement » qui figurent dans certains tableaux sont employées à des fins exclusivement statistiques et n'expriment pas nécessairement un jugement quant au niveau de développement atteint par tel pays ou telle région.

Les cotes des documents de l'Organisation des Nations Unies se composent de lettres majuscules et de chiffres.

ST/ESA/STAT/SER.S/38

PUBLICATION DES NATIONS UNIES
Numéro de vente: B.19.XVII.1.H

ISBN 978-92-1-259132-2
e-ISBN 978-92-1-004618-3
ISSN 0082-8459
eISSN : 2412-1436

Copyright © United Nations, 2019
Tous droits réservés

Preface

The 2019 edition of the United Nations *Statistical Yearbook* is the sixty-second issue of the publication, prepared by the Statistics Division of the Department of Economic and Social Affairs. Ever since the compilation of data for the *Statistical Yearbook* series was initiated in 1948, it has consistently provided a wide range of internationally available statistics on social, economic and environmental conditions and activities at the national, regional and world levels.

The contents of the *Yearbook* continue to be under review. Please send any comments or views to our email address, statistics@un.org. The tables include series covering an appropriate historical period, depending upon data availability and space constraints, for as many countries, territories and statistical areas of the world as available. The tables cover a period up to 2019, with some of the data being estimated.

The *Yearbook* tables are based on data which have been compiled by the Statistics Division mainly from official national and international sources as these are more authoritative and comprehensive, more generally available as time series and more comparable among countries than other sources. These sources include the United Nations Statistics Division in the fields of national accounts, industry, energy and international trade, the United Nations Statistics Division and the Population Division in the field of demographic statistics, and over 20 offices of the United Nations system and international organizations in other specialized fields. In some cases, official sources have been supplemented by other sources and estimates, where these have been subjected to professional scrutiny and debate and are consistent with other independent sources.

The United Nations agencies and other international, national and specialized organizations which furnished data are listed under "Source" at the end of each table. Acknowledgement is gratefully made for their generous and valuable cooperation in continually providing data.

After the first table, which presents key world aggregates and totals, the *Yearbook* is organized in three parts as follows; part one, relating to population and social topics; part two, relating to economic activity; and part three relating to energy, environment and infrastructure. The tables in the three parts are presented mainly by countries or areas, and world and regional aggregates are shown where available.

The four annexes contain information on country and area nomenclature (annex I), summary technical notes on statistical definitions, methods and sources for all tables of the *Yearbook* (annex II), the conversion coefficients and factors used in certain tables (annex III), and a list of those tables which were added, omitted or discontinued since the last issue of the *Yearbook* (annex IV).

The *Statistical Yearbook* is prepared by the Development Data Section, Development Data and Outreach Branch of the Statistics Division, Department of Economic and Social Affairs of the United Nations Secretariat. The programme manager is Matthias Reister, the chief editor is Anuradha Chimata and David Carter, Mohamed Nabassoua, Bradford Neidkowski and Zin Lin provide production assistance. Bogdan Dragovic provided IT support.

Comments on the present *Yearbook* and its future evolution are welcome. They may be sent via e-mail to statistics@un.org or to the United Nations Statistics Division, Development Data Section, New York, NY 10017, USA.

Préface

L'Annuaire statistique des Nations Unies 2019 est la soixante-deuxième édition de cette publication, préparée par la Division de statistique du Département des affaires économiques et sociales. Depuis son instauration en 1948 comme outil de compilation des données statistiques internationales, l'*Annuaire statistique* s'efforce de constamment diffuser un large éventail de statistiques disponibles sur les activités et conditions économiques et sociales, aux niveaux nationaux, régional et mondial.

Le contenu de l'Annuaire est actuellement en cours de révision. Pour tout commentaire, veuillez envoyer un courriel à notre adresse électronique : statistics@un.org. Les tableaux présentent des séries qui couvrent une période historique appropriée, en fonction de la disponibilité des données et des contraintes d'espace, pour autant de pays, territoires et zones statistiques du monde comme disponibles. Les tableaux couvrent généralement la période allant jusqu'en 2019.

Les tableaux de l'*Annuaire* sont construits essentiellement à partir des données compilées par la Division de statistique et provenant de sources officielles, nationales et internationales ; c'est en effet la meilleure source si l'on veut des données fiables, complètes et comparables, et si l'on a besoin de séries chronologiques. Ces sources sont: la Division de statistique du Secrétariat de l'Organisation des Nations Unies pour ce qui concerne la comptabilité nationale, l'industrie, l'énergie et le commerce extérieur, la Division de statistique et la Division de la population du Secrétariat de l'Organisation des Nations Unies pour les statistiques démographiques; et plus de 20 bureaux du système des Nations Unies et d'organisations internationales pour les autres domaines spécialisés. Dans quelques cas, les données officielles sont complétées par des informations et des estimations provenant d'autres sources qui ont été examinées par des spécialistes et confirmées par des sources indépendantes.

Les institutions spécialisées des Nations Unies et les autres organisations internationales, nationales et spécialisées qui ont fourni des données sont énumérées dans la "Source" sur chaque tableau. Les auteurs de l'*Annuaire statistique* les remercient de leur précieuse et généreuse collaboration.

Après le premier tableau qui fournit les principaux agrégats et totaux au niveau mondial, l'*Annuaire* est groupé en trois parties. La première partie est consacrée à la population et aux questions sociales, la deuxième est consacrée à l'activité économique, et la dernière est consacrée à l'énergie, environnement et infrastructures. Dans ces trois parties, les tableaux sont généralement présentés par pays ou régions, mais les agrégats mondiaux ou régionaux sont indiqués si disponibles.

Les quatre annexes donnent des renseignements sur la nomenclature des pays et des zones (annexe I), des notes récapitulatives sur les définitions, méthodes statistiques et techniques utilisées dans les sources de chaque tableau de l'*Annuaire* (annexe II), ainsi que sur les coefficients et facteurs de conversion employés dans les différents tableaux (annexe III), enfin une liste de nouveaux tableaux, de tableaux omis ou supprimés depuis la dernière édition est disponible (annexe IV).

L'Annuaire statistique est préparé par la Section des données de développement, Direction des données de développement et de liaison de la Division de statistique, Département des affaires économiques et sociales du Secrétariat de l'Organisation des Nations Unies. Les responsables du programme et Matthias Reister, le rédacteur en chef est Anuradha Chimata et David Carter, Mohamed Nabassoua, Bradford Neidkowski et Zin Lin fournissent une assistance à la production. Bogdan Dragovic est responsable du support en informatique.

Les observations sur la présente édition de l'*Annuaire* et les suggestions de modification pour l'avenir seront reçues avec intérêt. Elles peuvent être envoyées par message électronique à statistics@un.org, ou adressées à la Division de statistique des Nations Unies, Section des données de développement, New York, NY 10017 (États-Unis d'Amérique).

Explanatory notes

Symbols and conventions used in the tables

.   A point is used to indicate decimals.

-      A hyphen between years, for example, 2010-2015, indicates the full period involved, including the beginning and end

/   A slash indicates a financial year, school year or crop year, for example 2014/15.

...   Data are not available or not applicable.

*   Data are provisional, estimated or include a major revision.

\#   Marked break in the time series.

~0   Not zero, but less than half of the unit employed.

—~0   Not zero, but negative and less than half of the unit employed.

A space is used as a thousands separator, for example 1 000 is one thousand. Subtotals and percentages in the tables do not necessarily add to totals because of rounding.

Country notes and nomenclature

As a general rule, the data presented in the *Yearbook* relate to a given country or area as described in the complete list of countries and territories, see annex I.

References to statistical sources and methods in tables

For brevity the *Yearbook* omits specific information on the source or methodology for individual data points, and when a data point is estimated no distinction is made between whether the estimation was done by the international or national organization. See the technical notes to the tables in annex II for the primary source which may provide this information.

Units of measurement

The metric system of weights and measures has been employed throughout the *Yearbook*. For conversion coefficients and factors, see annex III.

Notes explicatives

Signes et conventions employés dans les tableaux

.   Les décimales sont précédées d'un point.

-      Un tiret entre des années, par exemple "2013-2014", indique que la période est embrassée dans sa totalité, y compris la première et la dernière année.

/   Une barre oblique renvoie à un exercice financier, à une année scolaire ou à une campagne agricole, par exemple

...   Données non disponibles ou non applicables.

*   Données provisoire, estimatif ou avec une révision majeure.

Discontinuité notable dans la série chronologique.

~0   Non nul mais inférieur à la moitié de l'unité employée

—~0 Non nul mais négatif et inférieur à la moitié de l'unité employée

Le séparateur utilisé pour les milliers est l'espace : par exemple, 1 000 correspond à un millier. Les chiffres étant arrondis, les sous-totaux ou pourcentages ne correspondent pas toujours à la somme exacte des éléments figurant dans les tableaux.

Notes sur les pays et nomenclature

En règle générale, les données renvoient au pays ou zone en question que décrite dans la liste complète des pays et territoires figure à l'annexe I.

Références à des sources et des méthodes statistiques dans les tableaux

Par souci de brièveté, l'*Annuaire* omet les informations relatives aux sources et méthodologies employées pour les points de données individuels. De plus, quand un point de données est estimé aucune distinction n'est faite entre une estimation provenant d'une organisation internationale ou d'une organisation nationale. Voir les notes techniques relatives aux tableaux dans l'annexe II ou se trouvent les références aux différentes sources contentant ces informations.

Unités de mesure

Le système métrique de poids et mesures a été utilisé dans tout l'*Annuaire*. On trouvera à l'annexe III les coefficients et facteurs de conversion.

Contents

Note: See **Annex IV** for table names presented in previous issues of the *Statistical Yearbook* which are not contained in the present issue.

Table des matières

Voir Annexe IV pour les tableaux publiés dans les éditions précédentes de l'Annuaire statistique mais qui n'ont pas été repris dans la présente édition.

Introduction

The 2019 edition of the United Nations *Statistical Yearbook* is the sixty-second issue of this publication, prepared by the Statistics Division, Department of Economic and Social Affairs of the United Nations Secretariat. The contents of the *Yearbook* continue to be under review. Please send any comments or views to our email address, statistics@un.org. The tables include series covering an appropriate historical period, depending upon data availability (as of 31 July 2019) and space constraints, for as many countries, territories and statistical areas of the world as available. The tables cover a period up to 2019, with some of the data being estimated.

Objective and content of the Statistical Yearbook

The main purpose of the *Statistical Yearbook* is to provide in a single volume a comprehensive compilation of internationally available statistics on social, economic and environmental conditions and activities, at world, regional and national levels, for an appropriate historical period.

Most of the statistics presented in the *Yearbook* are extracted from more detailed, specialized databases prepared by the Statistics Division and by many other international statistical services. Thus, while the specialized databases concentrate on monitoring topics and trends in particular social, economic and environmental fields, the *Statistical Yearbook* tables aim to provide data for a comprehensive, overall description of social, economic and environmental structures, conditions, changes and activities. The objective has been to collect, systematize, coordinate and present in a consistent way the most essential components of comparable statistical information which can give a broad picture of social, economic and environmental processes.

The content of the *Statistical Yearbook* is planned to serve a general readership. The *Yearbook* endeavours to provide information for various bodies of the United Nations system as well as for other international organizations, governments and non-governmental organizations, national statistical, economic and social policy bodies, scientific and educational institutions, libraries and the public. Data published in the *Statistical Yearbook* may also be of interest to companies and enterprises and to agencies engaged in market research. The *Statistical Yearbook* thus provides information on a wide range of social, economic and environmental issues which are of concern in the United Nations system and among the governments and peoples of the world. A particular value of the *Yearbook* is that it facilitates meaningful analysis of issues by systematizing and coordinating the data across many fields and shedding light on such interrelated issues as:

- General economic growth and related economic conditions;
- Gender equality;
- Population by sex and rate of increase, surface area and density;
- Unemployment, inflation and prices;
- Energy production and consumption;
- Expansion of trade;
- The financial situation of countries;
- Education;
- Improvement in general living conditions;
- Pollution and protection of the environment;
- Assistance provided to developing countries for social, economic and environmental development purposes.

Organization of the Yearbook

After the first table which presents key world aggregates and totals, the tables of the *Yearbook* are grouped into three parts as follows:

- Part One: Population and Social Statistics (chapters II-VI: tables 2-12);
- Part Two: Economic Activity (chapters VII-XI: tables 13-21);
- Part Three: Energy, environment and infrastructure (chapters XII-XVII: tables 22-32).

The first table provides a summary picture of development at the global level. More specific and detailed information for analysis concerning regions, individual countries or areas are presented in the three thematic parts.

Part One, Population and Social Statistics, comprises 11 tables which contain more detailed statistical series on population and migration, gender, education, health and crime.

Part Two, Economic Activity, comprises 9 tables on national accounts, finance, labour market, price and production indices and international merchandise trade.

Part Three, Energy, environment and infrastructure, comprises 11 tables on energy, environment, science and technology, international tourism and transport, communication and development assistance.

Annexes and regional groupings of countries or areas

The annexes to the *Statistical Yearbook*, and the section "Explanatory notes" preceding the Introduction, provide additional essential information on the *Yearbook*'s contents and presentation of data.

Annex I provides information on countries or areas covered in the *Yearbook* tables and on their arrangement in geographical regions and economic or other groupings. The geographical groupings shown in the *Yearbook* are generally based on continental regions unless otherwise indicated. However, strict consistency in this regard is impossible. A wide range of classifications is used for different purposes in the various international agencies and other sources of statistics for the *Yearbook*. These classifications vary in response to administrative and analytical requirements.

Annex II provides brief descriptions of major statistical concepts, definitions and classifications required for interpretation and analysis of the data.

Annex III provides detailed information on conversion coefficients and factors used in various tables, and Annex IV provides a list of tables added, omitted and discontinued in the present edition of the *Yearbook*. Some Tables do not feature in this edition of the *Yearbook* due to space limitations or an insufficient amount of new data being available. Their titles nevertheless are still listed in this Annex since it is planned that they will be published in a later issue as new data are compiled by the collecting agency and where space permits.

Data comparability, quality and relevance

The major challenge continuously facing the *Statistical Yearbook* is to present series which are as comparable across countries as the available statistics permit. Considerable efforts have already been made among the international suppliers of data and by the staff of the *Statistical Yearbook* to ensure the compatibility of various series by aligning time periods, base years, prices chosen for valuation, and so on. This is indispensable in relating various bodies of data to each other and in facilitating analysis across different sectors. In general, the data presented reflect the methodological recommendations of the United Nations Statistical Commission issued in various United Nations publications, and of other international bodies concerned with statistics. The use of international recommendations promotes international comparability of the data and ensures a degree of compatibility regarding the underlying concepts, definitions and classifications relating to different series. However, much work remains to be done in this area and, for this reason, some tables serve only as a first source of data and require further adjustment before being used for more in-depth analytical studies. While on the whole, a significant degree of comparability has been achieved in international statistics, there will remain some limitations, for a variety of reasons.

One common cause of non-comparability of economic data is different valuations of statistical aggregates such as national income, wages and salaries, output of industries and so forth. Conversion of these and similar series originally expressed in national prices into a common currency, for example into United States dollars, through the use of exchange rates, is not always satisfactory owing to frequent wide fluctuations in market rates and differences between official rates and rates which would be indicated by unofficial markets or purchasing power parities. The use of different kinds of sources for obtaining data is another cause of incomparability. This is true, for example, in the case of employment and unemployment, where data are obtained from different sources, namely household and labour force sample surveys, establishment censuses or surveys, official estimates, social insurance statistics and employment office statistics, which are not fully comparable in many cases. Non-comparability of data may also result from differences in the institutional patterns of countries. Certain variations in social, economic and environmental organization and institutions may have an impact on the comparability of the data even if the underlying concepts and definitions are identical. These and other causes of non-comparability of the data are briefly explained in the technical note associated with each table (see Annex II).

A further set of challenges relate to timeliness, quality and relevance of the data contained in the *Yearbook*. Users generally demand the most up-to-date statistics. However, due to the different development stages of statistical capacity in different countries, data for the most recent years may only be available for a small number of countries. For a global print publication, therefore, a balance has to be struck between presenting the most updated information and satisfactory country coverage. Of course, the United Nations Statistics Division's website offers greater flexibility in presenting continuously updated information and is therefore a useful complement to the annual print publication. Furthermore, as most of the information presented in this *Yearbook* is collected through specialized United Nations agencies and partners, the timeliness is continuously enhanced by improving the communication and data flow between countries and the specialized agencies on the one hand, and between the United Nations Statistics Division and the specialized agencies on the other. The development of new data transfer protocols will address this issue and is expected to make international data flows more efficient in the future.

Data quality at the international level is a function of the data quality at the national level. The United Nations Statistics Division in close cooperation with its partners among the UN agencies and the international statistical system continues to support countries' efforts to improve both the coverage and the quality of their data. Metadata, as for example reflected in the footnotes and technical notes of this publication, are an important service to the user to allow an informed assessment of the quality of the data. Given the wide variety of sources for the *Yearbook*, there is of course an equally wide variety of data formats and accompanying metadata. An important challenge for the United Nations Statistics Division and its partners for the future is to work further towards the standardization, or at least harmonization, of metadata.

A crucial challenge is to maintain the relevance of the series included in the *Yearbook*. As new policy concerns enter the developmental debate, the United Nations Statistics Division will need to introduce new series that describe concerns that have gained prominence as well as to prune data as they become outdated and continue to update the recurrent *Yearbook* series that still address those issues which are most pertinent. Often choosing the appropriate moment when the statistical information on new topics has matured sufficiently so as to be able to disseminate meaningful global data can be challenging. Furthermore, a balance has to continuously be found between the ever-increasing amount of information available for dissemination and the space limitations of the print version of the *Statistical Yearbook*. International comparability, data availability, data quality and relevance will remain the key criteria to guide the United Nations Statistics Division in its selection.

Needless to say, more can always be done to improve the *Statistical Yearbook*'s scope, coverage, design, metadata and timeliness. The *Yearbook* team continually strives to improve upon each of these aspects and to make its publication as responsive as possible to its users' needs and expectations, while at the same time focusing on a manageable body of data and metadata. Since data disseminated in digital form have clear advantages over those in print, as much of the *Yearbook* information as possible will continue to be included in the Statistics Division's online databases. Please feel welcome to provide feedback and suggestions to statistics@un.org.

Introduction

L'*Annuaire statistique* des Nations Unies 2019 est la soixante-deuxième édition de cette publication, établi par la Division de statistique du Département des affaires économiques et sociales du Secrétariat de l'Organisation des Nations Unies. Le contenu de l'*Annuaire* est actuellement en cours de révision, de ce fait le nombre de tableaux a été réduit. Des tableaux seront inclus dans les prochaines éditions. Pour tout commentaire, veuillez envoyer un courriel à notre adresse électronique : statistics@un.org. Les tableaux présentent des séries qui couvrent une période historique appropriée, en fonction de la disponibilité des données (à la date du 31 juillet 2019) et des contraintes d'espace, pour autant de pays, territoires et zones statistiques du monde comme disponibles. Les tableaux couvrent généralement pour la période jusqu'à 2019.

Objectif et contenu de l'Annuaire statistique

Le principal objectif de *l'Annuaire statistique* est de fournir en un seul volume un inventaire complet de statistiques internationales concernant la situation et les activités sociales, économiques et environnementales aux niveaux mondial, régional et national, sur une période adéquate.

La plupart des données qui figurent dans l'*Annuaire statistique* proviennent de bases de données spécialisées davantage détaillées, préparées par la Division de statistique et par bien d'autres services statistiques internationaux. Tandis que les bases de données spécialisées se concentrent sur le suivi de domaines socioéconomiques et environnementaux particuliers, les données de l'*Annuaire* sont présentées de telle sorte qu'elles fournissent une description globale et exhaustive des structures, conditions, transformations et activités socioéconomiques et environnementaux. On a cherché à recueillir, systématiser, coordonner et présenter de manière cohérente les principales informations statistiques comparables, de manière à dresser un tableau général des processus socioéconomiques et environnementaux.

Le contenu de l'*Annuaire statistique* a été élaboré en vue d'un lectorat large. Les renseignements fournis devraient ainsi pouvoir être utilisés par les divers organismes du système des Nations Unies, mais aussi par d'autres organisations internationales, les gouvernements et les organisations non gouvernementales, les organismes nationaux de statistique et de politique économique et sociale, les institutions scientifiques et les établissements d'enseignement, les bibliothèques et les particuliers. Les données publiées dans l'*Annuaire* peuvent également intéresser les sociétés et entreprises, et les organismes spécialisés dans les études de marché. L'*Annuaire* présente des informations sur un large éventail de questions socioéconomiques et environnementales liées aux préoccupations actuelles du système des Nations Unies, des gouvernements et des peuples du monde entier. Une qualité particulière de l'*Annuaire* est de faciliter une analyse approfondie de ces questions en systématisant et en articulant les données d'un domaine/secteur à l'autre, et en apportant un éclairage sur des sujets interdépendants, tels que :

- La croissance économique générale, et les conditions économiques qui lui sont liées;
- La situation de femmes;
- La population, taux d'accroissement, superficie et densité;
- Le chômage, l'inflation et les prix;
- La production et la consommation d'énergie;
- L'expansion des échanges;
- La situation financière des pays;
- L'éducation;
- L'amélioration des conditions de vie;
- La pollution et la protection de l'environnement;
- L'assistance aux pays en développement à des fins socioéconomiques et environnementaux.

Présentation de l'Annuaire

Après le premier tableau qui fournit les principaux agrégats et totaux au niveau mondial, l'Annuaire est groupés en trois parties comme suit:

- Première partie: Statistiques démographiques et sociales (chapitres II à VI, tableaux 2 à 12)
- Deuxième partie: Activité économique (chapitres VII à XI, tableaux 13 à 21)
- Troisième partie: Energie, environnement et infrastructures (chapitres XII à XVII, tableaux 22 à 32)

Le premier tableau donne un aperçu du développement à l'échelon mondial, tandis que les trois autres parties contiennent des renseignements plus précis et détaillés qui se prêtent mieux à une analyse par régions, pays ou par zones. Chacune de ces trois parties est subdivisée en unités thématiques.

La première partie, intitulée "Population et statistiques sociales", comporte 11 tableaux où figurent des séries plus détaillées concernant la population et la migration, la situation des femmes, l'éducation, la santé et la criminalité.

La deuxième partie, intitulée "Activité économique", comporte 9 tableaux qui présentent des statistiques concernant les comptes nationaux, le finances, le marché du travail, les indices des prix et de la production, et au commence international des marchandises. Les tableaux traitant de certains produits de base associent autant que possible les données relatives à la consommation aux valeurs concernant la production.

La troisième partie, intitulée "Energie, environnement et infrastructures", comprend 11 tableaux relatifs à l'énergie, l'environnement, la science et technologie, au tourisme et transport internationaux, à la communication et à l'aide au développement.

Annexes et groupements régionaux des pays et zones

Les annexes à l'*Annuaire statistique*, et la section intitulée "Notes explicatives" qui précède l'introduction, offrent d'importantes informations complémentaires quant à la teneur et à la présentation des données figurant dans le présent ouvrage.

L'annexe I donne des renseignements sur les pays ou zones couverts par les tableaux de l'*Annuaire* et sur leur regroupement en régions géographiques et groupements économiques ou autres. Sauf indication contraire, les groupements géographiques figurant dans l'*Annuaire* sont généralement fondés sur les régions continentales, mais une présentation absolument systématique est impossible à cet égard car les diverses institutions internationales et autres sources de statistiques employées pour la confection de l'*Annuaire* emploient, selon l'objet de l'exercice, des classifications fort différentes en réponse à diverses exigences d'ordre administratif ou analytique.

L'annexe II contient les notes techniques de chaque chapitre apportent une brève description des principales notions, définitions et classifications statistiques nécessaires pour interpréter et analyser les données.

L'annexe III fournit des renseignements sur les coefficients et facteurs de conversion employés dans les différents tableaux, et l'annexe IV contient la liste de tableaux qui ont été ajoutés omis ou supprimés dans la présente édition de l'*Annuaire*. Certains tableaux ne figurent pas dans cet *Annuaire* en raison du manque d'espace ou de données nouvelles. Comme ils seront repris dans une prochaine édition à mesure que des données nouvelles seront dépouillées par l'office statistique d'origine, ses titres figurent toujours dans la table des matières.

Comparabilité, qualité et pertinence des statistiques

Le défi majeur auquel l'*Annuaire Statistique* fait continuellement face est de présenter des séries aussi comparables entre les pays que la disponibilité des statistiques le permettent. Les sources internationales de données et les auteurs de l'*Annuaire* ont réalisé des efforts considérables pour faire en sorte que diverses séries soient compatibles, en harmonisant les périodes de référence, les années de base, les prix utilisés pour les évaluations, etc. Cette démarche est indispensable si l'on veut rapprocher divers ensembles de données, et faciliter l'analyse intersectorielle de l'économie. De façon générale, les données sont présentées selon les recommandations méthodologiques formulées par la Commission de statistique des Nations Unies, et par les autres entités internationales impliquées dans les statistiques. Le respect des recommandations internationales tend non seulement à promouvoir la comparabilité internationale des données, mais elle assure également une certaine comparabilité entre les concepts, les définitions et classifications utilisés. Mais comme il reste encore beaucoup à faire dans ce domaine, les données présentées dans certains tableaux n'ont qu'une valeur indicative, et nécessiteront des ajustements plus poussés avant de pouvoir servir à des analyses approfondies. Bien que l'on soit parvenu, dans l'ensemble, à un degré de comparabilité appréciable en matière de statistiques internationales, diverses raisons expliquent que subsistent encore de nombreuses limitations.

Une cause commune de non comparabilité des données économiques réside dans la diversité des méthodes d'évaluation employées pour comptabiliser des agrégats tels que le revenu national, les salaires et traitements, la production des différentes branches d'activité industrielle, etc. Il n'est pas toujours satisfaisant de ramener la valeur des séries de ce type—exprimée à l'origine en prix nationaux—à une monnaie commune (par exemple le dollar des États-Unis) car les taux de change du marché connaissent fréquemment de fortes fluctuations, et parce que les taux officiels ne coïncident pas avec ceux des marchés officieux ni avec les parités réelles de pouvoir d'achat. Le recours à des sources diverses pour la collecte des données est un autre facteur qui limite la comparabilité. C'est le cas, par exemple, des données d'emploi et de chômage, obtenues par des moyens aussi peu comparables que les sondages, le dépouillement des registres d'assurances sociales et les enquêtes auprès des entreprises. Dans certains cas, les données ne sont pas comparables en raison de différences entre les structures institutionnelles des pays. Des changements dans l'organisation et les institutions sociales, économiques et environnementales peuvent affecter la comparabilité des données, même si les concepts et définitions sont fondamentalement identiques. Ces causes, et d'autres, de non comparabilité des données sont brièvement expliquées dans les notes techniques associée à chaque tableau (voir annexe II).

Un autre ensemble de défis à relever concerne la fraîcheur, la qualité et la pertinence des données présentées dans l'*Annuaire*. Les utilisateurs exigent généralement des données les plus récentes possibles. Toutefois, selon le niveau de développement de la capacité statistique des pays, les données pour les dernières années peuvent n'être disponibles que pour un nombre limité de pays. Dans le cadre d'une publication mondiale, un équilibre doit être trouvé entre la présentation de l'information la plus récente et une couverture géographique satisfaisante. Bien entendu, le site Internet de la Division de statistique des Nations Unies offre une plus grande flexibilité, puisqu'il propose une information actualisée au fil de l'eau, et constitue ainsi un complément utile à la publication papier annuelle. Par ailleurs, étant donné que la plupart des informations présentées dans cet *Annuaire* sont collectées parmi les agences spécialisées des Nations Unies et autres partenaires, la fraîcheur des données est continuellement améliorée, grâce à une meilleure communication et un meilleur échange de données entre les pays et les agences spécialisées d'une part, et entre la Division de statistique des Nations Unies et les agences spécialisées d'autre part. Le développement de nouveaux protocoles de transfert de données basés sur le langage XML devrait contribuer à rendre, à l'avenir, les échanges de données internationales encore plus efficaces.

La qualité des données au niveau international est fonction de la qualité des données au niveau national. La Division de statistique des Nations Unies, en étroite collaboration avec ses partenaires dans les agences de l'ONU et dans le système statistique international, continue de soutenir les efforts des pays pour améliorer à la fois la couverture et la qualité de leurs données. Des métadonnées, comme l'illustrent les notes de bas de page et les notes techniques de cette publication, constituent un important service fourni à l'utilisateur pour lui permettre d'évaluer de manière avisée la qualité des données. Etant donné la grande variété des sources de l'*Annuaire*, il y a bien entendu une non moins grande variété de formats de données et de métadonnées associées. Un important défi que la Division de statistique des Nations Unies et ses partenaires doivent relever dans le futur est d'aboutir à la standardisation, ou au moins l'harmonisation, des métadonnées.

Le défi majeur reste la constance de la pertinence des séries présentées dans l'*Annuaire*. Au fur et à mesure que de nouvelles préoccupations politiques pénètrent le débat lié au développement, la Division de statistique des Nations Unies doit introduire dans l'*Annuaire* de nouvelles séries qui leur sont liées, et, ce faisant, effectuer une coupe sombre parmi les données qui lui semblent dépassées, tout en s'assurant de continuer à actualiser les séries récurrentes de qui paraissent encore pertinentes. Souvent, choisir le moment idoine auquel les données statistiques sur de nouveaux thèmes sont suffisamment matures pour qu'elles puissent, au niveau mondial, être diffusées sans hésitation, est un défi en soi. Par ailleurs, un équilibre doit continuellement être trouvé entre le volume toujours croissant d'informations disponibles à la diffusion, et les contraintes d'espace de la version papier de l'*Annuaire* statistique. La comparabilité internationale, la disponibilité, la qualité et la pertinence des données devront rester les principaux critères à considérer par la Division de statistique des Nations Unies dans sa sélection.

Inutile de dire qu'il est toujours possible d'améliorer l'*Annuaire* statistique en ce qui concerne son champ, sa couverture, sa conception générale, ses métadonnées et sa mise à jour. L'équipe en charge de l'*Annuaire* s'évertue en permanence à améliorer chacun de ces aspects, et de faire en sorte que cette publication réponde au plus près aux besoins et aux attentes de ses utilisateurs, sans toutefois oublier de mettre l'accent sur un corpus gérable de données et de métadonnées. Puisqu'il est avéré que les données diffusées de manière digitale ont des avantages comparés à celles diffusées sur papier, autant d'informations de l'*Annuaire* que possible continueront d'être inclues dans les bases de données électroniques de la Division de statistique. L'*Annuaire* statistique garde toujours une place de choix parmi les produits de la Division de statistique comme une ressource utile pour une compréhension général de la situation sociale, économique et environnementale globale. N'hésitez pas à nous faire part de vos commentaires et suggestions à statistics@un.org

1

World statistics: selected series
Population and social statistics, economic activity and energy, environment and infrastructure

Statistiques mondiales : séries principales
Population et statistiques sociales, activité économique et énergie, environnement et infrastructures

Series / Séries	Unit or base / Unité ou base	2005	2010	2015	2016	2017	2018	2019
Population and Migration • Population et migration								
Population [1]	million	6 541.9	6 956.8	7 379.8	...	7 547.9	7 631.1	7 713.5
Population density [1] / Densité de population [1]	per km² / pour km²	50.3	53.5	56.7	...	58.0	58.7	59.3
Population, male [1] / Population, hommes [1]	million	3 296.5	3 507.7	3 720.7	...	3 805.5	3 847.5	3 889.0
Population, female [1] / Population, femmes [1]	million	3 245.4	3 449.1	3 659.1	...	3 742.4	3 783.6	3 824.4
Sex ratio [1] / Rapport des sexes [1]	males per 100 females / hom. p. 100 fem.	101.4	101.6	101.7	...	101.7	101.7	101.7
Population age distribution, 0-14 [1] / Répartition par âge de la population, 0-14 [1]	percentage of pop. / pourcentage de la pop.	28.1	27.0	26.2	...	25.9	25.8	25.6
Population age distribution, 60+ [1] / Répartition par âge de la population, 60+ [1]	percentage of pop. / pourcentage de la pop.	10.3	11.0	12.2	...	12.7	13.0	13.5

Series / Séries	Unit or base / Unité ou base	2005	2010	2015	2016	2017	2018	2019
Urban population / Population urbaine	percentage of pop. / pourcentage de la pop.	49.2	51.7	53.9	...	...	55.3	
Total annual urban growth rate [2] / Taux d'accroissement urbaine annuel [2]	percentage of pop. / pourcentage de la pop.	2.3	2.2	2.0	...	...	...	...
Total annual rural growth rate [2] / Taux d'accroissement rurale annuel [2]	percentage of pop. / pourcentage de la pop.	0.3	0.2	0.2	...	...	...	...

Series / Séries	Unit or base / Unité ou base	2005	2010	2015	2016	2017	2018	2019
International migrant stock: total / Stock de migrants internationaux : total	thousand / millier	191 531	220 019	247 586	...	257 715	...	...
International migrant stock: total / Stock de migrants internationaux : total	percentage of pop. / pourcentage de la pop.	2.9	3.2	3.4	...	3.4	...	...
International migrant stock: male / Stock de migrants internationaux : hommes	percentage of pop. / pourcentage de la pop.	3.0	3.2	3.4	...	3.5	...	...
International migrant stock : female / Stock de migrants internationaux : fémmes	percentage of pop. / pourcentage de la pop.	2.9	3.1	3.3	...	3.3	...	...
Refugees / Réfugiés	thousand / millier	...	...	15 098	...	18 474	20 203	...
Asylum seekers / Demandeurs d'asile	thousand / millier	...	...	2 344	...	2 954	3 174	...
Other of concern to UNHCR / Autres personnes relevant de la comp. du HCR	thousand / millier	...	...	40 518	...	45 980	46 974	...
Total population of concern to UNHCR / Population totale de préoccupation pour le HCR	thousand / millier	...	...	57 960	...	67 408	70 351	...

Gender • Le genre

Series / Séries	Unit or base / Unité ou base	2005	2010	2015	2016	2017	2018	2019
Seats held by women in national parliament / Pro. de sièges occupés par les fem. au par. nat.	percentage of seats / pourcentage du sièges	15.9	19.0	22.3	22.7	23.4	23.4	24.3
Girls to boys in primary education / Filles/garçons dans l'enseigne. primaire	ratio / rapport	0.95	0.97	0.99	1.01	1.00	...	...
Girls to boys in secondary education / Filles/garçons dans l'enseigne. secondaire	ratio / rapport	0.94	0.97	0.99	.99	.99	...	...
Girls to boys in tertiary education / Filles/garçons dans l'enseigne. supérieur	ratio / rapport	1.05	1.07	1.12	1.12	1.12	...	...

1

World statistics: selected series *(continued)*
Population and social statistics, economic activity and energy, environment and infrastructure
Statistiques mondiales : séries principales *(suite)*
Population et statistiques sociales, activité économique et énergie, environnement et infrastructures

Education • Enseignement

Series Séries	Unit or base Unité ou base	2005	2010	2015	2016	2017	2018	2019
Students enrolled in primary education Les étudiants inscrits dans l'enseignement primaire	thousand millier	678 992	697 048	720 228	736 616	746 285	...	...
Gross enrollment ratio - primary, male Taux brut de scolarisation - primaire, hommes	percentage pourcentage	104.9	105.8	102.7	103.7	103.7	...	...
Gross enrollment ratio - primary, female Taux brut de scolarisation - primaire, fémmes	percentage pourcentage	99.9	103.0	102.6	104.5	104.5	...	...
Students enrolled in secondary education Les étudiants inscrits dans l'enseignement second.	thousand millier	509 245	546 102	583 316	588 197	590 725	...	...
Gross enrollment ratio - secondary, male Taux brut de scolarisation - secondaire, hommes	percentage pourcentage	65.7	72.3	76.9	77.2	77.0	...	...
Gross enrollment ratio - secondary, female Taux brut de scolarisation – secondaire, fémmes	percentage pourcentage	62.1	69.8	75.9	76.3	76.2	...	...
Students enrolled in tertiary education Les étudiants inscrits dans l'enseigne. supérieur	thousand millier	139 951	182 209	217 459	220 006	220 704	...	...
Gross enrollment ratio - tertiary, male Taux brut de scolarisation - tertiaire, hommes	percentage pourcentage	23.7	28.4	34.7	35.3	35.7	...	...
Gross enrollment ratio – tertiary, female Taux brut de scolarisation – tertiaire, féminin	percentage pourcentage	24.8	30.5	38.7	40.0	40.2	...	...
Teaching staff at the primary level Personnel enseignant au niveau primaire	thousand millier	26 891	28 669	31 185	31 386	31 573	...	...
Teaching staff at the secondary level Personnel enseignant au niveau secondaire	thousand millier	28 507	32 355	33 529	34 319	34 555	...	...
Teaching staff at the tertiary level Personnel enseignant au niveau supérieur	thousand millier	9 231	11 161	12 981	13 139	13 162	...	...
Pupils to teachers in the primary level Élèves/enseignant dans l'enseigne. primaire	ratio rapport	25.3	24.3	23.1	23.5	23.6	...	...
Pupils to teachers ratio in the secondary level Élèves/enseignant dans l'enseigne. secondaire	ratio rapport	17.9	16.9	17.4	17.1	17.1	...	...

Crime • La criminalité

Series Séries	Unit or base Unité ou base	2005	2010	2015	2016	2017	2018	2019
Intentional homicide rate [3] Homicides volontaires [3]	per 100,000 population pour 100,000 pop.	...	...	5.3	...	...	...	...

National Accounts • Comptes nationaux

Series Séries	Unit or base Unité ou base	2005	2010	2015	2016	2017	2018	2019
GDP in current prices PIB aux prix courants	billion US $ milliard $ E.-U.	47 550	66 146	74 757	75 840	80 501	...	...
GDP per capita PIB par habitant	US $ $ E.-U.	7 270	9 508	10 128	10 159	10 665	...	...
GDP in constant 2005 prices PIB aux prix constants	billion US $ milliard $ E.-U.	58 258	66 146	75 840	77 670	80 050	...	...
GDP real rates of growth Taux de croissance	percentage pourcentage	3.9	4.3	2.8	2.4	3.1	...	...

Labour market • Marché du travail

Series Séries	Unit or base Unité ou base	2005	2010	2015	2016	2017	2018	2019
Labour force - total Force de travail - total	percentage of pop. pourcentage de la pop.	63.7	62.4	61.7	61.6	61.6	61.4	61.2
Labour force - male Force de travail - hommes	percentage of pop. pourcentage de la pop.	77.3	76.0	75.3	75.1	75.0	74.9	74.7
Labour force - female Force de travail - femmes	percentage of pop. pourcentage de la pop.	50.3	48.8	48.1	48.1	48.2	47.9	47.7
Unemployment rate - total Chômage - total	percent. of active pop. pour. de la pop. active	5.9	5.7	5.5	5.5	5.5	5.4	5.4
Unemployment rate - male Chômage - mâle	percent. of active pop. pour. de la pop. active	5.5	5.4	5.2	5.2	5.1	5.0	5.0
Unemployment rate - female Chômage - femmes	percent. of active pop. pour. de la pop. active	6.4	6.2	5.9	6.0	6.0	5.9	5.9

1

World statistics: selected series *(continued)*
Population and social statistics, economic activity and energy, environment and infrastructure
Statistiques mondiales : séries principales *(suite)*
Population et statistiques sociales, activité économique et énergie, environnement et infrastructures

Series Séries	Unit or base Unité ou base	2005	2010	2015	2016	2017	2018	2019
Employment in agriculture - total L'emploi dans agriculture - total	percent. of employees pourcent. des employ.	35.2	30.8	27.2	26.7	26.5	25.9	25.5
Employment in agriculture - male L'emploi dans agriculture - hommes	percent. of employees pourcent. des employ.	34.0	30.2	26.7	26.2	25.9	25.4	24.9
Employment in agriculture - female L'emploi dans agriculture - femmes	percent. of employees pourcent. des employ.	37.1	31.8	28.0	27.5	27.2	26.7	26.3
Employment in industry - total L'emploi dans industrie - total	percent. of employees pourcent. des employ.	22.6	23.0	22.7	22.5	22.5	22.4	22.2
Employment in industry - male L'emploi dans industrie - hommes	percent. of employees pourcent. des employ.	25.5	26.8	27.2	27.0	27.0	27.0	27.0
Employment in industry - female L'emploi in industrie - femmes	percent. of employees pourcent. des employ.	18.3	17.1	15.7	15.5	15.3	15.1	14.8
Employment in services - total L'emploi dans services - total	percent. of employees pourcent. des employ.	42.1	46.2	50.1	50.8	51.1	51.7	52.3
Employment in services - male L'emploi dans services - hommes	percent. of employees pourcent. des employ.	40.5	43.1	46.1	46.7	47.0	47.6	48.1
Employment in services - female L'emploi dans services - femmes	percent. of employees pourcent. des employ.	44.7	51.1	56.2	57.0	57.4	58.2	58.9

Price and production indices • Indices de la production

Series Séries	Unit or base Unité ou base	2005	2010	2015	2016	2017	2018	2019
Agriculture (gross) Agriculture (brut)	2004-2006 = 100	99.9	112.9	125.9	127.3		...	...
Food (gross) Ailmentaires (brut)	2004-2006 = 100	99.9	113.4	126.4	127.8		...	...

International merchandise trade • Commerce international des marchandises

Series Séries	Unit or base Unité ou base	2005	2010	2015	2016	2017	2018	2019
Exports FOB Exportations FOB	billion US $ milliard $ E.-U.	10 373	15 100	16 371	15 844	17 353	18 662	...
Imports CIF Importations CIF	billion US $ milliard $ E.-U.	10 577	15 263	16 437	15 984	17 799	19 367	...
Balance Balance	billion US $ milliard $ E.-U.	-204	-162	-66	-141	-446	-705	...

Energy • Ènergie

Series Séries	Unit or base Unité ou base	2005	2010	2014	2015	2016	2017	2018
Primary energy production Production d'énergie primaire	petajoules pétajoules	476 738	530 597	567 032	570 980	568 988	...	...
Net imports Importations nettes	petajoules pétajoules	-13 751	-12 967	-16 188	-18 261	-21 853	...	...
Changes in stocks Variations des stocks	petajoules pétajoules	-313	138	3 372	2 540	-4 441	...	...
Total supply Approvisionnement total	petajoules pétajoules	463 000	517 492	547 472	550 179	551 577	...	...
Supply per capita Approvisionnement par habitant	gigajoules gigajoules	71	74	75	75	74	...	...

Environment • Environnement

Series Séries	Unit or base Unité ou base	2005	2010	2014	2015	2016	2017	2018
Land area Terres superficie	1,000 hectares	13 010 426	13 008 349	...	13 007 735	13 008 757	...	...
Arable land Terres arables	000 hectares	1 405 867	1 388 166	...	1 424 687	1 423 794	...	...
Arable land Terres arables	percentage of land pourcent. de la superf.	10.9	10.7	...	11.0	10.9	...	...
Forest cover Superficie forestière	1,000 hectares	4 032 743	4 015 673	...	3 999 133	3 995 825	...	...
Forest cover Superficie forestière	percentage of land pourcent. de la superf.	31.0	30.9	...	30.7	30.7	...	...

1

World statistics: selected series *(continued)*
Population and social statistics, economic activity and energy, environment and infrastructure

Statistiques mondiales : séries principales *(suite)*
Population et statistiques sociales, activité économique et énergie, environnement et infrastructures

Series	Unit or base							
Séries	Unité ou base	2005	2010	2014	2015	2016	2017	2018
Permanent crops								
Cultures permanentes	1,000 hectares	148 343	159 209		166 467	166 201	...	...
Permanent crops	percentage of land							
Cultures permanentes	pourcent. de la superf.	1.1	1.2		1.3	1.3	...	...
Sites protected for terrestrial biodiversity	percentage of sites							
Sites pour la bio. terre. dans aires protég	pourcentage du sites	40.1	44.4	46.3	46.5	46.6	46.7	46.7

Science and technology • Science et technologie

Series	Unit or base							
Séries	Unité ou base	2005	2010	2014	2015	2016	2017	2018
Grant of patents	per million population							
Brevets délivrés	par million d'habitants	633 100	914 800	1 173 900	1 240 200	1 352 300	1 404 600	...
Gross domestic expenditure on R & D	percentage of GDP							
Dépenses intérieures brutes de R-D	pourcentage du PIB	1.5	1.6	1.7	1.7	...	...	...

Communication • Internet users

Series	Unit or base							
Séries	Unité ou base	2005	2010	2014	2015	2016	2017	2018
Internet usage	% of individuals							
Utilisation d'internet	% de personnes	15.7	28.7	39.7	42.8	45.5	48.6	...

Development assistance • Aide au developpement

Series	Unit or base							
Séries	Unité ou base	2005	2010	2014	2015	2016	2017	2018
Net ODA received: bilateral	million US $							
APD nette reçue : bilatérale	million $ E.-U.	82 923	94 441	119 778	117 372	116 519	...	...
Net ODA received: multilateral	million US $							
APD nette reçue : multilatérale	million $ E.-U.	25 620	37 133	41 952	35 368	40 493	...	...
Net ODA received: total	million US $							
APD nette reçue : total	million $ E.-U.	108 542	131 574	161 730	152 740	157 011	...	...
Net ODA received: total	% of recipients' GNI							
APD nette reçue : total	% du RNB des bénéfic.	1.2	0.7	0.6	0.6	0.6	...	...

Source:
These data are presented in other tables of this Yearbook; please refer to the relevant table for source notes and last access data.

Source:
Ces données sont présentées dans d'autres tableaux du présent Annuaire, veuillez donc vous reporter au tableau correspondant pour les notes de source et la date du dernier accès.

1   Mid-year estimates and projections (medium fertility variant).

2   Data refers to a 5-year period preceding the reference year.

3   Data is for 2015, or latest available data from 2010 onwards.

1   Les estimations et projections approximative (variante moyenne fécondité) au milieu de l'année.

2   Les données se réfèrent a période de 5 ans précédant l'année de référence.

3   Données pour 2015, ou dernières données disponibles à partir de 2010.

Part One

Population and social statistics

Première partie

Population et statistiques sociales

2

Population, surface area and density

Population, superficie et densité

Country or area Pays ou zone	Year Année	Mid-year population estimates and projections (millions) Estimations et projections de population au milieu de l'année (millions)			Sex Ratio (males per 100 females) Rapport des sexes (hommes pour 100 femmes)	Population age distribution (percentage) Répartition par âge de la population (pourcentage)		Population density (per km²) Densité de population (pour km²)	Surface area Superficie (000 km²)
		Total	Male Hommes	Females Femmes		Aged 0 to 14 years old âgée de 0 à 14 ans	Aged 60+ years old âgée de 60 ans ou plus		
Total, all countries or areas	2005	6 541.91	3 296.49	3 245.42	101.6	28.1	10.3	50.3	...
Total, tous pays ou zones	2010	6 956.82	3 507.70	3 449.12	101.7	27.0	11.0	53.5	...
	2017	7 547.86	3 805.47	3 742.39	101.7	25.9	12.7	58.0	136 162
	2019	7 713.47	3 889.03	3 824.43	101.7	25.6	13.2	59.3	...
Africa	2005	916.15	456.65	459.51	99.4	41.9	5.1	30.9	...
Afrique	2010	1 039.30	518.25	521.05	99.5	41.5	5.1	35.1	...
	2017	1 244.22	621.39	622.84	99.8	40.9	5.4	42.0	30 311
	2019	1 308.06	653.51	654.55	99.8	40.6	5.5	44.1	...
Northern Africa	2005	186.42	93.70	92.72	101.1	33.5	7.0	24.0	...
Afrique septentrionale	2010	202.94	101.87	101.07	100.8	32.1	7.4	26.1	...
	2017	232.79	116.95	115.84	101.0	32.7	8.3	30.0	7 880
	2019	241.78	121.48	120.30	101.0	32.7	8.6	31.1	...
Sub-Saharan Africa	2005	729.73	362.95	366.79	99.0	44.0	4.6	33.4	...
Afrique subsaharienne	2010	836.36	416.39	419.98	99.1	43.8	4.6	38.2	...
	2017	1 011.43	504.44	506.99	99.5	42.8[1]	4.7	46.2	22 431[2]
	2019	1 066.28	532.04	534.25	99.6	42.3	4.7	48.7	...
Eastern Africa	2005	295.19	146.04	149.15	97.9	45.5	4.3	44.3	...
Afrique orientale	2010	339.32	167.97	171.35	98.0	44.9	4.3	50.9	...
	2017	411.40	204.01	207.39	98.4	42.9	4.5	61.7	7 005
	2019	433.90	215.28	218.62	98.5	42.2	4.5	65.1	...
Middle Africa	2005	112.01	55.69	56.32	98.9	45.7	4.6	17.2	...
Afrique centrale	2010	131.62	65.53	66.09	99.1	45.8	4.4	20.3	...
	2017	164.04	81.82	82.22	99.5	45.6	4.3	25.2	6 613
	2019	174.31	86.97	87.34	99.6	45.3	4.3	26.8	...
Southern Africa	2005	54.64	26.87	27.77	96.7	31.8	6.9	20.6	...
Afrique australe	2010	58.38	28.74	29.65	96.9	30.5	7.0	22.0	...
	2017	64.83	31.93	32.91	97.0	29.9	7.9	24.5	2 675
	2019	66.63	32.79	33.84	96.9	29.7	8.2	25.1	...
Western Africa	2005	267.89[3]	134.34[3]	133.55[3]	100.6[3]	44.1[3]	4.6[3]	44.2	...
Afrique occidentale	2010	307.04[3]	154.15[3]	152.89[3]	100.8[3]	44.2[3]	4.5[3]	50.6	...
	2017	371.16[3]	186.68[3]	184.48[3]	101.2[3]	43.7	4.5[3]	61.2[3]	6 138
	2019	391.44[3]	196.99[3]	194.45[3]	101.3[3]	43.4[3]	4.5[3]	64.6	...
Americas [2]	2005	884.79	436.52	448.26	97.4	26.5	11.9	20.9	...
Amériques [2]	2010	934.64	461.03	473.61	97.3	24.8	13.1	22.1	...
	2017	998.18	492.19	505.99	97.3	22.6	15.5	23.6	42 322
	2019	1 014.72	500.26	514.47	97.2	22.1	16.2	24.0	...
Northern America	2005	327.29	161.58[4]	165.71[4]	97.5[4]	20.6[4]	16.8[4]	17.5	...
Amérique septentrionale	2010	343.29	169.62[4]	173.67[4]	97.7[4]	19.8[4]	18.5[4]	18.4	...
	2017	361.94[4]	179.12[4]	182.82[4]	98.0[4]	18.6	21.7[4]	19.4[4]	21 776
	2019	366.60[4]	181.45[4]	185.15[4]	98.0[4]	18.3[4]	22.6[4]	19.7	...
Latin America & the Caribbean	2005	557.50	274.95	282.56	97.3	29.9	9.0	27.7	...
Amérique latine et Caraïbes	2010	591.35	291.42	299.94	97.2	27.7	10.0	29.4	...
	2017	636.23	313.07	323.17	96.9	24.9	12.0	31.6	20 546
	2019	648.12	318.80	329.32	96.8	24.2	12.6	32.2	...
Caribbean	2005	39.75	19.68[5]	20.07[5]	98.0[5]	28.2[5]	11.1[5]	175.9	...
Caraïbes	2010	41.22	20.39[5]	20.83[5]	97.9[5]	26.5[5]	12.0[5]	182.4	...
	2017	43.00[5]	21.25[5]	21.75[5]	97.7[5]	24.6	13.9[5]	190.3	234
	2019	43.34	21.40[5]	21.93[5]	97.6[5]	24.2[5]	14.5[5]	191.7	...
Central America	2005	145.95	71.51	74.44	96.1	33.4	7.8	59.5	...
Amérique centrale	2010	157.59	77.24	80.35	96.1	30.9	8.4	64.3	...
	2017	173.33	84.93	88.40	96.1	28.0	9.9	70.7	2 480
	2019	177.59	87.02	90.56	96.1	27.3	10.4	72.4	...
South America	2005	371.80	183.76[6]	188.05[6]	97.7[6]	28.8[6]	9.2[6]	21.3	...
Amérique du Sud	2010	392.54	193.79[6]	198.76[6]	97.5[6]	26.5[6]	10.4[6]	22.5	...
	2017	419.90[6]	206.89[6]	213.01[6]	97.1[6]	23.6	12.6[6]	24.0	17 832
	2019	427.20	210.38[6]	216.82[6]	97.0[6]	22.9[6]	13.3[6]	24.5	...

Country or area Pays ou zone	Year Année	Mid-year population estimates and projections (millions) Estimations et projections de population au milieu de l'année (millions)			Sex Ratio (males per 100 females) Rapport des sexes (hommes pour 100 femmes)	Population age distribution (percentage) Répartition par âge de la population (pourcentage)		Population density (per km²) Densité de population (pour km²)	Surface area Superficie (000 km²)
		Total	Male Hommes	Females Femmes		Aged 0 to 14 years old âgée de 0 à 14 ans	Aged 60+ years old âgée de 60 ans ou plus		
Asia	2005	3 977.99	2 035.22	1 942.76	104.8	27.6	9.1	128.2	...
Asie	2010	4 209.59	2 155.31	2 054.28	104.9	25.9	10.0	135.6	...
	2017	4 519.04	2 311.79	2 207.25	104.7	24.1	12.1	145.6	31 915
	2019	4 601.37	2 353.47	2 247.91	104.7	23.7	12.7	148.3	...
Central Asia	2005	58.45	28.82	29.63	97.2	30.9	7.3	14.9	...
Asie centrale	2010	62.81	31.02	31.79	97.6	28.7	7.0	16.0	...
	2017	70.87	35.07	35.80	98.0	29.9	8.1	18.0	4 103[2]
	2019	73.21	36.25	36.96	98.1	30.4	8.6	18.6	...
Eastern Asia	2005	1 564.19	798.71	765.49	104.3	19.8	12.2	135.3	...
Asie orientale	2010	1 604.86	819.65	785.21	104.4	18.2	13.8	138.8	...
	2017	1 659.77	846.78	812.98	104.2	17.4	17.5	143.6	11 799
	2019	1 672.61	852.92	819.69	104.1	17.2	18.4	144.7	...
South-central Asia	2005	1 647.07	851.43	795.64	107.0	33.5	7.0	159.5	...
Asie centrale et du Sud	2010	1 775.36	916.46	858.90	106.7	31.6	7.5	171.9	...
	2017	1 944.11	1 001.70	942.41	106.3	28.7	8.8	188.3	10 791
	2019	1 991.42	1 025.74	965.68	106.2	28.0	9.2	192.8	...
South-eastern Asia	2005	561.16	279.66	281.50	99.3	29.9	7.6	129.3	...
Asie du Sud-Est	2010	596.95	298.34	298.60	99.9	27.9	8.1	137.5	...
	2017	648.46	323.96	324.50	99.8	26.0	10.0	149.4	4 495
	2019	662.01	330.67	331.34	99.8	25.4	10.8	152.5	...
Southern Asia	2005	1 588.62	822.61	766.01	107.4	33.6	7.0	248.2	...
Asie méridionale	2010	1 712.56	885.44	827.11	107.1	31.7	7.5	267.6	...
	2017	1 873.24	966.63	906.61	106.6	28.6	8.8	292.7	6 688[2]
	2019	1 918.21	989.49	928.72	106.5	27.9	9.3	299.7	...
Western Asia	2005	205.56	105.43	100.13	105.3	33.5	7.2	42.8	...
Asie occidentale	2010	232.43	120.86	111.57	108.3	31.1	7.3	48.4	...
	2017	266.70	139.35	127.36	109.4	28.9	8.2	55.5	4 831
	2019	275.32	144.14	131.19	109.9	28.3	8.6	57.3	...
Europe	2005	729.29	351.22	378.06	92.9	15.9	20.6	32.9	...
Europe	2010	736.41	354.62	381.80	92.9	15.5	22.0	33.3	...
	2017	745.41	359.58	385.84	93.2	15.9	24.5	33.7	23 049
	2019	747.18	360.71	386.47	93.3	16.1	25.3	33.8	...
Eastern Europe	2005	297.50	140.21	157.29	89.1	15.4	18.2	16.5	...
Europe orientale	2010	294.87	138.61	156.26	88.7	14.9	19.3	16.3	...
	2017	294.06	138.30	155.76	88.8	16.5	22.4	16.3	18 814
	2019	293.44	138.02	155.42	88.8	16.9	23.3	16.3	...
Northern Europe	2005	96.31	47.13[7]	49.18[7]	95.8[7]	18.0[7]	21.1[7]	56.6	...
Europe septentrionale	2010	100.40	49.28[7]	51.12[7]	96.4[7]	17.4[7]	22.6[7]	59.0	...
	2017	104.68[7]	51.62[7]	53.06[7]	97.3[7]	17.5	24.0[7]	61.5	1 810
	2019	105.77	52.22[7]	53.55[7]	97.5[7]	17.6[7]	24.5[7]	62.1	...
Southern Europe	2005	149.68	73.24[8]	76.44[8]	95.8[8]	15.1[8]	22.5[8]	115.6	...
Europe méridionale	2010	153.02	74.75[8]	78.26[8]	95.5[8]	14.9[8]	24.0[8]	118.2	...
	2017	152.80[8]	74.56[8]	78.24[8]	95.3[8]	14.3	26.6[8]	118.0	1 317
	2019	152.45	74.45[8]	78.00[8]	95.5[8]	14.0[8]	27.4[8]	117.7	...
Western Europe	2005	185.80	90.64[9]	95.16[9]	95.2[9]	16.4[9]	22.6[9]	171.3	...
Europe occidentale	2010	188.13	91.96[9]	96.16[9]	95.6[9]	15.9[9]	24.3[9]	173.4	...
	2017	193.89[9]	95.10[9]	98.79[9]	96.3[9]	15.6	26.4[9]	178.7	1 108
	2019	195.52	96.02[9]	99.50[9]	96.5[9]	15.6[9]	27.0[9]	180.2	...
Oceania	2005	33.69	16.87	16.82	100.2	25.0	14.0	4.0	...
Océanie	2010	36.87	18.49	18.38	100.6	24.1	15.2	4.3	...
	2017	41.01	20.52	20.48	100.2	23.7[10]	16.7	4.8	8 564
	2019	42.13	21.09	21.04	100.2	23.7	17.2	5.0	...
Australia and New Zealand	2005	24.31	12.10	12.22	99.0	20.1	17.3	3.1	...
Australie et Nouvelle-	2010	26.52	13.23	13.30	99.4	19.3	18.8	3.3	...
Zélande	2017	29.29	14.56	14.73	98.8	19.2[11]	20.8	3.7	8 012
	2019	29.99	14.90	15.08	98.8	19.3	21.5	3.8	...

Country or area Pays ou zone	Year Année	Mid-year population estimates and projections (millions) Estimations et projections de population au milieu de l'année (millions)			Sex Ratio (males per 100 females) Rapport des sexes (hommes pour 100 femmes)	Population age distribution (percentage) Répartition par âge de la population (pourcentage)		Population density (per km²) Densité de population (pour km²)	Surface area Superficie (000 km²)
		Total	Male Hommes	Females Femmes		Aged 0 to 14 years old âgée de 0 à 14 ans	Aged 60+ years old âgée de 60 ans ou plus		
Melanesia	2005	8.23	4.19	4.04	103.6	38.1	5.3	15.5	...
Mélanésie	2010	9.19	4.67	4.51	103.6	37.2	5.7	17.3	...
	2017	10.51	5.36	5.16	103.9	35.6	6.1	19.9	541
	2019	10.92	5.57	5.35	104.0	35.0	6.4	20.6	...
Micronesia	2005	0.50	0.25[12]	0.25[12]	102.0[12]	33.4[12]	6.4[12]	157.2	...
Micronésie	2010	0.50	0.26[12]	0.25[12]	102.6[12]	32.1[12]	7.4[12]	158.9	...
	2017	0.53[12]	0.27[12]	0.26[12]	102.3[12]	30.0	9.7[12]	168.1	3
	2019	0.54	0.27[12]	0.27[12]	102.1[12]	29.6[12]	10.5[12]	171.4	...
Polynesia	2005	0.65[13]	0.33[14]	0.32[14]	104.6[14]	34.1[14]	7.6[14]	79.8[13]	...
Polynésie	2010	0.66[13]	0.33[14]	0.32[14]	104.0[14]	32.0[14]	8.4[14]	81.2[13]	...
	2017	0.67[14]	0.34[14]	0.33[14]	103.0[14]	30.2	10.2[14]	83.2[13]	8
	2019	0.68[13]	0.34[14]	0.34[14]	102.9[14]	29.6[14]	10.8[14]	84.0[13]	...
Afghanistan	2005	25.65	13.24	12.41	106.6	47.9	3.7	39.3	...
Afghanistan	2010	29.19	14.94	14.25	104.8	48.2	3.9	44.7	...
	2017	36.30	18.65	17.64	105.7	43.7	4.1	55.6	653
	2019	38.04	19.53	18.51	105.5	42.5	4.2	58.3	...
Albania	2005	3.09	1.55	1.53	101.1	26.5	12.3	112.7	...
Albanie	2010	2.95	1.49	1.46	101.5	22.5	15.0	107.6	...
	2017	2.88	1.47	1.41	103.9	18.0	19.1	105.3	29
	2019	2.88	1.47	1.41	103.7	17.4	20.5	105.1	...
Algeria	2005	33.15	16.77	16.38	102.3	29.2	7.0	13.9	...
Algérie	2010	35.98	18.16	17.82	101.9	27.3	7.8	15.1	...
	2017	41.39	20.91	20.48	102.1	29.6	9.3	17.4	2 382
	2019	43.05	21.75	21.30	102.1	30.6	9.7	18.1	...
American Samoa	2000	0.06	...	...	104.4[15,16]	38.8[15,16]	5.4[15,16]	287.6	...
Samoa américaines	2005	0.06	...	...	...	...	...	295.6	...
	2010	0.06	...	...	103.0[15,16]	35.0[15,16]	6.7[15,16]	278.2	...
	2016	0.06[17]	...	...	# 103.6	# 33.3	# 9.0	278.0[17]	~0
	2017	0.06[17]	...	...	...	...	...	278.2[17]	...
	2019	0.06	...	...	...	...	...	276.6	...
Andorra	2005	0.08	...	...	109.0[15,18]	15.1[15,18]	16.1[15,18]	167.8	...
Andorre	2010	0.08	...	...	108.5[15,18]	14.0[15,18]	18.6[15,18]	179.7	...
	2016	0.08[17]	...	...	102.3[15,18]	14.4[15,18]	19.0[15,18]	164.4[17]	...
	2017	0.08[17]	...	...	...	...	...	163.8[17]	~0
	2019	0.08	...	...	...	...	...	164.1	...
Angola	2005	19.43	9.64	9.79	98.4	46.9	4.0	15.6	...
Angola	2010	23.36	11.55	11.81	97.8	47.0	3.8	18.7	...
	2017	29.82	14.75	15.07	97.9	47.0	3.6	23.9	1 247
	2019	31.83	15.74	16.08	97.9	46.6	3.6	25.5	...
Anguilla	2001	0.01	...	...	97.3	27.7	10.2	126.4	...
Anguilla	2005	0.01	...	...	...	...	...	140.4	...
	2010	0.01	...	...	...	...	...	153.0	...
	2011	0.01	...	...	* 97.6	* 23.3	* 7.6[19]	155.0	...
	2017	0.01[17]	...	...	...	...	...	165.7[17]	~0
	2019	0.01	...	...	...	...	...	165.2	...
Antigua and Barbuda	2005	0.08	0.04	0.04	90.2	26.5	9.8	185.1	...
Antigua-et-Barbuda	2010	0.09	0.04	0.05	91.7	24.3	10.7	200.1	...
	2017	0.10	0.05	0.05	93.0	22.2	12.8	216.9	~0
	2019	0.10	0.05	0.05	93.2	22.0	13.6	220.7	...
Argentina	2005	38.89	18.90	20.00	94.5	27.3	13.6	14.2	...
Argentine	2010	40.90	19.90	21.00	94.8	26.0	14.2	14.9	...
	2017	43.94	21.42	22.52	95.1	24.9	15.1	16.1	2 780
	2019	44.78	21.84	22.94	95.2	24.6	15.4	16.4	...
Armenia	2005	2.98	1.40	1.58	88.8	21.5	14.4	104.7	...
Arménie	2010	2.88	1.35	1.53	87.9	19.5	14.8	101.1	...
	2017	2.94	1.39	1.56	88.8	20.5	16.8	103.4	30
	2019	2.96	1.39	1.57	88.8	20.8	17.9	103.9	...

Country or area Pays ou zone	Year Année	Mid-year population estimates and projections (millions) Estimations et projections de population au milieu de l'année (millions) Total	Male Hommes	Females Femmes	Sex Ratio (males per 100 females) Rapport des sexes (hommes pour 100 femmes)	Population age distribution (percentage) Répartition par âge de la population (pourcentage) Aged 0 to 14 years old âgée de 0 à 14 ans	Aged 60+ years old âgée de 60 ans ou plus	Population density (per km²) Densité de population (pour km²)	Surface area Superficie (000 km²)
Aruba	2005	0.10	0.05	0.05	90.7	21.5	12.6	555.7	...
Aruba	2010	0.10	0.05	0.05	91.1	20.9	15.5	564.8	...
	2017	0.11	0.05	0.06	90.4	18.0	19.7	585.4	~0
	2019	0.11	0.05	0.06	90.3	17.6	21.1	590.6	...
Australia	2005[11]	20.18	10.07	10.11	99.6	19.8	17.4	2.6	...
Australie	2010[11]	22.15	11.08	11.08	100.0	19.0	18.8	2.9	...
	2017	24.58[11]	12.24[11]	12.34[11]	99.2[11]	19.1	20.8[11]	3.2[11]	7 692[20]
	2019[11]	25.20	12.55	12.65	99.2	19.3	21.4	3.3	...
Austria	2005	8.25	4.01	4.24	94.6	16.0	22.1	100.2	...
Autriche	2010	8.41	4.10	4.31	95.1	14.7	23.3	102.1	...
	2017	8.82	4.33	4.49	96.4	14.2	24.7	107.0	84
	2019	8.96	4.41	4.55	97.0	14.4	25.3	108.7	...
Azerbaijan	2005[21]	8.54	4.21	4.33	97.1	26.2	8.5	103.3	...
Azerbaïdjan	2010[21]	9.03	4.48	4.56	98.2	22.8	8.1	109.3	...
	2017	9.85[21]	4.91[21]	4.94[21]	99.4[21]	23.3	10.1[21]	119.1[21]	87
	2019[21]	10.05	5.02	5.03	99.7	23.4	11.1	121.6	...
Bahamas	2005	0.32	0.16	0.17	94.4	28.1	8.6	32.5	...
Bahamas	2010	0.35	0.17	0.18	94.0	26.9	9.0	35.5	...
	2017	0.38	0.19	0.20	94.4	22.9[21]	10.9	38.1	14
	2019	0.39	0.19	0.20	94.5	22.1	11.7	38.9	...
Bahrain	2005	0.89	0.53	0.36	150.5	25.7	3.4	1 170.0	...
Bahreïn	2010	1.24	0.77	0.47	165.8	20.3	3.5	1 632.7	...
	2017	1.49	0.94	0.55	169.6	19.8	4.6	1 965.9	1
	2019	1.64	1.05	0.59	179.9	18.7	5.1	2 159.4	...
Bangladesh	2005	139.04	71.22	67.81	105.0	34.4	6.7	1 068.1	...
Bangladesh	2010	147.58	75.02	72.56	103.4	32.0	7.0	1 133.7	...
	2017	159.69	80.87	78.82	102.6	28.2	7.4	1 226.7	148
	2019	163.05	82.47	80.57	102.4	27.2	7.7	1 252.6	...
Barbados	2005	0.28	0.13	0.14	92.3	20.6	16.1	642.6	...
Barbade	2010	0.28	0.14	0.15	92.3	19.7	18.1	656.1	...
	2017	0.29	0.14	0.15	93.4	17.6	21.4	665.7	~0
	2019	0.29	0.14	0.15	93.7	17.1	22.5	667.5	...
Belarus	2005	9.56	4.46	5.10	87.6	15.6	18.5	47.1	...
Bélarus	2010	9.42	4.38	5.04	86.9	14.9	19.1	46.4	...
	2017	9.45	4.40	5.05	87.1	16.7	21.3	46.6	208
	2019	9.45	4.40	5.05	87.1	17.0	22.2	46.6	...
Belgium	2005	10.55	5.17	5.37	96.3	17.2	22.1	348.3	...
Belgique	2010	10.94	5.37	5.57	96.5	16.9	23.2	361.3	...
	2017	11.42	5.63	5.79	97.3	17.0	24.6	377.1	31
	2019	11.54	5.71	5.83	98.0	17.1	25.3	381.1	...
Belize	2005	0.28	0.14	0.14	101.1	38.9	4.8	12.4	...
Belize	2010	0.32	0.16	0.16	100.1	35.6	6.0	14.1	...
	2017	0.38	0.19	0.19	99.4	30.9	7.0	16.5	23
	2019	0.39	0.19	0.20	99.1	29.7	7.4	17.1	...
Benin	2005	7.98	3.96	4.03	98.2	44.4	5.0	70.8	...
Bénin	2010	9.20	4.57	4.63	98.7	43.8	4.9	81.6	...
	2017	11.18	5.57	5.60	99.5	42.7	5.0	99.1	115
	2019	11.80	5.89	5.91	99.7	42.2	5.0	104.7	...
Bermuda	2005	0.07	...	...	91.8[15,22]	18.4[15]	16.4[15]	1 302.6	...
Bermudes	2010	0.06	...	...	92.4[15,23]	17.4[15]	18.7[15]	1 279.1	...
	2017	0.06[17]	...	...	91.4[15,23]	14.8[15,23]	24.9[15,23]	1 227.0[17]	~0
	2019	0.06	...	...	...	...	...	1 250.1	...
Bhutan	2005	0.65	0.34	0.31	110.2	35.1	6.8	17.0	...
Bhoutan	2010	0.69	0.36	0.33	110.7	31.2	7.5	18.0	...
	2017	0.75	0.39	0.35	112.4	26.2	8.4	19.6[15,24]	38
	2019	0.76	0.41	0.36	113.1	25.3	8.8	20.0	...

Country or area Pays ou zone	Year Année	Mid-year population estimates and projections (millions) Estimations et projections de population au milieu de l'année (millions)			Sex Ratio (males per 100 females) Rapport des sexes (hommes pour 100 femmes)	Population age distribution (percentage) Répartition par âge de la population (pourcentage)		Population density (per km²) Densité de population (pour km²)	Surface area Superficie (000 km²)
		Total	Male Hommes	Females Femmes		Aged 0 to 14 years old âgée de 0 à 14 ans	Aged 60+ years old âgée de 60 ans ou plus		
Bolivia (Plurin. State of)	2005	9.23	4.65	4.58	101.4	36.3	8.1	8.5	...
Bolivie (État plurin. de)	2010	10.05	5.06	4.99	101.3	34.5	8.8	9.3	...
	2017	11.19	5.62	5.57	100.9	31.5[15,24]	9.8[15,24]	10.3	1 099[25]
	2019	11.51	5.78	5.73	100.8	30.6	10.2	10.6	...
Bonaire, St. Eustatius & Saba	2005	0.01	...	...	...	...	...	43.9	...
Bonaire, St-Eustache et	2010	0.02	...	...	...	...	...	63.8	...
Saba	2019	0.03	...	...	...	...	...	79.2	...
Bosnia and Herzegovina	2005	3.77	1.85	1.92	96.5	17.7	17.4	73.8	...
Bosnie-Herzégovine	2010	3.71	1.82	1.89	96.5	15.7	19.3	72.7	...
	2017	3.35	1.64	1.71	96.1	14.8	23.0	65.7	51
	2019	3.30	1.62	1.68	96.0	14.7	24.5	64.7	...
Botswana	2005	1.80	0.87	0.92	94.7	36.5	5.1	3.2	...
Botswana	2010	1.99	0.97	1.02	95.7	35.0	5.3	3.5	...
	2017	2.21	1.06	1.14	93.0	34.4	6.5	3.9	582
	2019	2.30	1.11	1.19	93.7	33.8	6.9	4.1	...
Brazil	2005	186.13	92.00	94.13	97.7	27.4	8.8	22.3	...
Brésil	2010	195.71	96.54	99.18	97.3	24.8	10.2	23.4	...
	2017	207.83	102.23	105.60	96.8	21.7	12.7	24.9	8 516
	2019	211.05	103.73	107.32	96.7	21.0	13.6	25.3	...
British Virgin Islands	2001	0.02	...	...	106.1	26.3	7.4	140.6	...
Îles Vierges britanniques	2005	0.02	...	...	...	...	...	154.5	...
	2010	0.03	...	...	97.1	22.3	9.7	181.5	...
	2017	0.03[17]	...	...	...	...	...	208.0[17]	~0
	2019	0.03	...	...	...	...	...	200.2	...
Brunei Darussalam	2005	0.37	0.19	0.18	104.3	27.8	4.8	69.3	...
Brunéi Darussalam	2010	0.39	0.20	0.19	106.8	26.0	5.4	73.7	...
	2017	0.42	0.22	0.20	108.3	23.5	7.9	80.5	6
	2019	0.43	0.23	0.21	108.0	22.6	9.0	82.2	...
Bulgaria	2005	7.69	3.74	3.95	94.8	13.6	23.1	70.8	...
Bulgarie	2010	7.43	3.62	3.81	94.9	13.5	25.3	68.4	...
	2017	7.10	3.45	3.65	94.6	14.4	27.6	65.4	111
	2019	7.00	3.40	3.60	94.4	14.7	28.0	64.5	...
Burkina Faso	2005	13.42	6.62	6.80	97.4	46.5	4.1	49.1	...
Burkina Faso	2010	15.61	7.74	7.87	98.3	46.2	3.9	57.0	...
	2017	19.19	9.57	9.62	99.5	45.2	3.9	70.2	273
	2019	20.32	10.15	10.17	99.7	44.7	3.9	74.3	...
Burundi	2005	7.36	3.63	3.74	97.2	47.0	3.4	286.8	...
Burundi	2010	8.68	4.29	4.39	97.7	45.1	3.3	337.8	...
	2017	10.83	5.37	5.46	98.2	45.6	3.8	421.6	28
	2019	11.53	5.72	5.81	98.4	45.4	4.0	449.0	...
Cabo Verde	2005	0.46	0.23	0.24	94.8	37.6	7.2	114.9	...
Cabo Verde	2010	0.49	0.25	0.25	99.8	32.3	6.5	122.2	...
	2017	0.54	0.27	0.27	100.7	29.2	7.0	133.4	4
	2019	0.55	0.28	0.27	100.8	28.4	7.3	136.5	...
Cambodia	2005	13.27	6.44	6.83	94.3	37.1	5.3	75.2	...
Cambodge	2010	14.31	6.97	7.34	95.0	33.3	5.9	81.1	...
	2017	16.01	7.81	8.20	95.3	31.3	7.1	90.7	181
	2019	16.49	8.05	8.44	95.4	31.1	7.4	93.4	...
Cameroon	2005	17.73	8.84	8.90	99.3	44.2	4.7	37.5	...
Cameroun	2010	20.34	10.15	10.19	99.7	43.7	4.4	43.0	...
	2017	24.57	12.28	12.29	99.9	42.9	4.3	52.0	476
	2019	25.88	12.94	12.94	100.0	42.4	4.3	54.7	...
Canada	2005	32.16	15.95	16.22	98.3	17.7	17.9	3.5	...
Canada	2010	34.15	16.94	17.21	98.5	16.5	19.9	3.8	...
	2017	36.73	18.22	18.51	98.4	15.9	23.3	4.0	9 985
	2019	37.41	18.56	18.85	98.5	15.8	24.3	4.1	...

Country or area Pays ou zone	Year Année	Mid-year population estimates and projections (millions) Estimations et projections de population au milieu de l'année (millions)			Sex Ratio (males per 100 females) Rapport des sexes (hommes pour 100 femmes)	Population age distribution (percentage) Répartition par âge de la population (pourcentage)		Population density (per km²) Densité de population (pour km²)	Surface area Superficie (000 km²)
		Total	**Male Hommes**	**Females Femmes**		**Aged 0 to 14 years old âgée de 0 à 14 ans**	**Aged 60+ years old âgée de 60 ans ou plus**		
Cayman Islands	2005	0.05	...	...	101.0[15]	...	...	202.6	...
Îles Caïmanes	2010	0.06	...	...	97.8[15,26]	18.1[15,26]	8.6[15,26]	231.3	...
	2015	0.06	...	...	100.4[15]	18.3[15]	6.7[15,19]	249.8	~0
	2017	0.06[17]	...	...	...	...	...	256.5[17]	~0
	2019	0.06	...	...	...	...	...	270.6	
Central African Republic	2005	4.04	2.00	2.04	97.7	43.5	5.0	6.5	...
République centrafricaine	2010	4.39	2.17	2.22	98.0	44.1	4.6	7.0	...
	2017	4.60	2.28	2.32	98.3	44.6	4.5	7.4	623
	2019	4.75	2.35	2.39	98.3	43.9	4.5	7.6	...
Chad	2005	10.10	5.03	5.07	99.3	49.1	4.2	8.0	...
Tchad	2010	11.95	5.96	5.99	99.5	48.8	3.9	9.5	...
	2017	15.02	7.50	7.52	99.6	47.4	3.9	11.9	1 284
	2019	15.95	7.96	7.99	99.7	46.8	3.9	12.7	...
Channel Islands	2005[27]	0.15	0.07	0.08	96.1	16.3	20.6	798.3	...
Îles Anglo-Normandes	2010[27]	0.16	0.08	0.08	97.1	15.5	21.5	840.7	...
	2017	0.17[27]	0.08[27]	0.09[27]	97.8[27]	15.3	22.9[27]	887.7[27]	~0[27]
	2019[27]	0.17	0.09	0.09	98.0	15.1	23.6	906.6	...
Chile	2005	16.18	7.96	8.22	96.9	24.7	11.9	21.8	...
Chili	2010	17.06	8.40	8.67	96.9	22.1	13.3	22.9	...
	2017	18.47	9.10	9.37	97.1	20.0[27]	16.1	24.8	756
	2019	18.95	9.34	9.61	97.2	19.5	16.9	25.5	...
China	2005[28]	1 330.78	683.49	647.29	105.6	20.4	10.8	141.7	...
Chine	2010[28]	1 368.81	703.41	665.40	105.7	18.7	12.2	145.8	...
	2017	1 421.02[28]	729.46[28]	691.56[28]	105.5[28]	17.9	16.0[28]	151.4[28]	9 600
	2019[28]	1 433.78	735.62	698.16	105.4	17.8	16.8	152.7	...
China, Hong Kong SAR	2005	6.77	3.25	3.52	92.5	14.3	15.6	6 447.2	...
Chine, RAS de Hong Kong	2010	6.97	3.28	3.69	88.8	11.9	18.4	6 634.6	...
	2017	7.31	3.37	3.93	85.8	11.5[28]	23.5	6 958.4	1
	2019	7.44	3.42	4.02	85.1	12.3	25.2	7 082.1	...
China, Macao SAR	2005	0.48	0.23	0.25	90.5	17.0	9.6	16 149.1	...
Chine, RAS de Macao	2010	0.54	0.26	0.28	92.3	13.0	10.9	18 000.6	...
	2017	0.62	0.30	0.32	92.3	13.3	16.1	20 822.2	~0[29]
	2019	0.64	0.31	0.33	92.5	14.0	17.9	21 419.6	...
Colombia	2005	42.65	20.90	21.75	96.1	30.3	8.4	38.4	...
Colombie	2010	45.22	22.16	23.06	96.1	27.3	9.7	40.8	...
	2017	48.91	23.99	24.92	96.3	23.6	12.1	44.1	1 142
	2019	50.34	24.71	25.63	96.4	22.6	12.8	45.4	...
Comoros	2005	0.61	0.31	0.30	101.4	42.3	4.6	328.7	...
Comores	2010	0.69	0.35	0.34	101.6	41.0	4.5	370.6	...
	2017	0.81	0.41	0.40	101.8	39.8	4.9	437.3	2
	2019	0.85	0.43	0.42	101.8	39.3	5.0	457.2	...
Congo	2005	3.62	1.80	1.83	98.3	41.8	4.1	10.6	...
Congo	2010	4.27	2.13	2.15	99.0	41.6	4.0	12.5	...
	2017	5.11	2.55	2.56	99.7	41.9	4.3	15.0	342
	2019	5.38	2.69	2.69	99.8	41.5	4.4	15.8	...
Cook Islands	2001	0.02	...	...	106.6	30.0	10.6	76.3	...
Îles Cook	2005	0.02	...	...	...	...	...	82.1	...
	2006	0.02	...	...	* 103.1	* 26.1	* 11.9	82.1	...
	2010	0.02	...	...	...	...	...	77.3	...
	2016	0.02[17]	...	...	# 97.4	# 26.9	# 14.2	72.4[17]	...
	2017	0.02[17]	...	...	...	...	...	72.4[17]	~0
	2019	0.02	...	...	...	...	...	73.1	...
Costa Rica	2005	4.29	2.15	2.14	100.5	27.4	9.2	83.9	...
Costa Rica	2010	4.58	2.29	2.28	100.4	24.3	10.8	89.6	...
	2017	4.95	2.48	2.47	100.0	21.6	13.5	96.9	51
	2019	5.05	2.52	2.53	99.9	21.1	14.5	98.9	...

Country or area Pays ou zone	Year Année	Mid-year population estimates and projections (millions) Estimations et projections de population au milieu de l'année (millions)			Sex Ratio (males per 100 females) Rapport des sexes (hommes pour 100 femmes)	Population age distribution (percentage) Répartition par âge de la population (pourcentage)		Population density (per km²) Densité de population (pour km²)	Surface area Superficie (000 km²)
		Total	Male Hommes	Females Femmes		Aged 0 to 14 years old âgée de 0 à 14 ans	Aged 60+ years old âgée de 60 ans ou plus		
Côte d'Ivoire	2005	18.35	9.38	8.98	104.5	44.1	4.7	57.7	...
Côte d'Ivoire	2010	20.53	10.43	10.11	103.2	43.6	4.5	64.6	...
	2017	24.44	12.34	12.09	102.1	42.2	4.6	76.8	322
	2019	25.72	12.97	12.74	101.8	41.7	4.7	80.9	...
Croatia	2005	4.38	2.11	2.27	92.9	15.7	21.9	78.2	...
Croatie	2010	4.33	2.08	2.24	92.9	15.4	23.8	77.3	...
	2017	4.18	2.01	2.17	92.7	14.4	27.1	74.7	57
	2019	4.13	1.99	2.14	93.0	14.6	27.9	73.8	...
Cuba	2005	11.26	5.61	5.65	99.4	19.2	15.4	105.8	...
Cuba	2010	11.23	5.58	5.64	99.0	17.7	17.3	105.5	...
	2017	11.34	5.63	5.71	98.7	16.4	20.0	106.5	110
	2019	11.33	5.63	5.71	98.6	16.0	20.7	106.5	...
Curaçao	2005	0.13	0.06	0.07	88.2	21.6	17.1	293.1	...
Curaçao	2010	0.15	0.07	0.08	85.0	20.7	18.6	336.0	...
	2017	0.16	0.07	0.09	84.7	19.3	22.7	364.9	~0
	2019	0.16	0.08	0.09	85.0	18.5	23.9	368.1	...
Cyprus	2005[30]	1.03	0.52	0.51	102.6	20.0	14.9	111.2	...
Chypre	2010[30]	1.11	0.56	0.56	99.7	17.8	16.1	120.4	...
	2017	1.18[30]	0.59[30]	0.59[30]	100.2[30]	16.8	18.5[30]	127.7[30]	9
	2019[30]	1.20	0.60	0.60	100.0	16.7	19.3	129.7	...
Czechia	2005	10.26	5.00	5.26	95.0	14.7	19.8	132.8	...
Tchéquie	2010	10.54	5.17	5.37	96.4	14.2	22.4	136.4	...
	2017	10.64	5.23	5.41	96.7	15.4[30]	25.5	137.8	79
	2019	10.69	5.26	5.43	96.9	15.7	25.9	138.4	...
Dem. People's Rep. Korea	2005	23.90	11.67	12.23	95.4	24.7	11.9	198.5	...
Rép. pop. dém. de Corée	2010	24.55	11.99	12.55	95.5	22.6	12.9	203.9	...
	2017	25.43	12.44	12.99	95.7	20.5	13.5	211.2	121
	2019	25.67	12.55	13.11	95.7	20.0	14.6	213.2	...
Dem. Rep. of the Congo	2005	54.79	27.22	27.56	98.8	45.8	4.7	24.2	...
Rép. dém. du Congo	2010	64.56	32.14	32.42	99.1	46.1	4.7	28.5	...
	2017	81.40	40.61	40.79	99.6	46.3	4.7	35.9	2 345
	2019	86.79	43.32	43.47	99.6	46.0	4.7	38.3	...
Denmark	2005	5.42	2.69	2.74	98.1	18.7	21.2	127.8	...
Danemark	2010	5.55	2.76	2.80	98.5	17.9	23.3	130.9	...
	2017	5.73	2.85	2.88	98.9	16.5	25.3	135.1	43
	2019	5.77	2.87	2.90	98.9	16.4	25.8	136.0	...
Djibouti	2005	0.78	0.39	0.39	101.0	37.9	5.2	33.8	...
Djibouti	2010	0.84	0.45	0.39	113.7	32.6	6.1	36.2	...
	2017	0.94	0.50	0.45	111.3	30.0	6.8	40.7	23
	2019	0.97	0.51	0.46	110.9	29.2	7.2	42.0	...
Dominica	2001	0.07	...	...	101.5[31]	29.0[32]	13.2[32]	92.9	...
Dominique	2005	0.07	...	...	101.4	...	...	94.2	...
	2006	0.07	...	...	103.7	29.5	13.3	94.4	...
	2010	0.07	...	...	101.4	...	...	95.3	...
	2014	0.07	...	...	103.0	...	...	97.0	1
	2017	0.07[17]	...	...	...	...	...	98.6[17]	1
	2019	0.07	...	...	...	...	...	95.7	...
Dominican Republic	2005	9.10	4.58	4.52	101.2	33.0	7.7	188.3	...
République dominicaine	2010	9.70	4.87	4.83	100.8	30.6	8.5	200.6	...
	2017	10.51	5.26	5.25	100.1	28.3	10.2	217.6	49
	2019	10.74	5.37	5.37	99.9	27.7	10.8	222.2	...
Ecuador	2005	13.83	6.93	6.89	100.6	33.1	7.8	55.7	...
Équateur	2010	15.01	7.52	7.49	100.4	31.0	8.6	60.4	...
	2017	16.79	8.40	8.39	100.2	28.4	10.2	67.6	257
	2019	17.37	8.69	8.68	100.1	27.7	10.7	70.0	...
Egypt	2005	75.52	38.10	37.43	101.8	33.8	7.1	75.9	...
Égypte	2010	82.76	41.81	40.96	102.1	32.6	7.6	83.1	...
	2017	96.44	48.74	47.71	102.2	33.8	7.9	96.9	1 002
	2019	100.39	50.72	49.67	102.1	33.8	8.1	100.8	...

2

Population, surface area and density *(continued)*

Population, superficie et densité *(suite)*

Country or area / Pays ou zone	Year / Année	Mid-year population estimates and projections (millions) / Estimations et projections de population au milieu de l'année (millions) Total	Male Hommes	Females Femmes	Sex Ratio (males per 100 females) Rapport des sexes (hommes pour 100 femmes)	Population age distribution (percentage) / Répartition par âge de la population (pourcentage) Aged 0 to 14 years old âgée de 0 à 14 ans	Aged 60+ years old âgée de 60 ans ou plus	Population density (per km²) Densité de population (pour km²)	Surface area Superficie (000 km²)
El Salvador	2005	6.05	2.89	3.16	91.3	34.8	9.1	292.1	...
El Salvador	2010	6.18	2.93	3.26	89.8	31.6	9.9	298.4	
	2017	6.39	3.00	3.39	88.4	27.4	11.4	308.3	21[33]
	2019	6.45	3.02	3.43	88.1	26.9	11.8	311.5	
Equatorial Guinea	2005	0.75	0.40	0.35	113.1	39.6	5.0	26.7	...
Guinée équatoriale	2010	0.94	0.51	0.43	119.3	38.5	4.4	33.6	
	2017	1.26	0.70	0.56	124.6	37.3	4.0	45.0	28
	2019	1.36	0.75	0.60	125.2	37.0	3.9	48.3	...
Eritrea	2005	2.83	1.41	1.42	99.6	38.6	6.1	28.0	...
Érythrée	2010	3.17	1.58	1.59	99.9	39.5	6.2	31.4	
	2017	3.41	1.71	1.70	100.4	42.0	6.5	33.8	118
	2019	3.50	1.75	1.74	100.5	41.6	6.4	34.6	...
Estonia	2005	1.36	0.63	0.73	86.8	15.2	21.9	32.0	...
Estonie	2010	1.33	0.62	0.71	87.2	15.1	23.2	31.4	
	2017	1.32	0.62	0.70	88.7	16.2	25.9	31.1	45
	2019	1.33	0.63	0.70	89.6	16.5	26.5	31.3	...
Eswatini	2005	1.03	0.49	0.54	90.4	41.3	5.1	59.9	...
Eswatini	2010	1.06	0.50	0.56	89.3	40.2	5.6	61.9	
	2017	1.12	0.55	0.58	94.8	38.3	5.7	65.4	17
	2019	1.15	0.56	0.59	96.1	37.8	5.7	66.8	...
Ethiopia	2005	76.35	38.07	38.27	99.5	46.5	4.9	76.3	...
Éthiopie	2010	87.64	43.73	43.91	99.6	44.9	5.1	87.6	
	2017	106.40	53.21	53.19	100.1	41.3	5.2	106.4	1 104
	2019	112.08	56.07	56.01	100.1	40.3	5.3	112.1	
Falkland Islands (Malvinas) [34]	2001	~0.00	...	...	121.5	15.0	12.0	0.2	...
Îles Falkland (Malvinas) [34]	2005	~0.00	...	...	...	...	...	0.2	
	2006	~0.00	...	...	113.2	15.9	14.0	0.2	
	2010	~0.00	...	...	...	...	...	0.2	
	2012	~0.00	...	...	110.5[35]	16.4[35]	15.7[35]	0.2	
	2017	~0.00[17]	...	...	...	...	...	0.2[17]	12
	2019	~0.00	...	...	...	...	...	0.3	
Faroe Islands	2005	0.05	...	...	108.0[15]	...	...	34.6	...
Îles Féroé	2008	0.05	...	...	108.1[15]	22.0[15]	19.3[15]	34.7	
	2010	0.05	...	...	108.0[15]	...	...	34.8	
	2015	0.05	...	...	107.2[15]	21.0[15]	22.5[15]	35.1	1
	2017	0.05[17]	...	...	...	...	...	35.3[17]	1
	2019	0.05	...	...	...	...	...	34.9	
Fiji	2005	0.82	0.42	0.40	104.1	30.5	6.9	45.0	...
Fidji	2010	0.86	0.44	0.42	104.3	29.0	7.9	47.1	...
	2017	0.88	0.45	0.43	103.0	29.7	8.7	48.0	18
	2019	0.89	0.45	0.44	102.7	29.3	9.3	48.7	...
Finland	2005[36]	5.26	2.57	2.68	95.9	17.3	21.5	17.3	...
Finlande	2010[36]	5.37	2.63	2.73	96.4	16.5	24.8	17.7	...
	2017	5.51[36]	2.71[36]	2.80[36]	97.1[36]	16.3	27.8[36]	18.1[36]	338[36]
	2019[36]	5.53	2.73	2.80	97.2	16.0	28.6	18.2	
France	2005	61.12	29.59	31.53	93.8	18.5	20.9	111.6	...
France	2010	62.88	30.46	32.42	93.9	18.5	23.1	114.8	
	2017	64.84	31.40	33.44	93.9	18.1[36]	25.7	118.4	552
	2019	65.13	31.52	33.61	93.8	17.8	26.5	118.9	...
French Guiana	2005	0.20	0.10	0.10	98.2	35.8	5.8	2.5	...
Guyane française	2010	0.23	0.12	0.12	99.9	34.9	6.6	2.8	
	2017	0.28	0.14	0.14	97.4	32.7	7.9	3.3	84
	2019	0.29	0.14	0.15	97.8	32.1	8.6	3.5	...
French Polynesia	2005	0.26	0.13	0.13	105.1	28.2	8.0	70.7	...
Polynésie française	2010	0.27	0.14	0.13	104.9	25.5	9.3	72.8	
	2017	0.28	0.14	0.14	102.8	22.9	12.2	75.4	4
	2019	0.28	0.14	0.14	102.7	22.6	13.1	76.3	...

20   **Statistical Yearbook** (Sixty-second issue) — **Annuaire statistique** (Soixante-deuxième édition)

Country or area Pays ou zone	Year Année	Mid-year population estimates and projections (millions) Estimations et projections de population au milieu de l'année (millions)			Sex Ratio (males per 100 females) Rapport des sexes (hommes pour 100 femmes)	Population age distribution (percentage) Répartition par âge de la population (pourcentage)		Population density (per km²) Densité de population (pour km²)	Surface area Superficie (000 km²)
		Total	Male Hommes	Females Femmes		Aged 0 to 14 years old âgée de 0 à 14 ans	Aged 60+ years old âgée de 60 ans ou plus		
Gabon Gabon	2005	1.39	0.70	0.70	100.0	39.3	6.8	5.4	...
	2010	1.62	0.82	0.80	102.4	37.4	6.0	6.3	...
	2017	2.06	1.05	1.01	103.8	36.8	5.4	8.0	268
	2019	2.17	1.11	1.07	103.7	37.2	5.3	8.4	...
Gambia Gambie	2005	1.54	0.77	0.78	98.7	46.3	4.3	152.5	...
	2010	1.79	0.89	0.90	98.5	45.1	4.3	177.2	...
	2017	2.21	1.10	1.12	98.4	44.4	4.0	218.8	11
	2019	2.35	1.16	1.18	98.4	44.1	3.9	232.0	...
Georgia Géorgie	2005[37]	4.21	2.01	2.20	91.1	19.0	18.4	60.6	...
	2010[37]	4.10	1.95	2.15	91.0	18.0	18.9	59.0	...
	2017	4.01[37]	1.91[37]	2.10[37]	91.3[37]	19.5	20.7[37]	57.7[37]	70
	2019[37]	4.00	1.91	2.09	91.1	20.0	21.2	57.5	...
Germany Allemagne	2005	81.60	39.87	41.73	95.6	14.4	24.9	234.1	...
	2010	80.83	39.62	41.21	96.1	13.6	26.1	231.9	...
	2017	82.66	40.74	41.92	97.2	13.5[37]	27.9	237.1	357
	2019	83.52	41.25	42.27	97.6	13.8	28.3	239.6	...
Ghana Ghana	2005	21.81	11.02	10.80	102.1	40.9	4.4	95.9	...
	2010	24.78	12.53	12.25	102.3	39.3	4.6	108.9	...
	2017	29.12	14.75	14.37	102.7	37.8	4.9	128.0	239
	2019	30.42	15.42	15.00	102.8	37.4	5.2	133.7	...
Gibraltar Gibraltar	2001	0.03	...	...	98.5[38]	18.4[38]	20.5[38]	3 137.4	...
	2005	0.03	...	...	97.3[39]	...	...	3 208.5	...
	2010	0.03	...	...	99.2[39]	...	...	3 318.9	...
	2012	0.03	...	...	99.6[15,39]	18.1[15,39]	22.4[15,39]	3 362.3	...
	2015	0.03	...	...	101.8[39]	...	...	3 422.8	~0
	2017	0.03[17]	...	...	...	...	...	3 457.1[17]	~0
	2019	0.03	...	...	...	...	...	3 370.1	...
Greece Grèce	2005	11.22	5.56	5.67	98.0	14.7	22.6	87.1	...
	2010	10.89	5.35	5.54	96.6	15.1	24.8	84.5	...
	2017	10.57	5.19	5.38	96.4	14.2	27.4	82.0	132
	2019	10.47	5.14	5.33	96.4	13.9	28.3	81.3	...
Greenland Groenland	2005	0.06	...	...	113.4[15,18]	25.0[15,18]	9.6[15,18]	0.1	...
	2010	0.06	...	...	112.6[15,18]	22.6[15,18]	10.9[15,18]	0.1	...
	2016	0.06[17]	...	...	112.1[15,18]	21.0[15,18]	13.2[15,18]	0.1[17]	...
	2017	0.06[17]	...	...	...	...	...	0.1[17]	2 166
	2019	0.06	...	...	...	...	...	0.1	...
Grenada Grenade	2005	0.10	0.05	0.05	100.6	28.1	11.5	307.8	...
	2010	0.11	0.05	0.05	102.1	24.0	13.3	312.5	...
	2017	0.11	0.06	0.06	101.7	23.4	14.0	326.1	~0
	2019	0.11	0.06	0.06	101.5	23.7	14.6	329.4	...
Guadeloupe Guadeloupe	2005	0.40	0.19	0.21	89.3	23.4	16.2	247.5	...
	2010	0.41	0.19	0.22	86.7	22.5	19.1	249.4	...
	2017	0.40	0.18	0.21	86.1	19.4	24.1	245.5	2
	2019	0.40	0.18	0.22	85.8	18.8	25.4	245.7	...
Guam Guam	2005	0.16	0.08	0.08	104.0	29.5	9.2	293.3	...
	2010	0.16	0.08	0.08	103.3	27.5	11.1	295.3	...
	2017	0.16	0.08	0.08	102.2	24.8	13.9	304.2	1
	2019	0.17	0.08	0.08	101.9	24.1	14.7	309.8	...
Guatemala Guatemala	2005	13.10	6.42	6.67	96.2	42.3	5.9	122.2	...
	2010	14.63	7.19	7.44	96.5	39.4	6.1	136.5	...
	2017	16.92	8.33	8.59	96.9	35.1	6.9	157.8	109
	2019	17.58	8.66	8.92	97.1	33.9	7.1	164.1	...
Guinea Guinée	2005	9.11	4.34	4.77	91.1	46.8	4.9	37.1	...
	2010	10.19	4.86	5.33	91.1	46.2	4.6	41.5	...
	2017	12.07	5.80	6.27	92.6	44.2	4.7	49.1	246
	2019	12.77	6.17	6.61	93.4	43.5	4.7	52.0	...

Country or area Pays ou zone	Year Année	Mid-year population estimates and projections (millions) Estimations et projections de population au milieu de l'année (millions)			Sex Ratio (males per 100 females) Rapport des sexes (hommes pour 100 femmes)	Population age distribution (percentage) Répartition par âge de la population (pourcentage)		Population density (per km²) Densité de population (pour km²)	Surface area Superficie (000 km²)
		Total	Male Hommes	Females Femmes		Aged 0 to 14 years old âgée de 0 à 14 ans	Aged 60+ years old âgée de 60 ans ou plus		
Guinea-Bissau	2005	1.34	0.65	0.70	93.2	44.1	4.4	47.8	...
Guinée-Bissau	2010	1.52	0.74	0.78	94.1	43.1	4.3	54.1	
	2017	1.83	0.89	0.94	95.3	42.5	4.6	65.0	36
	2019	1.92	0.94	0.98	95.6	42.2	4.6	68.3	
Guyana	2005	0.75	0.37	0.37	100.4	36.3	6.4	3.8	...
Guyana	2010	0.75	0.37	0.38	98.5	32.2	7.3	3.8	...
	2017	0.78	0.39	0.39	100.6	28.6	9.6	3.9	215
	2019	0.78	0.39	0.39	101.0	27.9	10.4	4.0	...
Haiti	2005	9.20	4.53	4.66	97.1	38.2	6.5	333.6	...
Haïti	2010	9.95	4.91	5.04	97.3	36.3	6.5	361.0	...
	2017	10.98	5.42	5.56	97.5	33.6	7.3	398.5	28
	2019	11.26	5.56	5.71	97.4	32.9	7.6	408.7	
Holy See	2000	~0.00	...	...	196.7[18,40]	...	...	1 784.1	...
Saint-Siège	2005	~0.00	...	...	...	...	...	1 813.6	...
	2009	~0.00	...	...	219.2	...	...	1 806.8	...
	2010	~0.00	...	...	...	...	...	1 804.5	...
	2017	~0.00[17]	...	...	...	...	...	1 800.0[17]	~0[41]
	2019	~0.00	...	...	...	...	...	1 815.9	...
Honduras	2005	7.46	3.71	3.74	99.2	40.6	5.4	66.7	...
Honduras	2010	8.32	4.15	4.17	99.5	37.6	5.8	74.3	...
	2017	9.43	4.71	4.72	99.8	32.3	6.8	84.3	112
	2019	9.75	4.87	4.88	99.8	31.2	7.2	87.1	
Hungary	2005	10.09	4.79	5.30	90.3	15.5	21.4	111.4	...
Hongrie	2010	9.93	4.71	5.22	90.3	14.9	22.1	109.7	...
	2017	9.73	4.63	5.10	90.7	14.4	26.0	107.5	93
	2019	9.68	4.61	5.08	90.8	14.4	26.6	107.0	
Iceland	2005	0.30	0.15	0.15	100.6	22.2	15.8	2.9	...
Islande	2010	0.32	0.16	0.16	101.5	20.8	16.9	3.2	...
	2017	0.33	0.17	0.17	100.7	20.0	20.1	3.3	103
	2019	0.34	0.17	0.17	100.8	19.6	21.1	3.4	...
India	2005	1 147.61	597.05	550.56	108.4	32.7	7.2	386.0	...
Inde	2010	1 234.28	642.16	592.12	108.5	30.8	7.8	415.1	...
	2017	1 338.68	695.88	642.80	108.3	27.5	9.4	450.2	3 287
	2019	1 366.42	710.13	656.29	108.2	26.6	9.9	459.6	
Indonesia	2005	226.29	113.59	112.70	100.8	29.9	7.4	124.9	...
Indonésie	2010	241.83	121.82	120.01	101.5	28.8	7.5	133.5	...
	2017	264.65	133.27	131.38	101.4	26.9	9.0	146.1	1 911
	2019	270.63	136.27	134.36	101.4	26.2	9.7	149.4	
Iran (Islamic Republic of)	2005	69.76	35.49	34.27	103.6	26.9	6.7	42.8	...
Iran (Rép. islamique d')	2010	73.76	37.18	36.58	101.6	24.0	7.5	45.3	...
	2017	80.67	40.82	39.85	102.4	24.2	9.4	49.5	1 629[42]
	2019	82.91	41.89	41.02	102.1	24.7	10.0	50.9	...
Iraq	2005	26.92	13.60	13.32	102.1	42.0	5.1	62.0	...
Iraq	2010	29.74	15.02	14.72	102.1	41.8	4.8	68.5	...
	2017	37.55	18.99	18.56	102.3	38.8	5.1	86.5	435
	2019	39.31	19.89	19.42	102.4	38.0	5.1	90.5	
Ireland	2005	4.14	2.07	2.07	99.7	20.2	14.7	60.1	...
Irlande	2010	4.55	2.26	2.29	98.8	20.8	15.9	66.1	...
	2017	4.75	2.35	2.40	98.1	21.6	18.6	69.0	70
	2019	4.88	2.42	2.46	98.5	21.2	19.3	70.9	
Isle of Man	2005	0.08	...	...	96.9[15]	17.3[15]	22.1[15]	133.5	...
Île de Man	2009	0.08	...	...	98.4[15]	16.4[15]	24.1[15]	139.2	...
	2010	0.08	...	...	98.6[15]	...	...	140.5	...
	2016	0.08[17]	...	...	98.2[15]	16.0[15]	26.9[15]	146.9[17]	...
	2017	0.08[17]	...	...	...	...	...	147.9[17]	1
	2019	0.08	...	...	...	...	...	148.4	...

Country or area Pays ou zone	Year Année	Mid-year population estimates and projections (millions) Estimations et projections de population au milieu de l'année (millions)			Sex Ratio (males per 100 females) Rapport des sexes (hommes pour 100 femmes)	Population age distribution (percentage) Répartition par âge de la population (pourcentage)		Population density (per km²) Densité de population (pour km²)	Surface area Superficie (000 km²)
		Total	Male Hommes	Females Femmes		Aged 0 to 14 years old âgée de 0 à 14 ans	Aged 60+ years old âgée de 60 ans ou plus		
Israel	2005	6.53	3.22	3.31	97.3	27.9	13.2	301.7	...
Israël	2010	7.35	3.63	3.72	97.6	27.3	14.9	339.5	...
	2017	8.24	4.09	4.15	98.7	27.9	16.1	381.0	22
	2019	8.52	4.24	4.28	99.0	27.9	16.3	393.7	...
Italy	2005	58.28	28.30	29.99	94.4	14.2	25.1	198.1	...
Italie	2010	59.33	28.70	30.62	93.7	14.1	26.7	201.7	...
	2017	60.67	29.48	31.19	94.5	13.5	28.6	206.3	302
	2019	60.55	29.46	31.09	94.8	13.2	29.4	205.9	...
Jamaica	2005	2.74	1.36	1.38	98.2	30.1	10.7	253.0	...
Jamaïque	2010	2.81	1.40	1.41	98.9	27.0	11.4	259.5	...
	2017	2.92	1.45	1.47	98.7	24.0	12.4	269.7	11
	2019	2.95	1.46	1.48	98.6	23.5	13.0	272.2	...
Japan	2005	128.33	62.89	65.44	96.1	13.8	26.3	352.0	...
Japon	2007	128.49	62.92	65.58	95.9	13.6	27.9	352.5	378[43]
	2010	128.54	62.87	65.67	95.7	13.4	30.3	352.6	...
	2019	126.86	61.95	64.91	95.4	12.6	34.0	348.0	...
Jordan	2005	5.77	2.97	2.79	106.6	38.2	5.2	64.9	...
Jordanie	2010	7.26	3.70	3.56	104.1	37.5	5.4	81.8	...
	2017	9.79	4.95	4.83	102.5	34.9	5.7	110.2	89
	2019	10.10	5.11	4.99	102.5	33.6	5.9	113.8	...
Kazakhstan	2005	15.40	7.42	7.98	92.9	24.5	10.1	5.7	...
Kazakhstan	2010	16.25	7.86	8.40	93.6	24.1	9.9	6.0	...
	2017	18.08	8.76	9.32	94.0	27.9	11.3	6.7	2 725
	2019	18.55	9.00	9.55	94.2	28.9	11.9	6.9	...
Kenya	2005	36.62	18.17	18.45	98.5	44.0	3.2	64.4	...
Kenya	2010	42.03	20.87	21.16	98.6	43.4	3.2	73.8	...
	2017	50.22	24.95	25.27	98.7	40.4	3.8	88.2	592
	2019	52.57	26.12	26.45	98.8	39.2	4.0	92.4	...
Kiribati	2005	0.09	0.05	0.05	97.1	36.9	5.4	114.0	...
Kiribati	2010	0.10	0.05	0.05	96.9	36.1	5.5	127.1	...
	2017	0.11	0.06	0.06	96.6	35.1	6.1	140.9	1[44]
	2019	0.12	0.06	0.06	96.7	35.8	6.5	145.2	...
Kuwait	2005	2.27	1.34	0.93	144.2	26.0	3.6	127.4	...
Koweït	2010	2.99	1.73	1.26	137.1	23.2	3.4	167.9	...
	2017	4.06	2.43	1.63	149.2	21.4	5.0	227.6	18
	2019	4.21	2.56	1.64	155.9	21.6	6.0	236.1	...
Kyrgyzstan	2005	5.08	2.52	2.56	98.3	31.0	7.1	26.5	...
Kirghizistan	2010	5.42	2.68	2.74	97.7	29.9	6.4	28.3	...
	2017	6.19	3.06	3.13	97.9	32.2	7.4	32.3	200
	2019	6.42	3.17	3.24	97.9	32.5	7.8	33.5	...
Lao People's Dem. Rep.	2005	5.75	2.85	2.91	97.9	40.3	5.5	24.9	...
Rép. dém. populaire lao	2010	6.25	3.10	3.15	98.4	36.4	5.6	27.1	...
	2017	6.95	3.49	3.46	100.9	32.9	6.4	30.1	237
	2019	7.17	3.60	3.57	100.8	32.3	6.6	31.1	...
Latvia	2005	2.25	1.03	1.22	84.7	14.7	22.5	36.2	...
Lettonie	2010	2.12	0.97	1.15	84.5	14.1	23.6	34.1	...
	2017	1.95	0.90	1.05	85.0	15.6	26.5	31.4	65
	2019	1.91	0.88	1.03	85.3	16.3	27.1	30.7	...
Lebanon	2005	4.70	2.39	2.31	103.6	30.3	8.1	459.3	...
Liban	2010	4.95	2.52	2.44	103.2	25.8	9.2	484.2	...
	2017	6.82	3.43	3.39	101.2	26.6	10.1	666.6	10
	2019	6.86	3.45	3.41	101.3	25.6	10.8	670.2	...
Lesotho	2005	2.00	0.96	1.03	93.4	37.2	6.5	65.7	...
Lesotho	2010	2.00	0.97	1.03	94.6	34.9	7.0	65.7	...
	2017	2.09	1.03	1.06	97.1	33.0	7.4	68.9	30
	2019	2.13	1.05	1.08	97.3	32.5	7.5	70.0	...

Country or area Pays ou zone	Year Année	Mid-year population estimates and projections (millions) Estimations et projections de population au milieu de l'année (millions)			Sex Ratio (males per 100 females) Rapport des sexes (hommes pour 100 femmes)	Population age distribution (percentage) Répartition par âge de la population (pourcentage)		Population density (per km²) Densité de population (pour km²)	Surface area Superficie (000 km²)
		Total	Male Hommes	Females Femmes		Aged 0 to 14 years old âgée de 0 à 14 ans	Aged 60+ years old âgée de 60 ans ou plus		
Liberia	2005	3.22	1.61	1.61	100.0	42.9	5.3	33.4	...
Libéria	2010	3.89	1.95	1.94	100.3	43.0	5.0	40.4	...
	2017	4.70	2.36	2.34	100.8	41.5	5.1	48.8	111
	2019	4.94	2.48	2.46	101.0	40.8	5.2	51.3	...
Libya	2005	5.80	2.99	2.81	106.4	30.2	5.9	3.3	...
Libye	2010	6.20	3.16	3.03	104.3	28.8	5.9	3.5	...
	2017	6.58	3.33	3.26	102.2	28.5	6.5	3.7	1 676
	2019	6.78	3.42	3.35	102.0	28.1	6.7	3.9	...
Liechtenstein	2005	0.03	...	...	97.0[15]	17.5[15]	16.8[15]	217.8	...
Liechtenstein	2010	0.04	...	...	97.9	16.0	20.1	225.0	...
	2016	0.04[17]	...	...	98.4[15]	14.9[15]	22.7[15]	235.4[17]	...
	2017	0.04[17]	...	...	...	...	...	237.0[17]	~0
	2019	0.04	...	...	...	...	...	237.6	...
Lithuania	2005	3.34	1.55	1.79	86.8	16.8	21.1	53.4	...
Lituanie	2010	3.12	1.44	1.69	85.3	14.8	22.4	49.8	...
	2017	2.85	1.31	1.53	85.7	14.7	25.7	45.4	65
	2019	2.76	1.28	1.48	86.1	15.1	26.9	44.0	...
Luxembourg	2005	0.46	0.23	0.23	97.4	18.6	19.0	176.8	...
Luxembourg	2010	0.51	0.25	0.26	98.7	17.6	19.0	196.1	...
	2017	0.59	0.30	0.29	101.5	16.1	19.4	228.5	3
	2019	0.62	0.31	0.30	102.1	15.7	19.7	237.7	...
Madagascar	2005	18.34	9.13	9.21	99.2	44.7	4.4	31.5	...
Madagascar	2010	21.15	10.54	10.62	99.3	43.5	4.3	36.4	...
	2017	25.57	12.75	12.82	99.5	41.0	4.8	44.0	587
	2019	26.97	13.45	13.52	99.5	40.4	4.9	46.4	...
Malawi	2005	12.63	6.21	6.41	96.9	46.4	4.5	133.9	...
Malawi	2010	14.54	7.15	7.39	96.9	46.4	4.2	154.2	...
	2017	17.67	8.71	8.96	97.2	44.3	4.1	187.4	118
	2019	18.63	9.19	9.44	97.3	43.5	4.1	197.6	...
Malaysia	2005[45]	25.69	13.17	12.52	105.2	30.5	7.1	78.2	...
Malaisie	2010[45]	28.21	14.55	13.66	106.5	28.0	7.9	85.9	...
	2017	31.10[45]	16.00[45]	15.10[45]	105.9[45]	24.3	9.9[45]	94.7[45]	330
	2019[45]	31.95	16.42	15.53	105.8	23.7	10.6	97.2	...
Maldives	2005	0.32	0.17	0.15	109.4	31.5	6.5	1 065.4	...
Maldives	2010	0.37	0.20	0.17	119.0	25.3	6.2	1 219.1	...
	2017	0.50	0.31	0.19	162.1	20.4[45]	5.8	1 654.7	~0
	2019	0.53	0.34	0.19	172.4	19.9	5.8	1 769.8	...
Mali	2005	12.78	6.36	6.42	99.1	46.9	4.6	10.5	...
Mali	2010	15.05	7.52	7.53	99.8	47.5	4.2	12.3	...
	2017	18.51	9.26	9.25	100.2	47.7	4.0	15.2	1 240
	2019	19.66	9.84	9.81	100.3	47.3	3.9	16.1	...
Malta	2005	0.40	0.20	0.20	98.4	17.4	18.9	1 264.5	...
Malte	2010	0.41	0.21	0.21	98.5	15.0	23.0	1 294.5	...
	2017	0.44	0.22	0.22	100.5	14.2	26.5	1 368.5	~0
	2019	0.44	0.22	0.22	100.5	14.3	27.6	1 376.2	...
Marshall Islands	2004	0.05	...	...	104.0[24,46]	40.6[24,46]	3.6[24,46]	289.3	...
Îles Marshall	2005	0.05	...	...	...	...	...	289.2	...
	2010	0.05	...	...	105.2[24,46]	40.9[24,46]	4.5[24,46]	291.3	...
	2016	0.05[17]	...	...	# 104.5	# 39.0	# 5.5	294.8[17]	...
	2017	0.05[17]	...	...	...	...	...	295.2[17]	~0
	2019	0.06	...	...	...	...	...	326.6	...
Martinique	2005	0.40	0.19	0.21	87.3	21.1	18.0	374.7	...
Martinique	2010	0.39	0.18	0.21	85.8	19.5	20.6	372.3	...
	2017	0.38	0.17	0.20	85.9	16.5	26.9	354.7	1
	2019	0.38	0.17	0.20	85.4	16.0	28.4	354.3	...
Mauritania	2005	3.02	1.51	1.52	99.5	42.2	4.9	2.9	...
Mauritanie	2010	3.49	1.75	1.75	100.0	41.2	4.8	3.4	...
	2017	4.28	2.15	2.13	100.6	40.3	4.9	4.2	1 031
	2019	4.53	2.27	2.25	100.8	39.9	5.0	4.4	...

Country or area Pays ou zone	Year Année	Mid-year population estimates and projections (millions) Estimations et projections de population au milieu de l'année (millions)			Sex Ratio (males per 100 females) Rapport des sexes (hommes pour 100 femmes)	Population age distribution (percentage) Répartition par âge de la population (pourcentage)		Population density (per km²) Densité de population (pour km²)	Surface area Superficie (000 km²)
		Total	Male Hommes	Females Femmes		Aged 0 to 14 years old âgée de 0 à 14 ans	Aged 60+ years old âgée de 60 ans ou plus		
Mauritius	2005[47]	1.22	0.61	0.62	98.3	24.7	9.6	602.0	...
Maurice	2010[47]	1.25	0.62	0.63	98.3	21.9	12.1	614.8	...
	2017	1.26[47]	0.63[47]	0.64[47]	97.9[47]	18.4	16.6[47]	622.9[47]	2[48]
	2019[47]	1.27	0.63	0.64	97.6	17.3	17.8	625.5	...
Mayotte	2005	0.18	0.09	0.09	97.2	42.4	4.8	474.9	...
Mayotte	2010	0.21	0.10	0.11	95.6	42.9	5.1	556.6	...
	2019	0.27	0.13	0.14	96.7	39.6	6.0	709.7	...
Mexico	2005	106.01	51.84	54.17	95.7	31.8	8.1	54.5	...
Mexique	2010	114.09	55.83	58.27	95.8	29.5	8.8	58.7	...
	2017	124.78	61.02	63.75	95.7	26.9	10.4	64.2	1 964
	2019	127.58	62.40	65.17	95.8	26.2	11.0	65.6	...
Micronesia (Fed. States of)	2005	0.11	0.05	0.05	103.3	38.9	5.4	151.6	...
Micronésie (États féd. de)	2010	0.10	0.05	0.05	103.1	35.7	5.4	147.0	...
	2017	0.11	0.06	0.05	103.4	32.0	7.0	159.2	1
	2019	0.11	0.06	0.06	103.4	31.5	7.6	162.6	...
Monaco	2000	0.03	...	...	94.3[15]	13.2[15]	28.9[15]	21 531.5	...
Monaco	2005	0.03	...	...	...	...	...	22 679.9	...
	2008	0.04	...	...	94.7[15]	12.7[15]	31.2[15]	24 062.4	...
	2010	0.04	...	...	...	...	...	24 895.3	...
	2017	0.04[17]	...	...	...	...	...	25 969.8[17]	~0
	2019	0.04	...	...	...	...	...	26 150.3	...
Mongolia	2005	2.53	1.26	1.27	99.0	28.9	5.6	1.6	...
Mongolie	2010	2.72	1.35	1.37	98.4	27.0	5.6	1.8	...
	2017	3.11	1.54	1.58	97.5	29.9	6.5	2.0	1 564
	2019	3.23	1.59	1.64	97.2	30.8	7.0	2.1	...
Montenegro	2005	0.62	0.30	0.31	96.9	20.2	17.0	45.8	...
Monténégro	2010	0.62	0.31	0.32	97.6	19.2	17.9	46.4	...
	2017	0.63	0.31	0.32	97.8	18.3	21.1	46.7	14
	2019	0.63	0.31	0.32	97.8	18.2	21.7	46.7	...
Montserrat	2001	~0.00	...	...	116.6	19.3	19.9	45.1	...
Montserrat	2004	~0.00	...	...	112.7			46.4	...
	2005	~0.00	...	...	...	...	...	47.8	...
	2006	~0.00	...	...	108.7[49]	19.6[49]	19.0[49]	48.5	...
	2010	~0.00	...	...	...	...	...	49.4	...
	2011	0.01	...	...	107.2[15]	19.7[15]	19.6[15]	49.9	...
	2016	0.01[17]	...	...	106.0	...	...	51.5[17]	...
	2017	0.01[17]	...	...	...	...	...	51.8[17]	~0
	2019	0.01	...	...	...	...	...	49.9	...
Morocco	2005	30.46	15.05	15.41	97.6	30.8	8.2	68.2	...
Maroc	2010	32.34	15.95	16.40	97.3	28.5	8.6	72.5	...
	2017	35.58	17.64	17.94	98.3	27.5	10.6	79.7	447
	2019	36.47	18.09	18.38	98.4	27.0	11.4	81.7	...
Mozambique	2005	20.49	9.85	10.65	92.5	45.2	4.9	26.1	...
Mozambique	2010	23.53	11.35	12.18	93.2	45.7	4.7	29.9	...
	2017	28.65	13.89	14.76	94.1	45.0	4.4	36.4	799
	2019	30.37	14.75	15.62	94.4	44.4	4.4	38.6	...
Myanmar	2005	48.95	23.67	25.28	93.6	31.2	6.9	74.9	...
Myanmar	2010	50.60	24.40	26.20	93.1	30.0	7.3	77.5	...
	2017	53.38	25.73	27.65	93.0	26.8	9.1	81.7	677
	2019	54.05	26.04	28.00	93.0	25.9	9.7	82.7	...
Namibia	2005	1.94	0.94	1.00	93.2	39.4	5.5	2.4	...
Namibie	2010	2.12	1.02	1.09	93.5	37.4	5.8	2.6	...
	2017	2.40	1.16	1.24	93.9	36.9	5.6	2.9	824
	2019	2.49	1.21	1.29	94.0	36.9	5.6	3.0	...

Country or area / Pays ou zone	Year / Année	Mid-year population estimates and projections (millions) / Estimations et projections de population au milieu de l'année (millions)			Sex Ratio (males per 100 females) / Rapport des sexes (hommes pour 100 femmes)	Population age distribution (percentage) / Répartition par âge de la population (pourcentage)		Population density (per km²) / Densité de population (pour km²)	Surface area / Superficie (000 km²)
		Total	Male / Hommes	Females / Femmes		Aged 0 to 14 years old / âgée de 0 à 14 ans	Aged 60+ years old / âgée de 60 ans ou plus		
Nauru	2002	0.01	...	...	104.2	38.1	2.5	504.0	...
Nauru	2005	0.01	...	...	...	...	...	505.7	...
	2010	0.01	...	...	...	...	...	501.3	...
	2016	0.01[17]	...	...	# 101.9	# 39.5	# 4.0	567.4[17]	...
	2017	0.01[17]	...	...	...	...	...	568.0[17]	~0
	2019	0.01	...	...	...	...	...	537.8	...
Nepal	2005	25.74	12.79	12.96	98.7	39.3	6.7	179.6	...
Népal	2010	27.01	13.30	13.72	96.9	36.3	7.5	188.4	...
	2017	27.63	12.56	15.08	83.3	31.3	8.5	192.8	147
	2019	28.61	13.05	15.56	83.8	29.6	8.6	199.6	...
Netherlands	2005	16.37	8.12	8.25	98.4	18.3	19.3	485.4	...
Pays-Bas	2010	16.68	8.28	8.40	98.6	17.5	22.0	494.7	...
	2017	17.02	8.47	8.55	99.0	16.4	25.0	504.8	42
	2019	17.10	8.51	8.58	99.2	15.9	26.1	507.0	...
New Caledonia	2005	0.24	0.12	0.12	101.7	27.9	9.5	12.9	...
Nouvelle-Calédonie	2010	0.25	0.13	0.13	101.5	25.8	11.0	13.9	...
	2017	0.28	0.14	0.14	101.5	23.0	13.0	15.2	19
	2019	0.28	0.14	0.14	101.2	22.4	13.8	15.5	...
New Zealand	2005	4.14	2.03	2.11	96.0	21.5	16.4	15.7	...
Nouvelle-Zélande	2010	4.37	2.15	2.22	96.5	20.5	18.4	16.6	...
	2017	4.70	2.31	2.39	96.7	19.7	20.9	17.9	268
	2019	4.78	2.35	2.43	96.7	19.6	21.7	18.2	...
Nicaragua	2005	5.44	2.68	2.75	97.4	36.2	6.0	45.2	...
Nicaragua	2010	5.82	2.87	2.96	97.1	33.3	6.3	48.4	...
	2017	6.38	3.15	3.24	97.2	30.5	7.9	53.1	130
	2019	6.55	3.23	3.32	97.2	29.9	8.4	54.4	...
Niger	2005	13.62	6.78	6.84	99.2	49.2	4.1	10.8	...
Niger	2010	16.46	8.23	8.24	99.9	50.0	4.2	13.0	...
	2017	21.60	10.84	10.76	100.8	50.1	4.1	17.1	1 267
	2019	23.31	11.71	11.60	101.0	49.8	4.1	18.4	...
Nigeria	2005	138.87	70.12	68.74	102.0	43.7	4.6	152.5	...
Nigéria	2010	158.50	80.16	78.34	102.3	44.0	4.5	174.0	...
	2017	190.87	96.69	94.19	102.7	44.0	4.5	209.6	924
	2019	200.96	101.83	99.13	102.7	43.7	4.5	220.7	...
Niue	2005	~0.00	...	...	94.8[15]	26.1[15]	15.1[15]	6.5	...
Nioué	2010	~0.00	...	...	101.9[15]	25.7[15]	16.8[15]	6.3	...
	2016	~0.00[17]	...	...	# 100.0	# 22.8	# 20.1	6.2[17]	...
	2017	~0.00[17]	...	...	...	...	...	6.2[17]	~0
	2019	~0.00	...	...	...	...	...	6.2	...
North Macedonia	2005	2.06	1.03	1.03	99.9	20.2	15.3	81.7	...
Macédoine du Nord	2010	2.07	1.03	1.04	99.9	17.9	16.4	82.1	...
	2017	2.08	1.04	1.04	100.2	16.7	19.4	82.6	26
	2019	2.08	1.04	1.04	100.1	16.4	20.3	82.6	...
Northern Mariana Islands	2005	0.06	...	...	83.3[24]	22.9[24,50]	3.7[24,50]	138.6	...
Îles Mariannes du Nord	2010	0.05	...	...	106.2	26.7	5.8	118.3	...
	2016	0.06[17]	...	...	# 107.1	# 23.5	# 10.0	119.6[17]	...
	2017	0.06[17]	...	...	...	...	...	119.9[17]	~0
	2019	0.06	...	...	...	...	...	124.4	...
Norway	2005[10]	4.63	2.30	2.33	98.5	19.6	19.8	12.7	...
Norvège	2010[10]	4.89	2.44	2.44	100.0	18.8	21.0	13.4	...
	2017	5.30[10]	2.67[10]	2.62[10]	101.8[10]	17.7	22.4[10]	14.5[10]	386[10]
	2019[10]	5.38	2.72	2.66	102.1	17.4	23.0	14.7	...
Oman	2005	2.51	1.42	1.09	130.2	32.5	4.1	8.1	...
Oman	2010	3.04	1.83	1.21	152.0	25.7	3.9	9.8	...
	2017	4.67	3.07	1.59	193.0	22.0	4.0	15.1	310
	2019	4.98	3.28	1.69	194.3	22.4	4.2	16.1	...
Other non-specified areas	2005	22.71	11.49	11.21	102.5	19.0	13.1	641.2	...
Autres zones non-spécifiées	2010	23.19	11.65	11.53	101.0	15.9	15.2	654.8	...
	2019	23.77	11.82	11.95	98.9	12.8	22.1	671.4	...

Population, surface area and density *(continued)*

Population, superficie et densité *(suite)*

Country or area Pays ou zone	Year Année	Mid-year population estimates and projections (millions) Estimations et projections de population au milieu de l'année (millions)			Sex Ratio (males per 100 females) Rapport des sexes (hommes pour 100 femmes)	Population age distribution (percentage) Répartition par âge de la population (pourcentage)		Population density (per km²) Densité de population (pour km²)	Surface area Superficie (000 km²)
		Total	Male Hommes	Females Femmes		Aged 0 to 14 years old âgée de 0 à 14 ans	Aged 60+ years old âgée de 60 ans ou plus		
Pakistan	2005	160.30	82.68	77.63	106.5	40.0	6.3	207.9	...
Pakistan	2010	179.42	92.43	87.00	106.2	37.7	6.3	232.8	...
	2017	207.91	106.99	100.91	106.0	35.5	6.5	269.7	796
	2019	216.57	111.45	105.12	106.0	35.1	6.6	280.9	...
Palau	2005	0.02	...	...	116.2[15]	24.1[15]	8.2[15]	43.3	...
Palaos	2010	0.02	...	...	...	...	...	44.5	...
	2016	0.02[17]	...	...	# 113.3	# 20.3	# 13.1	46.7[17]	...
	2017	0.02[17]	...	...	...	...	...	47.2[17]	~0
	2019	0.02	...	...	...	...	...	39.1	...
Panama	2005	3.33	1.68	1.65	101.3	30.4	8.8	44.8	...
Panama	2010	3.64	1.83	1.81	101.0	29.1	9.7	49.0	...
	2017	4.11	2.06	2.05	100.5	27.3	11.4	55.2	75
	2019	4.25	2.13	2.12	100.3	26.8	11.9	57.1	...
Papua New Guinea	2005	6.49	3.30	3.19	103.5	39.2	5.0	14.3	...
Papouasie-Nvl-Guinée	2010	7.31	3.72	3.59	103.6	38.3	5.3	16.1	...
	2017	8.44	4.31	4.13	104.2	36.1	5.7	18.6	463
	2019	8.78	4.48	4.30	104.3	35.5	5.9	19.4	...
Paraguay	2005	5.82	2.96	2.87	103.1	35.5	7.0	14.7	...
Paraguay	2010	6.25	3.18	3.07	103.5	32.9	7.8	15.7	...
	2017	6.87	3.49	3.37	103.5	29.7	9.3	17.3	407
	2019	7.04	3.58	3.46	103.4	29.2	9.7	17.7	...
Peru	2005	27.87	13.89	13.97	99.4	32.0	7.9	21.8	...
Pérou	2010	29.03	14.47	14.55	99.5	30.1	8.9	22.7	...
	2017	31.44	15.61	15.83	98.6	26.4	11.3	24.6	1 285
	2019	32.51	16.15	16.36	98.7	25.3	12.1	25.4	...
Philippines	2005	86.33	43.39	42.94	101.0	37.1	5.5	289.5	...
Philippines	2010	93.97	47.40	46.57	101.8	34.0	6.5	315.1	...
	2017	105.17	52.88	52.29	101.1	31.5	7.8	352.7	300
	2019	108.12	54.32	53.80	101.0	30.5	8.3	362.6	...
Poland	2005	38.37	18.58	19.79	93.9	16.6	17.0	125.3	...
Pologne	2010	38.33	18.53	19.80	93.6	15.2	19.4	125.2	...
	2017	37.95	18.40	19.55	94.1	14.9	24.2	123.9	313
	2019	37.89	18.36	19.53	94.0	15.2	25.4	123.7	...
Portugal	2005	10.51	5.08	5.43	93.6	15.4	22.4	114.7	...
Portugal	2010	10.60	5.07	5.53	91.8	15.0	24.7	115.7	...
	2017	10.29	4.87	5.42	89.7	13.7[13]	27.9	112.3	92
	2019	10.23	4.84	5.39	89.7	13.3	28.9	111.7	...
Puerto Rico	2005	3.63	1.74	1.89	92.1	22.3	16.9	409.5	...
Porto Rico	2010	3.58	1.72	1.86	92.4	20.6	18.3	403.6	...
	2017	3.16	1.51	1.66	91.0	17.4	23.5	356.7	9
	2019	2.93	1.39	1.54	90.3	16.3	26.2	330.7	...
Qatar	2005	0.87	0.58	0.28	208.2	21.7	2.5	74.5	...
Qatar	2010	1.86	1.42	0.44	324.8	12.9	1.6	159.9	...
	2017	2.72	2.06	0.66	311.0	13.5	2.7	234.7	12
	2019	2.83	2.13	0.70	305.4	13.6	3.3	243.9	...
Republic of Korea	2005	48.70	24.43	24.27	100.7	18.8	12.8	500.9	...
République de Corée	2010	49.55	24.82	24.72	100.4	16.1	15.3	509.6	...
	2017	51.10	25.60	25.50	100.4	13.2	20.1	525.5	100
	2019	51.23	25.65	25.58	100.3	12.7	22.1	526.8	...
Republic of Moldova	2005[51]	4.16	1.99	2.17	91.9	18.5	13.6	126.6	...
République de Moldova	2010[51]	4.09	1.96	2.12	92.6	16.5	14.1	124.4	...
	2017	4.06[51]	1.95[51]	2.11[51]	92.3[51]	15.8	17.5[51]	123.6[51]	34
	2019[51]	4.04	1.94	2.11	92.0	15.9	18.4	123.1	...
Réunion	2005	0.79	0.39	0.40	96.4	26.9	10.3	316.6	...
Réunion	2010	0.83	0.40	0.43	93.9	25.4	12.2	332.2	...
	2017	0.88	0.42	0.45	93.9	23.6[51]	16.4	350.5	3
	2019	0.89	0.43	0.46	93.8	22.8	17.6	355.6	...

Country or area Pays ou zone	Year Année	Mid-year population estimates and projections (millions) Estimations et projections de population au milieu de l'année (millions)			Sex Ratio (males per 100 females) Rapport des sexes (hommes pour 100 femmes)	Population age distribution (percentage) Répartition par âge de la population (pourcentage)		Population density (per km²) Densité de population (pour km²)	Surface area (000 km²) Superficie (000 km²)
		Total	Male Hommes	Females Femmes		Aged 0 to 14 years old âgée de 0 à 14 ans	Aged 60+ years old âgée de 60 ans ou plus		
Romania	2005	21.42	10.44	10.98	95.1	15.7	19.7	93.0	...
Roumanie	2010	20.47	9.94	10.53	94.4	15.8	21.3	88.9	...
	2017	19.65	9.57	10.09	94.8	15.4	24.9	85.4	238
	2019	19.36	9.42	9.95	94.7	15.6	25.7	84.1	...
Russian Federation	2005	143.67	66.85	76.82	87.0	15.2	17.2	8.8	...
Fédération de Russie	2010	143.48	66.54	76.94	86.5	14.9	18.0	8.8	...
	2017	145.53	67.43	78.10	86.3	17.6	21.0	8.9	17 098
	2019	145.87	67.60	78.27	86.4	18.2	22.0	8.9	...
Rwanda	2005	8.84	4.33	4.51	95.8	42.4	4.2	358.3	...
Rwanda	2010	10.04	4.92	5.12	96.1	41.5	4.1	406.9	...
	2017	11.98	5.89	6.09	96.6	40.1	4.7	485.6	26
	2019	12.63	6.21	6.42	96.7	39.8	5.0	511.8	...
Saint Barthélemy	2005	0.01	...	...	...	...	...	388.8	...
Saint-Barthélemy	2010	0.01	...	...	...	...	...	419.7	...
	2019	0.01	...	...	...	...	...	447.6	...
Saint Helena [52]	2005	~0.00	...	...	...	...	...	11.0	...
Sainte-Hélène [52]	2010	~0.00	...	...	...	...	...	10.7	...
	2017	~0.00[17]	...	...	...	...	...	10.4[17]	~0
	2019	0.01	...	...	...	...	...	15.5	...
Saint Kitts and Nevis	2000	0.05	...	...	101.9	28.0	9.9	174.5	...
Saint-Kitts-et-Nevis	2005	0.05	...	...	* 95.7	...	...	187.0	...
	2010	0.05	...	...	* 95.7	...	...	197.9	...
	2011	0.05	...	...	* 97.0	...	...	200.0	...
	2017	0.06[17]	...	...	...	...	...	212.9[17]	~0
	2019	0.05	...	...	...	...	...	203.2	...
Saint Lucia	2005	0.16	0.08	0.08	96.2	27.8	9.6	267.9	...
Sainte-Lucie	2010	0.17	0.09	0.09	96.9	23.2	11.9	285.4	...
	2017	0.18	0.09	0.09	97.0	18.9	13.6	296.6	1[53]
	2019	0.18	0.09	0.09	97.0	18.2	14.4	299.7	...
Saint Martin (French part)	2005	0.03	...	...	...	...	...	646.2	...
St-Martin (partie française)	2010	0.04	...	...	...	...	...	709.1	...
	2019	0.04	...	...	...	...	...	717.0	...
Saint Pierre and Miquelon	2005	0.01	...	...	...	...	...	27.2	...
Saint-Pierre-et-Miquelon	2006	0.01	...	...	98.2	19.1	17.8	27.2	...
	2010	0.01	...	...	...	...	...	27.3	...
	2017	0.01[17]	...	...	...	...	...	27.5[17]	~0
	2019	0.01	...	...	...	...	...	25.3	...
Saint Vincent & Grenadines	2005	0.11	0.05	0.05	102.1	28.6	9.3	278.5	...
Saint-Vincent-Grenadines	2010	0.11	0.06	0.05	103.7	25.8	11.3	277.6	...
	2017	0.11	0.06	0.05	103.4	22.9	13.7	281.6	~0
	2019	0.11	0.06	0.05	102.9	22.2	14.3	283.6	...
Samoa	2005	0.18	0.09	0.09	107.5	39.6	6.8	63.5	...
Samoa	2010	0.19	0.10	0.09	106.7	38.3	7.1	65.7	...
	2017	0.20	0.10	0.09	107.2	38.5	7.4	69.0	3
	2019	0.20	0.10	0.10	107.3	37.9	7.8	69.6	...
San Marino	2004	0.03	...	...	96.2[18]	15.2[18]	21.5[18]	481.1	...
Saint-Marin	2005	0.03	...	...	96.1[18]	...	...	487.3	...
	2010	0.03	...	...	* 93.5	* 20.9[54]	* 21.6[55]	518.5	...
	2015	0.03	...	...	94.9[18]	15.0[18]	24.1[18]	549.3	~0
	2017	0.03[17]	...	...	...	...	...	556.7[17]	~0
	2019	0.03	...	...	...	...	...	564.3	...
Sao Tome and Principe	2005	0.16	0.08	0.08	98.0	44.0	4.7	164.0	...
Sao Tomé-et-Principe	2010	0.18	0.09	0.09	99.9	43.4	4.4	187.9	...
	2017	0.21	0.10	0.10	100.1	42.9	4.7	215.7	1
	2019	0.22	0.11	0.11	100.2	42.1	4.9	224.0	...
Saudi Arabia	2005	23.82	13.26	10.56	125.6	33.9	4.4	11.1	...
Arabie saoudite	2010	27.42	15.43	11.99	128.6	29.7	4.5	12.8	...
	2017	33.10	18.98	14.13	134.3	25.3	5.4	15.4	2 207
	2019	34.27	19.78	14.49	136.6	24.9	5.7	15.9	...

Country or area Pays ou zone	Year Année	Mid-year population estimates and projections (millions) Estimations et projections de population au milieu de l'année (millions)			Sex Ratio (males per 100 females) Rapport des sexes (hommes pour 100 femmes)	Population age distribution (percentage) Répartition par âge de la population (pourcentage)		Population density (per km²) Densité de population (pour km²)	Surface area Superficie (000 km²)
		Total	Male Hommes	Females Femmes		Aged 0 to 14 years old âgée de 0 à 14 ans	Aged 60+ years old âgée de 60 ans ou plus		
Senegal	2005	11.09	5.42	5.67	95.5	43.7	4.9	57.6	...
Sénégal	2010	12.68	6.17	6.51	94.9	43.5	4.8	65.9	...
	2017	15.42	7.51	7.91	94.9	43.2	4.8	80.1	197[56]
	2019	16.30	7.95	8.35	95.2	42.8	4.8	84.6	...
Serbia	2005[57]	9.19	4.50	4.69	95.9	18.7	18.8	105.1	...
Serbie	2010[57]	8.99	4.41	4.58	96.1	17.3	21.1	102.8	...
	2017	8.83[57]	4.33[57]	4.50[57]	96.1[57]	15.8	24.9[57]	101.0[57]	88[58]
	2019[57]	8.77	4.30	4.47	96.0	15.5	25.2	100.3	...
Seychelles	2005	0.09	0.04	0.04	99.9	25.0	9.1	192.7	...
Seychelles	2010	0.09	0.05	0.04	106.6	22.8	9.9	198.4	...
	2017	0.10	0.05	0.05	105.7	23.5[57]	11.6	209.6	~0
	2019	0.10	0.05	0.05	105.5	23.7	12.5	212.5	...
Sierra Leone	2005	5.65	2.81	2.84	98.7	43.7	5.0	78.2	...
Sierra Leone	2010	6.42	3.19	3.22	99.1	43.0	4.8	88.9	...
	2017	7.49	3.73	3.75	99.5	41.4	4.6	103.7	72
	2019	7.81	3.90	3.91	99.6	40.7	4.6	108.2	...
Singapore	2005	4.27	2.16	2.11	102.2	17.2	10.7	6 093.8	...
Singapour	2010	5.13	2.68	2.46	108.9	14.0	12.7	7 330.2	...
	2017	5.71	2.99	2.72	109.8	12.2	17.8	8 154.3	1[59]
	2019	5.80	3.04	2.77	109.8	12.3	19.9	8 291.9	...
Sint Maarten (Dutch part)	2005	0.03	...	...	93.9[15]	...	...	956.8	...
St-Martin (partie néerland.)	2010	0.03	...	...	91.0[15]	...	...	974.2	...
	2013	0.04	...	...	95.8[15]	21.0[15]	10.4[15]	1 071.7	~0
	2014	0.04	...	...	95.7[15]	...	...	1 108.7	~0
	2017	0.04[17]	...	...	...	...	...	1 180.0[17]	~0
	2019	0.04	...	...	...	...	...	1 246.7	...
Slovakia	2005	5.40	2.62	2.78	94.1	16.8	16.1	112.3	...
Slovaquie	2010	5.40	2.62	2.78	94.2	15.3	17.8	112.4	...
	2017	5.45	2.65	2.80	94.7	15.3	21.8	113.3	49[60]
	2019	5.46	2.66	2.80	94.9	15.5	22.8	113.5	...
Slovenia	2005	2.00	0.98	1.02	95.7	14.0	20.8	99.1	...
Slovénie	2010	2.04	1.01	1.03	98.2	14.0	22.2	101.5	...
	2017	2.08	1.03	1.04	98.9	14.9	26.2	103.1	20
	2019	2.08	1.03	1.04	99.1	15.1	27.2	103.2	...
Solomon Islands	2005	0.47	0.24	0.23	104.4	41.3	4.9	16.8	...
Îles Salomon	2010	0.53	0.27	0.26	103.3	40.8	5.1	18.9	...
	2017	0.64	0.32	0.31	103.4	40.4	5.4	22.7	29
	2019	0.67	0.34	0.33	103.4	40.1	5.5	23.9	...
Somalia	2005	10.45	5.23	5.22	100.1	47.9	4.3	16.7	...
Somalie	2010	12.04	6.02	6.03	99.8	48.2	4.4	19.2	...
	2017	14.59	7.28	7.31	99.5	46.8	4.5	23.3	638
	2019	15.44	7.70	7.74	99.5	46.4	4.5	24.6	...
South Africa	2005	47.88	23.61	24.27	97.3	30.9	7.0	39.5	...
Afrique du Sud	2010	51.22	25.27	25.95	97.4	29.7	7.2	42.2	...
	2017	57.01	28.12	28.89	97.3	29.2	8.1	47.0	1 221
	2019	58.56	28.86	29.70	97.2	29.0	8.4	48.3	...
South Sudan	2005	7.54	3.76	3.78	99.6	44.3	5.1	12.3	...
Soudan du sud	2010	9.51	4.75	4.76	99.9	43.5	5.2	15.6	...
	2017	10.91	5.46	5.45	100.2	42.1	5.1	17.9	659
	2019	11.06	5.54	5.53	100.2	41.6	5.1	18.1	...
Spain	2005[61]	44.02	21.72	22.30	97.4	14.2	21.6	88.3	...
Espagne	2010[61]	46.93	23.20	23.73	97.7	14.8	22.2	94.1	...
	2017	46.65[61]	22.90[61]	23.75[61]	96.4[61]	14.7	24.8[61]	93.5[61]	506
	2019[61]	46.74	22.96	23.78	96.6	14.6	25.7	93.7	...
Sri Lanka	2005	19.55	9.64	9.91	97.3	25.6	10.4	311.7	...
Sri Lanka	2010	20.26	9.87	10.40	94.9	25.4	11.9	323.1	...
	2017	21.13	10.16	10.97	92.6	24.4[61]	15.0	336.9	66
	2019	21.32	10.23	11.09	92.3	24.0	15.9	340.0	...

Country or area Pays ou zone	Year Année	Total	Male Hommes	Females Femmes	Sex Ratio (males per 100 females) Rapport des sexes (hommes pour 100 femmes)	Aged 0 to 14 years old âgée de 0 à 14 ans	Aged 60+ years old âgée de 60 ans ou plus	Population density (per km²) Densité de population (pour km²)	Surface area Superficie (000 km²)
State of Palestine	2005[1]	3.58	1.82	1.76	103.2	45.5	4.0	594.3	...
État de Palestine	2010[1]	4.06	2.06	2.00	103.0	42.3	4.4	673.7	
	2017	4.75[1]	2.41[1]	2.34[1]	103.0[1]	39.3	4.7[1]	788.6[1]	6
	2019[1]	4.98	2.53	2.46	102.9	38.6	4.8	827.5	
Sudan	2005	30.95	15.52	15.43	100.5	43.5	4.8	17.5	...
Soudan	2010	34.55	17.23	17.31	99.5	43.0	5.1	19.6	
	2019	42.81	21.39	21.43	99.8	40.2	5.6	24.3	...
Suriname	2005	0.50	0.25	0.25	101.8	31.3	8.5	3.2	...
Suriname	2010	0.53	0.27	0.26	101.5	29.4	9.1	3.4	
	2017	0.57	0.29	0.28	101.2	27.4	10.0	3.7	164
	2019	0.58	0.29	0.29	101.1	26.9	10.5	3.7	
Sweden	2005	9.04	4.48	4.56	98.4	17.4	23.5	22.0	...
Suède	2010	9.39	4.68	4.71	99.2	16.5	24.9	22.9	
	2017	9.90	4.96	4.95	100.1	17.5	25.5	24.1	439
	2019	10.04	5.03	5.01	100.3	17.6	25.8	24.5	
Switzerland	2005	7.39	3.62	3.77	95.9	16.3	21.3	186.9	...
Suisse	2010	7.81	3.85	3.96	97.0	15.1	22.8	197.6	
	2017	8.46	4.19	4.27	98.2	14.9	24.1	214.0	41
	2019	8.59	4.26	4.33	98.4	14.9	24.8	217.4	
Syrian Arab Republic	2005	18.36	9.37	8.99	104.2	39.3	4.9	100.0	...
République arabe syrienne	2010	21.36	10.79	10.58	102.0	37.4	5.0	116.3	
	2017	17.10	8.59	8.50	101.0	31.8	6.8	93.1	185
	2019	17.07	8.55	8.52	100.5	31.1	7.3	93.0	
Tajikistan	2005	6.79	3.41	3.38	101.1	38.0	5.1	48.5	...
Tadjikistan	2010	7.53	3.80	3.73	101.8	35.7	4.8	53.8	
	2017	8.88	4.48	4.40	101.7	36.5	5.2	63.4	143
	2019	9.32	4.70	4.62	101.6	37.1	5.5	66.6	
Thailand	2005	65.42	32.17	33.24	96.8	21.3	11.1	128.0	...
Thaïlande	2010	67.20	32.93	34.26	96.1	19.2	12.9	131.5	
	2017	69.21	33.75	35.46	95.2	17.4	17.0	135.5	513
	2019	69.63	33.90	35.72	94.9	16.8	18.5	136.3	
Timor-Leste	2005	1.00	0.50	0.49	102.0	44.7	5.9	66.9	...
Timor-Leste	2010	1.09	0.55	0.54	102.2	42.5	6.3	73.5	...
	2017	1.24	0.63	0.61	102.2	38.3	6.4	83.6	15
	2019	1.29	0.65	0.64	102.2	37.3	6.5	87.0	
Togo	2005	5.61	2.78	2.83	97.9	42.8	4.5	103.2	...
Togo	2010	6.42	3.19	3.24	98.4	42.8	4.4	118.1	
	2017	7.70	3.83	3.87	98.9	41.6	4.6	141.5	57
	2019	8.08	4.02	4.06	99.0	41.0	4.7	148.6	...
Tokelau	2001	~0.00	...	...	98.1	40.7	9.5	150.3	
Tokélaou	2005	~0.00	...	...	...	...	...	120.8	...
	2006	~0.00	...	...	102.6	36.6	11.3	116.7	...
	2010	~0.00	...	...	...	...	...	114.0	...
	2016	~0.00[17]	...	...	# 100.0	# 28.3	# 12.2	128.2[17]	...
	2017	~0.00[17]	...	...	...	...	...	130.0[17]	~0
	2019	~0.00	...	...	...	...	...	134.0	
Tonga	2005	0.10	0.05	0.05	100.8	38.2	8.2	140.1	...
Tonga	2010	0.10	0.05	0.05	100.5	37.4	7.9	144.4	
	2017	0.10	0.05	0.05	100.0	35.8	8.7	141.7	1
	2019	0.10	0.05	0.05	100.1	35.1	8.7	145.1	
Trinidad and Tobago	2005	1.30	0.64	0.65	98.5	21.9	10.8	252.7	...
Trinité-et-Tobago	2010	1.33	0.66	0.67	98.1	20.7	12.4	258.9	
	2017	1.38	0.68	0.70	97.7	20.5	15.4	269.8	5
	2019	1.40	0.69	0.71	97.6	20.3	16.4	271.9	
Tunisia	2005	10.11	5.06	5.05	100.2	25.5	10.1	65.1	...
Tunisie	2010	10.64	5.30	5.33	99.5	23.3	10.4	68.5	...
	2017	11.43	5.67	5.77	98.2	24.1	12.4	73.6	164
	2019	11.69	5.80	5.90	98.3	24.2	13.1	75.3	...

Country or area Pays ou zone	Year Année	Mid-year population estimates and projections (millions) Estimations et projections de population au milieu de l'année (millions)			Sex Ratio (males per 100 females) Rapport des sexes (hommes pour 100 femmes)	Population age distribution (percentage) Répartition par âge de la population (pourcentage)		Population density (per km²) Densité de population (pour km²)	Surface area Superficie (000 km²)
		Total	Male Hommes	Females Femmes		Aged 0 to 14 years old âgée de 0 à 14 ans	Aged 60+ years old âgée de 60 ans ou plus		
Turkey	2005	67.90	33.42	34.48	96.9	28.6	9.6	88.2	...
Turquie	2010	72.33	35.56	36.76	96.7	26.9	10.4	94.0	...
	2017	81.12	39.98	41.14	97.2	25.0	12.1	105.4	784
	2019	83.43	41.17	42.26	97.4	24.3	12.7	108.4	...
Turkmenistan	2005	4.75	2.34	2.42	96.8	32.6	6.1	10.1	...
Turkménistan	2010	5.09	2.50	2.58	96.8	29.5	6.1	10.8	...
	2017	5.76	2.84	2.92	97.0	30.9	7.3	12.3	488
	2019	5.94	2.93	3.02	97.0	30.8	7.8	12.6	...
Turks and Caicos Islands	2001	0.02	...	...	99.1	28.6	5.2	21.2	...
Îles Turques-et-Caïques	2005	0.03	...	...	99.1[15,24]	...	...	27.8	...
	2010	0.03	...	...	106.7[15,24]	...	...	32.6	...
	2017	0.04[17]	...	...	104.1[15,24]	19.2[15,24]	7.6[15,24]	37.3[17]	1[62]
	2019	0.04	...	...	...	...	...	40.2	...
Tuvalu	2002	0.01	...	...	97.9	36.2	8.6	321.2	...
Tuvalu	2005	0.01	...	...	...	...	...	334.2	...
	2010	0.01	...	...	...	...	...	351.0	...
	2016	0.01[17]	...	...	102.0	31.1	9.9	369.9[17]	...
	2017	0.01[17]	...	...	...	...	...	373.1[17]	~0
	2019	0.01	...	...	...	...	...	388.2	...
Uganda	2005	27.68	13.64	14.05	97.1	49.7	3.2	138.6	...
Ouganda	2010	32.43	15.91	16.51	96.4	49.1	3.0	162.3	...
	2017	41.17	20.25	20.92	96.8	47.3	3.1	206.0	242
	2019	44.27	21.81	22.46	97.1	46.5	3.2	221.6	...
Ukraine	2005[63]	46.89	21.75	25.14	86.5	14.6	20.4	80.9	...
Ukraine	2010[63]	45.79	21.14	24.66	85.7	14.1	21.0	79.0	...
	2017	44.49[63]	20.60[63]	23.89[63]	86.2[63]	15.6	22.8[63]	76.8[63]	604
	2019[63]	43.99	20.38	23.61	86.3	15.9	23.4	75.9	...
United Arab Emirates	2005	4.59	3.23	1.36	237.7	18.3	1.6	54.9	...
Émirats arabes unis	2010	8.55	6.40	2.15	296.9	13.2	1.4	102.3	...
	2017	9.49	6.60	2.89	228.1	14.5[63]	2.2	113.5	84
	2019	9.77	6.77	3.00	225.3	14.7	2.8	116.9	...
United Kingdom	2005	60.29	29.52	30.77	95.9	18.0	21.2	249.2	...
Royaume-Uni	2010	63.46	31.18	32.28	96.6	17.5	22.6	262.3	...
	2017	66.73	32.92	33.80	97.4	17.6	23.7	275.8	242
	2019	67.53	33.35	34.18	97.6	17.7	24.1	279.1	...
United Rep. of Tanzania	2005[64]	38.45	19.14	19.31	99.1	44.8	4.1	43.4	...
Rép.-Unie de Tanzanie	2010[64]	44.35	22.12	22.23	99.5	44.9	4.0	50.1	...
	2017	54.66[64]	27.29[64]	27.37[64]	99.7[64]	44.3	4.1[64]	61.7[64]	947
	2019[64]	58.01	28.98	29.02	99.8	43.8	4.2	65.5	...
United States of America	2005	294.99	145.57	149.43	97.4	20.9	16.7	32.2	...
États-Unis d'Amérique	2010	309.01	152.61	156.40	97.6	20.2	18.4	33.8	...
	2017	325.08	160.84	164.24	97.9	18.9[64]	21.5	35.5	9 834
	2019	329.06	162.83	166.24	97.9	18.5	22.4	36.0	...
United States Virgin Islands	2005	0.11	0.05	0.06	93.5	22.4	16.6	308.0	...
Îles Vierges américaines	2010	0.11	0.05	0.06	91.8	20.7	20.4	303.1	...
	2017	0.10	0.05	0.05	90.8	19.9	25.5	299.3	~0
	2019	0.10	0.05	0.05	90.6	19.5	26.9	298.8	...
Uruguay	2005	3.32	1.60	1.72	93.2	23.7	17.9	19.0	...
Uruguay	2010	3.36	1.62	1.74	93.0	22.2	18.5	19.2	...
	2017	3.44	1.66	1.78	93.3	20.8	19.6	19.6	174
	2019	3.46	1.67	1.79	93.4	20.5	20.0	19.8	...
Uzbekistan	2005	26.43	13.13	13.30	98.7	32.6	6.5	62.1	...
Ouzbékistan	2010	28.52	14.18	14.33	98.9	29.1	6.2	67.0	...
	2017	31.96	15.93	16.03	99.4	28.5	7.4	75.1	449
	2019	32.98	16.45	16.53	99.5	28.8	8.0	77.5	...
Vanuatu	2005	0.21	0.11	0.10	104.1	39.7	5.1	17.2	...
Vanuatu	2010	0.24	0.12	0.12	103.1	38.2	5.7	19.4	...
	2017	0.29	0.14	0.14	102.9	38.9	5.7	23.4	12
	2019	0.30	0.15	0.15	102.8	38.7	5.8	24.6	...

Country or area Pays ou zone	Year Année	Mid-year population estimates and projections (millions) Estimations et projections de population au milieu de l'année (millions)			Sex Ratio (males per 100 females) Rapport des sexes (hommes pour 100 femmes)	Population age distribution (percentage) Répartition par âge de la population (pourcentage)		Population density (per km²) Densité de population (pour km²)	Surface area Superficie (000 km²)
		Total	Male Hommes	Females Femmes		Aged 0 to 14 years old âgée de 0 à 14 ans	Aged 60+ years old âgée de 60 ans ou plus		
Venezuela (Boliv. Rep. of)	2005	26.43	13.23	13.20	100.2	31.7	7.5	30.0	...
Venezuela (Rép. boliv. du)	2010	28.44	14.19	14.25	99.6	29.9	8.4	32.2	...
	2017	29.40	14.55	14.85	98.0	28.0	10.5	33.3	912
	2019	28.52	14.05	14.47	97.1	27.4	11.6	32.3	...
Viet Nam	2005	83.83	41.53	42.30	98.2	27.1	8.6	270.4	...
Viet Nam	2010	87.97	43.75	44.22	98.9	23.6	8.8	283.7	...
	2017	94.60	47.19	47.41	99.5	23.1	11.0	305.1	331
	2019	96.46	48.15	48.31	99.7	23.2	11.9	311.1	...
Wallis and Futuna Islands	2003	0.01	...	...	100.6	...	...	104.7	...
Îles Wallis-et-Futuna	2005	0.01	...	...	...	...	...	104.1	...
	2008	0.01	...	...	98.4	...	...	99.9	...
	2010	0.01	...	...	...	...	...	95.9	...
	2016	0.01[17]	...	...	# 93.4	25.5	15.4	85.0[17]	...
	2017	0.01[17]	...	...	...	...	...	84.1[17]	~0
	2019	0.01	...	...	...	...	...	81.7	...
Western Sahara	2005	0.44	0.23	0.21	111.5	31.5	3.6	1.6	...
Sahara occidental	2010	0.48	0.25	0.23	111.2	29.4	3.8	1.8	...
	2017	0.55	0.29	0.26	110.1	28.1	5.4	2.1	266[85]
	2019	0.58	0.30	0.28	109.7	27.4	6.0	2.2	...
Yemen	2005	20.11	10.13	9.97	101.6	46.1	4.2	38.1	...
Yémen	2010	23.15	11.67	11.48	101.6	42.7	4.3	43.9	...
	2017	27.83	14.03	13.81	101.6	40.0	4.5	52.7	528
	2019	29.16	14.69	14.47	101.5	39.2	4.6	55.2	...
Zambia	2005	11.86	5.86	6.00	97.8	47.0	3.5	15.9	...
Zambie	2010	13.61	6.72	6.89	97.5	47.3	3.3	18.3	...
	2017	16.85	8.34	8.51	98.0	45.4	3.3	22.7	753
	2019	17.86	8.84	9.02	98.1	44.5	3.4	24.0	...
Zimbabwe	2005	12.08	5.78	6.29	91.9	41.3	4.7	31.2	...
Zimbabwe	2010	12.70	6.05	6.65	91.0	41.6	4.4	32.8	...
	2017	14.24	6.78	7.46	90.9	42.6	4.5	36.8	391
	2019	14.65	6.98	7.66	91.1	42.2	4.6	37.9	...

Source:

United Nations Population Division, New York, World Population Prospects: The 2019 Revision, last accessed June 2019.
United Nations Population Division, New York, World Population Prospects: The 2019 Revision; supplemented by data from the United Nations Statistics Division, New York, Demographic Yearbook 2015 and Secretariat for the Pacific Community (SPC) for small countries or areas, last accessed June 2019.
United Nations Statistics Division, New York, "Demographic Yearbook 2015" and the demographic statistics database, last accessed June 2017.

Source:

Organisation des Nations Unies, Division de la population, New York, « World Population Prospects: The 2019 Revision », denier accès juin 2019.
Organisation des Nations Unies, Division de la population, New York, « World Population Prospects: The 2019 Revision »; complétées par des données de l'Organisation des Nations Unies, Division de statistique, New York, Annuaire démographique 2015 et Secrétariat de la Communauté du Pacifique (SCP) pour petits pays ou zones, denier accès juin 2019.
Organisation des Nations Unies, Division de statistique, New York, Annuaire démographique 2015 et recueil de statistiques démographiques, denier accès juin 2017.

1	Including East Jerusalem.
2	Calculated by the UN Statistics Division.
3	Including Saint Helena.
4	Including Bermuda, Greenland, and Saint Pierre and Miquelon.
5	Including Anguilla, Bonaire, Sint Eustatius and Saba, British Virgin Islands, Cayman Islands, Dominica, Montserrat, Saint Kitts and Nevis, Sint Maarten (Dutch part) and Turks and Caicos Islands.
6	Including Falkland Islands (Malvinas).
7	Including the Faroe Islands and the Isle of Man.
8	Including Andorra, Gibraltar, Holy See, and San Marino.

1	Y compris Jérusalem-Est.
2	Calculés par la Division de statistique des Nations Unies.
3	Y compris Sainte-Hélène.
4	Y compris les Bermudes, le Groenland et Saint-Pierre-et-Miquelon.
5	Y compris Anguilla, les îles Bonaire, Saint-Eustache et Saba, les îles Caïmans, la Dominique, Montserrat, Saint-Kitts-et-Nevis, Saint-Martin (partie néerlandaise), les îles Turques-et-Caïques et les îles Vierges britanniques.
6	Y compris les îles Falkland (Malvinas).
7	Y compris les îles Féroé et l'île de Man.
8	Y compris Andorre, Gibraltar, Saint-Siège, et Saint-Marin.

9	Including Liechtenstein and Monaco.	9	Y compris le Liechtenstein et Monaco.
10	Including Svalbard and Jan Mayen Islands.	10	Y compris les îles Svalbard-et-Jan Mayen.
11	Including Christmas Island, Cocos (Keeling) Islands and Norfolk Island.	11	Y compris l'île Christmas, les îles des Cocos (Keeling) et l'île Norfolk.
12	Including Marshall Islands, Nauru, Northern Mariana Islands and Palau.	12	Y compris les îles Mariannes du Nord, les îles Marshall, Nauru et Palaos.
13	Including Pitcairn.	13	Y compris Pitcairn.
14	Including American Samoa, Cook Islands, Niue, Pitcairn, Tokelau, Tuvalu, and Wallis and Futuna Islands.	14	Y compris les îles Cook, Nioué, Pitcairn, Samoa américaines, Tokélaou, Tuvalu, et les îles Wallis-et-Futuna.
15	De jure population.	15	Population de droit.
16	Including armed forces stationed in the area.	16	Y compris les militaires en garnison sur le territoire.
17	Projected estimate (medium fertility variant).	17	Projection approximative (variante moyenne fécondité).
18	Population statistics are compiled from registers.	18	Les statistiques de la population sont compilées à partir des registres.
19	Population aged 65 years and over.	19	Population âgée de 65 ans ou plus.
20	Including Norfolk Island.	20	Y compris l'île Norfolk.
21	Including Nagorno-Karabakh.	21	Y compris le Haut-Karabakh.
22	Data refer to projections based on the 2000 population census.	22	Les données se réfèrent aux projections basées sur le recensement de la population 2000.
23	Data refer to projections based on the 2010 Population Census.	23	Les données se réfèrent aux projections basées sur le recensement de la population de 2010.
24	Estimates should be viewed with caution as these are derived from scarce data.	24	Les montants estimatifs sont à prendre avec prudence, car calculés à partir de données peu nombreuses.
25	Data updated according to "Superintendencia Agraria". Interior waters correspond to natural or artificial bodies of water or snow.	25	Données actualisées d'après la « Superintendencia Agraria ». Les eaux intérieures correspondent aux étendues d'eau naturelles ou artificielles et aux étendues neigeuses.
26	Excluding the institutional population.	26	Non compris la population dans les institutions.
27	Refers to Guernsey and Jersey.	27	Se rapporte à Guernesey et Jersey.
28	For statistical purposes, the data for China do not include those for the Hong Kong Special Administrative Region (Hong Kong SAR), Macao Special Administrative Region (Macao SAR) and Taiwan Province of China.	28	Pour la présentation des statistiques, les données pour la Chine ne comprennent pas la région administrative spéciale de Hong Kong (RAS de Hong Kong), la région administrative spéciale de Macao (RAS de Macao) et la province chinoise de Taïwan.
29	Inland waters include the reservoirs.	29	Les eaux intérieures comprennent les réservoirs.
30	Refers to the whole country.	30	Ensemble du pays.
31	Excluding residents of institutions.	31	À l'exclusion de personnes en établissements de soins.
32	Data have not been adjusted for underenumeration, estimated at 1.4 per cent.	32	Les données n'ont pas été ajustées pour le sous-dénombrement, estimé à 1,4 pour cent.
33	The total surface is 21 040.79 square kilometres, without taking into account the last ruling of The Hague.	33	La superficie totale est égale à 21 040.79 km2, excluant la dernière décision de la Haye.
34	A dispute exists between the Governments of Argentina and the United Kingdom of Great Britain and Northern Ireland concerning sovereignty over the Falkland Islands (Malvinas).	34	La souveraineté sur les îles Falkland (Malvinas) fait l'objet d'un différend entre le Gouvernement argentin et le Gouvernement du Royaume-Uni de Grande-Bretagne et d'Irlande du Nord.
35	Excluding military personnel and their families, visitors and transients.	35	À l'exclusion des personnels militaires et leurs familles, les personnes de passage et les visiteurs.
36	Including Åland Islands.	36	Y compris les Îles d'Åland.
37	Including Abkhazia and South Ossetia.	37	Y compris l'Abkhazie et l'Ossétie du Sud.
38	Excluding families of military personnel, visitors and transients.	38	Non compris les familles des militaires, ni les visiteurs et voyageurs en transit.
39	Excluding military personnel, visitors and transients.	39	À l'exclusion des personnels militaires, les personnes de passage et les visiteurs.
40	Including nationals outside the country.	40	Y compris les ressortissants étrangers.
41	Surface area is 0.44 Km2.	41	Superficie: 0,44 Km2.
42	Land area only.	42	La superficie des terres seulement.
43	Data refer to 1 October.	43	Les données se réfèrent au 1er octobre.
44	Land area only. Excluding 84 square km of uninhabited islands.	44	La superficie des terres seulement. Exclut des îles inhabitées d'une superficie de 84 kilomètres carrés.
45	Including Sabah and Sarawak.	45	Y compris Sabah et Sarawak.
46	Projections are prepared by the Secretariat of the Pacific Community based on 1999 census of population and housing.	46	Les projections sont préparées par le Secrétariat de la Communauté du Pacifique en fonction du recensement de la population et du logement de 1999.
47	Including Agalega, Rodrigues and Saint Brandon.	47	Y compris Agalega, Rodrigues et Saint-Brandon.
48	Excluding the islands of Saint Brandon and Agalega.	48	Non compris les îles Saint-Brandon et Agalega.
49	Intercensus data.	49	Données intercensitaires.
50	Refers to the island of Saipan.	50	Fait référence seulement à l'île de Saipan.
51	Including the Transnistria region.	51	Y compris la région de Transnistrie.
52	Including Ascension and Tristan da Cunha.	52	Y compris Ascension et Tristan da Cunha.
53	Refers to habitable area. Excludes Saint Lucia's Forest Reserve.	53	S'applique à la zone habitable. Exclut la réserve forestière de Sainte-Lucie.

54	Population aged 0 to 20 years.	54	Population âgée de 0 à 20 ans.
55	Population aged 61 years and over.	55	Population âgée de 61 ans ou plus.
56	Surface area is based on the 2002 population and housing census.	56	La superficie est fondée sur les données provenant du recensement de la population et du logement de 2002.
57	Including Kosovo.	57	Y compris Kosovo.
58	Changes in total area per year are the result of new measuring and correcting of the administrative borders between former Yugoslavian countries.	58	Les changements des totaux par année résultent de nouvelles mesures et de corrections des frontières administratives entre pays ex-yougoslaves.
59	The land area of Singapore comprises the mainland and other islands.	59	La superficie terrestre de Singapour comprend l'île principale et les autres îles.
60	Excluding inland water.	60	Exception faite des eaux intérieures.
61	Including Canary Islands, Ceuta and Melilla.	61	Y compris les îles Canaries, Ceuta et Melilla.
62	Including low water level for all islands (area to shoreline).	62	Y compris le niveau de basses eaux pour toutes les îles.
63	Including Crimea.	63	Y compris Crimea.
64	Including Zanzibar.	64	Y compris Zanzibar.
65	Comprising the Northern Region (former Saguia el Hamra) and Southern Region (former Rio de Oro).	65	Comprend la région septentrionale (ancien Saguia el Hamra) et la région méridionale (ancien Rio de Oro).

Population growth and indicators of fertility and mortality

Croissance démographique et indicateurs de fécondité et mortalité

Country or area Pays ou zone	Year Année	Population rate of increase (annual %) Population taux d'accroissement (% annuel)	Fertility rate, total (live births per woman) Taux de fécondité (naissances vivantes) par femme	Mortality rates (per live births) Taux de mortalité (pour naissances vivantes)		Life expectancy at birth (years) Espérance de vie à la naissance (en années)		
				Infant Infantile p. 1 000	Maternal Maternelle p. 100 000	Total Totale	Male Hommes	Females Femmes
Total, all countries or areas	2005	1.3[1]	2.7[1]	49.2[1]	288	67.0[1]	64.8[1]	69.4[1]
Total, tous pays ou zones	2010	1.2[1]	2.6[1]	41.0[1]	246	68.9[1]	66.7[1]	71.3[1]
	2015	1.2[1]	2.5[1]	33.9[1]	216	70.9[1]	68.5[1]	73.3[1]
Africa [1]	2005	2.4	5.1	81.0	...	53.5	52.0	55.1
Afrique [1]	2010	2.5	4.9	67.7	...	56.8	55.2	58.3
	2015	2.6	4.7	55.9	...	60.2	58.6	61.9
Northern Africa	2005	1.7[1]	3.1[1]	38.7[1]	95[2]	68.0[1]	66.0[1]	70.0[1]
Afrique septentrionale	2010	1.7[1]	3.1[1]	31.7[1]	82[2]	69.8[1]	67.9[1]	71.7[1]
	2015	2.0[1]	3.3[1]	26.6[1]	70[2]	71.2[1]	69.4[1]	73.0[1]
Sub-Saharan Africa	2005	2.6[1]	5.6[1]	87.8[1]	717[3]	50.6[1]	49.1[1]	52.1[1]
Afrique subsaharienne	2010	2.7[1]	5.4[1]	73.5[1]	624[3]	54.0[1]	52.6[1]	55.5[1]
	2015	2.7[1]	5.1[1]	61.0[1]	546[3]	57.8[1]	56.2[1]	59.5[1]
Eastern Africa [1]	2005	2.7	5.8	77.8	...	51.5	49.7	53.3
Afrique orientale [1]	2010	2.8	5.4	62.6	...	56.1	54.4	57.7
	2015	2.8	4.9	50.4	...	61.0	59.0	62.9
Middle Africa [1]	2005	3.1	6.4	103.6	...	50.6	49.0	52.1
Afrique centrale [1]	2010	3.2	6.2	87.7	...	53.9	52.4	55.4
	2015	3.2	5.9	74.1	...	57.0	55.4	58.6
Southern Africa [1]	2005	1.2	2.7	56.0	...	53.0	50.6	55.6
Afrique australe [1]	2010	1.3	2.7	49.5	...	54.0	51.6	56.5
	2015	1.5	2.6	35.0	...	60.3	57.2	63.6
Western Africa [1]	2005	2.6	5.9[4]	95.3[4]	...	49.5[4]	48.6[4]	50.5[4]
Afrique occidentale [1]	2010	2.7	5.7[4]	81.2[4]	...	52.6[4]	51.6[4]	53.5[4]
	2015	2.7	5.5[4]	68.5[4]	...	55.1[4]	54.1[4]	56.0[4]
Northern America [1]	2005	0.9	2.0[5]	6.9[5]	...	77.4[5]	74.8[5]	80.0[5]
Amérique septentrionale [1]	2010	1.0	2.0[5]	6.7[5]	...	78.4[5]	75.9[5]	80.9[5]
	2015	0.8	1.8[5]	5.8[5]	...	79.2[5]	76.8[5]	81.6[5]
Latin America & the Caribbean	2005	1.3[1]	2.5[1]	25.0[1]	88	72.2[1]	69.0[1]	75.6[1]
Amérique latine et Caraïbes	2010	1.2[1]	2.3[1]	20.2[1]	81	73.5[1]	70.2[1]	76.8[1]
	2015	1.1[1]	2.1[1]	17.1[1]	67	74.4[1]	71.2[1]	77.7[1]
Caribbean [1]	2005	0.8	2.5[6]	37.5[6]	...	69.7[6]	67.3[6]	72.2[6]
Caraïbes [1]	2010	0.7	2.4[6]	34.8[6]	...	70.8[6]	68.4[6]	73.4[6]
	2015	0.7	2.3[6]	33.2[6]	...	71.6[6]	69.1[6]	74.2[6]
Central America [1]	2005	1.5	2.8	23.0	...	74.0	71.2	76.8
Amérique centrale [1]	2010	1.5	2.5	19.5	...	74.4	71.5	77.3
	2015	1.4	2.4	16.9	...	74.6	71.6	77.6
South America [1]	2005	1.3	2.4[7]	24.7[7]	...	71.9[7]	68.4[7]	75.5[7]
Amérique du Sud [1]	2010	1.1	2.1[7]	18.9[7]	...	73.4[7]	69.9[7]	76.9[7]
	2015	1.0	2.0[7]	15.4[7]	...	74.7[7]	71.3[7]	78.1[7]
Asia [1]	2005	1.2	2.4	45.8	...	68.3	66.6	70.1
Asie [1]	2010	1.1	2.3	37.1	...	70.0	68.2	72.0
	2015	1.0	2.2	29.5	...	71.8	69.8	74.0
Central Asia [1]	2005	1.1	2.5	47.1	...	65.6	61.6	69.8
Asie centrale [1]	2010	1.4	2.7	36.6	...	67.5	63.5	71.5
	2015	1.7	2.8	26.4	...	69.5	66.1	72.9
Eastern Asia	2005	0.6[1]	1.6[1]	24.8[1]	48[8]	73.5[1]	71.4[1]	75.7[1]
Asie orientale	2010	0.5[1]	1.6[1]	16.9[1]	36[8]	74.9[1]	72.7[1]	77.2[1]
	2015	0.5[1]	1.6[1]	11.5[1]	27[8]	76.3[1]	73.9[1]	78.9[1]
South-central Asia [1]	2005	1.7	3.2	61.1	...	64.0	63.0	65.1
Asie centrale et du Sud [1]	2010	1.5	2.9	51.1	...	65.9	64.8	67.1
	2015	1.3	2.5	41.7	...	68.0	66.8	69.4
South-eastern Asia	2005	1.3[1]	2.5[1]	34.3[1]	166	67.9[1]	65.3[1]	70.6[1]
Asie du Sud-Est	2010	1.2[1]	2.4[1]	28.6[1]	136	69.6[1]	66.8[1]	72.5[1]
	2015	1.2[1]	2.3[1]	24.0[1]	110	71.2[1]	68.2[1]	74.3[1]
Southern Asia	2005	1.7[1]	3.2[1]	61.5[1]	288	63.9[1]	63.1[1]	64.9[1]
Asie méridionale	2010	1.5[1]	2.9[1]	51.7[1]	221	65.9[1]	64.9[1]	66.9[1]
	2015	1.3[1]	2.5[1]	42.4[1]	176	68.0[1]	66.8[1]	69.2[1]

Country or area Pays ou zone	Year Année	Population rate of increase (annual %) Population taux d'accroissement (% annuel)	Fertility rate, total (live births per woman) Taux de fécondité (naissances vivantes par femme)	Mortality rates (per live births) Taux de mortalite (pour naissances vivantes) Infant Infantile p. 1 000	Maternal Maternale p. 100 000	Life expectancy at birth (years) Espérance de vie à la naissance (en années) Total Totale	Male Hommes	Females Femmes
Western Asia	2005	2.2[1]	3.2[1]	29.5[1]	110[9]	70.9[1]	68.4[1]	73.6[1]
Asie occidentale	2010	2.5[1]	3.0[1]	23.4[1]	96[9]	72.3[1]	69.6[1]	75.2[1]
	2015	2.1[1]	2.9[1]	20.5[1]	91[9]	73.4[1]	70.8[1]	76.3[1]
Europe [1]	2005	0.1	1.4	8.3	...	73.8	69.6	78.1
Europe [1]	2010	0.2	1.6	6.4	...	75.3	71.3	79.3
	2015	0.2	1.6	5.3	...	77.2	73.6	80.7
Eastern Europe [1]	2005	-0.4	1.3	13.8	...	67.9	62.4	73.8
Europe orientale [1]	2010	-0.2	1.4	9.8	...	69.5	64.1	75.1
	2015	~0.0	1.6	7.6	...	72.2	67.2	77.1
Northern Europe [1]	2005	0.4	1.7[10]	5.0[10]	...	77.9[10]	75.2[10]	80.5[10]
Europe septentrionale [1]	2010	0.8	1.8[10]	4.4[10]	...	79.2[10]	76.6[10]	81.6[10]
	2015	0.6	1.8[10]	3.7[10]	...	80.5[10]	78.3[10]	82.6[10]
Southern Europe [1]	2005	0.7	1.4[11]	5.5[11]	...	78.8[11]	75.6[11]	81.8[11]
Europe méridionale [1]	2010	0.4	1.5[11]	4.3[11]	...	80.0[11]	77.1[11]	82.9[11]
	2015	~0.0	1.4[11]	3.6[11]	...	81.2[11]	78.5[11]	83.8[11]
Western Europe [1]	2005	0.4	1.6[12]	4.3[12]	...	79.0[12]	75.8[12]	82.0[12]
Europe occidentale [1]	2010	0.2	1.6[12]	3.8[12]	...	80.2[12]	77.3[12]	83.0[12]
	2015	0.4	1.7[12]	3.4[12]	...	81.1[12]	78.4[12]	83.7[12]
Oceania [1]	2005	1.4	2.5	25.7	...	74.9	72.6	77.2
Océanie [1]	2010	1.8	2.5	23.1	...	76.2	74.1	78.4
	2015	1.6	2.4	20.5	...	77.4	75.4	79.4
Australia and New Zealand [1]	2005	1.2	1.8	5.0	...	80.1	77.6	82.6
Australie et Nouvelle-Zélande [1]	2010	1.7	2.0	4.5	...	81.3	79.0	83.5
	2015	1.5	1.9	3.7	...	82.2	80.2	84.2
Melanesia [1]	2005	1.9	4.2	51.4	...	61.3	60.0	62.8
Mélanésie [1]	2010	2.2	3.9	48.4	...	62.7	61.4	64.2
	2015	1.9	3.7	43.1	...	64.1	62.7	65.5
Micronesia [1]	2005	0.6	3.1[13]	32.6[13]	...	69.5[13]	67.3[13]	71.8[13]
Micronésie [1]	2010	0.2	3.1[13]	30.6[13]	...	70.6[13]	68.2[13]	73.2[13]
	2015	0.8	3.0[13]	28.7[13]	...	71.8[13]	69.1[13]	74.7[13]
Polynesia [1,14]	2005	0.9	3.3	15.6	...	71.2	69.0	73.6
Polynésie [1,14]	2010	0.3	3.2	14.7	...	72.6	70.4	74.9
	2015	0.3	2.9	13.2	...	73.7	71.6	75.9
Afghanistan	2005	4.2[1]	7.2[1]	84.6[1]	821	57.0[1]	55.8[1]	58.3[1]
Afghanistan	2010	2.6[1]	6.5[1]	72.2[1]	584	59.6[1]	58.3[1]	61.0[1]
	2015	3.3[1]	5.4[1]	60.1[1]	396	62.3[1]	60.9[1]	63.8[1]
Albania	2005	-0.3[1]	1.9[1]	21.2[1]	30	74.8[1]	72.3[1]	77.8[1]
Albanie	2010	-0.9[1]	1.6[1]	16.8[1]	30	75.6[1]	73.2[1]	78.5[1]
	2015	-0.4[1]	1.7[1]	9.2[1]	29	77.5[1]	75.2[1]	80.0[1]
Algeria	2005	1.3[1]	2.4[1]	33.6[1]	148	71.8[1]	70.5[1]	73.2[1]
Algérie	2010	1.6[1]	2.7[1]	29.4[1]	147	74.2[1]	73.0[1]	75.4[1]
	2015	2.0[1]	3.0[1]	24.9[1]	140	75.5[1]	74.4[1]	76.7[1]
American Samoa	2005[1]	0.5	...	...	...	...	...	...
Samoa américaines	2006	...	...	...	...	...	68.5	76.2
	2010[1]	-1.2	...	...	...	...	...	...
	2011	...	...	...	...	...	71.1	77.8
	2012[15]	...	...	9.6	...	...	...	...
	2013	...	2.6	...	...	...	...	...
	2015[1]	~0.0	...	...	...	...	...	...
Andorra	2005	3.7[1]	1.2	...	...	...	...	...
Andorre	2010	1.4[1]	1.2	...	...	...	...	...
	2012	...	1.2	...	...	...	...	...
	2015[1]	-1.6	...	...	...	...	...	...
Angola	2005	3.4[1]	6.6[1]	128.8[1]	705	48.1[1]	45.9[1]	50.4[1]
Angola	2010	3.7[1]	6.4[1]	104.2[1]	561	52.7[1]	50.3[1]	55.3[1]
	2015	3.5[1]	6.0[1]	78.2[1]	477	57.7[1]	55.2[1]	60.5[1]

Population growth and indicators of fertility and mortality *(continued)*

Croissance démographique et indicateurs de fécondité et mortalité *(suite)*

Country or area Pays ou zone	Year Année	Population rate of increase (annual %) Population taux d'accroissement (% annuel)	Fertility rate, total (live births per woman) Taux de fécondité (naissances vivantes par femme)	Mortality rates (per live births) Taux de mortalite (pour naissances vivantes)		Life expectancy at birth (years) Espérance de vie à la naissance (en années)		
				Infant Infantile p. 1 000	Maternal Maternale p. 100 000	Total Totale	Male Hommes	Females Femmes
Anguilla	2004	...	2.9	...	...	78.9[16]	76.5[16]	81.1[16]
Anguilla	2005	2.6[1]	1.8	...	...	...	...	...
	2006	...	2.0	...	...	...	...	...
	2010[1]	1.7	...	...	...	...	...	...
	2015[1]	1.2	...	...	...	...	...	...
Antigua and Barbuda [1]	2005	1.4	2.2	11.5	...	74.5	73.0	75.9
Antigua-et-Barbuda [1]	2010	1.6	2.0	9.0	...	75.5	74.1	76.8
	2015	1.2	2.0	6.8	...	76.1	74.8	77.4
Argentina	2005	1.1[1]	2.5[1]	16.7[1]	58	74.0[1]	70.6[1]	77.4[1]
Argentine	2010	1.0[1]	2.4[1]	14.2[1]	58	74.9[1]	71.4[1]	78.2[1]
	2015	1.0[1]	2.3[1]	12.1[1]	52	75.7[1]	72.2[1]	79.0[1]
Armenia	2005	-0.6[1]	1.7[1]	27.1[1]	40	72.4[1]	69.1[1]	75.3[1]
Arménie	2010	-0.7[1]	1.7[1]	21.0[1]	33	72.7[1]	69.4[1]	75.8[1]
	2015	0.3[1]	1.7[1]	13.2[1]	25	74.0[1]	70.6[1]	77.0[1]
Aruba [1]	2005	1.9	1.8	17.8	...	74.0	71.5	76.4
Aruba [1]	2010	0.3	1.8	16.2	...	74.7	72.2	77.1
	2015	0.5	1.8	14.8	...	75.4	72.9	77.8
Australia	2005	1.2[1,17]	1.8[1,17]	4.9[1,17]	7	80.3[1,17]	77.8[1,17]	82.8[1,17]
Australie	2010	1.9[1,17]	2.0[1,17]	4.4[1,17]	6	81.5[1,17]	79.2[1,17]	83.8[1,17]
	2015	1.5[1,17]	1.9[1,17]	3.6[1,17]	6	82.4[1,17]	80.3[1,17]	84.5[1,17]
Austria	2005	0.5[1]	1.4[1]	4.5[1]	5	78.9[1]	75.9[1]	81.7[1]
Autriche	2010	0.4[1]	1.4[1]	3.8[1]	4	80.1[1]	77.3[1]	82.8[1]
	2015	0.6[1]	1.4[1]	3.3[1]	4	81.0[1]	78.4[1]	83.5[1]
Azerbaijan	2005	1.0[1,18]	1.9[1,18]	54.2[1,18]	34	67.4[1,18]	64.6[1,18]	70.3[1,18]
Azerbaïdjan	2010	1.1[1,18]	1.8[1,18]	40.7[1,18]	27	70.1[1,18]	66.9[1,18]	73.4[1,18]
	2015	1.3[1,18]	2.1[1,18]	31.4[1,18]	25	71.6[1,18]	68.6[1,18]	74.6[1,18]
Bahamas	2005	1.7[1]	1.9[1]	13.1[1]	74	72.0[1]	69.0[1]	75.0[1]
Bahamas	2010	1.8[1]	1.9[1]	11.3[1]	85	72.0[1]	69.3[1]	74.7[1]
	2015	1.1[1]	1.8[1]	8.0[1]	80	72.5[1]	70.1[1]	74.8[1]
Bahrain	2005	5.8[1]	2.7[1]	9.8[1]	20	74.9[1]	74.2[1]	75.9[1]
Bahreïn	2010	6.7[1]	2.3[1]	7.9[1]	16	75.7[1]	74.9[1]	76.7[1]
	2015	2.0[1]	2.1[1]	6.9[1]	15	76.4[1]	75.6[1]	77.5[1]
Bangladesh	2005	1.7[1]	2.9[1]	55.5[1]	319	66.6[1]	66.0[1]	67.3[1]
Bangladesh	2010	1.2[1]	2.5[1]	43.3[1]	242	68.8[1]	67.8[1]	70.0[1]
	2015	1.1[1]	2.2[1]	33.2[1]	176	70.8[1]	69.4[1]	72.4[1]
Barbados	2005	0.4[1]	1.8[1]	13.0[1]	40	77.6[1]	75.9[1]	79.3[1]
Barbade	2010	0.4[1]	1.8[1]	12.6[1]	33	78.1[1]	76.5[1]	79.7[1]
	2015	0.2[1]	1.6[1]	11.5[1]	27	78.6[1]	77.1[1]	80.0[1]
Belarus	2005	-0.6[1]	1.3[1]	9.6[1]	13	67.8[1]	62.3[1]	73.7[1]
Bélarus	2010	-0.3[1]	1.4[1]	6.3[1]	5	69.3[1]	63.6[1]	75.2[1]
	2015	~0.0[1]	1.6[1]	3.4[1]	4	72.4[1]	66.8[1]	78.0[1]
Belgium	2005	0.5[1]	1.7[1]	4.2[1]	8	78.4[1]	75.3[1]	81.4[1]
Belgique	2010	0.7[1]	1.8[1]	3.8[1]	8	79.6[1]	76.8[1]	82.3[1]
	2015	0.6[1]	1.8[1]	3.5[1]	7	80.5[1]	78.0[1]	83.0[1]
Belize	2005	2.8[1]	3.4[1]	20.2[1]	52	69.6[1]	66.9[1]	72.5[1]
Belize	2010	2.6[1]	2.8[1]	17.3[1]	37	70.7[1]	68.0[1]	73.6[1]
	2015	2.3[1]	2.6[1]	15.0[1]	28	73.4[1]	71.1[1]	76.0[1]
Benin	2005	3.0[1]	5.8[1]	84.0[1]	502	56.2[1]	54.6[1]	57.7[1]
Bénin	2010	2.8[1]	5.5[1]	74.5[1]	446	58.6[1]	57.1[1]	60.0[1]
	2015	2.8[1]	5.2[1]	67.7[1]	405	59.9[1]	58.5[1]	61.4[1]
Bermuda	2005	0.3[1]	1.8	...	...	...	...	...
Bermudes	2010	-0.4[1]	1.7	...	...	79.3	76.9	82.3
	2015	-0.6[1]	1.5	...	...	...	77.3	84.9
	2016	...	1.5	...	...	...	77.5	85.1
Bhutan	2005	1.9[1]	3.1[1]	51.9[1]	308	63.2[1]	62.9[1]	63.5[1]
Bhoutan	2010	1.1[1]	2.6[1]	39.5[1]	204	67.0[1]	66.8[1]	67.3[1]
	2015	1.2[1]	2.1[1]	30.5[1]	148	69.4[1]	69.2[1]	69.6[1]

Country or area Pays ou zone	Year Année	Population rate of increase (annual %) Population taux d'accroissement (% annuel)	Fertility rate, total (live births per woman) Taux de fécondité (naissances vivantes par femme)	Mortality rates (per live births) Taux de mortalite (pour naissances vivantes)		Life expectancy at birth (years) Espérance de vie à la naissance (en années)		
				Infant Infantile p. 1 000	Maternal Maternale p. 100 000	Total Totale	Male Hommes	Females Femmes
Bolivia (Plurin. State of)	2005	1.8[1]	3.9[1]	52.0[1]	305	63.9[1]	62.0[1]	66.0[1]
Bolivie (État plurin. de)	2010	1.7[1]	3.4[1]	42.1[1]	253	66.6[1]	64.4[1]	69.0[1]
	2015	1.6[1]	3.1[1]	32.4[1]	206	69.3[1]	66.7[1]	71.9[1]
Bonaire, St. Eustatius & Saba [1]	2005	~0.0	...	...	...	...	...	...
Bonaire, St-Eustache et Saba [1]	2010	7.5	...	...	...	...	...	...
	2015	3.2	...	...	...	...	...	...
Bosnia and Herzegovina	2005	0.1[1]	1.3[1]	9.8[1]	14	74.8[1]	72.0[1]	77.4[1]
Bosnie-Herzégovine	2010	-0.3[1]	1.3[1]	9.0[1]	13	75.5[1]	72.9[1]	78.1[1]
	2015	-1.5[1]	1.3[1]	6.9[1]	11	76.5[1]	74.1[1]	78.9[1]
Botswana	2005	1.8[1]	3.2[1]	57.0[1]	276	50.1[1]	47.9[1]	52.5[1]
Botswana	2010	2.0[1]	3.0[1]	44.2[1]	169	55.9[1]	53.6[1]	58.1[1]
	2015	1.3[1]	3.0[1]	35.5[1]	129	64.4[1]	61.8[1]	67.0[1]
Brazil	2005	1.3[1]	2.1[1]	28.2[1]	67	71.0[1]	67.2[1]	74.9[1]
Brésil	2010	1.0[1]	1.9[1]	20.3[1]	65	72.8[1]	69.1[1]	76.6[1]
	2015	0.9[1]	1.8[1]	15.8[1]	44	74.3[1]	70.7[1]	78.0[1]
British Virgin Islands	2004	...	2.0	...	...	...	69.9	78.5
Îles Vierges britanniques	2005[1]	2.3	...	...	...	...	...	...
	2010[1]	3.2	...	...	...	...	...	...
	2015[1]	2.0	...	...	...	...	...	...
Brunei Darussalam	2005	1.8[1]	2.2[1]	9.7[1]	30	73.5[1]	72.4[1]	74.6[1]
Brunéi Darussalam	2010	1.2[1]	1.9[1]	9.3[1]	27	74.4[1]	73.4[1]	75.5[1]
	2015	1.3[1]	2.0[1]	8.8[1]	23	75.0[1]	73.8[1]	76.2[1]
Bulgaria	2005	-0.8[1]	1.3[1]	12.8[1]	15	72.2[1]	68.8[1]	75.8[1]
Bulgarie	2010	-0.7[1]	1.5[1]	9.5[1]	11	73.1[1]	69.7[1]	76.8[1]
	2015	-0.6[1]	1.5[1]	8.3[1]	11	74.3[1]	70.8[1]	77.8[1]
Burkina Faso	2005	2.9[1]	6.4[1]	90.0[1]	468	51.6[1]	50.5[1]	52.6[1]
Burkina Faso	2010	3.0[1]	6.1[1]	77.5[1]	417	55.3[1]	54.6[1]	55.8[1]
	2015	3.0[1]	5.6[1]	64.7[1]	371	58.7[1]	58.0[1]	59.3[1]
Burundi	2005	2.9[1]	6.8[1]	87.5[1]	863	51.4[1]	49.9[1]	52.9[1]
Burundi	2010	3.3[1]	6.4[1]	70.0[1]	808	55.3[1]	53.6[1]	57.0[1]
	2015	3.2[1]	6.0[1]	52.3[1]	712	58.9[1]	57.1[1]	60.7[1]
Cabo Verde	2005	1.6[1]	3.2[1]	24.5[1]	54	69.9[1]	66.2[1]	73.3[1]
Cabo Verde	2010	1.2[1]	2.7[1]	22.9[1]	51	70.6[1]	66.7[1]	74.2[1]
	2015	1.3[1]	2.5[1]	20.6[1]	42	71.5[1]	67.9[1]	75.0[1]
Cambodia	2005	1.8[1]	3.4[1]	65.8[1]	315	60.8[1]	58.5[1]	63.0[1]
Cambodge	2010	1.5[1]	3.1[1]	44.8[1]	202	65.1[1]	62.7[1]	67.4[1]
	2015	1.6[1]	2.7[1]	30.0[1]	161	67.6[1]	65.5[1]	69.6[1]
Cameroon	2005	2.7[1]	5.5[1]	92.2[1]	729	51.8[1]	50.5[1]	53.1[1]
Cameroun	2010	2.7[1]	5.3[1]	80.5[1]	676	54.0[1]	52.9[1]	55.0[1]
	2015	2.7[1]	5.0[1]	70.7[1]	596	56.3[1]	54.9[1]	57.7[1]
Canada	2005	1.0[1]	1.5[1]	5.3[1]	9	79.7[1]	77.2[1]	82.1[1]
Canada	2010	1.2[1]	1.6[1]	5.1[1]	8	80.8[1]	78.4[1]	83.0[1]
	2015	1.1[1]	1.6[1]	4.6[1]	7	81.8[1]	79.7[1]	83.9[1]
Cayman Islands	2005[1]	3.1	...	...	...	...	...	...
Îles Caïmanes	2006[19]	...	...	...	...	...	76.3	83.8
	2007	...	1.6	...	...	...	...	...
	2010[1]	2.6	...	...	...	...	...	...
	2015[1]	1.5	...	...	...	...	...	...
Central African Republic	2005	2.1[1]	5.5[1]	105.1[1]	1 058	44.1[1]	42.9[1]	45.3[1]
République centrafricaine	2010	1.7[1]	5.3[1]	99.7[1]	909	46.0[1]	44.6[1]	47.4[1]
	2015	0.5[1]	5.1[1]	90.3[1]	882	48.9[1]	47.3[1]	50.5[1]
Chad	2005	3.8[1]	7.2[1]	108.3[1]	1 168	48.0[1]	46.8[1]	49.2[1]
Tchad	2010	3.4[1]	6.9[1]	97.5[1]	1 036	49.5[1]	48.3[1]	50.7[1]
	2015	3.3[1]	6.3[1]	84.1[1]	856	52.3[1]	50.9[1]	53.7[1]
Channel Islands [1,20]	2005	0.4	1.5	8.8	...	79.6	77.2	82.0
Îles Anglo-Normandes [1,20]	2010	1.0	1.6	7.6	...	80.9	78.4	83.4
	2015	0.7	1.6	6.7	...	82.0	79.8	84.1

Country or area Pays ou zone	Year Année	Population rate of increase (annual %) Population taux d'accroissement (% annuel)	Fertility rate, total (live births per woman) Taux de fécondité (naissances vivantes par femme)	Mortality rates (per live births) Taux de mortalite (pour naissances vivantes)		Life expectancy at birth (years) Espérance de vie à la naissance (en années)		
				Infant Infantile p. 1 000	Maternal Maternale p. 100 000	Total Totale	Male Hommes	Females Femmes
Chile	2005	1.1[1]	2.0[1]	8.3[1]	27	77.0[1]	73.9[1]	80.0[1]
Chili	2010	1.1[1]	1.9[1]	7.7[1]	26	78.2[1]	75.1[1]	81.1[1]
	2015	1.0[1]	1.9[1]	7.2[1]	22	79.3[1]	76.3[1]	82.1[1]
China	2005	0.6[1,21]	1.6[1,21]	27.1[1,21]	48	72.3[1,21]	70.6[1,21]	74.1[1,21]
Chine	2010	0.6[1,21]	1.6[1,21]	18.1[1,21]	35	73.7[1,21]	71.9[1,21]	75.7[1,21]
	2015	0.5[1,21]	1.6[1,21]	12.3[1,21]	27	75.1[1,21]	73.1[1,21]	77.5[1,21]
China, Hong Kong SAR [1]	2005	0.5	1.0	2.5	...	81.4	78.5	84.5
Chine, RAS de Hong Kong [1]	2010	0.6	1.0	1.9	...	82.4	79.5	85.5
	2015	0.6	1.2	1.6	...	83.4	80.5	86.4
China, Macao SAR [1]	2005	2.4	0.9	4.9	...	81.0	78.2	83.6
Chine, RAS de Macao [1]	2010	2.2	1.0	3.8	...	82.1	79.1	84.9
	2015	2.2	1.2	3.1	...	83.3	80.3	86.2
Colombia	2005	1.5[1]	2.4[1]	19.5[1]	80	73.6[1]	70.4[1]	76.9[1]
Colombie	2010	1.2[1]	2.1[1]	16.9[1]	72	74.8[1]	71.7[1]	77.9[1]
	2015	1.0[1]	1.9[1]	14.4[1]	64	76.0[1]	73.1[1]	78.9[1]
Comoros	2005	2.4[1]	5.2[1]	72.5[1]	436	59.6[1]	58.0[1]	61.2[1]
Comores	2010	2.4[1]	4.9[1]	66.6[1]	388	60.9[1]	59.3[1]	62.5[1]
	2015	2.4[1]	4.6[1]	58.1[1]	335	62.8[1]	61.2[1]	64.5[1]
Congo	2005	2.9[1]	4.9[1]	72.2[1]	596	53.3[1]	52.3[1]	54.3[1]
Congo	2010	3.3[1]	4.8[1]	52.5[1]	509	58.2[1]	57.0[1]	59.2[1]
	2015	2.6[1]	4.7[1]	41.4[1]	442	61.7[1]	60.5[1]	62.7[1]
Cook Islands	2001	...	...	...	...	...	68.0	74.0
Îles Cook	2005[1]	1.7	...	...	...	...	...	...
	2006	...	...	...	...	...	69.5	76.2
	2010[1]	-1.2	...	...	...	...	...	...
	2011	...	2.6	...	...	...	...	...
	2013[22]	...	...	3.6	...	75.3	# 71.7	# 79.6
	2015[1]	-1.2	...	...	...	...	...	...
Costa Rica	2005	1.6[1]	2.2[1]	10.9[1]	31	77.8[1]	75.5[1]	80.2[1]
Costa Rica	2010	1.3[1]	1.9[1]	10.0[1]	29	78.4[1]	76.1[1]	80.8[1]
	2015	1.1[1]	1.9[1]	9.3[1]	25	79.2[1]	76.7[1]	81.7[1]
Côte d'Ivoire	2005	2.2[1]	5.7[1]	87.9[1]	742	49.5[1]	48.0[1]	51.2[1]
Côte d'Ivoire	2010	2.2[1]	5.3[1]	77.2[1]	717	51.4[1]	50.0[1]	53.0[1]
	2015	2.5[1]	5.0[1]	67.5[1]	645	54.6[1]	53.5[1]	55.9[1]
Croatia	2005	-0.2[1]	1.4[1]	6.5[1]	11	74.9[1]	71.4[1]	78.4[1]
Croatie	2010	-0.2[1]	1.5[1]	5.8[1]	10	76.1[1]	72.6[1]	79.5[1]
	2015	-0.4[1]	1.5[1]	4.3[1]	8	77.4[1]	74.2[1]	80.6[1]
Cuba	2005	0.2[1]	1.6[1]	6.1[1]	41	77.2[1]	75.3[1]	79.1[1]
Cuba	2010	-0.1[1]	1.6[1]	5.3[1]	44	78.1[1]	76.1[1]	80.1[1]
	2015	0.2[1]	1.7[1]	4.8[1]	39	78.5[1]	76.5[1]	80.4[1]
Curaçao [1]	2005	-0.3	2.3	14.7	...	75.0	71.2	78.6
Curaçao [1]	2010	2.7	2.2	13.0	...	76.1	72.7	79.4
	2015	1.4	2.1	10.3	...	77.8	74.5	80.7
Cyprus	2005	1.7[1,23]	1.6[1,23]	5.6[1,23]	12	78.3[1,23]	76.3[1,23]	80.5[1,23]
Chypre	2010	1.6[1,23]	1.5[1,23]	4.3[1,23]	8	79.0[1,23]	76.9[1,23]	81.1[1,23]
	2015	0.9[1,23]	1.4[1,23]	4.2[1,23]	7	79.9[1,23]	77.7[1,23]	82.2[1,23]
Czechia	2005	-0.1[1]	1.2[1]	4.0[1]	6	75.5[1]	72.2[1]	78.8[1]
Tchéquie	2010	0.5[1]	1.4[1]	3.1[1]	5	77.0[1]	73.8[1]	80.1[1]
	2015	0.1[1]	1.5[1]	2.5[1]	4	78.2[1]	75.1[1]	81.2[1]
Dem. People's Rep. Korea	2005	0.8[1]	2.0[1]	28.5[1]	105	68.1[1]	64.2[1]	71.5[1]
Rép. pop. dém. de Corée	2010	0.5[1]	2.0[1]	27.3[1]	97	68.4[1]	64.8[1]	71.8[1]
	2015	0.5[1]	1.9[1]	18.5[1]	82	70.8[1]	67.2[1]	74.1[1]
Dem. Rep. of the Congo	2005	3.0[1]	6.7[1]	99.5[1]	787	51.8[1]	50.4[1]	53.3[1]
Rép. dém. du Congo	2010	3.3[1]	6.6[1]	83.8[1]	794	55.5[1]	54.0[1]	56.9[1]
	2015	3.3[1]	6.4[1]	73.1[1]	693	58.1[1]	56.7[1]	59.5[1]
Denmark	2005	0.3[1]	1.8[1]	4.5[1]	8	77.3[1]	75.0[1]	79.6[1]
Danemark	2010	0.5[1]	1.9[1]	3.7[1]	7	78.6[1]	76.4[1]	80.8[1]
	2015	0.5[1]	1.7[1]	3.5[1]	6	80.1[1]	78.1[1]	82.2[1]

Country or area Pays ou zone	Year Année	Population rate of increase (annual %) Population taux d'accroissement (% annuel)	Fertility rate, total (live births per woman) Taux de fécondité (naissances vivantes par femme)	Mortality rates (per live births) Taux de mortalite (pour naissances vivantes) Infant Infantile p. 1 000	Maternal Maternale p. 100 000	Life expectancy at birth (years) Espérance de vie à la naissance (en années) Total Totale	Male Hommes	Females Femmes
Djibouti	2005	1.8[1]	4.2[1]	68.1[1]	341	57.3[1]	55.9[1]	58.8[1]
Djibouti	2010	1.4[1]	3.6[1]	63.4[1]	275	59.1[1]	57.6[1]	60.5[1]
	2015	1.7[1]	3.1[1]	55.7[1]	229	61.6[1]	60.0[1]	63.2[1]
Dominica	2001	...	3.0	...	...	...	...	...
Dominique	2005[1]	0.3	...	...	...	...	...	...
	2008	...	...	...	...	...	73.8	78.2
	2010[1]	0.2	...	...	...	...	...	...
	2015[1]	0.5	...	...	...	...	...	...
Dominican Republic	2005	1.4[1]	2.8[1]	34.9[1]	64	70.1[1]	67.2[1]	73.2[1]
République dominicaine	2010	1.3[1]	2.6[1]	29.5[1]	75	71.4[1]	68.5[1]	74.6[1]
	2015	1.2[1]	2.5[1]	27.5[1]	92	72.6[1]	69.6[1]	75.9[1]
Ecuador	2005	1.7[1]	2.9[1]	23.6[1]	74	73.5[1]	70.7[1]	76.5[1]
Équateur	2010	1.6[1]	2.7[1]	19.1[1]	75	74.6[1]	71.7[1]	77.6[1]
	2015	1.5[1]	2.6[1]	15.1[1]	64	75.6[1]	72.8[1]	78.5[1]
Egypt	2005	1.9[1]	3.2[1]	29.3[1]	52	69.0[1]	66.7[1]	71.4[1]
Égypte	2010	1.8[1]	3.0[1]	23.5[1]	40	69.9[1]	67.6[1]	72.2[1]
	2015	2.2[1]	3.5[1]	18.9[1]	33	70.8[1]	68.7[1]	73.1[1]
El Salvador	2005	0.6[1]	2.7[1]	23.6[1]	68	69.6[1]	65.0[1]	74.1[1]
El Salvador	2010	0.4[1]	2.4[1]	21.6[1]	59	70.6[1]	65.9[1]	75.1[1]
	2015	0.5[1]	2.2[1]	17.7[1]	54	71.8[1]	67.0[1]	76.3[1]
Equatorial Guinea	2005	4.2[1]	5.7[1]	95.4[1]	483	54.0[1]	52.8[1]	55.2[1]
Guinée équatoriale	2010	4.6[1]	5.4[1]	84.6[1]	379	54.9[1]	53.9[1]	56.0[1]
	2015	4.3[1]	5.0[1]	73.8[1]	342	56.5[1]	55.4[1]	57.8[1]
Eritrea	2005	4.2[1]	5.1[1]	59.4[1]	619	56.7[1]	54.7[1]	58.8[1]
Érythrée	2010	2.3[1]	4.8[1]	51.6[1]	579	60.7[1]	58.7[1]	62.7[1]
	2015	1.1[1]	4.4[1]	45.0[1]	501	63.4[1]	61.4[1]	65.6[1]
Estonia	2005	-0.6[1]	1.4[1]	7.3[1]	15	71.6[1]	66.0[1]	77.1[1]
Estonie	2010	-0.4[1]	1.7[1]	4.7[1]	8	73.8[1]	68.3[1]	79.0[1]
	2015	-0.3[1]	1.6[1]	3.2[1]	9	76.8[1]	71.9[1]	81.2[1]
Eswatini	2005	0.5[1]	3.8[1]	86.3[1]	595	43.6[1]	41.4[1]	46.0[1]
Eswatini	2010	0.7[1]	3.6[1]	74.2[1]	436	43.8[1]	42.0[1]	46.0[1]
	2015	0.7[1]	3.1[1]	51.6[1]	389	50.7[1]	47.8[1]	54.0[1]
Ethiopia	2005	2.8[1]	6.2[1]	77.9[1]	743	53.6[1]	52.3[1]	55.0[1]
Éthiopie	2010	2.8[1]	5.5[1]	59.8[1]	523	59.1[1]	57.6[1]	60.6[1]
	2015	2.8[1]	4.9[1]	45.8[1]	353	63.7[1]	61.9[1]	65.5[1]
Falkland Islands (Malvinas) [1]	2005	0.4	...	...	...	...	...	...
Îles Falkland (Malvinas) [1]	2010	-0.6	...	...	...	...	...	...
	2015	0.3	...	...	...	...	...	...
Faroe Islands	2005	0.4[1]	2.6	...	...	...	...	...
Îles Féroé	2008	...	2.6	...	...	...	76.8	82.3
	2010	0.1[1]	2.5	...	...	...	...	...
	2015	0.2[1]	2.4	...	...	...	...	...
	2016[15]	...	...	...	...	...	78.3	84.5
Fiji	2005	0.3[1]	3.0[1]	18.8[1]	39	66.2[1]	64.6[1]	67.9[1]
Fidji	2010	0.9[1]	2.8[1]	19.6[1]	34	66.4[1]	64.9[1]	68.0[1]
	2015	0.2[1]	2.8[1]	20.0[1]	30	66.9[1]	65.4[1]	68.6[1]
Finland	2005	0.3[1,24]	1.8[1,24]	3.2[1,24]	4	78.4[1,24]	74.9[1,24]	81.7[1,24]
Finlande	2010	0.4[1,24]	1.8[1,24]	2.7[1,24]	3	79.5[1,24]	76.1[1,24]	82.9[1,24]
	2015	0.4[1,24]	1.8[1,24]	2.1[1,24]	3	80.7[1,24]	77.7[1,24]	83.7[1,24]
France	2005	0.7[1]	1.9[1]	4.2[1]	10	79.6[1]	75.9[1]	83.2[1]
France	2010	0.6[1]	2.0[1]	3.7[1]	9	81.0[1]	77.5[1]	84.3[1]
	2015	0.5[1]	2.0[1]	3.5[1]	8	81.9[1]	78.7[1]	85.0[1]
French Guiana [1]	2005	4.4	3.7	13.2	...	76.3	73.1	80.2
Guyane française [1]	2010	2.8	3.6	10.5	...	78.0	75.0	81.5
	2015	2.3	3.4	9.1	...	79.3	76.2	82.8
French Polynesia [1]	2005	1.5	2.4	9.4	...	73.2	70.7	76.1
Polynésie française [1]	2010	0.6	2.2	8.8	...	75.0	72.8	77.5
	2015	0.5	2.0	6.9	...	76.1	74.0	78.6

Population growth and indicators of fertility and mortality *(continued)*

Croissance démographique et indicateurs de fécondité et mortalité *(suite)*

Country or area Pays ou zone	Year Année	Population rate of increase (annual %) Population taux d'accroissement (% annuel)	Fertility rate, total (live births per woman) Taux de fécondité (naissances vivantes par femme)	Mortality rates (per live births) Taux de mortalité (pour naissances vivantes)		Life expectancy at birth (years) Espérance de vie à la naissance (en années)		
				Infant Infantile p. 1 000	Maternal Maternale p. 100 000	Total Totale	Male Hommes	Females Femmes
Gabon Gabon	2005	2.5[1]	4.4[1]	59.7[1]	370	57.6[1]	56.3[1]	58.9[1]
	2010	3.1[1]	4.2[1]	49.9[1]	322	59.6[1]	58.2[1]	61.0[1]
	2015	3.6[1]	4.1[1]	41.9[1]	291	63.3[1]	61.9[1]	64.8[1]
Gambia Gambie	2005	3.2[1]	5.8[1]	59.4[1]	807	56.9[1]	55.9[1]	58.1[1]
	2010	3.0[1]	5.7[1]	52.4[1]	753	58.9[1]	57.6[1]	60.2[1]
	2015	3.0[1]	5.5[1]	49.8[1]	706	60.3[1]	59.1[1]	61.6[1]
Georgia Géorgie	2005	-0.7[1,25]	1.6[1,25]	26.5[1,25]	37	70.4[1,25]	66.7[1,25]	74.1[1,25]
	2010	-0.5[1,25]	1.8[1,25]	18.2[1,25]	40	70.7[1,25]	66.2[1,25]	75.3[1,25]
	2015	-0.4[1,25]	2.0[1,25]	12.9[1,25]	36	72.3[1,25]	67.8[1,25]	76.8[1,25]
Germany Allemagne	2005	0.1[1]	1.4[1]	4.2[1]	7	78.6[1]	75.6[1]	81.5[1]
	2010	-0.2[1]	1.4[1]	3.7[1]	7	79.7[1]	77.0[1]	82.4[1]
	2015	0.2[1]	1.4[1]	3.4[1]	6	80.4[1]	77.9[1]	82.9[1]
Ghana Ghana	2005	2.5[1]	4.6[1]	60.9[1]	376	57.5[1]	56.7[1]	58.3[1]
	2010	2.5[1]	4.4[1]	53.7[1]	325	60.1[1]	59.2[1]	61.1[1]
	2015	2.3[1]	4.2[1]	44.8[1]	319	61.8[1]	60.9[1]	62.7[1]
Gibraltar Gibraltar	2001	...	...	...	...	...	78.5	83.3
	2005[1]	0.6	...	...	...	...	...	...
	2010[1]	0.7	...	...	...	...	...	...
	2015[1]	0.6	...	...	...	...	...	...
Greece Grèce	2005	0.3[1]	1.3[1]	4.5[1]	3	79.1[1]	76.4[1]	81.9[1]
	2010	-0.6[1]	1.4[1]	3.5[1]	3	80.0[1]	77.3[1]	82.8[1]
	2015	-0.4[1]	1.3[1]	3.3[1]	3	81.1[1]	78.5[1]	83.7[1]
Greenland Groenland	2005	0.3[1]	2.3	...	...	...	...	...
	2010	-0.1[1]	2.3	...	...	...	65.7[22]	71.0[22]
	2014	...	2.0	...	...	...	67.8[22]	72.8[22]
	2015	-0.1[1]	...	...	...	...	68.2[22]	72.9[22]
	2018[22]	...	...	...	...	...	69.1	73.7
Grenada Grenade	2005	0.4[1]	2.4[1]	12.7[1]	25	73.0[1]	70.4[1]	75.6[1]
	2010	0.3[1]	2.3[1]	12.3[1]	27	73.1[1]	70.6[1]	75.7[1]
	2015	0.6[1]	2.2[1]	13.7[1]	27	72.6[1]	70.3[1]	75.2[1]
Guadeloupe [1] Guadeloupe [1]	2005	-0.9	2.2	8.8	...	77.9	74.3	81.4
	2010	0.2	2.2	7.0	...	79.4	75.7	82.9
	2015	-0.3	2.2	5.8	...	80.6	76.8	84.0
Guam [1] Guam [1]	2005	0.4	2.7	13.6	...	75.9	73.6	78.5
	2010	0.1	2.5	11.4	...	77.4	74.7	80.3
	2015	0.3	2.4	10.1	...	78.5	75.5	81.8
Guatemala Guatemala	2005	2.3[1]	4.3[1]	37.3[1]	120	68.9[1]	65.7[1]	72.1[1]
	2010	2.2[1]	3.6[1]	31.3[1]	109	70.5[1]	67.3[1]	73.7[1]
	2015	2.1[1]	3.2[1]	26.9[1]	88	72.4[1]	69.2[1]	75.6[1]
Guinea Guinée	2005	2.0[1]	5.9[1]	95.2[1]	831	51.3[1]	51.3[1]	51.3[1]
	2010	2.2[1]	5.5[1]	77.7[1]	720	55.6[1]	54.5[1]	56.4[1]
	2015	2.3[1]	5.1[1]	65.7[1]	679	58.0[1]	57.5[1]	58.4[1]
Guinea-Bissau Guinée-Bissau	2005	2.3[1]	5.6[1]	103.9[1]	714	51.4[1]	48.8[1]	53.8[1]
	2010	2.5[1]	5.2[1]	85.2[1]	570	53.3[1]	50.9[1]	55.6[1]
	2015	2.6[1]	4.9[1]	68.1[1]	549	55.9[1]	53.6[1]	58.2[1]
Guyana Guyana	2005	~0.0[1]	2.9[1]	35.3[1]	232	66.0[1]	63.0[1]	69.3[1]
	2010	0.1[1]	2.7[1]	32.0[1]	241	67.4[1]	64.2[1]	70.8[1]
	2015	0.5[1]	2.6[1]	31.7[1]	229	68.7[1]	65.5[1]	72.2[1]
Haiti Haïti	2005	1.7[1]	4.1[1]	68.9[1]	459	57.7[1]	55.8[1]	59.7[1]
	2010	1.6[1]	3.6[1]	63.8[1]	389	59.7[1]	57.7[1]	61.6[1]
	2015	1.4[1]	3.3[1]	61.0[1]	359	61.4[1]	59.3[1]	63.5[1]
Holy See [1] Saint-Siège [1]	2005	0.3	...	...	...	...	...	...
	2010	~0.0	...	...	...	...	...	...
	2015	~0.0	...	...	...	...	...	...
Honduras Honduras	2005	2.5[1]	3.9[1]	28.4[1]	150	71.4[1]	69.1[1]	73.7[1]
	2010	2.2[1]	3.2[1]	23.3[1]	155	72.7[1]	70.3[1]	75.0[1]
	2015	1.8[1]	2.7[1]	18.4[1]	129	73.9[1]	71.6[1]	76.3[1]

Country or area Pays ou zone	Year Année	Population rate of increase (annual %) Population taux d'accroissement (% annuel)	Fertility rate, total (live births per woman) Taux de fécondité (naissances vivantes par femme)	Infant Infantile p. 1 000	Maternal Maternale p. 100 000	Total Totale	Male Hommes	Females Femmes
				Mortality rates (per live births) **Taux de mortalite (pour naissances vivantes)**		**Life expectancy at birth (years)** **Espérance de vie à la naissance (en années)**		
Hungary	2005	-0.3[1]	1.3[1]	7.4[1]	14	72.5[1]	68.3[1]	76.7[1]
Hongrie	2010	-0.3[1]	1.3[1]	5.7[1]	15	73.7[1]	69.6[1]	77.8[1]
	2015	-0.3[1]	1.3[1]	5.0[1]	17	75.3[1]	71.6[1]	78.7[1]
Iceland	2005	1.0[1]	2.0[1]	2.5[1]	4	80.7[1]	78.8[1]	82.6[1]
Islande	2010	1.6[1]	2.1[1]	2.0[1]	4	81.4[1]	79.6[1]	83.2[1]
	2015	0.6[1]	2.0[1]	1.6[1]	3	82.2[1]	80.6[1]	83.8[1]
India	2005	1.7[1]	3.1[1]	60.0[1]	280	63.5[1]	62.7[1]	64.3[1]
Inde	2010	1.5[1]	2.8[1]	49.5[1]	215	65.5[1]	64.7[1]	66.4[1]
	2015	1.2[1]	2.4[1]	39.1[1]	174	67.8[1]	66.7[1]	69.0[1]
Indonesia	2005	1.4[1]	2.5[1]	37.3[1]	212	66.4[1]	64.8[1]	68.0[1]
Indonésie	2010	1.3[1]	2.5[1]	30.4[1]	165	68.3[1]	66.4[1]	70.3[1]
	2015	1.3[1]	2.5[1]	25.0[1]	126	70.0[1]	67.9[1]	72.2[1]
Iran (Islamic Republic of)	2005	1.2[1]	1.9[1]	24.8[1]	34	71.1[1]	70.0[1]	72.3[1]
Iran (Rép. islamique d')	2010	1.1[1]	1.8[1]	19.1[1]	27	72.7[1]	71.0[1]	74.6[1]
	2015	1.2[1]	1.9[1]	15.2[1]	25	75.0[1]	74.0[1]	76.2[1]
Iraq	2005	2.7[1]	4.7[1]	34.5[1]	54	68.8[1]	66.6[1]	71.1[1]
Iraq	2010	2.0[1]	4.4[1]	31.7[1]	51	68.0[1]	64.9[1]	71.3[1]
	2015	3.6[1]	4.3[1]	28.5[1]	50	69.4[1]	67.2[1]	71.6[1]
Ireland	2005	1.8[1]	1.9[1]	5.2[1]	8	77.8[1]	75.3[1]	80.4[1]
Irlande	2010	1.9[1]	2.0[1]	3.7[1]	7	79.7[1]	77.4[1]	82.0[1]
	2015	0.4[1]	2.0[1]	3.4[1]	8	80.6[1]	78.7[1]	82.5[1]
Isle of Man [1]	2005	1.0	...	...	...	...	...	...
Île de Man [1]	2010	1.0	...	...	...	...	...	...
	2015	0.8	...	...	...	...	...	...
Israel	2005	1.9[1]	2.9[1]	5.0[1]	7	79.6[1]	77.4[1]	81.6[1]
Israël	2010	2.4[1]	2.9[1]	4.0[1]	6	80.9[1]	79.0[1]	82.8[1]
	2015	1.7[1]	3.0[1]	3.4[1]	5	81.9[1]	80.0[1]	83.7[1]
Italy	2005	0.6[1]	1.3[1]	4.1[1]	4	80.3[1]	77.3[1]	83.1[1]
Italie	2010	0.4[1]	1.4[1]	3.4[1]	4	81.5[1]	78.8[1]	84.1[1]
	2015	0.4[1]	1.4[1]	3.0[1]	4	82.4[1]	79.9[1]	84.7[1]
Jamaica	2005	0.6[1]	2.5[1]	18.0[1]	92	74.1[1]	72.9[1]	75.4[1]
Jamaïque	2010	0.5[1]	2.3[1]	16.7[1]	93	74.2[1]	72.8[1]	75.6[1]
	2015	0.6[1]	2.1[1]	14.9[1]	89	74.0[1]	72.5[1]	75.5[1]
Japan	2005	0.1[1]	1.3[1]	3.0[1]	7	81.8[1]	78.3[1]	85.2[1]
Japon	2010	~0.0[1]	1.3[1]	2.6[1]	6	82.7[1]	79.2[1]	86.0[1]
	2015	-0.1[1]	1.4[1]	2.2[1]	5	83.3[1]	80.1[1]	86.5[1]
Jordan	2005	2.4[1]	4.0[1]	22.4[1]	62	72.2[1]	70.8[1]	73.8[1]
Jordanie	2010	4.6[1]	3.8[1]	19.7[1]	59	73.0[1]	71.5[1]	74.6[1]
	2015	4.9[1]	3.4[1]	17.1[1]	58	73.8[1]	72.2[1]	75.5[1]
Kazakhstan	2005	0.6[1]	2.0[1]	32.0[1]	44	64.6[1]	59.1[1]	70.4[1]
Kazakhstan	2010	1.1[1]	2.5[1]	23.9[1]	20	66.1[1]	60.6[1]	71.9[1]
	2015	1.6[1]	2.7[1]	14.1[1]	12	69.1[1]	64.3[1]	73.9[1]
Kenya	2005	2.7[1]	5.0[1]	62.8[1]	728	51.7[1]	49.6[1]	53.9[1]
Kenya	2010	2.8[1]	4.7[1]	51.1[1]	605	58.5[1]	56.7[1]	60.3[1]
	2015	2.6[1]	4.1[1]	41.6[1]	510	62.9[1]	60.6[1]	65.2[1]
Kiribati	2005	1.8[1]	4.0[1]	52.3[1]	135	63.9[1]	60.9[1]	66.8[1]
Kiribati	2010	2.2[1]	3.9[1]	51.4[1]	109	65.0[1]	61.5[1]	68.6[1]
	2015	1.5[1]	3.8[1]	47.9[1]	90	66.5[1]	62.5[1]	70.7[1]
Kuwait	2005	2.1[1]	2.6[1]	10.4[1]	6	73.3[1]	72.6[1]	74.5[1]
Koweït	2010	5.5[1]	2.4[1]	9.7[1]	5	73.8[1]	73.1[1]	74.9[1]
	2015	5.0[1]	2.1[1]	8.2[1]	4	74.9[1]	74.1[1]	75.9[1]
Kyrgyzstan	2005	0.6[1]	2.5[1]	37.8[1]	85	66.9[1]	63.0[1]	71.0[1]
Kirghizistan	2010	1.3[1]	2.8[1]	30.2[1]	84	67.5[1]	63.5[1]	71.7[1]
	2015	1.9[1]	3.3[1]	19.5[1]	76	70.3[1]	66.4[1]	74.3[1]
Lao People's Dem. Rep.	2005	1.5[1]	3.9[1]	70.0[1]	418	60.2[1]	58.4[1]	62.0[1]
Rép. dém. populaire lao	2010	1.7[1]	3.4[1]	57.5[1]	294	63.0[1]	61.2[1]	64.8[1]
	2015	1.5[1]	2.9[1]	47.0[1]	197	65.5[1]	63.7[1]	67.3[1]

Country or area Pays ou zone	Year Année	Population rate of increase (annual %) Population taux d'accroissement (% annuel)	Fertility rate, total (live births per woman) Taux de fécondité (naissances vivantes par femme)	Mortality rates (per live births) Taux de mortalite (pour naissances vivantes)		Life expectancy at birth (years) Espérance de vie à la naissance (en années)		
				Infant Infantile p. 1 000	Maternal Maternale p. 100 000	Total Totale	Male Hommes	Females Femmes
Latvia	2005	-1.1[1]	1.3[1]	9.9[1]	22	70.8[1]	65.2[1]	76.2[1]
Lettonie	2010	-1.2[1]	1.5[1]	7.8[1]	19	71.6[1]	66.0[1]	77.0[1]
	2015	-1.2[1]	1.5[1]	5.2[1]	18	74.1[1]	69.0[1]	78.8[1]
Lebanon	2005	4.0[1]	2.2[1]	13.8[1]	27	75.7[1]	73.9[1]	77.4[1]
Liban	2010	1.1[1]	1.9[1]	10.6[1]	19	77.8[1]	76.0[1]	79.7[1]
	2015	5.5[1]	2.1[1]	9.6[1]	15	78.6[1]	76.9[1]	80.6[1]
Lesotho	2005	-0.4[1]	3.7[1]	79.0[1]	746	44.2[1]	42.1[1]	46.6[1]
Lesotho	2010	~0.0[1]	3.4[1]	74.9[1]	587	43.1[1]	40.6[1]	45.8[1]
	2015	0.6[1]	3.3[1]	65.4[1]	487	48.2[1]	45.2[1]	51.3[1]
Liberia	2005	2.4[1]	5.7[1]	100.3[1]	1 020	52.8[1]	51.7[1]	53.9[1]
Libéria	2010	3.8[1]	5.2[1]	72.9[1]	811	58.1[1]	56.4[1]	59.8[1]
	2015	2.8[1]	4.8[1]	60.1[1]	725	60.7[1]	59.3[1]	62.2[1]
Libya	2005	1.6[1]	2.6[1]	21.5[1]	11	71.3[1]	69.6[1]	73.3[1]
Libye	2010	1.3[1]	2.5[1]	17.6[1]	9	72.3[1]	70.1[1]	74.9[1]
	2015	0.7[1]	2.5[1]	13.0[1]	9	71.7[1]	68.9[1]	74.9[1]
Liechtenstein	2005	0.9[1]	1.5	...	...	...	...	...
Liechtenstein	2010	0.7[1]	1.4	...	...	...	...	...
	2012	...	1.5	...	...	...	...	...
	2015[1]	0.8	...	...	...	...	...	...
Lithuania	2005	-0.9[1]	1.3[1]	7.7[1]	12	71.6[1]	65.7[1]	77.5[1]
Lituanie	2010	-1.4[1]	1.4[1]	6.0[1]	9	71.9[1]	66.0[1]	77.8[1]
	2015	-1.3[1]	1.6[1]	4.4[1]	10	74.0[1]	68.5[1]	79.3[1]
Luxembourg	2005	1.0[1]	1.7[1]	5.0[1]	13	78.3[1]	75.1[1]	81.4[1]
Luxembourg	2010	2.1[1]	1.6[1]	2.3[1]	11	79.5[1]	76.7[1]	82.2[1]
	2015	2.2[1]	1.5[1]	3.4[1]	10	81.1[1]	78.8[1]	83.5[1]
Madagascar	2005	3.0[1]	5.3[1]	58.0[1]	508	60.0[1]	58.8[1]	61.3[1]
Madagascar	2010	2.9[1]	4.8[1]	45.5[1]	436	62.2[1]	60.8[1]	63.7[1]
	2015	2.7[1]	4.4[1]	36.8[1]	353	64.5[1]	63.0[1]	66.0[1]
Malawi	2005	2.5[1]	6.0[1]	86.9[1]	648	45.6[1]	43.4[1]	48.0[1]
Malawi	2010	2.8[1]	5.7[1]	68.4[1]	629	51.3[1]	48.7[1]	54.0[1]
	2015	2.8[1]	4.9[1]	52.6[1]	634	59.6[1]	56.6[1]	62.5[1]
Malaysia	2005	2.0[1,26]	2.5[1,26]	7.6[1,26]	52	73.1[1,26]	71.0[1,26]	75.4[1,26]
Malaisie	2010	1.9[1,26]	2.2[1,26]	7.0[1,26]	48	74.0[1,26]	72.0[1,26]	76.3[1,26]
	2015	1.4[1,26]	2.1[1,26]	6.4[1,26]	40	75.0[1,26]	73.0[1,26]	77.2[1,26]
Maldives	2005	2.7[1]	2.4[1]	26.6[1]	101	72.1[1]	71.1[1]	73.3[1]
Maldives	2010	2.7[1]	2.3[1]	14.8[1]	87	74.8[1]	73.7[1]	76.2[1]
	2015	4.4[1]	2.1[1]	9.0[1]	68	76.8[1]	75.5[1]	78.5[1]
Mali	2005	3.1[1]	6.9[1]	106.5[1]	714	50.0[1]	49.3[1]	50.6[1]
Mali	2010	3.3[1]	6.7[1]	89.1[1]	630	54.0[1]	53.4[1]	54.7[1]
	2015	2.9[1]	6.4[1]	78.5[1]	587	56.2[1]	55.6[1]	56.9[1]
Malta	2005	0.6[1]	1.5[1]	5.7[1]	13	79.5[1]	77.2[1]	81.6[1]
Malte	2010	0.5[1]	1.4[1]	5.6[1]	11	80.3[1]	78.1[1]	82.4[1]
	2015	0.9[1]	1.4[1]	5.5[1]	9	81.4[1]	79.4[1]	83.4[1]
Marshall Islands	2004	...	...	...	...	...	67.0	70.6
Îles Marshall	2005[1]	~0.0	...	...	...	...	...	...
	2010[1]	0.1	...	...	...	...	...	...
	2011	...	4.1	25.4[16]	...	71.8	# 71.3	# 72.5
	2015[1]	0.2	...	...	...	...	...	...
Martinique [1]	2005	0.5	1.9	8.5	...	78.9	75.5	82.2
Martinique [1]	2010	-0.1	2.0	7.6	...	80.1	76.7	83.2
	2015	-0.8	2.0	6.4	...	81.2	77.8	84.4
Mauritania	2005	2.8[1]	5.3[1]	69.2[1]	750	60.9[1]	59.1[1]	62.8[1]
Mauritanie	2010	2.9[1]	5.1[1]	65.6[1]	723	61.9[1]	60.1[1]	63.7[1]
	2015	2.9[1]	4.9[1]	58.9[1]	602	63.2[1]	61.4[1]	65.0[1]
Mauritius	2005	0.6[1,27]	1.9[1,27]	13.3[1,27]	39	72.1[1,27]	68.9[1,27]	75.5[1,27]
Maurice	2010	0.4[1,27]	1.7[1,27]	13.2[1,27]	59	72.8[1,27]	69.4[1,27]	76.3[1,27]
	2015	0.2[1,27]	1.5[1,27]	12.0[1,27]	53	74.1[1,27]	70.7[1,27]	77.7[1,27]

Country or area Pays ou zone	Year Année	Population rate of increase (annual %) Population taux d'accroissement (% annuel)	Fertility rate, total (live births per woman) Taux de fécondité (naissances vivantes par femme)	Mortality rates (per live births) Taux de mortalite (pour naissances vivantes) Infant Infantile p. 1 000	Maternal Maternale p. 100 000	Life expectancy at birth (years) Espérance de vie à la naissance (en années) Total Totale	Male Hommes	Females Femmes
Mayotte [1]	2005	3.4	4.8	7.6	...	76.5	73.0	80.6
Mayotte [1]	2010	3.2	4.6	5.6	...	78.0	74.5	81.9
	2015	2.8	4.1	4.2	...	79.3	76.0	82.9
Mexico	2005	1.4[1]	2.6[1]	20.1[1]	54	75.1[1]	72.5[1]	77.7[1]
Mexique	2010	1.5[1]	2.4[1]	17.1[1]	45	75.2[1]	72.4[1]	78.0[1]
	2015	1.3[1]	2.3[1]	15.2[1]	38	74.9[1]	72.0[1]	77.9[1]
Micronesia (Fed. States of)	2005	-0.2[1]	4.1[1]	39.8[1]	134	65.0[1]	63.4[1]	66.6[1]
Micronésie (États féd. de)	2010	-0.6[1]	3.6[1]	35.0[1]	115	66.0[1]	64.5[1]	67.7[1]
	2015	1.1[1]	3.3[1]	30.3[1]	100	66.9[1]	65.3[1]	68.6[1]
Monaco [1]	2005	1.0	...	...	...	...	...	...
Monaco [1]	2010	1.9	...	...	...	...	...	...
	2015	0.6	...	...	...	...	...	...
Mongolia	2005	1.0[1]	2.1[1]	40.8[1]	95	64.1[1]	60.8[1]	67.7[1]
Mongolie	2010	1.5[1]	2.4[1]	30.5[1]	63	66.1[1]	62.4[1]	70.3[1]
	2015	2.0[1]	2.8[1]	22.8[1]	44	68.5[1]	64.5[1]	72.7[1]
Montenegro	2005	0.1[1]	1.9[1]	11.6[1]	9	73.4[1]	70.6[1]	76.2[1]
Monténégro	2010	0.3[1]	1.8[1]	10.9[1]	8	74.2[1]	71.9[1]	76.5[1]
	2015	0.1[1]	1.7[1]	4.3[1]	7	76.1[1]	73.6[1]	78.5[1]
Montserrat	2004	...	1.7					
Montserrat	2005[1]	-0.7	...	...	...	...	...	...
	2010[1]	0.7	...	...	...	...	...	...
	2015[1]	0.7	...	...	...	...	...	...
Morocco	2005	1.1[1]	2.7[1]	36.6[1]	190	70.0[1]	68.5[1]	71.4[1]
Maroc	2010	1.2[1]	2.5[1]	26.6[1]	153	73.4[1]	72.1[1]	74.7[1]
	2015	1.4[1]	2.6[1]	24.2[1]	121	75.0[1]	73.7[1]	76.3[1]
Mozambique	2005	2.9[1]	5.8[1]	98.8[1]	762	49.9[1]	47.8[1]	51.9[1]
Mozambique	2010	2.8[1]	5.5[1]	78.7[1]	619	51.1[1]	48.8[1]	53.3[1]
	2015	2.8[1]	5.2[1]	62.8[1]	489	54.2[1]	51.5[1]	56.8[1]
Myanmar	2005	0.9[1]	2.8[1]	57.8[1]	248	60.9[1]	57.9[1]	63.9[1]
Myanmar	2010	0.7[1]	2.5[1]	52.0[1]	205	62.4[1]	59.1[1]	65.8[1]
	2015	0.8[1]	2.3[1]	43.7[1]	178	64.7[1]	61.3[1]	68.0[1]
Namibia	2005	1.5[1]	3.6[1]	51.1[1]	390	50.6[1]	48.7[1]	52.5[1]
Namibie	2010	1.8[1]	3.6[1]	43.5[1]	319	53.0[1]	51.5[1]	54.4[1]
	2015	1.8[1]	3.6[1]	38.6[1]	265	60.4[1]	57.7[1]	63.0[1]
Nauru	2000	0.1[1]	...	...	...	...	57.0	64.0
Nauru	2005[1]	0.1	...	...	...	...	...	...
	2007[28]	...	...	...	...	55.0	52.5	58.2
	2010[1]	-0.2	...	...	...	...	...	...
	2013[16]	...	3.9	18.0	...	# 61.2	# 57.8	# 64.8
	2015[1]	2.3	...	...	...	...	...	...
Nepal	2005	1.5[1]	3.5[1]	53.7[1]	444	63.9[1]	62.7[1]	65.0[1]
Népal	2010	1.0[1]	2.8[1]	42.6[1]	349	66.5[1]	65.2[1]	67.8[1]
	2015	~0.0[1]	2.3[1]	33.8[1]	258	68.6[1]	67.3[1]	70.0[1]
Netherlands	2005	0.5[1]	1.7[1]	4.9[1]	11	78.7[1]	76.2[1]	81.0[1]
Pays-Bas	2010	0.4[1]	1.7[1]	4.1[1]	8	80.2[1]	78.0[1]	82.2[1]
	2015	0.3[1]	1.7[1]	3.5[1]	7	81.3[1]	79.4[1]	83.1[1]
New Caledonia [1]	2005	1.7	2.3	17.3	...	74.1	71.3	77.2
Nouvelle-Calédonie [1]	2010	1.4	2.3	15.1	...	75.2	72.4	78.3
	2015	1.3	2.2	13.0	...	76.3	73.7	79.3
New Zealand	2005	1.4[1]	1.9[1]	5.4[1]	14	79.1[1]	76.8[1]	81.3[1]
Nouvelle-Zélande	2010	1.1[1]	2.1[1]	5.0[1]	13	80.3[1]	78.3[1]	82.3[1]
	2015	1.1[1]	2.0[1]	4.4[1]	11	81.3[1]	79.5[1]	83.1[1]
Nicaragua	2005	1.4[1]	2.9[1]	26.4[1]	190	70.5[1]	67.5[1]	73.5[1]
Nicaragua	2010	1.4[1]	2.7[1]	23.1[1]	166	71.7[1]	68.6[1]	74.9[1]
	2015	1.3[1]	2.5[1]	17.8[1]	150	73.1[1]	69.8[1]	76.4[1]
Niger	2005	3.7[1]	7.7[1]	85.2[1]	723	51.6[1]	50.9[1]	52.3[1]
Niger	2010	3.8[1]	7.6[1]	67.6[1]	657	55.3[1]	54.5[1]	56.2[1]
	2015	3.9[1]	7.4[1]	55.9[1]	553	59.2[1]	58.1[1]	60.3[1]

Country or area Pays ou zone	Year Année	Population rate of increase (annual %) Population taux d'accroissement (% annuel)	Fertility rate, total (live births per woman) Taux de fécondité (naissances vivantes par femme)	Mortality rates (per live births) Taux de mortalite (pour naissances vivantes) Infant Infantile p. 1 000	Maternal Maternelle p. 100 000	Life expectancy at birth (years) Espérance de vie à la naissance (en années) Total Totale	Male Hommes	Females Femmes
Nigeria Nigéria	2005	2.5[1]	6.1[1]	104.0[1]	946	46.9[1]	46.1[1]	47.8[1]
	2010	2.6[1]	5.9[1]	89.3[1]	867	49.8[1]	49.0[1]	50.5[1]
	2015	2.7[1]	5.7[1]	75.0[1]	814	52.0[1]	51.2[1]	52.8[1]
Niue Nioué	2005[1]	-2.4	...	...	...	...	...	...
	2006	...	...	...	...	...	67.0	76.0
	2010[1]	-0.7	...	...	...	...	...	...
	2011	...	2.6[16]	8.1[22]	...	73.2[22]	# 70.1[22]	# 76.3[22]
	2015[1]	-0.1	...	...	...	...	...	...
Northern Mariana Islands Îles Mariannes du Nord	2000	4.1[1]	1.6	...	...	...	72.5	77.8
	2005	-1.6[1]	1.5	...	...	...	...	...
	2009	...	2.2	...	...	...	74.5	79.9
	2010	-3.2[1]	2.2	...	...	...	...	...
	2012	...	...	6.4	...	76.4	# 74.9	# 77.9
	2013	...	1.6	...	...	...	...	...
	2015[1]	0.1	...	...	...	...	...	...
Norway Norvège	2005	0.6[1,29]	1.8[1,29]	3.5[1,29]	7	79.3[1,29]	76.8[1,29]	81.8[1,29]
	2010	1.1[1,29]	1.9[1,29]	3.0[1,29]	6	80.6[1,29]	78.3[1,29]	82.8[1,29]
	2015	1.2[1,29]	1.8[1,29]	2.4[1,29]	5	81.6[1,29]	79.5[1,29]	83.6[1,29]
Oman Oman	2005	2.0[1]	3.2[1]	14.6[1]	20	73.2[1]	71.4[1]	75.5[1]
	2010	3.8[1]	2.9[1]	9.8[1]	18	75.1[1]	73.2[1]	77.5[1]
	2015	6.8[1]	2.9[1]	9.6[1]	17	76.2[1]	74.5[1]	78.7[1]
Other non-specified areas [1] Autres zones non-spécifiées [1]	2005	0.7	1.3	6.0	...	76.9	74.2	80.0
	2010	0.4	1.1	5.2	...	78.2	75.2	81.5
	2015	0.3	1.1	4.2	...	79.3	76.4	82.3
Pakistan Pakistan	2005	2.4[1]	4.7[1]	82.9[1]	249	63.4[1]	62.6[1]	64.4[1]
	2010	2.3[1]	4.2[1]	75.6[1]	211	64.5[1]	63.6[1]	65.5[1]
	2015	2.1[1]	3.8[1]	68.1[1]	178	66.0[1]	65.1[1]	67.0[1]
Palau Palaos	2000	2.1[1]	1.5	...	...	...	66.6	74.5
	2005	0.8[1]	...	...	...	...	66.3	72.1
	2010[1]	0.6	...	...	...	...	...	...
	2015	0.8[1]	# 2.2[30]	13.3	...	73.0	# 68.1	# 77.8
Panama Panama	2005	1.9[1]	2.7[1]	20.6[1]	87	75.5[1]	73.0[1]	78.1[1]
	2010	1.8[1]	2.6[1]	17.8[1]	101	76.3[1]	73.5[1]	79.3[1]
	2015	1.7[1]	2.6[1]	16.0[1]	94	77.3[1]	74.4[1]	80.4[1]
Papua New Guinea Papouasie-Nvl-Guinée	2005	2.1[1]	4.4[1]	58.2[1]	277	59.8[1]	58.5[1]	61.2[1]
	2010	2.4[1]	4.1[1]	54.5[1]	238	61.3[1]	60.0[1]	62.7[1]
	2015	2.1[1]	3.8[1]	48.3[1]	215	62.7[1]	61.4[1]	64.1[1]
Paraguay Paraguay	2005	1.8[1]	3.2[1]	27.1[1]	159	71.2[1]	69.2[1]	73.2[1]
	2010	1.4[1]	2.9[1]	24.1[1]	139	72.1[1]	70.2[1]	74.2[1]
	2015	1.4[1]	2.6[1]	20.8[1]	132	73.2[1]	71.3[1]	75.2[1]
Peru Pérou	2005	1.0[1]	2.7[1]	24.9[1]	114	72.1[1]	69.8[1]	74.4[1]
	2010	0.8[1]	2.7[1]	18.1[1]	92	73.7[1]	71.3[1]	76.1[1]
	2015	1.0[1]	2.4[1]	14.1[1]	68	75.1[1]	72.6[1]	77.7[1]
Philippines Philippines	2005	2.0[1]	3.7[1]	27.9[1]	127	68.9[1]	65.5[1]	72.4[1]
	2010	1.7[1]	3.3[1]	25.5[1]	129	69.4[1]	65.8[1]	73.4[1]
	2015	1.7[1]	3.1[1]	23.7[1]	114	70.2[1]	66.2[1]	74.6[1]
Poland Pologne	2005	-0.1[1]	1.3[1]	7.1[1]	6	74.6[1]	70.4[1]	78.8[1]
	2010	-~0.0[1]	1.4[1]	5.7[1]	4	75.6[1]	71.3[1]	79.8[1]
	2015	-0.2[1]	1.3[1]	4.4[1]	3	77.1[1]	73.1[1]	81.2[1]
Portugal Portugal	2005	0.4[1]	1.5[1]	4.5[1]	12	77.6[1]	74.1[1]	81.0[1]
	2010	0.2[1]	1.4[1]	3.3[1]	11	79.3[1]	76.0[1]	82.5[1]
	2015	-0.4[1]	1.3[1]	2.9[1]	10	80.6[1]	77.5[1]	83.7[1]
Puerto Rico Porto Rico	2005	-0.2[1]	1.9[1]	8.0[1]	19	76.8[1]	72.7[1]	80.9[1]
	2010	-0.3[1]	1.7[1]	7.2[1]	16	77.9[1]	74.0[1]	81.8[1]
	2015	-1.1[1]	1.5[1]	6.4[1]	14	79.1[1]	75.4[1]	82.7[1]
Qatar Qatar	2005	7.6[1]	3.0[1]	9.8[1]	21	77.8[1]	76.9[1]	79.4[1]
	2010	15.3[1]	2.2[1]	8.3[1]	16	78.7[1]	77.6[1]	80.3[1]
	2015	6.5[1]	2.0[1]	7.3[1]	13	79.5[1]	78.3[1]	81.1[1]

Country or area Pays ou zone	Year Année	Population rate of increase (annual %) Population taux d'accroissement (% annuel)	Fertility rate, total (live births per woman) Taux de fécondité (naissances vivantes par femme)	Infant Infantile p. 1 000	Maternal Maternale p. 100 000	Total Totale	Male Hommes	Females Femmes
Republic of Korea	2005	0.6[1]	1.2[1]	5.0[1]	14	77.2[1]	73.6[1]	80.6[1]
République de Corée	2010	0.3[1]	1.2[1]	3.5[1]	15	79.5[1]	76.0[1]	82.7[1]
	2015	0.5[1]	1.2[1]	3.0[1]	11	81.3[1]	77.9[1]	84.4[1]
Republic of Moldova	2005	-0.2[1,31]	1.2[1,31]	18.8[1,31]	39	67.6[1,31]	63.6[1,31]	71.6[1,31]
République de Moldova	2010	-0.4[1,31]	1.3[1,31]	15.6[1,31]	34	68.3[1,31]	64.4[1,31]	72.1[1,31]
	2015	-0.1[1,31]	1.3[1,31]	14.2[1,31]	23	71.0[1,31]	66.7[1,31]	75.2[1,31]
Réunion [1]	2005	1.4	2.4	7.6	...	76.8	73.0	80.6
Réunion [1]	2010	1.0	2.4	5.6	...	78.2	74.5	81.9
	2015	0.8	2.4	4.2	...	79.5	76.0	82.9
Romania	2005	-0.7[1]	1.3[1]	16.9[1]	33	71.5[1]	67.9[1]	75.2[1]
Roumanie	2010	-0.9[1]	1.5[1]	12.0[1]	30	73.1[1]	69.5[1]	76.7[1]
	2015	-0.5[1]	1.5[1]	8.4[1]	31	74.9[1]	71.5[1]	78.4[1]
Russian Federation	2005	-0.4[1]	1.3[1]	16.2[1]	42	65.0[1]	58.6[1]	72.0[1]
Fédération de Russie	2010	-~0.0[1]	1.5[1]	10.7[1]	29	67.1[1]	61.0[1]	73.7[1]
	2015	0.2[1]	1.7[1]	8.3[1]	25	70.3[1]	64.6[1]	76.0[1]
Rwanda	2005	2.2[1]	5.4[1]	94.3[1]	567	50.4[1]	49.4[1]	51.4[1]
Rwanda	2010	2.5[1]	4.9[1]	62.7[1]	381	60.0[1]	58.5[1]	61.5[1]
	2015	2.5[1]	4.3[1]	39.4[1]	290	65.8[1]	63.9[1]	67.6[1]
Saint Barthélemy [1]	2005	2.8	...	...	...	...	...	...
Saint-Barthélemy [1]	2010	1.5	...	...	...	...	...	...
	2015	1.0	...	...	...	...	...	...
Saint Helena [1,32]	2005	-3.6	...	...	...	...	...	...
Sainte-Hélène [1,32]	2010	-0.5	...	...	...	...	...	...
	2015	-0.7	...	...	...	...	...	...
Saint Kitts and Nevis [1]	2005	1.4	...	...	...	...	...	...
Saint-Kitts-et-Nevis [1]	2010	1.1	...	...	...	...	...	...
	2015	1.1	...	...	...	...	...	...
Saint Lucia	2005	0.8[1]	1.9[1]	15.7[1]	67	73.7[1]	72.2[1]	75.3[1]
Sainte-Lucie	2010	1.3[1]	1.6[1]	16.3[1]	54	74.5[1]	73.0[1]	76.0[1]
	2015	0.6[1]	1.5[1]	16.0[1]	48	75.2[1]	73.9[1]	76.6[1]
Saint Martin (French part) [1]	2005	3.4	...	...	...	...	...	...
St-Martin (partie française) [1]	2010	1.9	...	...	...	...	...	...
	2015	-0.9	...	...	...	...	...	...
Saint Pierre and Miquelon [1]	2005	-~0.0	...	...	...	...	...	...
Saint-Pierre-et-Miquelon [1]	2010	~0.0	...	...	...	...	...	...
	2015	~0.0	...	...	...	...	...	...
Saint Vincent & Grenadines	2005	0.2[1]	2.2[1]	19.6[1]	50	71.0[1]	68.8[1]	73.4[1]
Saint-Vincent-Grenadines	2010	-0.1[1]	2.1[1]	19.5[1]	50	71.6[1]	69.4[1]	74.1[1]
	2015	0.2[1]	2.0[1]	17.4[1]	45	71.9[1]	69.6[1]	74.5[1]
Samoa	2005	0.6[1]	4.4[1]	17.0[1]	77	69.7[1]	67.3[1]	72.3[1]
Samoa	2010	0.7[1]	4.5[1]	16.6[1]	64	71.0[1]	68.8[1]	73.5[1]
	2015	0.8[1]	4.2[1]	15.1[1]	51	72.3[1]	70.2[1]	74.5[1]
San Marino	2000	1.2[1]	1.3	...	...	...	77.4	84.0
Saint-Marin	2004	...	1.3	...	...	...	...	...
	2005[1]	1.3	...	...	...	...	...	...
	2010[1]	1.2	...	...	...	...	...	...
	2013	...	...	...	...	...	81.7	86.4
	2015[1]	1.2	...	...	...	...	...	...
Sao Tome and Principe	2005	2.0[1]	5.1[1]	56.1[1]	181	63.1[1]	61.0[1]	65.1[1]
Sao Tomé-et-Principe	2010	2.7[1]	4.9[1]	42.1[1]	162	66.1[1]	63.9[1]	68.3[1]
	2015	2.0[1]	4.6[1]	32.1[1]	156	68.5[1]	66.2[1]	70.8[1]
Saudi Arabia	2005	2.8[1]	3.7[1]	16.3[1]	18	73.0[1]	71.6[1]	74.7[1]
Arabie saoudite	2010	2.8[1]	3.2[1]	12.2[1]	14	73.5[1]	72.1[1]	75.1[1]
	2015	2.9[1]	2.7[1]	8.7[1]	12	74.4[1]	73.1[1]	76.0[1]
Senegal	2005	2.5[1]	5.3[1]	61.1[1]	427	58.9[1]	57.3[1]	60.6[1]
Sénégal	2010	2.7[1]	5.1[1]	47.5[1]	375	62.5[1]	61.1[1]	63.9[1]
	2015	2.8[1]	5.0[1]	38.3[1]	315	65.7[1]	63.8[1]	67.5[1]

Country or area Pays ou zone	Year Année	Population rate of increase (annual %) Population taux d'accroissement (% annuel)	Fertility rate, total (live births per woman) Taux de fécondité (naissances vivantes par femme)	Mortality rates (per live births) Taux de mortalite (pour naissances vivantes)		Life expectancy at birth (years) Espérance de vie à la naissance (en années)		
				Infant Infantile p. 1 000	Maternal Maternelle p. 100 000	Total Totale	Male Hommes	Females Femmes
Serbia	2005	-0.6[1,33]	1.7[1,33]	9.5[1,33]	15	72.3[1,33]	69.6[1,33]	75.1[1,33]
Serbie	2010	-0.4[1,33]	1.6[1,33]	7.1[1,33]	16	73.4[1,33]	70.8[1,33]	76.2[1,33]
	2015	-0.3[1,33]	1.5[1,33]	6.1[1,33]	17	74.8[1,33]	72.1[1,33]	77.4[1,33]
Seychelles [1]	2005	1.8	2.2	11.9	...	71.6	67.4	76.2
Seychelles [1]	2010	0.6	2.3	12.2	...	72.6	68.9	76.6
	2015	0.8	2.4	12.4	...	73.1	69.6	77.0
Sierra Leone	2005	4.2[1]	6.1[1]	141.9[1]	1 986	42.0[1]	41.3[1]	42.7[1]
Sierra Leone	2010	2.6[1]	5.6[1]	122.1[1]	1 633	47.0[1]	46.2[1]	47.8[1]
	2015	2.2[1]	4.8[1]	97.1[1]	1 360	51.4[1]	50.5[1]	52.3[1]
Singapore	2005	1.1[1]	1.3[1]	2.5[1]	16	79.2[1]	76.7[1]	81.8[1]
Singapour	2010	3.7[1]	1.3[1]	2.2[1]	11	81.2[1]	78.7[1]	83.7[1]
	2015	1.7[1]	1.2[1]	2.1[1]	10	82.3[1]	80.1[1]	84.5[1]
Sint Maarten (Dutch part)	2005[1]	0.4	...	...	...	...	...	...
St-Martin (partie néerland.)	2010	0.4[1]	...	...	...	...	72.0[16]	77.2[16]
	2013[15]	...	...	...	...	...	69.2	77.1
	2015[1]	3.1	...	...	...	...	...	...
Slovakia	2005	~0.0[1]	1.2[1]	7.3[1]	7	73.8[1]	69.8[1]	77.8[1]
Slovaquie	2010	~0.0[1]	1.3[1]	6.2[1]	6	74.8[1]	70.8[1]	78.6[1]
	2015	0.1[1]	1.4[1]	5.4[1]	6	76.2[1]	72.5[1]	79.8[1]
Slovenia	2005	0.1[1]	1.2[1]	4.0[1]	11	76.7[1]	72.8[1]	80.4[1]
Slovénie	2010	0.5[1]	1.4[1]	3.2[1]	9	78.6[1]	75.0[1]	82.0[1]
	2015	0.3[1]	1.6[1]	2.2[1]	9	80.1[1]	77.1[1]	83.1[1]
Solomon Islands	2005	2.6[1]	4.6[1]	24.6[1]	164	68.4[1]	67.0[1]	69.9[1]
Îles Salomon	2010	2.3[1]	4.4[1]	23.0[1]	136	69.9[1]	68.3[1]	71.7[1]
	2015	2.7[1]	4.4[1]	20.2[1]	114	71.4[1]	69.8[1]	73.3[1]
Somalia	2005	3.3[1]	7.5[1]	97.0[1]	939	51.5[1]	50.0[1]	53.1[1]
Somalie	2010	2.8[1]	7.1[1]	89.8[1]	820	53.2[1]	51.7[1]	54.8[1]
	2015	2.7[1]	6.6[1]	79.4[1]	732	54.9[1]	53.3[1]	56.5[1]
South Africa	2005	1.3[1]	2.6[1]	53.9[1]	112	53.9[1]	51.4[1]	56.6[1]
Afrique du Sud	2010	1.3[1]	2.6[1]	48.1[1]	154	54.7[1]	52.3[1]	57.3[1]
	2015	1.6[1]	2.6[1]	32.9[1]	138	61.0[1]	57.8[1]	64.2[1]
South Sudan	2005	3.9[1]	6.0[1]	101.3[1]	1 088	50.2[1]	49.1[1]	51.3[1]
Soudan du sud	2010	4.7[1]	5.6[1]	78.6[1]	876	53.3[1]	52.2[1]	54.4[1]
	2015	2.4[1]	5.2[1]	65.8[1]	789	56.1[1]	54.6[1]	57.5[1]
Spain	2005	1.5[1,34]	1.3[1,34]	4.0[1,34]	5	79.9[1,34]	76.5[1,34]	83.3[1,34]
Espagne	2010	1.3[1,34]	1.5[1,34]	3.4[1,34]	5	81.2[1,34]	78.1[1,34]	84.4[1,34]
	2015	-0.1[1,34]	1.3[1,34]	2.9[1,34]	5	82.5[1,34]	79.6[1,34]	85.3[1,34]
Sri Lanka	2005	0.8[1]	2.3[1]	11.8[1]	43	73.9[1]	70.5[1]	77.6[1]
Sri Lanka	2010	0.7[1]	2.3[1]	10.2[1]	35	74.9[1]	71.5[1]	78.5[1]
	2015	0.6[1]	2.2[1]	8.8[1]	30	75.9[1]	72.5[1]	79.3[1]
State of Palestine	2005	2.1[1,35]	5.0[1,35]	23.7[1,35]	62	71.5[1,35]	70.0[1,35]	73.1[1,35]
État de Palestine	2010	2.5[1,35]	4.6[1,35]	21.0[1,35]	54	72.5[1,35]	70.8[1,35]	74.2[1,35]
	2015	2.2[1,35]	4.3[1,35]	19.3[1,35]	45	73.1[1,35]	71.4[1,35]	74.9[1,35]
Sudan	2005	2.5[1]	5.3[1]	61.8[1]	440	59.5[1]	57.5[1]	61.5[1]
Soudan	2010	2.2[1]	5.0[1]	53.2[1]	349	61.6[1]	59.8[1]	63.5[1]
	2015	2.4[1]	4.8[1]	47.8[1]	311	63.8[1]	62.1[1]	65.5[1]
Suriname	2005	1.2[1]	2.8[1]	28.0[1]	223	68.1[1]	64.9[1]	71.6[1]
Suriname	2010	1.2[1]	2.7[1]	23.7[1]	169	69.8[1]	66.7[1]	73.2[1]
	2015	1.1[1]	2.6[1]	20.3[1]	155	70.9[1]	67.8[1]	74.3[1]
Sweden	2005	0.4[1]	1.7[1]	3.2[1]	5	80.1[1]	77.9[1]	82.3[1]
Suède	2010	0.8[1]	1.9[1]	2.6[1]	4	81.1[1]	79.0[1]	83.1[1]
	2015	0.8[1]	1.9[1]	2.4[1]	4	81.9[1]	80.0[1]	83.8[1]
Switzerland	2005	0.7[1]	1.4[1]	4.6[1]	7	80.5[1]	77.7[1]	83.1[1]
Suisse	2010	1.1[1]	1.5[1]	4.2[1]	6	81.8[1]	79.3[1]	84.1[1]
	2015	1.2[1]	1.5[1]	3.9[1]	5	82.7[1]	80.5[1]	84.8[1]
Syrian Arab Republic	2005	2.2[1]	3.9[1]	17.7[1]	58	73.6[1]	71.4[1]	75.9[1]
République arabe syrienne	2010	3.0[1]	3.7[1]	15.0[1]	49	74.5[1]	72.0[1]	77.3[1]
	2015	-3.4[1]	3.1[1]	17.9[1]	68	69.9[1]	64.4[1]	76.3[1]

Country or area Pays ou zone	Year Année	Population rate of increase (annual %) Population taux d'accroissement (% annuel)	Fertility rate, total (live births per woman) Taux de fécondité (naissances vivantes par femme)	Infant Infantile p. 1 000	Maternal Maternale p. 100 000	Total Totale	Male Hommes	Females Femmes
Tajikistan	2005	1.8[1]	3.7[1]	57.2[1]	46	64.1[1]	62.1[1]	66.2[1]
Tadjikistan	2010	2.1[1]	3.6[1]	39.0[1]	35	67.7[1]	65.6[1]	70.1[1]
	2015	2.3[1]	3.6[1]	34.1[1]	32	69.4[1]	67.2[1]	71.8[1]
Thailand	2005	0.8[1]	1.6[1]	16.7[1]	26	71.2[1]	67.7[1]	74.9[1]
Thaïlande	2010	0.5[1]	1.6[1]	13.4[1]	23	73.2[1]	69.8[1]	76.6[1]
	2015	0.4[1]	1.5[1]	10.1[1]	20	75.2[1]	71.6[1]	78.9[1]
North Macedonia	2005	0.2[1]	1.6[1]	12.9[1]	10	73.8[1]	71.3[1]	76.4[1]
Macédoine du Nord	2010	0.1[1]	1.5[1]	10.8[1]	8	74.2[1]	72.1[1]	76.3[1]
	2015	0.1[1]	1.5[1]	8.9[1]	8	75.2[1]	73.1[1]	77.2[1]
Timor-Leste	2005	2.4[1]	6.3[1]	69.0[1]	506	61.1[1]	59.4[1]	63.0[1]
Timor-Leste	2010	1.9[1]	5.3[1]	53.3[1]	317	66.2[1]	64.7[1]	67.6[1]
	2015	1.8[1]	4.4[1]	44.9[1]	215	67.7[1]	65.9[1]	69.5[1]
Togo	2005	2.6[1]	5.3[1]	77.3[1]	427	53.9[1]	53.0[1]	54.7[1]
Togo	2010	2.7[1]	5.0[1]	63.2[1]	393	55.8[1]	55.1[1]	56.5[1]
	2015	2.6[1]	4.7[1]	55.7[1]	368	59.1[1]	58.3[1]	59.8[1]
Tokelau	2005[1]	-5.0	...	...	...	...	...	...
Tokélaou	2010[1]	-1.3	...	...	...	...	...	...
	2012	...	2.1	...	...	...	...	...
	2015[1]	1.9	...	...	...	...	...	...
Tonga	2005	0.6[1]	4.2[1]	14.4[1]	114	69.8[1]	68.6[1]	71.0[1]
Tonga	2010	0.6[1]	4.0[1]	14.4[1]	130	69.9[1]	67.9[1]	71.8[1]
	2015	-0.6[1]	3.8[1]	14.7[1]	124	70.3[1]	68.4[1]	72.2[1]
Trinidad and Tobago	2005	0.5[1]	1.8[1]	28.8[1]	62	70.0[1]	67.7[1]	72.5[1]
Trinité-et-Tobago	2010	0.5[1]	1.8[1]	28.5[1]	65	71.3[1]	68.6[1]	74.2[1]
	2015	0.6[1]	1.8[1]	26.1[1]	63	72.5[1]	69.8[1]	75.2[1]
Tunisia	2005	0.8[1]	2.0[1]	23.0[1]	74	73.7[1]	71.4[1]	76.3[1]
Tunisie	2010	1.0[1]	2.0[1]	18.0[1]	67	74.6[1]	72.3[1]	77.2[1]
	2015	1.0[1]	2.3[1]	14.6[1]	62	75.5[1]	73.4[1]	77.6[1]
Turkey	2005	1.4[1]	2.4[1]	24.7[1]	57	71.4[1]	68.0[1]	74.9[1]
Turquie	2010	1.3[1]	2.2[1]	16.4[1]	23	73.4[1]	69.9[1]	76.9[1]
	2015	1.6[1]	2.1[1]	11.8[1]	16	75.6[1]	72.5[1]	78.7[1]
Turkmenistan	2005	1.0[1]	2.8[1]	62.0[1]	53	64.2[1]	60.3[1]	68.2[1]
Turkménistan	2010	1.4[1]	2.7[1]	54.1[1]	46	65.9[1]	62.2[1]	69.6[1]
	2015	1.8[1]	3.0[1]	46.9[1]	42	67.3[1]	63.9[1]	70.8[1]
Turks and Caicos Islands	2001	...	...	...	...	77.5	79.0	77.4
Îles Turques-et-Caïques	2002	...	...	...	...	...	75.1	77.3
	2005[1]	6.7	...	...	...	...	...	...
	2010[1]	3.2	...	...	...	...	...	...
	2012	...	...	...	...	...	75.8	77.8
	2015[1]	2.1	...	...	...	...	...	...
Tuvalu	2002	...	3.7	...	...	...	...	...
Tuvalu	2005[1]	1.2	...	...	...	...	...	...
	2010	1.0[1]	...	10.3	...	69.6	67.4	71.9
	#2012	...	3.6	...	...	...	...	...
	2015[1]	0.9	...	...	...	...	...	...
Uganda	2005	3.2[1]	6.7[1]	79.5[1]	504	49.0[1]	46.4[1]	51.7[1]
Ouganda	2010	3.2[1]	6.4[1]	70.7[1]	420	54.4[1]	52.5[1]	56.2[1]
	2015	3.3[1]	5.8[1]	59.0[1]	343	59.5[1]	57.7[1]	61.1[1]
Ukraine	2005	-0.8[1,36]	1.1[1,36]	14.8[1,36]	30	67.5[1,36]	61.9[1,36]	73.4[1,36]
Ukraine	2010	-0.5[1,36]	1.4[1,36]	12.6[1,36]	26	67.9[1,36]	62.3[1,36]	73.8[1,36]
	2015	-0.4[1,36]	1.5[1,36]	8.8[1,36]	24	70.9[1,36]	65.8[1,36]	75.9[1,36]
United Arab Emirates	2005	7.6[1]	2.4[1]	9.0[1]	6	74.9[1]	74.1[1]	76.3[1]
Émirats arabes unis	2010	12.4[1]	2.0[1]	7.7[1]	6	75.9[1]	75.1[1]	77.3[1]
	2015	1.6[1]	1.7[1]	6.5[1]	6	76.8[1]	76.1[1]	78.2[1]
United Kingdom	2005	0.5[1]	1.7[1]	5.3[1]	12	78.4[1]	76.1[1]	80.6[1]
Royaume-Uni	2010	1.0[1]	1.9[1]	4.8[1]	10	79.7[1]	77.5[1]	81.8[1]
	2015	0.7[1]	1.9[1]	4.1[1]	9	80.9[1]	78.9[1]	82.7[1]

Country or area Pays ou zone	Year Année	Population rate of increase (annual %) Population taux d'accroissement (% annuel)	Fertility rate, total (live births per woman) Taux de fécondité (naissances vivantes par femme)	Mortality rates (per live births) Taux de mortalite (pour naissances vivantes)		Life expectancy at birth (years) Espérance de vie à la naissance (en années)		
				Infant Infantile p. 1 000	Maternal Maternale p. 100 000	Total Totale	Male Hommes	Females Femmes
United Rep. of Tanzania	2005	2.8[1,37]	5.7[1,37]	71.0[1,37]	687	52.7[1,37]	50.9[1,37]	54.4[1,37]
Rép.-Unie de Tanzanie	2010	2.9[1,37]	5.6[1,37]	55.5[1,37]	514	56.3[1,37]	54.8[1,37]	57.7[1,37]
	2015	3.0[1,37]	5.2[1,37]	46.9[1,37]	398	60.9[1,37]	58.8[1,37]	63.11[1,37]
United States of America	2005	0.9[1]	2.0[1]	7.0[1]	13	77.2[1]	74.5[1]	79.7[1]
États-Unis d'Amérique	2010	0.9[1]	2.1[1]	6.8[1]	14	78.2[1]	75.7[1]	80.7[1]
	2015	0.8[1]	1.9[1]	6.0[1]	14	78.9[1]	76.5[1]	81.3[1]
United States Virgin Islands [1]	2005	-0.2	2.1	11.6	...	77.1	74.9	79.5
Îles Vierges américaines [1]	2010	-0.3	2.4	10.7	...	77.8	75.5	80.3
	2015	-0.2	2.3	9.0	...	79.4	76.7	82.2
Uruguay	2005	~0.0[1]	2.2[1]	14.5[1]	26	75.2[1]	71.5[1]	78.9[1]
Uruguay	2010	0.2[1]	2.0[1]	11.3[1]	19	76.4[1]	72.6[1]	80.0[1]
	2015	0.3[1]	2.0[1]	10.0[1]	15	77.0[1]	73.2[1]	80.7[1]
Uzbekistan	2005	1.3[1]	2.5[1]	49.4[1]	42	67.7[1]	64.5[1]	71.0[1]
Ouzbékistan	2010	1.5[1]	2.5[1]	40.7[1]	39	69.1[1]	66.1[1]	72.2[1]
	2015	1.6[1]	2.4[1]	27.7[1]	36	70.2[1]	67.8[1]	72.7[1]
Vanuatu	2005	2.5[1]	4.4[1]	23.7[1]	116	67.9[1]	66.7[1]	69.3[1]
Vanuatu	2010	2.4[1]	4.2[1]	24.0[1]	94	68.7[1]	67.3[1]	70.4[1]
	2015	2.8[1]	4.0[1]	24.3[1]	78	69.5[1]	68.0[1]	71.2[1]
Venezuela (Boliv. Rep. of)	2005	1.8[1]	2.7[1]	17.2[1]	93	72.6[1]	68.9[1]	76.5[1]
Venezuela (Rép. boliv. du)	2010	1.5[1]	2.5[1]	14.8[1]	99	73.0[1]	69.3[1]	77.0[1]
	2015	1.1[1]	2.4[1]	15.0[1]	95	73.1[1]	69.4[1]	77.0[1]
Viet Nam	2005	1.0[1]	1.9[1]	23.6[1]	61	73.5[1]	68.9[1]	78.1[1]
Viet Nam	2010	1.0[1]	1.9[1]	19.0[1]	58	74.6[1]	70.4[1]	78.7[1]
	2015	1.0[1]	2.0[1]	17.9[1]	54	75.0[1]	70.8[1]	79.1[1]
Wallis and Futuna Islands	2003	...	...	...	...	...	73.1	75.5
Îles Wallis-et-Futuna	2005[1]	0.1	...	...	...	...	...	...
	2008[38]	...	...	5.2	...	...	...	...
	2010[1]	-1.6	...	...	...	...	...	...
	2013	...	2.1	...	...	75.8	# 72.8	# 78.7
	2015[1]	-2.1	...	...	...	...	...	...
Western Sahara [1]	2005	6.6	2.9	52.9	...	63.9	62.3	65.8
Sahara occidental [1]	2010	1.9	2.6	43.0	...	66.2	64.7	68.1
	2015	1.8	2.6	34.1	...	68.4	66.9	70.3
Yemen	2005	2.9[1]	5.9[1]	61.6[1]	428	62.1[1]	60.6[1]	63.7[1]
Yémen	2010	2.8[1]	5.0[1]	48.6[1]	416	64.7[1]	63.1[1]	66.4[1]
	2015	2.7[1]	4.4[1]	43.3[1]	385	66.0[1]	64.3[1]	67.7[1]
Zambia	2005	2.6[1]	6.0[1]	88.4[1]	372	46.0[1]	44.0[1]	48.1[1]
Zambie	2010	2.8[1]	5.6[1]	64.7[1]	262	51.8[1]	49.6[1]	54.0[1]
	2015	3.1[1]	5.2[1]	53.3[1]	224	59.3[1]	57.0[1]	61.5[1]
Zimbabwe	2005	0.3[1]	3.7[1]	65.0[1]	629	43.7[1]	42.0[1]	45.6[1]
Zimbabwe	2010	1.0[1]	3.9[1]	62.7[1]	446	45.0[1]	43.3[1]	46.7[1]
	2015	1.7[1]	4.1[1]	51.2[1]	443	56.7[1]	54.9[1]	58.3[1]

Source:

United Nations Population Division, New York, World Population Prospects: The 2019 Revision, last accessed June 2019.

United Nations Population Division, New York, World Population Prospects: The 2019 Revision; supplemented by data from the United Nations Statistics Division, New York, Demographic Yearbook 2015 and Secretariat for the Pacific Community (SPC) for small countries or areas, last accessed June 2019.
United Nations Statistics Division, New York, "Demographic Yearbook 2015" and the demographic statistics database, last accessed June 2017.

Source:

Organisation des Nations Unies, Division de la population, New York, "World Population Prospects: The 2019 Revision" , denier accès juin 2019.
Organisation des Nations Unies, Division de la population, New York, "World Population Prospects: The 2019 Revision"; complétées par des données de l'Organisation des Nations Unies, Division de statistique, New York, Annuaire démographique 2015 et Secrétariat de la Communauté du Pacifique (SCP) pour petits pays ou zones, denier accès juin 2019.
Organisation des Nations Unies, Division de statistique, New York, "Annuaire démographique 2015" et recueil de statistiques démographiques, denier accès juin 2017.

World Health Organization (WHO), the United Nations Children's Fund (UNICEF), the United Nations Population Fund (UNFPA), the World Bank and the United Nations Population Division, "Trends in Maternal Mortality 1990 - 2015."

Organisation mondiale de la santé (OMS), le Fonds des Nations Unies pour l'enfance (UNICEF), le Fonds des Nations Unies pour la population (UNFPA), la Banque mondiale et la Division des Nations Unies pour la population, "Les tendances de la mortalité maternelle 1990-2015".

1	Data refers to a 5-year period preceding the reference year.	1	Les données se réfèrent a période de 5 ans précédant l'année de référence.
2	Excluding Sudan.	2	Exclut le Soudan.
3	Including Sudan.	3	Y compris le Soudan.
4	Including Saint Helena.	4	Y compris Sainte-Hélène.
5	Including Bermuda, Greenland, and Saint Pierre and Miquelon.	5	Y compris les Bermudes, le Groenland et Saint-Pierre-et-Miquelon.
6	Including Anguilla, Bonaire, Sint Eustatius and Saba, British Virgin Islands, Cayman Islands, Dominica, Montserrat, Saint Kitts and Nevis, Sint Maarten (Dutch part) and Turks and Caicos Islands.	6	Y compris Anguilla, les îles Bonaire, Saint-Eustache et Saba, les îles Caïmans, la Dominique, Montserrat, Saint-Kitts-et-Nevis, Saint-Martin (partie néerlandaise), les îles Turques-et-Caïques et les îles Vierges britanniques.
7	Including Falkland Islands (Malvinas).	7	Y compris les îles Falkland (Malvinas)
8	Excluding Japan.	8	Exclut le Japon.
9	Data excludes Armenia, Azerbaijan, Cyprus, Georgia, Israel and Turkey.	9	Les données excluent l'Arménie, l'Azerbaïdjan, Chypre, la Géorgie, l'Israël et la Turquie.
10	Including the Faroe Islands and the Isle of Man.	10	Y compris les îles Féroé et l'île de Man.
11	Including Andorra, Gibraltar, Holy See, and San Marino.	11	Y compris Andorre, Gibraltar, Saint-Siège, et Saint-Marin.
12	Including Liechtenstein and Monaco.	12	Y compris le Liechtenstein et Monaco.
13	Including Marshall Islands, Nauru, Northern Mariana Islands and Palau.	13	Y compris les îles Mariannes du Nord, les îles Marshall, Nauru et Palaos.
14	Including American Samoa, Cook Islands, Niue, Pitcairn, Tokelau, Tuvalu, and Wallis and Futuna Islands.	14	Y compris les îles Cook, Nioué, Pitcairn, Samoa américaines, Tokélaou, Tuvalu, et les îles Wallis-et-Futuna.
15	Data refers to a 2-year period up to and including the reference year.	15	Les données se réfèrent a période de 2 ans jusqu'à et y compris l'année de référence.
16	Data refers to a 3-year period up to and including the reference year.	16	Les données se réfèrent a période de 3 ans jusqu'à et y compris l'année de référence. .
17	Including Christmas Island, Cocos (Keeling) Islands and Norfolk Island.	17	Y compris l'île Christmas, les îles des Cocos (Keeling) et l'île Norfolk.
18	Including Nagorno-Karabakh.	18	Y compris le Haut-Karabakh.
19	Data are based on a small number of deaths.	19	Les données sont basées sur un nombre limité de décès.
20	Refers to Guernsey and Jersey.	20	Se rapporte à Guernesey et Jersey.
21	For statistical purposes, the data for China do not include those for the Hong Kong Special Administrative Region (Hong Kong SAR), Macao Special Administrative Region (Macao SAR) and Taiwan Province of China.	21	Pour la présentation des statistiques, les données pour la Chine ne comprennent pas la région administrative spéciale de Hong Kong (RAS de Hong Kong), la région administrative spéciale de Macao (RAS de Macao) et la province chinoise de Taïwan.
22	Data refers to a 5-year period up to and including the reference year.	22	Les données se réfèrent a période de 5 ans jusqu'à et y compris l'année de référence.
23	Refers to the whole country.	23	Ensemble du pays.
24	Including Åland Islands.	24	Y compris les Îles d'Åland.
25	Including Abkhazia and South Ossetia.	25	Y compris l'Abkhazie et l'Ossétie du Sud.
26	Including Sabah and Sarawak.	26	Y compris Sabah et Sarawak.
27	Including Agalega, Rodrigues and Saint Brandon.	27	Y compris Agalega, Rodrigues et Saint-Brandon.
28	Data refers to a 6-year period up to and including the reference year.	28	Les données se réfèrent a période de 6 ans jusqu'à et y compris l'année de référence.
29	Including Svalbard and Jan Mayen Islands.	29	Y compris les îles Svalbard-et-Jan Mayen.
30	Preliminary census results.	30	Résultats provisoires.
31	Including the Transnistria region.	31	Y compris la région de Transnistrie.
32	Including Ascension and Tristan da Cunha.	32	Y compris Ascension et Tristan da Cunha.
33	Including Kosovo.	33	Y compris Kosovo.
34	Including Canary Islands, Ceuta and Melilla.	34	Y compris les îles Canaries, Ceuta et Melilla.
35	Including East Jerusalem.	35	Y compris Jérusalem-Est.
36	Including Crimea.	36	Y compris Crimea.
37	Including Zanzibar.	37	Y compris Zanzibar.
38	Data refers to a 4-year period up to and including the reference year.	38	Les données se réfèrent a période de 4 ans jusqu'à et y compris l'année de référence.

4

International migrants and refugees
International migrant stock (number and percentage) and refugees and others of concern to UNHCR

Migrants internationaux et réfugiés
Stock de migrants internationaux (nombre et pourcentage) et réfugiés et autres personnes relevant de la compétence du HCR

Region, country or area Région, pays ou zone	Year Année	**International Migrant Stock (mid-year)** **Stock de migrants internationaux** **(milieu de l'année)**				**Refugees and others of concern to UNHCR (mid-year)** **Réfugiés et autres personnes relevant de la compétence du HCR** **(milieu de l'année)**			
		Total Total	% of total pop. % de la pop. totale			Refugees& Réfugiés&	Asylum seekers Demandeurs d'asile	Other&& Autres&&	Total pop. Pop. totale
			MF HF	M H	F				
Total, all countries or areas	2005	190 531 600	2.9	3.0	2.9	...	...	...	...
Total, tous pays ou zones	2010	220 019 266	3.2	3.2	3.1	...	...	...	...
	2015	247 585 744	3.4	3.4	3.3	15 097 633	2 343 919	40 518 150	57 959 702
	2017	257 715 425	3.4	3.5	3.3	18 473 853	2 954 666	45 979 852	67 408 371
	2018	...	...	...	...	20 203 120	3 174 042	46 974 012	70 351 174
Africa	2005	15 462 306	1.7	1.8	1.5	...	...	...	...
Afrique	2010	17 007 249	1.6	1.7	1.5	...	...	...	...
	2015	23 436 088	2.0	2.1	1.8	4 493 139	1 044 031	11 530 138	17 067 308
	2017	24 650 223	2.0	2.1	1.8	6 134 401	589 255	15 203 541	21 927 197
	2018	...	...	...	...	6 658 476	594 946	17 868 520	25 121 942
Northern Africa [1]	2005	1 731 939	0.9	1.1	0.7	...	...	...	...
Afrique septentrionale [1]	2010	1 893 613	0.9	1.1	0.8	...	...	...	...
	2015	2 354 732	1.0	1.2	0.9	...	...	...	...
	2017	2 410 056	1.0	1.2	0.9	...	...	...	...
Sub-Saharan Africa [2]	2005	14 272 361	1.9	2.0	1.7	...	...	...	...
Afrique subsaharienne [2]	2010	15 691 999	1.8	1.9	1.7	...	...	...	...
	2015	21 705 234	2.2	2.3	2.0	...	...	...	...
	2017	22 975 988	2.2	2.3	2.1	...	...	...	...
Eastern Africa	2005	4 745 792	1.6	1.7	1.5	...	...	...	...
Afrique orientale	2010	4 657 063	1.3	1.4	1.3	...	...	...	...
	2015	6 920 965	1.7	1.8	1.7	...	...	...	...
	2017	7 591 799	1.8	1.8	1.8	...	...	...	...
Middle Africa	2005	1 928 828	1.7	1.8	1.7	...	...	...	...
Afrique centrale	2010	2 139 979	1.6	1.7	1.6	...	...	...	...
	2015	3 436 978	2.2	2.3	2.2	...	...	...	...
	2017	3 539 697	2.2	2.2	2.1	...	...	...	...
Southern Africa	2005	1 439 426	2.6	3.1	2.1	...	...	...	...
Afrique australe	2010	2 357 093	4.0	4.7	3.3	...	...	...	...
	2015	4 112 793	6.5	7.3	5.7	...	...	...	...
	2017	4 338 205	6.7	7.5	5.8	...	...	...	...
Western Africa	2005	5 616 321	2.1	2.2	1.9	...	...	...	...
Afrique occidentale	2010	5 959 501	1.9	2.1	1.8	...	...	...	...
	2015	6 610 620	1.9	2.0	1.8	...	...	...	...
	2017	6 770 466	1.8	1.9	1.7	...	...	...	...
Northern America	2005	45 363 387	13.8	13.9	13.8	...	...	...	...
Amérique septentrionale	2010	50 970 996	14.9	14.7	15.0	...	...	...	...
	2015	55 766 224	15.7	15.4	16.0	416 385	238 989	...	655 374
	2017	57 664 154	16.0	15.6	16.3	380 675	725 314	...	1 105 989
	2018	...	...	...	...	409 776	721 060	3 790	1 134 626
Latin America & the Caribbean	2005	7 237 476	1.3	1.3	1.3	...	...	...	...
Amérique latine et Caraïbes	2010	8 246 652	1.4	1.4	1.4	...	...	...	...
	2015	9 272 027	1.5	1.5	1.5	336 552	37 378	6 697 290	7 071 220
	2017	9 508 189	1.5	1.5	1.5	323 973	117 507	7 774 202	8 215 682
	2018	...	...	...	...	255 038	326 870	8 676 855	9 258 763
Caribbean	2005	1 333 118	3.3	3.5	3.2	...	...	...	...
Caraïbes	2010	1 353 589	3.2	3.4	3.2	...	...	...	...
	2015	1 385 784	3.2	3.3	3.1	...	...	...	...
	2017	1 399 747	3.2	3.3	3.1	...	...	...	...
Central America	2005	1 385 713	0.9	0.9	0.9	...	...	...	...
Amérique centrale	2010	1 749 940	1.1	1.1	1.1	...	...	...	...
	2015	2 043 212	1.2	1.2	1.2	...	...	...	...
	2017	2 092 819	1.2	1.2	1.2	...	...	...	...
South America	2005	4 518 645	1.2	1.2	1.2	...	...	...	...
Amérique du Sud	2010	5 143 123	1.3	1.3	1.3	...	...	...	...
	2015	5 843 031	1.4	1.4	1.4	...	...	...	...
	2017	6 015 623	1.4	1.4	1.4	...	...	...	...

4

International migrants and refugees *(continued)*
International migrant stock (number and percentage) and refugees and others of concern to UNHCR

Migrants internationaux et réfugiés *(suite)*
Stock de migrants internationaux (nombre et pourcentage) et réfugiés et autres personnes relevant de la compétence du HCR

Region, country or area Région, pays ou zone	Year Année	International Migrant Stock (mid-year) Stock de migrants internationaux (milieu de l'année)				Refugees and others of concern to UNHCR (mid-year) Réfugiés et autres personnes relevant de la compétence du HCR (milieu de l'année)			
		Total Total	MF HF	M H	F	Refugees& Réfugiés&	Asylum seekers Demandeurs d'asile	Other&& Autres&&	Total pop. Pop. totale
			% of total pop. % de la pop. totale						
Asia Asie	2005	53 243 730	1.3	1.4	1.2	...	...	...	...
	2010	65 921 788	1.6	1.8	1.4	...	...	...	...
	2015	76 558 152	1.7	1.9	1.5	8 178 380	320 437	19 921 907	28 420 724
	2017	79 586 709	1.8	2.0	1.5	9 067 704	502 166	20 251 046	29 820 916
	2018	...	...	...	...	10 099 166	574 010	17 698 069	28 371 245
Central Asia Asie centrale	2005	5 238 699	8.9	8.3	9.5	...	...	...	...
	2010	5 262 414	8.3	8.0	8.7	...	...	...	...
	2015	5 393 504	7.9	7.6	8.1	...	...	...	...
	2017	5 462 972	7.7	7.5	7.9	...	...	...	...
Eastern Asia Asie orientale	2005	6 229 524	0.4	0.4	0.4	...	...	...	...
	2010	7 061 814	0.4	0.4	0.5	...	...	...	...
	2015	7 600 768	0.5	0.4	0.5	...	...	...	...
	2017	7 776 716	0.5	0.4	0.5	...	...	...	...
South-eastern Asia Asie du Sud-Est	2005	6 522 343	1.2	1.2	1.1	...	...	...	...
	2010	8 673 693	1.5	1.5	1.4	...	...	...	...
	2015	9 609 923	1.5	1.6	1.5	...	...	...	...
	2017	9 873 600	1.5	1.6	1.5	...	...	...	...
Southern Asia Asie méridionale	2005	13 722 011	0.9	0.9	0.9	...	...	...	...
	2010	14 307 646	0.8	0.9	0.8	...	...	...	...
	2015	14 173 830	0.8	0.8	0.8	...	...	...	...
	2017	13 582 402	0.7	0.7	0.7	...	...	...	...
Western Asia Asie occidentale	2005	21 531 153	10.5	12.6	8.2	...	...	...	...
	2010	30 616 221	13.2	16.5	9.5	...	...	...	...
	2015	39 780 127	15.4	18.9	11.6	...	...	...	...
	2017	42 891 019	16.0	19.6	12.1	...	...	...	...
Europe Europe	2005	63 201 280	8.7	8.7	8.6	...	...	...	...
	2010	70 747 947	9.6	9.6	9.6	...	...	...	...
	2015	74 501 508	10.1	10.0	10.1	1 626 214	678 737	2 368 815	4 673 766
	2017	77 895 217	10.5	10.4	10.6	2 508 981	983 967	2 751 063	6 244 011
	2018	...	...	...	...	2 715 811	907 165	2 726 732	6 349 708
Eastern Europe Europe orientale	2005	19 747 392	6.6	6.7	6.6	...	...	...	...
	2010	19 127 781	6.5	6.5	6.5	...	...	...	...
	2015	19 880 519	6.8	6.8	6.7	...	...	...	...
	2017	20 121 711	6.9	6.9	6.8	...	...	...	...
Northern Europe Europe septentrionale	2005	9 588 814	9.9	9.7	10.2	...	...	...	...
	2010	11 810 676	11.8	11.5	12.0	...	...	...	...
	2015	13 188 813	12.8	12.5	13.1	...	...	...	...
	2017	13 946 390	13.4	13.1	13.7	...	...	...	...
Southern Europe Europe méridionale	2005	11 974 334	8.0	7.9	8.0	...	...	...	...
	2010	16 205 444	10.5	10.5	10.6	...	...	...	...
	2015	15 830 496	10.4	10.0	10.8	...	...	...	...
	2017	15 957 631	10.5	10.1	10.9	...	...	...	...
Western Europe Europe occidentale	2005	21 890 740	11.8	11.9	11.7	...	...	...	...
	2010	23 604 046	12.5	12.4	12.6	...	...	...	...
	2015	25 601 680	13.3	13.2	13.4	...	...	...	...
	2017	27 869 485	14.4	14.4	14.5	...	...	...	...
Oceania Océanie	2005	6 023 421	17.9	17.9	18.2	...	...	...	...
	2010	7 124 634	19.4	19.4	19.8	...	...	...	...
	2015	8 051 745	20.4	20.1	20.8	46 963	24 347	...	71 310
	2017	8 410 933	20.7	20.4	21.2	58 119	36 457	...	94 576
	2018	...	...	...	...	64 853	49 991	46	114 890
Australia and New Zealand Australie et Nouvelle-Zélande	2005	5 717 982	23.5	23.3	23.6	...	...	...	...
	2010	6 830 423	25.8	25.6	26.0	...	...	...	...
	2015	7 750 276	27.3	26.9	27.7	...	...	...	...
	2017	8 102 983	27.8	27.3	28.3	...	...	...	...
Melanesia Mélanésie	2005	103 878	1.3	1.4	1.1	...	...	...	...
	2010	105 684	1.2	1.3	1.0	...	...	...	...
	2015	114 595	1.2	1.3	1.0	...	...	...	...
	2017	118 078	1.1	1.3	1.0	...	...	...	...

International migrants and refugees *(continued)*
International migrant stock (number and percentage) and refugees and others of concern to UNHCR

Migrants internationaux et réfugiés *(suite)*
Stock de migrants internationaux (nombre et pourcentage) et réfugiés et autres personnes relevant de la compétence du HCR

Region, country or area Région, pays ou zone	Year Année	International Migrant Stock (mid-year) Stock de migrants internationaux (milieu de l'année)				Refugees and others of concern to UNHCR (mid-year) Réfugiés et autres personnes relevant de la compétence du HCR (milieu de l'année)			
		Total Total	MF HF	M H	F	Refugees& Réfugiés&	Asylum seekers Demandeurs d'asile	Other&& Autres&&	Total pop. Pop. totale
			% of total pop. % de la pop. totale						
Micronesia	2005	128 390	25.5	35.4	36.6	...	...	...	...
Micronésie	2010	115 948	23.0	31.7	31.8	...	...	...	...
	2015	115 311	22.2	30.6	30.3	...	...	...	...
	2017	117 601	22.3	30.6	30.3	...	...	...	...
Polynesia	2005	73 171	11.4	14.4	12.8	...	...	...	...
Polynésie	2010	72 579	11.0	13.7	12.3	...	...	...	...
	2015	71 563	10.6	13.0	11.7	...	...	...	...
	2017	72 271	10.5	12.9	11.6	...	...	...	...
Afghanistan	2005	87 300	0.3	0.4	0.3	32[3]	14[3]	159 551[3]	159 597[3]
Afghanistan	2010	102 246	0.4	0.4	0.3	6 434[3]	30[3]	1 193 523[3]	1 199 987[3]
	2015	489 749	1.5	1.4	1.5	225 714	101	1 195 604	1 421 419
	2017	133 612	0.4	0.4	0.4	87 119	205	2 101 881[4]	2 189 205
	2018	...	...	...	...	78 384	365	2 458 314	2 537 063
Albania	2005	64 739	2.1	2.1	2.1	56[3]	35[3]	1[3]	92[3]
Albanie	2010	52 784	1.8	1.8	1.8	76[3]	23[3]	...	99[3]
	2015	52 031	1.8	1.8	1.8	154	501	7 443	8 098
	2017	52 484	1.8	1.8	1.8	113	2 743	4 860[5]	7 716
	2018	...	...	...	...	121	149	3 707[6]	3 977
Algeria	2005	197 422[7]	0.6[7]	0.6[7]	0.5[7]	94 101[3]	306[3]	...	94 407[3]
Algérie	2010	216 964[7]	0.6[7]	0.6[7]	0.6[7]	94 144[3]	304[3]	...	94 448[3]
	2015	239 473[7]	0.6[7]	0.6[7]	0.6[7]	94 144[8]	5 892	...	100 036
	2017	248 624[7]	0.6[7]	0.6[7]	0.6[7]	94 248[8]	5 986	...	100 234
	2018	...	...	...	...	177 881	7 886	...	185 767
American Samoa	2005	24 233	41.0	...	...	...	...	...	...
Samoa américaines	2010	23 555	42.3	...	...	...	...	...	...
	2015	23 513	42.3	...	...	...	...	...	...
	2017	23 561	42.3	...	...	...	...	...	...
Andorra [9]	2005	50 298	63.8	...	...	...	...	...	...
Andorre [9]	2010	52 053	61.6	...	...	...	...	...	...
	2015	42 082	53.9	...	...	...	...	...	...
	2017	41 039	53.3	...	...	...	...	...	...
Angola	2005	61 329[7]	0.3[7]	0.3[7]	0.3[7]	13 984[3]	885[3]	45[3]	14 914[3]
Angola	2010	76 549[7]	0.3[7]	0.3[7]	0.3[7]	15 155[3]	4 241[3]	...	19 396[3]
	2015	632 178[7]	2.3[7]	2.2[7]	2.3[7]	15 555[3]	30 143[3]	2 887	45 698[3]
	2017	638 499[7]	2.1[7]	2.1[7]	2.2[7]	48 232	30 192	...	78 424
	2018	...	...	...	...	37 933	30 143	...	68 076
Anguilla	2005	4 684	37.1	...	...	...	...	...	...
Anguilla	2010	5 103	37.1	...	...	...	...	...	...
	2015	5 470	37.4	...	...	...	...	...	...
	2017	5 579	37.4	...	...	...	...	...	...
	2018	...	...	...	...	1	...	...	1
Antigua and Barbuda	2005	24 741	27.7	25.8	29.5	...	...	...	...
Antigua-et-Barbuda	2010	26 412	27.9	26.0	29.7	...	...	...	...
	2015	28 083	28.1	26.1	29.9	...	10	...	10
	2017	28 646	28.1	26.1	29.9	1	...	...	1
	2018	...	...	...	...	1	1	...	2
Argentina	2005	1 673 088	4.3	4.0	4.5	3 074[3]	825[3]	2[3]	3 901[3]
Argentine	2010	1 805 957	4.4	4.1	4.6	3 276[3]	947[3]	...	4 223[3]
	2015	2 086 302	4.8	4.5	5.1	3 523	897	...	4 420
	2017	2 164 524	4.9	4.6	5.2	3 322	4 010	396	7 728
	2018	...	...	...	...	3 378	5 044	82 465	90 887
Armenia	2005	469 119[7]	15.7[7]	13.7[7]	17.6[7]	219 550[3]	70[3]	...	219 620[3]
Arménie	2010	221 560[7]	7.7[7]	6.7[7]	8.6[7]	3 296[3]	23[3]	82 525[3]	85 844[3]
	2015	191 199[7]	6.6[7]	5.6[7]	7.4[7]	15 690	114	238	16 042
	2017	190 719[7]	6.5[7]	5.6[7]	7.3[7]	17 922	71	613	18 606
	2018	...	...	...	...	17 996	110	791	18 897

4

International migrants and refugees *(continued)*
International migrant stock (number and percentage) and refugees and others of concern to UNHCR

Migrants internationaux et réfugiés *(suite)*
Stock de migrants internationaux (nombre et pourcentage) et réfugiés et autres personnes relevant de la compétence du HCR

Region, country or area / Région, pays ou zone	Year / Année	International Migrant Stock (mid-year) / Stock de migrants internationaux (milieu de l'année)				Refugees and others of concern to UNHCR (mid-year) / Réfugiés et autres personnes relevant de la compétence du HCR (milieu de l'année)			
		Total / Total	MF / HF	M / H	F	Refugees& / Réfugiés&	Asylum seekers / Demandeurs d'asile	Other&& / Autres&&	Total pop. / Pop. totale
Aruba / Aruba	2005	32 540	32.5	30.6	34.3	...	...	...	...
	2010	34 327	33.8	31.6	35.7	...	1[3]	...	1[3]
	2015	36 114	34.6	32.5	36.5	...	2	...	2
	2017	36 356	34.5	32.4	36.5	1	5	...	6
	2018	...	...	...	...	1	292	...	293
Australia / Australie	2005	4 878 030[10]	24.1[10]	24.0[10]	24.3[10]	64 964[3]	1 822[3]	8[3]	66 794[3]
	2010	5 882 980[10]	26.6[10]	26.4[10]	26.8[10]	21 805[3]	3 760[3]	15[3]	25 580[3]
	2015	6 710 540[10]	28.2[10]	27.8[10]	28.6[10]	35 582	22 837[11,12]	...	58 419
	2017	7 035 560[10]	28.8[10]	28.3[10]	29.3[10]	46 576	35 825[11]	...	82 401
	2018	...	...	...	...	52 729	49 482[11]	46	102 257
Austria / Autriche	2005	1 136 270	13.8	13.5	14.0	21 230[3]	40 710[3]	830[3]	62 770[3]
	2010	1 275 992	15.2	14.9	15.5	42 630[3]	25 625[3]	470[3]	68 725[3]
	2015	1 492 374	17.2	16.9	17.5	60 747[12]	30 900[12]	570[12]	92 217[12]
	2017	1 660 283	19.0	18.6	19.4	104 375	65 515	980	170 870
	2018	...	...	...	...	122 462	46 077	523	169 062
Azerbaijan / Azerbaïdjan	2005	302 220[7,13]	3.5[7,13]	3.2[7,13]	3.9[7,13]	3 004[3]	115[3]	581 194[3]	584 313[3]
	2010	276 901[7,13]	3.1[7,13]	2.9[7,13]	3.2[7,13]	1 891[3]	17[3]	594 969[3]	596 877[3]
	2015	264 241[7,13]	2.7[7,13]	2.6[7,13]	2.8[7,13]	1 357	262	626 477	628 096
	2017	259 241[7,13]	2.6[7,13]	2.5[7,13]	2.7[7,13]	1 196	358	616 714	618 268
	2018	...	...	...	...	1 114	172	616 370	617 656
Bahamas / Bahamas	2005	45 595	13.8	14.7	13.0	...	...	...	...
	2010	54 736	15.2	15.8	14.6	28[3]	9[3]	...	37[3]
	2015	59 306	15.3	15.8	14.8	7	19	30	56
	2016	...	...	...	...	11	17	97	125
	2017	61 806	15.6	16.1	15.1	14	23	...	37
	2018	...	...	...	...	14	17	...	31
Bahrain / Bahreïn	2005	404 018[9]	45.4[9]	54.0[9]	32.5[9]	...	15[3]	...	15[3]
	2010	657 856[9]	53.0[9]	61.5[9]	39.0[9]	165[3]	69[3]	...	234[3]
	2015	704 137[9]	51.3[9]	60.1[9]	37.2[9]	277	78	...	355
	2017	722 649[9]	48.4[9]	55.8[9]	36.0[9]	262	109	...	371
	2018	...	...	...	...	256	135	...	391
Bangladesh / Bangladesh	2005	1 166 700[7]	0.8[7]	0.9[7]	0.8[7]	21 098[3]	58[3]	250 094[3]	271 250[3]
	2010	1 345 546[7]	0.9[7]	0.9[7]	0.8[7]	229 253[3]	...	...	229 253[3]
	2015	1 422 805[7]	0.9[7]	0.9[7]	0.8[7]	232 975[14]	11	...	232 986
	2017	1 500 921[7]	0.9[7]	1.0[7]	0.9[7]	307 424[15]	104	2	307 530
	2018	...	...	...	...	943 240[16]	135	...	943 375
Barbados / Barbade	2005	30 624	11.2	10.3	12.0	...	...	...	...
	2010	32 825	11.7	11.0	12.4	...	...	...	...
	2015	34 475	12.1	11.4	12.8	1	...	...	1
	2017	34 660	12.1	11.4	12.8	...	5	...	5
	2018	...	...	...	...	1	1	...	2
Belarus / Bélarus	2005	1 106 982	11.5	11.3	11.7	725[3]	56[3]	12 421[3]	13 202[3]
	2010	1 090 378	11.5	11.3	11.7	589[3]	66[3]	7 734[3]	8 389[3]
	2015	1 082 905	11.4	11.2	11.6	1 369	257	6 302	7 928
	2017	1 078 652	11.4	11.2	11.5	1 930	112	5 915	7 957
	2018	...	...	...	...	2 677	178	5 781	8 636
Belgium / Belgique	2005	882 031[9]	8.4[9]	8.7[9]	8.0[9]	15 282[3]	18 913[3]	398[3]	34 593[3]
	2010	1 119 256[9]	10.2[9]	10.6[9]	9.9[9]	17 892[3]	18 288[3]	696[3]	36 876[3]
	2015	1 252 380[9]	11.1[9]	11.5[9]	10.7[9]	31 115	9 396	5 267	45 778
	2017[9]	1 268 411	11.1	11.4	10.8	...	...	...	...
	2018	...	...	...	...	59 208	15 275	8 984	83 467
Belize / Belize	2005	41 424[7]	14.6[7]	14.8[7]	14.5[7]	624[3]	14[3]	...	638[3]
	2010	46 360[7]	14.4[7]	14.6[7]	14.2[7]	134[3]	30[3]	2[3]	166[3]
	2015	54 674[7]	15.2[7]	15.4[7]	15.1[7]	...	146	...	146
	2017	59 998[7]	16.0[7]	16.2[7]	15.8[7]	...	2 666	2 442	5 108
	2018	...	...	...	...	28	3 414	2 774	6 216

International migrants and refugees *(continued)*
International migrant stock (number and percentage) and refugees and others of concern to UNHCR

Migrants internationaux et réfugiés *(suite)*
Stock de migrants internationaux (nombre et pourcentage) et réfugiés et autres personnes relevant de la compétence du HCR

Region, country or area Région, pays ou zone	Year Année	International Migrant Stock (mid-year) Stock de migrants internationaux (milieu de l'année)				Refugees and others of concern to UNHCR (mid-year) Réfugiés et autres personnes relevant de la compétence du HCR (milieu de l'année)			
		Total Total	MF HF	M H	F	Refugees& Réfugiés&	Asylum seekers Demandeurs d'asile	Other&& Autres&&	Total pop. Pop. totale
			% of total pop. % de la pop. totale						
Benin Bénin	2005	171 499[7,9]	2.1[7,9]	2.4[7,9]	1.9[7,9]	30 294[3]	1 695[3]	77[3]	32 066[3]
	2010	209 267[7,9]	2.3[7,9]	2.5[7,9]	2.0[7,9]	7 139[3]	101[3]	47[3]	7 287[3]
	2015	245 399[7,9]	2.3[7,9]	2.6[7,9]	2.0[7,9]	488	84	...	572
	2017	253 284[7,9]	2.3[7,9]	2.6[7,9]	2.0[7,9]	968	188	...	1 156
	2018	...	...	...	...	1 149	272	...	1 421
Bermuda Bermudes	2005	18 276	28.1	...	...	...	...	...	...
	2010	18 884	29.5	...	...	...	...	...	...
	2015	19 126	30.8	...	...	...	...	...	...
	2017	18 954	30.9	...	...	...	...	...	...
Bhutan Bhoutan	2005	40 279	6.1	9.5	2.4	...	...	...	...
	2010	48 420	6.7	10.2	2.7	...	...	...	...
	2015	51 106	6.5	9.9	2.6	...	...	...	...
	2017	52 296	6.5	9.9	2.6	...	...	...	...
Bolivia (Plurin. State of) Bolivie (État plurin. de)	2005	107 745	1.2	1.2	1.1	535[3]	3[3]	2[3]	540[3]
	2010	122 846	1.2	1.3	1.2	695[3]	41[3]	3[3]	739[3]
	2015	142 989	1.3	1.4	1.3	767	8	...	775
	2017	148 837	1.3	1.4	1.3	797	6	...	803
	2018	...				828	232	...	1 060
Bonaire, St. Eustatius & Saba Bonaire, St-Eustache et Saba	2010	11 445	54.7	...	...	...	1[3,17]	...	1[3,17]
	2015	13 002	52.9	...	...	...	...	...	...
	2017	13 508	53.2	...	...	...	...	...	...
Bosnia and Herzegovina Bosnie-Herzégovine	2005	* 47 272[7]	* 1.3[7]	* 1.2[7]	* 1.3[7]	10 568[3]	215[3]	188 735[3]	199 518[3]
	2010	* 38 792[7]	* 1.0[7]	* 1.0[7]	* 1.1[7]	7 016[3]	153[3]	171 790[3]	178 959[3]
	2015	* 38 574[7]	* 1.1[7]	* 1.1[7]	* 1.1[7]	6 805	11	137 035	143 851
	2017	* 37 100[7]	* 1.1[7]	* 1.0[7]	* 1.1[7]	5 265	92	151 064	156 421
	2018	...				5 229	438	147 124	152 791
Botswana Botswana	2005	88 829[9]	4.8[9]	5.4[9]	4.2[9]	3 109[3]	47[3]	592[3]	3 748[3]
	2010	120 912[9]	6.0[9]	6.7[9]	5.3[9]	2 986[3]	249[3]	111[3]	3 346[3]
	2015	160 644[9]	7.3[9]	8.0[9]	6.5[9]	2 164	248	...	2 412
	2017	166 430[9]	7.3[9]	8.0[9]	6.5[9]	2 149	86	635	2 870
	2018	...	...	...	...	2 081	51	271	2 403
Brazil Brésil	2005	638 582	0.3	0.4	0.3	3 458[3]	195[3]	4 093[3]	7 746[3]
	2010	592 568	0.3	0.3	0.3	4 357[3]	872[3]	8[3]	5 237[3]
	2015	716 568	0.3	0.4	0.3	7 762	17 902	40 338	66 002
	2017	735 557	0.4	0.4	0.3	10 129	53 949	43 875	107 953
	2018	...	...	...	...	10 850	113 152	19 910	143 912
British Virgin Islands Îles Vierges britanniques	2005	15 016	64.8	...	...	...	...	...	...
	2010	17 074	62.7	...	...	2[3]	...	...	2[3]
	2015	19 132	63.5	...	...	...	...	...	...
	2017	19 959	64.0	...	...	...	1	...	1
	2018	...	...	...	...	1	...	...	1
Brunei Darussalam Brunéi Darussalam	2005	98 441	27.0	29.6	24.2	...	...	...	...
	2010	100 587	25.9	28.3	23.3	...	...	20 992[3]	20 992[3]
	2015	102 733	24.6	27.0	22.0	...	...	20 524	20 524
	2017	108 612	25.3	27.9	22.6	...	...	20 524	20 524
	2018	...	...	...	...	...	...	20 524	20 524
Bulgaria Bulgarie	2005	61 074	0.8	0.7	0.9	4 413[3]	805[3]	...	5 218[3]
	2010	76 287	1.0	0.9	1.1	5 530[3]	1 412[3]	...	6 942[3]
	2015	133 803	1.9	1.7	2.0	11 046[12]	7 840	67	18 953
	2017	153 803	2.2	2.0	2.4	18 678	8 995	67	27 740
	2018	...	...	...	...	19 562	1 234	88	20 884
Burkina Faso Burkina Faso	2005	596 972[7]	4.4[7]	4.3[7]	4.6[7]	511[3]	784[3]	7[3]	1 302[3]
	2010	673 904[7]	4.3[7]	4.1[7]	4.5[7]	531[3]	534[3]	9[3]	1 074[3]
	2015	704 676[7]	3.9[7]	3.7[7]	4.1[7]	34 027	180	...	34 207
	2017	708 921[7]	3.7[7]	3.5[7]	3.9[7]	34 033	176	...	34 209
	2018	...	...	...	...	24 798	44	16 385	41 227

4 International migrants and refugees *(continued)*
International migrant stock (number and percentage) and refugees and others of concern to UNHCR

Migrants internationaux et réfugiés *(suite)*
Stock de migrants internationaux (nombre et pourcentage) et réfugiés et autres personnes relevant de la compétence du HCR

Region, country or area / Région, pays ou zone	Year / Année	International Migrant Stock (mid-year) / Stock de migrants internationaux (milieu de l'année)				Refugees and others of concern to UNHCR (mid-year) / Réfugiés et autres personnes relevant de la compétence du HCR (milieu de l'année)			
		Total / Total	MF / HF	M / H	F	Refugees[&] / Réfugiés[&]	Asylum seekers / Demandeurs d'asile	Other[&&] / Autres[&&]	Total pop. / Pop. totale
			% of total pop. / % de la pop. totale						
Burundi	2005	172 874[7]	2.3[7]	2.3[7]	2.3[7]	20 681[3]	19 900[3]	12 988[3]	53 569[3]
Burundi	2010	235 259[7]	2.7[7]	2.7[7]	2.7[7]	29 365[3]	12 062[3]	159 338[3]	200 765[3]
	2015	289 810[7]	2.8[7]	2.8[7]	2.8[7]	54 126	2 733	80 851	137 710
	2017	299 569[7]	2.8[7]	2.8[7]	2.8[7]	59 424	3 870	123 643[18]	186 937
	2018	...	...	...	...	67 963	4 646	80 357	152 966
Cabo Verde	2005	12 700	2.7	2.8	2.5	...	...	1[3]	1[3]
Cabo Verde	2010	14 373	2.9	2.9	2.8	...	...	...	...
	2015	14 924	2.8	2.8	2.8	...	...	115	115
	2017	15 295	2.8	2.8	2.8	...	...	115	115
	2018	...	...	...	...	...	...	115	115
Cambodia	2005	114 031	0.9	0.9	0.8	127[3]	68[3]	207[3]	402[3]
Cambodge	2010	81 977	0.6	0.6	0.5	129[3]	51[3]	...	180[3]
	2015	73 963	0.5	0.5	0.4	80	33	131	244
	2017	76 329	0.5	0.5	0.4	70	54	10	134
	2018	...	...	...	...	67	47	...	114
Cameroon	2005	258 737	1.5	1.6	1.3	52 042[3]	6 766[3]	7 444[3]	66 252[3]
Cameroun	2010	289 091	1.4	1.6	1.3	104 275[3]	2 383[3]	66[3]	106 724[3]
	2015	508 357	2.2	2.2	2.3	302 293	7 835	81 693	391 821
	2017	540 266	2.2	2.2	2.3	322 777	4 409	226 260	553 446
	2018	...	...	...	...	360 162	7 427	223 221	590 810
Canada	2005	6 078 985	18.8	18.2	19.4	147 171[3]	20 552[3]	12[3]	167 735[3]
Canada	2010	6 761 226	19.8	19.1	20.5	165 549[3]	51 025[3]	7[3]	216 581[3]
	2015	7 561 226	21.0	20.3	21.8	135 888[3]	19 951[3]	...	155 839[3]
	2017	7 861 226	21.5	20.7	22.2	101 256	33 261	...	134 517
	2018	...	...	...	...	110 123	63 830	3 790	177 743
Cayman Islands	2005[9]	21 655	44.5	...	...	...	...	...	...
Îles Caïmanes	2010	24 057[9]	43.3[9]	...	...	1[3]	4[3]	...	5[3]
	2015	23 726[9]	39.6[9]	...	...	6	1	100	107
	2017	24 355[9]	39.6[9]	...	...	25	32	...	57
	2018	...	...	...	...	33	32	...	65
Central African Republic	2005	94 449[9]	2.3[9]	2.5[9]	2.1[9]	24 569[3]	1 960[3]	2 167[3]	28 696[3]
République centrafricaine	2010	93 466[9]	2.1[9]	2.3[9]	1.9[9]	21 574[3]	1 219[3]	192 531[3]	215 324[3]
	2015	81 598[9]	1.8[9]	1.9[9]	1.7[9]	7 906	394	508 904	517 204
	2017	88 774[9]	1.9[9]	2.0[9]	1.8[9]	11 426	511	637 685	649 622
	2018	...	...	...	...	9 079	514	772 833	782 426
Chad	2005	352 062[7]	3.5[7]	3.2[7]	3.8[7]	275 412[3]	68[3]	...	275 480[3]
Tchad	2010	416 924[7]	3.5[7]	3.1[7]	3.9[7]	347 939[3]	110[3]	185 000[3]	533 049[3]
	2015	516 968[7]	3.7[7]	3.4[7]	4.0[7]	420 774	2 749	50 000	473 523
	2017	489 690[7]	3.3[7]	3.0[7]	3.5[7]	400 705	1 914	161 060	563 679
	2018	...	...	...	...	445 777	1 042	172 054	618 873
Channel Islands [19]	2005	70 941	46.0	44.3	47.6	...	...	...	...
Îles Anglo-Normandes [19]	2010	77 581	48.6	46.8	50.4	...	...	...	...
	2015	82 307	50.3	48.5	52.0	...	...	...	...
	2017	83 082	50.3	48.4	52.1	...	...	...	...
Chile	2005	273 384	1.7	1.6	1.8	806[3]	107[3]	...	913[3]
Chili	2010	369 436	2.2	2.1	2.3	1 621[3]	274[3]	...	1 895[3]
	2015	469 436	2.6	2.5	2.8	1 798	719	...	2 517
	2017	488 571	2.7	2.6	2.8	1 736	5 195	...	6 931
	2018	...	...	...	...	2 032	12 583	86 687	101 302
China [20]	2005	678 947[9]	0.1[9]	0.1[9]	~0.0[9]	301 041[3]	84[3]	1[3]	301 126[3]
Chine [20]	2010	849 861[9]	0.1[9]	0.1[9]	0.1[9]	300 986[3]	122[3]	...	301 108[3]
	2015	978 046[9]	0.1[9]	0.1[9]	0.1[9]	301 057[21]	564	...	301 621
	2017	999 527[9]	0.1[9]	0.1[9]	0.1[9]	317 238[21]	732	...	317 970
	2018	...	...	...	...	321 746[21]	685	...	322 431

International migrants and refugees *(continued)*
International migrant stock (number and percentage) and refugees and others of concern to UNHCR

Migrants internationaux et réfugiés *(suite)*
Stock de migrants internationaux (nombre et pourcentage) et réfugiés et autres personnes relevant de la compétence du HCR

Region, country or area Région, pays ou zone	Year Année	International Migrant Stock (mid-year) Stock de migrants internationaux (milieu de l'année)				Refugees and others of concern to UNHCR (mid-year) Réfugiés et autres personnes relevant de la compétence du HCR (milieu de l'année)			
		Total Total	MF HF	M H	F	Refugees& Réfugiés&	Asylum seekers Demandeurs d'asile	Other&& Autres&&	Total pop. Pop. totale
			% of total pop. % de la pop. totale						
China, Hong Kong SAR Chine, RAS de Hong Kong	2005	2 721 235	39.9	36.2	43.2	1 934[3]	1 097[3]	...	3 031[3]
	2010	2 779 950	39.6	34.8	43.8	154[3]	486[3]	3[3]	643[3]
	2015	2 838 665	39.2	33.4	44.1	151	9 940	1	10 092
	2016	...	...	...	...	140	2 315	1	2 456
	2017	2 883 051	39.1	33.6	43.9	93	...	1	94
	2018	...	...	...	...	106	...	...	106
China, Macao SAR Chine, RAS de Macao	2005	279 308	57.9	56.9	58.8	...	...	...	...
	2010	318 506	59.3	56.8	61.6	...	9[3]	1[3]	10[3]
	2015	342 703	57.0	54.0	59.8	...	6		6
	2017	353 654	56.8	53.8	59.6	...	5	...	5
	2018	...	...	...	...	...	2	...	2
Colombia Colombie	2005	107 612	0.2	0.3	0.2	155[3]	41[3]	2 000 009[3]	2 000 205[3]
	2010	124 271	0.3	0.3	0.3	212[3]	167[3]	3 672 065[3]	3 672 444[3]
	2015	139 134	0.3	0.3	0.3	219	56	6 520 304	6 520 579
	2017	142 319	0.3	0.3	0.3	258	542	7 524 010	7 524 810
	2018	...	...	...	...	282	2 101	7 869 597	7 871 980
Comoros Comores	2005	13 209	2.2	2.0	2.3	1[3]	...	...	1[3]
	2010	12 618	1.8	1.7	1.9	...	...	...	...
	2015	12 555	1.6	1.5	1.7	...	...	...	...
	2017	12 555	1.5	1.5	1.6	...	...	...	...
Congo Congo	2005	315 238	8.5	9.2	7.7	66 075[3]	3 486[3]	8 079[3]	77 640[3]
	2010	419 649	9.6	10.4	8.7	133 112[3]	5 524[3]	59[3]	138 695[3]
	2015	392 996	7.9	8.6	7.1	61 492	3 248	1 070	65 810
	2017	398 890	7.6	8.3	6.9	47 436	6 903	84 398	138 737
	2018	...	...	...	...	40 740	7 203	172 492	220 435
Cook Islands Îles Cook	2005	3 277	16.6	...	...	...	...	...	...
	2010	3 769	20.3	...	...	...	...	...	...
	2015	4 152	23.8	...	...	...	...	...	...
	2017	4 213	24.2	...	...	...	...	...	...
Costa Rica Costa Rica	2005	358 175[7]	8.4[7]	8.3[7]	8.6[7]	11 253[3]	223[3]	...	11 476[3]
	2010	405 404[7]	8.9[7]	8.6[7]	9.2[7]	19 505[3]	375[3]	40[3]	19 920[3]
	2015	411 697[7]	8.6[7]	8.2[7]	8.9[7]	3 475	1 819	2 613	7 907
	2017	414 214[7]	8.4[7]	8.1[7]	8.8[7]	4 414	5 594	216	10 224
	2018	...	...	...	...	4 600	12 913	627	18 140
Côte d'Ivoire Côte d'Ivoire	2005	2 010 824[9]	11.0[9]	11.8[9]	10.0[9]	41 627[3]	2 443[3]	71 050[3]	115 120[3]
	2010	2 095 185[9]	10.3[9]	11.1[9]	9.4[9]	26 218[3]	256[3]	538 068[3]	564 542[3]
	2015	2 175 399[9]	9.4[9]	10.3[9]	8.5[9]	1 972	667	724 131	726 770
	2017	2 197 152[9]	9.0[9]	9.9[9]	8.2[9]	1 468	342	698 343	700 153
	2018	...	...	...	...	1 714	254	692 813[22]	694 781
Croatia Croatie	2005	579 273[7]	13.2[7]	12.9[7]	13.6[7]	2 927[3]	8[3]	7 932[3]	10 867[3]
	2010	573 248[7]	13.2[7]	12.9[7]	13.6[7]	936[3]	81[3]	24 463[3]	25 480[3]
	2015	575 738[7]	13.6[7]	13.1[7]	14.1[7]	710	90	16 684	17 484
	2017	560 483[7]	13.4[7]	12.8[7]	13.9[7]	346	605	12 489	13 440
	2018	...	...	...	...	608	282	8 392	9 282
Cuba Cuba	2005	17 023	0.2	0.1	0.2	706[3]	32[3]	...	738[3]
	2010	14 818	0.1	0.1	0.1	411[3]	11[3]	1[3]	423[3]
	2015	13 336	0.1	0.1	0.1	313	12	...	325
	2017	13 136	0.1	0.1	0.1	325	20	...	345
	2018	...	...	...	...	282	25	1	308
Curaçao Curaçao	2010	34 627	23.5	21.0	25.6	7[3]	2[3]	...	9[3]
	2015	37 611	23.8	21.4	25.8	44	41		85
	2017	38 396	23.9	21.5	26.0	62	107	...	169
	2018					78	735	1	814
Cyprus Chypre	2005	117 165[23]	11.4[23]	9.7[23]	13.2[23]	701[3]	13 067[3]	1[3]	13 769[3]
	2010	188 472[23]	16.9[23]	14.8[23]	19.0[23]	3 394[3]	5 396[3]	...	8 790[3]
	2015	192 020[23]	16.5[23]	14.5[23]	18.6[23]	5 763	2 339	6 000	14 102
	2017	188 973[23]	16.0[23]	14.0[23]	18.0[23]	9 238	3 812	6 000	19 050
	2018	...	...	...	...	10 198	7 163	6 000	23 361

International migrants and refugees *(continued)*
International migrant stock (number and percentage) and refugees and others of concern to UNHCR

Migrants internationaux et réfugiés *(suite)*
Stock de migrants internationaux (nombre et pourcentage) et réfugiés et autres personnes relevant de la compétence du HCR

Region, country or area Région, pays ou zone	Year Année	International Migrant Stock (mid-year) Stock de migrants internationaux (milieu de l'année)				Refugees and others of concern to UNHCR (mid-year) Réfugiés et autres personnes relevant de la compétence du HCR (milieu de l'année)			
		Total Total	MF HF	M H	F	Refugees& Réfugiés&	Asylum seekers Demandeurs d'asile	Other&& Autres&&	Total pop. Pop. totale
			% of total pop. % de la pop. totale						
Czechia	2005	322 540[9]	3.1[9]	3.6[9]	2.7[9]	1 802[3]	924[3]	...	2 726[3]
Tchéquie	2010	398 493[9]	3.8[9]	4.6[9]	3.0[9]	2 449[3]	1 065[3]	1[3]	3 515[3]
	2015	416 454[9]	3.9[9]	4.6[9]	3.3[9]	3 137[12]	409	1 502	5 048
	2017	433 290[9]	4.1[9]	4.8[9]	3.4[9]	3 644	827	1 502	5 973
	2018	...	...	...	...	3 644	779	1 502	5 925
Dem. People's Rep. Korea	*2005	40 097	0.2	0.2	0.2	...	...	...	...
Rép. pop. dém. de Corée	*2010	44 010	0.2	0.2	0.2	...	...	...	...
	*2015	48 458	0.2	0.2	0.2	...	...	...	...
	*2017	48 939	0.2	0.2	0.2	...	...	...	...
Dem. Rep. of the Congo	2005	622 869[7]	1.1[7]	1.1[7]	1.2[7]	204 341[3]	140[3]	47 435[3]	251 916[3]
Rép. dém. du Congo	2010	588 950[7]	0.9[7]	0.9[7]	0.9[7]	166 336[3]	932[3]	2 196 591[3]	2 363 859[3]
	2015	824 492[7]	1.1[7]	1.1[7]	1.1[7]	* 160 271	1 124	1 839 611	2 001 006
	2017	879 223[7]	1.1[7]	1.1[7]	1.1[7]	533 656[24]	1 218	3 998 573	4 533 447
	2018	...	...	...	...	535 730	2 937	4 699 151	5 237 818
Denmark	2005	440 383	8.1	7.9	8.3	44 374[3]	510[3]	573[3]	45 457[3]
Danemark	2010	509 740	9.2	8.9	9.4	17 922[3]	3 363[3]	3 238[3]	24 523[3]
	2015	595 876	10.5	10.3	10.6	17 785[12]	4 566	4 984	27 335
	2017	656 789	11.5	11.4	11.5	34 977	4 502	7 610	47 089
	2018	...	...	...	...	36 100	3 445	7 990	47 535
Djibouti	2005	92 091[7]	11.8[7]	13.0[7]	10.5[7]	10 456[3]	19[3]	7 668[3]	18 143[3]
Djibouti	2010	101 575[7]	11.9[7]	12.5[7]	11.4[7]	15 104[3]	732[3]	7[3]	15 843[3]
	2015	112 351[7]	12.1[7]	12.7[7]	11.5[7]	14 787	2 586	...	17 373
	2017	116 089[7]	12.1[7]	12.7[7]	11.6[7]	18 548	8 579	97	27 224
	2018	...	...	...	...	17 302	10 129	50	27 481
Dominica	2005	4 744	6.7	...	...	...	...	...	...
Dominique	2010	5 765	8.1	...	...	...	...	...	...
	2015	6 720	9.2	...	...	...	...	...	...
	2017	6 782	9.2	...	...	...	...	...	...
Dominican Republic	2005	376 001	4.1	4.9	3.2	...	...	...	...
République dominicaine	2010	393 720	4.0	4.8	3.1	599[3]	1 759[3]	...	2 358[3]
	2015	415 564	3.9	4.8	3.1	609[25]	752[25]	133 770[25]	135 131[25]
	2017	424 964	3.9	4.8	3.1	592	835	...	1 427
	2018	...	...	...	...	583	865	25 872[26]	27 320
Ecuador	2005	187 404[7]	1.4[7]	1.4[7]	1.3[7]	10 063[3]	2 489[3]	250 001[3]	262 553[3]
Équateur	2010	325 366[7]	2.2[7]	2.2[7]	2.1[7]	121 249[3]	49 887[3]	...	171 136[3]
	2015	387 513[7]	2.4[7]	2.5[7]	2.3[7]	121 535[3]	11 583[3]	...	133 118[3]
	2017	399 068[7]	2.4[7]	2.5[7]	2.3[7]	102 610	19 006	...	121 616
	2018	...	...	...	...	93 822	14 076	120 000	227 898
Egypt	2005	274 001[7]	0.4[7]	0.4[7]	0.3[7]	88 946[3]	11 005[3]	203[3]	100 154[3]
Égypte	2010	295 714[7]	0.4[7]	0.4[7]	0.3[7]	95 056[3]	14 303[3]	570[3]	109 929[3]
	2015	565 931[7]	0.6[7]	0.7[7]	0.5[7]	226 344	30 019	21	256 384
	2017	478 310[7]	0.5[7]	0.5[7]	0.5[7]	223 964	54 465	18	278 447
	2018	...	...	...	...	239 741	60 629	...	300 370
El Salvador	2005	36 019[7]	0.6[7]	0.6[7]	0.6[7]	49[3]	1[3]	44[3]	94[3]
El Salvador	2010	40 324[7]	0.7[7]	0.7[7]	0.7[7]	38[3]	18[3]	...	56[3]
	2015	42 045[7]	0.7[7]	0.7[7]	0.7[7]	48	...	...	48
	2017	42 323[7]	0.7[7]	0.7[7]	0.7[7]	43	3	3 322	3 368
	2018	...	...	...	...	48	2	73 400	73 450
Equatorial Guinea [9]	2005	6 588	0.9	0.9	0.8	...	...	...	...
Guinée équatoriale [9]	2010	8 658	0.9	0.9	0.9	...	...	...	...
	2015	209 611	17.8	24.9	9.1	...	...	...	...
	2017	221 865	17.5	24.4	9.0	...	...	...	...
Eritrea	2005	* 14 314	* 0.4	* 0.4	* 0.3	4 418[3]	1 591[3]	31[3]	6 040[3]
Érythrée	2010	* 15 676	* 0.4	* 0.4	* 0.3	4 809[3]	137[3]	13[3]	4 959[3]
	2015	* 15 941	* 0.3	* 0.4	* 0.3	2 944	1	22	2 967
	2016	...	...	...	...	2 293	5	6	2 304
	2017	* 16 041	* 0.3	* 0.4	* 0.3	2 381	...	19	2 400
	2018	...	...	...	...	2 215	...	181	2 396

4

International migrants and refugees *(continued)*
International migrant stock (number and percentage) and refugees and others of concern to UNHCR

Migrants internationaux et réfugiés *(suite)*
Stock de migrants internationaux (nombre et pourcentage) et réfugiés et autres personnes relevant de la compétence du HCR

Region, country or area Région, pays ou zone	Year Année	International Migrant Stock (mid-year) Stock de migrants internationaux (milieu de l'année)				Refugees and others of concern to UNHCR (mid-year) Réfugiés et autres personnes relevant de la compétence du HCR (milieu de l'année)			
		Total Total	MF HF	M H	F	Refugees& Réfugiés&	Asylum seekers Demandeurs d'asile	Other&& Autres&&	Total pop. Pop. totale
Estonia	2005	233 701	17.2	15.0	19.2	7[3]	8[3]	136 000[3]	136 015[3]
Estonie	2010	217 890	16.4	14.1	18.3	39[3]	10[3]	100 983[3]	101 032[3]
	2015	194 664	14.8	13.0	16.4	117	117	86 522[27]	86 756
	2017	192 962	14.7	13.1	16.1	402	43	81 382[27]	81 827
	2018	...	...	...	...	403	3	79 026[27]	79 432
Eswatini	2005	27 097[7]	2.5[7]	2.8[7]	2.2[7]	760[3]	256[3]	...	1 016[3]
Eswatini	2010	30 476[7]	2.5[7]	2.7[7]	2.4[7]	759[3]	...	...	759[3]
	2015	31 993[7]	2.4[7]	2.6[7]	2.3[7]	539	321	4	864
	2017	33 263[7]	2.4[7]	2.6[7]	2.3[7]	770	462	10	1 242
	2018	...	...	...	...	849	635	...	1 484
Ethiopia	2005	514 242[7]	0.7[7]	0.7[7]	0.6[7]	100 817[3]	209[3]	4 110[3]	105 136[3]
Éthiopie	2010	567 720[7]	0.6[7]	0.7[7]	0.6[7]	154 295[3]	1 028[3]	47[3]	155 370[3]
	2015	1 162 576[7]	1.2[7]	1.2[7]	1.1[7]	702 467	2 871	348	705 686
	2017	1 227 143[7]	1.2[7]	1.2[7]	1.1[7]	841 285	1 929	536	843 750
	2018	...	...	...	...	920 961	2 360	1 205 119	2 128 440
Falkland Islands (Malvinas)	2005	1 166	39.7	...	...	...	...	...	...
Îles Falkland (Malvinas)	2010	1 436	50.4	...	...	...	...	...	...
	2015	1 571	54.2	...	...	...	...	...	...
	2017	1 579	54.3	...	...	...	...	...	...
Faroe Islands	2005	4 583	9.5	...	...	...	...	...	...
Îles Féroé	2010	5 096	10.5	...	...	...	...	...	...
	2015	5 517	11.3	...	...	...	...	...	...
	2017	5 735	11.6	...	...	...	...	...	...
Fiji	2005	12 435	1.5	1.6	1.5	...	...	...	...
Fidji	2010	13 351	1.6	1.6	1.5	1[3]	6[3]	...	7[3]
	2015	13 751	1.5	1.6	1.4	12	8	...	20
	2017	13 911	1.5	1.6	1.4	11	4	...	15
	2018	...	...	...	...	4	19	...	23
Finland	2005	192 169[28]	3.7[28]	3.7[28]	3.6[28]	11 809[3]	...	849[3]	12 658[3]
Finlande	2010	248 135[28]	4.6[28]	4.8[28]	4.5[28]	8 724[3]	2 097[3]	3 133[3]	13 954[3]
	2015	314 856[28]	5.7[28]	5.9[28]	5.6[28]	11 798[12]	2 622	1 928	16 348
	2017	343 582[28]	6.2[28]	6.4[28]	6.0[28]	19 939	3 520	2 671	26 130
	2018	...	...	...	...	21 599	13 897	2 749	38 245
France	2005	6 737 600	11.0	11.0	11.0	137 316[3]	41 279[3]	946[3]	179 541[3]
France	2010	7 196 481	11.4	11.3	11.5	200 687[3]	48 576[3]	1 171[3]	250 434[3]
	2015	7 918 382	12.3	12.1	12.5	264 972	53 827	1 290	320 089
	2017	7 902 783	12.2	11.9	12.4	321 119	55 606	1 363	378 088
	2018	...	...	...	...	355 222	67 350	1 449	424 021
French Guiana	2005	86 468	42.4	42.3	42.5	...	...	...	...
Guyane française	2010	96 288	41.1	39.8	42.4	...	...	...	...
	2015	106 108	39.5	37.5	41.5	...	...	...	...
	2017	111 718	39.5	37.5	41.5	...	...	...	...
French Polynesia	2005	32 286	12.7	14.1	11.2	...	...	...	...
Polynésie française	2010	31 640	11.8	13.2	10.4	...	...	...	...
	2015	30 058	10.8	12.1	9.5	...	...	...	...
	2017	30 687	10.8	12.1	9.5	...	...	...	...
Gabon	2005	214 123[9]	15.3[9]	17.4[9]	13.1[9]	8 545[3]	4 843[3]	291[3]	13 679[3]
Gabon	2010	243 992[9]	14.9[9]	16.7[9]	13.0[9]	9 015[3]	4 132[3]	84[3]	13 231[3]
	2015	268 384[9]	13.9[9]	15.4[9]	12.3[9]	1 008	1 886	...	2 894
	2017	280 197[9]	13.8[9]	15.4[9]	12.2[9]	957	105	3	1 065
	2018	...	...	...	...	833	89	...	922
Gambia	2005	181 905	12.6	13.4	11.8	7 330[3]	602[3]	42[3]	7 974[3]
Gambie	2010	185 763	11.0	11.7	10.3	8 378[3]	74[3]	31[3]	8 483[3]
	2015	192 540	9.7	10.4	9.1	11 773	2	...	11 775
	2017	205 063	9.8	10.4	9.1	7 973	5	33	8 011
	2018	...	...	...	...	8 487	301	38	8 826

International migrants and refugees *(continued)*
International migrant stock (number and percentage) and refugees and others of concern to UNHCR

Migrants internationaux et réfugiés *(suite)*
Stock de migrants internationaux (nombre et pourcentage) et réfugiés et autres personnes relevant de la compétence du HCR

Region, country or area Région, pays ou zone	Year Année	International Migrant Stock (mid-year) Stock de migrants internationaux (milieu de l'année) Total Total	% of total pop. % de la pop. totale MF HF	M H	F	Refugees and others of concern to UNHCR (mid-year) Réfugiés et autres personnes relevant de la compétence du HCR (milieu de l'année) Refugees& Réfugiés&	Asylum seekers Demandeurs d'asile	Other&& Autres&&	Total pop. Pop. totale
Georgia	2005	72 311[29]	1.6[29]	1.5[29]	1.7[29]	2 497[3]	8[3]	236 097[3]	238 602[3]
Géorgie	2010	73 034[29]	1.7[29]	1.6[29]	1.8[29]	639[3]	44[3]	361 547[3]	362 230[3]
	2015	76 685[29]	1.9[29]	1.8[29]	2.1[29]	1 659	587	266 060	268 306
	2017	78 218[29]	2.0[29]	1.8[29]	2.2[29]	2 167	344	276 271	278 782
	2018	...	...	...	...	2 019	509	280 585	283 113
Germany	2005	9 402 447	11.5	11.7	11.3	700 016[3]	71 624[3]	12 340[3]	783 980[3]
Allemagne	2010	9 812 263	12.1	12.2	12.0	594 269[3]	51 991[3]	24 378[3]	670 638[3]
	2015	10 220 418	12.5	12.5	12.5	250 299	311 551	11 978	573 828
	2017	12 165 083	14.8	15.0	14.7	864 686	459 503	12 957	1 337 146
	2018	...	...	...	...	1 021 706	394 131	14 386	1 430 223
Ghana	2005	304 436	1.4	1.5	1.3	53 537[3]	5 496[3]	1 212[3]	60 245[3]
Ghana	2010	337 017	1.4	1.4	1.3	13 828[3]	749[3]	184[3]	14 761[3]
	2015	399 471	1.4	1.5	1.4	18 476	2 855	...	21 331
	2016	...	...	...	...	16 409	2 048	8 871	27 328
	2017	417 642	1.4	1.5	1.4	11 976	1 376	...	13 352
	2018	...	...	...	...	11 940	1 174	...	13 114
Gibraltar	2005	9 211	28.7	...	...	...	...	...	...
Gibraltar	2010	10 369	31.2	...	...	...	...	...	...
	2015	11 065	32.3	...	...	...	...	...	...
	2017	11 152	32.3	...	...	...	...	...	...
Greece	2005	1 190 707	10.5	10.5	10.6	2 390[3]	8 867[3]	3 000[3]	14 257[3]
Grèce	2010	1 321 149	11.5	11.4	11.7	1 444[3]	55 724[3]	260[3]	57 428[3]
	2015	1 242 924	11.1	10.3	11.8	8 231	29 157	214	37 602
	2017	1 220 395	10.9	10.1	11.7	41 977	38 277	73	80 327
	2018	...	...	...	...	55 565	56 652	198	112 415
Greenland	2005	6 686	11.7	...	...	...	...	...	...
Groenland	2010	6 226	11.0	...	...	...	...	...	...
	2015	6 009	10.7	...	...	...	...	...	...
	2017	6 014	10.6	...	...	...	...	...	...
Grenada	2005	6 902	6.7	6.7	6.7	...	...	...	...
Grenade	2010	6 980	6.7	6.6	6.7	...	3[3]	...	3[3]
	2015	7 057	6.6	6.5	6.7	...	...	...	...
	2017	7 124	6.6	6.5	6.7	1	1	...	2
	2018	...	...	...	...	2	3	...	5
Guadeloupe [30]	2005	89 065	20.3	19.4	21.1	...	...	...	...
Guadeloupe [30]	2010	94 942	21.1	20.3	21.7	...	...	...	...
	2015	98 507	21.9	21.0	22.6	...	...	...	...
	2017	99 350	22.1	21.2	22.9	...	...	...	...
Guam	2005	74 743	47.2	47.8	46.5	...	...	...	...
Guam	2010	75 416	47.3	48.0	46.5	...	...	...	...
	2015	76 089	47.0	47.9	46.2	...	...	...	...
	2017	78 027	47.5	48.4	46.6	...	...	...	...
Guatemala	2005	57 252[7]	0.4[7]	0.4[7]	0.5[7]	391[3]	3[3]	...	394[3]
Guatemala	2010	66 384[7]	0.5[7]	0.4[7]	0.5[7]	138[3]	2[3]	...	140[3]
	2015	78 352[7]	0.5[7]	0.5[7]	0.5[7]	202	73	...	275
	2017	81 528[7]	0.5[7]	0.5[7]	0.5[7]	312	41	21 600	21 953
	2018	...	...	...	...	390	47	40 800	41 237
Guinea	2005	229 611[7,9]	2.4[7,9]	2.3[7,9]	2.4[7,9]	63 525[3]	3 808[3]	29 645[3]	96 978[3]
Guinée	2010	177 998[7,9]	1.6[7,9]	1.7[7,9]	1.6[7,9]	14 113[3]	764[3]	117[3]	14 994[3]
	2015	126 386[7,9]	1.0[7,9]	1.2[7,9]	0.9[7,9]	8 704	293	...	8 997
	2017	122 796[7,9]	1.0[7,9]	1.1[7,9]	0.8[7,9]	5 105	105	1	5 211
	2018	...	...	...	...	4 906	134	...	5 040
Guinea-Bissau	2005	20 736[7]	1.5[7]	1.5[7]	1.5[7]	7 616[3]	166[3]	...	7 782[3]
Guinée-Bissau	2010	21 061[7]	1.4[7]	1.4[7]	1.4[7]	7 679[3]	330[3]	5[3]	8 014[3]
	2015	22 333[7]	1.3[7]	1.2[7]	1.3[7]	8 684	123	...	8 807
	2017	23 405[7]	1.3[7]	1.2[7]	1.3[7]	9 323	27	...	9 350
	2018	...	...	...	...	11 151	24	...	11 175

4

International migrants and refugees *(continued)*
International migrant stock (number and percentage) and refugees and others of concern to UNHCR

Migrants internationaux et réfugiés *(suite)*
Stock de migrants internationaux (nombre et pourcentage) et réfugiés et autres personnes relevant de la compétence du HCR

Region, country or area / Région, pays ou zone	Year / Année	International Migrant Stock (mid-year) Stock de migrants internationaux (milieu de l'année)				Refugees and others of concern to UNHCR (mid-year) Réfugiés et autres personnes relevant de la compétence du HCR (milieu de l'année)			
		Total / Total	MF HF	M H	F	Refugees& / Réfugiés&	Asylum seekers Demandeurs d'asile	Other&& Autres&&	Total pop. Pop. totale
Guyana / Guyana	2005	10 868	1.4	1.5	1.3	...	...	...	...
	2010	13 126	1.8	1.9	1.6	7[3]	...	...	7[3]
	2015	15 384	2.0	2.1	1.9	11	1	...	12
	2017	15 530	2.0	2.1	1.9	11	...	...	11
	2018	...	...	...	...	14	10	...	24
Haiti / Haïti	2005	30 468	0.3	0.4	0.3	...	...	...	...
	2010	35 104	0.4	0.4	0.3	...	4[3]	...	4[3]
	2015	39 529	0.4	0.4	0.3	5	5	...	10
	2017	40 533	0.4	0.4	0.3	5	22	2 710[31]	2 737
	2018	...	...	...	...	6	11	2 992[31]	3 009
Holy See / Saint-Siège	*2005	798	100.0	...	...	...	...	...	...
	*2010	794	100.0	...	...	...	...	...	...
	*2015	803	100.0	...	...	...	...	...	...
	*2017	792	100.0	...	...	...	...	...	...
Honduras / Honduras	2005	27 875[7]	0.4[7]	0.4[7]	0.4[7]	22[3]	50[3]	...	72[3]
	2010	27 288[7]	0.3[7]	0.4[7]	0.3[7]	14[3]	...	1[3]	15[3]
	2015	38 317[7]	0.4[7]	0.5[7]	0.4[7]	23	19	...	42
	2017	38 700[7]	0.4[7]	0.4[7]	0.4[7]	22	12	175 600	175 634
	2018	...	...	...	...	27	23	176 500	176 550
Hungary / Hongrie	2005	366 787[7]	3.6[7]	3.6[7]	3.6[7]	8 046[3]	684[3]	192[3]	8 922[3]
	2010	436 616[7]	4.4[7]	4.5[7]	4.3[7]	5 414[3]	367[3]	62[3]	5 843[3]
	2015	475 508[7]	4.9[7]	5.1[7]	4.7[7]	4 192	24 431	128	28 751
	2017	503 787[7]	5.2[7]	5.4[7]	4.9[7]	5 069	754	137	5 960
	2018	...	...	...	...	5 983	140	143	6 266
Iceland / Islande	2005	25 492	8.6	8.4	8.9	293[3]	29[3]	53[3]	375[3]
	2010	35 091	11.0	10.9	11.0	83[3]	39[3]	113[3]	235[3]
	2015	39 072	11.8	11.5	12.2	104	225	119	448
	2017	41 853	12.5	12.3	12.7	308	366	85	759
	2018	...	...	...	...	439	318	85	842
India / Inde	2005	5 923 642[7]	0.5[7]	0.5[7]	0.5[7]	139 283[3]	303[3]	2 792[3]	142 378[3]
	2010	5 436 012[7]	0.4[7]	0.4[7]	0.4[7]	184 821[3]	3 746[3]	5 109[3]	193 676[3]
	2015	5 240 960[7]	0.4[7]	0.4[7]	0.4[7]	200 383	5 381	...	205 764
	2017	5 188 550[7]	0.4[7]	0.4[7]	0.4[7]	196 662	9 814	...	206 476
	2018	...	...	...	...	196 966	11 335	...	208 301
Indonesia / Indonésie	2005	289 568[7]	0.1[7]	0.1[7]	0.1[7]	89[3]	58[3]	263[3]	410[3]
	2010	305 416[7]	0.1[7]	0.1[7]	0.1[7]	811[3]	2 071[3]	12[3]	2 894[3]
	2015	338 124[7]	0.1[7]	0.2[7]	0.1[7]	5 277	7 911	...	13 188
	2017	345 930[7]	0.1[7]	0.2[7]	0.1[7]	8 819	5 274	...	14 093
	2018	...	...	...	...	11 031	2 898	...	13 929
Iran (Islamic Republic of) / Iran (Rép. islamique d')	2005	2 568 930[7]	3.6[7]	3.9[7]	3.4[7]	974 302[3]	140[3]	344 914[3]	1 319 356[3]
	2010	2 761 561[7]	3.7[7]	4.2[7]	3.2[7]	1 073 366[3]	1 775[3]	10 168[3]	1 085 309[3]
	2015	2 726 420[7]	3.4[7]	3.6[7]	3.3[7]	979 441	42	8	979 491
	2017	2 699 155[7]	3.3[7]	3.5[7]	3.1[7]	978 698	84	3	978 785
	2018	...	...	...	...	979 435	82	4	979 521
Iraq / Iraq	2005	132 915[7,9]	0.5[7,9]	0.6[7,9]	0.4[7,9]	50 177[3]	1 948[3]	1 526 104[3]	1 578 229[3]
	2010	117 389[7,9]	0.4[7,9]	0.5[7,9]	0.3[7,9]	34 655[3]	3 073[3]	1 758 603[3]	1 796 331[3]
	2015	359 381[7,9]	1.0[7,9]	1.1[7,9]	0.8[7,9]	288 035	7 420	4 016 205[32]	4 311 660
	2017	366 568[7,9]	1.0[7,9]	1.1[7,9]	0.8[7,9]	273 516	12 680	4 640 941[33]	4 927 137
	2018	...	...	...	...	281 905	13 813	2 667 951[33]	2 963 669
Ireland / Irlande	2005	589 046	14.0	14.7	13.2	7 113[3]	2 414[3]	4[3]	9 531[3]
	2010	730 542	15.8	15.6	15.9	9 107[3]	5 129[3]	1[3]	14 237[3]
	2015	749 943	16.0	15.4	16.5	6 125[3]	4 267[3]	100[3]	10 492[3]
	2017	806 549	16.9	16.7	17.2	5 731	5 123	100	10 954
	2018	...	...	...	...	6 405	6 556	99	13 060
Isle of Man / Île de Man	2005	41 475	54.5	...	...	...	...	...	...
	2010	43 447	54.3	...	...	...	...	...	...
	2015	45 221	54.4	...	...	...	...	...	...
	2017	45 872	54.4	...	...	...	...	...	...

4

International migrants and refugees *(continued)*
International migrant stock (number and percentage) and refugees and others of concern to UNHCR

Migrants internationaux et réfugiés *(suite)*
Stock de migrants internationaux (nombre et pourcentage) et réfugiés et autres personnes relevant de la compétence du HCR

Region, country or area / Région, pays ou zone	Year / Année	International Migrant Stock (mid-year) / Stock de migrants internationaux (milieu de l'année) Total / Total	MF HF	% of total pop. / % de la pop. totale M H	F	Refugees and others of concern to UNHCR (mid-year) / Réfugiés et autres personnes relevant de la compétence du HCR (milieu de l'année) Refugees& / Réfugiés&	Asylum seekers / Demandeurs d'asile	Other&& / Autres&&	Total pop. / Pop. totale
Israel Israël	2005	1 889 503[7]	28.6[7]	26.6[7]	30.5[7]	609[3]	939[3]	...	1 548[3]
	2010	1 950 615[7]	26.3[7]	24.3[7]	28.2[7]	25 471[3]	5 575[3]	9[3]	31 055[3]
	2015	2 011 727[7]	24.9[7]	22.8[7]	27.0[7]	38 500	6 591	88	45 179
	2017	1 962 123[7]	23.6[7]	21.5[7]	25.6[7]	35 851	27 759	42	63 652
	2018	...	...	...	...	17 958	35 917	42	53 917
Italy Italie	2005	3 954 785	6.7	6.4	7.1	20 675[3]	...	940[3]	21 615[3]
	2010	5 787 898	9.7	9.2	10.2	56 397[3]	4 076[3]	858[3]	61 331[3]
	2015	5 805 325	9.8	9.1	10.4	93 715[12]	48 307	606	142 628
	2017	5 907 461	10.0	9.3	10.6	157 839	134 327	715	292 881
	2018	...	...	...	...	180 829	131 937	732	313 498
Jamaica Jamaïque	2005	24 314	0.9	0.9	0.9	...	...	...	...
	2010	23 677	0.8	0.9	0.8	21[3]	...	...	21[3]
	2015	23 167	0.8	0.8	0.8	15	3	...	18
	2017	23 332	0.8	0.8	0.8	15	9	...	24
	2018					15	22	...	37
Japan Japon	2005	2 012 916[9]	1.6[9]	1.5[9]	1.7[9]	1 941[3]	533[3]	1 770[3]	4 244[3]
	2010	2 134 151[9]	1.7[9]	1.5[9]	1.8[9]	2 586[3]	3 047[3]	1 397[3]	7 030[3]
	2015	2 232 189[9]	1.7[9]	1.6[9]	1.9[9]	* 2 419	* 10 705	* 631	* 13 755
	2017	2 321 476[9]	1.8[9]	1.7[9]	2.0[9]	* 2 530	* 24 679	* 626	* 27 835
	*2018	...	...	...	...	1 972	31 736	585	34 293
Jordan Jordanie	2005	2 325 414[7,9]	40.7[7,9]	40.1[7,9]	41.3[7,9]	965[3]	16 570[3]	329[3]	17 864[3]
	2010	2 722 983[7,9]	37.9[7,9]	37.8[7,9]	38.0[7,9]	450 915[3]	2 159[3]	107[3]	453 181[3]
	2015	3 112 026[7,9]	34.0[7,9]	33.8[7,9]	34.2[7,9]	664 102[34]	20 693	...	684 795
	2017	3 233 553[7,9]	33.3[7,9]	33.1[7,9]	33.5[7,9]	692 240[34]	40 876	...	733 116[34]
	2018	...	...	...	...	705 762[34]	46 986	...	752 748
Kazakhstan Kazakhstan	2005	3 102 962	20.0	19.7	20.2	7 265[3]	65[3]	50 598[3]	57 928[3]
	2010	3 334 623	20.3	20.5	20.2	4 406[3]	314[3]	7 969[3]	12 689[3]
	2015	3 546 778	20.0	20.5	19.5	662	149	7 038	7 849
	2017	3 635 168	20.0	20.4	19.5	622	191	7 209	8 022
	2018	...	...	...	...	589	192	7 389	8 170
Kenya Kenya	2005	756 894[7]	2.1[7]	2.2[7]	2.0[7]	251 271[3]	16 460[3]	481[3]	268 212[3]
	2010	926 959[7]	2.2[7]	2.2[7]	2.2[7]	402 905[3]	27 966[3]	320 083[3]	750 954[3]
	2015	1 084 357[7]	2.3[7]	2.3[7]	2.3[7]	552 272	40 341	21 231	613 844
	2017	1 078 572[7]	2.2[7]	2.2[7]	2.2[7]	433 457	52 554	18 500	504 511
	2018	...	...	...	...	410 732	58 103	18 500	487 335
Kiribati Kiribati	2005	2 487	2.7	2.9	2.5	...	...	...	...
	2010	2 868	2.8	3.0	2.6	...	...	...	...
	2015	2 919	2.6	2.8	2.4	...	...	...	...
	2017	3 022	2.6	2.8	2.4	...	...	...	...
Kuwait Koweït	2005	1 333 327[7,9]	58.6[7,9]	68.3[7,9]	44.5[7,9]	1 523[3]	203[3]	101 000[3]	102 726[3]
	2010	1 871 537[7,9]	62.4[7,9]	75.6[7,9]	44.4[7,9]	184[3]	3 275[3]	93 000[3]	96 459[3]
	2015	2 866 136[7,9]	72.8[7,9]	83.5[7,9]	58.4[7,9]	593	1 040	93 000	94 633
	2017	3 123 431[7,9]	75.5[7,9]	89.4[7,9]	56.8[7,9]	844	810	93 000	94 654
	2018	...	...	...	...	620	988	92 016	93 624
Kyrgyzstan Kirghizistan	2005	312 897	6.2	5.1	7.2	2 598[3]	498[3]	100 004[3]	103 100[3]
	2010	231 511	4.3	3.5	5.0	2 458[3]	554[3]	301 164[3]	304 176[3]
	2015	204 382	3.5	2.8	4.1	433	168	13 678	14 279
	2017	200 294	3.3	2.7	3.9	350	102	2 272	2 724
	2018	...	...	...	...	339	88	1 190	1 617
Lao People's Dem. Rep. [7,9] Rép. dém. populaire lao [7,9]	2005	20 371	0.4	0.4	0.3	...	...	...	...
	2010	32 473	0.5	0.6	0.5	...	...	...	...
	2015	44 575	0.7	0.7	0.6	...	...	...	...
	2017	45 466	0.7	0.7	0.6	...	...	...	...
Latvia Lettonie	2005	376 725	16.7	15.0	18.2	11[3]	9[3]	418 638[3]	418 658[3]
	2010	313 786	14.8	12.8	16.5	68[3]	53[3]	326 906[3]	327 027[3]
	2015	265 418	13.3	11.4	15.0	195	171	262 802[35]	263 168
	2017	256 889	13.2	11.3	14.8	546	126	242 736[36]	243 408[36]
	2018	...	...	...	...	655	56	233 571[37]	234 282[37]

International migrants and refugees (continued)
International migrant stock (number and percentage) and refugees and others of concern to UNHCR

Migrants internationaux et réfugiés (suite)
Stock de migrants internationaux (nombre et pourcentage) et réfugiés et autres personnes relevant de la compétence du HCR

Region, country or area Région, pays ou zone	Year Année	International Migrant Stock (mid-year) Stock de migrants internationaux (milieu de l'année) % of total pop. % de la pop. totale				Refugees and others of concern to UNHCR (mid-year) Réfugiés et autres personnes relevant de la compétence du HCR (milieu de l'année)			
		Total Total	MF HF	M H	F	Refugees& Réfugiés&	Asylum seekers Demandeurs d'asile	Other&& Autres&&	Total pop. Pop. totale
Lebanon	2005	756 784[7]	19.0[7]	19.3[7]	18.7[7]	1 078[3]	1 450[3]	451[3]	2 979[3]
Liban	2010	820 655[7]	18.9[7]	19.3[7]	18.5[7]	8 063[3]	1 417[3]	40[3]	9 520[3]
	2015	1 973 204[7]	33.7[7]	32.3[7]	35.2[7]	1 172 388	10 851	5 813	1 189 052
	2017	1 939 212[7]	31.9[7]	30.6[7]	33.2[7]	1 003 076	13 630	4 314	1 021 020
	2018	...	...	...	...	974 629	16 071	3 818	994 518
Lesotho	2005[7,9]	6 290	0.3	0.4	0.3	...	...	...	...
Lesotho	2010[7,9]	6 414	0.3	0.4	0.3	...	...	...	...
	2015	6 572[7,9]	0.3[7,9]	0.3[7,9]	0.3[7,9]	44	1	...	45
	2017	6 749[7,9]	0.3[7,9]	0.3[7,9]	0.3[7,9]	59	3	...	62
	2018	...	...	...	...	79	40		119
Liberia	2005	87 188	2.7	3.1	2.2	10 168[3]	29[3]	498 604[3]	508 801[3]
Libéria	2010	99 129	2.5	2.9	2.2	24 743[3]	28[3]	1 855[3]	26 626[3]
	2015	113 779	2.5	2.9	2.2	38 904	18	1 486	40 408
	2017	98 630	2.1	2.4	1.8	13 380	22	374	13 776
	2018	...	...	...	...	9 529	33	374	9 936
Libya	2005	625 212[9]	10.8[9]	14.9[9]	6.4[9]	12 166[3]	200[3]	35[3]	12 401[3]
Libye	2010	683 998[9]	11.1[9]	15.5[9]	6.4[9]	7 923[3]	3 194[3]	37[3]	11 154[3]
	2015	771 146[9]	12.4[9]	17.4[9]	7.2[9]	27 948	8 904	434 869	471 721
	2017	788 419[9]	12.4[9]	17.5[9]	7.2[9]	9 450	32 430	300 019	341 899
	2018	...	...	...	...	9 365	43 714	242 176	295 255
Liechtenstein	2005	18 898	54.2	...	...	150[3]	60[3]	...	210[3]
Liechtenstein	2010	22 342	62.1	...	...	92[3]	44[3]	6[3]	142[3]
	2015	23 799	63.6	...	...	107	75	2	184
	2017	24 683	65.1	...	...	177	113	...	290
	2018	...	...	...	...	169	108	...	277
Lithuania	2005	201 209	6.0	6.1	6.0	531[3]	55[3]	8 709[3]	9 295[3]
Lituanie	2010	160 772	5.1	4.8	5.4	803[3]	71[3]	3 679[3]	4 553[3]
	2015	136 021	4.6	4.3	5.0	1 055	54	3 583	4 692
	2017	124 706	4.3	3.9	4.7	1 283	144	3 251	4 678
	2018	...	...	...	...	1 674	161	3 193	5 028
Luxembourg	2005	150 618	32.9	33.2	32.6	1 822[3]	...	74[3]	1 896[3]
Luxembourg	2010	248 888	49.0	50.0	48.0	3 254[3]	697[3]	173[3]	4 124[3]
	2015	260 573	46.0	46.6	45.4	1 192	831	81	2 104
	2017	264 073	45.3	45.8	44.7	...	...	...	...
	2018	...	...	...	...	2 046[38]	1 015	83	3 144
Madagascar	2005[9]	26 058	0.1	0.2	0.1	...	...	...	...
Madagascar	2010	28 905[9]	0.1[9]	0.2[9]	0.1[9]	...	...	1[3]	1[3]
	2015	32 075[9]	0.1[9]	0.2[9]	0.1[9]	10	9	...	19
	2017	33 844[9]	0.1[9]	0.2[9]	0.1[9]	43	46	...	89
	2018	...	...	...	...	44	84	...	128
Malawi	2005	221 661[7]	1.7[7]	1.6[7]	1.8[7]	4 240[3]	5 331[3]	49[3]	9 620[3]
Malawi	2010	217 722[7]	1.4[7]	1.4[7]	1.5[7]	5 740[3]	9 362[3]	131[3]	15 233[3]
	2015	232 803[7]	1.3[7]	1.3[7]	1.4[7]	8 963	13 669	...	22 632
	2017	237 104[7]	1.3[7]	1.2[7]	1.3[7]	8 904	23 066	395	32 365
	2018	...	...	...	...	13 660	23 645	359	37 664
Malaysia	2005	1 722 344[7,9,39]	6.7[7,9,39]	7.6[7,9,39]	5.8[7,9,39]	33 693[3]	10 838[3]	61 555[3]	106 086[3]
Malaisie	2010	2 406 011[7,9,39]	8.6[7,9,39]	9.9[7,9,39]	7.1[7,9,39]	81 516[3]	11 339[3]	120 015[3]	212 870[3]
	2015	2 650 617[7,9,39]	8.6[7,9,39]	10.1[7,9,39]	7.1[7,9,39]	97 573	54 400	120 000	271 973
	2017	2 703 629[7,9,39]	8.5[7,9,39]	10.0[7,9,39]	7.0[7,9,39]	95 903	51 764	90 558[40]	238 225
	2018	...	...	...	...	112 654	46 100	90 027[41]	248 781
Maldives [9]	2005	45 045	14.1	16.1	11.9	...	...	...	...
Maldives [9]	2010	54 659	15.0	20.9	7.9	...	...	...	...
	2015	64 273	15.4	23.8	4.4	...	...	...	...
	2017	67 026	15.4	23.7	4.4	...	...	...	...
Mali	2005	256 797[7]	2.0[7]	2.1[7]	1.9[7]	11 233[3]	1 833[3]	...	13 066[3]
Mali	2010	336 607[7]	2.2[7]	2.3[7]	2.2[7]	13 558[3]	1 703[3]	...	15 261[3]
	2015	365 145[7]	2.1[7]	2.1[7]	2.0[7]	14 970	386	132 953	148 309
	2017	383 721[7]	2.1[7]	2.1[7]	2.0[7]	17 586	373	65 895	83 854
	2018	...	...	...	...	24 366	601	64 972	89 939

4

International migrants and refugees *(continued)*
International migrant stock (number and percentage) and refugees and others of concern to UNHCR

Migrants internationaux et réfugiés *(suite)*
Stock de migrants internationaux (nombre et pourcentage) et réfugiés et autres personnes relevant de la compétence du HCR

Region, country or area / Région, pays ou zone	Year / Année	International Migrant Stock (mid-year) / Stock de migrants internationaux (milieu de l'année)				Refugees and others of concern to UNHCR (mid-year) / Réfugiés et autres personnes relevant de la compétence du HCR (milieu de l'année)			
		Total	MF HF	M H	F	Refugees& / Réfugiés&	Asylum seekers / Demandeurs d'asile	Other&& / Autres&&	Total pop. / Pop. totale
Malta / Malte	2005	24 560	6.0	5.9	6.2	1 939³	149³	...	2 088³
	2010	33 008	7.9	8.3	7.6	6 136³	1 295³	...	7 431³
	2015	42 430	9.9	10.6	9.3	6 095	425		6 520
	2017	45 539	10.6	11.2	9.9	8 314	1 307	...	9 621
	2018	...	...	...	...	8 218	1 610	11	9 839
Marshall Islands / Îles Marshall	2005	2 417	4.6	...	...	...	...	...	...
	2010	3 089	5.9	...					
	2015	3 284	6.2						
	2017	3 292	6.2						
Martinique / Martinique	2005	57 034	14.4	14.0	14.7	...			...
	2010	59 575	15.1	14.4	15.6	...			...
	2015	61 731	16.0	15.3	16.6	...			...
	2017	61 579	16.0	15.4	16.5	...			...
Mauritania / Mauritanie	2005	58 119⁷,⁹	1.9⁷,⁹	2.1⁷,⁹	1.6⁷,⁹	632³	92³	29 500³	30 224³
	2010	84 679⁷,⁹	2.3⁷,⁹	2.7⁷,⁹	2.0⁷,⁹	26 717³	241³	9³	26 967³
	2015	166 552⁷,⁹	4.0⁷,⁹	4.5⁷,⁹	3.5⁷,⁹	76 851	407		77 258
	2017	168 438⁷,⁹	3.8⁷,⁹	4.3⁷,⁹	3.3⁷,⁹	79 029	706	...	79 735
	2018	...	...	...	...	84 078	788	...	84 866
Mauritius / Maurice	2005⁹,⁴²	19 647	1.6	1.5	1.7	...	...	...	...
	2010⁹,⁴²	24 836	2.0	2.1	1.9	...	...	...	...
	2015⁹,⁴²	28 585	2.3	2.5	2.0	...	...	...	...
	2017	28 713⁹,⁴²	2.3⁹,⁴²	2.5⁹,⁴²	2.0⁹,⁴²	3	...	...	3
	2018					4			4
Mayotte / Mayotte	2005	63 176	35.5	35.7	35.2	...	...	...	...
	2010	72 757	34.9	33.8	35.9	...	...	...	...
	2015	73 992	30.8	29.0	32.6	...	...	...	...
	2017	74 399	29.4	27.7	31.1	...	...	...	...
Mexico / Mexique	2005	712 487⁷	0.7⁷	0.7⁷	0.6⁷	3 229³	161³	...	3 390³
	2010	969 538⁷	0.8⁷	0.8⁷	0.8⁷	1 395³	172³	6³	1 573³
	2015	1 193 155⁷	0.9⁷	1.0⁷	0.9⁷	2 158		68	2 226
	2017	1 224 169⁷	0.9⁷	1.0⁷	0.9⁷	7 186	6 653	13	13 852
	2018	...	...	...	...	9 143	19 760	70 992	99 895
Micronesia (Fed. States of) / Micronésie (États féd. de)	2005	2 905	2.7	2.9	2.6	...	...	...	...
	2010	2 805	2.7	2.8	2.6	...	...	...	...
	2015	2 756	2.6	2.8	2.5	...	34	...	34
	2016	...	...	...	...	3	1	...	4
	2017	2 785	2.6	2.8	2.5	4	...	...	4
Monaco / Monaco	2005	21 312	63.1	...	...	...	...	...	...
	2010	21 132	57.0	...	...	...	1³	...	1³
	2015	21 042	54.9			33	...		33
	2017	21 255	54.9						
	2018	...				25			25
Mongolia / Mongolie	2005	11 475⁹	0.5⁹	0.6⁹	0.3⁹	...	2³	581³	583³
	2010	16 061⁹	0.6⁹	0.9⁹	0.3⁹	12³	1³	260³	273³
	2015	17 620⁹	0.6⁹	0.9⁹	0.3⁹	11	5	16	32
	2017	18 204⁹	0.6⁹	0.9⁹	0.3⁹	8	3	19	30
	2018	...				7	2	22	31
Montenegro / Monténégro	2010	78 507	12.6	10.3	14.8	16 364³	5³	1 886³	18 255³
	2015	82 541	13.1	10.8	15.4	6 203	7	13 602	19 812
	2017	70 984	11.3	9.0	13.5	919	57	12 005	12 981
	2018	...	...			835	1 316	12 396	14 547
Montserrat / Montserrat	2005	1 244	26.0			...	...	...	...
	2010	1 277	25.8			...	14³	...	14³
	2015	1 351	26.4			...	...	...	...
	2017	1 364	26.3			...	...	...	...

4

International migrants and refugees *(continued)*
International migrant stock (number and percentage) and refugees and others of concern to UNHCR

Migrants internationaux et réfugiés *(suite)*
Stock de migrants internationaux (nombre et pourcentage) et réfugiés et autres personnes relevant de la compétence du HCR

Region, country or area Région, pays ou zone	Year Année	International Migrant Stock (mid-year) Stock de migrants internationaux (milieu de l'année)				Refugees and others of concern to UNHCR (mid-year) Réfugiés et autres personnes relevant de la compétence du HCR (milieu de l'année)			
		Total Total	MF HF	M H	F	Refugees[&] Réfugiés[&]	Asylum seekers Demandeurs d'asile	Other[&&] Autres[&&]	Total pop. Pop. totale
Morocco	2005	54 379[9]	0.2[9]	0.2[9]	0.2[9]	219[3]	1 843[3]	4[3]	2 066[3]
Maroc	2010	70 909[9]	0.2[9]	0.2[9]	0.2[9]	792[3]	280[3]	...	1 072[3]
	2015	92 424[9]	0.3[9]	0.3[9]	0.3[9]	2 144	2 216	...	4 360
	2017	95 835[9]	0.3[9]	0.3[9]	0.3[9]	5 167	1 887	...	7 054
	2018	...	...	...	...	5 069	2 135	...	7 204
Mozambique	2005	204 830[7]	1.0[7]	1.0[7]	0.9[7]	1 954[3]	4 015[3]	40[3]	6 009[3]
Mozambique	2010	214 612[7]	0.9[7]	0.9[7]	0.9[7]	4 077[3]	5 914[3]	1[3]	9 992[3]
	2015	238 930[7]	0.9[7]	0.9[7]	0.9[7]	4 552	14 257	7	18 816
	2017	246 954[7]	0.8[7]	0.8[7]	0.8[7]	4 787	16 324	21 543	42 654
	2018	...	...	...	...	4 993	21 072	21 359	47 424
Myanmar	2005	83 025[9]	0.2[9]	0.2[9]	0.2[9]	...	...	236 495[3]	236 495[3]
Myanmar	2010	76 414[9]	0.2[9]	0.2[9]	0.1[9]	...	...	859 403[3]	859 403[3]
	2015	73 308[9]	0.1[9]	0.2[9]	0.1[9]	...	...	1 466 501[43]	1 466 501
	2016	...	...	...	...	...	1	1 392 096[43]	1 392 097
	2017	74 660[9]	0.1[9]	0.2[9]	0.1[9]	...	...	1 277 777[44]	1 277 777
	2018	...	...	...	...	...	...	862 896[45]	862 896
Namibia	2005	106 274	5.2	5.8	4.7	5 307[3]	1 073[3]	2 752[3]	9 132[3]
Namibie	2010	102 405	4.7	5.2	4.2	7 254[3]	1 421[3]	93[3]	8 768[3]
	2015	96 888	4.0	4.4	3.6	1 659	1 100	1 684	4 443
	2017	95 067	3.8	4.2	3.4	1 972	1 860	77	3 909
	2018	...	...	...	...	2 182	1 510	39	3 731
Nauru	2005[9]	2 253	22.3	...	...	...	...	...	...
Nauru	2010[9]	2 112	21.1	...	...	...	...	...	...
	2015	3 678[9]	32.7[9]	...	...	506[3]	290	...	796
	2017	3 710[9]	32.7[9]	...	...	506	302	...	808
	2018	...	...	...	...	687	120	...	807
Nepal	2005	679 457[7]	2.7[7]	1.8[7]	3.4[7]	126 436[3]	1 272[3]	410 929[3]	538 637[3]
Népal	2010	578 657[7]	2.1[7]	1.4[7]	2.8[7]	89 808[3]	938[3]	800 571[3]	891 317[3]
	2015	509 855[7]	1.8[7]	1.1[7]	2.4[7]	36 287	57	409[46]	36 753
	2017	502 670[7]	1.7[7]	1.1[7]	2.3[7]	23 566	115	757[46]	24 438
	2018	...	...	...	...	20 949	91	565[46]	21 605
Netherlands	2005	1 736 127	10.6	10.4	10.8	118 189[3]	14 664[3]	6 872[3]	139 725[3]
Pays-Bas	2010	1 832 510	11.0	10.6	11.3	74 961[3]	13 053[3]	2 095[3]	90 109[3]
	2015	1 996 318	11.8	11.3	12.3	82 494[12]	8 097	1 951	92 542
	2017	2 056 520	12.1	11.6	12.5	...	...	...	...
	2018	...	...	...	...	102 899	7 048	1 951	111 898
New Caledonia	2005	55 405	23.8	25.6	22.0	...	...	...	...
Nouvelle-Calédonie	2010	61 158	24.4	25.8	22.9	...	...	...	...
	2015	64 290	23.9	25.5	22.3	...	...	...	...
	2017	66 001	23.9	25.5	22.2	...	...	...	...
New Zealand	2005	839 952	20.3	20.1	20.5	5 307[3]	396[3]	6[3]	5 709[3]
Nouvelle-Zélande	2010	947 443	21.7	21.4	22.0	2 307[3]	216[3]	1[3]	2 524[3]
	2015	1 039 736	22.5	22.2	22.9	1 349[12]	251	...	1 600
	2017	1 067 423	22.7	22.3	23.0	1 467	324	...	1 791
	2018	...	...	...	...	1 550	364	...	1 914
Nicaragua	2005	34 918[7]	0.6[7]	0.7[7]	0.6[7]	227[3]	1[3]	...	228[3]
Nicaragua	2010	37 333[7]	0.7[7]	0.7[7]	0.6[7]	64[3]	12[3]	...	76[3]
	2015	40 262[7]	0.7[7]	0.7[7]	0.6[7]	361	25	5	391
	2017	41 159[7]	0.7[7]	0.7[7]	0.6[7]	330	405	2	737
	2018	...	...	...	...	328	130	332	790
Niger	2005	124 461[7]	0.9[7]	0.9[7]	1.0[7]	301[3]	48[3]	37[3]	386[3]
Niger	2010	126 464[7]	0.8[7]	0.7[7]	0.8[7]	314[3]	18[3]	5[3]	337[3]
	2015	252 998[7]	1.3[7]	1.2[7]	1.3[7]	82 064	122	120 000	202 186
	2017	295 610[7]	1.4[7]	1.3[7]	1.5[7]	162 135	98	147 712	309 945
	2018	...	...	...	...	177 286	1 723	171 307	350 316

4 International migrants and refugees *(continued)*
International migrant stock (number and percentage) and refugees and others of concern to UNHCR

Migrants internationaux et réfugiés *(suite)*
Stock de migrants internationaux (nombre et pourcentage) et réfugiés et autres personnes relevant de la compétence du HCR

Region, country or area Région, pays ou zone	Year Année	International Migrant Stock (mid-year) Stock de migrants internationaux (milieu de l'année)				Refugees and others of concern to UNHCR (mid-year) Réfugiés et autres personnes relevant de la compétence du HCR (milieu de l'année)			
		Total Total	MF HF	M H	F	Refugees[&] Réfugiés[&]	Asylum seekers Demandeurs d'asile	Other[&&] Autres[&&]	Total pop. Pop. totale
			% of total pop. % de la pop. totale						
Nigeria Nigéria	2005	969 294[7,9]	0.7[7,9]	0.8[7,9]	0.6[7,9]	9 019[3]	420[3]	3 290[3]	12 729[3]
	2010	988 679[7,9]	0.6[7,9]	0.7[7,9]	0.5[7,9]	8 747[3]	1 815[3]	34[3]	10 596[3]
	2015	1 199 115[7,9]	0.7[7,9]	0.7[7,9]	0.6[7,9]	1 279	909	1 508 017	1 510 205
	2017	1 235 088[7,9]	0.6[7,9]	0.7[7,9]	0.6[7,9]	1 415	614	2 476 290	2 478 319
	2018	...	...	...	...	25 426	762	2 164 649	2 190 837
Niue Nioué	2005	522	31.0	...	...	...	...	...	...
	2010	545	33.4	...	...	...	...	...	...
	2015	557	34.2	...	...	...	...	...	...
	2017	553	34.2	...	...	...	...	...	...
North Macedonia Macédoine du Nord	2005	127 667	6.2	5.2	7.2	1 274[3]	723[3]	2 451[3]	4 448[3]
	2010	129 701	6.3	5.2	7.3	1 398[3]	161[3]	1 731[3]	3 290[3]
	2015	130 730	6.3	5.2	7.3	828	43	717	1 588
	2017	130 972	6.3	5.2	7.3	592	22	598	1 212
	2018	...	...	...	...	421	40	600	1 061
Northern Mariana Islands Îles Mariannes du Nord	2005	37 542	58.9	...	...	...	...	...	...
	2010	24 168	44.4	...	...	...	...	...	...
	2015	21 648	39.5	...	...	...	...	...	...
	2017	21 777	39.5	...	...	...	...	...	...
Norway Norvège	2005	361 144[47]	7.8[47]	7.7[47]	7.9[47]	43 034[3]	...	1 143[3]	44 177[3]
	2010	526 799[47]	10.8[47]	11.0[47]	10.6[47]	40 260[3]	12 473[3]	3 150[3]	55 883[3]
	2015	746 375[47]	14.4[47]	14.9[47]	13.8[47]	47 043[12]	5 885	1 997	54 925
	2017	798 944[47]	15.1[47]	15.6[47]	14.5[47]	60 118	4 861	3 251	68 230
	2018	...	...	...	...	58 107	2 256	3 282	63 645
Oman Oman	2005	666 160[9]	26.5[9]	37.2[9]	12.7[9]	7[3]	4[3]	...	11[3]
	2010	816 221[9]	26.8[9]	35.9[9]	13.0[9]	78[3]	13[3]	...	91[3]
	2015	1 814 591[9]	43.2[9]	55.1[9]	21.3[9]	122	268	...	390
	2017	2 073 292[9]	44.7[9]	57.0[9]	21.0[9]	315	366	...	681
	2018	...	...	...	...	309	422	...	731
Pakistan Pakistan	2005	3 171 132[7]	2.1[7]	2.2[7]	2.0[7]	1 084 694[3]	3 426[3]	461 123[3]	1 549 243[3]
	2010	3 941 586[7]	2.3[7]	2.4[7]	2.3[7]	1 900 621[3]	2 095[3]	2 248 308[3]	4 151 024[3]
	2015	3 628 956[7]	1.9[7]	1.9[7]	1.9[7]	1 540 854	6 103	1 893 008	3 439 965
	2017	3 398 154[7]	1.7[7]	1.7[7]	1.7[7]	1 406 794	3 233	452 131	1 862 158
	2018	...	...	...	...	1 397 629	4 545	177 872	1 580 046
Palau Palaos	2005	6 043	30.4	...	...	...	...	...	...
	2010	5 490	26.8	...	...	...	...	...	...
	2015	4 937	23.2	...	...	1	...	...	1
	2016	...	...	...	...	...	1	...	1
	2017	4 988	23.0	...	...	5	...	...	5
Panama Panama	2005	117 563	3.5	3.6	3.5	1 730[3]	433[3]	10 273[3]	12 436[3]
	2010	157 309	4.3	4.4	4.2	17 073[3]	479[3]	6[3]	17 558[3]
	2015	184 710	4.7	4.8	4.5	17 303	2 038	2	19 343
	2017	190 728	4.7	4.8	4.5	17 373	5 627	2	23 002
	2018	...	...	...	...	2 467	8 223	51 422	62 112
Papua New Guinea Papouasie-Nvl-Guinée	2005	29 967[7,9]	0.5[7,9]	0.6[7,9]	0.4[7,9]	9 999[3]	4[3]	135[3]	10 138[3]
	2010	25 424[7,9]	0.4[7,9]	0.5[7,9]	0.3[7,9]	9 698[3]	1[3]	...	9 699[3]
	2015	30 782[7,9]	0.4[7,9]	0.5[7,9]	0.3[7,9]	9 510	400	...	9 910
	2017	32 389[7,9]	0.4[7,9]	0.5[7,9]	0.3[7,9]	9 547	2	...	9 549
	2018	...	...	...	...	9 880	...	...	9 880
Paraguay Paraguay	2005	168 243	2.9	3.0	2.8	50[3]	8[3]	...	58[3]
	2010	160 299	2.6	2.6	2.5	107[3]	8[3]	...	115[3]
	2015	156 462	2.4	2.4	2.3	161	39	...	200
	2017	160 519	2.4	2.4	2.3	214	31	...	245
	2018	...	...	...	...	217	123	...	340
Peru Pérou	2005	77 541	0.3	0.3	0.3	848[3]	336[3]	1[3]	1 185[3]
	2010	84 066	0.3	0.3	0.3	1 146[3]	264[3]	1[3]	1 411[3]
	2015	91 481	0.3	0.3	0.3	1 407	366	...	1 773
	2017	93 780	0.3	0.3	0.3	1 746	10 436	...	12 182
	2018	...	...	...	...	1 978	122 644	46 299	170 921

4

International migrants and refugees *(continued)*
International migrant stock (number and percentage) and refugees and others of concern to UNHCR

Migrants internationaux et réfugiés *(suite)*
Stock de migrants internationaux (nombre et pourcentage) et réfugiés et autres personnes relevant de la compétence du HCR

Region, country or area / Région, pays ou zone	Year / Année	International Migrant Stock (mid-year) / Stock de migrants internationaux (milieu de l'année)				Refugees and others of concern to UNHCR (mid-year) / Réfugiés et autres personnes relevant de la compétence du HCR (milieu de l'année)			
		Total / Total	MF / HF	M / H	F	Refugees[&] / Réfugiés[&]	Asylum seekers / Demandeurs d'asile	Other[&&] / Autres[&&]	Total pop. / Pop. totale
				% of total pop. / % de la pop. totale					
Philippines Philippines	2005	257 468[7,9]	0.3[7,9]	0.3[7,9]	0.3[7,9]	96[3]	42[3]	775[3]	913[3]
	2010	208 599[7,9]	0.2[7,9]	0.2[7,9]	0.2[7,9]	243[3]	73[3]	139 577[3]	139 893[3]
	2015	211 862[7,9]	0.2[7,9]	0.2[7,9]	0.2[7,9]	254	163	385 746	386 163
	2017	218 530[7,9]	0.2[7,9]	0.2[7,9]	0.2[7,9]	451	227	510 506[48]	511 184
	2018	...	...	...	...	574	252	416 238[49]	417 064
Poland Pologne	2005	722 509	1.9	1.6	2.2	4 604[3]	1 627[3]	75[3]	6 306[3]
	2010	642 417	1.7	1.4	1.9	15 555[3]	2 126[3]	763[3]	18 444[3]
	2015	611 855	1.6	1.4	1.8	15 741[12]	2 470	10 825	29 036
	2017	640 937	1.7	1.5	1.9	12 002	2 902	10 825	25 729
	2018	...	...	...	...	12 381	3 109	10 825	26 315
Portugal Portugal	2005	771 184	7.3	7.4	7.2	363[3]	...	...	363[3]
	2010	762 825	7.2	7.3	7.0	384[3]	72[3]	31[3]	487[3]
	2015	864 814	8.3	8.1	8.5	699[12]	641	14	1 354
	2017	880 188	8.5	8.4	8.6	...	...	...	...
	2018	...	...	...	...	1 835	45	14	1 894
Puerto Rico Porto Rico	2005	352 144	9.4	9.2	9.5	...	...	...	...
	2010	304 969	8.2	8.0	8.4	...	...	...	...
	2015	280 494	7.6	7.4	7.8	...	...	...	...
	2017	273 494	7.5	7.2	7.7	...	...	...	...
Qatar Qatar	2005	646 026[9]	74.7[9]	85.3[9]	52.6[9]	46[3]	28[3]	...	74[3]
	2010	1 456 413[9]	81.8[9]	89.4[9]	58.1[9]	51[3]	16[3]	1 200[3]	1 267[3]
	2015	1 687 640[9]	68.0[9]	75.7[9]	44.4[9]	133	100	1 200	1 433
	2017	1 721 392[9]	65.2[9]	72.9[9]	42.1[9]	188	125	1 200	1 513
	2018	...	...	...	...	189	132	1 200	1 521
Republic of Korea République de Corée	2005	485 546[9]	1.0[9]	1.2[9]	0.8[9]	69[3]	519[3]	...	588[3]
	2010	919 275[9]	1.9[9]	2.1[9]	1.6[9]	358[3]	712[3]	179[3]	1 249[3]
	2015	1 143 087[9]	2.3[9]	2.5[9]	2.0[9]	1 313	5 102	200	6 615
	2017	1 151 865[9]	2.3[9]	2.5[9]	2.0[9]	2 051	7 107	196	9 354
	2018	...	...	...	...	2 379	16 393	197	18 969
Republic of Moldova République de Moldova	2005	173 957[50]	4.2[50]	3.8[50]	4.5[50]	84[3]	148[3]	1 543[3]	1 775[3]
	2010	157 668[50]	3.9[50]	3.1[50]	4.6[50]	148[3]	81[3]	2 032[3]	2 261[3]
	2015	142 904[50]	3.5[50]	2.6[50]	4.4[50]	389	164	6 233	6 786
	2017	140 045[50]	3.5[50]	2.5[50]	4.3[50]	408	70	4 692	5 170
	2018	...	...	...	...	404	90	4 507	5 001
Réunion Réunion	2005	115 076	14.5	15.2	13.9	...	...	...	...
	2010	123 029	14.8	15.6	14.1	...	...	...	...
	2015	127 209	14.7	15.4	14.1	...	...	...	...
	2017	129 153	14.7	15.4	14.1	...	...	...	...
Romania Roumanie	2005	145 162	0.7	0.6	0.7	2 056[3]	264[3]	400[3]	2 720[3]
	2010	166 126	0.8	0.8	0.8	1 021[3]	388[3]	321[3]	1 730[3]
	2015	281 048	1.4	1.5	1.3	2 426	138	294	2 858
	2017	370 753	1.9	2.1	1.7	3 423	101	240	3 764
	2018	...	...	...	...	4 072	373	217	4 662
Russian Federation Fédération de Russie	2005	11 667 588	8.1	8.7	7.6	1 523[3]	292[3]	481 282[3]	483 097[3]
	2010	11 194 710	7.8	8.3	7.4	4 922[3]	1 463[3]	126 170[3]	132 555[3]
	2015	11 643 276	8.1	8.5	7.7	315 313	2 423	113 474[51]	431 210
	2017	11 651 509	8.1	8.5	7.7	188 374	3 420	90 774[51]	282 568
	2018	...	...	...	...	104 644	1 175	79 334[51]	185 153
Rwanda Rwanda	2005	432 797[7]	4.8[7]	4.9[7]	4.7[7]	45 206[3]	4 301[3]	14 849[3]	64 356[3]
	2010	436 787[7]	4.3[7]	4.4[7]	4.2[7]	55 398[3]	290[3]	2[3]	55 690[3]
	2015	441 525[7]	3.8[7]	3.9[7]	3.7[7]	132 743	253	2 557	135 553
	2017	443 088[7]	3.6[7]	3.7[7]	3.6[7]	157 996	445	15 322	173 763
	2018	...	...	...	...	148 055	300	4 109	152 464
Saint Helena [52] Sainte-Hélène [52]	2005	487	11.4	...	...	...	...	...	...
	2010	569	13.6	...	...	...	...	...	...
	2015	604	15.0	...	...	...	...	...	...
	2017	606	15.0	...	...	...	...	...	...

4 International migrants and refugees *(continued)*
International migrant stock (number and percentage) and refugees and others of concern to UNHCR

Migrants internationaux et réfugiés *(suite)*
Stock de migrants internationaux (nombre et pourcentage) et réfugiés et autres personnes relevant de la compétence du HCR

Region, country or area Région, pays ou zone	Year Année	International Migrant Stock (mid-year) Stock de migrants internationaux (milieu de l'année)			% of total pop. % de la pop. totale	Refugees and others of concern to UNHCR (mid-year) Réfugiés et autres personnes relevant de la compétence du HCR (milieu de l'année)	Asylum seekers		
		Total Total	MF HF	M H	F	Refugees& Réfugiés&	Demandeurs d'asile	Other&& Autres&&	Total pop. Pop. totale
Saint Kitts and Nevis	2005	6 682	13.7	...	...	...	...	...	...
Saint-Kitts-et-Nevis	2010	7 245	14.1	...	...	...	...	...	...
	2015	7 443	13.7	...	...	1	...	...	1
	2017	7 587	13.7	...	...	...	...	...	...
Saint Lucia	2005	11 468	7.0	7.2	6.8	...	...	...	...
Sainte-Lucie	2010	12 100	7.0	7.2	6.8	...	6[3]	1[3]	7[3]
	2015	12 771	7.2	7.4	7.0	2	2	60	64
	2017	12 889	7.2	7.4	7.0	2	...	...	2
	2018	...	...	...	...	2	3	...	5
Saint Pierre and Miquelon	2005	1 147	18.3	...	...	...	...	...	...
Saint-Pierre-et-Miquelon	2010	1 017	16.2	...	...	...	...	...	...
	2015	986	15.7	...	...	...	...	...	...
	2017	990	15.7	...	...	...	...	...	...
Saint Vincent & Grenadines	2005	4 395	4.0	3.9	4.2	...	...	...	...
Saint-Vincent-Grenadines	2010	4 485	4.1	4.0	4.2	...	...	...	...
	2015	4 577	4.2	4.1	4.3	...	...	...	...
	2017	4 595	4.2	4.1	4.3	...	...	...	...
Samoa	2005	5 746	3.2	3.2	3.2	...	...	...	...
Samoa	2010	5 122	2.8	2.7	2.8	...	...	...	...
	2015	4 929	2.5	2.5	2.6	...	...	...	...
	2016	...	...	...	...	...	3	...	3
	2017	4 879	2.5	2.4	2.6	3	...	...	3
	2018	...	...	...	...	3	...	...	3
San Marino [9]	2005	4 218	14.4	...	...	...	...	...	...
Saint-Marin [9]	2010	4 399	14.1	...	...	...	...	...	...
	2015	5 174	15.7	...	...	...	...	...	...
	2017	5 243	15.7	...	...	...	...	...	...
Sao Tome and Principe [9]	2005	3 433	2.2	2.2	2.2	...	...	...	...
Sao Tomé-et-Principe [9]	2010	2 700	1.5	1.6	1.5	...	...	...	...
	2015	2 394	1.2	1.2	1.2	...	...	...	...
	2017	2 293	1.1	1.1	1.1	...	...	...	...
Saudi Arabia	2005	6 501 819[7,9]	27.2[7,9]	33.6[7,9]	19.2[7,9]	240 701[3]	212[3]	70 084[3]	310 997[3]
Arabie saoudite	2010	8 429 956[7,9]	30.7[7,9]	38.5[7,9]	20.8[7,9]	582[3]	87[3]	70 000[3]	70 669[3]
	2015	10 771 366[7,9]	34.1[7,9]	41.7[7,9]	24.2[7,9]	211	93	70 000	70 304
	2017	12 185 284[7,9]	37.0[7,9]	44.4[7,9]	27.2[7,9]	149	45	70 000	70 194
	2018	...	...	...	...	158	1 007	70 000	71 165
Senegal	2005	238 298[7]	2.1[7]	2.3[7]	2.0[7]	20 712[3]	2 629[3]	12[3]	23 353[3]
Sénégal	2010	256 092[7]	2.0[7]	2.1[7]	1.8[7]	20 672[3]	2 177[3]	1 401[3]	24 250[3]
	2015	263 242[7]	1.8[7]	1.9[7]	1.6[7]	14 304	2 956	...	17 260
	2017	265 601[7]	1.7[7]	1.8[7]	1.5[7]	14 565	3 313	...	17 878
	2018	...	...	...	...	14 686	3 434	...	18 120
Serbia [53]	2005	845 120	9.2	8.3	10.0	148 264[3]	33[3]	338 641[3]	486 938[3]
Serbie [53]	2010	826 066	9.1	8.3	10.0	73 608[3]	209[3]	238 810[3]	312 627[3]
	2015	807 441	9.1	8.2	10.0	35 309	464	223 949	259 722
	2017	801 903	9.1	8.2	10.0	33 704	205	220 378	254 287
	2018	...	...	...	...	30 935	140	219 601	250 676
Seychelles	2005	8 997	10.1	13.1	7.2	...	...	...	...
Seychelles	2010	11 420	12.5	16.6	8.2	...	...	...	...
	2015	12 791	13.6	19.3	8.1	...	...	...	...
	2017	12 926	13.6	19.4	8.1	...	1	...	1
	2018	...	...	...	...	...	1	...	1
Sierra Leone	2005	149 615[7]	2.6[7]	2.9[7]	2.4[7]	59 965[3]	177[3]	6 202[3]	66 344[3]
Sierra Leone	2010	97 452[7]	1.5[7]	1.7[7]	1.4[7]	8 363[3]	210[3]	38[3]	8 611[3]
	2015	91 213[7]	1.3[7]	1.4[7]	1.1[7]	1 371	16	...	1 387
	2017	95 248[7]	1.3[7]	1.4[7]	1.1[7]	693	1	...	694
	2018	...	...	...	...	686	...	...	686

International migrants and refugees *(continued)*
International migrant stock (number and percentage) and refugees and others of concern to UNHCR

Migrants internationaux et réfugiés *(suite)*
Stock de migrants internationaux (nombre et pourcentage) et réfugiés et autres personnes relevant de la compétence du HCR

Region, country or area / Région, pays ou zone	Year / Année	International Migrant Stock (mid-year) / Stock de migrants internationaux (milieu de l'année) Total / Total	% of total pop. / % de la pop. totale MF / HF	M / H	F	Refugees and others of concern to UNHCR (mid-year) / Réfugiés et autres personnes relevant de la compétence du HCR (milieu de l'année) Refugees[&] / Réfugiés[&]	Asylum seekers / Demandeurs d'asile	Other[&&] / Autres[&&]	Total pop. / Pop. totale
Singapore	2005	1 710 594	38.1	34.0	42.1	3[3]	1[3]	...	4[3]
Singapour	2010	2 164 794	42.7	38.2	47.0	7[3]	...	...	7[3]
	2015	2 543 638	46.0	41.1	50.7	...	...	1	1
	2017	2 623 404	46.0	41.1	50.7	...	...	1	1
	2018	...	...	...	...	...	...	1	1
Sint Maarten (Dutch part)	2005	13 100	40.3	...	...	...	...	...	...
St-Martin (partie néerland.)	2010	26 200	79.1	...	...	1[3]	3[3]	...	4[3]
	2015	27 295	70.4	...	...	3	5	...	8
	2017	28 260	70.4	...	...	5	6	...	11
	2018	...	...	...	...	5	2	...	7
Slovakia	2005	130 491	2.4	2.2	2.6	368[3]	2 707[3]	...	3 075[3]
Slovaquie	2010	146 319	2.7	2.6	2.9	461[3]	267[3]	911[3]	1 639[3]
	2015	177 624	3.3	3.4	3.2	799[12]	61	1 671	2 531
	2017	184 642	3.4	3.5	3.3	984	27	1 528	2 539
	2018	...	...	...	...	934	47	1 528	2 509
Slovenia	2005	197 276	9.9	11.0	8.8	251[3]	185[3]	715[3]	1 151[3]
Slovénie	2010	253 786	12.4	14.0	10.9	314[3]	121[3]	4 119[3]	4 554[3]
	2015	237 616	11.5	13.1	9.9	283	43	4	330
	2017	244 790	11.8	13.4	10.2	551	326	4	881
	2018	...	...	...	...	666	350	4	1 020
Solomon Islands	2005	3 271	0.7	0.8	0.6	...	...	...	...
Îles Salomon	2010	2 760	0.5	0.6	0.5	...	...	...	...
	2015	2 585	0.4	0.5	0.4	3	...	...	3
	2016	...	...	...	...	3	...	...	3
	2017	2 532	0.4	0.5	0.4	...	...	...	...
	2018	...	...	...	...	...	4	...	4
Somalia	2005	* 20 670[7]	* 0.2[7]	* 0.2[7]	* 0.2[7]	493[3]	98[3]	400 000[3]	400 591[3]
Somalie	2010	* 23 995[7]	* 0.2[7]	* 0.2[7]	* 0.2[7]	1 937[3]	24 111[3]	1 463 780[3]	1 489 828[3]
	2015	* 41 578[7]	* 0.3[7]	* 0.3[7]	* 0.3[7]	3 582	9 320	1 152 073	1 164 975
	2017	* 44 868[7]	* 0.3[7]	* 0.3[7]	* 0.3[7]	12 925	13 558	1 594 105	1 620 588
	2018	...	...	...	...	15 426	15 533	2 909 603	2 940 562
South Africa	2005	1 210 936[7]	2.5[7]	3.0[7]	2.0[7]	29 714[3]	140 095[3]	100[3]	169 909[3]
Afrique du Sud	2010	2 096 886[7]	4.1[7]	4.8[7]	3.4[7]	57 899[3]	171 702[3]	134[3]	229 735[3]
	2015	3 816 696[7]	6.9[7]	7.8[7]	6.0[7]	114 512	798 080	...	912 592
	2017	4 036 696[7]	7.1[7]	8.1[7]	6.2[7]	92 296	215 860[54]	...	308 156
	2018	...	...	...	...	89 285	184 203	...	273 488
South Sudan	2010[7]	257 905	2.6	2.6	2.5	...	...	...	...
Soudan du sud	2015	844 122[7]	7.1[7]	7.2[7]	7.0[7]	265 887	632	1 792 014[55]	2 058 533
	2017	845 239[7]	6.7[7]	6.8[7]	6.6[7]	274 920	2 400	1 944 735	2 222 055
	2018	...	...	...	...	297 150	2 207	1 859 835	2 159 192
Spain	2005	4 107 226[56]	9.3[56]	9.9[56]	8.8[56]	5 374[3]	...	27[3]	5 401[3]
Espagne	2010	6 280 065[56]	13.4[56]	14.0[56]	12.9[56]	3 820[3]	2 712[3]	31[3]	6 563[3]
	2015	5 891 208[56]	12.7[56]	12.7[56]	12.7[56]	5 798[12]	11 020	440	17 258
	2017	5 947 106[56]	12.8[56]	12.7[56]	12.9[56]	15 557	20 360	485	36 402
	2018	...	...	...	...	18 631	47 395	1 826	67 852
Sri Lanka	2005	39 526[7]	0.2[7]	0.2[7]	0.2[7]	106[3]	121[3]	351 884[3]	352 111[3]
Sri Lanka	2010	38 959[7]	0.2[7]	0.2[7]	0.2[7]	223[3]	138[3]	434 903[3]	435 264[3]
	2015	39 706[7]	0.2[7]	0.2[7]	0.2[7]	848	461	50 499[57]	51 808
	2017	40 018[7]	0.2[7]	0.2[7]	0.2[7]	651	634	40 445	41 730
	2018	...	...	...	...	802	626	40 550	41 978
State of Palestine	2005[58,59]	266 617	7.5	6.6	8.3	...	...	...	...
État de Palestine	2010[58,59]	258 032	6.3	5.6	7.2	...	...	...	...
	2015	255 507[58,59]	5.5[58,59]	4.8[58,59]	6.2[58,59]	...	...	3	3
	2017[58,59]	253 735	5.2	4.5	5.8	...	...	...	...
Sudan	2005[3]	...	...	...	...	147 256	4 425	878 067	1 029 748
Soudan	2010	578 363[7]	1.7[7]	1.7[7]	1.6[7]	178 308[3]	6 046[3]	1 767 167[3]	1 951 521[3]
	2015	623 878[7]	1.6[7]	1.6[7]	1.6[7]	356 191	11 448	2 400 270[60]	2 767 909
	2017	735 821[7]	1.8[7]	1.8[7]	1.8[7]	538 797	17 839	2 311 162	2 867 798
	2018	...	...	...	...	908 692	17 381	2 001 183	2 927 256

4 International migrants and refugees *(continued)*
International migrant stock (number and percentage) and refugees and others of concern to UNHCR

Migrants internationaux et réfugiés *(suite)*
Stock de migrants internationaux (nombre et pourcentage) et réfugiés et autres personnes relevant de la compétence du HCR

Region, country or area Région, pays ou zone	Year Année	International Migrant Stock (mid-year) Stock de migrants internationaux (milieu de l'année)				Refugees and others of concern to UNHCR (mid-year) Réfugiés et autres personnes relevant de la compétence du HCR (milieu de l'année)			
		Total Total	MF HF	M H	% of total pop. % de la pop. totale F	Refugees& Réfugiés&	Asylum seekers Demandeurs d'asile	Other&& Autres&&	Total pop. Pop. totale
Suriname	2005[9]	33 664	6.7	7.3	6.2	...	...	...	...
Suriname	2010	39 713[9]	7.5[9]	8.2[9]	6.9[9]	1[3]	7[3]	...	8[3]
	2015	46 836[9]	8.5[9]	9.2[9]	7.7[9]	1	...	...	1
	2017	47 699[9]	8.5[9]	9.2[9]	7.7[9]	15	72	1	88
	2018	...	...	...	...	47	70	2	119
Sweden	2005	1 125 790	12.5	12.0	12.9	74 915[3]	15 702[3]	5 785[3]	96 402[3]
Suède	2010	1 337 214	14.2	13.9	14.6	82 629[3]	18 635[3]	9 545[3]	110 809[3]
	2015	1 602 522	16.4	16.1	16.7	142 207[12]	56 135	27 167	225 509
	2017	1 747 710	17.6	17.4	17.9	235 853	67 140	36 036	339 029
	2018					242 725	43 494	35 101	321 320
Switzerland	2005	1 805 437	24.4	25.4	23.3	48 030[3]	14 428[3]	990[3]	63 448[3]
Suisse	2010	2 075 182	26.5	24.3	28.6	48 813[3]	12 916[3]	127[3]	61 856[3]
	2015	2 416 394	29.0	28.7	29.3	69 390	17 085	76	86 551
	2017	2 506 394	29.6	29.2	29.9	88 066	26 648	64	114 778
	2018	...	...	...	...	98 530	19 175	50	117 755
Syrian Arab Republic	2005	876 410[7,9]	4.8[7,9]	4.8[7,9]	4.8[7,9]	26 089[3]	1 898[3]	300 001[3]	327 988[3]
République arabe syrienne	2010	1 785 115[7,9]	8.5[7,9]	8.6[7,9]	8.4[7,9]	1 005 472[3]	2 446[3]	300 194[3]	1 308 112[3]
	2015	993 940[7,9]	5.3[7,9]	5.4[7,9]	5.3[7,9]	149 200[61]	4 839	7 792 500	7 946 539
	2017	1 013 818[7,9]	5.5[7,9]	5.6[7,9]	5.5[7,9]	19 006[61]	16 665	6 508 914[61]	6 544 585
	2018	...	...	...	...	18 490[62]	18 489	7 150 684[63]	7 187 663
Tajikistan	2005	280 444	4.1	3.5	4.7	1 018[3]	22[3]	25[3]	1 065[3]
Tadjikistan	2010	278 152	3.6	3.1	4.2	3 131[3]	1 656[3]	2 338[3]	7 125[3]
	2015	275 059	3.2	2.8	3.7	1 782	79	10 082[64]	11 943
	2017	273 259	3.1	2.6	3.5	2 612	474	15 047	18 133
	2018	...	...	...	...	2 647	167	7 353	10 167
Thailand	2005	2 163 447[7]	3.3[7]	3.4[7]	3.2[7]	117 053[3]	32 163[3]	136[3]	149 352[3]
Thaïlande	2010	3 224 131[7]	4.8[7]	4.9[7]	4.7[7]	96 675[3]	10 250[3]	542 505[3]	649 430[3]
	2015	3 486 526[7]	5.1[7]	5.2[7]	4.9[7]	110 372	8 166	506 718[65]	625 256
	2017	3 588 873[7]	5.2[7]	5.4[7]	5.1[7]	104 532	3 360	485 569[66]	593 461
	2018	...	...	...	...	102 223	1 461	479 394	583 078
Timor-Leste	2005	11 286	1.1	1.1	1.1	3[3]	10[3]	...	13[3]
Timor-Leste	2010	11 535	1.0	1.0	1.0	1[3]	4[3]	...	5[3]
	2015	11 784	0.9	0.9	1.0	...	...	5	5
	2017	12 063	0.9	0.9	0.9	...	...	2	2
	2018	...	...	...	...	...	...	2	2
Togo	2005	203 379[7,9]	3.6[7,9]	3.6[7,9]	3.5[7,9]	9 287[3]	420[3]	9 012[3]	18 719[3]
Togo	2010	255 262[7,9]	3.9[7,9]	4.0[7,9]	3.9[7,9]	14 051[3]	151[3]	5[3]	14 207[3]
	2015	276 844[7,9]	3.7[7,9]	3.8[7,9]	3.7[7,9]	21 877	687	...	22 564
	2017	283 966[7,9]	3.6[7,9]	3.7[7,9]	3.6[7,9]	12 558	726	1	13 285
	2018	...	...	...	...	12 426	723	...	13 149
Tokelau	2005	258	21.4	...	...	...	...	...	...
Tokélaou	2010	429	37.6	...	...	...	...	...	...
	2015	487	38.9	...	...	...	...	...	...
	2017	504	38.8	...	...	...	...	...	...
Tonga	2005	4 301	4.3	4.6	3.9	...	...	...	...
Tonga	2010	4 589	4.4	4.8	4.0	...	3[3]	...	3[3]
	2015	4 877	4.6	5.0	4.2	...	...	...	...
	2017	4 952	4.6	5.0	4.2	...	...	...	...
Trinidad and Tobago	2005	44 812	3.5	3.2	3.7	...	...	...	...
Trinité-et-Tobago	2010	48 226	3.6	3.5	3.7	29[3]	102[3]	...	131[3]
	2015	49 883	3.7	3.6	3.7	121	59	...	180
	2017	50 214	3.7	3.6	3.7	206	488	13	707
	2018	...	...	...	...	311	5 644	14	5 969
Tunisia	2005	35 040[9]	0.3[9]	0.4[9]	0.3[9]	87[3]	26[3]	...	113[3]
Tunisie	2010	43 172[9]	0.4[9]	0.4[9]	0.4[9]	89[3]	23[3]	3[3]	115[3]
	2015	56 701[9]	0.5[9]	0.5[9]	0.5[9]	824	156	3	983
	2017	57 663[7]	0.5[7]	0.5[7]	0.5[7]	601	34	3	638
	2018	...	...	...	...	877	125	6	1 008

International migrants and refugees *(continued)*
International migrant stock (number and percentage) and refugees and others of concern to UNHCR

Migrants internationaux et réfugiés *(suite)*
Stock de migrants internationaux (nombre et pourcentage) et réfugiés et autres personnes relevant de la compétence du HCR

Region, country or area / Région, pays ou zone	Year / Année	International Migrant Stock (mid-year) / Stock de migrants internationaux (milieu de l'année)				Refugees and others of concern to UNHCR (mid-year) / Réfugiés et autres personnes relevant de la compétence du HCR (milieu de l'année)			
		Total / Total	MF HF	M H	F	Refugees& / Réfugiés&	Asylum seekers Demandeurs d'asile	Other&& Autres&&	Total pop. Pop. totale
			% of total pop. / % de la pop. totale						
Turkey	2005	1 319 236[7]	1.9[7]	1.9[7]	2.0[7]	2 399[3]	4 872[3]	1 434[3]	8 705[3]
Turquie	2010	1 367 034[7]	1.9[7]	1.8[7]	2.0[7]	10 032[3]	6 715[3]	1 086[3]	17 833[3]
	2015	4 131 302[7]	5.3[7]	5.0[7]	5.5[7]	1 838 848[67]	145 335	1 086	1 985 269
	2017	4 881 966[7]	6.0[7]	5.8[7]	6.3[7]	3 203 785[67]	266 177	117	3 470 079
	2018	...	...	...	...	3 621 264[67]	301 940	118	3 923 322
Turkmenistan	2005	213 051	4.5	4.0	4.9	11 963[3]	2[3]	45[3]	12 010[3]
Turkménistan	2010	197 979	3.9	3.6	4.2	62[3]	...	20 000[3]	20 062[3]
	2015	196 386	3.5	3.3	3.7	27	...	7 144	7 171
	2017	195 061	3.4	3.2	3.6	22	...	3 390	3 412
	2018	...	...	...	...	23	...	4 314	4 337
Turks and Caicos Islands	2005	13 115	49.6	...	...	...	...	...	...
Îles Turques-et-Caïques	2010	17 216	55.5	...	...	...	...	...	...
	2015	22 719	66.2	...	...	4	4	...	8
	2017	24 534	69.2	...	...	5	...	...	5
	2018	...	...	...	...	5	...	...	5
Tuvalu [9]	2005	183	1.8	...	...	...	...	...	...
Tuvalu [9]	2010	154	1.5	...	...	...	...	...	...
	2015	141	1.3	...	...	...	...	...	...
	2017	143	1.3	...	...	...	...	...	...
Uganda	2005	652 968[7]	2.3[7]	2.3[7]	2.3[7]	257 256[3]	1 809[3]	1 636[3]	260 701[3]
Ouganda	2010	529 160[7]	1.6[7]	1.6[7]	1.6[7]	135 801[3]	20 804[3]	437 775[3]	594 380[3]
	2015	1 197 162[7]	3.0[7]	2.8[7]	3.1[7]	428 397	38 068	180 000	646 465
	2017	1 692 120[7]	3.9[7]	3.7[7]	4.2[7]	1 269 758	39 940	180 000	1 489 698
	2018	...	...	...	...	1 131 545	22 807	180 002	1 334 354
Ukraine	2005	5 050 302[68]	10.8[68]	10.0[68]	11.5[68]	2 346[3]	1 618[3]	72 896[3]	76 860[3]
Ukraine	2010	4 818 767[68]	10.5[68]	9.8[68]	11.1[68]	3 022[3]	2 981[3]	40 357[3]	46 360[3]
	2015	4 915 142[68]	11.0[68]	10.2[68]	11.7[68]	3 232	6 169	1 417 179	1 426 580
	2017	4 964 293[68]	11.2[68]	10.4[68]	11.9[68]	3 253	6 282	1 835 463[69]	1 844 998
	2018	...	...	...	...	3 225	6 286	1 835 574[69]	1 845 085
United Arab Emirates	2005	3 281 036[7,9]	71.6[7,9]	74.2[7,9]	65.5[7,9]	104[3]	79[3]	...	183[3]
Émirats arabes unis	2010	7 316 611[7,9]	88.5[7,9]	88.7[7,9]	87.9[7,9]	538[3]	86[3]	...	624[3]
	2015	7 995 126[7,9]	87.3[7,9]	89.2[7,9]	82.3[7,9]	424	378	...	802
	2017	8 312 524[7,9]	88.4[7,9]	91.2[7,9]	81.2[7,9]	807	872	...	1 679
	2018	...	...	...	...	969	4 814	30	5 813
United Kingdom	2005	5 926 156	9.8	9.5	10.1	303 181[3]	12 500[3]	909[3]	316 590[3]
Royaume-Uni	2010	7 604 583	12.0	11.8	12.2	238 150[3]	14 880[3]	229[3]	253 259[3]
	2015	8 411 021	12.9	12.5	13.2	117 234[12]	37 829	16	155 079
	2017	8 841 717	13.4	12.9	13.8	121 280	31 353	85	152 718
	2018	...	...	...	...	124 018	33 035	106	157 159
United Rep. of Tanzania	2005	770 846[7,70]	2.0[7,70]	2.5[7,70]	1.4[7,70]	548 824[3]	307[3]	81 519[3]	630 650[3]
Rép.-Unie de Tanzanie	2010	308 600[7,70]	0.7[7,70]	0.7[7,70]	0.7[7,70]	109 286[3]	1 247[3]	163 269[3]	273 802[3]
	2015	413 309[7,70]	0.8[7,70]	0.8[7,70]	0.8[7,70]	159 014	1 150	168 019	328 183
	2017	492 574[7,70]	0.9[7,70]	0.9[7,70]	0.9[7,70]	306 025	37 139	168 785	511 949
	2018	...	...	...	...	295 866	43 186	168 581	507 633
United States of America	2005	39 258 293	13.3	13.5	13.1	379 340[3]	169 743[3]	76[3]	549 159[3]
États-Unis d'Amérique	2010	44 183 643	14.3	14.2	14.4	264 569[3]	6 285[3]	89[3]	270 943[3]
	2015	48 178 877	15.1	14.8	15.3	* 267 222[12]	224 508	...	491 730
	2017	49 776 970	15.3	15.1	15.6	279 419	692 053[71]	...	971 472[71]
	2018	...	...	...	...	299 653	657 230	...	956 883
United States Virgin Islands	2005	56 647	52.6	51.3	53.7	...	...	...	...
Îles Vierges américaines	2010	56 684	53.4	52.6	54.1	...	...	...	...
	2015	56 721	54.0	53.4	54.6	...	...	...	...
	2017	56 745	54.1	53.5	54.7	...	...	...	...
Uruguay	2005	82 318	2.5	2.3	2.6	121[3]	9[3]	...	130[3]
Uruguay	2010	76 263	2.3	2.1	2.4	189[3]	40[3]	...	229[3]
	2015	78 799	2.3	2.2	2.4	289	68	...	357
	2017	79 586	2.3	2.2	2.4	318	772	...	1 090
	2018	...	...	...	...	344	4 026	6 157	10 527

International migrants and refugees *(continued)*
International migrant stock (number and percentage) and refugees and others of concern to UNHCR

Migrants internationaux et réfugiés *(suite)*
Stock de migrants internationaux (nombre et pourcentage) et réfugiés et autres personnes relevant de la compétence du HCR

Region, country or area Région, pays ou zone	Year Année	International Migrant Stock (mid-year) Stock de migrants internationaux (milieu de l'année) Total Total	MF HF	% of total pop. % de la pop. totale M H	F	Refugees and others of concern to UNHCR (mid-year) Réfugiés et autres personnes relevant de la compétence du HCR (milieu de l'année) Refugees& Réfugiés&	Asylum seekers Demandeurs d'asile	Other&& Autres&&	Total pop. Pop. totale
Uzbekistan	2005	1 329 345	5.0	4.5	5.5	43 950[3]	587[3]	5[3]	44 542[3]
Ouzbékistan	2010	1 220 149	4.3	3.9	4.6	311[3]	...	2[3]	313[3]
	2015	1 170 899	3.8	3.5	4.0	118	...	86 703[72]	86 821
	2017	1 159 190	3.6	3.4	3.9	22	...	86 425[73]	86 447
	2018	...	...	...	...	14	...	85 463[74]	85 477
Vanuatu	2005	2 800	1.3	1.3	1.4	...	...	...	...
Vanuatu	2010	2 991	1.3	1.2	1.3	4[3]	...	...	4[3]
	2015	3 187	1.2	1.2	1.2	...	1	...	1
	2017	3 245	1.2	1.2	1.2	...	...	...	...
	2018	...	...	...	...	...	2	...	2
Venezuela (Boliv. Rep. of)	2005	1 070 562	4.0	4.0	4.0	408[3]	5 912[3]	200 001[3]	206 321[3]
Venezuela (Rép. boliv. du)	2010	1 331 488	4.6	4.6	4.6	201 547[3]	15 859[3]	...	217 406[3]
	2015	1 404 448	4.5	4.5	4.5	174 191	704	...	174 895
	2017	1 426 336	4.5	4.5	4.4	171 878	933	...	172 811
	2018	...	...	...	...	122 874	644	11	123 529
Viet Nam	2005	51 768[7,9]	0.1[7,9]	0.1[7,9]	~0.0[7,9]	2 357[3]	...	15 000[3]	17 357[3]
Viet Nam	2010	61 756[7,9]	0.1[7,9]	0.1[7,9]	0.1[7,9]	1 928[3]	...	10 200[3]	12 128[3]
	2015	72 793[7,9]	0.1[7,9]	0.1[7,9]	0.1[7,9]	...	...	11 000	11 000
	2017	76 104[7,9]	0.1[7,9]	0.1[7,9]	0.1[7,9]	...	...	11 000	11 000
	2018	...	...	...	...	...	...	29 522	29 522
Wallis and Futuna Islands	2005	2 365	16.2	...	...	...	...	...	...
Îles Wallis-et-Futuna	2010	2 776	20.7	...	...	...	...	...	...
	2015	2 849	23.6	...	...	...	...	...	...
	2017	2 779	23.6	...	...	...	...	...	...
Western Sahara	*2005	3 891	0.9	1.0	0.8	...	...	...	...
Sahara occidental	*2010	4 493	0.9	1.0	0.8	...	...	...	...
	*2015	5 179	1.0	1.1	0.8	...	...	...	...
	*2017	5 384	1.0	1.1	0.8	...	...	...	...
Yemen	2005	171 073[7,9]	0.8[7,9]	0.9[7,9]	0.7[7,9]	81 937[3]	798[3]	48[3]	82 783[3]
Yémen	2010	285 837[7,9]	1.2[7,9]	1.3[7,9]	1.1[7,9]	190 092[3]	2 557[3]	315 929[3]	508 578[3]
	2015	379 899[7,9]	1.4[7,9]	1.5[7,9]	1.4[7,9]	263 047	9 902	1 267 590	1 540 539
	2017	384 321[7,9]	1.4[7,9]	1.4[7,9]	1.3[7,9]	270 905	9 306	2 926 569	3 206 780
	2018	...	...	...	...	271 554	8 140	2 126 042	2 405 736
Zambia	2005	252 749[7]	2.1[7]	2.2[7]	2.0[7]	155 718[3]	146[3]	29 833[3]	185 697[3]
Zambie	2010	149 637[7]	1.1[7]	1.1[7]	1.1[7]	47 857[3]	325[3]	9 687[3]	57 869[3]
	2015	155 428[7]	1.0[7]	1.0[7]	0.9[7]	25 737	2 606	23 415	51 758
	2017	156 982[7]	0.9[7]	0.9[7]	0.9[7]	29 509	3 871	25 088	58 468
	2018	...	...	...	...	45 870	4 551	22 690	73 111
Zimbabwe	2005	392 693[7]	3.0[7]	3.5[7]	2.5[7]	13 850[3]	118[3]	7[3]	13 975[3]
Zimbabwe	2010	397 891[7]	2.8[7]	3.3[7]	2.4[7]	4 435[3]	416[3]	...	4 851[3]
	2015	403 866[7]	2.6[7]	3.0[7]	2.2[7]	6 085	123	* 301 883	308 091
	2017	403 866[7]	2.4[7]	2.9[7]	2.1[7]	7 567	1 297	2 106[75]	10 970
	2018	...	...	...	...	7 707	8 391	3 696[75]	19 794

Source:

United Nations Population Division, New York, International migrant stock: The 2017 Revision, last accessed January 2018.

United Nations High Commissioner for Refugees (UNHCR), Geneva, UNHCR Population Statistics Database, last accessed March 2019.

& Number of refugees or persons in refugee-like situations as reported by the Office of the United Nations High Commissioner for Refugees (UNHCR). && Figure includes sum of returned refugees, internally

Source:

Organisation des Nations Unies, Division de la population, "New York, International migrant stock: The 2017 Revision", derniér accés janvier 2018.
Haut-Commissariat des Nations Unies pour les réfugiés (HCR), Genève, base de données statistique du HCR, dernier accès mars 2019.

&Nombre de réfugiés ou de personnes en situation analogue à celle de réfugiés, tel que donné par le Bureau des Nations Unies. && Les chiffres correspondent au total des réfugiés rapatriés, des personnes déplacées

4

International migrants and refugees *(continued)*
International migrant stock (number and percentage) and refugees and others of concern to UNHCR

Migrants internationaux et réfugiés *(suite)*
Stock de migrants internationaux (nombre et pourcentage) et réfugiés et autres personnes relevant de la compétence du HCR

displaced persons (IDPs) protected/assisted by UNHCR, including people in IDP like situations, returned IDPs, Persons under UNHCR's stateless mandate, and others of concern to UNHCR categories.

protégées ou assistées par le HCR, notamment celles se trouvant dans une situation analogue à celle des personnes déplacées, des personnes déplacées de retour, des apatrides relevant du mandat du HCR et d'autres catégories de personnes relevant de la compétence du HCR.

1	Excluding Sudan.	1	Exclut le Soudan.
2	Including Sudan.	2	Y compris le Soudan.
3	Data as at the end of December.	3	Données à la fin de décembre.
4	The number of IDPs in Afghanistan is decreased due to the revision of methodology.	4	Le nombre de personnes déplacées en Afghanistan est diminué en raison de la révision de la méthodologie.
5	The statelessness figure refers to a census from 2011 and has been adjusted to reflect the number of persons with undetermined nationality who had their nationality confirmed in 2011-mid 2017.	5	Le chiffre d'apatridie fait référence à un recensement de 2011 et a été ajusté pour refléter le nombre de personnes de nationalité indéterminée dont la nationalité a été confirmée en 2011-mi-2017.
6	The statelessness figure refers to a survey conducted in late 2017.	6	Le chiffre relatif à l'apatridie fait référence à une enquête menée fin 2017.
7	Including refugees.	7	Y compris les réfugiés.
8	According to the Government of Algeria, there are an estimated 165,000 Sahrawi refugees in the Tindouf camps.	8	Selon le Gouvernement algérien, les camps de Tindouf accueillent environ 165 000 réfugiés sahraouis.
9	Refers to foreign citizens.	9	Se rapportent aux citoyens étrangers.
10	Including Christmas Island, Cocos (Keeling) Islands and Norfolk Island.	10	Y compris l'île Christmas, les îles des Cocos (Keeling) et l'île Norfolk.
11	Asylum-seekers are based on the number of applications lodged for protection visas.	11	Les chiffres de l'Australie concernant les demandeurs d'asile sont établis sur la base du nombre de demandes de visa de protection présentées.
12	Data relates to the end of 2014.	12	Le nombre se rapporte à fin 2014.
13	Including Nagorno-Karabakh.	13	Y compris le Haut-Karabakh.
14	The refugee population includes 200,000 persons originating from Myanmar in a refugee-like situation. The Government of Bangladesh estimates the population to be between 300,000 and 500,000.	14	Au nombre des réfugiés figurent 200 000 personnes originaires du Myanmar se trouvant dans une situation analogue à celle des réfugiés. Le Gouvernement bangladais estime que le nombre de réfugiés se situe entre 300 000 et 500 000.
15	The refugee population includes 274,000 persons originating from Myanmar in a refugee-like situation. The Government of Bangladesh estimates the population to be between 300,000 and 500,000.	15	Au nombre des réfugiés figurent 274,000 personnes originaires du Myanmar se trouvant dans une situation analogue à celle des réfugiés. Le Gouvernement bangladais estime que le nombre de réfugiés se situe entre 300 000 et 500 000.
16	Refugee figure includes 943,228 stateless persons from Myanmar.	16	Le nombre de réfugiés comprend 943228 apatrides du Myanmar.
17	Bonaire only.	17	Bonaire seulement.
18	Refugee returnees in Burundi are cumulative as of June 2017. These include both registered and unregistered refugees.	18	Les réfugiés rapatriés au Burundi sont cumulatifs en juin 2017. Sont inclus les réfugiés enregistrés ou non enregistrés.
19	Refers to Guernsey and Jersey.	19	Se rapporte à Guernesey et Jersey.
20	For statistical purposes, the data for China do not include those for the Hong Kong Special Administrative Region (Hong Kong SAR), Macao Special Administrative Region (Macao SAR) and Taiwan Province of China.	20	Pour la présentation des statistiques, les données pour la Chine ne comprennent pas la région administrative spéciale de Hong Kong (RAS de Hong Kong), la région administrative spéciale de Macao (RAS de Macao) et la province chinoise de Taïwan.
21	The 300,000 Vietnamese refugees are well integrated and in practice receive protection from the Government of China.	21	Les 300 000 réfugiés vietnamiens sont bien intégrés et, dans la pratique, recoivent la protection du Gouvernement chinois.
22	The statelessness figure is based on a Government estimate of individuals or whose parents or grandparents migrated to Côte d'Ivoire before or just after independence and who did not establish their nationality at independence or before the nationality law changed in 1972. The estimation is adjusted to reflect the number of persons who acquired nationality through the special 'acquisition of nationality by declaration' procedure until mid of 2018. The estimate does not include individuals of unknown parentage who were abandoned as children and who are not considered as nationals under Ivorian law.	22	Le chiffre relatif à l'apatridie est basé sur une estimation gouvernementale des personnes qui ont émigré elles-mêmes ou dont les parents ou les grands-parents ont émigré en Côte d'Ivoire avant ou juste après l'indépendance et qui n'ont pas établi leur nationalité à l'indépendance ou avant que la loi sur la nationalité ne soit modifiée en 1972. ajusté pour refléter le nombre de personnes ayant acquis la nationalité par le biais de la procédure spéciale «acquisition de la nationalité par déclaration» jusqu'au milieu de 2018. L'estimation n'inclut pas les personnes de filiation inconnue qui ont été abandonnées dans leur enfance et qui ne sont pas considérées comme des ressortissants de droit ivoirien.
23	Including northern Cyprus.	23	Y compris la partie nord de Chypre.
24	Refugee population includes 60,280 refugee-like from Central African Rep. who are new arrivals from January to June 2017.	24	La population réfugiée comprend 60 280 qui se trouvent dans des situations semblables à celles de réfugiés en provenance de la République centrafricaine, qui sont de nouveaux arrivants de janvier à juin 2017.
25	Revised estimate includes only individuals born in the country where both parents were born abroad. This estimate does not include subsequent generations of individuals of foreign descent as such it does not include all persons without nationality.	25	Cette réestimation concerne uniquement les personnes nées dans le pays dont les deux parents sont nés à l'étranger. Cette estimation ne comprend pas les générations futures de personnes d'origine étrangère tels que les apatrides.

4   International migrants and refugees *(continued)*
International migrant stock (number and percentage) and refugees and others of concern to UNHCR

Migrants internationaux et réfugiés *(suite)*
Stock de migrants internationaux (nombre et pourcentage) et réfugiés et autres personnes relevant de la compétence du HCR

26	Since the adoption of Law 169-14 in May 2014, important steps have been taken by the Dominican Republic to confirm Dominican nationality through the validation of birth certificates of individuals born in the country to two migrant parents. Thousands of individuals also are believed to have been issued their Dominican civil documents in 2017 and 2018, although an official figure was not available for this report.
27	Almost all people recorded as being stateless have permanent residence and enjoy more rights than foreseen in the 1954 Convention relating to the Status of Stateless Persons.
28	Including Åland Islands.
29	Including Abkhazia and South Ossetia.
30	Including Saint Barthélemy and Saint Martin (French part).
31	Figure refers to individuals without a nationality who were born in the Dominican Republic prior to January 2010 and who were identified by UNHCR in Haiti since June 2015.
32	Including an estimate for stateless persons populations in line with Law 26 of 2006, which allows stateless persons to apply for nationality in certain circumstances.
33	Pending a more accurate study into stateless in Iraq, the estimate of stateless persons in Iraq has been adjusted to reflect the reduction of statelessness in line with Law 26 of 2006, which allows stateless persons to apply for nationality in certain circumstances.
34	Includes Iraqi refugees registered with UNHCR.
35	The figure of stateless persons includes persons covered by two separate Laws; Law on Stateless Persons dated 17 February 2004 and the Law on the Status of Those Former USSR Citizens who are not Citizens of Latvia or of Any Other State.
36	Non-citizens of Latvia is the only category of residents who are not Latvian citizens, but who enjoy the right to reside in Latvia ex lege (all others require a resident permit) and an immediate right to acquire citizenship through registration and/or naturalisation (depending on age).
37	Figure includes persons under UNHCR's statelessness mandate and covered by two separate Latvian laws.
38	Refugee figure related to the end of 2016.
39	Including Sabah and Sarawak.
40	The updated statelessness figure is based on a registration and community legal assistance programme undertaken in West Malaysia by a local NGO with technical support from UNHCR, which began in 2014. During 2016, 874 persons of those registered acquired Malaysian nationality.
41	Updated figure is based on a registration and community legal assistance programme undertaken in West Malaysia by a local NGO with technical support from UNHCR, which began in 2014. During 2017, 906 persons of those registered acquired Malaysian nationality.
42	Including Agalega, Rodrigues and Saint Brandon.
43	Stateless persons population refers to persons without citizenship in Rakhine State only.
44	This figure is an estimate of persons without any citizenship in Rakhine state derived from the 2014 census. It does not include an estimated 118,000 stateless IDPs, persons in an IDP-like situation who are also of concern under the statelessness mandate because they are already included within the figures on IDPs.

26	Depuis l'adoption de la loi 169-14 en mai 2014, la République dominicaine a pris d'importantes mesures pour confirmer la nationalité dominicaine en validant les actes de naissance des personnes nées dans le pays de deux parents migrants. Des milliers de personnes auraient également reçu leurs documents d'état civil dominicains en 2017 et 2018, bien qu'aucun chiffre officiel ne soit disponible pour ce rapport.
27	La quasi totalité des personnes enregistrées comme apatrides ont une résidence permanente et jouissent de davantage de droits que ceux prévus par la Convention de 1954 relative au statut des apatrides.
28	Y compris les Îles d'Åland.
29	Y compris l'Abkhazie et l'Ossétie du Sud.
30	Y compris Saint-Barthélemy et Saint-Martin (partie française).
31	Chiffre correspond aux individus sans nationalité qui sont nés en République Dominicaine avant Janvier 2010 et qui ont été identifiés par le HCR en Haïti depuis Juin 2015.
32	Y compris une estimation des populations apatrides conforme à la loi 26 de 2006, qui permet aux apatrides de demander la nationalité dans certaines circonstances.
33	En attendant une étude plus précise sur les apatrides en Irak, l'estimation des apatrides en Irak a été ajustée pour refléter la réduction de l'apatridie conformément à la loi 26 de 2006, qui permet aux apatrides de demander la nationalité dans certaines circonstances.
34	Y compris réfugiés iraquiens enregistrés par le HCR.
35	Le nombres d'apatrides comprend les personnes couvertes par deux lois distinctes: La loi sur les apatrides du 17 février 2004 et la loi relative au Statut des citoyens de l'ex-URSS qui ne sont pas citoyens de la Lettonie ou d'un autre État.
36	Les non-ressortissants de la Lettonie sont les seuls résidents qui, sans être des citoyens lettons, jouissent du droit de résider en Lettonie ex lege (tous les autres ont besoin d'un permis de séjour) et du droit d'acquérir immédiatement la nationalité par enregistrement ou naturalisation (en fonction de leur âge).
37	Le chiffre inclut les personnes relevant du mandat du HCR en matière d'apatridie et régies par deux lois lettones distinctes.
38	Chiffre de réfugié lié à la fin de 2016.
39	Y compris Sabah et Sarawak.
40	Le chiffre actualisé sur l'apatridie est basé sur un programme d'enregistrement et d'assistance juridique communautaire entrepris en Malaisie occidentale par une ONG locale avec le soutien technique du HCR, qui a débuté en 2014. En 2016, 874 personnes enregistrées ont acquis la nationalité malaisienne.
41	Le chiffre actualisé est basé sur un programme d'enregistrement et d'assistance juridique communautaire mis en place en Malaisie occidentale par une ONG locale avec l'assistance technique du HCR, qui a débuté en 2014. En 2017, 906 personnes enregistrées ont acquis la nationalité malaise.
42	Y compris Agalega, Rodrigues et Saint-Brandon.
43	Les apatrides s'entendent des personnes dépourvues de nationalité, dans l'État de Rakhine uniquement.
44	Ce chiffre est une estimation des personnes sans citoyenneté dans l'État de Rakhine dérivées du recensement de 2014. Il n'inclut pas environ 118 000 personnes déplacées apatrides, des personnes dans une situation de type PDI qui sont également préoccupantes dans le cadre du mandat sur l'apatridie parce qu'elles sont déjà incluses dans les chiffres sur les PDI.

4   International migrants and refugees *(continued)*
International migrant stock (number and percentage) and refugees and others of concern to UNHCR

Migrants internationaux et réfugiés *(suite)*
Stock de migrants internationaux (nombre et pourcentage) et réfugiés et autres personnes relevant de la compétence du HCR

45	The figure of stateless persons in Rakhine State (470,000) is based on an estimation exercise carried out by UNHCR and MIAG partners early 2018. It does not include an estimated 128,030 stateless IDPs who are also of concern under the statelessness mandate because they are already included within the IDP figures. Outside of Rakhine state, the figure of those with undetermined nationality (25,939) is based on government data released on 27 December 2016 indicating the number of persons who hold an Identity Card for National Verification, and whose citizenship has not yet been confirmed.
46	Various studies estimate that a large number of individuals lack citizenship certificates in Nepal. While these individuals are not all necessarily stateless, UNHCR has been working closely with the Government of Nepal and partners to address this situation.
47	Including Svalbard and Jan Mayen Islands.
48	The updated statelessness figure is based on a registration exercise covering 28 municipalities that has taken place between 2014 and 2016. 4,112 of the registered group were confirmed as Filipino, Indonesian or dual nationals during 2016.
49	By the end of 2017, a total of 6,072 persons out of the 8,745 persons of Indonesian descent registered by the Government of the Philippines between 2014-2016 were confirmed as Filipino, Indonesian or dual nationals.
50	Including the Transnistria region.
51	Stateless persons refers to census figure from 2010 adjusted to reflect the number of people who acquired nationality since 2011.
52	Including Ascension and Tristan da Cunha.
53	Including Kosovo.
54	An adjustment to 2015 and 2016 end of year figures, in particular for the number of asylum applications pending on appeal and review, has resulted in a substantially lower figure for numbers of asylum seekers reported in South Africa.
55	Internally displaced persons (IDP) figure in South Sudan includes 105,000 people who are in an IDP-like situation.
56	Including Canary Islands, Ceuta and Melilla.
57	The statistics of the remaining IDPs, while provided by the Government authorities at the district level, are being reviewed by the central authorities. Once this review has been concluded, the statistics will be changed accordingly.
58	Including East Jerusalem.
59	Refugees are not part of the foreign-born migrant stock in the State of Palestine.
60	Internally displaced persons (IDP) figure in Sudan includes 77,300 people who are in an IDP-like situation.
61	The figure for Iraqi refugees is a Government estimate.
62	Refugee figure for Iraqis was a Government estimate and UNHCR has registered and was assisting 15,400 Iraqis at mid-2018.
63	Figure for stateless persons was an estimate.
64	Figure refers to a registration exercise in three regions and 637 persons registered as stateless by the Ministry of Internal Affairs of Tajikistan.
65	Figure of stateless persons in Thailand refers to 2011.
66	The figure on the number of registered stateless persons has been updated by the Royal Thai Government. It includes an increase of 61,070 persons who are expected to form a large proportion of the group which will benefit from positive changes introduced to the nationality framework in December 2016. In addition, it reflects decreases as a result of 8,814 stateless persons acquiring Thai nationality in 2016 and 8,377 cases that were de-registered because of death or duplicate registration.
67	Refugee figure for Syrians in Turkey is a Government estimate.

45	Le chiffre des apatrides dans l'État de Rakhine (470 000) est basé sur un exercice d'estimation réalisé par le HCR et ses partenaires début 2018. Il n'inclut pas environ 128 030 personnes déplacées à l'intérieur apatrides qui sont également concernées par le mandat relatif à l'apatridie car elles sont déjà incluses dans les chiffres de PDI. En dehors de l'État de Rakhine, le nombre de personnes de nationalité indéterminée (25 939) est basé sur les données gouvernementales publiées le 27 décembre 2016 indiquant le nombre de personnes possédant une carte d'identité pour la vérification nationale et dont la citoyenneté n'a pas encore été confirmée.
46	Selon différentes études, un grand nombre de personnes ne disposeraient pas de certificat de nationalité au Népal. Elles ne sont pas nécessairement toutes apatrides, mais le HCR travaille en coopération étroite avec les autorités népalaises et des partenaires pour régler la situation.
47	Y compris les îles Svalbard-et-Jan Mayen.
48	Le chiffre mis à jour sur l'apatridie est basé sur un exercice d'enregistrement couvrant 28 municipalités qui a eu lieu entre 2014 et 2016. 4 112 du groupe enregistré ont été confirmés en tant que Philippins, Indonésiens ou binationaux en 2016.
49	À la fin de 2017, 6072 personnes sur les 8745 personnes d'ascendance indonésienne enregistrées par le gouvernement des Philippines entre 2014 et 2016 avaient été confirmées comme ressortissantes philippines, indonésiennes ou à double nationalité.
50	Y compris la région de Transnistrie.
51	Le nombre d'apatrides se rapporte aux données du recensement effectué en 2010, ajustées pour tenir compte du nombre de personnes ayant acquis la nationalité depuis 2011.
52	Y compris Ascension et Tristan da Cunha.
53	Y compris Kosovo.
54	Un ajustement des chiffres de fin d'année 2015 et 2016, en particulier pour le nombre de demandes d'asile pendantes en appel et en révision, a abouti à un chiffre sensiblement inférieur pour le nombre de demandeurs d'asile signalés en Afrique du Sud.
55	Au nombre des déplacés au Soudan du Sud figurent 105 000 personnes dans une situation analogue à celle des déplacés.
56	Y compris les îles Canaries, Ceuta et Melilla.
57	Les statistiques relatives au reste des déplacés ont été fournies par les autorités locales au niveau des districts, mais examinées par les autorités centrales, et seront ajustées en fonction des résultats de l'examen.
58	Y compris Jérusalem-Est.
59	Les réfugiés ne sont pas comptabilisés parmi les migrants nés à l'étranger qui se trouvent dans l'État de Palestine.
60	Au nombre des déplacés au Soudan figurent 77 300 personnes dans une situation analogue à celles des déplacés.
61	Le nombre de réfugiés iraquiens est une estimation du Gouvernement.
62	Le chiffre des réfugiés iraquiens était une estimation du gouvernement et le HCR s'est enregistré et a aidé 15 400 Iraquiens à la mi-2018.
63	Le chiffre relatif aux apatrides était une estimation.
64	Les chiffres se rapportent aux enregistrements effectués dans trois régions; 637 personnes ont été enregistrées comme apatrides par le Ministère de l'intérieur tadjik.
65	Les chiffres relatifs au nombre d'apatrides en Thaïlande remontent à 2011.
66	Le chiffre concernant le nombre d'apatrides enregistrés a été mis à jour par le gouvernement royal thaïlandais. Il comprend une augmentation de 61 070 personnes qui devraient former une grande partie du groupe qui bénéficiera des changements positifs introduits dans le cadre de la nationalité en décembre 2016. En outre, il reflète des diminutions dues au fait que 8 814 apatrides ayant acquis la nationalité thaïlandaise en 2016 et 8 377 cas qui ont été radiés en raison d'un décès ou d'un double enregistrement.
67	Le nombre de réfugiés syriens en Turquie est une estimation du Gouvernement.

4

International migrants and refugees *(continued)*
International migrant stock (number and percentage) and refugees and others of concern to UNHCR

Migrants internationaux et réfugiés *(suite)*
Stock de migrants internationaux (nombre et pourcentage) et réfugiés et autres personnes relevant de la compétence du HCR

68	Including Crimea.	68	Y compris Crimea.
69	Internally displaced persons (IDP) figure in Ukraine includes 800,000 people who are in an IDP-like situation.	69	Le chiffre sur les personnes déplacées à l'intérieur de leur propre pays (PDI) en Ukraine inclut 800000 personnes qui sont dans une situation similaire aux PDI.
70	Including Zanzibar.	70	Y compris Zanzibar.
71	Pending asylum applications for U.S. Citizenship and Immigration Services at start-2017 and mid-2017 are multiplied by inflation factor (1.518).	71	Les demandes d'asile pendantes pour les services de citoyenneté et d'immigration des États-Unis au début de 2017 et à la mi-2017 sont multipliées par le facteur d'inflation (1,518).
72	Figure of stateless persons refers to those with permanent residence reported in 2010 by the Government. Information on other categories of stateless persons is not available.	72	Le nombre d'apatrides renvoit au nombre de résidents permanents recensés en 2010 par le Gouvernement. On ne dispose d'aucune information sur d'autres catégories d'apatrides.
73	The statelessness figure refers to stateless persons with permanent residence reported by the Government in 2010. The figure has been adjusted to reflect the acquisition of nationality of 179 formerly stateless persons. Information on other categories of stateless persons is not available.	73	Le chiffre relatif à l'apatridie fait référence aux personnes apatrides avec résidence permanente déclarées par le gouvernement en 2010. Ce chiffre a été ajusté pour refléter l'acquisition de la nationalité de 179 anciens apatrides. Les informations sur les autres catégories d'apatrides ne sont pas disponibles.
74	The statelessness figure refers to stateless persons with permanent residence reported by the Government in 2010. The figure has been adjusted provided that citizenship of Uzbekistan was granted to 1,243 persons since December 2016. Information on other categories of stateless persons is not available.	74	Le chiffre d'apatridie concerne les apatrides ayant la résidence permanente déclarés par le gouvernement en 2010. Ce chiffre a été ajusté à la condition que la citoyenneté de l'Ouzbékistan ait été attribuée à 1243 personnes depuis décembre 2016. Aucune information sur les autres catégories d'apatrides n'est disponible.
75	A study is being pursued to provide a revised estimate of statelessness figure.	75	Une étude est en cours pour fournir une estimation révisée du chiffre d'apatridie.

5

Proportion of seats held by women in national parliament
Percentage, as of February each year

Proportion de sièges occupés par les femmes au parlement national
Pourcentage, données disponibles en février de chaque année

Region, country or area&	Last Election date Dernière date de l'élection	1990	2000	2005	2010	2015	2016	2017	2018	2019	Région, pays ou zone&
Total, all countries or areas	...		13.3	15.9	19.0	22.3	22.7	23.4	23.4	24.3	Total, tous pays ou zones
Africa	...		10.4	13.9	17.4	23.0	23.3	23.7	23.4	23.6	Afrique
Northern Africa	...		4.5	8.7	10.9	22.0	23.2	23.8	22.6	22.7	Afrique septentrionale
Sub-Saharan Africa	...		11.5	14.4	18.4	22.6	23.3	23.7	23.6	23.9	Afrique subsaharienne
Eastern Africa	...		11.9	16.6	21.6	27.2	28.9	29.7	30.0	30.2	Afrique orientale
Middle Africa	...		8.6	11.2	13.5	18.1	18.1	17.4	16.4	17.0	Afrique centrale
Southern Africa	...		22.5	24.6	33.4	33.4	33.4	33.4	33.7	34.0	Afrique australe
Western Africa	...		8.2	10.2	11.6	14.5	14.0	14.9	14.8	14.8	Afrique occidentale
Americas	...		15.4	18.8	22.1	26.5	27.3	28.3	28.5	30.6	Amériques
Northern America	...		16.3	17.5	19.0	21.8	22.3	22.2	22.8	25.0	Amérique septentrionale
Latin America & the Caribbean	...		15.2	19.0	22.7	27.4	28.2	29.4	29.5	31.6	Amérique latine et Caraïbes
Caribbean	...		20.6	26.0	29.4	33.1	33.0	33.8	33.7	36.1	Caraïbes
Central America	...		14.3	17.4	21.6	30.1	32.5	33.1	32.5	36.3	Amérique centrale
South America	...		12.5	15.8	19.2	22.2	22.7	24.5	24.8	26.1	Amérique du Sud
Asia	...		12.1	13.4	16.8	17.8	17.9	18.4	17.9	18.8	Asie
Central Asia	...		7.0	13.4	20.0	21.8	21.1	21.3	21.3	21.1	Asie centrale
Eastern Asia	...		18.2	18.1	18.7	20.4	20.4	20.5	20.9	21.4	Asie orientale
South-eastern Asia	...		12.3	15.5	19.3	17.8	18.3	19.3	19.1	19.6	Asie du Sud-Est
Southern Asia	...		6.8	8.8	18.2	17.6	17.7	18.0	13.9	15.8	Asie méridionale
Western Asia	...		5.2	5.7	9.3	12.8	13.2	13.8	14.3	15.3	Asie occidentale
Europe	...		16.8	20.5	23.2	26.7	27.2	28.0	28.9	29.8	Europe
Eastern Europe	...		9.5	14.1	15.2	16.9	17.6	19.4	20.0	20.5	Europe orientale
Northern Europe	...		27.0	28.0	29.6	30.4	32.5	33.3	33.8	35.1	Europe septentrionale
Southern Europe	...		11.0	17.1	23.0	30.0	29.0	29.4	29.9	31.5	Europe méridionale
Western Europe	...		23.0	25.8	28.4	32.0	32.2	32.1	34.0	34.2	Europe occidentale
Oceania	...		11.3	11.2	13.2	13.2	13.4	15.0	15.5	16.3	Océanie
Australia and New Zealand	...		25.5	26.3	30.1	28.8	28.8	31.1	33.0	34.4	Australie et Nouvelle-Zélande
Melanesia	...		3.9	3.2	1.4	4.2	4.6	4.6	3.5	4.3	Mélanésie
Micronesia	...		2.5	2.4	2.4	4.7	5.5	7.8	7.8	7.8	Micronésie
Polynesia	...		4.4	3.2	5.2	4.4	4.4	7.7	8.7	8.7	Polynésie
Afghanistan		3.7	...	...	27.3	27.7	27.7	27.7	27.7	...	Afghanistan
Albania	2017-06	28.8	5.2	6.4	16.4	20.7	20.7	22.9	27.9	29.3	Albanie
Algeria	2017-05	2.4	3.2	6.2	7.7	31.6	31.6	31.6	25.8	25.8	Algérie
Andorra	2015-03	...	7.1	14.3	35.7	50.0	39.3	32.1	32.1	32.1	Andorre
Angola	2017-08	14.5	15.5	15.0	38.6	36.8	36.8	38.2	30.5	30.0	Angola
Antigua and Barbuda	2018-03	0.0	...	10.5	10.5	11.1	11.1	11.1	11.1	11.1	Antigua-et-Barbuda
Argentina	2017-10	6.3	28.0	33.7	38.5	36.2	35.8	38.9	38.9	38.8	Argentine
Armenia	2017-04	35.6	3.1	5.3	9.2	10.7	10.7	9.9	18.1	24.2	Arménie
Australia	2016-07	6.1	22.4	24.7	27.3	26.7	26.7	28.7	28.7	30.0	Australie
Austria	2017-10	11.5	26.8	33.9	27.9	30.6	30.6	30.6	34.4	37.2	Autriche
Azerbaijan	2015-11	...	12.0	10.5	11.4	15.6	16.9	16.8	16.8	16.8	Azerbaïdjan
Bahamas	2017-05	4.1	15.0	20.0	12.2	13.2	13.2	13.2	12.8	12.8	Bahamas
Bahrain	2018-12	...	...	0.0	2.5	7.5	7.5	7.5	7.5	15.0	Bahreïn
Bangladesh	2018-12	10.3	9.1	2.0	18.6	20.0	20.0	20.3	20.3	20.7	Bangladesh
Barbados	2018-05	3.7	10.7	13.3	10.0	16.7	16.7	16.7	16.7	20.0	Barbade
Belarus	2016-09	...	4.5	29.4	31.8	27.3	27.3	34.5	34.5	34.6	Bélarus
Belgium	2014-05	8.5	23.3	34.7	38.0	39.3	39.3	38.0	38.0	38.0	Belgique
Belize	2015-11	0.0	6.9	6.7	0.0	3.1	3.1	9.4	9.4	9.4	Belize
Benin	2015-04	2.9	6.0	7.2	10.8	8.4	7.2	7.2	7.2	7.2	Bénin
Bhutan	2018-10	2.0	2.0	9.3	8.5	8.5	8.5	8.5	8.5	14.9	Bhoutan
Bolivia (Plurin. State of)	2014-10	9.2	11.5	19.2	22.3	53.1	53.1	53.1	53.1	53.1	Bolivie (État plurin. de)
Bosnia and Herzegovina	2018-10	...	28.6	16.7	19.0	21.4	21.4	21.4	21.4	21.4	Bosnie-Herzégovine
Botswana	2014-10	5.0	...	11.1	7.9	9.5	9.5	9.5	9.5	9.5	Botswana
Brazil	2018-10	5.3	5.7	8.6	8.8	9.0	9.9	10.7	10.7	15.0	Brésil
Brunei Darussalam	2017-01	...	...	...	...	...	...	9.1	9.1	9.1	Brunéi Darussalam

Proportion of seats held by women in national parliament *(continued)*
Percentage, as of February each year

Proportion de sièges occupés par les femmes au parlement national *(suite)*
Pourcentage, données disponibles en février de chaque année

Region, country or area[&]	Last Election date Dernière date de l'élection	1990	2000	2005	2010	2015	2016	2017	2018	2019	Région, pays ou zone[&]
Bulgaria	2017-03	21.0	10.8	26.3	20.8	20.4	20.4	19.2	23.8	25.8	Bulgarie
Burkina Faso	2015-11	...	8.1	11.7	15.3	13.3	9.4	11.0	11.0	13.4	Burkina Faso
Burundi	2015-06	...	6.0	18.4	31.4	30.5	36.4	36.4	36.4	36.4	Burundi
Cabo Verde	2016-03	12.0	11.1	11.1	18.1	20.8	20.8	23.6	23.6	23.6	Cabo Verde
Cambodia	2018-07	...	8.2	9.8	21.1	20.3	20.3	20.3	20.3	20.0	Cambodge
Cameroon	2013-09	14.4	5.6	8.9	13.9	31.1	31.1	31.1	31.1	31.1	Cameroun
Canada	2015-10	13.3	20.6	21.1	22.1	25.2	26.0	26.3	27.0	27.0	Canada
Central African Republic	2016-02	3.8	7.3	...	9.6	...	...	8.6	8.6	8.6	République centrafricaine
Chad	2011-02	...	2.4	6.5	5.2	14.9	14.9	12.8	12.8	14.9	Tchad
Chile	2017-11	...	10.8	12.5	14.2	15.8	15.8	15.8	...	22.6	Chili
China	2018-03	21.3	21.8	20.2	21.3	23.6	23.6	23.7	24.2	24.9	Chine
Colombia	2018-03	4.5	11.8	12.0	8.4	19.9	19.9	18.7	18.7	18.7	Colombie
Comoros	2015-01	0.0	...	3.0	3.0	...	3.0	6.1	6.1	6.1	Comores
Congo	2017-07	14.3	12.0	8.5	7.3	7.4	7.4	7.4	11.3	11.3	Congo
Costa Rica	2018-02	10.5	19.3	35.1	36.8	33.3	33.3	35.1	35.1	45.6	Costa Rica
Côte d'Ivoire	2016-12	5.7	...	8.5	8.9	9.2	9.2	11.5	10.6	11.0	Côte d'Ivoire
Croatia	2016-09	...	...	21.7	23.5	25.8	15.2	19.9	18.5	20.5	Croatie
Cuba	2018-03	33.9	27.6	36.0	43.2	48.9	48.9	48.9	48.9	53.2	Cuba
Cyprus	2016-05	1.8	5.4	16.1	12.5	12.5	12.5	17.9	17.9	17.9	Chypre
Czechia	2017-10	...	15.0	17.0	15.5	19.0	20.0	20.0	22.0	22.5	Tchéquie
Dem. People's Rep. Korea	2014-03	21.1	20.1	20.1	15.6	16.3	16.3	16.3	16.3	16.3	Rép. pop. dém. de Corée
Dem. Rep. of the Congo	2018-12	5.4	...	12.0	8.4	8.9	8.9	8.9	8.9	10.3	Rép. dém. du Congo
Denmark	2015-06	30.7	37.4	38.0	38.0	38.0	37.4	37.4	37.4	37.4	Danemark
Djibouti	2018-02	0.0	0.0	10.8	13.8	12.7	12.7	10.8	10.8	26.2	Djibouti
Dominica	2014-12	10.0	9.4	19.4	14.3	21.9	21.9	25.0	25.0	25.0	Dominique
Dominican Republic	2016-05	7.5	16.1	17.3	19.7	20.8	20.8	26.8	26.8	26.8	République dominicaine
Ecuador	2017-02	4.5	17.4	16.0	32.3	41.6	41.6	41.6	38.0	38.0	Équateur
Egypt	2015-10	3.9	2.0	2.9	1.8	...	14.9	14.9	14.9	14.9	Égypte
El Salvador	2018-03	11.7	16.7	10.7	19.0	27.4	32.1	32.1	32.1	31.0	El Salvador
Equatorial Guinea	2017-11	13.3	5.0	18.0	10.0	24.0	24.0	24.0	20.0	20.0	Guinée équatoriale
Eritrea	1994-02	...	14.7	22.0	22.0	22.0	22.0	22.0	22.0	22.0	Érythrée
Estonia	2015-03	...	17.8	18.8	22.8	19.8	23.8	26.7	26.7	28.7	Estonie
Eswatini	2018-09	3.6	3.1	10.8	13.6	6.2	6.2	6.2	6.2	7.3	Eswatini
Ethiopia	2015-05	...	2.0	7.7	21.9	27.8	38.8	38.8	38.8	38.8	Éthiopie
Fiji	2018-11	...	11.3	8.5	...	14.0	16.0	16.0	16.0	19.6	Fidji
Finland	2015-04	31.5	37.0	37.5	40.0	42.5	41.5	42.0	42.0	41.5	Finlande
France	2017-06	6.9	10.9	12.2	18.9	26.2	26.2	25.8	39.0	39.7	France
Gabon	2018-10	13.3	8.3	9.2	14.7	14.2	14.2	17.1	17.1	17.9	Gabon
Gambia	2017-04	7.8	2.0	13.2	7.5	9.4	9.4	9.4	10.3	10.3	Gambie
Georgia	2016-10	...	7.2	9.4	5.1	11.3	11.3	16.0	16.0	14.8	Géorgie
Germany	2017-09	...	30.9	32.8	32.8	36.5	36.5	37.0	30.7	30.9	Allemagne
Ghana	2016-12	...	9.0	10.9	8.3	10.9	10.9	12.7	12.7	13.1	Ghana
Greece	2015-09	6.7	6.3	14.0	17.3	23.0	19.7	18.3	18.3	18.7	Grèce
Grenada	2018-03	...	...	26.7	13.3	33.3	33.3	33.3	33.3	46.7	Grenade
Guatemala	2015-09	7.0	7.1	8.2	12.0	13.3	13.9	12.7	12.7	19.0	Guatemala
Guinea	2013-09	...	8.8	19.3	...	21.9	21.9	21.9	21.9	22.8	Guinée
Guinea-Bissau	2014-04	20.0	...	14.0	10.0	13.7	13.7	13.7	13.7	13.7	Guinée-Bissau
Guyana	2015-05	36.9	18.5	30.8	30.0	31.3	30.4	31.9	31.9	31.9	Guyana
Haiti	2015-08	...	3.6	3.6	4.1	4.2	0.0	2.6	2.5	2.5	Haïti
Honduras	2017-11	10.2	9.4	5.5	18.0	25.8	25.8	25.8	21.1	21.1	Honduras
Hungary	2018-04	20.7	8.3	9.1	11.1	10.1	10.1	10.1	10.1	12.6	Hongrie
Iceland	2017-10	20.6	34.9	30.2	42.9	41.3	41.3	47.6	38.1	38.1	Islande
India	2014-04	5.0	9.0	8.3	10.8	12.0	12.0	11.8	11.8	12.6	Inde
Indonesia	2014-04	12.4	...	11.3	18.0	17.1	17.1	19.8	19.8	18.2	Indonésie
Iran (Islamic Republic of)	2016-02	1.5	4.9	4.1	2.8	3.1	3.1	5.9	5.9	5.9	Iran (Rép. islamique d')
Iraq	2018-05	10.8	6.4	...	25.5	26.5	26.5	25.3	25.3	25.2	Iraq
Ireland	2016-02	7.8	12.0	13.3	13.9	16.3	16.3	22.2	22.2	22.2	Irlande
Israel	2015-03	6.7	11.7	15.0	19.2	22.5	26.7	27.5	27.5	29.2	Israël
Italy	2018-03	12.9	11.1	11.5	21.3	31.0	31.0	31.0	31.0	35.7	Italie

Proportion of seats held by women in national parliament *(continued)*
Percentage, as of February each year

Proportion de sièges occupés par les femmes au parlement national *(suite)*
Pourcentage, données disponibles en février de chaque année

Region, country or area&	Last Election date Dernière date de l'élection	1990	2000	2005	2010	2015	2016	2017	2018	2019	Région, pays ou zone&
Jamaica	2016-02	5.0	13.3	11.7	13.3	12.7	12.7	17.5	17.5	17.5	Jamaïque
Japan	2017-10	1.4	4.6	7.1	11.3	9.5	9.5	9.3	10.1	10.2	Japon
Jordan	2016-09	0.0	0.0	5.5	6.4	12.0	12.0	15.4	15.4	15.4	Jordanie
Kazakhstan	2016-03	...	10.4	10.4	17.8	26.2	26.2	27.1	27.1	27.1	Kazakhstan
Kenya	2017-07	1.1	3.6	7.1	9.8	19.7	19.7	19.4	21.8	21.8	Kenya
Kiribati	2015-12	0.0	4.9	4.8	4.3	8.7	6.5	6.5	6.5	6.5	Kiribati
Kuwait	2016-11	...	0.0	0.0	7.7	1.5	1.5	3.1	3.1	4.6	Koweït
Kyrgyzstan	2015-10	...	1.4	10.0	25.6	23.3	19.2	19.2	19.2	19.2	Kirghizistan
Lao People's Dem. Rep.	2016-03	6.3	21.2	22.9	25.2	25.0	25.0	27.5	27.5	27.5	Rép. dém. populaire lao
Latvia	2018-10	...	17.0	21.0	22.0	18.0	18.0	16.0	16.0	31.0	Lettonie
Lebanon	2018-05	0.0	2.3	2.3	3.1	3.1	3.1	3.1	3.1	4.7	Liban
Lesotho	2017-06	...	3.8	11.7	24.2	26.7	25.0	25.0	22.1	23.3	Lesotho
Liberia	2017-10	...	...	5.3	12.5	11.0	11.0	12.3	9.9	12.3	Libéria
Libya	2014-06	...	...	...	7.7	16.0	16.0	16.0	16.0	16.0	Libye
Liechtenstein	2017-02	4.0	4.0	12.0	24.0	20.0	20.0	12.0	12.0	12.0	Liechtenstein
Lithuania	2016-10	...	17.5	22.0	19.1	23.4	23.4	21.3	21.3	21.3	Lituanie
Luxembourg	2018-10	13.3	16.7	23.3	20.0	28.3	28.3	28.3	28.3	25.0	Luxembourg
Madagascar	2013-12	6.5	8.0	6.9	...	20.5	20.5	19.2	19.2	19.2	Madagascar
Malawi	2014-05	9.8	8.3	14.0	20.8	16.7	16.7	16.7	16.7	16.7	Malawi
Malaysia	2018-05	5.1	...	9.1	9.9	10.4	10.4	10.4	10.4	14.4	Malaisie
Maldives	2014-03	6.3	...	12.0	6.5	5.9	5.9	5.9	5.9	4.7	Maldives
Mali	2013-11	...	12.2	10.2	10.2	9.5	8.8	8.8	8.8	8.8	Mali
Malta	2017-06	2.9	9.2	9.2	8.7	12.9	12.9	12.5	11.9	11.9	Malte
Marshall Islands	2015-11	...	...	3.0	3.0	3.0	9.1	9.1	9.1	9.1	Îles Marshall
Mauritania	2018-09	...	3.8	3.7	22.1	25.2	25.2	25.2	25.2	20.3	Mauritanie
Mauritius	2014-12	7.1	7.6	5.7	17.1	11.6	11.6	11.6	11.6	11.6	Maurice
Mexico	2018-07	12.0	18.2	22.6	27.6	38.0	42.4	42.6	42.6	48.2	Mexique
Micronesia (Fed. States of)	2017-03	...	0.0	0.0	0.0	0.0	0.0	0.0	0.0	0.0	Micronésie (États féd. de)
Monaco	2018-02	11.1	22.2	20.8	26.1	20.8	20.8	20.8	20.8	33.3	Monaco
Mongolia	2016-06	24.9	7.9	6.8	3.9	14.9	14.5	17.1	17.1	17.1	Mongolie
Montenegro	2016-10	...	...	...	11.1	17.3	17.3	23.5	23.5	23.5	Monténégro
Morocco	2016-10	0.0	0.6	10.8	10.5	17.0	17.0	20.5	20.5	20.5	Maroc
Mozambique	2014-10	15.7	...	34.8	39.2	39.6	39.6	39.6	39.6	39.6	Mozambique
Myanmar	2015-11	...	...	...	...	6.2	9.9	10.2	10.2	11.3	Myanmar
Namibia	2014-11	6.9	22.2	25.0	26.9[1]	41.3	41.3	41.3	46.2	46.2	Namibie
Nauru	2016-07	5.6	0.0	0.0	0.0	5.3	5.3	10.5	10.5	10.5	Nauru
Nepal	2017-11	6.1	5.9	...	33.2	29.5	29.5	29.6	* 3.6	32.7	Népal
Netherlands	2017-03	21.3	36.0	36.7	42.0	37.3	37.3	38.0	36.0	31.3	Pays-Bas
New Zealand	2017-09	14.4	29.2	28.3	33.6	31.4	31.4	34.2	38.3	40.0	Nouvelle-Zélande
Nicaragua	2016-11	14.8	9.7	20.7	20.7	39.1	41.3	45.7	45.7	44.6	Nicaragua
Niger	2016-02	5.4	1.2	12.4	9.7	13.3	13.3	17.0	17.0	17.0	Niger
Nigeria	2015-03	...	...	4.7	7.0	6.7	5.6	5.6	5.6	5.6	Nigéria
North Macedonia	2016-12	...	7.5	19.2	32.5	33.3	33.3	31.7	37.5	38.3	Macédoine du Nord
Norway	2017-09	35.8	36.4	38.2	39.6	39.6	39.6	39.6	41.4	40.8	Norvège
Oman	2015-10	...	...	2.4	0.0	1.2	1.2	1.2	1.2	1.2	Oman
Pakistan	2018-08	10.1	...	21.3	22.2	20.7	20.6	20.6	20.6	20.2	Pakistan
Palau	2016-11	...	0.0	0.0	0.0	0.0	0.0	12.5	12.5	12.5	Palaos
Panama	2014-05	7.5	...	16.7	8.5	19.3	18.3	18.3	18.3	18.3	Panama
Papua New Guinea	2017-06	0.0	1.8	0.9	0.9	2.7	2.7	2.7	0.0	0.0	Papouasie-Nvl-Guinée
Paraguay	2018-04	5.6	2.5	10.0	12.5	15.0	15.0	13.8	13.8	15.0	Paraguay
Peru	2016-04	5.6	10.8	18.3	27.5	22.3	22.3	27.7	27.7	30.0	Pérou
Philippines	2016-05	9.1	12.4	15.3	21.0	27.2	27.2	29.5	29.5	29.5	Philippines
Poland	2015-10	13.5	13.0	20.2	20.0	24.1	27.4	28.0	28.0	29.1	Pologne
Portugal	2015-10	7.6	18.7	19.1	27.4	31.3	34.8	34.8	34.8	35.7	Portugal
Qatar	2013-07	...	...	...	0.0	0.0	0.0	0.0	0.0	9.8	Qatar
Republic of Korea	2016-04	2.0	3.7	13.0	14.7	16.3	16.3	17.0	17.0	17.1	République de Corée
Republic of Moldova	2014-11	...	8.9	15.8	23.8	20.8	21.8	22.8	22.8	22.8	République de Moldova
Romania	2016-12	34.4	7.3	11.4	11.4	13.7	13.7	20.7	20.7	20.7	Roumanie
Russian Federation	2016-09	...	7.7	9.8	14.0	13.6	13.6	15.8	15.8	15.8	Fédération de Russie

5

Proportion of seats held by women in national parliament *(continued)*
Percentage, as of February each year

Proportion de sièges occupés par les femmes au parlement national *(suite)*
Pourcentage, données disponibles en février de chaque année

Region, country or area[&]	Last Election date Dernière date de l'élection	1990	2000	2005	2010	2015	2016	2017	2018	2019	Région, pays ou zone[&]
Rwanda	2018-09	17.1	17.1	48.8	56.3	63.8	63.8	61.3	61.3	61.3	Rwanda
Saint Kitts and Nevis	2015-02	6.7	13.3	0.0	6.7	6.7	13.3	13.3	13.3	13.3	Saint-Kitts-et-Nevis
Saint Lucia	2016-06	0.0	11.1	11.1	11.1	16.7	16.7	16.7	16.7	16.7	Sainte-Lucie
Saint Vincent & Grenadines	2015-12	9.5	4.8	22.7	21.7	13.0	13.0	13.0	13.0	13.0	Saint-Vincent-Grenadines
Samoa	2016-03	0.0	8.2	6.1	8.2	6.1	6.1	10.0	10.0	10.0	Samoa
San Marino	2016-11	11.7	13.3	16.7	16.7	16.7	16.7	26.7	26.7	25.0	Saint-Marin
Sao Tome and Principe	2018-10	11.8	9.1	9.1	7.3	18.2	18.2	18.2	18.2	14.6	Sao Tomé-et-Principe
Saudi Arabia	2016-12	...	...	0.0	0.0	19.9	19.9	19.9	19.9	19.9	Arabie saoudite
Senegal	2017-07	12.5	12.1	19.2	22.7	42.7	42.7	42.7	41.8	41.8	Sénégal
Serbia	2016-04	...	...	...	21.6	34.0	34.0	34.4	34.4	37.7	Serbie
Serbia and Monten. [former]		...	5.1	7.9	...	...	...	...	...	...	Serbie-et-Monténégro [anc.]
Seychelles	2016-09	16.0	23.5	29.4	23.5	43.8	43.8	21.2	21.2	21.2	Seychelles
Sierra Leone	2018-03	...	8.8	14.5	13.2	12.4	12.4	12.4	12.4	12.3	Sierra Leone
Singapore	2015-09	4.9	4.3	16.0	23.4	25.3	23.1	23.8	23.0	23.0	Singapour
Slovakia	2016-03	...	12.7	16.7	18.0	18.7	18.7	20.0	20.0	20.0	Slovaquie
Slovenia	2018-06	...	7.8	12.2	14.4	36.7	36.7	36.7	36.7	24.4	Slovénie
Solomon Islands	2014-11	0.0	2.0	0.0	0.0	2.0	2.0	2.0	2.0	2.0	Îles Salomon
Somalia	2016-10	4.0	...	...	6.9	13.8	13.8	24.2	24.4	24.4	Somalie
South Africa	2014-05	2.8	30.0	32.8	44.5	41.5	42.0	42.2	42.4	42.8	Afrique du Sud
South Sudan	2016-08	...	...	...	...	26.5	26.5	28.5	28.5	28.5	Soudan du sud
Spain	2016-06	14.6	21.6	36.0	36.6	41.1	40.0	39.1	39.1	41.1	Espagne
Sri Lanka	2015-08	4.9	4.9	4.9	5.8	5.8	5.8	5.8	5.8	5.3	Sri Lanka
Sudan	2015-04	...	...	...	...	24.3	30.5	30.5	30.5	27.7	Soudan
Sudan [former]		...	...	9.7	18.9	...	...	...	...	...	Soudan [anc.]
Suriname	2015-05	7.8	15.7	19.6	25.5	11.8	25.5	25.5	25.5	29.4	Suriname
Sweden	2018-09	38.4	42.7	45.3	46.4	43.6	43.6	43.6	43.6	47.3	Suède
Switzerland	2015-10	14.0	22.5	25.0	29.0	30.5	32.0	32.5	32.5	32.5	Suisse
Syrian Arab Republic	2016-04	9.2	10.4	12.0	12.4	12.4	12.4	13.2	13.2	13.2	République arabe syrienne
Tajikistan	2015-03	...	2.8	12.7	17.5	16.9	19.0	19.0	19.0	19.1	Tadjikistan
Thailand	2014-08	2.8	5.6	8.8	13.3	6.1	6.1	4.9	4.8	5.4	Thaïlande
Timor-Leste	2018-05	...	...	25.3	29.2	38.5	38.5	38.5	32.3	40.0	Timor-Leste
Togo	2018-12	5.2	...	6.2	11.1	17.6	17.6	17.6	17.6	16.5	Togo
Tonga	2017-11	0.0	...	0.0	3.1	0.0	0.0	3.8	7.4	7.4	Tonga
Trinidad and Tobago	2015-09	16.7	11.1	19.4	26.8	28.6	31.0	31.0	31.0	31.0	Trinité-et-Tobago
Tunisia	2014-10	4.3	11.5	22.8	27.6	31.3	31.3	31.3	31.3	35.9	Tunisie
Turkey	2018-06	1.3	4.2	4.4	9.1	14.4	14.9	14.9	14.6	17.5	Turquie
Turkmenistan	2018-03	26.0	26.0	...	16.8	25.8	25.8	25.8	25.8	25.0	Turkménistan
Tuvalu	2015-03	7.7	0.0	0.0	0.0	6.7	6.7	6.7	6.7	6.7	Tuvalu
Uganda	2016-02	12.2	17.9	23.9	31.5	35.0	35.0	34.3	34.3	34.9	Ouganda
Ukraine	2014-10	...	7.8	5.3	8.0	11.8[2]	12.1[2]	12.3[2]	12.3[2]	11.6[2]	Ukraine
United Arab Emirates	2015-10	0.0	0.0	0.0	22.5	17.5	22.5	20.0	22.5	22.5	Émirats arabes unis
United Kingdom	2017-06	6.3	18.4	18.1	19.5	22.8	29.4	30.0	32.0	32.0	Royaume-Uni
United Rep. of Tanzania	2015-10	...	16.4	21.4	30.7	36.0	36.6	36.4	37.2	36.9	Rép.-Unie de Tanzanie
United States of America	2018-11	6.6	13.3	14.9	16.8	19.4	19.4	19.1	19.5	23.6	États-Unis d'Amérique
Uruguay	2014-10	6.1	12.1	12.1	14.1	13.1	16.2	20.2	20.2	22.2	Uruguay
Uzbekistan	2014-12	...	6.8	17.5	22.0	16.0	16.0	16.0	16.0	16.0	Ouzbékistan
Vanuatu	2016-01	4.3	0.0	3.8	3.8	0.0	0.0	0.0	0.0	0.0	Vanuatu
Venezuela (Boliv. Rep. of)	2015-12	10.0	12.1	9.7	17.5	17.0	14.4	22.2	22.2	22.2	Venezuela (Rép. boliv. du)
Viet Nam	2016-05	17.7	26.0	27.3	25.8	24.3	24.3	26.7	26.7	26.7	Viet Nam
Yemen	2003-04	4.1	0.7	0.3	0.3	0.3	0.0	0.0	0.0	0.3	Yémen
Zambia	2016-08	6.6	10.1	12.0	14.0	12.7	12.7	18.0	18.0	18.0	Zambie
Zimbabwe	2018-07	11.0	14.0	10.0	15.0	31.5	31.5	32.6	33.2	31.9	Zimbabwe

Source:

Inter-Parliamentary Union (IPU), Geneva, "Women in National Parliament" dataset and the Millennium Development Goals Indicators database, last accessed March 2019.

Source:

Union interparlementaire, Genève, données des "Les femmes dans les parlements nationaux" et la base de données des Objectifs du Millénaire pour le développement, dernier accès mars 2019.

5

Proportion of seats held by women in national parliament *(continued)*
Percentage, as of February each year

Proportion de sièges occupés par les femmes au parlement national *(suite)*
Pourcentage, données disponibles en février de chaque année

& The data are as at 1 February for 2015 – 2019, as at 31 January for 2005 and 2010, and as at 25 January for 2000.

1   Figure excludes 11 members yet to be sworn in.

2   Excludes the temporarily occupied territory of the Autonomous Republic of Crimea and Sevastopol.

& Les données sont au 1er février en 2015 – 2019, au 31 janvier en 2005 et 2010, et au 25 janvier en 2000.

1   Ce chiffre ne tient pas compte de 11 membres qui n'avaient pas encore été assermentés.

2   Excluent le territoire temporairement occupé de la République autonome de Crimée et de Sébastopol.

Ratio of girls to boys in primary, secondary and tertiary education

Rapport filles/garçons dans l'enseignement primaire, secondaire et supérieur

Region, country or area	1985	1995	2005	2010	2015	2016	2017	Région, pays ou zone
Total, all countries or areas								**Total, tous pays ou zones**
Primary education	**0.85**	**0.90**	**0.95**	**0.97**	**1.00**	**1.01**	*** 1.01**	**Enseignement primaire**
Secondary education	*** 0.81**	**0.88**	**0.94**	**0.97**	**0.99**	**0.99**	*** 0.99**	**Enseignement secondaire**
Tertiary education	*** 0.85**	*** 0.95**	**1.05**	**1.07**	**1.12**	**1.12**	*** 1.12**	**Enseignement supérieur**
Northern Africa								**Afrique septentrionale**
Primary education	0.78	0.86	0.93	0.95	* 0.97	0.97	0.97	Enseignement primaire
Secondary education	0.71	0.86	* 0.99	0.98	* 0.99	0.99	* 0.99	Enseignement secondaire
Tertiary education	* 0.62	* 0.76	0.96	1.07	1.10	1.15	* 1.13	Enseignement supérieur
Sub-Saharan Africa								**Afrique subsaharienne**
Primary education	0.81	0.84	0.88	0.93	0.96	0.95	* 0.96	Enseignement primaire
Secondary education	* 0.64	* 0.80	0.78	0.82	0.86	* 0.87	* 0.88	Enseignement secondaire
Tertiary education	* 0.46	* 0.59	0.67	0.67	* 0.71	* 0.72	* 0.72	Enseignement supérieur
Northern America								**Amérique septentrionale**
Primary education	1.01	0.99	0.99	0.99	1.00	1.00	* 1.00	Enseignement primaire
Secondary education	1.02	1.01	1.01	1.01	1.01	1.00	* 1.00	Enseignement secondaire
Tertiary education	1.13	1.28	1.42	1.39	1.35	1.34	* 1.34	Enseignement supérieur
Latin America & the Caribbean								**Amérique latine et Caraïbes**
Primary education	0.98	* 0.97	0.97	0.97	0.98	0.99	* 0.98	Enseignement primaire
Secondary education	* 1.03	* 1.08	1.08	1.08	1.06	1.05	* 1.05	Enseignement secondaire
Tertiary education	* 0.88	* 1.09	1.22	1.30	1.30	1.31	* 1.31	Enseignement supérieur
Central Asia								**Asie centrale**
Primary education	* 1.00	0.98	0.99	0.99	0.99	0.99	0.99	Enseignement primaire
Secondary education	...	* 1.00	0.96	0.98	0.99	0.98	0.98	Enseignement secondaire
Tertiary education	...	* 0.96	1.03	1.00	1.01	0.99	0.98	Enseignement supérieur
Eastern Asia								**Asie orientale**
Primary education	0.85	0.95	* 1.00	0.99	1.00	1.01	1.01	Enseignement primaire
Secondary education	0.77	0.89	* 0.98	1.00	1.02	1.02	1.02	Enseignement secondaire
Tertiary education	* 0.48	* 0.64	0.86	1.00	1.13	1.15	1.15	Enseignement supérieur
South-eastern Asia								**Asie du Sud-Est**
Primary education	0.95	0.97	0.97	1.01	0.97	0.97	0.97	Enseignement primaire
Secondary education	* 0.87	* 0.93	1.00	1.01	1.01	1.03	1.02	Enseignement secondaire
Tertiary education	* 0.87	0.95	* 1.00	1.08	* 1.19	* 1.22	1.22	Enseignement supérieur
Southern Asia								**Asie méridionale**
Primary education	0.69	0.81	* 0.95	1.00	1.06	1.09	* 1.09	Enseignement primaire
Secondary education	* 0.53	0.66	0.85	0.93	1.00	1.00	* 1.00	Enseignement secondaire
Tertiary education	0.43	0.54	0.74	0.76	0.95	0.96	* 0.96	Enseignement supérieur
Western Asia								**Asie occidentale**
Primary education	0.85	* 0.88	0.91	0.93	* 0.94	0.94	* 0.94	Enseignement primaire
Secondary education	* 0.69	* 0.75	0.86	0.90	* 0.91	0.91	* 0.92	Enseignement secondaire
Tertiary education	0.63	0.77	0.90	0.93	0.97	0.96	* 0.97	Enseignement supérieur
Europe								**Europe**
Primary education	* 0.99	0.99	0.99	0.99	1.00	1.00	* 1.00	Enseignement primaire
Secondary education	* 1.02	1.02	1.00	0.99	1.00	1.01	* 1.01	Enseignement secondaire
Tertiary education	* 1.08	1.14	1.28	1.29	1.23	1.22	* 1.22	Enseignement supérieur
Oceania								**Océanie**
Primary education	0.96	0.97	0.98	0.97	0.97	0.97	* 0.97	Enseignement primaire
Secondary education	* 0.99	0.99	* 0.97	* 0.93	0.89	0.88	* 0.88	Enseignement secondaire
Tertiary education	0.92	1.06	* 1.24	* 1.35	1.43	1.42	* 1.42	Enseignement supérieur
Afghanistan								**Afghanistan**
Primary education	0.49	0.51	0.59	0.69	0.69	...	0.69	Enseignement primaire
Secondary education	0.46	0.37	0.33	0.50	0.56	0.59	0.57	Enseignement secondaire
Albania								**Albanie**
Primary education	0.98	0.96	0.99	0.98	0.97	0.97	0.97	Enseignement primaire
Secondary education	0.91	0.98	0.95	0.99	0.93	0.93	0.94	Enseignement secondaire
Tertiary education	0.86	1.08	1.42	1.34	1.53	1.58	1.59	Enseignement supérieur
Algeria								**Algérie**
Primary education	0.79	0.88	0.92	0.94	0.95	0.95	0.95	Enseignement primaire
Secondary education	0.73	0.89	1.10	1.04	...	...	...	Enseignement secondaire
Tertiary education	...	...	1.28	1.44	1.56	1.67	1.49	Enseignement supérieur
Angola								**Angola**
Primary education	...	...	...	0.79	0.86	...	...	Enseignement primaire
Secondary education	...	...	...	0.67	...	0.63	...	Enseignement secondaire
Tertiary education	...	...	...	...	0.77	0.81	...	Enseignement supérieur

6 Ratio of girls to boys in primary, secondary and tertiary education *(continued)*

Rapport filles/garçons dans l'enseignement primaire, secondaire et supérieur *(suite)*

Region, country or area	1985	1995	2005	2010	2015	2016	2017	Région, pays ou zone
Antigua and Barbuda								**Antigua-et-Barbuda**
Primary education	...	...	...	0.92	0.94	...	0.97	Enseignement primaire
Secondary education	...	...	...	1.01	1.02	...	0.96	Enseignement secondaire
Tertiary education	...	...	...	2.53	...	...	...	Enseignement supérieur
Argentina								**Argentine**
Primary education	1.00	...	0.99	0.99	1.00	1.00	...	Enseignement primaire
Secondary education	1.12	...	1.10	1.10	1.06	1.04	...	Enseignement secondaire
Tertiary education	1.11	...	1.46	1.51	1.64	1.66	...	Enseignement supérieur
Armenia								**Arménie**
Primary education	...	1.02	1.02	1.03	1.02	1.01	1.00	Enseignement primaire
Secondary education	...	...	...	0.98	1.05	...	...	Enseignement secondaire
Tertiary education	...	...	1.40	1.22	1.19	1.27	1.27	Enseignement supérieur
Aruba								**Aruba**
Primary education	...	...	0.94	0.99	...	...	...	Enseignement primaire
Secondary education	...	...	1.00	1.05	...	...	...	Enseignement secondaire
Tertiary education	...	...	1.44	1.41	2.26	1.94	...	Enseignement supérieur
Australia								**Australie**
Primary education	0.99	1.00	1.02	1.00	1.00	1.00	1.00	Enseignement primaire
Secondary education	...	1.00	...	...	0.87	0.87	0.89	Enseignement secondaire
Tertiary education	0.95	1.05	...	...	1.45	1.43	1.42	Enseignement supérieur
Austria								**Autriche**
Primary education	0.99	0.99	1.00	0.99	0.99	0.99	1.00	Enseignement primaire
Secondary education	0.93	0.94	0.95	0.96	0.96	0.96	0.96	Enseignement secondaire
Tertiary education	0.84	0.94	...	...	1.19	1.19	1.18	Enseignement supérieur
Azerbaijan								**Azerbaïdjan**
Primary education	...	1.12	* 0.95	* 0.99	* 0.98	* 0.99	* 1.02	Enseignement primaire
Secondary education	...	1.02	...	...	...	...	...	Enseignement secondaire
Tertiary education	...	0.88	...	* 0.99	* 1.16	* 1.18	* 1.15	Enseignement supérieur
Bahamas								**Bahamas**
Primary education	1.01	1.00	0.99	1.02	...	1.05	...	Enseignement primaire
Secondary education	1.16	1.00	1.00	1.05	...	1.06	...	Enseignement secondaire
Tertiary education	...	2.71	...	...	...	...	...	Enseignement supérieur
Bahrain								**Bahreïn**
Primary education	1.00	1.01	1.04	...	1.01	1.02	1.00	Enseignement primaire
Secondary education	0.92	1.04	1.11	1.01	1.00	1.01	1.01	Enseignement secondaire
Tertiary education	1.39	1.62	3.06	...	1.92	1.87	1.95	Enseignement supérieur
Bangladesh								**Bangladesh**
Primary education	0.69	...	1.05	* 1.06	...	...	1.07	Enseignement primaire
Secondary education	0.40	...	1.07	1.12	1.13	1.10	1.17	Enseignement secondaire
Tertiary education	0.24	...	0.52	...	...	0.70	0.70	Enseignement supérieur
Barbados								**Barbade**
Primary education	0.96	...	1.00	* 1.02	1.00	1.01	0.98	Enseignement primaire
Secondary education	1.02	...	0.99	* 1.01	1.03	1.05	1.04	Enseignement secondaire
Tertiary education	0.98	...	...	2.18	...	...	...	Enseignement supérieur
Belarus								**Bélarus**
Primary education	...	0.96	0.97	1.00	1.00	1.00	1.00	Enseignement primaire
Secondary education	...	...	...	0.97	0.99	0.98	0.98	Enseignement secondaire
Tertiary education	...	...	1.37	* 1.45	1.33	1.29	1.24	Enseignement supérieur
Belgium								**Belgique**
Primary education	1.01	0.99	1.00	1.00	1.00	1.00	...	Enseignement primaire
Secondary education	1.03	1.08	1.12	1.14	1.14	1.12	...	Enseignement secondaire
Tertiary education	0.87	1.02	1.25	1.27	1.31	1.30	...	Enseignement supérieur
Belize								**Belize**
Primary education	...	0.96	0.96	0.96	0.95	0.95	0.95	Enseignement primaire
Secondary education	...	1.03	1.03	1.08	1.02	1.01	1.05	Enseignement secondaire
Tertiary education	...	...	1.58	1.60	1.61	1.62	1.62	Enseignement supérieur
Benin								**Bénin**
Primary education	0.50	0.57	0.79	0.89	0.93	0.94	0.94	Enseignement primaire
Secondary education	0.41	...	...	...	0.71	0.76	...	Enseignement secondaire
Tertiary education	* 0.21	0.21	...	0.35	0.40	0.42	...	Enseignement supérieur
Bermuda								**Bermudes**
Primary education	1.01	1.00	1.05	...	0.98	...	...	Enseignement primaire
Secondary education	...	...	1.13	1.18	1.12	...	...	Enseignement secondaire
Tertiary education	...	...	...	2.11	2.32	...	...	Enseignement supérieur

Region, country or area	1985	1995	2005	2010	2015	2016	2017	Région, pays ou zone
Bhutan								**Bhoutan**
Primary education	0.53	0.78	0.98	1.03	1.01	1.01	1.00	Enseignement primaire
Secondary education	...	...	0.89	1.02	1.06	1.10	1.10	Enseignement secondaire
Tertiary education	...	...	0.64	0.61	...	...	...	Enseignement supérieur
Bolivia (Plurin. State of)								**Bolivie (État plurin. de)**
Primary education	...	0.96	0.99	0.98	0.97	0.98	0.98	Enseignement primaire
Secondary education	...	...	0.94	0.99	0.98	0.98	0.97	Enseignement secondaire
Botswana								**Botswana**
Primary education	1.11	1.01	0.98	...	...	...	...	Enseignement primaire
Secondary education	1.13	1.10	1.03	...	...	...	...	Enseignement secondaire
Tertiary education	0.82	0.91	0.89	...	1.37	1.43	1.44	Enseignement supérieur
Brazil								**Brésil**
Primary education	...	...	* 0.94	...	* 0.96	* 0.97	...	Enseignement primaire
Secondary education	...	...	* 1.10	...	* 1.06	* 1.05	...	Enseignement secondaire
Tertiary education	...	...	* 1.29	...	* 1.34	* 1.38	...	Enseignement supérieur
Brunei Darussalam								**Brunéi Darussalam**
Primary education	...	0.95	0.96	1.00	0.99	0.99	0.99	Enseignement primaire
Secondary education	...	...	0.98	1.01	1.00	1.01	1.02	Enseignement secondaire
Tertiary education	...	...	1.99	1.87	1.65	1.59	1.56	Enseignement supérieur
Bulgaria								**Bulgarie**
Primary education	1.00	0.99	0.99	1.00	0.99	0.99	...	Enseignement primaire
Secondary education	0.99	1.00	0.96	0.96	0.97	0.97	...	Enseignement secondaire
Tertiary education	1.21	1.60	1.16	1.32	1.28	1.25	...	Enseignement supérieur
Burkina Faso								**Burkina Faso**
Primary education	0.60	0.66	0.80	0.91	0.97	0.98	0.98	Enseignement primaire
Secondary education	0.55	...	0.71	0.76	0.92	0.95	0.97	Enseignement secondaire
Tertiary education	0.29	0.28	0.45	0.48	0.52	0.51	0.52	Enseignement supérieur
Burundi								**Burundi**
Primary education	0.67	0.79	0.84	0.97	1.01	1.01	1.00	Enseignement primaire
Secondary education	0.50	...	* 0.71	0.68	0.91	0.97	1.02	Enseignement secondaire
Tertiary education	* 0.34	...	* 0.37	0.50	...	0.40	0.43	Enseignement supérieur
Cabo Verde								**Cabo Verde**
Primary education	0.97	...	0.96	0.93	0.93	0.93	0.93	Enseignement primaire
Secondary education	...	...	1.13	1.19	1.10	1.10	1.10	Enseignement secondaire
Tertiary education	...	...	1.07	1.29	1.42	1.45	1.45	Enseignement supérieur
Cambodia								**Cambodge**
Primary education	...	0.82	0.93	0.94	0.99	0.97	0.98	Enseignement primaire
Tertiary education	...	0.19	0.46	0.60	0.82	...	0.87	Enseignement supérieur
Cameroon								**Cameroun**
Primary education	0.84	0.90	* 0.84	0.86	0.90	0.90	0.90	Enseignement primaire
Secondary education	0.61	0.69	0.79	...	0.86	0.86	...	Enseignement secondaire
Tertiary education	...	...	* 0.66	0.82	0.81	0.79	...	Enseignement supérieur
Canada								**Canada**
Primary education	0.98	0.99	0.99	1.01	1.01	1.00	...	Enseignement primaire
Secondary education	1.00	1.00	0.98	0.98	1.01	1.01	...	Enseignement secondaire
Tertiary education	...	1.17	...	* 1.38	* 1.34	* 1.34	...	Enseignement supérieur
Central African Republic								**République centrafricaine**
Primary education	0.56	...	0.69	0.71	...	0.76	...	Enseignement primaire
Secondary education	...	...	...	...	...	0.64	0.66	Enseignement secondaire
Tertiary education	...	...	...	0.32	...	...	...	Enseignement supérieur
Chad								**Tchad**
Primary education	0.38	0.49	0.68	0.74	0.78	0.78	...	Enseignement primaire
Secondary education	0.18	0.24	* 0.35	0.42	0.45	0.46	...	Enseignement secondaire
Tertiary education	0.09	...	0.06	* 0.17	...	...	...	Enseignement supérieur
Chile								**Chili**
Primary education	0.97	...	0.95	0.97	0.97	0.97	0.97	Enseignement primaire
Secondary education	1.06	...	1.01	1.03	1.01	1.01	1.01	Enseignement secondaire
Tertiary education	0.78	0.86	0.96	1.08	1.13	1.14	1.16	Enseignement supérieur
China [1]								**Chine** [1]
Primary education	0.83	0.95	...	0.98	1.00	1.01	1.01	Enseignement primaire
Secondary education	0.70	0.85	...	1.00	...	...	...	Enseignement secondaire
Tertiary education	...	...	0.90	1.06	1.19	1.21	1.21	Enseignement supérieur
China, Hong Kong SAR								**Chine, RAS de Hong Kong**
Primary education	0.99	1.01	...	...	0.98	0.98	0.98	Enseignement primaire
Secondary education	1.08	...	1.01	1.00	0.97	0.97	0.96	Enseignement secondaire
Tertiary education	...	...	1.01	* 0.99	1.13	1.14	1.11	Enseignement supérieur

Region, country or area	1985	1995	2005	2010	2015	2016	2017	Région, pays ou zone
China, Macao SAR								**Chine, RAS de Macao**
Primary education	...	...	0.94	0.98	0.98	0.99	0.99	Enseignement primaire
Secondary education	...	...	0.93	0.97	0.99	1.00	1.00	Enseignement secondaire
Tertiary education	...	...	0.67	0.96	1.30	1.33	1.31	Enseignement supérieur
Colombia								**Colombie**
Primary education	1.03	0.99	0.98	0.98	0.97	0.97	0.97	Enseignement primaire
Secondary education	1.03	1.16	1.11	1.10	1.07	1.06	1.06	Enseignement secondaire
Tertiary education	0.96	1.05	1.08	1.10	1.16	1.16	1.16	Enseignement supérieur
Comoros								**Comores**
Primary education	0.90	...	...	...	...	...	0.96	Enseignement primaire
Secondary education	...	...	...	...	...	...	1.06	Enseignement secondaire
Tertiary education	...	...	...	0.74	...	...	...	Enseignement supérieur
Congo								**Congo**
Primary education	0.96	0.85	0.93	0.94	...	...	...	Enseignement primaire
Secondary education	0.75	...	...	...	...	...	...	Enseignement secondaire
Tertiary education	0.18	...	...	...	...	...	...	Enseignement supérieur
Cook Islands								**Îles Cook**
Primary education	...	...	* 1.03	* 0.99	* 0.91	* 0.94	...	Enseignement primaire
Secondary education	...	...	* 1.13	* 1.09	* 1.09	* 1.06	...	Enseignement secondaire
Costa Rica								**Costa Rica**
Primary education	0.97	0.99	0.97	0.98	0.99	1.01	...	Enseignement primaire
Secondary education	1.09	1.08	1.04	1.04	1.04	1.05	...	Enseignement secondaire
Tertiary education	...	...	...	...	1.31	1.24	1.26	Enseignement supérieur
Côte d'Ivoire								**Côte d'Ivoire**
Primary education	0.70	0.73	...	...	0.88	0.89	0.91	Enseignement primaire
Secondary education	...	...	...	...	0.71	0.73	0.75	Enseignement secondaire
Tertiary education	...	0.33	...	0.52	0.66	0.70	...	Enseignement supérieur
Croatia								**Croatie**
Primary education	...	1.00	1.00	1.00	1.00	1.01	...	Enseignement primaire
Secondary education	...	1.04	1.03	1.07	1.05	1.05	...	Enseignement secondaire
Tertiary education	...	1.01	1.21	1.34	1.35	1.38	...	Enseignement supérieur
Cuba								**Cuba**
Primary education	0.94	0.99	0.97	0.98	0.94	0.95	0.95	Enseignement primaire
Secondary education	1.06	1.12	1.02	1.01	1.04	1.04	1.03	Enseignement secondaire
Tertiary education	1.20	1.46	* 1.69	1.65	1.41	1.41	1.70	Enseignement supérieur
Cyprus								**Chypre**
Primary education	0.99	* 1.00	* 1.00	* 1.00	* 1.00	...	...	Enseignement primaire
Secondary education	1.05	* 1.01	* 1.02	* 1.01	* 0.99	...	...	Enseignement secondaire
Tertiary education	0.90	* 1.27	* 1.13	* 0.90	* 1.36	...	...	Enseignement supérieur
Czechia								**Tchéquie**
Primary education	0.97	1.00	0.99	1.00	1.00	1.01	...	Enseignement primaire
Secondary education	1.07	1.03	1.02	1.01	1.01	1.01	...	Enseignement secondaire
Tertiary education	0.74	0.96	1.16	1.40	1.41	1.41	...	Enseignement supérieur
Dem. People's Rep. Korea								**Rép. pop. dém. de Corée**
Primary education	...	...	...	...	1.00	...	...	Enseignement primaire
Secondary education	...	...	...	...	1.01	...	...	Enseignement secondaire
Tertiary education	...	...	...	...	0.55	...	...	Enseignement supérieur
Dem. Rep. of the Congo								**Rép. dém. du Congo**
Primary education	0.65	0.69	...	0.87	0.99	...	...	Enseignement primaire
Secondary education	0.41	0.61	...	0.58	0.64	...	...	Enseignement secondaire
Tertiary education	...	...	...	...	...	0.56	...	Enseignement supérieur
Denmark								**Danemark**
Primary education	1.00	1.00	1.00	1.00	0.99	0.99	...	Enseignement primaire
Secondary education	0.99	1.03	1.04	1.01	1.05	1.03	...	Enseignement secondaire
Tertiary education	1.02	1.12	1.38	1.45	1.40	1.36	...	Enseignement supérieur
Djibouti								**Djibouti**
Primary education	0.73	0.78	0.82	...	0.89	0.89	0.89	Enseignement primaire
Secondary education	0.61	0.69	0.67	...	0.80	0.82	0.83	Enseignement secondaire
Tertiary education	...	...	0.73	0.69	...	...	...	Enseignement supérieur
Dominica								**Dominique**
Primary education	...	1.14	1.00	0.98	0.98	0.97	...	Enseignement primaire
Secondary education	...	...	1.08	1.09	0.99	...	...	Enseignement secondaire
Tertiary education	2.04	...	...	...	...	...	...	Enseignement supérieur

Ratio of girls to boys in primary, secondary and tertiary education *(continued)*

Rapport filles/garçons dans l'enseignement primaire, secondaire et supérieur *(suite)*

Region, country or area	1985	1995	2005	2010	2015	2016	2017	Région, pays ou zone
Dominican Republic								**République dominicaine**
Primary education	* 1.03	...	* 0.95	* 0.88	* 0.91	* 0.92	* 0.93	Enseignement primaire
Secondary education	...	...	* 1.19	* 1.12	* 1.10	* 1.09	* 1.09	Enseignement secondaire
Tertiary education	...	...	...	...	* 1.83	* 1.79	* 1.79	Enseignement supérieur
Ecuador								**Équateur**
Primary education	0.99	0.99	1.00	1.00	1.00	1.01	...	Enseignement primaire
Secondary education	1.02	...	1.01	1.04	1.04	1.03	...	Enseignement secondaire
Tertiary education	...	...	...	...	1.16	...	...	Enseignement supérieur
Egypt								**Égypte**
Primary education	0.79	0.89	0.95	0.97	...	1.00	1.00	Enseignement primaire
Secondary education	0.68	0.88	...	0.97	...	0.98	0.98	Enseignement secondaire
Tertiary education	0.51	...	0.84	0.92	0.96	1.02	...	Enseignement supérieur
El Salvador								**El Salvador**
Primary education	...	0.98	0.97	0.95	0.96	0.96	0.97	Enseignement primaire
Secondary education	...	...	1.00	0.99	1.01	1.00	0.99	Enseignement secondaire
Tertiary education	0.73	0.97	1.12	1.11	1.11	1.12	1.12	Enseignement supérieur
Equatorial Guinea								**Guinée équatoriale**
Primary education	...	...	0.97	0.99	0.99	...	...	Enseignement primaire
Secondary education	...	...	0.74	...	...	...	...	Enseignement secondaire
Eritrea								**Érythrée**
Primary education	...	0.81	0.81	0.85	0.86	...	0.86	Enseignement primaire
Secondary education	...	0.72	0.60	0.77	0.85	...	0.90	Enseignement secondaire
Tertiary education	...	0.16	...	0.38	0.65	0.71	...	Enseignement supérieur
Estonia								**Estonie**
Primary education	0.98	0.97	0.97	0.99	1.00	1.00	...	Enseignement primaire
Secondary education	...	1.12	1.04	1.00	1.00	1.01	...	Enseignement secondaire
Tertiary education	...	1.10	1.68	1.66	1.52	1.51	...	Enseignement supérieur
Eswatini								**Eswatini**
Primary education	0.98	0.97	0.93	0.91	0.91	0.92	...	Enseignement primaire
Secondary education	...	...	1.01	0.99	0.99	0.98	...	Enseignement secondaire
Tertiary education	...	...	1.06	...	...	...	...	Enseignement supérieur
Ethiopia								**Éthiopie**
Primary education	0.65	0.60	0.84	0.92	0.91	...	...	Enseignement primaire
Secondary education	...	0.80	0.60	0.83	0.96	...	...	Enseignement secondaire
Tertiary education	...	0.26	0.32	0.43	...	...	...	Enseignement supérieur
Fiji								**Fidji**
Primary education	0.99	1.00	...	...	0.99	0.99	...	Enseignement primaire
Secondary education	1.03	...	...	...	...	...	...	Enseignement secondaire
Tertiary education	0.61	...	* 1.19	...	...	...	...	Enseignement supérieur
Finland								**Finlande**
Primary education	1.00	1.00	0.99	0.99	0.99	1.00	...	Enseignement primaire
Secondary education	1.17	1.15	1.05	1.05	1.10	1.10	...	Enseignement secondaire
Tertiary education	0.98	1.17	1.21	1.22	1.20	1.19	...	Enseignement supérieur
France								**France**
Primary education	0.98	0.98	* 0.99	* 0.99	* 0.99	* 0.99	...	Enseignement primaire
Secondary education	1.09	0.99	* 1.00	* 1.01	* 1.01	* 1.01	...	Enseignement secondaire
Tertiary education	1.03	1.26	* 1.25	* 1.26	* 1.24	* 1.24	...	Enseignement supérieur
French Guiana								**Guyane française**
Primary education	...	* 0.97	...	...	...	...	...	Enseignement primaire
Secondary education	...	1.04	...	...	...	...	...	Enseignement secondaire
French Polynesia								**Polynésie française**
Primary education	0.98	0.96	...	...	...	...	...	Enseignement primaire
Gabon								**Gabon**
Primary education	0.98	1.00	...	...	...	...	...	Enseignement primaire
Secondary education	0.71	0.84	...	...	...	...	...	Enseignement secondaire
Gambia								**Gambie**
Primary education	0.61	0.75	1.03	1.03	1.07	1.08	1.08	Enseignement primaire
Secondary education	0.41	0.54	...	* 0.95	...	...	...	Enseignement secondaire
Tertiary education	...	0.54	...	0.68	...	...	...	Enseignement supérieur
Georgia								**Géorgie**
Primary education	...	0.99	0.98	1.01	1.00	1.00	1.01	Enseignement primaire
Secondary education	...	0.92	0.98	...	1.03	1.02	1.02	Enseignement secondaire
Tertiary education	...	1.31	1.05	1.28	1.23	1.15	1.14	Enseignement supérieur

Ratio of girls to boys in primary, secondary and tertiary education *(continued)*

Rapport filles/garçons dans l'enseignement primaire, secondaire et supérieur *(suite)*

Region, country or area	1985	1995	2005	2010	2015	2016	2017	Région, pays ou zone
Germany								**Allemagne**
Primary education	...	0.99	1.00	1.00	0.99	0.99	...	Enseignement primaire
Secondary education	...	0.97	0.98	0.95	0.95	0.95	...	Enseignement secondaire
Tertiary education	...	0.80	...	...	0.98	1.00	...	Enseignement supérieur
Ghana								**Ghana**
Primary education	0.80	0.90	0.96	...	1.00	1.02	1.01	Enseignement primaire
Secondary education	0.63	0.72	* 0.83	...	0.95	0.97	0.97	Enseignement secondaire
Tertiary education	...	...	0.53	...	0.69	0.72	0.72	Enseignement supérieur
Greece								**Grèce**
Primary education	1.00	1.02	0.98	0.98	0.99	1.00	...	Enseignement primaire
Secondary education	0.99	1.01	0.95	0.94	0.93	0.94	...	Enseignement secondaire
Tertiary education	1.04	1.05	1.11	1.04	...	0.98	...	Enseignement supérieur
Grenada								**Grenade**
Primary education	0.94	0.93	0.97	0.97	0.96	0.97	0.95	Enseignement primaire
Secondary education	1.18	...	* 1.02	1.03	1.00	1.04	1.06	Enseignement secondaire
Tertiary education	...	...	...	...	1.16	1.28	1.24	Enseignement supérieur
Guadeloupe								**Guadeloupe**
Primary education	0.94	...	...	...	...	...	...	Enseignement primaire
Secondary education	...	1.10	...	...	...	...	...	Enseignement secondaire
Guatemala								**Guatemala**
Primary education	0.85	0.87	0.94	0.98	0.97	0.97	0.97	Enseignement primaire
Secondary education	...	...	0.92	0.94	0.94	0.95	0.95	Enseignement secondaire
Tertiary education	...	...	...	...	1.18	...	...	Enseignement supérieur
Guinea								**Guinée**
Primary education	0.46	0.51	0.80	0.82	...	0.82	...	Enseignement primaire
Secondary education	0.36	...	* 0.50	...	...	...	...	Enseignement secondaire
Tertiary education	0.34	...	0.23	0.33	...	...	...	Enseignement supérieur
Guinea-Bissau								**Guinée-Bissau**
Primary education	0.51	0.58	...	0.93				Enseignement primaire
Secondary education	0.27	...	...	...	...	...	...	Enseignement secondaire
Guyana								**Guyana**
Primary education	1.02	0.97	1.00	1.00	...	...	...	Enseignement primaire
Secondary education	1.00	...	1.03	1.06	...	...	...	Enseignement secondaire
Tertiary education	0.94	0.89	2.14	2.42	...	...	...	Enseignement supérieur
Haiti								**Haïti**
Primary education	0.87	0.95	...	...	...	...	...	Enseignement primaire
Honduras								**Honduras**
Primary education	1.00	1.01	1.00	1.00	0.99	0.99	1.00	Enseignement primaire
Secondary education	...	...	...	1.23	1.19	1.16	1.14	Enseignement secondaire
Tertiary education	...	...	...	1.15	1.36	...	...	Enseignement supérieur
Hungary								**Hongrie**
Primary education	1.00	0.99	0.98	0.99	1.00	1.00	...	Enseignement primaire
Secondary education	1.00	1.04	0.99	0.99	1.01	0.99	...	Enseignement secondaire
Tertiary education	1.18	1.13	1.46	1.36	1.26	1.25	...	Enseignement supérieur
Iceland								**Islande**
Primary education	...	1.00	0.98	1.01	1.00	1.00	...	Enseignement primaire
Secondary education	...	0.97	1.01	1.02	1.01	1.00	...	Enseignement secondaire
Tertiary education	...	1.40	1.92	1.79	1.79	1.87	...	Enseignement supérieur
India								**Inde**
Primary education	0.70	0.81	...	* 1.02	1.12	1.17	...	Enseignement primaire
Secondary education	...	0.64	* 0.82	0.93	1.01	1.02	...	Enseignement secondaire
Tertiary education	0.45	0.57	0.70	0.73	0.99	1.00	1.03	Enseignement supérieur
Indonesia								**Indonésie**
Primary education	0.95	0.97	* 0.97	1.04	0.97	0.96	0.96	Enseignement primaire
Secondary education	...	0.86	* 0.99	1.01	1.01	1.04	1.03	Enseignement secondaire
Tertiary education	0.49	0.63	...	0.90	...	...	1.13	Enseignement supérieur
Iran (Islamic Republic of)								**Iran (Rép. islamique d')**
Primary education	0.79	0.93	0.98	0.99	1.05	1.06	1.03	Enseignement primaire
Secondary education	0.70	0.83	0.96	0.98	1.00	1.02	1.02	Enseignement secondaire
Tertiary education	...	...	1.06	0.99	...	0.91	...	Enseignement supérieur
Iraq								**Iraq**
Primary education	0.86	...	...	...	...	...	...	Enseignement primaire
Secondary education	0.57	...	...	...	...	...	...	Enseignement secondaire
Tertiary education	0.41	...	* 0.60	...	...	...	...	Enseignement supérieur

6

Ratio of girls to boys in primary, secondary and tertiary education *(continued)*

Rapport filles/garçons dans l'enseignement primaire, secondaire et supérieur *(suite)*

Region, country or area	1985	1995	2005	2010	2015	2016	2017	Région, pays ou zone
Ireland								**Irlande**
Primary education	1.00	1.00	* 1.00	* 1.00	* 1.00	* 0.99	...	Enseignement primaire
Secondary education	1.10	1.06	* 1.09	* 1.06	* 1.03	* 1.03	...	Enseignement secondaire
Tertiary education	0.79	1.02	* 1.24	* 1.08	* 1.09	* 1.11	...	Enseignement supérieur
Israel								**Israël**
Primary education	1.03	...	1.01	1.00	1.01	1.01	1.01	Enseignement primaire
Secondary education	1.07	...	0.99	1.02	1.01	1.02	1.02	Enseignement secondaire
Tertiary education	...	...	1.33	...	1.38	1.40	1.41	Enseignement supérieur
Italy								**Italie**
Primary education	1.00	0.99	0.99	0.99	0.99	1.00	...	Enseignement primaire
Secondary education	0.99	1.00	0.99	0.99	0.98	0.98	...	Enseignement secondaire
Tertiary education	0.85	1.14	1.37	1.43	1.36	1.34	...	Enseignement supérieur
Jamaica								**Jamaïque**
Primary education	1.02	...	...	...	...	...	...	Enseignement primaire
Secondary education	1.09	...	1.06	1.08	1.07	1.05	1.06	Enseignement secondaire
Tertiary education	...	...	...	2.31	1.73	...	...	Enseignement supérieur
Japan								**Japon**
Primary education	1.00	1.00	...	...	1.00	1.00	...	Enseignement primaire
Secondary education	1.02	1.02	...	...	1.01	1.01	...	Enseignement secondaire
Tertiary education	0.55	0.83	...	...	...	...	...	Enseignement supérieur
Jordan								**Jordanie**
Primary education	1.05	1.01	...	...	...	...	...	Enseignement primaire
Secondary education	1.04	...	1.03	1.04	...	...	1.03	Enseignement secondaire
Tertiary education	0.95	...	1.09	1.14	1.09	1.07	1.15	Enseignement supérieur
Kazakhstan								**Kazakhstan**
Primary education	...	1.01	1.00	1.01	1.00	1.00	1.02	Enseignement primaire
Secondary education	...	...	...	1.01	1.04	1.03	1.01	Enseignement secondaire
Tertiary education	...	1.29	...	1.27	1.28	1.24	1.26	Enseignement supérieur
Kenya								**Kenya**
Primary education	0.96	0.98	0.96	...	1.00	1.00	...	Enseignement primaire
Secondary education	0.75	...	* 0.95	...	...	...	...	Enseignement secondaire
Tertiary education	0.35	...	* 0.60	...	0.72	0.70	...	Enseignement supérieur
Kiribati								**Kiribati**
Primary education	1.00	1.03	1.01	...	1.03	1.03	1.06	Enseignement primaire
Secondary education	1.01	1.24	1.15	...	...	...	...	Enseignement secondaire
Kuwait								**Koweït**
Primary education	0.94	1.01	1.04	0.99	1.04	1.04	1.00	Enseignement primaire
Secondary education	0.93	1.06	* 1.09	1.02	1.08	...	...	Enseignement secondaire
Tertiary education	1.16	1.58	...	...	...	...	...	Enseignement supérieur
Kyrgyzstan								**Kirghizistan**
Primary education	...	1.02	0.98	0.99	0.99	0.99	0.99	Enseignement primaire
Secondary education	...	...	1.00	1.00	1.02	1.00	1.00	Enseignement secondaire
Tertiary education	...	1.26	1.26	1.30	1.30	1.28	1.24	Enseignement supérieur
Lao People's Dem. Rep.								**Rép. dém. populaire lao**
Primary education	0.79	0.81	0.87	0.92	0.96	0.96	0.97	Enseignement primaire
Secondary education	...	0.66	0.75	0.83	0.93	0.93	0.93	Enseignement secondaire
Tertiary education	0.54	0.41	0.71	0.77	0.96	1.00	1.05	Enseignement supérieur
Latvia								**Lettonie**
Primary education	...	0.97	* 0.98	* 0.98	* 1.00	* 1.00	* 1.00	Enseignement primaire
Secondary education	...	1.07	* 0.99	* 0.99	* 0.98	* 0.99	* 0.99	Enseignement secondaire
Tertiary education	1.46	...	* 1.79	* 1.75	* 1.56	* 1.53	* 1.46	Enseignement supérieur
Lebanon								**Liban**
Primary education	0.92	0.99	* 0.92	0.91	0.91	0.91	0.92	Enseignement primaire
Secondary education	0.94	1.16	* 1.01	1.02	0.99	1.00	0.99	Enseignement secondaire
Tertiary education	0.60	...	1.05	1.04	...	...	...	Enseignement supérieur
Lesotho								**Lesotho**
Primary education	1.26	1.14	1.00	0.97	0.97	0.97	0.97	Enseignement primaire
Secondary education	1.46	...	1.29	1.41	1.34	1.35	1.36	Enseignement secondaire
Tertiary education	1.00	1.34	1.35	...	1.50	...	...	Enseignement supérieur
Liberia								**Libéria**
Primary education	...	...	...	...	0.90	0.92	...	Enseignement primaire
Secondary education	...	...	...	...	0.78	0.78	...	Enseignement secondaire
Tertiary education	...	...	...	0.53	...	...	...	Enseignement supérieur
Libya								**Libye**
Primary education	...	...	0.99	...	...	...	...	Enseignement primaire
Secondary education	...	...	* 1.19	...	...	...	...	Enseignement secondaire

Ratio of girls to boys in primary, secondary and tertiary education *(continued)*

Rapport filles/garçons dans l'enseignement primaire, secondaire et supérieur *(suite)*

Region, country or area	1985	1995	2005	2010	2015	2016	2017	Région, pays ou zone
Liechtenstein								**Liechtenstein**
Primary education	...	...	...	* 0.94	* 0.98	* 0.96	...	Enseignement primaire
Secondary education	...	...	...	* 0.85	* 0.78	* 0.78	...	Enseignement secondaire
Tertiary education	...	...	...	* 0.62	* 0.49	* 0.55	...	Enseignement supérieur
Lithuania								**Lituanie**
Primary education	...	0.97	* 0.99	* 0.99	* 1.00	* 1.00	...	Enseignement primaire
Secondary education	...	1.05	* 0.99	* 0.98	* 0.96	* 0.96	...	Enseignement secondaire
Tertiary education	...	1.44	* 1.56	* 1.51	* 1.44	* 1.37	...	Enseignement supérieur
Luxembourg								**Luxembourg**
Primary education	...	...	1.00	1.01	1.00	1.00	...	Enseignement primaire
Secondary education	...	1.01	1.05	1.03	1.04	1.03	...	Enseignement secondaire
Tertiary education	0.52	...	...	1.11	1.11	1.11	...	Enseignement supérieur
Madagascar								**Madagascar**
Primary education	0.93	1.04	0.96	0.98	1.00	1.00	...	Enseignement primaire
Secondary education	...	...	* 0.96	...	* 0.99	0.99	1.01	Enseignement secondaire
Tertiary education	...	0.83	0.89	0.91	0.90	0.92	...	Enseignement supérieur
Malawi								**Malawi**
Primary education	0.81	0.91	1.01	1.02	1.02	1.03	1.04	Enseignement primaire
Secondary education	0.49	0.68	0.80	0.90	* 0.92	0.89	0.94	Enseignement secondaire
Tertiary education	0.29	0.42	* 0.54	0.61	...	...	...	Enseignement supérieur
Malaysia								**Malaisie**
Primary education	0.99	1.00	1.00	1.01	1.00	1.01	1.01	Enseignement primaire
Secondary education	1.02	1.09	1.10	1.08	1.09	1.06	1.05	Enseignement secondaire
Tertiary education	0.84	...	1.32	1.37	1.34	1.20	1.18	Enseignement supérieur
Maldives								**Maldives**
Primary education	...	0.97	0.97	...	0.98	1.00	1.00	Enseignement primaire
Secondary education	...	1.05	...	...	...	...	...	Enseignement secondaire
Mali								**Mali**
Primary education	0.61	0.69	0.79	0.86	0.90	0.88	0.89	Enseignement primaire
Secondary education	...	0.49	* 0.62	0.69	0.79	0.74	0.81	Enseignement secondaire
Tertiary education	0.15	0.18	...	0.41	0.42	...	...	Enseignement supérieur
Malta								**Malte**
Primary education	0.94	0.97	0.98	1.01	1.02	1.04	...	Enseignement primaire
Secondary education	0.97	0.93	0.96	0.89	1.07	1.04	...	Enseignement secondaire
Tertiary education	0.45	0.99	1.35	1.35	1.37	1.37	...	Enseignement supérieur
Marshall Islands								**Îles Marshall**
Primary education	...	...	1.26	...	1.00	1.02	...	Enseignement primaire
Secondary education	...	...	1.00	...	1.10	1.10	...	Enseignement secondaire
Martinique								**Martinique**
Primary education	...	* 0.98	...	...	...	...	...	Enseignement primaire
Secondary education	...	1.06	...	...	...	...	...	Enseignement secondaire
Mauritania								**Mauritanie**
Primary education	0.69	0.84	1.03	1.04	1.05	1.06	1.06	Enseignement primaire
Secondary education	...	0.58	0.88	* 0.85	0.93	0.97	0.96	Enseignement secondaire
Tertiary education	...	0.21	0.34	0.41	0.50	0.51	0.50	Enseignement supérieur
Mauritius								**Maurice**
Primary education	0.99	1.00	1.00	1.01	1.02	1.02	1.02	Enseignement primaire
Secondary education	0.91	...	* 0.98	* 1.05	1.04	1.05	1.07	Enseignement secondaire
Tertiary education	0.60	1.00	* 1.03	1.21	1.31	...	1.29	Enseignement supérieur
Mexico								**Mexique**
Primary education	0.97	0.97	0.98	0.99	1.01	1.01	1.01	Enseignement primaire
Secondary education	0.90	1.01	1.09	1.09	1.07	1.09	1.09	Enseignement secondaire
Tertiary education	...	0.88	1.04	1.04	1.00	1.02	1.03	Enseignement supérieur
Micronesia (Fed. States of)								**Micronésie (États féd. de)**
Primary education	...	...	0.97	...	1.00	...	...	Enseignement primaire
Secondary education	...	...	1.08	...	...	...	...	Enseignement secondaire
Mongolia								**Mongolie**
Primary education	0.97	1.03	1.00	0.98	0.98	0.98	0.98	Enseignement primaire
Secondary education	...	1.33	1.11	1.07	...	...	...	Enseignement secondaire
Tertiary education	...	...	1.65	1.54	1.38	1.39	1.43	Enseignement supérieur
Montenegro								**Monténégro**
Primary education	...	...	1.00	0.99	0.99	0.97	0.99	Enseignement primaire
Secondary education	...	...	1.03	1.01	1.00	1.00	1.00	Enseignement secondaire
Tertiary education	...	...	1.58	1.25	...	1.25	1.28	Enseignement supérieur

Region, country or area	1985	1995	2005	2010	2015	2016	2017	Région, pays ou zone
Montserrat								**Montserrat**
Primary education	...	...	* 1.04	...	...	...	...	Enseignement primaire
Secondary education	...	...	* 1.10	...	...	...	...	Enseignement secondaire
Morocco								**Maroc**
Primary education	0.64	0.74	0.91	0.94	0.95	0.95	0.95	Enseignement primaire
Secondary education	0.68	0.74	0.85	0.87	...	...	0.89	Enseignement secondaire
Tertiary education	...	0.71	0.80	0.90	0.96	0.93	0.97	Enseignement supérieur
Mozambique								**Mozambique**
Primary education	0.77	0.71	0.84	0.90	* 0.92	0.93	0.93	Enseignement primaire
Secondary education	0.45	0.61	0.69	0.81	* 0.92	...	0.91	Enseignement secondaire
Tertiary education	0.29	0.30	0.48	0.65	0.73	0.79	0.81	Enseignement supérieur
Myanmar								**Myanmar**
Primary education	0.91	0.94	1.00	0.99	...	0.97	0.95	Enseignement primaire
Secondary education	...	...	0.97	1.05	...	1.10	1.10	Enseignement secondaire
Tertiary education	...	1.58	...	...	...	...	1.47	Enseignement supérieur
Namibia								**Namibie**
Primary education	...	0.99	0.99	0.97	...	...	0.97	Enseignement primaire
Secondary education	...	1.16	1.12	...	...	...	...	Enseignement secondaire
Tertiary education	...	1.53	0.85	...	1.75	1.75	...	Enseignement supérieur
Nauru								**Nauru**
Primary education	...	...	* 1.05	...	...	* 1.03	...	Enseignement primaire
Secondary education	...	...	* 1.13	...	...	* 1.03	...	Enseignement secondaire
Nepal								**Népal**
Primary education	0.45	0.69	0.92	1.07	1.08	1.08	1.06	Enseignement primaire
Secondary education	0.31	0.59	* 0.81	* 0.95	* 1.07	* 1.07	* 1.11	Enseignement secondaire
Tertiary education	...	...	0.54	0.61	1.02	1.07	1.12	Enseignement supérieur
Netherlands								**Pays-Bas**
Primary education	1.03	0.98	0.98	1.00	1.00	1.00	...	Enseignement primaire
Secondary education	0.97	0.95	0.98	0.99	1.02	1.02	...	Enseignement secondaire
Tertiary education	0.73	0.93	1.08	1.12	1.14	1.13	...	Enseignement supérieur
New Zealand								**Nouvelle-Zélande**
Primary education	0.98	1.00	0.99	1.00	1.01	1.01	1.00	Enseignement primaire
Secondary education	1.02	0.98	1.06	1.05	1.06	1.06	1.06	Enseignement secondaire
Tertiary education	0.88	1.25	...	...	1.41	1.41	1.43	Enseignement supérieur
Nicaragua								**Nicaragua**
Primary education	1.11	1.04	0.99	0.99	...	...	...	Enseignement primaire
Secondary education	2.09	...	1.16	1.13	...	...	...	Enseignement secondaire
Tertiary education	1.30	1.05	...	...	...	...	...	Enseignement supérieur
Niger								**Niger**
Primary education	0.58	0.62	0.72	0.81	0.85	0.86	0.87	Enseignement primaire
Secondary education	...	...	0.62	0.66	0.70	0.73	0.73	Enseignement secondaire
Tertiary education	0.17	...	0.34	0.36	0.41	...	0.43	Enseignement supérieur
Nigeria								**Nigéria**
Primary education	0.81	0.83	0.84	* 0.91	...	0.94	...	Enseignement primaire
Secondary education	...	...	0.83	0.87	0.91	0.90	...	Enseignement secondaire
Tertiary education	0.35	...	0.71	0.74	...	...	...	Enseignement supérieur
Niue								**Nioué**
Primary education	...	...	* 0.89	...	* 0.82	* 0.95	...	Enseignement primaire
Secondary education	...	...	* 1.63	...	* 1.10	...	...	Enseignement secondaire
North Macedonia								**Macédoine du Nord**
Primary education	...	0.99	0.98	0.99	1.00	...	...	Enseignement primaire
Secondary education	...	0.99	0.97	0.97	0.98	...	...	Enseignement secondaire
Tertiary education	...	1.23	1.38	1.16	1.25	...	...	Enseignement supérieur
Norway								**Norvège**
Primary education	1.00	1.00	1.00	1.00	1.00	1.00	1.00	Enseignement primaire
Secondary education	1.06	0.95	1.01	0.98	0.98	0.97	0.96	Enseignement secondaire
Tertiary education	1.05	1.25	1.52	1.62	1.46	1.48	1.49	Enseignement supérieur
Oman								**Oman**
Primary education	0.76	0.99	0.99	...	1.04	1.03	1.03	Enseignement primaire
Secondary education	0.46	0.95	0.96	...	0.98	0.94	0.97	Enseignement secondaire
Tertiary education	0.73	1.18	1.07	1.44	1.87	1.82	...	Enseignement supérieur
Pakistan								**Pakistan**
Primary education	0.52	...	0.77	0.85	0.85	0.85	0.86	Enseignement primaire
Secondary education	0.36	...	...	0.77	0.79	0.81	0.81	Enseignement secondaire
Tertiary education	...	...	0.87	...	0.87	0.87	0.87	Enseignement supérieur

Region, country or area	1985	1995	2005	2010	2015	2016	2017	Région, pays ou zone
Panama								**Panama**
Primary education	0.95	...	0.97	0.96	0.97	0.98	...	Enseignement primaire
Secondary education	1.12	...	1.07	1.06	1.05	1.03	...	Enseignement secondaire
Tertiary education	1.40	...	1.64	1.53	1.57	...	...	Enseignement supérieur
Papua New Guinea								**Papouasie-Nvl-Guinée**
Primary education	...	0.87	0.85	...	...	0.91	...	Enseignement primaire
Secondary education	...	0.68	...	...	...	0.73	...	Enseignement secondaire
Tertiary education	0.31	0.47	...	...	...	...	...	Enseignement supérieur
Paraguay								**Paraguay**
Primary education	0.94	0.97	0.97	0.96	...	...	...	Enseignement primaire
Secondary education	...	1.07	1.03	1.06	...	...	...	Enseignement secondaire
Tertiary education	...	...	1.13	1.42	...	...	...	Enseignement supérieur
Peru								**Pérou**
Primary education	0.96	0.97	1.01	1.01	1.00	1.00	1.00	Enseignement primaire
Secondary education	0.90	0.93	0.98	1.00	1.00	1.00	1.00	Enseignement secondaire
Tertiary education	...	...	1.03	...	...	1.12	...	Enseignement supérieur
Philippines								**Philippines**
Primary education	1.00	0.99	0.99	...	0.97	0.97	...	Enseignement primaire
Secondary education	1.07	...	1.12	...	1.09	1.10	...	Enseignement secondaire
Tertiary education	...	1.37	1.23	1.25	...	...	1.32	Enseignement supérieur
Poland								**Pologne**
Primary education	...	0.99	0.99	0.99	1.01	1.01	...	Enseignement primaire
Secondary education	...	1.01	0.99	0.99	0.97	0.97	...	Enseignement secondaire
Tertiary education	1.30	1.41	1.41	1.52	1.52	1.51	...	Enseignement supérieur
Portugal								**Portugal**
Primary education	0.95	0.95	0.95	0.97	0.96	0.97	...	Enseignement primaire
Secondary education	...	1.08	1.10	1.03	0.97	0.97	...	Enseignement secondaire
Tertiary education	1.14	1.34	1.31	1.18	1.13	1.12	...	Enseignement supérieur
Puerto Rico								**Porto Rico**
Primary education	...	...	...	1.04	1.02	1.02	...	Enseignement primaire
Secondary education	...	...	...	1.06	1.07	1.08	...	Enseignement secondaire
Tertiary education	...	...	...	1.48	1.41	1.41	...	Enseignement supérieur
Qatar								**Qatar**
Primary education	0.98	1.00	0.97	1.01	1.01	0.99	0.99	Enseignement primaire
Secondary education	0.94	0.97	0.94	1.04	1.26	1.17	1.25	Enseignement secondaire
Tertiary education	3.08	5.60	* 3.52	5.32	6.95	7.37	7.75	Enseignement supérieur
Republic of Korea								**République de Corée**
Primary education	1.01	1.03	0.99	1.00	1.00	1.00	...	Enseignement primaire
Secondary education	0.94	1.00	1.02	0.99	1.00	1.00	...	Enseignement secondaire
Tertiary education	0.47	0.57	0.64	0.74	0.77	0.78	...	Enseignement supérieur
Republic of Moldova								**République de Moldova**
Primary education	...	0.99	* 0.99	* 1.00	* 0.99	* 0.99	* 1.00	Enseignement primaire
Secondary education	...	1.04	* 1.04	* 1.02	* 1.01	* 1.00	* 0.99	Enseignement secondaire
Tertiary education	...	1.15	* 1.46	* 1.34	* 1.34	* 1.34	* 1.31	Enseignement supérieur
Réunion								**Réunion**
Primary education	0.94	...	...	...	...	...	...	Enseignement primaire
Secondary education	...	1.03	...	...	...	...	...	Enseignement secondaire
Romania								**Roumanie**
Primary education	...	1.00	0.99	0.98	0.98	0.99	...	Enseignement primaire
Secondary education	...	1.03	1.02	0.99	0.99	0.99	...	Enseignement secondaire
Tertiary education	0.81	0.94	1.26	1.37	1.23	1.24	...	Enseignement supérieur
Russian Federation								**Fédération de Russie**
Primary education	...	0.99	1.00	...	1.01	1.01	...	Enseignement primaire
Secondary education	...	...	0.99	...	0.98	0.99	...	Enseignement secondaire
Tertiary education	...	...	1.37	...	1.21	1.20	...	Enseignement supérieur
Rwanda								**Rwanda**
Primary education	0.95	...	1.01	1.03	1.01	1.00	0.99	Enseignement primaire
Secondary education	0.78	...	0.89	0.99	1.09	1.10	1.12	Enseignement secondaire
Tertiary education	0.16	...	...	0.78	0.78	0.76	0.88	Enseignement supérieur
Saint Lucia								**Sainte-Lucie**
Primary education	1.00	...	0.96	...	...	...	...	Enseignement primaire
Secondary education	1.64	...	1.18	0.99	0.99	1.01	1.01	Enseignement secondaire
Tertiary education	0.83	...	2.72	2.58	1.90	1.95	2.00	Enseignement supérieur
Saint Vincent & Grenadines								**Saint-Vincent-Grenadines**
Primary education	...	...	0.91	0.93	0.97	0.98	0.98	Enseignement primaire
Secondary education	1.49	...	1.25	1.02	0.97	0.99	0.96	Enseignement secondaire

Region, country or area	1985	1995	2005	2010	2015	2016	2017	Région, pays ou zone
Samoa								**Samoa**
Primary education	...	1.03	1.01	0.99	1.00	1.01	1.00	Enseignement primaire
Secondary education	...	1.12	1.13	1.14	1.11	1.10	...	Enseignement secondaire
San Marino								**Saint-Marin**
Primary education	...	...	...	* 1.13	...	...	...	Enseignement primaire
Secondary education	...	...	...	* 1.02	...	...	...	Enseignement secondaire
Tertiary education	...	...	...	* 1.46	...	...	...	Enseignement supérieur
Sao Tome and Principe								**Sao Tomé-et-Principe**
Primary education	...	...	0.96	0.99	0.96	0.95	0.96	Enseignement primaire
Secondary education	...	...	1.06	1.02	1.11	1.13	1.15	Enseignement secondaire
Tertiary education	...	...	...	0.97	1.03	...	...	Enseignement supérieur
Saudi Arabia								**Arabie saoudite**
Primary education	...	...	* 0.98	0.99	1.01	0.98	...	Enseignement primaire
Secondary education	...	...	* 0.94	...	...	...	...	Enseignement secondaire
Tertiary education	0.66	0.91	1.48	1.15	1.01	1.00	0.99	Enseignement supérieur
Senegal								**Sénégal**
Primary education	0.68	0.77	0.96	1.06	1.12	1.12	1.16	Enseignement primaire
Secondary education	0.50	...	0.75	0.87	...	...	1.09	Enseignement secondaire
Tertiary education	* 0.26	...	...	* 0.59	0.60	0.60	0.61	Enseignement supérieur
Serbia								**Serbie**
Primary education	...	...	* 1.01	* 1.00	* 1.00	* 1.00	* 1.00	Enseignement primaire
Secondary education	...	...	* 1.03	* 1.02	* 1.01	* 1.01	* 1.01	Enseignement secondaire
Tertiary education	...	...	* 1.30	* 1.30	* 1.33	* 1.31	* 1.35	Enseignement supérieur
Seychelles								**Seychelles**
Primary education	1.04	1.02	0.98	1.03	0.99	0.99	1.01	Enseignement primaire
Secondary education	1.02	1.00	1.07	* 1.06	1.05	1.07	1.07	Enseignement secondaire
Tertiary education	...	...	...	...	2.16	1.85	2.28	Enseignement supérieur
Sierra Leone								**Sierra Leone**
Primary education	0.67	...	...	...	1.01	1.01	1.01	Enseignement primaire
Secondary education	0.47	...	...	...	0.86	0.91	0.95	Enseignement secondaire
Tertiary education	0.30	...	...	...	...	...	...	Enseignement supérieur
Singapore								**Singapour**
Primary education	...	...	...	...	...	* 1.00	...	Enseignement primaire
Secondary education	...	...	...	...	...	* 0.99	...	Enseignement secondaire
Tertiary education	...	...	...	...	...	* 1.16	...	Enseignement supérieur
Slovakia								**Slovaquie**
Primary education	...	1.00	0.99	0.99	0.99	0.99	...	Enseignement primaire
Secondary education	...	1.05	1.01	1.01	1.01	1.01	...	Enseignement secondaire
Tertiary education	...	1.00	1.29	1.55	1.54	1.52	...	Enseignement supérieur
Slovenia								**Slovénie**
Primary education	...	1.00	0.98	0.99	1.00	1.00	...	Enseignement primaire
Secondary education	...	1.03	0.99	0.99	1.00	1.02	...	Enseignement secondaire
Tertiary education	1.06	1.34	1.42	1.49	1.47	1.43	...	Enseignement supérieur
Solomon Islands								**Îles Salomon**
Primary education	...	...	0.95	0.98	0.99	0.99	0.99	Enseignement primaire
Secondary education	...	...	0.83	0.86	...	...	...	Enseignement secondaire
Somalia								**Somalie**
Primary education	0.52	...	...	...	...	...	...	Enseignement primaire
Secondary education	0.55	...	...	...	...	...	...	Enseignement secondaire
South Africa								**Afrique du Sud**
Primary education	...	0.98	0.96	0.96	0.93	0.96	...	Enseignement primaire
Secondary education	...	...	1.07	1.06	0.99	1.09	...	Enseignement secondaire
Tertiary education	...	...	...	...	...	1.40	...	Enseignement supérieur
South Sudan								**Soudan du sud**
Primary education	...	...	...	...	0.71	...	...	Enseignement primaire
Secondary education	...	...	...	...	0.54	...	...	Enseignement secondaire
Spain								**Espagne**
Primary education	0.99	0.98	0.99	1.00	1.01	1.01	...	Enseignement primaire
Secondary education	1.05	1.09	1.07	1.02	1.00	1.01	...	Enseignement secondaire
Tertiary education	0.96	1.16	1.23	1.24	1.18	1.19	...	Enseignement supérieur
Sri Lanka								**Sri Lanka**
Primary education	0.96	0.97	0.99	0.98	0.98	0.98	0.99	Enseignement primaire
Secondary education	1.11	1.08	...	1.01	...	1.03	1.05	Enseignement secondaire
Tertiary education	0.70	...	...	1.79	1.54	1.55	1.51	Enseignement supérieur

Region, country or area	1985	1995	2005	2010	2015	2016	2017	Région, pays ou zone
State of Palestine								**État de Palestine**
Primary education	...	0.99	0.99	0.98	1.00	1.00	1.00	Enseignement primaire
Secondary education	...	0.96	1.05	1.08	1.10	1.10	1.10	Enseignement secondaire
Tertiary education	...	...	1.01	1.34	1.58	1.59	1.62	Enseignement supérieur
Sudan								**Soudan**
Primary education	...	...	0.88	0.90	0.92	0.94	0.94	Enseignement primaire
Secondary education	...	...	0.93	0.87	0.99	0.98	1.02	Enseignement secondaire
Tertiary education	...	...	1.13	1.17	1.02	...	...	Enseignement supérieur
Suriname								**Suriname**
Primary education	0.98	...	0.98	0.99	1.01	1.00	1.00	Enseignement primaire
Secondary education	...	...	1.33	1.28	1.32	...	...	Enseignement secondaire
Tertiary education	1.12	...	...	...	...	...	...	Enseignement supérieur
Sweden								**Suède**
Primary education	1.01	1.01	1.00	0.99	1.04	1.03	...	Enseignement primaire
Secondary education	1.13	1.15	1.00	0.99	1.14	1.12	...	Enseignement secondaire
Tertiary education	1.14	1.26	1.54	1.53	1.53	1.54	...	Enseignement supérieur
Switzerland								**Suisse**
Primary education	1.01	1.00	1.00	1.00	1.00	0.99	...	Enseignement primaire
Secondary education	0.91	0.94	0.94	0.97	0.97	0.96	...	Enseignement secondaire
Tertiary education	0.48	0.60	0.87	0.99	1.03	1.02	...	Enseignement supérieur
Syrian Arab Republic								**République arabe syrienne**
Primary education	0.86	0.91	0.97	0.97	...	...	...	Enseignement primaire
Secondary education	0.66	0.83	0.96	1.00	...	...	...	Enseignement secondaire
Tertiary education	0.52	0.72	0.90	0.86	1.14	1.19	...	Enseignement supérieur
Tajikistan								**Tadjikistan**
Primary education	...	0.97	0.97	0.98	0.99	0.99	0.99	Enseignement primaire
Secondary education	...	...	0.83	0.87	...	...	...	Enseignement secondaire
Tertiary education	...	...	0.48	0.53	0.67	0.71	0.75	Enseignement supérieur
Thailand								**Thaïlande**
Primary education	...	...	0.97	0.99	0.94	1.00	1.00	Enseignement primaire
Secondary education	...	...	* 1.05	1.07	0.96	0.99	0.96	Enseignement secondaire
Tertiary education	...	...	1.12	1.28	...	1.41	...	Enseignement supérieur
Timor-Leste								**Timor-Leste**
Primary education	...	...	0.91	0.96	0.99	0.98	0.97	Enseignement primaire
Secondary education	...	...	0.97	1.00	1.07	1.07	1.08	Enseignement secondaire
Tertiary education	...	...	...	0.72	...	...	...	Enseignement supérieur
Togo								**Togo**
Primary education	0.62	0.68	0.85	0.90	0.95	0.95	0.95	Enseignement primaire
Secondary education	0.31	0.35	0.53	...	...	...	0.73	Enseignement secondaire
Tertiary education	...	0.15	...	...	0.43	0.43	0.45	Enseignement supérieur
Tokelau								**Tokélaou**
Primary education	...	...	...	...	...	* 0.88	...	Enseignement primaire
Secondary education	...	...	...	...	...	* 1.02	...	Enseignement secondaire
Tonga								**Tonga**
Primary education	0.99	0.99	0.97	0.98	0.97	...	...	Enseignement primaire
Secondary education	1.09	...	...	1.07	1.06	...	...	Enseignement secondaire
Tertiary education	1.42	...	...	...	...	...	...	Enseignement supérieur
Trinidad and Tobago								**Trinité-et-Tobago**
Primary education	1.02	1.00	* 0.97	0.97	...	...	...	Enseignement primaire
Secondary education	1.02	...	...	...	...	...	...	Enseignement secondaire
Tertiary education	0.61	...	...	...	...	...	...	Enseignement supérieur
Tunisia								**Tunisie**
Primary education	0.82	0.92	0.96	0.97	0.97	0.97	...	Enseignement primaire
Secondary education	0.68	0.91	1.08	1.07	...	1.11	...	Enseignement secondaire
Tertiary education	0.59	0.78	1.23	1.53	1.64	1.71	1.77	Enseignement supérieur
Turkey								**Turquie**
Primary education	0.90	0.92	0.95	0.99	0.99	0.99	...	Enseignement primaire
Secondary education	...	0.65	0.83	0.92	0.97	0.98	...	Enseignement secondaire
Tertiary education	0.46	0.62	0.73	0.81	0.87	0.87	...	Enseignement supérieur
Tuvalu								**Tuvalu**
Primary education	...	...	* 0.96	...	* 0.99	* 0.97	...	Enseignement primaire
Secondary education	...	...	...	...	* 1.27	* 1.25	...	Enseignement secondaire
Uganda								**Ouganda**
Primary education	0.79	0.84	0.99	1.02	1.02	1.03	1.03	Enseignement primaire
Tertiary education	0.30	0.48	...	0.79	...	...	...	Enseignement supérieur

Region, country or area	1985	1995	2005	2010	2015	2016	2017	Région, pays ou zone
Ukraine								**Ukraine**
Primary education	...	...	1.00	1.01	...	...	...	Enseignement primaire
Secondary education	...	...	* 0.93	* 0.98	...	...	...	Enseignement secondaire
Tertiary education	...	...	1.24	1.26	...	...	...	Enseignement supérieur
United Arab Emirates								**Émirats arabes unis**
Primary education	0.95	0.98	...	...	1.01	0.97	...	Enseignement primaire
Secondary education	0.93	1.05	...	...	...	0.94	...	Enseignement secondaire
United Kingdom								**Royaume-Uni**
Primary education	1.00	...	1.00	0.99	1.00	1.00	...	Enseignement primaire
Secondary education	1.03	0.99	1.03	1.00	1.03	1.11	...	Enseignement secondaire
Tertiary education	0.84	1.06	1.39	1.34	1.34	1.35	...	Enseignement supérieur
United Rep. of Tanzania								**Rép.-Unie de Tanzanie**
Primary education	1.00	0.98	0.95	1.01	1.03	1.03	1.02	Enseignement primaire
Secondary education	0.59	0.80	...	0.79	...	...	1.01	Enseignement secondaire
Tertiary education	0.17	0.19	* 0.47	0.78	0.51	...	...	Enseignement supérieur
United States of America								**États-Unis d'Amérique**
Primary education	1.02	0.99	* 0.99	* 0.99	* 1.00	* 1.00	...	Enseignement primaire
Secondary education	1.03	1.01	* 1.02	* 1.01	* 1.01	* 0.99	...	Enseignement secondaire
Tertiary education	1.16	1.30	...	...	* 1.36	* 1.34	...	Enseignement supérieur
United States Virgin Islands								**Îles Vierges américaines**
Secondary education	* 0.96	* 0.95	...	...	...	...	...	Enseignement secondaire
Uruguay								**Uruguay**
Primary education	0.99	0.99	0.97	0.97	0.98	0.98	...	Enseignement primaire
Secondary education	...	1.20	1.15	1.17	...	...	...	Enseignement secondaire
Tertiary education	...	...	1.74	...	...	...	...	Enseignement supérieur
Uzbekistan								**Ouzbékistan**
Primary education	...	0.96	1.00	0.98	0.98	0.99	0.98	Enseignement primaire
Secondary education	...	...	0.97	1.00	0.99	0.99	0.99	Enseignement secondaire
Tertiary education	...	...	0.69	0.68	0.63	0.65	0.61	Enseignement supérieur
Vanuatu								**Vanuatu**
Primary education	...	...	0.97	0.99	0.98	...	...	Enseignement primaire
Secondary education	...	...	...	1.00	1.06	...	...	Enseignement secondaire
Venezuela (Boliv. Rep. of)								**Venezuela (Rép. boliv. du)**
Primary education	0.99	...	0.98	0.97	0.97	0.97	0.97	Enseignement primaire
Secondary education	1.26	...	1.13	1.10	1.08	1.08	1.08	Enseignement secondaire
Viet Nam								**Viet Nam**
Primary education	0.95	0.99	0.95	0.95	0.99	1.00	1.00	Enseignement primaire
Tertiary education	...	...	0.71	1.00	1.00	1.24	...	Enseignement supérieur
Yemen								**Yémen**
Primary education	...	...	0.74	0.82	...	0.87	...	Enseignement primaire
Secondary education	...	...	0.49	0.62	...	0.73	...	Enseignement secondaire
Tertiary education	...	...	0.36	0.44	...	...	...	Enseignement supérieur
Zambia								**Zambie**
Primary education	0.90	0.92	0.95	1.01	1.00	1.02	1.02	Enseignement primaire
Zimbabwe								**Zimbabwe**
Primary education	0.95	0.97	...	...	...	...	...	Enseignement primaire
Secondary education	0.68	0.84	...	...	...	...	...	Enseignement secondaire
Tertiary education	...	...	...	0.79	0.90	...	...	Enseignement supérieur

Source:

United Nations Educational, Scientific and Cultural Organization (UNESCO), Montreal, the UNESCO Institute for Statistics (UIS) statistics database, last accessed March 2019.

Source:

Organisation des Nations Unies pour l'éducation, la science et la culture (UNESCO), Montréal, base de données statistiques de l'Institut de statistique (ISU) de l'UNESCO, dernier accès mars 2019.

1   For statistical purposes, the data for China do not include those for the Hong Kong Special Administrative Region (Hong Kong SAR), Macao Special Administrative Region (Macao SAR) and Taiwan Province of China.

1   Pour la présentation des statistiques, les données pour la Chine ne comprennent pas la région administrative spéciale de Hong Kong (RAS de Hong Kong), la région administrative spéciale de Macao (RAS de Macao) et la province chinoise de Taïwan.

7 Enrollment in primary, secondary and tertiary education levels
Number of students enrolled (thousands) and gross enrollment ratio by sex

Inscriptions aux niveaux primaire, secondaire et supérieur
Nombre d'élèves inscrits (milliers) et taux brut de scolarisation par sexe

Region, country or area / Région, pays ou zone	Year & / Année &	Primary education / Enseignement primaire Total ('000)	Gross enrollment ratio Taux brut de scolarisation M/H	F	Secondary education / Enseignement secondaire Total ('000)	Gross enrollment ratio Taux brut de scolarisation M/H	F	Tertiary education / Enseignement supérieur Total ('000)	Gross enrollment ratio Taux brut de scolarisation M/H	F
Total, all countries or areas	2005	678 992	104.9	99.9	509 246	65.7	62.1	139 951	23.7	24.8
Total, tous pays ou zones	2010	697 049	105.8	103.0	546 102	72.3	69.8	182 209	28.4	30.5
	2014	715 017	103.2	102.8	580 925	76.8	75.8	212 931	33.7	37.5
	2015	720 228	102.7	102.6	583 316	77.0	75.9	217 459	34.7	38.7
	*2017	746 285	103.7	104.5	590 725	77.0	76.2	220 704	35.7	40.2
Northern Africa	2005	23 023	97.5	90.3	* 16 909	* 68.7	* 67.8	4 586	23.8	23.0
Afrique septentrionale	2010	23 598	101.4	96.0	17 399	72.2	70.4	5 515	25.8	27.7
	2014	25 150	100.1	96.8	18 618	* 78.8	* 77.7	5 884	28.0	30.2
	2015	* 25 787	* 100.7	* 97.2	* 18 902	* 79.3	* 78.8	6 353	30.1	33.2
	2017	27 431	102.2	99.2	* 19 607	* 80.5	* 79.8	* 6 621	* 31.7	* 35.9
Sub-Saharan Africa	2005	113 402	99.9	88.1	32 018	35.6	27.8	4 074	7.0	4.7
Afrique subsaharienne	2010	135 891	100.8	93.3	44 919	43.2	35.4	5 863	8.9	6.0
	2014	154 891	101.9	96.7	54 747	46.1	39.7	* 7 509	* 10.2	* 7.1
	2015	156 752	100.2	95.8	57 117	46.6	40.2	* 7 720	* 10.2	* 7.3
	*2017	164 726	100.2	95.8	59 298	45.6	39.9	8 034	10.4	7.5
Northern America	2005	26 780	102.0	101.0	27 039	94.9	96.3	18 631	67.0	94.9
Amérique septentrionale	2010	26 565	100.6	99.7	26 809	95.1	95.9	21 859	75.3	104.8
	2014	26 792	99.9	99.7	26 895	97.5	98.6	21 279	73.6	100.0
	2015	27 094	100.5	100.5	27 063	98.3	99.3	21 097	73.8	100.0
	*2017	27 846	101.3	101.4	27 403	100.2	99.8	20 883	74.2	99.8
Latin America & the Caribbean	2005	69 066	117.5	114.0	58 887	83.5	90.3	16 088	27.6	33.8
Amérique latine et Caraïbes	2010	67 190	115.4	111.9	61 100	85.7	92.8	22 055	35.4	46.0
	2014	65 267	110.0	107.8	64 190	90.7	96.7	25 509	41.3	53.8
	2015	64 580	109.2	107.2	64 042	91.6	96.8	26 217	42.4	55.0
	*2017	64 571	108.6	106.5	64 013	92.9	97.4	27 407	44.0	57.5
Eastern Asia	2005	* 126 355	* 104.7	* 104.6	* 115 226	* 69.7	* 68.6	28 737	25.1	21.6
Asie orientale	2010	113 593	107.5	106.0	113 534	89.1	89.1	39 209	27.6	27.7
	2014	106 544	99.1	99.2	102 399	91.9	93.8	50 194	41.9	46.3
	2015	107 284	99.1	99.4	99 600	91.0	93.1	51 555	45.0	50.8
	2017	111 862	101.1	102.1	96 500	89.3	91.1	52 223	49.5	56.8
South-eastern Asia	2005	68 305	106.9	103.9	40 839	62.6	62.4	11 323	* 21.1	* 21.0
Asie du Sud-Est	2010	68 390	107.1	107.7	45 570	69.8	70.8	14 475	25.5	27.4
	2014	68 911	108.1	106.0	50 105	78.6	79.5	17 649	28.8	34.2
	2015	68 744	108.2	105.2	51 424	81.1	81.5	* 18 072	* 29.6	* 35.1
	2017	68 525	107.6	104.3	52 096	81.5	83.0	18 724	30.6	37.3
Southern Asia	2005	* 181 476	* 106.1	* 100.6	120 739	55.3	46.8	16 055	11.7	8.7
Asie méridionale	2010	191 840	107.5	107.0	143 371	61.9	57.4	28 470	19.5	14.9
	2014	194 500	103.6	109.8	168 938	69.6	69.2	40 029	24.4	23.3
	2015	195 876	103.8	110.4	170 483	70.0	69.6	41 920	25.5	24.2
	*2017	204 902	106.8	116.8	175 186	71.1	71.4	42 158	25.4	24.4
Western Asia	2005	24 169	105.1	95.7	19 700	79.5	68.4	5 184	27.9	25.1
Asie occidentale	2010	25 425	105.7	98.3	22 391	79.9	72.0	7 514	36.1	33.7
	2014	* 26 143	* 104.6	* 97.6	* 25 143	* 85.8	* 78.3	10 570	48.8	47.0
	2015	* 26 701	* 104.6	* 98.3	* 25 328	* 85.8	* 78.3	11 219	51.6	50.0
	*2017	27 087	102.8	96.2	25 859	85.7	78.5	11 881	54.7	52.9
Europe	2005	38 463	101.9	101.1	65 271	97.6	97.5	32 142	55.3	70.7
Europe	2010	36 749	102.0	101.5	58 629	101.3	100.5	33 676	59.8	77.0
	2014	38 128	101.7	101.8	57 901	107.7	107.3	30 627	63.1	77.3
	2015	38 485	101.1	101.2	57 462	107.9	107.4	29 645	62.9	77.2
	*2017	39 681	101.4	101.5	58 803	109.7	110.4	29 100	64.0	78.2
Oceania	2005	3 142	91.7	89.7	* 3 575	* 112.8	* 109.5	* 1 643	* 58.4	* 72.4
Océanie	2010	3 556	100.4	97.4	* 3 776	* 115.9	* 108.2	* 2 014	* 62.5	* 84.5
	2014	4 081	107.9	104.4	* 3 889	* 117.9	* 105.6	* 2 172	* 63.4	* 89.6
	2015	4 101	106.1	103.0	3 913	118.7	105.2	2 207	64.2	91.6
	*2017	4 259	106.1	103.1	3 947	117.1	103.3	2 223	65.4	92.6

7

Enrollment in primary, secondary and tertiary education levels *(continued)*
Number of students enrolled (thousands) and gross enrollment ratio by sex

Inscriptions aux niveaux primaire, secondaire et supérieur *(suite)*
Nombre d'élèves inscrits (milliers) et taux brut de scolarisation par sexe

Region, country or area / Région, pays ou zone	Year & / Année &	Primary education / Enseignement primaire Total ('000)	Gross enrollment ratio Taux brut de scolarisation M H	F	Secondary education / Enseignement secondaire Total ('000)	Gross enrollment ratio Taux brut de scolarisation M H	F	Tertiary education / Enseignement supérieur Total ('000)	Gross enrollment ratio Taux brut de scolarisation M H	F
Afghanistan	2004	4 430	149.7	65.0	594	29.4	6.1	28	1.9	0.5
Afghanistan	2005	4 319	126.9	74.5	651	28.6	9.3	...	...	...
	2009	4 946	118.5	78.7	1 716	61.0	29.4	95	6.1	1.4
	2010	5 279	120.6	82.7	2 044	68.6	34.3	...	...	...
	2014	6 218	125.7	88.1	2 603	68.6	38.6	263	13.0	3.6
	2015	6 334	126.2	87.2	2 699	68.4	38.6	...	...	...
	2017	6 359	122.7	84.2	2 908	69.1	39.6	...	...	...
	2018	...	...	...	...	...	...	371	14.6	...
Albania	2005	238	101.6	100.6	407	80.2	76.4	63	19.1	27.2
Albanie	2010	225	94.6	93.0	356	89.1	88.1	122	38.6	51.6
	2014	196	108.6	106.7	333	99.9	92.5	174	56.7	86.3
	2015	188	111.2	108.2	315	99.3	92.0	161	53.3	81.7
	2017	175	111.5	108.6	280	99.0	93.1	140	44.4	70.8
Algeria	2005	4 362	111.8	103.4	3 654	75.2	82.4	792	18.2	23.3
Algérie	2010	3 312	118.9	111.4	4 616	95.3	98.7	1 144	24.4	35.3
	2011	3 363	120.1	112.6	4 573	97.8	101.5	1 189	25.5	37.0
	2014	3 765	121.3	115.3	...	...	...	1 245	27.4	41.9
	2015	3 925	118.5	112.8	...	...	...	1 289	28.8	45.1
	2017	4 283	114.5	108.8	...	...	...	1 546	38.5	57.3
American Samoa / Samoa américaines	2007	...	...	...	...	...	...	2	...	...
Andorra	2005	4	...	...	4	...	...	~0	...	...
Andorre	2008	4	...	...	4	...	...	~0	...	...
	2010	4	...	...	4	...	...	...	...	...
	2014	4	...	...	4	...	...	~0	...	...
	2015	4	...	...	4	...	...	1	...	...
	2017	4	...	...	4	...	...	1	...	...
Angola	2002	...	...	...	* 462	* 16.7	* 13.6	13	* 0.9	* 0.6
Angola	2005	...	...	...	...	...	...	48	...	...
	2006	...	...	...	...	...	...	49	...	...
	2010	4 273	117.6	92.8	850	31.9	21.2	...	...	...
	2011	5 027	146.7	91.2	885	32.9	20.7	143	9.3	3.4
	2013	...	...	...	...	...	...	219	10.1	7.9
	2015	5 621	121.6	105.2	...	...	...	221	9.6	7.4
	2016	...	...	...	2 034	62.0	39.3	253	10.4	8.5
Anguilla	2005	1	...	...	1	...	...	~0	...	...
Anguilla	2008	2	...	...	1	...	...	~0	...	...
	2010	2	...	...	1	...	...	...	...	...
	2011	2	...	...	1	...	...	...	...	...
Antigua and Barbuda	2000	13	...	...	5	* 72.6	* 65.7	...	...	...
Antigua-et-Barbuda	2010	11	98.1	89.9	8	98.8	100.0	1	8.3	20.9
	2012	10	91.7	85.7	8	90.4	104.2	2	14.1	29.2
	2014	10	91.1	84.4	8	93.1	94.0	...	...	...
	2015	10	90.2	85.1	8	92.7	94.6	...	...	...
	2017	10	89.2	86.1	8	94.4	90.6	...	...	...
Argentina	2005	4 873	117.7	116.6	3 884	89.8	98.4	2 083	52.1	75.8
Argentine	2010	4 947	117.5	115.9	4 213	97.1	106.6	2 521	59.1	89.2
	2014	4 780	110.2	109.7	4 451	103.4	110.3	2 869	63.5	102.9
	2015	4 784	110.1	109.7	4 502	104.0	110.2	2 966	65.4	107.1
	2016	4 776	109.7	109.2	4 583	105.7	110.4	3 061	67.2	111.6
Armenia	2000	180	98.0	99.3	409	87.8	96.5	93	31.5	39.3
Arménie	2005	125	94.6	96.3	370	...	...	115	32.8	46.0
	2010	102	97.7	100.7	306	105.6	103.7	146	47.6	58.0
	2014	143	96.1	97.4	245	83.7	88.4	113	43.9	50.1
	2015	145	94.1	95.5	240	84.0	88.4	106	42.4	50.5
	2017	152	94.0	94.3	...	...	...	105	46.1	58.7

7 Enrollment in primary, secondary and tertiary education levels *(continued)*
Number of students enrolled (thousands) and gross enrollment ratio by sex

Inscriptions aux niveaux primaire, secondaire et supérieur *(suite)*
Nombre d'élèves inscrits (milliers) et taux brut de scolarisation par sexe

Region, country or area Région, pays ou zone	Year & Année &	Primary education Enseignement primaire			Secondary education Enseignement secondaire			Tertiary education Enseignement supérieur		
		Total ('000)	Gross enrollment ratio Taux brut de scolarisation		Total ('000)	Gross enrollment ratio Taux brut de scolarisation		Total ('000)	Gross enrollment ratio Taux brut de scolarisation	
			M H	F		M H	F		M H	F
Aruba	2005	10	114.9	107.8	7	95.8	96.1	2	25.9	37.3
Aruba	2010	10	114.5	113.0	7	93.5	98.3	2	31.1	43.9
	2012	9	102.8	105.4	8	110.2	112.1	3	30.5	45.6
	2014	10	118.9	115.2	...	...	...	1	10.1	23.0
	2015	...	...	...	...	...	...	1	9.4	21.4
	2016	...	...	...	...	...	...	1	10.7	20.7
Australia	2005	1 935	101.8	103.3	...	...	...	...	...	...
Australie	2010	2 015	106.0	105.8	...	...	...	...	...	...
	2014	2 169	106.2	105.9	...	...	...	...	...	...
	2015	2 141	102.2	102.2	2 709	168.9	146.8	1 903	98.5	142.3
	2017	2 217	100.9	100.9	2 650	159.8	141.8	1 775	94.4	134.1
Austria	2005	363	100.9	100.8	781	102.8	97.8	...	...	...
Autriche	2010	328	100.5	99.1	744	100.8	96.8	385	...	...
	2014	327	101.7	101.1	697	101.2	97.5	421	72.2	86.1
	2015	328	102.2	101.4	691	101.9	98.3	426	73.6	87.9
	2017	335	104.2	103.7	687	104.1	99.5	430	79.4	93.6
Azerbaijan	2005	568	* 98.2	* 92.8	...	...	...	...	...	...
Azerbaïdjan	2010	482	* 94.2	* 93.2	...	...	...	181	* 19.4	* 19.2
	2014	518	* 106.6	* 105.5	...	...	...	195	* 21.7	* 24.8
	2015	551	* 107.4	* 105.6	...	...	...	204	* 23.6	* 27.5
	2017	607	* 102.5	* 104.2	...	...	...	206	* 25.3	* 29.0
Bahamas	2005	37	109.9	108.4	32	89.4	89.1	...	...	...
Bahamas	2010	34	106.9	109.0	34	90.2	95.1	...	...	...
	2016	31	92.9	97.9	28	87.9	93.1	...	...	...
Bahrain	2005	83	94.1	97.5	72	91.5	101.5	19	13.0	39.9
Bahreïn	2006	90	96.1	101.0	74	92.1	101.1	18	12.2	38.3
	2010	...	...	...	80	92.2	93.5	...	...	...
	2014	104	98.9	100.5	90	98.5	99.3	38	29.0	57.6
	2015	108	100.6	101.8	92	102.4	101.9	39	30.9	59.4
	2017	113	100.8	101.1	98	102.3	103.3	43	32.3	63.1
Bangladesh	2005	16 219	96.3	100.8	10 109	44.0	46.9	912	8.1	4.2
Bangladesh	2009	* 16 539	* 97.1	* 101.9	10 907	46.6	50.3	1 582	13.1	7.8
	2010	* 16 987	* 99.2	* 105.5	11 334	47.2	53.0	...	...	...
	2013	...	...	...	13 314	55.9	60.6	...	...	...
	2014	...	...	...	...	...	...	2 068	15.4	11.4
	2015	...	...	...	14 567	59.7	67.3	...	...	...
	2017	17 251	107.3	115.1	15 315	62.1	72.7	2 763	20.6	14.5
Barbados	2001	24	99.8	98.7	21	103.3	103.7	8	23.0	57.0
Barbade	2005	22	96.3	96.0	21	109.1	108.0	...	...	...
	2010	* 23	* 98.9	* 100.6	* 19	* 101.6	* 102.2	13	43.9	95.9
	2011	* 23	* 98.4	* 98.4	20	101.7	105.5	12	40.3	90.6
	2014	21	93.1	94.2	21	107.9	110.7	...	...	...
	2015	21	92.8	93.2	21	106.8	110.4	...	...	...
	2017	20	92.6	90.9	20	104.5	108.8	...	...	...
Belarus	2005	380	99.4	96.1	...	...	...	529	56.8	77.8
Bélarus	2010	358	103.8	103.6	763	109.3	105.8	569	* 65.0	* 94.0
	2014	369	98.1	98.5	649	105.7	103.8	518	77.6	103.6
	2015	387	99.5	99.6	644	105.6	104.1	477	76.2	101.0
	2017	423	101.8	101.4	644	103.7	102.1	419	77.5	96.4
Belgium	2005	739	100.7	100.2	1 200	151.1	169.1	390	54.5	67.9
Belgique	2010	732	102.0	101.8	1 203	146.9	167.3	445	60.0	75.9
	2014	774	103.7	103.6	1 210	152.3	172.7	496	63.5	82.8
	2015	783	103.2	103.1	1 218	153.6	174.7	505	64.8	84.7
	2016	797	103.4	103.3	1 196	152.1	170.4	508	66.1	86.0
Belize	2005	50	115.8	110.8	29	75.3	77.7	5	12.5	19.7
Belize	2010	53	114.8	110.3	33	72.5	78.2	7	16.8	26.9
	2014	52	114.4	109.0	37	78.1	81.7	9	18.1	29.9
	2015	52	115.8	110.4	38	79.8	81.8	9	17.9	28.7
	2017	52	116.1	110.3	40	82.2	86.2	9	18.9	30.5

Enrollment in primary, secondary and tertiary education levels *(continued)*
Number of students enrolled (thousands) and gross enrollment ratio by sex

Inscriptions aux niveaux primaire, secondaire et supérieur *(suite)*
Nombre d'élèves inscrits (milliers) et taux brut de scolarisation par sexe

| Region, country or area Région, pays ou zone | Year & Année & | Primary education Enseignement primaire | | | Secondary education Enseignement secondaire | | | Tertiary education Enseignement supérieur | | |
| | | Total ('000) | Gross enrollment ratio Taux brut de scolarisation | | Total ('000) | Gross enrollment ratio Taux brut de scolarisation | | Total ('000) | Gross enrollment ratio Taux brut de scolarisation | |
			M H	F		M H	F		M H	F
Benin	2001	1 055	106.7	74.4	* 257	* 32.1	* 15.2	28	* 7.2	* 1.8
Bénin	2004	1 320	117.2	89.9	345	39.2	18.4	41	...	...
	2005	1 318	112.4	89.0	...	...	...	42	...	...
	2010	1 788	126.9	113.2	...	...	...	114	20.3	7.2
	2014	2 133	134.6	124.4	897	66.4	45.8	150	23.3	8.5
	2015	2 238	137.2	127.6	964	68.5	48.9	131	19.3	7.7
	2016	2 268	135.1	126.5	993	67.1	50.7	129	18.2	7.6
	2017	2 252	130.8	122.3	...	...	...	...	...	...
Bermuda	2005	5	96.8	101.5	5	76.0	85.9	...	...	...
Bermudes	2006	5	93.7	100.7	5	74.4	81.0	1	18.7	41.6
	2010	4	72.3	...	4	72.3	85.4	1	19.3	40.6
	2014	4	88.8	86.1	4	68.0	77.4	1	19.1	36.1
	2015	4	91.3	89.4	4	67.7	75.5	1	14.7	34.1
Bhutan	2005	99	92.2	90.0	42	46.7	41.7	4	5.7	3.7
Bhoutan	2010	110	105.2	107.9	60	63.0	64.2	5	8.4	5.1
	2013	104	102.0	103.4	69	72.1	77.4	9	12.1	8.9
	2014	102	99.4	101.1	74	78.8	84.5	...	...	...
	2015	99	97.3	98.4	74	80.4	85.6	...	...	...
	2017	94	92.6	92.6	75	82.0	90.3	...	...	...
Bolivia (Plurin. State of)	2005	1 513	115.5	114.4	1 038	89.6	84.3	...	...	...
Bolivie (État plurin. de)	2010	1 429	105.7	103.6	1 058	83.6	82.6	...	...	...
	2014	1 346	98.8	95.8	1 132	85.8	84.9	...	...	...
	2015	1 344	98.5	95.7	1 153	87.1	85.7	...	...	...
	2017	1 369	99.6	97.6	1 237	93.2	90.4	...	...	...
Bosnia and Herzegovina	2005	...	...	...	...	...	...	84	...	...
Bosnie-Herzégovine	2010	175	...	...	323	...	...	105	...	...
	2014	161	...	...	297	...	...	112	...	...
	2015	163	...	...	278	...	...	108	...	...
	2017	161	...	...	253	...	...	102	...	...
Botswana	2005	329	109.5	107.8	173	80.0	82.4	20	9.7	8.6
Botswana	2006	330	110.3	107.9	177	80.6	85.0	22	11.1	9.1
	2008	327	109.7	106.6	168	75.0	81.9	31	...	...
	2009	331	111.4	107.4	...	...	...	48	...	...
	2010	...	...	...	...	...	...	42	...	...
	2014	341	107.2	103.5	...	...	...	55	22.9	28.5
	2015	...	...	...	...	...	...	61	23.9	32.6
	2017	...	...	...	...	...	...	49	18.9	27.2
Brazil	2005	18 661	* 137.2	* 129.2	24 863	* 96.5	* 106.2	4 572	* 22.8	* 29.3
Brésil	2009	17 452	* 133.9	* 128.2	23 617	* 91.5	* 102.1	6 115	* 31.9	* 42.2
	2010	16 893	...	...	23 539	...	...	6 553	...	...
	2014	16 630	* 116.7	* 111.7	24 225	* 96.8	* 105.2	8 072	* 42.3	* 57.6
	2015	16 299	* 115.1	* 110.4	23 502	* 97.4	* 102.9	8 285	* 43.7	* 58.5
	2016	16 119	* 115.4	* 112.4	23 538	* 99.2	* 103.9	8 319	* 42.5	* 58.8
British Virgin Islands	2004	3	...	...	2	...	...	1	...	...
Îles Vierges britanniques	2005	3	...	...	2	...	...	...	...	...
	2009	3	...	...	2	...	...	1	...	...
	2010	3	...	...	2	...	...	...	...	...
	2014	3	...	...	2	...	...	...	...	...
	2015	3	...	...	2	...	...	1	...	...
	2016	3	...	...	2	...	...	1	...	...
	2017	3	...	...	2	...	...	...	...	...
Brunei Darussalam	2005	46	112.9	108.4	44	97.3	95.8	5	9.7	19.4
Brunéi Darussalam	2010	44	106.8	106.3	49	98.9	99.5	6	10.9	20.4
	2014	41	105.4	105.0	49	99.0	98.9	11	23.7	40.1
	2015	40	105.5	104.7	47	95.6	96.0	11	23.5	38.6
	2017	40	105.3	104.3	44	91.5	93.0	12	25.9	40.3

7

Enrollment in primary, secondary and tertiary education levels *(continued)*
Number of students enrolled (thousands) and gross enrollment ratio by sex

Inscriptions aux niveaux primaire, secondaire et supérieur *(suite)*
Nombre d'élèves inscrits (milliers) et taux brut de scolarisation par sexe

Region, country or area Région, pays ou zone	Year & Année &	Primary education Enseignement primaire			Secondary education Enseignement secondaire			Tertiary education Enseignement supérieur		
		Total ('000)	Gross enrollment ratio Taux brut de scolarisation		Total ('000)	Gross enrollment ratio Taux brut de scolarisation		Total ('000)	Gross enrollment ratio Taux brut de scolarisation	
			M H	F		M H	F		M H	F
Bulgaria	2005	290	103.8	102.8	686	91.0	87.3	238	42.1	48.9
Bulgarie	2010	260	108.7	108.3	532	92.1	88.2	287	50.0	66.1
	2014	259	98.9	98.1	519	105.9	102.3	283	60.0	75.6
	2015	262	97.6	96.5	501	104.0	100.6	279	62.0	79.1
	2016	262	95.3	94.3	487	101.4	98.3	267	63.7	79.3
Burkina Faso	2005	1 271	64.6	51.8	295	16.7	11.8	28	3.2	1.4
Burkina Faso	2010	2 048	81.6	74.3	538	24.8	18.9	51	4.8	2.3
	2014	2 594	88.5	86.2	842	32.4	28.3	81	6.8	3.3
	2015	2 707	89.5	87.2	966	35.1	32.3	84	6.6	3.5
	2017	3 041	94.4	92.9	1 162	38.6	37.6	105	7.9	4.1
Burundi	2005	1 037	89.7	75.4	* 171	* 15.8	* 11.2	17	* 3.7	* 1.4
Burundi	2010	1 850	141.8	137.0	338	28.7	19.5	29	4.6	2.3
	2014	2 047	137.1	138.6	583	43.5	36.8	51	8.3	2.5
	2015	2 072	133.5	134.8	664	47.3	43.0	...	...	...
	2017	2 126	126.1	126.2	665	49.7	50.9	62	8.7	3.7
Cabo Verde	2005	83	114.7	110.1	53	66.7	75.3	4	7.3	7.8
Cabo Verde	2010	71	106.1	99.0	62	79.1	94.0	10	15.7	20.2
	2014	67	103.9	96.4	60	81.3	91.5	13	19.2	27.5
	2015	66	101.6	95.0	59	81.1	89.5	13	18.0	25.6
	2017	64	99.2	92.5	56	79.7	87.3	12	17.7	25.7
Cambodia	2004	2 763	137.3	126.4	* 630	* 36.7	* 25.7	45	3.9	1.8
Cambodge	2005	2 695	135.6	126.0	...	...	...	57	4.7	2.1
	2008	2 341	127.7	119.7	* 930	* 48.7	* 41.6	137	12.1	6.2
	2010	2 273	127.4	120.2	...	...	...	195	17.4	10.5
	2011	2 224	126.4	117.9	...	...	...	223	18.2	11.4
	2014	2 129	120.0	113.6	...	...	...	...	...	...
	2015	2 179	117.5	116.7	...	...	...	217	14.4	11.8
	2017	2 112	109.1	106.5	...	...	...	208	14.1	12.2
Cameroon	2005	2 978	* 115.1	* 96.6	784	31.0	24.5	* 100	* 7.2	* 4.7
Cameroun	2009	3 351	116.7	101.1	1 269	45.2	37.9	174	10.3	8.2
	2010	3 510	118.9	102.8	...	...	...	220	12.6	10.3
	2014	4 143	122.9	109.5	2 000	63.8	54.4	350	18.7	14.7
	2015	4 370	125.5	112.8	2 108	65.3	56.0	372	19.3	15.5
	2016	4 481	125.3	112.9	2 207	66.4	57.1	417	21.4	16.9
	2017	4 371	119.0	107.2	...	...	...	...	...	...
Canada	*2002	...	...	...	...	...	...	1 255	50.4	68.6
Canada	2005	2 321	97.4	96.6	2 602	102.1	99.8	...	...	...
	2010	2 168	98.4	98.9	2 612	103.5	101.1	* 1 430	* 52.1	* 71.9
	2014	2 249	101.2	102.4	2 661	109.5	110.1	* 1 578	* 56.7	* 75.7
	2015	2 304	102.4	103.2	2 642	110.4	111.4	* 1 564	* 56.0	* 75.0
	2016	2 319	101.4	101.5	2 641	112.2	113.9	* 1 593	* 57.5	* 77.1
Cayman Islands	2003	...	...	...	...	...	...	1	...	...
Îles Caïmanes	2005	3	...	...	3	...	...	...	...	...
	2008	4	...	...	3	...	...	1	...	...
	2013	4	...	...	3	...	...	...	...	...
	2018	4	...	...	3	...	...	...	...	...
Central African Republic	2000	...	...	...	...	...	...	6	3.1	0.6
République centrafricaine	*2001	459	91.8	62.7	70	15.5	8.1	...	...	...
	*2002	411	81.4	54.4	72	...	...	...	...	...
	2004	363	69.3	46.0	...	...	...	6	...	...
	2005	412	76.0	52.3	...	...	...	...	...	...
	2009	608	101.4	71.9	93	17.5	9.7	10	3.5	1.5
	2010	637	104.3	74.2	...	...	...	11	4.0	1.3
	2012	662	103.6	77.0	126	23.2	11.9	13	4.3	1.6
	2016	814	120.0	91.5	119	18.8	12.0	...	...	...
	2017	...	...	...	138	21.2	14.0	...	...	...

Enrollment in primary, secondary and tertiary education levels *(continued)*
Number of students enrolled (thousands) and gross enrollment ratio by sex

Inscriptions aux niveaux primaire, secondaire et supérieur *(suite)*
Nombre d'élèves inscrits (milliers) et taux brut de scolarisation par sexe

Region, country or area Région, pays ou zone	Year & Année &	Primary education Enseignement primaire			Secondary education Enseignement secondaire			Tertiary education Enseignement supérieur		
		Total ('000)	Gross enrollment ratio Taux brut de scolarisation M H	F	Total ('000)	Gross enrollment ratio Taux brut de scolarisation M H	F	Total ('000)	Gross enrollment ratio Taux brut de scolarisation M H	F
Chad	2005	1 262	85.5	58.0	* 245	* 23.2	* 8.1	12	2.7	0.2
Tchad	2010	1 727	94.9	69.8	430	31.7	13.4	* 22	* 3.6	* 0.6
	2014	2 443	116.4	88.9	509	31.8	14.4	* 42	* 5.7	* 1.1
	2015	2 270	104.4	81.0	513	31.0	14.0	...	...	...
	2016	2 213	99.0	77.0	535	31.0	14.3			
Chile	2005	1 721	109.2	104.3	1 630	94.8	96.0	664	49.7	47.7
Chili	2010	1 547	102.8	99.9	1 518	91.4	94.3	988	66.2	71.5
	2014	1 469	99.5	96.6	1 556	98.8	100.1	1 205	81.2	91.5
	2015	1 478	100.1	97.2	1 546	99.4	100.4	1 222	83.2	93.7
	2017	1 515	102.8	100.1	1 521	99.2	100.2	1 239	84.8	98.5
China [1]	2003	121 662	119.2	118.6	95 625	63.6	60.0	15 186	16.6	13.8
Chine [1]	2005	...	...	...	...	...	...	20 601	19.8	17.9
	2010	101 019	108.2	106.6	99 218	88.1	88.0	31 047	23.3	24.8
	2013	98 871	103.9	103.8	94 324	94.2	95.9	34 091	29.6	33.6
	2014	95 107	99.1	99.3	88 692	...	...	41 924	38.3	44.6
	2015	95 958	99.2	99.5	86 127	...	...	43 367	41.7	49.5
	2017	100 321	101.6	102.6	83 408	...	...	44 128	46.4	56.2
China, Hong Kong SAR	2005	451	...	...	498	81.3	81.9	152	33.0	33.3
Chine, RAS de Hong Kong	2010	349	...	...	508	87.5	87.1	265	* 59.2	* 58.9
	2014	324	109.4	107.1	416	102.1	99.0	305	65.0	72.5
	2015	333	110.5	107.9	394	102.9	99.9	299	64.9	73.1
	2017	352	107.8	105.8	357	106.7	102.0	300	70.1	77.5
China, Macao SAR	2005	37	102.8	96.6	47	89.3	83.2	23	65.7	44.2
Chine, RAS de Macao	2010	25	96.6	94.8	38	89.0	86.2	29	56.0	54.0
	2014	23	101.3	100.5	32	94.5	92.0	30	57.0	72.9
	2015	24	104.1	102.6	30	95.6	94.1	31	62.0	80.7
	2017	28	106.2	105.0	27	101.2	101.5	33	73.5	96.0
Colombia	2005	5 298	128.7	126.2	4 297	79.3	87.7	1 224	28.0	30.4
Colombie	2010	5 085	125.4	123.1	5 080	97.3	106.9	1 674	37.6	41.3
	2014	4 543	115.7	111.7	4 828	95.1	102.6	2 221	49.5	57.1
	2015	4 479	115.4	111.6	4 794	94.8	101.5	2 294	51.5	59.9
	2017	4 352	114.6	110.7	4 785	96.0	101.3	2 446	56.0	65.0
Comoros	2003	104	120.8	99.5	38	43.5	36.5	2	3.5	2.7
Comores	2004	104	114.5	101.6	43	49.8	38.0	...	...	...
	2008	111	113.0	104.1	...	...	...	...	...	...
	2010	...	...	...	...	...	...	4	6.6	4.9
	2014	120	108.6	101.2	70	59.1	63.1	6	9.9	8.0
	2017	122	101.6	97.2	67	53.9	57.2	...	...	...
Congo	2003	510	100.4	94.3	204	46.5	32.0	* 12	* 5.3	* 2.1
Congo	2004	584	112.0	105.0	* 235	* 48.2	* 40.7	...	...	...
	2005	597	111.4	103.5	...	...	...	...	...	...
	2009	672	109.0	101.5	...	...	...	23	10.3	2.2
	2010	705	110.0	103.8	...	...	...	...	...	...
	2012	734	100.6	107.8	339	55.8	48.4	39	12.2	7.7
	2013	...	...	...	...	...	...	37	10.6	8.0
Cook Islands	2005	2	* 110.2	* 113.0	2	* 75.1	* 84.9	...	...	...
Îles Cook	2010	2	* 104.6	* 103.6	2	* 80.7	* 88.1	...	...	...
	2012	2	* 111.5	* 105.8	2	* 94.6	* 101.2	1	* 41.2	* 50.1
	2014	2	* 109.8	* 105.0	2	* 85.0	* 93.6	...	...	...
	2015	2	* 109.1	* 99.8	2	* 85.8	* 93.3	...	...	...
	2016	2	* 111.7	* 105.2	2	* 84.9	* 90.1	...	...	...
Costa Rica	2004	558	116.7	114.0	340	80.8	84.3	109	24.5	30.2
Costa Rica	2005	542	114.4	111.5	347	82.6	86.2	...	...	...
	2010	521	118.1	115.8	414	100.1	104.3	...	...	...
	2014	476	111.3	110.3	460	117.2	123.6	217	47.5	58.8
	2015	473	110.1	109.5	460	120.7	125.6	218	46.6	60.9
	2016	476	109.7	110.3	463	122.8	129.5	218	48.4	59.8
	2017	...	...	...	...	...	...	221	49.3	62.2

7

Enrollment in primary, secondary and tertiary education levels *(continued)*
Number of students enrolled (thousands) and gross enrollment ratio by sex

Inscriptions aux niveaux primaire, secondaire et supérieur *(suite)*
Nombre d'élèves inscrits (milliers) et taux brut de scolarisation par sexe

Region, country or area Région, pays ou zone	Year & Année &	Primary education Enseignement primaire			Secondary education Enseignement secondaire			Tertiary education Enseignement supérieur		
		Total ('000)	Gross enrollment ratio Taux brut de scolarisation		Total ('000)	Gross enrollment ratio Taux brut de scolarisation		Total ('000)	Gross enrollment ratio Taux brut de scolarisation	
			M H	F		M H	F		M H	F
Côte d'Ivoire	*2003	2 046	79.3	63.5	...	...	...	...	...	...
Côte d'Ivoire	2009	2 383	79.4	64.8	...	...	...	* 153	* 11.3	* 6.0
	2010	...	...	...	...	...	...	144	10.4	5.4
	2014	3 177	94.2	82.0	1 418	46.4	32.7	177	10.8	6.3
	2015	3 371	97.6	85.9	1 587	50.4	36.1	193	10.8	7.2
	2016	3 617	102.1	91.3	1 727	53.3	38.8	203	10.8	7.5
	2017	3 772	103.6	94.0	1 898	56.8	42.6	...	...	...
Croatia	2005	196	103.3	103.4	400	91.7	94.8	135	40.5	49.2
Croatie	2010	167	91.9	92.0	389	96.5	103.4	150	46.3	62.1
	2014	161	99.1	98.8	370	97.0	100.6	166	57.2	78.4
	2015	162	97.9	98.2	360	96.0	100.6	162	57.1	77.3
	2016	163	95.0	95.8	349	95.6	100.0	162	57.0	78.5
Cuba	2005	895	99.7	96.8	937	91.6	93.1	472	* 46.6	* 78.8
Cuba	2010	853	104.0	102.2	809	90.8	91.4	801	72.4	119.2
	2013	772	101.4	100.0	787	91.8	92.8	373	36.9	61.5
	2014	763	104.1	99.0	830	97.8	100.3	302	...	...
	2015	746	103.8	97.9	825	98.6	102.2	261	29.9	42.2
	2017	734	104.4	99.2	816	103.0	105.7	287	30.1	51.2
Curaçao										
Curaçao	2013	21	176.3	169.2	11	84.1	91.1	2	13.0	29.6
Cyprus	2005	61	* 100.9	* 100.8	64	* 95.7	* 97.5	20	* 31.2	* 35.3
Chypre	2010	55	* 101.6	* 101.6	64	* 90.9	* 92.0	32	* 50.9	* 45.6
	2014	53	* 98.7	* 99.6	59	* 99.4	* 99.5	34	* 44.1	* 62.6
	2015	54	* 99.3	* 99.3	57	* 100.1	* 99.4	37	* 51.1	* 69.4
Czechia	2005	503	99.9	98.5	975	94.8	96.6	336	44.8	52.0
Tchéquie	2010	463	104.0	103.6	837	94.4	94.9	437	53.6	74.9
	2014	511	98.6	98.6	781	104.4	104.9	419	54.9	76.9
	2015	535	99.3	99.7	770	104.6	105.6	396	53.8	75.7
	2016	557	100.0	100.5	766	104.2	105.1	372	53.2	74.8
Dem. People's Rep. Korea	2009	1 547	99.4	99.4	...	...	...	593	40.8	20.6
Rép. pop. dém. de Corée	2011	...	...	...	...	...	...	600	...	...
	2015	1 358	93.5	93.7	2 148	92.4	93.5	565	36.1	20.0
	2018	1 508	88.1	88.1	...	...	...	526	35.4	...
Dem. Rep. of the Congo	2002	5 455	74.9	59.1	...	...	...	...	...	...
Rép. dém. du Congo	2009	10 244	108.2	92.8	3 399	53.1	29.9	378	10.3	3.2
	2010	10 572	107.0	93.1	3 484	52.2	30.1	...	...	...
	2013	12 601	111.8	101.3	3 996	52.9	32.8	443	9.5	4.3
	2014	13 535	115.5	105.0	4 388	56.1	34.9	...	...	...
	2015	13 763	108.4	107.6	4 619	56.3	36.0	...	...	...
	2016	...	...	...	...	...	...	465	8.5	4.7
Denmark	2005	414	98.8	98.7	465	121.9	126.5	232	67.7	93.4
Danemark	2010	403	99.5	99.7	504	119.0	120.0	241	60.4	87.4
	2014	467	101.9	100.7	554	126.7	132.1	301	67.4	95.3
	2015	469	102.1	100.8	553	127.3	133.4	314	68.7	96.3
	2016	472	102.4	101.2	541	127.3	131.0	315	68.8	94.0
Djibouti	2005	51	47.8	39.4	30	27.4	18.3	2	2.7	1.9
Djibouti	2009	56	58.9	53.0	44	38.5	28.4	3	4.0	2.8
	2010	...	...	...	...	...	...	3	4.1	2.8
	2011	61	64.2	58.4	51	42.1	33.8	5	6.0	4.0
	2014	64	69.5	60.6	59	47.3	38.2	...	...	...
	2015	63	68.0	60.4	59	48.0	38.5	...	...	...
	2018	63	69.3	60.8	65	51.4	43.2	...	...	...
Dominica	2005	9	99.4	99.4	7	103.3	111.7	...	...	...
Dominique	2010	8	110.0	107.6	7	92.8	101.4	...	...	...
	2014	8	117.9	118.0	6	98.0	96.2	...	...	...
	2015	8	117.2	114.8	6	101.2	99.8	...	...	...
	2016	7	114.1	110.5	...	...	...	...	...	...

Enrollment in primary, secondary and tertiary education levels *(continued)*
Number of students enrolled (thousands) and gross enrollment ratio by sex

Inscriptions aux niveaux primaire, secondaire et supérieur *(suite)*
Nombre d'élèves inscrits (milliers) et taux brut de scolarisation par sexe

Region, country or area / Région, pays ou zone	Year & / Année &	Primary education / Enseignement primaire Total ('000)	Gross enrollment ratio Taux brut de scolarisation M / H	F	Secondary education / Enseignement secondaire Total ('000)	Gross enrollment ratio Taux brut de scolarisation M / H	F	Tertiary education / Enseignement supérieur Total ('000)	Gross enrollment ratio Taux brut de scolarisation M / H	F
Dominican Republic	2003	1 375	* 115.4	* 116.3	...	...	...	287	* 26.5	* 41.6
République dominicaine	2005	1 290	* 111.1	* 105.5	808	* 64.9	* 77.5	...	...	...
	2010	1 318	* 117.3	* 103.4	905	* 73.6	* 82.8	...	...	...
	2014	1 268	* 112.7	* 102.2	931	* 76.2	* 84.2	456	* 37.8	* 60.9
	2015	1 307	* 116.4	* 106.2	929	* 76.2	* 83.8	480	* 36.6	* 67.0
	2017	1 253	* 111.5	* 104.0	925	* 76.5	* 83.0	557	* 43.0	* 77.0
Ecuador	2005	1 998	112.0	111.5	1 053	61.5	62.2	...	...	...
Équateur	2008	2 008	110.0	111.6	...	...	...	535	36.0	41.5
	2010	2 114	116.9	116.7	1 655	90.9	94.8	...	...	...
	2012	2 089	114.8	115.4	1 823	99.1	103.7	573	34.6	45.3
	2013	2 068	113.1	113.5	1 883	102.4	106.6	586	...	...
	2014	2 094	113.7	114.0	1 942	105.7	109.8	...	...	...
	2015	1 998	107.4	107.9	1 932	105.3	109.2	669	42.2	49.0
	2016	1 951	103.7	104.7	1 930	105.6	108.6	...	...	...
Egypt	2004	* 7 928	* 97.8	* 94.7	* 8 330	* 81.0	* 76.8	2 261	31.1	25.2
Égypte	2005	9 564	99.4	94.2	...	...	...	2 352	31.8	26.8
	2010	10 542	105.1	102.0	6 846	70.1	68.2	2 646	31.5	28.9
	2014	11 128	101.3	101.0	8 208	83.4	83.0	2 544	32.4	29.0
	2015	...	...	...	...	...	...	2 869	35.8	34.4
	2016	11 764	103.6	103.7	8 745	86.7	85.2	2 789	34.0	34.8
	2017	12 161	104.8	105.1	8 938	87.3	85.7	...	...	...
El Salvador	2005	1 045	120.7	116.6	524	68.0	68.0	122	21.8	24.3
El Salvador	2010	940	118.1	112.8	577	69.6	69.2	150	24.9	27.5
	2014	777	109.0	104.4	625	77.0	77.5	176	26.7	29.2
	2015	741	105.2	100.9	600	75.4	76.0	179	26.6	29.5
	2017	678	98.1	94.9	536	72.1	71.6	186	27.1	30.3
Equatorial Guinea	2000	73	111.9	92.3	21	32.2	14.4	1	2.4	1.2
Guinée équatoriale	2005	76	90.8	87.7	26	29.8	22.0	...	...	...
	2010	85	69.4	68.4	...	...	...	...	...	...
	2012	92	69.0	68.6	...	...	...	...	...	...
	2015	93	61.8	61.3	...	...	...	...	...	...
Eritrea	2004	375	84.0	67.4	194	35.3	20.1	5	1.9	0.3
Érythrée	2005	378	84.1	68.2	217	38.4	23.0	...	...	...
	2010	286	57.1	48.7	248	41.8	32.0	12	3.7	1.4
	2014	362	60.1	51.2	270	41.4	33.8	13	3.7	1.8
	2015	362	58.0	50.0	246	35.8	30.4	11	3.0	1.9
	2016	...	...	...	...	...	...	10	2.7	1.9
	2017	347	53.1	45.6	247	32.4	29.1	...	...	...
Estonia	2005	86	100.2	97.6	124	101.0	104.7	68	50.9	85.8
Estonie	2010	73	103.8	102.3	95	105.3	105.3	69	51.6	85.9
	2014	77	98.0	97.6	78	108.4	107.9	60	58.6	88.6
	2015	80	96.9	97.0	78	111.1	110.7	55	57.6	87.4
	2016	83	97.0	97.2	80	114.6	115.5	51	57.2	86.4
Eswatini	2005	222	106.2	99.1	71	46.9	47.5	6	4.6	4.9
Eswatini	2006	230	111.2	103.3	77	50.5	51.3	6	4.5	4.4
	2010	241	118.2	107.9	89	58.2	57.7	...	...	...
	2013	239	115.0	104.8	93	62.9	61.3	8	5.3	5.5
	2014	240	114.0	104.1	97	65.2	64.3	...	...	...
	2015	241	112.8	102.9	100	67.3	66.8	...	...	...
	2016	239	109.5	100.4	108	72.9	71.7	...	...	...
Ethiopia	2005	10 020	86.0	71.9	2 488	30.8	18.5	191	4.2	1.3
Éthiopie	2010	13 635	95.4	88.1	4 207	38.0	31.5	578	10.2	4.4
	2012	14 532	98.0	91.0	4 929	39.6	35.7	693	11.1	5.2
	2014	15 733	104.1	95.6	...	...	...	757	10.9	5.3
	2015	16 198	106.8	97.0	5 029	35.8	34.4	...	...	...

Enrollment in primary, secondary and tertiary education levels *(continued)*
Number of students enrolled (thousands) and gross enrollment ratio by sex

Inscriptions aux niveaux primaire, secondaire et supérieur *(suite)*
Nombre d'élèves inscrits (milliers) et taux brut de scolarisation par sexe

Region, country or area Région, pays ou zone	Year & Année &	Primary education Enseignement primaire			Secondary education Enseignement secondaire			Tertiary education Enseignement supérieur		
		Total ('000)	Gross enrollment ratio Taux brut de scolarisation		Total ('000)	Gross enrollment ratio Taux brut de scolarisation		Total ('000)	Gross enrollment ratio Taux brut de scolarisation	
			M H	F		M H	F		M H	F
Fiji Fidji	2004	113	113.4	111.8	102	88.0	93.9	13	14.6	17.4
	*2005	...	...	...	...	...	...	13	14.7	17.6
	2009	101	105.9	104.3	98	83.1	90.9	...	...	...
	2012	103	104.5	105.5	97	84.3	93.4	...	...	...
	2013	105	105.1	106.2	...	...	...	...	...	...
	2015	109	106.0	105.1	...	...	...	...	...	...
	2016	110	105.8	104.8	...	...	...	...	...	...
Finland Finlande	2005	382	98.8	98.0	431	109.3	114.3	306	83.3	100.5
	2010	347	99.8	99.2	427	105.2	110.1	304	84.3	103.1
	2014	352	100.8	100.4	537	139.7	153.5	306	80.8	97.3
	2015	355	100.8	100.2	540	142.9	157.4	302	79.9	95.8
	2016	360	100.6	100.2	540	145.0	159.7	297	79.8	94.5
France France	2005	4 015	* 105.1	* 104.1	6 036	* 106.6	* 107.0	2 187	* 47.9	* 60.0
	2010	4 159	* 103.4	* 102.1	5 873	* 105.9	* 107.0	2 245	* 48.7	* 61.2
	2014	4 189	* 102.3	* 101.9	5 947	* 103.3	* 105.0	2 389	* 55.2	* 68.6
	2015	4 256	* 102.3	* 101.7	5 983	* 102.9	* 104.0	2 424	* 56.1	* 69.7
	2016	4 284	* 102.2	* 101.7	6 017	* 102.7	* 103.5	2 480	* 57.7	* 71.5
Gabon Gabon	2002	282	142.9	142.0	* 105	...	...	...	...	...
	2003	280	139.5	138.5	...	...	...	10	10.5	6.1
	2011	318	140.8	136.6	...	...	...	...	...	...
Gambia Gambie	2004	205	92.7	93.5	...	...	...	2	1.9	0.4
	2005	205	88.7	91.5	...	...	...	...	...	...
	2010	229	82.6	84.9	* 124	* 58.5	* 55.7	3	2.6	1.8
	2012	244	81.6	85.4	...	...	...	5	3.7	2.5
	2014	275	85.9	90.7	...	...	...	...	...	...
	2015	294	88.5	94.5	...	...	...	...	...	...
	2018	350	95.8	104.8	...	...	...	...	...	...
Georgia Géorgie	2005	338	90.8	88.6	316	80.8	79.1	174	44.9	47.0
	2008	311	101.5	100.1	305	89.9	86.4	130	* 30.9	* 37.6
	2009	299	101.9	101.4	342	...	...	95	22.8	28.8
	2010	289	101.4	102.2	...	...	...	106	25.7	32.8
	2014	285	105.4	104.7	282	97.3	99.8	121	36.0	45.3
	2015	289	104.1	104.5	278	100.6	103.3	128	41.1	50.3
	2017	301	102.3	103.3	275	106.5	108.1	144	54.0	61.3
Germany Allemagne	2005	3 306	103.1	102.9	8 268	103.3	100.8	...	...	...
	2010	3 068	103.1	102.8	7 664	106.4	101.2	...	...	...
	2014	2 863	101.8	101.1	7 201	103.3	98.7	2 912	65.7	62.6
	2015	2 879	102.7	102.1	7 113	103.4	98.6	2 978	66.9	65.6
	2016	2 895	103.2	102.7	7 073	104.6	99.1	3 043	68.4	68.3
Ghana Ghana	2005	2 930	90.4	86.9	* 1 370	* 44.9	* 37.2	120	7.7	4.1
	2009	3 659	102.7	100.8	1 812	52.8	46.3	203	11.4	6.7
	2014	4 117	105.4	105.3	2 266	66.8	62.6	402	18.6	12.4
	2015	4 342	108.6	108.7	2 440	70.5	66.9	418	18.6	12.9
	2017	4 393	104.1	105.5	2 551	70.9	69.0	444	18.7	13.5
	2018	4 401	101.7	103.3	2 677	72.7	71.7	...	...	...
Gibraltar Gibraltar	2001	2	...	...	2	...	...	...	...	...
	2009	3	...	...	2	...	...	...	...	...
	2017	3	...	...	2	...	...	...	...	...
Greece Grèce	2005	650	96.4	94.3	716	100.4	95.8	647	80.8	90.0
	2010	643	96.4	94.7	717	105.4	99.0	642	100.0	103.7
	2014	629	94.5	93.4	668	101.9	96.2	677	118.0	116.9
	2015	644	95.5	94.6	663	102.6	95.9	...	...	...
	2016	647	94.4	94.0	662	103.2	97.1	709	127.4	125.4
Grenada Grenade	2005	14	98.4	95.5	* 13	* 96.9	* 98.7	...	...	...
	2009	14	107.6	101.5	11	100.7	100.8	7	44.9	60.9
	2010	14	105.1	101.5	12	106.2	109.4	...	...	...
	2014	13	103.9	102.2	10	101.2	100.5	...	...	...
	2015	13	106.7	102.9	9	99.3	99.0	9	84.6	97.9
	2017	13	104.7	99.3	9	96.7	102.0	9	84.6	104.7

Enrollment in primary, secondary and tertiary education levels *(continued)*
Number of students enrolled (thousands) and gross enrollment ratio by sex

Inscriptions aux niveaux primaire, secondaire et supérieur *(suite)*
Nombre d'élèves inscrits (milliers) et taux brut de scolarisation par sexe

Region, country or area Région, pays ou zone	Year & Année &	Primary education Enseignement primaire			Secondary education Enseignement secondaire			Tertiary education Enseignement supérieur		
		Total ('000)	Gross enrollment ratio Taux brut de scolarisation		Total ('000)	Gross enrollment ratio Taux brut de scolarisation		Total ('000)	Gross enrollment ratio Taux brut de scolarisation	
			M H	F		M H	F		M H	F
Guatemala	2002	2 076	107.3	98.8	608	37.8	33.8	112	10.6	7.8
Guatemala	2005	2 345	113.3	106.3	754	43.2	39.8	...	...	...
	2007	2 449	114.0	108.7	864	46.4	43.6	234	17.1	17.5
	2010	2 653	116.6	114.3	1 082	53.9	50.7	233	...	...
	2014	2 417	104.1	101.0	1 166	54.0	51.2	299	17.2	19.2
	2015	2 382	103.1	99.9	1 221	55.8	52.6	367	20.0	23.6
	2017	2 349	102.7	99.6	1 220	54.1	51.5	...	...	...
Guinea	2005	1 207	87.6	70.2	* 420	* 38.8	* 19.3	24	4.7	1.1
Guinée	2008	1 364	91.6	76.7	531	43.4	25.1	80	13.5	4.4
	2010	1 453	94.1	77.5	...	...	...	99	15.6	5.2
	2014	1 730	101.7	86.1	716	48.6	31.9	118	15.5	6.9
	2016	1 777	101.5	83.1	...	...	...	...	...	...
Guinea-Bissau	2000	150	87.8	58.9	26	22.8	12.4	...	...	...
Guinée-Bissau	2005	252	...	...	51	...	...	3	...	...
	2006	269	...	...	55	...	...	4	...	...
	2010	279	122.1	114.1	...	...	...	...	...	...
Guyana	2005	117	99.9	100.2	71	83.9	86.6	7	7.4	15.9
Guyana	2010	99	96.7	96.7	81	87.2	92.8	8	6.9	16.6
	2012	94	95.1	97.1	86	96.6	100.9	9	7.6	15.6
Honduras	2004	1 257	109.1	108.5	...	...	...	* 123	* 13.2	* 19.0
Honduras	2005	1 232	105.5	105.4	...	...	...	...	...	...
	2010	1 275	105.2	104.9	655	61.3	75.3	170	18.0	20.8
	2014	1 150	96.0	94.2	620	48.0	56.2	186	17.0	23.2
	2015	1 154	96.7	95.8	638	48.5	57.9	195	17.6	24.0
	2017	1 124	95.4	95.0	655	57.8	...	...	...	...
Hungary	2005	431	99.1	97.1	960	96.7	95.8	436	53.0	77.5
Hongrie	2010	388	101.2	100.5	905	97.7	96.4	389	54.1	73.8
	2014	393	102.2	101.5	858	103.9	104.5	329	45.5	58.9
	2015	396	102.5	102.1	827	102.7	103.3	308	43.5	54.7
	2016	394	102.0	101.7	809	103.1	102.3	295	42.8	53.5
Iceland	2005	31	98.0	95.7	33	110.5	112.1	15	48.1	92.5
Islande	2010	30	99.0	99.6	36	106.5	108.2	18	56.8	101.5
	2014	30	98.7	97.7	38	116.6	120.7	20	59.8	104.1
	2015	30	98.7	98.6	37	118.6	119.6	19	54.7	98.0
	2016	31	99.6	99.5	36	117.5	117.7	19	51.8	96.8
India	2003	125 569	104.3	101.5	81 050	55.0	44.2	11 295	12.7	8.5
Inde	2005	...	...	...	89 462	* 59.2	* 48.7	11 777	12.5	8.8
	2010	138 414	* 108.1	* 110.4	107 687	65.5	60.9	20 741	20.6	15.0
	2014	137 809	102.3	114.0	129 439	73.8	74.8	30 306	25.7	25.3
	2015	138 518	102.7	115.0	129 542	73.5	74.5	32 107	27.0	26.7
	2016	145 803	106.1	123.9	132 161	74.6	75.8	32 392	26.9	27.0
	2017	...	...	...	...	...	...	33 374	27.2	28.0
Indonesia	2004	29 142	109.6	108.0	16 354	62.1	61.6	3 551	18.5	14.7
Indonésie	2005	29 150	* 109.5	* 106.1	15 993	* 60.4	* 59.8	* 3 662	...	...
	2010	30 342	108.0	112.2	19 976	74.1	75.0	5 001	24.2	21.8
	2014	29 838	106.0	103.4	22 587	83.6	83.5	6 463	27.8	31.4
	2015	29 700	105.8	102.4	23 756	86.9	87.8	...	...	...
	2017	29 352	105.6	101.2	24 318	86.5	89.1	7 984	34.2	38.5
Iran (Islamic Republic of)	2005	6 207	100.7	98.2	9 066	76.9	74.1	2 126	22.2	23.5
Iran (Rép. islamique d')	2010	5 630	105.7	104.8	7 347	82.2	80.6	3 791	42.7	42.2
	2014	7 441	106.3	111.5	5 795	88.4	87.8	4 685	68.0	63.2
	2015	7 670	105.8	111.6	5 712	88.8	89.1	...	...	...
	2016	8 006	106.5	112.4	5 714	89.0	91.0	4 348	72.0	65.5
	2017	8 172	106.2	109.8	5 684	88.5	89.9	...	...	...
Iraq	2004	4 335	113.1	95.2	1 706	56.7	38.2	413	19.8	11.8
Iraq	*2005	...	...	...	...	...	...	425	20.0	11.9
	2007	4 864	117.0	98.7	2 038	61.0	45.6	...	...	...

Enrollment in primary, secondary and tertiary education levels *(continued)*
Number of students enrolled (thousands) and gross enrollment ratio by sex

Inscriptions aux niveaux primaire, secondaire et supérieur *(suite)*
Nombre d'élèves inscrits (milliers) et taux brut de scolarisation par sexe

Region, country or area Région, pays ou zone	Year & Année &	Primary education Enseignement primaire			Secondary education Enseignement secondaire			Tertiary education Enseignement supérieur		
		Total ('000)	Gross enrollment ratio Taux brut de scolarisation M H	F	Total ('000)	Gross enrollment ratio Taux brut de scolarisation M H	F	Total ('000)	Gross enrollment ratio Taux brut de scolarisation M H	F
Ireland	2005	454	* 103.3	* 102.9	317	* 105.2	* 114.6	187	* 52.5	* 65.3
Irlande	2010	506	* 103.2	* 103.3	336	* 114.8	* 121.7	194	* 60.8	* 65.4
	2014	536	* 101.8	* 101.3	348	* 115.3	* 118.3	204	* 71.8	* 75.9
	2015	545	* 101.4	* 101.0	355	* 115.4	* 118.7	215	* 74.0	* 80.6
	2016	554	* 101.6	* 101.0	360	* 115.5	* 118.6	218	* 73.7	* 81.6
Israel	2005	722	103.3	103.8	673	105.0	104.4	311	50.1	66.4
Israël	2009	786	102.6	103.2	694	100.9	103.1	343	54.5	70.7
	2010	807	104.0	104.5	708	100.9	103.3	360	...	...
	2014	862	103.8	104.2	768	101.1	102.6	377	56.7	76.2
	2015	884	104.2	104.8	785	102.0	103.0	374	54.6	75.5
	2017	917	103.4	104.3	819	103.1	104.8	377	52.2	73.6
Italy	2005	2 771	101.8	100.7	4 507	98.5	97.8	2 015	54.2	74.2
Italie	2010	2 822	102.4	101.4	4 626	102.7	101.3	1 980	54.7	78.0
	2014	2 863	102.0	101.1	4 597	103.9	101.6	1 854	53.5	73.8
	2015	2 856	101.6	100.8	4 606	104.3	102.0	1 826	53.6	72.7
	2016	2 832	100.5	100.2	4 590	103.7	101.9	1 816	54.1	72.4
Jamaica	2002	330	96.3	96.1	228	83.1	86.1	45	11.7	25.5
Jamaïque	2004	331	96.1	96.4	246	88.0	91.9	52	...	...
	2005	326	...	...	246	87.1	92.4	48	...	...
	2010	294	...	...	260	88.2	95.5	71	16.4	37.8
	2013	278	...	...	229	79.1	85.2	74	16.6	38.0
	2014	266	...	...	224	78.6	84.9	...	...	...
	2015	259	...	...	215	77.8	83.5	75	19.8	34.2
	2017	247	...	...	204	80.1	84.8			
Japan	2014	6 715	99.4	99.7	7 227	101.0	101.8	3 862	...	...
Japon	2015	6 638	98.6	99.0	7 221	101.8	102.5	3 845	...	...
	2016	6 582	98.0	98.4	7 157	102.0	102.7	3 847		...
Jordan	2004	800	99.0	100.0	616	83.8	86.2	214	35.2	39.8
Jordanie	2005	805	...	...	626	83.8	86.3	218	35.9	39.0
	2010	820	...	...	710	79.4	82.5	247	34.9	39.7
	2012	849	...	...	724	73.7	75.7	307	39.4	45.5
	2014	980	...	...	749	68.9	71.3	...	...	...
	2015	...	...	...	...	...	...	313	35.8	39.0
	2017	1 107	...	...	764	63.9	65.9	284	29.6	33.9
Kazakhstan	2000	1 208	95.6	95.9	1 994	90.3	95.2	418	28.9	34.4
Kazakhstan	2005	1 024	101.5	101.4	...	...	...	...	...	...
	2010	958	107.7	108.3	1 818	97.2	97.7	757	40.3	51.1
	2014	1 122	111.5	111.6	1 662	104.4	107.1	727	42.6	53.9
	2015	1 196	110.6	110.8	1 679	107.6	111.4	658	40.3	51.5
	2017	1 357	107.1	108.8	1 768	112.6	113.6	627	43.9	55.5
	2018	1 407	104.0	105.8	1 843	112.5	113.4	632	47.6	...
Kenya	2005	6 076	103.5	99.4	* 2 468	* 48.8	* 46.6	* 114	* 3.7	* 2.2
Kenya	2009	7 150	107.4	105.2	3 204	60.7	54.9	168	4.7	3.3
	*2014	8 158	107.8	108.5	...	...	...	...	...	...
	2015	8 169	106.0	105.9	...	...	...	421	10.9	7.9
	2016	8 290	105.1	105.5	...	...	...	540	13.7	9.6
Kiribati	2005	16	111.2	112.8	12	83.1	95.3	...	...	...
Kiribati	2008	16	108.3	113.1	12	82.9	91.5	...	...	...
	2009	16	108.0	113.7	...	...	...	...	...	...
	2014	16	111.2	115.2	...	...	...	...	...	...
	2015	16	102.8	106.2	...	...	...	...	...	...
	2017	17	97.0	103.0	...	...	...	...	...	...
Kuwait	2004	158	97.9	106.9	267	99.1	104.9	* 37	* 12.2	* 28.1
Koweït	2005	203	102.7	106.4	* 244	* 104.4	* 114.2	...	...	...
	2010	214	103.0	101.5	264	96.8	99.0	...	...	...
	2013	239	102.0	105.5	279	92.2	96.9	72	23.0	42.7
	2014	253	101.8	105.1	* 283	* 90.5	* 96.5	...	...	...
	2015	264	100.4	104.4	302	94.0	101.4	...	...	...
	2017	275	97.5	97.1	...	...	...	...	...	...

Enrollment in primary, secondary and tertiary education levels *(continued)*
Number of students enrolled (thousands) and gross enrollment ratio by sex

Inscriptions aux niveaux primaire, secondaire et supérieur *(suite)*
Nombre d'élèves inscrits (milliers) et taux brut de scolarisation par sexe

Region, country or area Région, pays ou zone	Year & Année &	Primary education Enseignement primaire			Secondary education Enseignement secondaire			Tertiary education Enseignement supérieur		
		Total ('000)	Gross enrollment ratio Taux brut de scolarisation M H	F	Total ('000)	Gross enrollment ratio Taux brut de scolarisation M H	F	Total ('000)	Gross enrollment ratio Taux brut de scolarisation M H	F
Kyrgyzstan	2005	434	99.6	98.1	721	86.4	86.8	220	37.8	47.5
Kirghizistan	2010	391	99.8	99.0	694	87.7	87.3	261	36.6	47.7
	2014	435	109.0	108.0	651	91.7	92.5	268	40.3	52.4
	2015	451	108.3	107.5	643	92.6	94.1	265	41.2	53.7
	2017	501	108.3	107.4	660	98.4	98.5	231	39.0	48.5
Lao People's Dem. Rep.	2005	891	119.6	104.6	394	49.5	37.4	47	9.1	6.4
Rép. dém. populaire lao	2010	916	128.6	118.7	435	51.1	42.4	118	18.8	14.4
	2014	871	121.7	116.0	601	61.7	56.3	132	18.9	17.7
	2015	850	117.1	112.5	640	66.0	61.1	130	18.5	17.7
	2017	809	108.7	105.2	677	70.2	65.5	111	15.4	16.1
Latvia	2005	84	* 106.1	* 103.5	272	* 103.0	* 102.4	131	* 54.4	* 97.3
Lettonie	2010	114	* 103.9	* 101.9	147	* 103.5	* 102.1	113	* 50.4	* 88.4
	2014	115	* 99.9	* 99.7	122	* 115.1	* 112.2	90	* 58.7	* 83.8
	2015	117	* 99.4	* 99.4	118	* 113.5	* 111.2	86	* 58.4	* 91.1
	2017	122	* 99.3	* 99.5	117	* 111.3	* 110.2	83	* 72.0	* 105.1
Lebanon	2005	* 476	* 107.8	* 99.0	* 378	* 80.2	* 80.8	166	43.0	45.2
Liban	2010	462	109.5	100.0	383	74.5	76.0	202	47.4	49.3
	2014	481	98.5	90.2	370	61.6	62.0	229	39.6	45.8
	2015	491	96.7	88.5	382	61.6	61.1	216	...	...
	2017	503	97.3	89.5	401	63.6	63.0	221	...	...
Lesotho	2005	422	117.2	117.0	94	34.5	44.4	8	3.1	4.2
Lesotho	2006	425	117.7	117.4	96	34.8	45.0	9	3.4	4.3
	2010	389	111.8	109.0	126	42.3	59.7	...	...	...
	2014	366	107.8	104.8	131	44.3	60.0	24	8.3	11.8
	2015	362	106.5	103.0	133	45.7	61.4	22	7.3	10.9
	2017	368	106.7	103.0	136	47.6	64.5	...	...	...
Liberia	2000	496	129.9	95.7	136	40.8	29.7	52	25.0	13.8
Libéria	2009	605	105.3	94.4	...	...	...	...	...	...
	2010	...	...	...	...	...	...	33	12.1	6.5
	2012	...	...	...	...	...	...	44	14.3	9.0
	2014	684	99.8	91.8	223	42.6	33.2	...	...	...
	2015	684	98.7	89.3	227	42.0	32.6	...	...	...
	2016	694	97.7	89.8	227	40.6	31.8	...	...	...
Libya	2003	739	104.9	101.7	* 798	* 100.7	* 107.2	* 375	* 57.5	* 63.6
Libye	2005	714	102.8	101.7	702	* 84.5	* 100.8	...	...	...
	2006	755	111.5	107.0	733	90.2	106.0	...	...	...
Liechtenstein	2004	2	* 109.9	* 108.5	3	* 117.2	* 103.9	1	* 35.7	* 13.3
Liechtenstein	2005	2	...	...	3	...	...	1	...	...
	2010	2	* 108.6	* 102.3	3	* 117.6	* 100.0	1	* 44.3	* 27.4
	2014	2	* 103.1	* 102.3	3	* 127.8	* 103.3	1	* 50.8	* 24.1
	2015	2	* 106.5	* 104.8	3	* 130.7	* 101.7	1	* 44.8	* 21.9
	2016	2	* 107.5	* 103.4	3	* 130.3	* 101.9	1	* 45.3	* 24.8
Lithuania	2005	158	* 103.2	* 102.4	424	* 104.8	* 104.2	195	* 62.5	* 97.5
Lituanie	2010	122	* 101.0	* 99.8	343	* 106.0	* 104.1	201	* 69.2	* 104.6
	2014	108	* 101.7	* 101.4	277	* 110.4	* 105.8	148	* 57.4	* 84.2
	2015	108	* 102.2	* 101.9	263	* 109.8	* 105.4	141	* 57.5	* 82.7
	2016	110	* 103.0	* 102.8	251	* 109.7	* 105.0	134	* 60.1	* 82.5
Luxembourg	2003	34	99.5	99.3	35	93.6	98.7	3	11.1	13.3
Luxembourg	2005	35	100.7	100.9	36	92.9	97.9	...	...	...
	2010	35	97.1	98.1	43	99.9	102.9	5	17.3	19.2
	2012	35	96.9	97.2	44	98.5	102.0	6	18.2	20.7
	2014	35	96.9	97.3	47	101.1	103.5	...	...	...
	2015	36	98.6	98.6	47	100.1	103.9	7	18.7	20.8
	2016	37	100.9	100.6	48	102.1	105.3	7	18.6	20.6

Enrollment in primary, secondary and tertiary education levels *(continued)*
Number of students enrolled (thousands) and gross enrollment ratio by sex

Inscriptions aux niveaux primaire, secondaire et supérieur *(suite)*
Nombre d'élèves inscrits (milliers) et taux brut de scolarisation par sexe

Region, country or area Région, pays ou zone	Year & Année &	Primary education Enseignement primaire			Secondary education Enseignement secondaire			Tertiary education Enseignement supérieur		
		Total ('000)	Gross enrollment ratio Taux brut de scolarisation		Total ('000)	Gross enrollment ratio Taux brut de scolarisation		Total ('000)	Gross enrollment ratio Taux brut de scolarisation	
			M H	F		M H	F		M H	F
Madagascar	2005	3 598	142.0	135.8	* 621	* 21.9	* 21.0	45	2.8	2.5
Madagascar	2009	4 324	151.0	147.6	* 1 022	* 31.6	29.7	68	3.7	3.3
	2010	4 242	145.0	142.4	...	...	...	74	3.8	3.5
	2014	4 611	145.4	145.0	1 494	38.7	38.0	113	5.0	4.6
	2015	4 764	147.3	147.3	* 1 536	* 38.7	* 38.3	117	5.0	4.6
	2016	4 734	143.7	144.0	1 561	38.4	38.2	122	5.0	4.6
	2017	...	...	...	1 534	36.7	37.1	...	...	...
Malawi	2005	2 868	123.5	125.1	516	29.6	23.8	6	* 0.6	* 0.3
Malawi	2010	3 417	131.5	134.6	692	33.8	30.3	10	0.8	0.5
	2011	3 564	133.4	136.9	736	34.8	31.4	12	0.9	0.6
	2014	4 097	140.8	143.7	920	40.0	36.2	...	...	...
	2015	4 205	139.6	142.8	* 962	* 40.4	* 37.1	...	...	...
	2017	4 434	137.5	142.4	999	39.3	37.0	...	...	...
Malaysia	2005	3 202	100.0	100.0	2 489	76.8	84.7	697	24.1	31.9
Malaisie	2010	3 234	99.8	100.7	2 616	74.8	80.6	1 061	31.6	43.3
	2014	3 178	104.5	104.7	2 846	81.4	88.2	1 128	31.1	43.1
	2015	3 108	103.4	103.2	2 801	81.5	88.6	1 302	36.4	48.8
	2017	3 085	102.6	103.6	2 745	84.1	88.4	1 249	38.6	45.5
Maldives	2003	66	128.2	124.1	29	64.0	73.2	~0	0.1	0.3
Maldives	2004	63	127.7	122.7	* 29	* 64.0	* 74.6	...	...	...
	2005	58	121.1	117.0	...	...	...	...	...	...
	2008	47	111.7	107.2	...	...	...	5	9.5	13.4
	2009	45	109.3	105.4	...	...	...	...	...	...
	2010	42	...	...	...	...	...	...	...	...
	2014	40	...	...	...	...	...	6	9.9	20.5
	2015	42	102.3	99.8	...	...	...	...	...	...
	2017	45	101.6	101.5	...	...	...	...	...	...
Mali	2002	1 227	75.2	56.6	...	...	...	23	2.8	1.4
Mali	2005	1 506	82.5	64.8	430	* 31.8	* 19.6	...	...	...
	2010	2 019	89.6	76.8	758	46.4	31.9	81	8.6	3.6
	2014	2 182	81.5	72.3	961	50.4	37.3	88	8.4	3.5
	2015	2 227	79.6	71.5	945	46.4	36.8	83	7.7	3.2
	2017	2 539	84.5	75.6	1 017	45.8	37.0	...	...	...
Malta	2005	30	98.0	95.7	40	104.5	100.3	9	27.5	37.3
Malte	2010	25	98.7	99.3	37	109.7	98.0	11	31.6	42.7
	2014	24	101.1	102.8	30	92.2	96.5	13	38.9	50.9
	2015	25	102.2	104.7	29	91.7	98.1	13	40.3	55.2
	2016	25	102.6	106.6	29	93.8	97.8	13	41.5	56.8
Marshall Islands	2002	9	124.6	116.1	6	71.7	74.4	1	14.2	18.3
Îles Marshall	2005	8	103.0	129.9	5	75.6	75.7	...	...	...
	2009	8	107.4	107.9	5	101.4	104.4	...	...	...
	2011	9	105.7	105.0	...	...	...	...	...	...
	2012	...	...	...	...	...	...	1	44.6	41.2
	2015	8	93.5	93.3	5	73.1	80.4	...	...	...
	2016	8	88.6	90.0	6	69.8	76.5	...	...	...
Mauritania	2005	444	89.4	91.9	93	23.6	20.7	9	4.3	1.5
Mauritanie	2010	531	94.2	98.3	* 110	* 21.8	* 18.6	15	6.2	2.5
	2013	569	93.5	98.0	171	30.1	28.1	19	7.3	3.3
	2014	592	94.5	99.8	179	31.0	28.3	...	...	...
	2015	633	98.8	103.7	188	31.4	29.2	21	7.2	3.6
	2017	627	92.8	98.0	209	32.9	31.5	19	6.4	3.2
Mauritius	2005	124	103.3	103.1	* 129	* 89.7	* 87.6	* 21	* 21.0	* 21.7
Maurice	2010	117	102.5	103.1	* 127	* 87.2	* 91.3	33	30.5	36.9
	2014	105	101.4	103.5	133	99.0	100.8	40	35.1	43.2
	2015	102	102.0	103.8	129	95.3	99.5	38	32.4	42.5
	2017	93	100.7	102.5	125	92.5	99.1	38	34.0	43.8

Enrollment in primary, secondary and tertiary education levels *(continued)*
Number of students enrolled (thousands) and gross enrollment ratio by sex

Inscriptions aux niveaux primaire, secondaire et supérieur *(suite)*
Nombre d'élèves inscrits (milliers) et taux brut de scolarisation par sexe

Region, country or area Région, pays ou zone	Year & Année &	Primary education Enseignement primaire			Secondary education Enseignement secondaire			Tertiary education Enseignement supérieur		
		Total ('000)	Gross enrollment ratio Taux brut de scolarisation		Total ('000)	Gross enrollment ratio Taux brut de scolarisation		Total ('000)	Gross enrollment ratio Taux brut de scolarisation	
			M H	F		M H	F		M H	F
Mexico	2005	14 700	105.6	103.7	10 564	76.5	83.3	2 385	23.0	23.8
Mexique	2010	14 906	105.6	104.6	11 682	80.9	87.9	2 847	25.8	26.8
	2014	14 627	104.8	105.5	12 993	89.1	94.7	3 419	30.1	30.3
	2015	14 398	103.8	104.5	13 473	91.9	98.7	3 515	30.8	30.8
	2017	14 182	103.3	103.9	14 035	95.8	104.2	4 430	37.6	38.8
Micronesia (Fed. States of)	*2000	...	...	...	...	...	...	2	...	...
Micronésie (États féd. de)	2005	19	112.7	109.8	14	80.1	86.7	...	...	...
	2007	19	111.0	112.4	...	...	...	...	...	...
	2014	14	98.0	97.2	...	...	...	...	...	...
	2015	14	95.4	95.7	...	...	...	...	...	...
Monaco	2004	2	...	...	3	...	...	...	...	...
Monaco	2010	2	...	...	3	...	...	...	...	...
	2014	2	...	...	3	...	...	...	...	...
	2015	2	...	...	3	...	...	...	...	...
	2017	2	...	...	3	...	...	1	...	...
Mongolia	2005	251	98.0	98.0	339	85.6	95.0	124	33.8	55.9
Mongolie	2010	274	127.1	124.2	276	88.4	94.8	166	42.5	65.3
	2014	239	102.9	100.8	...	...	...	175	52.9	75.9
	2015	251	102.2	100.3	...	...	...	180	57.7	79.7
	2017	291	105.6	103.3	...	...	...	157	53.5	76.4
Montenegro	2005	38	112.8	112.6	68	93.3	95.8	11	17.2	27.2
Monténégro	2010	35	111.2	109.6	70	99.7	101.0	24	46.5	58.3
	2012	38	96.9	97.8	63	92.8	93.6	...	...	...
	2015	38	96.1	94.8	61	92.7	92.7	...	...	...
	2017	39	98.9	97.5	58	90.1	89.7	25	51.4	65.6
Montserrat	2005	1	* 114.6	* 118.7	~0	* 111.0	* 122.5	...	...	...
Montserrat	2007	~0	* 101.2	* 112.9	~0	* 101.1	* 103.2	...	...	...
	2009	~0	...	...	~0	...	...	~0	...	...
	2010	...	...	...	...	...	...	~0	...	...
	2014	~0	...	...	~0	...	...	...	...	...
	2017	~0	...	...	~0	...	...	...	...	...
Morocco	2005	4 023	110.8	100.5	1 948	54.0	46.0	368	13.0	10.5
Maroc	2010	3 945	112.8	106.2	2 393	67.5	58.8	447	15.2	13.7
	2012	4 017	113.0	107.7	2 554	75.0	64.1	606	20.1	18.6
	2014	4 030	112.2	107.1	...	...	...	789	25.7	24.8
	2015	4 039	112.2	106.2	...	...	...	877	28.9	27.7
	2017	4 211	115.1	109.4	2 847	84.0	75.1	1 010	34.2	33.3
Mozambique	2005	3 943	105.7	88.9	306	15.6	10.8	28	1.9	0.9
Mozambique	2010	5 278	116.0	104.2	672	27.0	22.0	104	5.6	3.6
	2014	* 5 705	* 110.0	* 101.0	* 1 026	* 34.2	* 31.0	157	7.1	5.0
	2015	* 5 902	* 110.9	* 101.7	* 1 073	* 34.3	* 31.5	175	7.5	5.5
	2017	6 139	108.7	101.3	1 216	36.7	33.2	201	7.7	6.2
Myanmar	2001	4 782	101.0	98.9	2 302	39.6	37.2	553	...	...
Myanmar	2005	4 948	101.0	101.2	2 589	46.1	44.7	...	...	...
	2007	5 014	...	...	2 686	47.5	47.5	508	9.1	12.5
	2010	5 126	99.1	98.3	2 852	48.3	50.7	...	...	...
	2012	...	...	...	...	...	...	634	12.5	15.3
	2014	5 177	103.3	100.5	3 191	51.8	53.2	...	...	...
	2017	5 388	116.1	110.0	3 971	61.2	67.0	771	13.0	19.0
Namibia	2005	404	109.5	108.2	148	59.9	66.9	14	7.4	6.3
Namibie	2007	410	110.6	108.2	158	60.1	69.0	...	...	...
	2008	407	110.0	107.2	...	...	...	20	8.2	10.4
	2010	407	109.2	105.8	...	...	...	...	...	...
	2013	425	113.5	109.1	...	...	...	...	...	...
	2014	...	...	...	...	...	...	47	13.9	23.2
	2015	...	...	...	...	...	...	50	14.0	24.5
	2016	...	...	...	...	...	...	54	15.0	26.2
	2017	476	121.0	117.3	...	...	...	...	...	...

Enrollment in primary, secondary and tertiary education levels *(continued)*
Number of students enrolled (thousands) and gross enrollment ratio by sex

Inscriptions aux niveaux primaire, secondaire et supérieur *(suite)*
Nombre d'élèves inscrits (milliers) et taux brut de scolarisation par sexe

| Region, country or area Région, pays ou zone | Year & Année & | Primary education Enseignement primaire | | | Secondary education Enseignement secondaire | | | Tertiary education Enseignement supérieur | | |
		Total ('000)	Gross enrollment ratio Taux brut de scolarisation M H	F	Total ('000)	Gross enrollment ratio Taux brut de scolarisation M H	F	Total ('000)	Gross enrollment ratio Taux brut de scolarisation M H	F
Nauru Nauru	2005	2	* 122.3	* 128.5	1	* 44.4	* 50.3	...	...	...
	2008	1	* 90.1	* 96.0	1	* 57.6	* 68.9	...	...	...
	2014	2	* 110.4	* 101.1	1	* 81.7	* 83.9	...	...	...
	2016	2	* 105.7	* 108.5	1	* 76.5	* 79.0	...	...	...
Nepal Népal	2005	4 030	120.4	110.2	2 054	* 53.5	* 43.5	187	10.3	5.6
	2010	4 901	137.6	146.9	* 2 694	* 60.3	* 57.4	377	17.9	11.0
	2013	4 577	133.0	143.4	* 3 111	* 64.5	* 67.5	477	18.6	15.3
	2014	4 402	129.6	140.1	* 3 164	* 64.9	* 68.9	459	...	...
	2015	4 335	129.8	140.4	* 3 176	* 64.8	* 69.6	445	14.8	15.1
	2017	4 135	130.1	138.4	* 3 337	* 67.6	* 75.0	371	11.1	12.4
Netherlands Pays-Bas	2005	1 278	107.9	105.5	1 411	119.5	117.2	565	56.4	61.1
	2010	1 294	108.5	108.1	1 475	122.9	121.2	651	60.3	67.3
	2012	1 277	105.8	105.8	1 550	130.1	127.9	794	73.0	80.4
	2014	1 223	102.4	102.4	* 1 574	...	...	...	...	...
	2015	1 208	102.7	102.7	1 613	132.6	134.6	843	75.2	86.1
	2016	1 192	103.3	103.3	1 611	131.6	133.8	837	75.6	85.3
Netherlands Antilles [former] Antilles néerlandaises [anc.]	2002	23	...	...	15	...	...	2	...	...
New Zealand Nouvelle-Zélande	2005	353	100.1	99.3	526	117.1	123.6	...	...	...
	2010	348	101.0	101.3	512	116.4	121.8	...	...	...
	2014	360	97.5	97.8	492	111.9	119.1	261	64.4	92.6
	2015	368	97.7	98.2	487	111.5	118.1	270	67.3	94.9
	2017	384	99.8	100.2	486	111.1	118.2	269	67.8	97.1
Nicaragua Nicaragua	2002	923	116.4	116.6	383	55.3	65.8	100	16.8	18.7
	2005	945	121.9	120.2	438	63.7	74.1	...	...	...
	2010	924	123.8	122.7	465	69.8	78.8	...	...	...
Niger Niger	2005	1 064	56.2	40.2	182	12.0	7.4	11	1.7	0.6
	2010	1 726	69.1	56.0	307	16.1	10.7	17	2.2	0.8
	2012	2 051	74.5	62.3	389	18.6	12.3	22	2.6	0.9
	2014	2 277	75.3	64.1	515	22.0	15.3	...	...	...
	2015	2 445	77.4	66.0	595	24.1	17.0	52	5.1	2.1
	2017	2 768	80.1	69.9	787	28.4	20.8	65	5.8	2.5
Nigeria Nigéria	2005	22 115	109.8	92.6	6 398	38.1	31.7	1 392	12.3	8.7
	2010	* 21 558	* 89.1	* 80.9	9 057	47.1	41.2	1 395	11.0	8.1
	2011	23 669	93.7	87.4	9 591	49.1	41.9	1 513	12.0	8.3
	2014	25 801	90.7	89.4	10 496	48.1	43.0	...	...	...
	2015	...	...	...	11 116	48.8	44.6	...	...	...
	2016	25 591	87.1	82.2	10 315	44.1	39.8	...	...	...
Niue Nioué	2005	~0	* 118.9	* 105.9	~0	* 71.3	* 116.5	...	...	...
	2014	~0	* 127.4	* 125.3	~0	* 100.0	* 124.7	...	...	...
	2015	~0	* 147.2	* 120.2	~0	* 104.1	* 114.1	...	...	...
	2016	~0	* 132.5	* 125.3	...	...	...	...	...	...
North Macedonia Macédoine du Nord	2005	110	94.5	92.5	214	82.8	80.2	49	24.6	34.1
	2010	111	88.0	86.7	197	83.4	81.0	62	34.7	40.4
	2014	108	92.0	90.8	171	81.8	79.3	61	34.0	42.8
	2015	109	94.1	93.7	169	82.6	81.2	64	36.7	45.9
Norway Norvège	2005	430	98.4	98.7	403	113.2	114.3	214	62.4	95.1
	2010	424	98.9	99.2	435	113.5	111.7	225	56.5	91.2
	2014	426	99.9	99.8	439	114.6	110.8	264	63.7	92.2
	2015	431	100.0	99.8	443	116.1	113.2	268	63.8	92.9
	2017	445	100.3	100.2	448	119.4	114.2	284	66.3	98.7
Oman Oman	2005	312	93.2	92.1	302	89.3	86.0	48	17.9	19.1
	2009	302	104.9	100.7	322	101.8	97.1	76	19.7	27.4
	2010	...	...	...	...	...	...	78	19.7	28.5
	2013	320	106.5	112.5	293	99.1	100.5	105	23.1	41.2
	2014	337	107.4	113.5	...	...	...	118	25.4	49.3
	2015	351	106.9	111.3	287	104.3	102.3	127	29.2	54.5
	2016	368	107.2	110.1	294	110.4	103.9	132	32.8	59.7
	2017	384	105.7	108.8	296	104.1	100.9	...	...	...

Enrollment in primary, secondary and tertiary education levels *(continued)*
Number of students enrolled (thousands) and gross enrollment ratio by sex

Inscriptions aux niveaux primaire, secondaire et supérieur *(suite)*
Nombre d'élèves inscrits (milliers) et taux brut de scolarisation par sexe

Region, country or area Région, pays ou zone	Year & Année &	Primary education Enseignement primaire			Secondary education Enseignement secondaire			Tertiary education Enseignement supérieur		
		Total ('000)	Gross enrollment ratio Taux brut de scolarisation		Total ('000)	Gross enrollment ratio Taux brut de scolarisation		Total ('000)	Gross enrollment ratio Taux brut de scolarisation	
			M H	F		M H	F		M H	F
Pakistan	2005	17 258	98.9	76.1	6 852	...	...	783	5.3	4.6
Pakistan	2009	18 468	100.7	86.0	9 433	39.1	31.0	* 1 226	* 7.5	* 6.3
	2010	18 756	102.7	87.5	9 655	40.2	31.0	...	...	...
	2014	19 432	100.4	85.5	11 287	46.2	36.5	1 932	10.0	10.7
	2015	19 847	99.4	84.9	12 078	49.3	39.1	1 872	10.6	9.2
	2017	21 686	102.8	88.6	12 529	50.0	40.6	1 941	10.8	9.4
Palau	*2002	...	...	...	...	...	...	~0	25.6	52.3
Palaos	2004	2	* 104.6	* 101.1	2	* 97.7	* 99.9	...	...	...
	2005	2	...	...	2	...	...	...	...	...
	2007	2	...	...	2	...	...	...	...	...
	2013	2	* 115.9	* 113.5	2	* 115.4	* 118.3	1	* 50.6	* 78.1
	2014	2	* 117.0	* 112.5	2	* 112.3	* 118.3			
Panama	2005	430	109.1	105.3	256	65.7	70.3	126	32.1	52.5
Panama	2010	440	107.0	103.0	284	69.2	73.5	139	35.1	53.7
	2014	427	100.3	97.7	312	72.4	77.8	145	34.5	54.8
	2015	418	97.3	94.7	317	73.9	77.8	157	36.8	58.0
	2016	409	93.9	92.2	345	80.9	83.1	...	...	...
Papua New Guinea	2005	532	61.9	52.4	...	...	...	...	...	...
Papouasie-Nvl-Guinée	2008	601	63.2	55.9	...	...	...	...	...	...
	2012	1 132	110.9	98.5	378	45.2	34.0	...	...	...
	2016	1 275	116.5	106.5	507	56.2	40.9	...	...	...
Paraguay	2005	934	113.5	110.3	529	66.0	67.8	156	24.3	27.5
Paraguay	2010	839	105.9	101.8	561	66.5	70.2	225	29.1	41.2
	2012	838	107.6	104.3	631	74.2	79.1	...	...	...
	2016	727	...	...	611	...	...	...	...	...
Peru	2005	4 077	117.0	118.0	2 470	86.3	84.6	908	32.8	33.6
Pérou	2006	4 026	116.3	117.3	2 540	88.4	87.7	951	33.3	35.4
	2010	3 763	109.8	111.0	2 675	94.5	94.9	...	...	...
	2014	3 496	101.4	101.4	2 671	95.7	95.5	...	...	...
	2015	3 513	101.7	101.7	2 682	95.7	95.8	...	...	...
	2016	3 577	103.0	103.3	2 753	98.2	97.9	1 930	65.8	73.6
	2018	3 593	102.3	102.6	2 780	98.5	98.3	...	...	...
Philippines	2005	13 084	106.5	105.4	6 352	78.3	87.6	2 403	24.7	30.4
Philippines	2009	13 687	108.6	107.5	6 767	80.9	87.5	2 625	25.6	31.6
	2010	...	...	...	...	...	...	2 774	26.4	33.0
	2014	14 460	114.9	112.8	7 220	83.6	91.3	3 563	31.3	40.1
	2015	14 453	114.6	111.3	7 319	84.8	92.1	...	...	...
	2016	14 294	112.7	109.0	7 397	85.2	93.3	...	...	...
	2017	...	...	...	...	...	...	3 589	30.5	40.3
Poland	2005	2 724	94.8	94.3	3 445	99.9	99.3	2 118	52.9	74.7
Pologne	2010	2 235	97.0	96.2	2 842	96.2	95.8	2 149	59.6	90.8
	2014	2 153	99.2	99.4	2 641	107.9	104.3	1 763	54.2	83.2
	2015	2 306	104.6	105.4	2 548	108.3	104.8	1 665	53.3	80.7
	2016	2 481	109.6	110.6	2 463	108.5	105.5	1 600	53.2	80.6
Portugal	2005	753	120.3	114.6	670	92.8	102.1	381	47.9	62.6
Portugal	2010	734	112.7	109.4	721	104.8	107.7	384	59.9	70.7
	2014	674	109.8	105.3	769	116.9	114.1	362	60.4	69.9
	2015	657	108.5	104.4	779	120.0	116.4	338	57.6	65.3
	2016	639	107.1	103.3	766	119.1	115.9	343	59.5	66.4
Puerto Rico	2010	300	92.5	95.8	291	80.8	85.4	249	69.9	103.2
Porto Rico	2014	259	87.4	88.7	266	78.7	83.8	241	70.1	98.8
	2015	251	86.0	87.5	279	83.9	89.3	241	70.7	99.4
	2016	228	79.4	81.0	236	72.0	77.4	233	68.9	97.2
Qatar	2005	70	107.1	103.7	56	102.3	96.0	* 10	* 8.8	* 31.1
Qatar	2010	89	104.7	105.9	69	99.2	103.3	14	4.8	25.6
	2014	117	98.0	100.8	88	72.6	100.5	25	6.2	39.2
	2015	130	102.4	103.6	96	82.0	103.6	28	6.3	43.9
	2017	146	104.6	103.8	103	77.3	96.3	31	6.6	51.0

Enrollment in primary, secondary and tertiary education levels *(continued)*
Number of students enrolled (thousands) and gross enrollment ratio by sex

Inscriptions aux niveaux primaire, secondaire et supérieur *(suite)*
Nombre d'élèves inscrits (milliers) et taux brut de scolarisation par sexe

Region, country or area Région, pays ou zone	Year & Année &	Primary education Enseignement primaire			Secondary education Enseignement secondaire			Tertiary education Enseignement supérieur		
		Total ('000)	Gross enrollment ratio Taux brut de scolarisation		Total ('000)	Gross enrollment ratio Taux brut de scolarisation		Total ('000)	Gross enrollment ratio Taux brut de scolarisation	
			M H	F		M H	F		M H	F
Republic of Korea	2005	4 032	101.4	100.7	3 796	96.0	98.2	3 210	110.8	70.9
République de Corée	2010	3 306	101.7	101.7	3 959	96.6	96.1	3 270	116.7	86.8
	2014	2 736	96.8	97.3	3 579	100.5	100.5	3 318	105.2	80.2
	2015	2 722	97.4	97.8	3 397	100.1	100.3	3 268	104.6	80.6
	2016	2 680	96.9	97.1	3 232	99.7	99.8	3 204	104.7	81.7
Republic of Moldova	2005	184	* 98.6	* 97.2	394	* 86.2	* 90.0	130	* 29.5	* 42.9
République de Moldova	2010	141	* 93.7	* 93.3	308	* 87.0	* 89.0	130	* 32.7	* 43.7
	2014	138	* 93.3	* 92.9	246	* 86.8	* 87.9	116	* 35.9	* 47.3
	2015	139	* 92.9	* 91.9	233	* 85.8	* 86.5	109	* 35.3	* 47.4
	2017	139	* 91.4	* 91.1	227	* 87.1	* 86.5	96	* 35.7	* 46.7
Romania	2005	970	109.2	107.7	2 090	82.9	84.5	739	40.2	50.8
Roumanie	2010	842	98.3	96.8	1 822	97.6	96.8	1 000	55.3	75.9
	2012	807	97.0	95.1	1 714	96.8	95.6	705	45.0	56.9
	2014	...	...	...	1 609	93.2	92.2	579	42.7	52.7
	2015	947	91.1	89.7	1 563	91.2	90.6	542	42.2	51.8
	2016	939	90.0	88.9	1 515	89.3	88.6	535	43.0	53.3
Russian Federation	2005	5 309	95.2	95.4	12 433	83.4	82.5	9 003	61.3	84.3
Fédération de Russie	2009	5 015	99.0	99.5	9 614	85.7	84.3	9 330	64.3	86.9
	2014	5 726	98.3	99.0	9 061	101.5	99.5	6 996	71.6	86.3
	2015	5 983	100.3	101.1	9 385	105.5	103.3	6 592	73.0	88.4
	2016	6 199	101.8	102.3	9 567	105.6	104.0	6 182	74.7	89.3
Rwanda	2004	1 753	135.4	134.4	204	15.6	14.1	25	3.5	2.0
Rwanda	2005	1 858	137.2	138.1	219	17.3	15.4	28	...	...
	2010	2 299	143.3	146.9	426	33.1	32.8	63	6.4	5.0
	2014	2 399	134.9	138.0	587	38.0	41.6	78	8.4	6.9
	2015	2 451	134.7	136.3	568	35.8	38.9	80	9.0	7.0
	2017	2 540	134.1	132.8	611	35.9	40.3	81	8.1	7.2
Saint Kitts and Nevis	2005	6	...	...	* 4	...	...	...	...	...
Saint-Kitts-et-Nevis	2008	6	...	...	4	...	...	1	...	...
	2010	6	...	...	* 4	...	...	...	...	...
	2014	6	...	...	4	...	...	3	...	...
	2015	5	...	...	4	...	...	4	...	...
	2016	5	...	...	4	...	...	...	...	...
Saint Lucia	2005	24	105.1	100.5	14	71.5	84.0	2	7.0	19.0
Sainte-Lucie	2007	22	103.3	98.1	15	83.5	92.8	1	5.2	12.0
	2010	19	...	...	16	95.2	94.1	2	7.0	18.0
	2014	17	...	...	14	88.0	87.4	3	10.9	22.8
	2015	17	...	...	13	88.6	87.8	3	11.5	21.9
	2017	16	...	...	12	87.9	88.4	3	13.4	26.8
Saint Vincent & Grenadines	2005	18	123.9	112.3	10	79.5	99.5	...	...	...
Saint-Vincent-Grenadines	2010	14	108.8	101.2	11	106.3	108.8	...	...	...
	2014	13	106.4	103.0	10	106.2	103.2	...	...	...
	2015	13	105.9	103.2	10	107.8	105.0	...	...	...
	2017	13	103.8	101.9	10	111.7	106.9	...	...	...
Samoa	2000	28	95.9	97.3	22	73.7	83.9	1	7.8	7.2
Samoa	2005	31	109.0	109.8	24	78.2	88.2	...	...	...
	2010	31	111.5	109.9	26	82.3	93.6	...	...	...
	2014	31	105.9	106.2	26	81.9	92.2	...	...	...
	2015	32	106.5	106.6	26	80.7	89.5	...	...	...
	2016	33	107.0	108.3	26	80.3	88.6	...	...	...
	2017	33	108.5	108.8	...	...	...	...	...	...
San Marino	2000	1	...	...	1	...	...	1	...	...
Saint-Marin	2004	1	...	...	...	...	...	...	...	...
	2010	2	* 88.8	* 100.6	2	* 96.3	* 98.2	1	* 53.0	* 77.3
	2012	2	* 93.9	* 92.6	2	* 93.5	* 95.9	1	* 50.5	* 69.9
Sao Tome and Principe	2005	30	129.0	124.0	8	41.3	43.8	...	...	...
Sao Tomé-et-Principe	2010	34	118.3	117.1	10	51.1	52.0	1	4.3	4.2
	2014	34	109.1	104.7	19	* 71.0	* 77.8	2	10.2	8.8
	2015	36	110.9	106.0	22	77.9	86.2	2	12.8	13.3
	2017	37	112.4	108.1	26	83.5	96.0	...	...	...

7
Enrollment in primary, secondary and tertiary education levels *(continued)*
Number of students enrolled (thousands) and gross enrollment ratio by sex

Inscriptions aux niveaux primaire, secondaire et supérieur *(suite)*
Nombre d'élèves inscrits (milliers) et taux brut de scolarisation par sexe

Region, country or area Région, pays ou zone	Year & Année &	Primary education Enseignement primaire			Secondary education Enseignement secondaire			Tertiary education Enseignement supérieur		
		Total ('000)	Gross enrollment ratio Taux brut de scolarisation M H	F	Total ('000)	Gross enrollment ratio Taux brut de scolarisation M H	F	Total ('000)	Gross enrollment ratio Taux brut de scolarisation M H	F
Saudi Arabia	2005	* 3 098	* 96.2	* 94.7	* 2 610	* 89.7	* 84.4	604	23.8	35.2
Arabie saoudite	2009	3 255	105.5	102.8	* 2 997	* 100.0	* 88.6	758	27.8	35.3
	2010	3 321	106.5	105.6	...	...	...	904	34.0	39.1
	2014	3 737	120.0	116.4	* 3 419	* 131.3	* 101.5	1 497	58.2	57.7
	2015	3 845	120.2	121.1	...	...	...	1 528	60.3	60.9
	2016	3 735	117.3	115.2	...	...	...	1 622	66.5	66.7
	2017	...	...	...	...	...	...	1 681	69.4	68.5
Senegal	2005	1 444	80.6	77.5	406	25.2	18.9	* 59	...	...
Sénégal	2010	1 695	80.9	85.4	725	38.2	33.3	92	* 9.3	* 5.5
	2014	1 927	79.4	89.0	1 095	49.6	49.5	141	13.0	7.7
	2015	1 977	78.8	88.3	1 136	...	...	145	13.0	7.8
	2017	2 129	78.0	90.4	1 082	43.4	47.4	163	13.9	8.5
Serbia	2005	325	* 102.5	* 103.0	632	* 87.3	* 90.0	225	* 38.6	* 50.1
Serbie	2010	283	* 96.1	* 95.6	591	* 90.5	* 92.4	227	* 42.8	* 55.6
	2014	285	* 100.9	* 101.4	548	* 93.3	* 95.4	243	* 50.5	* 66.0
	2015	279	* 101.5	* 101.2	553	* 96.0	* 97.4	241	* 50.2	* 66.9
	2017	269	* 100.3	* 100.4	538	* 95.1	* 95.9	262	* 56.7	* 76.9
Seychelles	2005	9	110.1	108.0	9	79.0	84.8	...	...	...
Seychelles	2010	9	108.8	112.1	8	* 72.5	* 77.0	...	...	...
	2014	9	116.5	114.3	7	86.1	88.9	~0	4.0	10.5
	2015	9	116.5	115.7	7	90.2	94.3	1	10.4	22.5
	2017	9	108.7	110.3	7	88.6	94.8	1	13.8	31.5
Sierra Leone	2001	554	87.1	60.9	156	* 28.3	* 20.0	9	2.8	1.1
Sierra Leone	*2002	...	...	...	...	...	...	9	2.7	1.1
	2013	1 300	115.1	114.6	417	41.6	35.5	...	...	...
	2015	1 360	112.2	113.3	449	41.1	35.4	...	...	...
	2017	1 487	120.0	121.8	492	41.9	39.8	...	...	...
Singapore	2009	295	...	...	232	...	...	213	...	...
Singapour	2010	...	...	...	...	...	...	237	...	...
	2012	...	...	...	...	...	...	255	...	...
	2016	237	* 100.9	* 100.7	180	* 108.6	* 107.7	195	* 77.9	* 90.6
Sint Maarten (Dutch part)	2014	4	...	...	3	...	...	~0	...	...
St-Martin (partie néerland.)	2015	...	...	...	...	...	...	~0	...	...
Slovakia	2005	242	98.8	97.6	663	92.8	93.7	181	35.4	45.6
Slovaquie	2010	212	101.9	101.0	550	91.8	92.8	235	45.0	69.6
	2014	214	100.2	99.3	465	90.1	91.2	198	41.6	64.3
	2015	216	98.9	98.1	454	90.5	91.5	184	40.1	61.8
	2016	220	98.4	97.3	447	90.8	91.7	167	38.1	57.9
Slovenia	2005	93	101.0	99.3	181	97.4	96.8	112	65.6	93.4
Slovénie	2010	107	99.4	98.5	138	99.2	98.1	115	72.3	107.3
	2014	112	99.1	99.2	145	110.1	109.8	91	67.4	97.6
	2015	116	99.2	99.6	143	109.6	109.9	86	65.3	95.6
	2016	120	99.1	99.5	149	114.3	116.4	81	64.2	91.7
Solomon Islands	2005	75	103.2	97.8	22	33.2	27.4	...	...	...
Îles Salomon	2010	95	116.0	113.1	40	51.9	44.9	...	...	...
	2012	98	114.0	111.6	42	49.5	47.0	...	...	...
	2014	102	114.8	111.6	...	...	...	...	...	...
	2015	104	114.1	112.9	...	...	...	...	...	...
	2017	108	114.8	113.9	...	...	...	...	...	...
Somalia Somalie	2007	457	30.3	16.8	87	8.2	3.8	...	...	...
South Africa	2005	7 314	104.5	100.7	4 658	87.2	93.1	...	...	...
Afrique du Sud	2010	7 024	99.9	95.8	4 690	89.4	94.7	...	...	...
	2014	7 195	100.6	96.3	5 221	97.2	106.4	1 019	16.4	23.2
	2015	7 556	106.6	99.0	5 279	103.5	102.0	1 051	...	...
	2016	7 570	104.2	100.3	5 164	96.0	104.9	1 054	17.1	24.0
South Sudan	2011	1 451	101.8	67.4	134	12.0	6.1	...	...	...
Soudan du sud	2015	1 274	77.8	55.1	164	12.8	6.9	...	...	...

7

Enrollment in primary, secondary and tertiary education levels *(continued)*
Number of students enrolled (thousands) and gross enrollment ratio by sex

Inscriptions aux niveaux primaire, secondaire et supérieur *(suite)*
Nombre d'élèves inscrits (milliers) et taux brut de scolarisation par sexe

Region, country or area Région, pays ou zone	Year & Année &	Primary education Enseignement primaire			Secondary education Enseignement secondaire			Tertiary education Enseignement supérieur		
		Total ('000)	Gross enrollment ratio Taux brut de scolarisation		Total ('000)	Gross enrollment ratio Taux brut de scolarisation		Total ('000)	Gross enrollment ratio Taux brut de scolarisation	
			M H	F		M H	F		M H	F
Spain	2005	2 485	103.6	102.2	3 108	113.6	121.1	1 809	60.4	74.2
Espagne	2010	2 721	105.7	105.2	3 185	122.8	125.5	1 879	70.3	87.1
	2014	2 961	103.6	104.8	3 288	129.6	130.1	1 982	81.3	96.8
	2015	3 010	103.8	105.0	3 313	129.6	129.3	1 964	82.2	97.0
	2016	3 028	103.3	104.5	3 329	127.5	128.4	1 969	83.5	99.2
Sri Lanka	2005	1 611	99.9	99.3	...	...	...	...	...	...
Sri Lanka	2010	1 721	101.0	98.4	2 525	96.3	97.5	262	11.7	20.9
	2013	1 767	101.8	99.4	2 606	97.5	101.9	298	14.8	22.9
	2014	1 778	102.4	100.1	...	...	...	302	16.8	21.7
	2015	1 778	102.7	100.6	...	...	...	308	15.6	24.0
	2017	1 747	102.6	101.1	2 649	95.5	100.5	290	15.1	22.8
State of Palestine	2005	387	88.5	87.9	657	87.7	91.7	138	40.6	41.2
État de Palestine	2010	403	91.9	90.1	711	82.4	89.0	197	41.1	54.9
	2014	442	95.5	94.9	709	78.6	86.4	214	34.6	53.8
	2015	450	94.4	94.4	721	79.4	87.2	221	34.5	54.4
	2017	477	95.4	95.1	753	81.2	89.2	218	32.4	52.5
Sudan	2005	3 177	67.5	59.2	1 344	40.2	37.3	364	11.5	13.0
Soudan	2010	4 024	75.8	68.1	1 687	45.6	39.6	523	14.7	17.3
	2014	4 388	75.4	69.8	1 974	47.1	42.9	632	16.5	17.5
	2015	4 518	76.7	70.3	2 060	46.1	45.5	653	16.9	17.1
	2017	4 900	79.5	75.1	2 205	46.5	47.3	...	...	...
Sudan [former]	2000	2 567	...	...	980	...	...	* 204	...	...
Soudan [anc.]	2005	3 278	...	...	* 1 370	...	...	...	...	...
	2009	4 744	...	...	1 837	...	...	...	...	...
Suriname	2002	64	105.7	104.3	42	63.4	88.7	5	9.6	15.8
Suriname	2005	66	106.7	104.6	46	59.6	79.3	...	...	...
	2010	71	116.7	115.9	50	63.2	81.1	...	...	...
	2014	70	117.5	119.2	52	62.8	86.1	...	...	...
	2015	72	120.7	121.6	55	68.1	89.7	...	...	...
	2017	69	115.8	115.9	...	...	...	...	...	...
Sweden	2005	658	95.9	95.7	735	104.3	103.8	427	64.8	99.9
Suède	2010	576	101.7	101.2	731	98.6	97.6	455	58.5	89.6
	2014	757	117.7	124.2	827	124.8	141.6	429	49.3	75.7
	2015	792	120.5	125.5	844	131.5	150.0	429	49.6	75.6
	2016	827	123.3	126.5	856	137.1	153.3	426	50.3	77.5
Switzerland	2005	524	102.1	101.8	575	97.9	92.1	200	48.9	42.4
Suisse	2010	493	102.8	102.3	605	97.2	94.3	249	53.0	52.5
	2013	484	103.4	103.2	617	99.8	97.3	280	55.7	56.4
	2014	484	103.2	103.3	...	...	...	290	56.6	57.5
	2015	490	104.1	103.8	614	102.9	99.4	294	56.7	58.3
	2016	498	104.8	104.0	610	104.2	100.3	295	57.3	58.4
Syrian Arab Republic	2005	2 252	121.9	118.4	2 389	71.2	68.1	361	19.1	17.1
République arabe syrienne	2010	2 429	120.8	116.5	2 732	72.3	72.4	574	27.8	24.0
	2013	1 547	77.3	74.7	1 857	49.3	49.3	660	34.0	34.5
	2014	...	...	...	...	...	...	792	42.4	44.6
	2015	...	...	...	...	...	...	773	41.0	46.7
	2016	...	...	...	...	...	...	697	36.0	42.7
Tajikistan	2005	693	100.2	96.9	984	88.5	73.6	149	28.0	13.4
Tadjikistan	2010	682	100.4	98.0	1 032	89.7	78.3	196	29.9	15.8
	2013	665	99.5	97.5	1 063	92.0	82.7	195	29.1	16.3
	2014	662	96.5	95.3	...	...	...	209	30.4	18.4
	2015	683	95.8	94.5	...	...	...	225	31.5	21.0
	2017	771	99.5	98.1	...	...	...	265	35.2	26.4
Thailand	2005	5 975	103.3	100.4	4 533	* 71.9	* 75.4	2 359	42.0	47.2
Thaïlande	2010	5 147	97.4	96.2	4 807	79.6	85.3	2 427	44.3	56.5
	2014	5 182	101.3	102.8	6 792	117.2	123.5	2 433	42.7	57.8
	2015	5 081	103.5	97.5	6 757	123.0	118.1	...	...	...
	2016	5 063	100.5	100.9	6 571	118.9	118.3	2 411	41.1	57.7
	2017	4 953	99.7	99.5	6 335	119.1	114.3	...	...	...

Enrollment in primary, secondary and tertiary education levels *(continued)*
Number of students enrolled (thousands) and gross enrollment ratio by sex

Inscriptions aux niveaux primaire, secondaire et supérieur *(suite)*
Nombre d'élèves inscrits (milliers) et taux brut de scolarisation par sexe

Region, country or area Région, pays ou zone	Year & Année &	Primary education Enseignement primaire			Secondary education Enseignement secondaire			Tertiary education Enseignement supérieur		
		Total ('000)	Gross enrollment ratio Taux brut de scolarisation M H	F	Total ('000)	Gross enrollment ratio Taux brut de scolarisation M H	F	Total ('000)	Gross enrollment ratio Taux brut de scolarisation M H	F
Timor-Leste	2002	184	...	...	53	...	...	* 6	* 8.1	* 9.3
Timor-Leste	2005	178	93.2	85.2	75	53.2	51.8	...	...	...
	2010	230	121.4	116.3	102	60.6	60.8	19	21.9	15.8
	2014	246	122.5	120.7	119	60.3	64.8	...	...	...
	2015	244	117.3	115.5	129	65.7	70.3	...	...	...
	2017	223	102.0	99.1	150	76.2	82.6	...	...	...
Togo	2005	997	122.5	104.1	404	58.8	31.3	...	...	...
Togo	2007	1 022	118.7	102.8	409	* 57.9	* 30.7	33	...	...
	2010	1 287	133.7	120.6	...	...	...	56	...	...
	2011	1 300	130.2	118.5	546	...	...	63	...	...
	2014	1 413	126.6	119.4	...	...	...	67	14.4	6.0
	2015	1 414	123.0	116.5	...	...	...	71	15.0	6.4
	2017	1 524	125.9	120.1	728	71.4	51.9	89	17.7	8.0
Tokelau	2003	~0	* 101.8	* 132.6	~0	* 83.3	* 75.8	...	...	...
Tokélaou	2016	~0	* 107.7	* 95.2	~0	* 69.6	* 70.7	...	...	...
Tonga	2002	17	111.7	106.7	15	105.5	116.3	1	* 4.2	* 7.1
Tonga	2003	18	118.2	111.9	16	...	...	1	4.8	8.0
	2004	17	114.2	108.5	14	...	...	...	...	...
	2005	17	113.4	110.1	...	...	...	...	...	...
	2010	17	109.4	107.3	15	100.4	107.2	...	...	...
	2014	17	108.6	107.4	15	86.4	94.2	...	...	...
	2015	17	108.4	105.3	16	91.1	96.3	...	...	...
Trinidad and Tobago	2004	* 137	* 103.4	* 100.0	* 105	* 82.6	* 88.5	17	10.6	13.4
Trinité-et-Tobago	*2005	130	100.7	97.8	...	...	...	...	...	...
	2010	131	108.0	104.3	...	...	...	...	...	...
Tunisia	2005	1 184	114.0	109.3	1 239	81.4	88.3	327	28.6	35.1
Tunisie	2010	1 030	109.0	105.3	1 164	87.5	93.4	370	27.8	42.6
	2011	1 028	109.4	106.0	1 152	90.0	94.2	362	26.7	43.1
	2014	1 089	114.8	111.5	1 020	...	...	332	26.4	43.1
	2015	1 115	116.0	112.7	1 008	...	...	323	26.4	43.3
	2016	1 139	116.2	113.2	1 047	88.1	97.9	294	24.1	41.2
	2017	...	...	...	...	...	...	282	23.2	41.2
Turkey	2005	6 678	105.8	100.5	6 345	91.6	76.1	2 106	38.2	27.9
Turquie	2010	6 635	102.0	100.6	7 531	87.9	80.5	3 529	62.1	50.5
	2014	5 575	106.8	106.3	10 899	104.4	101.6	5 473	93.1	80.8
	2015	5 434	103.6	102.9	10 969	104.4	101.7	6 063	101.8	88.9
	2016	5 361	101.6	100.9	11 019	104.2	101.7	6 689	110.7	96.5
Turkmenistan Turkménistan	2014	359	89.2	87.5	651	87.6	84.0	44	9.7	6.2
Turks and Caicos Islands	2005	2	...	...	2	...	...	...	...	...
Îles Turques-et-Caïques	2009	3	...	...	2	...	...	...	...	...
	2010	...	...	...	...	...	...	~0	...	...
	2014	3	...	...	2	...	...	...	...	...
	2015	3	...	...	2	...	...	~0	...	...
Tuvalu	2001	1	* 94.9	* 106.9	1	* 67.4	* 74.1	...	...	...
Tuvalu	2005	1	* 101.4	* 97.6	...	...	...	...	...	...
	2006	1	* 102.4	* 97.6	...	...	...	...	...	...
	2014	1	* 114.2	* 112.9	1	* 78.4	* 96.5	...	...	...
	2015	1	* 119.6	* 118.8	1	* 85.0	* 108.2	...	...	...
	2016	1	* 108.3	* 104.7	1	* 76.4	* 95.8	...	...	...
Uganda	2004	7 377	127.3	125.4	733	21.1	17.0	88	4.4	2.7
Ouganda	2005	7 224	120.2	119.2	...	...	...	...	...	...
	2007	7 538	116.5	117.0	1 032	26.3	21.6	...	...	...
	2010	8 375	115.9	117.7	...	...	...	121	4.4	3.5
	2013	8 459	105.6	107.6	...	...	...	...	...	...
	2014	...	...	...	...	...	...	165	5.2	4.0
	2015	8 264	97.2	99.0	...	...	...	...	...	...
	2017	8 841	97.7	100.3	...	...	...	...	...	...

Enrollment in primary, secondary and tertiary education levels *(continued)*
Number of students enrolled (thousands) and gross enrollment ratio by sex

Inscriptions aux niveaux primaire, secondaire et supérieur *(suite)*
Nombre d'élèves inscrits (milliers) et taux brut de scolarisation par sexe

Region, country or area Région, pays ou zone	Year & Année &	Primary education Enseignement primaire			Secondary education Enseignement secondaire			Tertiary education Enseignement supérieur		
		Total ('000)	Gross enrollment ratio Taux brut de scolarisation		Total ('000)	Gross enrollment ratio Taux brut de scolarisation		Total ('000)	Gross enrollment ratio Taux brut de scolarisation	
			M H	F		M H	F		M H	F
Ukraine	2005	1 946	106.6	106.2	4 043	* 99.2	* 91.8	2 605	63.1	78.0
Ukraine	2010	1 540	98.5	99.1	3 133	* 96.7	* 94.3	2 635	71.2	89.5
	2014	1 685	98.9	100.9	2 714	97.8	95.7	2 146	77.6	89.5
	2015[2]	1 537	...	...	2 370	...	...	1 776	...	...
	2017[2]	1 644	...	...	2 335	...	...	1 667	...	...
United Arab Emirates	2005	263	...	...	...	...	...	...	...	...
Émirats arabes unis	2007	284	101.5	101.5	...	...	...	80	...	...
	2010	327	...	...	...	...	...	102	...	...
	2014	410	103.6	106.3	...	...	...	143	...	...
	2015	461	112.8	114.3	...	...	...	157	...	...
	2016	468	112.8	108.9	442	98.6	93.0	160	...	...
United Kingdom	2005	4 635	106.3	106.2	5 761	103.9	107.0	2 288	49.5	68.9
Royaume-Uni	2010	4 422	105.0	104.5	5 538	102.9	103.2	2 479	50.7	67.9
	2014	4 737	107.7	107.5	6 557	124.9	129.9	2 353	49.4	65.4
	2015	4 617	102.0	101.8	6 375	123.6	127.5	2 330	49.2	65.8
	2016	4 722	101.5	101.3	7 642	144.2	160.5	2 387	50.7	68.5
United Rep. of Tanzania	2005	7 541	104.9	99.7	...	...	...	* 52	* 2.0	* 0.9
Rép.-Unie de Tanzanie	2010	8 419	97.1	97.7	1 826	34.3	27.1	85	2.4	1.9
	2013	8 232	84.9	86.2	2 052	33.1	30.3	158	4.8	2.5
	2014	8 223	81.7	83.6	...	...	...	...	...	...
	2015	8 298	79.5	82.0	...	...	...	182	5.2	2.7
	2016	8 639	80.4	82.6	...	...	...	179	...	...
	2017	9 316	84.3	86.2	1 921	25.8	25.9	...	...	...
United States of America	2005	24 455	* 102.5	* 101.4	24 432	* 94.2	* 96.0	17 272	...	...
États-Unis d'Amérique	2010	24 393	* 100.8	* 99.8	24 193	* 94.3	* 95.4	20 428	...	...
	2014	24 538	* 99.8	* 99.5	24 230	* 96.4	* 97.5	19 700	* 75.4	* 102.6
	2015	24 786	* 100.3	* 100.3	24 417	* 97.2	* 98.2	19 532	* 75.8	* 102.7
	2016	25 019	* 101.4	* 101.3	24 708	* 99.1	* 98.5	19 288	* 76.1	* 102.3
United States Virgin Islands Îles Vierges américaines	2007	...	...	...	...	...	...	2	...	...
Uruguay	2005	366	115.3	112.4	323	94.2	108.5	111	33.2	57.9
Uruguay	2006	365	116.9	113.6	323	93.5	108.5	113	34.5	58.0
	2010	342	113.9	110.2	321	93.0	109.3	132	...	...
	2014	322	109.8	107.3	339	...	...	160	...	...
	2015	317	108.6	106.2	340	...	...	156	...	...
	2016	310	106.6	104.3	348	...	...	162	...	...
Uzbekistan	2005	2 383	96.8	96.7	4 516	89.9	87.3	266	11.9	8.2
Ouzbékistan	2010	1 971	94.5	92.8	4 449	89.6	89.6	289	11.1	7.6
	2014	2 034	98.9	97.3	4 083	92.2	91.2	260	9.9	6.2
	2015	2 135	100.1	98.6	3 964	92.1	91.0	262	10.0	6.3
	2017	2 391	103.9	102.3	3 893	93.6	92.4	281	11.3	6.9
Vanuatu	2004	39	122.4	120.0	14	45.8	39.5	* 1	* 5.9	* 3.5
Vanuatu	2005	39	119.2	116.1	...	...	...	...	...	...
	2010	42	123.0	121.9	20	59.6	59.5	...	...	...
	2013	44	125.2	122.2	...	...	...	...	...	...
	2015	46	120.7	118.7	21	53.4	56.4	...	...	...
Venezuela (Boliv. Rep. of)	2003	3 450	104.0	101.9	1 866	63.4	72.9	* 983	* 38.4	* 41.2
Venezuela (Rép. boliv. du)	2004	3 453	104.0	101.8	1 954	66.1	75.3	* 1 050	...	...
	2005	3 449	103.7	101.6	2 028	68.6	77.5	...	...	...
	2008	3 439	103.0	100.3	2 224	76.1	83.8	2 109	* 57.8	* 97.7
	2009	3 462	103.3	100.5	2 252	77.3	84.5	2 123	...	...
	2010	3 458	102.9	99.9	2 255	77.2	84.7	...	...	...
	2014	3 493	101.6	99.3	2 567	88.1	94.8	...	...	...
	2015	3 476	100.9	98.2	2 523	86.2	92.8	...	...	...
	2017	3 285	94.6	92.1	2 391	80.9	87.2	...	...	...

7

Enrollment in primary, secondary and tertiary education levels *(continued)*
Number of students enrolled (thousands) and gross enrollment ratio by sex

Inscriptions aux niveaux primaire, secondaire et supérieur *(suite)*
Nombre d'élèves inscrits (milliers) et taux brut de scolarisation par sexe

Region, country or area Région, pays ou zone	Year & Année &	Primary education Enseignement primaire			Secondary education Enseignement secondaire			Tertiary education Enseignement supérieur		
		Total ('000)	Gross enrollment ratio Taux brut de scolarisation M H	F	Total ('000)	Gross enrollment ratio Taux brut de scolarisation M H	F	Total ('000)	Gross enrollment ratio Taux brut de scolarisation M H	F
Viet Nam	2005	7 773	99.5	94.5	...	...	...	1 355	18.7	13.3
Viet Nam	2010	6 923	107.6	102.2	...	...	...	2 020	22.6	22.7
	2014	7 435	109.9	108.5	...	...	...	2 692	29.7	31.2
	2015	7 544	109.1	108.3	...	...	...	2 467	28.8	28.8
	2016	7 790	109.8	110.1	...	...	...	2 307	25.3	31.3
	2017	7 802	107.7	108.2	...	...	...	...	...	...
Yemen	2005	3 220	100.6	74.4	1 455	60.7	29.7	200	13.9	5.1
Yémen	2010	3 427	99.5	81.2	1 561	53.4	33.2	272	14.6	6.4
	2011	3 641	104.0	84.8	1 643	55.5	35.2	267	13.7	6.1
	2013	3 875	105.4	88.5	1 768	57.4	39.5	...	...	...
	2016	3 900	98.6	86.1	1 916	58.9	42.8	...	...	...
Zambia	2005	2 573	112.5	107.4	...	...	...	...	...	...
Zambie	2010	2 899	104.5	105.9	...	...	...	...	...	...
	2012	3 135	106.8	107.7	...	...	...	57	4.6	3.5
	2014	3 218	104.2	104.7	...	...	...	...	...	...
	2015	3 216	101.8	102.2	...	...	...	...	...	...
	2017	3 285	98.7	100.9	...	...	...	...	...	...
Zimbabwe	2003	2 362	98.5	97.2	758	40.8	36.8	...	...	...
Zimbabwe	2010	...	...	...	...	...	...	95	6.8	5.4
	2013	2 663	99.5	97.9	957	47.6	46.7	94	6.5	5.5
	2015	...	...	...	...	...	...	136	8.9	8.0

Source:

United Nations Educational, Scientific and Cultural Organization
(UNESCO), Montreal, the UNESCO Institute for Statistics (UIS) statistics
database, last accessed March 2019.

Source:

Organisation des Nations Unies pour l'éducation, la science et la culture
(UNESCO), Montréal, base de données statistiques de l'Institut de
statistique (ISU) de l'UNESCO, dernier accès mars 2019.

& Data relate to the calendar year in which the academic year ends.

& Les données se réfèrent à l'année civile durant laquelle l'année scolaire
se termine.

1   For statistical purposes, the data for China do not include those for
the Hong Kong Special Administrative Region (Hong Kong SAR),
Macao Special Administrative Region (Macao SAR) and Taiwan
Province of China.

2   The Government of Ukraine has informed the United Nations that it
is not in a position to provide statistical data concerning the
Autonomous Republic of Crimea and the city of Sevastopol.

1   Pour la présentation des statistiques, les données pour la Chine ne
comprennent pas la région administrative spéciale de Hong Kong
(RAS de Hong Kong), la région administrative spéciale de Macao
(RAS de Macao) et la province chinoise de Taïwan.

2   Le gouvernement Ukrainien a informé l'ONU qu'il n'est pas en
mesure de fournir des donnees statistiques concernant la République
autome de Crimée et la ville de Sébastopol.

Teaching staff at the primary, secondary and tertiary levels
Number of teachers and Pupil teacher ratio

Personnel enseignant au niveau primaire, secondaire et supérieur
Nombre d'enseignants et ratio élèves/enseignant par niveau d'enseignement

Region, country or area Région, pays ou zone	Year & Année &	Primary education Enseignant primaire		Secondary education Enseignant secondaire		Tertiary education Enseignant supérieur	
		Total Totale ('000)	Pupil-teacher ratio Ratio élèves/ enseignant	Total Totale ('000)	Pupil-teacher ratio Ratio élèves/ enseignant	Total Totale ('000)	Pupil-teacher ratio Ratio élèves/ enseignant
Total, all countries or areas	2005	* 26 891	* 25.2	* 28 507	* 17.9	9 231	...
Total, tous pays ou zones	2010	28 669	24.3	32 355	16.9	11 161	...
	2015	31 185	23.1	33 528	17.4	* 12 981	...
	*2017	31 573	23.6	34 555	17.1	13 162	...
Northern Africa	2005	944	24.4	* 994	* 17.0	* 173	...
Afrique septentrionale	2010	972	24.3	* 1 162	* 15.0	* 209	...
	*2015	1 176	21.9	1 202	15.7	258	...
	2017	1 197	22.9	1 218	* 16.1	* 262	...
Sub-Saharan Africa	2005	2 577	44.0	1 178	27.2	* 178	...
Afrique subsaharienne	2010	3 168	42.9	* 1 890	* 23.8	* 261	...
	2015	4 061	38.6	* 2 695	* 21.2	* 349	...
	*2017	4 280	38.5	2 731	21.7	...	...
Northern America	2005	1 865	14.4	1 774	15.2	1 386	...
Amérique septentrionale	2010	1 920	13.8	1 898	14.1	1 646	...
	2015	1 847	14.7	1 803	15.0	1 786	...
	*2016	1 864	14.7	1 822	15.0	1 735	...
Latin America & the Caribbean	2005	2 935	23.5	3 469	17.0	* 1 228	...
Amérique latine et Caraïbes	2010	2 908	23.1	3 542	17.3	* 1 689	...
	2015	2 985	21.6	3 907	16.4	1 850	...
	*2017	3 010	21.5	3 887	16.5	1 954	...
Central Asia	2005	242	19.8	793	11.4	* 102	...
Asie centrale	2010	226	18.8	747	11.5	113	...
	2015	253	19.1	784	10.2	117	...
	2017	252	21.5	840	9.5	113	...
Eastern Asia	2005	* 6 683	* 18.9	* 6 500	* 17.7	2 179	...
Asie orientale	2010	6 658	17.1	7 435	15.3	2 405	...
	2012	6 581	16.9	7 594	14.4	* 2 535	...
	2015	6 565	16.3	7 281	13.7	...	...
	2017	6 740	16.6	7 309	13.2	...	...
South-central Asia	*2005	4 826	38.6	4 949	26.2	844	...
Asie centrale et du Sud	2010	* 5 501	* 35.6	6 446	23.6	* 1 372	...
	2015	6 308	31.8	6 531	27.3	1 915	...
	*2017	6 170	34.1	7 278	25.2	1 952	...
South-eastern Asia	2005	2 941	23.2	2 239	18.2	580	...
Asie du Sud-Est	2010	3 248	21.1	* 2 701	* 16.9	* 691	...
	*2015	3 711	18.5	2 767	18.6	760	...
	2017	3 646	18.8	2 856	18.2	770	...
Southern Asia	*2005	4 583	39.6	4 156	29.0	742	...
Asie méridionale	2010	* 5 275	* 36.4	5 699	25.2	* 1 259	...
	2015	6 055	32.3	5 747	29.7	1 798	...
	*2017	5 919	34.6	6 438	27.2	1 839	...
Western Asia	2005	* 1 289	* 18.7	* 1 344	* 14.7	307	...
Asie occidentale	2010	* 1 445	* 17.6	* 1 595	* 14.0	372	...
	2015	* 1 613	* 16.6	* 1 795	* 14.1	480	...
	*2016	1 580	16.9	1 832	14.0	505	...
	*2017	1 601	16.9	...	...	...	...
Europe	2005	2 673	14.4	5 836	11.2	2 272	...
Europe	2010	2 673	13.7	* 5 470	* 10.7	* 2 412	...
	2015	2 724	14.1	5 328	10.8	2 377	...
	*2017	2 827	14.0	5 387	10.9	2 368	...
Oceania	*2005	159	19.8	...	...	...	...
Océanie	*2010	175	20.3	...	...	...	...
	*2015	195	21.1	...	...	...	...
	*2017	203	21.0	...	...	...	...

Teaching staff at the primary, secondary and tertiary levels *(continued)*
Number of teachers and Pupil teacher ratio

Personnel enseignant au niveau primaire, secondaire et supérieur *(suite)*
Nombre d'enseignants et ratio élèves/enseignant par niveau d'enseignement

Region, country or area Région, pays ou zone	Year & Année &	Primary education Enseignant primaire		Secondary education Enseignant secondaire		Tertiary education Enseignant supérieur	
		Total Totale ('000)	Pupil-teacher ratio Ratio élèves/ enseignant	Total Totale ('000)	Pupil-teacher ratio Ratio élèves/ enseignant	Total Totale ('000)	Pupil-teacher ratio Ratio élèves/ enseignant
Afghanistan	2004	...	...	...	...	2	15.5
Afghanistan	2007	110	42.8	33	31.6	...	...
	2009	115	42.8	...	...	3	28.5
	2010	119	44.4	...	...	...	...
	2014	...	...	...	...	11	23.9
	2015	143	44.3	72	37.7	...	...
	2017	144	44.0	75	38.7	...	...
	2018	...	...	...	...	17	21.5
Albania	2001	13	21.8	22	17.0	3	13.5
Albanie	2003	12	21.5	22	17.7	...	...
	2010	11	19.7	24	14.8	...	...
	2014	10	18.9	23	14.3	7	23.6
	2015	10	18.6	23	13.5	...	...
	2017	10	17.9	24	11.6	9	15.1
Algeria	2005	171	25.4	...	...	28	27.9
Algérie	2010	142	23.3	...	...	40	28.8
	2015	165	23.8	...	...	54	24.0
	2017	177	24.2	...	...	58	26.8
American Samoa Samoa américaines	2007	...	...	...	...	~0	15.3
Andorra	2004	~0	12.7	~0	7.1	~0	3.9
Andorre	2005	~0	11.5	~0	7.8	...	...
	2008	~0	10.0	...	...	~0	5.3
	2009	~0	10.3	...	...	~0	...
	2010	~0	9.6	...	...	...	...
	2015	~0	9.9	1	8.1	~0	4.6
	2017	~0	10.5	1	8.2	~0	3.9
Angola	*2001	...	...	22	19.0	...	...
Angola	*2002	...	...	...	...	1	9.8
	2006	...	...	...	...	1	37.9
	2010	94	45.6	...	...	...	...
	2011	118	42.5	32	27.4	8	18.2
	2015	112	50.0	73	...	9	25.5
	2016	96	...	76	26.8	...	...
Anguilla	2005	~0	15.4	* ~0	* 12.5	~0	1.4
Anguilla	2007	~0	16.1	~0	10.4	~0	3.9
	2008	~0	14.1	...	...	~0	3.9
	2010	~0	14.5	...	...	...	...
	2011	~0	14.8	~0	8.5	...	...
Antigua and Barbuda	2000	1	18.7	~0	13.4	...	...
Antigua-et-Barbuda	2010	1	15.1	1	12.2	~0	6.8
	2012	1	13.8	1	11.6	~0	8.2
	2015	1	14.3	1	11.5	...	...
	2017	1	12.1	1	9.6	...	...
Argentina	2004	274	18.0	254	15.4	142	14.9
Argentine	2005	279	17.4	257	15.1	...	...
	2008	289	17.2	324	12.2	...	...
	2009	...	...	...	...	142	16.8
Armenia	2005	6	21.2	...	...	17	6.8
Arménie	2007	7	19.3	...	...	16	8.3
	2010	...	...	...	...	16	9.2
	2015	...	...	...	...	16	6.8
	2017	...	...	...	...	15	6.9
Aruba	2005	1	18.1	1	14.2	~0	9.2
Aruba	2010	1	16.8	1	13.8	~0	10.4
	2012	1	14.8	1	15.1	~0	9.9
	2015	...	...	...	...	~0	13.6
	2016	...	...	...	...	~0	8.6
Austria	2005	29	12.4	71	11.0	...	...
Autriche	2010	30	11.0	75	10.0	47	8.3
	2015	31	10.6	72	9.6	61	7.0
	2017	33	10.0	74	9.3	60	7.2

8

Teaching staff at the primary, secondary and tertiary levels *(continued)*
Number of teachers and Pupil teacher ratio

Personnel enseignant au niveau primaire, secondaire et supérieur *(suite)*
Nombre d'enseignants et ratio élèves/enseignant par niveau d'enseignement

Region, country or area Région, pays ou zone	Year & Année &	Primary education Enseignant primaire		Secondary education Enseignant secondaire		Tertiary education Enseignant supérieur	
		Total Totale ('000)	Pupil-teacher ratio Ratio élèves/ enseignant	Total Totale ('000)	Pupil-teacher ratio Ratio élèves/ enseignant	Total Totale ('000)	Pupil-teacher ratio Ratio élèves/ enseignant
Azerbaijan	2005	42	13.4	...	...	...	...
Azerbaïdjan	2010	44	11.0	...	...	26	7.0
	2015	41	13.5	...	...	21	9.7
	2017	39	15.5	127	...	21	10.0
Bahamas	*2004	2	16.8	2	14.2	...	...
Bahamas	2005	...	...	2	13.6	...	...
	2010	2	14.1	3	12.1	...	...
	2016	2	19.0	2	11.8	...	...
Bahrain	2003	...	...	...	...	1	22.3
Bahreïn	*2004	...	...	...	...	1	...
	2015	9	11.7	9	9.9	3	15.4
	2017	9	12.2	10	10.1	2	19.4
Bangladesh	2005	345	47.0	423	23.9	52	17.4
Bangladesh	2009	361	* 45.8	387	28.2	59	26.9
	2010	395	* 43.0	400	28.3	...	...
	2013	...	...	378	35.2	...	...
	2014	...	...	...	...	90	22.9
	2015	528	...	...	...	...	...
	2017	574	30.1	451	34.0	91	30.3
Barbados	*2001	1	17.0	1	17.2	1	13.5
Barbade	2005	1	15.1	* 1	* 15.9	...	...
	2006	...	...	1	14.6	...	...
	2007	2	14.5	...	...	1	14.5
	*2010	2	13.0	...	...	...	...
	2015	2	13.4	1	17.5	...	...
	2017	1	14.1	1	18.5	...	...
Belarus	2005	24	16.0	...	...	42	12.7
Bélarus	2010	24	15.0	...	...	41	14.0
	2015	22	17.6	77	8.4	33	14.6
	2017	22	18.8	79	8.2	29	14.4
Belgium	2005	64	11.5	...	...	26	15.1
Belgique	2010	66	11.0	...	...	29	15.6
	2015	70	11.2	129	9.4	29	17.6
	2016	71	11.3	131	9.1	30	16.7
Belize	2005	2	23.6	* 2	* 18.7	...	...
Belize	2010	2	22.2	2	16.8	...	...
	2015	3	20.4	2	16.3	1	14.2
	2017	3	19.6	2	16.6	1	13.9
Benin	2001	20	53.5	* 12	* 21.6	* 1	* 29.4
Bénin	2004	26	51.6	* 14	* 23.9	...	...
	2005	28	46.8	...	...	...	...
	2010	39	46.4	...	...	6	17.8
	2011	42	44.2	...	...	6	17.3
	2015	50	45.0	93	10.3	...	...
	2016	54	41.6	90	11.0	...	...
	2017	52	43.6	...	...	...	...
Bermuda	2005	1	8.3	1	7.0	~0	...
Bermudes	2010	1	7.4	1	5.4	~0	15.3
	2015	~0	10.4	1	6.3	~0	18.7
	2016	~0	...	1	...	...	...
	2017	...	...	...	...	~0	...
Bhutan	2005	3	31.1	1	28.1	...	...
Bhoutan	2010	4	25.9	3	21.4	1	6.7
	2012	5	24.0	3	19.9	1	7.7
	2015	2	40.0	6	12.1	...	...
	2017	3	34.6	7	11.0	...	...
Bolivia (Plurin. State of)	2015	74	18.1	55	20.8	...	...
Bolivie (État plurin. de)	2017	73	18.8	60	20.6	...	...
Bosnia and Herzegovina	2010	...	...	...	...	8	12.4
Bosnie-Herzégovine	2015	9	17.2	27	10.1	10	11.3
	2017	9	17.2	27	9.3	10	10.2

Teaching staff at the primary, secondary and tertiary levels *(continued)*
Number of teachers and Pupil teacher ratio

Personnel enseignant au niveau primaire, secondaire et supérieur *(suite)*
Nombre d'enseignants et ratio élèves/enseignant par niveau d'enseignement

Region, country or area Région, pays ou zone	Year & Année &	Primary education Enseignant primaire		Secondary education Enseignant secondaire		Tertiary education Enseignant supérieur	
		Total Totale ('000)	Pupil-teacher ratio Ratio élèves/ enseignant	Total Totale ('000)	Pupil-teacher ratio Ratio élèves/ enseignant	Total Totale ('000)	Pupil-teacher ratio Ratio élèves/ enseignant
Botswana	2005	13	25.6	13	13.8	...	...
Botswana	2007	13	25.2	13	13.8	...	...
	2009	13	25.5	...	...	...	...
	2012	14	23.4	...	...	2	21.8
	2013	15	22.6	...	...	...	...
	2017	...	...	...	...	3	18.3
Brazil	2005	887	21.0	1 612	15.4	293	15.6
Brésil	2010	762	22.2	1 413	16.7	345	19.0
	2015	792	20.6	1 429	16.5	429	19.3
	2016	793	20.3	1 418	16.6	427	19.5
British Virgin Islands	2004	~0	13.9	~0	9.3	~0	10.9
Îles Vierges britanniques	2005	~0	14.9	~0	9.3	...	...
	2009	~0	13.5	~0	8.7	~0	11.5
	2010	~0	13.2	~0	8.7	...	...
	2015	~0	11.7	~0	8.1	~0	9.5
	2016	~0	10.5	~0	7.5	~0	9.3
	2017	~0	11.6	~0	8.7	...	...
Brunei Darussalam	2005	5	10.1	4	10.1	1	8.5
Brunéi Darussalam	2009	4	12.0	5	10.5	1	9.6
	2010	4	11.3	...	...	1	8.3
	2015	4	10.0	5	8.8	1	11.9
	2017	4	10.2	5	8.7	1	12.2
Bulgaria	2005	18	16.2	57	12.0	21	11.3
Bulgarie	2010	15	17.5	44	12.1	21	13.8
	2014	15	17.7	39	13.2	23	12.3
	2016	15	17.6	39	12.6	23	11.8
Burkina Faso	2003	23	44.7	8	31.3	...	...
Burkina Faso	2005	27	47.2	...	...	2	14.1
	2010	39	52.4	18	30.3	3	17.7
	2015	64	42.2	38	25.2	5	18.3
	2017	75	40.7	50	23.3	5	19.5
Burundi	2005	21	48.7	* 7	* 22.8	1	16.1
Burundi	2010	37	50.6	11	29.9	2	16.4
	2014	47	43.7	16	37.2	2	25.2
	2015	48	43.2	19	35.8	...	...
	2017	43	49.6	24	28.0	3	19.8
Cabo Verde	2005	3	26.0	2	23.5	~0	8.1
Cabo Verde	2010	3	23.6	4	17.5	1	11.0
	2015	3	21.9	4	16.4	1	9.2
	2017	3	21.1	4	15.6	1	8.8
Cambodia	2003	49	56.2	24	23.6	2	17.4
Cambodge	2005	51	53.2	...	...	2	22.7
	2006	51	50.4	27	30.0	3	29.0
	2007	49	50.9	30	28.9	...	...
	2010	47	48.4	...	...	...	...
	2015	48	45.5	...	...	12	17.7
	2017	51	41.7	...	...	15	13.9
Cameroon	2005	* 62	* 47.8	* 48	* 16.2	3	* 31.5
Cameroun	2008	70	46.0	43	26.3	4	38.5
	2010	77	45.8	...	...	* 4	* 52.0
	2014	94	44.2	98	20.4	* 7	* 52.3
	2015	105	41.5	106	19.9	...	...
	2016	105	42.7	115	19.3	...	...
	2017	98	44.6	...	...	...	...
Canada	2000	141	17.4	...	...	...	...
Canada	*2010	...	...	...	...	207	6.9
	*2015	...	...	...	...	205	7.6
	*2016	...	...	...	...	174	9.2

8

Teaching staff at the primary, secondary and tertiary levels *(continued)*
Number of teachers and Pupil teacher ratio

Personnel enseignant au niveau primaire, secondaire et supérieur *(suite)*
Nombre d'enseignants et ratio élèves/enseignant par niveau d'enseignement

Region, country or area Région, pays ou zone	Year & Année &	Primary education Enseignant primaire		Secondary education Enseignant secondaire		Tertiary education Enseignant supérieur	
		Total Totale ('000)	Pupil-teacher ratio Ratio élèves/ enseignant	Total Totale ('000)	Pupil-teacher ratio Ratio élèves/ enseignant	Total Totale ('000)	Pupil-teacher ratio Ratio élèves/ enseignant
Cayman Islands	2001	~0	15.2	* ~0	* 9.8	* ~0	* 18.8
Îles Caïmanes	2005	~0	12.8	* ~0	* 10.3	...	...
	2008	~0	12.1	~0	8.9	~0	26.8
	2012	~0	13.3	1	5.3	...	...
	2013	~0	13.0	...	...	...	...
	2018	~0	15.7	~0	11.0	...	...
Central African Republic	2000	...	...	...	...	~0	19.5
République centrafricaine	2005	5	88.6	...	...	...	...
	2009	6	94.6	1	80.1	~0	30.7
	2010	8	84.3	2	...	...	...
	2011	8	81.3	2	66.8	~0	34.6
	2012	8	80.1	2	68.1	...	...
	2016	10	83.4	3	34.6	...	...
	2017	...	...	4	31.6	...	...
Chad	2005	20	63.2	* 7	* 33.5	1	9.5
Tchad	2009	27	61.0	13	32.3	2	8.6
	2010	28	62.2	13	32.5	...	...
	2011	31	62.6	14	32.0	2	10.9
	2015	41	55.5	19	27.5	...	...
	2016	39	56.9	20	27.1	...	...
Chile	2005	66	26.1	66	24.8	...	...
Chili	2010	66	23.4	69	21.9	70	14.1
	2013	75	19.5	75	21.0	78	15.0
	2015	80	18.4	80	19.4	...	...
	2017	85	17.8	83	18.4	...	...
China	2003	5 779	21.1	5 138	18.6	* 742	* 20.5
Chine	2005	...	...	...	...	1 404	14.7
	2010	5 997	16.8	6 417	15.5	1 557	19.9
	2011	5 939	16.8	6 431	15.2	1 607	19.5
	2015	5 889	16.3	6 234	13.8	...	...
	2017	6 046	16.6	6 267	13.3	...	...
China, Hong Kong SAR	2005	25	18.3	* 28	* 18.1	...	...
Chine, RAS de Hong Kong	2010	23	15.2	* 30	* 16.7	...	...
	2015	24	13.7	* 30	* 13.0	...	...
	2017	26	13.8	31	11.5	...	...
China, Macao SAR	2005	2	23.2	2	22.4	2	15.4
Chine, RAS de Macao	2010	2	16.1	2	16.2	2	14.4
	2015	2	14.1	3	11.4	2	15.4
	2017	2	13.5	3	10.1	2	14.5
Colombia	2005	187	28.3	164	26.2	94	13.1
Colombie	2009	181	29.3	187	26.7	* 110	* 14.2
	2010	181	28.1	187	27.1	...	...
	2015	185	24.2	181	26.5	149	15.4
	2016	183	24.3	183	26.2	153	15.7
	2017	184	23.6	184	26.0	...	...
Comoros	2003	3	35.9	3	11.3	~0	13.7
Comores	2004	3	35.0	3	13.8	...	...
	2008	4	30.2	...	...	...	...
	2010	...	...	...	...	~0	17.1
	2013	4	27.8	8	8.7	~0	25.7
	2014	...	...	8	8.6	~0	26.3
	2017	6	18.9	13	5.3	...	...
Congo	2003	8	65.2	* 7	* 28.1	* 1	* 13.8
Congo	2004	7	82.8	* 7	* 34.3	...	...
	2009	10	64.4	...	...	1	20.0
	2010	14	49.1	...	...	...	...
	2012	17	44.4	18	18.7	3	11.8
	2013	...	...	...	...	3	12.3
Cook Islands	2005	~0	16.1	~0	15.6	...	...
Îles Cook	2010	~0	15.0	~0	16.2	...	...
	2015	~0	17.2	~0	13.9	~0	...
	2016	~0	17.4	~0	15.7	~0	...

Teaching staff at the primary, secondary and tertiary levels *(continued)*
Number of teachers and Pupil teacher ratio

Personnel enseignant au niveau primaire, secondaire et supérieur *(suite)*
Nombre d'enseignants et ratio élèves/enseignant par niveau d'enseignement

Region, country or area Région, pays ou zone	Year & Année &	Primary education Enseignant primaire		Secondary education Enseignant secondaire		Tertiary education Enseignant supérieur	
		Total Totale ('000)	Pupil-teacher ratio Ratio élèves/ enseignant	Total Totale ('000)	Pupil-teacher ratio Ratio élèves/ enseignant	Total Totale ('000)	Pupil-teacher ratio Ratio élèves/ enseignant
Costa Rica	2002	24	22.6	15	18.8	...	...
Costa Rica	2005	25	21.3	...	...	...	...
	2010	29	17.9	27	15.5	...	...
	2015	37	12.7	33	14.0	...	...
	2016	40	12.0	36	12.7	...	...
Côte d'Ivoire	*2003	48	42.4	...	...	...	...
Côte d'Ivoire	2009	57	42.1	...	...	...	...
	2010	...	...	...	...	10	14.2
	2014	75	42.5	64	22.3	19	9.1
	2015	80	42.1	...	...	19	10.3
	2016	85	42.5	67	25.8	18	11.5
	2017	89	42.4	72	26.3	...	...
Croatia	2005	11	17.5	39	10.1	...	...
Croatie	2010	12	14.3	48	8.1	16	9.5
	2015	12	13.7	51	7.0	16	10.1
	2016	12	13.5	52	6.7	17	9.8
Cuba	2005	87	10.3	85	11.1	91	5.2
Cuba	2010	93	9.1	85	9.5	153	5.2
	2015	84	8.9	91	9.0	57	4.6
	2017	83	8.8	86	9.5	62	4.6
Cyprus	2005	3	17.7	6	11.3	1	13.8
Chypre	2010	4	13.8	7	9.8	3	12.6
	2015	5	11.9	6	10.4	3	12.7
	2016	5	...	7	...	3	...
Czechia	2005	31	16.2	93	10.4	24	13.8
Tchéquie	2006	30	15.7	92	10.5	23	15.0
	2010	25	18.7	76	11.0	...	...
	2013	26	18.9	69	11.5	16	26.0
Dem. People's Rep. Korea	2009	70	22.0	124	...	69	8.6
Rép. pop. dém. de Corée	2015	66	20.5	123	17.5	63	9.0
	2018	74	20.3	124	...	...	...
Dem. Rep. of the Congo	2002	159	34.3	...	...	...	...
Rép. dém. du Congo	2009	274	37.3	212	16.0	23	16.4
	2010	286	37.0	218	16.0	...	...
	2013	340	37.1	281	14.2	29	15.3
	2015	415	33.2	324	14.2	...	...
Denmark	2001	40	9.9	44	10.1	...	...
Danemark	2014	44	10.7	49	11.3	28	10.7
	2015	...	...	...	...	37	8.5
Djibouti	2002	...	...	1	31.9	* ~0	* 15.2
Djibouti	2004	1	34.5	...	...	~0	12.3
	2005	...	...	...	...	~0	17.7
	2009	2	34.1	1	29.7	~0	20.1
	2010	...	...	...	...	~0	20.5
	2011	2	35.2	2	27.9	~0	19.2
	2015	2	33.0	3	22.8	...	...
	2018	2	29.4	3	25.4	...	...
Dominica	2005	1	18.2	~0	15.1	...	...
Dominique	2010	1	16.0	1	13.2	...	...
	2015	1	14.0	1	10.7	...	...
	2016	1	13.1	1	...	...	...
Dominican Republic	2003	...	...	...	...	11	25.8
République dominicaine	2005	53	24.3	31	26.4	...	...
	2010	52	25.5	32	28.2	...	...
	2015	71	18.3	42	22.1	19	25.5
	2017	66	18.9	50	18.6	20	27.4
Ecuador	2001	85	23.1	* 69	* 13.6	15	...
Équateur	2005	87	22.9	* 76	* 13.9	...	...
	2008	...	...	...	...	27	19.9
	2010	96	22.0	83	19.9	...	...
	2015	80	25.1	86	22.3	40	16.6
	2016	78	25.1	88	21.9	...	...

Teaching staff at the primary, secondary and tertiary levels *(continued)*
Number of teachers and Pupil teacher ratio

Personnel enseignant au niveau primaire, secondaire et supérieur *(suite)*
Nombre d'enseignants et ratio élèves/enseignant par niveau d'enseignement

Region, country or area Région, pays ou zone	Year & Année &	Primary education Enseignant primaire		Secondary education Enseignant secondaire		Tertiary education Enseignant supérieur	
		Total Totale ('000)	Pupil-teacher ratio Ratio élèves/ enseignant	Total Totale ('000)	Pupil-teacher ratio Ratio élèves/ enseignant	Total Totale ('000)	Pupil-teacher ratio Ratio élèves/ enseignant
Egypt Égypte	*2004	363	21.9	488	17.1	81	28.0
	*2005	373	25.6	...	...	...	...
	2009	382	27.2	549	12.1	...	...
	2010	380	27.7	...	...	...	...
	2014	...	...	...	...	107	23.9
	2017	511	23.8	588	15.2	...	...
El Salvador El Salvador	2005	24	43.2	* 18	* 28.9	8	15.2
	2009	31	31.0	23	24.4	9	16.2
	2010	...	...	...	...	9	16.5
	2015	25	29.7	19	30.8	10	18.1
	2017	24	28.3	19	27.8	11	17.7
Equatorial Guinea Guinée équatoriale	2000	2	43.4	* 1	* 23.2	~0	4.9
	2003	2	32.0	...	...	...	...
	2005	...	...	1	19.2	...	...
	2010	3	27.2	...	...	...	...
	2015	4	23.2	...	...	...	...
Eritrea Érythrée	2004	8	46.7	4	47.8	~0	10.8
	2005	8	47.5	4	51.3	...	...
	2010	8	38.0	6	38.7	1	19.2
	2015	8	43.3	6	38.9	1	19.5
	2016	9	...	6	...	1	14.1
	2017	9	39.2	7	36.6	...	...
Estonia Estonie	2001	8	14.1	12	10.1	7	8.8
	2005	...	...	...	...	6	10.7
	2006	8	10.6	...	...	* 6	* 10.7
	2010	6	11.7	11	8.8	...	...
	2013	7	11.5	10	8.1	...	...
	2016	7	11.3	9	8.8	4	11.4
Eswatini Eswatini	2005	7	32.9	4	16.7	~0	13.7
	2006	7	33.3	4	19.3	~0	12.3
	2010	7	32.3	5	18.1	...	...
	2013	9	28.1	6	16.0	~0	17.6
	2015	9	27.6	6	15.8	1	...
	2016	9	27.3	7	15.5	...	...
Ethiopia Éthiopie	2000	87	67.3	...	...	2	27.1
	2005	...	...	...	...	5	39.4
	2009	234	57.9	82	47.4	12	34.1
	2010	252	54.1	98	43.1	...	...
	2011	260	55.1	113	40.3	...	...
	*2012	...	...	122	40.4	...	...
	2014	...	...	...	...	24	31.2
Fiji Fidji	2004	4	28.2	* 5	* 22.4	...	...
	2008	4	26.0	5	18.7	...	...
	2012	4	28.0	5	19.3	...	...
	2016	6[1]	19.7	...	...	...	...
Finland Finlande	2005	25	15.5	42	10.3	19	16.4
	2010	25	14.0	43	9.9	15	19.7
	2014	26	13.3	42	12.8	16	19.3
	2016	27	13.3	41	13.2	15	19.9
France France	2004	203	18.6	511	11.4	136	15.9
	2005	216	18.6	528	11.4	...	...
	2010	234	17.8	463	12.7	...	...
	2013	229	18.2	457	12.9	110	21.3
Gabon Gabon	2003	8	36.0	...	...	...	...
	2011	13	24.5	...	...	...	...
Gambia Gambie	2004	5	38.5	...	...	~0	11.4
	2005	6	36.6	...	...	...	...
	*2010	6	37.5	...	...	...	...
	2012	7	33.9	...	...	~0	23.2
	2015	8	37.1	6	...	...	...
	2018	10	36.1	8	...	...	...

8   Teaching staff at the primary, secondary and tertiary levels *(continued)*
     Number of teachers and Pupil teacher ratio

     Personnel enseignant au niveau primaire, secondaire et supérieur *(suite)*
     Nombre d'enseignants et ratio élèves/enseignant par niveau d'enseignement

Region, country or area Région, pays ou zone	Year & Année &	Primary education Enseignant primaire		Secondary education Enseignant secondaire		Tertiary education Enseignant supérieur	
		Total Totale ('000)	Pupil-teacher ratio Ratio élèves/ enseignant	Total Totale ('000)	Pupil-teacher ratio Ratio élèves/ enseignant	Total Totale ('000)	Pupil-teacher ratio Ratio élèves/ enseignant
Georgia	2003	17	14.5	49	9.2	29	5.5
Géorgie	2005	...	...	...	...	29	5.9
	2009	* 34	* 8.9	* 45	* 7.6	12	7.7
	2010	...	...	...	...	13	7.9
	2015	32	9.0	38	7.2	18	7.1
	2017	33	9.0	37	7.4	20	7.3
Germany	2002	236	14.3	590	14.3	277	...
Allemagne	2005	234	14.1	596	13.9	...	...
	2010	242	12.7	594	12.9	...	...
	2015	236	12.2	586	12.1	396	7.5
	2016	238	12.1	589	12.0	402	7.6
Ghana	2005	89	32.8	* 73	* 18.8	...	...
Ghana	2009	111	33.1	99	18.3	...	...
	*2010	121	...	112	...	...	...
	2015	139	31.3	147	16.6	14	28.9
	2016	143	30.6	148	17.0	15	27.3
	2018	162	27.2	167	16.0	...	...
Gibraltar	2001	~0	20.7	~0	11.7	...	...
Gibraltar	2009	~0	16.0	~0	5.9	...	...
	2017	~0	14.2	~0	15.0	...	...
Greece	2005	59	11.1	86	8.3	27	23.8
Grèce	2007	62	10.3	87	7.9	29	20.8
	2014	67	9.4	80	8.3	15	44.5
	2015	67	9.6	76	8.7	...	...
	2016	70	9.3	79	8.4	18	39.7
Grenada	2004	1	17.7	* 1	* 20.1	...	...
Grenade	2005	1	18.2	...	...	...	...
	2010	1	16.1	1	15.5	...	...
	2015	1	17.0	1	11.9	2	4.3
	2017	1	16.2	1	11.8	8	1.2
Guatemala	2002	69	30.1	44	13.7	4	27.7
Guatemala	*2003	...	...	...	...	4	...
	2005	76	31.1	48	15.8	...	...
	2010	99	26.9	77	14.0	...	...
	2014	105	23.0	92	12.7	...	...
	2015	117	20.4	...	...	...	...
	2017	116	20.2	116	10.5	...	...
Guinea	2005	27	44.9	12	* 34.4	...	...
Guinée	2008	31	44.1	16	33.3	...	...
	2010	34	42.2	...	...	5	19.1
	2011	35	44.1	19	33.1	6	17.9
	2014	38	45.6	...	...	6	18.7
	2015	36	...	...	...	...	...
	2016	38	47.1	...	...	...	...
Guinea-Bissau	2000	3	44.1	* 2	* 15.0	...	...
Guinée-Bissau	2006	4	62.2	1	37.3	~0	147.6
	2010	5	51.9	...	...	...	...
Guyana	2005	4	28.0	* 4	* 18.0	1	12.6
Guyana	2010	4	24.6	4	21.4	1	10.6
	2012	4	23.2	4	20.3	1	13.1
Honduras	2004	38	32.9	17	...	* 7	* 17.1
Honduras	*2005	42	29.1	...	...	...	...
	2009	37	33.9	...	...	...	...
	2010	...	...	...	...	9	19.8
	2015	40	29.1	40	16.1	10	20.0
	2017	44	25.6	39	16.7	...	...
Hungary	2005	41	10.4	97	9.9	25	17.2
Hongrie	2010	37	10.6	89	10.2	25	15.8
	2015	36	11.0	80	10.3	21	14.6
	2016	37	10.8	81	10.0	22	13.6

Teaching staff at the primary, secondary and tertiary levels *(continued)*
Number of teachers and Pupil teacher ratio

Personnel enseignant au niveau primaire, secondaire et supérieur *(suite)*
Nombre d'enseignants et ratio élèves/enseignant par niveau d'enseignement

Region, country or area Région, pays ou zone	Year & Année &	Primary education Enseignant primaire		Secondary education Enseignant secondaire		Tertiary education Enseignant supérieur	
		Total Totale ('000)	Pupil-teacher ratio Ratio élèves/ enseignant	Total Totale ('000)	Pupil-teacher ratio Ratio élèves/ enseignant	Total Totale ('000)	Pupil-teacher ratio Ratio élèves/ enseignant
Iceland	2005	...	...	...	...	2	8.5
Islande	2010	...	...	...	...	2	8.6
	2012	3	9.9	...	...	2	8.7
	2015	3	10.1	...	...	...	...
India	2003	3 038	41.3	2 507	32.3	428	26.4
Inde	2004	...	...	2 586	32.7	539	22.0
	2010	...	...	4 252	25.3	...	...
	2015	4 399	31.5	4 093	31.7	1 322	24.3
	2016	4 140	35.2	4 639	28.5	1 364	23.7
	2017	4 373	...	...	...	1 366	24.4
Indonesia	2005	1 428	20.4	1 282	12.5	272	* 13.5
Indonésie	2010	1 596	19.0	1 641	12.2	271	18.4
	2014	1 802	16.6	1 460	15.5	258	25.0
	2017	1 827	16.1	1 586	15.3	289	27.6
Iran (Islamic Republic of)	2005	285	21.7	...	...	115	18.4
Iran (Rép. islamique d')	2009	278	20.5	...	...	164	20.5
	2010	...	...	...	...	174	21.8
	2014	287	25.9	331	17.5	288	16.3
	2015	286	26.8	...	...	...	...
	2016	293	27.3	306	18.7	311	14.0
	2017	286	28.5	299	19.0	...	...
Iraq	2004	211	20.5	91	18.8	19	22.1
Iraq	*2005	...	...	...	...	19	22.1
	2007	287	17.0	148	13.7	...	...
Ireland	2005	25	17.9	...	...	12	16.0
Irlande	2010	32	15.8	...	...	13	15.4
	2012	32	16.1	...	...	...	...
Israel	*2005	55	13.0	68	9.9	...	...
Israël	*2009	60	13.1	71	9.8	...	...
	2010	62	13.1	...	...	...	...
	2015	73	12.1	...	...	...	...
	2016	74	12.1	...	...	...	...
Italy	2005	264	10.5	428	10.5	94	21.4
Italie	2007	273	10.3	451	10.1	104	19.5
	2010	...	...	...	...	106	18.7
	2015	237	12.0	408	11.3	90	20.3
	2016	255	11.1	457	10.0	90	20.3
Jamaica	2002	...	...	* 12	* 19.3	2	22.8
Jamaïque	2004	12	27.5	13	19.1	...	...
	2010	...	...	18	14.3	...	...
	2015	12	22.0	13	16.4	...	...
	2017	11	22.1	13	15.5	...	...
Japan	2015	410	16.2	634	11.4	550[1]	7.0
Japon	2016	415	15.9	638	11.2	556[1]	6.9
Jordan	2003	* 39	* 19.9	* 34	* 17.9	7	26.8
Jordanie	2005	...	...	...	...	8	26.4
	2010	...	...	...	...	10	24.6
	2014	58	16.9	51	14.6	...	...
	2015	...	...	...	...	14	22.5
	2017	53	21.0	67	11.4	23	12.5
Kazakhstan	2000	...	...	...	...	31	13.4
Kazakhstan	2005	59	17.3	...	...	...	...
	2010	59	16.2	...	...	49	15.5
	2015	74	16.2	224	7.5	51	13.0
	2018	72	19.6	265	7.0	38	16.5
Kenya	*2005	145	42.0	91	27.2	...	...
Kenya	*2009	165	43.3	96	33.4	...	...
	*2015	267	30.7	199	...	...	...
	2016	...	...	...	...	16	33.1

8 Teaching staff at the primary, secondary and tertiary levels *(continued)*
Number of teachers and Pupil teacher ratio

Personnel enseignant au niveau primaire, secondaire et supérieur *(suite)*
Nombre d'enseignants et ratio élèves/enseignant par niveau d'enseignement

Region, country or area Région, pays ou zone	Year & Année &	Primary education Enseignant primaire		Secondary education Enseignant secondaire		Tertiary education Enseignant supérieur	
		Total Totale ('000)	Pupil-teacher ratio Ratio élèves/ enseignant	Total Totale ('000)	Pupil-teacher ratio Ratio élèves/ enseignant	Total Totale ('000)	Pupil-teacher ratio Ratio élèves/ enseignant
Kiribati Kiribati	2005	1	24.7	1	17.0	...	...
	2008	1	25.0	1	17.4	...	...
	2014	1	26.4	...	...	...	...
	2017	1	25.5	...	...	...	...
Kuwait Koweït	2004	12	12.8	25	10.6	* 2	* 17.0
	2005	17	12.1	...	...	...	...
	2009	25	8.6	* 31	* 8.2	...	...
	2010	26	8.4	...	...	...	...
	2015	30	8.9	40	7.6	...	...
	2017	31	8.9	44	...	...	...
Kyrgyzstan Kirghizistan	2005	18	24.5	54	13.4	13	16.5
	2010	16	24.3	48	14.3	17	14.9
	2015	17	26.2	60	10.8	21	12.8
	2017	20	24.9	63	10.4	18	12.7
Lao People's Dem. Rep. Rép. dém. populaire lao	2005	28	31.5	16	24.8	2	20.7
	2010	32	28.8	21	20.2	5	22.5
	2015	35	24.2	* 34	* 18.7	12	10.6
	2017	36	22.3	* 37	* 18.1	9	12.0
Latvia Lettonie	2005	7	12.2	25	10.8	6	20.9
	2010	10	11.9	16	9.0	7	16.3
	2015	11	11.1	15	8.0	7	12.6
	2016	11	11.3	14	8.1	7	12.3
Lebanon Liban	2005	* 33	* 14.6	* 42	* 9.0	21	8.0
	2010	33	14.1	43	8.9	25	8.0
	2014	39	12.3	48	7.7	46	5.0
	2017	40	12.5	51	7.9	...	...
Lesotho Lesotho	2005	10	41.6	3	27.0	1	14.2
	2006	10	40.8	4	25.8	1	13.3
	2010	12	33.8	* 5	* 24.5	...	...
	2014	11	32.8	* 6	* 23.5	1	29.3
	2015	11	33.1	6	24.0	...	...
	2017	11	32.9	5	25.3	...	...
Liberia Libéria	2000	13	38.3	...	...	1	72.3
	*2001	...	...	...	...	1	...
	2009	22	27.4	...	...	...	...
	2010	...	...	...	...	1	24.4
	2012	...	...	...	...	2	21.6
	2015	22	30.4	12	18.4	...	...
	2016	26	27.1	15	15.2	...	...
Libya Libye	*2003	...	...	...	...	16	23.9
Liechtenstein Liechtenstein	2005	~0	8.6	~0	9.6	...	...
	2009	~0	6.5	~0	9.3	...	...
	2010	~0	6.1	...	...	...	...
	2015	~0	7.8	~0	9.9	~0	6.3
	2016	~0	7.7	~0	9.7	~0	6.5
Lithuania Lituanie	2005	11	14.1	43	9.9	13	14.9
	2010	10	12.8	39	8.8	14	14.3
	2015	8	12.9	33	7.9	13	10.8
	2016	8	13.2	33	7.7	13	10.5
	2017	8	...	31	...	12	...
Luxembourg Luxembourg	2005	3	11.3	3	10.3	...	...
	2010	4	9.3	5	8.5	1	5.4
	2015	4	8.5	5	9.4	1	8.9
	2016	4	8.3	5[1]	8.8	1	9.2
Madagascar Madagascar	2005	67	53.6	* 29	* 21.6	2	25.5
	2009	90	47.9	44	* 23.5	4	16.3
	2010	106	40.1	...	...	4	16.6
	2014	111	41.7	65	23.1	6	18.8
	2015	116	41.2	...	...	6	18.7
	2016	117	40.6	...	...	5	24.4
	2017	120	...	77	20.0	...	...

Teaching staff at the primary, secondary and tertiary levels *(continued)*
Number of teachers and Pupil teacher ratio

Personnel enseignant au niveau primaire, secondaire et supérieur *(suite)*
Nombre d'enseignants et ratio élèves/enseignant par niveau d'enseignement

Region, country or area Région, pays ou zone	Year & Année &	Primary education Enseignant primaire		Secondary education Enseignant secondaire		Tertiary education Enseignant supérieur	
		Total Totale ('000)	Pupil-teacher ratio Ratio élèves/ enseignant	Total Totale ('000)	Pupil-teacher ratio Ratio élèves/ enseignant	Total Totale ('000)	Pupil-teacher ratio Ratio élèves/ enseignant
Malawi Malawi	2005	...	...	...	...	1	7.5
	2010	* 43	* 79.3	* 16	* 43.2	1	11.6
	2011	* 47	* 76.1	* 17	* 42.1	1	13.6
	*2015	60	69.5	25	37.9	...	...
Malaysia Malaisie	2005	190	16.9	153	16.3	45	15.4
	2010	257	12.6	191	13.7	75	14.2
	2013	274	11.8	207	13.3	69	16.2
	2015	270	11.5	...	...	82	15.9
	2017	265	11.7	224	12.3	90	13.9
Maldives Maldives	2003	4	18.2	2	13.7	~0	1.9
	2005	3	20.1	...	...	...	...
	2010	4	11.7	...	...	...	...
	2015	4	10.3	...	...	...	...
	2017	4	10.2	...	...	...	...
Mali Mali	2000	16	65.3	* 9	* 29.0	* 1	* 20.5
	2005	28	54.4	...	...	...	...
	2009	38	50.1	* 29	* 23.4	...	...
	2010	40	50.4	...	...	...	...
	2015	52	42.7	49	19.2	...	...
	2017	66	38.2	58	17.4	...	...
Malta Malte	2005	2	18.4	3	11.5	1	11.4
	2008	2	17.5	4	10.6	1	9.8
	2010	2	14.3	...	...	1	9.0
	2015	2	13.5	4	7.8	2	8.1
	2016	2	13.0	4	7.2	2	7.9
Marshall Islands Îles Marshall	2002	1	16.9	~0	16.7	~0	18.8
	*2003	...	...	~0	14.9	...	...
	2012	...	...	...	...	~0	19.6
Mauritania Mauritanie	2005	11	40.3	3	31.0	~0	24.6
	2006	11	41.4	* 4	* 26.2	~0	28.8
	2010	14	37.2	...	...	~0	38.4
	2013	16	35.4	...	...	~0	43.0
	2015	18	35.8	6	33.5	...	...
	2016	17	36.4	8	26.4	...	...
	2017	...	...	9	24.3	...	...
Mauritius Maurice	2005	6	22.3	7	* 17.4	...	...
	2010	5	21.5	8	* 15.3	1	30.4
	2015	5	18.8	10	12.9	...	...
	2017	5	17.9	10	12.7	...	...
Mexico Mexique	2005	519	28.3	593	17.8	251	9.5
	2010	530	28.1	652	17.9	310	9.2
	2015	535	26.9	838	16.1	364	9.7
	2017	534	26.6	833	16.9	387	11.4
Micronesia (Fed. States of) Micronésie (États féd. de)	*2000	...	...	...	...	~0	17.1
	*2015	1	19.7	...	...	...	...
Monaco Monaco	2001	~0	22.3	~0	10.8	...	...
	2004	...	...	~0	11.1	...	...
	2008	...	...	1	5.8	...	...
	2015	~0	12.6	~0	8.1	...	...
	2016	~0	13.7	...	...	~0	6.9
	2017	~0	10.5	* ~0	* 8.5	...	...
Mongolia Mongolie	2005	7	34.2	15	22.4	8	15.4
	2010	9	30.2	19	14.5	9	18.9
	2015	9	28.2	21	...	9	20.3
	2017	10	30.4	22[1]	...	8	18.9
Montenegro Monténégro	2017	...	...	...	...	2	15.6
Montserrat Montserrat	2005	~0	20.4	~0	11.5	...	...
	2009	~0	13.1	~0	13.3	...	...
	2014	~0	11.0	~0	12.7	...	...
	2017	~0	15.1	~0	9.1	...	...

8

Teaching staff at the primary, secondary and tertiary levels *(continued)*
Number of teachers and Pupil teacher ratio

Personnel enseignant au niveau primaire, secondaire et supérieur *(suite)*
Nombre d'enseignants et ratio élèves/enseignant par niveau d'enseignement

Region, country or area Région, pays ou zone	Year & Année &	Primary education Enseignant primaire		Secondary education Enseignant secondaire		Tertiary education Enseignant supérieur	
		Total Totale ('000)	Pupil-teacher ratio Ratio élèves/ enseignant	Total Totale ('000)	Pupil-teacher ratio Ratio élèves/ enseignant	Total Totale ('000)	Pupil-teacher ratio Ratio élèves/ enseignant
Morocco	2004	148	27.6	* 100	* 18.7	19	18.5
Maroc	2005	148	27.1	...	...	19	19.0
	2009	145	26.6	...	...	20	21.4
	2010	150	26.2	...	...	...	...
	2015	156	25.9	...	...	33	26.9
	2017	150	28.0	140	20.3	35	28.8
Mozambique	2005	59	66.3	* 10	* 32.2	3	9.4
Mozambique	2010	90	58.5	* 20	* 34.1	6	16.2
	2014	104	* 54.8	* 26	* 40.0	10	15.2
	2015	108	* 54.7	* 27	* 39.7	...	...
	2017	117	52.4	33	36.5	14	14.1
Myanmar	2001	148	32.3	75	30.8	11	52.6
Myanmar	2005	160	30.9	78	33.1	...	...
	2007	172	29.1	82	32.8	11	47.6
	2010	182	28.2	84	34.1	...	...
	2012	...	...	...	...	25	25.3
	2014	188	27.6	100	31.8	...	...
	2017	234	23.0	150	26.4	13	57.2
Namibia	2003	13	31.6	6	25.2	1	13.1
Namibie	2005	13	30.8	6	25.1	...	...
	2007	14	29.9	6	24.6	...	...
	2008	14	29.4	...	...	1	16.4
	2010	14	29.8	...	...	...	...
	2015	...	...	...	...	3	16.3
	2016	...	...	...	...	3	17.1
	2017	...	...	11	...	...	...
Nauru	2005	~0	27.9	~0	15.4	...	...
Nauru	2007	~0	19.9	~0	20.9	...	...
	2008	~0	22.4	...	...	...	...
	2014	~0	39.5	~0	22.8	...	...
	2016	~0	40.2	~0	24.8	...	...
Nepal	2003	110	35.7	53	34.7	...	...
Népal	2005	101	39.7	...	...	7	27.2
	2007	113	40.0	...	...	10	25.7
	2010	154	31.9	* 84	* 32.0	...	...
	2013	179	25.6	* 107	* 29.2	8	60.0
	2015	188	23.1	* 111	* 28.6	...	...
	2017	198	20.9	* 116	* 28.8	...	...
Netherlands	2005	...	...	107	13.1	45	12.7
Pays-Bas	2010	...	...	107	13.7	52	12.6
	2015	104	11.6	112	14.5	63	13.5
	2016	102	11.7	112	14.4	65	12.9
Netherlands Antilles [former] Antilles néerlandaises [anc.]	2002	1	20.0	1	12.8	* ~0	* 7.6
New Zealand	2005	22	16.3	36	14.7	...	...
Nouvelle-Zélande	2010	24	14.5	35	14.5	...	...
	2015	25	14.5	35	13.8	16	16.7
	2017	26	14.9	36	13.6	17	16.0
Nicaragua	2002	26	35.2	* 11	* 33.9	7	15.3
Nicaragua	2005	28	33.6	13	33.7	...	...
	2010	31	30.2	15	30.8	...	...
Niger	2005	24	43.7	7	27.4	1	14.9
Niger	2010	45	38.6	10	30.8	2	11.3
	2015	67	36.6	21	28.0	3	15.1
	2017	76	36.3	26	29.7	4	15.3
Nigeria	2004	598	35.8	155	40.6	37	34.8
Nigéria	2005	599	36.9	159	40.2	...	...
	2010	574	* 37.6	390	23.2	57	24.6
	2011	...	...	...	...	67	22.6

8

Teaching staff at the primary, secondary and tertiary levels *(continued)*
Number of teachers and Pupil teacher ratio

Personnel enseignant au niveau primaire, secondaire et supérieur *(suite)*
Nombre d'enseignants et ratio élèves/enseignant par niveau d'enseignement

Region, country or area Région, pays ou zone	Year & Année &	Primary education Enseignant primaire		Secondary education Enseignant secondaire		Tertiary education Enseignant supérieur	
		Total Totale ('000)	Pupil-teacher ratio Ratio élèves/ enseignant	Total Totale ('000)	Pupil-teacher ratio Ratio élèves/ enseignant	Total Totale ('000)	Pupil-teacher ratio Ratio élèves/ enseignant
Niue	2004	~0	11.5	~0	8.4	...	...
Nioué	2005	...	...	~0	8.2	...	...
	2015	~0	17.3	~0	7.9	...	...
	2016	~0	15.5	...	...	...	...
North Macedonia	2005	6	19.4	15	14.7	3	16.9
Macédoine du Nord	2010	7	15.9	17	11.9	3	17.8
	2015	8	14.4	18	9.4	* 4	* 17.7
Norway	2001	...	...	...	...	15	12.3
Norvège	2015	49	8.9	51	8.6	27	9.9
	2016	49	9.0	51	8.7	29	9.4
Oman	*2003	16	19.9	16	17.4	...	...
Oman	2005	...	...	...	...	3	16.2
	2010	...	...	...	...	5	16.8
	2015	...	...	...	...	8	16.2
	2016	...	...	...	...	8	16.2
	2017	38	10.1	30	10.0	...	...
Pakistan	2005	450	38.3	* 295	* 23.3	...	...
Pakistan	2010	464	40.5	...	...	...	...
	2015	428	46.3	* 572	* 21.1	...	...
	2017	484	44.8	* 646	* 19.4	59	33.1
Palau	2000	~0	15.7	~0	15.1	* ~0	* 10.9
Palaos	*2002	...	...	...	...	~0	10.5
	2013	...	...	...	...	~0	8.2
Panama	2005	18	24.2	16	15.6	11	11.0
Panama	2010	19	23.5	19	15.3	15	9.2
	2015	19	21.9	24	13.3	15	10.6
	2016	19	21.4	24	14.5	...	...
Papua New Guinea	*2001	14	36.2	...	...	...	...
Papouasie-Nvl-Guinée	2012	...	...	14	27.4	...	...
	2016	36	35.5	15	34.3	...	...
Paraguay	*2004	33	27.8	44	11.8	...	...
Paraguay	2012	35	24.2	34	18.4	...	...
Peru	2002	171	25.1	134	18.9	56	14.8
Pérou	2005	177	23.0	148	16.7	...	...
	2010	191	19.7	167	16.0	...	...
	2015	195	18.0	190	14.1	...	...
	2018	207	17.4	196	14.2	...	...
Philippines	2005	373	35.1	168	37.9	* 113	* 21.3
Philippines	2009	435	31.4	194	34.8	...	...
	2015	478	30.3	279	26.2	...	...
	2016	493	29.0	314	23.5	...	...
	2017	...	...	...	...	151	23.7
Poland	2005	236	11.5	296	11.6	95	22.3
Pologne	2010	240	9.3	273	10.4	103	20.9
	2015	220	10.5	273	9.3	97	17.1
	2016	229	10.8	268	9.2	...	...
Portugal	2005	72	10.5	94	7.1	37	10.4
Portugal	2010	68	10.8	98	7.3	36	10.6
	2015	49	13.3	78	9.9	32	10.4
	2016	50	12.8	79	9.6	33	10.5
	2017	51	...	81	...	33	...
Puerto Rico	2010	26	11.7	26	11.1	16	15.4
Porto Rico	2015	18	13.9	15	18.9	16	14.8
	2016	17	13.5	14	17.2	17	13.6
Qatar	2005	6	11.1	5	11.6	1	* 14.6
Qatar	2010	7	12.0	7	9.9	2	8.6
	2015	11	11.6	9	10.7	2	12.9
	2017	12	11.8	10	10.4	2	13.6

8

Teaching staff at the primary, secondary and tertiary levels *(continued)*
Number of teachers and Pupil teacher ratio

Personnel enseignant au niveau primaire, secondaire et supérieur *(suite)*
Nombre d'enseignants et ratio élèves/enseignant par niveau d'enseignement

Region, country or area Région, pays ou zone	Year & Année &	Primary education Enseignant primaire		Secondary education Enseignant secondaire		Tertiary education Enseignant supérieur	
		Total Totale ('000)	Pupil-teacher ratio Ratio élèves/ enseignant	Total Totale ('000)	Pupil-teacher ratio Ratio élèves/ enseignant	Total Totale ('000)	Pupil-teacher ratio Ratio élèves/ enseignant
Republic of Korea	2005	144	27.9	210	18.1	191	16.8
République de Corée	2010	158	20.9	225	17.6	223	14.7
	2015	164	16.6	236	14.4	225	14.5
	2016	164	16.3	233	13.8	220	14.6
Republic of Moldova	2005	10	18.0	31	12.8	8	16.7
République de Moldova	2010	9	15.4	29	10.5	8	16.8
	2015	8	17.5	25	9.3	7	16.5
	2017	8	17.7	23	9.9	6	14.9
Romania	2005	57	17.0	162	12.9	31	23.9
Roumanie	2010	52	16.1	146	12.5	31	32.1
	2015	50	18.9	129	12.1	28	19.5
	2016	49	19.3	125	12.1	27	19.9
	2017	48	...	124	...	27	...
Russian Federation	2005	* 317	* 16.7	* 1 306	* 9.5	625	14.4
Fédération de Russie	2009	278	18.1	1 136	8.5	670	13.9
	2012	282	19.6	1 046	8.8	554	14.4
	2015	297	20.1	...	...	627	10.5
	2016	301	20.6	...	...	601	10.3
Rwanda	2005	27	69.0	8	28.7	* 2	* 15.3
Rwanda	2009	33	68.3	15	22.6	3	18.7
	2010	36	64.6	...	...	3	22.2
	2015	42	58.3	30	19.2	3	23.9
	2017	44	57.9	30	20.1	3	23.4
Saint Kitts and Nevis	2005	~0	17.6	* ~0	* 9.9	...	...
Saint-Kitts-et-Nevis	2010	~0	14.1	~0	* 9.3	...	...
	2015	~0	15.1	1	8.3	~0	7.6
	2016	~0	13.9	1	7.9	...	...
Saint Lucia	2005	1	22.0	1	16.9	~0	12.6
Sainte-Lucie	2010	1	18.5	* 1	* 15.7	~0	9.3
	2015	1	15.5	1	11.7	~0	10.2
	2017	1	15.2	1	11.4	~0	10.6
Saint Vincent & Grenadines	*2004	1	17.2	1	18.1	...	...
Saint-Vincent-Grenadines	2010	1	16.3	1	16.8	...	...
	2015	1	14.9	1	15.0	...	...
	2017	1	14.4	1	14.4	...	...
Samoa	2000	1	24.0	1	21.2	~0	7.8
Samoa	2002	1	27.2	1	21.0	...	...
	2010	1	30.2	1	21.5	...	...
	2016	...	...	1	27.7	...	...
San Marino	2004	~0	6.3	...	...	...	...
Saint-Marin	2010	~0	6.5	~0	14.5	...	...
	2012	~0	6.3	...	...	...	...
Sao Tome and Principe	2005	1	30.8	* ~0	* 21.7	...	...
Sao Tomé-et-Principe	2009	1	26.2	...	...	...	...
	2010	...	...	...	...	~0	8.1
	2015	1	38.8	1	20.8	~0	8.0
	2016	1	32.2	1	24.8	...	...
	2017	1	31.2	...	...	...	...
Saudi Arabia	2005	* 273	* 11.3	* 234	* 11.1	27	22.5
Arabie saoudite	2009	* 285	* 11.4	* 264	* 11.3	39	19.2
	2010	298	11.2	...	...	50	18.2
	2014	347	10.8	312	* 11.0	74	20.3
	2015	353	10.9	...	...	77	19.8
	2016	320	11.7	...	...	80	20.3
	2017	...	...	...	...	84	20.0
Senegal	2005	35	41.7	* 15	* 26.4	...	...
Sénégal	2010	50	33.7	...	...	...	...
	2015	62	32.1	56	20.4	6	25.8
	2017	65	32.8	57	18.9	8	20.2
Serbia	2010	17	16.4	62	9.6	15	15.3
Serbie	2015	18	15.2	65	8.5	11	22.5
	2017	19	14.3	67	8.1	12	22.8

Teaching staff at the primary, secondary and tertiary levels *(continued)*
Number of teachers and Pupil teacher ratio

Personnel enseignant au niveau primaire, secondaire et supérieur *(suite)*
Nombre d'enseignants et ratio élèves/enseignant par niveau d'enseignement

Region, country or area Région, pays ou zone	Year & Année &	Primary education Enseignant primaire		Secondary education Enseignant secondaire		Tertiary education Enseignant supérieur	
		Total Totale ('000)	Pupil-teacher ratio Ratio élèves/ enseignant	Total Totale ('000)	Pupil-teacher ratio Ratio élèves/ enseignant	Total Totale ('000)	Pupil-teacher ratio Ratio élèves/ enseignant
Seychelles Seychelles	2005	1	13.7	1	14.4	...	...
	2010	1	12.5	1	12.8	...	...
	2015	1	13.7	1	12.0	~0	14.4
	2017	1	14.0	1	11.6	~0	21.2
Sierra Leone Sierra Leone	2001	15	37.3	6	26.6	1	7.7
	*2002	...	...	...	...	1	7.5
	2015	40	33.8	22	20.5	...	...
	2016	38	37.3	22	22.0	...	...
	2017	38	39.4	...	...	...	...
Singapore Singapour	2009	16	18.2	14	16.2	15	13.8
	2010	...	...	...	...	17	14.1
	2012	...	...	...	...	19	13.5
	2016	16	15.1	15	11.7	14	14.3
Sint Maarten (Dutch part) St-Martin (partie néerland.)	2012	~0	11.3	~0	11.8	~0	3.3
	2014	...	...	~0	7.6	~0	3.6
	2015	...	...	...	...	~0	3.6
Slovakia Slovaquie	2005	14	17.5	51	13.1	13	14.3
	2010	14	15.2	46	12.0	13	17.6
	2015	14	15.2	41	11.2	13	14.4
Slovenia Slovénie	2005	6	15.1	16	11.2	4	25.1
	2010	6	17.0	15	9.1	7	16.5
	2015	7	16.9	14	10.2	7	12.0
	2016	9	13.8	15	9.7	7	11.3
Solomon Islands Îles Salomon	*2000	...	...	1	10.1	...	...
	2010	5	19.9	1	28.1	...	...
	2012	5	19.1	2	25.9	...	...
	2015	4	25.7	2	...	...	...
	2017	4	25.8	...	...	...	...
Somalia Somalie	2007	13	35.5	5	19.3	...	...
South Africa Afrique du Sud	2005	* 233	* 31.4	142	32.9	...	...
	2009	* 212	* 33.6	187	25.0	...	...
	2010	238[1]	29.5	...	...	...	...
	2015	249	30.3	190	27.8	...	...
	2016	...	...	192	26.8	...	...
South Sudan Soudan du sud	*2015	27	46.8	6	27.5	...	...
Spain Espagne	2005	181	13.8	280	11.1	145	12.5
	2010	219	12.4	295	10.8	155	12.1
	2015	228	13.2	276	12.0	157	12.5
	2016	233	13.0	287	11.6	164	12.0
Sri Lanka Sri Lanka	2005	73	21.9	...	...	...	...
	2010	72	23.9	...	...	...	...
	2012	72	24.4	150	17.3	...	...
	2015	77	23.2	...	...	...	...
	2017	76	22.9	152	17.4	9	31.0
State of Palestine État de Palestine	2005	16	24.5	25	26.6	* 5	* 30.5
	2010	14	27.8	32	22.5	7	27.2
	2015	19	24.0	36	19.9	8	26.1
	2017	19	24.7	37	20.1	8	26.8
Sudan Soudan	2015	...	...	...	...	13	49.8
Sudan [former] Soudan [anc.]	*2000	...	...	...	...	4	45.5
	2005	113	29.0	64	* 21.5	...	...
	*2009	124	38.4	83	22.2	...	...
Suriname Suriname	2005	4	18.6	3	13.9	...	...
	2010	5	14.9	4	13.8	...	...
	2015	5	13.3	5	12.0	...	...
	2017	5	12.9	...	...	...	...

8

Teaching staff at the primary, secondary and tertiary levels *(continued)*
Number of teachers and Pupil teacher ratio

Personnel enseignant au niveau primaire, secondaire et supérieur *(suite)*
Nombre d'enseignants et ratio élèves/enseignant par niveau d'enseignement

Region, country or area Région, pays ou zone	Year & Année &	Primary education Enseignant primaire		Secondary education Enseignant secondaire		Tertiary education Enseignant supérieur	
		Total Totale ('000)	Pupil-teacher ratio Ratio élèves/ enseignant	Total Totale ('000)	Pupil-teacher ratio Ratio élèves/ enseignant	Total Totale ('000)	Pupil-teacher ratio Ratio élèves/ enseignant
Sweden	2005	66	10.1	76	9.7	38	11.3
Suède	2010	60	9.5	75	9.7	29	15.6
	2015	65	12.1	66	12.9	34	12.6
	2016	67	12.4	66	12.9	34	12.4
Switzerland	2005	...	...	...	...	34	5.9
Suisse	2010	...	...	...	...	40	6.2
	2013	46	10.4	67	9.3	...	...
	2014	48	10.1	64	...	33	8.9
	2016	49	10.1	62	9.8	34	8.7
Syrian Arab Republic	2002	115	25.3	65	18.1	...	...
République arabe syrienne	2015	...	...	...	...	12	64.4
Tajikistan	2005	32	21.3	60	16.4	10	14.9
Tadjikistan	2010	27	25.2	60	17.1	13	14.8
	2011	29	23.3	68	15.4	13	14.5
	2015	31	22.3	...	...	13	17.6
	2017	35	22.3	...	...	16	16.7
Thailand	2002	326	18.6	* 173	* 24.0	64	33.6
Thaïlande	*2003	...	...	...	...	66	33.6
	2008	348	16.0	223	21.2	* 76	* 32.1
	2010	317	16.3	...	...	...	...
	2014	337	15.4	230	29.5	104	23.5
	2015	301	16.9	240	28.2	104	...
	2016	304	16.7	247	26.6	98	24.6
	2017	305	16.2	262	24.2	...	...
Timor-Leste	2002	4	47.2	2	29.5	* ~0	* 51.6
Timor-Leste	2004	4	50.7	3	27.6	...	...
	2005	...	...	3	23.7	...	...
	2009	7	29.8	...	...	1	14.0
	2010	8	30.2	4	23.0	...	...
	2011	8	31.4	4	24.3	...	...
Togo	2005	30	33.6	13	30.5	~0	...
Togo	2007	26	39.1	* 12	* 35.5	~0	69.2
	2010	32	40.6	...	...	...	...
	2011	32	40.9	21	26.2	...	...
	2015	34	41.7	...	...	3	26.2
	2017	38	40.1	...	...	3	33.0
Tokelau	2003	~0	5.8	~0	7.1	...	...
Tokélaou	2016	~0	11.9	...	...	...	...
Tonga	2000	1	22.1	1	14.6	* ~0	* 5.1
Tonga	2002	1	22.1	1	14.4	...	...
	2005	1	20.3	...	...	...	...
	2010	1	24.9	1	14.9	...	...
	2015	1	21.6	1	14.5	...	...
Trinidad and Tobago	2004	* 8	* 17.5	...	...	2	9.7
Trinité-et-Tobago	*2005	8	16.5	...	...	...	...
	*2009	7	17.6	...	...	...	...
Tunisia	2005	59	20.0	72	17.2	17	19.6
Tunisie	2010	60	17.1	88	13.3	21	17.4
	2011	59	17.4	85	13.6	22	16.8
	2012	61	17.1	...	...	22	15.9
	2015	71	15.8	...	...	...	...
	2016	70	16.2	...	...	...	...
Turkey	2005	...	...	...	...	82	25.7
Turquie	2010	...	...	...	...	105	33.5
	2015	295	18.4	594	18.5	149	40.7
Turkmenistan Turkménistan	2014	...	...	...	...	8	5.4
Turks and Caicos Islands	2003	~0	15.2	~0	8.7	...	...
Îles Turques-et-Caïques	2014	~0	9.3	~0	8.8	...	...
	2015	...	...	~0	9.6	...	...

Teaching staff at the primary, secondary and tertiary levels *(continued)*
Number of teachers and Pupil teacher ratio

Personnel enseignant au niveau primaire, secondaire et supérieur *(suite)*
Nombre d'enseignants et ratio élèves/enseignant par niveau d'enseignement

Region, country or area Région, pays ou zone	Year & Année &	Primary education Enseignant primaire		Secondary education Enseignant secondaire		Tertiary education Enseignant supérieur	
		Total Totale ('000)	Pupil-teacher ratio Ratio élèves/ enseignant	Total Totale ('000)	Pupil-teacher ratio Ratio élèves/ enseignant	Total Totale ('000)	Pupil-teacher ratio Ratio élèves/ enseignant
Tuvalu	2004	~0	19.2	...	...	...	...
Tuvalu	2015	~0	12.7	~0	6.2	...	...
	2016	~0	17.2	~0	8.4	...	...
Uganda	2004	147	50.1	40	18.5	4	21.2
Ouganda	2005	140	51.7	* 40	...	...	...
	2007	152	49.6	56	18.5	...	...
	2010	172	48.6	66	...	5	22.6
	2011	170	47.8	...	...	6	24.5
	2014	191	...	64	...	...	...
	2015	193	42.9	...	...	...	...
	2017	207	42.7	...	...	...	...
Ukraine	2000	105	19.9	389	13.4	* 146	* 12.4
Ukraine	2005	104	18.7	...	...	187	13.9
	2010	98	15.7	...	...	201	13.1
	2015	124	12.4	340	7.0	169	10.5
	2017	127	13.0	324	7.2	160	10.4
United Arab Emirates	2005	17	15.2	...	...	...	...
Émirats arabes unis	2009	20	15.6	...	...	5	18.6
	2010	19	16.8	...	...	...	...
	2015	20	23.6	...	...	9	17.8
	2016	19	24.5	46	9.5	9	17.0
United Kingdom	2005	265	17.5	388	14.9	122	18.7
Royaume-Uni	2008	244	18.3	* 375	* 14.3	134	17.4
	2010	252	17.5	...	...	140	17.7
	2014	272	17.4	414	15.8	152	15.5
	2015	...	...	412	15.5	149	15.7
	2016	314	15.1	393	19.4	151	15.8
United Rep. of Tanzania	2005	135	55.9	...	...	3	* 18.8
Rép.-Unie de Tanzanie	2010	166	50.8	...	...	4	18.9
	2012	181	45.8	...	...	5	34.4
	2014	191	43.1	83	...	...	...
	2017	198	47.2	112	17.1	...	...
United States of America	2005	1 731	14.1	1 635	14.9	1 208	14.3
États-Unis d'Amérique	2010	1 795	13.6	1 758	13.8	1 439	14.2
	2015	1 714	14.5	1 661	14.7	1 581	12.4
	2017	1 769	...	1 695	...	1 581[1]	...
United States Virgin Islands Îles Vierges américaines	2007	...	...	...	...	~0	9.2
Uruguay	2005	18	20.2	22	14.6	12	9.3
Uruguay	2010	25	13.8	25	12.7	17	8.0
	2015	27	11.8	...	...	21	7.6
	2016	28	11.1	...	...	23	7.2
Uzbekistan	2005	119	19.9	339	13.3	20	13.3
Ouzbékistan	2010	111	17.8	342	13.0	23	12.5
	2015	112	19.0	371	10.7	24	10.7
	2017	113	21.2	377	10.3	24	11.7
Vanuatu	2001	2	23.7	1	15.1	~0	25.0
Vanuatu	2002	2	23.2	...	...	* ~0	* 24.9
	2004	2	20.0	...	...	...	...
	2010	2	21.7	...	...	...	...
	2015	2	26.6	1	20.6	...	...
Venezuela (Boliv. Rep. of)	*2004	...	...	...	...	82	12.8
Venezuela (Rép. boliv. du)	*2009	...	...	...	...	165	12.9
Viet Nam	2005	361	21.6	...	...	48	28.4
Viet Nam	2010	348	19.9	...	...	70	29.0
	2015	392	19.2	...	...	91	27.1
	2016	397	19.6	...	...	94	24.6
	2017	397	19.6	...	...	...	...

8

Teaching staff at the primary, secondary and tertiary levels *(continued)*
Number of teachers and Pupil teacher ratio

Personnel enseignant au niveau primaire, secondaire et supérieur *(suite)*
Nombre d'enseignants et ratio élèves/enseignant par niveau d'enseignement

Region, country or area Région, pays ou zone	Year & Année &	Primary education Enseignant primaire		Secondary education Enseignant secondaire		Tertiary education Enseignant supérieur	
		Total Totale ('000)	Pupil-teacher ratio Ratio élèves/ enseignant	Total Totale ('000)	Pupil-teacher ratio Ratio élèves/ enseignant	Total Totale ('000)	Pupil-teacher ratio Ratio élèves/ enseignant
Yemen	*2005	...	...	...	...	7	29.2
Yémen	2007	...	...	...	...	7	32.2
	2010	111	30.8	...	...	...	...
	*2012	122	30.3	...	...	...	...
	2016	145	26.9	...	...	...	...
Zambia	*2005	46	56.5	...	...	...	...
Zambie	*2010	55	53.0	...	...	...	...
	2015	75	42.7	...	...	...	...
	2017	78	42.1	...	...	...	...
Zimbabwe	2003	61	38.6	34	22.3	...	...
Zimbabwe	2010	...	...	...	...	4	23.2
	2013	73	36.4	43	22.5	6	17.0
	2015	...	...	...	...	8	17.9

Source:

United Nations Educational, Scientific and Cultural Organization (UNESCO), Montreal, the UNESCO Institute for Statistics (UIS) statistics database, last accessed March 2019.

& Data relate to the calendar year in which the academic year ends.

1 Data included elsewhere under another category.

Source:

Organisation des Nations Unies pour l'éducation, la science et la culture (UNESCO), Montréal, base de données statistiques de l'Institut de statistique (ISU) de l'UNESCO, dernier accès mars 2019.

& Les données se réfèrent à l'année civile durant laquelle l'année scolaire se termine.

1 Données incluses ailleurs dans une autre catégorie.

Public expenditure on education
By expenditure type, level of education, total government expenditure and GDP

Dépenses publiques afférentes à l'éducation
Par type de dépenses, niveau de scolarité, dépenses publiques totales et PIB

| Country or area Pays ou zone | Year Année | Percentage of total expenditure in public institutions Pourcentage des dépenses publiques totales en faveur de l'éducation | | | Percentage of government expenditure on education by level Pourcentage des dépenses publiques selon le niveau d'enseignement | | | | As % of Govt. Expenditure En % des dépenses du gouvt. | As % of GDP En % du PIB |
		Other expenditure Dépenses courantes	Staff Compensation Rémunération du personnel	Capital expenditure Dépenses en Capital	Pre-primary Préprimaire	Primary Primaire	Secondary Secondaire	Tertiary Tertiaire		
Afghanistan Afghanistan	2010	9.3	72.4	18.3	...	62.1	26.7	9.0	17.1	3.5
	2015	9.0	71.4	19.6	...	56.7	24.4	16.0	12.5	3.2
	*2017	...	...	...	...	44.2	22.3	...	15.7	3.9
Albania Albanie	2005	...	...	...	...	...	...	...	11.4	3.2
	2007	...	...	...	...	...	...	...	11.2	3.3
	2015	12.5	79.5	8.1	...	56.8	21.6	21.2	11.3	3.4
	2016	18.9	72.7	8.4	...	...	25.4	19.1	13.6	4.0
Algeria Algérie	2008	...	...	...	...	...	...	27.0	11.4	4.3
American Samoa Samoa américaines	2006	...	...	6.2	...	...	...	11.2	...	14.6
Andorra Andorre	2005	...	...	...	16.9	24.1	20.6	3.9	...	1.6
	2010	30.9	36.7	1.7	14.6	28.9	20.9	3.9	...	3.1
	2017	63.8	35.4	0.7	11.9	22.0	24.8	5.7	...	3.2
Angola Angola	2005	...	...	...	...	36.5	55.2	8.3	8.0	2.8
	2006	...	...	24.3	13.5	31.4	42.4	8.7	7.5	2.9
	2010	...	...	...	...	...	...	...	8.7	3.5
Anguilla Anguilla	2005	6.7	80.9	...	1.9	28.5	51.3	18.3	...	3.0
	2008	* 9.8	* 69.4	* 20.8	1.6	39.4	56.1	2.8	...	2.8
Antigua and Barbuda Antigua-et-Barbuda	2002	25.7	...	3.9	2.1	28.6	35.2	6.7	11.7	3.4
	2009	21.6	73.2	5.2	0.3	41.6	48.4	7.4	6.9	2.5
Argentina Argentine	2004	11.6	87.6	0.8	8.3	36.7	37.8	17.2	15.1	3.5
	2005	...	...	...	7.9	34.2	41.7	16.2	15.8	3.9
	2010	9.9	85.9	4.2	7.4	33.1	39.7	19.9	15.0	5.0
	2016	6.8	82.4	10.8	8.6	30.1	40.9	20.4	13.4	5.6
Armenia Arménie	2005	...	...	...	...	...	...	...	13.6	2.7
	2009	...	...	...	11.3	...	...	9.4	13.5	3.8
	2010	...	...	...	...	...	...	11.7	12.4	3.2
	2016	8.2	82.5	9.3	11.9	20.7	51.1	13.2	10.2	2.8
Aruba Aruba	2005	6.1	90.7	3.2	6.8	26.7	26.8	11.5	...	4.7
	2009	5.7	87.0	...	...	...	...	...	...	5.9
	2010	...	...	...	...	...	...	...	...	6.7
	2016	7.0	93.0	...	5.7	27.5	33.2	18.4	...	6.1
Australia Australie	2000	24.7	68.3	7.0	1.2	34.1	38.6	23.4	13.4	4.9
	2005	...	...	...	1.0	34.6	39.7	22.2	13.6	4.9
	2010	...	...	...	1.2	36.8	36.8	22.3	14.3	5.6
	2015	27.1	65.2	7.7	3.3	31.8	30.5	28.9	14.1	5.3
Austria Autriche	2005	23.2	72.1	4.7	7.4	19.0	45.9	27.3	10.3	5.2
	2010	24.9	70.2	4.9	10.3	17.1	44.4	27.7	10.8	5.7
	2015	26.2	68.3	5.5	8.8	16.6	39.9	32.6	10.7	5.5
Azerbaijan Azerbaïdjan	2005	31.6	66.8	1.6	6.9	...	...	6.9	13.2	3.0
	2010	32.6	64.8	2.5	7.1	...	...	14.0	8.7	2.8
	2016	42.0	56.1	2.0	10.5	...	72.4	17.1	8.2	2.9
Bahamas Bahamas	*2000	...	...	...	...	...	...	...	18.9	2.2
Bahrain Bahreïn	2008	...	...	...	...	...	...	...	10.6	2.5
	2012	13.8	82.3	3.8	...	...	...	...	8.3	2.6
	2013	...	...	...	...	32.1	43.4	24.4	7.2	2.5
	2015	...	...	...	...	33.0	44.2	...	7.3	2.7
	2017	...	...	...	...	...	...	...	7.2	2.3
Bangladesh Bangladesh	2004	...	...	...	...	40.0	48.5	11.5	16.0	1.9
	2009	21.2	59.8	19.0	...	44.7	40.2	13.5	14.0	1.9
	2012	4.3	95.2	0.5	...	44.6	39.1	14.7	15.6	2.2
	2016	12.9	73.0	14.2	...	...	64.3	33.3	11.4	1.5

9

Public expenditure on education *(continued)*
By expenditure type, level of education, total government expenditure and GDP

Dépenses publiques afférentes à l'éducation *(suite)*
Par type de dépenses, niveau de scolarité, dépenses publiques totales et PIB

Country or area Pays ou zone	Year Année	Percentage of total expenditure in public institutions Pourcentage des dépenses publiques totales en faveur de l'éducation			Percentage of government expenditure on education by level Pourcentage des dépenses publiques selon le niveau d'enseignement				As % of Govt. Expenditure En % des dépenses du gouvt.	As % of GDP En % du PIB
		Other expenditure Dépenses courantes	Staff Compensation Rémunération du personnel	Capital expenditure Dépenses en Capital	Pre-primary Préprimaire	Primary Primaire	Secondary Secondaire	Tertiary Tertiaire		
Barbados Barbade	2005	16.2	79.9	4.0	* 6.3	* 27.9	31.7	31.6	18.2	5.6
	2008	14.5	78.6	6.9	0.4	36.9	29.4	30.1	15.7	5.1
	2010	10.4	83.4	6.2	...	...	29.6	32.5	18.1	6.1
	2016	50.5	45.3	4.2	...	29.6	39.3	31.1	14.1	5.1
	2017	38.5	57.1	4.4	...	...	...	28.5	12.9	4.7
Belarus Bélarus	2005	30.1	65.2	4.8	17.4	...	...	25.5	12.6	5.9
	2010	26.5	62.6	10.9	19.0	...	...	17.1	11.8	5.2
	2017	27.4	67.0	5.6	24.0	...	50.5	16.5	12.3	4.8
Belgium Belgique	2005	11.7	85.5	2.8	9.6	...	...	21.7	11.2	...
	2010	11.9	84.3	3.8	9.5	...	...	22.2	12.0	...
	2013	13.0	81.4	5.6	10.6	23.4	42.1	21.8	11.9	...
	2015	13.9	81.0	5.0	10.7	23.5	...	22.1	12.2	6.6
Belize Belize	2003	* 18.3	* 62.3	* 19.3	...	...	...	...	16.2	5.2
	2004	...	...	...	0.6	42.6	39.2	10.8	16.8	5.3
	2010	...	...	...	1.5	46.1	41.1	8.7	23.1	6.6
	2017	...	...	...	4.6	31.8	41.0	10.9	21.7	7.1
Benin Bénin	2001	15.2	56.8	28.0	* 1.2	* 55.4	* 25.1	18.3	15.3	3.2
	2005	13.3	73.0	13.7	...	* 46.0	* 32.8	21.2	18.8	3.6
	2010	6.2	85.7	8.2	2.6	52.8	28.0	15.6	26.1	5.0
	2015	22.2	69.5	8.3	4.3	49.8	23.7	22.1	17.5	4.4
	*2016	...	...	...	...	...	...	...	18.8	4.0
Bermuda Bermudes	2005	...	...	...	* 7.0	* 40.7	* 52.3	...	...	2.0
	2010	...	...	...	8.9	30.8	45.4	13.5	...	2.6
	2015	18.6	79.9	1.5	7.0	30.7	44.3	...	...	1.7
	2017	...	...	...	6.5	32.2	44.4	17.0	...	1.5
Bhutan Bhoutan	2005	...	...	...	...	22.3	50.9	14.1	22.8	7.1
	2010	...	...	...	...	29.9	53.9	15.1	11.0	4.0
	2014	...	...	...	...	32.0	55.7	10.3	17.8	5.9
	2015	50.1	35.9	14.0	...	...	41.5	...	26.4	7.4
	*2017	...	...	...	...	...	...	...	24.0	7.1
Bolivia (Plurin. State of) Bolivie (État plurin. de)	2000	...	...	14.5	6.3	* 40.5	* 18.5	28.9	18.7	5.5
	2003	...	...	...	3.3	44.1	24.3	21.6	19.9	6.4
	2009	31.8	68.2	...	2.6	40.5	26.0	29.7	22.6	8.1
	2010	...	...	...	2.8	39.4	26.3	29.9	24.1	7.6
	2014	19.9	63.3	16.8	5.0	41.6	27.1	26.2	16.8	7.3
Botswana Botswana	2005	...	...	...	...	30.0	39.6	27.9	25.8	10.7
	2009	...	...	9.8	...	17.8	32.7	41.5	20.5	9.6
Brazil Brésil	2005	23.6	70.3	6.1	8.2	34.0	38.8	19.0	11.3	4.5
	2010	24.3	68.5	7.2	7.6	31.3	44.7	16.4	14.6	5.6
	2011	20.7	73.2	6.1	8.8	29.3	45.1	16.8	15.3	5.7
	2015	21.3	74.7	3.9	...	25.6	41.4	21.5	16.2	6.2
British Virgin Islands Îles Vierges britanniques	*2004	2.3	90.3	7.4	...	...	...	...	...	...
	2005	0.7	99.3	...	0.1	33.7	31.2	34.2	...	3.5
	2007	15.1	77.8	7.1	0.1	28.4	37.7	33.1	...	3.7
	2010	...	...	...	0.1	34.1	34.0	...	...	4.4
	2015	...	...	...	~0.0	16.6	19.0	22.1	...	6.3
	2017	...	...	...	...	29.9	35.1	35.1	...	...
Brunei Darussalam Brunéi Darussalam	2000	...	...	...	...	...	...	...	8.9	3.7
	2010	...	...	...	...	28.5	46.8	24.4	5.3	2.0
	2016	30.6	66.2	3.2	0.7	19.5	60.8	18.9	11.4	4.4
Bulgaria Bulgarie	2005	26.7	63.2	10.1	16.9	20.3	45.9	16.9	12.1	4.1
	2010	28.4	66.6	5.1	22.5	19.6	43.0	14.8	11.2	3.9
	2013	20.9	71.8	7.3	25.3	19.7	38.9	15.9	11.4	4.1
Burkina Faso Burkina Faso	2005	...	...	...	0.2	71.2	10.3	9.6	19.5	4.4
	2007	8.0	56.7	35.3	0.6	67.0	15.7	15.2	17.9	4.6
	2010	...	...	...	...	60.3	18.0	18.8	16.2	3.9
	2015	...	...	...	0.1	57.9	22.1	13.7	18.0	4.2

Dépenses publiques afférentes à l'éducation *(suite)*
Par type de dépenses, niveau de scolarité, dépenses publiques totales et PIB

Country or area Pays ou zone	Year Année	Percentage of total expenditure in public institutions Pourcentage des dépenses publiques totales en faveur de l'éducation			Percentage of government expenditure on education by level Pourcentage des dépenses publiques selon le niveau d'enseignement				As % of Govt. Expenditure En % des dépenses du gouv.	As % of GDP En % du PIB
		Other expenditure Dépenses courantes	Staff Compensation Rémunération du personnel	Capital expenditure Dépenses en Capital	Pre-primary Préprimaire	Primary Primaire	Secondary Secondaire	Tertiary Tertiaire		
Burundi Burundi	2004	15.7	57.8	26.6	~0.0	50.7	29.5	18.3	9.2	3.7
	2005	...	...	...	...	51.6	33.1	15.3	11.0	3.6
	2010	23.7	68.5	7.9	~0.0	45.4	27.9	18.0	16.6	6.8
	2012	20.5	77.6	1.9	~0.0	44.0	24.2	20.6	16.4	5.8
	2013	...	...	...	~0.0	45.4	26.8	24.2	17.2	5.4
	*2017	...	...	...	...	...	...	...	20.4	4.3
Cabo Verde Cabo Verde	2002	...	...	...	...	43.8	29.8	17.5	19.8	7.9
	2004	3.3	80.0	16.7	...	...	...	...	20.8	7.5
	*2005	2.1	82.4	16.7	...	...	...	...	...	...
	2008	...	...	15.9	0.3	36.3	36.6	11.3	18.2	5.5
	2009	...	...	...	...	44.1	33.0	14.0	15.9	5.3
	2010	15.6	77.1	7.3	...	...	...	...	14.2	5.6
	2016	12.2	82.8	4.9	1.1	39.1	40.8	17.6	17.8	5.4
	2017	...	...	...	1.0	38.1	39.9	17.2	16.4	5.2
Cambodia Cambodge	2001	...	...	...	1.1	74.4	11.2	...	11.4	1.7
	2002	...	...	...	1.0	64.6	...	...	10.1	1.7
	2004	...	...	...	...	...	...	...	12.4	1.7
	2010	...	...	...	1.7	50.0	42.5	5.8	7.3	1.5
	2012	57.3	42.7	...	2.0	49.2	44.1	...	7.2	1.6
	2013	...	...	...	2.7	49.7	41.5	6.1	9.6	2.1
	2014	...	...	0.5	2.6	48.5	44.1	...	8.8	1.9
Cameroon Cameroun	2005	...	...	...	...	35.1	52.0	12.6	21.4	2.9
	2010	6.5	80.2	13.4	3.9	34.2	52.7	9.0	18.8	3.0
	2012	...	...	...	3.5	36.2	52.6	7.8	15.2	2.7
	2013	10.7	75.7	13.6	4.0	33.9	...	10.2	13.8	2.8
	*2017	...	...	...	...	...	...	...	15.5	3.1
Canada Canada	2000	25.9	70.5	3.6	3.9	...	...	...	13.0	5.4
	2005	25.4	70.0	4.6	...	...	...	...	12.2	4.8
	2010	24.5	65.8	9.7	...	...	...	35.4	12.3	5.4
	2011	24.1	65.5	10.4	...	...	26.4	35.6	12.2	5.3
	2013	23.4	68.8	7.8	...	...	...	...	...	...
Cayman Islands Îles Caïmanes	2005	...	...	...	1.2	49.3	49.5	...	...	1.8
	2006	2.4	97.6	...	...	46.0	54.0	...	...	2.0
Central African Republic République centrafricaine	2005	...	79.2	2.2	...	...	...	...	9.7	1.7
	2008	13.5	84.2	2.3	...	...	25.9	17.5	7.9	1.3
	2010	...	...	1.1	2.3	53.3	24.0	20.5	6.5	1.2
	2011	...	...	...	...	...	...	27.3	7.8	1.2
Chad Tchad	2005	...	...	...	...	45.8	35.5	18.7	14.7	1.7
	2010	...	...	31.3	0.4	51.6	27.4	19.8	8.1	2.0
	2011	...	...	20.8	0.3	40.7	34.9	16.3	10.1	2.3
	2012	2.6	75.5	21.9	...	46.7	20.7	30.3	9.2	2.2
	2013	...	...	...	...	...	24.7	31.7	12.5	2.9
Chile Chili	2005	17.5	78.1	4.4	9.6	37.4	39.0	14.0	16.2	3.3
	2009	18.1	78.9	3.0	12.8	36.4	35.2	15.6	17.0	4.2
	2010	...	...	...	13.4	31.7	32.5	22.3	17.8	4.2
	2016	...	...	...	11.4	28.1	29.1	25.4	21.2	5.4
China, Hong Kong SAR Chine, RAS de Hong Kong	2005	...	...	...	2.3	23.1	33.8	28.4	22.5	4.1
	2010	...	...	12.7	3.8	20.9	35.5	27.8	19.9	3.5
	2012	...	...	18.2	3.9	18.7	33.6	32.8	18.6	3.5
	2017	...	...	...	5.3	21.7	32.7	28.5	17.8	3.3
China, Macao SAR Chine, RAS de Macao	2000	...	...	...	*7.6	*24.8	*25.0	28.4	...	3.3
	2003	...	...	...	...	*24.8	...	41.1	...	2.8
	2005	...	...	...	...	...	...	45.6	...	2.3
	2010	19.5	39.0	41.5	...	...	...	48.4	...	2.6
	2016	31.6	60.3	8.1	...	...	60.7	39.3	...	3.1

9

Public expenditure on education *(continued)*
By expenditure type, level of education, total government expenditure and GDP

Dépenses publiques afférentes à l'éducation *(suite)*
Par type de dépenses, niveau de scolarité, dépenses publiques totales et PIB

Country or area / Pays ou zone	Year / Année	Percentage of total expenditure in public institutions / Pourcentage des dépenses publiques totales en faveur de l'éducation			Percentage of government expenditure on education by level / Pourcentage des dépenses publiques selon le niveau d'enseignement				As % of Govt. Expenditure En % des dépenses du gouvt.	As % of GDP En % du PIB
		Other expenditure Dépenses courantes	Staff Compensation Rémunération du personnel	Capital expenditure Dépenses en Capital	Pre-primary Préprimaire	Primary Primaire	Secondary Secondaire	Tertiary Tertiaire		
Colombia	2004	23.3	71.0	5.7	* 2.7	* 48.3	* 35.7	13.3	15.4	4.1
Colombie	2005				2.6	47.4	36.1	13.8	15.5	4.0
	2010	6.8	71.0	22.3	5.8	35.9	34.8	22.1	16.4	4.8
	2017	5.2	70.9	23.8	5.8	36.4	38.7	18.5	15.2	4.4
Comoros	2002	...	...	...	* 0.4	* 45.2	* 40.1	* 7.7	15.8	3.9
Comores	2008	...	...	...	...	61.7	23.7	14.6	29.2	7.7
	2015	4.8	95.2		7.1	54.6	27.7	10.4	15.3	4.3
Congo	2005	...	...	...	* 2.9	* 27.3	* 41.2	* 25.9	7.6	1.8
Congo	2010	...	...	...	4.6	31.0	53.3	10.9	24.7	6.2
	*2015	...	...	...	...	...	...	...	8.0	4.6
Cook Islands	2000	...	...	...	7.1	50.6	36.5	...	...	2.1
Îles Cook	2013	...	...	...	11.4	40.4	40.6	7.6	...	3.0
	2016	34.0	63.3	2.6	...	...	...	11.5	...	4.7
Costa Rica	2004	...	...	...	7.9	45.5	27.8	18.8	...	4.9
Costa Rica	2010	...	...	...	5.4	41.9	31.5	18.4	...	6.6
	2017	39.7	55.9	4.4	6.0	28.9	31.7	23.6	...	7.4
Côte d'Ivoire	2000	...	...	...	* ~0.0	* 41.6	* 32.7	22.0	20.8	3.7
Côte d'Ivoire	2001	...	...	...	...	* 42.2	...	19.4	23.2	3.7
	2005	...	...	...	...	...	...	20.0	21.8	4.1
	2010	21.8	71.2	7.0	2.0	42.7	33.1	22.2	22.8	4.6
	*2015	21.4	72.7	5.9	3.0	41.4	34.2	21.4	21.2	4.8
	*2017								18.6	4.4
Croatia	2004	30.0	65.6	4.4	9.2	...	...	18.1	8.1	3.8
Croatie	2010	23.0	70.6	6.4	13.8	...	...	18.3	9.0	4.2
	2011	21.3	74.4	4.3	14.1	...	...	22.2	8.5	4.1
	2013	27.3	69.4	3.2	...	...	...	21.9	9.5	4.6
	2014	28.3	72.8	3.8	...	...	...	...	...	...
Cuba	2005	34.3	52.6	13.2	8.3	30.3	37.7	22.1	...	10.6
Cuba	2007	46.7	50.2	3.1	8.1	30.1	36.0	25.1	...	11.9
	2010	40.5	58.6	0.9	6.8	29.0	29.1	...	...	12.8
Curaçao										
Curaçao	2013	13.9	86.1	...	9.2	27.5	33.9	5.3	...	4.9
Cyprus	2005	9.8	76.9	13.4	4.9	27.3	44.9	22.9	15.8	6.2
Chypre	2010	11.5	77.5	11.0	5.5	31.0	43.0	20.5	15.6	6.6
	2015	13.0	82.9	4.1	5.5	32.2	41.3	20.7	16.3	6.4
Czechia	2005	34.4	56.0	9.7	9.8	14.5	51.3	21.0	9.2	3.9
Tchéquie	2010	38.4	51.5	10.1	11.4	16.2	45.7	22.5	9.3	4.1
	2015	56.6	35.5	7.9	9.0	13.3	29.8	13.3	13.9	5.8
Dem. Rep. of the Congo	2010	2.6	87.8	9.6	0.6	33.3	33.7	24.0	9.7	1.5
Rép. dém. du Congo	2013	1.7	81.4	16.9	1.0	61.6	14.4	22.0	16.3	2.1
	2015	...	...	...	...	...	...	23.8	11.7	2.2
	*2017	...	...	...	...	...	...	...	11.7	1.5
Denmark	2005	20.7	74.1	5.3	8.6	23.3	36.3	28.7	15.8	8.1
Danemark	2010	18.0	74.9	7.1	11.5	23.7	34.5	27.3	15.1	8.6
	2013	20.1	73.5	6.3	13.9	24.9	32.4	26.9	15.2	8.5
	2014	19.9	73.7	6.4	...	27.2	40.0	30.7	13.8	7.6
Djibouti	2005	...	42.2	2.7	...	...	...	...	22.7	8.4
Djibouti	2007	...	38.8	4.6	...	19.0	...	...	22.5	8.4
	2010	...	...	...	...	34.1	37.3	16.5	12.3	4.5
Dominica	2012	...	100.0	...	...	...	...	...	...	...
Dominique	2015	...	...	...	1.9	45.8	43.4	8.9	10.5	3.4
Dominican Republic	2002	16.6	76.7	6.7	2.1	62.8	...	...	12.1	1.9
République dominicaine	*2003	...	...	...	...	...	...	...	9.7	1.8
	2004	24.1	72.6	3.4	...	...	...	...	...	...
	2007	15.5	66.9	17.6	4.2	58.7	18.0	14.5	12.6	2.0
Ecuador	2000	16.7	78.1	5.2	...	38.3	34.6	5.2	5.0	1.2
Équateur	2010	...	...	...	21.4	32.4	10.4	35.8	13.0	4.5
	2015	...	...	...	21.1	23.3	12.1	43.5	12.6	5.0

9 Public expenditure on education *(continued)*
By expenditure type, level of education, total government expenditure and GDP

Dépenses publiques afférentes à l'éducation *(suite)*
Par type de dépenses, niveau de scolarité, dépenses publiques totales et PIB

Country or area Pays ou zone	Year Année	Percentage of total expenditure in public institutions Pourcentage des dépenses publiques totales en faveur de l'éducation			Percentage of government expenditure on education by level Pourcentage des dépenses publiques selon le niveau d'enseignement				As % of Govt. Expenditure En % des dépenses du gouvt.	As % of GDP En % du PIB
		Other expenditure Dépenses courantes	Staff Compensation Rémunération du personnel	Capital expenditure Dépenses en Capital	Pre-primary Préprimaire	Primary Primaire	Secondary Secondaire	Tertiary Tertiaire		
Egypt Égypte	2005	...	...	...	...	...	...	...	15.0	4.8
	2008	...	...	...	...	...	...	...	10.9	3.8
El Salvador El Salvador	2005	27.3	66.9	5.8	* 8.5	* 51.0	* 29.1	* 11.1	* 14.7	* 3.2
	2008	37.8	51.7	10.5	9.1	38.0	22.0	...	19.4	4.5
	2010	...	...	...	7.9	42.7	30.1	12.2	16.2	4.0
	2016	25.0	68.0	7.0	9.2	47.2	35.3	8.0	16.1	3.9
	2017	...	92.0	8.0	9.9	45.6	34.9	9.4	15.6	3.8
Eritrea Érythrée	2002	8.6	31.0	60.4	...	26.0	35.4	14.9	5.6	3.5
	2004	...	...	41.7	...	23.1	21.1	31.9	5.7	3.1
	2006	22.7	57.7	19.6	...	...	...	...	5.2	2.1
Estonia Estonie	2002	28.8	56.3	15.0	5.2	28.0	40.9	19.7	15.1	5.5
	2004	...	...	9.5	6.4	25.8	46.3	17.4	14.3	4.9
	2005	...	...	...	7.4	25.3	43.7	18.9	14.3	4.8
	2010	...	...	...	7.8	24.6	40.1	21.7	13.6	5.5
	2013	28.9	57.7	13.4	7.3	30.7	29.4	28.2	12.6	4.8
	2015	26.9	64.8	8.4	...	23.9	25.9	27.0	13.0	5.2
Eswatini Eswatini	2005	...	...	...	~0.0	39.9	34.9	23.9	20.9	6.5
	2010	...	...	...	0.2	47.2	35.5	16.6	18.3	6.1
	2014	36.2	59.3	4.5	1.1	50.8	34.1	13.3	24.9	7.1
Ethiopia Éthiopie	*2002	...	...	...	...	...	...	...	16.2	3.6
	2010	21.0	44.8	34.1	~0.0	28.4	25.0	43.9	26.3	4.5
	2015	19.4	45.2	35.4	1.9	27.5	18.1	47.9	27.1	4.7
Fiji Fidji	2004	...	...	...	0.2	39.1	32.6	15.9	23.7	6.2
	2005	...	...	...	...	...	...	...	20.3	5.1
	2009	...	...	...	...	...	...	...	15.9	4.5
	2011	...	...	...	0.4	44.4	15.9	13.0	14.4	4.2
	2013	1.2	98.7	0.1	...	38.6	...	22.6	14.3	3.9
Finland Finlande	2005	32.1	60.9	7.0	5.5	20.8	41.9	31.8	12.2	6.0
	2010	33.6	60.3	6.1	5.8	19.9	42.4	31.8	11.9	6.5
	2015	34.7	56.5	8.8	10.8	20.2	37.5	26.7	12.4	7.1
France France	2005	15.6	74.5	9.9	11.4	20.2	47.1	21.1	10.4	5.5
	2010	17.4	73.2	9.4	11.6	20.4	45.0	22.6	10.0	5.7
	2015	17.1	75.1	7.8	12.7	20.7	43.4	22.8	9.6	5.5
Gabon Gabon	*2000	...	...	...	...	...	...	...	17.7	3.8
	2010	...	...	...	3.6	29.6	28.3	37.8	13.3	3.1
	2014	...	45.5	...	3.8	29.2	28.9	37.8	11.2	2.7
Gambia Gambie	2005	...	...	...	...	61.4	23.1	14.3	5.3	1.1
	2010	10.8	46.4	42.8	...	65.3	23.4	9.9	17.6	4.2
	2012	7.4	50.4	42.2	...	60.0	31.4	7.4	13.8	4.1
	2014	...	...	...	...	55.2	30.2	14.6	11.8	3.3
	*2016	...	...	...	...	...	...	...	10.4	3.1
Georgia Géorgie	2005	...	...	...	...	...	...	...	11.2	2.5
	2008	...	...	...	10.7	36.0	37.0	11.6	8.9	2.9
	*2009	...	...	...	12.3	...	...	...	9.0	3.2
	2012	...	...	...	14.4	34.3	32.1	19.2	6.7	2.0
	2017	...	...	...	...	...	...	10.1	13.0	3.8
Germany Allemagne	2010	19.8	70.6	9.6	9.1	13.5	45.5	27.2	10.4	4.9
	2015	20.2	73.0	6.8	9.5	12.9	41.9	25.9	11.0	4.8
Ghana Ghana	2005	22.3	63.0	14.7	5.9	39.5	32.5	22.1	23.4	7.4
	2010	14.3	68.8	16.9	6.1	30.9	37.1	25.9	20.7	5.5
	2014	18.2	73.3	8.6	7.3	21.7	37.0	18.3	21.0	6.2
	*2017	...	...	...	...	...	...	...	20.1	4.5
Gibraltar Gibraltar	2017	42.3	54.2	3.5	...	...	...	...	...	...
Greece Grèce	2005	11.0	67.3	21.7	...	...	33.9	36.1	8.7	4.0
Grenada Grenade	2003	8.3	82.2	9.5	5.7	36.4	35.8	9.8	10.8	3.9
	2016	...	...	...	1.9	56.8	23.4	9.6	42.8	10.3

Public expenditure on education *(continued)*
By expenditure type, level of education, total government expenditure and GDP

Dépenses publiques afférentes à l'éducation *(suite)*
Par type de dépenses, niveau de scolarité, dépenses publiques totales et PIB

Country or area Pays ou zone	Year Année	Percentage of total expenditure in public institutions Pourcentage des dépenses publiques totales en faveur de l'éducation			Percentage of government expenditure on education by level Pourcentage des dépenses publiques selon le niveau d'enseignement				As % of Govt. Expenditure En % des dépenses du gouvt.	As % of GDP En % du PIB
		Other expenditure Dépenses courantes	Staff Compensation Rémunération du personnel	Capital expenditure Dépenses en Capital	Pre-primary Préprimaire	Primary Primaire	Secondary Secondaire	Tertiary Tertiaire		
Guatemala	2008	9.9	65.2	11.5	10.0	59.8	12.8	10.8	23.3	3.2
Guatemala	2010	...	...	0.1	11.2	55.6	14.8	11.3	19.3	2.8
	2017	23.6	72.0	4.4	12.7	56.5	13.1	13.2	23.1	2.8
Guinea	2005	...	...	...	...	...	...	30.6	10.9	1.8
Guinée	2010	...	...	7.7	...	38.9	24.9	36.2	12.4	2.6
	2017	12.6	75.1	12.3	0.1	40.5	22.7	36.7	13.4	2.2
Guinea-Bissau	2010	12.5	61.5	26.0	0.7	46.7	46.7	5.0	9.1	1.9
Guinée-Bissau	2013	0.9	48.3	50.8	0.8	64.4	30.4	3.9	16.2	2.1
Guyana	2004	37.6	51.8	10.6	11.6	32.1	26.5	6.2	11.1	5.5
Guyana	2005	23.1	62.3	14.6	...	...	...	...	13.8	8.1
	2010	22.8	68.4	8.7	11.5	29.1	33.4	5.3	11.8	3.6
	2012	22.5	62.9	14.6	11.6	30.6	33.3	5.1	10.2	3.2
	2017	...	...	...	...	...	...	...	18.3	6.3
Haiti										
Haïti	2016	...	...	...	...	...	...	...	13.1	2.4
Honduras	2013	15.6	79.7	4.7	7.3	48.9	25.3	18.5	19.9	5.9
Honduras	2015	...	...	...	...	...	...	13.7	24.6	6.4
	2017	...	...	...	...	...	...	...	22.0	6.0
Hungary	2005	21.0	71.6	7.4	14.2	20.1	40.4	18.9	10.8	5.3
Hongrie	2010	27.1	62.5	10.4	14.4	17.8	40.3	20.1	9.7	4.8
	2015	26.3	67.4	6.3	16.8	16.4	38.1	14.3	9.1	4.6
Iceland	2005	23.6	67.9	8.5	6.7	35.0	33.6	19.1	17.8	7.4
Islande	2010	20.8	72.6	6.6	9.6	32.4	31.2	21.5	14.6	7.2
	2015	29.7	64.8	5.5	11.5	28.6	28.1	18.9	18.2	7.7
India	2005	9.0	86.2	4.8	1.3	35.6	42.9	19.6	11.2	3.2
Inde	2010	...	...	...	1.1	25.2	37.0	36.1	11.8	3.4
	2013	...	...	...	1.6	28.4	41.4	28.5	14.1	3.8
Indonesia	*2005	...	...	...	...	...	...	...	15.1	2.9
Indonésie	2010	33.6	54.5	11.9	0.7	44.4	24.3	16.1	16.7	2.8
	2014	25.0	63.3	11.7	1.8	43.7	26.8	15.1	17.7	3.3
	2015	24.1	64.1	11.9	...	42.6	27.0	15.8	20.5	3.6
Iran (Islamic Republic of)	2002	...	...	8.2	0.9	25.9	36.3	18.5	26.3	4.5
Iran (Rép. islamique d')	2005	...	...	...	1.0	22.4	34.6	15.4	22.3	4.1
	2010	...	...	...	1.0	24.7	49.2	21.4	18.8	3.7
	2017	19.6	76.1	4.3	0.4	30.1	33.0	32.6	20.0	3.8
Ireland	2005	17.3	74.2	8.4	0.1	33.6	34.8	23.3	13.6	4.5
Irlande	2010	19.7	71.6	8.7	1.6	35.3	33.8	22.2	9.3	6.0
	2015	15.1	78.1	6.9	2.0	36.9	33.3	23.3	13.0	3.8
Israel	2005	25.1	68.8	6.1	10.7	37.5	28.9	16.6	12.7	5.8
Israël	2010	18.7	72.9	8.4	11.0	41.2	25.7	16.9	13.6	5.5
	2015	15.5	75.3	9.2	13.6	38.7	30.6	16.2	15.0	5.9
Italy	2005	20.9	71.9	7.2	10.3	24.6	46.5	17.2	9.0	4.2
Italie	2010	20.5	74.7	4.8	10.0	25.0	42.9	18.8	8.7	4.4
	2015	18.9	76.1	5.0	11.7	25.0	42.7	18.6	8.1	4.1
Jamaica	2004	7.5	88.1	4.5	5.6	32.6	41.9	18.8	11.7	3.9
Jamaïque	2005	...	...	...	4.9	* 34.2	* 38.0	22.1	14.3	4.6
	2008	4.9	85.6	9.4	5.5	30.2	42.6	15.7	19.1	6.2
	2009	7.0	93.0	...	8.2	33.2	37.1	20.3	17.6	6.2
	2010	...	...	...	4.0	36.3	36.6	21.8	16.1	6.4
	2017	19.6	77.6	2.8	3.8	37.9	36.3	19.3	18.4	5.3
Japan										
Japon	2016	23.4	64.5	12.1	2.8	33.0	38.8	18.8	9.1	3.5
Jordan										
Jordanie	2017	9.2	85.1	5.6	0.6	43.2	37.7	18.5	12.5	3.6
Kazakhstan	2005	40.6	53.2	6.2	3.8	...	...	12.3	10.2	2.3
Kazakhstan	2009	34.2	56.8	9.0	6.8	...	...	13.1	13.0	3.1
	2010	32.8	57.8	9.4	...	...	...	...	...	...
	2017	34.6	61.2	4.2	12.4	0.7	68.8	10.6	11.4	2.9

9

Public expenditure on education *(continued)*
By expenditure type, level of education, total government expenditure and GDP

Dépenses publiques afférentes à l'éducation *(suite)*
Par type de dépenses, niveau de scolarité, dépenses publiques totales et PIB

Country or area Pays ou zone	Year Année	Percentage of total expenditure in public institutions Pourcentage des dépenses publiques totales en faveur de l'éducation			Percentage of government expenditure on education by level Pourcentage des dépenses publiques selon le niveau d'enseignement				As % of Govt. Expenditure En % des dépenses du gouvt.	As % of GDP En % du PIB
		Other expenditure Dépenses courantes	Staff Compensation Rémunération du personnel	Capital expenditure Dépenses en Capital	Pre-primary Préprimaire	Primary Primaire	Secondary Secondaire	Tertiary Tertiaire		
Kenya	2004	...	...	...	1.6	62.1	23.4	12.9	26.7	6.8
Kenya	2005	...	...	...	...	...	...	...	27.5	7.3
	2006	...	...	...	0.1	54.1	21.7	15.4	25.1	7.0
	2010	...	...	...	...	...	...	...	20.6	5.5
	2015	31.6	60.9	7.5	1.8	36.3	41.8	13.1	16.7	5.3
	*2017	...	...	...	...	...	...	...	17.6	5.2
Kiribati										
Kiribati	2001	...	...	...		34.3	...		11.5	12.0
Kuwait	2005	17.4	74.9	7.7	9.8	19.8	36.2	32.6	13.9	4.7
Koweït	*2006	...	...	...	9.6	20.4	36.2	32.6	13.4	3.8
Kyrgyzstan	2005	28.4	66.2	5.4	6.2	...	...	19.2	16.8	4.9
Kirghizistan	2010	29.1	64.5	6.5	8.1	...	...	15.5	15.7	5.8
	2014	17.6	69.1	13.3	10.7	...	...	4.6	14.5	5.5
	2016	13.0	69.2	17.8	...	...	...	3.0	16.8	6.6
	*2017	...	...	...	...	...	...	...	18.6	7.2
Lao People's Dem. Rep.	2002	...	...	...	1.9	45.0	19.0	12.6	16.2	2.8
Rép. dém. populaire lao	2005	...	...	...	1.6	62.5	...	...	13.7	2.4
	2010	16.7	65.0	18.3	6.8	46.5	29.9	16.2	7.3	1.7
	2014	12.4	72.6	15.0	6.6	40.6	38.6	13.8	12.2	2.9
Latvia	2004	21.9	69.7	8.4	13.0	16.3	56.4	13.4	14.5	4.9
Lettonie	2010	21.6	65.7	12.7	16.8	28.5	38.4	15.9	11.8	5.1
	2015	23.8	60.5	15.6	15.1	30.1	31.4	22.1	14.1	5.3
Lebanon	2005	1.6	94.7	3.7	...	...	...	28.8	8.4	2.7
Liban	2010	0.1	88.0	11.9	...	...	...	27.2	5.5	1.6
	2011	0.1	86.8	13.1	...	...	...	26.5	5.7	1.6
	2013	2.4	97.6	...	...	...	17.1	28.7	8.6	2.5
Lesotho	2001	...	...	8.7	...	53.2	23.8	18.6	23.8	9.4
Lesotho	2005	...	...	...	...	* 43.0	* 18.3	* 36.4	32.4	12.1
	2008	...	...	* 1.7	0.1	36.0	20.5	36.4	24.7	11.4
	2018	3.6	92.9	3.5	0.2	56.0	30.1	7.4	13.8	6.4
Liberia	2008	47.4	41.4	11.2	...	...	...	...	6.5	3.2
Libéria	2012	...	...	...	...	30.7	34.5	* 31.6	5.2	2.8
	*2017	...	...	...	...	...	...	...	7.1	3.8
Liechtenstein	2004	...	...	...	6.5	29.0	42.6	13.9	...	2.4
Liechtenstein	2007	19.3	80.7	...	6.9	30.6	47.2	9.1	...	1.9
	2008	30.2	69.8	...	7.3	31.1	52.4	...	...	2.0
	2010	18.9	68.4	12.6	...	...	...	...	...	...
	2011	20.7	73.9	5.4	7.1	38.6	47.4	...	...	2.6
Lithuania	2005	20.1	73.0	6.8	12.1	14.9	50.6	21.0	14.6	4.9
Lituanie	2010	19.5	72.9	7.6	12.9	16.7	44.9	23.6	12.9	5.3
	2015	20.1	67.5	12.4	13.3	16.5	36.7	27.9	12.3	4.2
Luxembourg	2001	11.2	71.3	17.5	...	...	...	...	9.3	3.6
Luxembourg	2015	14.1	76.1	9.8	14.5	31.6	40.7	13.1	9.4	3.9
Madagascar	2005	* 24.4	* 43.8	31.8	...	57.3	18.9	10.1	18.0	3.8
Madagascar	2008	31.3	58.7	10.0	0.4	53.6	22.1	15.4	16.3	2.9
	2009	...	...	...	0.3	52.3	18.2	15.4	22.6	3.2
	2012	...	...	* 4.6	0.2	47.4	19.3	15.2	20.3	2.7
	2013	29.5	67.4	3.1	...	...	...	...	14.0	2.1
	*2014	...	...	...	...	...	...	...	19.0	2.8
Malawi	2001	...	...	...	...	45.2	22.5	15.3	...	4.5
Malawi	2003	...	...	...	...	54.9	21.1	...	16.6	3.2
	2010	...	...	4.9	~0.0	34.8	24.1	29.8	12.5	3.5
	2013	14.5	71.7	13.8	~0.0	36.7	24.4	28.4	20.4	5.4
	2016	...	...	3.1	...	43.9	28.8	23.1	17.1	4.7
	*2017	...	...	...	...	...	...	...	14.3	4.0

9

Public expenditure on education *(continued)*
By expenditure type, level of education, total government expenditure and GDP

Dépenses publiques afférentes à l'éducation *(suite)*
Par type de dépenses, niveau de scolarité, dépenses publiques totales et PIB

Country or area Pays ou zone	Year Année	Percentage of total expenditure in public institutions Pourcentage des dépenses publiques totales en faveur de l'éducation			Percentage of government expenditure on education by level Pourcentage des dépenses publiques selon le niveau d'enseignement				As % of Govt. Expend- iture En % des dépenses du gouvt.	As % of GDP En % du PIB
		Other expenditure Dépenses courantes	Staff Comp- ensation Rémun- ération du personnel	Capital expenditure Dépenses en Capital	Pre-primary Préprimaire	Primary Primaire	Secondary Secondaire	Tertiary Tertiaire		
Malaysia	2004	30.2	56.8	13.1	1.1	29.6	35.1	33.4	21.0	5.9
Malaisie	2009	15.7	68.8	15.5	1.2	27.7	32.8	35.9	18.5	6.0
	2010	...	...	...	1.2	28.6	33.7	34.5	18.4	5.0
	2017	21.5	70.5	7.9	3.2	33.8	42.1	21.0	21.1	4.7
Maldives	2005	...	...	...	...	54.1	...	...	13.0	5.0
Maldives	2010	20.5	78.3	1.2	12.7	42.5	25.0	7.3	12.5	4.1
	2016	38.4	60.8	0.7	10.8	36.4	21.6	20.6	11.3	4.3
Mali	2005	...	...	...	...	...	...	...	16.3	3.5
Mali	2010	40.9	54.1	5.0	0.2	25.3	53.8	20.7	16.5	3.3
	2016	38.5	57.8	3.6	0.3	39.6	37.4	21.7	13.9	3.1
Malta	2004	14.5	79.9	5.6	5.2	21.1	39.8	11.0	10.6	4.5
Malte	2010	17.5	72.4	10.1	7.4	21.6	45.7	22.8	15.7	6.5
	2015	13.7	72.7	13.6	9.7	24.3	37.5	25.3	13.2	5.3
Marshall Islands	2002	* 22.6	* 75.0	* 2.4	...	45.5	38.9	14.7	14.8	8.7
Îles Marshall	2003	...	...	...	...	...	...	...	22.5	12.2
	2006	42.8	35.8	21.4	...	...	...	...	...	...
Mauritania	*2004	...	...	...	...	...	...	...	8.2	2.5
Mauritanie	2010	...	...	...	0.5	47.5	23.2	18.8	16.0	3.6
	*2016	...	...	...	0.5	55.9	25.9	17.7	9.3	2.6
Mauritius	2005	...	...	...	1.5	27.2	44.2	11.3	17.1	4.2
Maurice	2010	...	...	13.5	1.4	27.0	52.6	9.4	14.6	3.6
	2017	...	...	...	1.2	23.1	63.1	5.9	19.9	5.0
Mexico	2005	11.2	85.7	3.1	10.4	39.1	30.3	17.5	21.9	4.8
Mexique	2010	10.3	85.7	3.9	10.2	36.0	30.3	19.7	18.6	5.2
	2011	10.6	85.5	3.9	10.4	35.5	30.7	18.1	18.4	5.1
	2015	11.9	85.1	3.1	...	32.5	32.3	21.5	19.0	5.2
Micronesia (Fed. States of)	*2000	...	...	...	...	...	...	...	10.0	6.7
Micronésie (États féd. de)	2015	...	...	...	...	...	...	...	22.3	12.5
Monaco	2004	2.1	90.9	7.0	4.3	15.4	45.8	4.4	...	1.2
Monaco	2010	8.4	90.7	0.9	3.2	15.3	37.7	...	...	1.3
	2016	8.5	80.8	10.7	3.0	12.7	31.5	...	...	1.4
Mongolia	2000	55.8	43.4	0.8	...	...	...	...	16.1	5.6
Mongolie	2002	...	...	4.9	14.1	...	...	15.5	20.3	7.2
	2004	...	...	...	18.5	25.1	32.8	18.4	13.6	4.3
	2010	...	...	...	22.0	26.9	33.7	6.7	14.7	4.6
	2017	21.8	69.3	8.9	26.3	32.2	29.2	6.4	13.5	4.1
Montserrat	2001	* 27.5	* 41.4	* 31.2	13.6	20.6	29.5	5.5	...	4.8
Montserrat	2004	...	...	...	...	20.5	...	...	...	3.8
	2009	...	...	...	...	...	...	...	...	5.1
Morocco	2008	...	...	...	~0.0	35.5	43.1	...	17.5	5.3
Maroc	2009	...	...	...	...	37.7	41.9	20.2	17.3	5.3
	2018	~0.0	99.8	0.2	...	...	...	...	...	...
Mozambique	2005	...	...	22.6	...	...	...	...	22.7	4.4
Mozambique	2006	...	...	26.8	...	57.7	29.3	12.1	18.6	4.3
	2013	22.2	58.5	19.3	...	49.2	30.6	13.7	19.0	6.5
Myanmar	2017	22.4	57.2	20.3	0.5	36.0	39.4	11.3	10.2	2.2
Myanmar	2018	...	...	...	...	39.3	41.0	14.8	9.4	...
Namibia	2000	19.3	73.6	7.2	0.2	58.8	27.2	12.0	21.9	7.0
Namibie	2003	...	...	...	0.5	63.1	25.8	9.1	20.3	6.1
	2008	...	* 79.9	...	0.4	47.6	18.7	9.9	24.9	6.5
	2010	22.1	77.0	0.8	...	40.0	23.5	23.1	26.1	8.3
	2014	3.5	89.1	7.4	1.3	16.9	15.3	50.6	7.6	3.1
Nauru	2002	...	...	...	...	67.5	...	...	...	...
Nauru	*2007	20.8	56.9	...	...	...	...	...	...	...

Public expenditure on education *(continued)*
By expenditure type, level of education, total government expenditure and GDP

Dépenses publiques afférentes à l'éducation *(suite)*
Par type de dépenses, niveau de scolarité, dépenses publiques totales et PIB

Country or area Pays ou zone	Year Année	Percentage of total expenditure in public institutions Pourcentage des dépenses publiques totales en faveur de l'éducation			Percentage of government expenditure on education by level Pourcentage des dépenses publiques selon le niveau d'enseignement				As % of Govt. Expend-iture En % des dépenses du gouvt.	As % of GDP En % du PIB
		Other expenditure Dépenses courantes	Staff Comp-ensation Rémun-ération du personnel	Capital expenditure Dépenses en Capital	Pre-primary Préprimaire	Primary Primaire	Secondary Secondaire	Tertiary Tertiaire		
Nepal	2003	...	...	...	...	* 56.5	22.1	10.3	21.3	3.1
Népal	2005	...	...	...	...	...	...	...	22.3	3.4
	2010	18.0	69.2	12.8	1.0	55.7	30.5	12.7	16.0	3.6
	2015	24.9	64.1	11.0	2.1	53.8	33.3	10.8	17.0	3.7
	*2017	...	...	...	...	...	...	...	15.7	5.1
Netherlands	2005	17.5	69.8	12.7	7.7	...	...	...	12.4	5.2
Pays-Bas	2010	18.5	69.6	11.9	6.9	...	...	...	11.7	5.6
	2015	20.8	67.8	11.4	6.6	22.3	40.9	30.1	12.3	5.4
New Zealand	2005	...	...	...	3.3	...	...	...	16.3	6.3
Nouvelle-Zélande	2010	...	...	...	6.7	...	...	...	15.7	7.0
	2016	...	...	...	7.3	24.6	35.9	25.3	16.6	6.3
Nicaragua	2002	10.7	80.1	9.2	...	...	...	...	...	2.4
Nicaragua	*2003	...	...	...	...	...	...	...	...	2.4
	2004	...	...	11.7	...	...	...	...	...	...
	2010	10.7	46.2	11.4	3.6	39.8	13.2	26.0	...	4.5
	2017	...	...	...	...	...	...	...	...	4.3
Niger	2003	...	...	...	...	72.6	...	...	13.8	2.4
Niger	2010	14.2	77.9	7.9	2.4	61.0	21.3	12.6	18.1	3.7
	2017	25.8	71.8	2.4	10.8	48.1	17.6	23.3	13.3	3.5
Niue	2002	...	...	...	...	28.8	50.7	...	...	...
Nioué	2016	10.3	89.7	...	5.2	37.0	56.9	...	...	...
	2017	...	...	...	5.7	33.4	60.1	...	...	...
North Macedonia										
Macédoine du Nord	2002	10.8	87.1	2.1	...	...	...	15.0	8.6	3.3
Norway	2005	22.4	66.9	10.7	4.1	25.0	35.7	32.4	16.5	6.9
Norvège	2010	21.3	67.4	11.3	4.9	26.7	35.3	29.6	15.2	6.7
	2015	18.1	69.7	12.3	8.8	23.7	29.4	25.9	15.7	7.6
Oman	2002	...	...	14.4	...	46.8	43.2	10.0	11.1	4.3
Oman	2005	...	...	...	...	50.5	41.8	7.6	10.1	3.5
	2009	...	...	...	...	33.0	40.2	26.9	10.9	4.2
	2017	18.9	77.5	3.5	...	37.9	33.3	28.7	15.3	6.7
Pakistan	2005	12.3	49.2	38.5	...	...	...	...	13.8	2.3
Pakistan	2007	14.8	59.1	26.1	...	...	...	...	15.4	2.6
	2010	...	...	...	...	...	...	...	11.9	2.3
	2016	...	...	13.7	16.6	43.7	29.0	10.7	12.6	2.5
	2017	...	...	...	...	...	...	10.2	13.8	2.8
Palau	2001	...	...	...	* 14.6	* 44.9	9.6	20.7	15.3	7.8
Palaos	*2002	...	...	...	...	...	...	...	15.5	7.6
Panama	2002	11.1	67.9	21.0	2.2	32.1	29.2	28.1	17.0	4.2
Panama	*2004	...	...	...	4.0	34.5	25.9	28.4	14.6	3.6
	2008	...	...	14.1	...	...	...	...	14.9	3.5
	2011	...	...	...	3.0	23.5	22.4	22.2	13.0	3.2
Paraguay	2004	6.2	89.4	4.4	7.6	46.6	29.8	15.9	...	3.4
Paraguay	2010	9.5	65.5	6.5	6.7	38.5	36.1	18.5	...	3.8
	2016	17.0	76.8	6.2	8.7	36.4	31.3	23.3	...	4.5
Peru	2005	9.3	81.3	9.4	8.1	35.6	31.4	10.7	14.3	2.8
Pérou	2010	14.5	64.6	20.9	12.0	39.9	34.2	13.8	13.6	2.9
	2017	28.4	53.5	18.1	16.0	33.5	33.8	16.7	18.2	3.9
Philippines	2005	11.1	85.5	3.4	0.1	52.0	26.8	13.3	12.4	2.4
Philippines	2009	18.4	73.4	8.2	1.7	55.0	29.7	12.0	13.2	2.7
Poland	2005	32.6	60.5	6.9	9.9	31.0	36.6	21.8	12.2	5.4
Pologne	2010	29.3	61.4	9.3	10.0	31.0	35.5	22.8	11.1	5.1
	2015	23.6	69.0	7.4	12.7	30.8	30.8	25.3	11.6	4.8
Portugal	2005	10.2	86.2	3.6	7.4	30.6	40.8	18.1	10.9	5.1
Portugal	2010	12.1	84.1	3.8	7.2	27.0	44.0	20.2	10.4	5.4
	2015	12.0	83.2	4.8	8.1	29.0	42.6	18.3	10.2	4.9
Puerto Rico										
Porto Rico	2014	37.4	58.0	4.6	7.4	22.0	24.6	36.8	...	6.1

9 Public expenditure on education *(continued)*
By expenditure type, level of education, total government expenditure and GDP

Dépenses publiques afférentes à l'éducation *(suite)*
Par type de dépenses, niveau de scolarité, dépenses publiques totales et PIB

Country or area / Pays ou zone	Year / Année	Percentage of total expenditure in public institutions / Pourcentage des dépenses publiques totales en faveur de l'éducation			Percentage of government expenditure on education by level / Pourcentage des dépenses publiques selon le niveau d'enseignement				As % of Govt. Expenditure / En % des dépenses du gouvt.	As % of GDP / En % du PIB
		Other expenditure / Dépenses courantes	Staff Compensation / Rémunération du personnel	Capital expenditure / Dépenses en Capital	Pre-primary / Préprimaire	Primary / Primaire	Secondary / Secondaire	Tertiary / Tertiaire		
Qatar	2005	...	...	...	...	...	...	...	13.7	4.0
Qatar	2009	...	...	...	4.4	17.6	14.7	...	14.8	3.4
	2010	...	...	...	...	...	...	...	13.8	4.5
	2017	24.9	52.7	22.4	...	...	...	...	8.9	2.9
Republic of Korea	2005	24.0	58.7	17.4	1.6	35.4	41.5	14.0	...	3.9
République de Corée	2009	27.2	55.8	17.0	2.2	32.6	38.2	17.1	...	4.7
	2015	24.8	64.2	11.0	9.4	31.8	39.8	18.9	...	5.3
Republic of Moldova	2005	...	...	...	...	...	...	...	19.3	7.2
République de Moldova	2010	29.1	62.6	8.2	19.5	18.0	37.3	18.0	22.3	9.1
	2017	24.9	62.8	12.3	23.1	22.7	35.3	14.7	18.3	6.7
Romania	2005	34.4	59.1	6.5	9.1	* 13.8	* 44.3	23.2	10.8	3.5
Roumanie	2010	27.1	62.2	10.8	10.0	16.4	35.8	28.5	9.1	3.5
	2015	31.8	62.5	5.7	10.7	13.3	41.1	21.2	9.1	3.1
Russian Federation	2005	...	...	...	13.9	...	...	21.1	12.0	3.8
Fédération de Russie	2008	...	...	...	15.0	...	...	23.1	12.0	4.1
	2015	21.9	70.9	7.2	...	...	...	21.1	10.9	3.8
Rwanda	2000	...	47.3	20.3	* 0.5	* 48.2	* 16.7	* 34.7	18.8	4.1
Rwanda	2001	24.4	33.8	41.8	...	...	...	...	25.3	5.7
	2010	25.1	58.7	16.1	0.2	36.7	30.7	22.7	17.5	4.9
	*2015	41.4	47.9	10.8	1.3	32.7	42.6	20.9	12.5	3.8
	*2016	44.8	42.2	13.0	7.7	34.6	52.8	...	12.3	3.5
	*2017	...	...	...	...	...	...	...	11.1	3.2
Saint Kitts and Nevis	2005	...	...	...	...	...	...	...	11.1	3.9
Saint-Kitts-et-Nevis	2007	...	...	...	...	...	...	...	13.1	4.3
	2015	...	...	...	15.6	21.4	40.2	15.4	8.6	2.8
	2016	18.6	61.7	19.8	...	...	...	...	...	...
Saint Lucia	2004	26.1	73.2	0.7	0.4	47.2	33.4	...	15.0	4.1
Sainte-Lucie	2005	...	...	...	...	...	...	...	16.3	5.1
	2006	28.4	45.3	26.3	...	...	...	...	19.0	5.3
	*2010	...	...	...	1.8	42.3	45.6	4.6	14.2	3.9
	2011	...	...	...	1.5	42.3	45.1	* 5.0	13.8	3.9
	2015	...	...	11.7	1.4	34.2	43.8	...	16.5	4.4
	2016	...	...	...	...	26.4	30.8	...	22.0	5.7
Saint Vincent & Grenadines	2005	14.6	51.9	33.6	0.3	41.0	31.7	3.7	22.6	6.4
Saint-Vincent-Grenadines	2010	5.6	94.4	...	2.0	41.4	36.3	7.0	15.5	5.1
	2017	...	...	...	...	36.6	31.8	...	19.0	5.8
Samoa	2001	...	...	...	* 0.7	* 36.2	* 29.8	33.2	12.8	3.8
Samoa	*2002	...	...	...	...	45.8	...	...	12.8	3.8
	2008	...	...	...	...	...	...	...	16.1	5.1
	2016	...	...	...	0.9	37.0	42.8	9.2	10.5	4.1
San Marino	2010	4.2	95.8	...	19.0	31.7	39.5	9.8	10.8	2.3
Saint-Marin	2011	5.0	95.0	...	20.2	33.3	35.8	10.8	10.6	2.4
Sao Tome and Principe	2005	...	...	...	...	...	...	...	12.1	5.3
Sao Tomé-et-Principe	2010	...	...	...	...	...	...	...	19.3	9.7
	2014	...	...	...	12.0	55.8	22.6	9.6	12.3	3.7
	2017	...	...	...	...	...	...	...	18.4	4.9
Saudi Arabia	2005	...	...	...	...	...	...	...	19.3	5.4
Arabie saoudite	2008	...	...	...	...	...	...	...	19.3	5.1
Senegal	2005	...	...	...	0.9	41.8	22.4	22.0	21.8	5.1
Sénégal	2010	18.3	72.6	9.1	1.1	43.2	27.9	26.8	24.0	6.5
	2016	27.2	67.8	5.0	0.5	31.3	16.7	28.1	21.3	6.6
	*2017	...	...	...	...	...	...	...	21.6	6.2
Serbia	2010	22.4	75.1	2.5	0.5	45.9	23.3	29.1	10.1	4.6
Serbie	2015	19.4	78.7	1.9	0.7	45.3	22.9	30.1	8.9	4.0
	2016	21.6	75.3	3.2	...	...	...	28.9	8.7	3.9

Public expenditure on education *(continued)*
By expenditure type, level of education, total government expenditure and GDP

Dépenses publiques afférentes à l'éducation *(suite)*
Par type de dépenses, niveau de scolarité, dépenses publiques totales et PIB

| Country or area Pays ou zone | Year Année | Percentage of total expenditure in public institutions Pourcentage des dépenses publiques totales en faveur de l'éducation | | | Percentage of government expenditure on education by level Pourcentage des dépenses publiques selon le niveau d'enseignement | | | | As % of Govt. Expend-iture En % des dépenses du gouvt. | As % of GDP En % du PIB |
		Other expenditure Dépenses courantes	Staff Comp-ensation Rémun-ération du personnel	Capital expenditure Dépenses en Capital	Pre-primary Préprimaire	Primary Primaire	Secondary Secondaire	Tertiary Tertiaire		
Seychelles Seychelles	2002	23.9	66.4	9.7	* 10.5	* 32.0	* 26.1	17.4	9.2	5.2
	2003	31.8	59.3	8.9	* 8.6	* 32.8	* 28.9	...	12.0	5.4
	2006	29.8	56.7	13.5	4.1	...	...	17.9	11.0	4.8
	2016	64.5	30.2	5.2	9.0	30.6	27.1	21.6	11.7	4.4
Sierra Leone Sierra Leone	*2005	...	...	...	...	...	...	...	15.5	2.8
	2010	28.3	69.1	2.5	...	50.7	26.4	19.6	12.8	2.6
	2011	24.5	74.3	1.2	...	52.6	26.3	17.9	12.4	2.7
	2014	...	...	0.5	...	43.1	23.4	30.7	15.1	2.7
	2017	...	...	...	...	20.4	20.2	59.0	19.9	4.6
Singapore Singapour	2005	...	...	...	...	...	...	...	19.8	3.2
	2010	...	...	9.2	...	20.8	25.0	35.1	17.2	3.1
	2013	...	...	8.2	...	22.0	23.0	35.3	20.0	2.9
Slovakia Slovaquie	2005	34.1	60.2	5.6	10.1	17.1	48.9	21.0	9.5	3.8
	2010	30.8	57.0	12.2	9.4	20.7	46.9	19.6	9.8	4.1
	2015	32.0	53.0	15.0	10.5	19.1	37.9	29.9	10.3	4.6
Slovenia Slovénie	2003	21.0	69.4	9.6	9.2	* 21.8	* 46.6	22.3	13.7	5.7
	2005	20.6	69.4	10.0	10.4	...	...	22.0	13.3	5.6
	2010	21.3	70.0	8.7	10.3	28.5	37.1	24.0	12.1	5.6
	2015	22.3	69.6	8.2	11.3	28.3	34.4	19.9	11.2	4.9
Solomon Islands Îles Salomon	2010	...	...	...	...	...	...	...	17.5	9.9
South Africa Afrique du Sud	2005	20.9	66.3	2.9	0.6	42.9	32.6	15.1	19.9	5.1
	2006	...	69.8	* 3.5	0.5	45.1	31.1	12.8	18.0	5.1
	2009	...	...	* 3.8	0.9	41.1	30.9	12.5	18.3	5.2
	2010	...	...	...	1.1	42.5	31.4	11.9	18.0	5.7
	2017	28.0	67.0	5.0	1.6	38.9	29.4	14.4	18.7	6.1
South Sudan Soudan du sud	2014	34.6	48.8	16.5	0.6	57.5	16.6	24.7	4.1	1.5
	2016	6.5	93.5	...	0.3	36.4	12.2	50.4	0.8	1.5
	2017	...	...	...	0.1	48.6	18.5	31.5	1.1	1.0
Spain Espagne	2005	16.7	73.5	9.8	12.4	25.8	39.5	22.4	10.8	4.1
	2010	17.7	71.6	10.8	14.1	25.5	37.0	23.4	10.6	4.8
	2015	18.2	76.5	5.3	11.0	26.6	36.8	22.4	9.8	4.3
Sri Lanka Sri Lanka	2010	9.9	75.5	14.6	...	25.0	53.2	16.4	8.6	1.7
	2017	26.6	53.4	20.0	...	33.4	51.2	13.0	14.5	2.8
State of Palestine État de Palestine	2010	...	...	...	...	...	...	...	...	6.7
	2017	14.2	83.5	2.2	...	...	...	...	...	5.3
Sudan Soudan	2005	...	...	...	...	...	...	...	6.0	1.6
	2009	...	...	...	...	...	...	...	10.8	2.2
Sweden Suède	2005	28.4	65.0	6.6	7.8	26.2	38.2	27.5	12.8	6.6
	2010	31.3	63.1	5.6	10.2	24.3	35.6	29.0	13.3	6.6
	2015	29.6	65.3	5.1	17.0	23.3	27.1	24.9	15.5	7.6
Switzerland Suisse	2005	15.5	75.3	9.1	3.6	29.7	37.7	26.0	15.8	5.2
	2010	16.2	75.2	8.6	3.7	28.0	41.3	25.3	15.4	4.9
	2015	15.4	74.3	10.2	7.9	28.5	35.6	26.3	15.5	5.1
	2016	15.3	74.1	10.6	8.0	28.9	...	26.0	15.5	5.1
Syrian Arab Republic République arabe syrienne	2002	...	...	...	...	44.4	33.4	21.0	16.8	5.0
	2004	...	...	...	...	...	...	24.8	17.1	5.4
	2009	...	...	...	...	38.9	36.9	24.2	19.2	5.1
Tajikistan Tadjikistan	2005	...	...	...	3.8	...	...	7.4	15.3	3.5
	2010	...	...	...	5.0	...	...	10.1	15.3	4.0
	2015	...	...	14.0	5.3	...	...	9.9	16.4	5.2
Thailand Thaïlande	2004	...	...	...	10.4	31.0	24.0	20.6	21.5	4.0
	2005	...	...	...	13.6	...	...	21.7	20.5	3.9
	2010	45.8	50.9	3.3	5.7	40.1	28.6	16.5	16.2	3.5
	2013	45.8	49.2	5.0	5.4	41.1	29.8	15.6	19.1	4.1
	2014	31.8	62.5	5.7	...	...	...	...	...	...
Timor-Leste Timor-Leste	2010	52.5	37.8	9.7	...	...	...	10.4	9.2	2.4
	2014	46.4	49.5	4.0	1.2	64.9	29.8	4.1	6.8	2.7

9

Public expenditure on education *(continued)*
By expenditure type, level of education, total government expenditure and GDP

Dépenses publiques afférentes à l'éducation *(suite)*
Par type de dépenses, niveau de scolarité, dépenses publiques totales et PIB

Country or area Pays ou zone	Year Année	Other expenditure Dépenses courantes	Staff Compensation Rémunération du personnel	Capital expenditure Dépenses en Capital	Pre-primary Préprimaire	Primary Primaire	Secondary Secondaire	Tertiary Tertiaire	As % of Govt. Expenditure En % des dépenses du gouvt.	As % of GDP En % du PIB
Togo	2000	20.9	69.1	10.0	...	48.6	29.3	17.4	24.4	4.5
Togo	2005	...	...	...	...	41.8	...	...	17.7	3.4
	2010	14.7	74.7	10.6	2.6	51.7	25.6	16.7	19.6	4.4
	2016	7.1	90.5	2.4	1.6	64.1	16.0	17.9	16.0	5.1
Tonga										
Tonga	2004	...	...	...	...	44.4	30.1	21.7	18.1	3.9
Trinidad and Tobago										
Trinité-et-Tobago	2003	...	...	...	0.6	39.2	36.8	...	13.9	3.1
Tunisia	2000	8.2	77.3	14.5	...	* 33.3	* 45.0	* 21.7	* 24.6	* 6.2
Tunisie	2002	...	...	11.6	...	* 32.9	* 44.4	22.8	22.9	5.8
	2005	...	...	...	...	* 34.3	* 41.6	24.1	26.7	6.5
	2008	...	...	10.0	...	27.7	47.3	25.0	25.3	6.3
	2010	...	...	10.4	...	...	...	28.2	24.8	6.3
	2015	...	...	...	...	...	71.6	23.9	22.9	6.6
Turkey	2004	12.6	66.3	21.1	0.6	...	...	27.9	8.7	3.0
Turquie	2006	14.9	74.6	10.6	...	...	...	31.9	8.0	2.8
	2015	15.9	71.6	12.5	...	22.9	37.8	34.6	12.8	4.3
Turkmenistan										
Turkménistan	2012	...	...	33.7	28.1	...	...	9.2	20.8	3.0
Turks and Caicos Islands	2002	9.8	61.1	29.2	* 5.0	* 21.1	31.7	22.9	...	5.1
Îles Turques-et-Caïques	2003	...	...	...	...	* 21.6	28.0	37.2	...	4.7
	2005	13.7	69.5	16.8	...	* 30.0	47.7	...	...	2.5
	2015	...	...	17.6	...	36.1	41.5	22.4	...	3.3
Uganda	2004	12.1	62.7	25.2	...	61.2	17.3	11.9	20.3	5.0
Ouganda	2010	51.1	35.5	13.4	...	47.3	39.4	13.3	10.1	2.4
	2014	48.3	39.1	12.6	...	59.2	24.6	16.3	10.9	2.3
	*2017	...	...	...	...	...	...	...	12.0	2.6
Ukraine	2000	...	...	8.3	11.1	...	...	32.3	11.4	4.2
Ukraine	2005	...	...	...	11.0	...	...	29.5	13.7	6.1
	2009	...	...	...	12.5	...	...	32.4	15.1	7.3
	2016	...	...	8.4	16.8	19.6	27.9	30.5	12.4	5.0
United Kingdom	2005	18.5	73.5	8.0	5.9	26.5	45.4	22.3	13.2	5.0
Royaume-Uni	2010	29.8	58.8	11.4	5.2	30.1	48.3	16.4	13.0	5.8
	2016	23.4	74.1	2.5	4.5	33.4	37.5	24.2	13.9	5.5
United Rep. of Tanzania	2005	...	...	...	5.8	56.0	12.9	21.7	18.1	4.6
Rép.-Unie de Tanzanie	2009	...	...	...	4.4	41.9	16.7	33.8	17.4	4.0
	2010	...	...	...	...	...	11.3	28.3	19.6	4.6
	2014	...	...	...	6.0	49.2	18.3	21.4	17.3	3.5
United States of America	2010	20.5	69.4	10.1	6.5	32.4	35.4	25.7	13.2	5.4
États-Unis d'Amérique	2014	21.6	69.7	8.7	6.6	31.0	34.6	27.5	13.6	5.0
Uruguay	2005	14.5	80.8	4.7	8.9	33.8	35.5	21.8	9.4	2.7
Uruguay	2006	14.1	80.2	5.7	8.7	33.3	36.0	22.0	9.9	2.9
	2011	14.9	80.5	4.6	10.2	27.9	33.2	26.8	14.9	4.4
	2016	23.0	73.3	3.7	...	...	...	...	...	...
Uzbekistan										
Ouzbékistan	*2017	...	...	...	...	...	...	...	20.0	6.4
Vanuatu	2001	1.1	51.7	47.2	0.1	27.9	57.4	10.5	40.1	9.0
Vanuatu	2003	...	...	...	...	...	...	...	44.8	8.4
	2008	11.4	87.4	1.2	0.5	49.7	32.9	5.9	21.4	5.8
	2009	8.8	89.5	1.7	0.1	54.3	29.7	...	18.7	5.0
	2017	20.8	78.0	1.2	0.1	44.6	32.9	...	11.8	4.7
Venezuela (Boliv. Rep. of) Venezuela (Rép. boliv. du)	2009	20.2	76.9	2.9	11.6	31.5	19.0	22.6	...	6.9
Viet Nam	2010	32.3	42.4	25.3	13.3	30.0	42.2	14.5	17.1	5.1
Viet Nam	2013	31.3	46.9	21.9	15.7	29.7	39.6	15.0	18.5	5.7
Yemen	*2001	...	...	...	...	...	...	...	30.3	9.2
Yémen	2008	...	...	25.7	...	...	...	...	12.5	5.2

9

Public expenditure on education *(continued)*
By expenditure type, level of education, total government expenditure and GDP

Dépenses publiques afférentes à l'éducation *(suite)*
Par type de dépenses, niveau de scolarité, dépenses publiques totales et PIB

Country or area Pays ou zone	Year Année	Percentage of total expenditure in public institutions Pourcentage des dépenses publiques totales en faveur de l'éducation			Percentage of government expenditure on education by level Pourcentage des dépenses publiques selon le niveau d'enseignement				As % of Govt. Expend-Iture En % des dépenses du gouvt.	As % of GDP En % du PIB
		Other expenditure Dépenses courantes	Staff Compensation Rémun-ération du personnel	Capital expenditure Dépenses en Capital	Pre-primary Préprimaire	Primary Primaire	Secondary Secondaire	Tertiary Tertiaire		
Zambia Zambie	2004	25.2	73.0	1.8	...	63.9	13.3	18.0	10.6	2.5
	2005	...	...	...	...	59.8	14.5	25.8	7.7	1.7
	2008	...	...	...	...	...	...	...	5.7	1.1
Zimbabwe Zimbabwe	2010	...	...	...	...	51.6	25.6	22.8	8.7	1.8
	2014	...	...	...	2.0	47.8	26.9	16.8	30.0	7.5

Source:

United Nations Educational, Scientific and Cultural Organization (UNESCO), Montreal, the UNESCO Institute for Statistics (UIS) statistics database, last accessed March 2019.

Source:

Organisation des Nations Unies pour l'éducation, la science et la culture (UNESCO), Montréal, base de données statistiques de l'Institut de statistique (ISU) de l'UNESCO, dernier accès mars 2019.

Country or area Pays ou zone	Year Année	Physicians Médecins		Dentists Dentistes		Pharmacists Pharmaciens		Nurses and midwives Infirmières et Sages-femmes	
		Number Nombre	Per 1 000 Pour 1 000	Number Nombre	Per 1 000 Pour 1 000	Number Nombre	Per 1 000 Pour 1 000	Number Nombre	Per 1 000 Pour 1 000
Afghanistan	2001	4 104	0.2	...	...	525	~0.0	...	...
Afghanistan	2005	...	...	...	...	900	~0.0	14 930	0.6
	2008	4 834	0.2	382	~0.0	829	~0.0	13 780	0.5
	2009	6 037	0.2	...	...	847	~0.0	17 257	0.6
	2010	6 901	0.2	...	...	814	~0.0	...	...
	2014	9 954	0.3	111	~0.0	1 711	0.1	10 482	0.3
	2015	9 808	0.3	123	~0.0	1 712	0.1	...	...
	2016	9 842	0.3	120	~0.0	1 675	~0.0	...	...
Albania	2006	...	...	1 035	0.3	...	...	...	...
Albanie	2010	3 640	1.2	...	...	1 324	0.5	...	...
	2013	3 709	1.3	...	...	2 441	0.8	13 334	4.6
	2016	3 511	1.2	...	...	...	...	10 534	3.6
Algeria	2002	35 368	1.1	8 861	0.3	5 413	0.2	69 749	2.2
Algérie	2005	33 952	1.0	9 022	0.3	6 104	0.2	...	...
	2007	40 857	1.2	10 621	0.3	7 417	0.2	65 919	1.9
	2016	74 309	1.8	...	...	...	...	90 958	2.2
Andorra	2003	244	3.3	44	0.6	68	0.9	...	...
Andorre	2015	260	3.3	64	0.8	79	1.0	313	4.0
Angola	2004	1 165	0.1	222	~0.0	919	~0.0	18 485	1.0
Angola	2009	2 956	0.1	...	...	...	...	29 592	1.3
	2017	6 400	0.2	...	...	...	...	...	...
Antigua and Barbuda	2007	144	1.6	...	...	15	0.2	277	3.0
Antigua-et-Barbuda	2017	282	2.8	...	...	...	...	318	3.1
Argentina	2004	122 623	3.2	35 592	0.9	19 510	0.5	18 685	0.5
Argentine	2013	166 187	3.9	...	...	...	...	179 175	4.2
	2017	175 313	4.0	...	...	...	...	114 219	2.6
Armenia	2010	8 177	2.8	1 257	0.4	123	~0.0	16 386	5.7
Arménie	2014	8 425	2.9	1 138	0.4	150	0.1	16 302	5.6
Australia	2001	47 875	2.5	8 200	0.4	13 956	0.7	187 837	9.7
Australie	2010	74 061	3.3	11 473	0.5	19 237	0.9	230 446	10.4
	2015	83 804	3.5	13 834	0.6	20 297	0.9	296 701	12.5
	2016	86 550	3.6	14 205	0.6	20 960	0.9	305 462	12.7
Austria	2010	40 105	4.8	4 685	0.6	5 579	0.7	65 698	7.8
Autriche	2015	44 002	5.1	4 906	0.6	6 104	0.7	70 955	8.2
	2016	44 816	5.1	4 954	0.6	6 194	0.7	71 246	8.2
	2017	...	...	5 009	0.6	...	...	...	...
Azerbaijan	2010	33 085	3.7	2 467	0.3	1 831	0.2	72 717	8.1
Azerbaïdjan	2014	32 756	3.4	2 601	0.3	1 897	0.2	66 166	7.0
Bahamas	2008	947	2.7	79	0.2	138	0.4	1 391	4.0
Bahamas	2011	830	2.3	84	0.2	202	0.6	1 458	4.0
	2017	766	1.9	102	0.3	...	...	1 241	3.1
Bahrain	2005	928	1.0	98	0.1	164	0.2	2 389	2.7
Bahreïn	2010	1 178	0.9	122	0.1	196	0.2	3 052	2.5
	2015	1 270	0.9	134	0.1	222	0.2	3 422	2.5
Bangladesh	2002	...	...	1 886	~0.0	7 622	0.1	...	...
Bangladesh	2005	42 881	0.3	2 344	~0.0	...	...	39 471	0.3
	2010	53 643	0.4	4 336	~0.0	12 172	0.1	27 005	0.2
	2015	75 915	0.5	6 520	~0.0	12 199	0.1	42 965	0.3
	2017	86 754	0.5	8 155	~0.0	25 692	0.2	50 510	0.3
Barbados	2005	489	1.8	83	0.3	251	0.9	1 311	4.8
Barbade	2017	711	2.5	88	0.3	...	...	1 722	6.0
Belarus	2010	33 325	3.5	5 087	0.5	2 731	0.3	104 872	11.1
Bélarus	2014	38 671	4.1	5 414	0.6	3 240	0.3	108 490	11.4
Belgium	2005	21 599	2.0	7 731	0.7	...	...	...	...
Belgique	2010	31 815	2.9	7 675	0.7	12 629	1.2	115 787	10.6
	2015	34 020	3.0	8 291	0.7	13 643	1.2	122 127	10.8
	2016	37 748	3.3	8 478	0.7	13 876	1.2	126 091	11.1

Country or area Pays ou zone	Year Année	Physicians Médecins Number Nombre	Per 1 000 Pour 1 000	Dentists Dentistes Number Nombre	Per 1 000 Pour 1 000	Pharmacists Pharmaciens Number Nombre	Per 1 000 Pour 1 000	Nurses and midwives Infirmières et Sages- femmes Number Nombre	Per 1 000 Pour 1 000
Belize Belize	2000	251	1.0	32	0.1	...	...	303	1.2
	2009	241	0.8	12	~0.0	112	0.4	570	1.8
	2010	...	...	12	~0.0	...	...	...	...
	2012	387	1.1	...	...	...	...	373	1.1
	2017	422	1.1	58	0.2	254	0.7	635	1.7
Benin Bénin	2004	311	~0.0	11	~0.0	11	~0.0	5 789	0.7
	2008	542	0.1	37	~0.0	20	~0.0	7 129	0.8
	2013	1 507	0.2	...	...	...	...	6 320	0.6
	2016	1 709	0.2	9	~0.0	13	~0.0	6 681	0.6
Bhutan Bhoutan	2004	118	0.2	10	~0.0	7	~0.0	515	0.8
	2007	144	0.2	7	~0.0	10	~0.0	545	0.8
	2008	171	0.2	...	...	14	~0.0	666	1.0
	2015	251	0.3	...	...	15	~0.0	1 070	1.4
	2017	300	0.4	67	0.1	37	~0.0	1 219	1.5
Bolivia (Plurin. State of) Bolivie (État plurin. de)	2001	10 329	1.2	...	...	2 593	0.3	18 091	2.1
	2010	4 406	0.4	976	0.1	567	0.1	8 366	0.8
	2011	4 771	0.5	1 130	0.1	660	0.1	10 139	1.0
	2016	17 542	1.6	2 428	0.2	2 477	0.2	8 010	0.7
Bosnia and Herzegovina Bosnie-Herzégovine	2010	6 665	1.8	797	0.2	371	0.1	21 560	5.8
	2013	7 211	2.0	809	0.2	429	0.1	22 052	6.1
	2014	...	...	825	0.2	441	0.1	22 465	6.3
Botswana Botswana	2004	715	0.4	38	~0.0	140	0.1	4 753	2.6
	2005	466	0.3	...	...	...	...	4 468	2.4
	2009	693	0.4	55	~0.0	107	0.1	5 816	2.9
	2010	819	0.4	55	~0.0	...	...	5 816	2.9
	2011	819	0.4	55	~0.0	430	0.2	5 816	2.8
	2012	819	0.4	55	~0.0	...	...	5 816	2.8
	2016	830	0.4	91	~0.0	...	...	7 427	3.3
Brazil Brésil	2005	310 138	1.7	207 904	1.1	99 696	0.5	703 813	3.8
	2010	355 006	1.8	223 021	1.1	107 564	0.5	1 446 403	7.3
	2013	378 354	1.9	...	...	...	...	1 520 533	7.5
	2017	450 009	2.2	258 842	1.2	141 968	0.7	1 246 347	6.0
	2018	453 351	2.1	...	...	...	...	2 047 172	9.7
Brunei Darussalam Brunéi Darussalam	2005	390	1.1	73	0.2	41	0.1	2 006	5.5
	2010	563	1.4	86	0.2	43	0.1	2 907	7.5
	2015	739	1.8	94	0.2	71	0.2	2 756	6.6
Bulgaria Bulgarie	2001	...	...	...	...	1 020	0.1	...	...
	2010	27 963	3.8	6 389	0.9	...	...	38 280	5.2
	2014	28 801	4.0	7 054	1.0	...	...	38 298	5.3
Burkina Faso Burkina Faso	2004	708	0.1	58	~0.0	227	~0.0	6 557	0.5
	2010	713	~0.0	32	~0.0	184	~0.0	8 645	0.6
	2012	787	~0.0	38	~0.0	203	~0.0	10 459	0.6
	2015	...	...	...	...	...	...	4 347	0.2
	2016	1 119	0.1	...	...	170	~0.0	10 620	0.6
Burundi Burundi	2004	200	~0.0	14	~0.0	73	~0.0	1 348	0.2
	2010	418	~0.0	2	~0.0	23	~0.0	5 973	0.7
	2011	...	...	...	...	101	~0.0	...	...
	2016	526	0.1	...	...	...	...	7 156	0.7
Cabo Verde Cabo Verde	2010	292	0.6	4	~0.0	4	~0.0	543	1.1
	2011	292	0.6	3	~0.0	3	~0.0	543	1.1
	2015	410	0.8	...	...	...	...	654	1.2
	2016	...	...	4	~0.0	4	~0.0	...	...
Cambodia Cambodge	2000	2 047	0.2	209	~0.0	564	~0.0	11 125	0.9
	2010	3 294	0.2	242	~0.0	548	~0.0	12 251	0.9
	2014	2 568	0.2	252	~0.0	526	~0.0	14 579	1.0
Cameroon Cameroun	2005	1 049	0.1	26	~0.0	27	~0.0	6 705	0.4
	2010	1 712	0.1	58	~0.0	42	~0.0	10 714	0.5
	2011	1 842	0.1	58	~0.0	162	~0.0	19 159	0.9
	2016	...	...	88	~0.0	199	~0.0	...	...

Country or area Pays ou zone	Year Année	Physicians Médecins Number Nombre	Per 1 000 Pour 1 000	Dentists Dentistes Number Nombre	Per 1 000 Pour 1 000	Pharmacists Pharmaciens Number Nombre	Per 1 000 Pour 1 000	Nurses and midwives Infirmières et Sages- femmes Number Nombre	Per 1 000 Pour 1 000
Canada Canada	2004	60 612	1.9	18 281	0.6	28 537	0.9	316 512	9.9
	2005	...	...	...	...	...	...	321 159	9.9
	2008	65 440	2.0	19 433	0.6	29 010	0.9	343 699	10.3
	2009	...	...	...	...	30 553	0.9	350 547	10.4
	2010	69 648	2.0	...	...	...	...	318 565	9.3
	2015	91 268	2.5	22 454	0.6	35 238	1.0	353 738	9.8
	2016	93 150	2.6	23 060	0.6	36 380	1.0	359 473	9.9
	2017	95 596	2.6	...	...	...	...	...	...
Central African Republic République centrafricaine	2004	331	0.1	6	~0.0	17	~0.0	1 613	0.4
	2009	205	~0.0	4	~0.0	10	~0.0	1 097	0.2
	2015	286	0.1	...	...	20	~0.0	927	0.2
Chad Tchad	2004	345	~0.0	7	~0.0	31	~0.0	2 499	0.3
	2006	368	~0.0	...	...	...	...	1 891	0.2
	2013	573	~0.0	...	...	72	~0.0	4 057	0.3
	2016	686	~0.0	...	...	...	...	5 255	0.4
Chile Chili	2005	15 865	1.0	12	~0.0	36	~0.0	2 103	0.1
	2009	17 382	1.0	15	~0.0	39	~0.0	2 443	0.1
	2016	19 342	1.1	2 865	0.2	...	...	15 402	0.9
China Chine	2002	1 463 573	1.1	...	...	357 659	0.3	1 246 545	1.0
	2005	...	...	51 012	~0.0	349 533	0.3	1 349 589	1.0
	2010	2 000 000	1.5	...	...	353 916	0.3	2 048 071	1.5
	2011	2 025 873	1.5	119 000	0.1	363 993	0.3	2 244 020	1.6
	2015	2 508 408	1.8	...	...	423 294	0.3	3 241 469	2.3
Colombia Colombie	2005	62 807	1.5	37 371	0.9	...	...	25 845	0.6
	2010	71 980	1.6	44 858	1.0	...	...	30 119	0.7
	2015	93 460	1.9	46 299	1.0	...	...	54 980	1.1
	2017	102 230	2.1	...	...	...	...	61 954	1.3
Comoros Comores	2005	116	0.2	17	~0.0	15	~0.0	344	0.6
	2009	128	0.2	21	~0.0	18	~0.0	473	0.7
	2012	123	0.2	18	~0.0	16	~0.0	667	0.9
Congo Congo	2004	756	0.2	...	...	95	~0.0	3 672	1.0
	2007	401	0.1	...	...	38	~0.0	3 492	0.9
	2011	523	0.1	133	~0.0	250	0.1	7 866	1.7
	2016	...	...	...	...	191	~0.0	...	...
Cook Islands Îles Cook	2004	20	1.0	10	0.5	2	0.1	80	4.1
	2009	24	1.3	4	0.2	1	0.1	116	6.1
	2014	25	1.4	22	1.3	1	0.1	102	5.8
Costa Rica Costa Rica	2000	5 204	1.3	1 467	0.4	1 144	0.3	3 653	0.9
	2013	5 411	1.1	599	0.1	891	0.2	3 745	0.8
	2017	...	...	49	~0.0	...	...	...	...
Côte d'Ivoire Côte d'Ivoire	2005	1 698	0.1	204	~0.0	128	~0.0	8 988	0.5
	2008	2 746	0.1	274	~0.0	413	~0.0	9 231	0.5
	2014	5 240	0.2	490	~0.0	2 430	0.1	19 190	0.9
Croatia Croatie	2010	12 304	2.8	3 158	0.7	2 851	0.7	26 553	6.1
	2014	13 302	3.1	3 327	0.8	3 024	0.7	27 714	6.5
	2015	...	...	3 614	0.9	2 797	0.7	...	...
	2016	12 624	3.0	...	...	...	...	34 184	8.1
Cuba Cuba	2002	67 079	6.0	9 955	0.9	...	...	83 880	7.5
	2005	70 594	6.3	10 554	0.9	...	...	...	...
	2010	76 506	6.8	12 144	1.1	...	...	103 014	9.1
	2014	85 563	7.5	16 630	1.5	...	...	90 765	7.9
	2017	94 059	8.2	19 064	1.7	...	...	89 465	7.8
Cyprus Chypre	2002	...	...	...	...	144	0.1	2 994	3.1
	2009	2 313	2.1	757	0.7	...	...	3 806	3.5
	2010	2 399	2.2	772	0.7	181	0.2	...	...
	2014	2 880	2.5	839	0.7	188	0.2	4 750	4.1
	2016	2 283	2.0	...	...	...	...	6 145	5.3

Country or area Pays ou zone	Year Année	Physicians Médecins Number Nombre	Per 1 000 Pour 1 000	Dentists Dentistes Number Nombre	Per 1 000 Pour 1 000	Pharmacists Pharmaciens Number Nombre	Per 1 000 Pour 1 000	Nurses and midwives Infirmières et Sages- femmes Number Nombre	Per 1 000 Pour 1 000
Czechia	2010	37 661	3.6	7 263	0.7	6 061	0.6	89 233	8.5
Tchéquie	2013	38 776	3.7	7 426	0.7	6 383	0.6	88 425	8.3
	2015	...	...	8 461	0.8	6 965	0.7	88 744	8.4
	2016	45 776	4.3	7 955	0.7	7 172	0.7	89 208	8.4
Dem. People's Rep. Korea	2003	74 597	3.2	3 955	0.2	7 303	0.3	93 414	4.0
Rép. pop. dém. de Corée	2008	79 931	3.3	4 314	0.2	8 622	0.4	100 768	4.1
	2012	85 470	3.4	4 615	0.2	9 215	0.4	...	...
	2014	87 839	3.5	...	...	9 404	0.4	118 692	4.7
	2017	93 667	3.7	5 595	0.2	10 094	0.4	113 135	4.4
Dem. Rep. of the Congo	2009	5 832	0.1	45	~0.0	283	~0.0	25 587	0.4
Rép. dém. du Congo	2013	6 418	0.1	...	...	...	...	33 518	0.5
Denmark	2005	17 350	3.2	4 634	0.9	...	...	81 219	15.0
Danemark	2010	19 881	3.6	4 485	0.8	2 623	0.5	89 431	16.1
	2015	20 902	3.7	4 205	0.7	2 918	0.5	97 924	17.2
	2016	25 456	4.5	...	...	...	...	58 835	10.3
Djibouti	2004	129	0.2	10	~0.0	18	~0.0	296	0.4
Djibouti	2005	140	0.2	...	...	18	~0.0	450	0.6
	2006	185	0.2	...	...	16	~0.0	...	...
	2008	...	...	...	...	266	0.3	...	...
	2014	201	0.2	19	~0.0	210	0.2	488	0.5
Dominica	2001	124	1.8	...	...	18	0.3	438	6.3
Dominique	2017	80	1.1	5	0.1	...	...	436	5.9
Dominican Republic	2000	15 670	1.8	7 000	0.8	3 330	0.4	15 352	1.8
République dominicaine	2008	10 385	1.1	1 205	0.1	...	...	...	...
	2009	...	...	1 785	0.2	...	...	12 686	1.3
	2011	14 983	1.5	1 910	0.2	...	...	13 374	1.3
	2017	16 796	1.6	2 261	0.2	...	...	3 337	0.3
Ecuador	2003	20 020	1.5	2 213	0.2	497	~0.0	20 372	1.5
Équateur	2009	23 614	1.6	3 363	0.2	664	~0.0	27 764	1.9
	2010	31 690	2.1	...	...	...	...	24 910	1.7
	2015	33 474	2.1	8 564	0.5	672	~0.0	40 171	2.5
	2016	33 589	2.1	5 243	0.3	...	...	19 662	1.2
Egypt	2003	38 485	0.5	...	...	...	...	...	...
Égypte	2004	...	...	8 193	0.1	...	...	146 761	1.9
	2006	...	...	...	...	...	...	179 590	2.3
	2015	75 960	0.8	16 880	0.2	36 573	0.4	140 667	1.5
	2017	77 083	0.8	19 111	0.2	42 067	0.4	136 470	1.4
El Salvador	2005	10 355	1.7	4 255	0.7	2 280	0.4	2 084	0.3
El Salvador	2008	11 542	1.9	4 669	0.8	2 316	0.4	2 929	0.5
	2016	9 955	1.6	...	...	...	...	14 453	2.3
	2017	...	...	...	...	4 181	0.7	...	...
Equatorial Guinea	2004	153	0.2	5	~0.0	12	~0.0	271	0.4
Guinée équatoriale	2017	507	0.4	...	...	...	...	634	0.5
Eritrea									
Érythrée	2004	215	0.1	16	~0.0	17	~0.0	2 505	0.6
Estonia	2000	6 118	4.4	909	0.6	274	0.2	12 087	8.6
Estonie	2010	4 319	3.2	1 198	0.9	842	0.6	8 894	6.7
	2015	4 492	3.4	1 239	0.9	948	0.7	8 355	6.4
	2016	4 548	3.5	1 257	1.0	963	0.7	8 469	6.5
Eswatini	2004	171	0.2	17	~0.0	46	~0.0	6 828	6.2
Eswatini	2009	173	0.1	13	~0.0	20	~0.0	1 626	1.4
	2011	109	0.1	46	~0.0	30	~0.0	1 292	1.1
	2015	...	...	...	...	...	...	2 638	2.0
	2016	107	0.1	...	...	...	...	...	...
Ethiopia	2003	1 936	~0.0	60	~0.0	172	~0.0	15 544	0.2
Éthiopie	2005	2 453	~0.0	...	...	191	~0.0	18 809	0.2
	2009	2 152	~0.0	...	...	632	~0.0	21 488	0.3
	2017	10 496	0.1	...	...	...	...	88 164	0.8
Fiji	2003	380	0.5	60	0.1	90	0.1	1 660	2.0
Fidji	2009	372	0.4	171	0.2	76	0.1	1 957	2.3
	2015	747	0.8	64	0.1	95	0.1	2 621	2.9

Country or area Pays ou zone	Year Année	Physicians Médecins Number Nombre	Per 1 000 Pour 1 000	Dentists Dentistes Number Nombre	Per 1 000 Pour 1 000	Pharmacists Pharmaciens Number Nombre	Per 1 000 Pour 1 000	Nurses and midwives Infirmières et Sages-femmes Number Nombre	Per 1 000 Pour 1 000
Finland Finlande	2002	16 446	3.2	4 658	0.9	5 829	1.1	78 402	15.0
	2010	16 030	3.0	4 234	0.8	5 944	1.1	78 666	14.7
	2014	17 511	3.2	3 925	0.7	5 988	1.1	82 368	15.1
	2016	20 956	3.8	...	...	...	...	81 022	14.7
France France	2003	...	...	40 648	0.7	63 909	1.1	439 115	7.3
	2005	...	...	...	...	...	...	469 036	7.7
	2007	227 683	3.7	41 444	0.7	70 498	1.1	500 863	8.1
	2008	...	...	41 422	0.7	72 160	1.2	494 895	7.9
	2015	207 789	3.2	42 602	0.7	70 247	1.1	705 181	10.9
	2016	209 367	3.2	43 026	0.7	70 025	1.1	627 062	9.7
Gabon Gabon	2004	395	0.3	14	~0.0	33	~0.0	6 778	5.0
	2016	715	0.4	9	~0.0	46	~0.0	5 109	2.6
Gambia Gambie	2005	166	0.1	10	~0.0	11	~0.0	732	0.5
	2008	175	0.1	12	~0.0	13	~0.0	1 411	0.9
	2015	213	0.1	17	~0.0	5	~0.0	3 222	1.6
Georgia Géorgie	2010	18 227	4.3	1 257	0.3	353	0.1	17 104	4.0
	2015	20 143	5.1	2 469	0.6	315	0.1	16 167	4.1
Germany Allemagne	2010	303 645	3.8	66 427	0.8	50 604	0.6	1 014 000	12.5
	2015	338 129	4.1	69 863	0.9	52 568	0.6	1 056 000	12.9
	2016	344 755	4.2	70 305	0.9	52 430	0.6	1 081 000	13.2
Ghana Ghana	2004	3 240	0.2	104	~0.0	...	...	19 707	0.9
	2008	2 587	0.1	45	~0.0	547	~0.0	22 834	1.0
	2010	2 325	0.1	...	...	...	...	22 507	0.9
	2013	4 443	0.2	...	...	9 564	0.4	41 922	1.6
	2017	5 190	0.2	...	...	...	...	34 600	1.2
Greece Grèce	2010	69 265	6.1	14 661	1.3	11 160	1.0	40 978	3.6
	2014	68 807	6.1	13 746	1.2	11 579	1.0	40 461	3.6
	2015	...	...	...	...	...	...	37 320	3.3
	2016	51 356	4.6	...	...	...	...	37 720	3.4
Grenada Grenade	2003	58	0.6	9	0.1	22	0.2	366	3.6
	2006	69	0.7	19	0.2	21	0.2	398	3.9
	2011	...	...	...	...	89	0.8	...	...
	2016	...	...	...	...	75	0.7	...	...
	2017	156	1.4	17	0.2	...	...	339	3.1
Guatemala Guatemala	2007	...	...	2 376	0.2	...	...	...	...
	2009	12 940	0.9	...	...	...	...	12 452	0.9
	2018	6 122	0.4	180	~0.0	68	~0.0	16 332	0.9
Guinea Guinée	2004	987	0.1	22	~0.0	...	...	4 408	0.5
	2005	940	0.1	17	~0.0	177	~0.0	...	...
	2016	977	0.1	...	...	142	~0.0	4 765	0.4
Guinea-Bissau Guinée-Bissau	2004	188	0.1	3	~0.0	...	...	1 072	0.8
	2009	124	0.1	7	~0.0	9	~0.0	1 042	0.7
	2015	354	0.2	...	...	...	...	2 479	1.4
Guyana Guyana	2000	366	0.5	30	~0.0	...	...	1 738	2.3
	2009	161	0.2	29	~0.0	15	~0.0	989	1.3
	2010	515	0.7	...	...	...	...	754	1.0
	2018	625	0.8	28	~0.0	7	~0.0	1 048	1.3
Haiti Haïti	2011	1 392	0.1	50	~0.0	85	~0.0	11 982	1.2
	2018	2 606	0.2	237	~0.0	336	~0.0	7 561	0.7
Honduras Honduras	2000	3 676	0.6	1 141	0.2	351	0.1	8 528	1.3
	2005	2 680	0.4	...	...	...	...	7 796	1.1
	2008	...	...	236	~0.0	...	...	...	...
	2013	8 657	1.0	...	...	...	...	3 289	0.4
	2017	2 913	0.3	308	~0.0	...	...	8 167	0.9
Hungary Hongrie	2005	32 563	3.2	...	...	...	...	...	...
	2010	28 686	2.9	5 257	0.5	5 821	0.6	65 659	6.6
	2015	30 486	3.1	5 936	0.6	7 039	0.7	65 367	6.7
	2016	31 515	3.2	6 083	0.6	7 353	0.8	64 786	6.6
Iceland Islande	2005	1 070	3.6	289	1.0	299	1.0	4 378	14.8
	2010	1 142	3.6	299	0.9	365	1.1	4 875	15.2
	2015	1 249	3.8	278	0.8	370	1.1	5 387	16.3
	2017	1 330	4.0	279	0.8	171	0.5	5 253	15.7

Country or area Pays ou zone	Year Année	Physicians Médecins Number Nombre	Per 1 000 Pour 1 000	Dentists Dentistes Number Nombre	Per 1 000 Pour 1 000	Pharmacists Pharmaciens Number Nombre	Per 1 000 Pour 1 000	Nurses and midwives Infirmières et Sages-femmes Number Nombre	Per 1 000 Pour 1 000
India	2004	645 825	0.6	55 058	~0.0	129 946	0.1	1 422 452	1.3
Inde	2005	660 801	0.6	55 344	~0.0	...	...	1 481 270	1.3
	2009	757 377	0.6	104 603	0.1	655 801	0.5	1 702 555	1.4
	2010	816 629	0.7	...	...	656 101	0.5	1 894 968	1.5
	2013	918 303	0.7	...	...	664 176	0.5	1 562 186	1.2
	2014	938 861	0.7	154 436	0.1	...	...	1 780 006	1.4
	2017	1 041 395	0.8	251 207	0.2	908 523	0.7	2 821 815	2.1
Indonesia	2003	29 499	0.1	5 267	~0.0	1 367	~0.0	179 959	0.8
Indonésie	2009	34 544	0.1	5 442	~0.0	2 007	~0.0	194 399	0.8
	2010	33 736	0.1	8 731	~0.0	...	...	256 625	1.1
	2015	70 735	0.3	12 740	~0.0	30 329	0.1	335 646	1.3
	2017	99 703	0.4	14 455	0.1	45 839	0.2	543 386	2.1
Iran (Islamic Republic of)	2005	61 870	0.9	13 210	0.2	13 900	0.2	98 020	1.4
Iran (Rép. islamique d')	2006	37 822	0.5	9 522	0.1	7 161	0.1	119 170	1.7
	2015	90 470	1.1	26 188	0.3	15 872	0.2	148 404	1.9
Iraq	2010	19 738	0.6	4 799	0.2	5 675	0.2	...	...
Iraq	2014	30 131	0.9	7 891	0.2	8 609	0.2	63 850	1.8
	2017	31 451	0.8	9 524	0.2	10 939	0.3	64 297	1.7
Ireland	2006	10 100	2.3	1 890	0.4	...	...	64 990	15.1
Irlande	2010	...	...	2 721	0.6	4 567	1.0	...	...
	2015	13 075	2.8	2 828	0.6	5 191	1.1	65 203	13.9
	2016	13 959	3.0	...	...	...	...	67 559	14.3
	2017	14 695	3.1	...	...	...	...	...	...
Israel	2010	25 333	3.4	6 367	0.9	5 733	0.8	39 086	5.3
Israël	2015	25 731	3.2	6 633	0.8	6 233	0.8	40 900	5.1
	2016	26 358	3.2	6 533	0.8	6 133	0.7	42 633	5.2
Italy	2010	...	...	34 023	0.6	51 832	0.9	...	...
Italie	2015	233 102	3.9	47 604	0.8	69 939	1.2	346 219	5.8
	2017	242 965	4.1	49 363	0.8	68 344	1.2	348 403	5.9
Jamaica	2003	2 253	0.8	212	0.1	...	...	4 374	1.6
Jamaïque	2008	1 103	0.4	46	~0.0	96	~0.0	2 930	1.1
	2015	1 199	0.4	37	~0.0	82	~0.0	4 188	1.5
	2016	1 322	0.5	45	~0.0	63	~0.0	4 669	1.6
	2017	3 815	1.3	260	0.1	...	...	3 294	1.1
Japan	2004	270 371	2.1	95 197	0.7	241 369	1.9	1 210 633	9.4
Japon	2010	288 850	2.2	98 739	0.8	205 716	1.6	1 320 623	10.3
	2014	300 075	2.3	100 994	0.8	216 077	1.7	1 425 322	11.1
	2016	308 105	2.4	101 584	0.8	230 186	1.8	1 471 455	11.5
Jordan	2005	12 909	2.3	4 194	0.7	7 100	1.2	17 428	3.1
Jordanie	2010	16 212	2.3	5 691	0.8	9 151	1.3	25 661	3.6
	2015	26 019	2.8	6 806	0.7	12 076	1.3	23 651	2.6
	2017	22 739	2.3	7 107	0.7	15 668	1.6	32 878	3.4
Kazakhstan	2010	57 179	3.5	6 657	0.4	11 265	0.7	135 125	8.2
Kazakhstan	2013	59 872	3.5	6 406	0.4	13 828	0.8	146 072	8.5
	2014	56 873	3.3	6 430	0.4	14 163	0.8	...	...
Kenya	2002	4 506	0.1	746	~0.0	...	...	...	...
Kenya	2004	...	...	...	...	1 773	0.1	16 146	0.5
	2010	7 129	0.2	898	~0.0	3 097	0.1	29 678	0.7
	2014	9 149	0.2	1 090	~0.0	2 355	0.1	70 975	1.5
Kiribati	2004	...	...	3	~0.0	2	~0.0	260	2.9
Kiribati	2010	41	0.4	4	~0.0	4	~0.0	404	3.9
	2013	22	0.2	7	0.1	3	~0.0	501	4.6
	2016	...	...	8	0.1	3	~0.0	552	4.8
Kuwait	2001	...	...	673	0.3	722	0.3	9 197	4.4
Koweït	2009	5 340	1.9	1 054	0.4	888	0.3	13 554	4.8
	2010	7 269	2.4	1 634	0.5	...	...	19 535	6.5
	2014	9 789	2.6	2 269	0.6	1 814	0.5	24 585	6.5
	2015	10 150	2.6	2 587	0.7	...	...	27 430	7.0
Kyrgyzstan	2010	10 277	1.9	1 022	0.2	169	~0.0	32 658	6.0
Kirghizistan	2013	10 838	1.9	981	0.2	317	0.1	36 546	6.4
	2014	10 833	1.9	965	0.2	242	~0.0	...	...

Country or area Pays ou zone	Year Année	Physicians Médecins Number Nombre	Per 1 000 Pour 1 000	Dentists Dentistes Number Nombre	Per 1 000 Pour 1 000	Pharmacists Pharmaciens Number Nombre	Per 1 000 Pour 1 000	Nurses and midwives Infirmières et Sages-femmes Number Nombre	Per 1 000 Pour 1 000
Lao People's Dem. Rep.	2005	1 614	0.3	...	...	...	...	5 724	1.0
Rép. dém. populaire lao	2009	1 211	0.2	228	~0.0	...	...	5 322	0.9
	2010	5 188	0.8	...	...	...	...	5 357	0.9
	2014	3 286	0.5	341	0.1	1 276	0.2	6 416	1.0
Latvia	2005	8 207	3.6	1 450	0.6	...	...	10 350	4.6
Lettonie	2010	6 517	3.1	1 488	0.7	1 433	0.7	10 922	5.2
	2015	6 324	3.2	1 419	0.7	1 574	0.8	9 661	4.8
	2016	6 295	3.2	1 411	0.7	1 643	0.8	9 489	4.8
Lebanon	2001	11 505	3.4	4 283	1.3	3 359	1.0	4 157	1.2
Liban	2005	...	...	...	...	4 105	1.0	4 720	1.2
	2010	11 583	2.7	5 395	1.2	5 508	1.3	8 791	2.0
	2015	13 738	2.3	5 527	0.9	7 590	1.3	14 300	2.4
	2017	13 813	2.3	6 727	1.1	8 368	1.4	16 087	2.6
Lesotho	2003	89	~0.0	3	~0.0	3	~0.0	1 123	0.6
Lesotho	2010	138	0.1	...	...	...	...	1 328	0.7
Liberia	2004	103	~0.0	3	~0.0	29	~0.0	1 035	0.3
Libéria	2010	90	~0.0	23	~0.0	46	~0.0	1 805	0.5
	2015	168	~0.0	...	...	...	...	453	0.1
Libya	2004	7 070	1.2	850	0.1	1 130	0.2	27 160	4.8
Libye	2009	12 009	2.0	3 792	0.6	2 275	0.4	42 982	7.0
	2014	13 095	2.1	4 583	0.7	3 928	0.6	43 216	7.0
	2015	12 158	2.0	4 987	0.8	3 117	0.5	...	...
	2017	13 757	2.2	5 776	0.9	3 956	0.6	42 975	6.7
Lithuania	2003	...	...	...	...	2 270	0.7	...	...
Lituanie	2010	12 226	3.9	2 456	0.8	...	...	24 609	7.9
	2015	12 605	4.3	2 644	0.9	...	...	23 172	7.9
	2016	12 613	4.3	2 787	1.0	...	...	23 020	7.9
	2017	...	...	...	...	2 673	0.9	...	...
Luxembourg	2010	1 404	2.8	422	0.8	374	0.7	5 970	11.8
Luxembourg	2015	1 656	2.9	506	0.9	396	0.7	6 990	12.3
	2017	1 766	3.0	581	1.0	416	0.7	7 206	12.3
Madagascar	2005	3 303	0.2	197	~0.0	8	~0.0	6 418	0.4
Madagascar	2010	4 130	0.2	195	~0.0	7	~0.0	4 724	0.2
	2012	3 188	0.1	181	~0.0	6	~0.0	4 858	0.2
	2014	4 275	0.2	...	...	...	...	2 500	0.1
	2016	...	...	...	...	4	~0.0	...	...
Malawi	2004	266	~0.0	...	...	...	...	7 264	0.6
Malawi	2008	257	~0.0	...	...	293	~0.0	3 896	0.3
	2009	265	~0.0	...	...	...	...	4 812	0.3
	2016	284	~0.0	...	...	...	...	4 573	0.3
Malaysia	2002	17 020	0.7	2 160	0.1	2 880	0.1	43 380	1.8
Malaisie	2010	32 979	1.2	3 810	0.1	7 759	0.3	90 199	3.2
	2015	46 491	1.5	10 596	0.3	10 511	0.3	125 100	4.1
Maldives	2004	302	1.0	10	~0.0	241	0.8	886	2.9
Maldives	2010	525	1.4	32	0.1	247	0.7	1 868	5.1
	2015	1 313	3.1	62	0.1	199	0.5	2 990	7.1
	2016	444	1.0	10	~0.0	...	...	1 690	4.0
Mali	2004	1 053	0.1	44	~0.0	351	~0.0	8 338	0.7
Mali	2010	1 536	0.1	35	~0.0	135	~0.0	6 715	0.4
	2012	1 711	0.1	...	...	...	...	6 027	0.4
	2016	2 506	0.1	...	...	...	...	6 874	0.4
Malta	2010	1 279	3.1	184	0.4	301	0.7	2 990	7.2
Malte	2015	1 636	3.8	206	0.5	558	1.3	3 827	9.0
Marshall Islands	2010	32	0.6	4	0.1	2	~0.0	127	2.4
Îles Marshall	2012	24	0.5	4	0.1	4	0.1	187	3.5
Mauritania	2004	313	0.1	47	~0.0	62	~0.0	1 893	0.6
Mauritanie	2009	445	0.1	70	~0.0	77	~0.0	2 303	0.7
	2010	547	0.2	...	...	...	...	2 803	0.8
	2015	692	0.2	...	...	...	...	4 137	1.0
	2017	791	0.2	...	...	...	...	4 571	1.0

Country or area Pays ou zone	Year Année	Physicians Médecins Number Nombre	Per 1 000 Pour 1 000	Dentists Dentistes Number Nombre	Per 1 000 Pour 1 000	Pharmacists Pharmaciens Number Nombre	Per 1 000 Pour 1 000	Nurses and midwives Infirmières et Sages-femmes Number Nombre	Per 1 000 Pour 1 000
Mauritius	2004	1 303	1.1	167	0.1	286	0.2	4 604	3.8
Maurice	2010	1 500	1.2	260	0.2	400	0.3	3 600	2.9
	2015	2 550	2.0	380	0.3	497	0.4	4 261	3.4
Mexico	2000	195 897	1.9	59 683	0.6	...	...	88 678	0.9
Mexique	2010	255 133	2.2	13 225	0.1	5 588	~0.0	275 171	2.3
	2015	283 414	2.3	15 915	0.1	...	...	335 959	2.7
	2016	286 685	2.2	12 754	0.1	...	...	369 867	2.9
Micronesia (Fed. States of)	2005	62	0.6	13	0.1	16	0.2	249	2.3
Micronésie (États féd. de)	2008	64	0.6	14	0.1	...	...	280	2.7
	2009	20	0.2	...	...	...	...	375	3.6
Monaco									
Monaco	2014	250	6.6	38	1.0	98	2.6	772	20.3
Mongolia	2002	6 732	2.8	315	0.1	901	0.4	8 826	3.6
Mongolie	2010	7 497	2.8	533	0.2	1 176	0.4	9 876	3.6
	2012	8 597	3.1	796	0.3	1 475	0.5	10 684	3.8
	2014	9 300	3.2	...	...	3 451	1.2	11 836	4.0
	2015	9 653	3.2	...	...	1 504	0.5	...	...
	2016	8 739	2.9	715	0.2	2 763	0.9	12 063	4.0
Montenegro	2010	1 268	2.0	26	~0.0	91	0.1	3 542	5.7
Monténégro	2015	1 466	2.3	25	~0.0	109	0.2	3 592	5.7
Morocco	2004	15 991	0.5	3 091	0.1	7 212	0.2	24 328	0.8
Maroc	2009	20 682	0.6	2 668	0.1	9 006	0.3	29 689	0.9
	2014	20 947	0.6	4 655	0.1	...	...	29 592	0.9
	2015	...	...	4 872	0.1	...	...	...	...
	2017	25 992	0.7	4 855	0.1	9 244	0.3	39 240	1.1
Mozambique	2004	514	~0.0	16	~0.0	14	~0.0	6 183	0.3
Mozambique	2010	1 145	~0.0	60	~0.0	48	~0.0	9 507	0.4
	2013	1 452	0.1	136	~0.0	103	~0.0	10 620	0.4
	2017	2 180	0.1	223	~0.0	220	~0.0	13 161	0.4
Myanmar	2004	17 791	0.4	1 329	~0.0	127	~0.0	...	...
Myanmar	2005	18 584	0.4	1 594	~0.0	...	...	36 521	0.8
	2010	26 435	0.5	2 562	0.1	...	...	45 200	0.9
	2012	29 832	0.6	3 011	0.1	...	...	48 871	1.0
	2015	...	...	3 270	0.1	...	...	20 038	0.4
	2017	46 110	0.9	4 301	0.1	2 063	~0.0	52 271	1.0
Namibia	2004	598	0.3	82	~0.0	194	0.1	6 145	3.1
Namibie	2007	774	0.4	90	~0.0	239	0.1	5 750	2.8
Nauru	2004	10	1.0	1	0.1	10	1.0	63	6.2
Nauru	2008	10	1.0	1	0.1	...	...	69	7.0
	2009	10	1.0	1	0.1	...	...	...	...
	2010	11	1.1	...	...	...	...	...	...
	2015	14	1.2	2	0.2	2	0.2	70	6.2
Nepal	2004	5 384	0.2	245	~0.0	266	~0.0	11 825	0.5
Népal	2012	13 925	0.5	...	...	1 200	~0.0	43 130	1.6
	2014	16 854	0.6	...	...	...	...	57 495	2.0
	2017	19 069	0.7	6 079	0.2	2 711	0.1	78 695	2.7
Netherlands	2010	49 242	3.0	8 345	0.5	3 308	0.2	...	...
Pays-Bas	2015	59 073	3.5	8 561	0.5	3 599	0.2	177 304	10.5
	2016	59 569	3.5	...	...	3 659	0.2	188 632	11.1
New Zealand	2001	9 027	2.3	1 431	0.4	...	...	33 249	8.5
Nouvelle-Zélande	2002	8 190	2.1	1 620	0.4	...	...	...	...
	2010	11 412	2.6	2 548	0.6	2 749	0.6	46 218	10.6
	2012	11 968	2.7	2 663	0.6	2 861	0.6	46 990	10.5
	2015	13 845	3.0	...	...	3 075	0.7	49 799	10.8
	2016	14 100	3.0	3 160	0.7	3 147	0.7	50 895	10.9
	2017	...	...	...	...	3 197	0.7	51 552	11.0
Nicaragua	2005	2 717	0.5	246	~0.0	...	...	6 294	1.2
Nicaragua	2010	4 239	0.7	258	~0.0	...	...	7 366	1.3
	2014	5 495	0.9	260	~0.0	1 141	0.2	8 323	1.4
	2018	6 320	1.0	254	~0.0	...	...	9 914	1.6

Country or area Pays ou zone	Year Année	Physicians Médecins Number Nombre	Per 1 000 Pour 1 000	Dentists Dentistes Number Nombre	Per 1 000 Pour 1 000	Pharmacists Pharmaciens Number Nombre	Per 1 000 Pour 1 000	Nurses and midwives Infirmières et Sages- femmes Number Nombre	Per 1 000 Pour 1 000
Niger Niger	2004	296	~0.0	15	~0.0	20	~0.0	2 818	0.2
	2009	439	~0.0	17	~0.0	22	~0.0	3 231	0.2
	2014	958	0.1	...	...	...	...	5 954	0.3
Nigeria Nigéria	2005	39 210	0.3	2 113	~0.0	12 072	0.1	213 425	1.5
	2010	29 120	0.2	8 359	0.1	11 598	0.1	215 055	1.4
	2011	...	...	...	...	15 377	0.1	...	...
	2013	65 759	0.4	...	...	...	...	249 566	1.5
Niue Nioué	2004	4	2.4	2	1.2	1	0.6	22	12.9
	2008	3	1.9	2	1.3	1	0.6	16	10.0
North Macedonia Macédoine du Nord	2010	5 541	2.7	1 599	0.8	692	0.3	9 899	4.8
	2015	5 975	2.9	1 824	0.9	1 029	0.5	7 884	3.8
Norway Norvège	2010	20 114	4.1	4 293	0.9	3 120	0.6	83 999	17.2
	2015	22 848	4.4	4 434	0.9	3 863	0.7	92 880	17.9
	2017	24 583	4.6	4 590	0.9	4 241	0.8	96 159	18.1
Oman Oman	2005	4 182	1.7	448	0.2	753	0.3	9 277	3.7
	2010	5 862	1.9	654	0.2	1 251	0.4	12 865	4.2
	2015	8 914	2.1	1 149	0.3	2 131	0.5	19 331	4.6
	2017	9 132	2.0	1 350	0.3	2 445	0.5	19 938	4.3
Pakistan Pakistan	2004	116 298	0.8	6 452	~0.0	8 102	0.1	71 764	0.5
	2005	126 350	0.8	...	...	...	...	...	...
	2010	144 901	0.8	10 508	0.1	...	...	100 397	0.6
	2012	...	...	...	...	24 907	0.1	...	...
	2015	184 711	1.0	16 652	0.1	...	...	94 766	0.5
Palau Palaos	2004	...	...	...	...	...	...	120	6.1
	2007	...	...	5	0.2	1	~0.0	...	...
	2010	29	1.4	...	...	2	0.1	119	5.8
	2014	25	1.2	...	...	...	...	111	5.3
Panama Panama	2005	4 488	1.3	938	0.3	...	...	6 675	2.0
	2010	5 121	1.4	1 091	0.3	...	...	9 021	2.5
	2011	5 551	1.5	1 114	0.3	...	...	8 579	2.3
	2013	6 068	1.6	1 037	0.3	...	...	...	...
	2016	6 333	1.6	1 129	0.3	...	...	5 688	1.4
Papua New Guinea Papouasie-Nvl-Guinée	2000	275	~0.0	90	~0.0	...	...	2 841	0.5
	2009	...	...	121	~0.0	...	...	...	...
	2010	376	0.1	...	...	...	...	3 643	0.5
	2012	...	...	...	...	354	~0.0	...	...
Paraguay Paraguay	2002	6 355	1.2	2 426	0.4	845	0.2	10 261	1.9
	2012	8 203	1.3	1 054	0.2	...	...	6 689	1.0
	2018	9 421	1.4	1 129	0.2	221	~0.0	8 048	1.2
Peru Pérou	2009	27 272	0.9	3 570	0.1	1 822	0.1	37 672	1.3
	2012	33 669	1.1	4 471	0.1	1 528	0.1	45 024	1.5
	2016	40 352	1.3	5 719	0.2	...	...	42 894	1.4
Philippines Philippines	2004	93 862	1.1	45 903	0.5	49 667	0.6	359 052	4.2
	2005	106 083	1.2	...	...	...	...	369 065	4.3
	2010	119 497	1.3	...	...	...	...	312 564	3.3
	2011	...	...	...	...	59 000	0.6	...	...
Poland Pologne	2010	83 201	2.2	12 549	0.3	25 203	0.7	246 001	6.4
	2015	88 437	2.3	12 603	0.3	28 121	0.7	219 845	5.7
	2016	91 730	2.4	13 308	0.3	29 268	0.8	218 723	5.7
Portugal Portugal	2005	36 138	3.4	5 056	0.5	9 494	0.9	48 155	4.6
	2010	40 672	3.8	8 105	0.8	7 674	0.7	64 760	6.1
	2014	46 036	4.4	9 125	0.9	8 653	0.8	68 888	6.6
	2015	...	...	...	...	8 711	0.8	...	...
	2016	34 595	3.3	...	...	8 788	0.8	66 093	6.4
Qatar Qatar	2005	2 150	2.5	690	0.8	1 100	1.3	4 880	5.6
	2006	2 313	2.3	486	0.5	1 056	1.0	6 185	6.1
	2010	6 919	3.9	...	...	...	...	10 615	6.0
	2014	4 267	1.8	1 662	0.7	2 136	0.9	13 771	5.8
	2016	7 152	2.8	2 155	0.8	2 757	1.1	16 968	6.6
	2017	2	~0.0	...	...	...	...	...	...

Country or area Pays ou zone	Year Année	Physicians Médecins Number Nombre	Per 1 000 Pour 1 000	Dentists Dentistes Number Nombre	Per 1 000 Pour 1 000	Pharmacists Pharmaciens Number Nombre	Per 1 000 Pour 1 000	Nurses and midwives Infirmières et Sages-femmes Number Nombre	Per 1 000 Pour 1 000
Republic of Korea	2005	85 369	1.8	21 581	0.4	54 829	1.1	222 301	4.6
République de Corée	2010	98 293	2.0	20 936	0.4	32 152	0.6	278 702	5.6
	2015	114 322	2.3	23 540	0.5	33 206	0.7	304 142	6.0
	2017	120 630	2.4	25 300	0.5	36 980	0.7	355 524	7.0
Republic of Moldova	2010	9 962	2.4	1 641	0.4	1 779	0.4	23 869	5.8
République de Moldova	2013	10 432	2.6	1 751	0.4	1 901	0.5	23 103	5.7
	2015	13 012	3.2	1 778	0.4	...	...	18 343	4.5
Romania	2002	43 093	2.0	8 274	0.4	7 316	0.3	...	...
Roumanie	2010	50 778	2.5	12 959	0.6	13 534	0.7	121 084	5.9
	2013	52 828	2.6	14 248	0.7	16 231	0.8	126 978	6.3
	2016	44 670	2.3	15 965	0.8	18 385	0.9	120 604	6.1
Russian Federation	2010	343 345	2.4	41 481	0.3	8 344	0.1	1 038 459	7.3
Fédération de Russie	2014	597 062	4.2	41 113	0.3	7 115	~0.0	1 286 791	9.0
	2015	570 260	4.0	...	...	...	...	1 245 594	8.7
	2016	577 856	4.0	...	...	...	...	1 241 151	8.6
Rwanda	2009	...	...	72	~0.0	36	~0.0	6 639	0.7
Rwanda	2015	1 638	0.1	127	~0.0	114	~0.0	9 661	0.8
	2017	1 643	0.1	...	...	...	...	...	...
Saint Kitts and Nevis	2001	49	1.1	15	0.3	...	...	294	6.4
Saint-Kitts-et-Nevis	2015	137	2.5	20	0.4	...	...	216	4.0
Saint Lucia	2001	...	...	27	0.2	23	0.1	371	2.3
Sainte-Lucie	2004	68	0.4	7	~0.0	...	...	375	2.3
	2005	83	0.5	...	...	...	...	326	2.0
	2009	18	0.1	5	~0.0	...	...	...	...
	2010	...	...	28	0.2	...	...	...	...
	2014	...	...	40	0.2	...	...	280	1.6
Saint Vincent & Grenadines	2004	101	0.9	13	0.1	36	0.3	504	4.6
Saint-Vincent-Grenadines	2010	72	0.7	...	...	...	...	282	2.6
Samoa	2003	50	0.3	10	0.1	20	0.1	310	1.7
Samoa	2005	50	0.3	...	...	...	...	...	...
	2008	85	0.5	17	0.1	16	0.1	348	1.9
	2010	64	0.3	45	0.2	...	...	286	1.5
	2013	92	0.5	12	0.1	14	0.1	...	...
	2014	...	...	...	...	...	...	357	1.9
	2016	67	0.3	29	0.1	...	...	...	...
San Marino Saint-Marin	2014	201	6.1	22	0.7	22	0.7	287	8.8
Sao Tome and Principe	2004	81	0.5	...	...	2	~0.0	308	2.0
Sao Tomé-et-Principe	2015	63	0.3	...	...	...	...	442	2.3
Saudi Arabia	2000	14 950	0.7	...	...	...	...	36 495	1.8
Arabie saoudite	2001	14 464	0.7	1 581	0.1	...	...	...	...
	2010	66 014	2.4	...	...	14 928	0.5	129 792	4.7
	2014	79 313	2.6	12 301	0.4	21 639	0.7	160 811	5.2
	2016	77 138	2.4	14 201	0.4	25 497	0.8	183 971	5.7
Senegal	2004	594	0.1	70	~0.0	63	~0.0	3 287	0.3
Sénégal	2008	741	0.1	105	~0.0	107	~0.0	5 254	0.4
	2013	4 381	0.3	54	~0.0	806	0.1	19 558	1.4
	2015	3 023	0.2	...	...	...	...	11 615	0.8
	2016	1 066	0.1	121	~0.0	170	~0.0	4 822	0.3
Serbia	2010	22 316	2.5	2 530	0.3	2 247	0.2	48 060	5.3
Serbie	2014	21 900	2.5	2 310	0.3	2 344	0.3	47 424	5.3
	2015	...	...	1 901	0.2	2 103	0.2	41 771	4.7
	2016	27 563	3.1	4 555	0.5	7 178	0.8	53 982	6.1
Seychelles	2005	104	1.2	10	0.1	7	0.1	390	4.4
Seychelles	2010	100	1.1	19	0.2	4	~0.0	412	4.5
	2012	93	1.0	14	0.2	4	~0.0	419	4.5
	2016	89	0.9	20	0.2	3	~0.0	307	3.3
Sierra Leone	2004	168	~0.0	5	~0.0	84	~0.0	2 510	0.5
Sierra Leone	2010	136	~0.0	6	~0.0	33	~0.0	1 842	0.3
	2011	165	~0.0	...	...	197	~0.0	1 828	0.3
	2014	...	...	...	...	...	...	7 052	1.0

Health Personnel *(continued)*
Number of health workers and workforce density (per 1 000 population)

Le personnel de santé *(suite)*
Personnel de santé et densité (pour 1 000 habitants)

Country or area Pays ou zone	Year Année	Physicians Médecins Number Nombre	Per 1 000 Pour 1 000	Dentists Dentistes Number Nombre	Per 1 000 Pour 1 000	Pharmacists Pharmaciens Number Nombre	Per 1 000 Pour 1 000	Nurses and midwives Infirmières et Sages-femmes Number Nombre	Per 1 000 Pour 1 000
Singapore	2005	6 748	1.5	1 277	0.3	1 330	0.3	20 167	4.5
Singapour	2010	8 819	1.7	1 568	0.3	1 814	0.4	29 340	5.8
	2013	10 339	1.9	1 804	0.3	2 186	0.4	30 533	5.7
	2014	11 120	2.0	...	...	...	...	31 746	5.8
	2016	12 967	2.3	2 198	0.4	2 875	0.5	40 561	7.2
Slovakia	2009	17 798	3.3	2 633	0.5	2 917	0.5	34 477	6.4
Slovaquie	2010	...	...	...	...	...	...	36 493	6.8
	2015	18 719	3.4	2 647	0.5	3 826	0.7	32 664	6.0
	2016	13 416	2.5	...	...	...	...	49 938	9.2
Slovenia	2010	4 979	2.4	1 259	0.6	1 102	0.5	16 871	8.2
Slovénie	2015	5 830	2.8	1 392	0.7	1 295	0.6	18 277	8.8
	2016	6 224	3.0	1 421	0.7	1 356	0.7	20 114	9.7
Solomon Islands	2005	89	0.2	52	0.1	53	0.1	694	1.5
Îles Salomon	2008	89	0.2	...	...	...	...	...	...
	2009	...	...	...	...	...	...	1 080	2.1
	2013	107	0.2	27	~0.0	75	0.1	998	1.8
	2016	120	0.2	29	~0.0	74	0.1	1 277	2.1
Somalia	2006	300	~0.0	...	...	...	...	965	0.1
Somalie	2014	309	~0.0	...	...	...	...	825	0.1
South Africa	2004	34 829	0.7	5 577	0.1	11 097	0.2	184 459	3.8
Afrique du Sud	2005	...	...	...	...	...	...	191 269	3.9
	2010	37 599	0.7	5 296	0.1	...	...	231 086	4.5
	2015	43 277	0.8	5 985	0.1	15 784	0.3	278 617	5.0
	2017	51 616	0.9	8 586	0.2	8 624	0.2	199 482	3.5
Spain	2005	199 123	4.5	22 150	0.5	59 498	1.4	231 001	5.2
Espagne	2010	175 033	3.7	27 826	0.6	43 000	0.9	239 867	5.1
	2014	176 665	3.8	33 286	0.7	54 567	1.2	256 395	5.5
	2015	178 600	3.8	...	...	55 400	1.2	245 533	5.3
	2016	188 595	4.1	...	...	56 167	1.2	256 333	5.5
Sri Lanka	2004	10 479	0.5	771	~0.0	907	~0.0	33 233	1.7
Sri Lanka	2005	10 198	0.5	954	~0.0	...	...	27 514	1.4
	2007	11 023	0.6	1 314	0.1	886	~0.0	40 678	2.1
	2010	14 668	0.7	1 046	0.1	...	...	35 367	1.8
	2015	20 188	1.0	1 340	0.1	1 504	0.1	51 516	2.5
	2016	22 000	1.1	1 900	0.1	1 600	0.1	44 000	2.1
	2017	20 000	1.0	...	...	...	...	...	...
Sudan	2004	7 552	0.3	701	~0.0	1 336	~0.0	31 496	1.0
Soudan	2008	10 813	0.3	772	~0.0	386	~0.0	32 439	1.0
	2015	15 845	0.4	8 116	0.2	17 005	0.4	32 077	0.8
Suriname	2004	400	0.8	42	0.1	...	...	2 580	5.2
Suriname	2009	369	0.7	25	~0.0	31	0.1	1 602	3.1
	2017	...	...	...	...	25	~0.0	2 309	4.1
	2018	697	1.2	...	...	...	...	...	...
Sweden	2010	36 501	3.9	7 546	0.8	7 135	0.8	111 000	11.8
Suède	2015	41 848	4.3	7 813	0.8	7 427	0.8	115 702	11.9
	2016	53 119	5.4	...	...	...	...	113 558	11.5
Switzerland	2010	29 803	3.8	4 109	0.5	4 230	0.5	129 891	16.6
Suisse	2015	34 762	4.2	4 200	0.5	4 498	0.5	139 899	16.8
	2016	35 592	4.2	4 217	0.5	...	...	145 205	17.3
Syrian Arab Republic	2005	28 247	1.5	15 725	0.9	13 218	0.7	34 604	1.9
République arabe syrienne	2010	31 194	1.5	15 984	0.8	16 554	0.8	40 053	1.9
	2014	29 025	1.5	16 585	0.9	27 715	1.4	43 210	2.3
	2016	22 485	1.2	12 532	0.7	18 614	1.0	26 908	1.5
Tajikistan	2003	12 688	1.9	...	...	680	0.1	...	...
Tadjikistan	2005	13 272	1.9	...	...	...	...	...	...
	2010	12 778	1.7	1 234	0.2	...	...	33 764	4.4
	2014	14 219	1.7	1 289	0.2	...	...	43 762	5.2
Thailand	2004	18 918	0.3	4 129	0.1	7 413	0.1	96 704	1.5
Thaïlande	2010	26 244	0.4	11 847	0.2	8 700	0.1	138 710	2.1
	2015	31 959	0.5	...	...	12 231	0.2	162 734	2.4
	2017	55 890	0.8	11 575	0.2	28 896	0.4	204 675	3.0

Country or area Pays ou zone	Year Année	Physicians Médecins		Dentists Dentistes		Pharmacists Pharmaciens		Nurses and midwives Infirmières et Sages- femmes	
		Number Nombre	Per 1 000 Pour 1 000	Number Nombre	Per 1 000 Pour 1 000	Number Nombre	Per 1 000 Pour 1 000	Number Nombre	Per 1 000 Pour 1 000
Timor-Leste Timor-Leste	2004	...	...	2	~0.0	1	~0.0	1 795	1.8
	2010	...	...	7	~0.0	15	~0.0	1 255	1.1
	2015	831	0.7	18	~0.0	10	~0.0	1 773	1.4
	2017	933	0.7	85	0.1	...	...	2 165	1.7
Togo Togo	2004	244	~0.0	18	~0.0	49	~0.0	1 937	0.4
	2008	349	0.1	15	~0.0	11	~0.0	1 816	0.3
	2010	1 315	0.2	66	~0.0	...	...	9 386	1.4
	2015	361	~0.0	18	~0.0	17	~0.0	2 210	0.3
Tonga Tonga	2001	35	0.4	33	0.3	17	0.2	341	3.5
	2002	30	0.3	...	...	...	...	350	3.5
	2003	...	...	23	0.2	...	...	...	...
	2010	58	0.6	10	0.1	4	~0.0	400	3.8
	2013	55	0.5	12	0.1	4	~0.0	408	3.9
	2016	...	...	...	...	...	...	421	3.9
Trinidad and Tobago Trinité-et-Tobago	2003	1 038	0.8	249	0.2	525	0.4	3 980	3.1
	2010	2 402	1.8	343	0.3	641	0.5	3 905	2.9
	2011	2 431	1.8	343	0.3	650	0.5	4 379	3.3
	2015	3 631	2.7	489	0.4	...	...	4 773	3.5
	2016	...	...	...	...	690	0.5	...	...
Tunisia Tunisie	2004	13 330	1.3	2 100	0.2	2 779	0.3	28 537	2.8
	2005	9 422	0.9	1 850	0.2	2 114	0.2	...	...
	2010	12 996	1.2	3 130	0.3	3 236	0.3	23 836	2.2
	2015	14 655	1.3	3 494	0.3	2 592	0.2	29 851	2.6
	2016	14 507	1.3	...	...	2 593	0.2	30 049	2.6
Turkey Turquie	2005	100 853	1.5	18 149	0.3	22 756	0.3	121 723	1.8
	2010	123 447	1.7	21 432	0.3	26 506	0.4	215 458	3.0
	2014	135 616	1.8	22 996	0.3	27 199	0.4	248 108	3.2
	2015	...	...	24 834	0.3	27 530	0.4	205 889	2.6
Turkmenistan Turkménistan	2002	20 032	4.3	876	0.2	1 626	0.4	43 359	9.4
	2010	11 570	2.3	586	0.1	928	0.2	23 994	4.7
	2014	12 161	2.2	631	0.1	926	0.2	25 312	4.6
Tuvalu Tuvalu	2003	10	1.0	2	0.2	2	0.2	50	5.1
	2008	10	1.0	2	0.2	1	0.1	64	6.2
	2009	12	1.2	...	...	...	...	...	...
	2014	10	0.9	5	0.5	3	0.3	41	3.8
Uganda Ouganda	2005	3 361	0.1	98	~0.0	162	~0.0	37 625	1.3
	2015	3 645	0.1	276	~0.0	45	~0.0	25 305	0.6
Ukraine Ukraine	2010	159 495	3.5	30 147	0.7	1 818	~0.0	362 236	7.9
	2014	134 986	3.0	26 954	0.6	1 521	~0.0	316 771	7.1
United Arab Emirates Émirats arabes unis	2005	6 971	1.5	1 414	0.3	2 790	0.6	13 764	3.0
	2010	12 137	1.5	3 081	0.4	1 528	0.2	22 682	2.7
	2015	20 481	2.2	4 916	0.5	5 247	0.6	46 155	5.0
	2016	22 195	2.4	5 165	0.6	6 871	0.7	51 777	5.6
United Kingdom Royaume-Uni	2010	169 179	2.7	32 423	0.5	40 641	0.6	630 394	10.0
	2015	181 673	2.8	34 621	0.5	54 380	0.8	577 269	8.8
	2017	185 692	2.8	34 760	0.5	58 261	0.9	548 498	8.3
United Rep. of Tanzania Rép.-Unie de Tanzanie	2002	822	~0.0	147	~0.0	111	~0.0	13 292	0.4
	2006	...	...	43	~0.0	...	...	9 440	0.2
	2014	2 086	~0.0	104	~0.0	707	~0.0	21 552	0.4
United States of America États-Unis d'Amérique	2005	867 712	2.9	179 414	0.6	259 259	0.9	2 927 000	9.9
	2010	752 572	2.4	178 559	0.6	285 794	0.9	3 891 298	12.6
	2015	827 261	2.6	195 156	0.6	336 398	1.1	2 735 394	8.6
	2016	835 987	2.6	...	...	...	...	...	...
Uruguay Uruguay	2002	12 384	3.7	3 936	1.2	...	...	2 880	0.9
	2008	13 197	3.9	2 476	0.7	...	...	19 595	5.8
	2017	17 456	5.0	5 115	1.5	...	...	6 671	1.9
Uzbekistan Ouzbékistan	2010	72 522	2.5	4 693	0.2	1 074	~0.0	349 800	12.2
	2014	72 237	2.4	4 520	0.1	1 243	~0.0	368 250	12.1
Vanuatu Vanuatu	2004	30	0.1	...	...	...	...	360	1.8
	2008	26	0.1	3	~0.0	2	~0.0	380	1.7
	2012	46	0.2	17	0.1	29	0.1	459	1.9
	2016	46	0.2	...	...	...	...	374	1.4

Country or area Pays ou zone	Year Année	Physicians Médecins		Dentists Dentistes		Pharmacists Pharmaciens		Nurses and midwives Infirmières et Sages-femmes	
		Number Nombre	Per 1 000 Pour 1 000	Number Nombre	Per 1 000 Pour 1 000	Number Nombre	Per 1 000 Pour 1 000	Number Nombre	Per 1 000 Pour 1 000
Venezuela (Boliv. Rep. of) Venezuela (Rép. boliv. du)	2001	48 000	1.9	13 680	0.5	...	...	28 000	1.1
Viet Nam Viet Nam	2005	51 466	0.6	...	...	15 090	0.2	69 665	0.8
	2010	62 458	0.7	...	...	23 494	0.3	108 435	1.2
	2015	73 797	0.8	...	...	31 535	0.3	131 858	1.4
	2016	77 539	0.8	...	...	31 719	0.3	135 432	1.4
Yemen Yémen	2004	6 739	0.3	478	~0.0	925	~0.0	13 746	0.7
	2009	7 127	0.3	...	...	...	...	...	...
	2010	...	...	573	~0.0	1 010	~0.0	16 590	0.7
	2014	8 148	0.3	543	~0.0	2 716	0.1	19 159	0.7
Zambia Zambie	2004	1 499	0.1	269	~0.0	...	...	...	...
	2005	646	0.1	...	...	...	...	8 369	0.7
	2010	836	0.1	246	~0.0	317	~0.0	9 932	0.7
	2012	2 399	0.2	77	~0.0	409	~0.0	...	...
	2016	1 514	0.1	312	~0.0	1 159	0.1	14 807	0.9
Zimbabwe Zimbabwe	2004	2 086	0.2	...	...	605	~0.0	...	...
	2009	827	0.1	182	~0.0	678	~0.0	16 668	1.2
	2010	916	0.1	239	~0.0	...	...	17 029	1.2
	2014	1 176	0.1	250	~0.0	392	~0.0	17 795	1.2

Source:

World Health Organisation (WHO), Geneva, WHO Global Health Workforce statistics database, last accessed March 2019.

Source:

Organisation mondiale de la santé (OMS), Genève, base de données de l'OMS sur les statistiques relatives aux personnels de santé, dernier accès mars 2019.

11

Expenditure on health
Percentage of GDP and of government expenditure

Dépenses de santé
Pourcentage du PIB et des dépenses du gouvernement

Region, country or area[&]	2000	2005	2010	2014	2015	2016	Région, pays ou zone[&]
Afghanistan							**Afghanistan**
Current expenditure (% GDP)	...	9.9	8.6	9.5	10.1	10.2	Dépenses courantes (% du PIB)
Domestic General govt.(% expend. total)	...	3.4	2.3	1.9	2.0	2.0	Dépenses intérieures (en % du totale)
Albania							**Albanie**
Current expenditure (% GDP)	6.8	6.3	5.0	6.9	6.8	6.7	Dépenses courantes (% du PIB)
Domestic General govt.(% expend. total)	7.1	9.7	8.5	9.6	9.5	9.5	Dépenses intérieures (en % du totale)
Algeria							**Algérie**
Current expenditure (% GDP)	3.5	3.2	5.1	6.5	7.0	6.6	Dépenses courantes (% du PIB)
Domestic General govt.(% expend. total)	8.8	8.3	9.5	11.6	10.7	10.7	Dépenses intérieures (en % du totale)
Andorra							**Andorre**
Current expenditure (% GDP)	9.3	8.6	9.4	10.3	10.3	10.4	Dépenses courantes (% du PIB)
Domestic General govt.(% expend. total)	13.0	11.0	10.9	15.0	15.2	14.0	Dépenses intérieures (en % du totale)
Angola							**Angola**
Current expenditure (% GDP)	2.3	3.7	2.7	2.8	3.0	2.9	Dépenses courantes (% du PIB)
Domestic General govt.(% expend. total)	2.7	4.8	4.2	3.6	4.6	5.4	Dépenses intérieures (en % du totale)
Antigua and Barbuda							**Antigua-et-Barbuda**
Current expenditure (% GDP)	3.9	4.5	5.4	5.8	4.7	4.3	Dépenses courantes (% du PIB)
Domestic General govt.(% expend. total)	11.3	11.9	17.0	17.9	12.3	10.8	Dépenses intérieures (en % du totale)
Argentina							**Argentine**
Current expenditure (% GDP)	8.5	7.6	8.6	8.2	8.7	7.5	Dépenses courantes (% du PIB)
Domestic General govt.(% expend. total)	17.8	16.0	16.7	16.3	16.6	13.6	Dépenses intérieures (en % du totale)
Armenia							**Arménie**
Current expenditure (% GDP)	6.5	7.0	5.3	10.2	10.1	9.9	Dépenses courantes (% du PIB)
Domestic General govt.(% expend. total)	4.2	7.4	6.4	6.3	6.1	6.1	Dépenses intérieures (en % du totale)
Australia							**Australie**
Current expenditure (% GDP)	* 7.6	* 8.0	* 8.4	* 9.1	* 9.3	* 9.3	Dépenses courantes (% du PIB)
Domestic General govt.(% expend. total)	* 15.2	* 16.3	* 16.3	* 16.6	* 17.2	* 17.4	Dépenses intérieures (en % du totale)
Austria							**Autriche**
Current expenditure (% GDP)	* 9.2	* 9.6	* 10.2	* 10.4	* 10.3	* 10.4	Dépenses courantes (% du PIB)
Domestic General govt.(% expend. total)	* 13.4	* 13.7	* 14.0	* 14.4	* 14.8	* 14.9	Dépenses intérieures (en % du totale)
Azerbaijan							**Azerbaïdjan**
Current expenditure (% GDP)	* 3.8	* 7.4	* 4.9	* 5.6	* 6.8	* 6.9	Dépenses courantes (% du PIB)
Domestic General govt.(% expend. total)	* 4.8	* 3.9	* 3.6	* 3.4	* 3.7	* 3.9	Dépenses intérieures (en % du totale)
Bahamas							**Bahamas**
Current expenditure (% GDP)	4.0	4.6	5.9	5.9	6.0	6.4	Dépenses courantes (% du PIB)
Domestic General govt.(% expend. total)	15.9	16.2	17.3	14.8	15.9	16.0	Dépenses intérieures (en % du totale)
Bahrain							**Bahreïn**
Current expenditure (% GDP)	3.6	3.2	3.8	4.4	5.0	4.9	Dépenses courantes (% du PIB)
Domestic General govt.(% expend. total)	10.2	8.6	8.5	10.1	8.8	8.4	Dépenses intérieures (en % du totale)
Bangladesh [1]							**Bangladesh** [1]
Current expenditure (% GDP)	* 2.0	* 2.3	* 2.5	* 2.5	* 2.5	* 2.4	Dépenses courantes (% du PIB)
Domestic General govt.(% expend. total)	* 5.2	* 4.4	* 4.4	* 3.6	* 3.4	* 3.4	Dépenses intérieures (en % du totale)
Barbados							**Barbade**
Current expenditure (% GDP)	5.2	6.6	6.8	7.1	7.0	7.0	Dépenses courantes (% du PIB)
Domestic General govt.(% expend. total)	9.4	13.2	10.7	9.9	9.1	9.3	Dépenses intérieures (en % du totale)
Belarus							**Bélarus**
Current expenditure (% GDP)	5.5	6.3	5.7	5.4	6.1	6.3	Dépenses courantes (% du PIB)
Domestic General govt.(% expend. total)	12.1	10.1	8.7	8.7	8.5	8.5	Dépenses intérieures (en % du totale)
Belgium							**Belgique**
Current expenditure (% GDP)	* 7.9	* 9.0	* 9.8	* 10.3	* 10.1	* 10.0	Dépenses courantes (% du PIB)
Domestic General govt.(% expend. total)	* 12.9	* 14.3	* 15.2	* 15.5	* 15.7	* 15.8	Dépenses intérieures (en % du totale)
Belize							**Belize**
Current expenditure (% GDP)	3.9	4.2	5.8	5.7	5.9	6.1	Dépenses courantes (% du PIB)
Domestic General govt.(% expend. total)	6.6	8.6	13.0	10.4	11.4	12.4	Dépenses intérieures (en % du totale)
Benin							**Bénin**
Current expenditure (% GDP)	4.2	4.0	4.1	3.6	4.0	3.9	Dépenses courantes (% du PIB)
Domestic General govt.(% expend. total)	5.2	4.8	5.1	4.0	3.2	3.7	Dépenses intérieures (en % du totale)
Bhutan [1]							**Bhoutan** [1]
Current expenditure (% GDP)	* 4.3	* 4.0	* 3.5	* 3.5	* 3.7	* 3.5	Dépenses courantes (% du PIB)
Domestic General govt.(% expend. total)	* 7.6	* 6.8	* 5.6	* 8.0	* 10.0	* 8.3	Dépenses intérieures (en % du totale)
Bolivia (Plurin. State of)							**Bolivie (État plurin. de)**
Current expenditure (% GDP)	4.3	5.0	5.1	5.8	6.4	6.9	Dépenses courantes (% du PIB)
Domestic General govt.(% expend. total)	8.4	8.6	9.9	8.7	9.8	11.3	Dépenses intérieures (en % du totale)

Region, country or area[&]	2000	2005	2010	2014	2015	2016	Région, pays ou zone[&]
Bosnia and Herzegovina							**Bosnie-Herzégovine**
Current expenditure (% GDP)	7.7	9.1	9.0	9.6	9.3	9.2	Dépenses courantes (% du PIB)
Domestic General govt.(% expend. total)	7.3	10.8	12.4	14.4	15.2	15.4	Dépenses intérieures (en % du totale)
Botswana							**Botswana**
Current expenditure (% GDP)	5.8	5.3	6.0	5.3	6.0	5.5	Dépenses courantes (% du PIB)
Domestic General govt.(% expend. total)	10.8	10.5	7.9	8.3	8.8	9.1	Dépenses intérieures (en % du totale)
Brazil							**Brésil**
Current expenditure (% GDP)	6.6	8.3	9.7	10.8	11.5	11.8	Dépenses courantes (% du PIB)
Domestic General govt.(% expend. total)	4.9	8.9	8.8	9.7	9.9	9.9	Dépenses intérieures (en % du totale)
Brunei Darussalam [2]							**Brunéi Darussalam [2]**
Current expenditure (% GDP)	2.5	2.2	2.3	1.9	2.4	2.3	Dépenses courantes (% du PIB)
Domestic General govt.(% expend. total)	5.7	6.4	5.8	5.2	5.9	5.7	Dépenses intérieures (en % du totale)
Bulgaria [3]							**Bulgarie [3]**
Current expenditure (% GDP)	5.9	6.9	7.1	8.5	8.2	8.2	Dépenses courantes (% du PIB)
Domestic General govt.(% expend. total)	8.5	11.2	10.9	10.7	10.3	11.9	Dépenses intérieures (en % du totale)
Burkina Faso							**Burkina Faso**
Current expenditure (% GDP)	3.3	4.4	5.9	5.6	5.8	6.8	Dépenses courantes (% du PIB)
Domestic General govt.(% expend. total)	4.8	6.0	6.0	7.8	7.2	11.0	Dépenses intérieures (en % du totale)
Burundi							**Burundi**
Current expenditure (% GDP)	* 6.2	* 8.4	* 11.3	* 7.2	* 6.6	* 7.7	Dépenses courantes (% du PIB)
Domestic General govt.(% expend. total)	* 5.9	* 6.2	* 4.9	* 8.1	* 9.2	* 8.5	Dépenses intérieures (en % du totale)
Cabo Verde							**Cabo Verde**
Current expenditure (% GDP)	4.4	4.3	4.5	5.3	5.3	5.3	Dépenses courantes (% du PIB)
Domestic General govt.(% expend. total)	7.5	8.8	7.2	10.0	10.0	9.9	Dépenses intérieures (en % du totale)
Cambodia [1,4]							**Cambodge [1,4]**
Current expenditure (% GDP)	6.5	6.9	6.9	6.7	6.2	6.1	Dépenses courantes (% du PIB)
Domestic General govt.(% expend. total)	8.6	9.9	6.8	5.9	6.6	6.2	Dépenses intérieures (en % du totale)
Cameroon							**Cameroun**
Current expenditure (% GDP)	* 4.0	* 4.1	* 4.5	* 4.5	* 4.7	* 4.7	Dépenses courantes (% du PIB)
Domestic General govt.(% expend. total)	* 4.4	* 5.2	* 5.1	* 2.6	* 3.3	* 3.0	Dépenses intérieures (en % du totale)
Canada							**Canada**
Current expenditure (% GDP)	8.3	9.1	10.6	10.0	10.4	10.5	Dépenses courantes (% du PIB)
Domestic General govt.(% expend. total)	14.8	17.1	17.9	19.1	19.2	19.0	Dépenses intérieures (en % du totale)
Central African Republic							**République centrafricaine**
Current expenditure (% GDP)	* 5.0	* 4.8	* 3.7	* 4.9	* 6.3	* 4.3	Dépenses courantes (% du PIB)
Domestic General govt.(% expend. total)	* 11.2	* 10.1	* 6.0	* 7.2	* 4.3	* 5.1	Dépenses intérieures (en % du totale)
Chad							**Tchad**
Current expenditure (% GDP)	* 5.5	* 4.8	* 4.1	* 4.6	* 4.5	* 4.5	Dépenses courantes (% du PIB)
Domestic General govt.(% expend. total)	* 11.3	* 12.4	* 3.5	* 5.7	* 5.8	* 5.9	Dépenses intérieures (en % du totale)
Chile							**Chili**
Current expenditure (% GDP)	7.0	6.6	6.8	7.8	8.3	8.5	Dépenses courantes (% du PIB)
Domestic General govt.(% expend. total)	16.3	17.3	17.1	19.4	19.6	19.7	Dépenses intérieures (en % du totale)
China							**Chine**
Current expenditure (% GDP)	* 4.5	* 4.1	* 4.2	* 4.8	* 4.9	* 5.0	Dépenses courantes (% du PIB)
Domestic General govt.(% expend. total)	* 6.1	* 7.5	* 8.8	* 9.6	* 9.4	* 9.1	Dépenses intérieures (en % du totale)
Colombia							**Colombie**
Current expenditure (% GDP)	5.5	5.5	6.3	5.8	6.0	5.9	Dépenses courantes (% du PIB)
Domestic General govt.(% expend. total)	16.2	15.5	15.0	12.6	12.8	13.4	Dépenses intérieures (en % du totale)
Comoros							**Comores**
Current expenditure (% GDP)	* 12.2	* 9.9	* 8.5	* 7.6	* 7.7	* 7.6	Dépenses courantes (% du PIB)
Domestic General govt.(% expend. total)	* 9.7	* 6.7	* 3.5	* 3.8	* 3.8	* 3.6	Dépenses intérieures (en % du totale)
Congo							**Congo**
Current expenditure (% GDP)	1.7	1.9	2.0	2.5	3.4	4.6	Dépenses courantes (% du PIB)
Domestic General govt.(% expend. total)	2.3	2.0	4.2	2.1	2.9	3.9	Dépenses intérieures (en % du totale)
Cook Islands [1]							**Îles Cook [1]**
Current expenditure (% GDP)	3.2	4.2	3.5	3.3	2.9	3.4	Dépenses courantes (% du PIB)
Domestic General govt.(% expend. total)	9.6	9.6	9.3	5.7	5.2	5.7	Dépenses intérieures (en % du totale)
Costa Rica							**Costa Rica**
Current expenditure (% GDP)	6.6	6.7	8.1	7.8	7.8	7.6	Dépenses courantes (% du PIB)
Domestic General govt.(% expend. total)	25.6	26.0	32.1	29.3	29.9	29.2	Dépenses intérieures (en % du totale)
Côte d'Ivoire							**Côte d'Ivoire**
Current expenditure (% GDP)	5.7	5.4	6.1	5.0	5.3	4.4	Dépenses courantes (% du PIB)
Domestic General govt.(% expend. total)	4.5	3.9	4.1	4.1	5.0	4.9	Dépenses intérieures (en % du totale)
Croatia							**Croatie**
Current expenditure (% GDP)	7.7	6.9	8.1	7.1	7.2	7.2	Dépenses courantes (% du PIB)
Domestic General govt.(% expend. total)	14.6	12.5	14.3	11.7	11.7	12.0	Dépenses intérieures (en % du totale)

Region, country or area[&]	2000	2005	2010	2014	2015	2016	Région, pays ou zone[&]
Cuba							**Cuba**
Current expenditure (% GDP)	6.6	8.8	10.7	12.1	12.8	12.2	Dépenses courantes (% du PIB)
Domestic General govt.(% expend. total)	10.8	11.7	13.9	18.0	18.2	17.3	Dépenses intérieures (en % du totale)
Cyprus							**Chypre**
Current expenditure (% GDP)	5.3	5.3	6.3	6.8	6.8	6.9	Dépenses courantes (% du PIB)
Domestic General govt.(% expend. total)	6.4	5.4	7.2	6.1	7.1	7.5	Dépenses intérieures (en % du totale)
Czechia							**Tchéquie**
Current expenditure (% GDP)	* 5.7	* 6.4	* 6.9	* 7.7	* 7.2	* 7.1	Dépenses courantes (% du PIB)
Domestic General govt.(% expend. total)	* 12.4	* 12.9	* 13.2	* 14.9	* 14.3	* 14.8	Dépenses intérieures (en % du totale)
Dem. Rep. of the Congo							**Rép. dém. du Congo**
Current expenditure (% GDP)	1.6	4.3	4.0	4.0	4.0	3.9	Dépenses courantes (% du PIB)
Domestic General govt.(% expend. total)	2.5	2.5	2.5	3.0	4.0	3.7	Dépenses intérieures (en % du totale)
Denmark							**Danemark**
Current expenditure (% GDP)	8.1	9.1	10.3	* 10.2	10.3	10.4	Dépenses courantes (% du PIB)
Domestic General govt.(% expend. total)	12.8	14.9	15.3	* 15.5	15.8	16.2	Dépenses intérieures (en % du totale)
Djibouti							**Djibouti**
Current expenditure (% GDP)	4.1	4.5	4.3	* 4.1	4.4	3.5	Dépenses courantes (% du PIB)
Domestic General govt.(% expend. total)	6.1	5.3	7.0	* 6.1	4.1	3.1	Dépenses intérieures (en % du totale)
Dominica							**Dominique**
Current expenditure (% GDP)	5.1	5.2	5.6	5.5	5.5	5.3	Dépenses courantes (% du PIB)
Domestic General govt.(% expend. total)	8.4	9.5	8.2	10.4	10.6	8.0	Dépenses intérieures (en % du totale)
Dominican Republic							**République dominicaine**
Current expenditure (% GDP)	4.9	4.4	5.6	5.9	6.0	6.2	Dépenses courantes (% du PIB)
Domestic General govt.(% expend. total)	11.8	9.2	15.9	14.3	14.0	16.0	Dépenses intérieures (en % du totale)
Ecuador							**Équateur**
Current expenditure (% GDP)	3.3	5.6	7.1	8.6	8.6	8.4	Dépenses courantes (% du PIB)
Domestic General govt.(% expend. total)	4.1	7.9	9.2	10.2	10.8	11.0	Dépenses intérieures (en % du totale)
Egypt							**Égypte**
Current expenditure (% GDP)	4.9	4.9	4.2	4.7	4.6	4.6	Dépenses courantes (% du PIB)
Domestic General govt.(% expend. total)	6.7	5.2	4.4	4.2	5.0	4.2	Dépenses intérieures (en % du totale)
El Salvador							**El Salvador**
Current expenditure (% GDP)	8.1	7.2	6.9	6.9	6.9	7.0	Dépenses courantes (% du PIB)
Domestic General govt.(% expend. total)	18.4	19.6	17.7	20.1	20.8	20.9	Dépenses intérieures (en % du totale)
Equatorial Guinea							**Guinée équatoriale**
Current expenditure (% GDP)	* 2.4	* 1.4	* 1.5	* 1.8	* 2.7	* 3.4	Dépenses courantes (% du PIB)
Domestic General govt.(% expend. total)	* 2.5	* 2.1	* 1.0	* 1.3	* 1.4	* 2.6	Dépenses intérieures (en % du totale)
Eritrea							**Érythrée**
Current expenditure (% GDP)	* 4.5	* 5.3	* 3.4	* 2.9	* 3.0	* 3.0	Dépenses courantes (% du PIB)
Domestic General govt.(% expend. total)	* 2.1	* 1.1	* 1.5	* 1.1	* 1.2	* 2.9	Dépenses intérieures (en % du totale)
Estonia							**Estonie**
Current expenditure (% GDP)	5.2	5.0	6.3	6.2	6.5	6.7	Dépenses courantes (% du PIB)
Domestic General govt.(% expend. total)	10.8	11.1	11.6	12.2	12.1	12.4	Dépenses intérieures (en % du totale)
Eswatini							**Eswatini**
Current expenditure (% GDP)	4.5	5.6	8.4	7.6	7.8	7.7	Dépenses courantes (% du PIB)
Domestic General govt.(% expend. total)	10.5	12.6	18.8	13.7	14.9	15.2	Dépenses intérieures (en % du totale)
Ethiopia							**Éthiopie**
Current expenditure (% GDP)	4.4	4.1	5.5	4.0	4.0	4.0	Dépenses courantes (% du PIB)
Domestic General govt.(% expend. total)	7.0	7.6	5.1	4.1	5.9	6.0	Dépenses intérieures (en % du totale)
Fiji							**Fidji**
Current expenditure (% GDP)	* 3.7	* 3.6	* 3.7	* 3.6	* 3.6	* 3.5	Dépenses courantes (% du PIB)
Domestic General govt.(% expend. total)	* 10.6	* 10.4	* 8.6	* 7.1	* 7.0	* 7.7	Dépenses intérieures (en % du totale)
Finland							**Finlande**
Current expenditure (% GDP)	6.8	8.0	8.9	9.5	9.7	9.5	Dépenses courantes (% du PIB)
Domestic General govt.(% expend. total)	10.5	12.7	12.5	12.7	13.3	13.1	Dépenses intérieures (en % du totale)
France							**France**
Current expenditure (% GDP)	9.5	10.2	11.2	11.6	11.5	11.5	Dépenses courantes (% du PIB)
Domestic General govt.(% expend. total)	14.7	15.1	15.1	15.5	15.5	17.0	Dépenses intérieures (en % du totale)
Gabon							**Gabon**
Current expenditure (% GDP)	2.9	2.9	2.5	2.5	2.7	3.1	Dépenses courantes (% du PIB)
Domestic General govt.(% expend. total)	5.2	5.1	6.8	6.4	7.0	9.2	Dépenses intérieures (en % du totale)
Gambia							**Gambie**
Current expenditure (% GDP)	4.7	4.9	5.7	5.3	4.8	4.4	Dépenses courantes (% du PIB)
Domestic General govt.(% expend. total)	6.9	10.2	7.8	4.1	2.8	2.8	Dépenses intérieures (en % du totale)
Georgia [5]							**Géorgie [5]**
Current expenditure (% GDP)	7.4	8.3	9.5	8.4	7.9	8.4	Dépenses courantes (% du PIB)
Domestic General govt.(% expend. total)	4.9	5.6	6.2	7.8	9.6	10.3	Dépenses intérieures (en % du totale)

Expenditure on health *(continued)*
Percentage of GDP and of government expenditure

Dépenses de santé *(suite)*
Pourcentage du PIB et des dépenses du gouvernement

Region, country or area	2000	2005	2010	2014	2015	2016	Région, pays ou zone
Germany							**Allemagne**
Current expenditure (% GDP)	9.8	10.2	11.0	11.0	11.1	11.1	Dépenses courantes (% du PIB)
Domestic General govt.(% expend. total)	17.2	16.8	19.4	20.9	21.3	21.4	Dépenses intérieures (en % du totale)
Ghana							**Ghana**
Current expenditure (% GDP)	4.0	5.3	6.1	5.6	6.1	4.4	Dépenses courantes (% du PIB)
Domestic General govt.(% expend. total)	6.0	10.6	12.0	6.7	8.6	6.5	Dépenses intérieures (en % du totale)
Greece							**Grèce**
Current expenditure (% GDP)	7.2	9.0	9.6	8.0	8.2	8.5	Dépenses courantes (% du PIB)
Domestic General govt.(% expend. total)	9.5	12.0	12.4	9.1	8.8	10.3	Dépenses intérieures (en % du totale)
Grenada							**Grenade**
Current expenditure (% GDP)	5.1	5.3	6.1	5.2	4.9	5.2	Dépenses courantes (% du PIB)
Domestic General govt.(% expend. total)	6.8	10.0	9.8	7.1	7.4	9.0	Dépenses intérieures (en % du totale)
Guatemala							**Guatemala**
Current expenditure (% GDP)	5.7	6.3	6.1	5.9	5.5	5.8	Dépenses courantes (% du PIB)
Domestic General govt.(% expend. total)	14.0	14.3	14.1	16.6	15.7	17.9	Dépenses intérieures (en % du totale)
Guinea							**Guinée**
Current expenditure (% GDP)	3.7	2.9	3.1	4.8	5.8	5.5	Dépenses courantes (% du PIB)
Domestic General govt.(% expend. total)	2.9	3.0	1.9	3.0	2.0	4.1	Dépenses intérieures (en % du totale)
Guinea-Bissau							**Guinée-Bissau**
Current expenditure (% GDP)	* 7.1	* 6.4	* 6.3	* 6.8	* 6.5	* 6.1	Dépenses courantes (% du PIB)
Domestic General govt.(% expend. total)	* 13.7	* 13.7	* 5.9	* 8.8	* 9.4	* 12.9	Dépenses intérieures (en % du totale)
Guyana							**Guyana**
Current expenditure (% GDP)	2.8	3.4	4.6	5.1	4.5	4.2	Dépenses courantes (% du PIB)
Domestic General govt.(% expend. total)	7.1	6.3	5.6	8.6	7.8	7.7	Dépenses intérieures (en % du totale)
Haiti							**Haïti**
Current expenditure (% GDP)	6.9	5.5	8.1	7.8	5.4	5.4	Dépenses courantes (% du PIB)
Domestic General govt.(% expend. total)	16.1	6.6	6.0	3.2	4.0	4.4	Dépenses intérieures (en % du totale)
Honduras							**Honduras**
Current expenditure (% GDP)	6.4	7.7	8.6	8.0	7.7	8.4	Dépenses courantes (% du PIB)
Domestic General govt.(% expend. total)	13.7	12.4	14.0	11.5	11.4	14.0	Dépenses intérieures (en % du totale)
Hungary							**Hongrie**
Current expenditure (% GDP)	* 6.8	* 8.0	* 7.5	* 7.1	* 7.1	* 7.4	Dépenses courantes (% du PIB)
Domestic General govt.(% expend. total)	* 9.9	* 11.4	* 10.2	* 9.6	* 9.4	* 10.4	Dépenses intérieures (en % du totale)
Iceland							**Islande**
Current expenditure (% GDP)	* 9.0	* 9.2	* 8.8	* 8.5	* 8.3	* 8.3	Dépenses courantes (% du PIB)
Domestic General govt.(% expend. total)	* 17.6	* 18.0	* 14.4	* 15.2	* 15.9	* 14.9	Dépenses intérieures (en % du totale)
India [2]							**Inde** [2]
Current expenditure (% GDP)	# 4.0	# 3.8	# 3.3	# 3.6	# 3.6	# 3.6	Dépenses courantes (% du PIB)
Domestic General govt.(% expend. total)	* 3.3	* 3.0	* 3.2	* 3.0	* 3.1	* 3.1	Dépenses intérieures (en % du totale)
Indonesia							**Indonésie**
Current expenditure (% GDP)	* 1.9	* 2.6	* 3.0	* 3.1	* 3.0	* 3.1	Dépenses courantes (% du PIB)
Domestic General govt.(% expend. total)	* 3.8	* 4.2	* 4.5	* 5.8	* 6.9	* 8.3	Dépenses intérieures (en % du totale)
Iran (Islamic Republic of)							**Iran (Rép. islamique d')**
Current expenditure (% GDP)	* 4.7	* 5.3	* 6.8	* 6.9	* 7.8	* 8.1	Dépenses courantes (% du PIB)
Domestic General govt.(% expend. total)	* 11.0	* 9.4	* 11.9	* 22.6	* 22.6	* 22.6	Dépenses intérieures (en % du totale)
Iraq							**Iraq**
Current expenditure (% GDP)	...	2.9	3.2	2.8	3.1	3.3	Dépenses courantes (% du PIB)
Domestic General govt.(% expend. total)	...	3.2	4.8	2.4	1.7	1.7	Dépenses intérieures (en % du totale)
Ireland							**Irlande**
Current expenditure (% GDP)	5.9	7.6	10.5	9.7	7.4	7.4	Dépenses courantes (% du PIB)
Domestic General govt.(% expend. total)	14.8	18.1	12.3	18.2	18.4	19.7	Dépenses intérieures (en % du totale)
Israel							**Israël**
Current expenditure (% GDP)	6.8	7.1	7.1	7.2	7.4	7.3	Dépenses courantes (% du PIB)
Domestic General govt.(% expend. total)	8.9	9.3	10.7	11.2	11.6	11.6	Dépenses intérieures (en % du totale)
Italy							**Italie**
Current expenditure (% GDP)	7.6	8.4	9.0	9.0	9.0	8.9	Dépenses courantes (% du PIB)
Domestic General govt.(% expend. total)	12.1	13.7	14.1	13.4	13.3	13.5	Dépenses intérieures (en % du totale)
Jamaica							**Jamaïque**
Current expenditure (% GDP)	6.0	4.6	5.0	5.2	5.7	6.1	Dépenses courantes (% du PIB)
Domestic General govt.(% expend. total)	11.8	7.7	9.0	11.2	12.9	12.8	Dépenses intérieures (en % du totale)
Japan							**Japon**
Current expenditure (% GDP)	* 7.2	* 7.8	* 9.2	* 10.8	* 10.9	* 10.9	Dépenses courantes (% du PIB)
Domestic General govt.(% expend. total)	* 15.3	* 17.8	* 18.9	* 22.6	* 23.2	* 23.4	Dépenses intérieures (en % du totale)
Jordan							**Jordanie**
Current expenditure (% GDP)	9.6	8.9	8.4	7.4	6.3	5.5	Dépenses courantes (% du PIB)
Domestic General govt.(% expend. total)	12.8	11.6	18.4	12.6	12.0	12.0	Dépenses intérieures (en % du totale)

Region, country or area[&]	2000	2005	2010	2014	2015	2016	Région, pays ou zone[&]
Kazakhstan							**Kazakhstan**
Current expenditure (% GDP)	* 4.2	* 3.9	* 2.7	* 2.7	* 3.1	* 3.5	Dépenses courantes (% du PIB)
Domestic General govt.(% expend. total)	* 9.2	* 11.4	* 8.2	* 8.8	* 8.4	* 9.4	Dépenses intérieures (en % du totale)
Kenya							**Kenya**
Current expenditure (% GDP)	4.7	5.3	6.1	5.3	4.9	* 4.5	Dépenses courantes (% du PIB)
Domestic General govt.(% expend. total)	7.1	6.9	7.3	6.7	6.3	* 6.1	Dépenses intérieures (en % du totale)
Kiribati [1,6]							**Kiribati** [1,6]
Current expenditure (% GDP)	8.6	11.5	9.2	10.0	8.1	11.9	Dépenses courantes (% du PIB)
Domestic General govt.(% expend. total)	11.4	11.4	10.3	7.0	6.3	5.5	Dépenses intérieures (en % du totale)
Kuwait							**Koweït**
Current expenditure (% GDP)	2.5	2.4	2.8	3.2	4.0	3.9	Dépenses courantes (% du PIB)
Domestic General govt.(% expend. total)	5.2	6.8	5.2	6.2	6.2	6.2	Dépenses intérieures (en % du totale)
Kyrgyzstan							**Kirghizistan**
Current expenditure (% GDP)	4.4	7.5	7.0	8.3	7.2	6.6	Dépenses courantes (% du PIB)
Domestic General govt.(% expend. total)	7.1	12.8	9.2	10.6	7.3	6.6	Dépenses intérieures (en % du totale)
Lao People's Dem. Rep. [7]							**Rép. dém. populaire lao** [7]
Current expenditure (% GDP)	4.3	3.3	# 2.9	2.3	2.5	2.4	Dépenses courantes (% du PIB)
Domestic General govt.(% expend. total)	6.2	5.7	2.7	2.8	3.8	3.7	Dépenses intérieures (en % du totale)
Latvia							**Lettonie**
Current expenditure (% GDP)	* 5.4	* 5.9	* 6.1	* 5.5	* 5.7	* 6.2	Dépenses courantes (% du PIB)
Domestic General govt.(% expend. total)	* 7.4	* 9.6	* 8.1	* 8.6	* 8.5	* 9.2	Dépenses intérieures (en % du totale)
Lebanon							**Liban**
Current expenditure (% GDP)	10.7	7.6	7.4	8.0	7.8	8.0	Dépenses courantes (% du PIB)
Domestic General govt.(% expend. total)	7.5	9.2	10.3	13.7	14.3	14.3	Dépenses intérieures (en % du totale)
Lesotho							**Lesotho**
Current expenditure (% GDP)	* 5.9	* 5.1	* 7.7	* 8.6	* 8.3	* 8.1	Dépenses courantes (% du PIB)
Domestic General govt.(% expend. total)	* 7.7	* 5.8	* 8.6	* 11.7	* 11.3	* 10.9	Dépenses intérieures (en % du totale)
Liberia							**Libéria**
Current expenditure (% GDP)	* 4.0	* 8.8	* 8.8	* 8.9	* 10.2	* 9.6	Dépenses courantes (% du PIB)
Domestic General govt.(% expend. total)	* 5.0	* 4.5	* 2.4	* 2.4	* 3.1	* 3.9	Dépenses intérieures (en % du totale)
Libya							**Libye**
Current expenditure (% GDP)	* 3.4	* 2.6	* 3.6	...	...	...	Dépenses courantes (% du PIB)
Domestic General govt.(% expend. total)	* 6.0	* 5.8	* 4.3	...	...	...	Dépenses intérieures (en % du totale)
Lithuania							**Lituanie**
Current expenditure (% GDP)	* 6.2	* 5.6	* 6.8	* 6.2	* 6.5	* 6.7	Dépenses courantes (% du PIB)
Domestic General govt.(% expend. total)	* 10.6	* 10.1	* 11.5	* 11.9	* 12.3	* 12.8	Dépenses intérieures (en % du totale)
Luxembourg							**Luxembourg**
Current expenditure (% GDP)	5.9	7.2	7.0	6.4	6.2	6.2	Dépenses courantes (% du PIB)
Domestic General govt.(% expend. total)	13.0	13.9	13.7	12.7	12.2	11.9	Dépenses intérieures (en % du totale)
Madagascar							**Madagascar**
Current expenditure (% GDP)	* 5.4	* 5.5	* 5.3	* 5.1	* 5.5	* 6.0	Dépenses courantes (% du PIB)
Domestic General govt.(% expend. total)	* 12.4	* 8.3	* 15.2	* 13.9	* 15.6	* 17.8	Dépenses intérieures (en % du totale)
Malawi							**Malawi**
Current expenditure (% GDP)	3.4	6.1	7.2	9.7	9.3	9.8	Dépenses courantes (% du PIB)
Domestic General govt.(% expend. total)	7.1	6.1	5.8	8.5	9.7	9.8	Dépenses intérieures (en % du totale)
Malaysia							**Malaisie**
Current expenditure (% GDP)	2.6	2.8	3.2	3.8	* 3.9	* 3.8	Dépenses courantes (% du PIB)
Domestic General govt.(% expend. total)	4.6	5.6	6.3	7.9	* 8.2	* 8.2	Dépenses intérieures (en % du totale)
Maldives							**Maldives**
Current expenditure (% GDP)	7.7	8.8	# * 8.5	7.9	8.9	10.6	Dépenses courantes (% du PIB)
Domestic General govt.(% expend. total)	8.8	7.7	# * 13.6	14.4	18.2	20.2	Dépenses intérieures (en % du totale)
Mali							**Mali**
Current expenditure (% GDP)	5.1	5.0	4.4	4.5	4.1	3.8	Dépenses courantes (% du PIB)
Domestic General govt.(% expend. total)	5.4	8.4	3.2	4.4	4.4	5.3	Dépenses intérieures (en % du totale)
Malta							**Malte**
Current expenditure (% GDP)	6.5	8.7	8.2	9.4	9.4	9.3	Dépenses courantes (% du PIB)
Domestic General govt.(% expend. total)	11.8	14.2	12.9	14.0	14.2	15.8	Dépenses intérieures (en % du totale)
Marshall Islands [7,8]							**Îles Marshall** [7,8]
Current expenditure (% GDP)	25.2	26.3	19.3	18.8	22.6	23.3	Dépenses courantes (% du PIB)
Domestic General govt.(% expend. total)	26.1	11.7	14.2	19.0	20.2	20.7	Dépenses intérieures (en % du totale)
Mauritania							**Mauritanie**
Current expenditure (% GDP)	4.5	4.5	3.3	4.2	4.6	4.2	Dépenses courantes (% du PIB)
Domestic General govt.(% expend. total)	2.5	3.9	4.2	5.2	5.5	5.5	Dépenses intérieures (en % du totale)
Mauritius							**Maurice**
Current expenditure (% GDP)	3.0	3.7	4.7	5.6	5.8	5.7	Dépenses courantes (% du PIB)
Domestic General govt.(% expend. total)	6.9	7.4	8.3	10.5	9.5	10.0	Dépenses intérieures (en % du totale)

Region, country or area&	2000	2005	2010	2014	2015	2016	Région, pays ou zone&
Mexico							**Mexique**
Current expenditure (% GDP)	4.4	5.8	5.8	5.5	5.7	5.5	Dépenses courantes (% du PIB)
Domestic General govt.(% expend. total)	10.0	11.2	10.9	10.3	10.9	10.4	Dépenses intérieures (en % du totale)
Micronesia (Fed. States of) [7]							**Micronésie (États féd. de)** [7]
Current expenditure (% GDP)	7.7	11.5	12.9	11.5	12.2	12.6	Dépenses courantes (% du PIB)
Domestic General govt.(% expend. total)	2.6	4.5	3.4	6.2	5.8	5.7	Dépenses intérieures (en % du totale)
Monaco							**Monaco**
Current expenditure (% GDP)	* 1.7	* 2.1	* 2.3	* 2.1	* 2.0	* 1.7	Dépenses courantes (% du PIB)
Domestic General govt.(% expend. total)	* 6.9	* 7.9	* 9.2	* 8.3	* 8.1	* 6.7	Dépenses intérieures (en % du totale)
Mongolia							**Mongolie**
Current expenditure (% GDP)	* 5.3	* 3.2	* 3.4	* 3.7	* 3.9	* 3.8	Dépenses courantes (% du PIB)
Domestic General govt.(% expend. total)	* 12.3	* 9.0	* 6.5	* 4.9	* 6.1	* 5.3	Dépenses intérieures (en % du totale)
Morocco							**Maroc**
Current expenditure (% GDP)	4.0	4.8	5.9	5.7	5.4	5.8	Dépenses courantes (% du PIB)
Domestic General govt.(% expend. total)	4.0	4.0	7.5	7.7	7.7	9.1	Dépenses intérieures (en % du totale)
Mozambique							**Mozambique**
Current expenditure (% GDP)	* 3.9	* 6.4	* 5.1	* 5.9	* 5.2	* 5.1	Dépenses courantes (% du PIB)
Domestic General govt.(% expend. total)	* 14.5	* 15.9	* 1.4	* 4.4	* 1.2	* 8.3	Dépenses intérieures (en % du totale)
Myanmar [2,9]							**Myanmar** [2,9]
Current expenditure (% GDP)	* 1.8	* 2.0	* 1.9	* 5.0	* 5.2	* 5.1	Dépenses courantes (% du PIB)
Domestic General govt.(% expend. total)	* 1.2	* 1.1	* 1.2	* 4.4	* 4.9	* 4.8	Dépenses intérieures (en % du totale)
Namibia							**Namibie**
Current expenditure (% GDP)	10.3	12.4	9.5	8.2	9.9	9.1	Dépenses courantes (% du PIB)
Domestic General govt.(% expend. total)	20.5	20.9	15.4	12.9	12.4	13.8	Dépenses intérieures (en % du totale)
Nauru [1,6,10]							**Nauru** [1,6,10]
Current expenditure (% GDP)	13.5	12.6	10.4	8.8	11.4	11.1	Dépenses courantes (% du PIB)
Domestic General govt.(% expend. total)	9.7	18.0	7.3	6.6	5.0	5.0	Dépenses intérieures (en % du totale)
Nepal [11]							**Népal** [11]
Current expenditure (% GDP)	3.6	4.5	5.0	5.8	6.2	6.3	Dépenses courantes (% du PIB)
Domestic General govt.(% expend. total)	4.2	6.2	4.8	5.3	5.1	5.3	Dépenses intérieures (en % du totale)
Netherlands							**Pays-Bas**
Current expenditure (% GDP)	* 7.1	* 9.3	* 10.4	* 10.9	* 10.4	* 10.4	Dépenses courantes (% du PIB)
Domestic General govt.(% expend. total)	* 11.2	* 14.7	* 17.8	* 19.0	* 18.8	* 19.3	Dépenses intérieures (en % du totale)
New Zealand							**Nouvelle-Zélande**
Current expenditure (% GDP)	* 7.5	* 8.3	* 9.6	* 9.4	* 9.3	* 9.2	Dépenses courantes (% du PIB)
Domestic General govt.(% expend. total)	* 17.1	* 20.0	* 20.1	* 22.2	* 22.1	* 22.5	Dépenses intérieures (en % du totale)
Nicaragua							**Nicaragua**
Current expenditure (% GDP)	5.2	5.5	6.5	7.7	7.9	8.7	Dépenses courantes (% du PIB)
Domestic General govt.(% expend. total)	10.0	11.0	13.3	18.0	17.9	20.0	Dépenses intérieures (en % du totale)
Niger							**Niger**
Current expenditure (% GDP)	6.2	7.5	6.5	5.9	7.1	6.2	Dépenses courantes (% du PIB)
Domestic General govt.(% expend. total)	8.3	12.3	7.9	5.4	4.6	5.7	Dépenses intérieures (en % du totale)
Nigeria							**Nigéria**
Current expenditure (% GDP)	2.6	3.8	3.3	3.3	3.6	3.6	Dépenses courantes (% du PIB)
Domestic General govt.(% expend. total)	2.1	3.6	2.7	3.5	5.3	5.0	Dépenses intérieures (en % du totale)
Niue [1,6,10]							**Nioué** [1,6,10]
Current expenditure (% GDP)	7.9	10.1	9.8	7.7	6.4	7.3	Dépenses courantes (% du PIB)
Domestic General govt.(% expend. total)	6.3	2.7	2.1	2.1	2.2	2.0	Dépenses intérieures (en % du totale)
North Macedonia							**Macédoine du Nord**
Current expenditure (% GDP)	8.9	7.7	6.7	6.3	6.4	6.3	Dépenses courantes (% du PIB)
Domestic General govt.(% expend. total)	14.7	13.6	12.5	12.7	12.8	13.1	Dépenses intérieures (en % du totale)
Norway							**Norvège**
Current expenditure (% GDP)	* 7.7	* 8.3	* 8.9	* 9.3	* 10.1	* 10.5	Dépenses courantes (% du PIB)
Domestic General govt.(% expend. total)	* 15.0	* 16.5	* 16.8	* 17.4	* 17.7	* 17.6	Dépenses intérieures (en % du totale)
Oman							**Oman**
Current expenditure (% GDP)	3.1	2.6	2.7	3.5	4.3	4.3	Dépenses courantes (% du PIB)
Domestic General govt.(% expend. total)	7.0	6.1	6.7	6.7	7.6	7.6	Dépenses intérieures (en % du totale)
Pakistan							**Pakistan**
Current expenditure (% GDP)	2.9	2.7	2.6	2.7	2.7	2.8	Dépenses courantes (% du PIB)
Domestic General govt.(% expend. total)	5.9	3.7	2.8	3.5	3.7	3.9	Dépenses intérieures (en % du totale)
Palau [7]							**Palaos** [7]
Current expenditure (% GDP)	* 8.8	* 9.0	* 11.6	* 12.0	* 10.5	* 11.7	Dépenses courantes (% du PIB)
Domestic General govt.(% expend. total)	* 8.2	* 8.7	* 8.5	* 13.3	* 13.3	* 18.7	Dépenses intérieures (en % du totale)
Panama							**Panama**
Current expenditure (% GDP)	7.0	6.2	7.0	6.7	6.8	7.3	Dépenses courantes (% du PIB)
Domestic General govt.(% expend. total)	20.3	10.0	13.1	11.9	11.6	21.4	Dépenses intérieures (en % du totale)

Region, country or area&	2000	2005	2010	2014	2015	2016	Région, pays ou zone&
Papua New Guinea							**Papouasie-Nvl-Guinée**
Current expenditure (% GDP)	2.1	2.5	2.1	3.6	2.5	2.0	Dépenses courantes (% du PIB)
Domestic General govt.(% expend. total)	8.3	7.8	7.1	8.2	8.2	7.2	Dépenses intérieures (en % du totale)
Paraguay							**Paraguay**
Current expenditure (% GDP)	5.8	5.0	6.2	7.6	7.8	8.0	Dépenses courantes (% du PIB)
Domestic General govt.(% expend. total)	6.9	5.9	9.0	11.2	10.9	16.2	Dépenses intérieures (en % du totale)
Peru							**Pérou**
Current expenditure (% GDP)	4.6	4.6	4.7	5.1	5.1	5.1	Dépenses courantes (% du PIB)
Domestic General govt.(% expend. total)	11.2	12.4	11.7	13.7	14.5	15.7	Dépenses intérieures (en % du totale)
Philippines							**Philippines**
Current expenditure (% GDP)	* 3.2	* 3.9	* 4.3	* 4.1	* 4.3	* 4.4	Dépenses courantes (% du PIB)
Domestic General govt.(% expend. total)	* 6.5	* 6.6	* 7.2	* 6.3	* 7.3	* 7.1	Dépenses intérieures (en % du totale)
Poland							**Pologne**
Current expenditure (% GDP)	* 5.3	* 5.8	* 6.4	* 6.2	* 6.3	* 6.5	Dépenses courantes (% du PIB)
Domestic General govt.(% expend. total)	* 8.6	* 9.0	* 10.0	* 10.4	* 10.7	* 11.0	Dépenses intérieures (en % du totale)
Portugal							**Portugal**
Current expenditure (% GDP)	8.4	9.4	9.8	9.0	9.0	9.1	Dépenses courantes (% du PIB)
Domestic General govt.(% expend. total)	13.8	14.4	13.2	11.5	12.3	13.4	Dépenses intérieures (en % du totale)
Qatar							**Qatar**
Current expenditure (% GDP)	2.0	2.6	1.8	2.4	3.1	3.1	Dépenses courantes (% du PIB)
Domestic General govt.(% expend. total)	3.9	6.6	4.1	6.3	6.3	6.3	Dépenses intérieures (en % du totale)
Republic of Korea							**République de Corée**
Current expenditure (% GDP)	* 4.0	* 4.9	* 6.2	* 6.8	* 7.0	* 7.3	Dépenses courantes (% du PIB)
Domestic General govt.(% expend. total)	* 8.0	* 9.7	* 12.2	* 12.5	* 12.9	* 13.5	Dépenses intérieures (en % du totale)
Republic of Moldova [12]							**République de Moldova [12]**
Current expenditure (% GDP)	5.9	9.6	12.2	10.3	10.2	9.0	Dépenses courantes (% du PIB)
Domestic General govt.(% expend. total)	8.5	13.6	13.6	12.8	12.2	12.1	Dépenses intérieures (en % du totale)
Romania							**Roumanie**
Current expenditure (% GDP)	* 4.2	* 5.5	* 5.8	* 5.0	* 4.9	* 5.0	Dépenses courantes (% du PIB)
Domestic General govt.(% expend. total)	* 8.7	* 13.2	* 11.5	* 11.4	* 10.8	* 11.3	Dépenses intérieures (en % du totale)
Russian Federation							**Fédération de Russie**
Current expenditure (% GDP)	5.0	4.8	5.0	5.2	5.3[13]	5.3[13]	Dépenses courantes (% du PIB)
Domestic General govt.(% expend. total)	9.7	9.9	8.6	9.2	8.8[13]	8.2[13]	Dépenses intérieures (en % du totale)
Rwanda							**Rwanda**
Current expenditure (% GDP)	* 4.3	* 8.8	* 8.6	* 6.9	* 6.5	* 6.8	Dépenses courantes (% du PIB)
Domestic General govt.(% expend. total)	* 3.5	* 8.1	* 8.6	* 8.0	* 7.9	* 8.9	Dépenses intérieures (en % du totale)
Saint Kitts and Nevis							**Saint-Kitts-et-Nevis**
Current expenditure (% GDP)	4.8	4.8	5.8	5.2	5.2	5.7	Dépenses courantes (% du PIB)
Domestic General govt.(% expend. total)	5.8	6.4	5.9	6.7	6.6	8.1	Dépenses intérieures (en % du totale)
Saint Lucia							**Sainte-Lucie**
Current expenditure (% GDP)	5.3	5.4	5.7	5.8	5.4	5.3	Dépenses courantes (% du PIB)
Domestic General govt.(% expend. total)	8.1	6.2	7.0	8.2	8.6	8.5	Dépenses intérieures (en % du totale)
Saint Vincent & Grenadines							**Saint-Vincent-Grenadines**
Current expenditure (% GDP)	3.7	3.3	3.7	3.7	3.5	3.6	Dépenses courantes (% du PIB)
Domestic General govt.(% expend. total)	11.7	9.0	8.2	8.3	9.2	9.6	Dépenses intérieures (en % du totale)
Samoa [1]							**Samoa [1]**
Current expenditure (% GDP)	4.4	4.8	5.5	6.2	5.7	5.5	Dépenses courantes (% du PIB)
Domestic General govt.(% expend. total)	11.8	10.4	10.4	10.1	11.5	12.5	Dépenses intérieures (en % du totale)
San Marino							**Saint-Marin**
Current expenditure (% GDP)	5.1	4.5	6.0	7.1	6.8	6.4	Dépenses courantes (% du PIB)
Domestic General govt.(% expend. total)	11.7	11.7	13.1	13.5	13.3	12.2	Dépenses intérieures (en % du totale)
Sao Tome and Principe							**Sao Tomé-et-Principe**
Current expenditure (% GDP)	* 11.5	* 11.2	* 6.8	* 6.7	* 5.3	* 6.0	Dépenses courantes (% du PIB)
Domestic General govt.(% expend. total)	* 31.7	* 11.5	* 4.1	* 7.7	* 4.9	* 7.4	Dépenses intérieures (en % du totale)
Saudi Arabia							**Arabie saoudite**
Current expenditure (% GDP)	4.2	3.4	3.7	5.2	6.0	5.7	Dépenses courantes (% du PIB)
Domestic General govt.(% expend. total)	9.2	8.8	6.8	9.3	10.1	10.1	Dépenses intérieures (en % du totale)
Senegal							**Sénégal**
Current expenditure (% GDP)	4.5	4.6	4.9	5.8	5.7	5.6	Dépenses courantes (% du PIB)
Domestic General govt.(% expend. total)	8.9	8.2	4.9	6.0	5.7	6.0	Dépenses intérieures (en % du totale)
Serbia [14]							**Serbie [14]**
Current expenditure (% GDP)	6.5	8.7	10.1	9.8	9.4	9.1	Dépenses courantes (% du PIB)
Domestic General govt.(% expend. total)	13.6	14.2	14.1	12.5	12.3	12.2	Dépenses intérieures (en % du totale)
Seychelles							**Seychelles**
Current expenditure (% GDP)	4.7	3.9	3.6	3.4	3.3	3.9	Dépenses courantes (% du PIB)
Domestic General govt.(% expend. total)	6.8	9.3	9.0	9.7	10.0	10.0	Dépenses intérieures (en % du totale)

Expenditure on health *(continued)*
Percentage of GDP and of government expenditure

Dépenses de santé *(suite)*
Pourcentage du PIB et des dépenses du gouvernement

Region, country or area[&]	2000	2005	2010	2014	2015	2016	Région, pays ou zone[&]
Sierra Leone							**Sierra Leone**
Current expenditure (% GDP)	11.5	11.0	10.9	19.7	20.4	16.5	Dépenses courantes (% du PIB)
Domestic General govt.(% expend. total)	12.7	9.5	6.3	7.6	7.9	7.9	Dépenses intérieures (en % du totale)
Singapore [2,15]							**Singapour [2,15]**
Current expenditure (% GDP)	3.4	3.0	3.2	3.9	4.2	4.5	Dépenses courantes (% du PIB)
Domestic General govt.(% expend. total)	6.7	6.9	8.9	12.3	12.4	13.6	Dépenses intérieures (en % du totale)
Slovakia							**Slovaquie**
Current expenditure (% GDP)	* 5.3	* 6.6	* 7.8	* 6.9	* 6.9	* 7.1	Dépenses courantes (% du PIB)
Domestic General govt.(% expend. total)	* 9.0	* 12.3	* 13.3	* 13.1	* 12.0	* 13.7	Dépenses intérieures (en % du totale)
Slovenia							**Slovénie**
Current expenditure (% GDP)	* 7.8	* 8.0	* 8.6	* 8.5	* 8.5	* 8.5	Dépenses courantes (% du PIB)
Domestic General govt.(% expend. total)	* 12.0	* 12.8	* 12.6	* 12.0	* 12.7	* 13.5	Dépenses intérieures (en % du totale)
Solomon Islands							**Îles Salomon**
Current expenditure (% GDP)	* 5.5	* 10.1	* 7.3	* 5.9	* 5.2	* 5.2	Dépenses courantes (% du PIB)
Domestic General govt.(% expend. total)	* 23.1	* 20.0	* 7.5	* 7.4	* 7.3	* 8.0	Dépenses intérieures (en % du totale)
South Africa [16]							**Afrique du Sud [16]**
Current expenditure (% GDP)	7.4	6.7	7.4	7.9	8.2	8.1	Dépenses courantes (% du PIB)
Domestic General govt.(% expend. total)	10.9	9.8	12.4	13.4	13.3	13.3	Dépenses intérieures (en % du totale)
Spain							**Espagne**
Current expenditure (% GDP)	6.8	7.7	9.0	9.0	9.1	9.0	Dépenses courantes (% du PIB)
Domestic General govt.(% expend. total)	12.4	14.4	14.8	14.2	14.9	15.1	Dépenses intérieures (en % du totale)
Sri Lanka							**Sri Lanka**
Current expenditure (% GDP)	# 4.2	# 4.0	# 3.9	# 3.6	# 3.9	# 3.9	Dépenses courantes (% du PIB)
Domestic General govt.(% expend. total)	# 10.1	# 10.1	# 7.8	# 9.0	# 8.4	# 8.6	Dépenses intérieures (en % du totale)
Sudan							**Soudan**
Current expenditure (% GDP)	* 3.6[17]	* 4.1[17]	* 5.0[17]	* 5.5	* 6.8	* 5.7	Dépenses courantes (% du PIB)
Domestic General govt.(% expend. total)	* 11.8[17]	* 8.1[17]	* 9.5[17]	* 11.5	* 18.1	* 10.7	Dépenses intérieures (en % du totale)
Suriname							**Suriname**
Current expenditure (% GDP)	6.3	6.5	5.5	* 5.6	* 6.7	6.1	Dépenses courantes (% du PIB)
Domestic General govt.(% expend. total)	11.6	11.9	8.6	* 6.6	* 12.7	16.6	Dépenses intérieures (en % du totale)
Sweden							**Suède**
Current expenditure (% GDP)	7.4	8.3	8.5	11.1	11.0	10.9	Dépenses courantes (% du PIB)
Domestic General govt.(% expend. total)	11.7	12.9	13.7	18.2	18.5	18.5	Dépenses intérieures (en % du totale)
Switzerland							**Suisse**
Current expenditure (% GDP)	9.8	10.8	10.7	11.5	11.9	12.2	Dépenses courantes (% du PIB)
Domestic General govt.(% expend. total)	16.2	19.4	20.0	21.5	22.1	22.4	Dépenses intérieures (en % du totale)
Syrian Arab Republic							**République arabe syrienne**
Current expenditure (% GDP)	4.3	4.1	3.3	...	...	...	Dépenses courantes (% du PIB)
Domestic General govt.(% expend. total)	5.6	7.3	5.1	...	...	...	Dépenses intérieures (en % du totale)
Tajikistan							**Tadjikistan**
Current expenditure (% GDP)	4.3	5.2	5.7	6.7	6.9	7.0	Dépenses courantes (% du PIB)
Domestic General govt.(% expend. total)	4.6	4.3	4.5	7.0	6.1	5.0	Dépenses intérieures (en % du totale)
Thailand [7]							**Thaïlande [7]**
Current expenditure (% GDP)	* 3.1	* 3.2	* 3.4	* 3.7	* 3.7	* 3.7	Dépenses courantes (% du PIB)
Domestic General govt.(% expend. total)	* 13.3	* 13.6	* 14.8	* 14.8	* 15.3	* 15.3	Dépenses intérieures (en % du totale)
Timor-Leste							**Timor-Leste**
Current expenditure (% GDP)	...	* 1.3	* 1.4	* 2.4	* 3.5	* 4.0	Dépenses courantes (% du PIB)
Domestic General govt.(% expend. total)	...	* 3.6	* 2.7	* 3.7	* 4.5	* 3.2	Dépenses intérieures (en % du totale)
Togo							**Togo**
Current expenditure (% GDP)	3.3	3.9	5.9	6.4	6.2	6.6	Dépenses courantes (% du PIB)
Domestic General govt.(% expend. total)	2.4	3.8	7.4	5.1	4.2	4.3	Dépenses intérieures (en % du totale)
Tonga [1]							**Tonga [1]**
Current expenditure (% GDP)	2.9	4.2	4.7	5.1	4.7	5.3	Dépenses courantes (% du PIB)
Domestic General govt.(% expend. total)	11.4	10.6	9.0	8.1	6.8	8.0	Dépenses intérieures (en % du totale)
Trinidad and Tobago							**Trinité-et-Tobago**
Current expenditure (% GDP)	4.3	4.5	5.2	5.3	6.2	6.5	Dépenses courantes (% du PIB)
Domestic General govt.(% expend. total)	6.8	8.9	8.0	7.5	8.3	9.7	Dépenses intérieures (en % du totale)
Tunisia							**Tunisie**
Current expenditure (% GDP)	5.0	5.4	5.9	6.8	7.0	7.0	Dépenses courantes (% du PIB)
Domestic General govt.(% expend. total)	10.5	11.4	13.0	13.3	13.9	13.7	Dépenses intérieures (en % du totale)
Turkey							**Turquie**
Current expenditure (% GDP)	* 4.6	* 4.9	* 5.1	* 4.3	* 4.1	* 4.3	Dépenses courantes (% du PIB)
Domestic General govt.(% expend. total)	* 7.2	* 10.3	* 10.9	* 10.1	* 9.7	* 9.6	Dépenses intérieures (en % du totale)
Turkmenistan							**Turkménistan**
Current expenditure (% GDP)	6.9	9.6	5.0	5.5	6.3	6.6	Dépenses courantes (% du PIB)
Domestic General govt.(% expend. total)	13.3	10.3	8.7	8.7	8.7	8.7	Dépenses intérieures (en % du totale)

Expenditure on health *(continued)*
Percentage of GDP and of government expenditure

Dépenses de santé *(suite)*
Pourcentage du PIB et des dépenses du gouvernement

Region, country or area&	2000	2005	2010	2014	2015	2016	Région, pays ou zone&
Tuvalu							**Tuvalu**
Current expenditure (% GDP)	* 24.2	* 11.3	* 15.7	* 15.4	* 14.1	* 15.5	Dépenses courantes (% du PIB)
Domestic General govt.(% expend. total) [6]	11.9	11.6	14.8	12.9	10.3	9.0	Dépenses intérieures (en % du totale) [6]
Uganda [18]							**Ouganda** [18]
Current expenditure (% GDP)	7.6	11.4	10.5	6.7	6.3	6.2	Dépenses courantes (% du PIB)
Domestic General govt.(% expend. total)	9.3	14.9	7.6	5.6	5.1	5.1	Dépenses intérieures (en % du totale)
Ukraine [19]							**Ukraine** [19]
Current expenditure (% GDP)	5.3	6.1	7.0	6.6	7.0	6.7	Dépenses courantes (% du PIB)
Domestic General govt.(% expend. total)	7.1	8.4	7.5	6.5	6.6	7.0	Dépenses intérieures (en % du totale)
United Arab Emirates							**Émirats arabes unis**
Current expenditure (% GDP)	2.4	2.3	3.9	3.6	3.6	3.5	Dépenses courantes (% du PIB)
Domestic General govt.(% expend. total)	7.6	8.4	8.5	7.8	7.9	7.9	Dépenses intérieures (en % du totale)
United Kingdom							**Royaume-Uni**
Current expenditure (% GDP)	6.0	7.2	8.5	9.7	9.8	9.8	Dépenses courantes (% du PIB)
Domestic General govt.(% expend. total)	13.8	14.5	15.0	18.1	18.5	18.9	Dépenses intérieures (en % du totale)
United Rep. of Tanzania [20]							**Rép.-Unie de Tanzanie** [20]
Current expenditure (% GDP)	* 3.4	* 6.4	* 5.3	* 4.2	* 3.8	* 4.1	Dépenses courantes (% du PIB)
Domestic General govt.(% expend. total)	* 6.1	* 12.6	* 7.3	* 6.9	* 7.3	* 9.5	Dépenses intérieures (en % du totale)
United States of America							**États-Unis d'Amérique**
Current expenditure (% GDP)	12.5	14.5	16.4	16.5	16.8	17.1	Dépenses courantes (% du PIB)
Domestic General govt.(% expend. total)	16.4	18.1	18.6	* 35.3	* 36.6	* 39.5	Dépenses intérieures (en % du totale)
Uruguay							**Uruguay**
Current expenditure (% GDP)	10.0	8.4	8.6	8.8	9.0	9.1	Dépenses courantes (% du PIB)
Domestic General govt.(% expend. total)	14.3	13.2	16.9	18.5	19.0	19.5	Dépenses intérieures (en % du totale)
Uzbekistan							**Ouzbékistan**
Current expenditure (% GDP)	* 5.4	* 5.0	* 5.4	* 5.7	* 6.1	* 6.3	Dépenses courantes (% du PIB)
Domestic General govt.(% expend. total)	* 6.1	* 6.5	* 8.0	* 9.3	* 9.0	* 9.2	Dépenses intérieures (en % du totale)
Vanuatu [21]							**Vanuatu** [21]
Current expenditure (% GDP)	3.3	3.3	3.4	3.5	4.2	3.7	Dépenses courantes (% du PIB)
Domestic General govt.(% expend. total)	9.7	11.7	6.8	2.0	4.9	5.4	Dépenses intérieures (en % du totale)
Venezuela (Boliv. Rep. of)							**Venezuela (Rép. boliv. du)**
Current expenditure (% GDP)	5.0	4.8	6.1	5.8	5.1	3.2	Dépenses courantes (% du PIB)
Domestic General govt.(% expend. total)	6.5	5.2	6.2	4.3	4.1	1.9	Dépenses intérieures (en % du totale)
Viet Nam							**Viet Nam**
Current expenditure (% GDP)	* 4.8	* 5.1	* 6.0	* 5.8	* 5.7	* 5.7	Dépenses courantes (% du PIB)
Domestic General govt.(% expend. total)	* 9.5	* 8.7	* 8.6	* 8.5	* 7.9	* 8.9	Dépenses intérieures (en % du totale)
Yemen							**Yémen**
Current expenditure (% GDP)	* 4.7	* 5.2	* 5.2	* 4.8	* 5.6	...	Dépenses courantes (% du PIB)
Domestic General govt.(% expend. total)	* 7.5	* 4.5	* 3.8	* 2.8	* 2.2	...	Dépenses intérieures (en % du totale)
Zambia							**Zambie**
Current expenditure (% GDP)	* 7.2	* 6.9	* 3.7	* 3.8	* 4.4	* 4.5	Dépenses courantes (% du PIB)
Domestic General govt.(% expend. total)	* 14.9	* 8.2	* 4.7	* 7.7	* 7.4	* 7.1	Dépenses intérieures (en % du totale)
Zimbabwe							**Zimbabwe**
Current expenditure (% GDP)	...	...	11.8	8.7	9.3	9.4	Dépenses courantes (% du PIB)
Domestic General govt.(% expend. total)	...	...	14.6	12.1	15.9	14.5	Dépenses intérieures (en % du totale)

Source:

World Health Organization (WHO), Geneva, WHO Global Health Expenditure database, last accessed April 2019.

& These estimates are in line with the 2011 System of Health Accounts (SHA).

1   Data refer to fiscal years beginning 1 July.

2   Data refer to fiscal years beginning 1 April.

Source:

Organisation mondiale de la santé (OMS), Genève, base de données de l'OMS sur les dépenses de santé mondiales, dernier accès avril 2019.

& Ces estimations sont conformes au Système de comptes de la santé (SCS) de 2011.

1   Les données se réfèrent aux exercices budgétaires commençant le 1er juillet.

2   Les données se réfèrent aux exercices budgétaires commençant le 1er avril.

3	Health expenditure data do not include funds from foreign origin flowing in the health financing system.
4	2012 data are based on a health accounts study based on SHA2011. Numbers were converted to SHA 1.0 format for comparability.
5	As a result of recent health-care reforms, public compulsory insurance has since 2008 been implemented by private insurance companies. The voucher cost of this insurance is treated as general government health expenditure.
6	General government expenditure (GGE) can be larger than the Gross domestic product (GDP) because government accounts for a very large part of domestic consumption and because a large part of domestic consumption in the country is accounted for by imports.
7	Data refer to fiscal years ending 30 September.
8	Health expenditure indicators are high as they spend a lot on health using direct funding from the United States and also from their domestic funds. Current health expenditure is mostly government.
9	Country is still reporting data based on SHA 1.0.
10	Indicators are sensitive to external funds flowing in to the country.
11	Data refer to fiscal years ending 15 July.
12	Excluding the Transnistria region.
13	From 2015 the data is adjusted by WHO in accordance with UN General Assembly Resolution A/RES/68/262.
14	Excluding Kosovo and Metohija.
15	Medisave is classified as Social insurance scheme, considering that it is a compulsory payment.
16	Data refer to fiscal years ending 31 March.
17	Including South Sudan.
18	Unlike other countries, in Uganda Fiscal Years starting on July 1 and ending in June 30 are converted to the previous year and that is a special request from the country.
19	Excludes the temporarily occupied territory of the Autonomous Republic of Crimea and Sevastopol.
20	Tanzania mainland only, excluding Zanzibar.
21	Government expenditures show fluctuations due to variations in capital investment.

3	Les données sur les dépenses de santé n'incluent pas les fonds d'origine étrangère qui entrent dans le système de financement de la santé.
4	Les données de 2012 sont basées sur une étude sur les comptes de santé basée sur SCS2011. Les nombres ont été convertis au format SCS 1.0 pour la comparabilité.
5	L'assurance publique obligatoire est réalisée depuis 2008 par des sociétés privées dont le coût des coupons est traité comme dépense publique de santé du fait des réformes des soins de santé.
6	Les dépenses publiques peuvent être supérieure au produit intérieur brut (PIB) parce que le gouvernement contribue très largement à la consommation intérieure et aussi une grande partie de la consommation intérieure du pays et représentée par les importations.
7	Les données se réfèrent aux exercices budgétaires finissant le 30 septembre.
8	Les indicateurs de dépenses de santé sont élevés car ils dépensent beaucoup pour la santé en utilisant le financement direct de - États-Unis et aussi de leurs fonds nationaux. Dépenses de santé est principalement le gouvernement.
9	Le pays rapporte toujours des données basées sur SCS 1.0.
10	Les indicateurs sont sensibles aux fonds externes vers le pays.
11	Les données se réfèrent aux exercices budgétaires finissant le 15 juillet.
12	Non compris la région de Transnistrie.
13	À partir de 2015 les données sont ajustées conformes à la résolution A/RES/68/262.
14	Non compris Kosovo et Metohija.
15	Medisave est classé comme régime d'assurance sociale, considérant qu'il s'agit d'un paiement obligatoire.
16	Les données se réfèrent aux exercices budgétaires finissant le 31 mars.
17	Y compris le Sud Soudan.
18	Contrairement aux autres pays, en Ouganda, les années fiscales commençant le 1er juillet et se terminant le 30 juin sont converties en années précédentes et il s'agit d'une demande spéciale du pays.
19	Excluent le territoire temporairement occupé de la République autonome de Crimée et de Sébastopol.
20	Tanzanie continentale seulement, Zanzibar non compris.
21	Les dépenses publiques manifestent des fluctuations du fait de variations des investissements.

12

Intentional homicides and other crimes
By type of crime per 100 000 population and homicide victims by sex

Homicides intentionnels et autres crimes
Par type de crime pour 100 000 habitants et victimes d'homicides par sexe

Country or area / Pays ou zone	Year / Année	Intentional homicides / Homicides volontaires — Per 100 000 / Pour 100 000	Victims (%) / Victimes (%) — Male / Hommes	Victims (%) / Victimes (%) — Female / Femmes	Other crimes (per 100 000 pop.) / Autres infractions (pour 100 000 hab.) — Assault / Agression	Other crimes (per 100 000 pop.) / Autres infractions (pour 100 000 hab.) — Theft / Vol simple
Total, all countries or areas [1] Total, tous pays ou zones [1]	2015	5.3	...	...	...	...
Sub-Saharan Africa [1] Afrique subsaharienne [1]	2015	9.6			...	...
Latin America & the Caribbean [1] Amérique latine et Caraïbes [1]	2015	22.3	...	...	...	...
South-central Asia [1] Asie centrale et du Sud [1]	2015	3.7	...	...	...	...
Oceania [1,2] Océanie [1,2]	2015	8.8	...	...		
Australia and New Zealand [1] Australie et Nouvelle-Zélande [1]	2015	1.0	...	...	...	...
Afghanistan Afghanistan	2010	3.4	...	...	...	...
	2012	6.3	* 11.8	* 0.6	...	...
Albania Albanie	2005	5.0	8.6	1.4	5.4	97.0
	2010	4.3	7.3	1.3	6.1	135.3
	2015	2.3	3.5	1.0	5.8	245.8
	2016	2.7	4.3	1.0	4.0	192.4
Algeria Algérie	2005	0.6	...	...	98.9	...
	2010	0.7	...	...	114.6	141.4
	2015	1.4	2.3	0.4	123.1	124.3
American Samoa Samoa américaines	2005	10.1	...	...	...	...
	2010	9.0	...	...	...	...
	2016	5.4	...	...	...	...
Andorra Andorre	2004	1.3	...	...	...	...
	2008	1.2	0.0	2.4	125.2	1 165.0
	2010	...	0.0	0.0	116.0	1 322.7
	2011	1.2	2.3	0.0	171.9	1 269.2
	2014	...	0.0	0.0	155.3	1 181.5
	2015	...	0.0	0.0	170.5	1 340.8
Angola Angola	2012	4.8	* 7.8	* 2.1	...	...
Anguilla Anguilla	2004	8.1	...	...	...	...
	2009	7.4	...	...	...	...
	2014	27.7	...	...	...	...
Antigua and Barbuda Antigua-et-Barbuda	2002	5.8	9.2	2.8	...	...
	2005	3.4	...	...	...	...
	2008	17.3	24.8	10.4	...	...
	2010	6.3	...	...	...	...
	2012	10.3	...	...	...	...
Argentina Argentine	2005	...	...	...	363.0	775.7
	2008	...	...	...	359.7	703.8
	2015	6.5	11.5	1.7	417.6	626.3
	2016	5.9	...	...	326.2	616.2
Armenia Arménie	2005	1.9	3.4	0.7	6.0	82.6
	2010	1.9	3.4	0.7	5.4	127.3
	2015	2.6	3.9	1.4	5.6	183.9
	2016	3.0	5.2	1.0	6.4	194.3
Aruba Aruba	2005	6.0	10.5	1.9	...	...
	2010	3.9	8.3	0.0	...	...
	2014	1.9	4.1	0.0	...	...
Australia Australie	2005	1.3	1.6	1.0	...	2 561.1
	2010	1.0	1.2	0.8	310.4	2 157.6
	2015	1.0	1.3	0.7	284.7	2 357.9
	2016	0.9	1.2	0.7	293.3	2 460.1

12 Intentional homicides and other crimes *(continued)*
By type of crime per 100 000 population and homicide victims by sex

Homicides intentionnels et autres crimes *(suite)*
Par type de crime pour 100 000 habitants et victimes d'homicides par sexe

Country or area Pays ou zone	Year Année	Intentional homicides Homicides volontaires			Other crimes (per 100 000 pop.) Autres infractions (pour 100 000 hab.)	
		Per 100 000 Pour 100 000	Victims (%) Victims (%) Male Hommes	Female Femmes	Assault Agression	Theft Vol simple
Austria	2005	0.7	0.7	0.6	43.8	2 144.8
Autriche	2010	0.7	0.7	0.7	42.9	1 853.2
	2015	0.5	0.7	0.4	35.4	1 616.1
	2016	0.7	0.6	0.7	37.8	1 649.9
Azerbaijan	2005	2.2	...	...	1.9	25.2
Azerbaïdjan	2010	2.3	3.2	1.4	1.9	42.8
	2014	2.5	3.2	1.8	1.7	61.7
	2016	2.1	2.5	1.8	3.4	24.8
Bahamas	2005	15.8	27.4	4.7	...	440.4
Bahamas	2010	26.1	45.4	7.6	848.9	545.7
	2012	29.8	55.5	5.3	841.8	533.5
	2016	28.4	...	...	...	...
Bahrain	2005	0.4	...	...	396.8	1 086.3
Bahreïn	2007	0.4	...	...	254.3	700.5
	2008	0.5	...	...	327.8	681.7
	2010	0.9	...	...	...	...
	2011	0.5	* 0.7	* 0.3	...	...
	2014	0.5	...	...	...	...
Bangladesh	2005	2.5	...	...	0.4	8.7
Bangladesh	2006	2.9	...	...	0.4	8.9
	2010	2.6	...	...	...	...
	2015	2.5	* 3.9	* 1.0	...	...
Barbados	2005	10.6	15.1	6.4	631.7	412.4
Barbade	2010	11.1	17.1	5.5	540.5	739.4
	2015	10.9	20.6	2.0	518.6	596.0
	2016	...	...	...	547.2	597.1
Belarus	2005	8.6	...	...	19.9	1 072.6
Bélarus	2010	4.2	6.0	2.7	12.2	776.8
	2014	3.6	5.1	2.3	8.8	427.3
Belgium	2005	2.1[3]	2.5	1.7	639.2	2 061.0
Belgique	2010	1.7[3]	2.2	1.2	710.8	2 087.6
	2014	1.9[3]	2.3	1.4	626.1	1 857.9
	2015	1.9[3]	...	...	600.6	1 653.0
Belize	2004	28.6	46.8	10.2	...	...
Belize	2005	28.6	...	...	...	592.4
	2009	30.9	56.0	5.7	165.3	375.6
	2010	40.1	70.2	10.0	...	259.9
	2014	35.0	63.3	6.8	296.3	234.9
	2015	33.1	61.4	5.0	...	219.6
	2016	37.6	67.2	8.1	...	204.9
Benin	*2005	7.2	...	...	...	...
Bénin	*2010	6.6	...	...	...	...
	*2015	6.2	10.0	2.4	...	...
Bermuda	2004	1.5	0.0	2.9	668.6	1 541.5
Bermudes	2005	3.1	6.5	0.0	...	...
	2010	10.9	23.0	0.0	964.7	950.7
	2015	6.5	13.6	0.0	93.5	2 272.5
	2016	13.0	27.2	0.0	74.5	2 190.3
Bhutan	2005	1.7	...	...	...	...
Bhoutan	2010	2.2	...	...	...	67.2
	2013	3.1	...	...	...	75.4
	2014	...	...	...	67.1	68.5
	2016	1.1	1.2	1.1	50.2	...
	2017	...	...	...	121.3	...
Bolivia (Plurin. State of)	2005	5.2	...	...	66.0	41.6
Bolivie (État plurin. de)	2008	8.6	14.4	2.9	72.8	50.3
	2010	12.8	...	...	85.2	50.9
	2012	11.9	...	...	72.5	50.8
	2016	6.3	8.3	4.3	74.5	...

Intentional homicides and other crimes *(continued)*
By type of crime per 100 000 population and homicide victims by sex

Homicides intentionnels et autres crimes *(suite)*
Par type de crime pour 100 000 habitants et victimes d'homicides par sexe

Country or area Pays ou zone	Year Année	Intentional homicides Homicides volontaires			Other crimes (per 100 000 pop.) Autres infractions (pour 100 000 hab.)	
		Per 100 000 Pour 100 000	Victims (%) Victimes (%)		Assault Agression	Theft Vol simple
			Male Hommes	Female Femmes		
Bosnia and Herzegovina	2002	2.4	3.5	1.3	...	...
Bosnie-Herzégovine	2005	1.9	...	...	36.2	487.0
	2008	1.8	...	...	39.2	171.5
	2010	1.5	2.5	0.5	13.6	305.3
	2015	1.6	2.2	1.0	28.1	137.8
	2016	1.3	1.7	0.8	28.6	127.3
Botswana	2005	15.7	...	...		
Botswana	2010	15.0	* 27.9	* 2.5	866.4	1 474.8
	2014	...	...	...	776.9	1 367.5
Brazil	2005	23.3	43.5	3.8	...	...
Brésil	2010	22.0	40.8	3.7	363.7	702.6
	2013	26.8	49.8	4.4	326.8	881.8
	2015	28.4	53.1	4.4	...	...
	2016	29.5	...	...	...	...
British Virgin Islands	2004	17.7	...	...	...	...
Îles Vierges britanniques	2006	8.4	...	...	...	...
Brunei Darussalam	2000	1.2	1.2	1.2	...	...
Brunéi Darussalam	2004	0.6	...	...	149.4	292.6
	2005	0.5	...	...	145.1	329.2
	2006	0.8	...	...	121.8	306.8
	2010	0.3	...	...	...	...
	2013	0.5	...	...	...	...
Bulgaria	2005	2.6	3.9	1.3	47.6	561.2
Bulgarie	2010	2.0	3.4	0.7	41.0	681.7
	2015	1.8	2.9	0.8	35.1	533.8
	2016	1.1	1.7	0.6	34.6	459.0
Burkina Faso	2005	0.5	...	...	...	...
Burkina Faso	2010	0.6	...	...	...	...
	2015	0.4	* 0.6	* 0.2	...	...
Burundi	2010	4.0	...	...	3.5	...
Burundi	2014	5.7	9.5	2.0	5.6	8.2
	2016	6.0	9.9	2.3	...	...
Cabo Verde	2005	9.3	...	...	...	...
Cabo Verde	2010	7.8	...	...	814.1	746.6
	2015	8.6	14.7	2.6	789.1	780.8
	2016	11.5	...	...	...	...
Cambodia	2005	3.4	...	...	...	...
Cambodge	2010	2.3	...	...	...	...
	2011	1.8	* 3.2	* 0.6	...	...
Cameroon	2003	6.1	...	...	18.2	71.7
Cameroun	2005	...	...	...	18.0	69.0
	2010	5.0	...	...	24.6	82.2
	2012	4.2	* 6.8	* 1.5	27.3	74.7
	2014	...	...	...	32.3	113.6
	2015	...	...	...	21.0	71.3
Canada	2005	2.1	3.0	1.1	165.5	2 031.4
Canada	2010	1.6	2.4	0.9	162.2	1 592.8
	2015	1.7	2.4	1.0	141.1	1 398.1
	2016	1.7	2.6	0.8	143.4	1 408.6
Cayman Islands	2005	6.2	...	...	...	...
Îles Caïmanes	2010	16.2	...	...	...	...
	2014	8.4	...	...	...	...
Central African Republic						
République centrafricaine	2016	19.8	29.4	10.4	...	...
Chad	2005	10.7	...	...	...	...
Tchad	2010	9.7	...	...	...	...
	2015	9.0	14.4	3.6	...	...
Channel Islands	2005	0.6	...	...	...	...
Îles Anglo-Normandes	2010	0.0	...	...	...	...

12 Intentional homicides and other crimes *(continued)*
By type of crime per 100 000 population and homicide victims by sex

Homicides intentionnels et autres crimes *(suite)*
Par type de crime pour 100 000 habitants et victimes d'homicides par sexe

| Country or area
Pays ou zone | Year
Année | Intentional homicides
Homicides volontaires | | | Other crimes (per 100 000 pop.)
Autres infractions (pour 100 000 hab.) | |
| | | Per 100 000
Pour 100 000 | Victims (%)
Victimes (%) | | Assault
Agression | Theft
Vol simple |
			Male Hommes	Female Femmes		
Chile	2005	3.6	6.2	1.0	...	961.6
Chili	2010	3.2	5.3	1.1	131.0	1 100.3
	2015	3.0	5.3	0.7	69.3	1 044.6
	2016	3.5	6.0	1.0	67.1	969.2
China [4]	2005	1.6	...	...	...	...
Chine [4]	2010	1.0	...	...	...	...
	2014	0.7	* 0.9	* 0.5	...	...
	2016	0.6	...	...	...	...
China, Hong Kong SAR	2005	0.5	0.6	0.4	118.5	515.7
Chine, RAS de Hong Kong	2010	0.5	0.5	0.5	108.2	488.9
	2013	0.9	0.8	1.0	92.6	442.0
	2016	0.4	...	...	...	...
China, Macao SAR	2005	0.8	...	...	...	...
Chine, RAS de Macao	2010	0.4	0.8	0.0	341.9	523.7
	2015	0.2	0.0	0.3	269.6	440.5
	2016	0.2	0.3	0.0	280.3	479.8
Colombia	2005	41.8	77.7	6.8	70.3	158.8
Colombie	2010	33.7	62.9	5.3	115.7	200.0
	2015	26.5	49.3	4.4	363.1	163.0
	2016	25.5	47.5	4.2	369.4	178.0
Comoros	*2005	9.5	...	...	...	...
Comores	*2010	8.5	...	...	...	...
	*2015	7.7	11.6	3.7	...	...
Congo	*2005	10.6	...	...	...	...
Congo	*2010	9.9	...	...	...	...
	*2015	9.3	14.1	4.5	...	...
Cook Islands						
Îles Cook	2012	3.5	...	...	...	...
Costa Rica	2005	7.9	12.9	2.9	...	196.8
Costa Rica	2010	11.6	20.5	2.7	175.0	445.5
	2013	8.7	15.9	1.5	174.7	696.6
	2014	10.0	17.9	2.1	...	...
	2016	11.9	...	...	...	...
Côte d'Ivoire	*2005	14.7	...	...	...	...
Côte d'Ivoire	2008	...	...	...	51.9	...
	*2010	12.6	...	...	...	...
	*2015	11.6	15.6	7.5	...	...
Croatia	2005	1.6	1.9	1.2	26.3	694.3
Croatie	2010	1.4	1.4	1.4	22.8	313.6
	2015	0.9	1.1	0.7	19.0	319.8
	2016	1.0	1.2	0.9	18.8	302.4
Cuba	2005	6.1	9.1	3.0	...	...
Cuba	2010	4.5	6.7	2.2	...	...
	2016	5.0	7.9	2.1	...	...
Curaçao	2005	20.1	33.0	8.7	...	...
Curaçao	2007	19.2	36.5	4.1	...	...
Cyprus	2005	1.9	3.5	0.4	12.8	116.9
Chypre	2010	0.7	1.3	0.2	15.5	150.1
	2015	1.3	2.2	0.3	12.1	79.1
	2016	1.1	1.4	0.9	12.4	61.7
Czechia	2005	1.1	1.3	0.9	211.4	1 502.5
Tchéquie	2010	1.0	1.0	1.0	171.5	1 198.8
	2015	0.8	0.7	0.9	147.8	799.7
	2016	0.6	0.6	0.7	134.2	677.4
Dem. People's Rep. Korea	*2005	5.0	...	...	...	...
Rép. pop. dém. de Corée	*2010	4.8	...	...	...	...
	*2015	4.4	...	...	...	...
Dem. Rep. of the Congo	*2005	14.6	...	...	...	...
Rép. dém. du Congo	*2010	14.3	...	...	...	...
	*2015	13.5	22.0	5.1	...	...

12 Intentional homicides and other crimes *(continued)*
By type of crime per 100 000 population and homicide victims by sex

Homicides intentionnels et autres crimes *(suite)*
Par type de crime pour 100 000 habitants et victimes d'homicides par sexe

| Country or area
Pays ou zone | Year
Année | Intentional homicides
Homicides volontaires | | | Other crimes (per 100 000 pop.)
Autres infractions (pour 100 000 hab.) | |
		Per 100 000 Pour 100 000	Victims (%) Victimes (%) Male Hommes	Female Femmes	Assault Agression	Theft Vol simple
Denmark	2005	1.0	1.4	0.6	205.0	3 100.9
Danemark	2010	0.8	0.7	0.8	31.6	4 351.2
	2015	1.0	1.2	0.8	25.7	3 970.5
	2016	1.0	1.2	0.8	30.3	3 949.2
Djibouti	*2005	8.1	...	...	...	...
Djibouti	*2010	7.4	...	...	...	...
	*2015	6.5	10.6	2.3	...	...
Dominica	2005	11.3	...	...	...	...
Dominique	2010	21.0	...	...	...	...
	2011	8.4	...	...	...	...
Dominican Republic	2005	25.9	47.2	4.6	...	...
République dominicaine	2006	22.9	41.9	3.8	...	...
	2010	25.0	45.8	4.2	...	...
	2014	17.4	31.3	3.6	41.1	7.7
	2016	15.2	27.3	3.2	29.5	8.2
Ecuador	2005	15.4	28.4	2.4	56.5	43.4
Équateur	2010	17.6	31.9	3.2	30.2	33.6
	2014	8.2	14.1	2.4	46.7	152.8
	2016	5.9	9.5	2.2	43.7	194.0
Egypt	2005	0.7	1.2	0.2	...	45.6
Égypte	2010	2.2	3.9	0.5	0.2	91.7
	2011	3.1	5.5	0.8	0.4	101.4
	2012	2.5	4.4	0.6	...	...
El Salvador	2005	64.4	121.0	12.6	76.8	177.8
El Salvador	2010	64.7	117.4	17.3	63.1	157.0
	2015	105.4	204.8	17.2	93.3	135.3
	2016	82.8	158.4	15.7	...	...
Equatorial Guinea	*2005	2.9	...	...	...	...
Guinée équatoriale	*2010	2.6	...	...	...	...
	*2015	2.3	3.4	0.9	...	...
Eritrea	*2005	9.6	...	...	...	...
Érythrée	*2010	8.9	...	...	...	...
	*2015	8.0	12.6	3.4	...	...
Estonia	2005	8.3	13.4	3.9	9.7	2 246.3
Estonie	2010	5.3	8.6	2.3	7.7	1 895.7
	2015	3.2	5.2	1.4	7.5	863.2
Eswatini	2004	13.3	...	...	1 332.1	1 904.1
Eswatini	2005	13.7	...	...	...	...
	2010	17.3	* 30.9	* 4.5	...	...
Ethiopia	*2005	9.4	...	...	...	...
Éthiopie	*2010	8.5	...	...	...	...
	*2015	7.6	11.3	3.9	...	...
Fiji	2005	2.8	3.3	2.2	...	...
Fidji	2010	2.3	3.2	1.4	...	...
	2014	2.3	1.8	2.8	...	...
Finland	2005	2.3	3.3	1.3	579.3	2 378.5
Finlande	2010	2.2	3.5	1.0	37.2	1 853.1
	2015	1.5	2.4	0.6	28.5	2 229.6
	2016	1.4	2.0	0.9	28.9	2 081.0
France	2005	1.6	...	...	242.8	1 363.7
France	2010	1.3	...	...	368.0	1 860.4
	2015	1.6	2.0	1.2	375.7	2 167.9
	2016	1.4	1.7	1.0	375.4	2 134.8
French Guiana	2005	22.1	...	...	...	...
Guyane française	2009	13.2	21.6	4.8	...	...
French Polynesia						
Polynésie française	2009	0.4	...	...	...	...
Gabon	*2005	11.0	...	...	...	...
Gabon	*2010	8.7	...	...	...	...
	*2015	8.0	12.6	3.2	...	...

12

Intentional homicides and other crimes *(continued)*
By type of crime per 100 000 population and homicide victims by sex

Homicides intentionnels et autres crimes *(suite)*
Par type de crime pour 100 000 habitants et victimes d'homicides par sexe

| Country or area
Pays ou zone | Year
Année | Intentional homicides
Homicides volontaires | | | Other crimes (per 100 000 pop.)
Autres infractions (pour 100 000 hab.) | |
| | | Per 100 000
Pour 100 000 | Victims (%)
Victimes (%) | | Assault
Agression | Theft
Vol simple |
			Male Hommes	Female Femmes		
Gambia	*2005	9.8	...	...	...	...
Gambie	*2010	9.8	...	...	...	...
	*2015	9.1	16.6	1.8	...	...
Georgia	2005	9.0	15.6	3.0	8.2	362.3
Géorgie	2010	4.4	7.9	1.3	3.0	268.7
	2014	2.7	3.9	1.6	5.7	239.4
	2016	1.0	0.3	1.7	...	...
Germany	2005	1.1	1.2	0.9	605.3	2 735.9
Allemagne	2010	1.0	1.0	1.0	176.7	1 508.1
	2015	0.8	0.9	0.8	155.9	1 651.0
	2016	1.2	1.2	1.1	171.0	1 576.2
Ghana	2005	1.8	...	...	...	...
Ghana	2010	1.7	...	...	...	...
	2011	1.7	* 2.4	* 1.0	...	...
Gibraltar						
Gibraltar	2010	3.0	...	...	...	...
Greece	2005	1.2	1.6	0.8	68.8	545.5
Grèce	2010	1.5	2.5	0.6	9.6	1 035.5
	2015	0.8	1.1	0.5	14.5	898.6
	2016	0.8	1.1	0.5	13.5	909.1
Greenland	2005	17.6	...	...	...	...
Groenland	2010	19.4	...	...	...	...
	2016	5.3	...	...	...	...
Grenada	2005	10.7	15.6	5.8	1 839.7	1 761.1
Grenade	2010	9.6	15.3	3.8	1 100.5	918.1
	2015	5.6	7.5	3.8	462.4	1 948.1
	2016	10.2	14.9	5.6	1 721.9	2 307.0
Guadeloupe	2005	5.2	10.1	0.7	...	...
Guadeloupe	2009	8.0	14.5	2.3	...	...
Guam	2005	4.4	...	...	...	...
Guam	2010	1.9	...	...	...	...
	2011	2.5	* 3.6	* 1.4	...	...
Guatemala	2005	40.8	75.0	7.8	46.5	32.9
Guatemala	2010	40.7	73.3	9.3	50.9	44.5
	2012	33.8	61.0	7.4	39.9	59.7
	2014	31.4	55.8	7.8	15.2	285.6
	2015	29.4	...	...	14.5	290.1
	2016	27.3	...	...	11.1	296.2
Guinea	2005	* 10.1	...	...	3.0	...
Guinée	2007	...	...	...	2.9	13.4
	2008	...	...	...	...	...
	*2010	9.4	...	...	...	...
	*2015	8.8	13.8	3.8	...	...
Guinea-Bissau	*2005	11.7	...	...	...	...
Guinée-Bissau	*2010	10.5	...	...	...	...
	*2015	9.5	10.6	8.6	...	...
Guyana	2005	18.9	30.3	7.5	...	...
Guyana	2010	18.8	29.2	8.3	1 497.8	523.2
	2015	19.4	31.3	7.3	1 206.1	672.9
	2016	18.4	33.9	2.6	149.3	623.1
Haiti	2010	6.8	...	...	...	...
Haïti	2012	10.0	* 15.7	* 4.5	...	...
Holy See	2010	0.0	...	...	0.0	0.0
Saint-Siège	2015	0.0	...	...	0.0	0.0
Honduras	2005	43.6	...	...	...	...
Honduras	2010	76.1	143.3	9.4	...	54.6
	2015	57.5	104.5	10.6	14.8	32.5
	2016	56.5	103.1	10.2	14.8	33.9

Intentional homicides and other crimes *(continued)*
By type of crime per 100 000 population and homicide victims by sex

Homicides intentionnels et autres crimes *(suite)*
Par type de crime pour 100 000 habitants et victimes d'homicides par sexe

Country or area Pays ou zone	Year Année	Intentional homicides Homicides volontaires Per 100 000 Pour 100 000	Victims (%) Victimes (%) Male Hommes	Female Femmes	Other crimes (per 100 000 pop.) Autres infractions (pour 100 000 hab.) Assault Agression	Theft Vol simple
Hungary	2005	1.6	1.8	1.4	122.3	1 251.7
Hongrie	2010	1.4	1.6	1.2	146.7	1 351.7
	2014	1.5	1.7	1.3	137.3	1 089.7
	2015	2.3	2.6	2.0	127.5	1 137.8
	2016	2.1	2.6	1.6	...	959.8
Iceland	2005	1.0	2.0	0.0	...	1 078.4
Islande	2010	0.6	1.2	0.0	17.8	1 535.9
	2015	0.9	1.8	0.0	25.7	1 220.9
	2016	0.3	0.0	0.6	22.2	1 043.2
India	2005	3.9	5.0	2.8	23.7	23.9
Inde	2010	3.8	4.5	3.0	23.5	26.8
	2013	3.6	4.2	2.9	26.2	29.1
	2016	3.2	3.7	2.7	...	...
Indonesia	2004	0.6	...	...		
Indonésie	2010	0.4	...	...	13.2	10.1
	2014	0.5	* 0.7	* 0.3	14.5	9.6
	2015	0.6	...	...	5.6	10.2
	2016	0.5	...	...	5.5	10.2
Iran (Islamic Republic of)	2004	2.9	...	...	...	157.8
Iran (Rép. islamique d')	2009	3.0	...	...	...	...
	2014	2.5	4.3	0.6	...	...
Iraq	2010	8.7[5]	14.2[5]	3.2[5]	98.3[6]	31.1[6]
Iraq	2013	9.9[5]	16.3[5]	3.2[5]	96.2[6]	36.7[6]
	2014[6]	...	...	...	83.2	34.8
Ireland	2005	1.2	2.1	0.4	296.2	1 397.6
Irlande	2010	1.1	2.0	0.3	325.0	1 413.8
	2013	1.1	1.9	0.3	66.0	1 681.7
	2015	0.6	...	...	74.8	1 614.1
	2016	0.8	...	...	73.9	1 371.6
Isle of Man						
Île de Man	2016	0.0	...	...	...	...
Israel	2005	2.5	3.5	1.5	774.1	1 897.5
Israël	2010	2.0	3.1	0.9	619.5	974.2
	2011	2.0	3.1	0.9	569.0	935.5
	2014	1.5	2.4	0.6	...	...
	2015	1.4	...	...	...	...
Italy	2005	1.0	1.7	0.5	96.3	1 866.0
Italie	2010	0.9	1.3	0.5	108.6	1 580.5
	2015	0.8	1.2	0.4	107.6	1 756.8
	2016	0.7	0.9	0.5	...	...
Jamaica	2005	61.0	109.5	13.4	...	...
Jamaïque	2008	58.0	105.1	11.7	...	...
	2010	51.4	93.1	10.2	49.9	...
	2015	42.1	76.4	8.0	102.1	11.7
	2016	47.0	85.1	9.3	78.5	6.5
Japan	2005	0.5	0.5	0.5	47.0	719.4
Japon	2010	0.4	0.4	0.4	20.7	480.8
	2014	0.3	0.3	0.3	20.8	352.4
	2016	0.3	0.3	0.3	19.1	293.3
Jordan	2005	1.2	...	...	256.9	123.7
Jordanie	2006	1.7	...	...	264.5	150.7
	2010	1.6	2.1	1.1	...	169.9
	2012	2.0	3.3	0.6	...	169.0
	2016	1.5	2.3	0.8	...	...
Kazakhstan	#2004	13.6	...	...	...	...
Kazakhstan	2005	...	...	...	...	406.3
	2010	# 8.5	13.2	4.1	9.7	365.8
	2015	# 4.8	7.0	2.7	5.1	1 177.0

12

Intentional homicides and other crimes *(continued)*
By type of crime per 100 000 population and homicide victims by sex

Homicides intentionnels et autres crimes *(suite)*
Par type de crime pour 100 000 habitants et victimes d'homicides par sexe

Country or area Pays ou zone	Year Année	Intentional homicides Homicides volontaires Per 100 000 Pour 100 000	Victims (%) Victimes (%) Male Hommes	Female Femmes	Other crimes (per 100 000 pop.) Autres infractions (pour 100 000 hab.) Assault Agression	Theft Vol simple
Kenya	2005	3.0	...	...	35.3	33.8
Kenya	2010	4.7	...	...	34.0	29.0
	2015	4.8	7.0	2.6	31.6	2.4
	2016	4.9	7.2	2.6	32.4	2.8
Kiribati	2001	4.7	...	...	...	...
Kiribati	2010	3.9	...	...	...	...
	2012	7.5	* 12.2	* 2.9	...	...
Kosovo	2010	6.0	9.6	2.3	211.7	857.9
Kosovo	2014	2.3	3.8	0.7	50.0	856.7
	2016	1.6	2.7	0.4	57.7	693.4
Kuwait	2005	1.8	1.9	1.7	26.1	430.0
Koweït	2009	1.7	2.3	1.0	24.3	288.4
	2010	2.0	2.7	1.0	...	...
	2012	1.8	2.6	0.7	...	...
Kyrgyzstan	2005	8.3	13.1	3.5	5.2	243.0
Kirghizistan	2009	7.8	10.9	4.9	6.7	204.8
	2010	19.8	...	...	9.9	182.3
	2015	5.2	...	...	6.1	168.7
	2016	4.5	...	...	4.8	156.1
Lao People's Dem. Rep.	*2005	9.6	...	...	...	...
Rép. dém. populaire lao	*2010	8.0	...	...	...	...
	*2015	7.0	10.8	3.2	...	...
Latvia	2005	5.6	...	...	48.8	1 078.5
Lettonie	2010	3.3	...	...	57.9	1 211.0
	2015	3.4	4.1	2.7	26.8	972.9
	2016	...	...	...	33.3	738.6
Lebanon	2010	3.8	...	...	218.9	662.1
Liban	2015	3.9	* 6.6	* 1.2	132.8	427.8
	2016	4.0	...	...	127.3	...
Lesotho	2009	35.8	...	...	363.1	222.7
Lesotho	2010	37.4	...	...	...	...
	2015	41.2	* 75.6	* 8.9	...	...
Liberia	2010	3.3	...	...	...	...
Libéria	2012	3.2	* 5.1	* 1.4	...	...
Libya	*2005	3.7	...	...	...	...
Libye	*2010	3.1	...	...	...	...
	*2015	2.5	4.0	1.0	...	...
Liechtenstein	2005	0.0	...	...	203.7	502.1
Liechtenstein	2010	2.8	...	...	213.9	483.3
	2015	0.0	...	...	328.9	516.0
	2016	0.0	...	...	188.6	520.6
Lithuania	2005	11.1	17.5	5.6	12.2	825.8
Lituanie	2010	7.0	10.0	4.4	7.8	849.3
	2015	5.9	9.1	3.1	7.3	777.1
	2016	5.2	8.0	2.9	7.4	684.6
Luxembourg	2004	0.4	0.4	0.4	...	...
Luxembourg	2005	0.9	...	...	...	...
	2010	2.0	2.0	2.0	487.3	1 421.2
	2014	0.7	0.7	0.7	572.9	1 844.1
Madagascar	*2005	10.0	...	...	...	...
Madagascar	2010	* 9.2	...	...	16.3	0.3
	2015	* 7.7	* 12.1	* 3.3	9.0	0.9
Malawi	2005	1.5	...	...	...	...
Malawi	2010	3.4	...	...	...	...
	2012	1.7	* 2.7	* 0.8	...	...
Malaysia	2005	2.4	...	...	16.5	133.7
Malaisie	2006	2.2	...	...	21.9	142.0
	2010	1.9	* 3.0	* 0.7	...	...
	2013	2.1	...	...	...	...

12

Intentional homicides and other crimes *(continued)*
By type of crime per 100 000 population and homicide victims by sex

Homicides intentionnels et autres crimes *(suite)*
Par type de crime pour 100 000 habitants et victimes d'homicides par sexe

Country or area Pays ou zone	Year Année	Intentional homicides Homicides volontaires			Other crimes (per 100 000 pop.) Autres infractions (pour 100 000 hab.)	
		Per 100 000 Pour 100 000	Victims (%) Victimes (%) Male Hommes	Female Femmes	Assault Agression	Theft Vol simple
Maldives Maldives	2003	1.3	...	...	...	...
	2004	...	...	...	...	...
	2010	1.6	...	...	405.5	1 097.6
	2013	0.8	* 1.1	* 0.3	324.4	1 681.7
Mali Mali	*2005	12.7	...	...	...	...
	*2010	12.2	...	...	...	...
	*2015	10.9	16.7	5.1	...	...
Malta Malte	2005	1.0	1.0	1.0	...	2 362.9
	2010	1.0	1.4	0.5	43.3	1 867.1
	2015	0.9	0.9	0.9	42.8	2 023.5
Martinique Martinique	2005	4.8	...	...	...	...
	2009	2.8	4.4	1.4	...	...
Mauritania Mauritanie	*2005	12.4	...	...	...	...
	*2010	10.9	...	...	...	...
	*2015	9.9	14.6	5.2	...	...
Mauritius Maurice	2005	3.0	3.9	2.1	10.0	1 172.3
	2010	2.6	4.0	1.3	19.1	864.0
	2011	2.7	4.2	1.3	18.4	731.1
	2016	1.8	2.1	1.6	...	...
Mayotte Mayotte	2009	5.9	...	...	...	...
Mexico Mexique	2005	9.1	16.0	2.4	220.5	78.2
	2010	22.0	40.0	4.1	196.6	112.6
	2015	16.5	29.3	3.8	36.7	210.5
	2016	19.3	34.2	4.4	49.9	242.9
Micronesia (Fed. States of) Micronésie (États féd. de)	*2005	4.6	...	...	...	...
	*2010	4.5	...	...	...	...
	*2015	4.7	6.9	2.4	...	...
Monaco Monaco	2005	3.0	...	...	458.7	958.8
	2006	2.9	...	...	406.9	1 005.6
	2010	0.0	...	...	...	...
	2015	0.0	...	...	514.3	1 420.1
	2016	...	...	...	...	1 080.2
Mongolia Mongolie	2005	15.8	...	...	118.4	264.5
	2010	8.8	12.8	4.9	214.6	213.0
	2015	6.2	9.6	2.9	270.9	308.0
	2016	5.7	8.8	2.6	62.6	299.8
Montenegro Monténégro	2005	3.6	...	...	25.1	249.8
	2010	2.4	2.6	2.2	30.9	84.9
	2015	2.7	4.5	0.9	22.3	131.7
	2016	4.5	8.1	0.9	20.4	80.5
Montserrat Montserrat	2005	20.9	...	...	...	...
	2008	20.4	...	...	...	...
	2012	19.9	...	...	...	...
Morocco Maroc	2005	1.5	...	...	106.9	203.4
	2009	1.4	2.4	0.3	97.2	245.1
	2010	1.4	...	...	...	...
	2013	1.3	2.2	0.4	200.3	318.8
	2015	1.2	1.9	0.6	161.7	139.6
Mozambique Mozambique	2005	5.2	...	...	6.1	26.5
	2009	3.5	...	...	2.2	20.2
	2010	3.6	...	...	...	...
	2011	3.4	* 5.8	* 1.1	...	...
Myanmar Myanmar	2005	1.4	...	...	...	...
	2010	1.6	2.7	0.6	5.3	3.4
	2013	2.4	4.1	0.8	9.7	5.3
	2016	2.3	3.8	0.8	8.7	5.9
Namibia Namibie	2004	17.5	...	...	...	...
	2010	14.4	...	...	...	...
	2012	17.1	* 31.7	* 3.5	...	...

12
Intentional homicides and other crimes *(continued)*
By type of crime per 100 000 population and homicide victims by sex

Homicides intentionnels et autres crimes *(suite)*
Par type de crime pour 100 000 habitants et victimes d'homicides par sexe

Country or area Pays ou zone	Year Année	Intentional homicides Homicides volontaires			Other crimes (per 100 000 pop.) Autres infractions (pour 100 000 hab.)	
		Per 100 000 Pour 100 000	Victims (%) Victimes (%)			
			Male Hommes	Female Femmes	Assault Agression	Theft Vol simple
Nauru Nauru	*2012	0.0	...	...	...	...
Nepal Népal	2005	3.4	...	...	4.1	2.0
	2006	2.4	...	...	4.0	2.1
	2010	3.0	...	...	...	...
	2014	2.0	* 3.1	* 0.9	...	...
	2016	2.2			0.2	4.4
Netherlands Pays-Bas	2005	1.1	1.4	0.7	409.7	4 631.5
	2010	0.9	1.1	0.6	361.3	3 968.8
	2015	0.6	0.7	0.5	30.1	1 978.6
	2016	0.6	0.8	0.4	29.5	1 791.2
New Caledonia Nouvelle-Calédonie	2009	3.2	...	...	...	...
New Zealand Nouvelle-Zélande	2005	1.5[3]	1.7	1.3	234.2	3 087.9
	2010	1.0	1.0	1.0	257.7	2 676.0
	2013	1.0	1.5	0.5	198.1	2 253.8
	2014	1.0	1.4	0.6	216.8	...
Nicaragua Nicaragua	2005	13.6	...	...	359.4	269.8
	2010	13.7	25.0	2.7	319.7	182.2
	2015	8.6	15.3	2.1	...	...
	2016	7.4	...	...	...	...
Niger Niger	2012	4.4	* 6.9	* 2.0	...	...
Nigeria Nigéria	*2005	11.8	...	...	...	...
	2010	* 10.7	...	...	11.4	12.9
	2013	...	...	...	9.6	14.0
	*2015	9.8	14.6	5.0	...	...
Niue Nioué	2012	0.0	...	...	...	...
North Macedonia Macédoine du Nord	2005	2.1	3.4	0.9	...	...
	2010	2.1	2.7	1.4	12.0	236.4
	2014	1.6	2.2	1.0	10.3	239.9
Norway Norvège	2005	0.7	0.8	0.6	63.9	2 991.6
	2010	0.6	0.6	0.6	59.9	2 592.9
	2014	0.6	0.6	0.5	46.2	2 568.3
	2016	0.5	0.6	0.4	41.9	1 990.7
Oman Oman	2005	2.1	...	...	...	...
	2008	1.7	...	...	75.5	199.9
	2010	1.6	...	...	...	...
	2014	0.7	* 0.8	* 0.4	...	...
Other non-specified areas Autres zones non-spécifiées	2001	1.4	...	...	...	...
	2010	0.8	...	...	...	...
	2015	0.8	1.2	0.5	...	...
Pakistan Pakistan	2005	6.4	...	...	...	...
	2010	7.7	...	...	20.9	28.9
	2015	5.0	* 7.5	* 2.3	15.3	20.5
	2016	4.4	...	...	15.4	20.9
Palau Palaos	*2012	3.1	...	...	...	...
Panama Panama	2005	10.9	19.6	2.2	...	419.7
	2010	12.6	23.4	1.7	166.3	501.3
	2015	11.3	20.0	2.5	71.6	475.6
	2016	9.7	17.1	2.2	62.3	396.3
Papua New Guinea Papouasie-Nvl-Guinée	2000	8.3	...	...	...	...
	2007	7.8	11.9	3.6	...	...
Paraguay Paraguay	2005	15.3	...	...	38.6	...
	2010	11.9	21.2	2.4	31.4	502.1
	2015	9.3	16.6	1.7	10.3	572.7
	2016	...	...	...	9.9	630.2

Intentional homicides and other crimes *(continued)*
By type of crime per 100 000 population and homicide victims by sex

Homicides intentionnels et autres crimes *(suite)*
Par type de crime pour 100 000 habitants et victimes d'homicides par sexe

Country or area Pays ou zone	Year Année	Intentional homicides Homicides volontaires Per 100 000 Pour 100 000	Victims (%) Victimes (%) Male Hommes	Female Femmes	Other crimes (per 100 000 pop.) Autres infractions (pour 100 000 hab.) Assault Agression	Theft Vol simple
Peru	2005	...	...	...	53.2	189.9
Pérou	2010	...	...	...	64.9	190.1
	2015	7.2	11.7	2.6	79.0	301.1
	2016	7.7	12.1	3.3	71.5	298.8
Philippines	2005	7.5	...	...	...	12.9
Philippines	2010	9.5	16.2	2.7	...	77.8
	2012	8.8	15.1	2.3	...	45.0
	2016	11.0	...	...	...	48.0
Poland	2005	1.4	2.2	0.7	...	726.9
Pologne	2010	1.1	1.6	0.7	28.7	532.1
	2015	0.8	...	...	18.2	379.5
	2016	0.7[3]	1.0	0.4	19.9	330.9
Portugal	2005	1.3	2.0	0.6	371.2	869.0
Portugal	2010	1.2	1.6	0.8	8.1	892.4
	2014	0.9	0.9	0.9	5.2	869.4
	2015	1.0	...	...	4.5	829.5
	2016	0.6	...	...	5.0	749.4
Puerto Rico	2005	20.5	39.5	2.9	...	...
Porto Rico	2010	27.4	53.5	3.2	73.0	720.3
	2016	18.5	35.3	3.0	98.0	631.3
Qatar	2004	0.7	0.8	0.4	39.3	96.7
Qatar	2005	0.7	0.3	1.4	...	103.7
	2006	0.5	0.6	0.3	...	103.2
	2010	0.2	0.3	0.0	...	...
	2014	0.4	0.4	0.3	...	...
Republic of Korea	2005	...	...	...	...	387.6
République de Corée	2010	...	...	...	590.0	543.7
	2014	0.7	0.7	0.8	99.8	528.4
	2016	0.7	0.6	0.8	98.5	399.9
Republic of Moldova	2005	7.1	9.8	4.6	9.5	276.7
République de Moldova	2010	6.5	10.8	2.5	10.2	334.1
	2014	3.2	4.2	2.3	7.9	411.0
Réunion	2005	3.2	4.5	1.8	...	...
Réunion	2009	1.8	2.3	1.4	...	...
Romania	2005	2.1[3]	3.0	1.2	41.5	201.5
Roumanie	2010	2.0[3]	2.7	1.3	60.2	238.9
	2015	1.5[3]	2.0	1.0	1.5	545.6
	2016	1.2[3]	...	...	1.5	465.6
Russian Federation	2005	# 24.8	40.1	11.5	40.3	1 095.3
Fédération de Russie	2009	# 14.9	24.1	7.0	30.1	830.6
	2010	...	...	...	21.2	774.3
	2015	11.5[7]	...	...	18.9	772.8
	2016	10.8[7]	...	...	17.5	511.6
Rwanda	2010	2.8	...	...	19.6	...
Rwanda	2013	3.2	...	...	29.8	...
	2015	2.5	* 4.0	* 1.1	...	...
Saint Helena	2005	0.0	...	...	...	...
Sainte-Hélène	2009	0.0	...	...	...	...
Saint Kitts and Nevis	2005	16.5	...	...	...	...
Saint-Kitts-et-Nevis	2010	40.8	...	...	301.3	1 036.1
	2011	65.4	...	...	263.4	944.1
	2012	34.2	...	...	...	...
Saint Lucia	2004	22.8	41.7	4.7	...	...
Sainte-Lucie	2005	25.0	...	...	...	...
	2010	25.5	45.5	6.3	...	...
	2014	19.3	39.3	0.0	...	...
Saint Pierre and Miquelon Saint-Pierre-et-Miquelon	2009	15.9	...	...	...	...

12

Intentional homicides and other crimes *(continued)*
By type of crime per 100 000 population and homicide victims by sex

Homicides intentionnels et autres crimes *(suite)*
Par type de crime pour 100 000 habitants et victimes d'homicides par sexe

Country or area Pays ou zone	Year Année	Intentional homicides Homicides volontaires			Other crimes (per 100 000 pop.) Autres infractions (pour 100 000 hab.)	
		Per 100 000 Pour 100 000	Victims (%) Victimes (%)		Assault Agression	Theft Vol simple
			Male Hommes	Female Femmes		
Saint Vincent & Grenadines	2005	23.9	34.6	13.0	1 151.3	1 777.6
Saint-Vincent-Grenadines	2010	22.9	39.9	5.5	1 197.5	1 739.0
	2012	25.6	...	...	1 017.1	1 923.6
	2013	...	...	...	...	...
	2016	36.5	65.0	7.4	748.3	...
Samoa	2010	8.6	...	...	...	...
Samoa	2013	3.1	* 4.8	* 1.4	...	...
San Marino	2005	0.0	...	...	...	...
Saint-Marin	2010	0.0	...	...	...	...
	2011	0.0	...	...	...	...
Sao Tome and Principe	2004	...	...	...	0.7	...
Sao Tomé-et-Principe	2010	3.4	...	...	0.0	9.2
	2011	3.4	* 5.2	* 1.5	2.2	11.2
Saudi Arabia	2005	1.2	...	...	...	...
Arabie saoudite	2007	1.0	...	...	...	...
	2015	1.5	* 1.8	* 1.1	1.4	...
Senegal	2005	* 9.3	...	...	2.5	...
Sénégal	2010	* 8.5	...	...	2.4	19.4
	2015	* 7.4	* 12.3	* 2.7	...	16.7
	2016	...	...	...	...	1.0
Serbia	2005	1.6	2.3	1.0	17.5	181.9
Serbie	2010	1.4	2.0	0.9	15.4	176.2
	2015	1.2	1.7	0.7	16.1	276.6
	2016	1.4	1.9	0.9	15.2	254.4
Seychelles	2004	11.4	18.8	4.1	...	...
Seychelles	2010	9.8	16.4	2.9	...	...
	2014	17.2	29.1	5.3	...	...
	2016	12.7	...	...	...	...
Sierra Leone	2005	1.7	...	...	...	...
Sierra Leone	2008	3.0	...	...	322.3	170.4
	2010	2.5	...	...	...	...
	2015	1.7	* 2.7	* 0.8	...	...
Singapore	2005	0.5	...	...	13.5	471.3
Singapour	2010	0.4	0.6	0.1	8.5	360.1
	2011	0.3	0.4	0.2	7.8	333.3
	2015	0.3	0.4	0.1	8.5	274.7
	2016	0.3	0.4	0.2	8.8	243.4
Slovakia	2005	1.7	2.3	1.2	72.2	350.0
Slovaquie	2010	1.5	1.9	1.1	44.9	452.7
	2015	0.8	1.1	0.5	34.9	442.9
	2016	1.0	1.4	0.7	30.0	291.6
Slovenia	2005	1.0	1.0	1.0	115.4	1 477.2
Slovénie	2010	0.7	0.7	0.8	106.7	1 413.6
	2015	1.0	0.9	1.1	74.2	1 098.8
	2016	0.5	0.8	0.2	71.8	1 030.5
Solomon Islands	2005	5.5	...	...	258.1	219.0
Îles Salomon	2008	3.8	* 5.7	* 1.8	217.5	174.0
Somalia	*2005	5.0	...	...	...	...
Somalie	*2010	5.3	...	...	...	...
	*2015	4.3	6.5	2.2	...	...
South Africa	2005	38.0	...	...	...	...
Afrique du Sud	2010	30.8	51.9	10.4	...	...
	2011	29.8	51.3	9.0	...	...
	2016	34.0	...	...	...	...
South Sudan						
Soudan du sud	2012	13.9	* 21.6	* 6.2	...	...
Spain	2005	1.2	1.8	0.6	392.4	...
Espagne	2010	0.9	1.1	0.7	53.6	309.1
	2015	0.7	0.8	0.5	62.6	443.5
	2016	0.6	0.8	0.5	37.3	351.4

12

Intentional homicides and other crimes *(continued)*
By type of crime per 100 000 population and homicide victims by sex

Homicides intentionnels et autres crimes *(suite)*
Par type de crime pour 100 000 habitants et victimes d'homicides par sexe

Country or area Pays ou zone	Year Année	Intentional homicides Homicides volontaires Per 100 000 Pour 100 000	Victims (%) Victims (%) Male Hommes	Female Femmes	Other crimes (per 100 000 pop.) Autres infractions (pour 100 000 hab.) Assault Agression	Theft Vol simple
Sri Lanka	2004	7.1	...	...	109.3	135.8
Sri Lanka	2005	6.2	...	...	...	...
	2010	3.8	6.1	1.6	319.9	62.8
	2013	3.0	4.8	1.4	20.0	55.8
	2016	2.5	4.0	1.2	17.1	29.6
State of Palestine	2005	2.4	...	...	183.8	122.4
État de Palestine	2010	0.8	1.1	0.5	7.0	67.4
	2012	0.6	1.0	0.2	8.1	45.3
	2013	0.5	...	...	...	...
	2016	0.7	...	...	...	...
Sudan						
Soudan	2008	5.2	* 8.0	* 2.4	...	227.9
Suriname	2004	9.3	...	...	...	2 754.5
Suriname	2005	13.8	...	...	...	...
	2008	8.3	12.7	3.9	...	...
Sweden	2005	0.9	1.2	0.7	803.7	4 921.4
Suède	2010	1.0	1.4	0.6	59.6	3 918.6
	2015	1.1	1.7	0.6	47.4	4 093.2
	2016	1.1	1.6	0.6	50.1	3 816.9
Switzerland	2005	1.0	1.0	1.0	109.3	1 921.9
Suisse	2010	0.7	0.7	0.7	6.2	2 059.2
	2015	0.7	0.7	0.7	7.4	1 863.1
	2016	0.5	0.5	0.6	6.8	1 712.4
Syrian Arab Republic	2004	2.4	...	...	35.7	64.8
République arabe syrienne	2005	2.4	...	...	33.7	...
	2008	2.6	...	...	2.8	32.0
	2010	2.2	* 3.4	* 1.0	...	...
Tajikistan	2005	2.3	...	...	...	51.9
Tadjikistan	2010	2.4	4.1	0.6	71.8	46.6
	2011	1.6	2.8	0.4	47.8	46.9
Thailand	2005	7.3	13.0	1.9	43.2	93.1
Thaïlande	2010	5.4	9.7	1.3	13.6	80.8
	2014	3.9	6.7	1.2	18.5	58.3
	2015	3.5	...	...	19.9	57.3
	2016	3.2	...	...	...	48.0
Timor-Leste	2005	4.5	...	...	...	...
Timor-Leste	2010	3.5	...	...	...	...
	2015	3.9	* 6.2	* 1.6	...	...
Togo	*2005	10.7	...	...	...	...
Togo	*2010	9.6	...	...	...	...
	*2015	9.0	14.9	3.2	...	...
Tonga	2005	4.0	7.9	0.0	...	...
Tonga	2010	1.0	1.9	0.0	...	...
	2012	1.0	0.0	1.9	...	...
Trinidad and Tobago	2005	29.8	54.0	6.0	61.8	212.2
Trinité-et-Tobago	2010	35.6	63.9	7.9	46.4	307.9
	2015	30.9	58.3	4.2	44.1	137.5
Tunisia	2005	2.6	...	...	...	...
Tunisie	2010	2.7	...	...	...	...
	2012	3.0	* 5.1	* 1.0	...	...
Turkey	2005	4.9	8.1	1.8	155.7	152.8
Turquie	2010	4.2	6.8	1.7	305.4	248.3
	2012	4.3	7.1	1.6	351.8	280.2
	2016	...	...	...	88.0	214.0
Turkmenistan	2004	4.4	...	...	...	...
Turkménistan	2005	4.3	...	...	1.9	35.0
	2006	4.2	* 6.8	* 1.7	1.7	29.7
Turks and Caicos Islands	2005	0.0	...	...	...	...
Îles Turques-et-Caïques	2009	6.6	...	...	...	...
	2014	5.9	...	...	...	...

12 Intentional homicides and other crimes *(continued)*
By type of crime per 100 000 population and homicide victims by sex

Homicides intentionnels et autres crimes *(suite)*
'Par type de crime pour 100 000 habitants et victimes d'homicides par sexe

Country or area Pays ou zone	Year Année	Intentional homicides Homicides volontaires Per 100 000 Pour 100 000	Victims (%) Victimes (%) Male Hommes	Female Femmes	Other crimes (per 100 000 pop.) Autres infractions (pour 100 000 hab.) Assault Agression	Theft Vol simple
Tuvalu	2005	0.0	...	...	...	...
Tuvalu	2010	9.5	...	...	...	...
	2012	18.6	...	...	...	...
Uganda	2005	8.7	...	...	122.9	192.9
Ouganda	2010	9.3	15.2	3.5	67.8	69.1
	2014	11.5	18.8	4.3	37.4	43.9
Ukraine	2005	6.5	9.5	3.8	14.3	398.1
Ukraine	2010	4.3	6.6	2.4	8.8	556.3
	2014	6.3	...	...	...	...
United Arab Emirates	2004	0.7	...	...	...	270.0
Émirats arabes unis	2005	1.2	...	...	15.7	...
	2006	0.7	...	...	14.5	...
	2010	0.8	0.8	0.9	...	...
	2015	0.7	0.7	0.4	3.5	67.8
	2016	0.9	...	...	3.7	51.7
United Kingdom	2005	1.4	1.8	1.0	1 010.6[8]	3 368.8[8]
Royaume-Uni	2010	1.2	1.5	0.9	658.8[8]	2 654.9[8]
	2014	0.9	1.1	0.7	649.3[8]	2 208.6[8]
	2016	1.2	1.5	0.9	798.4[8]	2 283.0[8]
United Rep. of Tanzania	2004	7.6	...	...	...	...
Rép.-Unie de Tanzanie	2010	8.4	14.7	2.4	...	...
	2015	7.0	11.5	2.5	4.4	0.3
United States of America	2005	5.7	9.1	2.4	292.1	2 298.5
États-Unis d'Amérique	2010	4.8	7.5	2.1	253.3	2 010.3
	2016	5.4	8.5	2.3	249.2	1 749.8
United States Virgin Islands	2005	34.3	65.3	5.4	...	...
Îles Vierges américaines	2010	52.8	96.5	12.6	...	...
	2012	49.3	99.2	3.6	...	...
Uruguay	2003	5.9	...	...	...	2 904.9
Uruguay	2004	6.0	...	...	...	3 179.5
	2005	5.7	...	...	...	...
	2010	6.1	10.1	2.3	15.4	2 823.3
	2015	8.5	14.7	2.8	13.6	3 043.6
	2016	7.7	13.4	2.4	16.5	3 205.5
Uzbekistan	2005	3.4	...	...	...	...
Ouzbékistan	2008	3.0	* 4.9	* 1.2	...	...
Vanuatu	*2005	2.5	...	...	...	...
Vanuatu	*2010	2.3	...	...	...	...
	*2015	2.1	3.2	1.1	...	...
Venezuela (Boliv. Rep. of)	2005	37.2	70.2	4.2	...	...
Venezuela (Rép. boliv. du)	2010	45.1	84.8	5.4	...	...
	2012	53.8	101.5	6.3	...	...
	2016	56.3	...	...	...	...
Viet Nam	2005	1.2	...	...	...	...
Viet Nam	2010	1.5	...	...	...	...
	2011	1.5	* 2.6	* 0.4	...	...
Yemen	2005	4.6	...	...	...	...
Yémen	2009	4.3	...	...	0.1	...
	2010	4.7	...	...	...	...
	2013	6.7	* 10.3	* 3.0	...	...
Zambia	2000	7.6	...	...	...	...
Zambie	2010	5.9	...	...	...	...
	2015	5.3	* 8.6	* 2.1	...	...
Zimbabwe	2005	10.4	...	...	714.9	854.0
Zimbabwe	2008	...	...	...	378.0	674.5
	2010	5.0	...	...	...	...
	2012	6.7	* 11.5	* 2.0	...	...

12

Intentional homicides and other crimes *(continued)*
By type of crime per 100 000 population and homicide victims by sex

Homicides intentionnels et autres crimes *(suite)*
Par type de crime pour 100 000 habitants et victimes d'homicides par sexe

Source:

United Nations Office on Drugs and Crime (UNODC), Vienna, UNODC Statistics database, last accessed March 2019.

Source:

Office des Nations Unies contre la drogue et le crime (ONUDC), Vienne, base de données statistiques de l'ONUDC, dernier accès mars 2019.

1	Data is for 2015, or latest available data from 2010 onwards.
2	Excludes Australia and New Zealand.
3	Data refer to offences, not victims, of intentional homicide.
4	For statistical purposes, the data for China do not include those for the Hong Kong Special Administrative Region (Hong Kong SAR), Macao Special Administrative Region (Macao SAR) and Taiwan Province of China.
5	Excluding victims of terrorist attacks.
6	Data refer to Central Iraq.
7	Include victims of attempted homicide.
8	England and Wales only.

1	Données pour 2015, ou dernières données disponibles à partir de 2010.
2	Exclut l'Australie et la Nouvelle-Zélande.
3	Les données concernent les infractions, et non les victimes, d'homicides volontaires.
4	Pour la présentation des statistiques, les données pour la Chine ne comprennent pas la région administrative spéciale de Hong Kong (RAS de Hong Kong), la région administrative spéciale de Macao (RAS de Macao) et la province chinoise de Taïwan.
5	À l'exclusion des victimes d'attaques terroristes.
6	Les données se réfèrent l'Iraq central.
7	Inclure les victimes de tentative d'homicide.
8	Se rapporte seulement a l'Angleterre et au pays de Galles.

Part Two

Economic activity

Chapter VII   National accounts (tables 13 and 14)

Chapter VIII   Finance (tables 15 and 16)

Chapter IX   Labour market (tables 17 and 18)

Chapter X   Price and production indices (tables 19)

Chapter XI   International merchandise trade (tables 20 and 21)

Deuxième partie

Activité économique

Chapitre VII   Compatibilités nationales (tableaux 13 et 14)

Chapitre VIII   Finances (tableaux 15 et 16)

Chapitre IX   Marché du travail (tableaux 17 et 18)

Chapitre X   Indices des prix et de la production (tableaux 19)

Chapitre XI   Commerce international des marchandises (tableaux 20 et 21)

Part Two

Economic activity

Deuxième partie

Activité économique

13

Gross domestic product and gross domestic product per capita
In millions of US dollars at current and constant 2010 prices; per capita US dollars; real rates of growth

Produit intérieur brut et produit intérieur brut par habitant
En millions de dollars É.-U. aux prix courants et constants de 2010; par habitant en dollars É.U.; taux de croissance réels

Country or area	1985	1995	2005	2010	2015	2016	2017	Pays ou zone
Total, all countries or areas								**Total, tous pays ou zones**
GDP at current prices	13 518 851	31 084 222	47 550 129	66 145 612	74 757 288	75 840 177	80 501 414	PIB aux prix courants
GDP per capita	2 776	5 406	7 270	9 508	10 128	10 159	10 665	PIB par habitant
GDP at constant prices	31 826 492	42 246 915	58 258 483	66 145 612	75 839 510	77 669 298	80 050 391	PIB aux prix constants
Growth rates	3.5	3.1	3.9	4.3	2.8	2.4	3.1	Taux de croissance
Africa								**Afrique**
GDP at current prices	517 301	582 440	1 128 718	1 966 483	2 293 977	2 138 916	2 215 906	PIB aux prix courants
GDP per capita	937	807	1 222	1 877	1 923	1 748	1 766	PIB par habitant
GDP at constant prices	798 216	975 000	1 526 210	1 966 483	2 290 892	2 330 484	2 397 256	PIB aux prix constants
Growth rates	3.6	3.2	6.0	5.3	2.7	1.7	2.9	Taux de croissance
Northern Africa								**Afrique septentrionale**
GDP at current prices	142 523	207 392	373 106	648 507	728 806	682 558	657 861	PIB aux prix courants
GDP per capita	1 103	1 270	1 908	3 182	3 245	2 983	2 823	PIB par habitant
GDP at constant prices	264 050	333 874	519 909	648 507	665 365	686 921	714 839	PIB aux prix constants
Growth rates	5.8	1.7	5.7	4.6	2.6	3.2	4.1	Taux de croissance
Sub-Saharan Africa								**Afrique subsaharienne**
GDP at current prices	374 778	375 048	755 612	1 317 975	1 565 171	1 456 357	1 558 044	PIB aux prix courants
GDP per capita	886	671	1 038	1 561	1 617	1 464	1 525	PIB par habitant
GDP at constant prices	534 166	641 126	1 006 302	1 317 975	1 625 527	1 643 563	1 682 416	PIB aux prix constants
Growth rates	2.6	3.9	6.1	5.7	2.8	1.1	2.4	Taux de croissance
Eastern Africa								**Afrique orientale**
GDP at current prices	64 114	67 938	111 482	214 641	315 078	321 275	350 941	PIB aux prix courants
GDP per capita	388	309	382	620	791	785	834	PIB par habitant
GDP at constant prices	71 192	95 016	143 547	214 641	283 341	297 113	313 742	PIB aux prix constants
Growth rates	2.2	4.6	6.4	7.2	5.9	4.9	5.6	Taux de croissance
Middle Africa								**Afrique centrale**
GDP at current prices	35 267	36 081	99 548	189 045	237 337	222 542	250 577	PIB aux prix courants
GDP per capita	572	429	889	1 439	1 544	1 403	1 533	PIB par habitant
GDP at constant prices	92 743	83 536	139 063	189 045	233 260	231 174	230 035	PIB aux prix constants
Growth rates	1.6	6.6	8.7	4.9	1.0	-0.9	-0.5	Taux de croissance
Southern Africa								**Afrique australe**
GDP at current prices	62 927	168 964	279 562	406 242	350 139	328 716	386 563	PIB aux prix courants
GDP per capita	1 645	3 518	5 013	6 884	5 521	5 113	5 934	PIB par habitant
GDP at constant prices	214 759	249 548	347 279	406 242	457 976	461 285	467 187	PIB aux prix constants
Growth rates	-1.0	3.3	5.2	3.3	1.3	0.7	1.3	Taux de croissance
Western Africa								**Afrique occidentale**
GDP at current prices	212 470	102 064	265 020	508 048	662 617	583 825	569 962	PIB aux prix courants
GDP per capita	1 346	494	987	1 651	1 879	1 612	1 532	PIB par habitant
GDP at constant prices	155 472	213 026	376 413	508 048	650 950	653 991	671 453	PIB aux prix constants
Growth rates	8.9	3.3	6.0	7.3	3.1	0.5	2.7	Taux de croissance
Americas								**Amériques**
GDP at current prices	5 491 739	10 213 265	17 070 406	21 951 438	25 261 020	25 492 004	26 896 468	PIB aux prix courants
GDP per capita	8 185	13 078	19 223	23 370	25 590	25 584	26 748	PIB par habitant
GDP at constant prices	11 167 542	14 727 486	20 316 809	21 951 438	24 436 405	24 635 134	25 113 358	PIB aux prix constants
Growth rates	4.1	2.4	3.7	3.4	1.9	0.8	1.9	Taux de croissance
Northern America								**Amérique septentrionale**
GDP at current prices	4 705 619	8 247 641	14 212 748	16 613 872	19 780 210	20 242 949	21 141 574	PIB aux prix courants
GDP per capita	17 637	27 948	43 392	48 447	55 563	56 452	58 531	PIB par habitant
GDP at constant prices	8 537 958	11 325 523	15 864 996	16 613 872	18 520 758	18 808 282	19 240 424	PIB aux prix constants
Growth rates	4.2	2.7	3.5	2.6	2.7	1.6	2.3	Taux de croissance
Latin America & the Caribbean								**Amérique latine et Caraïbes**
GDP at current prices	786 120	1 965 625	2 857 658	5 337 566	5 480 810	5 249 055	5 754 894	PIB aux prix courants
GDP per capita	1 945	4 046	5 098	8 950	8 684	8 230	8 931	PIB par habitant
GDP at constant prices	2 629 584	3 401 963	4 451 813	5 337 566	5 915 647	5 826 853	5 872 934	PIB aux prix constants
Growth rates	3.6	1.5	4.3	5.8	-0.5	-1.5	0.8	Taux de croissance
Caribbean								**Caraïbes**
GDP at current prices	69 195	119 686	221 390	288 896	341 075	346 934	354 606	PIB aux prix courants
GDP per capita	2 222	3 369	5 654	7 089	8 055	8 137	8 262	PIB par habitant
GDP at constant prices	151 318	183 368	263 011	288 896	313 919	316 894	319 330	PIB aux prix constants
Growth rates	0.8	4.0	3.4	1.8	2.3	0.9	0.8	Taux de croissance
Central America								**Amérique centrale**
GDP at current prices	258 698	412 184	972 224	1 210 291	1 401 962	1 321 864	1 416 752	PIB aux prix courants
GDP per capita	2 496	3 250	6 560	7 538	8 121	7 554	7 990	PIB par habitant
GDP at constant prices	652 279	793 168	1 106 744	1 210 291	1 412 539	1 455 557	1 488 924	PIB aux prix constants
Growth rates	2.6	-5.2	2.5	5.0	3.4	3.0	2.3	Taux de croissance

13

Gross domestic product and gross domestic product per capita *(continued)*
In millions of US dollars at current and constant 2010 prices; per capita US dollars; real rates of growth

Produit intérieur brut et produit intérieur brut par habitant *(suite)*
En millions de dollars É.-U. aux prix courants et constants de 2010; par habitant en dollars É.-U.; taux de croissance réels

Country or area	1985	1995	2005	2010	2015	2016	2017	Pays ou zone
South America								**Amérique du Sud**
GDP at current prices	458 228	1 433 755	1 664 043	3 838 379	3 737 774	3 580 257	3 983 536	PIB aux prix courants
GDP per capita	1 701	4 433	4 460	9 716	8 981	8 521	9 393	PIB par habitant
GDP at constant prices	1 825 986	2 425 428	3 082 058	3 838 379	4 189 190	4 054 401	4 064 679	PIB aux prix constants
Growth rates	4.2	3.7	5.0	6.4	-1.9	-3.2	0.3	Taux de croissance
Asia								**Asie**
GDP at current prices	2 880 324	9 195 635	12 338 718	20 892 982	26 598 242	27 563 610	29 477 988	PIB aux prix courants
GDP per capita	1 010	2 636	3 113	4 982	6 018	6 177	6 545	PIB par habitant
GDP at constant prices	6 803 983	11 050 094	16 373 075	20 892 982	26 343 440	27 525 475	28 810 433	PIB aux prix constants
Growth rates	4.6	5.1	5.6	7.3	4.5	4.5	4.7	Taux de croissance
Central Asia								**Asie centrale**
GDP at current prices	...	38 937	90 468	220 593	301 877	254 659	261 710	PIB aux prix courants
GDP per capita	...	729	1 540	3 493	4 394	3 649	3 694	PIB par habitant
GDP at constant prices	...	89 429	157 606	220 593	297 786	306 560	320 870	PIB aux prix constants
Growth rates	...	-6.9	9.2	7.5	3.2	2.9	4.7	Taux de croissance
Eastern Asia								**Asie orientale**
GDP at current prices	1 922 987	7 177 176	8 524 913	13 619 284	17 750 809	18 479 876	19 634 506	PIB aux prix courants
GDP per capita	1 506	4 904	5 483	8 535	10 857	11 256	11 914	PIB par habitant
GDP at constant prices	4 683 137	7 469 938	10 723 064	13 619 284	17 002 833	17 708 096	18 532 899	PIB aux prix constants
Growth rates	6.2	4.8	5.2	7.5	4.2	4.1	4.7	Taux de croissance
South-eastern Asia								**Asie du Sud-Est**
GDP at current prices	243 805	703 488	958 893	1 980 866	2 460 015	2 574 987	2 767 984	PIB aux prix courants
GDP per capita	609	1 449	1 707	3 316	3 876	4 012	4 266	PIB par habitant
GDP at constant prices	524 229	1 052 745	1 526 165	1 980 866	2 528 012	2 644 528	2 780 478	PIB aux prix constants
Growth rates	0.7	7.9	5.7	7.8	4.6	4.6	5.1	Taux de croissance
Southern Asia								**Asie méridionale**
GDP at current prices	370 097	616 292	1 270 195	2 542 992	3 128 656	3 323 136	3 726 063	PIB aux prix courants
GDP per capita	349	467	802	1 491	1 716	1 800	1 994	PIB par habitant
GDP at constant prices	722 264	1 104 851	1 893 853	2 542 992	3 261 710	3 516 335	3 730 638	PIB aux prix constants
Growth rates	4.3	6.1	6.7	7.3	6.2	7.8	6.1	Taux de croissance
Western Asia								**Asie occidentale**
GDP at current prices	343 435	659 741	1 494 249	2 529 247	2 956 885	2 930 952	3 087 724	PIB aux prix courants
GDP per capita	2 967	3 959	7 273	10 881	11 469	11 161	11 550	PIB par habitant
GDP at constant prices	874 354	1 333 132	2 072 386	2 529 247	3 253 100	3 349 955	3 445 547	PIB aux prix constants
Growth rates	-0.7	4.3	6.9	5.7	4.0	3.0	2.9	Taux de croissance
Europe								**Europe**
GDP at current prices	4 415 032	10 619 622	16 112 496	19 854 417	19 133 917	19 107 907	20 253 103	PIB aux prix courants
GDP per capita	5 732	14 557	22 012	26 868	25 763	25 705	27 222	PIB par habitant
GDP at constant prices	12 381 279	14 580 951	18 743 794	19 854 417	21 061 693	21 435 436	21 936 347	PIB aux prix constants
Growth rates	2.5	2.3	2.5	2.3	1.8	1.8	2.3	Taux de croissance
Eastern Europe								**Europe orientale**
GDP at current prices	1 124 317	789 180	1 628 697	2 863 393	2 625 765	2 556 626	2 999 690	PIB aux prix courants
GDP per capita	3 023	2 549	5 474	9 722	8 954	8 729	10 257	PIB par habitant
GDP at constant prices	2 232 778	1 692 395	2 428 848	2 863 393	3 125 437	3 164 279	3 257 826	PIB aux prix constants
Growth rates	1.6	-1.0	5.6	3.4	-0.3	1.2	3.0	Taux de croissance
Northern Europe								**Europe septentrionale**
GDP at current prices	810 121	2 164 279	3 977 645	4 256 951	4 715 832	4 510 787	4 608 254	PIB aux prix courants
GDP per capita	9 783	23 267	41 391	42 559	45 873	43 648	44 352	PIB par habitant
GDP at constant prices	2 306 583	2 987 002	4 127 663	4 256 951	4 749 867	4 852 040	4 967 407	PIB aux prix constants
Growth rates	4.0	4.0	3.2	2.1	3.7	2.2	2.4	Taux de croissance
Southern Europe								**Europe méridionale**
GDP at current prices	783 494	2 120 827	3 606 052	4 304 395	3 620 250	3 691 053	3 873 340	PIB aux prix courants
GDP per capita	5 514	14 667	23 983	27 967	23 754	24 261	25 490	PIB par habitant
GDP at constant prices	2 694 159	3 319 243	4 243 040	4 304 395	4 174 239	4 243 555	4 333 303	PIB aux prix constants
Growth rates	2.5	3.0	1.9	0.6	1.9	1.7	2.1	Taux de croissance
Western Europe								**Europe occidentale**
GDP at current prices	1 697 100	5 545 336	6 900 101	8 429 679	8 172 070	8 349 442	8 771 820	PIB aux prix courants
GDP per capita	9 784	30 415	36 699	44 254	42 072	42 823	44 828	PIB par habitant
GDP at constant prices	5 147 759	6 582 311	7 944 244	8 429 679	9 012 149	9 175 562	9 377 812	PIB aux prix constants
Growth rates	2.2	2.0	1.5	2.9	1.6	1.8	2.2	Taux de croissance
Oceania								**Océanie**
GDP at current prices	214 454	473 260	899 792	1 480 293	1 470 130	1 537 740	1 657 949	PIB aux prix courants
GDP per capita	8 673	16 369	27 046	40 723	37 450	38 608	41 037	PIB par habitant
GDP at constant prices	675 471	913 384	1 298 596	1 480 293	1 707 081	1 742 769	1 792 997	PIB aux prix constants
Growth rates	3.6	3.9	2.9	2.4	3.0	2.1	2.9	Taux de croissance

13

Gross domestic product and gross domestic product per capita *(continued)*
In millions of US dollars at current and constant 2010 prices; per capita US dollars; real rates of growth

Produit intérieur brut et produit intérieur brut par habitant *(suite)*
En millions de dollars É.-U. aux prix courants et constants de 2010; par habitant en dollars É.U.; taux de croissance réels

Country or area	1985	1995	2005	2010	2015	2016	2017	Pays ou zone
Australia and New Zealand								**Australie et Nouvelle-Zélande**
GDP at current prices	206 320	454 246	875 117	1 443 843	1 424 009	1 492 274	1 610 720	PIB aux prix courants
GDP per capita	10 860	20 883	35 903	54 505	50 116	51 839	55 244	PIB par habitant
GDP at constant prices	658 811	887 882	1 267 594	1 443 843	1 663 631	1 698 849	1 748 706	PIB aux prix constants
Growth rates	3.6	4.0	2.9	2.3	3.0	2.1	2.9	Taux de croissance
Melanesia								**Mélanésie**
GDP at current prices	5 971	13 533	17 353	28 167	38 317	37 435	38 850	PIB aux prix courants
GDP per capita	1 179	2 118	2 156	3 135	3 857	3 697	3 764	PIB par habitant
GDP at constant prices	11 431	18 798	22 505	28 167	34 965	35 245	35 444	PIB aux prix constants
Growth rates	2.5	0.8	3.6	8.0	5.3	0.8	0.6	Taux de croissance
Micronesia								**Micronésie**
GDP at current prices	257	544	718	863	1 046	1 112	1 139	PIB aux prix courants
GDP per capita	1 222	2 066	2 560	2 983	3 461	3 643	3 695	PIB par habitant
GDP at constant prices	714	844	863	863	1 050	1 071	1 086	PIB aux prix constants
Growth rates	2.4	3.9	1.5	2.8	5.8	2.0	1.4	Taux de croissance
Polynesia								**Polynésie**
GDP at current prices	1 906	4 937	6 603	7 420	6 758	6 919	7 241	PIB aux prix courants
GDP per capita	4 184	9 689	11 674	12 636	11 148	11 325	11 754	PIB par habitant
GDP at constant prices	4 516	5 859	7 634	7 420	7 435	7 603	7 762	PIB aux prix constants
Growth rates	5.4	0.8	1.6	-1.6	1.7	2.3	2.1	Taux de croissance
Afghanistan								**Afghanistan**
GDP at current prices	3 322	3 236	6 622	16 078	20 608	20 235	21 993	PIB aux prix courants
GDP per capita	282	189	264	558	611	584	619	PIB par habitant
GDP at constant prices	11 604	7 011	10 244	16 078	20 890	21 634	22 175	PIB aux prix constants
Growth rates	0.3	49.9	9.9	3.2	-1.8	3.6	2.5	Taux de croissance
Albania								**Albanie**
GDP at current prices	2 324	2 393	8 052	11 927	11 387	11 884	13 039	PIB aux prix courants
GDP per capita	783	770	2 615	4 056	3 895	4 061	4 450	PIB par habitant
GDP at constant prices	5 911	5 424	9 222	11 927	13 033	13 470	13 988	PIB aux prix constants
Growth rates	1.8	13.3	5.5	3.7	2.2	3.4	3.8	Taux de croissance
Algeria								**Algérie**
GDP at current prices	57 866	41 971	103 198	161 207	165 979	160 130	167 555	PIB aux prix courants
GDP per capita	2 564	1 452	3 100	4 463	4 163	3 943	4 055	PIB par habitant
GDP at constant prices	88 592	93 203	142 230	161 207	189 797	195 871	198 613	PIB aux prix constants
Growth rates	3.7	3.8	5.9	3.6	3.7	3.2	1.4	Taux de croissance
Andorra								**Andorre**
GDP at current prices	439	1 491	3 256	3 355	2 812	2 877	3 013	PIB aux prix courants
GDP per capita	9 837	23 359	41 281	39 734	36 040	37 230	39 153	PIB par habitant
GDP at constant prices	1 602	2 151	3 851	3 355	3 258	3 320	3 377	PIB aux prix constants
Growth rates	2.3	2.8	7.4	-5.4	0.8	1.9	1.7	Taux de croissance
Angola								**Angola**
GDP at current prices	9 109	6 642	36 971	83 799	116 194	101 124	126 506	PIB aux prix courants
GDP per capita	859	466	1 891	3 586	4 171	3 510	4 247	PIB par habitant
GDP at constant prices	27 369	26 858	55 997	83 799	104 520	101 823	99 277	PIB aux prix constants
Growth rates	3.5	15.0	15.0	4.9	0.9	-2.6	-2.5	Taux de croissance
Anguilla								**Anguilla**
GDP at current prices	27	104	229	268	331	317	281	PIB aux prix courants
GDP per capita	4 072	10 583	18 129	19 459	22 622	21 480	18 861	PIB par habitant
GDP at constant prices	62	145	256	268	281	277	256	PIB aux prix constants
Growth rates	12.9	-2.3	13.1	-4.5	3.1	-1.3	-7.7	Taux de croissance
Antigua and Barbuda								**Antigua-et-Barbuda**
GDP at current prices	245	577	1 022	1 152	1 359	1 465	1 510	PIB aux prix courants
GDP per capita	3 508	7 841	11 453	12 175	13 602	14 507	14 803	PIB par habitant
GDP at constant prices	504	769	1 148	1 152	1 270	1 341	1 382	PIB aux prix constants
Growth rates	7.7	-4.4	6.4	-7.2	4.0	5.6	3.0	Taux de croissance
Argentina								**Argentine**
GDP at current prices	95 530	279 701	200 622	426 487	644 903	554 862	637 486	PIB aux prix courants
GDP per capita	3 144	7 993	5 125	10 346	14 853	12 654	14 400	PIB par habitant
GDP at constant prices	204 283	268 814	335 871	426 487	458 903	450 539	463 442	PIB aux prix constants
Growth rates	-7.0	-2.8	8.9	10.1	2.7	-1.8	2.9	Taux de croissance
Armenia								**Arménie**
GDP at current prices	...	1 372	5 226	9 875	10 553	10 546	11 537	PIB aux prix courants
GDP per capita	...	426	1 753	3 432	3 618	3 606	3 937	PIB par habitant
GDP at constant prices	...	3 520	8 172	9 875	12 236	12 257	13 175	PIB aux prix constants
Growth rates	...	6.9	13.9	2.2	3.2	0.2	7.5	Taux de croissance

13

Gross domestic product and gross domestic product per capita *(continued)*
In millions of US dollars at current and constant 2010 prices; per capita US dollars; real rates of growth

Produit intérieur brut et produit intérieur brut par habitant *(suite)*
En millions de dollars É.-U. aux prix courants et constants de 2010; par habitant en dollars É.U.; taux de croissance réels

Country or area	1985	1995	2005	2010	2015	2016	2017	Pays ou zone
Aruba								**Aruba**
GDP at current prices	385	1 321	2 331	2 391	2 692	2 647	2 701	PIB aux prix courants
GDP per capita	6 108	16 442	23 303	23 513	25 796	25 252	25 655	PIB par habitant
GDP at constant prices	881	2 099	2 702	2 391	2 554	2 548	2 582	PIB aux prix constants
Growth rates	9.1	2.5	1.2	-3.4	-0.5	-0.2	1.3	Taux de croissance
Australia								**Australie**
GDP at current prices	182 212	391 094	760 397	1 297 259	1 246 800	1 304 420	1 408 676	PIB aux prix courants
GDP per capita	11 584	21 635	37 571	58 646	52 388	54 067	57 613	PIB par habitant
GDP at constant prices	577 296	791 349	1 131 642	1 297 259	1 493 121	1 522 350	1 567 225	PIB aux prix constants
Growth rates	3.9	3.9	2.8	2.5	2.8	2.0	2.9	Taux de croissance
Austria								**Autriche**
GDP at current prices	69 388	241 054	315 967	391 893	381 806	394 053	416 836	PIB aux prix courants
GDP per capita	9 112	30 169	38 282	46 599	43 994	45 230	47 718	PIB par habitant
GDP at constant prices	224 101	290 414	367 273	391 893	413 555	421 989	432 754	PIB aux prix constants
Growth rates	2.5	2.7	2.2	1.8	1.1	2.0	2.6	Taux de croissance
Azerbaijan								**Azerbaïdjan**
GDP at current prices	...	3 081	13 245	52 906	53 076	37 867	40 749	PIB aux prix courants
GDP per capita	...	396	1 551	5 857	5 519	3 894	4 146	PIB par habitant
GDP at constant prices	...	9 499	24 742	52 906	58 515	56 722	56 782	PIB aux prix constants
Growth rates	...	-11.8	28.0	4.8	1.0	-3.1	0.1	Taux de croissance
Bahamas								**Bahamas**
GDP at current prices	2 880	5 117	9 836	10 096	11 240	11 262	11 792	PIB aux prix courants
GDP per capita	12 271	18 264	29 875	27 979	29 056	28 786	29 825	PIB par habitant
GDP at constant prices	6 551	7 344	10 214	10 096	9 967	9 983	10 163	PIB aux prix constants
Growth rates	4.8	4.4	3.4	1.5	-3.1	0.2	1.8	Taux de croissance
Bahrain								**Bahreïn**
GDP at current prices	4 475	6 787	15 969	25 713	31 126	32 228	35 326	PIB aux prix courants
GDP per capita	10 669	12 040	17 959	20 722	22 689	22 614	23 668	PIB par habitant
GDP at constant prices	7 940	12 142	19 620	25 713	30 781	31 843	33 039	PIB aux prix constants
Growth rates	-16.1	1.9	6.8	4.3	2.9	3.5	3.8	Taux de croissance
Bangladesh								**Bangladesh**
GDP at current prices	19 169	37 866	57 628	114 508	194 466	220 316	245 633	PIB aux prix courants
GDP per capita	206	319	402	753	1 206	1 352	1 492	PIB par habitant
GDP at constant prices	33 762	50 806	85 320	114 508	155 582	166 649	178 788	PIB aux prix constants
Growth rates	3.0	4.9	6.0	5.6	6.6	7.1	7.3	Taux de croissance
Barbados								**Barbade**
GDP at current prices	1 425	2 275	3 897	4 365	4 463	4 572	4 713	PIB aux prix courants
GDP per capita	5 569	8 585	14 223	15 613	15 704	16 043	16 494	PIB par habitant
GDP at constant prices	3 197	3 422	4 209	4 365	4 448	4 521	4 561	PIB aux prix constants
Growth rates	1.1	2.0	4.0	0.3	0.9	1.6	0.9	Taux de croissance
Belarus								**Bélarus**
GDP at current prices	...	14 324	31 232	57 232	56 455	47 724	54 441	PIB aux prix courants
GDP per capita	...	1 412	3 246	6 042	5 952	5 034	5 750	PIB par habitant
GDP at constant prices	...	20 655	40 278	57 232	60 712	59 216	60 667	PIB aux prix constants
Growth rates	...	-10.4	9.4	7.8	-3.8	-2.5	2.4	Taux de croissance
Belgium								**Belgique**
GDP at current prices	86 728	289 571	387 356	483 548	455 838	469 739	494 764	PIB aux prix courants
GDP per capita	8 746	28 427	36 727	44 205	40 383	41 356	43 289	PIB par habitant
GDP at constant prices	283 438	357 103	450 521	483 548	509 186	516 766	525 514	PIB aux prix constants
Growth rates	1.7	2.4	2.1	2.7	1.7	1.5	1.7	Taux de croissance
Belize								**Belize**
GDP at current prices	209	587	1 114	1 397	1 779	1 820	1 902	PIB aux prix courants
GDP per capita	1 268	2 834	3 933	4 344	4 950	4 960	5 077	PIB par habitant
GDP at constant prices	358	708	1 235	1 397	1 611	1 603	1 610	PIB aux prix constants
Growth rates	1.0	4.2	3.0	3.3	3.8	-0.5	0.5	Taux de croissance
Benin								**Bénin**
GDP at current prices	1 130	2 345	4 804	6 970	8 454	8 572	9 236	PIB aux prix courants
GDP per capita	264	397	602	758	799	788	826	PIB par habitant
GDP at constant prices	2 604	3 727	5 773	6 970	9 108	9 563	10 041	PIB aux prix constants
Growth rates	7.5	10.1	1.7	2.1	6.5	5.0	5.0	Taux de croissance
Bermuda								**Bermudes**
GDP at current prices	1 428	2 557	4 868	5 853	5 891	6 093	6 269	PIB aux prix courants
GDP per capita	24 241	40 780	74 745	91 516	95 006	98 809	102 192	PIB par habitant
GDP at constant prices	3 726	4 273	5 840	5 853	5 244	5 238	5 369	PIB aux prix constants
Growth rates	4.2	5.4	1.7	-2.5	0.4	-0.1	2.5	Taux de croissance

13

Gross domestic product and gross domestic product per capita *(continued)*
In millions of US dollars at current and constant 2010 prices; per capita US dollars; real rates of growth

Produit intérieur brut et produit intérieur brut par habitant *(suite)*
En millions de dollars É.-U. aux prix courants et constants de 2010; par habitant en dollars É.U.; taux de croissance réels

Country or area	1985	1995	2005	2010	2015	2016	2017	Pays ou zone
Bhutan								**Bhoutan**
GDP at current prices	172	289	819	1 585	2 059	2 213	2 562	PIB aux prix courants
GDP per capita	369	562	1 247	2 179	2 615	2 774	3 173	PIB par habitant
GDP at constant prices	214	491	1 008	1 585	2 069	2 235	2 369	PIB aux prix constants
Growth rates	5.7	6.8	7.1	11.7	6.6	8.0	6.0	Taux de croissance
Bolivia (Plurin. State of)								**Bolivie (État plurin. de)**
GDP at current prices	4 122	6 715	9 549	19 650	33 000	33 941	37 509	PIB aux prix courants
GDP per capita	664	887	1 046	1 981	3 077	3 117	3 394	PIB par habitant
GDP at constant prices	8 325	11 383	15 697	19 650	25 664	26 759	27 881	PIB aux prix constants
Growth rates	-1.0	4.7	4.4	4.1	4.9	4.3	4.2	Taux de croissance
Bosnia and Herzegovina								**Bosnie-Herzégovine**
GDP at current prices	...	2 034	11 223	17 176	16 210	16 911	18 169	PIB aux prix courants
GDP per capita	...	529	2 968	4 615	4 584	4 809	5 181	PIB par habitant
GDP at constant prices	...	4 249	14 922	17 176	18 351	18 928	19 502	PIB aux prix constants
Growth rates	...	20.8	3.9	0.9	3.1	3.1	3.0	Taux de croissance
Botswana								**Botswana**
GDP at current prices	838	4 731	9 931	12 787	14 421	15 649	17 407	PIB aux prix courants
GDP per capita	704	3 015	5 351	6 346	6 528	6 954	7 596	PIB par habitant
GDP at constant prices	2 856	6 649	10 231	12 787	16 146	16 843	17 241	PIB aux prix constants
Growth rates	9.2	7.0	4.6	8.6	-1.7	4.3	2.4	Taux de croissance
Brazil								**Brésil**
GDP at current prices	187 460	778 053	891 634	2 208 838	1 802 212	1 792 800	2 055 512	PIB aux prix courants
GDP per capita	1 382	4 794	4 770	11 224	8 750	8 634	9 821	PIB par habitant
GDP at constant prices	1 102 866	1 400 990	1 774 773	2 208 838	2 331 897	2 251 150	2 273 334	PIB aux prix constants
Growth rates	7.8	4.2	3.2	7.5	-3.8	-3.5	1.0	Taux de croissance
British Virgin Islands								**Îles Vierges britanniques**
GDP at current prices	45	389	853	876	955	971	996	PIB aux prix courants
GDP per capita	3 396	21 114	36 802	32 183	31 698	31 677	31 917	PIB par habitant
GDP at constant prices	100	563	921	876	889	892	897	PIB aux prix constants
Growth rates	1.4	24.1	15.5	-0.1	0.3	0.3	0.5	Taux de croissance
Brunei Darussalam								**Brunéi Darussalam**
GDP at current prices	4 425	5 245	10 561	13 707	12 930	11 400	12 128	PIB aux prix courants
GDP per capita	19 712	17 650	28 923	35 267	30 968	26 939	28 291	PIB par habitant
GDP at constant prices	10 494	11 205	13 264	13 707	13 639	13 301	13 478	PIB aux prix constants
Growth rates	-1.5	4.5	0.4	2.6	-0.4	-2.5	1.3	Taux de croissance
Bulgaria								**Bulgarie**
GDP at current prices	16 486	14 433	29 636	50 610	50 201	53 240	58 222	PIB aux prix courants
GDP per capita	1 837	1 723	3 857	6 835	6 994	7 465	8 218	PIB par habitant
GDP at constant prices	37 424	35 336	42 593	50 610	54 636	56 787	58 951	PIB aux prix constants
Growth rates	2.7	2.9	7.1	1.3	3.5	3.9	3.8	Taux de croissance
Burkina Faso								**Burkina Faso**
GDP at current prices	1 569	2 404	5 463	8 980	10 416	10 864	12 325	PIB aux prix courants
GDP per capita	203	238	407	575	575	583	642	PIB par habitant
GDP at constant prices	2 627	3 681	6 872	8 980	11 688	12 379	13 162	PIB aux prix constants
Growth rates	8.5	5.7	8.7	8.4	3.9	5.9	6.3	Taux de croissance
Burundi								**Burundi**
GDP at current prices	1 171	1 000	1 117	2 032	2 811	2 916	3 155	PIB aux prix courants
GDP per capita	249[1]	168	150	232	276	277	290	PIB par habitant
GDP at constant prices	1 461	1 563	1 629	2 032	2 404	2 472	2 472	PIB aux prix constants
Growth rates	11.7	-7.0	0.9	5.1	-0.4	2.8	~0.0	Taux de croissance
Cabo Verde								**Cabo Verde**
GDP at current prices	157	558	1 105	1 664	1 596	1 663	1 773	PIB aux prix courants
GDP per capita	497	1 434	2 329	3 313	2 995	3 082	3 245	PIB par habitant
GDP at constant prices	430	671	1 302	1 664	1 792	1 876	1 951	PIB aux prix constants
Growth rates	8.6	7.5	6.5	1.5	1.0	4.7	4.0	Taux de croissance
Cambodia								**Cambodge**
GDP at current prices	1 059	3 309	6 293	11 242	18 050	20 017	22 121	PIB aux prix courants
GDP per capita	137	311	474	786	1 163	1 270	1 382	PIB par habitant
GDP at constant prices	1 824	3 688	8 138	11 242	15 904	16 998	18 189	PIB aux prix constants
Growth rates	4.7	5.9	13.2	6.0	7.0	6.9	7.0	Taux de croissance
Cameroon								**Cameroun**
GDP at current prices	9 597	9 641	17 944	26 144	30 905	32 618	34 924	PIB aux prix courants
GDP per capita	955	716	1 030	1 309	1 353	1 392	1 452	PIB par habitant
GDP at constant prices	19 199	14 338	22 022	26 144	33 558	35 118	36 365	PIB aux prix constants
Growth rates	2.4	3.5	2.0	3.4	5.7	4.6	3.5	Taux de croissance

Gross domestic product and gross domestic product per capita *(continued)*
In millions of US dollars at current and constant 2010 prices; per capita US dollars; real rates of growth

Produit intérieur brut et produit intérieur brut par habitant *(suite)*
En millions de dollars É.-U. aux prix courants et constants de 2010; par habitant en dollars É.U.; taux de croissance réels

Country or area	1985	1995	2005	2010	2015	2016	2017	Pays ou zone
Canada								**Canada**
GDP at current prices	364 761	604 014	1 169 393	1 613 463	1 552 523	1 526 954	1 647 120	PIB aux prix courants
GDP per capita	14 098	20 594	36 218	47 221	43 186	42 077	44 974	PIB par habitant
GDP at constant prices	890 993	1 102 814	1 524 530	1 613 463	1 802 512	1 828 001	1 883 707	PIB aux prix constants
Growth rates	4.7	2.7	3.2	3.1	1.0	1.4	3.0	Taux de croissance
Cayman Islands								**Îles Caïmanes**
GDP at current prices	416	1 296	3 042	3 267	3 753	3 900	4 030	PIB aux prix courants
GDP per capita	21 544	40 930	62 559	58 859	62 592	64 179	65 472	PIB par habitant
GDP at constant prices	995	1 993	3 366	3 267	3 577	3 704	3 789	PIB aux prix constants
Growth rates	3.5	4.8	6.5	-2.7	2.8	3.5	2.3	Taux de croissance
Central African Republic								**République centrafricaine**
GDP at current prices	905	1 167	1 413	2 034	1 632	1 810	1 993	PIB aux prix courants
GDP per capita	344	348	342	457	359	394	428	PIB par habitant
GDP at constant prices	1 426	1 591	1 723	2 034	1 431	1 496	1 561	PIB aux prix constants
Growth rates	3.3	5.2	2.4	3.6	4.8	4.5	4.3	Taux de croissance
Chad								**Tchad**
GDP at current prices	987	1 643	6 681	10 970	11 733	10 953	10 717	PIB aux prix courants
GDP per capita	194	235	664	923	838	758	719	PIB par habitant
GDP at constant prices	2 353	3 269	7 449	10 970	13 101	12 747	12 346	PIB aux prix constants
Growth rates	7.9	1.4	7.9	15.0	3.8	-2.7	-3.1	Taux de croissance
Chile								**Chili**
GDP at current prices	18 985	75 099	122 965	218 538	243 999	250 036	277 081	PIB aux prix courants
GDP per capita	1 559	5 253	7 615	12 860	13 737	13 961	15 347	PIB par habitant
GDP at constant prices	56 647	118 979	181 652	218 538	264 555	267 904	271 896	PIB aux prix constants
Growth rates	2.0	10.6	6.2	5.8	2.3	1.3	1.5	Taux de croissance
China [2]								**Chine** [2]
GDP at current prices	309 839	734 485	2 285 960	6 100 648	11 064 687	11 191 030	12 237 782	PIB aux prix courants
GDP per capita	289	592	1 730	4 487	7 920	7 974	8 682	PIB par habitant
GDP at constant prices	566 341	1 479 036	3 569 998	6 100 648	8 908 435	9 507 063	10 158 897	PIB aux prix constants
Growth rates	13.4	11.0	11.4	10.6	6.9	6.7	6.9	Taux de croissance
China, Hong Kong SAR								**Chine, RAS de Hong Kong**
GDP at current prices	35 700	144 652	181 569	228 639	309 386	320 874	341 659	PIB aux prix courants
GDP per capita	6 688	23 559	26 593	32 545	42 699	43 938	46 390	PIB par habitant
GDP at constant prices	71 743	134 780	188 650	228 639	264 388	270 039	280 363	PIB aux prix constants
Growth rates	0.8	2.4	7.4	6.8	2.4	2.1	3.8	Taux de croissance
China, Macao SAR								**Chine, RAS de Macao**
GDP at current prices	1 349	6 996	12 092	28 124	45 362	45 311	50 361	PIB aux prix courants
GDP per capita	4 756	18 139	25 059	52 375	75 485	74 018	80 893	PIB par habitant
GDP at constant prices	4 967	9 852	16 526	28 124	32 199	31 921	34 824	PIB aux prix constants
Growth rates	0.7	3.3	8.1	25.3	-21.6	-0.9	9.1	Taux de croissance
Colombia								**Colombie**
GDP at current prices	49 322	110 292	146 566	287 018	291 520	280 091	309 191	PIB aux prix courants
GDP per capita	1 590	2 946	3 386	6 251	6 045	5 757	6 302	PIB par habitant
GDP at constant prices	118 422	183 904	229 937	287 018	359 120	366 457	372 936	PIB aux prix constants
Growth rates	3.1	5.2	4.7	4.0	3.1	2.0	1.8	Taux de croissance
Comoros								**Comores**
GDP at current prices	240	483	787	907	988	1 021	1 082	PIB aux prix courants
GDP per capita	675	1 016	1 287	1 315	1 271	1 283	1 330	PIB par habitant
GDP at constant prices	633	747	907	907	1 179	1 227	1 269	PIB aux prix constants
Growth rates	2.0	3.6	2.8	4.8	2.0	4.1	3.4	Taux de croissance
Congo								**Congo**
GDP at current prices	2 339	2 207	6 350	13 678	11 092	10 100	11 292	PIB aux prix courants
GDP per capita	1 099	789	1 708	3 118	2 220	1 970	2 147	PIB par habitant
GDP at constant prices	6 860	6 844	9 410	13 678	14 081	13 683	13 258	PIB aux prix constants
Growth rates	-1.2	4.0	7.6	15.0	-13.2	-2.8	-3.1	Taux de croissance
Cook Islands								**Îles Cook**
GDP at current prices	28	106	183	255	285	288	309	PIB aux prix courants
GDP per capita	1 591	5 588	9 262	13 758	16 350	16 572	17 798	PIB par habitant
GDP at constant prices	140	201	257	255	293	310	316	PIB aux prix constants
Growth rates	8.8	-4.4	-1.1	-3.0	3.8	5.9	1.9	Taux de croissance
Costa Rica								**Costa Rica**
GDP at current prices	4 989	11 507	19 952	37 269	54 776	56 989	57 565	PIB aux prix courants
GDP per capita	1 827	3 278	4 697	8 199	11 393	11 733	11 734	PIB par habitant
GDP at constant prices	12 177	19 824	29 540	37 269	44 694	46 551	48 037	PIB aux prix constants
Growth rates	0.7	4.1	3.9	5.0	3.6	4.2	3.2	Taux de croissance

Gross domestic product and gross domestic product per capita *(continued)*
In millions of US dollars at current and constant 2010 prices; per capita US dollars; real rates of growth

Produit intérieur brut et produit intérieur brut par habitant *(suite)*
En millions de dollars É.-U. aux prix courants et constants de 2010; par habitant en dollars É.U.; taux de croissance réels

Country or area	1985	1995	2005	2010	2015	2016	2017	Pays ou zone
Côte d'Ivoire								**Côte d'Ivoire**
GDP at current prices	6 978	11 105	17 085	24 885	33 119	35 293	38 055	PIB aux prix courants
GDP per capita	683[1]	764[1]	932	1 220	1 433	1 489	1 566	PIB par habitant
GDP at constant prices	15 125	18 833	22 299	24 885	33 960	36 667	39 491	PIB aux prix constants
Growth rates	4.5	7.1	1.7	2.0	8.8	8.0	7.7	Taux de croissance
Croatia								**Croatie**
GDP at current prices	...	22 388	45 347	59 866	49 519	51 624	55 201	PIB aux prix courants
GDP per capita	...	4 849	10 358	13 832	11 690	12 253	13 177	PIB par habitant
GDP at constant prices	...	39 561	58 176	59 866	59 343	61 442	63 237	PIB aux prix constants
Growth rates	...	6.8	4.1	-1.5	2.4	3.5	2.9	Taux de croissance
Cuba								**Cuba**
GDP at current prices	22 921	30 428	42 644	64 328	87 206	91 370	96 851	PIB aux prix courants
GDP per capita	2 273	2 790	3 779	5 676	7 609	7 962	8 433	PIB par habitant
GDP at constant prices	45 176	31 019	49 481	64 328	73 869	74 248	75 572	PIB aux prix constants
Growth rates	1.6	2.5	11.2	2.4	4.4	0.5	1.8	Taux de croissance
Curaçao								**Curaçao**
GDP at current prices	...	...	2 345	2 951	3 152	3 122	...	PIB aux prix courants
GDP per capita	...	...	18 120	19 994	19 948	19 591	...	PIB par habitant
GDP at constant prices	...	...	2 786	2 951	2 916	2 888	2 837	PIB aux prix constants
Growth rates	...	...	...	0.1	0.3	-1.0	-1.7	Taux de croissance
Cyprus [3]								**Chypre [3]**
GDP at current prices	2 682	9 827	18 967	25 561	19 681	20 453	22 054	PIB aux prix courants
GDP per capita	4 957	15 102	25 682	30 817	23 236	24 110	25 790	PIB par habitant
GDP at constant prices	8 351	15 096	22 568	25 561	23 627	24 763	25 811	PIB aux prix constants
Growth rates	4.7	9.9	4.9	1.3	2.0	4.8	4.2	Taux de croissance
Czechia								**Tchéquie**
GDP at current prices	...	59 774	136 281	207 478	186 830	195 090	215 825	PIB aux prix courants
GDP per capita	...	5 771	13 285	19 692	17 619	18 386	20 326	PIB par habitant
GDP at constant prices	...	139 036	183 918	207 478	225 493	231 018	240 919	PIB aux prix constants
Growth rates	...	6.2	6.5	2.3	5.3	2.5	4.3	Taux de croissance
Dem. People's Rep. Korea								**Rép. pop. dém. de Corée**
GDP at current prices	12 075	4 849	13 031	13 945	16 283	16 789	17 365	PIB aux prix courants
GDP per capita	722	222	548	570	648	665	685	PIB par habitant
GDP at constant prices	16 158	12 982	14 023	13 945	14 377	14 933	14 413	PIB aux prix constants
Growth rates	3.7	-4.4	3.8	-0.5	-1.1	3.9	-3.5	Taux de croissance
Dem. Rep. of the Congo								**Rép. dém. du Congo**
GDP at current prices	7 524	8 947	11 965	21 566	37 918	40 338	37 642	PIB aux prix courants
GDP per capita	252	215	219	334	498	512	463	PIB par habitant
GDP at constant prices	24 387	16 680	16 467	21 566	31 338	32 090	33 278	PIB aux prix constants
Growth rates	0.5	0.7	6.1	7.1	6.9	2.4	3.7	Taux de croissance
Denmark								**Danemark**
GDP at current prices	62 659	185 008	264 467	321 995	302 673	311 988	329 866	PIB aux prix courants
GDP per capita	12 252	35 356	48 779	57 967	53 206	54 621	57 533	PIB par habitant
GDP at constant prices	213 347	257 078	318 623	321 995	343 294	351 532	359 485	PIB aux prix constants
Growth rates	4.0	3.0	2.3	1.9	2.3	2.4	2.3	Taux de croissance
Djibouti								**Djibouti**
GDP at current prices	360	497	674	1 015	1 634	1 764	1 845	PIB aux prix courants
GDP per capita	846	788	861	1 192	1 762	1 872	1 928	PIB par habitant
GDP at constant prices	551	632	748	1 015	1 394	1 516	1 578	PIB aux prix constants
Growth rates	-0.2	5.6	3.2	3.5	9.7	8.7	4.1	Taux de croissance
Dominica								**Dominique**
GDP at current prices	117	260	370	494	541	575	497	PIB aux prix courants
GDP per capita	1 586	3 639	5 245	6 912	7 392	7 825	6 719	PIB par habitant
GDP at constant prices	243	344	413	494	495	507	459	PIB aux prix constants
Growth rates	1.3	2.0	-0.3	1.2	-2.6	2.5	-9.5	Taux de croissance
Dominican Republic								**République dominicaine**
GDP at current prices	5 618	15 747	35 510	53 160	68 802	72 343	75 932	PIB aux prix courants
GDP per capita	866	1 995	3 844	5 371	6 535	6 794	7 052	PIB par habitant
GDP at constant prices	15 876	23 630	39 230	53 160	68 042	72 541	75 843	PIB aux prix constants
Growth rates	-2.1	5.5	9.3	8.3	7.0	6.6	4.6	Taux de croissance
Ecuador								**Équateur**
GDP at current prices	17 141	24 421	41 507	69 555	99 290	98 614	104 296	PIB aux prix courants
GDP per capita	1 895	2 135	3 022	4 657	6 150	6 019	6 273	PIB par habitant
GDP at constant prices	33 225	44 018	58 876	69 555	86 419	85 057	87 606	PIB aux prix constants
Growth rates	3.9	2.3	5.3	3.5	0.1	-1.6	3.0	Taux de croissance

13 Gross domestic product and gross domestic product per capita *(continued)*
In millions of US dollars at current and constant 2010 prices; per capita US dollars; real rates of growth

Produit intérieur brut et produit intérieur brut par habitant *(suite)*
En millions de dollars É.-U. aux prix courants et constants de 2010; par habitant en dollars É.U.; taux de croissance réels

Country or area	1985	1995	2005	2010	2015	2016	2017	Pays ou zone
Egypt								**Égypte**
GDP at current prices	23 801	65 758	94 456	214 630	317 745	270 255	195 136	PIB aux prix courants
GDP per capita	474	1 032	1 230	2 552	3 388	2 824	2 000	PIB par habitant
GDP at constant prices	63 151	102 915	159 056	214 630	245 076	255 728	266 421	PIB aux prix constants
Growth rates	6.8	4.6	4.5	5.1	4.4	4.3	4.2	Taux de croissance
El Salvador								**El Salvador**
GDP at current prices	5 183	8 922	14 698	18 448	23 166	23 912	24 805	PIB aux prix courants
GDP per capita	1 053	1 590	2 438	2 993	3 670	3 769	3 889	PIB par habitant
GDP at constant prices	8 894	13 169	17 193	18 448	20 318	20 842	21 325	PIB aux prix constants
Growth rates	2.0	6.4	3.6	1.4	2.4	2.6	2.3	Taux de croissance
Equatorial Guinea								**Guinée équatoriale**
GDP at current prices	88	215	8 520	16 299	13 176	11 253	12 487	PIB aux prix courants
GDP per capita	246	427	11 250	17 136	11 209	9 213	9 850	PIB par habitant
GDP at constant prices	574	926	12 349	16 299	16 457	15 046	14 561	PIB aux prix constants
Growth rates	12.9	11.7	8.9	-8.9	-9.1	-8.6	-3.2	Taux de croissance
Eritrea								**Érythrée**
GDP at current prices	...	640	1 098	2 117	4 442	5 005	5 813	PIB aux prix courants
GDP per capita	...	207	277	482	916	1 010	1 147	PIB par habitant
GDP at constant prices	...	1 844	2 201	2 117	2 719	2 770	2 909	PIB aux prix constants
Growth rates	...	20.9	1.5	2.2	2.6	1.9	5.0	Taux de croissance
Estonia								**Estonie**
GDP at current prices	...	4 423	14 003	19 503	22 567	23 338	25 921	PIB aux prix courants
GDP per capita	...	3 086	10 330	14 640	17 157	17 782	19 793	PIB par habitant
GDP at constant prices	...	10 494	19 902	19 503	23 341	23 823	24 979	PIB aux prix constants
Growth rates	...	4.3	9.6	2.3	1.7	2.1	4.9	Taux de croissance
Eswatini								**Eswatini**
GDP at current prices	539	1 902	3 178	4 439	4 020	3 721	4 409	PIB aux prix courants
GDP per capita	764	1 979	2 874	3 690	3 048	2 770	3 224	PIB par habitant
GDP at constant prices	1 427	2 799	3 773	4 439	5 176	5 246	5 351	PIB aux prix constants
Growth rates	1.9	4.8	6.0	3.8	0.4	1.4	2.0	Taux de croissance
Ethiopia								**Éthiopie**
GDP at current prices	...	7 587	12 164	26 311	63 079	70 314	75 605	PIB aux prix courants
GDP per capita	...	132	159	300	632	687	720	PIB par habitant
GDP at constant prices	...	9 196	15 699	26 311	43 538	46 831	52 035	PIB aux prix constants
Growth rates	...	6.1	11.8	12.6	10.4	7.6	11.1	Taux de croissance
Fiji								**Fidji**
GDP at current prices	1 143	1 993	2 980	3 140	4 362	4 575	4 874	PIB aux prix courants
GDP per capita	1 605	2 570	3 627	3 652	4 890	5 090	5 382	PIB par habitant
GDP at constant prices	1 753	2 423	3 033	3 140	3 756	3 781	3 895	PIB aux prix constants
Growth rates	-3.9	2.5	0.7	3.0	3.8	0.7	3.0	Taux de croissance
Finland								**Finlande**
GDP at current prices	55 914	134 196	204 431	247 800	232 465	239 052	252 247	PIB aux prix courants
GDP per capita	11 385	26 215	38 873	46 181	42 405	43 439	45 670	PIB par habitant
GDP at constant prices	141 128	163 434	237 928	247 800	247 409	253 539	260 631	PIB aux prix constants
Growth rates	3.5	4.2	2.8	3.0	0.1	2.5	2.8	Taux de croissance
France [4]								**France** [4]
GDP at current prices	553 143	1 600 997	2 196 071	2 642 610	2 438 208	2 465 134	2 582 492	PIB aux prix courants
GDP per capita	9 737	26 707	34 724	40 565	36 574	36 822	38 415	PIB par habitant
GDP at constant prices	1 604 225	2 019 538	2 536 821	2 642 610	2 781 288	2 813 858	2 874 672	PIB aux prix constants
Growth rates	1.6	2.1	1.7	1.9	1.1	1.2	2.2	Taux de croissance
French Polynesia								**Polynésie française**
GDP at current prices	1 716	4 421	5 703	6 081	5 262	5 368	5 606	PIB aux prix courants
GDP per capita	9 795	20 542	22 374	22 704	18 950	19 156	19 807	PIB par habitant
GDP at constant prices	3 751	4 934	6 344	6 081	5 982	6 070	6 212	PIB aux prix constants
Growth rates	5.4	0.5	1.4	-2.5	1.3	1.5	2.3	Taux de croissance
Gabon								**Gabon**
GDP at current prices	4 639	5 519	9 579	14 359	14 372	13 992	14 623	PIB aux prix courants
GDP per capita	5 589	5 081	6 827	8 754	7 446	7 068	7 221	PIB par habitant
GDP at constant prices	10 467	12 922	13 498	14 359	18 527	18 913	19 121	PIB aux prix constants
Growth rates	-2.3	5.0	1.1	7.1	3.9	2.1	1.1	Taux de croissance
Gambia								**Gambie**
GDP at current prices	990	1 189	944	1 441	1 394	1 442	1 489	PIB aux prix courants
GDP per capita	1 352	1 115	654	851	705	708	709	PIB par habitant
GDP at constant prices	602	792	1 147	1 441	1 603	1 610	1 683	PIB aux prix constants
Growth rates	3.4	0.9	-0.9	6.5	5.9	0.4	4.6	Taux de croissance

Gross domestic product and gross domestic product per capita *(continued)*
In millions of US dollars at current and constant 2010 prices; per capita US dollars; real rates of growth

Produit intérieur brut et produit intérieur brut par habitant *(suite)*
En millions de dollars É.-U. aux prix courants et constants de 2010; par habitant en dollars É.U.; taux de croissance réels

Country or area	1985	1995	2005	2010	2015	2016	2017	Pays ou zone
Georgia								**Géorgie**
GDP at current prices	...	2 703	6 411	11 638	13 993	14 378	15 159	PIB aux prix courants
GDP per capita	...	539	1 429	2 750	3 541	3 663	3 875	PIB par habitant
GDP at constant prices	...	4 766	9 011	11 638	14 768	15 189	15 923	PIB aux prix constants
Growth rates	...	2.6	9.6	6.2	2.9	2.8	4.8	Taux de croissance
Germany								**Allemagne**
GDP at current prices	729 751	2 591 447	2 861 339	3 417 095	3 381 389	3 495 163	3 693 204	PIB aux prix courants
GDP per capita	9 390	31 898	35 035	42 241	41 384	42 668	44 976	PIB par habitant
GDP at constant prices	2 183 636	2 840 972	3 213 777	3 417 095	3 718 482	3 801 859	3 883 870	PIB aux prix constants
Growth rates	2.3	1.7	0.7	4.1	1.7	2.2	2.2	Taux de croissance
Ghana								**Ghana**
GDP at current prices	8 743	13 714	22 765	42 587	49 182	55 010	58 996	PIB aux prix courants
GDP per capita	688	818	1 057	1 737	1 783	1 950	2 046	PIB par habitant
GDP at constant prices	12 673	19 742	31 614	42 587	59 891	61 956	67 001	PIB aux prix constants
Growth rates	5.1	4.0	6.2	7.9	2.2	3.4	8.1	Taux de croissance
Greece								**Grèce**
GDP at current prices	47 816	136 886	247 777	299 362	196 591	195 222	203 086	PIB aux prix courants
GDP per capita	4 794	12 687	21 925	26 154	17 525	17 456	18 198	PIB par habitant
GDP at constant prices	185 846	210 286	304 331	299 362	244 719	244 251	247 927	PIB aux prix constants
Growth rates	2.5	2.1	0.6	-5.5	-0.4	-0.2	1.5	Taux de croissance
Greenland								**Groenland**
GDP at current prices	451	1 321	1 850	2 503	2 499	2 714	2 790	PIB aux prix courants
GDP per capita	8 482	23 671	32 481	44 196	44 329	48 102	49 398	PIB par habitant
GDP at constant prices	1 416	1 573	2 127	2 503	2 544	2 695	2 722	PIB aux prix constants
Growth rates	3.7	3.7	5.0	1.7	-2.5	6.0	1.0	Taux de croissance
Grenada								**Grenade**
GDP at current prices	136	278	695	771	997	1 062	1 127	PIB aux prix courants
GDP per capita	1 359	2 775	6 755	7 366	9 333	9 892	10 451	PIB par habitant
GDP at constant prices	325	470	807	771	898	932	979	PIB aux prix constants
Growth rates	8.1	2.1	13.3	-0.5	6.4	3.7	5.1	Taux de croissance
Guatemala								**Guatemala**
GDP at current prices	9 967	13 066	27 211	41 338	63 767	68 663	75 620	PIB aux prix courants
GDP per capita	1 210	1 255	2 078	2 825	3 924	4 141	4 471	PIB par habitant
GDP at constant prices	17 225	24 523	34 551	41 338	49 879	51 421	52 841	PIB aux prix constants
Growth rates	-0.6	5.0	3.3	2.9	4.1	3.1	2.8	Taux de croissance
Guinea								**Guinée**
GDP at current prices	2 848	5 260	4 063	6 853	8 794	8 694	10 208	PIB aux prix courants
GDP per capita	560	668	420	635	727	701	803	PIB par habitant
GDP at constant prices	2 771	4 122	5 964	6 853	8 579	9 475	10 257	PIB aux prix constants
Growth rates	5.0	4.7	3.0	4.8	3.8	10.5	8.2	Taux de croissance
Guinea-Bissau								**Guinée-Bissau**
GDP at current prices	415	800	587	849	1 047	1 178	1 347	PIB aux prix courants
GDP per capita	462	703	425	546	592	649	724	PIB par habitant
GDP at constant prices	459	644	720	849	998	1 061	1 123	PIB aux prix constants
Growth rates	4.3	4.0	4.3	4.6	6.1	6.3	5.9	Taux de croissance
Guyana								**Guyana**
GDP at current prices	737	991	1 315	2 259	3 166	3 504	3 543	PIB aux prix courants
GDP per capita	956	1 302	1 752	3 026	4 120	4 531	4 555	PIB par habitant
GDP at constant prices	1 232	1 541	1 826	2 259	2 813	2 908	2 971	PIB aux prix constants
Growth rates	2.4	5.0	-2.0	4.1	3.1	3.4	2.2	Taux de croissance
Haiti								**Haïti**
GDP at current prices	2 665	2 696	4 154	6 708	8 355	7 598	8 521	PIB aux prix courants
GDP per capita	417	345	448	671	780	700	776	PIB par habitant
GDP at constant prices	6 649	5 865	6 462	6 708	7 899	8 013	8 107	PIB aux prix constants
Growth rates	0.6	9.9	1.8	-5.5	1.2	1.5	1.2	Taux de croissance
Honduras								**Honduras**
GDP at current prices	4 342	4 724	9 757	15 839	20 980	21 644	22 979	PIB aux prix courants
GDP per capita	1 014	828	1 323	1 933	2 341	2 375	2 480	PIB par habitant
GDP at constant prices	6 557	9 104	13 268	15 839	18 839	19 546	20 481	PIB aux prix constants
Growth rates	4.2	4.1	6.1	3.7	3.8	3.8	4.8	Taux de croissance
Hungary								**Hongrie**
GDP at current prices	23 709	46 432	113 035	130 923	123 074	126 008	139 761	PIB aux prix courants
GDP per capita	2 244	4 486	11 207	13 187	12 579	12 920	14 376	PIB par habitant
GDP at constant prices	101 587	92 506	132 407	130 923	144 236	147 526	153 629	PIB aux prix constants
Growth rates	-0.3	1.5	4.4	0.7	3.5	2.3	4.1	Taux de croissance

13 Gross domestic product and gross domestic product per capita *(continued)*
In millions of US dollars at current and constant 2010 prices; per capita US dollars; real rates of growth

Produit intérieur brut et produit intérieur brut par habitant *(suite)*
En millions de dollars É.-U. aux prix courants et constants de 2010; par habitant en dollars É.U.; taux de croissance réels

Country or area	1985	1995	2005	2010	2015	2016	2017	Pays ou zone
Iceland								**Islande**
GDP at current prices	2 940	7 018	16 813	13 684	17 344	20 716	24 477	PIB aux prix courants
GDP per capita	12 169	26 223	56 996	42 718	52 519	62 309	73 060	PIB par habitant
GDP at constant prices	6 769	8 017	12 948	13 684	15 682	16 835	17 507	PIB aux prix constants
Growth rates	3.3	0.1	6.3	-3.4	4.5	7.4	4.0	Taux de croissance
India								**Inde**
GDP at current prices	222 557	362 877	823 612	1 669 620	2 145 537	2 270 060	2 575 667	PIB aux prix courants
GDP per capita	285	378	720	1 356	1 639	1 714	1 923	PIB par habitant
GDP at constant prices	371 307	649 063	1 189 601	1 669 620	2 290 085	2 452 971	2 616 859	PIB aux prix constants
Growth rates	5.5	7.6	7.9	8.5	8.2	7.1	6.7	Taux de croissance
Indonesia								**Indonésie**
GDP at current prices	102 171	236 456	304 372	755 094	860 854	932 256	1 015 539	PIB aux prix courants
GDP per capita	617	1 195	1 343	3 113	3 335	3 570	3 847	PIB par habitant
GDP at constant prices	214 637	437 210	571 205	755 094	988 129	1 037 864	1 090 459	PIB aux prix constants
Growth rates	2.5	8.2	5.7	6.2	4.9	5.0	5.1	Taux de croissance
Iran (Islamic Republic of)								**Iran (Rép. islamique d')**
GDP at current prices	76 257	114 364	226 452	491 099	393 436	425 403	460 976	PIB aux prix courants
GDP per capita	1 611	1 888	3 216	6 586	4 958	5 299	5 680	PIB par habitant
GDP at constant prices	222 796	262 362	403 657	491 099	480 662	545 053	565 521	PIB aux prix constants
Growth rates	1.9	2.4	3.2	5.8	-1.3	13.4	3.8	Taux de croissance
Iraq								**Iraq**
GDP at current prices	12 074	3 477	36 268	117 138	161 316	161 530	182 024	PIB aux prix courants
GDP per capita	775	172	1 343	3 808	4 467	4 342	4 756	PIB par habitant
GDP at constant prices	49 034	29 296	88 107	117 138	190 599	208 842	210 990	PIB aux prix constants
Growth rates	-~0.0	-18.3	4.4	5.5	3.8	9.6	1.0	Taux de croissance
Ireland								**Irlande**
GDP at current prices	21 296	69 225	211 644	222 134	291 092	302 243	331 430	PIB aux prix courants
GDP per capita	5 974	18 958	50 236	48 009	61 933	63 952	69 604	PIB par habitant
GDP at constant prices	66 270	104 604	214 526	222 134	316 887	332 635	358 589	PIB aux prix constants
Growth rates	3.1	9.6	6.0	1.8	25.8	5.0	7.8	Taux de croissance
Israel								**Israël**
GDP at current prices	27 379	100 239	142 411	233 733	300 471	319 378	353 268	PIB aux prix courants
GDP per capita	6 706	18 793	21 568	31 475	37 258	38 987	42 452	PIB par habitant
GDP at constant prices	76 059	133 128	188 895	233 733	279 247	290 439	300 480	PIB aux prix constants
Growth rates	4.0	8.7	4.1	5.5	2.6	4.0	3.5	Taux de croissance
Italy								**Italie**
GDP at current prices	450 706	1 170 824	1 852 616	2 125 058	1 832 273	1 869 117	1 943 835	PIB aux prix courants
GDP per capita	7 905	20 449	31 503	35 578	30 792	31 451	32 747	PIB par habitant
GDP at constant prices	1 499 984	1 866 192	2 158 722	2 125 058	2 062 368	2 085 992	2 118 779	PIB aux prix constants
Growth rates	2.8	2.9	0.9	1.7	0.9	1.1	1.6	Taux de croissance
Jamaica								**Jamaïque**
GDP at current prices	2 605	6 578	11 244	13 219	14 187	14 077	14 827	PIB aux prix courants
GDP per capita	1 114	2 592	4 097	4 692	4 940	4 886	5 130	PIB par habitant
GDP at constant prices	8 555	12 565	13 545	13 219	13 643	13 837	13 972	PIB aux prix constants
Growth rates	-4.6	1.0	0.9	-1.5	0.9	1.4	1.0	Taux de croissance
Japan								**Japon**
GDP at current prices	1 398 893	5 449 118	4 755 410	5 700 098	4 394 978	4 949 273	4 872 415	PIB aux prix courants
GDP per capita	11 476	43 118	37 054	44 341	34 342	38 742	38 220	PIB par habitant
GDP at constant prices	3 700 733	5 063 812	5 672 307	5 700 098	5 996 414	6 052 672	6 157 659	PIB aux prix constants
Growth rates	5.2	2.7	1.7	4.2	1.4	0.9	1.7	Taux de croissance
Jordan								**Jordanie**
GDP at current prices	5 173	6 802	12 720	26 520	37 923	39 197	40 708	PIB aux prix courants
GDP per capita	1 786	1 488	2 226	3 692	4 140	4 145	4 196	PIB par habitant
GDP at constant prices	9 373	12 369	19 725	26 520	30 218	30 844	31 496	PIB aux prix constants
Growth rates	-2.7	6.2	8.1	2.7	2.6	2.1	2.1	Taux de croissance
Kazakhstan								**Kazakhstan**
GDP at current prices	...	20 563	57 124	148 047	184 388	137 278	159 407	PIB aux prix courants
GDP per capita	...	1 282	3 676	9 028	10 388	7 632	8 756	PIB par habitant
GDP at constant prices	...	59 128	109 540	148 047	188 652	190 714	198 400	PIB aux prix constants
Growth rates	...	-8.2	9.7	7.3	1.2	1.1	4.0	Taux de croissance
Kenya								**Kenya**
GDP at current prices	9 110	13 428	21 506	40 000	64 008	70 875	74 938	PIB aux prix courants
GDP per capita	464	491	597	967	1 355	1 463	1 508	PIB par habitant
GDP at constant prices	16 538	23 533	31 367	40 000	52 339	55 410	58 117	PIB aux prix constants
Growth rates	4.3	4.4	5.9	8.4	5.7	5.9	4.9	Taux de croissance

Gross domestic product and gross domestic product per capita *(continued)*
In millions of US dollars at current and constant 2010 prices; per capita US dollars; real rates of growth

Produit intérieur brut et produit intérieur brut par habitant *(suite)*
En millions de dollars É.-U. aux prix courants et constants de 2010; par habitant en dollars É.U.; taux de croissance réels

Country or area	1985	1995	2005	2010	2015	2016	2017	Pays ou zone
Kiribati								**Kiribati**
GDP at current prices	30	56	112	156	169	182	197	PIB aux prix courants
GDP per capita	468	720	1 215	1 521	1 505	1 587	1 694	PIB par habitant
GDP at constant prices	106	124	157	156	190	192	198	PIB aux prix constants
Growth rates	-4.6	-0.6	5.0	-0.9	10.3	1.1	3.1	Taux de croissance
Kosovo								**Kosovo**
GDP at current prices	...	5 304	3 680	5 830	6 440	6 714	7 228	PIB aux prix courants
GDP per capita	...	2 351	2 074	3 354	3 668	3 811	4 116	PIB par habitant
GDP at constant prices	...	4 213	4 536	5 830	6 819	7 096	7 396	PIB aux prix constants
Growth rates	...	8.1	3.9	3.3	4.1	4.1	4.2	Taux de croissance
Kuwait								**Koweït**
GDP at current prices	21 446	26 554	80 798	115 416	114 586	109 407	119 534	PIB aux prix courants
GDP per capita	12 333	16 487	35 490	38 497	29 114	26 997	28 897	PIB par habitant
GDP at constant prices	42 081	65 562	108 938	115 416	137 959	141 997	137 054	PIB aux prix constants
Growth rates	-4.3	1.4	10.6	-2.4	0.6	2.9	-3.5	Taux de croissance
Kyrgyzstan								**Kirghizistan**
GDP at current prices	...	1 492	2 460	4 794	6 678	6 813	7 565	PIB aux prix courants
GDP per capita	...	327	485	884	1 139	1 144	1 251	PIB par habitant
GDP at constant prices	...	2 440	3 859	4 794	6 083	6 347	6 638	PIB aux prix constants
Growth rates	...	-5.4	-0.2	-0.5	3.9	4.3	4.6	Taux de croissance
Lao People's Dem. Rep.								**Rép. dém. populaire lao**
GDP at current prices	626	1 852	2 946	7 313	14 390	15 806	16 853	PIB aux prix courants
GDP per capita	170	382	512	1 171	2 159	2 339	2 457	PIB par habitant
GDP at constant prices	1 616	2 692	4 982	7 313	10 631	11 378	12 162	PIB aux prix constants
Growth rates	5.1	7.5	6.8	8.1	7.3	7.0	6.9	Taux de croissance
Latvia								**Lettonie**
GDP at current prices	...	5 404	16 922	23 765	26 973	27 695	30 463	PIB aux prix courants
GDP per capita	...	2 154	7 514	11 216	13 536	14 055	15 625	PIB par habitant
GDP at constant prices	...	12 742	24 316	23 765	28 257	28 840	30 177	PIB aux prix constants
Growth rates	...	-1.1	10.7	-3.9	3.0	2.1	4.6	Taux de croissance
Lebanon								**Liban**
GDP at current prices	2 275	11 506	21 490	38 420	49 974	51 239	53 394	PIB aux prix courants
GDP per capita	850	3 793	5 390	8 858	8 540	8 530	8 778	PIB par habitant
GDP at constant prices	20 297	20 531	26 598	38 420	41 813	42 484	42 719	PIB aux prix constants
Growth rates	24.3	6.5	2.7	8.0	0.4	1.6	0.6	Taux de croissance
Lesotho								**Lesotho**
GDP at current prices	297	955	1 560	2 386	2 506	2 291	2 632	PIB aux prix courants
GDP per capita	202	542	800	1 169	1 152	1 040	1 178	PIB par habitant
GDP at constant prices	807	1 340	1 888	2 386	2 911	2 981	2 934	PIB aux prix constants
Growth rates	9.4	4.6	2.7	6.1	2.5	2.4	-1.6	Taux de croissance
Liberia								**Libéria**
GDP at current prices	1 076	209	706	1 292	2 669	2 757	2 763	PIB aux prix courants
GDP per capita	491	101	217	327	593	598	584	PIB par habitant
GDP at constant prices	1 197	174	662	1 292	1 871	1 862	1 908	PIB aux prix constants
Growth rates	-2.0	-4.3	5.3	7.3	9.3	-0.5	2.5	Taux de croissance
Libya								**Libye**
GDP at current prices	29 887	28 292	45 451	80 942	17 666	15 320	25 127	PIB aux prix courants
GDP per capita	7 715	5 717	7 846	13 121	2 833	2 434	3 942	PIB par habitant
GDP at constant prices	45 138	44 062	60 808	80 942	9 171	7 695	12 621	PIB aux prix constants
Growth rates	8.3	-2.2	10.3	4.3	-45.5	-16.1	64.0	Taux de croissance
Liechtenstein								**Liechtenstein**
GDP at current prices	681	2 695	4 046	5 621	6 269	6 215	6 296	PIB aux prix courants
GDP per capita	24 995	87 414	116 095	156 127	167 594	164 994	166 022	PIB par habitant
GDP at constant prices	2 441	3 456	5 047	5 621	5 892	6 007	6 049	PIB aux prix constants
Growth rates	7.0	1.9	4.8	7.4	~0.0	2.0	0.7	Taux de croissance
Lithuania								**Lituanie**
GDP at current prices	...	6 702	26 141	37 130	41 517	42 973	47 544	PIB aux prix courants
GDP per capita	...	1 848	7 817	11 886	14 160	14 776	16 450	PIB par habitant
GDP at constant prices	...	19 321	35 022	37 130	44 693	45 745	47 639	PIB aux prix constants
Growth rates	...	3.3	7.7	1.6	2.0	2.4	4.1	Taux de croissance
Luxembourg								**Luxembourg**
GDP at current prices	4 738	21 588	37 346	53 212	57 204	58 961	62 316	PIB aux prix courants
GDP per capita	12 915	52 894	81 571	104 772	100 936	102 408	106 806	PIB par habitant
GDP at constant prices	17 554	30 556	47 158	53 212	61 082	62 555	63 522	PIB aux prix constants
Growth rates	2.8	1.4	3.2	4.9	3.9	2.4	1.5	Taux de croissance

13

Gross domestic product and gross domestic product per capita *(continued)*
In millions of US dollars at current and constant 2010 prices; per capita US dollars; real rates of growth

Produit intérieur brut et produit intérieur brut par habitant *(suite)*
En millions de dollars É.-U. aux prix courants et constants de 2010; par habitant en dollars É.U.; taux de croissance réels

Country or area	1985	1995	2005	2010	2015	2016	2017	Pays ou zone
Madagascar								**Madagascar**
GDP at current prices	2 791	3 726	5 942	10 250	11 243	11 487	13 208	PIB aux prix courants
GDP per capita	277	277	324	485	464	461	517	PIB par habitant
GDP at constant prices	5 847	6 586	8 896	10 250	11 659	12 129	12 275	PIB aux prix constants
Growth rates	1.2	1.7	4.6	0.7	3.5	4.0	1.2	Taux de croissance
Malawi								**Malawi**
GDP at current prices	2 028	2 474	3 656	6 868	6 430	5 310	6 339	PIB aux prix courants
GDP per capita	281	250	280	453	366	294	340	PIB par habitant
GDP at constant prices	3 029	3 653	4 867	6 868	8 453	8 681	9 122	PIB aux prix constants
Growth rates	4.7	9.0	3.3	5.5	3.3	2.7	5.1	Taux de croissance
Malaysia								**Malaisie**
GDP at current prices	31 200	88 833	143 534	255 018	296 636	296 753	314 707	PIB aux prix courants
GDP per capita	2 000	4 334	5 594	9 071	9 655	9 515	9 951	PIB par habitant
GDP at constant prices	59 287	128 614	204 864	255 018	330 323	344 274	364 575	PIB aux prix constants
Growth rates	-1.1	9.8	5.3	7.4	5.1	4.2	5.9	Taux de croissance
Maldives								**Maldives**
GDP at current prices	166	566	1 163	2 588	4 109	4 414	4 866	PIB aux prix courants
GDP per capita	875	2 229	3 649	7 100	9 822	10 319	11 151	PIB par habitant
GDP at constant prices	513	1 169	1 749	2 588	3 413	3 661	3 914	PIB aux prix constants
Growth rates	13.0	7.1	-13.1	7.3	2.9	7.3	6.9	Taux de croissance
Mali								**Mali**
GDP at current prices	1 260	2 837	6 245	10 679	13 095	14 032	15 236	PIB aux prix courants
GDP per capita	161	295	488	708	750	780	822	PIB par habitant
GDP at constant prices	1 276	2 762	6 457	10 679	15 885	17 275	18 474	PIB aux prix constants
Growth rates	8.5	37.2	10.4	10.9	7.6	8.8	6.9	Taux de croissance
Malta								**Malte**
GDP at current prices	1 156	3 697	6 393	8 741	10 563	11 261	12 553	PIB aux prix courants
GDP per capita	3 311	9 722	15 716	21 005	24 703	26 227	29 137	PIB par habitant
GDP at constant prices	3 159	5 562	7 909	8 741	11 272	11 860	12 653	PIB aux prix constants
Growth rates	2.6	6.3	3.8	3.5	9.5	5.2	6.7	Taux de croissance
Marshall Islands								**Îles Marshall**
GDP at current prices	44	121	138	165	179	194	199	PIB aux prix courants
GDP per capita	1 155	2 379	2 651	3 143	3 386	3 665	3 753	PIB par habitant
GDP at constant prices	83	160	152	165	177	179	183	PIB aux prix constants
Growth rates	-6.3	8.2	2.9	6.4	0.6	0.9	2.5	Taux de croissance
Mauritania								**Mauritanie**
GDP at current prices	1 085	1 681	2 184	4 338	4 833	4 747	4 992	PIB aux prix courants
GDP per capita	613	722	698	1 202	1 155	1 104	1 129	PIB par habitant
GDP at constant prices	1 775	2 332	3 387	4 338	5 432	5 524	5 716	PIB aux prix constants
Growth rates	3.4	-2.4	9.0	4.8	0.9	1.7	3.5	Taux de croissance
Mauritius								**Maurice**
GDP at current prices	1 152	4 273	6 775	10 004	11 692	12 221	13 366	PIB aux prix courants
GDP per capita	1 134	3 786	5 544	8 016	9 284	9 683	10 565	PIB par habitant
GDP at constant prices	2 806	5 131	7 939	10 004	11 965	12 425	12 906	PIB aux prix constants
Growth rates	6.9	4.4	1.8	4.4	3.6	3.8	3.9	Taux de croissance
Mexico								**Mexique**
GDP at current prices	224 593	360 073	877 477	1 057 801	1 170 567	1 077 830	1 158 229	PIB aux prix courants
GDP per capita	2 903	3 829	8 089	9 016	9 298	8 451	8 967	PIB par habitant
GDP at constant prices	591 937	707 431	982 737	1 057 801	1 223 115	1 258 850	1 284 904	PIB aux prix constants
Growth rates	2.8	-6.3	2.3	5.1	3.3	2.9	2.1	Taux de croissance
Micronesia (Fed. States of)								**Micronésie (États féd. de)**
GDP at current prices	108	222	251	297	315	330	336	PIB aux prix courants
GDP per capita	1 262	2 063	2 360	2 862	3 018	3 144	3 188	PIB par habitant
GDP at constant prices	192	293	301	297	296	296	302	PIB aux prix constants
Growth rates	16.6	4.2	2.1	2.0	4.9	-0.1	2.0	Taux de croissance
Monaco								**Monaco**
GDP at current prices	1 059	3 070	4 203	5 362	6 259	6 468	6 401	PIB aux prix courants
GDP per capita	36 724	100 041	124 374	144 561	163 394	168 003	165 421	PIB par habitant
GDP at constant prices	3 101	3 903	4 890	5 362	7 146	7 375	7 376	PIB aux prix constants
Growth rates	1.6	2.1	1.6	2.2	4.9	3.2	~0.0	Taux de croissance
Mongolia								**Mongolie**
GDP at current prices	1 218	1 678	2 926	7 189	11 750	11 187	11 135	PIB aux prix courants
GDP per capita	634	730	1 158	2 650	3 947	3 695	3 620	PIB par habitant
GDP at constant prices	3 185	3 338	5 253	7 189	11 680	11 817	12 416	PIB aux prix constants
Growth rates	5.7	6.3	7.3	6.4	2.4	1.2	5.1	Taux de croissance

13 Gross domestic product and gross domestic product per capita *(continued)*
In millions of US dollars at current and constant 2010 prices; per capita US dollars; real rates of growth

Produit intérieur brut et produit intérieur brut par habitant *(suite)*
En millions de dollars É.-U. aux prix courants et constants de 2010; par habitant en dollars É.U.; taux de croissance réels

Country or area	1985	1995	2005	2010	2015	2016	2017	Pays ou zone
Montenegro								**Monténégro**
GDP at current prices	...	1 215	2 279	4 139	4 053	4 374	4 845	PIB aux prix courants
GDP per capita	...	1 958	3 697	6 630	6 452	6 958	7 703	PIB par habitant
GDP at constant prices	...	2 005	3 440	4 139	4 529	4 663	4 882	PIB aux prix constants
Growth rates	...	14.3	4.2	2.7	3.4	2.9	4.7	Taux de croissance
Montserrat								**Montserrat**
GDP at current prices	44	69	49	56	61	63	60	PIB aux prix courants
GDP per capita	3 850	6 728	10 229	11 228	11 979	12 197	11 582	PIB par habitant
GDP at constant prices	101	113	54	56	64	64	62	PIB aux prix constants
Growth rates	5.9	-8.8	3.1	-2.8	-1.9	0.5	-2.8	Taux de croissance
Morocco [5]								**Maroc** [5]
GDP at current prices	15 111	38 728	62 545	93 217	101 179	103 346	109 709	PIB aux prix courants
GDP per capita	670	1 430	2 049	2 876	2 907	2 930	3 070	PIB par habitant
GDP at constant prices	35 111	45 626	70 187	93 217	116 048	119 853	126 561	PIB aux prix constants
Growth rates	6.3	-6.6	3.0	4.0	4.9	3.3	5.6	Taux de croissance
Mozambique								**Mozambique**
GDP at current prices	8 103	2 572	7 724	10 154	14 798	10 897	12 652	PIB aux prix courants
GDP per capita	624	163	369	419	528	378	426	PIB par habitant
GDP at constant prices	1 914	2 688	7 096	10 154	14 308	14 846	15 401	PIB aux prix constants
Growth rates	-8.8	2.2	8.7	6.7	6.6	3.8	3.7	Taux de croissance
Myanmar								**Myanmar**
GDP at current prices	6 607	7 764	11 931	41 445	62 543	64 560	67 102	PIB aux prix courants
GDP per capita	177	180	246	826	1 193	1 221	1 257	PIB par habitant
GDP at constant prices	7 496	8 935	24 375	41 445	58 845	62 312	66 575	PIB aux prix constants
Growth rates	2.9	6.9	13.6	10.2	7.0	5.9	6.8	Taux de croissance
Namibia								**Namibie**
GDP at current prices	1 606	3 942	7 121	11 282	11 657	11 309	13 245	PIB aux prix courants
GDP per capita	1 399	2 382	3 504	5 192	4 806	4 561	5 227	PIB par habitant
GDP at constant prices	4 418	6 059	9 159	11 282	14 846	14 950	14 835	PIB aux prix constants
Growth rates	0.5	3.9	2.5	6.0	6.1	0.7	-0.8	Taux de croissance
Nauru								**Nauru**
GDP at current prices	33	35	26	62	90	103	114	PIB aux prix courants
GDP per capita	4 043	3 496	2 600	6 234	7 955	9 119	10 045	PIB par habitant
GDP at constant prices	212	93	40	62	162	178	186	PIB aux prix constants
Growth rates	-2.8	-7.9	-12.1	20.1	2.8	10.4	4.0	Taux de croissance
Nepal								**Népal**
GDP at current prices	2 741	4 534	8 259	16 281	20 801	20 929	24 870	PIB aux prix courants
GDP per capita	164	212	322	602	726	722	849	PIB par habitant
GDP at constant prices	5 401	8 694	13 101	16 281	20 119	20 202	21 717	PIB aux prix constants
Growth rates	6.1	3.5	3.5	4.8	3.3	0.4	7.5	Taux de croissance
Netherlands								**Pays-Bas**
GDP at current prices	143 847	452 287	685 076	846 555	765 265	783 528	830 573	PIB aux prix courants
GDP per capita	9 911	29 240	41 857	50 744	45 179	46 124	48 754	PIB par habitant
GDP at constant prices	455 443	601 444	794 651	846 555	881 474	900 954	929 444	PIB aux prix constants
Growth rates	2.6	3.1	2.2	1.4	2.3	2.2	3.2	Taux de croissance
Netherlands Antilles [former]								**Antilles néerlandaises [anc.]**
GDP at current prices	1 190	2 571	3 053	3 848	...	...	...	PIB aux prix courants
GDP per capita	7 024	14 734	18 852	21 290	...	...	...	PIB par habitant
GDP at constant prices	2 818	3 522	3 569	3 848	...	...	...	PIB aux prix constants
Growth rates	-2.1	1.6	1.1	-0.3	...	...	...	Taux de croissance
New Caledonia								**Nouvelle-Calédonie**
GDP at current prices	855	3 628	6 236	9 355	9 174	9 446	9 894	PIB aux prix courants
GDP per capita	5 480	19 024	26 801	37 266	34 094	34 641	35 815	PIB par habitant
GDP at constant prices	3 302	6 162	7 713	9 355	10 834	11 157	11 458	PIB aux prix constants
Growth rates	4.5	5.9	3.6	6.9	3.6	3.0	2.7	Taux de croissance
New Zealand								**Nouvelle-Zélande**
GDP at current prices	24 108	63 151	114 721	146 584	177 208	187 854	202 044	PIB aux prix courants
GDP per capita	7 376	17 184	27 741	33 543	38 402	40 305	42 935	PIB par habitant
GDP at constant prices	81 515	96 534	135 952	146 584	170 509	176 499	181 482	PIB aux prix constants
Growth rates	1.6	4.6	3.3	1.0	4.5	3.5	2.8	Taux de croissance
Nicaragua								**Nicaragua**
GDP at current prices	3 598	4 118	6 300	8 759	12 611	13 184	13 814	PIB aux prix courants
GDP per capita	970	893	1 171	1 526	2 073	2 144	2 222	PIB par habitant
GDP at constant prices	5 563	5 135	7 663	8 759	11 423	11 955	12 537	PIB aux prix constants
Growth rates	-4.1	5.9	4.3	4.4	4.8	4.7	4.9	Taux de croissance

13 Gross domestic product and gross domestic product per capita *(continued)*
In millions of US dollars at current and constant 2010 prices; per capita US dollars; real rates of growth

Produit intérieur brut et produit intérieur brut par habitant *(suite)*
En millions de dollars É.-U. aux prix courants et constants de 2010; par habitant en dollars É.U.; taux de croissance réels

Country or area	1985	1995	2005	2010	2015	2016	2017	Pays ou zone
Niger								**Niger**
GDP at current prices	1 531	1 786	3 369	5 719	7 249	7 606	8 120	PIB aux prix courants
GDP per capita	221	188	247	348	364	368	378	PIB par habitant
GDP at constant prices	2 795	3 044	4 445	5 719	7 726	8 107	8 504	PIB aux prix constants
Growth rates	7.7	3.3	7.4	8.4	4.3	4.9	4.9	Taux de croissance
Nigeria								**Nigéria**
GDP at current prices	178 821	49 030	180 502	369 062	494 583	404 649	375 770	PIB aux prix courants
GDP per capita	2 139	454	1 299	2 327	2 730	2 176	1 969	PIB par habitant
GDP at constant prices	99 925	139 274	266 817	369 062	464 282	456 775	460 496	PIB aux prix constants
Growth rates	11.3	2.1	6.5	7.8	2.7	-1.6	0.8	Taux de croissance
North Macedonia								**Macédoine du Nord**
GDP at current prices	...	4 707	6 259	9 407	10 065	10 672	11 280	PIB aux prix courants
GDP per capita	...	2 373	3 038	4 543	4 840	5 128	5 415	PIB par habitant
GDP at constant prices	...	6 063	7 736	9 407	10 616	10 918	10 944	PIB aux prix constants
Growth rates	...	-1.1	4.7	3.4	3.9	2.8	0.2	Taux de croissance
Norway								**Norvège**
GDP at current prices	65 417	152 028	308 722	429 131	386 663	371 337	399 470	PIB aux prix courants
GDP per capita	15 751	34 813	66 645	87 831	74 361	70 668	75 295	PIB par habitant
GDP at constant prices	235 051	307 138	409 135	429 131	467 661	473 214	482 586	PIB aux prix constants
Growth rates	5.6	4.2	2.6	0.7	2.0	1.2	2.0	Taux de croissance
Oman								**Oman**
GDP at current prices	10 281	13 650	31 082	57 048	68 921	65 941	70 784	PIB aux prix courants
GDP per capita	6 861	6 193	12 377	18 757	16 411	14 903	15 267	PIB par habitant
GDP at constant prices	23 487	35 967	44 279	57 048	71 221	74 768	74 075	PIB aux prix constants
Growth rates	14.5	4.8	2.5	2.0	4.7	5.0	-0.9	Taux de croissance
Pakistan								**Pakistan**
GDP at current prices	38 840	77 266	117 708	174 508	267 035	277 779	302 139	PIB aux prix courants
GDP per capita	421	629	765	1 023	1 410	1 438	1 534	PIB par habitant
GDP at constant prices	59 288	98 511	147 540	174 508	212 404	224 026	236 748	PIB aux prix constants
Growth rates	7.6	5.0	7.7	1.6	4.7	5.5	5.7	Taux de croissance
Palau								**Palaos**
GDP at current prices	41	110	191	183	293	303	292	PIB aux prix courants
GDP per capita	3 006	6 398	9 611	8 932	13 768	14 077	13 417	PIB par habitant
GDP at constant prices	121	176	213	183	225	225	217	PIB aux prix constants
Growth rates	5.4	10.0	0.2	-0.9	10.1	0.1	-3.7	Taux de croissance
Panama								**Panama**
GDP at current prices	5 817	9 188	15 714	29 440	54 316	57 821	61 838	PIB aux prix courants
GDP per capita	2 621	3 354	4 718	8 081	13 684	14 333	15 088	PIB par habitant
GDP at constant prices	9 569	13 274	20 557	29 440	42 661	44 789	47 188	PIB aux prix constants
Growth rates	5.1	1.8	7.2	5.8	5.6	5.0	5.4	Taux de croissance
Papua New Guinea								**Papouasie-Nvl-Guinée**
GDP at current prices	3 682	7 274	7 312	14 251	22 962	21 480	22 006	PIB aux prix courants
GDP per capita	970	1 486	1 158	2 005	2 899	2 657	2 667	PIB par habitant
GDP at constant prices	5 740	9 257	10 693	14 251	18 771	18 648	18 373	PIB aux prix constants
Growth rates	3.6	-3.3	3.9	10.1	6.9	-0.7	-1.5	Taux de croissance
Paraguay								**Paraguay**
GDP at current prices	4 017	8 066[6]	8 735	20 048	27 283	27 424	29 435	PIB aux prix courants
GDP per capita	1 094[7]	1 694[7]	1 507	3 228	4 109	4 078	4 322	PIB par habitant
GDP at constant prices	8 524[7]	12 183[7]	15 707	20 048	25 402	26 423	27 553	PIB aux prix constants
Growth rates	4.0[7]	5.4[7]	2.1	13.1	3.0	4.0	4.3	Taux de croissance
Peru								**Pérou**
GDP at current prices	14 529	53 371	76 080	147 528	189 924	191 642	211 403	PIB aux prix courants
GDP per capita	743	2 220	2 755	5 022	6 053	6 031	6 572	PIB par habitant
GDP at constant prices	64 566	75 500	105 785	147 528	186 291	193 652	198 546	PIB aux prix constants
Growth rates	2.1	7.4	6.3	8.3	3.3	4.0	2.5	Taux de croissance
Philippines								**Philippines**
GDP at current prices	34 052	82 121	103 072	199 591	292 774	304 889	313 595	PIB aux prix courants
GDP per capita	627	1 176	1 195	2 130	2 878	2 951	2 989	PIB par habitant
GDP at constant prices	75 004	105 213	156 874	199 591	266 056	284 349	303 356	PIB aux prix constants
Growth rates	-7.3	4.7	4.8	7.6	6.1	6.9	6.7	Taux de croissance
Poland								**Pologne**
GDP at current prices	73 333	142 138	306 127	479 321	477 577	472 030	526 212	PIB aux prix courants
GDP per capita	1 975	3 696	7 980	12 507	12 481	12 349	13 786	PIB par habitant
GDP at constant prices	231 201	252 409	379 769	479 321	556 361	573 400	600 956	PIB aux prix constants
Growth rates	3.6	7.0	3.5	3.6	3.8	3.1	4.8	Taux de croissance

13

Gross domestic product and gross domestic product per capita *(continued)*
In millions of US dollars at current and constant 2010 prices; per capita US dollars; real rates of growth

Produit intérieur brut et produit intérieur brut par habitant *(suite)*
En millions de dollars É.-U. aux prix courants et constants de 2010; par habitant en dollars É.U.; taux de croissance réels

Country or area	1985	1995	2005	2010	2015	2016	2017	Pays ou zone
Portugal								**Portugal**
GDP at current prices	27 118	118 132	197 300	238 303	199 420	188 344	195 041	PIB aux prix courants
GDP per capita	2 716	11 639	18 674	22 371	19 141	18 160	18 882	PIB par habitant
GDP at constant prices	126 436	181 279	231 124	238 303	228 052	221 988	223 971	PIB aux prix constants
Growth rates	2.8	4.3	0.8	1.9	1.8	-2.7	0.9	Taux de croissance
Puerto Rico								**Porto Rico**
GDP at current prices	20 574	43 246	83 915	98 381	103 376	103 961	104 219	PIB aux prix courants
GDP per capita	6 106	11 721	22 286	26 470	28 139	28 343	28 451	PIB par habitant
GDP at constant prices	49 122	78 847	105 342	98 381	95 579	94 311	92 067	PIB aux prix constants
Growth rates	2.1	4.5	-2.0	-0.4	-1.0	-1.3	-2.4	Taux de croissance
Qatar								**Qatar**
GDP at current prices	6 153	8 138	44 530	125 122	164 641	152 452	167 605	PIB aux prix courants
GDP per capita	16 582	15 849	51 489	70 306	66 347	59 324	63 506	PIB par habitant
GDP at constant prices	15 791	21 719	54 659	125 122	166 430	170 130	172 845	PIB aux prix constants
Growth rates	-2.1	2.4	7.5	16.7	3.6	2.2	1.6	Taux de croissance
Republic of Korea								**République de Corée**
GDP at current prices	100 273	556 129	898 137	1 094 499	1 382 764	1 414 804	1 530 751	PIB aux prix courants
GDP per capita	2 457	12 277	18 439	22 088	27 331	27 855	30 025	PIB par habitant
GDP at constant prices	220 570	543 606	894 708	1 094 499	1 268 781	1 305 948	1 345 946	PIB aux prix constants
Growth rates	7.7	9.6	3.9	6.5	2.8	2.9	3.1	Taux de croissance
Republic of Moldova								**République de Moldova**
GDP at current prices	...	1 767	2 988	5 812	6 513	6 796	8 128	PIB aux prix courants
GDP per capita	...	407	719	1 423	1 602	1 674	2 006	PIB par habitant
GDP at constant prices	...	3 992	4 960	5 812	7 034	7 349	7 681	PIB aux prix constants
Growth rates	...	-1.4	7.5	7.1	-0.4	4.5	4.5	Taux de croissance
Romania								**Roumanie**
GDP at current prices	50 742	37 657	99 699	166 658	177 913	187 807	211 804	PIB aux prix courants
GDP per capita	2 196	1 640	4 652	8 153	8 951	9 496	10 763	PIB par habitant
GDP at constant prices	136 139	111 623	145 789	166 658	191 009	200 217	214 126	PIB aux prix constants
Growth rates	-0.1	7.1	4.2	-2.8	4.0	4.8	6.9	Taux de croissance
Russian Federation								**Fédération de Russie**
GDP at current prices	...	402 316	771 495	1 539 845	1 368 402	1 284 727	1 577 524	PIB aux prix courants
GDP per capita	...	2 713	5 372	10 757	9 510	8 924	10 956	PIB par habitant
GDP at constant prices	...	887 588	1 293 864	1 539 845	1 663 126	1 659 801	1 685 454	PIB aux prix constants
Growth rates	...	-4.1	6.4	4.5	-2.5	-0.2	1.5	Taux de croissance
Rwanda								**Rwanda**
GDP at current prices	1 813	1 230	2 581	5 772	8 278	8 475	9 136	PIB aux prix courants
GDP per capita	296	208	287	563	712	711	748	PIB par habitant
GDP at constant prices	2 344	1 587	3 874	5 772	8 307	8 804	9 342	PIB aux prix constants
Growth rates	4.4	33.5	9.4	7.3	8.9	6.0	6.1	Taux de croissance
Saint Kitts and Nevis								**Saint-Kitts-et-Nevis**
GDP at current prices	106	300	543	705	865	900	931	PIB aux prix courants
GDP per capita	2 524	6 987	11 178	13 708	15 937	16 413	16 818	PIB par habitant
GDP at constant prices	262	455	689	705	840	859	869	PIB aux prix constants
Growth rates	8.6	5.8	8.8	-2.2	4.0	2.2	1.2	Taux de croissance
Saint Lucia								**Sainte-Lucie**
GDP at current prices	249	617	935	1 382	1 622	1 636	1 718	PIB aux prix courants
GDP per capita	1 970	4 199	5 714	8 008	9 156	9 188	9 607	PIB par habitant
GDP at constant prices	539	909	1 127	1 382	1 439	1 488	1 532	PIB aux prix constants
Growth rates	7.5	1.1	-1.7	0.2	-0.9	3.4	3.0	Taux de croissance
Saint Vincent & Grenadines								**Saint-Vincent-Grenadines**
GDP at current prices	133	312	551	681	757	767	780	PIB aux prix courants
GDP per capita	1 277	2 887	5 065	6 232	6 915	6 994	7 099	PIB par habitant
GDP at constant prices	295	436	637	681	720	729	734	PIB aux prix constants
Growth rates	6.2	7.5	2.5	-3.3	1.8	1.3	0.7	Taux de croissance
Samoa								**Samoa**
GDP at current prices	85	196	434	679	774	822	856	PIB aux prix courants
GDP per capita	532	1 151	2 414	3 648	3 995	4 213	4 356	PIB par habitant
GDP at constant prices	373	405	644	679	725	772	769	PIB aux prix constants
Growth rates	3.9	6.0	5.1	4.3	2.9	6.5	-0.4	Taux de croissance
San Marino								**Saint-Marin**
GDP at current prices	318	1 020	2 027	2 139	1 570	1 612	1 690	PIB aux prix courants
GDP per capita	14 017	39 407	69 338	68 767	47 627	48 560	50 588	PIB par habitant
GDP at constant prices	998	1 515	2 355	2 139	1 729	1 767	1 800	PIB aux prix constants
Growth rates	2.8	9.3	2.3	-4.6	0.5	2.2	1.9	Taux de croissance

13

Gross domestic product and gross domestic product per capita *(continued)*
In millions of US dollars at current and constant 2010 prices; per capita US dollars; real rates of growth

Produit intérieur brut et produit intérieur brut par habitant *(suite)*
En millions de dollars É.-U. aux prix courants et constants de 2010; par habitant en dollars É.U.; taux de croissance réels

Country or area	1985	1995	2005	2010	2015	2016	2017	Pays ou zone
Sao Tome and Principe								**Sao Tomé-et-Principe**
GDP at current prices	79	99	126	197	316	354	393	PIB aux prix courants
GDP per capita	759	780	811	1 130	1 613	1 772	1 921	PIB par habitant
GDP at constant prices	108	110	148	197	247	257	267	PIB aux prix constants
Growth rates	9.3	2.0	7.1	6.7	3.9	4.2	3.9	Taux de croissance
Saudi Arabia								**Arabie saoudite**
GDP at current prices	103 894	143 152	328 461	528 207	654 270	644 935	683 827	PIB aux prix courants
GDP per capita	7 877	7 641	13 740	19 260	20 733	19 982	20 761	PIB par habitant
GDP at constant prices	207 527	349 402	461 602	528 207	678 730	690 069	684 994	PIB aux prix constants
Growth rates	-9.8	0.2	5.6	5.0	4.1	1.7	-0.7	Taux de croissance
Senegal								**Sénégal**
GDP at current prices	3 632	6 306	11 267	16 725	17 761	18 972	21 126	PIB aux prix courants
GDP per capita	560	721	1 001	1 295	1 186	1 231	1 333	PIB par habitant
GDP at constant prices	7 074	8 878	14 060	16 725	20 351	21 619	23 061	PIB aux prix constants
Growth rates	3.8	4.7	5.6	4.2	6.4	6.2	6.7	Taux de croissance
Serbia								**Serbie**
GDP at current prices	...	21 823[8]	26 252[9]	39 460[9]	37 160[9]	38 300[9]	41 590[9]	PIB aux prix courants
GDP per capita	...	2 208[8]	3 528[9]	5 412[9]	5 237[9]	5 426[9]	5 912[9]	PIB par habitant
GDP at constant prices	...	24 046[8]	34 596[9]	39 460[9]	40 184[9]	41 308[9]	42 155[9]	PIB aux prix constants
Growth rates	...	5.7[8]	5.5[9]	0.6[9]	0.8[9]	2.8[9]	2.0[9]	Taux de croissance
Seychelles								**Seychelles**
GDP at current prices	204	614	919	970	1 377	1 428	1 487	PIB aux prix courants
GDP per capita	2 922	8 005	10 357	10 612	14 695	15 150	15 693	PIB par habitant
GDP at constant prices	392	596	783	970	1 232	1 288	1 368	PIB aux prix constants
Growth rates	10.3	-0.6	9.0	5.9	4.9	4.5	6.3	Taux de croissance
Sierra Leone								**Sierra Leone**
GDP at current prices	1 376	1 179	1 650	2 578	4 248	3 863	3 740	PIB aux prix courants
GDP per capita	362	276	292	399	587	522	495	PIB par habitant
GDP at constant prices	2 087	1 874	1 998	2 578	3 168	3 369	3 497	PIB aux prix constants
Growth rates	2.3	-10.0	4.5	5.3	-20.5	6.3	3.8	Taux de croissance
Singapore								**Singapour**
GDP at current prices	18 555	87 892	127 418	236 420	304 092	309 753	323 901	PIB aux prix courants
GDP per capita	6 858	25 265	28 372	46 592	54 937	55 092	56 737	PIB par habitant
GDP at constant prices	44 696	102 240	170 716	236 420	292 165	299 168	309 994	PIB aux prix constants
Growth rates	-0.7	7.0	7.5	15.2	2.2	2.4	3.6	Taux de croissance
Sint Maarten (Dutch part)								**St-Martin (partie néerland.)**
GDP at current prices	...	...	708	896	1 066	1 072	...	PIB aux prix courants
GDP per capita	...	...	21 762	27 065	27 521	27 116	...	PIB par habitant
GDP at constant prices	...	...	805	896	942	947	867	PIB aux prix constants
Growth rates	...	...	...	1.1	0.5	0.4	-8.4	Taux de croissance
Slovakia								**Slovaquie**
GDP at current prices	...	19 959	48 965	89 501	87 770	89 848	95 618	PIB aux prix courants
GDP per capita	...	3 713	9 069	16 561	16 136	16 503	17 552	PIB par habitant
GDP at constant prices	...	46 643	70 976	89 501	101 628	104 804	108 145	PIB aux prix constants
Growth rates	...	5.8	6.8	5.0	4.2	3.1	3.2	Taux de croissance
Slovenia								**Slovénie**
GDP at current prices	...	21 274	36 345	48 014	43 102	44 641	48 456	PIB aux prix courants
GDP per capita	...	10 683	18 206	23 477	20 774	21 484	23 296	PIB par habitant
GDP at constant prices	...	29 973	44 069	48 014	48 978	50 481	52 945	PIB aux prix constants
Growth rates	...	4.1	4.0	1.2	2.3	3.1	4.9	Taux de croissance
Solomon Islands								**Îles Salomon**
GDP at current prices	160	365	429	720	1 059	1 131	1 212	PIB aux prix courants
GDP per capita	591	1 015	914	1 363	1 803	1 886	1 982	PIB par habitant
GDP at constant prices	303	510	516	720	849	878	909	PIB aux prix constants
Growth rates	2.8	10.0	12.8	10.6	2.5	3.5	3.5	Taux de croissance
Somalia								**Somalie**
GDP at current prices	810	1 122	2 316	1 093	1 455	1 435	1 535	PIB aux prix courants
GDP per capita	119	146	222	91	105	100	104	PIB par habitant
GDP at constant prices	1 031	747	963	1 093	1 257	1 287	1 311	PIB aux prix constants
Growth rates	9.5	...	3.0	2.6	2.7	2.4	1.8	Taux de croissance
South Africa								**Afrique du Sud**
GDP at current prices	59 648	157 434	257 772	375 348	317 536	295 746	348 872	PIB aux prix courants
GDP per capita	1 768	3 741	5 280	7 276	5 743	5 280	6 151	PIB par habitant
GDP at constant prices	205 250	232 702	322 227	375 348	418 897	421 265	426 826	PIB aux prix constants
Growth rates	-1.2	3.1	5.3	3.0	1.3	0.6	1.3	Taux de croissance

13
Gross domestic product and gross domestic product per capita *(continued)*
In millions of US dollars at current and constant 2010 prices; per capita US dollars; real rates of growth

Produit intérieur brut et produit intérieur brut par habitant *(suite)*
En millions de dollars É.-U. aux prix courants et constants de 2010; par habitant en dollars É.U.; taux de croissance réels

Country or area	1985	1995	2005	2010	2015	2016	2017	Pays ou zone
South Sudan								**Soudan du sud**
GDP at current prices	...	...	...	15 206	13 408	6 534	5 694	PIB aux prix courants
GDP per capita	...	...	...	1 510	1 128	534	453	PIB par habitant
GDP at constant prices	...	...	...	15 206	12 556	12 596	12 755	PIB aux prix constants
Growth rates	...	...	...	-1.8	5.1	0.3	1.3	Taux de croissance
Spain								**Espagne**
GDP at current prices	180 305	612 943	1 157 248	1 431 617	1 199 084	1 237 499	1 314 314	PIB aux prix courants
GDP per capita	4 643	15 366	26 276	30 598	25 844	26 700	28 354	PIB par habitant
GDP at constant prices	700 750	940 937	1 358 050	1 431 617	1 420 987	1 466 069	1 509 746	PIB aux prix constants
Growth rates	2.3	2.8	3.7	~0.0	3.6	3.2	3.0	Taux de croissance
Sri Lanka								**Sri Lanka**
GDP at current prices	6 873	15 293	27 932	56 726	80 604	81 787	87 357	PIB aux prix courants
GDP per capita	425	838	1 431	2 808	3 891	3 932	4 184	PIB par habitant
GDP at constant prices	17 380	26 744	41 633	56 726	76 486	79 904	82 548	PIB aux prix constants
Growth rates	5.0	5.5	6.2	8.0	5.0	4.5	3.3	Taux de croissance
State of Palestine								**État de Palestine**
GDP at current prices	1 005	3 283	4 832	8 913	12 673	13 426	14 498	PIB aux prix courants
GDP per capita	571	1 254	1 351	2 192	2 718	2 802	2 946	PIB par habitant
GDP at constant prices	2 115	4 804	6 983	8 913	11 238	11 767	12 137	PIB aux prix constants
Growth rates	-0.6	7.1	10.8	8.1	3.4	4.7	3.1	Taux de croissance
Sudan								**Soudan**
GDP at current prices	...	...	...	54 459	83 085	91 701	120 266	PIB aux prix courants
GDP per capita	...	...	...	1 584	2 150	2 317	2 967	PIB par habitant
GDP at constant prices	...	...	...	54 459	57 686	59 705	61 615	PIB aux prix constants
Growth rates	...	...	...	8.8	3.0	3.5	3.2	Taux de croissance
Sudan [former]								**Soudan [anc.]**
GDP at current prices	6 624	12 847	35 183	69 665	...	...	...	PIB aux prix courants
GDP per capita	292	435	902	1 567	...	...	...	PIB par habitant
GDP at constant prices	16 497	26 296	52 248	69 665	...	...	...	PIB aux prix constants
Growth rates	5.4	6.0	9.0	6.6	...	...	...	Taux de croissance
Suriname								**Suriname**
GDP at current prices	1 196	844	2 193	4 368	4 826	3 278	3 807	PIB aux prix courants
GDP per capita	3 221	1 903	4 395	8 303	8 725	5 871	6 757	PIB par habitant
GDP at constant prices	2 507	2 478	3 483	4 368	4 773	4 527	4 496	PIB aux prix constants
Growth rates	14.0	~0.0	3.9	5.2	-2.6	-5.1	-0.7	Taux de croissance
Sweden								**Suède**
GDP at current prices	112 640	264 346	389 489	488 909	498 118	512 205	535 607	PIB aux prix courants
GDP per capita	13 477	29 915	43 092	52 066	51 018	52 066	54 043	PIB par habitant
GDP at constant prices	285 573	333 105	451 913	488 909	543 061	557 637	569 373	PIB aux prix constants
Growth rates	2.2	4.0	2.8	6.0	4.5	2.7	2.1	Taux de croissance
Switzerland								**Suisse**
GDP at current prices	107 765	342 626	408 697	583 783	679 832	670 181	678 938	PIB aux prix courants
GDP per capita	16 692	48 817	55 153	74 538	81 713	79 767	80 101	PIB par habitant
GDP at constant prices	373 821	434 925	524 104	583 783	634 045	644 197	654 612	PIB aux prix constants
Growth rates	3.7	0.5	3.1	3.0	1.3	1.6	1.6	Taux de croissance
Syrian Arab Republic								**République arabe syrienne**
GDP at current prices	10 050	13 547	28 397	60 465	19 090	12 377	15 183	PIB aux prix courants
GDP per capita	944	944	1 552	2 877	1 019	672	831	PIB par habitant
GDP at constant prices	22 117	31 119	47 588	60 465	27 492	26 398	26 899	PIB aux prix constants
Growth rates	6.1	7.0	6.2	3.4	-6.1	-4.0	1.9	Taux de croissance
Tajikistan								**Tadjikistan**
GDP at current prices	...	1 218	2 312	5 642	7 855	6 953	7 146	PIB aux prix courants
GDP per capita	...	211	337	738	919	796	801	PIB par habitant
GDP at constant prices	...	2 597	4 126	5 642	7 547	8 072	8 643	PIB aux prix constants
Growth rates	...	-12.4	6.7	6.5	6.0	6.9	7.1	Taux de croissance
Thailand								**Thaïlande**
GDP at current prices	40 313	169 279	189 318	341 105	401 399	411 755	455 303	PIB aux prix courants
GDP per capita	775	2 845	2 894	5 075	5 846	5 979	6 595	PIB par habitant
GDP at constant prices	85 565	210 023	283 767	341 105	394 078	407 015	422 941	PIB aux prix constants
Growth rates	4.6	8.1	4.2	7.5	3.0	3.3	3.9	Taux de croissance
Timor-Leste								**Timor-Leste**
GDP at current prices	...	438	1 814	3 999	3 104	2 521	2 955	PIB aux prix courants
GDP per capita	...	503	1 767	3 604	2 502	1 987	2 279	PIB par habitant
GDP at constant prices	...	1 416	2 627	3 999	3 734	3 765	3 464	PIB aux prix constants
Growth rates	...	9.5	35.9	-1.2	20.9	0.8	-8.0	Taux de croissance

13

Gross domestic product and gross domestic product per capita *(continued)*
In millions of US dollars at current and constant 2010 prices; per capita US dollars; real rates of growth

Produit intérieur brut et produit intérieur brut par habitant *(suite)*
En millions de dollars É.-U. aux prix courants et constants de 2010; par habitant en dollars É.U.; taux de croissance réels

Country or area	1985	1995	2005	2010	2015	2016	2017	Pays ou zone
Togo								**Togo**
GDP at current prices	860	1 663	2 281	3 426	4 178	4 483	4 786	PIB aux prix courants
GDP per capita	264	389	401	527	563	589	614	PIB par habitant
GDP at constant prices	2 053	2 476	2 898	3 426	4 616	4 872	5 087	PIB aux prix constants
Growth rates	3.7	6.8	-4.7	6.1	5.7	5.6	4.4	Taux de croissance
Tonga								**Tonga**
GDP at current prices	73	203	262	374	402	401	427	PIB aux prix courants
GDP per capita	779	2 115	2 589	3 590	3 778	3 748	3 950	PIB par habitant
GDP at constant prices	242	297	360	374	398	411	422	PIB aux prix constants
Growth rates	6.6	4.0	1.6	3.6	3.7	3.4	2.7	Taux de croissance
Trinidad and Tobago								**Trinité-et-Tobago**
GDP at current prices	7 355	5 314	15 938	22 062	24 402	22 304	22 105	PIB aux prix courants
GDP per capita	6 282	4 235	12 289	16 611	17 942	16 340	16 145	PIB par habitant
GDP at constant prices	8 967	8 579	18 214	22 062	22 784	21 426	20 926	PIB aux prix constants
Growth rates	-4.1	4.0	6.2	3.3	1.5	-6.0	-2.3	Taux de croissance
Tunisia								**Tunisie**
GDP at current prices	9 234	19 795	32 272	44 051	43 152	41 808	40 069	PIB aux prix courants
GDP per capita	1 261	2 172	3 194	4 140	3 828	3 666	3 475	PIB par habitant
GDP at constant prices	15 561	21 771	35 380	44 051	47 587	48 069	49 008	PIB aux prix constants
Growth rates	5.7	2.3	4.0	3.0	1.2	1.0	2.0	Taux de croissance
Turkey								**Turquie**
GDP at current prices	92 554	233 085	501 423	771 877	859 794	863 712	851 542	PIB aux prix courants
GDP per capita	1 884	3 985	7 384	10 672	10 985	10 863	10 546	PIB par habitant
GDP at constant prices	277 716	426 265	658 107	771 877	1 087 840	1 122 475	1 206 001	PIB aux prix constants
Growth rates	4.2	7.2	9.0	8.5	6.1	3.2	7.4	Taux de croissance
Turkmenistan								**Turkménistan**
GDP at current prices	...	2 190	14 176	22 583	36 052	36 169	37 915	PIB aux prix courants
GDP per capita	...	520	2 982	4 439	6 478	6 387	6 585	PIB par habitant
GDP at constant prices	...	8 641	13 784	22 583	37 230	39 538	42 096	PIB aux prix constants
Growth rates	...	-7.2	13.0	9.2	6.5	6.2	6.5	Taux de croissance
Turks and Caicos Islands								**Îles Turques-et-Caïques**
GDP at current prices	58	191	579	687	894	950	1 017	PIB aux prix courants
GDP per capita	6 142	12 425	21 879	22 159	26 020	27 231	28 689	PIB par habitant
GDP at constant prices	102	279	627	687	802	838	874	PIB aux prix constants
Growth rates	10.7	7.3	14.4	1.0	5.9	4.4	4.3	Taux de croissance
Tuvalu								**Tuvalu**
GDP at current prices	4	12	22	31	35	40	44	PIB aux prix courants
GDP per capita	406	1 274	2 162	2 981	3 185	3 564	3 924	PIB par habitant
GDP at constant prices	10	22	29	31	38	40	42	PIB aux prix constants
Growth rates	-1.8	-5.0	-4.1	-3.3	9.2	5.9	5.9	Taux de croissance
Uganda								**Ouganda**
GDP at current prices	4 743	7 148	11 158	19 683	25 098	25 423	27 699	PIB aux prix courants
GDP per capita	324	348	391	580	625	613	646	PIB par habitant
GDP at constant prices	3 578	6 775	13 326	19 683	24 893	25 536	26 812	PIB aux prix constants
Growth rates	-0.3	9.4	10.0	8.2	5.7	2.6	5.0	Taux de croissance
Ukraine								**Ukraine**
GDP at current prices	...	50 379	89 239	136 012[10]	91 031[10]	93 356[10]	112 154[10]	PIB aux prix courants
GDP per capita	...	990	1 903	2 970[10]	2 038[10]	2 101[10]	2 536[10]	PIB par habitant
GDP at constant prices	...	102 606	134 293	136 012[10]	121 203[10]	124 161[10]	127 296[10]	PIB aux prix constants
Growth rates	...	-12.2	3.1	0.3[10]	-9.8[10]	2.4[10]	2.5[10]	Taux de croissance
United Arab Emirates								**Émirats arabes unis**
GDP at current prices	41 134	66 603	182 978	289 787	358 135	357 045	382 575	PIB aux prix courants
GDP per capita	29 571	27 198	39 955	35 038	39 122	38 518	40 699	PIB par habitant
GDP at constant prices	103 869	144 762	257 284	289 787	373 073	384 222	387 259	PIB aux prix constants
Growth rates	-2.4	8.2	4.9	1.6	5.1	3.0	0.8	Taux de croissance
United Kingdom								**Royaume-Uni**
GDP at current prices	489 256	1 335 930	2 525 013	2 452 900	2 896 421	2 659 239	2 631 228	PIB aux prix courants
GDP per capita	8 665	23 042	41 883	38 746	44 290	40 421	39 758	PIB par habitant
GDP at constant prices	1 358 445	1 771 069	2 403 352	2 452 900	2 719 581	2 768 241	2 816 441	PIB aux prix constants
Growth rates	4.2	3.9	3.1	1.7	2.3	1.8	1.7	Taux de croissance
United Rep. of Tanzania [11]								**Rép.-Unie de Tanzanie** [11]
GDP at current prices	11 654	7 575	18 072	31 105	45 628	47 388	52 090	PIB aux prix courants
GDP per capita	534	260	471	694	870	876	934	PIB par habitant
GDP at constant prices	9 123	13 412	23 158	31 105	43 307	46 326	...	PIB aux prix constants
Growth rates	4.6	3.6	7.4	6.4	7.0	7.0	...	Taux de croissance

13

Gross domestic product and gross domestic product per capita *(continued)*
In millions of US dollars at current and constant 2010 prices; per capita US dollars; real rates of growth

Produit intérieur brut et produit intérieur brut par habitant *(suite)*
En millions de dollars É.-U. aux prix courants et constants de 2010; par habitant en dollars É.U.; taux de croissance réels

Country or area	1985	1995	2005	2010	2015	2016	2017	Pays ou zone
United States of America								**États-Unis d'Amérique**
GDP at current prices	4 338 979	7 639 749	13 036 637	14 992 052	18 219 297	18 707 189	19 485 394	PIB aux prix courants
GDP per capita	18 017	28 758	44 173	48 574	56 948	58 064	60 055	PIB par habitant
GDP at constant prices	7 641 823	10 216 863	14 332 499	14 992 052	16 710 458	16 972 347	17 348 626	PIB aux prix constants
Growth rates	4.2	2.7	3.5	2.6	2.9	1.6	2.2	Taux de croissance
Uruguay								**Uruguay**
GDP at current prices	5 226	21 312	17 363	40 285	53 274	52 688	59 180	PIB aux prix courants
GDP per capita	1 735	6 609	5 221	11 938	15 525	15 298	17 120	PIB par habitant
GDP at constant prices	18 302	26 841	30 157	40 285	47 559	48 363	49 648	PIB aux prix constants
Growth rates	1.5	-1.5	7.5	7.8	0.4	1.7	2.7	Taux de croissance
Uzbekistan								**Ouzbékistan**
GDP at current prices	...	13 474	14 396	39 526	66 904	67 446	49 677	PIB aux prix courants
GDP per capita	...	589	543	1 382	2 160	2 145	1 557	PIB par habitant
GDP at constant prices	...	16 623	26 297	39 526	58 274	61 890	65 093	PIB aux prix constants
Growth rates	...	-0.9	7.0	8.5	7.9	6.2	5.2	Taux de croissance
Vanuatu								**Vanuatu**
GDP at current prices	133	273	395	701	760	804	864	PIB aux prix courants
GDP per capita	1 020	1 621	1 886	2 966	2 871	2 975	3 128	PIB par habitant
GDP at constant prices	334	447	550	701	754	780	808	PIB aux prix constants
Growth rates	1.1	4.7	5.3	1.6	0.2	3.5	3.5	Taux de croissance
Venezuela (Boliv. Rep. of)								**Venezuela (Rép. boliv. du)**
GDP at current prices	59 963	74 889	145 514	393 806	344 375	291 376	255 093	PIB aux prix courants
GDP per capita	3 425	3 375	5 433	13 566	11 054	9 230	7 977	PIB par habitant
GDP at constant prices	207 087	278 797	328 294	393 806	395 794	330 663	284 370	PIB aux prix constants
Growth rates	0.2	4.0	10.3	-1.5	-6.2	-16.5	-14.0	Taux de croissance
Viet Nam								**Viet Nam**
GDP at current prices	4 797	20 736	57 633	115 932	193 241	205 276	223 780	PIB aux prix courants
GDP per capita	79	276	684	1 310	2 065	2 171	2 342	PIB par habitant
GDP at constant prices	23 610	42 924	85 352	115 932	154 509	164 105	175 284	PIB aux prix constants
Growth rates	5.6	9.5	7.5	6.4	6.7	6.2	6.8	Taux de croissance
Yemen								**Yémen**
GDP at current prices	...	5 936	19 041	30 907	26 660	24 841	27 957	PIB aux prix courants
GDP per capita	...	387	925	1 309	990	901	990	PIB par habitant
GDP at constant prices	...	13 186	25 507	30 907	17 313	14 744	13 868	PIB aux prix constants
Growth rates	...	16.7	5.1	3.3	-30.3	-14.8	-5.9	Taux de croissance
Zambia								**Zambie**
GDP at current prices	2 772	3 807	8 332	20 265	21 243	20 954	25 868	PIB aux prix courants
GDP per capita	399	417	691	1 463	1 319	1 263	1 513	PIB par habitant
GDP at constant prices	7 820	8 274	13 350	20 265	26 058	27 037	27 990	PIB aux prix constants
Growth rates	-~0.0	2.9	7.2	10.3	2.9	3.8	3.5	Taux de croissance
Zanzibar								**Zanzibar**
GDP at current prices	...	186	438	746	1 160	1 207	1 391	PIB aux prix courants
GDP per capita	...	235	408	587	795	823	920	PIB par habitant
GDP at constant prices	...	294	572	746	1 044	1 115	1 198	PIB aux prix constants
Growth rates	...	0.5	1.7	0.8	0.6	6.2	4.3	Taux de croissance
Zimbabwe								**Zimbabwe**
GDP at current prices	7 548	9 576	6 223	10 142	16 305	16 620	18 037	PIB aux prix courants
GDP per capita	872	846	481	720	1 033	1 029	1 091	PIB par habitant
GDP at constant prices	5 847	7 760	6 171	10 142	14 728	14 819	15 265	PIB aux prix constants
Growth rates	6.9	0.2	-4.1	12.6	1.7	0.6	3.0	Taux de croissance

Source:

United Nations Statistics Division, New York, National Accounts Statistics: Analysis of Main Aggregates (AMA) database, last accessed February 2018.

Source:

Organisation des Nations Unies, Division de statistique, New York, base de données des statistiques des comptes nationaux : Analyse des principaux agrégats, denier accès février 2018.

1 Data compiled in accordance with the System of National Accounts 1968 (1968 SNA).
2 For statistical purposes, the data for China do not include those for the Hong Kong Special Administrative Region (Hong Kong SAR), Macao Special Administrative Region (Macao SAR) and Taiwan Province of China.

1 Données compilées selon le Système de comptabilité nationale de 1968 (SCN 1968).
2 Pour la présentation des statistiques, les données pour la Chine ne comprennent pas la région administrative spéciale de Hong Kong (RAS de Hong Kong), la région administrative spéciale de Macao (RAS de Macao) et la province chinoise de Taïwan.

13

Gross domestic product and gross domestic product per capita *(continued)*
In millions of US dollars at current and constant 2010 prices; per capita US dollars; real rates of growth

Produit intérieur brut et produit intérieur brut par habitant *(suite)*
En millions de dollars É.-U. aux prix courants et constants de 2010; par habitant en dollars É.U.; taux de croissance réels

3	Excluding northern Cyprus.	3	Chypre du nord non compris.
4	Including French Guiana, Guadeloupe, Martinique and Réunion.	4	Y compris Guadeloupe, Guyane française, Martinique et Réunion.
5	Including Western Sahara.	5	Y compris les données de Sahara occidental.
6	Does not incorporate value added generated by binational hydroelectric plants.	6	Ne comprend pas la valeur ajoutée produite par les centrales hydroélectriques binationales.
7	Does not incorporate export of binational hydroelectric power at market prices.	7	Ne comprend pas l'exportation d'énergie hydroélectrique binationale aux prix du marché.
8	Including Kosovo and Metohija.	8	Y compris Kosovo et Metohija.
9	Excluding Kosovo and Metohija.	9	Non compris Kosovo et Metohija.
10	Excludes the temporarily occupied territory of the Autonomous Republic of Crimea and Sevastopol.	10	Excluent le territoire temporairement occupé de la République autonome de Crimée et de Sébastopol.
11	Tanzania mainland only, excluding Zanzibar.	11	Tanzanie continentale seulement, Zanzibar non compris.

14

Gross value added by kind of economic activity
Percentage distribution, current prices

Valeur ajoutée brute par type d'activité économique
Répartition en pourcentage, aux prix courants

Country or area [&]	1985	1995	2005	2010	2015	2016	2017	Pays ou zone [&]
Afghanistan								**Afghanistan**
Agriculture	51.2	65.7	35.2	28.8	24.9	22.7	24.1	Agriculture
Industry	24.9	10.5	26.0	21.3	21.4	22.7	22.0	Industrie
Services	23.9	23.8	38.8	49.8	53.6	54.7	53.9	Services
Albania [1]								**Albanie** [1]
Agriculture	38.7	54.3	21.5	20.7	22.9	22.5	22.7	Agriculture
Industry	43.1	26.5	28.7	28.7	24.6	24.8	24.1	Industrie
Services	18.3	19.2	49.8	50.7	52.5	52.7	53.2	Services
Algeria								**Algérie**
Agriculture	8.4	10.4	8.0	8.6	10.7	12.1	12.7	Agriculture
Industry	49.8	47.9	59.7	51.4	43.9	37.3	36.1	Industrie
Services	41.9	41.7	32.3	40.0	45.5	50.6	51.2	Services
Andorra [1]								**Andorre** [1]
Agriculture	0.5	0.5	0.4	0.5	0.6	0.5	0.6	Agriculture
Industry	18.3	18.8	17.3	14.6	11.0	11.1	11.3	Industrie
Services	81.2	80.7	82.3	84.8	88.4	88.3	88.1	Services
Angola								**Angola**
Agriculture	13.6	7.4	5.0	6.2	7.5	9.1	9.9	Agriculture
Industry	43.4	67.4	59.7	52.1	45.9	42.1	42.9	Industrie
Services	43.0	25.2	35.3	41.7	46.6	48.8	47.2	Services
Anguilla								**Anguilla**
Agriculture	5.6	3.3	2.7	2.0	2.2	2.3	3.0	Agriculture
Industry	16.6	14.5	19.3	15.8	15.1	15.3	13.5	Industrie
Services	77.8	82.2	78.0	82.2	82.7	82.4	83.4	Services
Antigua and Barbuda								**Antigua-et-Barbuda**
Agriculture	2.2	1.9	2.0	1.8	1.8	1.8	1.7	Agriculture
Industry	11.4	14.4	16.3	18.2	17.8	18.2	19.8	Industrie
Services	86.4	83.7	81.7	80.0	80.4	80.0	78.5	Services
Argentina								**Argentine**
Agriculture	7.4	5.3	9.3	8.5	8.0	6.1	7.5	Agriculture
Industry	37.7	26.0	33.7	30.1	28.9	27.5	26.3	Industrie
Services	54.9	68.7	57.0	61.4	63.1	66.3	66.2	Services
Armenia [1]								**Arménie** [1]
Agriculture	...	40.3	19.9	17.8	19.9	18.9	17.8	Agriculture
Industry	...	28.4	43.8	34.7	27.8	28.2	27.8	Industrie
Services	...	31.3	36.3	47.4	52.2	52.9	54.3	Services
Aruba								**Aruba**
Agriculture [2]	0.5	0.5	0.4	0.5	0.5	0.5	0.5	Agriculture [2]
Industry	15.9	15.6	19.6	15.4	15.4	15.4	15.4	Industrie
Services	83.5	83.9	80.0	84.2	84.2	84.1	84.2	Services
Australia [1]								**Australie** [1]
Agriculture	4.5	3.7	3.0	2.4	2.5	2.6	3.0	Agriculture
Industry	35.5	28.4	27.8	28.2	25.2	23.9	24.8	Industrie
Services	60.1	67.9	69.2	69.4	72.2	73.4	72.2	Services
Austria [1]								**Autriche** [1]
Agriculture	3.6	2.4	1.4	1.4	1.3	1.3	1.2	Agriculture
Industry	34.5	32.1	30.5	28.7	28.4	28.2	28.3	Industrie
Services	61.9	65.5	68.1	69.9	70.2	70.5	70.5	Services
Azerbaijan [1]								**Azerbaïdjan** [1]
Agriculture	...	26.9	9.8	5.9	5.7	6.7	6.1	Agriculture
Industry	...	32.9	63.2	64.0	57.6	48.9	51.4	Industrie
Services	...	40.3	27.0	30.1	36.7	44.3	42.5	Services
Bahamas [1]								**Bahamas** [1]
Agriculture	2.2	2.0	1.1	1.2	0.9	0.9	1.0	Agriculture
Industry	13.9	10.4	11.7	12.4	15.3	11.2	12.8	Industrie
Services	84.0	87.6	87.1	86.4	83.8	87.8	86.2	Services
Bahrain [3]								**Bahreïn** [3]
Agriculture	0.8	0.7	0.3	0.3	0.3	0.3	0.3	Agriculture
Industry	38.9	36.1	42.8	45.5	46.9	40.7	39.7	Industrie
Services	60.2	63.2	56.9	54.2	52.8	59.0	60.0	Services
Bangladesh								**Bangladesh**
Agriculture	35.7	26.4	20.1	17.8	16.1	15.3	14.8	Agriculture
Industry	21.5	24.6	27.2	26.1	27.6	27.8	28.8	Industrie
Services	42.8	49.1	52.6	56.0	56.3	57.0	56.5	Services

Gross value added by kind of economic activity *(continued)*
Percentage distribution, current prices

Valeur ajoutée brute par type d'activité économique *(suite)*
Répartition en pourcentage, aux prix courants

Country or area [&]	1985	1995	2005	2010	2015	2016	2017	Pays ou zone [&]
Barbados								**Barbade**
Agriculture	4.5	3.5	1.8	1.5	1.6	1.5	1.6	Agriculture
Industry	23.0	16.6	16.9	15.5	15.6	15.2	15.5	Industrie
Services	72.5	79.9	81.3	83.0	82.8	83.3	83.0	Services
Belarus [1]								**Bélarus** [1]
Agriculture	...	16.8	9.7	10.1	8.3	7.2	8.0	Agriculture
Industry	...	37.5	43.8	40.3	40.1	37.7	35.8	Industrie
Services	...	45.6	46.5	49.5	51.7	55.1	56.2	Services
Belgium [1]								**Belgique** [1]
Agriculture	2.6	1.4	0.9	0.9	0.7	0.8	0.7	Agriculture
Industry	31.4	29.0	25.1	23.2	22.0	22.1	21.9	Industrie
Services	66.0	69.6	74.0	76.0	77.3	77.1	77.4	Services
Belize								**Belize**
Agriculture	19.8	19.8	14.7	12.6	15.1	14.5	12.2	Agriculture
Industry	24.3	23.5	16.5	20.7	18.2	16.3	16.3	Industrie
Services	55.9	56.8	68.8	66.7	66.7	69.3	71.5	Services
Benin								**Bénin**
Agriculture	32.4	23.7	27.1	25.4	23.0	22.7	27.7	Agriculture
Industry	15.5	32.5	30.3	24.7	22.7	24.4	24.0	Industrie
Services	52.0	43.8	42.5	49.9	54.3	52.9	48.4	Services
Bermuda								**Bermudes**
Agriculture	0.8	0.8	0.8	0.7	0.6	0.7	0.8	Agriculture
Industry [4,5]	10.4	10.4	9.7	7.1	5.3	5.5	5.6	Industrie [4,5]
Services	88.9	88.8	89.5	92.2	94.1	93.9	93.6	Services
Bhutan								**Bhoutan**
Agriculture	42.3	33.2	23.2	17.5	17.7	17.5	17.3	Agriculture
Industry	21.4	33.5	37.3	44.6	42.9	43.2	43.5	Industrie
Services	36.4	33.3	39.5	37.9	39.4	39.3	39.2	Services
Bolivia (Plurin. State of)								**Bolivie (État plurin. de)**
Agriculture	28.7	16.4	13.9	12.4	12.4	12.6	12.9	Agriculture
Industry	28.5	32.1	30.9	35.8	35.0	31.0	29.4	Industrie
Services	42.8	51.5	55.2	51.8	52.6	56.5	57.7	Services
Bosnia and Herzegovina								**Bosnie-Herzégovine**
Agriculture	...	22.0	9.8[1]	8.0[1]	7.0[1]	7.3[1]	7.5[1]	Agriculture
Industry	...	31.8	25.3[1]	26.4[1]	26.0[1]	26.5[1]	27.3[1]	Industrie
Services	...	46.2	64.9[1]	65.6[1]	67.0[1]	66.2[1]	65.3[1]	Services
Botswana								**Botswana**
Agriculture	7.4	4.9	2.0	2.8	2.3	2.4	2.2	Agriculture
Industry	54.3	46.5	47.6	35.7	36.4	33.2	35.2	Industrie
Services	38.3	48.6	50.3	61.6	61.3	64.4	62.5	Services
Brazil								**Brésil**
Agriculture	11.0	5.5[1]	5.5[1]	4.8[1]	5.0[1]	5.0[1]	5.5[1]	Agriculture
Industry	42.2	26.0[1]	28.5[1]	27.4[1]	23.8[1]	22.5[1]	21.4[1]	Industrie
Services	46.7	68.5[1]	66.0[1]	67.8[1]	71.2[1]	72.5[1]	73.1[1]	Services
British Virgin Islands [1]								**Îles Vierges britanniques** [1]
Agriculture	0.7	0.3	0.2	0.2	0.2	0.2	0.2	Agriculture
Industry	4.9	7.0	6.1	5.3	6.7	6.4	6.5	Industrie
Services	94.5	92.7	93.7	94.5	93.1	93.5	93.3	Services
Brunei Darussalam [1]								**Brunéi Darussalam** [1]
Agriculture	0.4	1.1	0.9	0.7	0.8	1.1	1.2	Agriculture
Industry	78.5	53.4	72.0	67.4	66.8	60.2	56.5	Industrie
Services	21.1	45.5	27.1	31.9	32.3	38.7	42.4	Services
Bulgaria [1]								**Bulgarie** [1]
Agriculture	13.0	13.4	8.6	4.8	5.3	4.8	4.7	Agriculture
Industry	53.9	25.6	28.4	27.4	27.3	27.9	28.3	Industrie
Services	33.0	61.0	63.0	67.8	67.5	67.3	67.0	Services
Burkina Faso								**Burkina Faso**
Agriculture	34.9	34.3	38.5	35.2	34.3	33.2	31.6	Agriculture
Industry	19.8	24.8	17.7	22.7	21.6	20.8	20.6	Industrie
Services	45.4	40.9	43.8	42.0	44.1	46.0	47.7	Services
Burundi								**Burundi**
Agriculture	55.8[6]	48.2	43.0	40.7	37.7	37.5	37.3	Agriculture
Industry	16.9[6]	19.2	17.8	16.3	16.7	16.4	16.8	Industrie
Services	27.2[6]	32.6	39.1	43.0	45.7	46.1	45.8	Services

Gross value added by kind of economic activity *(continued)*
Percentage distribution, current prices

Valeur ajoutée brute par type d'activité économique *(suite)*
Répartition en pourcentage, aux prix courants

Country or area &	1985	1995	2005	2010	2015	2016	2017	Pays ou zone &
Cabo Verde [1]								**Cabo Verde** [1]
Agriculture	17.3	15.6	11.7	9.2	9.1	10.0	9.2	Agriculture
Industry	25.5	29.9	22.8	20.8	21.3	20.7	19.7	Industrie
Services	57.2	54.5	65.5	70.1	69.6	69.3	71.1	Services
Cambodia								**Cambodge**
Agriculture	47.0	51.4	32.4	36.0	30.7	28.2	26.3	Agriculture
Industry	13.6	12.9	26.4	23.3	27.2	29.4	31.3	Industrie
Services	39.4	35.7	41.2	40.7	42.2	42.3	42.4	Services
Cameroon [1]								**Cameroun** [1]
Agriculture	14.8	17.5	15.2	15.1	15.3	16.1	16.0	Agriculture
Industry	31.2	28.6	30.3	29.1	29.1	27.4	26.9	Industrie
Services	54.0	53.8	54.6	55.8	55.6	56.6	57.1	Services
Canada								**Canada**
Agriculture	3.5	2.9	1.8	1.4[1]	1.5[1]	1.8[1]	1.7[1]	Agriculture
Industry	35.1	30.7	32.4	28.6[1]	28.7[1]	25.9[1]	27.6[1]	Industrie
Services	61.4	66.4	65.8	70.0[1]	69.7[1]	72.2[1]	70.7[1]	Services
Cayman Islands [1]								**Îles Caïmanes** [1]
Agriculture	0.3	0.2	0.2	0.3	0.4	0.4	0.4	Agriculture
Industry	9.8	9.2	9.1	7.7	7.4	7.6	8.0	Industrie
Services	89.9	90.5	90.6	92.0	92.2	92.1	91.7	Services
Central African Republic								**République centrafricaine**
Agriculture	35.7	36.1	45.0	41.2	30.8	31.4	31.9	Agriculture
Industry	22.2	26.9	18.6	24.0	27.4	26.0	25.5	Industrie
Services	42.1	37.0	36.5	34.8	41.9	42.6	42.6	Services
Chad								**Tchad**
Agriculture	31.7	27.7	26.0	31.8	28.9	29.8	32.9	Agriculture
Industry	14.9	15.0	35.1	32.9	32.8	32.0	25.5	Industrie
Services	53.4	57.3	38.9	35.3	38.3	38.3	41.5	Services
Chile [1]								**Chili** [1]
Agriculture	5.9	5.9	4.5	3.9	4.3	4.1	4.4	Agriculture
Industry	37.3	41.4	40.3	38.8	33.7	32.5	31.6	Industrie
Services	56.7	52.7	55.2	57.3	62.0	63.4	64.0	Services
China [7,8]								**Chine** [7,8]
Agriculture	28.2	19.8	12.0	9.8	9.3	9.1	8.9	Agriculture
Industry	42.8	46.9	47.2	46.6	43.3	41.1	40.0	Industrie
Services [1]	29.0	33.3	40.9	43.6	47.4	49.8	51.1	Services [1]
China, Hong Kong SAR [1]								**Chine, RAS de Hong Kong** [1]
Agriculture [2,9]	0.6	0.2	0.1	0.1	0.1	0.1	0.1	Agriculture [2,9]
Industry [4,10]	26.8	14.1	8.7	7.0	7.2	7.3	7.7	Industrie [4,10]
Services [11]	72.6	85.7	91.3	93.0	92.7	92.7	92.2	Services [11]
China, Macao SAR								**Chine, RAS de Macao**
Industry	24.3	14.8	14.9	7.4	7.5	10.5	8.9	Industrie
Services	75.7	85.2	85.1	92.6	92.5	89.5	91.1	Services
Colombia								**Colombie**
Agriculture	12.3	9.3	8.4	7.1	6.2	6.6	7.3	Agriculture
Industry	31.2	30.0	32.8	35.0	35.7	33.4	32.4	Industrie
Services	56.5	60.7	58.8	57.9	58.1	59.9	60.3	Services
Comoros								**Comores**
Agriculture	26.5	31.9	37.3	31.6	31.3	31.1	30.9	Agriculture
Industry	17.5	11.7	10.9	12.2	12.1	11.8	12.2	Industrie
Services	56.0	56.3	51.8	56.1	56.6	57.1	56.9	Services
Congo								**Congo**
Agriculture	7.8	10.2	5.5	4.1	4.8	7.6	9.0	Agriculture
Industry	40.6	34.3	59.7	68.4	59.4	48.1	43.9	Industrie
Services	51.6	55.5	34.8	27.6	35.8	44.4	47.1	Services
Cook Islands [3]								**Îles Cook** [3]
Agriculture	6.8	7.4	6.9	4.9	9.0	8.3	7.9	Agriculture
Industry	8.8	7.8	9.6	8.5	7.5	9.0	7.6	Industrie
Services	84.5	84.8	83.5	86.6	83.5	82.7	84.5	Services
Costa Rica [1]								**Costa Rica** [1]
Agriculture	14.4	14.0	9.6	7.2	5.6	5.4	5.7	Agriculture
Industry	33.5	29.2	26.9	25.4	22.0	21.2	20.6	Industrie
Services	52.1	56.8	63.6	67.4	72.4	73.4	73.7	Services

Country or area &	1985	1995	2005	2010	2015	2016	2017	Pays ou zone &
Côte d'Ivoire								**Côte d'Ivoire**
Agriculture	28.1[6]	26.6[6]	24.3	26.0	22.9	24.9	24.6	Agriculture
Industry	20.5[6]	22.3[6]	24.5	23.8	29.8	28.2	27.7	Industrie
Services	51.4[6]	51.1[6]	51.3	50.2	47.3	46.9	47.7	Services
Croatia [1]								**Croatie** [1]
Agriculture	...	7.2	4.7	4.4	3.5	3.6	3.8	Agriculture
Industry	...	32.3	29.2	27.0	26.8	26.8	26.6	Industrie
Services	...	60.5	66.1	68.6	69.6	69.6	69.6	Services
Cuba								**Cuba**
Agriculture	9.5	6.4	4.4	3.7	4.0	3.9	4.0	Agriculture
Industry	20.7	25.9	21.8	23.1	22.4	22.6	23.2	Industrie
Services	69.9	67.7	73.8	73.2	73.6	73.5	72.8	Services
Curaçao								**Curaçao**
Agriculture [5]	...	...	0.6	0.5	0.3	0.5	0.4	Agriculture [5]
Industry	...	...	16.4	16.2	18.4	20.2	20.1	Industrie
Services	...	...	83.0	83.3	81.3	79.3	79.5	Services
Cyprus [1]								**Chypre** [1]
Agriculture	7.6	5.2	3.1	2.4	2.1	2.1	2.2	Agriculture
Industry [12]	27.0	22.0	20.5	16.7	10.7	11.1	11.8	Industrie [12]
Services [12]	65.4	72.8	76.4	80.9	87.2	86.8	86.0	Services [12]
Czechia [1]								**Tchéquie** [1]
Agriculture	...	4.4	2.4	1.7	2.7	2.5	2.3	Agriculture
Industry	...	38.9	37.7	36.8	37.9	37.8	37.3	Industrie
Services	...	56.7	59.8	61.5	59.4	59.7	60.4	Services
Dem. People's Rep. Korea								**Rép. pop. dém. de Corée**
Agriculture	28.3	27.6	25.0	20.8	21.8	21.6	21.7	Agriculture
Industry	48.5	42.0	42.8	48.2	46.9	46.2	47.2	Industrie
Services	23.2	30.3	32.2	31.0	31.3	32.2	31.1	Services
Dem. Rep. of the Congo								**Rép. dém. du Congo**
Agriculture	31.8	57.0	22.3	22.4	19.9	19.7	20.6	Agriculture
Industry	31.0	17.0	32.9	40.5	46.1	44.8	43.1	Industrie
Services	37.1	26.0	44.9	37.0	34.0	35.5	36.2	Services
Denmark [1]								**Danemark** [1]
Agriculture	4.9	3.3	1.3	1.4	1.6	1.1	1.1	Agriculture
Industry	26.5	25.5	26.2	22.8	22.8	23.0	23.7	Industrie
Services	68.6	71.2	72.5	75.8	75.6	75.9	75.2	Services
Djibouti								**Djibouti**
Agriculture	1.4[13]	1.5[13]	1.7	2.3	2.4	2.3	2.5	Agriculture
Industry	20.9[14]	16.4[14]	16.2	20.1	22.3	22.0	20.3	Industrie
Services	77.7	82.1	82.2	77.5	75.3	75.7	77.2	Services
Dominica								**Dominique**
Agriculture	22.7	13.7	13.2	13.8	14.9	15.9	18.4	Agriculture
Industry	13.7	16.0	15.0	14.4	14.7	13.4	13.0	Industrie
Services	63.6	70.3	71.9	71.8	70.4	70.7	68.5	Services
Dominican Republic [1]								**République dominicaine** [1]
Agriculture	13.4	10.7	7.7	6.5	5.6	6.0	6.3	Agriculture
Industry	41.9	35.1	32.5	29.9	31.7	30.3	28.9	Industrie
Services	44.7	54.3	59.8	63.6	62.7	63.6	64.8	Services
Ecuador [1]								**Équateur** [1]
Agriculture	19.6	22.6	10.0	10.2	9.6	10.2	10.2	Agriculture
Industry	30.7	28.0	33.4	36.3	38.6	34.4	34.7	Industrie
Services	49.7	49.4	56.6	53.5	51.8	55.4	55.1	Services
Egypt [15]								**Égypte** [15]
Agriculture	18.4	16.8	14.4	14.0	10.9	11.3	11.9	Agriculture
Industry	31.8	32.7	36.9	37.5	38.5	36.2	32.9	Industrie
Services	49.9	50.9	48.8	48.5	50.5	52.5	55.2	Services
El Salvador [1]								**El Salvador** [1]
Agriculture	18.4	12.6	6.8	7.6	6.4	6.4	6.6	Agriculture
Industry	20.8[16]	27.9	26.8	27.5	28.3	26.9	26.6	Industrie
Services	60.8	59.5	66.4	64.8	65.3	66.7	66.8	Services
Equatorial Guinea								**Guinée équatoriale**
Agriculture	14.5	12.5	1.5	1.1	1.3	1.9	2.4	Agriculture
Industry	20.6	35.8	81.3	74.3	69.8	59.0	52.0	Industrie
Services	64.9	51.6	17.2	24.6	28.9	39.1	45.6	Services

Gross value added by kind of economic activity *(continued)*
Percentage distribution, current prices

Valeur ajoutée brute par type d'activité économique *(suite)*
Répartition en pourcentage, aux prix courants

Country or area &	1985	1995	2005	2010	2015	2016	2017	Pays ou zone &
Eritrea								**Érythrée**
Agriculture	...	20.9	24.2	19.1	17.2	17.2	17.3	Agriculture
Industry	...	16.8	21.9	23.1	23.6	23.5	23.5	Industrie
Services	...	62.3	53.9	57.8	59.2	59.3	59.1	Services
Estonia [1]								**Estonie** [1]
Agriculture	...	5.7	3.5	3.2	3.5	3.1	2.6	Agriculture
Industry	...	31.9	29.8	28.0	28.6	27.8	26.9	Industrie
Services	...	62.4	66.7	68.8	67.9	69.1	70.5	Services
Eswatini [1]								**Eswatini** [1]
Agriculture	14.5	7.9	11.3	10.4	9.9	10.1	9.9	Agriculture
Industry	24.8	41.2	40.8	38.7	37.7	37.6	37.0	Industrie
Services	60.7	51.0	47.9	50.9	52.4	52.3	53.1	Services
Ethiopia								**Éthiopie**
Agriculture	...	55.0	45.6	45.6	41.5	38.8	36.8	Agriculture
Industry	...	9.8	13.2	10.4	14.5	17.5	21.0	Industrie
Services	...	35.1	42.1	44.5	44.0	43.7	42.2	Services
Fiji [1]								**Fidji** [1]
Agriculture	16.4	16.4	12.8	10.2	11.8	11.3	13.8	Agriculture
Industry	16.1	17.8	17.9	19.9	18.1	17.9	18.1	Industrie
Services	67.5	65.8	69.2	69.9	70.1	70.7	68.1	Services
Finland [1]								**Finlande** [1]
Agriculture	7.8	4.3	2.6	2.7	2.8	2.6	2.8	Agriculture
Industry	35.1	33.7	33.5	30.0	26.8	27.0	27.3	Industrie
Services	57.1	62.0	63.8	67.3	70.4	70.4	69.9	Services
France [1,17]								**France** [1,17]
Agriculture	3.7	2.7	1.9	1.8	1.7	1.8	1.6	Agriculture
Industry	28.8	24.9	21.8	19.8	19.8	19.8	19.7	Industrie
Services	67.5	72.4	76.3	78.4	78.5	78.5	78.7	Services
French Polynesia								**Polynésie française**
Agriculture	4.7	5.2	3.4	2.5	3.0	3.1	3.1	Agriculture
Industry	21.0[2]	12.5	12.7	12.3	11.8	11.8	11.8	Industrie
Services	74.3	82.3	83.9	85.2	85.2	85.1	85.1	Services
Gabon								**Gabon**
Agriculture	5.0	7.3	5.2	4.2	3.9	4.7	5.3	Agriculture
Industry	58.5	54.5	62.6	59.6	56.7	51.9	47.7	Industrie
Services	36.5	38.2	32.2	36.2	39.4	43.4	47.0	Services
Gambia [1]								**Gambie** [1]
Agriculture	24.2	21.7	32.3	35.1	24.0	25.6	27.2	Agriculture
Industry	9.6	13.1	12.4	10.4	14.7	16.5	15.3	Industrie
Services	66.3	65.1	55.3	54.4	61.3	57.8	57.5	Services
Georgia								**Géorgie**
Agriculture	...	44.4	16.5	8.3	9.1	9.0	8.8	Agriculture
Industry	...	14.3	26.5	22.0	23.6	24.2	24.5	Industrie
Services	...	41.3	57.0	69.8	67.3	66.8	66.7	Services
Germany [1]								**Allemagne** [1]
Agriculture	1.6	1.0	0.8	0.7	1.0	0.7	0.7	Agriculture
Industry	39.4	32.9	29.4	30.2	30.3	30.5	30.9	Industrie
Services	59.0	66.0	69.8	69.1	68.7	68.8	68.3	Services
Ghana [1]								**Ghana** [1]
Agriculture	34.1	30.6	29.1	28.9	22.0	22.1	22.7	Agriculture
Industry	30.7	35.0	33.2	28.2	38.1	34.6	30.6	Industrie
Services	35.2	34.4	37.7	43.0	39.8	43.2	46.7	Services
Greece [1]								**Grèce** [1]
Agriculture	10.2	8.1	4.8	3.3	3.8	4.3	4.1	Agriculture
Industry	27.0	21.6	19.8	15.7	16.0	16.1	17.0	Industrie
Services	62.7	70.3	75.4	81.1	80.1	79.6	78.9	Services
Greenland								**Groenland**
Agriculture	17.5	17.5	17.5	13.8	17.9	17.6	19.2	Agriculture
Industry	15.5	15.5	16.8	18.6	16.3	17.6	18.4	Industrie
Services	67.1	67.1	65.8	67.6	65.8	64.9	62.4	Services
Grenada								**Grenade**
Agriculture	16.1	9.5	3.4	5.2	7.0	8.6	7.3	Agriculture
Industry	16.3	18.6	26.1	16.8	14.7	14.2	14.3	Industrie
Services	67.7	71.9	70.5	78.1	78.3	77.2	78.5	Services

Country or area [&]	1985	1995	2005	2010	2015	2016	2017	Pays ou zone [&]
Guatemala								**Guatemala**
Agriculture	27.2	25.4	13.1	11.4	11.0	10.8	10.3	Agriculture
Industry	20.7	20.7	28.6	28.0	28.1	27.2	26.7	Industrie
Services	52.2	53.9	58.3	60.6	60.9	62.0	63.0	Services
Guinea								**Guinée**
Agriculture	18.3	25.7	14.9	18.6	19.0	20.4	19.6	Agriculture
Industry	31.9	27.2	34.9	34.3	32.3	28.3	33.8	Industrie
Services	49.9	47.1	50.3	47.1	48.7	51.2	46.6	Services
Guinea-Bissau								**Guinée-Bissau**
Agriculture	46.5	55.1	45.4	46.2	42.2	49.0	48.7	Agriculture
Industry	15.6	12.2	14.7	13.5	14.8	12.8	13.2	Industrie
Services	37.9	32.7	39.9	40.3	43.0	38.2	38.1	Services
Guyana								**Guyana**
Agriculture	20.0	37.1	25.7	17.6	18.0	18.9	14.6	Agriculture
Industry	31.6	33.3	28.7	34.5	32.8	33.3	40.1	Industrie
Services	48.4	29.6	45.6	47.9	49.2	47.9	45.3	Services
Haiti								**Haïti**
Agriculture	33.3	24.3	18.9	25.7	18.0	17.3	17.7	Agriculture
Industry	24.7	31.4	36.7	27.4	32.7	34.7	33.5	Industrie
Services	42.0	44.3	44.3	46.9	49.2	48.1	48.8	Services
Honduras								**Honduras**
Agriculture	20.4	20.4	13.1	11.9	12.9	12.6	12.6	Agriculture
Industry	23.8	29.9	27.6	26.2	25.2	26.5	26.6	Industrie
Services	55.8	49.7	59.3	62.0	61.9	60.8	60.8	Services
Hungary [1]								**Hongrie** [1]
Agriculture	16.0	8.4	4.3	3.5	4.7	4.5	4.6	Agriculture
Industry	42.8	30.4	31.3	29.9	30.6	31.7	30.4	Industrie
Services	41.3	61.3	64.5	66.6	64.7	63.9	65.0	Services
Iceland [1]								**Islande** [1]
Agriculture	11.3	11.0	5.7	7.1	6.0	6.0	5.2	Agriculture
Industry	34.1	28.4	24.9	24.1	22.6	22.3	22.3	Industrie
Services	54.5	60.6	69.4	68.8	71.5	71.7	72.5	Services
India [1]								**Inde** [1]
Agriculture	32.6	27.4	19.2	18.4	18.2	17.7	17.9	Agriculture
Industry	29.9	31.7	32.2	33.1	30.0	29.8	29.3	Industrie
Services	37.5	40.9	48.5	48.5	51.8	52.5	52.8	Services
Indonesia [1]								**Indonésie** [1]
Agriculture	19.8	14.2	12.1	14.3	13.7	13.9	14.0	Agriculture
Industry	33.1	38.3	43.1	43.9	43.0	41.4	40.8	Industrie
Services	47.1	47.6	44.8	41.8	43.3	44.7	45.3	Services
Iran (Islamic Republic of)								**Iran (Rép. islamique d')**
Agriculture	13.1	12.4	6.2	6.4	9.9	10.6	9.8	Agriculture
Industry	31.4	38.7	47.7	43.4	39.9	33.2	34.3	Industrie
Services	55.4	48.9	46.1	50.2	50.3	56.3	55.9	Services
Iraq								**Iraq**
Agriculture	13.9[18]	12.3	6.9	5.1	4.9	4.1	3.8	Agriculture
Industry	42.2[18,19]	66.0	63.3	55.4	55.1	46.4	44.2	Industrie
Services	43.9[19,20]	21.7	29.9	39.4	40.0	49.6	52.0	Services
Ireland [1]								**Irlande** [1]
Agriculture	9.1	6.2	1.2	1.0	1.3	0.9	1.0	Agriculture
Industry	30.6	32.1	34.3	25.6	27.1	40.8	38.5	Industrie
Services	60.3	61.8	64.5	73.3	71.6	58.3	60.5	Services
Israel [1]								**Israël** [1]
Agriculture	4.3	2.0	1.8	1.7	1.3	1.3	1.3	Agriculture
Industry	28.7	28.1	24.1	23.6	22.7	22.4	21.9	Industrie
Services	67.0	70.0	74.1	74.7	75.9	76.2	76.7	Services
Italy [1]								**Italie** [1]
Agriculture	4.6	3.3	2.2	2.0	2.2	2.2	2.1	Agriculture
Industry	33.0	29.1	25.8	24.4	23.4	23.6	24.0	Industrie
Services	62.4	67.6	71.9	73.7	74.5	74.2	73.9	Services
Jamaica								**Jamaïque**
Agriculture	5.4	9.2	5.7	5.9	6.8	7.2	7.6	Agriculture
Industry	28.4	29.4	23.9	20.0	20.8	21.9	22.0	Industrie
Services	66.2	61.4	70.4	74.1	72.4	70.9	70.5	Services

Gross value added by kind of economic activity *(continued)*
Percentage distribution, current prices

Valeur ajoutée brute par type d'activité économique *(suite)*
Répartition en pourcentage, aux prix courants

Country or area &	1985	1995	2005	2010	2015	2016	2017	Pays ou zone &
Japan [1]								**Japon** [1]
Agriculture [3]	2.9	1.7	1.1	1.1	1.1	1.1	1.2	Agriculture [3]
Industry [3]	39.5	34.7	30.1	28.5	27.9	29.1	29.5	Industrie [3]
Services	57.5	63.6	68.8	70.4	71.0	69.7	69.3	Services
Jordan [1]								**Jordanie** [1]
Agriculture	7.0	5.8	4.0	4.5	4.9	5.4	5.5	Agriculture
Industry	27.3	28.3	28.2	31.0	30.1	29.9	29.2	Industrie
Services	65.7	65.8	67.8	64.5	65.0	64.7	65.2	Services
Kazakhstan [1]								**Kazakhstan** [1]
Agriculture	...	12.9	6.6	4.7	4.7	5.0	4.8	Agriculture
Industry	...	30.2	39.2	41.9	35.9	32.5	33.9	Industrie
Services	...	56.9	54.2	53.4	59.4	62.5	61.3	Services
Kenya [1]								**Kenya** [1]
Agriculture	28.7	27.6	23.2	27.1	29.6	32.2	34.1	Agriculture
Industry	25.2	20.9	22.3	20.3	18.8	18.5	18.5	Industrie
Services	46.1	51.5	54.5	52.6	51.7	49.3	47.4	Services
Kiribati [15]								**Kiribati** [15]
Agriculture	44.0	26.9	21.8	24.2	23.9	22.6	25.4	Agriculture
Industry	9.4	9.1	9.3	11.9	14.6	15.7	15.8	Industrie
Services	46.6	64.0	68.9	63.9	61.5	61.7	58.9	Services
Kosovo [1]								**Kosovo** [1]
Agriculture	...	7.2	17.2	16.2	14.3	12.6	13.0	Agriculture
Industry	...	32.6	26.6	28.4	26.7	29.1	29.6	Industrie
Services	...	60.2	56.2	55.4	59.0	58.2	57.4	Services
Kuwait								**Koweït**
Agriculture	0.6	0.4	0.3	0.4	0.4	0.5	0.5	Agriculture
Industry	56.4	52.8	60.2	58.2	62.3	48.7	46.0	Industrie
Services	43.0	46.7	39.5	41.4	37.3	50.9	53.6	Services
Kyrgyzstan [1]								**Kirghizistan** [1]
Agriculture	...	43.1	31.3	18.8	16.5	15.4	14.3	Agriculture
Industry	...	21.8	22.1	28.2	26.8	27.5	29.7	Industrie
Services	...	35.1	46.6	53.0	56.7	57.1	56.0	Services
Lao People's Dem. Rep. [1]								**Rép. dém. populaire lao** [1]
Agriculture	39.1	42.8	29.1	23.6	19.7	19.7	19.5	Agriculture
Industry	16.2	15.7	26.2	30.9	31.7	31.0	32.5	Industrie
Services	44.7	41.5	44.7	45.5	48.6	49.4	48.0	Services
Latvia [1]								**Lettonie** [1]
Agriculture	...	8.9	4.3	4.4	3.8	4.1	3.7	Agriculture
Industry	...	30.3	22.9	23.4	22.4	22.3	21.6	Industrie
Services	...	60.8	72.8	72.2	73.8	73.6	74.7	Services
Lebanon [1]								**Liban** [1]
Agriculture	3.7	5.7	4.0	4.3	4.3	3.7	3.1	Agriculture
Industry	23.5	32.3	16.7	15.7	17.2	16.6	16.6	Industrie
Services	72.8	62.0	79.3	80.1	78.5	79.8	80.2	Services
Lesotho [1]								**Lesotho** [1]
Agriculture	16.8	9.2	6.2	5.6	6.2	5.5	6.5	Agriculture
Industry	15.7	32.4	37.7	32.9	34.0	36.2	36.1	Industrie
Services	67.5	58.4	56.1	61.5	59.9	58.3	57.4	Services
Liberia								**Libéria**
Agriculture	35.9	80.5	68.8	70.2	70.3	70.3	72.5	Agriculture
Industry	24.7	5.2	9.8	11.9	11.9	11.9	9.3	Industrie
Services	39.4	14.3	21.5	17.9	17.8	17.8	18.3	Services
Libya								**Libye**
Agriculture	3.5	6.7	2.2	2.5	0.9	0.9	0.9	Agriculture
Industry	58.8	40.3	75.7	74.0	67.1	67.1	67.1	Industrie
Services	37.7	53.0	22.2	23.5	32.0	32.0	32.0	Services
Liechtenstein [1]								**Liechtenstein** [1]
Agriculture	2.5	1.6	5.2	5.2	4.8	4.7	4.4	Agriculture
Industry	32.5	30.1	38.6	39.0	41.0	38.9	43.2	Industrie
Services	65.0	68.4	56.1	55.9	54.2	56.4	52.4	Services
Lithuania [1]								**Lituanie** [1]
Agriculture	...	11.1	4.8	3.3	3.8	3.8	3.4	Agriculture
Industry	...	31.5	32.7	29.1	30.4	29.6	28.7	Industrie
Services [21]	...	57.4	62.5	67.6	65.8	66.6	67.9	Services [21]

Country or area &	1985	1995	2005	2010	2015	2016	2017	Pays ou zone &
Luxembourg [1]								**Luxembourg** [1]
Agriculture	2.0	1.0	0.4	0.3	0.3	0.3	0.2	Agriculture
Industry	28.1	21.2	16.5	12.7	11.8	12.4	13.0	Industrie
Services	70.0	77.8	83.1	87.0	87.9	87.3	86.8	Services
Madagascar								**Madagascar**
Agriculture	37.8	36.6	31.5	29.6	28.3	27.6	27.4	Agriculture
Industry	9.0	9.6	12.2	13.6	13.8	13.5	13.2	Industrie
Services	53.1	53.8	56.3	56.8	57.9	58.9	59.4	Services
Malawi [1]								**Malawi** [1]
Agriculture	50.0	31.9	37.1	31.9	33.6	32.4	31.6	Agriculture
Industry	28.1	21.9	16.8	16.4	16.3	16.4	16.3	Industrie
Services	21.8	46.1	46.1	51.7	50.1	51.2	52.1	Services
Malaysia								**Malaisie**
Agriculture	20.3	12.7[1]	8.4[1]	10.2[1]	9.0[1]	8.6[1]	8.8[1]	Agriculture
Industry	39.2	40.5[1,3]	46.9[1,3]	40.9[1,3]	40.4[1,3]	39.6[1,3]	38.8[1,3]	Industrie
Services	40.5	46.8[1,3]	44.7[1,3]	48.9[1,3]	50.7[1,3]	51.9[1,3]	52.4[1,3]	Services
Maldives [1]								**Maldives** [1]
Agriculture	10.7	7.5	8.7	6.1	6.0	6.3	6.5	Agriculture
Industry	8.2	9.8	13.2	10.2	9.4	12.1	13.7	Industrie
Services	81.1	82.7	78.1	83.8	84.6	81.7	79.8	Services
Mali								**Mali**
Agriculture	36.1	38.8	34.4	34.9	39.3	40.2	40.9	Agriculture
Industry	14.7	18.0	25.9	25.3	20.8	19.5	18.4	Industrie
Services	49.3	43.2	39.6	39.7	39.9	40.3	40.7	Services
Malta [1]								**Malte** [1]
Agriculture	4.4	2.8	2.2	1.7	1.3	1.3	1.2	Agriculture
Industry	33.3	28.5	23.0	19.0	15.0	13.5	12.9	Industrie
Services	62.4	68.7	74.7	79.4	83.7	85.2	85.9	Services
Marshall Islands								**Îles Marshall**
Agriculture	9.7	10.5	9.2	15.6	15.9	14.3	17.0	Agriculture
Industry	12.5	14.0	9.2	11.6	10.7	10.6	10.7	Industrie
Services	77.7	75.6	81.6	72.9	73.4	75.1	72.3	Services
Mauritania								**Mauritanie**
Agriculture	36.1	43.6	29.8	21.3	23.8	26.7	25.7	Agriculture
Industry	27.0	24.7	32.4	40.9	35.8	29.1	30.2	Industrie
Services	36.9	31.6	37.9	37.8	40.5	44.2	44.1	Services
Mauritius								**Maurice**
Agriculture	14.8	9.8	5.7	4.1[1]	3.7[1]	3.6[1]	3.6[1]	Agriculture
Industry	32.2	31.3	26.6	25.3[1]	22.3[1]	21.7[1]	20.9[1]	Industrie
Services	53.1	58.9	67.8	70.7[1]	74.0[1]	74.7[1]	75.6[1]	Services
Mexico								**Mexique**
Agriculture [1]	7.3	4.6	3.2	3.4	3.3	3.4	3.6	Agriculture [1]
Industry	44.3	34.2[1]	34.3[1]	33.7[1]	33.2[1]	31.8[1]	31.5[1]	Industrie
Services [1]	48.4	61.2	62.5	62.9	63.5	64.8	65.0	Services [1]
Micronesia (Fed. States of)								**Micronésie (États féd. de)**
Agriculture	24.5	24.9	24.2	26.7	26.1	27.7	28.8	Agriculture
Industry	7.4	7.2	5.7	7.8	6.4	6.5	6.5	Industrie
Services	68.1	68.0	70.2	65.5	67.5	65.8	64.8	Services
Monaco [1,3]								**Monaco** [1,3]
Industry	12.8	12.8	12.2	12.9	12.6	17.6	18.3	Industrie
Services	87.2	87.2	87.8	87.1	87.4	82.4	81.7	Services
Mongolia [1]								**Mongolie** [1]
Agriculture	9.9	28.5	17.8	13.1	14.7	14.5	12.7	Agriculture
Industry	32.5	33.8	37.4	37.0	34.7	33.8	37.0	Industrie
Services	57.6	37.7	44.8	50.0	50.5	51.7	50.3	Services
Montenegro [1]								**Monténégro** [1]
Agriculture	...	12.1	10.3	9.2	10.0	9.8	9.0	Agriculture
Industry	...	25.3	22.1	20.5	17.7	17.4	19.1	Industrie
Services	...	62.6	67.6	70.3	72.3	72.9	71.8	Services
Montserrat								**Montserrat**
Agriculture	4.0	4.9	0.9	1.1	1.6	1.4	1.5	Agriculture
Industry	17.7	12.3	16.7	13.3	15.9	12.4	14.0	Industrie
Services	78.3	82.8	82.5	85.7	82.5	86.3	84.5	Services

Gross value added by kind of economic activity *(continued)*
Percentage distribution, current prices

Valeur ajoutée brute par type d'activité économique *(suite)*
Répartition en pourcentage, aux prix courants

Country or area &	1985	1995	2005	2010	2015	2016	2017	Pays ou zone &
Morocco [22]								**Maroc [22]**
Agriculture	17.4	15.1	13.1	14.4	13.0	14.3	13.6	Agriculture
Industry	32.8	29.6	28.9	28.6	29.5	29.5	29.4	Industrie
Services	49.8	55.3	58.0	56.9	57.5	56.2	56.9	Services
Mozambique								**Mozambique**
Agriculture	47.5	33.5[1]	25.4[1]	28.9[1]	24.5[1]	24.6[1]	24.3[1]	Agriculture
Industry	13.2	14.4[1]	20.7[1]	18.6[1]	20.2[1]	21.0[1]	21.2[1]	Industrie
Services	39.3	52.1[1]	53.8[1]	52.5[1]	55.3[1]	54.4[1]	54.6[1]	Services
Myanmar [3]								**Myanmar [3]**
Agriculture	48.2	60.0	46.7	36.9	27.8	26.8	25.5	Agriculture
Industry	13.1	9.9	17.5	26.5	34.5	34.5	35.0	Industrie
Services [23]	38.7	30.1	35.8	36.7	37.7	38.8	39.5	Services [23]
Namibia								**Namibie**
Agriculture	7.9	10.5	11.4	9.2	7.1	6.3	6.5	Agriculture
Industry	39.7	24.2	27.3	29.8	31.1	30.5	31.3	Industrie
Services	52.4	65.2	61.3	61.1	61.7	63.2	62.1	Services
Nauru [3]								**Nauru [3]**
Agriculture	6.0	6.4	7.8	4.3	3.2	3.1	3.2	Agriculture
Industry	32.9	27.7	-6.5	48.0	58.8	60.5	58.5	Industrie
Services	61.1	65.8	98.7	47.7	38.0	36.5	38.3	Services
Nepal								**Népal**
Agriculture	49.0	38.9	35.2	35.4	32.6	31.7	31.6	Agriculture
Industry	11.5	17.7	17.1	15.1	14.9	14.8	14.2	Industrie
Services	39.5	43.4	47.7	49.5	52.5	53.4	54.2	Services
Netherlands [1]								**Pays-Bas [1]**
Agriculture	4.1	3.4	2.1	2.0	1.9	1.9	2.0	Agriculture
Industry	32.7	26.5	23.6	21.9	20.4	20.2	19.7	Industrie
Services	63.2	70.1	74.3	76.1	77.6	77.9	78.3	Services
Netherlands Antilles [former]								**Antilles néerlandaises [anc.]**
Agriculture [5]	1.1	0.9	0.8	0.6	...	...	...	Agriculture [5]
Industry	20.5	18.4	15.6	15.7	...	...	...	Industrie
Services	78.4	80.7	83.7	83.7	...	...	...	Services
New Caledonia								**Nouvelle-Calédonie**
Agriculture	1.8	1.8	1.7	1.4	1.4	1.4	1.4	Agriculture
Industry	25.9	22.0	26.6	25.5	26.4	26.0	26.2	Industrie
Services	72.2	76.2	71.7	73.1	72.2	72.6	72.4	Services
New Zealand [1]								**Nouvelle-Zélande [1]**
Agriculture	7.4	7.0	4.9	7.1	5.2	4.9	6.2	Agriculture
Industry	34.1	27.8	25.8	23.0	23.4	23.2	22.0	Industrie
Services	58.5	65.3	69.3	69.9	71.4	71.9	71.8	Services
Nicaragua								**Nicaragua**
Agriculture	14.9	22.4	17.8	18.7	18.5	17.7	16.6	Agriculture
Industry	33.7	22.0	22.9	24.2	27.8	27.2	27.0	Industrie
Services	51.4	55.6	59.3	57.0	53.7	55.2	56.5	Services
Niger [1]								**Niger [1]**
Agriculture	37.0	35.9	45.5	43.8	39.2	38.7	41.4	Agriculture
Industry	20.2	14.3	11.8	16.7	20.7	19.4	17.7	Industrie
Services	42.8	49.7	42.7	39.4	40.2	41.9	41.0	Services
Nigeria [1]								**Nigéria [1]**
Agriculture	23.2	27.0	25.6	23.9	20.2	20.9	21.2	Agriculture
Industry	18.2	25.1	23.7	25.3	24.9	20.4	18.4	Industrie
Services	58.6	47.9	50.7	50.8	54.8	58.8	60.4	Services
North Macedonia [1]								**Macédoine du Nord [1]**
Agriculture	...	12.5	11.3	11.7	11.7	11.1	10.6	Agriculture
Industry	...	24.7	23.7	24.4	26.3	27.4	27.6	Industrie
Services	...	62.8	64.9	63.9	62.0	61.5	61.8	Services
Norway [1]								**Norvège [1]**
Agriculture	3.2	3.0	1.6	1.8	1.6	1.7	2.3	Agriculture
Industry	40.6	33.2	42.6	39.0	38.0	34.8	31.4	Industrie
Services	56.2	63.8	55.8	59.2	60.4	63.5	66.3	Services
Oman								**Oman**
Agriculture	2.3	2.9	1.6	1.4	1.2	1.9	2.2	Agriculture
Industry	63.3	49.7	62.1	62.7	60.3	51.0	46.1	Industrie
Services	34.4	47.4	36.3	36.0	38.5	47.2	51.7	Services

Gross value added by kind of economic activity *(continued)*
Percentage distribution, current prices

Valeur ajoutée brute par type d'activité économique *(suite)*
Répartition en pourcentage, aux prix courants

Country or area [&]	1985	1995	2005	2010	2015	2016	2017	Pays ou zone [&]
Pakistan [1]								**Pakistan** [1]
Agriculture	30.5	28.1	24.5	24.3	24.9	25.1	24.6	Agriculture
Industry	16.7	17.9	21.2	20.6	21.0	20.1	19.4	Industrie
Services	52.8	54.0	54.3	55.1	54.2	54.9	56.0	Services
Palau [1]								**Palaos** [1]
Agriculture	16.7	8.1	4.4	4.2	3.7	3.1	3.2	Agriculture
Industry	25.4	11.1	16.6	11.0	8.4	7.9	10.4	Industrie
Services	57.9	80.8	79.1	84.8	87.9	88.9	86.3	Services
Panama								**Panama**
Agriculture	7.0	7.1	6.6	3.8	3.0	2.8	2.6	Agriculture
Industry	21.9	19.6	16.1	20.1	27.7	28.9	29.4	Industrie
Services	71.1	73.2	77.3	76.2	69.3	68.3	68.0	Services
Papua New Guinea								**Papouasie-Nvl-Guinée**
Agriculture	18.6	22.0	22.7	20.2	18.8	19.6	19.5	Agriculture
Industry	14.4	23.0	34.0	34.2	33.7	29.9	30.4	Industrie
Services	67.0	55.0	43.3	45.5	47.5	50.5	50.2	Services
Paraguay								**Paraguay**
Agriculture	26.5	22.8	19.6	22.5	20.5	19.2	20.0	Agriculture
Industry	24.2[24]	25.7[24]	34.8	30.1	28.8	29.6	30.3	Industrie
Services	49.3	51.5	45.7	47.4	50.6	51.2	49.7	Services
Peru [1]								**Pérou** [1]
Agriculture	8.7	8.9	7.5	7.5	7.5	7.7	7.6	Agriculture
Industry	45.4	32.3	37.7	39.1	34.8	33.1	33.1	Industrie
Services	45.9	58.8	54.7	53.5	57.7	59.2	59.4	Services
Philippines [1]								**Philippines** [1]
Agriculture	21.2	18.8	12.7	12.3	11.3	10.3	9.7	Agriculture
Industry [8]	38.0	35.0	33.8	32.6	31.3	30.9	30.8	Industrie [8]
Services [8]	40.8	46.1	53.5	55.1	57.3	58.8	59.6	Services [8]
Poland [1]								**Pologne** [1]
Agriculture	14.6	5.6	3.3	2.9	2.9	2.5	2.7	Agriculture
Industry	51.4	37.4	32.8	33.2	33.2	34.1	33.5	Industrie
Services	34.0	57.0	63.9	63.9	63.9	63.4	63.8	Services
Portugal [1]								**Portugal** [1]
Agriculture	13.3	5.4	2.6	2.2	2.3	2.4	2.2	Agriculture
Industry	26.8	28.2	24.6	22.6	21.6	22.4	22.4	Industrie
Services	59.9	66.4	72.7	75.2	76.0	75.3	75.3	Services
Puerto Rico [3]								**Porto Rico** [3]
Agriculture	2.5	1.0	0.6	0.8	0.8	0.8	0.8	Agriculture
Industry	45.3	47.6	47.3	50.7	50.0	51.1	50.9	Industrie
Services	52.2	51.4	52.1	48.4	49.1	48.0	48.3	Services
Qatar [1]								**Qatar** [1]
Agriculture	1.0	1.0	0.1	0.1	0.1	0.2	0.2	Agriculture
Industry [3]	57.8	53.0	74.6	67.5	67.9	56.4	49.7	Industrie [3]
Services [3]	41.3	46.0	25.3	32.4	32.0	43.5	50.1	Services [3]
Republic of Korea [1]								**République de Corée** [1]
Agriculture	13.0	5.9	3.1	2.5	2.3	2.3	2.1	Agriculture
Industry	37.2	39.5	37.5	38.3	38.1	38.3	38.7	Industrie
Services	49.7	54.6	59.4	59.3	59.6	59.4	59.2	Services
Republic of Moldova [1]								**République de Moldova** [1]
Agriculture	...	32.2	19.1	14.1	15.1	13.9	14.0	Agriculture
Industry	...	31.3	22.3	20.0	21.6	21.4	21.3	Industrie
Services	...	36.5	58.6	65.9	63.2	64.7	64.7	Services
Romania [1]								**Roumanie** [1]
Agriculture	15.5	19.2	9.5	6.1	5.3	4.8	4.6	Agriculture
Industry	54.0	38.4	36.0	42.0	35.6	34.1	33.7	Industrie
Services	30.4	42.5	54.5	51.8	59.0	61.2	61.8	Services
Russian Federation								**Fédération de Russie**
Agriculture	...	7.1	4.9	3.8	4.1	4.6	4.6	Agriculture
Industry	...	39.5	38.2	34.8	32.1	33.1	32.5	Industrie
Services	...	53.4	56.9	61.4	63.9	62.3	62.9	Services
Rwanda [1]								**Rwanda** [1]
Agriculture	50.7	42.9	39.3	30.2	30.9	30.1	31.5	Agriculture
Industry	19.2	13.7	13.8	15.8	18.5	18.3	17.6	Industrie
Services	30.1	43.4	46.9	53.9	50.6	51.6	50.9	Services

Gross value added by kind of economic activity *(continued)*
Percentage distribution, current prices

Valeur ajoutée brute par type d'activité économique *(suite)*
Répartition en pourcentage, aux prix courants

Country or area &	1985	1995	2005	2010	2015	2016	2017	Pays ou zone &
Saint Kitts and Nevis								**Saint-Kitts-et-Nevis**
Agriculture	5.7	3.3	1.9	1.6	1.4	1.2	1.1	Agriculture
Industry	19.1	24.0	25.4	28.1	27.2	28.1	28.0	Industrie
Services	75.2	72.6	72.6	70.3	71.4	70.7	70.9	Services
Saint Lucia								**Sainte-Lucie**
Agriculture	12.0	7.5	3.5	2.5	2.4	2.4	2.4	Agriculture
Industry	16.0	16.2	18.7	13.8	11.9	12.1	12.4	Industrie
Services	72.1	76.3	77.8	83.7	85.7	85.5	85.2	Services
Saint Vincent & Grenadines								**Saint-Vincent-Grenadines**
Agriculture	15.1	11.2	6.2	7.1	7.7	7.3	8.2	Agriculture
Industry	19.6	20.9	18.6	19.2	17.2	18.0	17.6	Industrie
Services	65.3	67.9	75.1	73.7	75.1	74.6	74.2	Services
Samoa [3]								**Samoa** [3]
Agriculture	22.4	20.1	12.3	9.1	9.2	9.4	10.5	Agriculture
Industry	27.3	27.1	30.6	25.8	25.0	24.5	23.0	Industrie
Services	50.3	52.7	57.2	65.1	65.8	67.4	67.9	Services
San Marino [1]								**Saint-Marin** [1]
Agriculture	~0.0	~0.0	~0.0	~0.0	~0.0	~0.0	~0.0	Agriculture
Industry	40.9	40.9	38.2	35.4	32.8	34.4	34.9	Industrie
Services	59.0	59.1	61.8	64.6	67.2	65.6	65.0	Services
Sao Tome and Principe								**Sao Tomé-et-Principe**
Agriculture	27.6	26.4	18.3	11.8	11.6	12.3	12.1	Agriculture
Industry	17.9	19.6	14.9	18.2	17.3	14.9	15.8	Industrie
Services	54.5	53.9	66.8	70.1	71.1	72.7	72.1	Services
Saudi Arabia [1]								**Arabie saoudite** [1]
Agriculture	3.6	5.9	3.2	2.6	2.2	2.6	2.7	Agriculture
Industry	41.2	48.9	61.8	58.2	57.2	45.3	43.2	Industrie
Services	55.2	45.3	35.0	39.1	40.6	52.0	54.1	Services
Senegal [1]								**Sénégal** [1]
Agriculture	17.3	18.3	16.0	16.6	14.8	16.0	16.4	Agriculture
Industry	27.1	28.9	26.3	25.6	25.7	26.4	25.9	Industrie
Services	55.6	52.8	57.7	57.8	59.5	57.6	57.7	Services
Serbia [1]								**Serbie** [1]
Agriculture	...	20.9	12.0[25]	10.2[25]	9.3[25]	8.2[25]	7.9[25]	Agriculture
Industry	...	35.5	29.3[25]	28.4[25]	30.2[25]	31.4[25]	31.3[25]	Industrie
Services	...	43.6	58.7[25]	61.4[25]	60.5[25]	60.5[25]	60.8[25]	Services
Seychelles [1]								**Seychelles** [1]
Agriculture	6.7	5.9	3.8	2.7	2.8	2.4	2.4	Agriculture
Industry	9.2	13.5	19.4	16.5	14.5	14.0	13.5	Industrie
Services	84.1	80.6	76.8	80.8	82.6	83.6	84.2	Services
Sierra Leone								**Sierra Leone**
Agriculture	41.0	48.1	51.0	55.2	53.3	60.5	59.4	Agriculture
Industry	20.4	9.1	11.6	8.1	16.1	4.6	7.0	Industrie
Services	38.7	42.8	37.4	36.7	30.7	34.9	33.7	Services
Singapore [1]								**Singapour** [1]
Agriculture	1.0	0.2	0.1	~0.0	~0.0	~0.0	~0.0	Agriculture
Industry [4]	33.4	33.8	32.4	27.6	25.4	25.7	25.3	Industrie [4]
Services	65.6	66.1	67.6	72.3	74.5	74.2	74.7	Services
Sint Maarten (Dutch part)								**St-Martin (partie néerland.)**
Agriculture	...	...	0.3	0.1	0.1	0.1	0.1	Agriculture
Industry	...	...	16.4	13.4	11.6	9.8	9.2	Industrie
Services	...	...	83.3	86.5	88.3	90.1	90.7	Services
Slovakia [1]								**Slovaquie** [1]
Agriculture	...	5.6	3.6	2.8	4.5	3.7	3.7	Agriculture
Industry	...	36.8	36.1	35.2	34.6	34.8	34.4	Industrie
Services	...	57.5	60.3	62.0	61.0	61.4	61.9	Services
Slovenia [1]								**Slovénie** [1]
Agriculture	...	4.3	2.6	2.0	2.3	2.4	2.2	Agriculture
Industry	...	34.7	34.1	30.6	32.8	32.6	32.4	Industrie
Services	...	61.0	63.3	67.4	64.9	65.1	65.3	Services
Solomon Islands								**Îles Salomon**
Agriculture	50.4	44.7	30.4	28.7	26.3	25.0	25.6	Agriculture
Industry	8.3	14.4	7.5	13.3	15.2	15.5	15.0	Industrie
Services	41.3	41.0	62.1	57.9	58.6	59.5	59.4	Services

Country or area [&]	1985	1995	2005	2010	2015	2016	2017	Pays ou zone [&]
Somalia								**Somalie**
Agriculture	66.1	60.1	60.1	60.2	60.2	60.2	60.2	Agriculture
Industry	7.6	7.3	7.4	7.4	7.4	7.4	7.4	Industrie
Services	26.3	32.6	32.6	32.5	32.5	32.5	32.5	Services
South Africa								**Afrique du Sud**
Agriculture	5.1	3.8	2.7	2.6	2.4	2.3	2.4	Agriculture
Industry	42.8	33.9	30.3	30.2	29.6	29.1	29.2	Industrie
Services	52.1	62.4	67.1	67.2	68.0	68.6	68.4	Services
South Sudan [1]								**Soudan du sud** [1]
Agriculture	...	...	...	5.1	4.9	4.1	3.8	Agriculture
Industry	...	...	...	55.4	55.1	46.4	44.2	Industrie
Services	...	...	...	39.4	40.0	49.6	52.0	Services
Spain [1]								**Espagne** [1]
Agriculture	5.7	4.2	3.0	2.6	2.7	2.9	3.0	Agriculture
Industry	34.9	30.7	30.4	26.0	23.2	23.3	23.5	Industrie
Services	59.4	65.1	66.5	71.4	74.1	73.9	73.6	Services
Sri Lanka [1]								**Sri Lanka** [1]
Agriculture	22.2	16.6	8.8	9.5	8.6	8.8	8.2	Agriculture
Industry	31.8	32.8	31.0	29.7	30.4	29.3	29.8	Industrie
Services	46.0	50.6	60.1	60.9	61.0	61.9	62.1	Services
State of Palestine [1]								**État de Palestine** [1]
Agriculture	13.2	12.6	5.8	6.4	4.4	4.1	3.7	Agriculture
Industry	30.7	31.6	25.8	23.3	22.7	21.8	22.7	Industrie
Services	56.1	55.8	68.3	70.2	72.9	74.0	73.6	Services
Sudan								**Soudan**
Agriculture	...	...	...	42.8	32.1	32.4	31.7	Agriculture
Industry	...	...	...	13.9	21.3	20.1	20.8	Industrie
Services	...	...	...	43.4	46.6	47.6	47.6	Services
Sudan [former]								**Soudan [anc.]**
Agriculture	36.7	37.1	34.5	34.6	...	...	...	Agriculture
Industry	13.2	9.9	21.7	22.9	...	...	...	Industrie
Services	50.1	53.0	43.7	42.5	...	...	...	Services
Suriname								**Suriname**
Agriculture	8.6[15]	29.9	11.3	10.2	10.0	9.9	9.7	Agriculture
Industry	28.5[15]	27.5	37.4	37.9	32.7	27.9	31.8	Industrie
Services	62.9[15]	42.6	51.3	51.9	57.3	62.2	58.4	Services
Sweden [1]								**Suède** [1]
Agriculture	4.5	2.8	1.1	1.6	1.3	1.4	1.3	Agriculture
Industry	33.7	31.3	29.7	28.9	25.7	24.5	24.4	Industrie
Services	61.9	65.9	69.2	69.5	72.9	74.2	74.3	Services
Switzerland [1]								**Suisse** [1]
Agriculture	2.4	1.5	0.9	0.7	0.7	0.7	0.7	Agriculture
Industry	32.6	30.1	27.0	26.6	26.0	25.9	25.6	Industrie
Services	64.9	68.3	72.1	72.7	73.2	73.4	73.7	Services
Syrian Arab Republic [8]								**République arabe syrienne** [8]
Agriculture	21.0	28.2	20.3	19.7	20.6	20.7	20.5	Agriculture
Industry	21.9	18.1	31.2	30.7	30.2	30.0	30.2	Industrie
Services	57.1	53.7	48.5	49.6	49.2	49.3	49.3	Services
Tajikistan								**Tadjikistan**
Agriculture	...	31.6	23.8	21.8	26.8	24.7	22.7	Agriculture
Industry	...	48.4	30.7	27.9	25.5	27.5	30.3	Industrie
Services	...	20.0	45.6	50.3	47.6	47.8	47.0	Services
Thailand [1]								**Thaïlande** [1]
Agriculture [3]	15.8	9.1	9.2	10.5	10.1	9.0	8.5	Agriculture [3]
Industry [3]	31.8	37.5	38.6	40.0	36.8	36.2	35.8	Industrie [3]
Services	52.3	53.4[3]	52.2[3]	49.5[3]	53.1[3]	54.8[3]	55.7[3]	Services
Timor-Leste [1]								**Timor-Leste** [1]
Agriculture	...	20.6	7.4	5.7	7.4	9.1	11.4	Agriculture
Industry	...	47.8	76.1	79.1	69.9	57.7	45.1	Industrie
Services	...	31.6	16.4	15.2	22.7	33.2	43.5	Services
Togo								**Togo**
Agriculture	30.9	34.2	34.0	33.8	29.1	28.2	27.8	Agriculture
Industry [26]	25.7	27.5	16.5	16.0	18.3	18.0	19.6	Industrie [26]
Services [27]	43.4	38.3	49.5	50.3	52.6	53.8	52.6	Services [27]

Country or area [&]	1985	1995	2005	2010	2015	2016	2017	Pays ou zone [&]
Tonga								**Tonga**
Agriculture	37.8	22.1	20.2	18.2	19.4	19.9	19.3	Agriculture
Industry	14.9	22.0	19.1	19.9	18.3	19.1	19.4	Industrie
Services	47.3	55.9	60.6	61.8	62.3	60.9	61.3	Services
Trinidad and Tobago [1]								**Trinité-et-Tobago** [1]
Agriculture	2.9	1.9	0.5	0.4	0.4	0.5	0.5	Agriculture
Industry	42.1	42.7	56.3	51.8	48.2	38.1	36.2	Industrie
Services	55.0	55.4	43.2	47.8	51.4	61.4	63.3	Services
Tunisia [15]								**Tunisie** [15]
Agriculture	14.4	10.5	10.0	8.1	9.7	10.9	10.2	Agriculture
Industry	34.7	29.6	28.8	31.1	28.5	26.5	25.8	Industrie
Services	50.8	59.9	61.3	60.8	61.7	62.5	64.1	Services
Turkey [1]								**Turquie** [1]
Agriculture	16.2	12.4	10.6	10.3	7.5	7.8	7.0	Agriculture
Industry	34.1	38.3	29.0	28.0	31.9	31.7	32.0	Industrie
Services	49.7	49.3	60.4	61.8	60.7	60.5	61.0	Services
Turkmenistan								**Turkménistan**
Agriculture	...	16.9	18.8	11.5	8.4	9.4	8.8	Agriculture
Industry	...	65.3	37.6	60.0	61.6	57.8	61.3	Industrie
Services	...	17.9	43.6	28.5	30.0	32.7	29.9	Services
Turks and Caicos Islands								**Îles Turques-et-Caïques**
Agriculture	1.3	1.3	1.2	0.6	0.6	0.6	0.6	Agriculture
Industry	16.3	16.4	19.7	12.4	10.7	10.5	10.6	Industrie
Services	82.4	82.3	79.1	86.9	88.8	88.9	88.8	Services
Tuvalu								**Tuvalu**
Agriculture	10.8	24.0	22.2	27.3	23.0	21.4	20.7	Agriculture
Industry	13.5	14.0	8.3	5.7[28]	8.6[28]	12.7[28]	15.4[28]	Industrie
Services	75.6	62.0	69.4	67.0	68.4	65.9	63.9	Services
Uganda [1]								**Ouganda** [1]
Agriculture	50.2	40.2	28.7	26.3	27.1	25.8	25.4	Agriculture
Industry	9.5	17.0	22.2	20.5	21.7	22.2	22.7	Industrie
Services	40.2	42.8	49.1	53.2	51.2	52.0	51.9	Services
Ukraine [1]								**Ukraine** [1]
Agriculture	...	14.5	10.0	8.4[29]	11.7[29]	14.2[29]	13.8[29]	Agriculture
Industry	...	41.8	34.1	29.3[29]	26.2[29]	25.6[29]	27.3[29]	Industrie
Services	...	43.7	55.8	62.3[29]	62.2[29]	60.2[29]	58.8[29]	Services
United Arab Emirates								**Émirats arabes unis**
Agriculture	0.9	1.6	1.3	0.8	0.6	0.7	0.8	Agriculture
Industry	60.8	47.5	54.0	52.5	52.8	43.9	41.4	Industrie
Services	38.4	50.9	44.7	46.7	46.6	55.3	57.8	Services
United Kingdom [1]								**Royaume-Uni** [1]
Agriculture	1.3	1.4	0.6	0.7	0.7	0.7	0.7	Agriculture
Industry	33.3	27.5	21.8	19.9	20.0	20.0	19.8	Industrie
Services	65.4	71.1	77.6	79.4	79.3	79.3	79.6	Services
United Rep. of Tanzania [1,30]								**Rép.-Unie de Tanzanie** [1,30]
Agriculture	27.6	34.2	30.1	31.7	31.0	31.1	31.3	Agriculture
Industry	13.0	16.7	20.8	21.5	25.0	26.1	26.7	Industrie
Services	59.4	49.2	49.1	46.8	44.0	42.9	42.0	Services
United States of America [1,8]								**États-Unis d'Amérique** [1,8]
Agriculture	1.6	1.2	1.0	1.0	1.1	1.0	0.9	Agriculture
Industry	28.3	24.3	21.5	19.7	19.6	18.8	18.2	Industrie
Services	70.0	74.5	77.5	79.3	79.2	80.2	80.9	Services
Uruguay								**Uruguay**
Agriculture	12.5	8.1	9.8	8.0	7.4	6.7	6.5	Agriculture
Industry	30.8	25.9	26.6	27.3	27.3	28.0	28.0	Industrie
Services	56.7	66.0	63.6	64.7	65.3	65.3	65.5	Services
Uzbekistan								**Ouzbékistan**
Agriculture	...	31.4	29.5	19.8	18.9	18.3	18.2	Agriculture
Industry	...	30.9	29.1	33.3	32.6	33.0	33.0	Industrie
Services	...	37.7	41.4	46.9	48.5	48.8	48.9	Services
Vanuatu [1]								**Vanuatu** [1]
Agriculture	32.6	30.5	24.1	21.9	26.8	23.1	22.2	Agriculture
Industry	5.9	9.1	8.5	13.0	8.7	11.5	11.1	Industrie
Services	61.5	60.4	67.4	65.0	64.5	65.4	66.6	Services

Country or area [&]	1985	1995	2005	2010	2015	2016	2017	Pays ou zone [&]
Venezuela (Boliv. Rep. of)								**Venezuela (Rép. boliv. du)**
Agriculture	6.4	5.9	4.0	5.7	5.4	6.3	5.6	Agriculture
Industry	51.9	47.1	56.9	51.0	39.6	30.5	39.2	Industrie
Services	41.7	47.0	39.2	43.4	55.0	63.2	55.3	Services
Viet Nam [1]								**Viet Nam [1]**
Agriculture [3]	39.0	24.5	19.3	21.0	19.7	18.9	18.1	Agriculture [3]
Industry	21.4[3]	26.1[3]	38.1[3]	36.7	36.9[3]	37.0	36.4	Industrie
Services	39.6[3]	49.4[3]	42.6[3]	42.2[3]	43.4[3]	44.2	45.5[3]	Services
Yemen								**Yémen**
Agriculture	...	17.3	9.6	12.1	14.0	17.6	18.6	Agriculture
Industry	...	27.4	43.8	38.7	36.0	20.3	20.7	Industrie
Services	...	55.3	46.5	49.2	50.0	62.1	60.6	Services
Zambia [1]								**Zambie [1]**
Agriculture	13.3	15.1	15.5	10.0	7.3	5.3	6.5	Agriculture
Industry	50.8	36.8	28.6	34.1	35.3	35.3	36.6	Industrie
Services	35.9	48.1	55.9	55.9	57.4	59.4	56.9	Services
Zanzibar [1]								**Zanzibar [1]**
Agriculture	...	21.3	23.0	32.5	30.7	28.3	28.4	Agriculture
Industry	...	22.5	17.5	19.2	18.6	19.8	20.5	Industrie
Services	...	56.2	59.5	48.3	50.7	51.8	51.1	Services
Zimbabwe								**Zimbabwe**
Agriculture	20.1	13.5	11.6	13.3	12.2	11.7	11.0	Agriculture
Industry	26.9	27.6	39.7	28.1	25.7	24.4	22.9	Industrie
Services	53.0	58.9	48.7	58.6	62.1	64.0	66.1	Services

Source:

United Nations Statistics Division, New York, National Accounts
Statistics: Analysis of Main Aggregates (AMA) database, last accessed
February 2019.

Source:

Organisation des Nations Unies, Division de statistique, New York, base
de données des statistiques des comptes nationaux : Analyse des
principaux agrégats, denier accès février 2019.

[&] Table is in ISIC Rev. 3 unless otherwise indicated.

[&] Sauf indication contraire la classification utilisée dans ce tableau est la
CITI Rev. 3.

1	Data classified according to ISIC Rev. 4.
2	Including mining and quarrying.
3	At producers' prices.
4	Excluding mining and quarrying.
5	Includes mining and handicrafts.
6	Data compiled in accordance with the System of National Accounts 1968 (1968 SNA).
7	For statistical purposes, the data for China do not include those for the Hong Kong Special Administrative Region (Hong Kong SAR) and Macao Special Administrative Region (Macao SAR).
8	Including taxes less subsidies on production and imports.
9	Excluding hunting and forestry.
10	Includes waste management.
11	Excluding waste management.
12	Excluding northern Cyprus.
13	Excludes hunting.
14	Excludes gas.
15	At factor cost.
16	Restaurants and hotels only.
17	Including French Guiana, Guadeloupe, Martinique and Réunion.
18	Agricultural services and related activities such as cotton ginning and pressing are included in Manufacturing.
19	Gas distribution is included in Wholesale and retail trade.

1	Classifiées selon la CITI, Rév. 4.
2	Y compris les industries extractives.
3	Aux prix à la production.
4	Non compris les industries extractives.
5	Y compris l'extraction et l'artisanat.
6	Données compilées selon le Système de comptabilité nationale de 1968 (SCN 1968).
7	Pour la présentation des statistiques, les données pour la Chine ne comprennent pas la Région Administrative Spéciale de Hong Kong (RAS de Hong Kong) et la Région Administrative Spéciale de Macao (RAS de Macao).
8	Y compris les impôts moins les subventions sur la production et les importations.
9	Non compris la chasse et la sylviculture.
10	Y compris la gestion des déchets.
11	Gestion des déchets non-compris.
12	Chypre du nord non compris.
13	Non compris la chasse.
14	Non compris le gaz.
15	Au coût des facteurs.
16	Les restaurants et hôtels seulement.
17	Y compris Guadeloupe, Guyane française, Martinique et Réunion.
18	Les services agricoles et les activités connexes (par exemple l'égrenage du coton, tressage) figurent sous l'industrie manufacturière.
19	La distribution de gaz est incluse dans le commerce de gros et de detail.

14

Gross value added by kind of economic activity *(continued)*
Percentage distribution, current prices

Valeur ajoutée brute par type d'activité économique *(suite)*
Répartition en pourcentage, aux prix courants

20	Distribution of petroleum products is included in Wholesale and retail trade.
21	Includes publishing activities and landscaping care.
22	Including Western Sahara.
23	Excludes Hotels and restaurants.
24	Does not incorporate value added generated by binational hydroelectric plants.
25	Excluding Kosovo and Metohija.
26	Construction refers to buildings and public works.
27	Refers to trade only.
28	Includes Electricity, gas and water supply.
29	Excludes the temporarily occupied territory of the Autonomous Republic of Crimea and Sevastopol.
30	Tanzania mainland only, excluding Zanzibar.

20 La distribution des produits pétroliers est comprise dans le commerce de gros et de détail.
21 Y compris les activités d'édition et l'aménagement paysager.
22 Y compris les données de Sahara occidental.
23 Non compris les hôtels et restaurants.
24 Ne comprend pas la valeur ajoutée produite par les centrales hydroélectriques binationales.
25 Non compris Kosovo et Metohija.
26 Construction se rapporte aux bâtiments et travaux publics.
27 Se rapporte seulement au commerce
28 Y compris la production et la distribution d'électricité, de gaz et d'eau.
29 Excluent le territoire temporairement occupé de la République autonome de Crimée et de Sébastopol.
30 Tanzanie continentale seulement, Zanzibar non compris.

Balance of payments summary
Millions of US dollars

Résumé de la balance des paiements
Millions de dollars É.-U.

Country or area&	1985	1995	2005	2010	2016	2017	2018	Pays ou zone&
Afghanistan								**Afghanistan**
Current account	-243	...	...	-1 732	-3 323	-4 227	...	Compte des transac. cour.
Capital account	...	...	...	2 999	1 771	1 733	...	Compte de capital
Financial account	-75	...	...	1 061	697	420	...	Compte financier
Albania								**Albanie**
Current account	-36	-12	-571	-1 356	-900	-981	-1 008	Compte des transac. cour.
Capital account	...	389	123	113	72	139	122	Compte de capital
Financial account	-30	432	-245	-797	-686	-1 082	-919	Compte financier
Algeria								**Algérie**
Current account	1 015	...	21 180	12 220	-26 204	-22 059	...	Compte des transac. cour.
Capital account	...	...	-3	4	1	1	...	Compte de capital
Financial account	1 141	...	20 988	10 921	-26 179	-22 015	...	Compte financier
Angola								**Angola**
Current account	195	-295	5 138	7 506	-3 085	-633	7 502	Compte des transac. cour.
Capital account	...	8	8	1	1	3	3	Compte de capital
Financial account	-460	-314	4 571	7 219	-4 892	-748	4 721	Compte financier
Anguilla								**Anguilla**
Current account	...	-10	-52	-51	-86	-62	...	Compte des transac. cour.
Capital account	...	1	2	4	1	11	...	Compte de capital
Financial account	...	4	-42	-35	-20	-7	...	Compte financier
Antigua and Barbuda								**Antigua-et-Barbuda**
Current account	-23	-1	-171	-167	-39	34	...	Compte des transac. cour.
Capital account	...	4	211	17	28	40	...	Compte de capital
Financial account	-23	24	32	-158	-57	103	...	Compte financier
Argentina								**Argentine**
Current account	-952	-5 118	5 274	-1 623	-15 105	-31 598	-28 003	Compte des transac. cour.
Capital account	...	14	89	78	366	139	86	Compte de capital
Financial account	-1 484	-7 777	5 699	-3 803	-13 951	-31 297	-28 480	Compte financier
Armenia								**Arménie**
Current account	...	-221	-124	-1 261	-238	-280	-1 131	Compte des transac. cour.
Capital account	...	8	84	99	35	46	68	Compte de capital
Financial account	...	-198	-203	-1 318	-429	-542	-687	Compte financier
Aruba								**Aruba**
Current account	...	-~0	105	-460	141	...	...	Compte des transac. cour.
Capital account	...	0	16	4	8	...	...	Compte de capital
Financial account	...	1	148	-446	133	...	...	Compte financier
Australia								**Australie**
Current account	...	-18 669	-43 343	-44 714	-41 197	-35 758	-30 508	Compte des transac. cour.
Capital account	...	-300	-121	-287	-605	-388	-384	Compte de capital
Financial account	...	-18 866	-42 174	-44 105	-39 252	-35 672	-33 743	Compte financier
Austria								**Autriche**
Current account	...	...	6 245	11 478	9 752	7 996	10 801	Compte des transac. cour.
Capital account	...	...	-84	268	-411	-290	-355	Compte de capital
Financial account	...	...	168	4 758	11 752	10 232	9 207	Compte financier
Azerbaijan								**Azerbaïdjan**
Current account	...	-401	167	15 040	-1 363	1 685	6 051	Compte des transac. cour.
Capital account	...	-2	-~0	...	-40	100	1	Compte de capital
Financial account	...	-342	83	14 065	2 222	2 173	6 699	Compte financier
Bahamas								**Bahamas**
Current account	-3	-146	-701	-814	-1 106	-1 981	...	Compte des transac. cour.
Financial account	30	-107	-910	-1 097	58	-1 643	...	Compte financier
Bahrain								**Bahreïn**
Current account	39	237	1 474	770	-1 493	-1 600	...	Compte des transac. cour.
Capital account	...	157	50	50	874	604	...	Compte de capital
Financial account	834	1 896	1 674	927	1 693	77	...	Compte financier
Bangladesh								**Bangladesh**
Current account	-455	-824	-174	2 109	931	-5 985	-7 593	Compte des transac. cour.
Capital account	...	...	262	603	427	293	291	Compte de capital
Financial account	-523	-691	-480	-1 745	135	-6 186	-8 693	Compte financier
Barbados								**Barbade**
Current account	60	10	-466	-218	...	...	...	Compte des transac. cour.
Financial account	23	69	-395	-284	...	...	...	Compte financier

15   Balance of payments summary *(continued)*
Millions of US dollars

Résumé de la balance des paiements *(suite)*
Millions de dollars É.-U.

Country or area[&]	1985	1995	2005	2010	2016	2017	2018	Pays ou zone[&]
Belarus								**Bélarus**
Current account	...	-458	459	-8 280	-1 612	-945	-266	Compte des transac. cour.
Capital account	...	7	...	...	7	2	20	Compte de capital
Financial account	...	-282	585	-7 578	-746	-366	-75	Compte financier
Belgium								**Belgique**
Current account	...	...	7 703	7 977	-2 809	3 567	-6 819	Compte des transac. cour.
Capital account	...	...	-922	-1 142	441	441	-85	Compte de capital
Financial account	...	...	9 221	6 567	-1 570	-4 537	-6 332	Compte financier
Belize								**Belize**
Current account	9	-17	-151	-46	-163	-131	-155	Compte des transac. cour.
Capital account	...	...	3	5	33	16	24	Compte de capital
Financial account	-7	5	-156	-22	-107	-119	-126	Compte financier
Benin								**Bénin**
Current account	-39	-167	-226	-530	-809	-927	...	Compte des transac. cour.
Capital account	...	88	102	122	138	196	...	Compte de capital
Financial account	-23	-79	-95	-375	-670	-712	...	Compte financier
Bermuda								**Bermudes**
Current account	...	...	...	696	846	940	...	Compte des transac. cour.
Financial account	...	...	...	714	831	824	...	Compte financier
Bhutan								**Bhoutan**
Current account	...	...	...	-323	-623	-540	-498	Compte des transac. cour.
Capital account	...	...	...	150	192	186	166	Compte de capital
Financial account	...	...	...	-105	-462	-263	-186	Compte financier
Bolivia (Plurin. State of)								**Bolivie (État plurin. de)**
Current account	-285	-303	622	874	-1 907	-1 871	-1 990	Compte des transac. cour.
Capital account	...	...	...	...	31	15	11	Compte de capital
Financial account	-92	-413	257	64	-2 254	-2 603	-2 943	Compte financier
Bosnia and Herzegovina								**Bosnie-Herzégovine**
Current account	...	...	-1 844	-1 031	-787	-851	-829	Compte des transac. cour.
Capital account	...	...	276	264	168	174	187	Compte de capital
Financial account	...	...	-1 336	-647	-532	-571	-517	Compte financier
Botswana								**Botswana**
Current account	82	300	1 598	-804	1 213	929	345	Compte des transac. cour.
Capital account	0	12	...	...	...	...	...	Compte de capital
Financial account	131	240	2 795	-871	490	666	-376	Compte financier
Brazil								**Brésil**
Current account	-280	-18 136	13 985	-79 014	-24 009	-7 235	-14 509	Compte des transac. cour.
Capital account	...	...	52	242	274	379	440	Compte de capital
Financial account	-803	-16 337	14 423	-69 970	-10 268	-447	-7 732	Compte financier
Brunei Darussalam								**Brunéi Darussalam**
Current account	...	...	4 033	5 016	1 470	1 984	1 068	Compte des transac. cour.
Capital account	...	...	-8	...	...	...	...	Compte de capital
Financial account	...	...	19	4 918	6 563	1 171	202	Compte financier
Bulgaria								**Bulgarie**
Current account	-136	-26	-3 347	-965	1 413	1 847	2 959	Compte des transac. cour.
Capital account	...	...	290	398	1 188	605	696	Compte de capital
Financial account	463	118	-4 277	861	4 578	1 363	2 374	Compte financier
Burkina Faso								**Burkina Faso**
Current account	...	...	-634	-181	-780	-894	...	Compte des transac. cour.
Capital account	...	...	209	180	253	297	...	Compte de capital
Financial account	...	...	-431	16	-534	-594	...	Compte financier
Burundi								**Burundi**
Current account	-41	10	-6	-301	-340	-360	...	Compte des transac. cour.
Capital account	...	...	32	78	70	79	...	Compte de capital
Financial account	-50	16	-58	-226	-249	-226	...	Compte financier
Cabo Verde								**Cabo Verde**
Current account	-9	-62	-41	-223	-64	-138	-104	Compte des transac. cour.
Capital account	...	21	21	38	13	16	15	Compte de capital
Financial account	-4	-76	-18	-270	-55	-125	-133	Compte financier
Cambodia								**Cambodge**
Current account	...	-186	-307	-981	-1 687	-1 743	-2 773	Compte des transac. cour.
Capital account	...	92	102	434	283	279	293	Compte de capital
Financial account	...	-82	-238	-632	-1 344	-1 473	-2 435	Compte financier

Balance of payments summary *(continued)*
Millions of US dollars

Résumé de la balance des paiements *(suite)*
Millions de dollars É.-U.

Country or area&	1985	1995	2005	2010	2016	2017	2018	Pays ou zone&
Cameroon								**Cameroun**
Current account	-562	90	-495	-856	-1 037	-949	...	Compte des transac. cour.
Capital account	...	20	204	147	99	120	...	Compte de capital
Financial account	-453	-16	-319	-521	-922	-1 121	...	Compte financier
Canada								**Canada**
Current account	-5 839	-5 061	21 933	-58 163	-49 054	-46 381	-45 323	Compte des transac. cour.
Capital account	-1	-433	-191	-121	-68	-58	-60	Compte de capital
Financial account	-9 987	-1 621	20 410	-58 302	-49 607	-40 550	-36 633	Compte financier
Central African Republic								**République centrafricaine**
Current account	-49	...	...	...	...	...	...	Compte des transac. cour.
Financial account	-56	...	...	...	...	...	...	Compte financier
Chad								**Tchad**
Current account	-87	...	...	...	...	...	...	Compte des transac. cour.
Financial account	-93	...	...	...	...	...	...	Compte financier
Chile								**Chili**
Current account	-1 413	-1 350	1 825	3 069	-3 960	-5 965	-9 157	Compte des transac. cour.
Capital account	...	...	41	6 240	7	67	42	Compte de capital
Financial account	-1 483	-1 218	919	8 480	-2 566	-4 685	-8 035	Compte financier
China [1]								**Chine** [1]
Current account	-11 417	1 618	132 378	237 810	202 203	195 117	49 092	Compte des transac. cour.
Capital account			4 102	4 630	-344	-91	-569	Compte de capital
Financial account	-11 411	-16 205	159 727	189 424	-27 555	-18 011	-111 690	Compte financier
China, Hong Kong SAR								**Chine, RAS de Hong Kong**
Current account	...	...	21 575	16 012	12 711	15 885	15 556	Compte des transac. cour.
Capital account	...	...	-74	-571	-48	-83	-194	Compte de capital
Financial account	...	...	19 369	10 867	12 972	9 706	23 290	Compte financier
China, Macao SAR								**Chine, RAS de Macao**
Current account	...	...	2 902	11 089	12 341	16 662	...	Compte des transac. cour.
Capital account	...	...	515	20	-68	-45	...	Compte de capital
Financial account	...	...	1 446	6 809	12 673	16 701	...	Compte financier
Colombia								**Colombie**
Current account	-1 809	-4 516	-1 891	-8 732	-12 008	-10 341	-12 908	Compte des transac. cour.
Financial account	-2 082	-4 564	-1 508	-9 344	-12 263	-9 608	-12 147	Compte financier
Comoros								**Comores**
Current account	-14	-19	-27	-39	...	...	...	Compte des transac. cour.
Capital account	...	...	15	71	...	...	...	Compte de capital
Financial account	-12	-21	-5	35	...	...	...	Compte financier
Congo								**Congo**
Current account	-161	-625	696	900	-3 594	...	...	Compte des transac. cour.
Capital account	...	45	11	2 667	58	...	...	Compte de capital
Financial account	-120	-635	737	3 314	-430	...	...	Compte financier
Costa Rica								**Costa Rica**
Current account	-126	-358	-860	-1 214	-1 257	-1 815	-1 878	Compte des transac. cour.
Capital account	...	...	15	54	87	41	31	Compte de capital
Financial account	17	-301	-1 158	-1 642	-1 547	-2 144	-1 393	Compte financier
Côte d'Ivoire								**Côte d'Ivoire**
Current account	...	...	40	465	-414	-1 047	...	Compte des transac. cour.
Capital account	...	...	185	1 178	187	192	...	Compte de capital
Financial account	...	...	167	1 590	-318	-776	...	Compte financier
Croatia								**Croatie**
Current account	...	-1 442	-2 479	-894	1 390	2 997	1 459	Compte des transac. cour.
Capital account	...	...	64	77	574	346	888	Compte de capital
Financial account	...	-1 102	-3 749	-1 867	1 287	2 183	1 600	Compte financier
Curaçao								**Curaçao**
Current account	...	...	...	...	-585	-681	-899	Compte des transac. cour.
Capital account	...	...	...	...	1	~0	4	Compte de capital
Financial account	...	...	...	...	-544	-652	-863	Compte financier
Cyprus								**Chypre**
Current account	-180	-205	-971	-2 906	-1 014	-1 852	-1 685	Compte des transac. cour.
Capital account	...	...	35	78	41	120	172	Compte de capital
Financial account	-142	-150	-719	-2 265	-954	-1 224	-1 009	Compte financier
Czechia								**Tchéquie**
Current account	...	-1 374	-2 810	-7 351	3 016	3 148	860	Compte des transac. cour.
Capital account	...	6	1 028	1 953	2 208	1 830	625	Compte de capital
Financial account	...	-771	-2 113	-6 445	4 739	4 795	765	Compte financier

15 Balance of payments summary *(continued)*
Millions of US dollars

Résumé de la balance des paiements *(suite)*
Millions de dollars É.-U.

Country or area&	1985	1995	2005	2010	2016	2017	2018	Pays ou zone&
Dem. Rep. of the Congo								**Rép. dém. du Congo**
Current account	...	...	-389	-2 174	-1 504	-1 241	-2 169	Compte des transac. cour.
Capital account	...	...	-93	10 084	-46	465	245	Compte de capital
Financial account	...	...	-377	9 059	-1 238	-844	-1 738	Compte financier
Denmark								**Danemark**
Current account	-2 767	1 855	11 007	21 051	24 695	26 270	19 977	Compte des transac. cour.
Capital account	...	...	404	84	25	152	31	Compte de capital
Financial account	-3 071	2 929	9 060	-1 005	15 830	23 796	11 110	Compte financier
Djibouti								**Djibouti**
Current account	...	78	20	50	-170	-294	...	Compte des transac. cour.
Capital account	...	5	27	55	34	26	...	Compte de capital
Financial account	...	-5	1	-17	-290	-255	...	Compte financier
Dominica								**Dominique**
Current account	-6	-40	-76	-80	-49	202	...	Compte des transac. cour.
Capital account	...	22	15	30	147	126	...	Compte de capital
Financial account	-7	-34	-46	-54	93	328	...	Compte financier
Dominican Republic								**République dominicaine**
Current account	-108	-183	-473	-4 024	-815	-133	-1 160	Compte des transac. cour.
Capital account	...	1	...	4	2	2	2	Compte de capital
Financial account	48	-107	-893	-4 983	-1 558	-1 396	-1 863	Compte financier
Ecuador								**Équateur**
Current account	76	-1 000	474	-1 582	1 324	-481	-1 358	Compte des transac. cour.
Capital account	...	2 078	73	105	-794	87	-175	Compte de capital
Financial account	244	645	1 168	-1 581	430	-410	-1 690	Compte financier
Egypt								**Égypte**
Current account	-1 816	-254	2 103	-4 504	-20 494	-7 940	-6 293	Compte des transac. cour.
Capital account	...	...	-40	-39	-103	-156	-133	Compte de capital
Financial account	-1 231	18	-364	-6 688	-27 824	-15 007	-10 097	Compte financier
El Salvador								**El Salvador**
Current account	-29	-262	-622	-533	-550	-465	-1 242	Compte des transac. cour.
Capital account	...	...	94	232	70	85	203	Compte de capital
Financial account	-6	-290	-977	-264	-787	-552	-850	Compte financier
Equatorial Guinea								**Guinée équatoriale**
Current account	...	-123	...	...	...	...	...	Compte des transac. cour.
Capital account	...	53	...	...	...	...	...	Compte de capital
Financial account	...	-60	...	...	...	...	...	Compte financier
Eritrea								**Érythrée**
Current account	...	-31	...	...	...	...	...	Compte des transac. cour.
Financial account	...	-72	...	...	...	...	...	Compte financier
Estonia								**Estonie**
Current account	...	-158	-1 386	344	475	861	571	Compte des transac. cour.
Capital account	...	-1	103	681	249	267	385	Compte de capital
Financial account	...	-150	-1 135	1 098	313	1 143	884	Compte financier
Eswatini								**Eswatini**
Current account	-38	-30	-103	-388	541	554	...	Compte des transac. cour.
Capital account	...	~0	-3	14	~0	6	...	Compte de capital
Financial account	-27	49	-147	-318	470	588	...	Compte financier
Ethiopia								**Éthiopie**
Current account	106	39	-1 568	-425	-8 269	-5 566	...	Compte des transac. cour.
Capital account	...	11	...	...	...	...	...	Compte de capital
Financial account	-63	-72	-1 081	-3 355	-4 933	-9 196	...	Compte financier
Faroe Islands								**Îles Féroé**
Current account	...	...	31	144	...	...	...	Compte des transac. cour.
Fiji								**Fidji**
Current account	19	-113	-206	-149	-194	-372	-493	Compte des transac. cour.
Capital account	...	116	3	3	4	4	5	Compte de capital
Financial account	-2	5	-303	221	-316	-337	-670	Compte financier
Finland								**Finlande**
Current account	-806	5 231	7 788	2 792	-1 785	-706	-5 190	Compte des transac. cour.
Capital account	...	66	324	234	272	204	193	Compte de capital
Financial account	-849	3 913	3 787	4 364	-13 915	-6 332	-10 397	Compte financier
France								**France**
Current account	-35	10 840	-137	-22 034	-12 202	-16 465	-19 014	Compte des transac. cour.
Capital account	...	442	1 161	1 637	1 248	350	2 441	Compte de capital
Financial account	256	8 230	-11 143	782	-19 226	-33 642	-34 338	Compte financier

Balance of payments summary *(continued)*
Millions of US dollars

Résumé de la balance des paiements *(suite)*
Millions de dollars É.-U.

Country or area&	1985	1995	2005	2010	2016	2017	2018	Pays ou zone&
French Polynesia								**Polynésie française**
Current account	...	...	9	-18	412	...	...	Compte des transac. cour.
Capital account	...	...	-1	-1	-3	...	...	Compte de capital
Financial account	...	...	32	-119	374	...	...	Compte financier
Gabon								**Gabon**
Current account	-162	515	1 983	2 453	...	...	...	Compte des transac. cour.
Capital account	...	5	...	1	...	...	...	Compte de capital
Financial account	-225	287	1 568	1 121	...	...	...	Compte financier
Gambia								**Gambie**
Current account	8	-8	-43	17	-96	-111	...	Compte des transac. cour.
Capital account	...	...	1	38	18	55	...	Compte de capital
Financial account	-4	-22	-77	36	-31	-117	...	Compte financier
Georgia								**Géorgie**
Current account	...	...	-696	-1 199	-1 890	-1 331	-1 249	Compte des transac. cour.
Capital account	...	...	56	198	56	108	76	Compte de capital
Financial account	...	...	-613	-1 065	-1 754	-1 288	-1 222	Compte financier
Germany								**Allemagne**
Current account	17 994	-32 191	133 161	196 220	293 670	296 172	291 199	Compte des transac. cour.
Capital account	-741	-3 119	-2 998	1 617	2 274	-2 154	2 318	Compte de capital
Financial account	20 714	-37 877	120 502	123 738	286 842	319 882	270 798	Compte financier
Ghana								**Ghana**
Current account	-134	-144	-1 105	-2 747	-2 832	-2 003		Compte des transac. cour.
Capital account	...	...	331	338	274	241	...	Compte de capital
Financial account	-71	-276	-710	-3 586	-2 022	-1 777	...	Compte financier
Greece								**Grèce**
Current account	-3 276	-2 864	-18 233	-30 275	-3 260	-3 325	-6 370	Compte des transac. cour.
Capital account	...	...	2 563	2 776	1 130	1 042	419	Compte de capital
Financial account	-3 320	-3 185	-15 737	-28 117	-917	-1 660	-4 782	Compte financier
Grenada								**Grenade**
Current account	3	-42	-193	-204	-108	-144	...	Compte des transac. cour.
Capital account	...	9	24	36	44	113	...	Compte de capital
Financial account	1	-1	-171	-141	-36	-1	...	Compte financier
Guatemala								**Guatemala**
Current account	-246	-572	-1 241	-563	1 023	1 189	638	Compte des transac. cour.
Capital account	...	62	...	3	...	...	...	Compte de capital
Financial account	-203	-647	-443	-907	332	909	893	Compte financier
Guinea								**Guinée**
Current account	...	-216	-160	-327	-2 745	519	...	Compte des transac. cour.
Capital account	...	45	21	47	164	146	...	Compte de capital
Financial account	...	-137	-20	-241	-2 567	679	...	Compte financier
Guinea-Bissau								**Guinée-Bissau**
Current account	-76	-35	-10	-71	10	4	...	Compte des transac. cour.
Capital account	31	49	45	980	30	104	...	Compte de capital
Financial account	-55	3	30	907	27	95	...	Compte financier
Guyana								**Guyana**
Current account	-97	-135	-96	-246	128	...	...	Compte des transac. cour.
Capital account	...	11	52	65	70	...	...	Compte de capital
Financial account	-101	-113	-112	-317	167	...	...	Compte financier
Haiti								**Haïti**
Current account	-95	-87	7	-102	-72	-265	...	Compte des transac. cour.
Capital account	...	50	...	1 474	62	28	...	Compte de capital
Financial account	-48	88	18	1 738	172	-422	...	Compte financier
Honduras								**Honduras**
Current account	-220	-201	-304	-682	-567	-409	-1 003	Compte des transac. cour.
Capital account	...	17	848	48	11	45	15	Compte de capital
Financial account	-259	-139	367	-896	-594	-325	-1 203	Compte financier
Hungary								**Hongrie**
Current account	-455	-1 577	-7 883	346	7 760	3 848	806	Compte des transac. cour.
Capital account	...	60	740	2 365	-17	1 579	2 762	Compte de capital
Financial account	-530	403	-10 073	1 380	4 116	2 533	-130	Compte financier
Iceland								**Islande**
Current account	-115	13	-2 653	-881	1 593	913	764	Compte des transac. cour.
Capital account	...	-4	-6	-11	-12	-13	-15	Compte de capital
Financial account	-168	-33	-2 336	-680	1 890	505	1 674	Compte financier

15 Balance of payments summary *(continued)*
Millions of US dollars

Résumé de la balance des paiements *(suite)*
Millions de dollars É.-U.

Country or area&	1985	1995	2005	2010	2016	2017	2018	Pays ou zone&
India								**Inde**
Current account	-4 141	-5 563	-10 284	-54 516	-12 114	-38 168	-64 855	Compte des transac. cour.
Capital account	...	...	...	50	137	37	-123	Compte de capital
Financial account	-3 641	-4 594	-10 730	-55 470	-13 601	-39 559	-64 125	Compte financier
Indonesia								**Indonésie**
Current account	-1 923	-6 431	278	5 144	-16 952	-16 196	-31 051	Compte des transac. cour.
Capital account	...	...	334	50	41	46	97	Compte de capital
Financial account	-1 272	-8 686	475	3 866	-17 217	-17 101	-32 352	Compte financier
Iran (Islamic Republic of)								**Iran (Rép. islamique d')**
Current account	-476	3 358	...	...	...	...	...	Compte des transac. cour.
Financial account	11	3 641	...	...	...	...	...	Compte financier
Iraq								**Iraq**
Current account	...	...	-3 335	6 488	2 158	14 892	35 270	Compte des transac. cour.
Capital account	...	...	20 489	25	-1	-1	-6	Compte de capital
Financial account	...	...	17 604	-2 637	-2 846	6 288	22 145	Compte financier
Ireland								**Irlande**
Current account	...	...	-7 150	2 319	14 349	29 099	34 638	Compte des transac. cour.
Capital account	...	...	418	-827	-6 129	-31 053	-25 590	Compte de capital
Financial account	...	...	724	-8 419	6 238	13 339	32 330	Compte financier
Israel								**Israël**
Current account	988	-4 790	4 540	8 687	11 938	10 058	9 671	Compte des transac. cour.
Capital account	151	285	253	336	302	341	364	Compte de capital
Financial account	22	-3 831	11 351	8 475	9 232	10 057	1 675	Compte financier
Italy								**Italie**
Current account	-4 088	25 096	-17 023	-73 018	47 506	51 595	50 559	Compte des transac. cour.
Capital account	222	1 721	1 301	69	-3 390	639	-741	Compte de capital
Financial account	-7 735	5 625	-39 697	-106 243	66 627	58 887	34 687	Compte financier
Jamaica								**Jamaïque**
Current account	-271	-99	-1 071	-934	-43	-386	-461	Compte des transac. cour.
Capital account	...	21	~0	4	21	7	20	Compte de capital
Financial account	-285	-81	-1 080	-785	324	-1 432	-1 350	Compte financier
Japan								**Japon**
Current account	...	...	170 123	220 888	197 049	201 639	174 719	Compte des transac. cour.
Capital account	...	...	-4 878	-4 964	-6 580	-2 499	-1 942	Compte de capital
Financial account	...	...	148 988	244 200	264 759	166 203	181 852	Compte financier
Jordan								**Jordanie**
Current account	-260	-259	-2 271	-1 882	-3 689	-4 301	-2 969	Compte des transac. cour.
Capital account	...	...	8	~0	75	42	77	Compte de capital
Financial account	-290	-401	-1 588	-1 117	-3 269	-3 239	-3 935	Compte financier
Kazakhstan								**Kazakhstan**
Current account	...	-213	-1 036	1 386	-8 132	-5 102	-52	Compte des transac. cour.
Capital account	...	...	5	7 898	270	347	203	Compte de capital
Financial account	...	-864	350	15 338	-7 966	-6 844	1 032	Compte financier
Kenya								**Kenya**
Current account	-115	-1 578	-252	-2 369	-3 697	-5 018	...	Compte des transac. cour.
Capital account	0	124	103	240	206	184	...	Compte de capital
Financial account	-82	252	-394	-1 987	-4 017	-4 741	...	Compte financier
Kiribati								**Kiribati**
Current account	-2	...	...	~0	19	71	...	Compte des transac. cour.
Capital account	7	...	...	13	50	32	...	Compte de capital
Financial account	~0	...	...	2	73	101	...	Compte financier
Kosovo								**Kosovo**
Current account	...	...	-308	-678	-530	-449	-634	Compte des transac. cour.
Capital account	...	...	20	28	15	-13	-13	Compte de capital
Financial account	...	...	-67	-419	-221	-349	-306	Compte financier
Kuwait								**Koweït**
Current account	4 798	5 016	30 071	36 989	642	7 757	23 428	Compte des transac. cour.
Capital account	...	-194	710	2 096	-646	-448	-196	Compte de capital
Financial account	2 879	-298	33 381	46 187	-3 566	27 493	25 422	Compte financier
Kyrgyzstan								**Kirghizistan**
Current account	...	-235	-37	-475	-792	-524	-700	Compte des transac. cour.
Capital account	...	2	43	-11	113	131	335	Compte de capital
Financial account	...	-341	8	-394	-279	-307	-401	Compte financier

15 Balance of payments summary *(continued)*
Millions of US dollars

Résumé de la balance des paiements *(suite)*
Millions de dollars É.-U.

Country or area&	1985	1995	2005	2010	2016	2017	2018	Pays ou zone&
Lao People's Dem. Rep.								**Rép. dém. populaire lao**
Current account	-114	-237	-174	29	-1 385	-1 260	-1 430	Compte des transac. cour.
Capital account	...	...	...	...	22	22	12	Compte de capital
Financial account	-75	-131	-168	-374	-2 705	-1 962	-2 349	Compte financier
Latvia								**Lettonie**
Current account	...	-16	-1 988	494	377	-246	-296	Compte des transac. cour.
Capital account	...	...	211	471	275	240	610	Compte de capital
Financial account	...	-669	-2 073	1 428	489	202	743	Compte financier
Lebanon								**Liban**
Current account	...	...	-2 748	-7 552	-10 474	-12 396	...	Compte des transac. cour.
Capital account	...	...	27	39	1 588	1 567	...	Compte de capital
Financial account	...	...	-3 329	-457	-11 782	-7 548	...	Compte financier
Lesotho								**Lesotho**
Current account	142	-165	166	-158	-198	-182	-114	Compte des transac. cour.
Capital account	8	296	26	108	49	39	37	Compte de capital
Financial account	170	254	178	-9	-285	-59	152	Compte financier
Liberia								**Libéria**
Current account	1	...	-184	-853	-276	-566	...	Compte des transac. cour.
Capital account	...	...	...	2 136	63	65	...	Compte de capital
Financial account	6	...	-223	-1 488	-503	-676	...	Compte financier
Libya								**Libye**
Current account	1 906	1 672	14 945	16 801	-4 705	...	...	Compte des transac. cour.
Financial account	1 578	1 908	13 448	14 509	-5 911	...	...	Compte financier
Lithuania								**Lituanie**
Current account	...	-614	-1 888	-488	-345	463	817	Compte des transac. cour.
Capital account	...	-39	250	1 412	628	574	781	Compte de capital
Financial account	...	-366	-1 239	1 130	51	1 497	1 321	Compte financier
Luxembourg								**Luxembourg**
Current account	...	...	4 107	3 585	3 013	3 067	3 389	Compte des transac. cour.
Capital account	...	...	1 278	-263	-253	-245	784	Compte de capital
Financial account	...	...	5 384	3 298	2 333	2 824	4 188	Compte financier
Madagascar								**Madagascar**
Current account	-184	-276	-725	-909	28	-53	...	Compte des transac. cour.
Capital account	...	40	332	351	148	123	...	Compte de capital
Financial account	-173	-132	-263	-734	315	170	...	Compte financier
Malawi								**Malawi**
Current account	-126	-78	-507	-969	-912	-1 021	...	Compte des transac. cour.
Capital account	...	...	363	710	238	229	...	Compte de capital
Financial account	-21	-162	-109	-6	-696	-664	...	Compte financier
Malaysia								**Malaisie**
Current account	-600	-8 644	19 980	25 644	7 133	8 960	7 590	Compte des transac. cour.
Capital account	...	...	...	-34	27	-6	-23	Compte de capital
Financial account	-781	-9 405	13 425	5 924	1 329	4 990	-2 685	Compte financier
Maldives								**Maldives**
Current account	-6	-18	-273	-196	-1 032	-1 059	-1 338	Compte des transac. cour.
Capital account	...	...	...	9	...	...	...	Compte de capital
Financial account	6	-50	-246	-71	-769	-848	-1 293	Compte financier
Mali								**Mali**
Current account	-210	-284	-438	-1 190	-1 015	-1 210	...	Compte des transac. cour.
Capital account	81	130	206	252	209	258	...	Compte de capital
Financial account	-147	-167	-261	-907	-873	-876	...	Compte financier
Malta								**Malte**
Current account	-26	-380	-418	-420	435	1 346	1 433	Compte des transac. cour.
Capital account	...	13	197	171	35	70	132	Compte de capital
Financial account	-42	-346	-137	-64	900	1 438	711	Compte financier
Marshall Islands								**Îles Marshall**
Current account	...	...	-3	-14	-16	...	...	Compte des transac. cour.
Capital account	...	...	6	19	11	...	...	Compte de capital
Financial account	...	...	-4	19	32	...	...	Compte financier
Mauritania								**Mauritanie**
Current account	-116	22	...	...	-707	-709	...	Compte des transac. cour.
Capital account	...	...	...	...	8	11	...	Compte de capital
Financial account	-122	4	...	...	-531	-753	...	Compte financier
Mauritius								**Maurice**
Current account	-30	-22	-324	-1 006	-491	-574	-815	Compte des transac. cour.
Financial account	22	84	-307	-856	-586	-432	-899	Compte financier

15

Balance of payments summary *(continued)*
Millions of US dollars

Résumé de la balance des paiements *(suite)*
Millions de dollars É.-U.

Country or area[&]	1985	1995	2005	2010	2016	2017	2018	Pays ou zone[&]
Mexico								**Mexique**
Current account	800	-1 576	-9 053	-5 269	-24 252	-19 401	-22 186	Compte des transac. cour.
Capital account	...	...	...	-167	39	150	-65	Compte de capital
Financial account	-2 117	-5 824	-5 267	-26 492	-35 525	-29 006	-35 914	Compte financier
Micronesia (Fed. States of)								**Micronésie (États féd. de)**
Current account	...	...	...	-25	...	...	...	Compte des transac. cour.
Capital account	...	...	...	64	...	...	...	Compte de capital
Financial account	...	...	...	29	...	...	...	Compte financier
Mongolia								**Mongolie**
Current account	-814	39	88	-885	-700	-1 155	-2 207	Compte des transac. cour.
Capital account	...	...	...	152	91	78	92	Compte de capital
Financial account	-730	49	-107	-794	-823	-1 133	-2 233	Compte financier
Montenegro								**Monténégro**
Current account	...	...	...	-852	-707	-761	-943	Compte des transac. cour.
Capital account	...	...	...	-1	1	~0	...	Compte de capital
Financial account	...	...	...	-849	-615	-754	-820	Compte financier
Montserrat								**Montserrat**
Current account	...	-2	-16	-19	-13	-6	...	Compte des transac. cour.
Capital account	...	7	7	13	5	6	...	Compte de capital
Financial account	...	-1	-10	-6	-10	-6	...	Compte financier
Morocco								**Maroc**
Current account	-891	-1 186	1 041	-3 925	-4 180	-3 677	-6 445	Compte des transac. cour.
Financial account	-847	-801	629	-4 092	-3 496	-2 843	-5 093	Compte financier
Mozambique								**Mozambique**
Current account	...	...	-761	-1 679	-3 846	-2 586	-4 362	Compte des transac. cour.
Capital account	...	...	193	357	206	203	164	Compte de capital
Financial account	...	...	-543	-1 267	-3 634	-2 318	-4 169	Compte financier
Myanmar								**Myanmar**
Current account	-205	-258	582	1 574	-1 776	-4 504	...	Compte des transac. cour.
Capital account	...	...	...	...	~0	1	...	Compte de capital
Financial account	-164	-275	-22	-559	-3 853	-4 784	...	Compte financier
Namibia								**Namibie**
Current account	...	176	333	-382	-1 769	-689	-312	Compte des transac. cour.
Capital account	...	40	80	187	132	183	131	Compte de capital
Financial account	...	229	541	-494	-1 436	-520	-309	Compte financier
Nepal								**Népal**
Current account	-122	-356	153	-128	-168	-815	...	Compte des transac. cour.
Capital account	...	...	40	185	165	149	...	Compte de capital
Financial account	-119	-354	332	-123	553	-250	...	Compte financier
Netherlands								**Pays-Bas**
Current account	4 248	25 773	41 600	61 820	62 915	87 393	99 063	Compte des transac. cour.
Capital account	-39	-497	82	-4 123	-1 291	-725	-599	Compte de capital
Financial account	3 144	16 928	32 359	51 355	63 265	84 942	104 996	Compte financier
Netherlands Antilles [former]								**Antilles néerlandaises [anc.]**
Current account	403	128	-106	...	...	...	...	Compte des transac. cour.
Capital account	...	63	96	...	...	...	...	Compte de capital
Financial account	396	203	22	...	...	...	...	Compte financier
New Caledonia								**Nouvelle-Calédonie**
Current account	...	...	-112	-1 360	-654	...	...	Compte des transac. cour.
Capital account	...	...	9	2	-12	...	...	Compte de capital
Financial account	...	...	-19	-1 279	-860	...	...	Compte financier
New Zealand								**Nouvelle-Zélande**
Current account	...	...	-8 025	-3 429	-4 196	-5 870	-7 396	Compte des transac. cour.
Capital account	...	...	-1	4 824	951	179	-29	Compte de capital
Financial account	...	...	-8 950	1 219	-6 954	-3 780	-465	Compte financier
Nicaragua								**Nicaragua**
Current account	-771	-722	-784	-780	-871	-675	83	Compte des transac. cour.
Capital account	45	1 707	479	264	202	178	111	Compte de capital
Financial account	-913	1 127	-369	-351	-1 017	-839	-198	Compte financier
Niger								**Niger**
Current account	-64	-152	-312	-1 136	-1 181	-1 271	...	Compte des transac. cour.
Capital account	...	65	49	196	387	407	...	Compte de capital
Financial account	-37	28	-141	-925	-803	-874	...	Compte financier

15

Balance of payments summary *(continued)*
Millions of US dollars

Résumé de la balance des paiements *(suite)*
Millions de dollars É.-U.

Country or area&	1985	1995	2005	2010	2016	2017	2018	Pays ou zone&
Nigeria								**Nigéria**
Current account	2 604	-802	36 529	13 111	2 714	10 381	...	Compte des transac. cour.
Capital account	...	-14	7 336	...	...	...	...	Compte de capital
Financial account	2 469	-848	26 520	-1 802	-2 931	4 320	...	Compte financier
North Macedonia								**Macédoine du Nord**
Current account	...	...	-159	-198	-310	-94	-46	Compte des transac. cour.
Capital account	...	...	~0	4	12	20	8	Compte de capital
Financial account	...	...	-165	-193	-304	-85	-19	Compte financier
Norway								**Norvège**
Current account	3 030	5 233	49 967	50 258	14 766	22 367	35 182	Compte des transac. cour.
Capital account	...	-170	-279	-164	-93	-96	-106	Compte de capital
Financial account	1 954	1 116	49 596	43 365	38 159	10 448	33 373	Compte financier
Oman								**Oman**
Current account	-10	-801	5 178	4 634	-12 335	-10 764	...	Compte des transac. cour.
Capital account	...	...	-16	-65	515	260	...	Compte de capital
Financial account	-336	-413	4 310	5 926	-13 093	-11 662	...	Compte financier
Pakistan								**Pakistan**
Current account	-1 067	-3 349	-3 606	-1 354	-7 094	-16 251	-18 250	Compte des transac. cour.
Capital account	9	...	202	109	232	436	347	Compte de capital
Financial account	-1 027	-3 653	-3 551	-2 433	-6 112	-16 263	-18 350	Compte financier
Palau								**Palaos**
Current account	...	...	-40	-19	-46	-52	...	Compte des transac. cour.
Capital account	...	...	51	30	23	14	...	Compte de capital
Financial account	...	...	7	6	-7	-33	...	Compte financier
Panama								**Panama**
Current account	75	-471	-1 064	-3 113	-4 634	-4 941	-5 067	Compte des transac. cour.
Capital account	...	9	16	43	24	25	23	Compte de capital
Financial account	-46	-447	-1 288	-2 803	-6 803	-6 277	-6 515	Compte financier
Papua New Guinea								**Papouasie-Nvl-Guinée**
Current account	-122	674	539	-633	5 181	5 532	...	Compte des transac. cour.
Capital account	0	...	33	37	2	9	...	Compte de capital
Financial account	-125	587	575	-672	5 163	5 322	...	Compte financier
Paraguay								**Paraguay**
Current account	-252	-217	-68	49	1 276	1 206	175	Compte des transac. cour.
Capital account	...	11	20	40	163	166	153	Compte de capital
Financial account	-178	-964	-402	-82	1 135	678	-665	Compte financier
Peru								**Pérou**
Current account	102	-4 625	1 148	-3 782	-5 304	-2 720	...	Compte des transac. cour.
Capital account	32	93	106	26	14	18	...	Compte de capital
Financial account	-1 394	-4 280	1 488	-2 402	-6 219	-2 367	...	Compte financier
Philippines								**Philippines**
Current account	-36	-1 980	1 990	7 179	-1 199	-2 143	-7 879	Compte des transac. cour.
Capital account	...	...	79	88	62	69	65	Compte de capital
Financial account	510	-4 074	4 244	3 753	-861	-3 662	-10 137	Compte financier
Poland								**Pologne**
Current account	-982	854	-7 981	-25 875	-2 458	602	-3 929	Compte des transac. cour.
Capital account	...	285	996	8 612	4 884	6 798	11 802	Compte de capital
Financial account	-864	575	-7 028	-31 020	1 407	-1 381	6 379	Compte financier
Portugal								**Portugal**
Current account	380	-132	-19 538	-24 202	1 201	1 167	-1 508	Compte des transac. cour.
Capital account	...	...	2 782	3 318	2 073	2 070	2 498	Compte de capital
Financial account	127	-3 325	-17 307	-20 336	3 359	3 743	1 772	Compte financier
Qatar								**Qatar**
Current account	...	...	...	...	-8 270	6 426	16 652	Compte des transac. cour.
Capital account	...	...	...	...	-823	-468	-240	Compte de capital
Financial account	...	...	...	...	-10 260	7 109	15 332	Compte financier
Republic of Korea								**République de Corée**
Current account	-2 079	-10 230	12 209	27 951	97 924	75 231	76 409	Compte des transac. cour.
Capital account	...	...	-1	-63	-46	-27	189	Compte de capital
Financial account	-3 660	-11 380	18 058	21 449	99 919	84 520	71 081	Compte financier
Republic of Moldova								**République de Moldova**
Current account	...	-85	-226	-481	-285	-562	-1 187	Compte des transac. cour.
Capital account	...	...	13	5	-18	-21	-39	Compte de capital
Financial account	...	-103	-51	-402	-373	-508	-1 132	Compte financier

15 Balance of payments summary *(continued)*
Millions of US dollars

Résumé de la balance des paiements *(suite)*
Millions de dollars É.-U.

Country or area[&]	1985	1995	2005	2010	2016	2017	2018	Pays ou zone[&]
Romania								**Roumanie**
Current account	1 381	-1 774	-8 541	-8 478	-3 961	-6 755	-10 757	Compte des transac. cour.
Capital account	...	242	714	259	4 729	2 563	2 843	Compte de capital
Financial account	1 263	-1 076	-7 358	-7 548	1 737	-3 553	-6 823	Compte financier
Russian Federation								**Fédération de Russie**
Current account	...	7 438	84 389	67 452	24 469	33 156	113 811	Compte des transac. cour.
Capital account	...	786	-12 387	-41	-764	-192	-1 114	Compte de capital
Financial account	...	-7 560	67 015	58 278	18 305	35 544	115 262	Compte financier
Rwanda								**Rwanda**
Current account	...	...	...	-427	-1 336	-628	...	Compte des transac. cour.
Capital account	...	...	...	286	190	190	...	Compte de capital
Financial account	...	...	...	-207	-1 078	-537	...	Compte financier
Saint Kitts and Nevis								**Saint-Kitts-et-Nevis**
Current account	-7	-45	-65	-139	-120	-86	...	Compte des transac. cour.
Capital account	...	6	12	56	37	34	...	Compte de capital
Financial account	-7	-23	-36	-109	-88	-91	...	Compte financier
Saint Lucia								**Sainte-Lucie**
Current account	-13	-36	-129	-203	-57	-47	...	Compte des transac. cour.
Capital account	...	12	4	42	10	19	...	Compte de capital
Financial account	-11	-25	-139	-136	-32	-5	...	Compte financier
Saint Vincent & Grenadines								**Saint-Vincent-Grenadines**
Current account	4	-40	-102	-208	-117	-135	...	Compte des transac. cour.
Capital account	...	5	12	52	6	11	...	Compte de capital
Financial account	6	-35	-111	-148	-106	-104	...	Compte financier
Samoa								**Samoa**
Current account	2	9	-48	-44	-38	-3	...	Compte des transac. cour.
Capital account	...	...	35	31	31	41	...	Compte de capital
Financial account	6	8	-9	-21	-42	57	...	Compte financier
Sao Tome and Principe								**Sao Tomé-et-Principe**
Current account	-16	...	-36	-88	-61	-73	-62	Compte des transac. cour.
Capital account	...	...	66	42	30	30	30	Compte de capital
Financial account	-10	...	35	-61	-66	-45	-73	Compte financier
Saudi Arabia								**Arabie saoudite**
Current account	-12 932	-5 318	89 990	66 751	-23 843	10 464	72 337	Compte des transac. cour.
Capital account	...	...	...	...	-897	-1 848	-1 469	Compte de capital
Financial account	-12 931	-5 318	55 563	32 598	-91 083	6 917	66 234	Compte financier
Senegal								**Sénégal**
Current account	-360	-244	-676	-589	-795	-1 522	...	Compte des transac. cour.
Capital account	88	209	200	302	362	384	...	Compte de capital
Financial account	-269	-55	-479	-305	-435	-1 099	...	Compte financier
Serbia								**Serbie**
Current account	...	...	...	-2 693	-1 190	-2 322	-2 630	Compte des transac. cour.
Capital account	...	...	...	-1	-11	6	-7	Compte de capital
Financial account	...	...	...	-2 079	-593	-1 864	-1 993	Compte financier
Seychelles								**Seychelles**
Current account	-19	1	-174	-214	-286	-295	-269	Compte des transac. cour.
Capital account	...	1	30	275	54	52	50	Compte de capital
Financial account	-17	-26	-144	138	-215	-262	-192	Compte financier
Sierra Leone								**Sierra Leone**
Current account	3	-118	-105	-585	-163	-535	...	Compte des transac. cour.
Capital account	...	...	68	118	165	148	...	Compte de capital
Financial account	-6	-97	-96	-445	-47	-911	...	Compte financier
Singapore								**Singapour**
Current account	-4	14 445	28 105	55 421	55 542	53 913	63 910	Compte des transac. cour.
Financial account	639	14 175	29 123	59 958	54 974	54 065	62 816	Compte financier
Sint Maarten (Dutch part)								**St-Martin (partie néerland.)**
Current account	...	...	...	...	-27	47	63	Compte des transac. cour.
Capital account	...	...	...	...	~0	...	17	Compte de capital
Financial account	...	...	...	...	-20	74	164	Compte financier
Slovakia								**Slovaquie**
Current account	...	390	-5 125	-4 211	-1 923	-1 939	-2 614	Compte des transac. cour.
Capital account	...	46	-13	1 392	1 801	900	1 699	Compte de capital
Financial account	...	580	-4 741	-3 140	-1 773	-2 556	-1 935	Compte financier

15 Balance of payments summary *(continued)*
Millions of US dollars

Résumé de la balance des paiements *(suite)*
Millions de dollars É.-U.

Country or area[&]	1985	1995	2005	2010	2016	2017	2018	Pays ou zone[&]
Slovenia								**Slovénie**
Current account	...	-75	-681	-55	2 465	3 483	3 785	Compte des transac. cour.
Capital account	...	-6	-137	72	-334	-360	-245	Compte de capital
Financial account	...	-276	-637	-1 911	1 279	1 965	2 501	Compte financier
Solomon Islands								**Îles Salomon**
Current account	-28	8	-90	-144	-49	-46	-51	Compte des transac. cour.
Capital account	...	1	28	50	53	60	60	Compte de capital
Financial account	-29	8	-9	-116	-34	10	62	Compte financier
South Africa								**Afrique du Sud**
Current account	2 261	-2 493	-8 015	-5 492	-8 353	-8 908	-13 381	Compte des transac. cour
Capital account	...	...	30	31	16	18	18	Compte de capital
Financial account	1 350	-3 385	-6 846	-7 508	-8 760	-8 189	-11 043	Compte financier
South Sudan								**Soudan du sud**
Current account	...	...	...	...	-216	282	455	Compte des transac. cour.
Capital account	...	...	...	...	81	117	153	Compte de capital
Financial account	...	...	...	...	-298	-71	616	Compte financier
Spain								**Espagne**
Current account	2 785	-1 967	-87 005	-56 363	27 901	25 008	12 924	Compte des transac. cour.
Capital account	...	5 861	9 047	6 500	2 800	3 067	7 407	Compte de capital
Financial account	942	261	-75 438	-57 066	27 306	25 776	25 629	Compte financier
Sri Lanka								**Sri Lanka**
Current account	-418	-770	-650	-1 075	-1 742	-2 309	...	Compte des transac. cour.
Capital account	...	116	242	150	25	11	...	Compte de capital
Financial account	-461	-491	-473	-1 778	-2 182	-2 184	...	Compte financier
State of Palestine								**État de Palestine**
Current account	...	-984	-1 365	-1 307	-1 941	-1 564	-1 659	Compte des transac. cour.
Capital account	...	262	386	828	682	397	389	Compte de capital
Financial account	...	-557	-885	-201	-1 019	-998	-1 414	Compte financier
Sudan								**Soudan**
Current account	154	-500	-2 473	-1 725	-4 213	-4 611	-4 679	Compte des transac. cour.
Capital account	...	...	165	378	148	152	163	Compte de capital
Financial account	5	-481	-1 448	-1 633	-3 440	-3 401	-2 981	Compte financier
Suriname								**Suriname**
Current account	...	...	-144	651	-170	-2	-189	Compte des transac. cour.
Capital account	...	...	15	54	19	...	-~0	Compte de capital
Financial account	...	...	40	537	-413	-154	-222	Compte financier
Sweden								**Suède**
Current account	-1 010	4 940	23 583	29 196	19 219	15 015	9 458	Compte des transac. cour.
Capital account	...	...	290	-681	-395	-376	-68	Compte de capital
Financial account	-1 758	3 388	27 989	34 610	-24 202	20 517	3 114	Compte financier
Switzerland								**Suisse**
Current account	6 039	20 703	55 102	85 822	63 280	45 360	72 186	Compte des transac. cour.
Capital account	...	-462	-2 289	-4 437	2 400	1 160	4 608	Compte de capital
Financial account	8 500	11 260	79 876	109 086	82 428	39 898	75 420	Compte financier
Syrian Arab Republic								**République arabe syrienne**
Current account	-958	263	299	-367	...	...	...	Compte des transac. cour.
Capital account	...	20	18	50	...	...	...	Compte de capital
Financial account	-974	318	180	824	...	...	...	Compte financier
Tajikistan								**Tadjikistan**
Current account	...	...	-296	-581	-291	159	-378	Compte des transac. cour.
Capital account	...	...	...	69	179	135	176	Compte de capital
Financial account	...	...	-259	-245	-263	151	-469	Compte financier
Thailand								**Thaïlande**
Current account	-1 537	-13 582	-7 642	11 486	48 208	50 211	35 159	Compte des transac. cour.
Capital account	...	...	...	245	13	...	-611	Compte de capital
Financial account	-1 434	-14 778	-2 435	7 751	33 683	38 386	29 179	Compte financier
Timor-Leste								**Timor-Leste**
Current account	...	...	...	1 671	-533	-339	...	Compte des transac. cour.
Capital account	...	...	...	31	30	34	...	Compte de capital
Financial account	...	...	...	1 703	-656	-212	...	Compte financier
Togo								**Togo**
Current account	-27	-122	-204	-200	-436	-96	...	Compte des transac. cour.
Capital account	...	3	51	1 388	276	243	...	Compte de capital
Financial account	-28	-139	-141	1 191	-159	165	...	Compte financier

15 Balance of payments summary *(continued)*
Millions of US dollars

Résumé de la balance des paiements *(suite)*
Millions de dollars É.-U.

Country or area[&]	1985	1995	2005	2010	2016	2017	2018	Pays ou zone[&]
Tonga								**Tonga**
Current account	-2	...	-24	-87	-27	-30	-29	Compte des transac. cour.
Capital account	...	...	12	72	31	54	49	Compte de capital
Financial account	-1	...	-25	120	-15	40	-6	Compte financier
Trinidad and Tobago								**Trinité-et-Tobago**
Current account	-48	294	3 881	4 172	-858	1 089	...	Compte des transac. cour.
Capital account	...	...	~0	...	~0	1	...	Compte de capital
Financial account	-322	298	2 897	4 199	-1 722	-552	...	Compte financier
Tunisia								**Tunisie**
Current account	-581	-774	-299	-2 104	-3 694	-4 080	...	Compte des transac. cour.
Capital account	...	47	127	82	95	184	...	Compte de capital
Financial account	-607	-861	-200	-1 927	-3 448	-3 673	...	Compte financier
Turkey								**Turquie**
Current account	-1 013	-2 338	-20 980	-44 616	-33 139	-47 347	-27 125	Compte des transac. cour.
Capital account	...	...	...	-51	23	17	58	Compte de capital
Financial account	-1 849	17	-19 509	-45 128	-22 012	-46 716	-9 864	Compte financier
Turks and Caicos Islands								**Îles Turques-et-Caïques**
Current account	...	...	...	...	247	35	173	Compte des transac. cour.
Capital account	...	...	...	...	...	17	...	Compte de capital
Financial account	...	...	...	...	270	30	107	Compte financier
Tuvalu								**Tuvalu**
Current account	...	...	-4	-14	...	...	...	Compte des transac. cour.
Capital account	...	...	2	9	...	...	...	Compte de capital
Financial account	...	...	~0	-~0	...	...	...	Compte financier
Uganda								**Ouganda**
Current account	5	-281	49	-1 610	-831	-1 491	-2 565	Compte des transac. cour.
Capital account	...	48	...	...	139	122	95	Compte de capital
Financial account	-48	-204	-398	-1 113	-779	-932	-2 015	Compte financier
Ukraine [2]								**Ukraine [2]**
Current account	...	-1 152	2 534	-3 016	-1 340	-2 442	-4 287	Compte des transac. cour.
Capital account	...	6	-43	188	92	-4	37	Compte de capital
Financial account	...	-1 098	2 598	-1 463	-1 801	-1 969	-2 622	Compte financier
United Kingdom								**Royaume-Uni**
Current account	3 314	-13 436	-51 038	-83 113	-140 271	-87 895	-108 745	Compte des transac. cour.
Capital account	...	486	-1 439	-1 130	-2 171	-2 233	-3 254	Compte de capital
Financial account	4 358	-4 522	-71 565	-108 764	-148 594	-116 982	-83 907	Compte financier
United Rep. of Tanzania								**Rép.-Unie de Tanzanie**
Current account	-375	-590	-1 093	-2 211	-2 155	-1 634	...	Compte des transac. cour.
Capital account	...	191	393	538	420	351	...	Compte de capital
Financial account	-415	-369	-1 539	-2 712	-1 983	-731	...	Compte financier
United States of America								**États-Unis d'Amérique**
Current account	-124 455	-113 561	-745 246	-431 271	-432 874	-449 137	-488 480	Compte des transac. cour.
Capital account	...	-222	13 115	-158	-59	24 746	9 408	Compte de capital
Financial account	-104 677	-82 815	-714 071	-446 430	-385 064	-331 869	-519 545	Compte financier
Uruguay								**Uruguay**
Current account	-98	-213	42	-731	324	465	-374	Compte des transac. cour.
Capital account	...	...	4	...	17	5	31	Compte de capital
Financial account	141	-194	-127	-1 418	-247	1 691	-1 006	Compte financier
Uzbekistan								**Ouzbékistan**
Current account	...	...	...	...	295	1 480	-3 577	Compte des transac. cour.
Capital account	...	...	...	...	14	100	143	Compte de capital
Financial account	...	...	...	...	381	-444	-4 373	Compte financier
Vanuatu								**Vanuatu**
Current account	-10	-18	-34	-42	...	...	...	Compte des transac. cour.
Capital account	10	31	22	21	...	...	...	Compte de capital
Financial account	-5	-20	-29	-149	...	...	...	Compte financier
Venezuela (Boliv. Rep. of)								**Venezuela (Rép. boliv. du)**
Current account	3 327	2 014	25 447	5 585	-3 870	...	...	Compte des transac. cour.
Capital account	...	...	...	-211	...	...	...	Compte de capital
Financial account	2 328	1 520	21 855	1 644	-6 665	...	...	Compte financier
Viet Nam								**Viet Nam**
Current account	...	...	-560	-4 276	8 235	6 124	...	Compte des transac. cour.
Financial account	...	...	-957	-7 966	-2 568	-7 658	...	Compte financier

15

Balance of payments summary *(continued)*
Millions of US dollars

Résumé de la balance des paiements *(suite)*
Millions de dollars É.-U.

Country or area&	1985	1995	2005	2010	2016	2017	2018	Pays ou zone&
Yemen								**Yémen**
Current account	...	...	624	-1 054	-2 419	...	...	Compte des transac. cour.
Capital account	...	...	202	88	...	...	...	Compte de capital
Financial account	...	...	1 040	-900	-1 147	...	...	Compte financier
Zambia								**Zambie**
Current account	-395	...	-232	1 525	-954	-1 006	-342	Compte des transac. cour.
Capital account	...	...	2 560	150	55	58	66	Compte de capital
Financial account	-544	...	2 206	1 646	-1 032	-1 001	-252	Compte financier
Zimbabwe								**Zimbabwe**
Current account	-64	...	...	-1 444	-718	-308	...	Compte des transac. cour.
Capital account	...	...	...	231	242	278	...	Compte de capital
Financial account	-38	...	...	-411	-451	-384	...	Compte financier
Euro Area								**Zone euro**
Current account	...	...	19 191	-7 825	369 868	415 251	393 981	Compte des transac. cour.
Capital account	...	...	14 237	16 526	1 673	-23 287	-2 934	Compte de capital
Financial account	...	...	48 521	-18 162	372 512	428 485	375 357	Compte financier

Source:

International Monetary Fund (IMF), Washington, D.C., Balance of Payment (BOP) Statistics database, last accessed June 2019.

& Financial account includes reserves and related items.

1 For statistical purposes, the data for China do not include those for the Hong Kong Special Administrative Region (Hong Kong SAR), Macao Special Administrative Region (Macao SAR) and Taiwan Province of China.
2 Excludes the temporarily occupied territory of the Autonomous Republic of Crimea and Sevastopol.

Source:

Fonds monétaire international (FMI), Washington, D.C., base de données des statistiques Balance des Paiements (BDP), dernier accès juin 2019.

& Compte financier inclut les réserves et les éléments connexes.

1 Pour la présentation des statistiques, les données pour la Chine ne comprennent pas la région administrative spéciale de Hong Kong (RAS de Hong Kong), la région administrative spéciale de Macao (RAS de Macao) et la province chinoise de Taïwan.
2 Excluent le territoire temporairement occupé de la République autonome de Crimée et de Sébastopol.

16
Exchange rates
National currency per US dollar
Cours des changes
Valeur du dollar E.-U. en monnaie nationale

Country or area National currency Monnaie nationale		1985	1995	2005	2010	2015	2016	2017	2018	Pays ou zone
Afghanistan										**Afghanistan**
End of period	Afghani (AFN)	42.8	47.5	50.4	45.3	68.1	66.8	69.5	75.0	Fin de période
Period average		39.3	36.6	49.5	46.5	61.1	67.9	68.0	72.1	Moy. sur période
Åland Islands										**Îles d'Åland**
End of period	Euro (EUR)	...	...	0.8	0.7	0.9	0.9	0.8	0.9	Fin de période
Period average		...	...	0.8	0.8	0.9	0.9	0.9	0.8	Moy. sur période
Albania										**Albanie**
End of period	Lek (ALL)	...	94.2	103.6	104.0	125.8	128.2	111.1	107.8	Fin de période
Period average		...	92.7	99.9	103.9	126.0	124.1	119.1	108.0	Moy. sur période
Algeria										**Algérie**
End of period	Algerian Dinar (DZD),	4.8	52.2	73.4	74.9	107.1	110.5	114.9	118.3	Fin de période
Period average	dinar algérien (DZD)	5.0	47.7	73.3	74.4	100.7	109.4	111.0	116.6	Moy. sur période
Andorra										**Andorre**
End of period	Euro (EUR)	...	...	0.8	0.7	0.9	0.9	0.8	0.9	Fin de période
Period average		...	...	0.8	0.8	0.9	0.9	0.9	0.8	Moy. sur période
Angola										**Angola**
End of period	Kwanza (AOA)	0.0	~0.0	80.8	92.6	135.3	165.9	165.9	308.6	Fin de période
Period average		0.0	~0.0	87.2	91.9	120.1	163.7	165.9	252.9	Moy. sur période
Anguilla										**Anguilla**
End of period	E. Caribbean Dollar (XCD),	2.7	2.7	2.7	2.7	2.7	2.7	2.7	2.7	Fin de période
Period average	dollar des Caraïb. (XCD) [1]	2.7	2.7	2.7	2.7	2.7	2.7	2.7	2.7	Moy. sur période
Antigua and Barbuda										**Antigua-et-Barbuda**
End of period	E. Caribbean Dollar (XCD),	2.7	2.7	2.7	2.7	2.7	2.7	2.7	2.7	Fin de période
Period average	dollar des Caraïb. (XCD) [1]	2.7	2.7	2.7	2.7	2.7	2.7	2.7	2.7	Moy. sur période
Argentina										**Argentine**
End of period	Argentine Peso (ARS),	~0.0	1.0	3.0	4.0	13.1	15.9	18.6	37.6	Fin de période
Period average	peso argentin (ARS)	~0.0	1.0	2.9	3.9	9.2	14.8	16.6	28.1	Moy. sur période
Armenia										**Arménie**
End of period	Armenian Dram (AMD),	...	402.0	450.2	363.4	483.8	483.9	484.1	483.8	Fin de période
Period average	dram arménien (AMD)	...	405.9	457.7	373.7	477.9	480.5	482.7	483.0	Moy. sur période
Aruba										**Aruba**
End of period	Aruban Florin (AWG),	...	1.8	1.8	1.8	1.8	1.8	1.8	1.8	Fin de période
Period average	florin de Aruba (AWG)	...	1.8	1.8	1.8	1.8	1.8	1.8	1.8	Moy. sur période
Australia										**Australie**
End of period	Australian Dollar (AUD),	1.5	1.3	1.4	1.0	1.4	1.4	1.3	1.4	Fin de période
Period average	dollar australien (AUD)	1.4	1.3	1.3	1.1	1.3	1.3	1.3	1.3	Moy. sur période
Austria										**Autriche**
End of period	Euro (EUR)	...	...	0.8	0.7	0.9	0.9	0.8	0.9	Fin de période
Period average		...	...	0.8	0.8	0.9	0.9	0.9	0.8	Moy. sur période
Azerbaijan										**Azerbaïdjan**
End of period	Azerbaijan manat (AZN),	...	0.9	0.9	0.8	1.6	1.8	1.7	1.7	Fin de période
Period average	manat azerbaïdjanais (AZN)	...	0.9	0.9	0.8	1.0	1.6	1.7	1.7	Moy. sur période
Bahamas										**Bahamas**
End of period	Bahamian Dollar (BSD),	1.0	1.0	1.0	1.0	1.0	1.0	1.0	1.0	Fin de période
Period average	dollar des Bahamas (BSD)	1.0	1.0	1.0	1.0	1.0	1.0	1.0	1.0	Moy. sur période
Bahrain										**Bahreïn**
End of period	Bahraini Dinar (BHD),	0.4	0.4	0.4	0.4	0.4	0.4	0.4	0.4	Fin de période
Period average	dinar de Bahreïn (BHD)	0.4	0.4	0.4	0.4	0.4	0.4	0.4	0.4	Moy. sur période
Bangladesh										**Bangladesh**
End of period	Taka (BDT)	31.0	40.8	66.2	70.7	78.5	78.7	82.7	83.9	Fin de période
Period average		28.0	40.3	64.3	69.6	77.9	78.5	80.4	83.5	Moy. sur période
Barbados										**Barbade**
End of period	Barbados Dollar (BBD),	2.0	2.0	2.0	2.0	2.0	2.0	2.0	2.0	Fin de période
Period average	dollar de la Barbade (BBD)	2.0	2.0	2.0	2.0	2.0	2.0	2.0	2.0	Moy. sur période
Belarus										**Bélarus**
End of period	Belarusian Ruble (BYN),	...	0.0	0.2	0.3	1.9	2.0	2.0	2.2	Fin de période
Period average	rouble bélarussien (BYN)	...	~0.0	0.2	0.3	1.6	2.0	1.9	2.0	Moy. sur période
Belgium										**Belgique**
End of period	Euro (EUR)	...	...	0.8	0.7	0.9	0.9	0.8	0.9	Fin de période
Period average		...	...	0.8	0.8	0.9	0.9	0.9	0.8	Moy. sur période
Belize										**Belize**
End of period	Belize Dollar (BZD),	2.0	2.0	2.0	2.0	2.0	2.0	2.0	2.0	Fin de période
Period average	dollar du Belize (BZD)	2.0	2.0	2.0	2.0	2.0	2.0	2.0	2.0	Moy. sur période

16

Exchange rates *(continued)*
National currency per US dollar

Cours des changes *(suite)*
Valeur du dollar E.-U. en monnaie nationale

Country or area	National currency Monnaie nationale	1985	1995	2005	2010	2015	2016	2017	2018	Pays ou zone
Benin										**Bénin**
End of period	CFA Franc, BCEAO (XOF),	378.1	490.0	556.0	490.9	602.5	622.3	546.9	572.9	Fin de période
Period average	franc CFA, BCEAO (XOF) [2]	449.3	499.1	527.5	495.3	591.4	593.0	582.1	555.7	Moy. sur période
Bermuda										**Bermudes**
End of period	Bermudian Dollar (BMD),	1.0	1.0	1.0	1.0	1.0	1.0	1.0	1.0	Fin de période
Period average	dollar des Bermudes (BMD)	1.0	1.0	1.0	1.0	1.0	1.0	1.0	1.0	Moy. sur période
Bhutan										**Bhoutan**
End of period	Ngultrum (BTN)	12.2	35.2	45.1	44.8	66.3	68.0	63.9	69.8	Fin de période
Period average		12.4	32.4	44.1	45.7	64.2	67.2	65.1	68.4	Moy. sur période
Bolivia (Plurin. State of)										**Bolivie (État plurin. de)**
End of period	Boliviano (BOB)	1.7	4.9	8.0	7.0	6.9	6.9	6.9	6.9	Fin de période
Period average		0.4	4.8	8.1	7.0	6.9	6.9	6.9	6.9	Moy. sur période
Bosnia and Herzegovina										**Bosnie-Herzégovine**
End of period	Convertible Mark (BAM),	...	...	1.7	1.5	1.8	1.9	1.6	1.7	Fin de période
Period average	marka convertible (BAM)	...	...	1.6	1.5	1.8	1.8	1.7	1.7	Moy. sur période
Botswana										**Botswana**
End of period	Pula (BWP)	1.9	2.8	5.5	6.4	11.2	10.6	9.9	10.7	Fin de période
Period average			2.8	5.1	6.8	10.1	10.9	10.3	10.2	Moy. sur période
Bouvet Island										**Île Bouvet**
End of period	Norwegian Krone (NOK),	7.6	6.3	6.8	5.9	8.8	8.6	8.2	8.7	Fin de période
Period average	couronne norvégienne (NOK)	8.6	6.3	6.4	6.0	8.1	8.4	8.3	8.1	Moy. sur période
Brazil										**Brésil**
End of period	Brazilian Real (BRL),	0.0	1.0	2.3	1.7	3.9	3.3	3.3	3.9	Fin de période
Period average	real brésilien (BRL)	0.0	0.9	2.4	1.8	3.3	3.5	3.2	3.7	Moy. sur période
Brunei Darussalam										**Brunéi Darussalam**
End of period	Brunei Dollar (BND),	2.1	1.4	1.7	1.3	1.4	1.4	1.3	1.4	Fin de période
Period average	dollar du Brunéi (BND)	2.2	1.4	1.7	1.4	1.4	1.4	1.4	1.3	Moy. sur période
Bulgaria										**Bulgarie**
End of period	Bulgarian Lev (BGN),	...	0.1	1.7	1.5	1.8	1.9	1.6	1.7	Fin de période
Period average	lev bulgare (BGN)	...	0.1	1.6	1.5	1.8	1.8	1.7	1.7	Moy. sur période
Burkina Faso										**Burkina Faso**
End of period	CFA Franc, BCEAO (XOF),	378.0	490.0	556.0	490.9	602.5	622.3	546.9	572.9	Fin de période
Period average	franc CFA, BCEAO (XOF) [2]	449.3	499.1	527.5	495.3	591.4	593.0	582.1	555.7	Moy. sur période
Burundi										**Burundi**
End of period	Burundi Franc (BIF),	112.0	277.9	997.8	1 232.5	1 617.1	1 688.6	1 766.7	1 808.3	Fin de période
Period average	franc burundais (BIF)	120.7	249.8	1 081.6	1 230.7	1 571.9	1 654.6	1 729.1	1 782.9	Moy. sur période
Cabo Verde										**Cabo Verde**
End of period	Cabo Verde Escudo (CVE),	85.4	77.5	93.2	83.0	100.9	105.5	92.4	96.3	Fin de période
Period average	escudo du Cabo Verde (CVE)	91.6	76.9	88.6	83.3	99.4	99.7	97.8	93.4	Moy. sur période
Cambodia										**Cambodge**
End of period	Riel (KHR)	...	2 526.0	4 112.0	4 051.0	4 051.5	4 044.5	4 041.5	4 033.0	Fin de période
Period average		...	2 450.8	4 092.5	4 184.9	4 067.8	4 058.7	4 050.6	4 051.2	Moy. sur période
Cameroon										**Cameroun**
End of period	CFA Franc, BEAC (XAF),	378.1	490.0	556.0	490.9	602.5	622.3	546.9	572.9	Fin de période
Period average	franc CFA, BEAC (XAF) [3]	449.3	499.1	527.5	495.3	591.4	593.0	582.1	555.7	Moy. sur période
Canada										**Canada**
End of period	Canadian Dollar (CAD),	1.4	1.4	1.2	1.0	1.4	1.3	1.3	1.4	Fin de période
Period average	dollar canadien (CAD)	1.4	1.4	1.2	1.0	1.3	1.3	1.3	1.3	Moy. sur période
Cayman Islands										**Îles Caïmanes**
End of period	Cayman Islands Dollar (KYD),	0.8	0.8	0.8	0.8	0.8	0.8	0.8	0.8	Fin de période
Period average	dollar des Îles Caïmanes (KYD)	0.8	0.8	0.8	0.8	0.8	0.8	0.8	0.8	Moy. sur période
Central African Republic										**République centrafricaine**
End of period	CFA Franc, BEAC (XAF),	378.0	490.0	556.0	490.9	602.5	622.3	546.9	572.9	Fin de période
Period average	franc CFA, BEAC (XAF) [3]	449.3	499.1	527.5	495.3	591.4	593.0	582.1	555.7	Moy. sur période
Chad										**Tchad**
End of period	CFA Franc, BEAC (XAF),	378.1	490.0	556.0	490.9	602.5	622.3	546.9	572.9	Fin de période
Period average	franc CFA, BEAC (XAF) [3]	449.3	499.1	527.5	495.3	591.4	593.0	582.1	555.7	Moy. sur période
Channel Islands										**Îles Anglo-Normandes**
End of period	Pound Sterling (GBP),	0.7	0.6	0.6	0.6	0.7	0.8	0.7	0.8	Fin de période
Period average	livre sterling (GBP)	0.8	0.6	0.6	0.6	0.7	0.7	0.8	0.7	Moy. sur période
Chile										**Chili**
End of period	Chilean Peso (CLP),	183.7	407.1	514.2	468.4	707.3	667.3	615.2	695.7	Fin de période
Period average	peso chilien (CLP)	160.9	396.8	559.8	510.2	654.1	677.0	648.8	641.3	Moy. sur période

Country or area	National currency Monnaie nationale	1985	1995	2005	2010	2015	2016	2017	2018	Pays ou zone
China [4]										**Chine** [4]
End of period	Yuan Renminbi (CNY),	3.2	8.3	8.1	6.6	6.5	6.9	6.5	6.9	Fin de période
Period average	yuan (CNY)	2.9	8.4	8.2	6.8	6.2	6.6	6.8	6.6	Moy. sur période
China, Hong Kong SAR										**Chine, RAS de Hong Kong**
End of period	Hong Kong Dollar (HKD),	7.8	7.7	7.8	7.8	7.8	7.8	7.8	7.8	Fin de période
Period average	dollar de Hong Kong (HKD)	7.8	7.7	7.8	7.8	7.8	7.8	7.8	7.8	Moy. sur période
China, Macao SAR										**Chine, RAS de Macao**
End of period	Pataca (MOP)	8.0	8.0	8.0	8.0	8.0	8.0	8.1	8.1	Fin de période
Period average		8.0	8.0	8.0	8.0	8.0	8.0	8.0	8.1	Moy. sur période
Christmas Island										**Île Christmas**
End of period	Australian dollar (AUD),	1.5	1.3	1.4	1.0	1.4	1.4	1.3	1.4	Fin de période
Period average	dollar australien (AUD)	1.4	1.3	1.3	1.1	1.3	1.3	1.3	1.3	Moy. sur période
Cocos (Keeling) Islands										**Îles des Cocos (Keeling)**
End of period	Australian dollar (AUD),	1.5	1.3	1.4	1.0	1.4	1.4	1.3	1.4	Fin de période
Period average	dollar australien (AUD)	1.4	1.3	1.3	1.1	1.3	1.3	1.3	1.3	Moy. sur période
Colombia										**Colombie**
End of period	Colombian Peso (COP),	172.2	987.7	2 284.2	1 989.9	3 149.5	3 000.7	2 971.6	3 275.0	Fin de période
Period average	peso colombien (COP)	142.3	912.8	2 320.8	1 898.6	2 741.9	3 054.1	2 951.3	2 955.7	Moy. sur période
Comoros										**Comores**
End of period	Comorian Franc (KMF),	378.0	367.5	417.0	368.2	451.9	466.7	410.2	429.7	Fin de période
Period average	franc comorien (KMF)	449.3	374.4	395.6	371.5	443.6	444.8	436.6	416.8	Moy. sur période
Congo										**Congo**
End of period	CFA Franc, BEAC (XAF),	378.0	490.0	556.0	490.9	602.5	622.3	546.9	572.9	Fin de période
Period average	franc CFA, BEAC (XAF) [3]	449.3	499.1	527.5	495.3	591.4	593.0	582.1	555.7	Moy. sur période
Cook Islands										**Îles Cook**
End of period	New Zealand Dollar (NZD),	2.0	1.5	1.5	1.3	1.5	1.4	1.4	1.5	Fin de période
Period average	dollar néo-zélandais (NZD)	2.0	1.5	1.4	1.4	1.4	1.4	1.4	1.4	Moy. sur période
Costa Rica										**Costa Rica**
End of period	Costa Rican Colon (CRC),	53.7	194.9	496.7	513.0	538.4	554.6	569.5	608.1	Fin de période
Period average	colon costaricien (CRC)	50.5	179.7	477.8	525.8	534.6	544.7	567.5	577.0	Moy. sur période
Côte d'Ivoire										**Côte d'Ivoire**
End of period	CFA Franc, BCEAO (XOF),	378.0	490.0	556.0	490.9	602.5	622.3	546.9	572.9	Fin de période
Period average	franc CFA, BCEAO (XOF) [2]	449.3	499.1	527.5	495.3	591.4	593.0	582.1	555.7	Moy. sur période
Croatia										**Croatie**
End of period	Kuna (HRK)	...	5.3	6.2	5.6	7.0	7.2	6.3	6.5	Fin de période
Period average		...	5.2	5.9	5.5	6.9	6.8	6.6	6.3	Moy. sur période
Cuba [5]										**Cuba** [5]
End of period	Cuban Peso (CUP),					1.0	1.0	1.0	1.0	Fin de période
	peso cubain (CUP) [6]									Moy. sur période
Curaçao										**Curaçao**
End of period	Neth. Ant. Guilder (ANG),	...	...	...	1.8	1.8	1.8	1.8	1.8	Fin de période
Period average	florin des Ant. néer. (ANG) [7]	...	...	...	...	1.8	1.8	1.8	1.8	Moy. sur période
Cyprus										**Chypre**
End of period	Euro (EUR)	...	...	...	0.7	0.9	0.9	0.8	0.9	Fin de période
Period average		...	...	...	0.8	0.9	0.9	0.9	0.8	Moy. sur période
Czechia										**Tchéquie**
End of period	Czech Koruna (CZK),	...	26.6	24.6	18.8	24.8	25.6	21.3	...	Fin de période
Period average	couronne tchèque (CZK)	...	26.5	24.0	19.1	24.6	24.4	23.4	21.7	Moy. sur période
Dem. People's Rep. Korea [5]										**Rép. pop. dém. de Corée** [5]
End of period	North Korean Won (KPW), won nord-coréen (KPW)	...	...	...	...	109.0	110.9	105.0	106.8	Fin de période
Dem. Rep. of the Congo										**Rép. dém. du Congo**
End of period	Congolese Franc (CDF),	0.0	0.1	431.3	915.1	926.8	1 215.6	1 592.2	1 635.6	Fin de période
Period average	franc congolais (CDF)	0.0	0.1	473.9	905.9	926.0	1 010.3	1 464.4	1 622.5	Moy. sur période
Denmark										**Danemark**
End of period	Danish Krone (DKK),	9.0	5.5	6.3	5.6	6.8	7.1	6.2	6.5	Fin de période
Period average	couronne danoise (DKK)	10.6	5.6	6.0	5.6	6.7	6.7	6.6	6.3	Moy. sur période
Djibouti										**Djibouti**
End of period	Djibouti Franc (DJF),	177.7	177.7	177.7	177.7	177.7	177.7	177.7	177.7	Fin de période
Period average	franc Djibouti (DJF)	177.7	177.7	177.7	177.7	177.7	177.7	177.7	177.7	Moy. sur période
Dominica										**Dominique**
End of period	E. Caribbean Dollar (XCD), dollar des	2.7	2.7	2.7	2.7	2.7	2.7	2.7	2.7	Fin de période
Period average	Caraïb. (XCD) [1]	2.7	2.7	2.7	2.7	2.7	2.7	2.7	2.7	Moy. sur période

Country or area / National currency Monnaie nationale		1985	1995	2005	2010	2015	2016	2017	2018	Pays ou zone
Dominican Republic										**République dominicaine**
End of period	Dominican Peso (DOP),	2.9	12.9	34.5	37.5	45.6	46.7	48.3	50.3	Fin de période
Period average	peso dominicain (DOP)	3.1	12.9	30.3	36.8	45.0	46.1	47.5	49.5	Moy. sur période
Ecuador										**Équateur**
End of period	US Dollar (USD),	...	...	1.0	1.0	1.0	1.0	1.0	1.0	Fin de période
Period average	dollar des É.-U. (USD)	...	...	1.0	1.0	1.0	1.0	1.0	1.0	Moy. sur période
Egypt										**Égypte**
End of period	Egyptian Pound (EGP),	0.7	3.4	5.7	5.8	7.8	18.1	17.7	17.9	Fin de période
Period average	livre égyptienne (EGP)	0.7	3.4	5.8	5.6	7.7	10.0	17.8	17.8	Moy. sur période
El Salvador										**El Salvador**
End of period	US Dollar (USD),	...	...	1.0	1.0	1.0	1.0	1.0	1.0	Fin de période
Period average	dollar des É.-U. (USD)	...	...	1.0	1.0	1.0	1.0	1.0	1.0	Moy. sur période
Equatorial Guinea										**Guinée équatoriale**
End of period	CFA Franc, BEAC (XAF),	378.0	490.0	556.0	490.9	602.5	622.3	546.9	572.9	Fin de période
Period average	franc CFA, BEAC (XAF) [3]	449.3	499.1	527.5	495.3	591.4	593.0	582.1	555.7	Moy. sur période
Eritrea										**Érythrée**
End of period	Nakfa (ERN)	2.1	6.3	15.4	15.4	15.4	15.1	15.1	15.1	Fin de période
Period average		2.1	6.2	15.4	15.4	15.4	15.4	15.1	15.1	Moy. sur période
Estonia										**Estonie**
End of period	Euro (EUR)	...	...	...	...	0.9	0.9	0.8	0.9	Fin de période
Period average		...	...	...	...	0.9	0.9	0.9	0.8	Moy. sur période
Eswatini										**Eswatini**
End of period	Lilangeni (SZL)	2.2	3.6	6.3	6.6	15.5	13.7	12.3	14.4	Fin de période
Period average			3.6	6.4	7.3	12.8	14.7	13.3	13.2	Moy. sur période
Ethiopia										**Éthiopie**
End of period	Ethiopian Birr (ETB),	2.1	6.3	8.7	16.6	21.1	22.4	27.2	28.0	Fin de période
Period average	birr éthiopien (ETB)	2.1	6.2	8.7	14.4	20.6	21.7	23.9	27.4	Moy. sur période
Falkland Islands (Malvinas)										**Îles Falkland (Malvinas)**
End of period	Falkland Islands Pound (FKP),	0.7	0.6	0.6	0.6	0.7	0.8	0.7	...	Fin de période
Period average	livre de Îles Falkland (FKP)	0.8	0.6	0.6	0.6	0.7	0.7	0.8	...	Moy. sur période
Faroe Islands										**Îles Féroé**
End of period	Danish Krone (DKK),	9.0	5.5	6.3	5.6	6.8	7.1	...	...	Fin de période
Period average	couronne danoise (DKK)	10.6	5.6	6.0	5.6	6.7	6.7	...	...	Moy. sur période
Fiji										**Fidji**
End of period	Fiji Dollar (FJD),	1.1	1.4	1.7	1.8	2.1	2.1	2.1	2.1	Fin de période
Period average	dollar des Fidji (FJD)	1.2	1.4	1.7	1.9	2.1	2.1	2.1	2.1	Moy. sur période
Finland										**Finlande**
End of period	Euro (EUR)	...	...	0.8	0.7	0.9	0.9	0.8	0.9	Fin de période
Period average		...	...	0.8	0.8	0.9	0.9	0.9	0.8	Moy. sur période
France										**France**
End of period	Euro (EUR)	...	...	0.8	0.7	0.9	0.9	0.8	0.9	Fin de période
Period average		...	...	0.8	0.8	0.9	0.9	0.9	0.8	Moy. sur période
French Guiana										**Guyane française**
End of period	Euro (EUR)	...	...	0.8	0.7	0.9	0.9	0.8	0.9	Fin de période
Period average		...	...	0.8	0.8	0.9	0.9	0.9	0.8	Moy. sur période
French Polynesia										**Polynésie française**
End of period	CFP Franc (XPF),	137.5	89.1	101.2	89.3	109.6	113.2	99.5	104.2	Fin de période
Period average	franc CFP (XPF) [8]	163.4	90.8	96.0	90.1	107.6	107.9	105.9	101.1	Moy. sur période
French Southern Territories										**Terres australes françaises**
End of period	Euro (EUR)	...	...	0.8	0.7	0.9	0.9	0.8	0.9	Fin de période
Period average		...	...	0.8	0.8	0.9	0.9	0.9	0.8	Moy. sur période
Gabon										**Gabon**
End of period	CFA Franc, BEAC (XAF),	378.0	490.0	556.0	490.9	602.5	622.3	546.9	572.9	Fin de période
Period average	franc CFA, BEAC (XAF) [3]	449.3	499.1	527.5	495.3	591.4	593.0	582.1	555.7	Moy. sur période
Gambia										**Gambie**
End of period	Dalasi (GMD)	3.9	9.6	28.1	28.4	39.8	43.9	47.9	49.5	Fin de période
Period average			9.5	28.6	28.0	42.5	43.9	46.6	48.2	Moy. sur période
Georgia										**Géorgie**
End of period	Lari (GEL)	...	1.2	1.8	1.8	2.4	2.6	2.6	2.7	Fin de période
Period average		...	...	1.8	1.8	2.3	2.4	2.5	2.5	Moy. sur période
Germany										**Allemagne**
End of period	Euro (EUR)	...	...	0.8	0.7	0.9	0.9	0.8	0.9	Fin de période
Period average		...	...	0.8	0.8	0.9	0.9	0.9	0.8	Moy. sur période

Country or area National currency Monnaie nationale		1985	1995	2005	2010	2015	2016	2017	2018	Pays ou zone
Ghana										**Ghana**
End of period	Ghana Cedi (GHS),	~0.0	0.1	0.9	1.5	3.8	4.2	4.4	4.8	Fin de période
Period average	cedi ghanéen (GHS)	~0.0	0.1	0.9	1.4	3.7	3.9	4.4	4.6	Moy. sur période
Gibraltar										**Gibraltar**
End of period	Gibraltar Pound (GIP),	0.7	0.6	0.6	0.6	0.7	0.8	0.7	0.8	Fin de période
Period average	livre de Gibraltar (GIP)	0.8	0.6	0.6	0.6	0.7	0.7	0.8	0.7	Moy. sur période
Greece										**Grèce**
End of period	Euro (EUR)	...	...	...	0.8	0.7	0.9	0.9	0.8	0.9	Fin de période
Period average		...	...	...	0.8	0.8	0.9	0.9	0.9	0.8	Moy. sur période
Greenland										**Groenland**
End of period	Danish Krone (DKK),	9.0	5.5	6.3	5.6	6.8	7.1	...	...	Fin de période
Period average	couronne danoise (DKK)	10.6	5.6	6.0	5.6	6.7	6.7	...	...	Moy. sur période
Grenada										**Grenade**
End of period	E. Caribbean Dollar (XCD),	2.7	2.7	2.7	2.7	2.7	2.7	2.7	2.7	Fin de période
Period average	dollar des Caraïb. (XCD) [1]	2.7	2.7	2.7	2.7	2.7	2.7	2.7	2.7	Moy. sur période
Guadeloupe										**Guadeloupe**
End of period	Euro (EUR)	...	...	...	0.8	0.7	0.9	0.9	0.8	0.9	Fin de période
Period average		...	...	...	0.8	0.8	0.9	0.9	0.9	0.8	Moy. sur période
Guatemala										**Guatemala**
End of period	Quetzal (GTQ)	1.0	6.0	7.6	8.0	7.7	7.5	7.3	7.7	Fin de période
Period average		1.0	5.8	7.6	8.1	7.7	7.6	7.3	7.5	Moy. sur période
Guernsey										**Guernesey**
End of period	Pound Sterling (GBP),	0.7	0.6	0.6	0.6	0.7	0.8	0.7	0.8	Fin de période
Period average	livre sterling (GBP)	0.8	0.6	0.6	0.6	0.7	0.7	0.8	0.7	Moy. sur période
Guinea										**Guinée**
End of period	Guinean Franc (GNF),	22.5	998.0	4 500.0	6 083.9	8 003.7	9 225.3	9 006.4	9 084.8	Fin de période
Period average	franc guinéen (GNF)	24.3	991.4	3 644.3	5 726.1	7 485.5	8 959.7	9 088.3	9 011.1	Moy. sur période
Guinea-Bissau										**Guinée-Bissau**
End of period	CFA Franc, BCEAO (XOF),	378.1	490.0	556.0	490.9	602.5	622.3	546.9	572.9	Fin de période
Period average	franc CFA, BCEAO (XOF) [2]	449.3	499.1	527.5	495.3	591.4	593.0	582.1	555.7	Moy. sur période
Guyana										**Guyana**
End of period	Guyana Dollar (GYD),	4.2	140.5	200.3	203.5	206.5	206.5	206.5	208.5	Fin de période
Period average	dollar guyanien (GYD)	4.3	142.0	199.9	203.6	206.5	206.5	206.5	207.7	Moy. sur période
Haiti										**Haïti**
End of period	Gourde (HTG)	5.0	16.2	43.0	39.9	56.7	67.4	63.7	77.2	Fin de période
Period average		5.0	15.1	40.4	39.8	50.7	63.3	64.8	68.0	Moy. sur période
Heard Is. and McDonald Is.										**Île Heard-et-Îles MacDonald**
End of period	Australian Dollar (AUD),	1.5	1.3	1.4	1.0	1.4	1.4	1.3	1.4	Fin de période
Period average	dollar australien (AUD)	1.4	1.3	1.3	1.1	1.3	1.3	1.3	1.3	Moy. sur période
Holy See										**Saint-Siège**
End of period	Euro (EUR)	...	...	...	0.8	0.7	0.9	0.9	0.8	0.9	Fin de période
Period average		...	...	...	0.8	0.8	0.9	0.9	0.9	0.8	Moy. sur période
Honduras										**Honduras**
End of period	Lempira (HNL)	2.0	10.3	18.9	18.9	22.4	23.5	23.6	24.3	Fin de période
Period average		2.0	...	18.8	18.9	21.9	22.8	23.5	23.9	Moy. sur période
Hungary										**Hongrie**
End of period	Forint (HUF)	47.3	139.5	213.6	208.7	286.6	293.7	258.8	280.9	Fin de période
Period average		50.1	125.7	199.6	207.9	279.3	281.5	274.4	270.2	Moy. sur période
Iceland										**Islande**
End of period	Iceland Krona (ISK),	42.1	65.2	63.0	115.1	129.6	112.8	104.4	116.3	Fin de période
Period average	couronne islandaise (ISK)	41.5	64.7	63.0	122.2	131.9	120.8	106.8	108.3	Moy. sur période
India										**Inde**
End of period	Indian Rupee (INR),	12.2	35.2	45.1	44.8	66.3	68.0	63.9	69.8	Fin de période
Period average	roupie indienne (INR)	12.4	32.4	44.1	45.7	64.2	67.2	65.1	68.4	Moy. sur période
Indonesia										**Indonésie**
End of period	Rupiah (IDR)	1 125.0	2 308.0	9 830.0	8 991.0	13 795.0	13 436.0	13 548.0	14 481.0	Fin de période
Period average		1 110.6	2 248.6	9 704.7	9 090.4	13 389.4	13 308.3	13 380.8	14 236.9	Moy. sur période
Iran (Islamic Republic of)										**Iran (Rép. islamique d')**
End of period	Iranian Rial (IRR),	84.2	1 747.5	9 091.0	10 353.0	30 130.0	32 376.0	36 074.0	42 000.0	Fin de période
Period average	rial iranien (IRR)	91.1	1 748.4	8 964.0	10 254.2	29 011.5	30 914.9	33 226.3	40 864.3	Moy. sur période
Iraq										**Iraq**
End of period	Iraqi Dinar (IQD),	1 938.7	1 938.7	1 487.0	1 170.0	1 182.0	1 182.0	1 184.0	1 182.0	Fin de période
Period average	dinar iraquien (IQD)	2 002.4	2 002.4	1 472.0	1 170.0	1 167.3	1 182.0	1 184.0	1 182.8	Moy. sur période

Country or area	National currency Monnaie nationale	1985	1995	2005	2010	2015	2016	2017	2018	Pays ou zone
Ireland										**Irlande**
End of period	Euro (EUR)	...	...	0.8	0.7	0.9	0.9	0.8	0.9	Fin de période
Period average		...	...	0.8	0.8	0.9	0.9	0.9	0.8	Moy. sur période
Isle of Man										**Île de Man**
End of period	Pound Sterling (GBP),	0.7	0.6	0.6	0.6	0.7	0.8	0.7	0.8	Fin de période
Period average	livre sterling (GBP)	0.8	0.6	0.6	0.6	0.7	0.7	0.8	0.7	Moy. sur période
Israel										**Israël**
End of period	New Israeli Sheqel (ILS),	1.5	3.1	4.6	3.5	3.9	3.8	3.5	3.7	Fin de période
Period average	nouv. shekel israélien (ILS)	1.2	3.0	4.5	3.7	3.9	3.8	3.6	3.6	Moy. sur période
Italy										**Italie**
End of period	Euro (EUR)	...	...	0.8	0.7	0.9	0.9	0.8	0.9	Fin de période
Period average		...	...	0.8	0.8	0.9	0.9	0.9	0.8	Moy. sur période
Jamaica										**Jamaïque**
End of period	Jamaican Dollar (JMD),	5.5	39.6	64.4	85.6	120.0	127.8	124.3	126.8	Fin de période
Period average	dollar jamaïcain (JMD)	5.6	35.1	62.3	87.2	117.0	125.1	128.0	128.9	Moy. sur période
Japan										**Japon**
End of period	Yen (JPY)	200.5	102.8	118.0	81.5	120.5	116.8	112.9	110.8	Fin de période
Period average		238.5	94.1	110.2	87.8	121.0	108.8	112.2	110.4	Moy. sur période
Jersey										**Jersey**
End of period	Pound Sterling (GBP),	0.7	0.6	0.6	0.6	0.7	0.8	0.7	0.8	Fin de période
Period average	livre sterling (GBP)	0.8	0.6	0.6	0.6	0.7	0.7	0.8	0.7	Moy. sur période
Jordan										**Jordanie**
End of period	Jordanian Dinar (JOD),	0.4	0.7	0.7	0.7	0.7	0.7	0.7	0.7	Fin de période
Period average	dinar jordanien (JOD)	0.4	0.7	0.7	0.7	0.7	0.7	0.7	0.7	Moy. sur période
Kazakhstan										**Kazakhstan**
End of period	Tenge (KZT)	...	64.0	134.0	147.5	340.0	333.3	332.3	384.2	Fin de période
Period average		...	61.0	132.9	147.4	221.7	342.2	326.0	344.7	Moy. sur période
Kenya										**Kenya**
End of period	Kenyan Shilling (KES),	16.3	55.9	72.4	80.8	102.3	102.5	103.2	101.8	Fin de période
Period average	shilling kényan (KES)	16.4	51.4	75.6	79.2	98.2	101.5	103.4	101.3	Moy. sur période
Kiribati										**Kiribati**
End of period	Australian Dollar (AUD),	1.5	1.3	1.4	1.0	1.4	1.4	1.3	1.4	Fin de période
Period average	dollar australien (AUD)	1.4	1.3	1.3	1.1	1.3	1.3	1.3	1.3	Moy. sur période
Kosovo										**Kosovo**
End of period	Euro (EUR)	...	...	...	0.7	0.9	0.9	0.8	0.9	Fin de période
Period average		...	...	...	0.8	0.9	0.9	0.9	0.8	Moy. sur période
Kuwait										**Koweït**
End of period	Kuwaiti Dinar (KWD),	0.3	0.3	0.3	0.3	0.3	0.3	0.3	0.3	Fin de période
Period average	dinar koweïtien (KWD)	0.3	0.3	0.3	0.3	0.3	0.3	0.3	0.3	Moy. sur période
Kyrgyzstan										**Kirghizistan**
End of period	Som (KGS)	...	11.2	41.3	47.1	75.9	69.2	68.8	69.9	Fin de période
Period average		...	10.8	41.0	46.0	64.5	69.9	68.9	68.8	Moy. sur période
Lao People's Dem. Rep.										**Rép. dém. populaire lao**
End of period	Lao Kip (LAK)	95.0	923.0	10 743.0	8 058.8	8 172.6	8 337.8	8 307.3	8 596.2	Fin de période
Period average		55.0	804.7	10 655.2	8 258.8	8 147.9	8 179.3	8 351.5	8 489.2	Moy. sur période
Latvia										**Lettonie**
End of period	Euro (EUR)	...	...	...	...	0.9	0.9	0.8	0.9	Fin de période
Period average		...	...	...	...	0.9	0.9	0.9	0.8	Moy. sur période
Lebanon										**Liban**
End of period	Lebanese Pound (LBP),	18.1	1 596.0	1 507.5	1 507.5	1 507.5	1 507.5	1 507.5	1 507.5	Fin de période
Period average	livre libanaise (LBP)	16.4	1 621.4	1 507.5	1 507.5	1 507.5	1 507.5	1 507.5	1 507.5	Moy. sur période
Lesotho										**Lesotho**
End of period	Loti (LSL)	2.6	3.6	6.3	6.6	15.5	13.7	12.3	14.4	Fin de période
Period average		2.2	3.6	6.4	7.3	12.8	14.7	13.3	13.2	Moy. sur période
Liberia										**Libéria**
End of period	Liberian Dollar (LRD),	43.3	43.8	56.5	71.5	88.5	102.5	125.5	157.6	Fin de période
Period average	dollar libérien (LRD)	46.4	49.8	57.1	71.4	86.2	94.4	112.7	144.1	Moy. sur période
Libya										**Libye**
End of period	Libyan Dinar (LYD),	0.3	0.4	1.4	1.3	1.4	1.4	1.4	1.4	Fin de période
Period average	dinar libyen (LYD)	0.3	0.4	1.3	1.3	1.4	1.4	1.4	1.4	Moy. sur période
Liechtenstein										**Liechtenstein**
End of period	Swiss Franc (CHF),	2.1	1.2	1.3	0.9	1.0	1.0	1.0	1.0	Fin de période
Period average	franc suisse (CHF)	2.5	1.2	1.2	1.0	1.0	1.0	1.0	1.0	Moy. sur période

Country or area	National currency Monnaie nationale	1985	1995	2005	2010	2015	2016	2017	2018	Pays ou zone
Lithuania										**Lituanie**
End of period	Euro (EUR)	...	...	...	...	0.9	0.9	0.8	0.9	Fin de période
Period average		...	...	...	...	0.9	0.9	0.9	0.8	Moy. sur période
Luxembourg										**Luxembourg**
End of period	Euro (EUR)	...	...	0.8	0.7	0.9	0.9	0.8	0.9	Fin de période
Period average		...	...	0.8	0.8	0.9	0.9	0.9	0.8	Moy. sur période
Madagascar										**Madagascar**
End of period	Malagasy Ariary (MGA),	127.2	684.6	2 159.8	2 146.1	3 199.2	3 347.9	3 230.2	3 470.2	Fin de période
Period average	ariary malgache (MGA)	132.5	853.1	2 003.0	2 090.0	2 933.5	3 176.5	3 116.1	3 334.8	Moy. sur période
Malawi										**Malawi**
End of period	Malawi Kwacha (MWK),	1.7	15.3	123.8	150.8	672.7	728.6	732.0	733.7	Fin de période
Period average	kwacha malawien (MWK)	1.7	15.3	118.4	150.5	499.6	718.0	730.3	732.3	Moy. sur période
Malaysia										**Malaisie**
End of period	Malaysian Ringgit (MYR),	2.4	2.5	3.8	3.1	4.3	4.5	4.1	4.1	Fin de période
Period average	ringgit malaisien (MYR)	2.5	2.5	3.8	3.2	3.9	4.1	4.3	4.0	Moy. sur période
Maldives										**Maldives**
End of period	Rufiyaa (MVR)	7.1	11.8	12.8	12.8	15.4	15.4	15.4	15.4	Fin de période
Period average		7.1	11.8	12.8	12.8	15.4	15.4	15.4	15.4	Moy. sur période
Mali										**Mali**
End of period	CFA Franc, BCEAO (XOF),	378.0	490.0	556.0	490.9	602.5	622.3	546.9	572.9	Fin de période
Period average	franc CFA, BCEAO (XOF) [2]	449.3	499.1	527.5	495.3	591.4	593.0	582.1	555.7	Moy. sur période
Malta										**Malte**
End of period	Euro (EUR)	...	...	...	0.7	0.9	0.9	0.8	0.9	Fin de période
Period average		...	...	...	0.8	0.9	0.9	0.9	0.8	Moy. sur période
Martinique										**Martinique**
End of period	Euro (EUR)	...	...	0.8	0.7	0.9	0.9	0.8	0.9	Fin de période
Period average		...	...	0.8	0.8	0.9	0.9	0.9	0.8	Moy. sur période
Mauritania										**Mauritanie**
End of period	Ouguiya (MRU)	7.7	13.7	27.1	28.2	33.9	35.6	35.3	36.4	Fin de période
Period average		7.7	13.0	26.6	27.6	32.5	35.2	35.8	35.7	Moy. sur période
Mauritius										**Maurice**
End of period	Mauritius Rupee (MUR),	14.3	17.7	30.7	30.4	35.9	36.0	33.5	34.2	Fin de période
Period average	roupie mauricienne (MUR)	15.4	17.4	29.5	30.8	35.1	35.5	34.5	33.9	Moy. sur période
Mayotte										**Mayotte**
End of period	Euro (EUR)	...	...	0.8	0.7	0.9	0.9	0.8	0.9	Fin de période
Period average		...	...	0.8	0.8	0.9	0.9	0.9	0.8	Moy. sur période
Mexico										**Mexique**
End of period	Mexican Peso (MXN),	0.4	7.6	10.8	12.4	17.2	20.7	19.8	19.7	Fin de période
Period average	peso mexicain (MXN)	0.3	6.4	10.9	12.6	15.8	18.7	18.9	19.2	Moy. sur période
Monaco										**Monaco**
End of period	Euro (EUR)	...	...	0.8	0.7	0.9	0.9	0.8	0.9	Fin de période
Period average		...	...	0.8	0.8	0.9	0.9	0.9	0.8	Moy. sur période
Mongolia										**Mongolie**
End of period	Tugrik (MNT)	...	473.6	1 221.0	1 256.5	1 996.0	2 489.5	2 427.1	2 643.7	Fin de période
Period average		...	448.6	1 205.2	1 357.1	1 970.3	2 140.3	2 439.8	2 472.5	Moy. sur période
Montenegro										**Monténégro**
End of period	Euro (EUR)	...	...	0.8	0.7	0.9	0.9	0.8	0.9	Fin de période
Period average		...	...	0.8	0.8	0.9	0.9	0.9	0.8	Moy. sur période
Montserrat										**Montserrat**
End of period	E. Caribbean Dollar (XCD),	2.7	2.7	2.7	2.7	2.7	2.7	2.7	2.7	Fin de période
Period average	dollar des Caraïb. (XCD) [1]	2.7	2.7	2.7	2.7	2.7	2.7	2.7	2.7	Moy. sur période
Morocco										**Maroc**
End of period	Moroccan Dirham (MAD),	9.6	8.5	9.2	8.4	9.9	10.1	9.3	9.6	Fin de période
Period average	dirham marocain (MAD)	10.1	8.5	8.9	8.4	9.8	9.8	9.7	9.4	Moy. sur période
Mozambique										**Mozambique**
End of period	Mozambique Metical (MZN),	~0.0	10.9	24.2	32.6	45.9	71.4	59.0	61.5	Fin de période
Period average	metical de Mozambique (MZN)	~0.0	9.0	23.1	34.0	40.0	63.1	63.6	60.3	Moy. sur période
Myanmar										**Myanmar**
End of period	Kyat (MMK)	7.8	5.8	6.0	5.6	1 304.0	1 357.5	1 362.0	1 550.0	Fin de période
Period average		8.5	5.7	5.8	5.6	1 162.6	1 234.9	1 360.4	1 429.8	Moy. sur période
Namibia										**Namibie**
End of period	Namibia Dollar (NAD),	2.6	3.6	6.3	6.6	15.5	13.6	12.4	14.4	Fin de période
Period average	dollar namibien (NAD)	2.2	3.6	6.4	7.3	12.9	14.7	13.3	13.2	Moy. sur période

Country or area	National currency Monnaie nationale	1985	1995	2005	2010	2015	2016	2017	2018	Pays ou zone
Nauru										**Nauru**
End of period	Australian Dollar (AUD),	1.5	1.3	1.4	1.0	1.4	1.4	1.3	1.4	Fin de période
Period average	dollar australien (AUD)	1.4	1.3	1.3	1.1	1.3	1.3	1.3	1.3	Moy. sur période
Nepal										**Népal**
End of period	Nepalese Rupee (NPR),	20.7	56.0	74.1	71.7	107.3	108.0	103.0	115.0	Fin de période
Period average	roupie népalaise (NPR)	18.2	51.9	71.4	73.3	102.4	107.4	104.5	108.9	Moy. sur période
Netherlands										**Pays-Bas**
End of period	Euro (EUR)	...	...	0.8	0.7	0.9	0.9	0.8	0.9	Fin de période
Period average		...	...	0.8	0.8	0.9	0.9	0.9	0.8	Moy. sur période
New Caledonia										**Nouvelle-Calédonie**
End of period	CFP Franc (XPF),	137.5	89.1	101.2	89.3	109.6	113.2	99.5	104.2	Fin de période
Period average	franc CFP (XPF) [8]	163.4	90.8	96.0	90.1	107.6	107.9	105.9	101.1	Moy. sur période
New Zealand										**Nouvelle-Zélande**
End of period	New Zealand Dollar (NZD),	2.0	1.5	1.5	1.3	1.5	1.4	1.4	1.5	Fin de période
Period average	dollar néo-zélandais (NZD)	2.0	1.5	1.4	1.4	1.4	1.4	1.4	1.4	Moy. sur période
Nicaragua										**Nicaragua**
End of period	Cordoba Oro (NIO)	0.0	8.0	17.1	21.9	27.9	29.3	30.8	32.3	Fin de période
Period average		0.0	7.5	16.7	21.4	27.3	28.6	30.1	31.6	Moy. sur période
Niger										**Niger**
End of period	CFA Franc, BCEAO (XOF),	378.0	490.0	556.0	490.9	602.5	622.3	546.9	572.9	Fin de période
Period average	franc CFA, BCEAO (XOF) [2]	449.3	499.1	527.5	495.3	591.4	593.0	582.1	555.7	Moy. sur période
Nigeria										**Nigéria**
End of period	Naira (NGN)	1.0	21.9	129.0	150.7	197.0	305.0	306.0	307.0	Fin de période
Period average		0.9	21.9	131.3	150.3	192.4	253.5	305.8	306.1	Moy. sur période
Niue										**Nioué**
End of period	New Zealand Dollar (NZD),	2.0	1.5	1.5	1.3	1.5	1.4	1.4	1.5	Fin de période
Period average	dollar néo-zélandais (NZD)	2.0	1.5	1.4	1.4	1.4	1.4	1.4	1.4	Moy. sur période
Norfolk Island										**Île Norfolk**
End of period	Australian dollar (AUD),	1.5	1.3	1.4	1.0	1.4	1.4	1.3	1.4	Fin de période
Period average	dollar australien (AUD)	1.4	1.3	1.3	1.1	1.3	1.3	1.3	1.3	Moy. sur période
North Macedonia										**Macédoine du Nord**
End of period	Denar (MKD)	...	38.0	51.9	46.3	56.4	58.3	51.3	53.7	Fin de période
Period average		...	37.9	49.3	46.5	55.5	55.7	54.7	52.1	Moy. sur période
Norway										**Norvège**
End of period	Norwegian Krone (NOK),	7.6	6.3	6.8	5.9	8.8	8.6	8.2	8.7	Fin de période
Period average	couronne norvégienne (NOK)	8.6	6.3	6.4	6.0	8.1	8.4	8.3	8.1	Moy. sur période
Oman										**Oman**
End of period	Rial Omani (OMR),	0.3	0.4	0.4	0.4	0.4	0.4	0.4	0.4	Fin de période
Period average	rial omanais (OMR)	0.3	0.4	0.4	0.4	0.4	0.4	0.4	0.4	Moy. sur période
Other non-specified areas										**Autres zones non-spécifiées**
End of period	New Taiwan Dollar (TWD),	39.9	27.3	32.9	30.4	33.1	32.3	29.8	30.7	Fin de période
Period average	nouv. dollar de Taïwan (TWD)	39.8	26.5	32.2	31.6	31.9	32.3	30.4	30.2	Moy. sur période
Pakistan										**Pakistan**
End of period	Pakistan Rupee (PKR),	16.0	34.3	59.8	85.7	104.9	104.8	110.4	138.8	Fin de période
Period average	roupie pakistanaise (PKR)	15.9	31.6	59.5	85.2	102.8	104.8	105.5	121.8	Moy. sur période
Panama										**Panama**
End of period	Balboa (PAB)	1.0	1.0	1.0	1.0	1.0	1.0	1.0	1.0	Fin de période
Period average		1.0	1.0	1.0	1.0	1.0	1.0	1.0	1.0	Moy. sur période
Papua New Guinea										**Papouasie-Nvl-Guinée**
End of period	Kina (PGK)	1.0	1.3	3.1	2.6	3.0	3.2	3.2	3.4	Fin de période
Period average		1.0	1.3	3.1	2.7	2.8	3.1	3.2	3.3	Moy. sur période
Paraguay										**Paraguay**
End of period	Guarani (PYG),	320.0	1 979.7	6 120.0	4 573.8	5 806.9	5 766.9	5 590.5	5 960.5	Fin de période
Period average	guaraní (PYG)	306.7	1 963.0	6 178.0	4 735.5	5 204.9	5 670.5	5 618.9	5 732.1	Moy. sur période
Peru										**Pérou**
End of period	Sol (PEN)	0.0	2.3	3.4	2.8	3.4	3.4	3.2	3.4	Fin de période
Period average		0.0	2.3	3.3	2.8	3.2	3.4	3.3	3.3	Moy. sur période
Philippines										**Philippines**
End of period	Philippine Piso (PHP),	19.0	26.2	53.1	43.9	47.2	49.8	49.9	52.7	Fin de période
Period average	piso philippin (PHP)	18.6	25.7	55.1	45.1	45.5	47.5	50.4	52.7	Moy. sur période
Pitcairn										**Pitcairn**
End of period	New Zealand dollar (NZD),	2.0	1.5	1.5	1.3	1.5	1.4	1.4	1.5	Fin de période
Period average	dollar néo-zélandais (NZD)	2.0	1.5	1.4	1.4	1.4	1.4	1.4	1.4	Moy. sur période

Country or area	National currency Monnaie nationale	1985	1995	2005	2010	2015	2016	2017	2018	Pays ou zone
Poland										**Pologne**
End of period	Zloty (PLN)	~0.0	2.5	3.3	3.0	3.9	4.2	3.5	3.8	Fin de période
Period average		~0.0	2.4	3.2	3.0	3.8	3.9	3.8	3.6	Moy. sur période
Portugal										**Portugal**
End of period	Euro (EUR)	...	...	0.8	0.7	0.9	0.9	0.8	0.9	Fin de période
Period average		...	...	0.8	0.8	0.9	0.9	0.9	0.8	Moy. sur période
Qatar										**Qatar**
End of period	Qatari Rial (QAR),	3.6	3.6	3.6	3.6	3.6	3.6	3.6	3.6	Fin de période
Period average	riyal qatari (QAR)	3.6	3.6	3.6	3.6	3.6	3.6	3.6	3.6	Moy. sur période
Republic of Korea										**République de Corée**
End of period	South Korean Won (KRW),	890.2	774.7	1 011.6	1 134.8	1 172.5	1 207.7	1 070.5	1 115.7	Fin de période
Period average	won sud-coréen (KRW)	870.0	771.3	1 024.1	1 156.1	1 131.2	1 160.4	1 130.4	1 100.6	Moy. sur période
Republic of Moldova										**République de Moldova**
End of period	Moldovan Leu (MDL),	...	4.5	12.8	12.2	19.7	20.0	17.1	17.1	Fin de période
Period average	leu moldove (MDL)	...	4.5	12.6	12.4	18.8	19.9	18.5	16.8	Moy. sur période
Réunion										**Réunion**
End of period	Euro (EUR)	...	...	0.8	0.7	0.9	0.9	0.8	0.9	Fin de période
Period average		...	...	0.8	0.8	0.9	0.9	0.9	0.8	Moy. sur période
Romania										**Roumanie**
End of period	Romanian Leu (RON),	~0.0	0.3	3.1	3.2	4.1	4.3	3.9	4.1	Fin de période
Period average	leu roumain (RON)	~0.0	0.2	2.9	3.2	4.0	4.1	4.1	3.9	Moy. sur période
Russian Federation										**Fédération de Russie**
End of period	Russian Ruble (RUB),	...	4.6	28.8	30.5	72.9	60.7	57.6	69.5	Fin de période
Period average	ruble russe (RUB)	...	...	28.3	30.4	60.9	67.1	58.3	62.7	Moy. sur période
Rwanda										**Rwanda**
End of period	Rwanda Franc (RWF),	93.5	299.8	553.7	594.5	747.4	819.8	843.3	879.1	Fin de période
Period average	franc rwandais (RWF)	101.2	262.2	557.8	583.1	721.0	787.3	831.5	861.1	Moy. sur période
Saint Barthélemy										**Saint-Barthélemy**
End of period	Euro (EUR)	...	...	0.8	0.7	0.9	0.9	0.8	0.9	Fin de période
Period average		...	...	0.8	0.8	0.9	0.9	0.9	0.8	Moy. sur période
Saint Helena										**Sainte-Hélène**
End of period	Saint Helena Pound (SHP),	0.7	0.6	0.6	0.6	0.7	0.8	0.7	...	Fin de période
Period average	livre de Sainte-Hélène (SHP)	0.8	0.6	0.6	0.6	0.7	0.7	0.8	...	Moy. sur période
Saint Kitts and Nevis										**Saint-Kitts-et-Nevis**
End of period	E. Caribbean Dollar (XCD),	2.7	2.7	2.7	2.7	2.7	2.7	2.7	2.7	Fin de période
Period average	dollar des Caraïb. (XCD) [1]	2.7	2.7	2.7	2.7	2.7	2.7	2.7	2.7	Moy. sur période
Saint Lucia										**Sainte-Lucie**
End of period	E. Caribbean Dollar (XCD),	2.7	2.7	2.7	2.7	2.7	2.7	2.7	2.7	Fin de période
Period average	dollar des Caraïb. (XCD) [1]	2.7	2.7	2.7	2.7	2.7	2.7	2.7	2.7	Moy. sur période
Saint Martin (French part)										**St-Martin (partie française)**
End of period	Euro (EUR)	...	...	0.8	0.7	0.9	0.9	0.8	0.9	Fin de période
Period average		...	...	0.8	0.8	0.9	0.9	0.9	0.8	Moy. sur période
Saint Pierre and Miquelon										**Saint-Pierre-et-Miquelon**
End of period	Euro (EUR)	...	...	0.8	0.7	0.9	0.9	0.8	0.9	Fin de période
Period average		...	...	0.8	0.8	0.9	0.9	0.9	0.8	Moy. sur période
Saint Vincent & Grenadines										**Saint-Vincent-Grenadines**
End of period	E. Caribbean Dollar (XCD),	2.7	2.7	2.7	2.7	2.7	2.7	2.7	2.7	Fin de période
Period average	dollar des Caraïb. (XCD) [1]	2.7	2.7	2.7	2.7	2.7	2.7	2.7	2.7	Moy. sur période
Samoa										**Samoa**
End of period	Tala (WST)	2.3	2.5	2.8	2.3	2.6	2.6	2.5	2.6	Fin de période
Period average		2.2	2.5	2.7	2.5	2.6	2.6	2.6	2.6	Moy. sur période
San Marino										**Saint-Marin**
End of period	Euro (EUR)	...	...	0.8	0.7	0.9	0.9	0.8	0.9	Fin de période
Period average		...	...	0.8	0.8	0.9	0.9	0.9	0.8	Moy. sur période
Sao Tome and Principe										**Sao Tomé-et-Principe**
End of period	Dobra (STN)	~0.0	1.8	11.9	18.3	22.4	23.4	20.5	21.5	Fin de période
Period average		~0.0	1.4	10.6	18.5	22.1	22.1	21.7	20.8	Moy. sur période
Saudi Arabia										**Arabie saoudite**
End of period	Saudi Riyal (SAR),	3.6	3.8	3.8	3.8	3.8	3.8	3.8	3.8	Fin de période
Period average	rial saoudien (SAR)	3.6	3.8	3.8	3.8	3.8	3.8	3.8	3.8	Moy. sur période
Senegal										**Sénégal**
End of period	CFA Franc, BCEAO (XOF),	378.0	490.0	556.0	490.9	602.5	622.3	546.9	572.9	Fin de période
Period average	franc CFA, BCEAO (XOF) [2]	449.3	499.1	527.5	495.3	591.4	593.0	582.1	555.7	Moy. sur période

Country or area	National currency Monnaie nationale	1985	1995	2005	2010	2015	2016	2017	2018	Pays ou zone
Serbia										**Serbie**
End of period	Serbian Dinar (RSD),	...	...	72.2	79.3	111.2	117.1	99.1	103.4	Fin de période
Period average	dinar de Serbie (RSD)	...	...	66.7	77.7	108.8	111.3	107.8	100.2	Moy. sur période
Seychelles										**Seychelles**
End of period	Seychelles Rupee (SCR),	6.6	4.9	5.5	12.1	13.2	13.5	13.8	14.0	Fin de période
Period average	roupie seychelloise (SCR)	7.1	4.8	5.5	12.1	13.3	13.3	13.6	13.9	Moy. sur période
Sierra Leone										**Sierra Leone**
End of period	Leone (SLL)	5.2	943.4	2 932.5	4 198.0	5 639.1	7 195.4	7 537.0	8 396.1	Fin de période
Period average		5.1	755.2	2 889.6	3 978.1	5 080.7	6 289.9	7 384.4	7 931.6	Moy. sur période
Singapore										**Singapour**
End of period	Singapore Dollar (SGD),	2.1	1.4	1.7	1.3	1.4	1.4	1.3	1.4	Fin de période
Period average	dollar singapourien (SGD)	2.2	1.4	1.7	1.4	1.4	1.4	1.4	1.3	Moy. sur période
Sint Maarten (Dutch part)										**St-Martin (partie néerland.)**
End of period	Neth. Ant. Guilder (ANG),	...	...	...	1.8	1.8	1.8	1.8	1.8	Fin de période
Period average	florin des Ant. néer. (ANG) [7]	...	...	...	...	1.8	1.8	1.8	1.8	Moy. sur période
Slovakia										**Slovaquie**
End of period	Euro (EUR)	...				0.9	0.9	0.8	0.9	Fin de période
Period average		...				0.9	0.9	0.9	0.8	Moy. sur période
Slovenia										**Slovénie**
End of period	Euro (EUR)	...	...	...	0.7	0.9	0.9	0.8	0.9	Fin de période
Period average		...	...	...	0.8	0.9	0.9	0.9	0.8	Moy. sur période
Solomon Islands										**Îles Salomon**
End of period	Solomon Is. Dollar (SBD),	1.6	3.5	7.6	8.1	8.1	8.2	7.9	8.1	Fin de période
Period average	dollar des Îl. Salomon (SBD) [9]	1.5	3.4	7.5	8.1	7.9	7.9	7.9	8.0	Moy. sur période
Somalia										**Somalie**
End of period	Somali Shilling (SOS)	42.5	...	...	30 900.0	22 285.0	24 005.0	23 605.0	...	Fin de période
Period average	shilling somalien (SOS)	39.5	...	...	31 269.7	22 254.2	23 061.8	23 098.0	...	Moy. sur période
South Africa										**Afrique du Sud**
End of period	Rand (ZAR)	2.6	3.6	6.3	6.6	15.5	13.7	12.3	14.4	Fin de période
Period average		2.2	3.6	6.4	7.3	12.8	14.7	13.3	13.2	Moy. sur période
South Georgia & Sandwich Is.										**Géorgie du S.-Îles Sandwich**
End of period	Pound Sterling (GBP),	0.7	0.6	0.6	0.6	0.7	0.8	0.7	0.8	Fin de période
Period average	livre sterling (GBP)	0.8	0.6	0.6	0.6	0.7	0.7	0.8	0.7	Moy. sur période
South Sudan										**Soudan du sud**
End of period	S. Sudanese Pound (SSP),	...	...	...	...	16.6	83.9	127.9	154.0	Fin de période
Period average	livre s.-soudanaise (SSP) [10]	...	...	...	...	3.6	46.7	113.6	141.4	Moy. sur période
Spain										**Espagne**
End of period	Euro (EUR)	...	...	0.8	0.7	0.9	0.9	0.8	0.9	Fin de période
Period average		...	...	0.8	0.8	0.9	0.9	0.9	0.8	Moy. sur période
Sri Lanka										**Sri Lanka**
End of period	Sri Lanka Rupee (LKR),	27.4	54.0	102.1	111.0	144.1	149.8	152.9	182.3	Fin de période
Period average	roupie sri-lankaise (LKR)	27.2	51.3	100.5	113.1	135.9	145.6	152.4	162.5	Moy. sur période
Sudan										**Soudan**
End of period	Sudanese Pound (SDG),	~0.0	0.5	2.3	2.5	6.1	6.6	6.7	...	Fin de période
Period average	livre soudanaise (SDG)	~0.0	0.6	2.4	2.3	6.0	6.2	6.7	...	Moy. sur période
Suriname										**Suriname**
End of period	Surinam Dollar (SRD),	~0.0	0.4	2.7	2.7	4.0	7.4	7.5	7.5	Fin de période
Period average	dollar surinamais (SRD)	~0.0	0.4	2.7	2.7	3.4	6.2	7.5	7.5	Moy. sur période
Svalbard and Jan Mayen Is.										**Îles Svalbard-et-Jan Mayen**
End of period	Norwegian Krone (NOK),	7.6	6.3	6.8	5.9	8.8	8.6	8.2	8.7	Fin de période
Period average	couronne norvégienne (NOK)	8.6	6.3	6.4	6.0	8.1	8.4	8.3	8.1	Moy. sur période
Sweden										**Suède**
End of period	Swedish Krona (SEK),	7.6	6.7	8.0	6.7	8.4	9.1	8.2	9.0	Fin de période
Period average	couronne suédoise (SEK)	8.6	7.1	7.5	7.2	8.4	8.6	8.5	8.7	Moy. sur période
Switzerland										**Suisse**
End of period	Swiss Franc (CHF),	2.1	1.2	1.3	0.9	1.0	1.0	1.0	1.0	Fin de période
Period average	franc suisse (CHF)	2.5	1.2	1.2	1.0	1.0	1.0	1.0	1.0	Moy. sur période
Syrian Arab Republic [5]										**République arabe syrienne [5]**
End of period		...	...	...	46.6	338.0	514.9	434.0	434.0	Fin de période
Tajikistan										**Tadjikistan**
End of period	Somoni (TJS)	...	0.3	3.2	4.4	7.0	7.9	8.8	9.4	Fin de période
Period average		...	0.1	3.1	4.4	6.2	7.8	8.5	9.2	Moy. sur période
Thailand										**Thaïlande**
End of period	Baht (THB)	26.7	25.2	41.0	30.2	36.1	35.8	32.7	32.4	Fin de période
Period average		27.2	24.9	40.2	31.7	34.2	35.3	33.9	32.3	Moy. sur période

Country or area	National currency Monnaie nationale	1985	1995	2005	2010	2015	2016	2017	2018	Pays ou zone
Togo										**Togo**
End of period	CFA Franc, BCEAO (XOF),	378.1	490.0	556.0	490.9	602.5	622.3	546.9	572.9	Fin de période
Period average	franc CFA, BCEAO (XOF) [2]	449.3	499.1	527.5	495.3	591.4	593.0	582.1	555.7	Moy. sur période
Tokelau										**Tokélaou**
End of period	New Zealand Dollar (NZD),	2.0	1.5	1.5	1.3	1.5	1.4	1.4	1.5	Fin de période
Period average	dollar néo-zélandais (NZD)	2.0	1.5	1.4	1.4	1.4	1.4	1.4	1.4	Moy. sur période
Tonga										**Tonga**
End of period	Pa'anga (TOP)	1.5	1.3	2.1	1.8	2.2	2.2	2.2	2.3	Fin de période
Period average		1.4	1.3	1.9	1.9	2.1	2.2	2.2	2.2	Moy. sur période
Trinidad and Tobago										**Trinité-et-Tobago**
End of period	TT Dollar (TTD),	3.6	6.0	6.3	6.4	6.4	6.8	6.8	6.8	Fin de période
Period average	dollar de la T-et-T (TTD) [11]	2.5	5.9	6.3	6.4	6.4	6.7	6.8	6.8	Moy. sur période
Tunisia										**Tunisie**
End of period	Tunisian Dinar (TND),	0.8	1.0	1.4	1.4	2.0	2.3	2.5	3.0	Fin de période
Period average	dinar tunisien (TND)	0.8	0.9	1.3	1.4	2.0	2.1	2.4	2.6	Moy. sur période
Turkey										**Turquie**
End of period	Turkish Lira (TRY),	~0.0	0.1	1.3	1.5	2.9	3.5	3.8	5.3	Fin de période
Period average	livre turque (TRY)	~0.0	~0.0	1.3	1.5	2.7	3.0	3.6	4.8	Moy. sur période
Turkmenistan [5]										**Turkménistan** [5]
End of period		...	...	...	3.5	3.5	3.5	3.5	3.5	Fin de période
Tuvalu										**Tuvalu**
End of period	Australian Dollar (AUD),	1.5	1.3	1.4	1.0	1.4	1.4	1.3	1.4	Fin de période
Period average	dollar australien (AUD)	1.4	1.3	1.3	1.1	1.3	1.3	1.3	1.3	Moy. sur période
Uganda										**Ouganda**
End of period	Uganda Shilling (UGX),	14.0	1 009.5	1 816.9	2 308.3	3 377.0	3 610.5	3 635.1	3 713.4	Fin de période
Period average	shilling ougandais (UGX)	6.7	968.9	1 780.5	2 177.6	3 240.6	3 420.1	3 611.2	3 727.1	Moy. sur période
Ukraine [12]										**Ukraine** [12]
End of period	Hryvnia (UAH)	...	1.8	5.1	8.0	24.0	27.2	28.1	28.0	Fin de période
Period average		...	1.5	5.1	7.9	21.8	25.6	26.6	27.2	Moy. sur période
United Arab Emirates										**Émirats arabes unis**
End of period	UAE Dirham (AED),	3.7	3.7	3.7	3.7	3.7	3.7	3.7	3.7	Fin de période
Period average	dirham des É.A.U. (AED) [13]	3.7	3.7	3.7	3.7	3.7	3.7	3.7	3.7	Moy. sur période
United Kingdom										**Royaume-Uni**
End of period	Pound Sterling (GBP),	0.7	0.6	0.6	0.6	0.7	0.8	0.7	0.8	Fin de période
Period average	livre sterling (GBP)	0.8	0.6	0.6	0.6	0.7	0.7	0.8	0.7	Moy. sur période
United Rep. of Tanzania										**Rép.-Unie de Tanzanie**
End of period	Tanzanian Shilling (TZS),	16.5	550.4	1 165.5	1 453.5	2 148.5	2 172.6	2 230.1	2 281.2	Fin de période
Period average	shilling tanzanien (TZS)	17.5	574.8	1 128.9	1 395.6	1 991.4	2 177.1	2 228.9	2 263.8	Moy. sur période
Uruguay										**Uruguay**
End of period	Peso Uruguayo (UYU),	0.1	7.1	24.1	20.1	29.9	29.3	28.8	32.4	Fin de période
Period average	peso uruguayen (UYU)	0.1	6.3	24.5	20.1	27.3	30.2	28.7	30.7	Moy. sur période
Uzbekistan [5]										**Ouzbékistan** [5]
End of period	Uzbekistan Sum (UZS), sum ouzbek (UZS)	...	...	...	1 640.0	2 780.1	3 218.0	8 125.0	8 345.0	Fin de période
Vanuatu										**Vanuatu**
End of period	Vatu (VUV)	100.3	113.7	112.3	93.2	110.5	112.3	107.5	112.6	Fin de période
Period average		106.0	112.1	109.2	96.9	109.0	108.5	107.8	110.2	Moy. sur période
Venezuela (Boliv. Rep. of)										**Venezuela (Rép. boliv. du)**
End of period	Bolívar (VEF),	~0.0	0.3	2.1	2.6	6.3	10.0	10.0	...	Fin de période
Period average	bolivar (VEF)	~0.0	0.2	2.1	2.6	6.3	9.3	10.0	...	Moy. sur période
Viet Nam										**Viet Nam**
End of period	Dong (VND)	22.4	11 015.0	15 916.0	18 932.0	21 890.0	22 159.0	22 425.0	22 825.0	Fin de période
Period average		...	11 038.3	15 858.9	18 612.9	21 697.6	21 935.0	22 370.1	22 602.1	Moy. sur période
Wallis and Futuna Islands										**Îles Wallis-et-Futuna**
End of period	CFP Franc (XPF),	137.5	89.1	101.2	89.3	109.6	113.2	99.5	104.2	Fin de période
Period average	franc CFP (XPF) [8]	163.4	90.8	96.0	90.1	107.6	107.9	105.9	101.1	Moy. sur période
Western Sahara										**Sahara occidental**
End of period	Moroccan Dirham (MAD),	9.6	8.5	9.2	8.4	9.9	10.1	9.3	9.6	Fin de période
Period average	dirham marocain (MAD)	10.1	8.5	8.9	8.4	9.8	9.9	9.7	9.4	Moy. sur période
Zambia										**Zambie**
End of period	Zambian Kwacha (ZMW),	~0.0	1.0	3.5	4.8	11.0	9.9	9.9	11.9	Fin de période
Period average	kwacha zambien (ZMW)	~0.0	0.9	4.5	4.8	8.6	10.3	9.5	10.5	Moy. sur période
Zimbabwe										**Zimbabwe**
End of period	Zimbabwe Dollar (ZWL),	~0.0	~0.0	80.8	...	...	...	...	...	Fin de période
Period average	dollar du Zimbabwe (ZWL)	~0.0	~0.0	22.4	...	...	...	...	...	Moy. sur période

16

Exchange rates *(continued)*
National currency per US dollar

Cours des changes *(suite)*
Valeur du dollar E.-U. en monnaie nationale

Country or area	National currency Monnaie nationale	1985	1995	2005	2010	2015	2016	2017	2018	Pays ou zone
Euro Area										**Zone euro**
End of period	Euro (EUR)	...	...	0.8	0.7	0.9	0.9	0.8	0.9	Fin de période
Period average		...	...	0.8	0.8	0.9	0.9	0.9	0.8	Moy. sur période

Source:

International Monetary Fund (IMF), Washington, D.C., the database on International Financial Statistics supplemented by operational rates of exchange for United Nations programmes, last accessed June 2019.

Source:

Fonds monétaire international (FMI), Washington, D.C., base de données des Statistiques Financières Internationales, complétée par les taux de change opérationnels de la Trésorerie de l'ONU, dernier accès juin 2019.

1   East Caribbean Dollar.
2   African Financial Community (CFA) Franc, Central Bank of West African States (BCEAO).
3   African Financial Community (CFA) Franc, Bank of Central African States (BEAC).
4   For statistical purposes, the data for China do not include those for the Hong Kong Special Administrative Region (Hong Kong SAR), Macao Special Administrative Region (Macao SAR) and Taiwan Province of China.
5   UN operational exchange rate.
6   The national currency of Cuba is the Cuban Peso (CUP). The convertible peso (CUC) is used by foreigners and tourists in Cuba.
7   Netherlands Antillean Guilder.
8   Communauté financière du Pacifique (CFP) Franc.
9   Solomon Islands Dollar.
10 South Sudanese Pound.
11 Trinidad and Tobago Dollar.
12 Excludes the temporarily occupied territory of the Autonomous Republic of Crimea and Sevastopol.
13 United Arab Emirates Dirham.

1   dollar des Caraïbes orientales.
2   franc Communauté financière africaine (CFA), Banque centrale des États de l'Afrique de l'Ouest (BCEAO).
3   franc Communauté financière africaine (CFA), Banque des États de l'Afrique centrale (BEAC).
4   Pour la présentation des statistiques, les données pour la Chine ne comprennent pas la région administrative spéciale de Hong Kong (RAS de Hong Kong), la région administrative spéciale de Macao (RAS de Macao) et la province chinoise de Taïwan.
5   Taux de change opérationnel des Nations Unies.
6   La monnaie nationale du Cuba est le Peso Cubain (CUP). Le Peso Cubain Convertible (CUC) est utilisé par les touristes et les étrangers à Cuba.
7   florin des Antilles néerlandaises.
8   franc Communauté financière du Pacifique (CFP).
9   dollar des Îles Salomon.
10 livre sud-soudanaise.
11 dollar de la Trinité-et-Tobago.
12 Excluent le territoire temporairement occupé de la République autonome de Crimée et de Sébastopol.
13 dirham des Émirats arabes unis.

17

Labour force participation rate and unemployment rate
Labour force (LF) participation rate and unemployment rate by sex (percent)

Taux d'activité et taux de chômage
Taux d'activité et taux de chômage par sexe (pourcentage)

Region, country or area & Région, pays ou zone &	Year Année	Male and Female Hommes et femmes		Male Hommes		Female Femmes	
		LF particip. rate Taux d'activité	Unemployment rate Taux de Chômage	LF particip. rate Taux d'activité	Unemployment rate Taux de Chômage	LF particip. rate Taux d'activité	Unemployment rate Taux de Chômage
Total, all countries or areas Total, tous pays ou zones	*2005	63.7	5.9	77.3	5.5	50.3	6.4
	*2010	62.4	5.7	76.0	5.4	48.8	6.2
	*2015	61.7	5.5	75.3	5.2	48.1	5.9
	*2019	61.2	5.4	74.7	5.0	47.7	5.9
Africa Afrique	*2005	64.0	8.4	74.8	7.2	53.5	10.0
	*2010	63.6	7.9	74.0	6.7	53.5	9.4
	*2015	63.3	7.5	72.9	6.6	53.9	8.8
	*2019	63.4	7.8	72.6	6.8	54.5	9.1
Northern Africa Afrique septentrionale	*2005	46.9	12.5	73.2	9.9	20.8	21.8
	*2010	47.7	11.5	73.9	8.6	21.8	20.9
	*2015	46.8	12.4	72.0	9.7	21.7	21.1
	*2019	46.3	11.4	71.1	8.7	21.6	20.3
Sub-Saharan Africa Afrique subsaharienne	*2005	69.2	7.5	75.3	6.3	63.4	8.8
	*2010	68.3	7.1	74.1	6.1	62.7	8.2
	*2015	67.9	6.6	73.2	5.7	62.7	7.6
	*2019	68.0	7.2	73.0	6.3	63.1	8.1
Eastern Africa Afrique orientale	*2005	78.2	6.8	83.5	5.1	73.2	8.6
	*2010	77.8	7.1	83.1	5.5	72.7	8.8
	*2015	76.8	6.4	81.9	4.9	71.8	8.0
	*2019	76.7	6.5	81.5	4.9	72.1	8.2
Middle Africa Afrique centrale	*2005	73.7	7.9	76.6	7.1	71.0	8.9
	*2010	70.3	5.7	74.0	5.0	66.7	6.5
	*2015	69.2	5.1	72.9	4.4	65.6	5.8
	*2019	68.9	5.5	72.5	4.8	65.3	6.2
Southern Africa Afrique australe	*2005	55.2	24.2	63.3	20.7	47.7	28.5
	*2010	53.2	24.4	61.3	22.5	45.7	26.9
	*2015	55.8	24.7	63.0	22.7	48.9	27.1
	*2019	56.6	27.0	63.7	25.2	49.9	29.2
Western Africa Afrique occidentale	*2005	61.1	4.5	68.8	4.4	53.5	4.6
	*2010	60.5	4.3	67.3	4.1	53.8	4.5
	*2015	59.9	4.0	65.8	4.0	54.1	4.0
	*2019	59.9	5.3	65.5	5.4	54.3	5.1
Americas Amériques	*2005	64.7	6.9	76.3	6.1	53.6	8.1
	*2010	64.1	7.9	75.1	7.4	53.7	8.5
	*2015	63.4	6.2	74.1	5.7	53.2	6.9
	*2019	63.3	6.4	73.6	5.8	53.4	7.2
Northern America Amérique septentrionale	*2005	65.2	5.3	72.2	5.3	58.5	5.2
	*2010	63.9	9.5	70.1	10.3	58.0	8.5
	*2015	62.4	5.5	68.6	5.6	56.3	5.3
	*2019	62.1	4.3	68.1	4.3	56.3	4.2
Latin America & the Caribbean Amérique latine et Caraïbes	*2005	64.4	8.0	79.0	6.5	50.3	10.3
	*2010	64.3	6.9	78.3	5.8	50.9	8.6
	*2015	64.1	6.6	77.5	5.7	51.2	7.9
	*2019	64.0	7.6	76.9	6.6	51.7	9.1
Caribbean Caraïbes	*2005	57.4	8.1	69.8	6.6	45.3	10.3
	*2010	58.4	8.6	70.0	7.4	47.2	10.4
	*2015	59.6	8.2	70.4	6.6	49.3	10.2
	*2019	59.9	7.9	70.4	6.5	49.8	9.8
Central America Amérique centrale	*2005	61.5	4.0	81.8	3.7	42.0	4.6
	*2010	61.6	5.4	80.5	5.3	43.5	5.5
	*2015	61.7	4.4	80.0	4.1	44.2	4.9
	*2019	61.7	3.6	79.7	3.3	44.4	4.0
South America Amérique du Sud	*2005	66.1	9.4	79.0	7.6	53.9	11.9
	*2010	65.9	7.3	78.2	5.8	54.1	9.4
	*2015	65.5	7.3	77.3	6.2	54.2	8.7
	*2019	65.3	9.2	76.5	8.0	54.7	10.7

17

Labour force participation rate and unemployment rate *(continued)*
Labour force (LF) participation rate and unemployment rate by sex (percent)

Taux d'activité et taux de chômage *(suite)*
Taux d'activité et taux de chômage par sexe (pourcentage)

Region, country or area [&] Région, pays ou zone [&]	Year Année	Male and Female Hommes et femmes		Male Hommes		Female Femmes	
		LF particip. rate Taux d'activité	Unemployment rate Taux de Chômage	LF particip. rate Taux d'activité	Unemployment rate Taux de Chômage	LF particip. rate Taux d'activité	Unemployment rate Taux de Chômage
Central Asia Asie centrale	*2005	63.0	8.1	72.8	7.7	53.7	8.7
	*2010	63.5	7.5	73.7	7.4	53.8	7.7
	*2015	64.0	7.0	75.1	6.7	53.5	7.2
	*2019	63.9	6.5	75.4	6.1	52.9	6.9
Eastern Asia Asie orientale	*2005	71.7	4.2	78.9	4.5	64.3	3.7
	*2010	69.6	4.3	77.1	4.7	61.9	3.8
	*2015	68.8	4.5	76.2	4.9	61.1	3.9
	*2019	67.4	4.5	75.0	4.8	59.6	4.2
South-eastern Asia Asie du Sud-Est	*2005	67.6	4.4	81.1	4.1	54.5	5.0
	*2010	68.5	3.5	80.9	3.4	56.4	3.6
	*2015	68.3	2.9	80.6	3.0	56.2	2.7
	*2019	67.4	2.8	79.4	2.9	55.7	2.7
Southern Asia Asie méridionale	*2005	57.6	5.0	83.0	4.6	30.9	6.0
	*2010	54.1	3.7	80.4	3.4	26.5	4.5
	*2015	52.9	4.0	79.2	3.6	25.4	5.2
	*2019	52.9	4.1	78.8	3.7	25.8	5.2
Western Asia [1] Asie occidentale [1]	*2005	48.3	8.7	75.0	7.1	16.7	16.8
	*2010	49.7	8.0	75.8	6.1	17.0	17.7
	*2015	51.0	7.7	77.2	5.9	18.0	17.0
	*2019	51.2	7.8	77.2	6.0	18.3	16.9
Caucasus [2] Caucase [2]	*2005	50.3	10.7	69.9	10.5	31.9	10.9
	*2010	51.8	10.4	69.7	10.3	35.1	10.8
	*2015	54.5	9.6	71.4	8.9	38.6	10.9
	*2019	55.4	10.1	72.0	9.3	39.8	11.5
Eastern Europe Europe orientale	*2005	57.9	8.5	65.1	8.5	51.6	8.5
	*2010	58.8	7.8	66.7	8.3	52.0	7.3
	*2015	59.2	6.4	67.6	6.7	52.0	6.1
	*2019	58.5	5.1	66.9	5.3	51.3	4.8
Northern Europe Europe septentrionale	*2005	62.0	5.5	68.9	5.7	55.5	5.2
	*2010	62.0	8.6	68.1	9.5	56.2	7.5
	*2015	62.2	6.1	67.7	6.3	57.0	5.8
	*2019	62.2	4.7	67.2	4.9	57.4	4.5
Southern Europe Europe méridionale	*2005	53.4	10.4	64.4	8.5	43.0	13.1
	*2010	53.5	14.3	62.9	13.5	44.6	15.4
	*2015	53.1	17.3	61.4	16.3	45.4	18.7
	*2019	52.8	12.3	60.6	11.3	45.5	13.6
Western Europe Europe occidentale	*2005	58.2	9.0	65.8	8.8	51.1	9.3
	*2010	58.9	7.2	65.4	7.3	52.7	7.1
	*2015	59.0	6.9	64.7	7.2	53.6	6.6
	*2019	58.8	5.4	64.1	5.6	53.7	5.3
Oceania Océanie	*2005	64.1	4.5	71.1	4.5	57.2	4.5
	*2010	62.8	5.0	69.0	4.9	56.6	5.0
	*2015	62.2	5.5	67.6	5.5	56.8	5.4
	*2019	62.0	5.1	67.0	5.1	57.1	5.0
Afghanistan Afghanistan	2005	* 64.3	8.5	* 83.1	7.6	* 44.0	13.6
	*2010	63.3	7.8	82.7	7.1	42.7	12.4
	*2015	65.3	8.9	82.3	8.0	47.0	13.4
	*2019	66.0	8.8	82.1	8.1	48.8	12.2
Albania Albanie	*2005	57.9	17.5	67.9	15.9	48.1	19.6
	2010	* 54.3	14.2	* 63.0	14.6	* 45.7	13.7
	2015	* 56.5	17.1	* 65.2	17.0	* 47.7	17.1
	*2019	55.9	15.1	64.8	15.2	47.1	14.9
Algeria Algérie	2005	* 42.5	15.3	* 71.8	13.6	* 12.8	25.0
	2010	* 42.4	10.0	* 70.0	8.1	* 14.4	19.1
	2015	* 41.5	11.2	* 67.4	10.0	* 15.2	16.7
	*2019	41.2	9.9	67.2	8.2	14.9	17.4
American Samoa [3] Samoa américaines [3]	2000	52.9	5.1	58.8	4.9	41.2	6.0
	#2005	59.9	...	...	...	...	...
	2010	52.8	# 9.2	...	...	...	...

17

Labour force participation rate and unemployment rate *(continued)*
Labour force (LF) participation rate and unemployment rate by sex (percent)

Taux d'activité et taux de chômage *(suite)*
Taux d'activité et taux de chômage par sexe (pourcentage)

Region, country or area & Région, pays ou zone &	Year Année	Male and Female Hommes et femmes		Male Hommes		Female Femmes	
		LF particip. rate Taux d'activité	Unemployment rate Taux de Chômage	LF particip. rate Taux d'activité	Unemployment rate Taux de Chômage	LF particip. rate Taux d'activité	Unemployment rate Taux de Chômage
Angola Angola	*2005	77.7	21.4	80.5	19.6	75.1	23.2
	*2010	77.8	9.9	80.5	9.3	75.3	10.4
	*2015	77.8	7.3	80.4	6.9	75.5	7.6
	*2019	77.6	8.9	80.0	8.3	75.4	9.5
Anguilla Anguilla	2002	72.3	7.8	77.2	6.3	67.2	9.5
Antigua and Barbuda Antigua-et-Barbuda	2001	71.7	8.4	78.4	8.0	65.9	8.8
Argentina Argentine	2005	* 62.1	11.5	* 75.6	10.1	* 49.4	13.6
	2010	* 60.6	7.7	* 74.3	6.7	* 47.8	9.2
	2015	* 60.1	7.2	* 73.4	6.4	* 47.8	8.2
	*2019	60.4	7.9	72.7	7.3	48.8	8.9
Armenia Arménie	*2005	55.9	16.1	65.9	13.8	47.5	18.7
	2010	* 59.5	19.0	* 71.6	17.1	* 49.6	21.3
	2015	* 59.8	18.3	* 70.2	17.4	* 51.2	19.3
	*2019	58.9	18.4	69.9	17.8	49.7	19.0
Aruba Aruba	2001	...	6.9	...	6.5	...	7.4
	#2010[4]	63.9[5]	10.6	68.9[5]	10.8	59.5[5]	10.4
	#2011	63.8	...	69.6	...	58.8	...
Australia Australie	2005	* 64.5	5.0	* 72.2	4.9	* 57.1	5.2
	2010	* 65.5	5.2	* 72.5	5.1	* 58.7	5.4
	2015	* 65.0	6.1	* 71.1	6.1	* 59.1	6.1
	*2019	64.9	5.5	70.3	5.5	59.6	5.7
Austria Autriche	2005	* 58.1	5.6	* 66.1	5.4	* 50.7	5.9
	2010	* 60.0	4.8	* 66.9	5.0	* 53.5	4.6
	2015	* 60.1	5.7	* 66.0	6.1	* 54.5	5.3
	*2019	60.1	5.4	65.6	5.8	54.7	5.0
Azerbaijan Azerbaïdjan	2005	* 62.8	7.3	* 68.4	7.3	* 57.7	7.4
	2010	* 63.8	5.6	* 67.5	4.4	* 60.2	6.9
	2015	* 65.5	5.0	* 68.7	4.1	* 62.5	5.9
	*2019	66.1	5.0	69.4	4.7	62.9	5.4
Bahamas Bahamas	2005	* 75.0	10.2	* 81.3	9.4	* 69.2	11.1
	*2010	75.1	14.3	81.9	14.5	68.7	14.2
	2015	* 74.7	12.0	* 82.1	11.4	* 67.7	12.7
	*2019	74.5	11.4	82.0	10.5	67.5	12.3
Bahrain Bahreïn	*2005	68.6	1.3	86.2	0.5	38.9	4.1
	2010	* 72.2	1.1	* 87.4	0.4	* 43.8	3.7
	*2015	71.6	1.2	87.0	0.5	43.8	3.9
	*2019	73.3	1.2	87.4	0.5	44.6	4.1
Bangladesh Bangladesh	2005	* 57.2	4.3	* 85.5	3.4	* 27.8	7.0
	2010	* 56.7	3.4	* 83.1	3.1	* 29.9	4.2
	*2015	56.5	4.4	80.4	3.3	32.4	7.2
	*2019	58.7	4.4	81.2	3.4	36.1	6.8
Barbados Barbade	2005	* 69.5	9.1	* 75.4	7.9	* 64.2	10.3
	2010	* 68.0	10.7	* 73.1	11.0	* 63.5	10.4
	2015	* 65.7	11.4	* 69.9	12.1	* 61.9	10.6
	*2019	65.1	9.4	69.2	8.9	61.5	9.9
Belarus Bélarus	*2005	60.9	0.9	67.3	0.9	55.4	0.9
	2010	* 63.0	1.2	* 69.6	1.2	* 57.5	1.2
	*2015	64.3	0.5	71.0	0.5	58.6	0.5
	*2019	63.3	0.5	70.0	0.4	57.8	0.5
Belgium Belgique	2005	* 53.2	8.4	* 61.3	7.6	* 45.5	9.5
	2010	* 54.0	8.3	* 60.8	8.1	* 47.5	8.5
	2015	* 53.4	8.5	* 59.1	9.1	* 48.0	7.8
	*2019	53.2	5.4	58.6	6.5	47.9	6.4
Belize Belize	2005	* 64.0	11.0	* 82.0	7.5	* 45.9	17.3
	*2010	67.2	11.4	82.7	7.3	51.9	17.8
	2015	* 66.4	10.0	* 80.9	6.6	* 52.2	15.1
	*2019	67.4	9.3	81.5	5.7	53.6	14.5

17

Labour force participation rate and unemployment rate *(continued)*
Labour force (LF) participation rate and unemployment rate by sex (percent)

Taux d'activité et taux de chômage *(suite)*
Taux d'activité et taux de chômage par sexe (pourcentage)

Region, country or area & Région, pays ou zone &	Year Année	Male and Female Hommes et femmes		Male Hommes		Female Femmes	
		LF particip. rate Taux d'activité	Unemployment rate Taux de Chômage	LF particip. rate Taux d'activité	Unemployment rate Taux de Chômage	LF particip. rate Taux d'activité	Unemployment rate Taux de Chômage
Benin	*2005	71.9	0.9	76.6	1.0	67.3	0.8
Bénin	2010	* 71.0	1.0	* 73.0	0.9	* 69.2	1.2
	*2015	71.0	2.6	73.4	2.4	68.7	2.8
	*2019	71.3	2.3	73.3	2.1	69.3	2.5
Bermuda	2000	73.8	2.7[3]	79.2	3.1[3]	67.4	2.3[3]
Bermudes	#2009[3]	82.0	4.5	86.0	6.0	79.0	3.0
	2010[3]	84.0	...	87.0	...	81.0	...
	2012[3,6]	76.1	8.4	80.0	8.7	72.6	8.2
	2013[3,6]	...	6.7	...	...	...	...
Bhutan	2005	* 70.3	3.1	* 75.1	2.6	* 64.7	3.7
Bhoutan	2010	* 69.8	3.3	* 74.3	2.7	* 64.6	4.2
	2015	* 66.6	2.5	* 74.1	1.8	* 57.8	3.4
	*2019	67.1	2.5	74.6	1.9	58.4	3.3
Bolivia (Plurin. State of)	2005	* 72.5	5.1	* 82.6	4.4	* 62.5	6.0
Bolivie (État plurin. de)	*2010	72.0	2.5	82.0	2.1	62.0	3.1
	2015	* 67.0	3.1	* 79.7	2.6	* 54.5	3.8
	*2019	67.9	3.2	79.4	2.6	56.6	4.1
Bosnia and Herzegovina	*2005	48.9	30.1	60.5	27.6	37.8	33.8
Bosnie-Herzégovine	2010	* 48.2	27.2	* 59.9	25.5	* 37.1	29.8
	2015	* 46.7	27.7	* 58.4	25.8	* 35.7	30.7
	*2019	46.7	26.5	58.5	23.9	35.5	30.5
Botswana	*2005	62.8	20.8	71.5	18.7	54.4	23.4
Botswana	2010	* 60.3	17.9	* 67.3	14.7	* 53.5	21.6
	*2015	71.7	17.0	78.4	13.8	65.2	20.7
	*2019	72.6	17.8	78.8	14.7	66.5	21.3
Brazil	2005	* 66.4	9.3	* 78.3	7.1	* 55.1	12.3
Brésil	2010	* 64.8	7.3	* 76.6	5.3	* 53.6	9.9
	2015	* 64.1	8.4	* 75.4	7.2	* 53.4	10.1
	*2019	63.8	11.6	74.3	10.3	53.9	13.4
Brunei Darussalam	*2005	67.1	5.9	77.6	5.1	56.2	7.0
Brunéi Darussalam	*2010	66.4	6.2	75.3	5.5	56.9	7.2
	*2015	65.8	6.8	73.1	6.0	58.0	7.9
	*2019	64.9	6.8	71.3	6.0	58.1	7.9
Bulgaria	2005	* 50.4	10.1	* 56.4	10.3	* 44.7	9.8
Bulgarie	2010	* 53.4	10.3	* 59.5	10.9	* 47.7	9.6
	2015	* 54.2	9.1	* 60.1	9.8	* 48.6	8.4
	*2019	55.2	4.4	61.5	4.6	49.4	4.3
Burkina Faso	2005	* 74.2	4.0	* 86.8	3.8	* 62.4	4.3
Burkina Faso	*2010	70.4	4.7	81.7	3.5	59.7	6.2
	*2015	66.7	6.5	75.5	4.1	58.4	9.5
	*2019	66.5	6.2	75.0	4.1	58.3	8.8
Burundi	*2005	81.1	1.7	80.2	2.2	82.1	1.2
Burundi	*2010	79.3	1.6	78.2	2.1	80.4	1.1
	*2015	78.5	1.6	77.0	2.1	79.8	1.1
	*2019	79.0	1.5	77.6	1.9	80.4	1.1
Cabo Verde	*2005	64.2	11.2	75.0	10.6	54.3	12.3
Cabo Verde	2010	* 66.5	10.7	* 74.4	* 10.1	* 58.7	* 11.6
	*2015	68.4	10.3	73.3	9.7	63.5	11.1
	*2019	69.3	10.4	73.2	9.7	65.5	11.2
Cambodia	*2005	81.5	2.0	86.7	2.2	76.9	1.8
Cambodge	2010	* 85.4	0.4	* 89.3	0.4	* 81.8	0.3
	*2015	81.0	0.2	87.3	0.2	75.3	0.2
	*2019	81.3	0.3	87.9	0.3	75.2	0.2
Cameroon	*2005	* 81.7	4.4	* 85.3	4.2	* 78.1	4.6
Cameroun	2010	* 75.9	4.1	* 81.4	3.4	* 70.6	4.9
	*2015	76.3	4.3	81.5	3.5	71.2	5.3
	*2019	76.1	4.2	81.3	3.4	71.0	5.1
Canada	2005	* 66.7	6.8	* 72.6	7.0	* 60.9	6.5
Canada	2010	* 66.6	8.1	* 71.4	8.8	* 61.9	7.2
	2015	* 65.5	6.9	* 70.5	7.5	* 60.8	6.3
	*2019	65.0	5.9	69.4	6.3	60.7	5.4

Labour force participation rate and unemployment rate *(continued)*
Labour force (LF) participation rate and unemployment rate by sex (percent)

Taux d'activité et taux de chômage *(suite)*
Taux d'activité et taux de chômage par sexe (pourcentage)

Region, country or area [&] / Région, pays ou zone [&]	Year / Année	Male and Female / Hommes et femmes		Male / Hommes		Female / Femmes	
		LF particip. rate / Taux d'activité	Unemployment rate / Taux de Chômage	LF particip. rate / Taux d'activité	Unemployment rate / Taux de Chômage	LF particip. rate / Taux d'activité	Unemployment rate / Taux de Chômage
Cayman Islands	2005	...	3.5	...	...	...	...
Îles Caïmanes	#2009	84.2[5]	6.0	88.0[5]	7.0	80.6[5]	5.0
	2010	81.8	6.7	...	...	...	...
	2013	83.1	6.3	85.6	6.7	80.6	5.8
Central African Republic	*2005	72.5	6.2	79.5	5.7	65.8	6.8
République centrafricaine	*2010	72.5	6.3	79.7	5.8	65.7	6.9
	*2015	72.4	6.4	80.4	5.9	64.6	7.0
	*2019	72.1	5.6	79.8	5.0	64.7	6.3
Chad	*2005	71.8	5.7	79.8	4.8	63.9	6.8
Tchad	*2010	71.5	5.8	79.1	4.8	64.1	6.9
	*2015	71.3	5.7	78.1	4.8	64.5	6.7
	*2019	71.3	5.9	77.8	5.0	64.8	7.1
Channel Islands	*2005	59.4	9.3	69.1	10.5	50.2	7.8
Îles Anglo-Normandes	*2010	58.8	9.7	67.6	11.1	50.3	7.8
	*2015	58.0	9.6	66.3	10.9	49.9	7.8
	*2019	57.1	9.2	65.1	9.8	49.4	8.5
Chile	2005	* 57.5	8.0	* 74.2	7.0	* 41.4	9.8
Chili	2010	* 60.8	8.4	* 75.0	7.5	* 47.1	9.9
	2015	* 62.3	6.5	* 74.8	6.1	* 50.1	7.1
	*2019	62.5	7.1	74.2	6.7	51.1	7.8
China [7]	*2005	73.4	4.1	79.7	4.5	66.8	3.7
Chine [7]	*2010	71.0	4.2	77.9	4.6	63.8	3.7
	*2015	69.9	4.6	76.9	5.1	62.6	4.0
	*2019	68.2	4.8	75.4	5.0	60.6	4.5
China, Hong Kong SAR	2005	* 60.9	5.6	* 71.1	6.5	* 51.7	4.4
Chine, RAS de Hong Kong	2010	* 59.1	4.3	* 68.1	5.0	* 51.4	3.5
	2015	* 60.7	3.3	* 68.5	3.4	* 54.2	3.2
	*2019	60.0	2.9	67.5	3.2	53.8	2.6
China, Macao SAR	2005	* 64.4	4.2	* 72.5	4.5	* 57.3	3.8
Chine, RAS de Macao	2010	* 70.8	2.8	* 76.9	3.6	* 65.3	2.1
	2015	* 71.6	1.8	* 77.2	2.0	* 66.6	1.6
	*2019	70.5	2.0	76.4	2.4	65.2	1.6
Colombia	2005	* 67.1	11.9	* 82.0	9.2	* 53.0	16.1
Colombie	2010	* 69.2	10.9	* 82.7	8.5	* 56.5	14.2
	2015	* 70.8	8.2	* 83.0	6.2	* 59.2	10.9
	*2019	70.0	9.2	81.9	7.2	58.6	11.8
Comoros	*2005	41.9	4.5	50.3	4.4	33.5	4.8
Comores	*2010	42.6	4.4	50.1	4.3	35.1	4.7
	*2015	43.6	4.4	50.5	4.1	36.6	4.6
	*2019	44.2	4.3	50.8	4.1	37.6	4.7
Congo	2005	* 68.7	19.8	* 70.6	18.5	* 66.7	21.2
Congo	*2010	69.5	14.6	71.5	13.6	67.4	15.6
	*2015	69.5	10.0	71.9	9.4	67.1	10.7
	*2019	69.1	11.5	71.4	10.8	66.8	12.3
Cook Islands	2001	74.5[8]	13.1	75.5[8]	11.7	63.0[8]	14.8
Îles Cook	#2006[5]	70.2	6.9	76.1	6.7	64.2	7.3
	2011[5]	71.0	8.2	76.6	8.2	65.4	8.1
Costa Rica	2005	* 62.5	6.6	* 80.5	5.0	* 44.7	9.3
Costa Rica	2010	* 61.6	8.9	* 76.6	7.7	* 46.6	11.1
	2015	* 61.8	9.3	* 75.4	7.6	* 48.3	11.8
	*2019	60.1	7.9	74.4	6.6	45.9	10.1
Côte d'Ivoire	*2005	63.2	3.5	76.9	2.9	48.3	4.6
Côte d'Ivoire	*2010	60.6	3.1	72.3	2.5	48.2	4.0
	*2015	57.9	2.7	67.3	2.1	48.0	3.5
	*2019	57.3	2.6	65.9	2.1	48.3	3.3
Croatia	2005	* 53.3	12.6	* 61.1	11.6	* 46.2	13.8
Croatie	2010	* 52.7	11.6	* 59.8	11.0	* 46.2	12.3
	2015	* 52.9	16.2	* 59.4	15.6	* 47.0	16.9
	*2019	51.5	8.4	57.9	8.0	45.6	8.9

17

Labour force participation rate and unemployment rate *(continued)*
Labour force (LF) participation rate and unemployment rate by sex (percent)

Taux d'activité et taux de chômage *(suite)*
Taux d'activité et taux de chômage par sexe (pourcentage)

Region, country or area [&] Région, pays ou zone [&]	Year Année	Male and Female Hommes et femmes		Male Hommes		Female Femmes	
		LF particip. rate Taux d'activité	Unemployment rate Taux de Chômage	LF particip. rate Taux d'activité	Unemployment rate Taux de Chômage	LF particip. rate Taux d'activité	Unemployment rate Taux de Chômage
Cuba Cuba	2005	* 52.8	2.0	* 67.4	1.8	* 38.3	2.2
	2010	* 55.5	2.5	* 68.9	2.4	* 42.3	2.7
	2015	* 54.3	2.4	* 67.8	2.3	* 40.9	2.6
	*2019	53.5	2.6	67.3	2.4	39.8	2.9
Curaçao Curaçao	2005	59.4	18.2	65.4	17.1	54.8	19.2
	2008	59.0	10.3	66.5	8.0	53.2	12.5
	#2009[6]	...	9.6	...	7.8	...	11.2
	2013[6]	...	13.0	...	10.5	...	15.4
Cyprus Chypre	2005	* 63.0	5.3	* 72.7	4.4	* 53.2	6.5
	2010	* 64.1	6.3	* 70.6	6.1	* 57.6	6.4
	2015	* 62.6	14.9	* 67.4	15.0	* 57.9	14.8
	*2019	62.0	9.9	66.9	9.3	57.2	10.5
Czechia Tchéquie	2005	* 59.5	7.9	* 68.9	6.5	* 50.8	9.8
	2010	* 58.3	7.3	* 68.0	6.4	* 49.2	8.5
	2015	* 59.6	5.1	* 68.2	4.2	* 51.4	6.1
	*2019	60.0	2.1	68.1	1.6	52.3	2.6
Dem. People's Rep. Korea Rép. pop. dém. de Corée	*2005	81.6	4.5	88.2	5.3	75.5	3.6
	*2010	81.0	4.6	87.5	5.4	74.9	3.7
	*2015	80.7	4.5	87.3	5.3	74.5	3.7
	*2019	80.5	4.7	87.2	5.3	74.2	4.1
Dem. Rep. of the Congo Rép. dém. du Congo	2005	* 71.6	3.7	* 72.8	* 3.0	* 70.5	* 4.3
	*2010	66.3	3.7	68.7	3.0	63.9	4.4
	*2015	63.9	3.7	66.8	3.1	61.1	4.4
	*2019	63.4	3.7	66.3	3.1	60.5	4.3
Denmark Danemark	2005	* 65.9	4.8	* 71.4	4.4	* 60.5	5.3
	2010	* 64.4	7.5	* 69.1	8.4	* 59.8	6.5
	2015	* 62.0	6.2	* 66.4	5.9	* 57.7	6.5
	*2019	61.9	5.3	65.8	5.2	58.0	5.5
Djibouti Djibouti	*2005	62.0	6.4	75.0	5.8	49.1	7.4
	*2010	62.3	6.2	73.3	5.6	51.3	7.1
	*2015	62.8	5.9	71.7	5.3	54.0	6.7
	*2019	63.0	5.8	71.1	5.1	54.9	6.7
Dominica Dominique	2001	57.7	11.0	70.2	12.0	45.0	9.5
Dominican Republic République dominicaine	2005	* 56.9	6.5	* 74.6	4.7	* 39.6	9.5
	2010	* 57.6	5.0	* 74.0	3.8	* 41.6	7.0
	2015	* 63.6	5.9	* 77.9	3.8	* 49.6	9.0
	*2019	64.1	5.5	77.6	3.7	51.0	8.0
Ecuador Équateur	2005	* 68.1	7.7	* 83.8	5.6	* 52.5	10.9
	2010	* 65.1	4.1	* 80.5	3.5	* 49.9	5.0
	2015	* 66.6	3.6	* 81.2	3.0	* 52.2	4.5
	*2019	69.0	4.2	81.7	3.4	56.6	5.4
Egypt Égypte	2005	* 46.6	11.2	* 73.0	7.1	* 20.2	26.1
	2010	* 49.2	11.9	* 75.7	7.7	* 22.6	25.7
	2015	* 48.3	13.1	* 74.1	9.1	* 22.6	26.1
	*2019	48.1	11.6	73.2	7.8	22.9	24.0
El Salvador El Salvador	2005	* 60.9	7.2	* 79.0	8.9	* 45.5	4.8
	2010	* 59.9	4.9	* 76.5	5.4	* 45.9	4.2
	2015	* 58.8	4.0	* 75.2	4.4	* 45.1	3.5
	*2019	61.1	4.6	78.9	5.2	46.3	3.7
Equatorial Guinea Guinée équatoriale	*2005	60.3	5.8	67.1	5.4	52.1	6.3
	*2010	61.9	5.6	67.8	5.3	54.1	6.0
	*2015	62.7	5.5	68.0	5.1	55.4	6.0
	*2019	62.3	8.1	67.4	8.0	55.3	8.3
Eritrea Érythrée	*2005	78.9	7.0	85.0	6.5	73.0	7.5
	*2010	80.0	6.8	86.6	6.3	73.5	7.3
	*2015	80.6	6.6	87.4	6.1	73.8	7.1
	*2019	80.5	6.2	87.0	5.8	74.2	6.7

17
Labour force participation rate and unemployment rate *(continued)*
Labour force (LF) participation rate and unemployment rate by sex (percent)

Taux d'activité et taux de chômage *(suite)*
Taux d'activité et taux de chômage par sexe (pourcentage)

Region, country or area & Région, pays ou zone &	Year Année	Male and Female Hommes et femmes		Male Hommes		Female Femmes	
		LF particip. rate Taux d'activité	Unemployment rate Taux de Chômage	LF particip. rate Taux d'activité	Unemployment rate Taux de Chômage	LF particip. rate Taux d'activité	Unemployment rate Taux de Chômage
Estonia	2005	* 58.6	8.0	* 64.7	9.1	* 53.5	6.9
Estonie	2010	* 60.5	16.7	* 67.1	19.3	* 55.0	14.1
	2015	* 62.2	6.2	* 69.5	6.2	* 56.0	6.1
	*2019	63.1	5.5	70.5	5.9	56.7	5.0
Ethiopia	2005	* 82.1	5.4	* 90.0	2.8	* 74.4	8.3
Éthiopie	*2010	81.3	5.2	88.9	3.0	73.8	7.8
	*2015	80.5	5.0	87.3	3.0	73.8	7.2
	*2019	80.4	5.4	86.5	3.2	74.4	7.9
Falkland Islands (Malvinas) [9] Îles Falkland (Malvinas) [9]	2013	# 81.9	1.2	# 86.0	1.1	# 77.2	1.4
Faroe Islands	2005[3]	...	3.2	...	2.6	...	3.9
Îles Féroé	2010[6,10]	81.7	# 6.4	85.3	# 5.1	77.5	# 8.0
	2013[6,10]	82.9	4.0	86.0	3.4	79.4	4.9
Fiji	2005	* 57.0	4.6	* 78.4	3.7	* 34.9	6.5
Fidji	2010	* 61.4	8.9	* 79.2	7.2	* 43.1	12.3
	*2015	58.1	6.1	76.3	4.9	39.6	8.4
	*2019	57.2	6.2	75.8	5.0	38.2	8.5
Finland	2005	* 60.6	8.4	* 64.8	8.2	* 56.6	8.6
Finlande	2010	* 59.8	8.4	* 63.9	9.1	* 56.0	7.6
	2015	* 58.8	9.4	* 62.3	9.9	* 55.5	8.8
	*2019	58.3	8.1	62.0	8.3	54.9	7.9
France	2005	* 56.2	8.5	* 62.6	7.8	* 50.1	9.3
France	2010	* 56.3	8.9	* 62.0	8.7	* 50.9	9.1
	2015	* 55.6	10.4	* 60.7	10.8	* 50.7	9.9
	*2019	54.9	8.6	59.8	8.7	50.2	8.6
French Guiana [6]	2005	42.1	24.8	48.2	22.8	36.3	27.0
Guyane française [6]	2010	48.9	21.0	54.9	17.8	43.2	25.1
	#2013	53.4	21.3	58.8	16.7	48.4	26.3
French Polynesia	*2005	56.7	11.8	65.7	10.9	47.2	13.2
Polynésie française	*2010	56.2	18.0	63.8	17.3	48.2	18.9
	*2015	55.4	21.4	62.3	20.8	48.2	22.2
	*2019	54.2	20.2	60.9	19.4	47.4	21.1
Gabon	2005	* 46.8	16.9	* 56.7	12.9	* 37.0	23.0
Gabon	2010	* 49.2	20.4	* 58.1	14.7	* 39.9	29.1
	*2015	51.3	20.0	59.3	14.2	42.7	28.7
	*2019	52.3	19.2	60.2	13.6	43.7	27.4
Gambia	*2005	58.5	9.4	68.8	6.9	48.5	12.8
Gambie	*2010	59.3	9.4	68.7	6.8	50.3	12.8
	*2015	59.5	9.4	68.1	6.8	51.3	12.7
	*2019	59.6	9.5	67.7	6.9	51.8	12.7
Georgia	2005	* 63.4	13.8	* 72.9	14.8	* 55.2	12.7
Géorgie	2010	* 64.8	16.3	* 75.1	17.9	* 56.0	14.5
	2015	* 68.1	12.0	* 78.7	13.5	* 58.9	10.2
	*2019	67.6	11.6	78.8	13.5	57.9	9.4
Germany	2005	* 58.5	11.2	* 66.7	11.4	* 50.7	10.9
Allemagne	2010	* 59.4	7.0	* 66.5	7.4	* 52.8	6.5
	2015	* 60.3	4.6	* 66.2	5.0	* 54.6	4.2
	*2019	60.6	3.6	66.1	3.9	55.3	3.2
Ghana	*2005	71.6	4.7	74.0	4.4	69.4	5.0
Ghana	2010	* 69.4	5.3	* 72.5	4.9	* 66.5	5.7
	*2015	67.4	2.2	71.5	2.0	63.4	2.3
	*2019	67.4	2.5	71.5	2.3	63.5	2.7
Gibraltar Gibraltar	2001	68.4	...	78.8	...	57.5	...
Greece	2005	* 53.6	10.0	* 64.9	6.3	* 42.7	15.5
Grèce	2010	* 54.4	12.7	* 64.5	10.1	* 44.7	16.4
	2015	* 53.1	24.9	* 61.1	21.8	* 45.5	28.9
	*2019	52.5	19.5	60.3	16.1	45.1	23.7

17

Labour force participation rate and unemployment rate *(continued)*
Labour force (LF) participation rate and unemployment rate by sex (percent)

Taux d'activité et taux de chômage *(suite)*
Taux d'activité et taux de chômage par sexe (pourcentage)

Region, country or area & Région, pays ou zone &	Year Année	Male and Female Hommes et femmes		Male Hommes		Female Femmes	
		LF particip. rate Taux d'activité	Unemployment rate Taux de Chômage	LF particip. rate Taux d'activité	Unemployment rate Taux de Chômage	LF particip. rate Taux d'activité	Unemployment rate Taux de Chômage
Greenland	2005	...	9.3	...	10.4	...	8.0
Groenland	2006	...	8.4	...	10.0	...	6.7
	#2013[11,12]	...	9.7	...	9.6	...	9.8
Grenada							
Grenade	2001	...	10.2	...	9.6	...	10.9
Guadeloupe [6]	2005	41.8	25.9	46.8	22.4	37.7	29.5
Guadeloupe [6]	2010	41.6	23.8	44.2	21.4	39.5	26.0
	#2013	52.7	26.1	56.5	23.8	49.6	28.3
Guam	2005	* 68.1	7.0	* 79.8	6.5	* 56.1	7.8
Guam	2010	* 66.7	8.2	* 78.4	7.4	* 54.7	9.4
	2015	* 65.5	6.9	* 77.3	6.5	* 53.5	7.5
	*2019	64.6	6.5	76.5	6.2	52.5	6.8
Guatemala	*2005	62.5	2.5	85.3	1.9	41.7	3.4
Guatemala	2010	* 61.5	3.7	* 84.3	3.4	* 40.5	4.3
	2015	* 61.4	2.7	* 85.5	2.1	* 39.1	4.0
	*2019	62.3	2.6	85.1	2.1	41.1	3.7
Guinea	*2005	65.2	4.6	67.4	5.6	62.9	3.5
Guinée	*2010	65.0	4.6	66.7	5.6	63.2	3.5
	*2015	64.8	4.5	65.7	5.5	63.8	3.5
	*2019	64.6	4.5	65.1	5.5	64.1	3.4
Guinea-Bissau	*2005	72.1	6.5	79.5	5.9	65.2	7.1
Guinée-Bissau	*2010	72.2	6.3	78.7	5.8	66.1	6.9
	*2015	72.7	6.2	78.9	5.7	66.9	6.8
	*2019	73.0	6.0	78.9	5.5	67.5	6.6
Guyana	*2005	55.8	12.4	78.0	10.9	34.0	16.0
Guyana	*2010	56.1	10.9	75.4	9.2	37.2	14.4
	*2015	57.1	11.8	73.8	9.9	40.5	15.4
	*2019	57.5	11.8	73.5	9.9	41.3	15.3
Haiti	*2005	64.5	15.0	70.1	13.0	59.2	17.3
Haïti	*2010	65.6	16.0	71.5	14.0	60.1	18.2
	*2015	67.1	14.1	72.0	12.3	62.5	16.0
	*2019	68.1	13.8	72.9	12.0	63.5	15.6
Honduras	2005	* 63.9	4.9	* 85.5	4.2	* 43.0	6.5
Honduras	2010	* 64.3	4.1	* 84.8	3.4	* 44.5	5.5
	2015	* 65.7	4.6	* 84.7	3.5	* 47.2	6.4
	*2019	65.2	4.3	83.6	3.9	47.3	5.1
Hungary	2005	* 50.1	7.2	* 58.4	7.0	* 42.9	7.4
Hongrie	2010	* 50.5	11.2	* 58.2	11.6	* 43.8	10.7
	2015	* 54.8	6.8	* 63.4	6.6	* 47.3	7.0
	*2019	56.1	3.5	64.8	3.2	48.3	3.8
Iceland	2005	* 75.8	2.6	* 80.7	2.6	* 70.9	2.5
Islande	2010	* 74.9	7.6	* 79.1	8.3	* 70.6	6.7
	2015	* 77.0	4.0	* 80.9	3.9	* 73.1	4.1
	*2019	76.0	2.9	80.2	3.0	71.8	2.9
India	2005	* 58.5	4.4	* 83.3	4.1	* 32.2	5.0
Inde	2010	* 54.1	3.5	* 80.7	3.3	* 25.8	4.4
	2015	* 52.2	3.5	* 79.3	3.3	* 23.5	4.2
	*2019	51.8	3.5	78.6	3.3	23.4	4.2
Indonesia	2005	* 63.9	7.7	* 82.4	6.6	* 45.5	9.7
Indonésie	2010	* 67.0	5.6	* 82.8	5.1	* 51.1	6.4
	2015	* 66.6	4.5	* 82.5	4.6	* 50.8	4.4
	*2019	67.1	4.5	81.8	4.5	52.3	4.3
Iran (Islamic Republic of)	2005	* 47.4	12.1	* 74.3	10.6	* 19.4	18.2
Iran (Rép. islamique d')	2010	* 43.2	13.5	* 70.0	11.9	* 15.9	20.7
	2015	* 42.8	11.1	* 70.3	9.3	* 15.2	19.4
	*2019	43.8	12.2	70.9	10.5	16.6	19.6
Iraq	*2005	42.3	8.6	73.2	8.9	11.5	7.1
Iraq	*2010	42.3	8.3	72.6	7.8	12.1	10.5
	*2015	42.5	8.1	72.8	7.1	12.2	12.1
	*2019	42.6	8.3	72.6	7.4	12.4	11.6

Labour force participation rate and unemployment rate *(continued)*
Labour force (LF) participation rate and unemployment rate by sex (percent)

Taux d'activité et taux de chômage *(suite)*
Taux d'activité et taux de chômage par sexe (pourcentage)

Region, country or area & Région, pays ou zone &	Year Année	Male and Female Hommes et femmes		Male Hommes		Female Femmes	
		LF particip. rate Taux d'activité	Unemployment rate Taux de Chômage	LF particip. rate Taux d'activité	Unemployment rate Taux de Chômage	LF particip. rate Taux d'activité	Unemployment rate Taux de Chômage
Ireland	2005	* 65.0	4.3	* 75.8	4.6	* 54.5	4.0
Irlande	2010	* 63.0	13.9	* 70.6	17.0	* 55.5	9.8
	2015	* 62.0	9.4	* 69.4	10.8	* 54.8	7.7
	*2019	61.1	6.0	67.6	6.8	54.8	5.0
Isle of Man	2001	63.3	1.6	71.4	1.7	55.7	1.5
Île de Man	2006	62.8	2.4	69.9	2.8	56.3	2.0
	#2011[3]	63.3	3.3[11]	69.3	3.8[11]	57.5	2.8[11]
	#2013[13]	...	2.6	...	3.4	...	1.7
Israel	2005	* 61.7	11.3	* 68.8	11.1	* 55.0	11.6
Israël	2010	* 63.0	8.5	* 69.4	8.9	* 57.0	8.0
	2015	* 64.1	5.3	* 69.5	5.1	* 59.0	5.4
	*2019	64.0	3.8	69.0	3.7	59.2	3.9
Italy	2005	* 49.0	7.7	* 61.0	6.2	* 37.9	10.1
Italie	2010	* 48.0	8.4	* 58.9	7.5	* 37.8	9.6
	2015	* 48.4	11.9	* 58.4	11.3	* 39.0	12.7
	*2019	48.7	10.4	58.1	9.6	39.9	11.4
Jamaica	2005	* 65.5	10.9	* 75.0	8.3	* 56.5	14.3
Jamaïque	2010	* 64.7	12.4	* 73.0	9.6	* 56.6	16.1
	2015	* 65.4	13.5	* 72.8	10.1	* 58.2	18.0
	*2019	67.2	11.9	74.0	9.1	60.6	15.6
Japan	2005	* 60.6	4.4	* 73.5	4.6	* 48.4	4.2
Japon	2010	* 60.1	5.1	* 72.1	5.4	* 48.7	4.6
	2015	* 60.0	3.3	* 70.8	3.6	* 49.9	3.0
	*2019	60.6	2.4	70.4	2.5	51.4	2.2
Jordan	2005	* 40.9	14.8	* 67.6	13.0	* 12.2	25.8
Jordanie	2010	* 41.9	12.5	* 67.3	10.5	* 15.3	21.9
	2015	* 39.3	13.1	* 64.0	11.0	* 14.0	22.7
	*2019	39.2	14.5	63.7	12.1	14.2	25.5
Kazakhstan	2005	* 69.5	8.1	* 75.2	6.8	* 64.4	9.6
Kazakhstan	2010	* 70.3	5.8	* 75.8	4.9	* 65.4	6.6
	2015	* 70.9	4.9	* 77.0	4.1	* 65.4	5.8
	*2019	70.5	5.2	76.9	4.4	64.8	6.2
Kenya	*2005	64.8	10.5	69.7	7.5	60.1	13.9
Kenya	*2010	66.1	12.1	70.7	8.6	61.7	16.0
	*2015	66.3	11.6	69.7	8.1	63.1	15.4
	*2019	66.3	11.4	69.1	7.8	63.6	15.2
Kiribati	2005	# 26.4[14]	14.7[15]	# 32.8[14]	12.3[15]	# 20.4[14]	18.2[15]
Kiribati	2010	# 59.3[14]	30.6[15]	66.8[14]	27.6[15]	52.3[14]	34.1[15]
Kosovo [13]	2005	48.7	41.4	68.3	32.9	29.7	60.5
Kosovo [13]	2009	47.7	# 45.4	66.9	# 56.4	28.7	# 40.7
	#2012	37.1	30.9	55.5	28.1	17.9	40.0
	#2013	40.6	...	60.2	...	21.1	...
Kuwait	2005	* 69.7	2.0	* 82.7	2.0	* 49.0	1.8
Koweït	2010	* 72.1	1.8	* 84.5	1.4	* 53.6	2.8
	2015	* 75.0	2.2	* 86.5	1.3	* 58.5	4.6
	*2019	73.8	2.0	85.3	1.2	57.3	4.1
Kyrgyzstan	2005	* 64.8	8.1	* 76.1	7.4	* 54.1	9.1
Kirghizistan	2010	* 64.1	8.6	* 76.6	7.7	* 52.2	9.9
	2015	* 62.4	7.6	* 75.6	6.5	* 49.8	9.0
	*2019	61.4	7.4	75.8	6.4	47.7	9.0
Lao People's Dem. Rep.	2005	* 78.8	1.4	* 79.8	1.4	* 77.9	1.3
Rép. dém. populaire lao	2010	* 78.1	0.7	* 79.3	0.8	* 76.8	0.7
	*2015	78.1	0.7	79.6	0.7	76.7	0.6
	*2019	78.3	0.7	79.8	0.8	76.8	0.6
Latvia	2005	* 57.3	10.0	* 65.6	10.1	* 50.4	10.0
Lettonie	2010	* 59.0	19.5	* 65.3	22.7	* 53.9	16.3
	2015	* 60.2	9.9	* 67.6	11.1	* 54.3	8.6
	*2019	60.7	8.5	67.6	9.5	55.2	7.5

Labour force participation rate and unemployment rate *(continued)*
Labour force (LF) participation rate and unemployment rate by sex (percent)

Taux d'activité et taux de chômage *(suite)*
Taux d'activité et taux de chômage par sexe (pourcentage)

Region, country or area [&] Région, pays ou zone [&]	Year Année	Male and Female Hommes et femmes		Male Hommes		Female Femmes	
		LF particip. rate Taux d'activité	Unemployment rate Taux de Chômage	LF particip. rate Taux d'activité	Unemployment rate Taux de Chômage	LF particip. rate Taux d'activité	Unemployment rate Taux de Chômage
Lebanon	*2005	46.2	8.1	70.7	7.7	20.4	9.7
Liban	*2010	45.6	6.4	67.9	5.1	22.0	10.5
	*2015	46.8	6.6	70.4	5.4	23.0	10.6
	*2019	47.3	6.7	71.0	5.6	23.5	10.3
Lesotho	*2005	70.4	37.2	77.4	34.9	64.1	39.7
Lesotho	*2010	67.7	25.9	75.4	22.4	60.7	29.8
	*2015	66.4	27.0	74.3	24.7	59.3	29.5
	*2019	67.1	28.2	75.1	25.6	59.8	31.1
Liberia	*2005	56.1	5.6	59.1	6.9	53.1	4.2
Libéria	2010	* 56.4	2.3	* 59.3	2.2	* 53.6	2.3
	*2015	56.2	2.3	58.1	2.3	54.3	2.3
	*2019	56.0	2.5	57.4	2.5	54.7	2.4
Libya	*2005	49.3	20.0	75.3	17.4	21.5	27.7
Libye	*2010	50.4	18.6	77.2	16.3	22.5	25.0
	*2015	52.6	18.4	78.8	15.6	26.3	26.9
	*2019	52.4	15.0	79.0	12.1	25.7	23.7
Liechtenstein	2005	63.0	...	73.7	...	52.8	...
Liechtenstein	2010	61.6	2.6[13]	70.9	2.3[13]	52.6	3.1[13]
	2013	61.9	2.6[13]	70.6	2.3[13]	53.5	3.1[13]
Lithuania	2005	* 56.2	8.3	* 62.9	8.1	* 50.6	8.5
Lituanie	2010	* 57.0	17.8	* 62.3	21.2	* 52.5	14.5
	2015	* 59.3	9.1	* 65.0	10.1	* 54.5	8.2
	*2019	61.1	6.8	66.7	8.1	56.4	5.6
Luxembourg	2005	* 54.8	4.5	* 64.7	3.5	* 45.4	5.8
Luxembourg	2010	* 57.0	4.4	* 65.4	3.8	* 48.8	5.1
	2015	* 59.4	6.7	* 65.2	6.1	* 53.6	7.4
	*2019	58.0	5.2	62.5	5.1	53.5	5.4
Madagascar	2005	* 86.6	2.3	* 89.1	2.2	* 84.2	2.4
Madagascar	2010	* 89.1	3.8	* 91.0	3.7	* 87.1	4.0
	2015	* 86.5	1.8	* 89.6	1.7	* 83.5	1.9
	*2019	86.5	1.8	89.3	1.7	83.7	1.9
Malawi	2005	* 77.1	7.8	* 80.1	5.5	* 74.2	10.2
Malawi	*2010	77.3	6.7	81.8	5.3	73.1	8.3
	*2015	77.3	5.9	82.2	4.9	72.6	6.9
	*2019	77.4	6.0	82.3	4.9	72.9	7.1
Malaysia	2005	* 61.1	3.5	* 77.4	3.3	* 44.0	4.0
Malaisie	2010	* 60.3	3.3	* 76.2	3.1	* 43.5	3.5
	2015	* 64.3	3.1	* 77.4	2.9	* 50.3	3.4
	*2019	64.8	3.3	77.6	3.0	51.1	3.8
Maldives	*2005	58.1	3.8	73.5	3.7	40.4	4.2
Maldives	*2010	62.9	4.6	77.6	4.2	44.1	5.3
	*2015	66.4	5.1	81.9	4.7	45.0	6.0
	*2019	65.6	4.9	82.2	4.6	42.0	6.0
Mali	*2005	70.6	9.5	81.0	8.5	60.6	11.4
Mali	2010	* 71.1	8.1	* 82.0	6.2	* 60.5	11.1
	2015	* 71.1	7.7	* 81.2	7.2	* 61.2	8.5
	*2019	71.0	8.1	80.9	7.5	61.3	8.9
Malta	2005	* 48.4	6.9	* 67.5	6.3	* 29.6	8.4
Malte	2010	* 50.1	6.9	* 66.4	6.7	* 34.1	7.1
	2015	* 54.2	5.4	* 66.8	5.5	* 41.6	5.2
	*2019	54.6	3.8	66.0	3.7	43.2	4.1
Marshall Islands	2006[3]	44.6	...	...	...	...	...
Îles Marshall	2011	41.3	# 4.7	53.3	# 4.9	29.0	# 4.5
Martinique [6]	2005	43.6	18.7	48.5	16.9	39.6	20.4
Martinique [6]	2010	45.9	21.0	49.1	19.7	43.3	22.2
	#2013	53.1	22.8	53.8	22.8	52.6	22.8
Mauritania	*2005	48.6	10.6	68.7	9.2	28.7	13.7
Mauritanie	*2010	46.5	10.2	65.0	8.9	28.2	13.1
	*2015	46.1	9.9	63.4	8.6	28.8	12.6
	*2019	46.3	9.9	63.2	8.7	29.2	12.7

17 Labour force participation rate and unemployment rate *(continued)*
Labour force (LF) participation rate and unemployment rate by sex (percent)

Taux d'activité et taux de chômage *(suite)*
Taux d'activité et taux de chômage par sexe (pourcentage)

Region, country or area [&] Région, pays ou zone [&]	Year Année	Male and Female Hommes et femmes		Male Hommes		Female Femmes	
		LF particip. rate Taux d'activité	Unemployment rate Taux de Chômage	LF particip. rate Taux d'activité	Unemployment rate Taux de Chômage	LF particip. rate Taux d'activité	Unemployment rate Taux de Chômage
Mauritius Maurice	2005	* 58.9	9.6	* 77.1	5.8	* 41.3	16.5
	2010	* 58.3	7.7	* 74.1	4.6	* 43.0	12.9
	2015	* 59.3	7.9	* 73.4	5.5	* 45.7	11.6
	*2019	57.9	7.0	71.4	4.7	44.9	10.5
Mexico Mexique	2005	* 61.0	3.6	* 81.5	3.4	* 41.3	3.9
	2010	* 61.4	5.3	* 80.1	5.4	* 43.2	5.2
	2015	* 61.3	4.3	* 79.3	4.3	* 43.9	4.5
	*2019	61.1	3.3	78.8	3.2	43.9	3.5
Monaco [16] Monaco [16]	2000	45.7	3.6	57.3	2.5	35.1	5.2
Mongolia Mongolie	2005	* 59.2	3.3	* 64.9	3.5	* 53.7	3.1
	2010	* 59.0	6.6	* 65.1	7.1	* 53.1	5.9
	2015	* 60.3	4.9	* 67.2	5.3	* 53.7	4.3
	*2019	59.7	6.2	66.6	6.9	53.2	5.4
Montenegro Monténégro	2005	* 50.6	30.3	* 59.1	26.2	* 42.7	35.6
	2010	* 49.5	19.7	* 56.7	18.9	* 42.6	20.6
	2015	* 50.9	17.5	* 57.6	18.2	* 44.5	16.7
	*2019	50.5	16.2	57.8	15.4	43.5	17.2
Montserrat Montserrat	#2001	85.2	9.5	89.2	...	80.6	...
	2011	...	5.6	...	7.7	...	3.3
Morocco Maroc	2005	* 50.6	11.0	* 76.1	10.8	* 26.5	11.6
	2010	* 49.8	9.1	* 75.6	8.8	* 25.6	9.8
	2015	* 47.1	9.7	* 72.4	9.4	* 23.0	10.4
	*2019	45.2	9.3	70.2	9.1	21.3	10.1
Mozambique Mozambique	*2005	85.0	21.7	83.1	19.1	86.6	23.9
	*2010	82.5	22.2	82.0	20.0	82.9	24.0
	*2015	78.9	25.3	80.0	23.1	77.8	27.1
	*2019	78.4	24.8	79.5	22.6	77.3	26.6
Myanmar Myanmar	*2005	69.7	0.9	84.1	0.7	56.3	1.0
	*2010	67.4	0.8	82.3	0.7	53.6	0.9
	2015	* 65.6	0.8	* 80.5	0.7	* 51.8	0.9
	*2019	61.8	0.8	77.0	0.7	47.5	0.9
Namibia Namibie	*2005	57.2	22.2	63.9	19.9	51.1	24.9
	2010	* 57.6	22.1	* 62.9	19.9	* 52.9	24.4
	*2015	60.5	19.6	65.1	17.9	56.4	21.3
	*2019	61.2	23.2	66.2	21.5	56.7	24.9
Nauru Nauru	2002[3]	78.0	22.7	86.8	17.1	69.6	29.6
	2011	64.0	# 23.0	78.9	# 21.4	49.3	# 25.5
Nepal Népal	*2005	84.2	1.5	88.7	1.7	79.9	1.2
	*2010	82.9	2.1	86.9	2.5	79.3	1.8
	*2015	83.1	3.1	85.3	3.6	81.1	2.6
	*2019	82.9	2.7	84.3	3.2	81.7	2.2
Netherlands Pays-Bas	2005	* 64.4	4.7	* 72.3	4.4	* 56.6	5.1
	2010	* 64.7	4.5	* 71.3	4.4	* 58.2	4.5
	2015	* 64.1	6.9	* 70.1	6.5	* 58.2	7.3
	*2019	63.2	3.4	68.6	3.2	57.9	3.7
Netherlands Antilles [former] [6,14,17] Antilles néerlandaises [anc.] [6,14,17]	#2009	56.3	...	61.1	...	52.6	...
	2011	57.9	...	62.2	...	54.5	...
New Caledonia Nouvelle-Calédonie	*2005	65.5	15.8	70.5	14.8	60.5	17.0
	*2010	63.1	14.2	68.0	13.3	58.1	15.3
	*2015	63.0	14.6	68.2	13.7	57.7	15.6
	*2019	62.4	14.8	67.8	13.9	57.1	15.8
New Zealand Nouvelle-Zélande	2005	* 67.2	3.8	* 74.7	3.5	* 60.1	4.1
	2010	* 67.2	6.1	* 73.8	5.9	* 61.0	6.4
	2015	* 68.3	5.4	* 74.1	4.9	* 62.8	5.9
	*2019	69.9	5.2	75.6	4.8	64.5	5.6
Nicaragua Nicaragua	2005	* 62.5	5.4	* 82.1	5.1	* 44.1	5.8
	2010	* 64.4	7.8	* 82.9	7.4	* 47.1	8.6
	*2015	66.2	4.5	84.0	3.8	49.5	5.5
	*2019	66.8	4.5	83.6	4.0	50.9	5.3

17 Labour force participation rate and unemployment rate *(continued)*
Labour force (LF) participation rate and unemployment rate by sex (percent)

Taux d'activité et taux de chômage *(suite)*
Taux d'activité et taux de chômage par sexe (pourcentage)

Region, country or area & Région, pays ou zone &	Year Année	Male and Female Hommes et femmes LF particip. rate Taux d'activité	Unemployment rate Taux de Chômage	Male Hommes LF particip. rate Taux d'activité	Unemployment rate Taux de Chômage	Female Femmes LF particip. rate Taux d'activité	Unemployment rate Taux de Chômage
Niger	2005	* 79.3	3.1	* 91.0	3.4	* 68.2	2.7
Niger	*2010	79.2	0.9	91.1	1.3	67.8	0.3
	*2015	78.9	0.3	90.8	0.4	67.4	0.2
	*2019	78.7	0.4	90.4	0.5	67.2	0.2
Nigeria	*2005	54.8	4.3	61.7	4.3	47.8	4.4
Nigéria	*2010	55.0	3.9	60.7	4.0	49.2	3.8
	2015	* 55.1	4.3	* 59.8	4.7	* 50.4	3.9
	*2019	55.2	7.0	59.7	7.6	50.6	6.3
Niue	2001	75.5	2.2	76.7	2.3	74.8	2.1
Nioué	#2002	...	9.7	...	...	...	...
North Macedonia	2005	* 53.9	37.3	* 66.0	36.5	* 42.0	38.4
Macédoine du Nord	2010	* 55.6	32.0	* 68.6	31.9	* 42.8	32.2
	2015	* 55.5	26.1	* 67.6	26.7	* 43.5	25.1
	*2019	54.9	22.0	67.3	22.3	42.7	21.4
Northern Mariana Islands [3]	2003	81.8	4.6	82.5	5.0	81.3	4.3
Îles Mariannes du Nord [3]	2005	...	6.5	...	7.3	...	5.8
	#2010	72.3	11.2	77.6	9.7	66.6	13.0
Norway	2005	* 65.4	4.4	* 70.3	4.6	* 60.7	4.2
Norvège	2010	* 65.7	3.5	* 69.6	4.0	* 61.8	2.9
	2015	* 64.9	4.3	* 68.4	4.6	* 61.3	4.0
	*2019	63.4	3.9	66.5	4.2	60.2	3.4
Oman	*2005	55.8	4.2	77.4	3.3	24.7	8.6
Oman	*2010	62.0	4.0	82.2	2.9	27.0	9.2
	*2015	70.0	3.3	88.1	1.9	30.2	12.5
	*2019	72.2	3.2	89.4	1.9	30.9	12.1
Pakistan	2005	* 51.2	7.7	* 82.3	6.5	* 18.4	13.0
Pakistan	2010	* 51.6	0.7	* 80.1	0.7	* 21.7	0.7
	2015	* 53.2	3.6	* 81.2	2.8	* 23.9	6.2
	*2019	53.4	4.3	81.5	3.4	24.1	7.5
Palau [3]							
Palaos [3]	2005	67.5	4.2	75.4	3.7	58.1	4.9
Panama	2005	* 64.5	10.3	* 81.1	8.2	* 48.0	14.0
Panama	2010	* 63.5	6.5	* 80.0	5.3	* 47.1	8.5
	2015	* 64.9	4.5	* 79.2	3.7	* 50.7	5.8
	*2019	66.4	4.7	80.4	3.7	52.5	6.2
Papua New Guinea	*2005	61.0	2.5	62.5	3.3	59.6	1.6
Papouasie-Nvl-Guinée	2010	* 48.2	2.0	* 49.3	2.7	* 47.1	1.3
	*2015	47.1	2.6	47.8	3.6	46.4	1.7
	*2019	46.6	2.7	47.5	3.7	45.7	1.7
Paraguay	2005	* 70.9	4.8	* 85.4	3.9	* 56.1	6.3
Paraguay	2010	* 69.0	4.6	* 83.7	3.6	* 53.9	6.1
	2015	* 69.6	4.6	* 82.9	4.3	* 55.9	5.0
	*2019	70.8	4.6	84.0	4.0	57.2	5.5
Peru	2005	* 72.7	4.9	* 81.5	4.9	* 64.0	4.9
Pérou	2010	* 79.1	3.5	* 86.3	3.2	* 72.0	3.8
	2015	* 76.1	3.0	* 84.2	3.0	* 68.1	3.0
	*2019	77.4	3.7	84.8	3.5	70.2	3.8
Philippines	2005	* 61.9	3.8	* 76.4	3.6	* 47.6	4.2
Philippines	2010	* 62.2	3.6	* 76.0	3.5	* 48.5	3.8
	2015	* 62.5	3.0	* 76.0	2.9	* 49.1	3.3
	*2019	59.9	1.8	74.1	1.6	45.9	1.9
Poland	2005	* 55.1	17.8	* 63.0	16.6	* 47.8	19.2
Pologne	2010	* 55.9	9.6	* 64.3	9.3	* 48.3	10.0
	2015	* 56.7	7.5	* 65.1	7.3	* 49.0	7.7
	*2019	56.6	4.4	65.2	4.4	48.7	4.4
Portugal	2005	* 62.0	7.6	* 69.3	6.7	* 55.3	8.6
Portugal	2010	* 61.0	10.8	* 66.9	9.8	* 55.8	11.9
	2015	* 58.6	12.4	* 64.2	12.2	* 53.8	12.7
	*2019	58.3	6.7	63.8	6.3	53.6	7.0

Labour force participation rate and unemployment rate (continued)
Labour force (LF) participation rate and unemployment rate by sex (percent)

Taux d'activité et taux de chômage (suite)
Taux d'activité et taux de chômage par sexe (pourcentage)

Region, country or area & Région, pays ou zone &	Year Année	Male and Female Hommes et femmes		Male Hommes		Female Femmes	
		LF particip. rate Taux d'activité	Unemployment rate Taux de Chômage	LF particip. rate Taux d'activité	Unemployment rate Taux de Chômage	LF particip. rate Taux d'activité	Unemployment rate Taux de Chômage
Puerto Rico	2005	* 47.4	11.4	* 59.1	12.2	* 36.9	10.1
Porto Rico	2010	* 44.7	16.4	* 55.0	18.0	* 35.6	14.1
	2015	* 41.7	12.0	* 51.2	13.2	* 33.2	10.3
	*2019	41.1	10.3	51.1	11.3	32.2	8.8
Qatar	*2005	80.3	1.2	94.0	0.7	45.4	3.7
Qatar	2010	* 86.7	0.5	* 95.8	0.1	* 51.1	2.7
	2015	* 87.6	0.2	* 95.0	0.1	* 58.9	0.8
	*2019	87.0	0.1	95.0	0.1	57.7	0.5
Republic of Korea	2005	* 62.1	3.7	* 74.0	4.0	* 50.4	3.4
République de Corée	2010	* 60.8	3.7	* 72.1	4.0	* 49.5	3.3
	2015	* 62.5	3.6	* 73.1	3.7	* 51.9	3.6
	*2019	63.0	3.6	73.3	3.8	52.7	3.5
Republic of Moldova	2005	* 48.4	7.3	* 50.8	8.6	* 46.3	6.0
République de Moldova	2010	* 41.7	7.5	* 45.2	9.1	* 38.6	5.8
	2015	* 44.1	3.7	* 47.3	4.4	* 41.3	2.9
	*2019	41.7	4.3	45.4	5.7	38.4	3.0
Réunion [6]	2005	50.1	30.1	60.3	27.6	41.1	33.3
Réunion [6]	2010	52.1	28.9	59.9	28.0	45.3	30.0
	#2013	54.9	28.9	61.3	28.3	49.1	29.7
Romania	2005	* 53.5	7.2	* 61.2	7.8	* 46.3	6.4
Roumanie	2010	* 55.0	7.0	* 64.3	7.6	* 46.3	6.2
	2015	* 54.3	6.8	* 64.2	7.5	* 45.2	5.9
	*2019	54.1	5.0	63.8	5.7	45.2	4.1
Russian Federation	2005	* 61.0	7.2	* 67.8	7.3	* 55.2	7.0
Fédération de Russie	2010	* 62.5	7.4	* 70.3	7.9	* 55.9	6.8
	2015	* 62.7	5.6	* 71.2	5.8	* 55.6	5.3
	*2019	61.6	4.9	70.0	5.0	54.5	4.8
Rwanda	*2005	84.7	1.7	85.4	1.4	84.0	2.0
Rwanda	*2010	84.8	3.0	85.2	2.5	84.4	3.5
	*2015	84.1	1.2	84.2	1.1	84.1	1.3
	*2019	83.8	1.4	83.5	1.3	84.2	1.5
Saint Helena	2005	...	5.2	...	...	...	...
Sainte-Hélène	2010	...	2.0	...	...	...	...
Saint Kitts and Nevis Saint-Kitts-et-Nevis	2001	# 68.8	5.1	# 62.8	4.3	# 74.9	5.9
Saint Lucia	2005	* 66.0	18.7	* 75.4	16.4	* 57.2	21.5
Sainte-Lucie	2010	* 66.3	20.6	* 74.9	18.3	* 58.1	23.5
	2015	* 67.1	24.1	* 75.2	21.5	* 59.5	27.1
	*2019	67.6	19.8	75.3	18.2	60.4	21.7
Saint Vincent & Grenadines	*2005	67.2	18.9	80.0	17.6	54.1	20.8
Saint-Vincent-Grenadines	*2010	68.4	18.8	80.1	17.6	56.4	20.6
	*2015	68.4	18.0	79.6	16.9	57.1	19.5
	*2019	68.2	18.2	79.0	17.2	57.3	19.6
Samoa	*2005	32.9	2.1	40.8	1.8	24.6	2.5
Samoa	*2010	32.6	4.8	40.4	4.4	24.3	5.5
	*2015	32.0	8.8	39.6	7.8	23.9	10.5
	*2019	31.2	8.0	38.5	7.1	23.6	9.5
San Marino	2003	66.2	...	79.2	...	53.8	...
Saint-Marin	2010	...	4.4	...	2.1	...	7.3
	#2014[4]	...	6.6	...	4.3	...	9.5
Sao Tome and Principe	2005	* 57.0	16.5	* 74.4	11.3	* 40.3	25.9
Sao Tomé-et-Principe	*2010	58.7	14.6	76.5	10.0	41.5	23.1
	*2015	59.6	13.4	76.8	9.0	42.8	21.5
	*2019	59.5	13.5	76.1	9.0	43.2	21.7
Saudi Arabia	2005	* 50.5	6.1	* 74.0	4.7	* 17.7	14.2
Arabie saoudite	2010	* 51.1	5.6	* 74.4	3.5	* 18.2	17.5
	2015	* 55.6	5.6	* 79.2	2.5	* 22.1	21.6
	*2019	56.8	5.3	79.5	2.4	23.5	20.7

17

Labour force participation rate and unemployment rate *(continued)*
Labour force (LF) participation rate and unemployment rate by sex (percent)

Taux d'activité et taux de chômage *(suite)*
Taux d'activité et taux de chômage par sexe (pourcentage)

		Male and Female Hommes et femmes		Male Hommes		Female Femmes	
Region, country or area & Région, pays ou zone &	Year Année	LF particip. rate Taux d'activité	Unemployment rate Taux de Chômage	LF particip. rate Taux d'activité	Unemployment rate Taux de Chômage	LF particip. rate Taux d'activité	Unemployment rate Taux de Chômage
Senegal	*2005	50.9	9.0	69.5	7.3	33.8	12.2
Sénégal	*2010	48.8	10.2	64.7	8.0	34.3	13.6
	2015	* 46.2	4.9	* 58.6	4.8	* 34.8	4.9
	*2019	46.5	4.8	58.5	4.6	35.3	5.1
Serbia	2005	* 54.6	20.9	* 64.5	17.1	* 45.4	25.9
Serbie	2010	50.9	19.2	* 59.4	18.5	* 42.9	20.2
	2015	* 52.0	17.9	* 60.5	17.1	* 44.1	19.0
	*2019	53.9	12.2	61.8	11.4	46.6	13.1
Seychelles	2005	72.1	5.5	...	6.1	...	4.9
Seychelles	#2011[6,18]	65.0	4.1	68.3	3.8	61.9	4.5
Sierra Leone	*2005	65.0	3.6	65.7	4.7	64.4	2.4
Sierra Leone	*2010	61.2	4.3	61.9	5.3	60.5	3.3
	*2015	58.3	4.7	59.1	5.6	57.5	3.9
	*2019	57.9	4.3	58.3	5.0	57.6	3.5
Singapore	2005	* 64.2	5.6	* 76.3	5.3	* 52.4	6.1
Singapour	2010	* 66.9	3.2	* 77.1	3.1	* 57.0	3.3
	2015	* 68.9	1.7	* 77.3	1.7	* 60.8	1.7
	*2019	68.1	1.7	76.1	1.7	60.4	1.8
Slovakia	2005	* 59.6	16.3	* 68.6	15.5	* 51.3	17.2
Slovaquie	2010	* 58.8	14.4	* 67.6	14.2	* 50.6	14.6
	2015	* 59.6	11.5	* 67.8	10.3	* 52.0	12.9
	*2019	59.5	7.0	67.0	6.8	52.5	7.2
Slovenia	2005	* 59.2	6.5	* 66.0	6.1	* 52.8	7.0
Slovénie	2010	* 59.2	7.2	* 65.5	7.4	* 53.2	7.0
	2015	* 57.4	9.0	* 62.8	8.1	* 52.0	10.0
	*2019	57.4	6.0	62.0	5.3	52.9	6.8
Solomon Islands	*2005	72.8	2.2	81.6	2.1	63.8	2.3
Îles Salomon	*2010	72.3	2.1	81.3	2.0	63.3	2.2
	*2015	71.5	2.0	80.4	2.0	62.5	2.1
	*2019	71.4	2.1	80.2	2.0	62.4	2.2
Somalia	*2005	46.6	5.9	75.9	5.7	17.4	6.7
Somalie	*2010	46.0	6.0	74.9	5.8	17.6	6.8
	*2015	46.2	6.1	74.3	5.9	18.7	6.9
	*2019	46.5	5.9	74.4	5.7	19.2	6.6
South Africa	2005	* 54.5	23.8	* 62.5	20.2	* 47.0	28.4
Afrique du Sud	2010	* 52.4	24.7	* 60.5	22.9	* 44.7	27.0
	2015	* 54.6	25.2	* 61.9	23.2	* 47.8	27.5
	*2019	55.5	27.6	62.6	25.8	48.8	29.8
South Sudan	*2005	73.7	12.2	77.1	11.2	70.5	13.2
Soudan du sud	*2010	73.4	12.1	76.0	11.2	70.8	13.2
	*2015	73.0	12.0	74.7	11.0	71.4	13.0
	*2019	73.1	11.5	74.3	10.1	71.9	13.0
Spain	2005	* 56.8	9.2	* 68.0	7.1	* 46.1	12.0
Espagne	2010	* 59.3	19.9	* 67.3	19.6	* 51.5	20.2
	2015	* 58.3	22.1	* 64.7	20.8	* 52.3	23.6
	*2019	57.0	13.4	62.8	12.2	51.4	14.7
Sri Lanka	2005	* 56.3	7.7	* 76.7	5.6	* 36.9	11.8
Sri Lanka	2010	* 54.7	4.9	* 76.3	3.6	* 34.8	7.7
	2015	* 53.5	4.7	* 74.4	3.1	* 34.7	7.7
	*2019	52.3	4.2	71.9	2.9	34.8	6.7
State of Palestine	2005	* 40.6	23.5	* 67.1	23.8	* 13.6	22.2
État de Palestine	2010	* 40.7	23.7	* 66.2	23.1	* 14.8	26.7
	2015	* 45.4	25.8	* 71.3	22.4	* 19.0	39.0
	*2019	45.7	26.4	71.5	21.3	19.5	45.0
Sudan	*2005	49.1	13.1	74.0	9.3	24.5	24.5
Soudan	*2010	47.5	12.8	72.8	9.3	23.0	23.7
	*2015	47.2	12.8	71.0	9.2	24.1	23.3
	*2019	47.1	12.7	70.2	9.2	24.5	23.1

17

Labour force participation rate and unemployment rate *(continued)*
Labour force (LF) participation rate and unemployment rate by sex (percent)

Taux d'activité et taux de chômage *(suite)*
Taux d'activité et taux de chômage par sexe (pourcentage)

Region, country or area &	Year	Male and Female Hommes et femmes		Male Hommes		Female Femmes	
Région, pays ou zone &	Année	LF particip. rate Taux d'activité	Unemployment rate Taux de Chômage	LF particip. rate Taux d'activité	Unemployment rate Taux de Chômage	LF particip. rate Taux d'activité	Unemployment rate Taux de Chômage
Suriname	*2005	51.2	9.8	65.5	6.0	37.0	16.3
Suriname	2010	* 51.9	7.6	* 64.8	4.5	* 39.3	12.4
	2015	* 52.0	7.2	* 64.3	4.4	* 39.9	11.5
	*2019	51.6	8.0	64.0	4.4	39.3	12.4
Eswatini	*2005	49.1	22.1	65.1	21.5	34.9	23.0
Eswatini	*2010	50.1	27.8	63.9	27.3	37.5	28.5
	*2015	52.0	26.3	65.0	25.9	40.2	27.0
	*2019	53.2	26.5	66.1	26.1	41.6	27.1
Sweden	2005	* 62.9	7.7	* 67.0	7.8	* 58.8	7.6
Suède	2010	* 63.1	8.6	* 67.4	8.7	* 58.9	8.5
	2015	* 64.0	7.4	* 67.3	7.5	* 60.7	7.3
	*2019	64.4	6.3	67.6	6.5	61.2	6.1
Switzerland	2005	* 67.0	4.4	* 75.0	3.9	* 59.5	5.1
Suisse	2010	* 66.9	4.8	* 74.3	4.5	* 59.9	5.2
	2015	* 68.2	4.8	* 74.2	4.7	* 62.4	4.9
	*2019	68.1	4.7	73.8	4.4	62.6	5.0
Syrian Arab Republic	*2005	46.6	9.2	76.2	6.5	16.2	22.3
République arabe syrienne	2010	* 43.0	8.6	* 72.8	6.2	* 13.2	21.9
	*2015	41.6	14.7	71.0	10.8	12.0	38.1
	*2019	40.8	14.9	69.8	11.1	11.7	38.2
Tajikistan	*2005	42.5	11.2	54.9	10.9	30.2	11.6
Tadjikistan	*2010	43.2	11.7	57.0	11.7	29.5	11.7
	*2015	43.5	10.4	58.9	9.9	28.3	11.1
	*2019	43.6	10.3	59.9	9.9	27.7	11.0
Thailand	2005	* 73.4	1.4	* 81.5	1.5	* 65.7	1.2
Thaïlande	2010	* 71.7	0.6	* 80.0	0.6	* 63.8	0.6
	2015	* 69.1	0.6	* 77.8	0.6	* 61.0	0.6
	*2019	67.2	1.4	75.9	1.4	59.2	1.5
Timor-Leste	*2005	49.2	7.2	66.4	6.5	31.6	8.7
Timor-Leste	2010	* 41.5	3.3	* 56.2	2.8	* 26.5	4.4
	*2015	39.3	3.3	53.0	2.8	25.3	4.4
	*2019	38.8	3.5	52.5	3.0	24.9	4.6
Togo	*2005	80.6	1.9	80.7	2.2	80.5	1.6
Togo	*2010	78.6	1.9	80.3	2.2	77.0	1.6
	*2015	78.0	1.8	79.7	2.1	76.2	1.6
	*2019	77.5	1.9	79.3	2.1	75.8	1.6
Tonga	*2005	60.2	3.1	75.3	2.3	45.7	4.5
Tonga	*2010	59.9	1.1	75.1	0.8	45.3	1.5
	*2015	59.6	1.1	74.5	0.8	45.2	1.6
	*2019	59.5	1.2	74.1	0.9	45.2	1.7
Trinidad and Tobago	2005	* 64.7	8.0	* 76.2	5.8	* 53.5	11.0
Trinité-et-Tobago	2010	* 62.3	5.9	* 73.9	5.2	* 51.0	7.0
	2015	* 62.0	3.4	* 73.5	2.9	* 50.8	4.1
	*2019	60.2	5.1	70.7	4.2	50.1	6.5
Tunisia	2005	* 45.1	12.9	* 67.6	12.1	* 23.3	15.2
Tunisie	2010	* 46.7	13.1	* 69.7	10.9	* 24.5	19.0
	2015	* 47.0	15.2	* 70.2	12.6	* 24.7	22.4
	*2019	46.3	15.1	69.7	12.5	23.9	22.5
Turkey	2005	* 46.0	10.6	* 70.1	10.5	* 23.3	11.0
Turquie	2010	* 47.7	10.7	* 69.6	10.4	* 27.0	11.2
	2015	* 51.0	10.2	* 71.7	9.2	* 31.5	12.5
	*2019	52.4	11.2	72.4	9.9	33.5	14.0
Turkmenistan	*2005	63.3	3.8	75.2	3.7	52.1	3.9
Turkménistan	2010	* 64.0	4.0	* 76.2	4.0	* 52.4	4.0
	*2015	65.2	3.6	78.1	3.4	53.0	3.8
	*2019	65.0	3.3	78.1	3.1	52.6	3.5
Turks and Caicos Islands	2005	# 62.0	8.0	...	...	...	...
Îles Turques-et-Caïques	#2008	64.0	8.3	...	...	...	...
Tuvalu							
Tuvalu	2005	58.2	6.5	69.6	4.9	47.9	8.6

17 Labour force participation rate and unemployment rate *(continued)*
Labour force (LF) participation rate and unemployment rate by sex (percent)

Taux d'activité et taux de chômage *(suite)*
Taux d'activité et taux de chômage par sexe (pourcentage)

Region, country or area & Région, pays ou zone &	Year Année	Male and Female Hommes et femmes		Male Hommes		Female Femmes	
		LF particip. rate Taux d'activité	Unemployment rate Taux de Chômage	LF particip. rate Taux d'activité	Unemployment rate Taux de Chômage	LF particip. rate Taux d'activité	Unemployment rate Taux de Chômage
Uganda	2005	* 70.4	1.9	* 76.1	1.6	* 65.0	2.3
Ouganda	*2010	70.8	4.0	76.0	3.3	65.9	4.8
	*2015	71.0	1.9	75.4	1.4	66.7	2.5
	*2019	71.1	2.3	75.0	1.5	67.3	3.1
Ukraine	2005	* 55.1	7.2	* 62.9	7.5	* 48.6	6.8
Ukraine	2010	* 55.0	8.1	* 63.0	9.3	* 48.4	6.8
	2015	* 54.6	9.1	* 63.3	10.1	* 47.4	8.1
	*2019	53.7	8.6	62.5	9.8	46.4	7.2
United Arab Emirates	2005	* 78.4	3.1	* 92.5	2.6	* 37.2	7.2
Émirats arabes unis	*2010	83.5	3.7	94.5	2.7	44.0	11.8
	*2015	84.1	1.9	94.7	1.4	49.4	5.7
	*2019	82.9	1.7	93.4	1.3	51.1	4.7
United Kingdom	2005	* 61.7	4.8	* 69.2	5.1	* 54.7	4.3
Royaume-Uni	2010	* 61.8	7.8	* 68.6	8.6	* 55.5	6.9
	2015	* 62.2	5.3	* 68.2	5.5	* 56.6	5.1
	*2019	62.3	3.9	67.7	4.0	57.1	3.8
United Rep. of Tanzania	*2005	88.2	4.4	89.8	3.0	86.6	5.9
Rép.-Unie de Tanzanie	*2010	86.3	3.0	88.9	2.1	83.9	3.8
	*2015	83.4	2.1	87.4	1.6	79.6	2.7
	*2019	83.1	2.3	87.1	1.7	79.2	2.9
United States of America	2005	* 65.1	5.1	* 72.2	5.1	* 58.2	5.1
États-Unis d'Amérique	2010	* 63.6	9.6	* 69.9	10.5	* 57.5	8.6
	2015	* 62.0	5.3	* 68.4	5.4	* 55.8	5.2
	*2019	61.7	4.1	67.9	4.1	55.8	4.0
United States Virgin Islands	*2005	64.0	7.7	69.6	6.7	58.9	8.7
Îles Vierges américaines	*2010	62.5	7.3	67.8	6.5	57.9	8.1
	*2015	60.1	7.3	64.9	6.8	55.9	7.9
	*2019	59.1	7.0	63.3	6.5	55.4	7.5
Uruguay	2005	* 62.5	12.2	* 73.7	9.6	* 52.4	15.5
Uruguay	2010	* 65.5	7.2	* 76.7	5.3	* 55.3	9.5
	2015	* 64.9	7.5	* 75.1	6.4	* 55.7	8.9
	*2019	64.5	8.2	73.8	6.7	55.9	10.0
Uzbekistan	*2005	63.2	8.3	74.6	8.4	52.3	8.1
Ouzbékistan	*2010	64.0	8.2	75.6	8.3	52.7	8.0
	*2015	65.2	7.9	77.4	8.1	53.3	7.8
	*2019	65.5	6.7	78.0	6.7	53.4	6.7
Vanuatu	*2005	70.3	5.6	79.0	5.1	61.4	6.4
Vanuatu	*2010	70.4	5.4	79.5	4.8	61.2	6.2
	*2015	70.6	5.3	79.6	4.7	61.6	6.0
	*2019	70.6	5.2	79.7	4.6	61.5	5.9
Venezuela (Boliv. Rep. of)	2005	* 65.0	11.5	* 80.6	10.5	* 49.7	13.1
Venezuela (Rép. boliv. du)	2010	* 64.8	8.5	* 79.3	7.8	* 50.6	9.4
	2015	* 63.9	6.8	* 78.0	6.2	* 50.1	7.7
	*2019	62.1	7.7	76.9	7.0	47.8	8.9
Viet Nam	*2005	76.1	2.3	80.8	2.1	71.7	2.5
Viet Nam	2010	* 76.2	2.6	* 81.3	2.6	* 71.3	2.6
	2015	* 77.8	2.1	* 83.0	2.2	* 72.9	2.0
	*2019	77.3	2.1	82.3	2.3	72.5	2.0
Western Sahara	*2005	53.9	8.1	79.2	6.6	24.4	13.3
Sahara occidental	*2010	54.7	7.9	79.7	6.4	26.0	13.0
	*2015	55.1	7.6	79.9	6.1	26.8	12.4
	*2019	55.1	7.2	79.7	5.9	27.4	11.1
Yemen	2005	* 42.2	16.1	* 69.9	10.8	* 14.4	41.8
Yémen	2010	* 39.5	17.8	* 68.8	12.5	* 10.0	54.8
	*2015	37.6	13.8	68.8	12.7	6.1	26.6
	*2019	38.4	14.0	70.9	12.6	5.8	31.6
Zambia	*2005	79.5	10.4	85.7	10.8	73.7	9.9
Zambie	2010	* 76.5	13.2	* 82.2	12.6	* 71.1	13.8
	*2015	75.2	7.8	80.2	7.2	70.4	8.4
	*2019	75.2	7.8	79.7	7.4	70.8	8.3

Taux d'activité et taux de chômage *(suite)*
Taux d'activité et taux de chômage par sexe (pourcentage)

Region, country or area & Région, pays ou zone &	Year Année	Male and Female Hommes et femmes		Male Hommes		Female Femmes	
		LF particip. rate Taux d'activité	Unemployment rate Taux de Chômage	LF particip. rate Taux d'activité	Unemployment rate Taux de Chômage	LF particip. rate Taux d'activité	Unemployment rate Taux de Chômage
Zimbabwe Zimbabwe	*2005	82.4	4.5	88.2	4.3	77.1	4.7
	*2010	82.6	5.3	88.4	4.7	77.4	5.8
	*2015	83.2	5.1	88.9	4.4	78.1	5.8
	*2019	83.7	5.0	89.0	4.3	78.7	5.6
European Union (EU) Union européenne (UE)	*2005	56.7	8.9	65.2	8.3	48.8	9.7
	*2010	57.3	9.5	64.9	9.5	50.1	9.5
	*2015	57.4	9.4	64.2	9.3	51.0	9.5
	*2019	57.3	6.7	63.7	6.5	51.2	6.9

Source:

International Labour Organization (ILO), Geneva, Key Indicators of the Labour Market (KILM 9th edition) and the ILOSTAT database, last accessed January 2019.

& Population aged 15 years and over, unless otherwise footnoted.

1   Data excludes Armenia, Azerbaijan, Cyprus, Georgia, Israel and Turkey.
2   Caucasus refers to Armenia, Azerbaijan, Cyprus, Georgia, Israel and Turkey.
3   Population aged 16 years and over.
4   Population aged 14 years and over.
5   Resident population (de jure).
6   Excluding the institutional population.
7   For statistical purposes, the data for China do not include those for the Hong Kong Special Administrative Region (Hong Kong SAR), Macao Special Administrative Region (Macao SAR) and Taiwan Province of China.
8   Population aged 15 to 69 years.
9   Population aged 16 to 65 years.
10   Population aged 15 to 74 years.
11   Nationals, residents.
12   Population aged 18 to 64 years.
13   Population aged 15 to 64 years.
14   Persons present (de facto).
15   De facto population.
16   Population aged 17 years and over.
17   Main city or metropolitan area.
18   Excluding some areas.

Source:

Organisation internationale du Travail (OIT), Genève, Indicateurs Clés du Marché du Travail (ICMT 9e édition) et ILOSTAT base de données, dernier accès janvier 2019.

& Sauf indication contraire, population âgée de 15 ans et plus.

1   Les données excluent l'Arménie, l'Azerbaïdjan, Chypre, la Géorgie, l'Israël et la Turquie.
2   Le Caucase se rapporte à l'Arménie, l'Azerbaïdjan, Chypre, la Géorgie, l'Israël et la Turquie.
3   Population âgée de 16 ans et plus.
4   Population âgée de 14 ans et plus.
5   Population résidente (de droit).
6   Non compris la population dans les institutions.
7   Pour la présentation des statistiques, les données pour la Chine ne comprennent pas la région administrative spéciale de Hong Kong (RAS de Hong Kong), la région administrative spéciale de Macao (RAS de Macao) et la province chinoise de Taïwan.
8   Population âgée de 15 à 69 ans.
9   Population âgée de 16 à 65 ans.
10   Population âgée de 15 à 74 ans.
11   Ressortissants, résidents.
12   Population âgée de 18 à 64 ans.
13   Population âgée de 15 à 64 ans.
14   Personnes présentes (de facto).
15   Population de fait.
16   Population âgée de 17 ans et plus.
17   Ville principale ou zone métropolitaine.
18   Certaines régions sont exclues.

Employment by economic activity
Percentage of persons employed by sex and ISIC 4 categories; agriculture (agr.), industry (ind.) and services (ser.)

Emploi par activité économique
Personnes employées par sexe et branches de la CITI rév. 4; agriculture (agr.), industrie (ind.) et services (ser.), pourcentage

Region, country or area [+] Région, pays ou zone [+]	Year Année	Male and Female Hommes et femmes			Male Hommes			Female Femmes		
		Agr.	Ind.	Ser.	Agr.	Ind.	Ser.	Agr.	Ind.	Ser.
Total, all countries or areas	*2005	35.2	22.6	42.1	34.0	25.5	40.5	37.1	18.3	44.7
Total, tous pays ou zones	*2010	30.8	23.0	46.2	30.2	26.8	43.1	31.8	17.1	51.1
	*2015	27.2	22.7	50.1	26.7	27.2	46.1	28.0	15.7	56.2
	*2019	25.5	22.2	52.3	24.9	27.0	48.1	26.3	14.8	58.9
Africa	*2005	58.7	12.0	29.3	55.5	14.7	29.8	63.3	8.3	28.5
Afrique	*2010	54.1	13.3	32.6	51.6	16.3	32.2	57.6	9.2	33.2
	*2015	53.3	13.6	33.1	51.3	16.8	31.9	56.0	9.4	34.6
	*2019	52.5	13.6	33.9	50.7	16.8	32.5	54.9	9.2	35.8
Northern Africa	*2005	34.0	24.0	42.1	31.6	25.1	43.3	43.4	19.1	37.5
Afrique septentrionale	*2010	30.4	27.5	42.1	27.9	29.5	42.6	39.9	19.9	40.2
	*2015	29.0	28.1	42.9	26.5	29.9	43.6	38.3	21.1	40.6
	*2019	27.7	28.0	44.3	25.5	29.9	44.6	36.1	20.7	43.2
Sub-Saharan Africa	*2005	63.6	9.7	26.8	62.4	11.6	26.0	65.0	7.3	27.7
Afrique subsaharienne	*2010	58.7	10.6	30.8	58.3	12.6	29.2	59.1	8.3	32.6
	*2015	57.6	11.1	31.4	57.8	13.3	28.9	57.4	8.5	34.1
	*2019	56.7	11.1	32.2	57.0	13.5	29.5	56.4	8.4	35.3
Eastern Africa	*2005	74.5	7.2	18.3	71.8	8.8	19.4	77.5	5.4	17.1
Afrique orientale	*2010	71.2	7.6	21.2	69.1	9.5	21.4	73.5	5.5	21.0
	*2015	67.4	8.7	23.9	66.2	10.9	22.9	68.8	6.3	24.9
	*2019	65.7	9.1	25.2	64.6	11.6	23.8	66.8	6.3	26.8
Middle Africa	*2005	70.8	11.1	18.1	66.2	13.4	20.4	75.6	8.7	15.7
Afrique centrale	*2010	70.5	10.5	19.0	65.3	13.0	21.8	76.2	7.9	16.0
	*2015	70.9	10.7	18.4	66.2	13.5	20.3	76.0	7.7	16.3
	*2019	71.4	10.1	18.5	66.6	12.9	20.5	76.6	7.2	16.2
Southern Africa	*2005	10.6	24.9	64.5	12.1	32.8	55.0	8.5	13.7	77.8
Afrique australe	*2010	8.1	23.9	67.9	9.1	32.2	58.7	6.9	12.9	80.2
	*2015	8.7	23.5	67.9	9.9	32.7	57.4	7.2	11.6	81.2
	*2019	8.3	23.2	68.5	9.7	31.9	58.4	6.5	11.8	81.7
Western Africa	*2005	54.8	9.6	35.6	58.0	10.6	31.4	50.7	8.4	41.0
Afrique occidentale	*2010	43.9	12.5	43.6	49.2	13.1	37.7	37.2	11.9	51.0
	*2015	45.0	12.6	42.5	50.3	13.4	36.4	38.6	11.6	49.8
	*2019	43.5	12.7	43.8	49.1	13.7	37.2	37.0	11.5	51.5
Americas	*2005	12.2	21.3	66.4	15.7	28.0	56.3	7.3	12.0	80.7
Amériques	*2010	11.2	20.4	68.5	14.8	27.5	57.7	6.2	10.8	83.0
	*2015	9.5	20.7	69.8	13.0	28.0	59.0	4.7	10.7	84.5
	*2019	9.3	20.4	70.3	12.8	27.7	59.5	4.6	10.5	84.9
Northern America	*2005	1.7	21.2	77.2	2.4	30.8	66.8	0.9	9.8	89.3
Amérique septentrionale	*2010	1.7	18.6	79.7	2.4	28.0	69.6	0.9	8.0	91.1
	*2015	1.7	18.9	79.4	2.4	27.9	69.7	0.9	8.4	90.7
	*2019	1.6	18.7	79.6	2.3	27.7	70.0	0.9	8.2	91.0
Latin America & the Caribbean	*2005	19.5	21.5	59.1	23.9	26.3	49.8	12.5	13.8	73.6
Amérique latine et Caraïbes	*2010	16.9	21.5	61.6	21.5	27.2	51.3	10.0	12.8	77.2
	*2015	14.2	21.8	64.0	18.9	28.1	53.1	7.4	12.4	80.2
	*2019	13.9	21.4	64.7	18.5	27.7	53.8	7.2	12.0	80.8
Caribbean	*2005	22.4	18.7	58.9	29.0	23.5	47.5	12.5	11.3	76.2
Caraïbes	*2010	21.8	16.1	62.1	28.6	20.9	50.5	11.9	9.2	78.9
	*2015	20.9	16.3	62.9	27.9	21.3	50.9	11.0	9.3	79.7
	*2019	19.9	16.2	63.9	26.8	21.4	51.8	10.3	8.9	80.8
Central America	*2005	18.3	24.4	57.2	24.9	27.5	47.7	6.0	18.7	75.3
Amérique centrale	*2010	18.0	22.8	59.2	25.0	26.7	48.4	5.6	16.0	78.4
	*2015	16.7	23.7	59.6	23.6	27.8	48.6	4.6	16.4	79.0
	*2019	15.8	24.3	59.9	22.4	28.8	48.8	4.5	16.6	78.9
South America	*2005	19.6	20.7	59.7	23.0	26.1	50.9	14.5	12.6	72.9
Amérique du Sud	*2010	16.1	21.5	62.4	19.5	28.0	52.5	11.3	12.1	76.6
	*2015	12.7	21.5	65.8	16.0	28.8	55.1	8.0	11.3	80.7
	*2019	12.6	20.6	66.8	16.0	27.8	56.2	7.8	10.7	81.5
Central Asia	*2005	35.1	25.4	39.5	32.4	33.0	34.7	38.5	15.8	45.7
Asie centrale	*2010	29.0	29.0	42.0	26.6	37.3	36.1	32.1	18.2	49.7
	*2015	23.6	29.9	46.5	21.3	39.2	39.5	26.8	17.7	55.6
	*2019	22.1	30.2	47.7	19.9	39.9	40.3	25.1	17.4	57.5

Employment by economic activity *(continued)*
Percentage of persons employed by sex and ISIC 4 categories; agriculture (agr.), industry (ind.) and services (ser.)

Emploi par activité économique *(suite)*
Personnes employées par sexe et branches de la CITI rév. 4; agriculture (agr.), industrie (ind.) et services (ser.), pourcentage

Region, country or area [+] Région, pays ou zone [+]	Year Année	Male and Female Hommes et femmes			Male Hommes			Female Femmes		
		Agr.	Ind.	Ser.	Agr.	Ind.	Ser.	Agr.	Ind.	Ser.
Eastern Asia	*2005	32.8	29.2	38.1	29.9	29.9	40.3	36.4	28.4	35.3
Asie orientale	*2010	24.4	29.5	46.1	21.7	32.0	46.3	27.8	26.2	46.0
	*2015	18.5	26.8	54.7	16.2	30.9	52.9	21.5	21.6	56.9
	*2019	15.0	25.8	59.2	13.1	30.5	56.3	17.4	19.8	62.8
South-eastern Asia	*2005	46.4	18.1	35.5	46.7	20.1	33.2	46.0	15.2	38.8
Asie du Sud-Est	*2010	41.1	18.9	40.0	41.9	21.5	36.6	40.0	15.3	44.7
	*2015	34.8	21.4	43.8	35.8	24.8	39.5	33.4	16.7	49.9
	*2019	30.9	21.5	47.6	32.3	25.3	42.4	28.9	16.3	54.8
Southern Asia	*2005	53.5	18.6	27.9	47.3	20.4	32.3	69.5	14.0	16.5
Asie méridionale	*2010	49.7	21.3	29.0	44.1	23.4	32.5	66.7	15.0	18.4
	*2015	43.7	23.3	33.0	38.4	25.3	36.3	59.7	17.1	23.3
	*2019	40.2	23.5	36.4	34.7	25.6	39.6	56.7	16.9	26.4
Western Asia [1]	*2005	13.9	22.7	63.4	12.8	25.7	61.6	20.6	5.6	73.8
Asie occidentale [1]	*2010	10.7	25.7	63.6	9.7	28.9	61.4	17.3	6.0	76.7
	*2015	11.7	26.0	62.3	11.0	29.4	59.6	16.0	6.0	78.1
	*2019	12.5	26.4	61.2	11.9	29.9	58.2	15.8	6.0	78.1
Caucasus [2]	*2005	27.6	22.7	49.7	21.1	28.0	50.9	40.6	12.0	47.4
Caucase [2]	*2010	25.0	22.8	52.2	19.3	28.7	52.0	35.6	11.9	52.4
	*2015	21.8	23.5	54.6	17.4	29.9	52.8	29.8	12.3	58.0
	*2019	20.1	23.5	56.5	16.2	29.7	54.1	27.0	12.2	60.8
Eastern Europe	*2005	13.8	29.9	56.3	15.2	38.4	46.5	12.4	20.8	66.8
Europe orientale	*2010	11.7	28.7	59.7	13.1	38.5	48.4	10.1	18.0	72.0
	*2015	9.8	28.2	62.1	11.3	38.4	50.2	8.1	16.8	75.1
	*2019	9.0	28.0	63.0	10.5	38.4	51.1	7.2	16.5	76.2
Northern Europe	*2005	2.8	23.1	74.1	3.8	34.0	62.2	1.6	10.5	87.9
Europe septentrionale	*2010	2.2	19.9	77.9	3.1	30.3	66.6	1.2	8.3	90.6
	*2015	2.1	19.3	78.6	3.0	29.1	67.9	1.1	8.3	90.6
	*2019	1.9	18.8	79.3	2.7	28.5	68.8	1.0	7.9	91.1
Southern Europe	*2005	8.7	29.3	62.0	8.8	38.6	52.6	8.4	15.5	76.1
Europe méridionale	*2010	7.7	25.6	66.8	8.3	35.1	56.6	6.9	12.6	80.5
	*2015	7.0	23.5	69.4	8.2	32.2	59.6	5.5	12.3	82.2
	*2019	6.6	22.8	70.6	7.8	31.7	60.5	5.0	11.5	83.5
Western Europe	*2005	3.1	26.3	70.7	3.8	36.8	59.4	2.2	13.4	84.5
Europe occidentale	*2010	2.4	24.7	72.9	3.1	35.7	61.3	1.7	11.7	86.7
	*2015	2.1	23.6	74.2	2.7	34.5	62.8	1.5	11.2	87.4
	*2019	2.0	23.1	74.9	2.7	33.9	63.5	1.3	10.8	87.9
Oceania	*2005	14.6	18.3	67.1	15.9	26.6	57.5	13.2	8.1	78.7
Océanie	*2010	9.7	18.3	72.0	11.4	27.1	61.5	7.7	7.7	84.6
	*2015	8.5	17.3	74.2	10.1	26.2	63.7	6.5	7.1	86.4
	*2019	8.4	16.6	75.0	10.2	25.1	64.6	6.4	6.7	86.9
Afghanistan	*2005	71.8	6.6	21.7	70.2	6.5	23.3	81.4	6.8	11.8
Afghanistan	*2010	64.5	6.1	29.4	62.8	6.2	31.0	75.6	5.5	18.8
	*2015	61.1	6.7	32.2	59.0	6.9	34.1	72.4	5.7	21.9
	*2019	61.7	6.8	31.5	59.3	7.1	33.6	73.5	5.5	21.1
Albania	*2005	54.0	19.9	26.2	44.7	25.1	30.2	67.5	12.2	20.4
Albanie	*2010	43.9	19.4	36.7	36.3	25.7	38.0	54.1	10.9	35.0
	*2015	41.4	18.6	40.0	36.7	22.1	41.3	47.8	13.9	38.3
	*2019	37.8	18.8	43.4	32.8	22.5	44.7	44.6	13.7	41.7
Algeria	*2005	20.0	29.8	50.2	20.8	28.9	50.3	14.2	36.0	49.8
Algérie	*2010	16.5	39.4	44.0	17.9	37.5	44.6	8.7	50.3	41.0
	*2015	13.1	47.6	39.3	13.8	45.9	40.4	9.8	55.8	34.4
	*2019	12.6	46.7	40.7	13.4	44.8	41.8	8.8	55.8	35.5
American Samoa [3,4]	2000	3.1	41.7	51.9	...	...	...	...	...	...
Samoa américaines [3,4]	#2010	3.0	23.2	73.8	...	...	...	...	...	...
Angola	*2005	37.5	8.8	53.7	30.0	15.6	54.4	45.5	1.6	53.0
Angola	*2010	47.2	8.8	44.0	40.2	16.2	43.7	54.4	1.2	44.4
	*2015	48.9	8.9	42.2	41.8	16.6	41.6	56.0	1.3	42.8
	*2019	50.0	8.7	41.3	43.1	16.1	40.8	57.0	1.3	41.7
Anguilla [4]										
Anguilla [4]	#2001	2.9	18.9	76.7	4.8	32.1	61.7	0.7	3.7	93.9
Antigua and Barbuda [4]	2005	2.8	15.6	81.6	4.4	26.1	69.5	1.2	5.0	93.8
Antigua-et-Barbuda [4]	2008	2.8	15.6	81.6	4.4	26.1	69.5	1.2	5.0	93.8

18

Employment by economic activity *(continued)*
Percentage of persons employed by sex and ISIC 4 categories; agriculture (agr.), industry (ind.) and services (ser.)

Emploi par activité économique *(suite)*
Personnes employées par sexe et branches de la CITI rév. 4; agriculture (agr.), industrie (ind.) et services (ser.), pourcentage

Region, country or area [+] Région, pays ou zone [+]	Year Année	Male and Female Hommes et femmes			Male Hommes			Female Femmes		
		Agr.	Ind.	Ser.	Agr.	Ind.	Ser.	Agr.	Ind.	Ser.
Argentina	*2005	1.3	23.3	75.5	1.7	31.8	66.6	0.7	10.6	88.7
Argentine	*2010	1.3	23.3	75.4	1.9	32.6	65.6	0.4	9.3	90.3
	*2015	0.5	23.8	75.7	0.8	34.3	64.9	0.2	8.1	91.8
	*2019	0.5	23.1	76.4	0.8	33.4	65.8	0.1	7.5	92.4
Armenia	*2005	40.6	17.7	41.7	35.2	25.3	39.6	47.1	8.7	44.2
Arménie	*2010	38.6	17.4	44.0	31.7	26.7	41.7	47.3	5.8	46.9
	*2015	35.3	15.9	48.8	31.3	23.1	45.7	40.1	7.5	52.4
	*2019	32.6	16.2	51.2	28.9	23.2	47.9	37.1	7.8	55.1
Aruba [4]	#2000	0.5	16.4	82.3	0.8	26.7	71.6	0.2	4.5	94.7
Aruba [4]	#2010[5]	0.6	14.5	84.4	1.0	24.4	74.1	0.3	4.5	94.8
	#2011	0.6	14.0	85.1	0.8	24.4	74.4	0.4	3.3	96.1
Australia	*2005	3.6	21.1	75.3	4.5	30.7	64.9	2.5	9.3	88.2
Australie	*2010	3.2	21.0	75.8	4.0	31.1	64.9	2.3	8.6	89.1
	*2015	2.6	19.5	77.9	3.3	29.4	67.3	1.9	7.7	90.5
	*2019	2.5	18.8	78.7	3.3	28.5	68.2	1.6	7.5	91.0
Austria	*2005	5.3	27.6	67.2	5.3	39.7	55.1	5.3	12.9	81.8
Autriche	*2010	5.2	24.9	69.9	5.4	36.5	58.1	5.0	11.5	83.5
	*2015	4.5	25.8	69.7	4.8	37.8	57.4	4.2	12.1	83.7
	*2019	4.2	25.3	70.6	4.6	37.4	58.0	3.7	11.7	84.6
Azerbaijan	*2005	40.5	12.6	46.9	36.5	20.2	43.3	44.6	4.8	50.6
Azerbaïdjan	*2010	38.2	13.7	48.1	32.3	21.0	46.8	44.4	6.2	49.4
	*2015	36.4	14.1	49.6	31.0	21.8	47.2	42.1	5.9	52.1
	*2019	37.3	13.8	48.9	31.4	21.3	47.3	43.6	5.8	50.6
Bahamas	*2005	3.5	17.8	78.7	6.3	29.4	64.3	0.3	5.1	94.6
Bahamas	*2010	3.3	14.7	82.0	5.5	24.7	69.9	1.0	3.8	95.2
	*2015	3.9	12.1	84.0	5.7	19.5	74.8	1.9	3.9	94.3
	*2019	4.0	11.7	84.3	5.9	18.8	75.3	1.9	3.8	94.4
Bahrain	*2005	1.3	30.7	68.0	1.5	35.2	63.3	0.1	9.4	90.6
Bahreïn	*2010	1.1	35.7	63.2	1.4	42.6	56.0	0.1	9.1	90.9
	*2015	0.9	35.4	63.7	1.2	42.4	56.4	~0.0	9.2	90.8
	*2019	1.1	36.1	62.9	1.3	42.5	56.2	0.1	9.5	90.5
Bangladesh	*2005	48.1	14.5	37.4	42.0	15.1	42.9	68.2	12.5	19.3
Bangladesh	*2010	47.3	17.6	35.1	40.9	19.2	39.8	65.5	13.1	21.4
	*2015	42.7	20.5	36.9	34.7	22.2	43.1	63.5	15.9	20.7
	*2019	36.4	21.6	42.0	27.7	23.5	48.8	58.2	16.7	25.2
Barbados	*2005	2.4	20.6	77.0	4.3	32.3	63.4	0.4	7.9	91.7
Barbade	*2010	2.8	28.0	69.2	3.7	44.4	51.9	2.0	11.1	86.9
	*2015	2.9	19.3	77.8	4.2	28.6	67.1	1.6	10.0	88.4
	*2019	2.9	19.1	78.1	3.9	28.9	67.2	1.8	9.2	89.0
Belarus	*2005	13.9	35.6	50.5	17.4	44.5	38.0	10.2	26.5	63.3
Bélarus	*2010	10.8	34.6	54.6	13.5	45.4	41.1	8.1	23.7	68.2
	*2015	9.5	32.4	58.1	12.5	44.0	43.6	6.5	20.7	72.8
	*2019	9.4	30.8	59.8	12.4	42.6	45.0	6.4	18.9	74.7
Belgium	*2005	2.0	24.7	73.3	2.5	35.0	62.6	1.5	11.3	87.2
Belgique	*2010	1.4	23.4	75.3	1.7	34.3	64.0	0.9	10.1	89.0
	*2015	1.2	21.4	77.4	1.6	32.8	65.7	0.7	8.4	90.9
	*2019	1.2	21.2	77.6	1.7	32.3	66.1	0.7	8.1	91.1
Belize	*2005	19.6	17.9	62.6	27.8	21.7	50.5	3.3	10.3	86.5
Belize	*2010	17.2	18.0	64.8	25.0	22.3	52.7	3.6	10.5	85.9
	*2015	15.9	16.2	67.9	22.7	21.0	56.4	4.8	8.2	87.1
	*2019	15.3	15.3	69.5	22.7	19.4	57.9	3.2	8.6	88.2
Benin	*2005	47.5	11.9	40.6	54.9	14.8	30.3	39.5	8.8	51.7
Bénin	*2010	45.3	10.5	44.2	53.3	13.8	32.9	37.2	7.1	55.6
	*2015	41.8	18.2	40.0	49.2	19.8	31.0	34.2	16.4	49.4
	*2019	41.5	18.7	39.8	49.0	20.3	30.7	33.7	17.1	49.2
Bermuda	2004[6]	1.7	12.1	86.2	3.0	20.5	76.6	0.3	3.1	96.6
Bermudes	#2010[3,4]	1.4	12.9	85.7	2.4	22.6	75.0	0.4	3.2	96.4
	#2012[4,7]	1.7	9.6	88.7	3.0	16.5	80.5	0.3	2.6	97.1
	#2013[3,4,8]	1.6	10.3	87.6	...	...	...	...	...	...
Bhutan	*2005	70.3	4.8	24.9	62.8	6.1	31.1	80.3	3.1	16.6
Bhoutan	*2010	59.6	6.6	33.8	55.0	6.6	38.5	65.9	6.7	27.3
	*2015	58.0	9.7	32.4	52.5	9.9	37.6	66.4	9.3	24.3
	*2019	54.8	9.7	35.5	49.0	10.3	40.7	63.3	8.9	27.8

18

Employment by economic activity *(continued)*
Percentage of persons employed by sex and ISIC 4 categories; agriculture (agr.), industry (ind.) and services (ser.)

Emploi par activité économique *(suite)*
Personnes employées par sexe et branches de la CITI rév. 4; agriculture (agr.), industrie (ind.) et services (ser.), pourcentage

Region, country or area [+] Région, pays ou zone [+]	Year Année	Male and Female Hommes et femmes			Male Hommes			Female Femmes		
		Agr.	Ind.	Ser.	Agr.	Ind.	Ser.	Agr.	Ind.	Ser.
Bolivia (Plurin. State of)	*2005	35.2	20.4	44.4	34.6	27.3	38.1	36.0	11.2	52.8
Bolivie (État plurin. de)	*2010	30.1	20.6	49.3	29.7	28.3	42.1	30.6	10.5	58.9
	*2015	27.9	22.5	49.6	27.5	30.4	42.1	28.3	11.0	60.7
	*2019	26.0	22.5	51.5	26.1	30.7	43.2	25.9	10.9	63.3
Bosnia and Herzegovina	*2005	24.6	28.4	47.1	21.9	36.3	41.8	28.9	15.4	55.8
Bosnie-Herzégovine	*2010	19.7	29.1	51.2	18.5	37.3	44.3	21.6	15.6	62.7
	*2015	17.9	37.5	44.6	18.7	42.7	38.6	16.7	29.9	53.4
	*2019	18.1	32.1	49.8	18.3	38.6	43.1	17.6	19.0	63.4
Botswana	*2005	27.0	17.2	55.9	32.5	20.7	46.8	19.4	12.3	68.3
Botswana	*2010	26.4	13.8	59.8	30.6	20.6	48.8	21.0	4.7	74.3
	*2015	26.9	13.8	59.3	31.1	21.0	48.0	21.7	4.8	73.5
	*2019	25.2	13.7	61.1	29.5	20.9	49.7	19.9	4.8	75.4
Brazil	*2005	20.5	21.5	58.1	23.7	27.2	49.1	15.9	13.2	70.9
Brésil	*2010	16.0	22.3	61.7	19.3	29.1	51.6	11.2	12.6	76.1
	*2015	10.2	22.2	67.6	14.0	29.8	56.2	5.1	11.7	83.3
	*2019	10.0	20.9	69.1	13.8	28.3	58.0	4.7	10.7	84.6
British Virgin Islands [4]										
Îles Vierges britanniques [4]	2010	0.5	11.1	87.4	...	...	...	...	...	...
Brunei Darussalam	*2005	1.0	19.2	79.8	1.5	26.2	72.4	0.3	9.0	90.7
Brunéi Darussalam	*2010	0.7	19.3	80.0	1.0	25.7	73.4	0.4	10.0	89.6
	*2015	0.6	18.6	80.9	0.7	24.1	75.3	0.5	11.0	88.5
	*2019	0.5	17.1	82.4	0.6	22.7	76.7	0.4	9.6	90.0
Bulgaria	*2005	8.9	34.2	56.8	10.7	38.9	50.4	6.8	28.8	64.3
Bulgarie	*2010	6.8	33.0	60.2	8.2	40.7	51.0	5.2	24.1	70.7
	*2015	6.9	29.9	63.3	9.1	36.2	54.7	4.3	22.7	72.9
	*2019	5.9	28.9	65.3	8.0	35.9	56.2	3.5	20.8	75.7
Burkina Faso	*2005	82.0	5.1	12.9	80.3	6.1	13.7	84.2	3.9	11.9
Burkina Faso	*2010	60.9	11.4	27.7	62.5	12.2	25.3	58.7	10.3	30.9
	*2015	29.4	32.0	38.5	36.0	31.2	32.8	20.9	33.1	46.0
	*2019	27.0	31.9	41.1	33.3	32.0	34.8	18.7	31.9	49.4
Burundi	*2005	91.8	2.6	5.6	86.7	4.4	8.9	96.6	0.9	2.6
Burundi	*2010	91.4	2.6	6.1	85.9	4.5	9.6	96.3	0.8	2.9
	*2015	91.6	2.4	6.1	86.1	4.2	9.7	96.5	0.7	2.8
	*2019	91.4	2.5	6.1	85.9	4.3	9.8	96.5	0.8	2.7
Cabo Verde	*2005	73.2	6.8	20.0	68.2	8.8	23.0	81.3	3.6	15.1
Cabo Verde	*2010	69.7	7.3	23.0	64.6	9.5	25.9	77.8	3.8	18.5
	*2015	68.7	7.0	24.4	63.1	9.3	27.6	76.8	3.6	19.7
	*2019	66.8	6.9	26.3	61.1	9.3	29.6	74.8	3.5	21.7
Cambodia	*2005	70.8	9.8	19.4	69.4	8.8	21.8	72.2	10.8	17.0
Cambodge	*2010	54.2	16.3	29.6	53.0	17.0	30.1	55.4	15.5	29.1
	*2015	28.8	26.8	44.4	29.3	27.4	43.4	28.3	26.3	45.4
	*2019	24.7	26.8	48.5	25.3	28.5	46.2	24.2	25.1	50.7
Cameroon	*2005	64.9	9.6	25.5	62.0	11.4	26.5	68.3	7.5	24.2
Cameroun	*2010	64.9	9.3	25.8	62.0	11.1	26.9	68.3	7.2	24.6
	*2015	62.4	9.2	28.5	59.5	11.1	29.4	65.7	6.9	27.4
	*2019	61.2	9.3	29.5	58.4	11.3	30.3	64.4	7.0	28.6
Canada	*2005	2.7	22.1	75.2	3.7	32.1	64.2	1.6	10.6	87.9
Canada	*2010	2.3	19.8	77.9	3.2	30.0	66.8	1.3	8.5	90.2
	*2015	2.0	19.4	78.6	2.8	29.3	67.9	1.2	8.4	90.4
	*2019	1.9	19.3	78.8	2.6	29.1	68.3	1.1	8.6	90.4
Cayman Islands	2005[4]	1.7	22.2	75.5	2.6	39.3	57.3	0.6	3.3	95.7
Îles Caïmanes	#2010	0.6	14.9	84.2	1.1	26.2	72.5	0.1	3.2	96.4
	#2013	0.8	15.5	83.6	1.5	29.0	69.5	0.2	2.0	97.7
Central African Republic	*2005	86.4	7.0	6.6	82.1	8.6	9.3	91.5	5.1	3.4
République centrafricaine	*2010	86.2	7.1	6.8	81.9	8.7	9.4	91.3	5.1	3.6
	*2015	85.6	8.0	6.4	81.7	9.4	8.9	90.5	6.3	3.2
	*2019	85.6	7.9	6.6	81.6	9.3	9.1	90.5	6.1	3.4
Chad	*2005	87.3	5.3	7.5	83.1	6.8	10.1	92.4	3.4	4.2
Tchad	*2010	86.8	6.1	7.1	82.7	7.7	9.6	91.8	4.1	4.1
	*2015	85.9	6.4	7.7	81.5	8.2	10.3	91.3	4.2	4.5
	*2019	87.0	5.0	8.1	82.7	6.5	10.9	92.2	3.1	4.7

Employment by economic activity *(continued)*
Percentage of persons employed by sex and ISIC 4 categories; agriculture (agr.), industry (ind.) and services (ser.)

Emploi par activité économique *(suite)*
Personnes employées par sexe et branches de la CITI rév. 4; agriculture (agr.), industrie (ind.) et services (ser.), pourcentage

Region, country or area [+] Région, pays ou zone [+]	Year Année	Male and Female Hommes et femmes			Male Hommes			Female Femmes		
		Agr.	Ind.	Ser.	Agr.	Ind.	Ser.	Agr.	Ind.	Ser.
Channel Islands	*2005	20.9	30.2	48.9	26.7	35.4	37.9	13.6	23.6	62.8
Îles Anglo-Normandes	*2010	21.0	30.0	49.0	26.9	35.1	38.0	13.6	23.5	62.9
	*2015	20.2	29.9	49.9	26.0	35.4	38.6	12.8	23.1	64.1
	*2019	19.7	29.6	50.6	25.6	35.1	39.3	12.2	22.7	65.1
Chile	*2005	13.2	23.0	63.9	17.1	29.0	53.9	5.8	11.5	82.8
Chili	*2010	10.6	23.0	66.4	14.1	31.0	54.9	5.1	10.2	84.7
	*2015	9.4	23.3	67.3	12.7	31.6	55.7	4.5	11.2	84.3
	*2019	9.2	22.7	68.2	12.3	31.0	56.7	4.7	10.7	84.6
China [9]	*2005	35.8	29.6	34.6	32.8	29.4	37.8	39.5	30.0	30.5
Chine [9]	*2010	26.2	30.2	43.6	23.3	32.0	44.6	29.9	27.8	42.3
	*2015	19.6	27.1	53.4	17.0	30.7	52.4	22.8	22.6	54.6
	*2019	15.5	26.0	58.5	13.4	30.3	56.3	18.2	20.6	61.3
China, Hong Kong SAR	*2005	0.3	15.1	84.7	0.3	22.1	77.5	0.2	6.5	93.3
Chine, RAS de Hong Kong	*2010	0.2	13.3	86.5	0.3	20.6	79.1	0.2	5.1	94.7
	*2015	0.2	13.3	86.5	0.3	21.2	78.6	0.2	5.0	94.8
	*2019	0.2	12.9	87.0	0.3	20.8	79.0	0.1	4.8	95.1
China, Macao SAR	*2005	0.1	25.0	74.8	0.1	26.8	73.1	0.1	23.2	76.7
Chine, RAS de Macao	*2010	0.2	13.7	86.1	0.2	20.3	79.5	0.2	6.9	92.9
	*2015	0.3	16.8	83.0	0.2	26.5	73.3	0.3	6.6	93.2
	*2019	0.5	19.6	79.8	0.4	29.9	69.7	0.7	9.0	90.4
Colombia	*2005	20.7	20.0	59.3	28.8	22.0	49.2	7.0	16.8	76.3
Colombie	*2010	18.3	19.6	62.1	26.3	22.3	51.4	6.5	15.5	78.0
	*2015	16.0	19.6	64.4	22.8	23.8	53.4	6.5	13.7	79.8
	*2019	15.8	19.2	65.1	22.2	23.6	54.2	6.8	13.0	80.2
Comoros	*2005	55.8	14.3	29.9	50.9	15.7	33.4	63.3	12.2	24.6
Comores	*2010	55.9	14.7	29.5	51.0	16.0	33.0	63.0	12.7	24.3
	*2015	55.4	15.1	29.5	50.5	16.5	33.0	62.2	13.2	24.6
	*2019	54.6	15.5	30.0	49.7	17.1	33.2	61.4	13.2	25.4
Congo	*2005	40.0	23.4	36.6	38.6	23.7	37.7	41.5	23.1	35.4
Congo	*2010	39.1	23.3	37.6	37.6	23.9	38.5	40.8	22.7	36.6
	*2015	36.9	25.2	37.9	35.8	25.6	38.6	38.2	24.8	37.1
	*2019	37.1	25.9	37.1	36.0	25.7	38.3	38.3	26.1	35.7
Cook Islands [10]										
Îles Cook [10]	2011	4.3	11.7	84.0	6.4	17.7	75.9	1.8	5.0	93.3
Costa Rica	*2005	15.3	21.6	63.1	20.9	26.5	52.7	4.8	12.6	82.7
Costa Rica	*2010	15.1	19.6	65.3	20.9	24.2	55.0	4.7	11.5	83.8
	*2015	12.3	19.2	68.5	17.4	25.1	57.6	4.2	9.6	86.2
	*2019	11.2	18.5	70.3	15.7	24.4	59.9	3.7	8.8	87.5
Côte d'Ivoire	*2005	50.6	6.1	43.3	53.0	8.0	39.0	46.2	2.9	51.0
Côte d'Ivoire	*2010	49.5	5.9	44.6	52.4	7.9	39.8	45.0	2.6	52.4
	*2015	50.0	5.6	44.4	55.2	7.1	37.6	42.3	3.4	54.4
	*2019	46.5	6.3	47.2	52.0	8.2	39.9	38.8	3.6	57.7
Croatia	*2005	17.3	28.6	54.1	16.0	37.2	46.8	18.9	18.1	63.0
Croatie	*2010	14.3	27.5	58.3	13.2	38.0	48.8	15.5	14.9	69.6
	*2015	9.2	26.7	64.1	10.8	36.7	52.5	7.4	15.0	77.5
	*2019	7.1	26.6	66.2	8.9	37.4	53.7	5.1	14.2	80.8
Cuba	*2005	20.3	19.1	60.6	26.4	22.5	51.1	9.4	13.1	77.5
Cuba	*2010	18.6	17.1	64.3	24.9	20.5	54.6	8.5	11.5	80.0
	*2015	18.3	16.8	64.9	24.8	20.7	54.6	7.9	10.7	81.4
	*2019	18.2	16.5	65.3	24.7	20.3	55.0	7.6	10.4	82.0
Curaçao [4]	2000	1.1	18.0	80.9	2.0	28.6	69.4	0.2	5.6	94.2
Curaçao [4]	2005	0.9	15.3	83.8	...	...	...	...	...	...
	2008	1.1	17.6	81.3	...	...	...	...	...	...
Cyprus	*2005	4.7	24.1	71.2	5.7	33.7	60.6	3.5	10.4	86.2
Chypre	*2010	3.8	20.4	75.8	4.9	29.7	65.5	2.5	9.2	88.3
	*2015	4.0	16.2	79.8	5.7	24.9	69.5	2.1	6.3	91.6
	*2019	3.4	16.8	79.8	5.1	26.0	68.9	1.5	6.2	92.3
Czechia	*2005	4.0	39.5	56.5	4.9	49.4	45.7	2.8	26.5	70.7
Tchéquie	*2010	3.1	38.0	58.9	4.0	49.0	47.0	1.9	23.2	74.9
	*2015	2.9	38.0	59.1	3.9	49.1	47.0	1.6	23.8	74.6
	*2019	2.7	37.1	60.2	3.6	48.3	48.0	1.6	23.0	75.5

Employment by economic activity *(continued)*
Percentage of persons employed by sex and ISIC 4 categories; agriculture (agr.), industry (ind.) and services (ser.)

Emploi par activité économique *(suite)*
Personnes employées par sexe et branches de la CITI rév. 4; agriculture (agr.), industrie (ind.) et services (ser.), pourcentage

Region, country or area [+] Région, pays ou zone [+]	Year Année	Male and Female Hommes et femmes			Male Hommes			Female Femmes		
		Agr.	Ind.	Ser.	Agr.	Ind.	Ser.	Agr.	Ind.	Ser.
Dem. People's Rep. Korea	*2005	67.6	16.3	16.1	63.9	16.4	19.7	71.4	16.2	12.3
Rép. pop. dém. de Corée	*2010	66.8	17.4	15.8	63.6	17.0	19.4	70.3	17.8	11.9
	*2015	67.2	17.1	15.8	63.8	16.9	19.3	70.8	17.3	11.9
	*2019	66.9	17.5	15.6	63.8	17.3	19.0	70.2	17.8	12.0
Dem. Rep. of the Congo	*2005	81.4	13.0	5.7	77.2	14.4	8.4	85.5	11.6	2.9
Rép. dém. du Congo	*2010	79.6	11.7	8.7	73.7	13.0	13.3	85.6	10.5	4.0
	*2015	81.5	11.8	6.7	76.9	13.5	9.6	86.3	10.1	3.7
	*2019	82.0	11.0	7.0	77.1	12.8	10.1	87.0	9.2	3.9
Denmark	*2005	3.2	23.9	72.9	4.6	33.9	61.6	1.6	12.4	86.0
Danemark	*2010	2.4	19.6	78.0	3.9	29.1	67.1	0.9	9.2	89.9
	*2015	2.5	19.3	78.2	3.8	27.8	68.4	1.1	9.7	89.3
	*2019	2.5	18.5	79.0	3.8	26.8	69.4	1.0	9.2	89.8
Djibouti	*2005	36.1	24.4	39.6	38.3	18.1	43.7	32.5	34.4	33.0
Djibouti	*2010	33.2	27.4	39.4	35.9	21.1	43.0	29.1	36.9	33.9
	*2015	30.7	30.1	39.2	32.1	25.2	42.8	28.8	37.2	34.0
	*2019	28.3	30.2	41.5	30.4	25.3	44.4	25.4	37.1	37.4
Dominica [6] Dominique [6]	#2001	21.0	20.0	58.8	29.4	26.8	43.9	8.3	9.7	81.5
Dominican Republic	*2005	15.3	23.4	61.3	22.3	27.6	50.1	3.1	16.1	80.8
République dominicaine	*2010	14.5	18.2	67.4	21.7	23.3	55.1	2.8	10.0	87.3
	*2015	13.3	18.1	68.6	20.6	23.3	56.1	2.2	10.1	87.8
	*2019	11.4	17.7	71.0	17.9	23.5	58.6	1.8	9.0	89.3
Ecuador	*2005	29.1	18.5	52.4	34.0	22.7	43.3	21.5	12.0	66.6
Équateur	*2010	27.9	18.5	53.6	32.2	23.1	44.7	20.9	11.1	68.0
	*2015	26.2	19.7	54.2	28.5	25.1	46.4	22.6	11.2	66.3
	*2019	26.5	18.6	54.9	29.4	23.8	46.9	22.3	10.8	66.9
Egypt	*2005	30.9	21.5	47.6	27.5	25.2	47.4	46.7	4.9	48.4
Égypte	*2010	29.1	24.0	46.9	25.5	28.6	46.0	43.9	5.2	50.9
	*2015	25.8	25.1	49.1	22.3	29.9	47.9	40.2	5.6	54.2
	*2019	24.0	25.8	50.3	20.9	30.7	48.4	36.5	5.9	57.5
El Salvador	*2005	20.0	22.2	57.8	30.5	23.7	45.8	4.7	20.1	75.2
El Salvador	*2010	20.8	21.4	57.9	31.8	23.4	44.8	5.3	18.4	76.3
	*2015	18.1	22.2	59.7	28.5	24.1	47.4	3.9	19.5	76.6
	*2019	18.3	21.1	60.6	28.8	24.2	47.0	4.0	16.8	79.2
Equatorial Guinea	*2005	57.2	6.8	36.1	51.5	10.1	38.4	65.0	2.1	32.9
Guinée équatoriale	*2010	54.9	8.0	37.1	49.2	11.8	39.0	63.3	2.5	34.2
	*2015	56.9	7.7	35.4	51.0	11.0	38.0	66.0	2.6	31.4
	*2019	60.8	6.2	33.0	54.8	8.8	36.4	70.1	2.2	27.7
Eritrea	*2005	83.7	7.6	8.7	78.5	9.4	12.1	89.6	5.6	4.7
Érythrée	*2010	84.3	7.3	8.4	79.3	9.0	11.7	90.2	5.3	4.5
	*2015	84.0	7.1	8.9	78.8	8.9	12.3	90.0	5.0	5.0
	*2019	83.8	7.0	9.2	78.4	8.9	12.7	89.9	4.8	5.3
Estonia	*2005	5.2	34.1	60.7	7.2	44.1	48.8	3.2	24.2	72.6
Estonie	*2010	4.2	30.3	65.5	5.7	43.1	51.2	2.8	18.0	79.2
	*2015	3.9	30.7	65.4	5.2	43.2	51.6	2.5	17.5	80.0
	*2019	3.7	29.3	67.0	5.5	41.5	53.1	1.9	16.7	81.4
Eswatini	*2005	69.1	14.5	16.4	63.0	18.0	19.0	78.8	8.8	12.4
Eswatini	*2010	68.3	13.7	18.0	61.9	17.4	20.7	78.0	8.1	14.0
	*2015	68.1	13.2	18.7	61.5	17.1	21.4	77.6	7.6	14.9
	*2019	69.5	12.3	18.2	63.0	16.0	21.0	78.7	7.0	14.3
Ethiopia	*2005	80.2	6.7	13.1	84.3	5.2	10.6	75.4	8.4	16.2
Éthiopie	*2010	77.2	6.3	16.6	81.9	5.6	12.5	71.5	7.1	21.4
	*2015	69.9	8.6	21.5	77.3	8.5	14.3	61.3	8.8	29.9
	*2019	66.5	9.8	23.7	74.4	10.3	15.3	57.3	9.3	33.4
Faroe Islands [3,6] Îles Féroé [3,6]	2005	11.1	22.2	66.7	20.0	33.3	53.3	8.3	8.3	83.3
Fiji	*2005	44.2	13.4	42.4	44.2	15.5	40.3	44.1	9.2	46.7
Fidji	*2010	42.9	13.7	43.4	43.0	15.8	41.2	42.6	9.4	48.0
	*2015	39.4	13.1	47.5	39.7	15.5	44.7	38.7	8.4	52.9
	*2019	37.8	13.3	49.0	38.2	15.8	46.0	36.9	8.4	54.8
Finland	*2005	4.8	25.8	69.4	6.6	38.3	55.1	2.9	12.3	84.8
Finlande	*2010	4.4	23.3	72.3	6.0	35.9	58.1	2.8	9.9	87.3
	*2015	4.2	21.7	74.1	6.1	34.0	59.9	2.2	8.7	89.1
	*2019	3.7	21.8	74.5	5.4	34.1	60.5	2.0	8.6	89.5

Employment by economic activity *(continued)*
Percentage of persons employed by sex and ISIC 4 categories; agriculture (agr.), industry (ind.) and services (ser.)

Emploi par activité économique *(suite)*
Personnes employées par sexe et branches de la CITI rév. 4; agriculture (agr.), industrie (ind.) et services (ser.), pourcentage

Region, country or area [+] Région, pays ou zone [+]	Year Année	Male and Female Hommes et femmes			Male Hommes			Female Femmes		
		Agr.	Ind.	Ser.	Agr.	Ind.	Ser.	Agr.	Ind.	Ser.
France	*2005	3.6	23.8	72.6	4.8	33.7	61.6	2.3	12.0	85.8
France	*2010	2.9	22.3	74.8	3.9	32.8	63.3	1.8	10.1	88.2
	*2015	2.8	20.4	76.9	3.7	30.3	66.0	1.6	9.3	89.1
	*2019	2.8	20.2	77.1	3.9	30.1	66.1	1.5	9.1	89.4
French Guiana [8,11]	2010	...	14.1	51.5	...	...	...	...	...	...
Guyane française [8,11]	2012	...	14.9	58.3	...	...	...	...	...	...
French Polynesia	*2005	9.2	17.5	73.3	11.7	24.3	64.0	5.4	7.2	87.3
Polynésie française	*2010	9.2	18.2	72.6	11.6	25.9	62.6	5.8	7.4	86.9
	*2015	8.7	17.2	74.1	11.1	25.1	63.8	5.4	6.5	88.1
	*2019	8.4	17.4	74.2	10.8	25.5	63.7	5.2	6.4	88.4
Gabon	*2005	43.3	12.2	44.5	31.1	18.0	50.9	62.6	3.0	34.4
Gabon	*2010	43.1	12.6	44.3	32.1	17.8	50.1	63.3	3.1	33.5
	*2015	41.2	12.7	46.1	30.3	17.9	51.8	60.9	3.3	35.8
	*2019	41.7	12.7	45.7	30.4	18.1	51.6	61.1	3.4	35.5
Gambia	*2005	34.2	16.2	49.6	28.5	24.3	47.3	42.6	4.4	53.0
Gambie	*2010	32.8	14.7	52.5	27.0	22.6	50.3	40.9	3.7	55.5
	*2015	28.4	15.5	56.1	23.5	24.0	52.5	35.1	4.1	60.9
	*2019	26.6	15.5	57.9	22.0	24.0	54.0	32.8	4.2	63.0
Georgia	*2005	54.3	9.3	36.4	51.8	13.7	34.5	57.2	4.4	38.4
Géorgie	*2010	48.2	10.4	41.5	47.4	16.3	36.3	49.1	3.7	47.2
	*2015	41.8	12.2	46.0	41.1	19.5	39.4	42.6	4.0	53.4
	*2019	38.8	12.9	48.3	38.1	20.7	41.3	39.7	4.1	56.3
Germany	*2005	2.4	29.8	67.8	2.9	41.1	56.0	1.7	16.0	82.3
Allemagne	*2010	1.7	28.3	70.0	2.0	40.2	57.8	1.2	14.3	84.5
	*2015	1.4	27.7	70.9	1.8	39.7	58.5	1.0	13.9	85.2
	*2019	1.2	26.8	72.0	1.6	38.7	59.7	0.8	13.2	86.0
Ghana	*2005	49.0	15.8	35.2	52.2	16.6	31.2	45.8	14.9	39.3
Ghana	*2010	42.0	15.2	42.8	45.9	17.1	37.1	38.1	13.4	48.5
	*2015	42.5	14.0	43.5	46.3	17.5	36.3	38.7	10.4	50.9
	*2019	38.3	14.3	47.3	42.3	18.4	39.3	34.3	10.1	55.6
Greece	*2005	12.2	22.4	65.5	11.3	30.0	58.7	13.5	9.9	76.6
Grèce	*2010	12.4	19.6	68.0	12.3	27.5	60.2	12.6	7.8	79.6
	*2015	12.9	14.9	72.2	13.3	19.9	66.8	12.4	8.0	79.7
	*2019	11.7	15.3	73.0	12.1	20.6	67.3	11.0	8.1	80.9
Greenland [11,12]										
Groenland [11,12]	2011	4.6	12.6	82.5	8.1	20.3	71.3	0.3	3.3	96.2
Guadeloupe [8,11]	2010	...	13.8	64.4	...	...	...	...	...	...
Guadeloupe [8,11]	2012	3.3	13.5	65.5	...	...	...	...	...	...
Guam	*2005	10.1	15.4	74.5	13.3	23.7	63.0	5.6	3.4	91.0
Guam	*2010	9.6	16.6	73.9	12.6	25.5	62.0	5.4	3.8	90.9
	*2015	8.9	15.9	75.2	11.8	24.6	63.6	4.7	3.4	91.9
	*2019	8.6	16.0	75.4	11.4	24.7	63.9	4.5	3.4	92.1
Guatemala	*2005	36.0	20.9	43.1	47.3	21.2	31.6	15.5	20.4	64.1
Guatemala	*2010	37.0	19.8	43.2	48.1	19.8	32.2	16.0	19.8	64.2
	*2015	31.9	18.9	49.2	42.6	19.5	38.0	9.8	17.7	72.5
	*2019	28.7	21.1	50.3	38.6	22.5	38.9	9.0	18.2	72.8
Guernsey										
Guernesey	2013	1.5	13.6	84.8	1.0	12.2	40.9	0.5	1.4	44.3
Guinea	*2005	70.1	5.8	24.0	66.4	9.6	24.0	74.0	1.9	24.1
Guinée	*2010	70.3	6.0	23.8	66.1	9.9	24.0	74.6	1.9	23.6
	*2015	68.0	5.8	26.3	64.0	9.6	26.4	72.0	1.9	26.1
	*2019	67.7	6.0	26.2	63.8	10.1	26.1	71.7	1.9	26.4
Guinea-Bissau	*2005	84.6	6.9	8.5	79.5	8.9	11.6	90.5	4.6	4.8
Guinée-Bissau	*2010	84.5	6.6	9.0	79.2	8.6	12.2	90.5	4.3	5.2
	*2015	83.7	7.1	9.3	78.4	9.2	12.4	89.7	4.6	5.6
	*2019	83.3	6.9	9.9	77.9	9.0	13.1	89.4	4.4	6.2
Guyana	*2005	23.5	23.9	52.6	30.0	29.1	41.0	7.8	11.5	80.7
Guyana	*2010	17.0	25.1	58.0	22.5	31.5	46.1	5.1	11.1	83.8
	*2015	15.2	24.8	60.0	20.5	32.0	47.5	4.5	10.2	85.3
	*2019	12.9	26.3	60.8	17.6	34.6	47.9	3.6	9.8	86.6
Haiti	*2005	49.8	10.4	39.9	62.9	13.6	23.5	34.3	6.7	59.0
Haïti	*2010	47.2	10.3	42.5	60.1	13.9	26.0	32.1	6.0	61.9
	*2015	42.6	12.1	45.4	55.2	16.8	28.0	28.2	6.7	65.1
	*2019	39.9	12.8	47.3	52.5	18.0	29.5	25.7	6.9	67.4

Employment by economic activity *(continued)*
Percentage of persons employed by sex and ISIC 4 categories; agriculture (agr.), industry (ind.) and services (ser.)

Emploi par activité économique *(suite)*
Personnes employées par sexe et branches de la CITI rév. 4; agriculture (agr.), industrie (ind.) et services (ser.), pourcentage

Region, country or area [+] Région, pays ou zone [+]	Year Année	Male and Female Hommes et femmes			Male Hommes			Female Femmes		
		Agr.	Ind.	Ser.	Agr.	Ind.	Ser.	Agr.	Ind.	Ser.
Honduras Honduras	*2005	39.3	20.9	39.8	51.0	19.8	29.2	12.9	23.4	63.7
	*2010	37.8	18.6	43.6	51.4	18.4	30.3	12.3	19.1	68.6
	*2015	28.7	21.8	49.5	41.0	22.3	36.7	7.7	20.9	71.4
	*2019	27.8	21.3	50.9	39.7	22.2	38.1	8.0	19.8	72.2
Hungary Hongrie	*2005	4.9	32.5	62.7	6.7	41.9	51.4	2.6	21.2	76.2
	*2010	4.5	30.7	64.8	6.5	40.2	53.4	2.3	19.8	77.9
	*2015	4.9	30.3	64.8	6.8	39.9	53.3	2.7	18.9	78.4
	*2019	4.6	29.7	65.7	6.4	39.4	54.2	2.5	18.2	79.3
Iceland Islande	*2005	6.5	21.7	71.8	9.6	31.5	58.9	3.1	10.6	86.3
	*2010	5.6	18.4	76.0	8.6	28.1	63.4	2.2	7.8	90.0
	*2015	4.2	17.8	77.9	6.5	27.7	65.8	1.8	6.9	91.3
	*2019	3.0	15.0	82.1	4.2	23.6	72.2	1.5	5.4	93.1
India Inde	*2005	56.0	18.8	25.2	49.9	20.9	29.2	70.7	13.8	15.5
	*2010	51.5	21.8	26.7	46.5	23.8	29.7	66.8	15.7	17.6
	*2015	44.4	23.9	31.7	40.1	25.8	34.2	57.7	18.0	24.3
	*2019	40.5	24.1	35.4	36.1	26.1	37.8	54.4	17.7	27.9
Indonesia Indonésie	*2005	44.0	18.8	37.2	43.8	20.4	35.8	44.5	15.9	39.7
	*2010	39.2	18.7	42.2	39.6	20.9	39.5	38.4	15.0	46.6
	*2015	33.0	22.0	44.9	33.3	25.8	40.9	32.6	15.8	51.7
	*2019	29.4	21.1	49.6	30.6	25.0	44.4	27.5	14.7	57.8
Iran (Islamic Republic of) Iran (Rép. islamique d')	*2005	24.8	30.4	44.9	22.7	30.8	46.5	33.6	28.4	38.0
	*2010	19.2	32.2	48.6	17.5	33.8	48.8	28.0	24.4	47.6
	*2015	18.0	32.5	49.4	17.1	34.2	48.7	22.8	23.8	53.3
	*2019	15.9	32.4	51.7	15.2	33.9	50.9	19.7	25.2	55.2
Iraq Iraq	*2005	23.0	18.3	58.7	18.8	20.5	60.8	47.8	5.2	46.9
	*2010	23.1	18.7	58.3	17.1	21.9	61.1	51.3	3.6	45.1
	*2015	20.3	19.6	60.1	14.2	23.2	62.6	46.9	3.9	49.3
	*2019	18.7	19.7	61.7	12.7	23.5	63.9	43.6	3.9	52.5
Ireland Irlande	*2005	6.0	27.7	66.3	9.4	39.4	51.2	1.4	11.9	86.7
	*2010	4.6	19.6	75.9	7.5	28.8	63.7	1.1	8.8	90.2
	*2015	5.6	19.1	75.3	9.1	27.8	63.1	1.4	8.5	90.1
	*2019	5.2	18.8	76.0	8.5	27.8	63.8	1.2	8.1	90.7
Isle of Man [4] Île de Man [4]	2001	1.4	16.1	82.5	2.2	25.0	72.9	0.5	5.5	94.0
	2006	1.9	14.8	83.3	2.9	24.0	73.0	0.7	3.9	95.4
Israel Israël	*2005	2.0	21.6	76.4	3.0	31.0	66.0	0.8	10.4	88.8
	*2010	1.6	20.2	78.2	2.3	29.7	68.0	0.8	9.5	89.8
	*2015	1.0	17.7	81.2	1.4	26.3	72.3	0.6	8.1	91.3
	*2019	1.0	17.0	82.0	1.4	25.5	73.1	0.6	7.5	91.9
Italy Italie	*2005	4.2	30.7	65.1	4.8	39.2	56.0	3.3	17.4	79.4
	*2010	3.8	28.6	67.6	4.5	38.4	57.1	2.7	14.1	83.2
	*2015	3.8	26.6	69.7	4.7	36.0	59.3	2.4	13.2	84.3
	*2019	3.8	26.0	70.2	4.8	35.4	59.8	2.4	12.8	84.8
Jamaica Jamaïque	*2005	18.1	17.8	64.1	25.0	26.7	48.3	8.4	5.2	86.4
	*2010	20.3	15.9	63.8	28.0	22.3	49.7	9.1	6.8	84.1
	*2015	18.5	15.5	66.0	25.5	22.2	52.3	8.2	5.8	86.0
	*2019	18.1	15.4	66.5	25.3	22.3	52.4	8.0	5.7	86.3
Japan Japon	*2005	4.5	27.8	67.7	4.4	35.1	60.5	4.6	17.4	78.0
	*2010	4.1	25.7	70.2	4.2	33.5	62.3	3.9	14.9	81.1
	*2015	3.6	25.9	70.5	3.9	34.3	61.8	3.2	14.8	82.0
	*2019	3.4	25.2	71.5	3.7	33.7	62.6	2.9	14.1	83.0
Jersey Jersey	2013	4.1	11.7	70.2	...	...	...	...	...	...
Jordan Jordanie	*2005	3.9	26.6	69.5	4.3	27.8	67.9	1.2	17.7	81.1
	*2010	3.7	26.4	69.9	4.2	28.2	67.7	1.3	17.0	81.8
	*2015	3.7	26.8	69.5	4.1	28.5	67.4	1.2	17.8	81.0
	*2019	3.6	26.9	69.5	4.1	28.6	67.3	1.2	17.5	81.3
Kazakhstan Kazakhstan	*2005	32.4	18.0	49.6	33.4	24.6	42.0	31.3	10.9	57.8
	*2010	28.3	18.7	53.0	29.1	25.6	45.3	27.4	11.4	61.2
	*2015	18.0	20.6	61.4	18.9	29.0	52.1	17.1	11.5	71.4
	*2019	17.4	20.8	61.8	18.3	29.3	52.5	16.6	11.5	71.9
Kenya Kenya	*2005	41.5	14.6	44.0	33.7	19.4	46.9	50.8	8.8	40.4
	*2010	39.1	15.3	45.6	31.4	20.6	48.1	48.4	9.0	42.6
	*2015	37.8	14.6	47.7	29.8	20.3	49.9	47.0	7.9	45.1
	*2019	36.4	14.3	49.3	28.6	20.3	51.1	45.5	7.4	47.2

18 Employment by economic activity *(continued)*
Percentage of persons employed by sex and ISIC 4 categories; agriculture (agr.), industry (ind.) and services (ser.)

Emploi par activité économique *(suite)*
Personnes employées par sexe et branches de la CITI rév. 4; agriculture (agr.), industrie (ind.) et services (ser.), pourcentage

Region, country or area [+] Région, pays ou zone [+]	Year Année	Male and Female Hommes et femmes			Male Hommes			Female Femmes		
		Agr.	Ind.	Ser.	Agr.	Ind.	Ser.	Agr.	Ind.	Ser.
Kiribati	2005[6]	7.1	8.4	81.1	8.7	10.9	77.3	4.7	4.5	87.8
Kiribati	2010	22.1	16.1	61.8	32.1	9.1	58.8	9.0	25.3	65.7
Kosovo [11,13]										
Kosovo [11,13]	2012	4.6	28.4	67.1	4.3	33.3	62.3	5.4	10.1	84.7
Kuwait	*2005	2.7	20.7	76.6	3.6	27.1	69.3	0.1	2.3	97.7
Koweït	*2010	3.1	25.7	71.2	4.3	33.9	61.8	0.1	4.2	95.8
	*2015	3.4	26.6	70.1	4.6	35.2	60.2	0.1	4.5	95.4
	*2019	3.4	26.4	70.2	4.6	34.9	60.5	0.1	4.5	95.4
Kyrgyzstan	*2005	38.5	17.6	43.9	39.3	22.9	37.8	37.3	10.3	52.4
Kirghizistan	*2010	29.9	22.8	47.3	31.3	29.3	39.4	27.9	13.3	58.7
	*2015	29.3	20.9	49.8	27.5	27.7	44.8	31.9	10.8	57.3
	*2019	25.6	22.3	52.1	24.8	29.2	46.0	26.8	11.4	61.8
Lao People's Dem. Rep.	*2005	78.5	5.3	16.2	75.6	6.4	18.0	81.4	4.2	14.4
Rép. dém. populaire lao	*2010	71.5	8.3	20.2	69.3	10.0	20.7	73.6	6.7	19.7
	*2015	63.1	9.5	27.4	61.1	11.8	27.1	65.1	7.2	27.7
	*2019	58.4	10.0	31.6	56.7	12.8	30.5	60.2	7.1	32.7
Latvia	*2005	12.1	26.5	61.5	15.9	35.2	48.9	8.0	17.2	74.8
Lettonie	*2010	8.6	23.1	68.3	11.8	33.5	54.8	5.7	13.6	80.7
	*2015	7.9	23.7	68.4	10.9	34.7	54.5	5.0	12.7	82.2
	*2019	7.1	23.6	69.3	9.7	35.0	55.4	4.5	12.5	83.0
Lebanon	*2005	3.4	18.8	77.8	4.3	21.8	73.9	~0.0	7.4	92.5
Liban	*2010	2.5	19.2	78.3	3.2	22.9	73.9	~0.0	7.0	93.0
	*2015	3.2	21.9	74.9	4.2	25.8	70.0	0.1	9.2	90.7
	*2019	3.0	20.2	76.8	4.0	24.1	71.9	~0.0	7.8	92.1
Lesotho	*2005	25.8	27.3	46.9	36.4	28.5	35.1	13.5	26.0	60.6
Lesotho	*2010	12.9	39.3	47.8	18.6	48.1	33.4	5.8	28.5	65.7
	*2015	11.1	39.8	49.1	16.1	51.3	32.6	4.9	25.9	69.1
	*2019	10.0	40.3	49.7	14.6	52.2	33.3	4.3	25.6	70.1
Liberia	*2005	53.0	9.3	37.7	51.4	13.7	35.0	54.8	4.6	40.6
Libéria	*2010	47.3	10.8	41.9	47.1	15.6	37.2	47.5	5.5	47.1
	*2015	43.4	11.9	44.7	43.8	17.6	38.7	42.9	6.0	51.2
	*2019	41.6	12.0	46.4	42.2	17.7	40.1	41.0	5.9	53.1
Libya	*2005	8.7	28.3	63.1	9.2	30.6	60.3	7.1	20.6	72.4
Libye	*2010	7.3	31.6	61.0	7.7	34.8	57.6	6.3	22.1	71.6
	*2015	16.6	28.8	54.6	17.2	27.9	54.9	14.6	32.1	53.3
	*2019	10.6	24.7	64.7	11.4	24.7	63.8	7.7	24.5	67.8
Lithuania	*2005	14.3	29.1	56.7	16.9	37.0	46.0	11.5	20.8	67.7
Lituanie	*2010	8.8	24.6	66.6	11.4	33.4	55.2	6.5	16.6	76.9
	*2015	9.1	25.1	65.9	11.6	34.0	54.4	6.6	16.5	76.9
	*2019	7.3	24.4	68.3	9.8	34.7	55.5	4.9	14.7	80.4
Luxembourg	*2005	1.7	17.3	81.0	2.2	25.5	72.3	1.1	5.8	93.1
Luxembourg	*2010	1.1	13.4	85.6	1.4	19.8	78.8	0.7	4.8	94.5
	*2015	1.1	12.5	86.4	1.3	19.1	79.6	0.8	4.4	94.9
	*2019	0.9	11.5	87.6	1.3	17.4	81.4	0.5	4.4	95.1
Madagascar	*2005	82.0	3.4	14.6	81.5	5.1	13.4	82.5	1.6	15.9
Madagascar	*2010	74.0	5.5	20.5	75.8	6.0	18.2	72.1	5.0	22.9
	*2015	74.5	9.1	16.4	76.7	8.6	14.7	72.2	9.7	18.2
	*2019	73.9	9.3	16.8	76.3	8.9	14.8	71.5	9.7	18.9
Malawi	*2005	85.0	9.1	5.9	80.9	10.4	8.7	89.4	7.7	3.0
Malawi	*2010	84.8	8.8	6.5	80.6	10.2	9.3	89.3	7.2	3.4
	*2015	84.9	8.3	6.9	80.4	9.8	9.8	89.8	6.6	3.6
	*2019	84.6	8.4	7.0	80.2	10.0	9.9	89.6	6.6	3.8
Malaysia	*2005	14.6	29.7	55.6	17.1	32.6	50.3	10.1	24.4	65.5
Malaisie	*2010	14.2	27.7	58.1	17.1	31.6	51.3	8.9	20.5	70.7
	*2015	12.5	27.5	60.0	15.2	32.5	52.3	7.9	19.2	72.9
	*2019	10.3	27.0	62.7	13.0	31.9	55.1	6.0	19.0	74.9
Maldives	*2005	14.4	26.1	59.5	17.8	20.7	61.5	8.5	35.4	56.1
Maldives	*2010	15.0	16.1	68.8	19.4	15.3	65.3	6.3	17.8	76.0
	*2015	8.0	24.8	67.2	10.0	25.1	65.0	2.7	24.3	73.0
	*2019	7.0	24.5	68.5	8.7	25.0	66.2	2.2	23.1	74.7
Mali	*2005	44.8	15.1	40.1	51.2	16.2	32.6	33.2	13.0	53.8
Mali	*2010	57.5	11.1	31.5	60.8	11.9	27.3	51.9	9.7	38.4
	*2015	62.3	8.3	29.5	62.5	10.0	27.5	61.9	6.0	32.1
	*2019	56.1	8.6	35.4	56.8	10.8	32.4	55.1	5.6	39.3

18

Employment by economic activity *(continued)*
Percentage of persons employed by sex and ISIC 4 categories; agriculture (agr.), industry (ind.) and services (ser.)

Emploi par activité économique *(suite)*
Personnes employées par sexe et branches de la CITI rév. 4; agriculture (agr.), industrie (ind.) et services (ser.), pourcentage

Region, country or area [+] Région, pays ou zone [+]	Year Année	Male and Female Hommes et femmes			Male Hommes			Female Femmes		
		Agr.	Ind.	Ser.	Agr.	Ind.	Ser.	Agr.	Ind.	Ser.
Malta	*2005	2.1	29.9	68.1	2.8	35.6	61.7	0.6	16.8	82.6
Malte	*2010	1.3	25.5	73.2	1.9	31.9	66.2	0.3	13.2	86.5
	*2015	1.6	19.8	78.6	2.4	26.7	71.0	0.4	8.9	90.7
	*2019	1.2	18.9	79.9	1.8	25.5	72.7	0.2	8.5	91.3
Marshall Islands [4] Îles Marshall [4]	#2010	11.0	9.4	79.6	...	...	...	...	...	...
Martinique [8,11]	2010	4.1	11.9	65.3	...	...	...	...	...	...
Martinique [8,11]	2012	3.9	11.8	69.0	...	...	...	...	...	...
Mauritania	*2005	77.9	8.9	13.3	74.7	10.5	14.9	85.5	5.1	9.4
Mauritanie	*2010	77.3	7.6	15.1	73.8	9.2	17.0	85.4	3.9	10.7
	*2015	75.9	7.6	16.5	72.2	9.3	18.5	84.2	3.9	12.0
	*2019	75.3	7.2	17.5	71.6	8.8	19.6	83.7	3.5	12.8
Mauritius	*2005	10.0	32.4	57.6	10.6	34.2	55.2	8.9	28.8	62.4
Maurice	*2010	8.5	28.8	62.7	9.1	32.8	58.2	7.4	21.6	71.0
	*2015	7.5	25.4	67.1	8.7	30.4	60.9	5.7	17.0	77.3
	*2019	6.9	25.5	67.7	7.6	31.5	61.0	5.8	15.6	78.7
Mexico	*2005	14.8	25.7	59.5	20.1	29.4	50.6	4.7	18.8	76.6
Mexique	*2010	13.9	24.1	62.0	19.4	28.8	51.7	3.8	15.7	80.5
	*2015	13.5	25.1	61.4	19.2	29.9	50.8	3.5	16.5	80.0
	*2019	12.9	25.9	61.2	18.3	31.0	50.7	3.5	17.0	79.5
Mongolia	*2005	45.7	11.9	42.5	46.8	13.9	39.3	44.3	9.5	46.2
Mongolie	*2010	33.5	16.2	50.2	34.7	20.2	45.1	32.2	11.6	56.2
	*2015	28.5	20.3	51.3	29.7	26.5	43.8	26.9	12.9	60.2
	*2019	28.9	19.4	51.7	30.9	25.4	43.7	26.5	12.4	61.1
Montenegro	*2005	8.6	19.2	72.1	8.5	26.9	64.6	8.9	9.5	81.7
Monténégro	*2010	6.2	19.0	74.8	7.1	26.7	66.2	5.1	9.4	85.5
	*2015	7.8	17.6	74.7	7.3	26.0	66.7	8.3	7.4	84.3
	*2019	7.2	17.9	74.9	6.7	26.6	66.8	7.7	7.4	84.9
Morocco	*2005	45.5	19.5	35.0	39.6	20.8	39.5	61.5	15.9	22.7
Maroc	*2010	40.2	22.0	37.8	33.0	25.1	42.0	60.7	13.2	26.1
	*2015	38.6	19.2	42.3	31.8	21.6	46.6	58.1	12.1	29.9
	*2019	36.4	19.6	44.0	29.6	22.1	48.3	56.1	12.2	31.7
Mozambique	*2005	79.3	3.3	17.4	67.9	6.6	25.5	89.4	0.3	10.3
Mozambique	*2010	77.3	3.4	19.3	65.0	7.0	28.0	88.0	0.3	11.7
	*2015	73.6	4.3	22.2	60.4	8.8	30.8	85.0	0.4	14.7
	*2019	73.2	4.8	22.0	60.7	9.8	29.5	84.3	0.4	15.4
Myanmar	*2005	69.5	11.7	18.8	69.7	12.2	18.1	69.2	11.1	19.7
Myanmar	*2010	60.6	15.0	24.4	61.4	15.7	22.9	59.5	13.9	26.6
	*2015	51.8	16.8	31.5	52.8	18.3	28.9	50.2	14.6	35.2
	*2019	46.8	17.1	36.1	48.1	19.1	32.8	45.0	14.2	40.9
Namibia	*2005	26.8	15.3	57.9	31.9	20.3	47.9	20.7	9.4	70.0
Namibie	*2010	31.7	12.7	55.6	32.9	19.1	48.0	30.4	5.5	64.2
	*2015	24.3	17.1	58.5	24.9	27.6	47.4	23.7	6.0	70.3
	*2019	19.6	19.8	60.7	21.5	31.4	47.1	17.5	7.4	75.1
Nepal	*2005	76.0	4.7	19.3	68.0	4.7	27.3	84.4	4.8	10.8
Népal	*2010	74.8	7.5	17.7	64.2	9.2	26.7	85.2	5.8	9.0
	*2015	72.3	7.9	19.8	60.5	9.7	29.9	83.3	6.3	10.4
	*2019	70.6	8.3	21.1	58.2	10.1	31.7	82.0	6.7	11.3
Netherlands	*2005	3.3	20.5	76.1	4.3	30.2	65.5	2.2	8.5	89.3
Pays-Bas	*2010	3.1	17.6	79.3	4.1	26.9	69.0	1.8	6.6	91.5
	*2015	2.3	16.4	81.3	3.0	25.2	71.8	1.5	6.1	92.5
	*2019	2.1	16.2	81.7	2.9	24.9	72.2	1.3	5.9	92.8
Netherlands Antilles [former]	2009	0.8	16.0	83.2	1.6	28.2	70.1	0.2	4.4	95.4
Antilles néerlandaises [anc.]	2011	0.7	15.3	84.0	1.4	27.7	71.0	0.2	4.1	95.7
	2013	0.2	15.9	83.2	...	...	...	...	...	...
New Caledonia	*2005	4.6	31.8	63.7	6.0	44.8	49.1	2.8	16.1	81.1
Nouvelle-Calédonie	*2010	4.0	33.1	63.0	5.3	45.7	49.0	2.4	17.5	80.1
	*2015	3.5	31.7	64.8	4.8	45.0	50.3	2.1	15.4	82.5
	*2019	3.3	31.5	65.2	4.4	45.0	50.6	1.9	15.0	83.1
New Zealand	*2005	7.2	22.2	70.7	9.0	32.2	58.9	5.0	10.5	84.5
Nouvelle-Zélande	*2010	6.9	21.0	72.2	9.0	30.8	60.2	4.4	9.7	85.9
	*2015	6.1	22.0	71.9	8.0	32.5	59.5	4.0	10.1	85.9
	*2019	6.5	19.9	73.7	8.4	29.9	61.8	4.3	8.8	87.0

18

Employment by economic activity *(continued)*
Percentage of persons employed by sex and ISIC 4 categories; agriculture (agr.), industry (ind.) and services (ser.)

Emploi par activité économique *(suite)*
Personnes employées par sexe et branches de la CITI rév. 4; agriculture (agr.), industrie (ind.) et services (ser.), pourcentage

Region, country or area [+] Région, pays ou zone [+]	Year Année	Male and Female Hommes et femmes			Male Hommes			Female Femmes		
		Agr.	Ind.	Ser.	Agr.	Ind.	Ser.	Agr.	Ind.	Ser.
Nicaragua Nicaragua	*2005	28.9	19.7	51.4	40.7	20.1	39.2	8.1	19.0	72.9
	*2010	32.2	16.5	51.3	46.2	17.3	36.6	9.0	15.2	75.9
	*2015	30.7	18.0	51.3	44.0	20.4	35.6	9.0	14.1	76.9
	*2019	28.2	17.7	54.1	41.2	20.8	38.0	7.8	13.0	79.3
Niger Niger	*2005	77.6	6.9	15.5	79.9	4.2	15.9	74.7	10.4	14.9
	*2010	77.8	7.2	15.1	80.6	4.3	15.1	74.0	10.9	15.0
	*2015	76.1	7.5	16.5	79.1	4.5	16.5	72.3	11.3	16.5
	*2019	74.8	7.7	17.4	78.0	4.7	17.3	70.7	11.7	17.6
Nigeria Nigéria	*2005	51.2	8.5	40.4	56.3	8.9	34.8	44.5	7.9	47.6
	*2010	30.6	14.2	55.3	39.5	13.5	46.9	19.5	14.9	65.6
	*2015	36.4	11.8	51.8	44.8	11.5	43.7	26.3	12.2	61.5
	*2019	36.1	11.8	52.2	44.9	11.4	43.7	25.8	12.2	62.1
Niue [4] Nioué [4]	2001	9.0	20.4	70.1	11.4	28.7	59.4	5.8	8.7	85.1
	#2002	4.8	9.3	85.9	...	...	...	...	...	...
North Macedonia Macédoine du Nord	*2005	19.5	32.4	48.1	19.4	34.6	46.0	19.6	29.2	51.2
	*2010	19.3	29.6	51.1	19.4	32.3	48.3	19.2	25.3	55.5
	*2015	17.9	30.5	51.6	18.1	34.5	47.4	17.5	24.5	58.1
	*2019	15.7	29.5	54.8	16.1	33.4	50.5	15.1	23.5	61.5
Northern Mariana Islands [3,6] Îles Mariannes du Nord [3,6]	#2000	1.5	47.2	45.8	...	...	...	...	...	...
Norway Norvège	*2005	3.3	20.9	75.9	4.8	32.3	62.9	1.6	8.1	90.4
	*2010	2.6	19.7	77.8	3.9	31.2	64.9	1.0	7.0	92.0
	*2015	2.0	20.1	77.9	3.0	31.7	65.3	0.9	7.2	91.9
	*2019	2.0	19.5	78.5	3.0	30.9	66.2	0.9	6.9	92.2
Oman Oman	*2005	6.8	17.8	75.5	7.7	19.2	73.2	1.2	9.2	89.6
	*2010	5.2	36.9	58.0	5.9	41.8	52.4	0.5	5.9	93.7
	*2015	6.0	38.9	55.1	6.6	42.9	50.4	0.6	6.4	93.0
	*2019	6.5	38.3	55.3	7.2	41.8	51.0	0.6	6.5	92.9
Pakistan Pakistan	*2005	43.1	20.3	36.6	38.2	21.4	40.5	67.4	15.0	17.6
	*2010	43.4	21.4	35.2	35.4	24.0	40.6	74.1	11.5	14.4
	*2015	41.0	24.0	35.0	32.6	26.6	40.8	72.1	14.5	13.4
	*2019	40.5	24.0	35.5	31.7	26.6	41.7	72.0	14.5	13.6
Palau [3] Palaos [3]	2000[6]	7.1	13.8	79.1	9.6	20.7	69.7	3.1	2.6	94.4
	2008[4]	2.4	11.8	85.9	...	...	...	...	...	...
Panama Panama	*2005	15.7	17.2	67.1	22.1	21.7	56.2	4.3	9.1	86.6
	*2010	17.4	18.7	63.9	23.1	23.9	53.0	7.5	9.7	82.8
	*2015	15.7	19.0	65.3	20.0	24.7	55.3	8.9	9.8	81.3
	*2019	14.0	17.9	68.2	17.9	23.5	58.6	7.8	9.0	83.2
Papua New Guinea Papouasie-Nvl-Guinée	*2005	52.6	5.8	41.7	56.9	9.5	33.6	48.0	1.9	50.1
	*2010	25.8	7.5	66.7	31.2	12.1	56.7	20.1	2.7	77.2
	*2015	20.7	7.5	71.8	25.8	12.4	61.8	15.5	2.5	82.0
	*2019	20.1	7.6	72.4	25.1	12.5	62.3	14.9	2.5	82.6
Paraguay Paraguay	*2005	32.4	15.7	51.9	38.7	19.9	41.4	22.1	9.0	68.9
	*2010	25.6	19.2	55.2	30.2	25.6	44.2	18.1	8.7	73.2
	*2015	19.7	19.7	60.6	23.4	26.3	50.2	14.0	9.7	76.4
	*2019	20.5	19.5	60.0	24.8	26.8	48.4	13.9	8.3	77.9
Peru Pérou	*2005	34.8	14.1	51.1	36.6	18.2	45.2	32.6	8.9	58.5
	*2010	27.7	16.9	55.4	28.7	22.6	48.7	26.6	10.1	63.3
	*2015	28.3	16.6	55.2	29.3	22.8	47.9	27.0	9.0	64.0
	*2019	27.5	15.9	56.5	29.2	21.9	48.9	25.5	8.8	65.7
Philippines Philippines	*2005	36.0	15.6	48.5	43.6	17.8	38.6	23.7	12.0	64.3
	*2010	33.2	15.0	51.8	40.5	18.2	41.3	21.7	9.9	68.4
	*2015	29.2	16.2	54.7	35.8	20.3	43.9	19.0	10.0	71.0
	*2019	24.7	18.0	57.4	30.8	23.5	45.8	15.5	9.8	74.8
Poland Pologne	*2005	17.4	29.3	53.4	18.0	39.0	43.1	16.6	17.1	66.3
	*2010	13.1	30.3	56.6	13.4	41.8	44.8	12.7	16.1	71.2
	*2015	11.5	30.5	57.9	12.5	42.1	45.5	10.4	16.5	73.1
	*2019	10.0	30.9	59.1	11.1	42.9	46.0	8.7	16.2	75.1
Portugal Portugal	*2005	12.1	30.4	57.6	11.2	40.6	48.3	13.1	18.4	68.5
	*2010	11.2	27.3	61.6	11.5	37.5	51.0	10.9	16.0	73.1
	*2015	7.5	24.4	68.1	9.6	33.0	57.5	5.4	15.2	79.4
	*2019	6.5	24.3	69.2	8.5	33.4	58.1	4.5	14.8	80.7

Employment by economic activity *(continued)*
Percentage of persons employed by sex and ISIC 4 categories; agriculture (agr.), industry (ind.) and services (ser.)

Emploi par activité économique *(suite)*
Personnes employées par sexe et branches de la CITI rév. 4; agriculture (agr.), industrie (ind.) et services (ser.), pourcentage

Region, country or area [+] Région, pays ou zone [+]	Year Année	Male and Female Hommes et femmes			Male Hommes			Female Femmes		
		Agr.	Ind.	Ser.	Agr.	Ind.	Ser.	Agr.	Ind.	Ser.
Puerto Rico	*2005	2.1	19.0	78.9	3.3	24.9	71.8	0.4	10.9	88.8
Porto Rico	*2010	1.6	13.8	84.7	2.6	18.0	79.4	0.2	8.3	91.5
	*2015	3.0	16.7	80.3	5.0	19.3	75.7	0.4	13.3	86.3
	*2019	3.2	17.1	79.7	5.3	19.4	75.3	0.4	14.0	85.6
Qatar	*2005	3.1	40.4	56.5	3.6	47.1	49.3	0.1	3.5	96.4
Qatar	*2010	1.5	57.2	41.3	1.7	64.1	34.2	~0.0	5.2	94.7
	*2015	1.2	54.1	44.6	1.4	61.9	36.7	~0.0	6.0	94.0
	*2019	1.2	54.7	44.1	1.4	62.6	36.0	~0.0	6.7	93.3
Republic of Korea	*2005	7.9	26.9	65.2	7.3	34.0	58.7	8.9	16.6	74.5
République de Corée	*2010	6.6	25.0	68.5	6.4	32.4	61.3	6.9	14.3	78.8
	*2015	5.2	25.1	69.7	5.2	33.3	61.6	5.2	13.7	81.1
	*2019	4.7	24.4	70.9	4.8	32.8	62.4	4.6	12.7	82.7
Republic of Moldova	*2005	40.7	16.0	43.3	41.1	20.8	38.1	40.2	11.5	48.4
République de Moldova	*2010	27.5	18.7	53.8	30.5	24.9	44.6	24.5	12.3	63.2
	*2015	34.2	17.9	48.0	38.5	23.9	37.7	29.7	11.8	58.5
	*2019	31.8	17.2	51.0	35.2	22.5	42.3	28.4	11.7	59.9
Réunion [8]	2010[11]	4.2	14.1	67.1	...	...	...	...	...	...
Réunion [8]	#2012	4.3	12.7	81.7	6.3	20.0	72.0	2.1	4.1	93.0
Romania	*2005	32.3	30.5	37.3	31.7	35.1	33.2	33.1	24.8	42.2
Roumanie	*2010	31.0	28.3	40.7	30.0	35.0	35.1	32.4	19.9	47.8
	*2015	25.6	28.5	46.0	25.6	35.0	39.4	25.6	20.0	54.4
	*2019	21.9	28.1	50.0	22.6	34.9	42.5	21.0	19.3	59.8
Russian Federation	*2005	10.2	29.8	60.0	12.3	38.2	49.6	8.0	21.3	70.7
Fédération de Russie	*2010	7.8	27.7	64.5	9.9	37.3	52.8	5.6	17.8	76.6
	*2015	6.7	27.2	66.1	8.2	37.7	54.1	5.1	16.2	78.7
	*2019	6.5	26.7	66.8	8.1	37.1	54.8	4.9	15.9	79.3
Rwanda	*2005	85.6	3.4	11.0	79.1	6.1	14.9	91.9	0.9	7.2
Rwanda	*2010	79.6	5.5	14.8	70.8	9.5	19.7	88.1	1.7	10.2
	*2015	67.3	8.1	24.6	56.6	13.8	29.5	77.4	2.7	19.9
	*2019	64.8	8.4	26.8	53.8	14.4	31.8	75.1	2.7	22.1
Saint Helena [4,14] Sainte-Hélène [4,14]	2008	7.3	20.0	72.7	11.8	33.9	54.3	1.7	2.9	95.4
Saint Kitts and Nevis [6] Saint-Kitts-et-Nevis [6]	#2001	0.2	48.8	42.1	0.4	51.6	34.7	0.1	45.5	50.6
Saint Lucia	*2005	13.8	20.3	65.9	17.8	27.5	54.7	8.5	10.8	80.6
Sainte-Lucie	*2010	14.6	18.4	67.0	18.7	25.9	55.5	9.4	8.7	82.0
	*2015	14.7	17.0	68.3	18.8	24.2	57.0	9.5	8.0	82.6
	*2019	15.2	17.5	67.3	19.4	25.2	55.5	10.0	8.2	81.8
Saint Vincent & Grenadines	*2005	7.2	12.6	80.3	10.8	16.4	72.9	1.5	6.7	91.9
Saint-Vincent-Grenadines	*2010	6.9	13.1	80.0	10.4	17.3	72.3	1.5	6.9	91.7
	*2015	6.3	12.4	81.2	9.8	16.7	73.6	1.4	6.3	92.3
	*2019	5.9	12.6	81.6	9.1	17.0	73.9	1.3	6.2	92.6
Samoa	*2005	7.1	14.8	78.1	8.4	18.8	72.8	4.8	7.7	87.5
Samoa	*2010	5.9	15.3	78.8	7.0	19.4	73.6	3.8	8.2	88.0
	*2015	5.4	14.7	80.0	6.4	18.8	74.8	3.4	7.3	89.3
	*2019	5.8	14.2	80.0	6.9	18.2	74.9	3.8	7.0	89.2
San Marino	2005[4]	0.5	39.3	60.2	0.6	50.4	49.1	0.3	23.4	76.3
Saint-Marin	#2010	0.3	34.3	65.4	0.4	45.6	54.0	0.2	18.7	81.1
Sao Tome and Principe	*2005	27.9	17.2	54.9	34.1	24.1	41.8	16.0	3.9	80.1
Sao Tomé-et-Principe	*2010	23.9	16.1	60.0	28.6	20.8	50.7	15.0	7.1	77.9
	*2015	18.8	14.0	67.2	22.9	18.7	58.4	11.0	5.4	83.7
	*2019	15.2	13.8	70.9	19.1	18.8	62.1	8.2	4.6	87.2
Saudi Arabia	*2005	4.0	20.0	75.9	4.6	22.9	72.6	0.4	1.0	98.6
Arabie saoudite	*2010	4.3	21.4	74.4	4.9	24.3	70.8	0.2	1.6	98.3
	*2015	6.1	22.7	71.2	7.0	26.1	67.0	0.6	1.6	97.9
	*2019	6.2	22.6	71.2	7.1	26.0	66.8	0.6	1.6	97.8
Senegal	*2005	40.6	17.4	42.0	39.9	23.1	37.0	42.1	6.2	51.8
Sénégal	*2010	53.3	19.7	27.0	49.0	25.1	25.8	60.2	10.9	28.9
	*2015	54.0	20.0	26.0	49.7	25.7	24.6	60.1	11.8	28.1
	*2019	52.1	20.4	27.5	47.8	26.5	25.7	58.2	11.7	30.1
Serbia	*2005	23.3	27.6	49.1	23.3	34.4	42.3	23.3	17.5	59.2
Serbie	*2010	22.7	22.3	55.0	23.8	27.9	48.3	21.1	14.9	64.0
	*2015	19.5	24.5	56.1	21.9	30.2	47.9	16.3	16.9	66.8
	*2019	18.2	24.4	57.3	20.1	30.9	49.1	15.9	16.2	67.9

18

Employment by economic activity *(continued)*
Percentage of persons employed by sex and ISIC 4 categories; agriculture (agr.), industry (ind.) and services (ser.)

Emploi par activité économique *(suite)*
Personnes employées par sexe et branches de la CITI rév. 4; agriculture (agr.), industrie (ind.) et services (ser.), pourcentage

Region, country or area [+] Région, pays ou zone [+]	Year Année	Male and Female Hommes et femmes			Male Hommes			Female Femmes		
		Agr.	Ind.	Ser.	Agr.	Ind.	Ser.	Agr.	Ind.	Ser.
Seychelles [8,15] Seychelles [8,15]	2011	3.6	17.9	78.2	6.4	25.3	68.1	0.7	10.4	88.5
Sierra Leone Sierra Leone	*2005	65.9	6.1	28.0	66.2	11.4	22.4	65.6	1.0	33.4
	*2010	63.7	6.4	29.8	64.7	12.1	23.2	62.8	1.0	36.2
	*2015	60.9	6.2	33.0	61.7	11.6	26.8	60.1	0.9	39.1
	*2019	59.0	6.3	34.7	60.4	11.8	27.8	57.8	0.9	41.4
Singapore Singapour	*2005	0.9	21.8	77.3	1.2	25.4	73.5	0.6	16.8	82.6
	*2010	0.1	30.4	69.5	0.2	37.2	62.6	0.1	21.5	78.5
	*2015	0.9	16.4	82.7	1.2	20.1	78.7	0.6	11.8	87.6
	*2019	0.1	16.1	83.8	0.2	19.8	80.0	0.1	11.5	88.5
Slovakia Slovaquie	*2005	4.8	38.8	56.4	6.4	49.6	43.9	2.6	25.2	72.1
	*2010	3.2	37.1	59.7	4.4	50.1	45.5	1.8	21.1	77.1
	*2015	3.2	36.1	60.7	4.7	48.4	46.9	1.3	20.8	77.9
	*2019	2.8	35.8	61.4	4.0	48.4	47.6	1.3	20.4	78.2
Slovenia Slovénie	*2005	9.1	37.1	53.8	9.1	46.9	44.0	9.1	25.4	65.5
	*2010	8.8	32.6	58.6	9.1	42.7	48.2	8.5	20.5	70.9
	*2015	7.1	32.0	60.9	7.1	43.5	49.5	7.1	18.2	74.7
	*2019	4.7	31.1	64.2	5.5	43.3	51.2	3.7	17.0	79.3
Solomon Islands Îles Salomon	*2005	71.2	8.4	20.5	69.5	10.0	20.5	73.3	6.2	20.5
	*2010	69.5	9.1	21.4	67.7	11.2	21.1	71.8	6.3	21.8
	*2015	69.0	9.4	21.6	67.6	11.6	20.8	70.8	6.6	22.6
	*2019	69.3	9.8	20.9	68.0	11.8	20.2	70.9	7.2	21.9
Somalia Somalie	*2005	86.7	7.2	6.1	85.4	7.7	6.9	92.4	5.0	2.7
	*2010	86.4	7.4	6.2	85.1	8.0	7.0	92.1	5.2	2.7
	*2015	86.1	7.7	6.2	84.7	8.2	7.1	91.8	5.4	2.8
	*2019	86.2	7.6	6.3	84.7	8.2	7.1	91.8	5.4	2.9
South Africa Afrique du Sud	*2005	7.5	25.7	66.8	8.6	34.3	57.1	6.0	13.5	80.5
	*2010	4.9	24.4	70.7	5.7	32.8	61.5	3.8	13.0	83.2
	*2015	5.6	23.8	70.6	6.7	33.2	60.2	4.2	11.8	84.0
	*2019	5.4	23.4	71.3	6.6	32.1	61.3	3.7	11.9	84.4
South Sudan Soudan du sud	*2005	56.5	18.9	24.6	57.2	16.0	26.9	55.8	22.0	22.2
	*2010	54.1	19.8	26.1	54.6	17.6	27.8	53.5	22.2	24.3
	*2015	62.4	19.4	18.2	64.6	14.1	21.3	60.1	25.0	14.9
	*2019	65.4	19.7	14.9	68.3	13.2	18.5	62.4	26.5	11.0
Spain Espagne	*2005	5.3	29.6	65.1	6.5	41.1	52.5	3.5	12.4	84.1
	*2010	4.2	23.0	72.8	5.6	33.6	60.9	2.4	9.5	88.0
	*2015	4.1	19.9	76.0	5.8	29.2	65.1	2.1	8.7	89.2
	*2019	4.0	19.1	76.9	5.6	28.5	65.8	2.0	8.0	90.0
Sri Lanka Sri Lanka	*2005	33.8	27.3	38.9	32.0	26.5	41.6	37.8	29.0	33.3
	*2010	33.6	24.9	41.5	31.4	24.7	43.8	38.2	25.2	36.6
	*2015	28.1	25.5	46.4	26.5	25.7	47.9	31.4	25.3	43.3
	*2019	25.6	25.5	48.9	24.1	26.0	49.9	28.5	24.6	47.0
State of Palestine État de Palestine	*2005	14.6	26.3	59.2	10.7	30.2	59.1	32.0	8.6	59.4
	*2010	12.8	25.7	61.5	9.6	29.1	61.3	27.9	9.5	62.6
	*2015	8.7	29.2	62.2	7.7	32.8	59.5	13.1	11.7	75.2
	*2019	9.5	29.5	61.0	8.3	33.9	57.9	14.1	12.6	73.3
Sudan Soudan	*2005	54.8	21.4	23.8	57.4	17.1	25.5	46.1	35.6	18.2
	*2010	49.2	22.6	28.2	51.4	19.2	29.5	42.0	34.3	23.7
	*2015	52.8	18.9	28.3	54.9	15.1	30.0	46.3	31.0	22.7
	*2019	53.0	19.2	27.8	55.2	15.3	29.5	46.1	31.8	22.1
Suriname Suriname	*2005	7.0	24.2	68.8	8.7	32.6	58.8	3.8	8.4	87.8
	*2010	4.2	23.0	72.8	5.4	32.6	62.0	2.2	6.4	91.3
	*2015	2.4	23.8	73.7	3.4	34.1	62.6	0.9	7.1	92.0
	*2019	2.6	24.6	72.9	3.6	34.8	61.7	1.0	7.8	91.3
Sweden Suède	*2005	2.0	22.1	75.9	3.0	33.7	63.3	0.9	9.2	89.8
	*2010	2.1	19.9	78.0	3.1	30.9	66.0	1.0	7.6	91.4
	*2015	2.0	18.3	79.7	3.0	28.7	68.3	1.0	6.9	92.1
	*2019	1.8	17.9	80.3	2.6	28.1	69.3	1.0	6.7	92.4
Switzerland Suisse	*2005	3.9	22.5	73.6	4.8	32.0	63.2	2.8	11.0	86.2
	*2010	3.5	22.5	74.1	4.1	32.3	63.6	2.7	10.7	86.6
	*2015	3.4	20.8	75.8	3.9	30.0	66.1	2.9	10.1	87.0
	*2019	3.4	20.4	76.2	3.8	29.7	66.5	2.9	9.8	87.3

Employment by economic activity *(continued)*
Percentage of persons employed by sex and ISIC 4 categories; agriculture (agr.), industry (ind.) and services (ser.)

Emploi par activité économique *(suite)*
Personnes employées par sexe et branches de la CITI rév. 4; agriculture (agr.), industrie (ind.) et services (ser.), pourcentage

Region, country or area [+] Région, pays ou zone [+]	Year Année	Male and Female Hommes et femmes			Male Hommes			Female Femmes		
		Agr.	Ind.	Ser.	Agr.	Ind.	Ser.	Agr.	Ind.	Ser.
Syrian Arab Republic	*2005	21.2	26.5	52.2	19.3	29.7	51.0	33.2	7.2	59.6
République arabe syrienne	*2010	15.2	34.3	50.6	14.2	38.0	47.8	21.4	10.0	68.6
	*2015	20.8	32.4	46.8	20.9	34.6	44.5	19.8	13.4	66.8
	*2019	22.8	33.3	43.9	22.9	35.3	41.8	21.7	14.4	63.9
Tajikistan	*2005	56.7	16.2	27.1	44.1	24.1	31.8	75.1	4.6	20.3
Tadjikistan	*2010	53.1	15.5	31.4	42.4	22.3	35.3	69.4	5.1	25.6
	*2015	51.8	16.1	32.1	40.6	23.5	35.9	69.7	4.4	26.0
	*2019	50.7	16.7	32.6	39.6	24.3	36.2	68.7	4.4	26.9
Thailand	*2005	42.6	20.3	37.1	44.2	21.6	34.2	40.7	18.7	40.6
Thaïlande	*2010	38.2	20.6	41.1	40.1	22.7	37.2	36.1	18.2	45.7
	*2015	32.3	23.7	44.0	34.4	26.1	39.6	29.8	20.8	49.4
	*2019	31.2	22.5	46.3	33.5	25.4	41.2	28.5	19.1	52.4
Timor-Leste	*2005	60.4	7.9	31.8	60.7	7.9	31.4	59.8	7.7	32.5
Timor-Leste	*2010	50.8	9.3	39.9	51.1	10.2	38.7	50.2	7.4	42.5
	*2015	39.1	13.1	47.8	36.5	15.9	47.6	44.7	7.1	48.2
	*2019	24.9	15.8	59.3	23.4	20.1	56.5	28.1	6.5	65.4
Togo	*2005	42.5	17.9	39.6	47.1	16.0	37.0	38.1	19.8	42.1
Togo	*2010	38.4	18.3	43.4	43.6	16.4	40.0	33.0	20.2	46.8
	*2015	39.4	17.3	43.3	43.9	16.6	39.5	34.9	17.9	47.2
	*2019	36.0	17.3	46.7	40.3	17.2	42.4	31.6	17.4	51.0
Tonga	*2005	31.9	30.3	37.7	49.3	13.5	37.1	4.2	57.2	38.7
Tonga	*2010	31.6	30.7	37.8	48.8	14.3	36.8	4.3	56.5	39.2
	*2015	31.0	30.8	38.2	47.9	14.2	37.9	4.0	57.3	38.7
	*2019	31.5	31.8	36.7	48.5	14.8	36.6	4.0	59.2	36.8
Trinidad and Tobago	*2005	4.3	31.1	64.5	6.1	41.5	52.4	1.7	16.0	82.3
Trinité-et-Tobago	*2010	3.7	30.2	66.1	5.1	41.1	53.8	1.7	14.8	83.5
	*2015	3.7	27.7	68.6	5.1	37.7	57.3	1.8	13.8	84.4
	*2019	3.5	26.8	69.7	4.9	36.6	58.6	1.6	13.2	85.2
Tunisia	*2005	20.8	42.2	37.0	20.1	43.3	36.6	23.0	38.8	38.2
Tunisie	*2010	17.7	44.9	37.3	17.1	46.6	36.3	19.7	39.8	40.4
	*2015	13.2	44.7	42.1	13.8	45.6	40.6	11.4	42.1	46.5
	*2019	13.3	42.6	44.1	13.8	43.9	42.3	11.8	38.7	49.5
Turkey	*2005	25.7	26.3	48.0	18.5	29.7	51.8	46.2	16.7	37.1
Turquie	*2010	23.7	26.2	50.1	17.4	30.4	52.2	39.2	16.0	44.9
	*2015	20.4	27.2	52.4	15.7	32.1	52.2	31.0	16.3	52.8
	*2019	18.3	27.0	54.7	14.5	32.0	53.6	26.8	16.1	57.1
Turkmenistan	*2005	19.1	36.6	44.2	15.7	47.3	37.0	23.8	22.2	54.0
Turkménistan	*2010	12.6	45.1	42.3	9.9	56.9	33.2	16.4	29.0	54.7
	*2015	8.9	45.1	46.1	6.8	57.9	35.3	11.8	27.2	61.1
	*2019	7.6	44.8	47.6	5.8	58.1	36.1	10.1	26.2	63.7
Turks and Caicos Islands [4]	2005	1.4	16.8	70.9	...	...	...	...	...	...
Îles Turques-et-Caïques [4]	#2008	1.2	23.1	74.0	...	...	...	...	...	...
Uganda	*2005	75.3	5.7	19.0	69.3	8.3	22.4	82.1	2.7	15.2
Ouganda	*2010	71.1	7.1	21.8	67.3	9.2	23.5	75.4	4.7	20.0
	*2015	71.0	6.8	22.2	66.2	10.0	23.8	76.4	3.3	20.3
	*2019	67.8	7.1	25.1	63.0	10.6	26.4	73.1	3.2	23.7
Ukraine	*2005	19.4	26.0	54.6	18.8	34.9	46.3	20.0	16.5	63.5
Ukraine	*2010	20.3	25.7	54.0	21.0	35.5	43.5	19.6	15.4	65.0
	*2015	15.3	24.7	60.1	17.2	34.7	48.1	13.1	13.9	73.0
	*2019	14.0	26.0	60.0	15.6	36.4	48.0	12.3	14.7	73.0
United Arab Emirates	*2005	4.9	40.1	55.0	5.6	44.6	49.8	0.1	6.1	93.8
Émirats arabes unis	*2010	0.8	29.3	69.9	0.9	32.0	67.1	~0.0	6.4	93.6
	*2015	0.2	33.6	66.2	0.2	37.4	62.4	~0.0	4.5	95.5
	*2019	0.3	38.6	61.1	0.4	43.1	56.6	~0.0	6.6	93.4
United Kingdom	*2005	1.4	22.2	76.4	1.9	33.1	65.0	0.7	9.4	89.9
Royaume-Uni	*2010	1.2	19.2	79.6	1.8	29.5	68.8	0.6	7.4	92.0
	*2015	1.1	18.7	80.2	1.6	28.2	70.2	0.7	7.7	91.7
	*2019	1.1	18.1	80.8	1.5	27.5	71.0	0.6	7.4	92.1
United Rep. of Tanzania	*2005	74.7	4.9	20.5	71.3	7.0	21.7	78.1	2.7	19.2
Rép.-Unie de Tanzanie	*2010	72.2	5.4	22.4	69.1	7.8	23.1	75.4	2.9	21.7
	*2015	67.7	6.2	26.2	64.9	9.3	25.8	70.6	2.9	26.5
	*2019	65.3	6.1	28.6	62.5	9.4	28.1	68.3	2.6	29.1

18

Employment by economic activity *(continued)*
Percentage of persons employed by sex and ISIC 4 categories; agriculture (agr.), industry (ind.) and services (ser.)

Emploi par activité économique *(suite)*
Personnes employées par sexe et branches de la CITI rév. 4; agriculture (agr.), industrie (ind.) et services (ser.), pourcentage

Region, country or area [+] / Région, pays ou zone [+]	Year / Année	Male and Female Hommes et femmes			Male Hommes			Female Femmes		
		Agr.	Ind.	Ser.	Agr.	Ind.	Ser.	Agr.	Ind.	Ser.
United States of America États-Unis d'Amérique	*2005	1.6	21.1	77.4	2.2	30.7	67.1	0.8	9.7	89.5
	*2010	1.6	18.5	79.9	2.3	27.7	70.0	0.8	7.9	91.3
	*2015	1.7	18.9	79.5	2.3	27.7	69.9	0.9	8.4	90.8
	*2019	1.6	18.7	79.7	2.3	27.6	70.2	0.8	8.1	91.0
United States Virgin Islands Îles Vierges américaines	*2005	2.3	11.0	86.7	3.7	17.7	78.6	0.7	3.9	95.5
	*2010	2.2	11.1	86.7	3.6	18.0	78.4	0.7	3.9	95.4
	*2015	2.9	12.0	85.2	4.8	18.9	76.3	1.0	4.9	94.1
	*2019	2.6	11.7	85.7	4.4	18.6	77.0	0.8	4.7	94.5
Uruguay Uruguay	*2005	5.7	22.9	71.5	8.4	30.3	61.3	1.9	12.8	85.4
	*2010	11.6	21.4	67.0	16.5	28.8	54.7	5.1	11.8	83.1
	*2015	8.8	20.5	70.7	12.3	29.0	58.7	4.5	9.7	85.8
	*2019	7.8	19.8	72.4	11.2	28.5	60.3	3.6	8.9	87.5
Uzbekistan Ouzbékistan	*2005	34.7	32.2	33.1	30.9	39.6	29.5	39.9	22.0	38.1
	*2010	27.2	37.1	35.7	23.7	45.8	30.5	32.0	25.2	42.8
	*2015	22.9	37.8	39.3	19.7	47.5	32.9	27.3	24.4	48.3
	*2019	20.7	37.7	41.6	17.8	47.9	34.4	24.8	23.4	51.8
Vanuatu Vanuatu	*2005	64.2	5.5	30.3	63.0	8.0	29.0	65.7	2.2	32.1
	*2010	61.4	6.9	31.7	60.1	10.1	29.8	63.2	2.6	34.3
	*2015	63.2	6.0	30.8	62.0	8.9	29.0	64.8	2.2	33.0
	*2019	64.5	5.9	29.6	63.3	8.7	28.0	66.0	2.3	31.7
Venezuela (Boliv. Rep. of) Venezuela (Rép. boliv. du)	*2005	9.8	21.0	69.3	14.5	26.9	58.6	2.0	11.2	86.8
	*2010	9.1	23.9	67.0	13.8	31.2	55.0	1.9	12.6	85.5
	*2015	9.1	23.7	67.3	13.4	31.0	55.6	2.5	12.6	84.9
	*2019	9.7	23.7	66.6	14.3	30.2	55.5	2.7	13.8	83.5
Viet Nam Viet Nam	*2005	54.6	18.9	26.5	52.7	22.6	24.8	56.7	14.9	28.4
	*2010	48.9	21.4	29.7	46.7	25.7	27.6	51.1	16.9	32.0
	*2015	43.9	23.3	32.8	42.4	26.9	30.7	45.6	19.3	35.1
	*2019	38.4	25.4	36.2	37.1	29.5	33.4	39.7	21.1	39.3
Western Sahara Sahara occidental	*2005	38.0	29.2	32.9	40.2	24.8	35.0	30.0	45.1	24.9
	*2010	34.6	30.2	35.2	36.5	26.2	37.3	27.7	44.4	27.9
	*2015	31.8	31.0	37.2	33.6	27.2	39.2	25.6	43.8	30.6
	*2019	30.1	31.0	38.9	32.1	27.3	40.7	23.8	43.2	33.0
Yemen Yémen	*2005	30.1	15.7	54.2	28.2	17.1	54.8	40.0	8.6	51.3
	*2010	24.1	19.0	56.9	23.8	19.4	56.8	28.0	14.6	57.4
	*2015	34.7	14.4	50.9	33.0	14.4	52.6	56.7	14.6	28.8
	*2019	41.5	13.4	45.0	40.1	13.4	46.5	62.8	13.6	23.6
Zambia Zambie	*2005	72.8	6.8	20.4	65.7	10.7	23.6	80.6	2.5	17.0
	*2010	63.4	8.8	27.9	55.4	13.9	30.7	72.4	3.0	24.6
	*2015	53.7	11.5	34.8	45.1	18.3	36.6	63.2	4.0	32.9
	*2019	52.5	12.1	35.4	43.9	19.4	36.8	62.1	4.1	33.8
Zimbabwe Zimbabwe	*2005	72.6	10.4	17.0	65.3	15.8	18.9	80.2	4.8	15.0
	*2010	69.0	9.4	21.6	62.9	15.1	22.0	75.4	3.5	21.2
	*2015	67.2	7.3	25.5	62.9	12.3	24.8	71.6	2.2	26.2
	*2019	68.7	7.3	24.0	64.3	12.3	23.4	73.1	2.3	24.5
European Union (EU) Union européenne (UE)	*2005	6.2	27.6	66.3	6.9	37.6	55.5	5.3	14.8	79.9
	*2010	5.2	25.2	69.6	5.9	35.7	58.4	4.3	12.4	83.2
	*2015	4.5	24.1	71.4	5.5	34.2	60.4	3.4	12.1	84.5
	*2019	4.1	23.5	72.4	5.0	33.7	61.3	2.9	11.5	85.6

Source:

International Labour Organization (ILO), Geneva, Key Indicators of the Labour Market (KILM 9th edition) and the ILOSTAT database, last accessed January 2019.

Source:

Organisation internationale du Travail (OIT), Genève, Indicateurs Clés du Marché du Travail (ICMT 9e édition) et ILOSTAT base de données, dernier accès janvier 2019.

[+] Ages 15 years and over unless indicated otherwise. Table is in ISIC Rev. 4 unless otherwise indicated.

[+] Sauf indication contraire, Age 15 ans et plus. Sauf indication contraire, la classification utilisée dans ce tableau est la CITI Rév. 4.

18

Employment by economic activity *(continued)*
Percentage of persons employed by sex and ISIC 4 categories; agriculture (agr.), industry (ind.) and services (ser.)

Emploi par activité économique *(suite)*
Personnes employées par sexe et branches de la CITI rév. 4; agriculture (agr.), industrie (ind.) et services (ser.), pourcentage

1	Data excludes Armenia, Azerbaijan, Cyprus, Georgia, Israel and Turkey.	1	Les données excluent l'Arménie, l'Azerbaïdjan, Chypre, la Géorgie, l'Israël et la Turquie.
2	Caucasus refers to Armenia, Azerbaijan, Cyprus, Georgia, Israel and Turkey.	2	Le Caucase se rapportent à l'Arménie, l'Azerbaïdjan, Chypre, la Géorgie, l'Israël et la Turquie.
3	Population aged 16 years and over.	3	Population âgée de 16 ans et plus.
4	Data classified according to ISIC Rev. 3.	4	Données classifiées selon la CITI, Rév. 3.
5	Population aged 14 years and over.	5	Population âgée de 14 ans et plus.
6	Data classified according to ISIC Rev. 2.	6	Données classifiées selon la CITI, Rév. 2.
7	Population aged 13 years and over.	7	Population âgée de 13 ans et plus.
8	Excluding the institutional population.	8	Non compris la population dans les institutions.
9	For statistical purposes, the data for China do not include those for the Hong Kong Special Administrative Region (Hong Kong SAR), Macao Special Administrative Region (Macao SAR) and Taiwan Province of China.	9	Pour la présentation des statistiques, les données pour la Chine ne comprennent pas la région administrative spéciale de Hong Kong (RAS de Hong Kong), la région administrative spéciale de Macao (RAS de Macao) et la province chinoise de Taïwan.
10	Resident population (de jure).	10	Population résidente (de droit).
11	Population aged 15 to 64 years.	11	Population âgée de 15 à 64 ans.
12	Nationals, residents.	12	Ressortissants, résidents.
13	Civilians only.	13	Civils uniquement.
14	Population aged 15 to 69 years.	14	Population âgée de 15 à 69 ans.
15	Excluding some areas.	15	Certaines régions sont exclues.

Consumer price indices
General and food (Index base: 2010 = 100)

Indices des prix à la consommation
Généraux et alimentation (Indices base: 2010 = 100)

Country or area	1995	2005	2010	2015	2016	2017	2018	Pays ou zone
Afghanistan								**Afghanistan**
General	...	71.1	100.0	132.1	137.9	144.8	...	Généraux
Food	...	...	100.0	* 100.8	* 106.5	* 113.9	...	Alimentation
Åland Islands								**Îles d'Åland**
General	# 80.0[1]	# 90.8[1]	# 100.0	108.6	109.2	111.1	112.5	Généraux
Food	...	# 90.3[1]	100.0	114.3	113.1	113.7	115.6	Alimentation
Albania [1]								**Albanie** [1]
General	40.7	86.7	100.0	111.4	112.8	115.1	117.4	Généraux
Food	...	82.8	100.0	118.8	122.6	127.3	130.8	Alimentation
Algeria [2]								**Algérie** [2]
General	51.9	81.8	100.0	126.7	134.8	142.4	148.5[1]	Généraux
Food [1]	...	...	100.0	131.3	135.7	142.5	147.3	Alimentation [1]
Andorra [1]								**Andorre** [1]
General	...	89.6	100.0	103.3	102.8	105.5	105.8	Généraux
Food	...	92.0	100.0	108.2	109.1	112.3	114.5	Alimentation
Angola [3]								**Angola** [3]
General	* # ~0.0	* 53.7	* 100.0	* 161.1	* 213.2	* 280.8	* 337.5	Généraux
Food	...	* 45.5	* 100.0	* 167.3	* 222.6	* 286.6	...	Alimentation
Anguilla								**Anguilla**
General	61.0	81.9	# 100.0	105.1	104.5	105.9	...	Généraux
Food [1]	...	...	100.0	111.4	111.0	112.3	113.4	Alimentation [1]
Antigua and Barbuda								**Antigua-et-Barbuda**
General	...	89.5	100.0	110.3	109.8	112.5	...	Généraux
Argentina [4]								**Argentine** [4]
General	...	...	...	...	...	112.9	151.6	Généraux
Food	...	...	...	...	...	111.7	148.2	Alimentation
Armenia								**Arménie**
General	* 44.3	* 76.4	* # 100.0	* 124.8	* 123.0	* 124.2	* 127.3	Généraux
Food [1]	...	...	* 100.0	* 127.1	* 122.9	* 127.9	...	Alimentation [1]
Aruba [1]								**Aruba** [1]
General	62.5	84.1	100.0	103.4	102.5	102.0	105.6	Généraux
Food	...	73.6	100.0	111.9	111.8	112.5	120.9	Alimentation
Australia [1,5]								**Australie** [1,5]
General	67.6	86.3	# 100.0	112.0	113.5	115.7	117.9	Généraux
Food	...	...	100.0	107.6	108.4	109.2	110.3	Alimentation
Austria								**Autriche**
General	77.1	91.4	100.0	110.7	111.7	114.0	116.3	Généraux
Food	76.4	88.1	100.0	114.4	115.2	118.0	119.7	Alimentation
Azerbaijan								**Azerbaïdjan**
General	42.7	61.1	100.0	117.7	132.4	149.5	152.9	Généraux
Food [6]	...	...	100.0	119.6	136.2	159.8	163.0	Alimentation [6]
Bahamas								**Bahamas**
General	* # 75.3[7]	* 88.2	* 100.0	* 109.6	* 109.2	* 110.9	* 113.4	Généraux
Food [7,8]	...	...	...	106.5	...	...	...	Alimentation [7,8]
Bahrain [1]								**Bahreïn** [1]
General	83.8	87.5	100.0	110.6	113.7	115.2	117.6	Généraux
Food	...	...	100.0	114.5	115.9	117.1	119.6	Alimentation
Bangladesh								**Bangladesh**
General	42.5	69.2	100.0	144.5	152.4	161.1	...	Généraux
Food [9]	...	...	...	...	* 239.1	* 257.9	...	Alimentation [9]
Barbados [10,11]								**Barbade** [10,11]
General	...	...	...	# 167.6	169.7	177.6	184.1	Généraux
Food	...	...	...	200.7	217.5	230.9	234.6	Alimentation
Belarus								**Bélarus**
General	* 0.4	* 61.7	* 100.0	387.0	433.1	459.0	480.1	Généraux
Food	...	...	100.0	389.9	424.1	...	471.0	Alimentation
Belgium								**Belgique**
General	75.0[1]	90.4[1]	100.0[1]	108.6[1]	110.8[1]	112.8[1]	115.5	Généraux
Food	71.9	86.3	100.0	110.4	112.9	114.3	116.8	Alimentation
Belize [1]								**Belize** [1]
General	73.5	88.3	100.0	103.8	104.5	105.7	106.0	Généraux
Food [6]	74.0	82.7	100.0	104.8	104.8	103.6	103.1	Alimentation [6]
Benin								**Bénin**
General [12]	* 61.1	* 84.3	* 100.0	* 109.8	* 108.9	* 109.0	* 110.1	Généraux [12]
Food [1]	...	...	* 100.0	* 113.0	* 112.5	* 112.5	...	Alimentation [1]

Country or area	1995	2005	2010	2015	2016	2017	2018	Pays ou zone
Bhutan								**Bhoutan**
General	56.7	74.8	100.0	146.2	152.5	158.4	162.7	Généraux
Food [13]	...	...	...	* 121.5	* 138.7	* 135.8	...	Alimentation [13]
Bolivia (Plurin. State of) [1]								**Bolivie (État plurin. de)** [1]
General	46.2	73.0	100.0	133.7	138.5	142.4	145.6	Généraux
Food	...		100.0	145.8	153.8	159.0	163.0	Alimentation
Bosnia and Herzegovina								**Bosnie-Herzégovine**
General	...	84.9	100.0	103.7	102.6	103.8	...	Généraux
Food	...	* 81.4	* 100.0	* 104.1	* 102.9	...	...	Alimentation
Botswana [1]								**Botswana** [1]
General	29.5	64.3	100.0	132.9	136.6	141.1	145.7	Généraux
Food		56.1	100.0	126.9	130.3	134.8	134.1	Alimentation
Brazil [1]								**Brésil** [1]
General	36.6	79.5	100.0	138.4	150.4	155.7	161.4	Généraux
Food [14]	...	...	100.0	154.4	173.6	175.3	176.8	Alimentation [14]
Brunei Darussalam								**Brunéi Darussalam**
General	90.9	# 95.5	100.0	100.0	99.3	99.1	99.3	Généraux
Food	...		* 100.0	* 100.7	* 99.8	* 100.0	...	Alimentation
Bulgaria [1]								**Bulgarie** [1]
General	1.6	72.7	100.0	106.6	105.8	107.9	111.0	Généraux
Food	2.1	72.4	100.0	112.5	112.2	116.7	119.2	Alimentation
Burkina Faso [15]								**Burkina Faso** [15]
General	66.6	86.9	100.0	108.0	107.7	108.1	110.1	Généraux
Food [16]	...	...	...	...	...	* 117.6	...	Alimentation [16]
Burundi								**Burundi**
General [17]	17.5	61.3	100.0	154.0	162.6	188.7	183.4	Généraux [17]
Food	...	* 57.7	* 100.0	* 147.1	* 157.6	* 195.4	...	Alimentation
Cabo Verde [1]								**Cabo Verde** [1]
General	64.4	82.6	100.0	108.6	107.1	107.9	109.3	Généraux
Food	...	...	100.0	109.0	108.3	108.1	108.6	Alimentation
Cambodia [18]								**Cambodge** [18]
General	43.1	67.8	100.0	117.5	121.1	124.6	...	Généraux
Food [19]	...	...	...	...	* 200.0	* 206.7	...	Alimentation [19]
Cameroon								**Cameroun**
General	* 67.0	* 85.7	* 100.0	* 112.9	* 113.9	* 114.6	* 115.8	Généraux
Food [20]	...	...	...	* 109.8	* 110.9	* 111.0	...	Alimentation [20]
Canada [1]								**Canada** [1]
General	75.2	91.9	100.0	108.7	110.2	112.0	114.5	Généraux
Food	70.6	86.5	100.0	114.2	115.9	115.9	118.1	Alimentation
Cayman Islands [1]								**Îles Caïmanes** [1]
General	...	...	100.0	103.6	102.9	105.0	...	Généraux
Food	...	...	100.0	115.8	115.9	116.9	...	Alimentation
Central African Republic [21]								**République centrafricaine** [21]
General	* 69.0	* 80.9	* 100.0	* 186.9	...	...	...	Généraux
Chad [22]								**Tchad** [22]
General	* 61.7	* 85.6	* 100.0	* 115.9	...	...	...	Généraux
Chile								**Chili**
General	...	...	101.4[23]	108.9[24]	113.1[24]	115.5[24]	118.3[24]	Généraux
Food	...	...	102.2[23]	114.6[24]	119.0[24]	121.4[24]	125.1[24]	Alimentation
China [25]								**Chine** [25]
General	...	...	100.0	114.9	# 102.0[26]	103.6[26]	105.8[26]	Généraux
Food	...	...	100.0	129.4	# 104.6[6,26]	103.0[6,26]	104.9[6,26]	Alimentation
China, Hong Kong SAR								**Chine, RAS de Hong Kong**
General	89.6	89.5	100.0	123.0	125.9	127.8	130.8	Généraux
Food	...	...	100.0	127.9	132.2	135.1	139.7	Alimentation
China, Macao SAR								**Chine, RAS de Macao**
General	* 77.8	79.7	100.0	131.3[1]	134.4[1]	136.1[1]	140.2[1]	Généraux
Food [1]	...	...	100.0	139.2	143.3	145.5	149.5	Alimentation [1]
Colombia [1]								**Colombie** [1]
General	28.3	79.7	100.0	117.6	126.4	132.0	136.2	Généraux
Food	...	...	100.0	121.5	137.4	138.3	139.5	Alimentation
Comoros								**Comores**
General	...	84.4	100.0	...	...	...	...	Généraux
Food [1]	...	...	* 100.0	...	...	...	...	Alimentation [1]
Congo [27]								**Congo** [27]
General	* 55.5	* 78.9	* 100.0	* 118.5	...	...	...	Généraux

Country or area	1995	2005	2010	2015	2016	2017	2018	Pays ou zone
Cook Islands [1,28]								**Îles Cook [1,28]**
General	...	...	100.0	111.6	111.3	111.2	111.3	Généraux
Food	...	...	100.0	111.7	113.2	113.5	114.0	Alimentation
Costa Rica [1,29]								**Costa Rica [1,29]**
General	20.6	# 63.5	100.0	121.5	121.5	123.5	126.2	Généraux
Food	...		100.0	122.1	121.1	123.2	125.2	Alimentation
Côte d'Ivoire [30]								**Côte d'Ivoire [30]**
General	* 65.3	* 88.1	* 100.0	* 110.9	* 111.7	* 112.5	* 112.9	Généraux
Food [1,31]	...	* 75.5	* 100.0	* 111.9	* 115.3	* 115.7	...	Alimentation [1,31]
Croatia								**Croatie**
General	60.3	85.8	100.0	107.4	106.2	107.4	109.0	Généraux
Food	...		# 116.6⁹	# 109.3	108.8	112.0	113.1	Alimentation
Curaçao [1]								**Curaçao [1]**
General	66.9	84.3	100.0	108.1	108.1	109.8	112.6	Généraux
Food [32]	...	...	100.0	124.8	126.8	128.9	134.6	Alimentation [32]
Cyprus [1,33]								**Chypre [1,33]**
General	...	88.6	100.0	101.7	100.3	100.8	102.3	Généraux
Food	...		100.0	103.6	103.2	102.8	103.6	Alimentation
Czechia								**Tchéquie**
General	56.1	87.0	100.0	107.5	108.2	110.9	113.3	Généraux
Food [1]	77.0	89.9	100.0	118.4	117.3	123.4	125.1	Alimentation [1]
Dem. Rep. of the Congo								**Rép. dém. du Congo**
General	~0.0	58.6	100.0	130.1	133.9	...	...	Généraux
Food	...	...	...	* 122.0	* 125.7	...	...	Alimentation
Denmark [1]								**Danemark [1]**
General	72.8	90.0	100.0	107.1	107.4	108.6	109.5	Généraux
Food	...	86.4	100.0	109.1	109.2	112.2	112.3	Alimentation
Djibouti								**Djibouti**
General	...	77.8	100.0	112.5	115.6	116.2	...	Généraux
Dominica								**Dominique**
General	74.7	86.0	100.0	102.5	102.7	103.1	...	Généraux
Food [34]	...	...		* 110.9	* 110.9	* 111.1	...	Alimentation [34]
Dominican Republic [1]								**République dominicaine [1]**
General	23.2	73.4	100.0	122.5	124.4	128.5	133.1	Généraux
Food	...	74.6	100.0	133.0	135.9	139.0	144.0	Alimentation
Ecuador								**Équateur**
General	6.9	80.2	100.0	121.5	123.6	124.1	123.8	Généraux
Food [1]	...	70.7	100.0	125.2	128.4	129.0	126.9	Alimentation [1]
Egypt								**Égypte**
General [35]	36.6	57.8	100.0	156.8	178.5	231.1	...	Généraux [35]
Food [36]	...			* 194.1	* 226.4	* 313.9	* 355.7	Alimentation [36]
El Salvador								**El Salvador**
General [35]	59.2	84.2	100.0	108.2	108.8	109.9	111.1	Généraux [35]
Food [37]	...	...	...	...	* 119.3	* 119.4	...	Alimentation [37]
Equatorial Guinea								**Guinée équatoriale**
General	45.8	77.5	# 100.0	118.6	120.3	121.2	...	Généraux
Food [1]	...	...	* 100.0	* 123.4	* 118.4	* 120.3	...	Alimentation [1]
Estonia								**Estonie**
General	42.0	79.1	100.0	111.5	111.6	115.5	119.4	Généraux
Food [1]	...	77.1	100.0	118.0	117.7	124.8	128.6	Alimentation [1]
Eswatini								**Eswatini**
General	34.3	69.5	100.0	135.4	146.0	155.1	...	Généraux
Food [13]	...	...	...	* 113.6	* 130.7	* 140.0	...	Alimentation [13]
Ethiopia								**Éthiopie**
General	* 36.6	* # 44.8	* 100.0	* 211.4	* 226.8	* 249.3	...	Généraux
Food [1]	...	43.0	100.0	222.9	237.5	267.1	...	Alimentation [1]
Fiji [1]								**Fidji [1]**
General	60.4	# 80.8	100.0	116.4	120.9	124.9	130.0	Généraux
Food	...	...	100.0	127.5	135.2	132.3	136.9	Alimentation
Finland								**Finlande**
General	80.0¹	91.2¹	100.0¹	108.8¹	109.2¹	110.0¹	111.2	Généraux
Food	80.9¹	90.3¹	100.0¹	115.7¹	114.4¹	113.3¹	115.5	Alimentation
France [1,38,39]								**France [1,38,39]**
General	79.5	92.8	100.0	105.6	105.8	106.8	108.9	Généraux
Food	76.3	91.5	100.0	105.7	106.3	107.3	109.7	Alimentation

Country or area	1995	2005	2010	2015	2016	2017	2018	Pays ou zone
Gabon								**Gabon**
General [31,40]	* 77.9	* 88.7	* 100.0	* 109.0	* 111.3	* 114.3	* 119.7	Généraux [31,40]
Food [1]	...	...	* 100.0	* 115.9	* 115.8	...	...	Alimentation [1]
Gambia								**Gambie**
General [41]	46.3	81.1	100.0	130.7	140.1	151.4	161.3	Généraux [41]
Food [42]	...	...	...	* 186.0	* 201.3	...	...	Alimentation [42]
Georgia [43]								**Géorgie** [43]
General	28.6	70.0	100.0	114.7	117.1	124.2	127.4	Généraux
Food	...	...	100.0	120.5	122.5	130.8	133.7	Alimentation
Germany								**Allemagne**
General	80.5	92.5	100.0	106.9	107.4	109.3	111.4	Généraux
Food	84.1	89.1	100.0	112.3	113.2	116.4	119.2	Alimentation
Ghana								**Ghana**
General	7.0	52.9	100.0	176.0	206.7	232.3	255.1	Généraux
Food [44]	...	...	...	* 123.2	* 133.8	* 143.6	* 154.8	Alimentation [44]
Greece [1]								**Grèce** [1]
General	57.0	85.3	100.0	100.8	99.9	101.1	101.7	Généraux
Food	60.9	86.9	100.0	104.8	104.5	104.9	105.3	Alimentation
Grenada								**Grenade**
General	68.3	82.9	100.0	103.9	105.6	106.6	...	Généraux
Food [1]	...	* 74.0	* 100.0	* 110.5	* 108.0	* 108.6	...	Alimentation [1]
Guadeloupe [1]								**Guadeloupe** [1]
General	...	...	100.0	106.1	106.0	...	...	Généraux
Food	...	...	* 100.0	* 109.3	* 110.5	...	...	Alimentation
Guam [1]								**Guam** [1]
General	...	...	100.0	106.3	112.7	115.5	118.5	Généraux
Food [14,45]	...	...	100.0	125.2	123.2	121.4	127.2	Alimentation [14,45]
Guatemala								**Guatemala**
General	36.0	74.6	# 100.0	121.8	127.2	132.8	137.8	Généraux
Food [46]	...	...	...	147.0	161.6	176.0	188.7	Alimentation [46]
Guinea								**Guinée**
General [47]	...	42.2	100.0	185.6	200.8	218.7	240.2	Généraux [47]
Food [1]	...	...	* 100.0	* 204.5	* 228.0	* 256.4	...	Alimentation [1]
Guinea-Bissau [48]								**Guinée-Bissau** [48]
General	30.4	84.2	100.0	108.4	110.2	111.7	...	Généraux
Food [16,49]	...	...	...	...	115.5	117.6	...	Alimentation [16,49]
Guyana [50]								**Guyana** [50]
General	* 43.3	* 72.4	* 100.0	* 109.4	* 110.3	* 112.4	* 113.8	Généraux
Haiti								**Haïti**
General	13.5	66.8	100.0	139.0	158.3	181.5	...	Généraux
Food [51]	...	...	100.0	142.2	163.1	186.3	...	Alimentation [51]
Honduras								**Honduras**
General	* 22.9	* 72.0	* 100.0	* 129.3	* 132.8	* 138.1	* 144.1	Généraux
Food [1]	...	* 70.8	* 100.0	* 126.6	* 127.8	* 129.8	...	Alimentation [1]
Hungary								**Hongrie**
General	28.7	76.9	100.0	111.4	111.8	114.5	117.7	Généraux
Food	...	...	100.0	116.6	117.4	120.6	125.6	Alimentation
Iceland								**Islande**
General	47.6	67.1	100.0	117.8	119.8	122.0	125.3	Généraux
Food	52.4	65.9	100.0	119.6	121.2	118.3	121.3	Alimentation
India								**Inde**
General [52]	37.6	65.8	100.0	147.7	155.0	160.1	...	Généraux [52]
Food [44]	...	...	...	127.7	134.5	136.9	139.2	Alimentation [44]
Indonesia								**Indonésie**
General	19.4	68.7	100.0	132.3	137.0	142.2	146.7	Généraux
Food [32,44]	...	...	...	128.0	137.3	139.9	145.6	Alimentation [32,44]
Iran (Islamic Republic of) [53]								**Iran (Rép. islamique d')** [53]
General	...	...	...	91.6	98.3	106.2	125.3	Généraux
Food	...	...	...	91.5	97.5	109.7	135.3	Alimentation
Iraq								**Iraq**
General	13.0	58.6	100.0	118.5	119.2	119.4	...	Généraux
Food [1]	...	...	100.0	112.8	...	...	...	Alimentation [1]
Ireland [1]								**Irlande** [1]
General	69.0	93.1	100.0	104.7	104.7	105.1	105.6	Généraux
Food	77.3	97.7	100.0	98.3	97.0	95.0	93.1	Alimentation

Country or area	1995	2005	2010	2015	2016	2017	2018	Pays ou zone
Israel								**Israël**
General	59.5	87.8	100.0	106.7	106.1	106.4	107.2	Généraux
Food	52.1	79.3	100.0	108.8	107.8	108.0	109.1	Alimentation
Italy								**Italie**
General	71.6[1]	91.0[1]	100.0	107.5	107.4[1]	108.7[1]	109.9[1]	Généraux
Food	72.8[1]	88.9[1]	100.0	108.8	109.0[1]	111.1[1]	112.4[1]	Alimentation
Jamaica [1]								**Jamaïque** [1]
General	19.6	56.0	100.0	141.1	144.4	150.8	156.4	Généraux
Food	...	51.7	100.0	157.2	163.6	170.7	177.7	Alimentation
Japan [1]								**Japon** [1]
General	101.1	100.4	100.0	103.6	103.5	104.0	105.0	Généraux
Food [14]	97.8	96.8	100.0	106.6	108.4	110.6	110.7	Alimentation [14]
Jordan								**Jordanie**
General	57.7	74.5	100.0	116.4	115.5	119.3	124.7	Généraux
Food	...	...	100.0	115.2	111.2	110.8	114.4	Alimentation
Kazakhstan								**Kazakhstan**
General	20.4	61.5	100.0	137.8	157.6	169.3	...	Généraux
Food [1]	...	* 58.6	* 100.0	* 136.8	* 154.4	* 167.7	...	Alimentation [1]
Kenya								**Kenya**
General	25.3	55.5	100.0	150.2	159.6	172.4	180.5	Généraux
Food [1]	...	...	* 100.0	* 172.1	* 189.5	* 214.8	...	Alimentation [1]
Kiribati								**Kiribati**
General	...	...	* 100.0	* 99.5	...	...	...	Généraux
Food [1]	...	...	* 100.0	* 94.1	...	...	...	Alimentation [1]
Kuwait								**Koweït**
General	63.9	* 76.1	* 100.0	* 118.1	* 121.9	* 124.6	...	Généraux
Food	...	...	* 100.0	* 124.7	* 127.1	* 126.7	...	Alimentation
Kyrgyzstan								**Kirghizistan**
General	16.7	59.8	100.0	146.4	146.9	151.6	153.9	Généraux
Food	...	55.9	100.0	141.7	132.5	135.8	132.9	Alimentation
Lao People's Dem. Rep.								**Rép. dém. populaire lao**
General	* 6.2	* # 78.5	* # 100.0	* 125.8	* 127.8	* 128.9	...	Généraux
Food [1]	...	...	* 100.0	* 146.6	* 152.9	* 152.7	...	Alimentation [1]
Latvia								**Lettonie**
General	42.2	72.1	100.0	107.6	107.7	110.9	113.7	Généraux
Food	45.6	69.1	100.0	110.7	111.9	118.1	118.8	Alimentation
Lebanon								**Liban**
General	...	...	* 100.0	* 115.0	* 114.1	* 119.1	...	Généraux
Food [1]	...	...	* 100.0	* 118.5	* 117.1	* 121.3	...	Alimentation [1]
Lesotho								**Lesotho**
General	69.7	70.9	100.0	127.1	135.5	142.7	148.4	Généraux
Food [1]	...	* 61.9	* 100.0	* 138.4	* 154.8	* 165.5	...	Alimentation [1]
Liberia								**Libéria**
General	...	61.8	100.0	147.6	160.6	180.6	...	Généraux
Food	...	...	* 100.0	* 162.5	* 175.3	* 186.5	...	Alimentation
Libya								**Libye**
General	88.7	79.8	100.0	...	...	...	...	Généraux
Lithuania [1]								**Lituanie** [1]
General	51.3	77.7	100.0	107.6	108.6	112.6	115.7	Généraux
Food	54.2	72.2	100.0	113.3	114.7	118.8	120.5	Alimentation
Luxembourg [1]								**Luxembourg** [1]
General	74.2	89.7	100.0	109.2	109.5	111.5	113.1	Généraux
Food	70.6	87.7	100.0	110.5	112.2	115.3	117.9	Alimentation
Madagascar								**Madagascar**
General	23.2	62.9	100.0	139.5	148.8	161.2	...	Généraux
Food [1,51,54]	...	...	...	140.4	149.4	161.8	...	Alimentation [1,51,54]
Malawi								**Malawi**
General	* 8.9	* 64.2	* 100.0	* 250.6	* 305.0	* 340.2	* 382.5	Généraux
Food [44]	...	...	...	* 185.1	* 230.9	* 262.4	...	Alimentation [44]
Malaysia								**Malaisie**
General	69.0	87.7	100.0	112.8	115.2	119.6	120.7	Généraux
Food	...	...	100.0	119.4	124.0	129.2	130.9	Alimentation
Maldives								**Maldives**
General	...	* # 73.3	* 100.0	* 132.0	* 132.7	* 136.4	...	Généraux
Food [1]	...	...	* 100.0	* 153.0	* 153.9	* 163.3	...	Alimentation [1]

Country or area	1995	2005	2010	2015	2016	2017	2018	Pays ou zone
Mali [55]								**Mali [55]**
General	70.3	85.9	100.0	110.3	108.3	110.2	...	Généraux
Food [1,49]	...	...	* 100.0	* 112.9	* 109.2	* 112.0	...	Alimentation [1,49]
Malta								**Malte**
General	70.0	88.9	100.0	108.2	# 108.9	110.3	111.6	Généraux
Food [4]	...	...	...	...	* # 96.5	* 99.8	...	Alimentation [4]
Martinique [1]								**Martinique [1]**
General			100.0	106.3	106.1	...	...	Généraux
Food	...	...	* 100.0	* 110.3	* 111.7	...	...	Alimentation
Mauritania								**Mauritanie**
General	41.8	75.2	100.0	# 123.4	102.6[56]	104.8[56]	108.0[56]	Généraux
Food	...	...	* 100.0[1]	* 128.6[1]	104.0[56]	107.2[56]	111.7[56]	Alimentation
Mauritius [1]								**Maurice [1]**
General	42.0	72.9	100.0	119.8	121.0	125.4	129.4	Généraux
Food	...	...	100.0	120.8	122.1	126.6	134.0	Alimentation
Mexico [1]								**Mexique [1]**
General	26.4	80.5	100.0	119.4	122.8	130.2	136.6	Généraux
Food [51]	23.8	74.4	100.0	129.9	135.2	144.4	151.3	Alimentation [51]
Micronesia (Fed. States of)								**Micronésie (États féd. de)**
General		77.8	100.0	112.5	...	...	...	Généraux
Mongolia								**Mongolie**
General	15.8[1]	57.3[1]	100.0[1]	163.8[1]	165.6[1]	172.0[1]	# 112.3[26]	Généraux
Food	...	...	100.0[1]	161.4[1]	157.9[1]	164.3[1]	# 110.1[26]	Alimentation
Montenegro								**Monténégro**
General		82.2	100.0	111.0	110.7[1]	113.4[1]	116.3[1]	Généraux
Food	...	...	100.0	114.3	113.4[1]	115.4[1]	115.8[1]	Alimentation
Montserrat								**Montserrat**
General	...	* 86.8	* 100.0	* 107.9	* 107.6	* 108.9	...	Généraux
Food [56]	...	...	...	* 99.1	* 99.0	* 98.6	...	Alimentation [56]
Morocco [1]								**Maroc [1]**
General	76.3	89.7	100.0	106.2	108.0	108.8	110.7	Généraux
Food	...	...	100.0	107.4	110.5	110.5	111.6	Alimentation
Mozambique [1]								**Mozambique [1]**
General	...	...	100.0	126.3	148.3	170.7	177.4	Généraux
Food	...	...	100.0	134.4	170.9	199.0	199.0	Alimentation
Myanmar								**Myanmar**
General	5.5	44.5	100.0	129.3	138.3	144.6	154.5	Généraux
Food [44]	...	...	...	* 127.9	* 139.7	* 145.9	...	Alimentation [44]
Namibia [1]								**Namibie [1]**
General	...	71.4	100.0	128.9	137.6	145.9	152.3	Généraux
Food	...	63.0	100.0	139.4	154.4	162.9	168.2	Alimentation
Nepal [57]								**Népal [57]**
General	...	...	...	103.7	112.8	116.9	121.7	Généraux
Food	...	...	...	104.4	113.3	114.8	117.1	Alimentation
Netherlands								**Pays-Bas**
General	73.7	92.7	100.0	109.3	109.5	111.0	112.9	Généraux
Food [1]	81.4	91.3	100.0	107.4	108.4	111.3	112.2	Alimentation [1]
New Caledonia [1]								**Nouvelle-Calédonie [1]**
General	...	...	100.0	106.3	107.0	...	109.9	Généraux
Food	...	...	100.0	110.6	112.5	...	113.9	Alimentation
New Zealand [1]								**Nouvelle-Zélande [1]**
General	71.7	87.0	100.0	107.9	108.6	110.7	112.4	Généraux
Food	...	...	100.0	106.0	105.3	107.7	107.5	Alimentation
Nicaragua								**Nicaragua**
General	...	62.9	100.0	136.9	141.7	147.2	154.4	Généraux
Food [1]	...	57.0	100.0	146.5	148.7	149.5	155.8	Alimentation [1]
Niger								**Niger**
General	68.5[31,58]	88.5[31,58]	100.0[31,58]	107.3[16,49,58]	107.5[16,49,58]	110.1[16,49,58]	# 104.1[49,56]	Généraux
Food [49]	...	...	...	122.4[16,58]	120.9[16,58]	121.8[16,58]	# 102.2[56]	Alimentation [49]
Nigeria [59]								**Nigéria [59]**
General	17.0	61.9	100.0	158.9	183.9	214.2	240.1	Généraux
Food [1]			100.0	161.3	185.2	221.3	253.0	Alimentation [1]
North Macedonia								**Macédoine du Nord**
General	72.8	86.8	100.0	109.7	109.4	110.9	112.6	Généraux
Food [1]	...	83.1	100.0	111.6	109.9	110.1	111.1	Alimentation [1]

Country or area	1995	2005	2010	2015	2016	2017	2018	Pays ou zone
Norway								**Norvège**
General	73.1	89.3	100.0	108.6	112.5	114.6	117.7	Généraux
Food	74.3	88.3	100.0	108.4	111.2	111.2	114.0	Alimentation
Oman								**Oman**
General	...	76.1	100.0	109.4	110.6	112.4	...	Généraux
Food [1]	...	...	* 100.0	* 110.8	* 109.5	* 110.1	...	Alimentation [1]
Pakistan								**Pakistan**
General	30.3	55.3	# 100.0	145.3	150.8	156.9	164.9	Généraux
Food [1]	...	...	100.0	143.0	146.5	151.3	154.6	Alimentation [1]
Palau								**Palaos**
General	...	80.5	100.0	117.9	116.7	118.2	...	Généraux
Food [1]	...	* 73.6	* 100.0	* 116.4	* 112.9	* 115.1	...	Alimentation [1]
Panama								**Panama**
General [35]	72.9	81.3	100.0	119.6	120.5	121.6	122.5	Généraux [35]
Food [1]	...	* 74.0	* 100.0	* 122.6	* 124.2	* 123.6	...	Alimentation [1]
Papua New Guinea								**Papouasie-Nvl-Guinée**
General	30.2	77.1	# 100.0	127.8	136.3	...	...	Généraux
Food [1]	...	...	# 100.0	* 106.4	* 111.8	...	...	Alimentation [1]
Paraguay [1,60]								**Paraguay [1,60]**
General	31.0	71.4	100.0	124.8	129.9	134.6	140.0	Généraux
Food	...	58.2	100.0	125.8	133.1	140.8	146.3	Alimentation
Peru [61]								**Pérou [61]**
General	56.8	87.1	100.0	117.8	122.0	125.4	127.1	Généraux
Food [9,14,45]	...	...	...	...	...	163.1	...	Alimentation [9,14,45]
Philippines								**Philippines**
General	...	100.0	...	107.0[44]	108.4[44]	111.5[44]	117.3[44]	Généraux
Food	...	100.0	...	110.5[44]	112.3[44]	115.7[44]	123.6[44]	Alimentation
Poland [1]								**Pologne [1]**
General	...	...	100.0	108.1	107.6	109.6	111.5	Généraux
Food	...	...	100.0	109.1	110.3	114.9	117.9	Alimentation
Portugal [1]								**Portugal [1]**
General [62]	69.0	91.8	100.0	107.0	107.7	109.2	110.3	Généraux [62]
Food	77.4	95.1	100.0	107.0	107.6	109.2	110.0	Alimentation
Puerto Rico [1]								**Porto Rico [1]**
General	...	...	100.0	105.2	104.8	106.7	...	Généraux
Food [14]	...	...	100.0	111.1	112.0	112.4	...	Alimentation [14]
Qatar [24]								**Qatar [24]**
General	...	...	...	105.2	108.0	108.5	108.8	Généraux
Food	...	...	...	101.1	99.2	101.1	101.1	Alimentation
Republic of Korea [1]								**République de Corée [1]**
General	60.2	86.2	100.0	109.8	110.9	113.1	114.8	Généraux
Food	50.6	80.8	100.0	115.6	118.3	122.3	125.9	Alimentation
Republic of Moldova [63,64]								**République de Moldova [63,64]**
General	...	...	100.0	135.8	144.5	153.9	158.7	Généraux
Food [14]	...	...	100.0	137.1	147.1	159.1	167.8	Alimentation [14]
Romania								**Roumanie**
General	2.7	74.1	# 100.0	# 114.2	112.4	113.9	119.2[21]	Généraux
Food	...	...	...	131.0[9,14]	# 97.4[26]	99.8[26]	103.6[26]	Alimentation
Russian Federation								**Fédération de Russie**
General	6.3	61.4	100.0	151.5	162.2	168.2	173.0	Généraux
Food	...	58.4	100.0	161.7	171.0	175.6	178.5	Alimentation
Rwanda [1,35]								**Rwanda [1,35]**
General	...	...	100.0	122.1	129.1	135.4	137.2	Généraux
Food	...	...	100.0	132.2	146.5	160.4	156.1	Alimentation
Saint Kitts and Nevis								**Saint-Kitts-et-Nevis**
General	* 59.6	* 81.7	100.0[1]	105.7[1]	104.9[1]	105.7[1]	...	Généraux
Food [1]	...	...	100.0	102.2	95.9	95.7	...	Alimentation [1]
Saint Lucia								**Sainte-Lucie**
General	* 69.8	* 87.3	100.0[1]	111.4[1]	107.9[1]	108.0[1]	110.1[1]	Généraux
Food	...	...	* 100.0[1]	102.4	99.1	97.6	101.2	Alimentation
Saint Vincent & Grenadines								**Saint-Vincent-Grenadines**
General	* 67.9	* 80.9	* # 100.0	* 105.1	* 104.9	* 107.2	...	Généraux
Food [1]	...	...	* 100.0	* 109.5	* 108.8	* 111.5	...	Alimentation [1]
Samoa [62]								**Samoa [62]**
General	* 49.3	* 76.4	* 100.0	* 108.4	* 109.8	* 111.6	...	Généraux

Country or area	1995	2005	2010	2015	2016	2017	2018	Pays ou zone
San Marino [46]								**Saint-Marin** [46]
General	...	...	...	107.7	108.4	109.5	111.4	Généraux
Food	...	...	...	121.3	123.7	126.7	133.2	Alimentation
Sao Tome and Principe								**Sao Tomé-et-Principe**
General	...	39.2	100.0	154.0	162.3	171.6	185.1	Généraux
Food [56]	...	...	...	...	* 105.0	* 111.9	...	Alimentation [56]
Saudi Arabia [1]								**Arabie saoudite** [1]
General	...	81.4	100.0	114.4	116.7	115.7	118.6	Généraux
Food	...	73.0	100.0	118.6	117.1	116.2	123.6	Alimentation
Senegal [1,65]								**Sénégal** [1,65]
General	...	...	100.0	105.3	106.9	108.9	...	Généraux
Food	...	...	100.0	110.9	113.6	117.2	...	Alimentation
Serbia								**Serbie**
General	2.6	65.2	100.0	133.0	134.5	138.7	141.4	Généraux
Food	...	...	100.0	133.2	132.8	137.2	139.7	Alimentation
Seychelles [1]								**Seychelles** [1]
General	40.8	54.1	100.0	120.9	119.6	123.1	127.7	Généraux
Food [66]	...	...	100.0	116.7	116.7	117.7	117.9	Alimentation [66]
Sierra Leone [1]								**Sierra Leone** [1]
General	...	...	100.0	134.1	148.7	175.8	205.4	Généraux
Food	...	...	100.0	137.8	155.1	185.3	219.2	Alimentation
Singapore								**Singapour**
General	81.5	88.0	100.0	113.2	112.6	113.3	113.8	Généraux
Food [1]	77.4	85.6	100.0	112.9	115.3	116.9	118.6	Alimentation [1]
Slovakia								**Slovaquie**
General	44.1	86.8	100.0	108.7	108.2	109.6	112.3	Généraux
Food	61.9	89.6	100.0	113.2	110.0	114.4	118.8	Alimentation
Slovenia								**Slovénie**
General	# 44.8	86.8	100.0	105.9	105.9	107.4	109.3	Généraux
Food	...	81.3	100.0	113.2	114.2	116.8	119.9	Alimentation
Solomon Islands								**Îles Salomon**
General	28.2	65.8[67]	100.0[67]	125.3[67]	125.9[67]	126.5[67]	...	Généraux
Food [67]	...	...	...	* 552.5	* 555.4	* 551.6	...	Alimentation [67]
South Africa [1]								**Afrique du Sud** [1]
General	43.4[35]	74.3	100.0[35]	130.1[35]	# 138.4[35]	145.7[35]	152.4[35]	Généraux
Food	34.9[35]	67.1	100.0[35]	137.2[35]	# 151.7[35]	162.2[35]	168.0[35]	Alimentation
South Sudan								**Soudan du sud**
General	...	...	100.0	331.9	1 592.4	4 583.7	...	Généraux
Food [1]	...	...	* 100.0	* 349.4	* 1 660.9	* 4 574.0	...	Alimentation [1]
Spain [1]								**Espagne** [1]
General	66.7	# 89.0	100.0	106.5	106.3	108.4	110.2	Généraux
Food	67.0	89.2	100.0	108.2	109.7	111.1	112.9	Alimentation
Sri Lanka								**Sri Lanka**
General	23.6[1,68]	# 58.3[1,68]	100.0[1,68]	109.5[24]	113.8[24]	122.6[24]	125.2[24]	Généraux
Food	...	...	100.0[1,68]	110.7[24]	114.1[24]	127.0[24]	126.8[24]	Alimentation
State of Palestine								**État de Palestine**
General	...	80.7	100.0	111.0	110.7	111.0	110.8	Généraux
Food	...	71.8	100.0	107.8	106.2	105.2	104.4	Alimentation
Sudan								**Soudan**
General	8.3	* 60.0	* 100.0	* 349.8	...	...	...	Généraux
Food [69]	...	...	...	* 501.5	...	...	...	Alimentation [69]
Suriname								**Suriname**
General	7.2	69.0[1]	100.0[1]	139.2[1]	216.4[1]	264.1[1]	282.8[1,70]	Généraux
Food [1]	...	...	100.0	141.8	206.7	264.7	289.5[70]	Alimentation [1]
Sweden								**Suède**
General	84.3	92.7	100.0	103.6	104.6	106.5	108.6	Généraux
Food [1]	86.3	87.2	100.0	107.9	109.0	111.4	114.0	Alimentation [1]
Switzerland [1]								**Suisse** [1]
General	88.4	95.7	100.0	98.2	97.7	98.3	99.2	Généraux
Food	90.4	97.8	100.0	97.1	97.5	97.9	99.1	Alimentation
Syrian Arab Republic								**République arabe syrienne**
General	...	...	100.0	448.8	662.9	...	...	Généraux
Food	...	...	100.0	512.1	807.3	...	...	Alimentation
Tajikistan [1]								**Tadjikistan** [1]
General	...	...	100.0	140.2	148.7	159.5	165.7	Généraux
Food [14]	...	...	100.0	146.8	154.4	168.6	173.1	Alimentation [14]

Country or area	1995	2005	2010	2015	2016	2017	2018	Pays ou zone
Thailand [1]								**Thaïlande [1]**
General	62.9	86.6	100.0	110.3	110.6	111.3	112.5	Généraux
Food	...	...	100.0	123.0	124.9	124.9	125.5	Alimentation
Timor-Leste								**Timor-Leste**
General	...	* 74.4	* 100.0	* 142.8	* 140.9	* 141.6	...	Généraux
Food [13]	...	...	...	* 105.7	* 103.5	* 104.4	...	Alimentation [13]
Togo [49]								**Togo [49]**
General	65.2	77.6[71]	100.0[71]	110.3[71]	111.3[71]	110.4[71]	...	Généraux
Food [1,71]	...	* 81.5	* 100.0	* 106.6	* 109.9	* 105.4	...	Alimentation [1,71]
Tonga								**Tonga**
General	* 39.5	* 76.7	* 100.0	* 109.9	* 112.7	...	...	Généraux
Food [1]	...	* 75.7	* 100.0	* 116.3	* 117.8	...	...	Alimentation [1]
Trinidad and Tobago [10]								**Trinité-et-Tobago [10]**
General	42.1	64.6	100.0	133.6	137.7	140.3	...	Généraux
Food [1]	...	* 39.9	* 100.0	* 170.9	* 183.6	* 189.0	...	Alimentation [1]
Tunisia								**Tunisie**
General	* 61.2	* 81.6	* # 100.0	* 126.7	* 131.4	* 138.4	...	Généraux
Food	...	...	100.0	135.0	138.5	146.2	...	Alimentation
Turkey								**Turquie**
General	* 1.3[1]	* # 65.9	* 100.0	* 146.1	* 157.4	175.0	202.1	Généraux
Food	1.5[1]	60.2[1]	100.0	157.3	166.4	187.5	219.9	Alimentation
Uganda [72]								**Ouganda [72]**
General	...	...	...	150.8	159.0	167.9	172.3	Généraux
Food	...	...	...	160.7	169.7	186.8	184.6	Alimentation
Ukraine								**Ukraine**
General [73]	9.6	51.2	100.0	180.5	205.6	235.3	261.1	Généraux [73]
Food	...	...	100.0	166.6	181.6	204.9	227.8	Alimentation
United Arab Emirates								**Émirats arabes unis**
General	...	...	# 100.0	109.3	111.1	113.3	116.8	Généraux
Food [1]	...	...	* 100.0	* 118.3	* 119.5	* 121.0	...	Alimentation [1]
United Kingdom [1]								**Royaume-Uni [1]**
General	...	87.4	100.0	111.9	112.6	115.6	118.4	Généraux
Food	...	78.5	100.0	109.8	107.2	109.5	111.8	Alimentation
United Rep. of Tanzania [74]								**Rép.-Unie de Tanzanie [74]**
General	28.6	66.3	100.0	# 158.0	166.2	175.0	181.2	Généraux
Food [75]	...	...	...	* 96.6	* 103.8	* 113.3	...	Alimentation [75]
United States of America [35]								**États-Unis d'Amérique [35]**
General	69.9	89.6	100.0	108.7	110.1	112.4	115.2	Généraux
Food [1]	68.9	87.9	100.0	112.2	110.8	110.5	111.0	Alimentation [1]
Uruguay [1]								**Uruguay [1]**
General	23.0	70.5	100.0	150.1	164.6	174.8	188.1	Généraux
Food	...	64.3	100.0	158.8	174.1	179.0	193.9	Alimentation
Vanuatu								**Vanuatu**
General	# 67.0	83.9	100.0	107.1	108.0	...	...	Généraux
Food [1]	...	...	* 100.0	* 109.2	* 111.6	...	...	Alimentation [1]
Venezuela (Boliv. Rep. of) [1]								**Venezuela (Rép. boliv. du) [1]**
General	...	...	100.0	772.0	...	...	...	Généraux
Food	...	...	100.0	1 487.2	...	...	...	Alimentation
Viet Nam								**Viet Nam**
General	40.2	59.9	100.0	145.8	150.5	155.8	161.3	Généraux
Food [56]	...	...	...	...	* 104.1	* 103.0	...	Alimentation [56]
Yemen								**Yémen**
General	* 21.3	* # 60.0	* 100.0	...	...	...	...	Généraux
Zambia								**Zambie**
General	6.7	59.9	# 100.0	144.0	169.8	180.9	194.5	Généraux
Food [23]	...	...	...	* 151.2	* 183.3	* 193.9	...	Alimentation [23]
Zimbabwe								**Zimbabwe**
General	...	...	100.0	106.2	104.6	105.5	...	Généraux
Food [1]	...	...	* 100.0	* 103.6	* 100.2	* 102.7	...	Alimentation [1]

Source:

United Nations Statistics Division (UNSD), New York, Monthly Bulletin of Statistics (MBS), last accessed June 2019.

Source:

Organisation des Nations Unies (ONU), Division de statistique, New York, Bulletin mensuel de statistique (BMS), dernier accès juin 2019.

1	Calculated by the UN Statistics Division from national indices.
2	Algiers
3	Luanda
4	Index base: December 2016=100.
5	Weighted average of index values computed for the 8 capital cities.
6	Including tobacco.
7	New Providence
8	Index base: November 2014=100.
9	Index base: 2005=100.
10	Data refer to the Retail Price Index.
11	Index base: July 2001=100.
12	Cotonou
13	Index base: December 2012=100.
14	Including alcoholic beverages.
15	Ouagadougou
16	Index base: 2008=100.
17	Bujumbura
18	Phnom Penh
19	Index Base: October to December 2006=100.
20	Base: 2011=100.
21	Bangui
22	N'Djamena
23	Index base: 2009=100.
24	Index base: 2013=100.
25	For statistical purposes, the data for China do not include those for the Hong Kong Special Administrative Region (Hong Kong SAR), Macao Special Administrative Region (Macao SAR) and Taiwan Province of China.
26	Index base: 2015=100.
27	Brazzaville
28	Rarotonga
29	Central area.
30	Abidjan
31	African population.
32	Food only.
33	Excluding northern Cyprus.
34	Index base: June 2010=100.
35	Urban areas.
36	Index base: January 2010=100.
37	Index base: December 2009=100.
38	All households.
39	Including French Guiana, Guadeloupe, Martinique and Réunion.
40	Libreville and Owendo.
41	Banjul, Kombo St. Mary
42	Index base: August 2004=100.
43	Data refer to 5 cities only.
44	Index base: 2012=100.
45	Including food and beverages consumed away from home.
46	Index base: December 2010=100.
47	Conakry
48	Bissau
49	WAEMU harmonized consumer price index.
50	Georgetown
51	Including alcoholic beverages and tobacco.
52	Industrial workers.
53	Index base: fiscal (solar) year 2016 (21 March 2016 - 20 March 2017)=100.
54	Data refer to 7 cities only.
55	Bamako
56	Index base: 2014=100.

1	Les indices ont été calculés par la Division de statistique de l'ONU à partir des indices nationaux.
2	Alger
3	Luanda
4	Indices base: 2016 décembre=100.
5	Moyenne pondérée des données d'index calculées pour les 8 capitales.
6	Y compris le tabac.
7	Nouvelle Providence
8	Indices base: 2014 novembre=100.
9	Indices base: 2005=100.
10	Les données se rapporte à l'index des prix en détail.
11	Indices base: 2001 juillet=100.
12	Cotonou
13	Indices base: 2012 décembre=100.
14	Y compris les boissons alcoolisées.
15	Ouagadougou
16	Indices base: 2008=100.
17	Bujumbura
18	Phnom Penh
19	Indices base: octobre au décembre 2006=100.
20	Base : 2011=100.
21	Bangui
22	N'Djamena
23	Indices base: 2009=100.
24	Indices base: 2013=100.
25	Pour la présentation des statistiques, les données pour la Chine ne comprennent pas la région administrative spéciale de Hong Kong (RAS de Hong Kong), la région administrative spéciale de Macao (RAS de Macao) et la province chinoise de Taïwan.
26	Indices base: 2015=100.
27	Brazzaville
28	Rarotonga
29	Région centrale.
30	Abidjan
31	Population Africaine.
32	Alimentation seulement.
33	Chypre du nord non compris.
34	Indices base: 2010 juin=100.
35	Zones urbaines.
36	Indices base: 2010 janvier=100.
37	Indices base: 2009 décembre=100.
38	Tous ménages.
39	Y compris Guadeloupe, Guyane française, Martinique et Réunion.
40	Libreville et Owendo.
41	Banjul, Kombo St. Mary
42	Indices base: 2004 août=100.
43	Les données se réfère à 5 villes seulement.
44	Indices base: 2012=100.
45	Y compris les aliments et de boissons loin de la maison.
46	Indices base: 2000 décembre=100.
47	Conakry
48	Bissau
49	UEMOA harmonisé l'indice des prix à la consommation.
50	Georgetown
51	Y compris les boissons alcoolisées et le tabac.
52	Ouvriers industriels.
53	Indices base: année fiscale (solaire) 2016 (21 mars 2016 - 20 mars 2017) = 100.
54	Les données se réfère à 7 villes seulement.
55	Bamako
56	Indices base: 2014=100.

57	Index base: 2014/2015=100.	57	Indices base: 2014/2015=100.
58	Niamey	58	Niamey
59	Rural and urban areas.	59	Régions rurales et urbaines.
60	Refers to the metropolitan area of Asunción.	60	Fait référence à la zone métropolitaine d'Asunción.
61	Metropolitan Lima.	61	Lima métropolitaine.
62	Excluding rent.	62	Sans le loyer.
63	Excluding the left side of the river Nistru and the municipality of Bender.	63	La rive gauche de la rivière Nistru et la municipalité de Bender sont exclues.
64	Data refer to 8 cities only.	64	Les données se réfère à 8 villes seulement.
65	Data refer to the national index.	65	Les données se rapporte à l'indice national.
66	Excluding fresh fish.	66	Non compris le poisson frais.
67	Honiara	67	Honiara
68	Colombo	68	Colombo
69	Index base: 2007=100.	69	Indices base: 2007=100.
70	Average for 10 months excluding data for May and June.	70	Moyenne sur 10 mois à l'exclusion des données de mai et juin.
71	For Lome only.	71	Pour Lome seulement.
72	Index base: 1 July 2009 - 30 June 2010=100.	72	Indices base: 1 juillet 2009 - 30 juin 2010=100.
73	Excludes the temporarily occupied territory of the Autonomous Republic of Crimea and Sevastopol.	73	Excluent le territoire temporairement occupé de la République autonome de Crimée et de Sébastopol.
74	Tanzania mainland only, excluding Zanzibar.	74	Tanzanie continentale seulement, Zanzibar non compris.
75	Index base: December 2015=100.	75	Indices base: 2015 décembre=100.

Total imports, exports and balance of trade
Imports CIF, exports FOB and balance: millions of US dollars

Total des importations, des exportations et balance commerciale
Importations CAF, exportations FAB et balance: en millions de dollars É.-U.

Region, country or area	Sys.&	1995	2005	2010	2015	2016	2017	2018	Région, pays ou zone
Total, all countries or areas									**Total, tous pays ou zones**
Imports		5 099 057	10 577 013	15 262 545	16 437 277	15 984 051	17 799 382	19 366 965	Importations
Exports		5 050 238	10 373 445	15 100 194	16 371 462	15 843 503	17 353 362	18 661 823	Exportations
Balance		-48 819	-203 568	-162 352	-65 815	-140 548	-446 020	-705 141	Balance
Africa									**Afrique**
Imports		114 352	246 228	468 297	541 791	474 356	501 889	535 885	Importations
Exports		103 460	306 656	496 503	397 465	346 523	395 199	439 921	Exportations
Balance		-10 892	60 428	28 206	-144 326	-127 833	-106 690	-95 964	Balance
Northern Africa									**Afrique septentrionale**
Imports		45 062	87 571	181 147	205 345	182 480	194 069	210 159	Importations
Exports		33 043	114 104	165 544	108 661	99 289	107 472	116 995	Exportations
Balance		-12 019	26 533	-15 603	-96 684	-83 191	-86 597	-93 164	Balance
Sub-Saharan Africa									**Afrique subsaharienne**
Imports		69 290	158 657	287 151	336 446	291 875	307 819	325 726	Importations
Exports		70 417	192 552	330 959	288 804	247 234	287 727	322 926	Exportations
Balance		1 127	33 895	43 809	-47 642	-44 641	-20 093	-2 800	Balance
Eastern Africa									**Afrique orientale**
Imports		17 980	31 243	62 688	102 677	83 571	87 427	87 923	Importations
Exports		9 499	16 297	31 652	42 957	37 507	40 942	44 537	Exportations
Balance		-8 481	-14 945	-31 036	-59 721	-46 064	-46 485	-43 387	Balance
Middle Africa									**Afrique centrale**
Imports		5 412	18 680	43 623	45 015	37 019	38 035	38 131	Importations
Exports		10 954	48 958	90 717	64 086	51 678	57 500	57 029	Exportations
Balance		5 542	30 278	47 094	19 071	14 659	19 465	18 898	Balance
Southern Africa									**Afrique australe**
Imports		26 745	63 786	97 723	103 707	90 115	98 767	111 531	Importations
Exports		28 214	56 076	95 232	93 563	88 325	101 870	108 471	Exportations
Balance		1 470	-7 711	-2 491	-10 144	-1 790	3 103	-3 060	Balance
Western Africa									**Afrique occidentale**
Imports		19 153	44 948	83 116	85 047	81 171	83 591	88 141	Importations
Exports		21 750	71 221	113 358	88 199	69 723	87 414	112 889	Exportations
Balance		2 597	26 273	30 241	3 152	-11 447	3 823	24 748	Balance
Americas									**Amériques**
Imports		1 178 848	2 557 150	3 229 231	3 739 935	3 560 750	3 821 128	4 131 697	Importations
Exports		997 709	1 835 325	2 550 328	2 827 271	2 716 488	2 935 711	3 164 266	Exportations
Balance		-181 139	-721 825	-678 903	-912 664	-844 262	-885 417	-967 431	Balance
Northern America									**Amérique septentrionale**
Imports		936 343	2 048 668	2 362 939	2 736 892	2 655 399	2 844 608	3 047 075	Importations
Exports		774 525	1 265 374	1 665 222	1 911 586	1 840 742	1 967 582	2 115 701	Exportations
Balance		-161 818	-783 295	-697 718	-825 306	-814 657	-877 026	-931 374	Balance
Latin America & the Caribbean									**Amérique latine et Caraïbes**
Imports		242 505	508 481	866 292	1 003 043	905 351	976 520	1 084 622	Importations
Exports		223 184	569 951	885 107	915 685	875 746	968 129	1 048 565	Exportations
Balance		-19 321	61 470	18 815	-87 358	-29 606	-8 391	-36 056	Balance
Caribbean									**Caraïbes**
Imports		20 945	36 923	51 812	58 006	55 207	55 849	57 169	Importations
Exports		8 346	21 331	24 161	26 508	22 501	23 116	24 493	Exportations
Balance		-12 598	-15 592	-27 651	-31 498	-32 706	-32 734	-32 676	Balance
Central America									**Amérique centrale**
Imports		87 084	259 847	366 171	464 284	454 772	492 913	545 688	Importations
Exports		87 067	233 506	336 529	426 823	419 936	459 317	489 018	Exportations
Balance		-17	-26 340	-29 642	-37 461	-34 836	-33 597	-56 670	Balance
South America									**Amérique du Sud**
Imports		134 476	211 711	448 308	480 752	395 372	427 757	481 765	Importations
Exports		127 771	315 113	524 416	462 353	433 308	485 697	535 054	Exportations
Balance		-6 706	103 402	76 108	-18 399	37 936	57 940	53 290	Balance
Asia									**Asie**
Imports		1 500 432	3 172 210	5 444 293	6 191 376	5 960 162	6 841 611	7 610 235	Importations
Exports		1 557 385	3 569 857	5 893 442	6 845 829	6 552 219	7 153 892	7 734 304	Exportations
Balance		56 953	397 647	449 149	654 453	592 057	312 281	124 069	Balance
Central Asia									**Asie centrale**
Imports		9 375	25 644	40 686	53 042	46 769	52 300	63 767	Importations
Exports		10 782	36 890	74 861	64 827	55 406	67 678	82 847	Exportations
Balance		1 407	11 246	34 175	11 785	8 636	15 378	19 080	Balance

20 Total imports, exports and balance of trade *(continued)*
Imports CIF, exports FOB and balance: millions of US dollars

Total des importations, des exportations et balance commerciale *(suite)*
Importations CAF, exportations FAB et balance: en millions de dollars É.-U.

Region, country or area	Sys.&	1995	2005	2010	2015	2016	2017	2018	Région, pays ou zone
Eastern Asia									**Asie orientale**
Imports		804 190	1 744 378	2 967 424	3 317 929	3 163 173	3 599 760	4 136 761	Importations
Exports		894 718	1 937 757	3 219 271	3 942 643	3 761 758	4 093 595	4 471 633	Exportations
Balance		90 528	193 379	251 847	624 714	598 585	493 836	334 871	Balance
South-eastern Asia									**Asie du Sud-Est**
Imports		353 943	584 010	950 429	1 088 724	1 087 896	1 258 901	1 460 313	Importations
Exports		320 454	655 071	1 051 556	1 158 886	1 148 376	1 311 607	1 451 432	Exportations
Balance		-33 489	71 061	101 127	70 162	60 480	52 706	-8 880	Balance
Southern Asia									**Asie méridionale**
Imports		74 082	229 179	497 340	560 507	534 659	642 975	723 350	Importations
Exports		65 912	193 182	354 892	394 653	408 558	467 407	469 892	Exportations
Balance		-8 171	-35 997	-142 448	-165 854	-126 102	-175 568	-253 458	Balance
Western Asia									**Asie occidentale**
Imports		155 335	407 407	737 099	942 666	896 734	1 027 769	939 430	Importations
Exports		154 177	557 564	919 156	1 004 801	897 643	896 025	922 479	Exportations
Balance		-1 159	150 158	182 058	62 135	909	-131 745	-16 952	Balance
Europe									**Europe**
Imports		2 228 669	4 439 990	5 873 573	5 712 661	5 748 467	6 349 901	6 793 183	Importations
Exports		2 320 042	4 527 059	5 907 021	6 065 793	5 991 866	6 585 500	7 011 026	Exportations
Balance		91 373	87 068	33 447	353 132	243 399	235 599	217 843	Balance
Eastern Europe									**Europe orientale**
Imports		161 835	490 657	867 387	847 830	854 735	1 004 455	952 641	Importations
Exports		176 871	594 285	993 297	1 024 049	976 844	1 137 907	1 131 024	Exportations
Balance		15 036	103 628	125 910	176 219	122 110	133 452	178 383	Balance
Northern Europe									**Europe septentrionale**
Imports		470 870	937 990	1 122 240	1 133 060	1 140 543	1 204 374	1 300 233	Importations
Exports		494 552	913 599	1 045 978	1 046 686	980 714	1 067 795	1 198 094	Exportations
Balance		23 682	-24 391	-76 262	-86 374	-159 829	-136 579	-102 139	Balance
Southern Europe									**Europe méridionale**
Imports		400 631	861 881	1 039 442	925 618	922 645	1 048 651	1 164 305	Importations
Exports		372 435	660 817	830 354	887 637	899 540	1 000 611	1 081 203	Exportations
Balance		-28 196	-201 064	-209 088	-37 981	-23 105	-48 040	-83 103	Balance
Western Europe									**Europe occidentale**
Imports		1 195 333	2 149 462	2 844 504	2 806 152	2 830 544	3 092 421	3 376 004	Importations
Exports		1 276 184	2 358 357	3 037 392	3 107 421	3 134 768	3 379 187	3 600 706	Exportations
Balance		80 851	208 895	192 888	301 269	304 224	286 766	224 702	Balance
Oceania									**Océanie**
Imports		76 756	161 435	247 151	251 515	240 316	284 853	295 964	Importations
Exports		71 642	134 548	252 899	235 103	236 407	283 060	312 306	Exportations
Balance		-5 114	-26 888	5 748	-16 411	-3 909	-1 793	16 341	Balance
Australia and New Zealand									**Australie et Nouvelle-Zélande**
Imports		71 338	151 453	231 861	236 642	225 619	268 570	278 363	Importations
Exports		66 374	127 740	243 041	222 150	223 500	268 213	295 524	Exportations
Balance		-4 965	-23 714	11 179	-14 493	-2 119	-357	17 160	Balance
Melanesia									**Mélanésie**
Imports		3 432	5 397	9 665	7 968	7 505	8 476	9 194	Importations
Exports		4 039	5 199	8 112	10 998	10 856	12 774	14 693	Exportations
Balance		607	-197	-1 553	3 030	3 351	4 298	5 499	Balance
Micronesia [1]									**Micronésie** [1]
Imports		897	2 379	3 292	4 627	4 949	5 368	5 515	Importations
Exports		1 028	1 295	1 508	1 737	1 785	1 833	1 868	Exportations
Balance		131	-1 084	-1 783	-2 890	-3 164	-3 535	-3 646	Balance
Polynesia									**Polynésie**
Imports		1 089	2 206	2 333	2 277	2 242	2 439	2 892	Importations
Exports		201	314	238	219	265	240	220	Exportations
Balance		-887	-1 893	-2 095	-2 058	-1 977	-2 199	-2 671	Balance
Afghanistan									**Afghanistan**
Imports	G	...	...	5 154	7 723	6 534	* 7 384	* 8 345	Importations
Exports	G	...	...	388	571	596	* 700	* 822	Exportations
Balance	G	...	...	-4 766	-7 151	-5 938	-6 684	-7 523	Balance
Albania									**Albanie**
Imports	G	* 713	2 614	4 603	4 320	4 669	5 294	* 5 942	Importations
Exports	G	* 202	658	1 550	1 930	1 962	2 301	* 2 876	Exportations
Balance	G	-511	-1 956	-3 053	-2 391	-2 707	-2 993	-3 066	Balance

20

Total imports, exports and balance of trade *(continued)*
Imports CIF, exports FOB and balance: millions of US dollars

Total des importations, des exportations et balance commerciale *(suite)*
Importations CAF, exportations FAB et balance: en millions de dollars É.-U.

Region, country or area	Sys.&	1995	2005	2010	2015	2016	2017	2018	Région, pays ou zone
Algeria									**Algérie**
Imports	S	10 782	20 357	41 000	51 803	47 091	46 053	* 49 214	Importations
Exports	S	9 357	46 002	57 051	34 796	29 992	35 191	* 41 347	Exportations
Balance	S	-1 426	25 645	16 051	-17 007	-17 099	-10 862	-7 867	Balance
Andorra									**Andorre**
Imports	S	1 025	* 1 796	1 541	* 1 295	* 1 355	* 1 480	* 1 623	Importations
Exports	S	48	143	92	* 87	* 100	* 120	* 129	Exportations
Balance	S	-978	-1 653	-1 448	-1 209	-1 255	-1 360	-1 494	Balance
Angola [1]									**Angola** [1]
Imports	S	* 1 466	* 8 321	18 143	16 758	* 12 310	* 13 540	* 18 019	Importations
Exports	S	* 3 592	* 23 835	52 612	33 048	* 29 198	* 32 265	* 38 953	Exportations
Balance	S	2 126	15 514	34 469	16 290	16 888	18 725	20 935	Balance
Anguilla									**Anguilla**
Imports	S	* 53	* 133	* 150	* 204	* 193	* 181	* 283	Importations
Exports	S	* 1	* 7	* 12	* 11	* 7	* 4	* 5	Exportations
Balance	S	-52	-126	-137	-193	-186	-176	-278	Balance
Antigua and Barbuda									**Antigua-et-Barbuda**
Imports	G	* 344	525	501	465	491	630	* 829	Importations
Exports	G	* 53	121	35	26	61	62	* 46	Exportations
Balance	G	-291	-405	-466	-439	-429	-567	-783	Balance
Argentina									**Argentine**
Imports	S	20 122	28 689	56 792	59 757	55 610	66 899	* 66 306	Importations
Exports	S	20 963	40 106	68 174	56 788	57 733	58 384	* 66 319	Exportations
Balance	S	841	11 418	11 382	-2 969	2 124	-8 515	13	Balance
Armenia									**Arménie**
Imports	S	* 674	1 692	3 782	3 257	3 218	3 893	4 796	Importations
Exports	S	* 271	937	1 011	1 483	1 808	2 145	2 382	Exportations
Balance	S	-403	-755	-2 770	-1 774	-1 411	-1 748	-2 414	Balance
Aruba									**Aruba**
Imports	S	* 566	1 030	1 071	1 165	1 117	1 189	* 1 262	Importations
Exports	S	* 15	106	125	80	95	89	* 67	Exportations
Balance	S	-551	-924	-947	-1 085	-1 022	-1 099	-1 195	Balance
Australia									**Australie**
Imports	G	* 57 381	125 221	201 703	200 114	189 406	228 442	* 234 678	Importations
Exports	G	* 52 628	106 011	212 109	187 792	189 630	230 163	* 255 727	Exportations
Balance	G	-4 752	-19 210	10 405	-12 322	224	1 721	21 049	Balance
Austria									**Autriche**
Imports	S	* 66 331	119 950	150 593	147 935	149 987	166 475	* 188 616	Importations
Exports	S	* 53 460	117 722	144 882	145 277	144 701	159 971	* 181 666	Exportations
Balance	S	-12 871	-2 228	-5 711	-2 658	-5 287	-6 505	-6 951	Balance
Azerbaijan									**Azerbaïdjan**
Imports	G	* 666	4 211	6 597	9 211	8 516	8 767	* 11 318	Importations
Exports	G	* 637	4 347	21 278	11 327	9 067	13 798	* 20 555	Exportations
Balance	G	-30	136	14 682	2 116	551	5 031	9 236	Balance
Bahamas [2]									**Bahamas** [2]
Imports	G	* 1 243	2 567	2 862	3 161	* 2 931	* 3 428	* 3 743	Importations
Exports	G	* 176	271	620	443	* 403	* 469	* 482	Exportations
Balance	G	-1 067	-2 296	-2 242	-2 719	-2 528	-2 959	-3 262	Balance
Bahrain									**Bahreïn**
Imports	G	3 679	9 339	16 002	16 378	14 749	* 17 449	* 19 019	Importations
Exports	G	3 475	10 239	16 059	16 684	12 892	* 15 506	* 18 493	Exportations
Balance	G	-204	899	58	307	-1 856	-1 943	-526	Balance
Bangladesh									**Bangladesh**
Imports	G	5 438	12 631	30 504	48 059	* 50 210	* 47 743	* 56 216	Importations
Exports	G	3 407	9 332	19 231	31 734	* 32 013	* 31 367	* 32 777	Exportations
Balance	G	-2 031	-3 299	-11 273	-16 325	-18 197	-16 376	-23 438	Balance
Barbados									**Barbade**
Imports	G	766	1 672	1 196	1 618	1 621	1 600	1 594	Importations
Exports	G	238	361	314	483	517	485	458	Exportations
Balance	G	-528	-1 311	-883	-1 135	-1 104	-1 114	-1 136	Balance
Belarus									**Bélarus**
Imports	G	* 5 382	16 699	34 884	30 291	27 610	34 235	38 202	Importations
Exports	G	* 4 623	15 977	25 283	26 660	23 537	29 240	33 461	Exportations
Balance	G	-759	-722	-9 601	-3 631	-4 073	-4 995	-4 741	Balance

20

Total imports, exports and balance of trade *(continued)*
Imports CIF, exports FOB and balance: millions of US dollars

Total des importations, des exportations et balance commerciale *(suite)*
Importations CAF, exportations FAB et balance: en millions de dollars É.-U.

Region, country or area	Sys.&	1995	2005	2010	2015	2016	2017	2018	Région, pays ou zone
Belgium									**Belgique**
Imports	S	...	319 085	391 256	371 025	372 713	406 412	* 450 888	Importations
Exports	S	...	335 692	407 596	397 739	398 033	429 980	* 468 529	Exportations
Balance	S	...	16 606	16 340	26 714	25 321	23 568	17 641	Balance
Belize									**Belize**
Imports	G	259	439	700	996	952	913	* 958	Importations
Exports	G	162	208	282	314	246	278	* 179	Exportations
Balance	G	-97	-231	-418	-682	-706	-636	-780	Balance
Benin									**Bénin**
Imports	S	* 745	899	2 134	2 475	2 630	3 060	* 3 132	Importations
Exports	S	* 415	288	534	626	410	726	* 287	Exportations
Balance	S	-329	-611	-1 600	-1 849	-2 220	-2 334	-2 845	Balance
Bermuda									**Bermudes**
Imports	G	633	988	970	929	971	1 078	1 070	Importations
Exports	G	63	* 49	* 15	9	8	12	23	Exportations
Balance	G	-570	-939	-955	-920	-963	-1 066	-1 047	Balance
Bhutan									**Bhoutan**
Imports	G	* 113	387	854	* 1 062	* 1 003	* 1 030	* 1 052	Importations
Exports	G	* 103	258	413	* 549	* 525	* 573	* 622	Exportations
Balance	G	-9	-129	-440	-512	-478	-457	-430	Balance
Bolivia (Plurin. State of)									**Bolivie (État plurin. de)**
Imports	G	1 396	2 343	5 604	9 766	8 427	9 302	9 994	Importations
Exports	G	1 181	2 797	6 965	8 726	7 082	7 852	8 965	Exportations
Balance	G	-215	454	1 361	-1 041	-1 345	-1 450	-1 030	Balance
Bosnia and Herzegovina									**Bosnie-Herzégovine**
Imports	S	* 1 068	7 054	9 223	8 994	9 142	10 444	* 11 529	Importations
Exports	S	* 152	2 388	4 803	5 099	5 328	6 367	* 7 124	Exportations
Balance	S	-917	-4 665	-4 420	-3 895	-3 814	-4 078	-4 405	Balance
Botswana									**Botswana**
Imports	G	...	3 162	5 657	7 626	6 103	5 284	* 6 040	Importations
Exports	G	...	4 431	4 693	6 319	7 321	5 898	* 5 803	Exportations
Balance	G	...	1 268	-964	-1 307	1 218	614	-236	Balance
Brazil									**Brésil**
Imports	G	53 734	73 600	181 768	171 446	137 552	150 749	* 185 357	Importations
Exports	G	46 505	118 529	201 915	191 127	185 235	217 739	* 236 466	Exportations
Balance	G	-7 229	44 928	20 147	19 681	47 683	66 990	51 108	Balance
British Virgin Islands									**Îles Vierges britanniques**
Imports	G	* 122	* 227	* 313	* 430	* 457	* 486	* 341	Importations
Exports	G	* 11	* ~0	* ~0	* ~0	* ~0	* ~0	* 0	Exportations
Balance	G	-110	-226	-313	-430	-457	-486	-341	Balance
Brunei Darussalam									**Brunéi Darussalam**
Imports	S	2 078	* 1 447	2 539	3 229	2 679	3 085	* 3 233	Importations
Exports	S	2 379	* 6 242	8 908	6 353	4 875	5 571	* 6 200	Exportations
Balance	S	301	4 794	6 369	3 124	2 197	2 486	2 967	Balance
Bulgaria									**Bulgarie**
Imports	S	5 469	18 162	25 360	29 265	28 958	34 264	* 37 970	Importations
Exports	S	5 220	11 739	20 608	25 779	26 688	31 588	* 33 332	Exportations
Balance	S	-249	-6 423	-4 752	-3 486	-2 270	-2 675	-4 638	Balance
Burkina Faso									**Burkina Faso**
Imports	G	484	1 161	2 048	2 980	3 343	3 717	* 4 562	Importations
Exports	G	171	332	1 288	2 177	2 520	2 790	* 2 527	Exportations
Balance	G	-313	-828	-760	-802	-823	-927	-2 035	Balance
Burundi									**Burundi**
Imports	S	270	258	404	561	625	783	* 798	Importations
Exports	S	179	114	118	114	123	149	* 140	Exportations
Balance	S	-92	-144	-286	-447	-502	-634	-658	Balance
Cabo Verde									**Cabo Verde**
Imports	G	* 252	438	731	606	672	794	* 930	Importations
Exports	G	* 9	89	220	215	60	50	* 51	Exportations
Balance	G	-243	-349	-511	-391	-612	-744	-880	Balance
Cambodia									**Cambodge**
Imports	S	* 217	2 552	4 903	10 669	12 371	* 13 155	* 17 316	Importations
Exports	S	* 76	3 019	5 590	8 542	10 069	* 13 195	* 18 682	Exportations
Balance	S	-142	467	688	-2 126	-2 302	40	1 366	Balance

20

Total imports, exports and balance of trade *(continued)*
Imports CIF, exports FOB and balance: millions of US dollars

Total des importations, des exportations et balance commerciale *(suite)*
Importations CAF, exportations FAB et balance: en millions de dollars É.-U.

Region, country or area	Sys.&	1995	2005	2010	2015	2016	2017	2018	Région, pays ou zone
Cameroon									**Cameroun**
Imports	S	1 079	2 800	5 133	6 037	4 899	5 184	* 4 453	Importations
Exports	S	1 539	2 849	3 878	4 053	2 130	3 264	* 2 651	Exportations
Balance	S	460	49	-1 255	-1 984	-2 768	-1 919	-1 802	Balance
Canada [1]									**Canada** [1]
Imports	G	164 371	314 444	392 109	419 693	402 966	432 405	* 466 895	Importations
Exports	G	191 118	360 552	386 580	408 804	389 071	420 632	* 451 085	Exportations
Balance	G	26 747	46 108	-5 529	-10 889	-13 895	-11 773	-15 811	Balance
Cayman Islands									**Îles Caïmanes**
Imports	G	* 390	* 1 191	* 828	915	* 941	* 1 051	* 1 291	Importations
Exports	G	* 4	* 52	* 13	* 99	* 88	* 33	* 13	Exportations
Balance	G	-386	-1 138	-815	-817	-853	-1 018	-1 279	Balance
Central African Republic									**République centrafricaine**
Imports	S	265	185	210	457	401	419	* 359	Importations
Exports	S	120	111	90	97	88	197	* 231	Exportations
Balance	S	-146	-75	-120	-360	-313	-222	-128	Balance
Chad									**Tchad**
Imports	S	* 214	* 953	* 2 507	* 2 200	* 1 373	* 844	* 523	Importations
Exports	S	* 243	* 3 095	* 3 410	* 2 900	* 1 990	* 1 344	* 915	Exportations
Balance	S	28	2 142	904	700	617	499	392	Balance
Chile									**Chili**
Imports	S	14 903	32 927	59 007	62 387	58 761	65 062	74 187	Importations
Exports	S	15 901	41 973	71 106	62 033	60 733	69 229	75 482	Exportations
Balance	S	998	9 046	12 099	-354	1 972	4 168	1 294	Balance
China [3]									**Chine** [3]
Imports	S	* 131 353	659 953	1 396 002	1 679 564	1 587 921	1 843 793	* 2 215 158	Importations
Exports	S	148 616	761 953	1 577 764	2 273 468	2 097 637	2 263 371	* 2 528 426	Exportations
Balance	S	17 263	102 001	181 762	593 904	509 716	419 578	313 268	Balance
China, Hong Kong SAR									**Chine, RAS de Hong Kong**
Imports	G	196 072	300 160	441 369	559 306	547 124	589 317	627 327	Importations
Exports	G	173 871	292 119	400 692	510 553	516 588	549 861	569 106	Exportations
Balance	G	-22 201	-8 042	-40 677	-48 753	-30 536	-39 456	-58 221	Balance
China, Macao SAR									**Chine, RAS de Macao**
Imports	G	2 025	4 514	5 629	10 603	8 924	* 9 449	* 11 394	Importations
Exports	G	2 025	2 474	870	1 339	1 257	* 1 406	* 1 255	Exportations
Balance	G	-1	-2 040	-4 760	-9 264	-7 668	-8 043	-10 139	Balance
Colombia									**Colombie**
Imports	G	13 883	21 204	40 683	54 036	44 831	46 050	* 47 063	Importations
Exports	G	10 201	21 190	39 820	35 691	31 045	37 766	* 46 892	Exportations
Balance	G	-3 682	-14	-863	-18 345	-13 786	-8 284	-171	Balance
Comoros									**Comores**
Imports	S	62	85	181	* 227	* 193	* 167	* 150	Importations
Exports	S	11	4	14	* 22	* 20	* 18	* 17	Exportations
Balance	S	-51	-81	-167	-205	-173	-149	-133	Balance
Congo									**Congo**
Imports	S	556	* 1 342	4 369	* 4 183	* 3 602	4 553	* 2 117	Importations
Exports	S	1 090	* 4 744	6 918	* 3 536	* 2 540	8 148	* 4 451	Exportations
Balance	S	534	3 402	2 548	-647	-1 062	3 595	2 334	Balance
Cook Islands									**Îles Cook**
Imports	G	* 49	81	91	* 109	* 107	* 130	* 137	Importations
Exports	G	* 5	5	5	* 14	* 13	* 21	* 15	Exportations
Balance	G	-44	-76	-85	-95	-93	-109	-122	Balance
Costa Rica									**Costa Rica**
Imports	S	3 205	9 173	13 920	15 504	15 322	16 352	* 17 144	Importations
Exports	S	2 702	7 151	9 045	9 578	9 908	11 297	* 11 915	Exportations
Balance	S	-504	-2 023	-4 875	-5 926	-5 414	-5 056	-5 230	Balance
Côte d'Ivoire									**Côte d'Ivoire**
Imports	S	2 472	5 865	7 849	9 532	8 404	9 605	* 10 999	Importations
Exports	S	* 3 736	7 248	10 284	11 845	10 605	12 560	* 11 923	Exportations
Balance	S	1 264	1 383	2 434	2 313	2 201	2 955	925	Balance
Croatia									**Croatie**
Imports	G	7 509	18 560	20 067	20 580	21 830	24 513	* 30 812	Importations
Exports	G	4 633	8 773	11 811	12 844	13 648	15 732	* 17 720	Exportations
Balance	G	-2 877	-9 788	-8 256	-7 737	-8 182	-8 780	-13 092	Balance

Total imports, exports and balance of trade *(continued)*
Imports CIF, exports FOB and balance: millions of US dollars

Total des importations, des exportations et balance commerciale *(suite)*
Importations CAF, exportations FAB et balance: en millions de dollars É.-U.

Region, country or area	Sys.&	1995	2005	2010	2015	2016	2017	2018	Région, pays ou zone
Cuba									**Cuba**
Imports	S	* 2 874	8 084	* 11 488	* 12 637	* 11 085	* 9 734	* 8 543	Importations
Exports	S	* 1 491	2 319	* 4 914	* 3 618	* 2 502	* 1 731	* 1 197	Exportations
Balance	S	-1 384	-5 766	-6 574	-9 019	-8 582	-8 004	-7 346	Balance
Cyprus									**Chypre**
Imports	G	3 694	6 382	8 645	5 699	6 604	9 308	* 10 740	Importations
Exports	G	1 231	1 546	1 506	1 935	1 920	3 360	* 5 065	Exportations
Balance	G	-2 463	-4 836	-7 138	-3 764	-4 684	-5 948	-5 675	Balance
Czechia									**Tchéquie**
Imports	S	25 303	76 527	125 691	140 716	142 328	162 899	15 670	Importations
Exports	S	21 686	78 209	132 141	157 194	162 087	182 231	17 169	Exportations
Balance	S	-3 618	1 681	6 450	16 478	19 760	19 332	1 499	Balance
Dem. People's Rep. Korea									**Rép. pop. dém. de Corée**
Imports	G	* 3 122	* 1 466	* 1 957	* 2 604	* 2 758	* 2 920	* 3 092	Importations
Exports	G	* 1 739	* 787	* 882	* 987	* 1 010	* 1 033	* 1 056	Exportations
Balance	G	-1 382	-679	-1 075	-1 617	-1 748	-1 887	-2 036	Balance
Dem. Rep. of the Congo									**Rép. dém. du Congo**
Imports	S	* 869	* 2 268	* 4 500	* 6 197	* 5 907	* 5 655	* 5 401	Importations
Exports	S	* 1 562	* 2 190	* 5 300	* 5 800	* 5 114	* 4 491	* 3 951	Exportations
Balance	S	693	-78	800	-397	-793	-1 165	-1 450	Balance
Denmark									**Danemark**
Imports	S	43 142	72 716	82 724	85 327	84 428	92 121	101 114	Importations
Exports	S	48 789	82 278	96 217	94 619	94 729	* 101 443	107 633	Exportations
Balance	S	5 648	9 562	13 492	9 291	10 301	9 322	6 520	Balance
Djibouti									**Djibouti**
Imports	G	* 176	* 277	* 603	* 890	* 987	* 1 094	* 1 212	Importations
Exports	G	* 13	* 39	* 470	* 132	* 134	* 137	* 140	Exportations
Balance	G	-163	-238	-133	-758	-852	-956	-1 072	Balance
Dominica									**Dominique**
Imports	S	117	165	225	* 214	* 214	* 198	* 275	Importations
Exports	S	45	42	34	* 30	* 23	* 21	* 18	Exportations
Balance	S	-72	-124	-190	-184	-191	-177	-257	Balance
Dominican Republic [1,4]									**République dominicaine** [1,4]
Imports	G	* 3 155	6 804	15 138	17 348	17 789	19 524	* 22 481	Importations
Exports	G	* 872	6 183	4 767	8 384	8 745	8 856	* 9 178	Exportations
Balance	G	-2 283	-621	-10 371	-8 964	-9 044	-10 669	-13 303	Balance
Ecuador									**Équateur**
Imports	G	4 195	9 609	20 591	21 387	16 189	19 845	23 020	Importations
Exports	G	4 361	9 869	17 490	18 331	16 798	19 122	21 606	Exportations
Balance	G	166	261	-3 101	-3 057	609	-722	-1 414	Balance
Egypt									**Égypte**
Imports	G	11 739	19 812	53 003	74 361	58 053	66 339	* 84 010	Importations
Exports	G	3 444	10 646	26 332	21 967	22 507	25 943	* 29 564	Exportations
Balance	G	-8 295	-9 166	-26 672	-52 394	-35 545	-40 396	-54 446	Balance
El Salvador									**El Salvador**
Imports	S	2 628	6 809	8 416	10 293	9 829	10 593	* 11 350	Importations
Exports	S	985	3 436	4 499	5 509	5 420	5 760	* 6 275	Exportations
Balance	S	-1 642	-3 373	-3 917	-4 784	-4 410	-4 833	-5 075	Balance
Equatorial Guinea									**Guinée équatoriale**
Imports	G	* 50	* 1 309	* 5 679	* 6 010	* 5 457	* 4 887	* 4 402	Importations
Exports	G	* 86	* 7 062	* 9 964	* 9 570	* 7 753	* 6 196	* 4 980	Exportations
Balance	G	36	5 753	4 285	3 560	2 297	1 309	578	Balance
Eritrea									**Érythrée**
Imports	G	* 432	* 503	* 1 187	* 2 800	* 3 326	* 3 949	* 4 688	Importations
Exports	G	* 73	* 11	* 13	* 15	* 16	* 16	* 17	Exportations
Balance	G	-359	-493	-1 175	-2 785	-3 310	-3 932	-4 671	Balance
Estonia									**Estonie**
Imports	S	2 546	11 018	13 197	15 732	15 682	17 358	19 826	Importations
Exports	S	1 840	8 247	12 811	13 908	13 967	15 384	17 830	Exportations
Balance	S	-706	-2 770	-385	-1 824	-1 715	-1 974	-1 996	Balance
Eswatini									**Eswatini**
Imports	G	...	1 656	* 1 710	1 464	1 299	1 608	* 1 299	Importations
Exports	G	...	1 278	* 1 557	1 747	1 572	1 802	* 1 849	Exportations
Balance	G	...	-378	-153	282	273	193	550	Balance

20

Total imports, exports and balance of trade *(continued)*
Imports CIF, exports FOB and balance: millions of US dollars

Total des importations, des exportations et balance commerciale *(suite)*
Importations CAF, exportations FAB et balance: en millions de dollars É.-U.

Region, country or area	Sys.&	1995	2005	2010	2015	2016	2017	2018	Région, pays ou zone
Ethiopia									**Éthiopie**
Imports	G	1 141	4 095	8 602	25 815	19 121	* 15 739	* 9 116	Importations
Exports	G	422	926	2 330	5 028	1 724	* 1 350	* 1 394	Exportations
Balance	G	-719	-3 169	-6 272	-20 788	-17 397	-14 389	-7 722	Balance
Falkland Islands (Malvinas)									**Îles Falkland (Malvinas)**
Imports	G	* 27	* 8	* 50	* 21	* 17	* 13	* 10	Importations
Exports	G	* 4	* 11	* 9	* 4	* 4	* 3	* 2	Exportations
Balance	G	-23	2	-41	-17	-13	-10	-8	Balance
Faroe Islands									**Îles Féroé**
Imports	G	* 314	747	* 780	* 911	* 978	* 1 066	* 1 161	Importations
Exports	G	* 362	602	* 839	* 1 024	* 1 192	* 1 405	* 1 655	Exportations
Balance	G	48	-145	59	113	214	338	494	Balance
Fiji									**Fidji**
Imports	G	* 891	1 607	1 808	2 081	2 316	2 420	2 720	Importations
Exports	G	* 619	702	841	895	926	956	1 041	Exportations
Balance	G	-273	-906	-967	-1 186	-1 391	-1 464	-1 679	Balance
Finland									**Finlande**
Imports	G	29 520	58 473	68 767	60 174	60 502	70 100	78 352	Importations
Exports	G	40 409	65 238	70 117	59 682	57 326	67 281	75 258	Exportations
Balance	G	10 889	6 766	1 349	-492	-3 176	-2 820	-3 094	Balance
France									**France**
Imports	S	273 387	475 857	599 172	563 398	560 555	613 133	* 660 511	Importations
Exports	S	277 079	434 354	511 651	493 941	488 885	523 385	* 568 451	Exportations
Balance	S	3 692	-41 503	-87 520	-69 457	-71 670	-89 748	-92 059	Balance
French Guiana [5]									**Guyane française** [5]
Imports	S	783	...	...	...	...	...	...	Importations
Exports	S	158	...	...	...	...	...	...	Exportations
Balance	S	-625	...	...	...	...	...	...	Balance
French Polynesia									**Polynésie française**
Imports	S	* 848	1 702	1 726	1 527	* 1 491	* 1 638	* 2 023	Importations
Exports	S	* 173	210	153	130	* 173	* 153	* 156	Exportations
Balance	S	-675	-1 491	-1 573	-1 397	-1 319	-1 485	-1 868	Balance
Gabon									**Gabon**
Imports	S	* 884	1 451	* 2 969	* 3 033	* 2 931	* 2 805	* 2 693	Importations
Exports	S	* 2 718	5 068	* 8 539	* 5 074	* 2 854	* 1 584	* 884	Exportations
Balance	S	1 834	3 617	5 570	2 041	-77	-1 220	-1 809	Balance
Gambia									**Gambie**
Imports	G	215	260	284	402	384	549	* 531	Importations
Exports	G	19	7	68	90	94	22	* 27	Exportations
Balance	G	-196	-252	-215	-312	-290	-527	-504	Balance
Georgia									**Géorgie**
Imports	G	396	2 490	5 236	7 730	7 236	7 939	9 122	Importations
Exports	G	152	865	1 677	2 205	2 114	2 735	3 362	Exportations
Balance	G	-245	-1 624	-3 558	-5 525	-5 122	-5 204	-5 760	Balance
Germany									**Allemagne**
Imports	S	464 145	779 819	1 066 817	1 057 616	1 060 672	1 167 753	* 1 250 895	Importations
Exports	S	518 224	977 132	1 271 096	1 328 549	1 340 752	1 446 642	* 1 479 187	Exportations
Balance	S	54 079	197 313	204 280	270 933	280 080	278 889	228 292	Balance
Ghana									**Ghana**
Imports	G	* 1 897	4 878	8 057	* 12 450	11 361	12 718	11 880	Importations
Exports	G	* 1 755	3 060	5 233	* 12 132	10 656	14 359	17 100	Exportations
Balance	G	-142	-1 819	-2 824	-318	-705	1 640	5 219	Balance
Gibraltar									**Gibraltar**
Imports		* 408	* 501	* 627	* 776	* 861	* 955	* 528	Importations
Exports		* 114	* 195	* 259	* 295	* 327	* 362	* 400	Exportations
Balance		-294	-306	-368	-481	-535	-593	-128	Balance
Greece									**Grèce**
Imports	S	25 805	54 894	66 453	47 264	47 595	55 301	65 090	Importations
Exports	S	* 10 896	17 434	27 586	28 289	27 811	32 155	39 450	Exportations
Balance	S	-14 909	-37 459	-38 867	-18 975	-19 784	-23 146	-25 640	Balance
Greenland									**Groenland**
Imports	G	421	700	854	586	623	* 743	* 778	Importations
Exports	G	364	402	391	395	553	* 549	* 669	Exportations
Balance	G	-57	-297	-463	-191	-71	-194	-110	Balance

20

Total imports, exports and balance of trade *(continued)*
Imports CIF, exports FOB and balance: millions of US dollars

Total des importations, des exportations et balance commerciale *(suite)*
Importations CAF, exportations FAB et balance: en millions de dollars É.-U.

Region, country or area	Sys.&	1995	2005	2010	2015	2016	2017	2018	Région, pays ou zone
Grenada									**Grenade**
Imports	S	129	334	* 306	* 372	* 350	* 420	* 504	Importations
Exports	S	22	28	* 25	* 33	* 30	* 25	* 27	Exportations
Balance	S	-107	-306	-281	-339	-321	-395	-478	Balance
Guadeloupe 5									**Guadeloupe 5**
Imports	S	1 901	...	...	...	...	...	...	Importations
Exports	S	162	...	...	...	...	...	...	Exportations
Balance	S	-1 739	...	...	...	...	...	...	Balance
Guatemala									**Guatemala**
Imports	S	3 292	10 500	13 830	17 637	16 979	18 378	* 19 776	Importations
Exports	S	1 936	5 381	8 460	10 677	10 591	11 011	* 10 731	Exportations
Balance	S	-1 357	-5 119	-5 370	-6 960	-6 387	-7 367	-9 045	Balance
Guinea									**Guinée**
Imports	S	819	1 648	* 1 405	2 139	* 2 122	* 2 065	* 2 049	Importations
Exports	S	702	796	* 1 471	1 574	* 1 743	* 1 942	* 2 152	Exportations
Balance	S	-117	-852	66	-565	-378	-123	103	Balance
Guinea-Bissau									**Guinée-Bissau**
Imports	G	* 134	112	* 197	* 221	* 212	* 204	* 196	Importations
Exports	G	* 45	23	* 120	* 548	* 885	* 1 430	* 2 310	Exportations
Balance	G	-89	-88	-77	327	673	1 226	2 114	Balance
Guyana									**Guyana**
Imports	S	* 472	778	1 452	2 186	1 625	1 762	3 998	Importations
Exports	S	* 455	539	901	1 286	1 453	1 790	1 487	Exportations
Balance	S	-17	-239	-551	-900	-172	28	-2 511	Balance
Haiti									**Haïti**
Imports	G	650	* 1 449	* 3 147	* 3 523	* 3 405	* 3 463	* 3 601	Importations
Exports	G	35	* 470	* 579	* 1 018	* 982	* 939	* 917	Exportations
Balance	G	-615	-979	-2 568	-2 505	-2 423	-2 524	-2 683	Balance
Honduras									**Honduras**
Imports	S	1 728	4 419	6 895	8 381	7 912	8 612	* 9 562	Importations
Exports	S	656	1 294	3 104	4 201	4 085	4 970	* 4 750	Exportations
Balance	S	-1 072	-3 125	-3 791	-4 179	-3 827	-3 642	-4 812	Balance
Hungary									**Hongrie**
Imports	S	15 186	65 920	87 432	90 761	92 044	104 284	* 115 807	Importations
Exports	S	12 452	62 272	94 749	100 297	103 071	113 382	* 122 450	Exportations
Balance	S	-2 734	-3 648	7 317	9 536	11 027	9 098	6 643	Balance
Iceland									**Islande**
Imports	G	1 751	4 979	3 914	5 285	5 703	6 971	7 865	Importations
Exports	G	1 803	3 091	4 603	4 722	4 450	4 883	5 718	Exportations
Balance	G	51	-1 888	689	-563	-1 254	-2 088	-2 147	Balance
India									**Inde**
Imports	G	36 592	140 862	350 029	390 745	356 705	444 052	* 519 677	Importations
Exports	G	31 699	100 353	220 408	264 381	260 327	294 364	* 321 093	Exportations
Balance	G	-4 893	-40 509	-129 621	-126 364	-96 378	-149 688	-198 584	Balance
Indonesia									**Indonésie**
Imports	S	40 629	57 701	135 663	142 695	135 653	156 925	188 711	Importations
Exports	S	45 418	85 660	157 779	150 366	144 490	168 810	180 215	Exportations
Balance	S	4 789	27 959	22 116	7 671	8 837	11 885	-8 496	Balance
Iran (Islamic Republic of) 6,7									**Iran (Rép. islamique d') 6,7**
Imports	S	* 13 882	* 38 869	54 697	* 41 453	42 702	51 612	* 43 014	Importations
Exports	S	* 18 360	60 012	83 785	* 64 084	83 148	105 844	* 76 724	Exportations
Balance	S	4 478	21 143	29 088	22 631	40 446	54 232	33 710	Balance
Iraq									**Iraq**
Imports	S	* 445	* 12 861	31 764	32 667	45 831	* 40 370	* 35 481	Importations
Exports	S	* 555	19 773	52 483	49 403	43 774	* 24 266	* 8 402	Exportations
Balance	S	110	6 912	20 718	16 736	-2 056	-16 104	-27 079	Balance
Ireland									**Irlande**
Imports	G	32 321	70 284	64 601	77 795	82 029	88 828	106 931	Importations
Exports	G	43 789	110 003	120 645	124 731	132 010	138 072	167 018	Exportations
Balance	G	11 468	39 719	56 045	46 935	49 981	49 244	60 087	Balance
Israel 8									**Israël 8**
Imports	S	* 28 328	45 032	59 194	62 068	65 803	69 116	76 584	Importations
Exports	S	* 19 046	42 771	58 413	64 062	60 571	61 150	61 906	Exportations
Balance	S	-9 282	-2 262	-781	1 994	-5 232	-7 966	-14 678	Balance

20

Total imports, exports and balance of trade *(continued)*
Imports CIF, exports FOB and balance: millions of US dollars

Total des importations, des exportations et balance commerciale *(suite)*
Importations CAF, exportations FAB et balance: en millions de dollars É.-U.

Region, country or area	Sys.&	1995	2005	2010	2015	2016	2017	2018	Région, pays ou zone
Italy									**Italie**
Imports	S	200 320	384 836	486 984	410 933	404 578	451 416	* 488 740	Importations
Exports	S	230 441	372 957	446 840	456 989	461 529	503 054	* 529 067	Exportations
Balance	S	30 122	-11 878	-40 145	46 055	56 951	51 638	40 327	Balance
Jamaica									**Jamaïque**
Imports	G	2 773	4 885	5 225	4 993	4 767	5 818	* 7 067	Importations
Exports	G	1 424	1 514	1 328	1 263	1 202	1 310	* 1 456	Exportations
Balance	G	-1 349	-3 370	-3 898	-3 730	-3 565	-4 508	-5 611	Balance
Japan									**Japon**
Imports	G	336 094	515 866	694 059	625 568	606 924	671 474	* 759 925	Importations
Exports	G	442 937	594 941	769 774	624 874	644 932	698 097	* 739 755	Exportations
Balance	G	106 843	79 074	75 715	-695	38 008	26 623	-20 170	Balance
Jordan									**Jordanie**
Imports	G	3 696	10 455	15 262	20 475	19 207	20 407	* 20 797	Importations
Exports	G	1 769	4 284	7 023	7 833	7 509	7 469	* 7 754	Exportations
Balance	G	-1 928	-6 170	-8 239	-12 642	-11 698	-12 938	-13 043	Balance
Kazakhstan									**Kazakhstan**
Imports	G	3 805	17 333	24 024	30 567	25 175	29 346	* 33 885	Importations
Exports	G	5 227	27 846	57 244	45 954	36 775	48 342	* 61 439	Exportations
Balance	G	1 422	10 513	33 220	15 387	11 601	18 996	27 554	Balance
Kenya									**Kenya**
Imports	G	2 818	5 846	12 093	* 16 097	* 14 107	16 690	* 19 191	Importations
Exports	G	1 826	3 420	5 169	* 5 908	* 5 695	5 747	* 6 241	Exportations
Balance	G	-992	-2 426	-6 924	-10 189	-8 412	-10 943	-12 950	Balance
Kiribati									**Kiribati**
Imports	G	34	74	73	111	117	* 183	* 356	Importations
Exports	G	7	4	4	10	11	* 11	* 10	Exportations
Balance	G	-27	-70	-69	-101	-107	-172	-347	Balance
Kuwait									**Koweït**
Imports	S	7 790	* 15 801	22 691	31 907	30 820	33 590	* 37 593	Importations
Exports	S	12 944	* 44 869	62 698	55 162	46 242	54 807	* 62 041	Exportations
Balance	S	5 155	29 068	40 007	23 254	15 422	21 217	24 448	Balance
Kyrgyzstan									**Kirghizistan**
Imports	S	522	1 108	3 223	4 068	3 844	4 487	4 830	Importations
Exports	S	412	672	1 488	1 441	1 423	1 757	1 690	Exportations
Balance	S	-110	-436	-1 734	-2 627	-2 421	-2 730	-3 139	Balance
Lao People's Dem. Rep.									**Rép. dém. populaire lao**
Imports	S	* 588	* 874	1 837	3 778	4 107	* 4 804	* 6 177	Importations
Exports	S	* 311	* 552	1 909	2 985	3 124	* 2 759	* 1 611	Exportations
Balance	S	-277	-322	72	-793	-983	-2 045	-4 566	Balance
Latvia									**Lettonie**
Imports	S	1 818	8 770	11 143	13 854	13 593	15 897	18 310	Importations
Exports	S	1 305	5 303	8 851	11 493	11 470	13 030	14 632	Exportations
Balance	S	-513	-3 468	-2 292	-2 361	-2 123	-2 867	-3 679	Balance
Lebanon									**Liban**
Imports	G	* 7 295	9 327	17 970	18 600	18 703	140 412	* 129 793	Importations
Exports	G	* 826	1 879	4 254	2 953	2 977	8 739	* 9 336	Exportations
Balance	G	-6 469	-7 448	-13 716	-15 646	-15 726	-131 673	-120 457	Balance
Lesotho									**Lesotho**
Imports	G	...	* 1 410	1 277	1 410	* 1 248	2 066	* 1 870	Importations
Exports	G	...	* 650	503	604	* 506	673	* 577	Exportations
Balance	G	...	-760	-773	-806	-742	-1 392	-1 293	Balance
Liberia									**Libéria**
Imports	S	* 358	* 309	* 710	* 899	* 768	* 661	* 292	Importations
Exports	S	* 452	* 130	* 222	* 627	* 649	* 697	* 519	Exportations
Balance	S	94	-179	-488	-272	-120	36	227	Balance
Libya									**Libye**
Imports	G	* 4 912	* 6 058	17 674	* 12 999	* 8 789	* 5 743	* 3 786	Importations
Exports	G	* 9 363	* 31 272	36 440	* 10 200	* 4 902	* 2 273	* 1 064	Exportations
Balance	G	4 451	25 215	18 766	-2 799	-3 887	-3 470	-2 722	Balance
Lithuania									**Lituanie**
Imports	G	3 649	15 704	23 378	28 176	27 349	30 979	36 514	Importations
Exports	G	2 706	12 070	20 814	25 411	25 023	29 350	33 405	Exportations
Balance	G	-943	-3 634	-2 564	-2 765	-2 326	-1 629	-3 109	Balance

Total imports, exports and balance of trade *(continued)*
Imports CIF, exports FOB and balance: millions of US dollars

Total des importations, des exportations et balance commerciale *(suite)*
Importations CAF, exportations FAB et balance: en millions de dollars É.-U.

Region, country or area	Sys.&	1995	2005	2010	2015	2016	2017	2018	Région, pays ou zone
Luxembourg									**Luxembourg**
Imports	S	...	17 586	20 400	19 296	19 124	21 071	* 23 583	Importations
Exports	S	...	12 715	13 911	12 626	12 838	13 959	* 15 776	Exportations
Balance	S	...	-4 871	-6 489	-6 671	-6 285	-7 112	-7 807	Balance
Madagascar									**Madagascar**
Imports	S	550	1 686	2 546	2 961	2 972	3 654	* 3 427	Importations
Exports	S	360	836	1 082	2 164	2 261	2 847	* 2 885	Exportations
Balance	S	-190	-850	-1 464	-796	-710	-807	-542	Balance
Malawi									**Malawi**
Imports	G	500	1 165	2 173	2 312	2 210	2 547	* 1 549	Importations
Exports	G	433	495	1 066	1 080	1 022	884	* 836	Exportations
Balance	G	-67	-670	-1 107	-1 232	-1 188	-1 663	-712	Balance
Malaysia									**Malaisie**
Imports	G	77 046	114 290	164 586	176 175	168 375	193 856	* 218 764	Importations
Exports	G	73 778	141 624	198 791	200 211	189 414	216 428	* 246 670	Exportations
Balance	G	-3 267	27 334	34 204	24 036	21 039	22 572	27 906	Balance
Maldives									**Maldives**
Imports	G	268	745	1 095	1 897	2 128	2 360	* 2 790	Importations
Exports	G	50	154	74	144	140	199	* 174	Exportations
Balance	G	-218	-591	-1 021	-1 753	-1 988	-2 160	-2 616	Balance
Mali									**Mali**
Imports	S	* 774	1 544	4 704	* 3 169	3 845	4 337	* 5 622	Importations
Exports	S	* 443	1 075	1 996	* 2 530	2 848	1 903	* 1 269	Exportations
Balance	S	-331	-468	-2 707	-639	-998	-2 434	-4 353	Balance
Malta									**Malte**
Imports	G	2 942	3 865	5 732	6 788	7 182	* 6 868	* 7 219	Importations
Exports	G	1 913	2 431	3 717	3 915	4 039	* 3 784	* 3 863	Exportations
Balance	G	-1 029	-1 435	-2 015	-2 873	-3 143	-3 084	-3 357	Balance
Marshall Islands									**Îles Marshall**
Imports	G	* 75	* 68	* 76	* 84	* 86	* 88	* 57	Importations
Exports	G	* 23	* 11	* 17	* 25	* 28	* 25	* 16	Exportations
Balance	G	-52	-57	-60	-59	-59	-62	-41	Balance
Martinique [5]									**Martinique** [5]
Imports	S	1 970	...	...	...	...	...	...	Importations
Exports	S	242	...	...	...	...	...	...	Exportations
Balance	S	-1 728	...	...	...	...	...	...	Balance
Mauritania									**Mauritanie**
Imports	S	* 326	1 342	1 708	* 3 677	2 174	3 522	* 3 414	Importations
Exports	S	* 550	556	1 819	* 1 522	1 623	1 989	* 2 134	Exportations
Balance	S	225	-786	111	-2 156	-551	-1 533	-1 280	Balance
Mauritius									**Maurice**
Imports	G	2 000	3 160	4 402	4 458	4 655	5 269	* 6 280	Importations
Exports	G	1 538	2 144	1 850	2 481	2 194	2 103	* 2 156	Exportations
Balance	G	-462	-1 016	-2 553	-1 977	-2 461	-3 167	-4 124	Balance
Mayotte									**Mayotte**
Imports	G	...	309	...	...	...	...	...	Importations
Exports	G	...	6	...	...	...	...	...	Exportations
Balance	G	...	-303	...	...	...	...	...	Balance
Mexico [1,9]									**Mexique** [1,9]
Imports	G	72 453	221 819	301 482	395 232	387 064	420 369	464 268	Importations
Exports	G	79 541	214 207	298 305	380 527	373 900	409 451	450 532	Exportations
Balance	G	7 088	-7 612	-3 177	-14 705	-13 164	-10 918	-13 737	Balance
Micronesia (Fed. States of)									**Micronésie (États féd. de)**
Imports	S	* 100	128	168	* 67	* 40	* 23	* 14	Importations
Exports	S	* 43	13	23	* 11	* 6	* 3	* 2	Exportations
Balance	S	-56	-115	-145	-56	-34	-20	-12	Balance
Mongolia									**Mongolie**
Imports	G	* 415	1 183	* 3 200	3 797	3 340	4 337	* 6 317	Importations
Exports	G	* 473	1 064	* 2 908	4 669	4 916	6 201	* 7 071	Exportations
Balance	G	58	-118	-291	873	1 577	1 863	754	Balance
Montenegro									**Monténégro**
Imports	S	...	...	2 182	2 050	2 263	2 611	* 3 069	Importations
Exports	S	...	...	437	353	354	421	* 447	Exportations
Balance	S	...	...	-1 745	-1 697	-1 908	-2 190	-2 622	Balance

Total imports, exports and balance of trade *(continued)*
Imports CIF, exports FOB and balance: millions of US dollars

Total des importations, des exportations et balance commerciale *(suite)*
Importations CAF, exportations FAB et balance: en millions de dollars É.-U.

Region, country or area	Sys.&	1995	2005	2010	2015	2016	2017	2018	Région, pays ou zone
Montserrat									**Montserrat**
Imports	S	* 51	30	* 29	* 39	* 36	* 31	* 33	Importations
Exports	S	* 2	1	1	* 3	* 4	* 6	* 5	Exportations
Balance	S	-49	-28	-28	-36	-32	-25	-28	Balance
Morocco									**Maroc**
Imports	S	8 540	20 803	35 379	37 546	41 696	45 039	* 38 058	Importations
Exports	S	4 719	11 185	17 765	22 037	22 858	25 624	* 24 446	Exportations
Balance	S	-3 822	-9 618	-17 614	-15 509	-18 838	-19 415	-13 612	Balance
Mozambique									**Mozambique**
Imports	S	727	2 408	3 564	7 908	5 295	5 702	6 786	Importations
Exports	S	174	1 745	2 243	3 196	3 352	4 719	5 196	Exportations
Balance	S	-553	-663	-1 321	-4 712	-1 943	-983	-1 590	Balance
Myanmar									**Myanmar**
Imports	G	* 1 346	* 1 907	4 164	16 907	15 696	19 253	* 23 335	Importations
Exports	G	* 860	* 3 776	7 625	12 197	11 673	13 879	* 16 581	Exportations
Balance	G	-487	1 869	3 461	-4 710	-4 023	-5 375	-6 754	Balance
Namibia									**Namibie**
Imports	G	...	2 525	5 980	7 697	6 721	6 778	* 6 845	Importations
Exports	G	...	2 726	5 848	4 628	4 816	5 229	* 5 517	Exportations
Balance	G	...	201	-131	-3 069	-1 905	-1 549	-1 328	Balance
Nepal									**Népal**
Imports	G	* 1 330	* 2 282	5 116	6 612	8 879	10 038	* 9 502	Importations
Exports	G	* 345	* 863	874	660	729	741	* 684	Exportations
Balance	G	-985	-1 419	-4 242	-5 952	-8 150	-9 297	-8 818	Balance
Netherlands									**Pays-Bas**
Imports	S	157 929	310 591	439 987	393 728	398 336	450 076	* 522 846	Importations
Exports	S	177 626	349 813	492 646	437 329	444 867	505 941	* 576 573	Exportations
Balance	S	19 697	39 222	52 659	43 601	46 531	55 866	53 728	Balance
Netherlands Antilles [former]									**Antilles néerlandaises [anc.]**
Imports	S	* 1 830	894	* 1 254	...	...	...	...	Importations
Exports	S	* 1 354	91	* 109	...	...	...	...	Exportations
Balance	S	-476	-803	-1 145	...	...	...	...	Balance
New Caledonia									**Nouvelle-Calédonie**
Imports	S	* 840	1 774	3 303	2 529	* 2 257	* 2 515	* 2 733	Importations
Exports	S	* 570	1 114	1 268	1 239	* 1 267	* 1 460	* 2 057	Exportations
Balance	S	-270	-660	-2 036	-1 291	-989	-1 055	-676	Balance
New Zealand									**Nouvelle-Zélande**
Imports	G	13 958	26 232	30 158	36 528	36 213	40 128	43 685	Importations
Exports	G	13 745	21 729	30 932	34 357	33 870	38 050	39 797	Exportations
Balance	G	-212	-4 504	774	-2 171	-2 343	-2 078	-3 888	Balance
Nicaragua									**Nicaragua**
Imports	G	1 009	2 536	4 191	5 866	7 476	7 704	* 8 831	Importations
Exports	G	509	866	1 848	4 667	4 592	4 926	* 3 927	Exportations
Balance	G	-500	-1 670	-2 343	-1 199	-2 884	-2 778	-4 903	Balance
Niger									**Niger**
Imports	S	345	736	2 273	2 458	1 861	* 1 617	* 1 314	Importations
Exports	S	273	486	479	790	927	* 639	* 342	Exportations
Balance	S	-71	-250	-1 794	-1 669	-933	-978	-972	Balance
Nigeria									**Nigéria**
Imports	G	* 8 221	* 21 314	44 235	* 34 912	35 194	31 270	* 32 071	Importations
Exports	G	* 12 342	* 55 145	86 568	* 50 108	32 883	44 466	* 67 934	Exportations
Balance	G	4 121	33 831	42 333	15 196	-2 311	13 196	35 863	Balance
North Macedonia									**Macédoine du Nord**
Imports	S	1 719	3 228	5 474	6 400	6 757	7 719	9 052	Importations
Exports	S	1 204	2 041	3 351	4 490	4 785	5 670	6 906	Exportations
Balance	S	-515	-1 187	-2 123	-1 910	-1 972	-2 049	-2 145	Balance
Northern Mariana Islands									**Îles Mariannes du Nord**
Imports	G	* 628	* 1 952	* 2 867	* 4 215	* 4 553	* 4 917	* 4 930	Importations
Exports	G	* 941	* 1 254	* 1 453	* 1 685	* 1 735	* 1 787	* 1 839	Exportations
Balance	G	313	-699	-1 414	-2 530	-2 818	-3 130	-3 091	Balance
Norway									**Norvège**
Imports	G	32 706	55 488	77 330	77 193	72 810	85 526	* 90 413	Importations
Exports	G	41 740	103 759	130 657	104 800	89 628	101 976	* 121 917	Exportations
Balance	G	9 034	48 271	53 327	27 607	16 819	16 450	31 503	Balance

20

Total imports, exports and balance of trade *(continued)*
Imports CIF, exports FOB and balance: millions of US dollars

Total des importations, des exportations et balance commerciale *(suite)*
Importations CAF, exportations FAB et balance: en millions de dollars É.-U.

Region, country or area	Sys.&	1995	2005	2010	2015	2016	2017	2018	Région, pays ou zone
Oman									**Oman**
Imports	G	4 249	8 970	19 775	29 007	23 260	26 435	* 25 154	Importations
Exports	G	5 917	18 692	36 600	31 927	24 455	32 904	* 43 938	Exportations
Balance	G	1 669	9 722	16 825	2 919	1 195	6 469	18 784	Balance
Other non-specified areas									**Autres zones non-spécifiées**
Imports		103 506	181 592	251 315	228 508	230 930	* 259 906	* 286 613	Importations
Exports		111 343	189 393	273 706	280 019	280 479	* 317 579	* 336 021	Exportations
Balance		7 838	7 801	22 391	51 511	49 549	* 57 673	49 408	Balance
Pakistan									**Pakistan**
Imports	G	11 704	25 097	37 537	43 990	46 998	57 440	60 163	Importations
Exports	G	8 158	16 050	21 413	22 089	20 534	21 878	23 631	Exportations
Balance	G	-3 546	-9 046	-16 124	-21 901	-26 464	-35 562	-36 532	Balance
Palau									**Palaos**
Imports	S	* 60	* 156	107	150	154	158	* 158	Importations
Exports	S	* 14	* 14	* 12	6	7	6	* 2	Exportations
Balance	S	-47	-143	-96	-144	-147	-151	-156	Balance
Panama									**Panama**
Imports	S	2 511	4 152	16 737	10 375	9 238	* 9 992	* 13 798	Importations
Exports	S	577	963	10 987	11 348	11 195	* 11 624	* 710	Exportations
Balance	S	-1 933	-3 189	-5 751	973	1 957	1 632	-13 088	Balance
Papua New Guinea									**Papouasie-Nvl-Guinée**
Imports	G	* 1 451	* 1 728	* 3 950	* 2 537	* 2 101	* 2 598	* 2 893	Importations
Exports	G	* 2 653	* 3 276	* 5 742	* 8 425	* 8 176	* 9 798	* 10 906	Exportations
Balance	G	1 202	1 548	1 792	5 888	6 074	7 200	8 013	Balance
Paraguay									**Paraguay**
Imports	S	3 136	3 274	10 033	10 291	9 753	11 873	13 334	Importations
Exports	S	919	3 153	6 517	8 328	8 502	8 680	9 045	Exportations
Balance	S	-2 217	-121	-3 517	-1 964	-1 251	-3 194	-4 289	Balance
Peru [1]									**Pérou** [1]
Imports	S	7 584	12 502	29 966	38 026	36 148	39 764	* 45 297	Importations
Exports	S	5 440	17 114	35 807	33 667	36 310	44 238	* 51 004	Exportations
Balance	S	-2 144	4 612	5 842	-4 359	162	4 474	5 707	Balance
Philippines									**Philippines**
Imports	G	28 487	49 487	58 468	70 153	85 909	101 889	115 038	Importations
Exports	G	17 447	41 255	51 498	58 648	56 313	68 713	67 488	Exportations
Balance	G	-11 040	-8 233	-6 970	-11 505	-29 596	-33 177	-47 550	Balance
Poland									**Pologne**
Imports	S	29 019	101 539	174 128	189 696	188 518	217 979	* 250 313	Importations
Exports	S	22 862	89 378	157 065	194 461	196 455	221 308	* 247 643	Exportations
Balance	S	-6 157	-12 161	-17 063	4 765	7 937	3 329	-2 670	Balance
Portugal									**Portugal**
Imports	S	33 565	63 904	77 682	66 871	67 953	77 834	88 958	Importations
Exports	S	23 370	38 672	49 414	55 259	55 372	62 170	68 652	Exportations
Balance	S	-10 195	-25 232	-28 268	-11 612	-12 581	-15 664	-20 307	Balance
Qatar									**Qatar**
Imports	S	3 398	10 061	23 240	32 610	32 060	* 29 451	* 29 075	Importations
Exports	S	3 557	25 762	74 964	77 971	57 311	* 67 444	* 77 360	Exportations
Balance	S	159	15 702	51 725	45 361	25 250	37 993	48 285	Balance
Republic of Korea									**République de Corée**
Imports	G	135 109	261 236	425 208	436 487	406 182	478 469	* 513 548	Importations
Exports	G	* 125 056	284 418	466 381	526 753	495 418	573 627	* 624 964	Exportations
Balance	G	-10 052	23 183	41 173	90 266	89 236	95 158	111 416	Balance
Republic of Moldova									**République de Moldova**
Imports	G	841	2 292	3 855	3 987	4 020	4 831	* 6 216	Importations
Exports	G	746	1 091	1 541	1 967	2 045	2 425	* 3 114	Exportations
Balance	G	-95	-1 201	-2 314	-2 020	-1 976	-2 406	-3 103	Balance
Réunion [5]									**Réunion** [5]
Imports	S	2 711	...	...	...	...	...	...	Importations
Exports	S	209	...	...	...	...	...	...	Exportations
Balance	S	-2 502	...	...	...	...	...	...	Balance
Romania									**Roumanie**
Imports	S	10 278	40 463	62 007	69 858	74 605	85 318	* 98 026	Importations
Exports	S	7 910	27 730	49 413	60 605	63 581	70 627	* 80 710	Exportations
Balance	S	-2 368	-12 733	-12 593	-9 253	-11 024	-14 691	-17 316	Balance

20 Total imports, exports and balance of trade *(continued)*
Imports CIF, exports FOB and balance: millions of US dollars

Total des importations, des exportations et balance commerciale *(suite)*
Importations CAF, exportations FAB et balance: en millions de dollars É.-U.

Region, country or area	Sys.&	1995	2005	2010	2015	2016	2017	2018	Région, pays ou zone
Russian Federation									**Fédération de Russie**
Imports	G	* 46 710	98 707	228 912	182 782	182 257	228 213	* 239 459	Importations
Exports	G	* 79 869	241 452	397 068	343 908	285 491	359 152	* 452 571	Exportations
Balance	G	33 159	142 744	168 156	161 126	103 234	130 939	213 112	Balance
Rwanda									**Rwanda**
Imports	G	* 241	374	1 405	1 858	1 778	* 1 963	* 3 256	Importations
Exports	G	* 8	150	242	579	622	* 820	* 1 121	Exportations
Balance	G	-233	-224	-1 163	-1 279	-1 157	-1 143	-2 135	Balance
Saint Helena [10]									**Sainte-Hélène** [10]
Imports	G	* 13	* 12	* 20	* 41	* 48	* 55	* 63	Importations
Exports	G	* 1	* 1	* ~0	* ~0	* ~0	* ~0	* ~0	Exportations
Balance	G	-12	-12	-20	-40	-48	-55	-63	Balance
Saint Kitts and Nevis									**Saint-Kitts-et-Nevis**
Imports	S	132	210	270	297	334	309	* 430	Importations
Exports	S	19	34	32	32	37	33	* 35	Exportations
Balance	S	-113	-176	-238	-265	-297	-276	-395	Balance
Saint Lucia									**Sainte-Lucie**
Imports	S	* 306	486	647	583	669	664	* 622	Importations
Exports	S	* 109	64	215	181	120	142	* 91	Exportations
Balance	S	-197	-422	-432	-403	-549	-522	-531	Balance
Saint Pierre and Miquelon									**Saint-Pierre-et-Miquelon**
Imports	S	* 96	* 216	* 747	* 2 259	* 2 629	* 2 991	* 3 402	Importations
Exports	S	* 16	* 31	* 137	* 533	* 653	* 780	* 931	Exportations
Balance	S	-80	-185	-610	-1 726	-1 976	-2 211	-2 471	Balance
Saint Vincent & Grenadines									**Saint-Vincent-Grenadines**
Imports	S	134	240	379	334	335	330	* 378	Importations
Exports	S	59	40	42	47	43	42	* 42	Exportations
Balance	S	-75	-201	-338	-287	-292	-288	-336	Balance
Samoa									**Samoa**
Imports	S	* 95	239	310	371	350	356	* 381	Importations
Exports	S	* 9	87	70	59	56	44	* 30	Exportations
Balance	S	-86	-151	-240	-312	-294	-312	-351	Balance
Sao Tome and Principe									**Sao Tomé-et-Principe**
Imports	S	* 29	50	112	142	139	147	* 164	Importations
Exports	S	* 5	3	6	9	10	11	* 12	Exportations
Balance	S	-24	-46	-106	-133	-129	-136	-152	Balance
Saudi Arabia									**Arabie saoudite**
Imports	S	28 085	57 233	103 622	163 821	140 170	* 134 475	* 129 442	Importations
Exports	S	49 030	180 278	250 577	201 492	183 608	* 221 634	* 308 998	Exportations
Balance	S	20 944	123 045	146 955	37 671	43 438	87 159	179 556	Balance
Senegal									**Sénégal**
Imports	G	* 1 413	3 498	4 782	5 595	5 478	6 729	* 8 011	Importations
Exports	G	* 412	1 471	2 088	2 612	2 640	2 989	* 3 419	Exportations
Balance	G	-1 001	-2 027	-2 694	-2 984	-2 838	-3 740	-4 592	Balance
Serbia									**Serbie**
Imports	S	...	...	16 735	18 210	19 231	22 146	25 882	Importations
Exports	S	...	...	9 795	13 379	14 852	16 959	19 226	Exportations
Balance	S	...	...	-6 940	-4 831	-4 379	-5 187	-6 656	Balance
Serbia and Monten. [former]									**Serbie-et-Monténégro [anc.]**
Imports	S	* 2 666	* 11 393	...	...	...	...	...	Importations
Exports	S	* 1 531	* 4 430	...	...	...	...	...	Exportations
Balance	S	-1 135	-6 963	...	...	...	...	...	Balance
Seychelles									**Seychelles**
Imports	G	255	675	1 180	975	1 648	1 348	* 2 186	Importations
Exports	G	53	340	418	474	484	592	* 758	Exportations
Balance	G	-202	-335	-763	-501	-1 164	-757	-1 428	Balance
Sierra Leone									**Sierra Leone**
Imports	S	* 131	341	* 776	1 759	958	1 074	* 985	Importations
Exports	S	* 42	154	* 319	93	466	103	* 20	Exportations
Balance	S	-89	-187	-457	-1 666	-492	-971	-965	Balance
Singapore									**Singapour**
Imports	G	124 503	200 724	310 791	296 745	291 908	327 710	* 370 541	Importations
Exports	G	118 263	230 344	351 867	346 638	338 082	373 255	* 412 522	Exportations
Balance	G	-6 240	29 619	41 076	49 893	46 174	45 545	41 981	Balance

20

Total imports, exports and balance of trade *(continued)*
Imports CIF, exports FOB and balance: millions of US dollars

Total des importations, des exportations et balance commerciale *(suite)*
Importations CAF, exportations FAB et balance: en millions de dollars É.-U.

Region, country or area	Sys.&	1995	2005	2010	2015	2016	2017	2018	Région, pays ou zone
Slovakia									**Slovaquie**
Imports	S	8 162	34 226	64 382	72 958	75 145	82 994	* 92 983	Importations
Exports	S	8 374	* 32 210	63 999	75 051	77 527	84 525	* 93 226	Exportations
Balance	S	212	-2 016	-383	2 094	2 382	1 532	244	Balance
Slovenia									**Slovénie**
Imports	S	9 492	19 626	26 592	25 870	26 690	31 149	* 36 100	Importations
Exports	S	8 316	17 896	24 435	26 587	27 658	31 894	* 36 400	Exportations
Balance	S	-1 176	-1 730	-2 157	717	967	744	299	Balance
Solomon Islands									**Îles Salomon**
Imports	S	* 154	139	328	466	454	572	* 495	Importations
Exports	S	* 168	70	215	400	437	500	* 626	Exportations
Balance	S	14	-68	-112	-65	-17	-72	131	Balance
Somalia									**Somalie**
Imports	G	* 38	* 469	* 496	* 525	* 531	* 537	* 543	Importations
Exports	G	* 38	* 379	* 568	* 853	* 925	* 1 003	* 1 087	Exportations
Balance	G	-~0	-90	72	328	394	466	545	Balance
South Africa [1,11]									**Afrique du Sud** [1,11]
Imports	G	...	55 033	83 100	85 510	74 744	83 031	* 95 478	Importations
Exports	G	...	46 991	82 631	80 265	74 111	88 268	* 94 725	Exportations
Balance	G	...	-8 042	-469	-5 244	-633	5 237	-753	Balance
South Sudan									**Soudan du sud**
Imports	G	...	...	...	* 635	* 750	* 886	* 1 048	Importations
Exports	G	...	...	...	* 3 103	* 2 389	* 1 840	* 1 417	Exportations
Balance	G	...	...	...	2 468	1 639	953	369	Balance
Spain									**Espagne**
Imports	S	113 399	289 611	315 547	305 266	302 539	350 922	* 389 760	Importations
Exports	S	89 616	192 798	246 265	278 122	281 777	319 622	* 348 943	Exportations
Balance	S	-23 783	-96 812	-69 282	-27 144	-20 762	-31 300	-40 817	Balance
Sri Lanka									**Sri Lanka**
Imports	G	* 4 756	8 307	12 354	18 967	19 501	21 316	* 22 592	Importations
Exports	G	* 3 790	6 160	8 304	10 440	10 546	11 741	* 13 365	Exportations
Balance	G	-966	-2 147	-4 050	-8 528	-8 955	-9 575	-9 227	Balance
State of Palestine									**État de Palestine**
Imports	S	...	2 668	3 959	5 225	5 364	* 5 624	* 5 661	Importations
Exports	S	...	335	576	958	926	* 1 035	* 1 087	Exportations
Balance	S	...	-2 332	-3 383	-4 268	-4 437	-4 589	-4 574	Balance
Sudan									**Soudan**
Imports	G	...	...	...	8 413	* 7 365	10 277	* 12 578	Importations
Exports	G	...	...	...	5 588	* 5 455	4 241	* 4 908	Exportations
Balance	G	...	...	...	-2 826	-1 910	-6 036	-7 669	Balance
Sudan [former]									**Soudan [anc.]**
Imports	G	1 185	7 367	11 875	...	...	...	...	Importations
Exports	G	685	4 506	11 529	...	...	...	...	Exportations
Balance	G	-500	-2 861	-346	...	...	...	...	Balance
Suriname									**Suriname**
Imports	G	583	1 050	1 397	* 1 826	1 174	1 209	* 1 150	Importations
Exports	G	483	997	2 026	* 1 468	1 235	1 441	* 2 025	Exportations
Balance	G	-100	-53	628	-359	61	232	875	Balance
Sweden									**Suède**
Imports	G	61 647	111 351	148 788	138 361	141 101	154 195	170 107	Importations
Exports	G	77 436	130 264	158 411	140 001	139 456	152 907	165 959	Exportations
Balance	G	15 790	18 912	9 622	1 641	-1 645	-1 288	-4 148	Balance
Switzerland									**Suisse**
Imports	S	80 152	126 574	176 281	253 152	269 157	267 501	278 666	Importations
Exports	S	81 641	130 930	195 609	291 959	304 691	299 309	310 524	Exportations
Balance	S	1 489	4 356	19 329	38 807	35 534	31 807	31 859	Balance
Syrian Arab Republic									**République arabe syrienne**
Imports	S	* 4 645	7 898	17 562	* 3 206	* 2 383	* 1 773	* 1 319	Importations
Exports	S	* 3 561	6 450	11 353	* 1 685	* 1 265	* 949	* 712	Exportations
Balance	S	-1 084	-1 448	-6 209	-1 521	-1 118	-824	-607	Balance
Tajikistan									**Tadjikistan**
Imports	G	* 809	* 1 329	* 2 659	* 3 435	* 3 031	* 2 775	* 2 774	Importations
Exports	G	* 748	* 905	* 1 206	* 891	* 899	* 1 198	* 1 573	Exportations
Balance	G	-61	-424	-1 453	-2 544	-2 132	-1 577	-1 201	Balance

20

Total imports, exports and balance of trade *(continued)*
Imports CIF, exports FOB and balance: millions of US dollars

Total des importations, des exportations et balance commerciale *(suite)*
Importations CAF, exportations FAB et balance: en millions de dollars É.-U.

Region, country or area	Sys.&	1995	2005	2010	2015	2016	2017	2018	Région, pays ou zone
Thailand									**Thaïlande**
Imports	S	70 781	118 164	182 393	202 019	195 714	* 224 421	* 250 524	Importations
Exports	S	56 439	110 110	195 312	210 883	213 593	* 233 856	* 253 430	Exportations
Balance	S	-14 341	-8 054	12 918	8 864	17 879	9 435	2 905	Balance
Timor-Leste									**Timor-Leste**
Imports	S	* 112	102	* 246	* 578	* 506	588	* 552	Importations
Exports	S	* 34	43	* 42	* 45	* 162	24	* 45	Exportations
Balance	S	-78	-58	-205	-533	-345	-564	-507	Balance
Togo									**Togo**
Imports	S	556	593	1 205	1 731	1 716	1 615	* 2 091	Importations
Exports	S	383	360	648	710	715	749	* 877	Exportations
Balance	S	-174	-233	-557	-1 021	-1 001	-866	-1 214	Balance
Tokelau									**Tokélaou**
Imports	G	* 1	* 1	* 1	* 1	* 1	* 1	* 1	Importations
Exports	G	* ~0	* ~0	* ~0	* ~0	* ~0	* ~0	* ~0	Exportations
Balance	G	-~0	-1	-1	-1	-1	-1	-1	Balance
Tonga									**Tonga**
Imports	G	* 77	120	159	* 208	* 229	* 246	* 277	Importations
Exports	G	* 15	10	8	* 15	* 21	* 19	* 17	Exportations
Balance	G	-63	-110	-151	-194	-208	-226	-260	Balance
Trinidad and Tobago									**Trinité-et-Tobago**
Imports	S	* 1 386	5 694	6 480	9 298	* 8 084	* 6 425	* 3 540	Importations
Exports	S	* 2 007	9 611	10 982	10 756	* 7 639	* 8 863	* 10 454	Exportations
Balance	S	622	3 918	4 502	1 458	-446	2 439	6 914	Balance
Tunisia									**Tunisie**
Imports	G	* 7 903	13 174	22 215	20 223	19 487	20 618	* 22 513	Importations
Exports	G	* 5 475	10 494	16 427	14 073	13 575	14 200	* 15 666	Exportations
Balance	G	-2 428	-2 681	-5 789	-6 149	-5 912	-6 418	-6 848	Balance
Turkey									**Turquie**
Imports	S	35 707	116 774	185 544	207 207	198 618	233 800	* 222 444	Importations
Exports	S	21 599	73 476	113 883	143 850	142 530	156 993	* 167 933	Exportations
Balance	S	-14 109	-43 298	-71 661	-63 356	-56 089	-76 807	-54 512	Balance
Turkmenistan									**Turkménistan**
Imports	G	* 1 364	* 2 217	* 2 400	* 2 558	* 2 618	* 2 679	* 2 721	Importations
Exports	G	* 677	* 3 009	* 3 335	* 3 670	* 3 741	* 3 813	* 3 887	Exportations
Balance	G	-687	792	935	1 112	1 123	1 135	1 166	Balance
Turks and Caicos Islands									**Îles Turques-et-Caïques**
Imports	G	* 51	304	* 302	* 410	* 389	* 370	* 351	Importations
Exports	G	* 5	15	* 16	* 5	* 4	* 4	* 4	Exportations
Balance	G	-46	-289	-286	-405	-385	-366	-347	Balance
Tuvalu									**Tuvalu**
Imports	G	* 6	13	* 12	* 12	* 12	* 12	* 12	Importations
Exports	G	* ~0	~0	* ~0	* ~0	* ~0	* ~0	* ~0	Exportations
Balance	G	-6	-13	-12	-12	-12	-12	-12	Balance
Uganda									**Ouganda**
Imports	G	1 038	2 054	4 664	5 528	4 829	5 596	* 3 230	Importations
Exports	G	575	813	1 619	2 267	2 482	2 901	* 2 911	Exportations
Balance	G	-462	-1 241	-3 046	-3 261	-2 347	-2 694	-319	Balance
Ukraine [12]									**Ukraine** [12]
Imports	G	* 15 484	36 122	60 737	37 516	39 250	49 439	* 57 993	Importations
Exports	G	* 13 128	34 228	51 430	38 127	36 361	43 428	* 47 348	Exportations
Balance	G	-2 356	-1 894	-9 307	611	-2 889	-6 011	-10 645	Balance
United Arab Emirates									**Émirats arabes unis**
Imports	G	* 20 776	80 814	187 001	287 025	270 882	* 237 797	* 155 599	Importations
Exports	G	* 27 691	115 453	198 362	333 362	298 651	* 220 453	* 106 586	Exportations
Balance	G	6 915	34 639	11 361	46 338	27 769	-17 345	-49 013	Balance
United Kingdom									**Royaume-Uni**
Imports	G	261 456	528 461	627 618	630 251	636 368	641 332	669 640	Importations
Exports	G	234 372	392 744	422 014	466 296	411 463	442 066	487 069	Exportations
Balance	G	-27 084	-135 717	-205 603	-163 955	-224 905	-199 267	-182 571	Balance
United Rep. of Tanzania									**Rép.-Unie de Tanzanie**
Imports	G	1 653	3 247	8 013	14 706	7 876	7 765	* 8 744	Importations
Exports	G	685	1 672	4 051	5 854	4 742	4 178	* 5 132	Exportations
Balance	G	-968	-1 575	-3 962	-8 852	-3 134	-3 587	-3 612	Balance

20

Total imports, exports and balance of trade *(continued)*
Imports CIF, exports FOB and balance: millions of US dollars

Total des importations, des exportations et balance commerciale *(suite)*
Importations CAF, exportations FAB et balance: en millions de dollars É.-U.

Region, country or area	Sys.&	1995	2005	2010	2015	2016	2017	2018	Région, pays ou zone
United States of America [13]									**États-Unis d'Amérique** [13]
Imports	G	770 821	1 732 321	1 968 260	2 313 425	2 248 209	2 407 390	* 2 574 930	Importations
Exports	G	582 965	904 339	1 278 099	1 501 846	1 450 457	1 545 609	* 1 662 993	Exportations
Balance	G	-187 857	-827 981	-690 161	-811 579	-797 752	-861 781	-911 937	Balance
Uruguay									**Uruguay**
Imports	G	2 866	3 879	8 622	9 489	8 137	8 458	* 9 381	Importations
Exports	G	2 106	3 422	6 724	7 670	6 964	7 889	* 9 148	Exportations
Balance	G	-760	-457	-1 898	-1 820	-1 173	-568	-233	Balance
Uzbekistan									**Ouzbékistan**
Imports	G	* 2 874	* 3 657	* 8 381	* 12 414	* 12 102	* 13 013	* 19 557	Importations
Exports	G	* 3 718	* 4 458	* 11 587	* 12 871	* 12 568	* 12 568	* 14 258	Exportations
Balance	G	844	801	3 206	457	466	-446	-5 300	Balance
Vanuatu									**Vanuatu**
Imports	G	* 95	* 149	276	* 355	* 377	* 371	* 355	Importations
Exports	G	* 28	* 38	46	* 39	* 50	* 61	* 63	Exportations
Balance	G	-67	-111	-230	-316	-327	-310	-291	Balance
Venezuela (Boliv. Rep. of)									**Venezuela (Rép. boliv. du)**
Imports	G	10 791	21 848	32 343	* 40 133	* 17 150	* 6 771	* 2 667	Importations
Exports	G	19 093	55 413	66 963	* 37 236	* 20 215	* 11 563	* 6 614	Exportations
Balance	G	8 302	33 565	34 620	-2 897	3 065	4 792	3 947	Balance
Viet Nam									**Viet Nam**
Imports	G	* 8 155	36 761	84 839	165 776	174 978	213 215	* 266 122	Importations
Exports	G	* 5 449	32 447	72 237	162 017	176 581	215 119	* 247 989	Exportations
Balance	G	-2 706	-4 314	-12 602	-3 759	1 602	1 903	-18 133	Balance
Wallis and Futuna Islands									**Îles Wallis-et-Futuna**
Imports	S	* 13	51	* 35	* 49	* 53	* 57	* 60	Importations
Exports	S	* ~0	* 1	* 1	* 1	* 1	* 1	* 1	Exportations
Balance	S	-13	-50	-34	-48	-51	-55	-59	Balance
Yemen									**Yémen**
Imports	S	* 1 812	5 400	9 255	6 573	* 3 311	* 7 162	* 15 493	Importations
Exports	S	* 1 917	5 608	6 437	510	* 24	* 637	* 16 569	Exportations
Balance	S	105	208	-2 818	-6 063	-3 286	-6 525	1 076	Balance
Zambia									**Zambie**
Imports	S	708	2 558	5 321	8 420	* 7 457	8 774	9 462	Importations
Exports	S	1 055	1 810	7 200	6 983	* 6 490	8 158	9 052	Exportations
Balance	S	347	-748	1 879	-1 437	-967	-616	-410	Balance
Zimbabwe									**Zimbabwe**
Imports	G	2 659	2 072	5 852	6 002	5 212	4 962	6 259	Importations
Exports	G	1 846	1 394	3 199	2 704	2 832	3 480	4 037	Exportations
Balance	G	-813	-679	-2 653	-3 298	-2 379	-1 482	-2 222	Balance

Source:

United Nations Statistics Division, New York, Commodity Trade Statistics Database (UN COMTRADE), last accessed May 2019.

Source:

Organisation des Nations Unies, Division de statistique, New York, Comtrade base de données de l'ONU, dernier accès mai 2019.

& Systems of trade: Two systems of recording trade, the General trade system (G) and the Special trade system (S), are in common use. They differ mainly in the way warehoused and re-exported goods are recorded. See the Technical notes for an explanation of the trade systems.

& Systèmes de commerce : Deux systèmes d'enregistrement du commerce sont couramment utilisés, le Commerce général (G) et le Commerce spécial (S). Ils ne diffèrent que par la façon dont sont enregistrées les marchandises entreposées et les marchandises réexportées. Voir les Notes techniques pour une explication des Systèmes de commerce.

1 Imports FOB.
2 Trade statistics exclude certain oil and chemical products.
3 For statistical purposes, the data for China do not include those for the Hong Kong Special Administrative Region (Hong Kong SAR), Macao Special Administrative Region (Macao SAR) and Taiwan Province of China.
4 Export and import values exclude trade in the processing zone.

1 Importations FAB.
2 Les statistiques commerciales font exclusion de certains produits pétroliers et chimiques.
3 Pour la présentation des statistiques, les données pour la Chine ne comprennent pas la région administrative spéciale de Hong Kong (RAS de Hong Kong), la région administrative spéciale de Macao (RAS de Macao) et la province chinoise de Taïwan.
4 Les valeurs à l'exportation et à l'importation excluent le commerce de la zone de transformation.

20

Total imports, exports and balance of trade *(continued)*
Imports CIF, exports FOB and balance: millions of US dollars

Total des importations, des exportations et balance commerciale *(suite)*
Importations CAF, exportations FAB et balance: en millions de dollars É.-U.

5	After 1995, import and exports included in France.
6	Data include oil and gas. The value of oil exports and total exports are rough estimates based on information published in various petroleum industry journals.
7	Year ending 20 March of the year stated.
8	Imports and exports net of returned goods. The figures also exclude Judea and Samaria and the Gaza area.
9	Trade data include maquiladoras and exclude goods from customs-bonded warehouses. Total exports include revaluation and exports of silver.
10	Year ending 31 March of the following year.
11	Exports include gold.
12	Excludes the temporarily occupied territory of the Autonomous Republic of Crimea and Sevastopol.
13	Including the trade of the U.S. Virgin Islands and Puerto Rico but excluding shipments of merchandise between the United States and its other possessions (Guam and American Samoa). Data include imports and exports of non-monetary gold.

5	Après 1995, importations et exportations incluses en France.
6	Les données comprennent le pétrole et le gaz. La valeur des exportations de pétrole et des exportations totales sont des évaluations grossières basées sur l'information publiée à divers journaux d'industrie de pétrole.
7	Année finissant le 20 mars de l'année indiquée.
8	Importations et exportations nettes des marchandises retournées excluant les régions de Judée et Samarie et Gaza.
9	Les statistiques du commerce extérieur comprennent maquiladoras et ne comprennent pas les marchandises provenant des entrepôts en douane. Les exportations comprennent la réévaluation et les données sur les exportations d'argent.
10	Année finissant le 31 Mars de l'année suivante.
11	Les exportations comprennent l'or.
12	Excluent le territoire temporairement occupé de la République autonome de Crimée et de Sébastopol.
13	Incluant les Iles Vierges américaines et Porto Rico excluant l'expédition de marchandises avec Guam et les Samoa américaines. Incluant le commerce d'or non-monétaire.

21

Major trading partner
Three largest trade partners as a percentage of total international merchandise trade in US dollars, as at 2018

Partenaire commercial principal
Trois principaux partenaires commerciaux en pourcentage du total de commerce international de marchandises en dollars américains, en 2018

Country or area / Major trading partner	Percentage of exports 2005	2010	2018	Major trading partner	Percentage of imports 2005	2010	2018	Pays ou zone
Afghanistan								**Afghanistan**
Partner 1	Pakistan	...	39.0	* 47.5	Iran (Islamic Rep.), Iran (Rép. islamique)	...	7.5	* 19.4	Partenaire 1
Partner 2	India, Inde	...	16.8	* 38.6	Pakistan	...	11.6	* 18.3	Partenaire 2
Partner 3	Iran (Islamic Rep.), Iran (Rép. islamique)	...	8.2	* 3.2	China, Chine	...	13.7	* 16.7	Partenaire 3
Albania								**Albanie**
Partner 1	Italy, Italie	72.4	50.8	* 53.5	Italy, Italie	29.3	28.2	* 28.6	Partenaire 1
Partner 2	Serbia, Serbie	...	8.3	* 9.4	Turkey, Turquie	7.5	5.7	* 8.1	Partenaire 2
Partner 3	Spain, Espagne	0.1	3.4	* 5.5	Germany, Allemagne	5.4	5.6	* 8.1	Partenaire 3
Algeria								**Algérie**
Partner 1	Italy, Italie	16.4	15.4	* 16.0	China, Chine	6.5	11.2	* 18.1	Partenaire 1
Partner 2	France	10.0	6.6	* 12.6	France	22.0	14.9	* 9.3	Partenaire 2
Partner 3	Spain, Espagne	11.0	10.4	* 11.7	Italy, Italie	7.5	10.0	* 8.2	Partenaire 3
Andorra								**Andorre**
Partner 1	Spain, Espagne	59.2	67.4	* 28.1	Spain, Espagne	* 51.5	59.9	* 68.6	Partenaire 1
Partner 2	France	17.0	16.8	* 14.1	France	* 22.3	17.6	* 17.9	Partenaire 2
Partner 3	Sri Lanka	...	...	* 13.9	Germany, Allemagne	* 5.3	4.5	* 2.9	Partenaire 3
Angola								**Angola**
Partner 1	China, Chine	* 29.8	39.8	* 58.1	China, Chine	* 4.8	10.1	* 20.7	Partenaire 1
Partner 2	India, Inde	* ~0.0	9.7	* 11.3	Portugal	* 12.9	14.4	* 14.8	Partenaire 2
Partner 3	United States, États-Unis	* 40.1	18.9	* 6.7	United States, États-Unis	* 12.0	9.3	* 7.2	Partenaire 3
Anguilla								**Anguilla**
Partner 1	Thailand, Thaïlande	...	...	* 23.7	United States, États-Unis	* 61.7	* 59.4	* 61.7	Partenaire 1
Partner 2	United States, États-Unis	* 26.5	* 17.0	* 22.9	France	* 3.2	* 1.5	* 17.7	Partenaire 2
Partner 3	Chile, Chili	...	...	* 13.0	Poland, Pologne	* ~0.0	* ~0.0	* 3.9	Partenaire 3
Antigua and Barbuda								**Antigua-et-Barbuda**
Partner 1	Spain, Espagne	~0.0	0.7	* 22.3	United States, États-Unis	48.9	34.5	* 43.2	Partenaire 1
Partner 2	United Kingdom, Royaume-Uni	16.7	19.7	* 20.9	Areas nes, Zones nsa [1]	0.1	0.1	* 16.2	Partenaire 2
Partner 3	Bermuda, Bermudes	~0.0	...	* 13.9	United Kingdom, Royaume-Uni	6.8	4.7	* 5.5	Partenaire 3
Argentina								**Argentine**
Partner 1	Brazil, Brésil	15.8	21.2	* 15.9	Brazil, Brésil	37.0	* 32.5	* 26.7	Partenaire 1
Partner 2	United States, États-Unis	12.1	5.4	* 7.7	China, Chine	5.3	* 13.5	* 18.4	Partenaire 2
Partner 3	China, Chine	7.9	8.5	* 7.4	United States, États-Unis	16.3	* 11.8	* 11.4	Partenaire 3
Armenia								**Arménie**
Partner 1	Russian Federation, Fédération de Russie	12.4	17.5	26.9	Russian Federation, Fédération de Russie	14.8	22.0	26.2	Partenaire 1
Partner 2	Switzerland, Suisse	3.7	1.7	14.1	China, Chine	1.5	10.6	13.8	Partenaire 2
Partner 3	Bulgaria, Bulgarie	0.1	15.5	9.0	Iran (Islamic Rep.), Iran (Rép. islamique)	6.0	5.8	5.6	Partenaire 3
Aruba								**Aruba**
Partner 1	Areas nes, Zones nsa [1]	0.2	3.0	* 45.6	United States, États-Unis	* 55.7	50.0	* 52.3	Partenaire 1
Partner 2	Colombia, Colombie	11.9	27.2	* 19.5	Areas nes, Zones nsa [1]	0.1	2.0	* 21.5	Partenaire 2
Partner 3	United States, États-Unis	* 11.3	* 6.1	* 14.4	Netherlands, Pays-Bas	* 12.7	11.3	* 12.0	Partenaire 3
Australia								**Australie**
Partner 1	China, Chine	11.6	* 25.4	* 29.6	China, Chine	13.8	* 18.7	* 21.9	Partenaire 1
Partner 2	Areas nes, Zones nsa [1]	0.1	* 0.4	* 15.0	United States, États-Unis	13.9	* 12.4	* 10.3	Partenaire 2
Partner 3	Japan, Japon	20.5	* 18.5	* 10.4	Japan, Japon	11.0	* 8.7	* 7.2	Partenaire 3
Austria								**Autriche**
Partner 1	Germany, Allemagne	31.8	* 31.0	* 29.7	Germany, Allemagne	42.2	* 38.7	* 36.5	Partenaire 1
Partner 2	United States, États-Unis	5.6	* 4.4	* 6.6	Italy, Italie	6.6	* 6.6	* 6.1	Partenaire 2
Partner 3	Italy, Italie	8.6	* 7.7	* 6.2	China, Chine	3.1	* 4.7	* 5.7	Partenaire 3
Azerbaijan								**Azerbaïdjan**
Partner 1	Italy, Italie	30.3	* 33.1	* 31.9	Russian Federation, Fédération de Russie	17.0	17.4	* 16.8	Partenaire 1
Partner 2	Turkey, Turquie	6.3	* 0.8	* 9.9	Turkey, Turquie	7.4	11.7	* 14.7	Partenaire 2
Partner 3	Israel, Israël	4.5	8.2	* 4.6	China, Chine	4.1	8.9	* 11.2	Partenaire 3
Bahamas								**Bahamas**
Partner 1	United States, États-Unis	60.9	76.0	* 38.2	United States, États-Unis	* 85.9	* 90.9	* 33.1	Partenaire 1
Partner 2	Poland, Pologne	...	...	* 21.6	Rep. of Korea, République de Corée	~0.0	...	* 19.1	Partenaire 2
Partner 3	Nicaragua	...	...	* 6.4	Colombia, Colombie	~0.0	~0.0	* 10.0	Partenaire 3
Bahrain								**Bahreïn**
Partner 1	Saudi Arabia, Arabie saoudite	* 6.3	7.2	* 18.1	Areas nes, Zones nsa [1]	44.6	36.6	* 21.4	Partenaire 1
Partner 2	United Arab Emirates, Émirats arabes unis	* 1.6	* 2.7	* 17.3	China, Chine	4.1	7.4	* 9.7	Partenaire 2
Partner 3	United States, États-Unis	* 2.7	1.5	* 11.0	United States, États-Unis	3.7	4.5	* 8.6	Partenaire 3

Major trading partner *(continued)*
Three largest trade partners as a percentage of total international merchandise trade in US dollars, as at 2018

Partenaire commercial principal *(suite)*
Trois principaux partenaires commerciaux en pourcentage du total de commerce international de marchandises en dollars américains, en 2018

Country or area Major trading partner		Percentage of exports			Major trading partner	Percentage of imports			Pays ou zone
		2005	2010	2018		2005	2010	2018	
Bangladesh									**Bangladesh**
Partner 1	Germany, Allemagne	* 15.7	* 13.8	* 14.9	China, Chine	* 15.9	17.5	* 30.9	Partenaire 1
Partner 2	United States, États-Unis	* 28.5	* 24.3	* 14.4	India, Inde	* 10.9	11.5	* 14.4	Partenaire 2
Partner 3	United Kingdom, Royaume-Uni	* 10.1	* 8.9	* 8.5	Singapore, Singapour	* 3.5	5.4	* 5.8	Partenaire 3
Barbados									**Barbade**
Partner 1	Areas nes, Zones nsa [1]	~0.0	...	23.8	United States, États-Unis	35.9	43.9	39.6	Partenaire 1
Partner 2	United States, États-Unis	* 13.4	24.9	22.7	Trinidad and Tobago, Trinité-et-Tobago	21.2	7.2	17.9	Partenaire 2
Partner 3	Trinidad and Tobago, Trinité-et-Tobago	10.6	8.4	6.9	China, Chine	2.9	4.8	5.9	Partenaire 3
Belarus									**Bélarus**
Partner 1	Russian Federation, Fédération de Russie	35.8	39.4	38.5	Russian Federation, Fédération de Russie	60.4	55.8	58.6	Partenaire 1
Partner 2	Ukraine	5.7	10.1	12.1	China, Chine	1.7	4.6	7.9	Partenaire 2
Partner 3	United Kingdom, Royaume-Uni	7.0	3.7	9.2	Germany, Allemagne	6.7	6.8	4.7	Partenaire 3
Belgium									**Belgique**
Partner 1	Germany, Allemagne	19.2	18.6	* 16.6	Netherlands, Pays-Bas	17.6	18.6	* 17.2	Partenaire 1
Partner 2	France	17.2	16.6	* 14.9	Germany, Allemagne	17.1	16.1	* 13.8	Partenaire 2
Partner 3	Netherlands, Pays-Bas	11.7	11.9	* 12.0	France	11.3	11.0	* 9.5	Partenaire 3
Belize									**Belize**
Partner 1	United Kingdom, Royaume-Uni	19.9	26.1	* 27.7	United States, États-Unis	40.3	47.9	* 35.6	Partenaire 1
Partner 2	United States, États-Unis	53.9	49.1	* 26.3	China, Chine	2.2	9.7	* 11.2	Partenaire 2
Partner 3	Jamaica, Jamaïque	4.6	2.6	* 5.4	Mexico, Mexique	11.6	10.0	* 11.2	Partenaire 3
Benin									**Bénin**
Partner 1	Viet Nam	1.5	2.1	* 13.9	India, Inde	1.6	* 0.9	* 19.0	Partenaire 1
Partner 2	Bangladesh	0.4	0.6	* 12.6	Thailand, Thaïlande	6.7	8.6	* 14.4	Partenaire 2
Partner 3	Malaysia, Malaisie	2.8	1.5	* 11.4	China, Chine	8.8	10.2	* 7.9	Partenaire 3
Bermuda									**Bermudes**
Partner 1	United States, États-Unis	* 7.0	* 69.1	62.6	United States, États-Unis	77.0	71.7	69.4	Partenaire 1
Partner 2	Areas nes, Zones nsa [1]	* 0.7	* 5.6	18.4	Canada	4.0	8.0	9.1	Partenaire 2
Partner 3	United Kingdom, Royaume-Uni	* 1.1	* 8.2	6.2	United Kingdom, Royaume-Uni	3.3	3.7	3.5	Partenaire 3
Bhutan									**Bhoutan**
Partner 1	India, Inde	87.6	82.4	* 85.2	India, Inde	75.1	75.1	* 77.1	Partenaire 1
Partner 2	United Kingdom, Royaume-Uni	~0.0	~0.0	* 3.0	United States, États-Unis	0.5	0.4	* 6.6	Partenaire 2
Partner 3	Nepal, Népal	0.4	0.2	* 2.7	Thailand, Thaïlande	1.6	2.5	* 5.0	Partenaire 3
Bolivia (Plurin. State of)									**Bolivie (État plurin. de)**
Partner 1	Brazil, Brésil	36.3	* 34.6	19.2	China, Chine	5.8	11.7	20.7	Partenaire 1
Partner 2	Argentina, Argentine	* 9.5	* 8.0	16.0	Brazil, Brésil	21.9	* 18.0	16.1	Partenaire 2
Partner 3	India, Inde	~0.0	0.1	8.1	Argentina, Argentine	16.7	12.7	11.6	Partenaire 3
Bosnia and Herzegovina									**Bosnie-Herzégovine**
Partner 1	Germany, Allemagne	11.3	* 15.8	* 14.4	Germany, Allemagne	14.4	10.5	* 11.6	Partenaire 1
Partner 2	Croatia, Croatie	20.5	* 15.3	* 11.6	Italy, Italie	8.9	8.9	* 11.4	Partenaire 2
Partner 3	Italy, Italie	13.1	* 12.2	* 10.9	Serbia, Serbie	...	10.5	* 11.2	Partenaire 3
Botswana									**Botswana**
Partner 1	Belgium, Belgique	0.2	3.3	* 22.8	South Africa, Afrique du Sud	84.1	72.8	* 64.3	Partenaire 1
Partner 2	India, Inde	0.1	0.9	* 19.7	Canada	0.5	0.1	* 8.8	Partenaire 2
Partner 3	United Arab Emirates, Émirats arabes unis	0.1	0.1	* 16.6	Namibia, Namibie	0.5	1.2	* 6.7	Partenaire 3
Brazil									**Brésil**
Partner 1	China, Chine	5.8	15.2	* 21.8	China, Chine	7.3	14.1	* 18.1	Partenaire 1
Partner 2	United States, États-Unis	19.9	10.0	* 12.5	United States, États-Unis	17.5	15.0	* 16.7	Partenaire 2
Partner 3	Argentina, Argentine	8.4	9.2	* 8.1	Argentina, Argentine	8.5	7.9	* 6.3	Partenaire 3
British Virgin Islands									**Îles Vierges britanniques**
Partner 1	Mexico, Mexique	* 1.3	* 0.1	* 20.8	Areas nes, Zones nsa [1]	...	...	* 48.4	Partenaire 1
Partner 2	Rwanda	...	...	* 8.2	United States, États-Unis	* 8.9	* 9.9	* 31.1	Partenaire 2
Partner 3	Australia, Australie	* 1.0	* 2.4	* 5.7	Switzerland, Suisse	* 2.0	* 3.9	* 4.5	Partenaire 3
Brunei Darussalam									**Brunéi Darussalam**
Partner 1	Japan, Japon	* 37.7	43.5	* 29.3	China, Chine	* 6.2	7.8	* 20.8	Partenaire 1
Partner 2	Rep. of Korea, République de Corée	* 12.9	16.7	* 14.2	Singapore, Singapour	* 18.3	19.1	* 18.5	Partenaire 2
Partner 3	Malaysia, Malaisie	* 1.4	1.5	* 11.2	Malaysia, Malaisie	* 20.1	23.6	* 18.2	Partenaire 3
Bulgaria									**Bulgarie**
Partner 1	Germany, Allemagne	9.8	10.6	* 12.9	Germany, Allemagne	13.6	11.7	* 12.2	Partenaire 1
Partner 2	Turkey, Turquie	10.5	* 8.7	* 8.9	Russian Federation, Fédération de Russie	15.6	16.1	* 10.2	Partenaire 2
Partner 3	Italy, Italie	12.0	* 9.7	* 7.9	Italy, Italie	9.0	7.4	* 7.2	Partenaire 3

21 Major trading partner *(continued)*
Three largest trade partners as a percentage of total international merchandise trade in US dollars, as at 2018

Partenaire commercial principal *(suite)*
Trois principaux partenaires commerciaux en pourcentage du total de commerce international de marchandises en dollars américains, en 2018

Country or area / Major trading partner		Percentage of exports			Major trading partner	Percentage of imports			Pays ou zone
		2005	2010	2018		2005	2010	2018	
Burkina Faso									**Burkina Faso**
Partner 1	Switzerland, Suisse	9.4	63.5	* 58.8	China, Chine	2.7	9.7	* 14.0	Partenaire 1
Partner 2	India, Inde	~0.0	0.1	* 9.9	Côte d'Ivoire	* 17.9	16.0	* 10.8	Partenaire 2
Partner 3	Singapore, Singapour	2.2	4.9	* 9.3	France	* 18.7	10.3	* 8.6	Partenaire 3
Burundi									**Burundi**
Partner 1	United Arab Emirates, Émirats arabes unis	25.3	8.8	* 25.6	India, Inde	4.1	6.0	* 14.0	Partenaire 1
Partner 2	Dem.Rep. of the Congo, Rép. Dém. du Congo	0.9	6.2	* 17.8	China, Chine	4.2	12.0	* 13.8	Partenaire 2
Partner 3	Pakistan	~0.0	...	* 9.2	Saudi Arabia, Arabie saoudite	0.3	0.6	* 9.4	Partenaire 3
Cabo Verde									**Cabo Verde**
Partner 1	Spain, Espagne	8.1	* 32.2	* 70.8	Portugal	40.4	* 45.5	* 42.9	Partenaire 1
Partner 2	Portugal	* 22.9	* 24.4	* 24.8	Spain, Espagne	7.0	6.8	* 12.6	Partenaire 2
Partner 3	United States, États-Unis	6.0	* 0.4	* 2.3	Italy, Italie	4.3	2.0	* 6.1	Partenaire 3
Cambodia									**Cambodge**
Partner 1	United States, États-Unis	52.9	34.1	* 21.3	China, Chine	16.6	24.2	* 36.8	Partenaire 1
Partner 2	United Kingdom, Royaume-Uni	4.1	4.2	* 9.5	Thailand, Thaïlande	* 11.4	14.1	* 15.4	Partenaire 2
Partner 3	Germany, Allemagne	7.5	2.0	* 9.0	Viet Nam	* 7.1	9.9	* 11.4	Partenaire 3
Cameroon									**Cameroun**
Partner 1	Italy, Italie	16.3	9.7	* 13.9	China, Chine	4.4	10.6	* 17.2	Partenaire 1
Partner 2	China, Chine	2.4	8.5	* 12.1	France	18.0	14.6	* 9.8	Partenaire 2
Partner 3	France	12.3	6.3	* 10.5	Thailand, Thaïlande	2.4	3.0	* 5.7	Partenaire 3
Canada									**Canada**
Partner 1	United States, États-Unis	83.8	74.9	* 75.9	United States, États-Unis	56.5	50.4	* 51.3	Partenaire 1
Partner 2	China, Chine	1.7	3.3	* 4.3	China, Chine	7.8	11.0	* 12.6	Partenaire 2
Partner 3	United Kingdom, Royaume-Uni	1.9	4.1	* 3.2	Mexico, Mexique	3.8	5.5	* 6.3	Partenaire 3
Cayman Islands									**Îles Caïmanes**
Partner 1	Malta, Malte	* 0.1	* 4.9	* 50.7	United States, États-Unis	* 50.8	* 11.7	* 20.5	Partenaire 1
Partner 2	Netherlands, Pays-Bas	* ~0.0	* ~0.0	* 38.5	Netherlands, Pays-Bas	* 1.2	* 5.2	* 17.0	Partenaire 2
Partner 3	United States, États-Unis	* 67.0	* 1.0	* 4.0	Germany, Allemagne	* 1.9	* 10.9	* 15.9	Partenaire 3
Central African Republic									**République centrafricaine**
Partner 1	France	* 19.6	16.0	* 61.1	France	* 14.0	24.1	* 26.1	Partenaire 1
Partner 2	Benin, Bénin	...	...	* 9.9	Cameroon, Cameroun	* 16.0	7.1	* 12.1	Partenaire 2
Partner 3	China, Chine	0.3	8.0	* 7.0	Belgium, Belgique	* 3.1	3.1	* 8.1	Partenaire 3
Chad									**Tchad**
Partner 1	United States, États-Unis	* 72.7	* 68.0	* 39.3	China, Chine	* 3.7	* 22.5	* 20.7	Partenaire 1
Partner 2	China, Chine	* 8.8	* 16.0	* 22.7	France	* 23.5	* 12.2	* 17.2	Partenaire 2
Partner 3	Netherlands, Pays-Bas	* ~0.0	* 0.7	* 16.1	Cameroon, Cameroun	* 6.5	* 24.7	* 8.9	Partenaire 3
Chile									**Chili**
Partner 1	China, Chine	11.7	24.4	33.5	China, Chine	9.6	* 16.8	23.6	Partenaire 1
Partner 2	United States, États-Unis	16.0	* 9.9	13.8	United States, États-Unis	15.5	* 17.7	18.9	Partenaire 2
Partner 3	Japan, Japon	* 11.9	10.9	9.3	Brazil, Brésil	11.6	* 8.3	9.0	Partenaire 3
China									**Chine**
Partner 1	United States, États-Unis	21.4	18.0	* 19.0	Rep. of Korea, République de Corée	11.6	9.9	* 9.6	Partenaire 1
Partner 2	China, Hong Kong SAR, Chine, RAS Hong Kong	16.3	13.8	* 12.3	Japan, Japon	15.2	12.7	* 9.0	Partenaire 2
Partner 3	Japan, Japon	11.0	7.7	* 6.1	Asia nes, Asie nsa [2]	11.3	8.3	* 8.5	Partenaire 3
China, Hong Kong SAR									**Chine, RAS de Hong Kong**
Partner 1	China, Chine	44.6	52.5	55.2	China, Chine	45.0	44.7	44.8	Partenaire 1
Partner 2	United States, États-Unis	15.9	10.7	8.1	Asia nes, Asie nsa [2]	7.2	6.6	6.9	Partenaire 2
Partner 3	India, Inde	1.0	2.5	3.1	Singapore, Singapour	5.8	7.0	6.4	Partenaire 3
China, Macao SAR									**Chine, RAS de Macao**
Partner 1	Areas nes, Zones nsa [1]	4.1	69.5	* 61.9	China, Chine	37.4	29.1	* 31.4	Partenaire 1
Partner 2	China, Hong Kong SAR, Chine, RAS Hong Kong	9.8	9.6	* 29.8	Areas nes, Zones nsa [1]	...	...	* 11.6	Partenaire 2
Partner 3	China, Chine	14.9	5.5	* 5.9	China, Hong Kong SAR, Chine, RAS Hong Kong	8.6	10.4	* 8.5	Partenaire 3
Colombia									**Colombie**
Partner 1	United States, États-Unis	* 41.8	* 43.1	* 29.2	United States, États-Unis	28.5	25.9	* 26.3	Partenaire 1
Partner 2	Panama	* 1.2	* 2.4	* 6.8	China, Chine	7.6	13.5	* 19.0	Partenaire 2
Partner 3	China, Chine	1.1	* 4.9	* 5.3	Mexico, Mexique	8.3	9.5	* 7.5	Partenaire 3
Comoros									**Comores**
Partner 1	India, Inde	6.1	5.2	* 36.4	United Rep. of Tanzania, Rép.-Unie Tanzanie	1.7	1.6	* 27.3	Partenaire 1
Partner 2	France	74.9	22.0	* 17.9	China, Chine	1.6	7.7	* 19.2	Partenaire 2
Partner 3	Germany, Allemagne	9.3	3.6	* 7.7	France	17.9	20.6	* 9.9	Partenaire 3

Major trading partner *(continued)*
Three largest trade partners as a percentage of total international merchandise trade in US dollars, as at 2018

Partenaire commercial principal *(suite)*
Trois principaux partenaires commerciaux en pourcentage du total de commerce international de marchandises en dollars américains, en 2018

Country or area	Major trading partner	Percentage of exports			Major trading partner	Percentage of imports			Pays ou zone
		2005	2010	2018		2005	2010	2018	
Congo									**Congo**
Partner 1	China, Chine	* 36.1	20.9	* 33.9	Namibia, Namibie	...	...	* 8.7	Partenaire 1
Partner 2	Spain, Espagne	* 0.5	1.1	* 12.4	France	* 1.0	1.4	* 8.0	Partenaire 2
Partner 3	Angola	...	13.1	* 6.4	Angola	* 20.9	12.2	* 8.0	Partenaire 3
Cook Islands									**Îles Cook**
Partner 1	Japan, Japon	30.8	49.7	* 41.9	New Zealand, Nouvelle-Zélande	* 73.9	76.4	* 52.2	Partenaire 1
Partner 2	China, Chine	33.8	14.2	* 14.7	Fiji, Fidji	1.2	9.4	* 9.3	Partenaire 2
Partner 3	Thailand, Thaïlande	...	...	* 11.2	Italy, Italie	~0.0	~0.0	* 5.6	Partenaire 3
Costa Rica									**Costa Rica**
Partner 1	United States, États-Unis	42.8	37.4	* 40.9	United States, États-Unis	41.1	46.8	* 38.4	Partenaire 1
Partner 2	Belgium, Belgique	1.8	3.4	* 6.5	China, Chine	3.8	7.1	* 13.1	Partenaire 2
Partner 3	Netherlands, Pays-Bas	6.3	7.0	* 5.6	Mexico, Mexique	4.7	6.4	* 7.0	Partenaire 3
Côte d'Ivoire									**Côte d'Ivoire**
Partner 1	Netherlands, Pays-Bas	11.0	14.2	* 11.9	China, Chine	3.1	* 7.0	* 13.5	Partenaire 1
Partner 2	United States, États-Unis	14.1	* 10.3	* 9.4	France	27.7	* 11.9	* 11.1	Partenaire 2
Partner 3	Viet Nam	0.2	1.0	* 6.2	Nigeria, Nigéria	24.5	* 26.3	* 9.2	Partenaire 3
Croatia									**Croatie**
Partner 1	Italy, Italie	21.2	18.7	* 13.6	Germany, Allemagne	14.8	12.5	* 15.8	Partenaire 1
Partner 2	Germany, Allemagne	10.7	10.3	* 12.3	Italy, Italie	16.0	15.2	* 12.9	Partenaire 2
Partner 3	Slovenia, Slovénie	8.1	7.8	* 10.7	Slovenia, Slovénie	6.8	5.8	* 10.7	Partenaire 3
Cuba									**Cuba**
Partner 1	China, Chine	4.9	* 27.4	* 23.0	China, Chine	11.5	* 18.6	* 21.3	Partenaire 1
Partner 2	Canada	20.3	* 22.7	* 21.1	Spain, Espagne	* 8.7	* 13.6	* 15.6	Partenaire 2
Partner 3	Spain, Espagne	6.9	* 6.1	* 10.2	Mexico, Mexique	* 3.6	* 5.4	* 5.9	Partenaire 3
Cyprus									**Chypre**
Partner 1	Libya, Libye	* 0.5	0.7	* 9.0	Greece, Grèce	17.1	18.7	* 18.9	Partenaire 1
Partner 2	Bunkers, Com. de soute	15.7	0.1	* 8.2	Italy, Italie	10.1	9.3	* 7.4	Partenaire 2
Partner 3	Greece, Grèce	* 11.4	* 21.5	* 7.7	China, Chine	3.8	5.3	* 7.2	Partenaire 3
Czechia									**Tchéquie**
Partner 1	Germany, Allemagne	33.5	33.4	33.3	Germany, Allemagne	30.0	26.9	24.7	Partenaire 1
Partner 2	Slovakia, Slovaquie	8.6	8.2	7.0	China, Chine	5.1	12.1	15.1	Partenaire 2
Partner 3	Poland, Pologne	5.5	6.0	6.2	Poland, Pologne	5.0	6.1	7.4	Partenaire 3
Dem. People's Rep. Korea									**Rép. pop. dém. de Corée**
Partner 1	China, Chine	* 35.0	* 56.2	* 90.2	China, Chine	* 45.0	* 62.8	* 92.7	Partenaire 1
Partner 2	India, Inde	* 0.6	* 6.9	* 1.8	Russian Federation, Fédération de Russie	* 9.3	* 1.3	* 2.4	Partenaire 2
Partner 3	Zambia, Zambie	* ~0.0	* ~0.0	* 0.9	India, Inde	* 1.6	* 11.8	* 1.7	Partenaire 3
Dem. Rep. of the Congo									**Rép. dém. du Congo**
Partner 1	China, Chine	* 11.6	* 43.3	* 46.6	China, Chine	* 3.1	* 10.8	* 18.1	Partenaire 1
Partner 2	Zambia, Zambie	* 1.4	* 21.9	* 16.4	South Africa, Afrique du Sud	* 17.0	* 19.3	* 15.8	Partenaire 2
Partner 3	Rep. of Korea, République de Corée	* ~0.0	* 1.7	* 7.6	Zambia, Zambie	* 6.0	* 7.6	* 14.5	Partenaire 3
Denmark									**Danemark**
Partner 1	Undisclosed, Non divulgués [3]	3.1	1.4	15.9	Germany, Allemagne	21.0	20.7	22.5	Partenaire 1
Partner 2	Germany, Allemagne	* 17.2	* 19.8	14.5	Sweden, Suède	14.1	13.3	11.8	Partenaire 2
Partner 3	Sweden, Suède	* 14.8	* 14.2	10.5	Netherlands, Pays-Bas	6.7	7.1	7.6	Partenaire 3
Djibouti									**Djibouti**
Partner 1	United States, États-Unis	* 1.0	* 0.4	* 27.9	China, Chine	* 11.0	* 3.2	* 49.2	Partenaire 1
Partner 2	Saudi Arabia, Arabie saoudite	* 0.1	* 0.8	* 20.0	India, Inde	* 19.2	* 3.2	* 6.1	Partenaire 2
Partner 3	United Arab Emirates, Émirats arabes unis	* 5.3	* 1.0	* 4.9	Saudi Arabia, Arabie saoudite	* 3.1	* 6.0	* 4.9	Partenaire 3
Dominica									**Dominique**
Partner 1	Indonesia, Indonésie	...	...	* 16.2	United States, États-Unis	36.6	41.8	* 48.1	Partenaire 1
Partner 2	Saudi Arabia, Arabie saoudite	...	...	* 12.6	China, Chine	2.2	4.0	* 13.8	Partenaire 2
Partner 3	Belarus, Bélarus	...	...	* 8.9	Mexico, Mexique	0.5	0.5	* 7.3	Partenaire 3
Dominican Republic									**République dominicaine**
Partner 1	United States, États-Unis	70.3	57.7	* 53.3	United States, États-Unis	54.8	39.0	* 44.4	Partenaire 1
Partner 2	Haiti, Haïti	2.7	16.8	* 9.6	China, Chine	5.4	10.7	* 13.2	Partenaire 2
Partner 3	Canada	0.6	0.5	* 8.9	Mexico, Mexique	2.8	6.0	* 4.6	Partenaire 3
Ecuador									**Équateur**
Partner 1	United States, États-Unis	* 50.1	* 34.7	30.9	United States, États-Unis	19.2	* 27.9	21.8	Partenaire 1
Partner 2	Peru, Pérou	8.8	* 7.6	7.5	China, Chine	6.5	7.8	18.9	Partenaire 2
Partner 3	China, Chine	* 0.1	1.9	6.9	Colombia, Colombie	14.4	* 9.8	7.9	Partenaire 3

21 Major trading partner *(continued)*
Three largest trade partners as a percentage of total international merchandise trade in US dollars, as at 2018

Partenaire commercial principal *(suite)*
Trois principaux partenaires commerciaux en pourcentage du total de commerce international de marchandises en dollars américains, en 2018

Country or area / Major trading partner	Percentage of exports			Major trading partner	Percentage of imports			Pays ou zone
	2005	2010	2018		2005	2010	2018	
Egypt								**Égypte**
Partner 1 United Arab Emirates, Émirats arabes unis	2.9	2.3	* 10.6	China, Chine	5.0	9.2	* 12.2	Partenaire 1
Partner 2 Italy, Italie	10.1	8.4	* 8.5	Germany, Allemagne	10.4	7.6	* 6.8	Partenaire 2
Partner 3 Turkey, Turquie	3.1	3.7	* 7.2	Italy, Italie	4.2	5.6	* 6.3	Partenaire 3
El Salvador								**El Salvador**
Partner 1 United States, États-Unis	52.9	48.4	* 44.9	United States, États-Unis	36.5	33.0	* 31.8	Partenaire 1
Partner 2 Honduras	14.1	12.9	* 13.8	China, Chine	3.2	10.4	* 13.7	Partenaire 2
Partner 3 Guatemala	12.4	14.0	* 13.8	Guatemala	8.7	8.7	* 9.9	Partenaire 3
Equatorial Guinea								**Guinée équatoriale**
Partner 1 China, Chine	* 21.7	* 6.2	* 28.1	Spain, Espagne	* 11.2	* 5.8	* 21.0	Partenaire 1
Partner 2 India, Inde	* ~0.0	* 1.3	* 11.2	China, Chine	* 1.9	* 8.9	* 20.2	Partenaire 2
Partner 3 Portugal	* 5.6	* 2.5	* 9.1	United States, États-Unis	* 24.8	* 5.3	* 13.1	Partenaire 3
Eritrea								**Érythrée**
Partner 1 China, Chine	* 0.7	* 5.8	* 52.8	Egypt, Égypte	* 2.3	* 10.9	* 28.9	Partenaire 1
Partner 2 Rep. of Korea, République de Corée	...	* 0.1	* 23.1	China, Chine	* 2.7	* 7.6	* 11.8	Partenaire 2
Partner 3 United Arab Emirates, Émirats arabes unis	* 0.3	* 13.3	* 13.9	Italy, Italie	* 11.6	* 4.9	* 8.2	Partenaire 3
Estonia								**Estonie**
Partner 1 Finland, Finlande	24.6	15.3	15.1	Germany, Allemagne	12.8	10.6	10.0	Partenaire 1
Partner 2 Sweden, Suède	12.2	14.0	10.4	Russian Federation, Fédération de Russie	11.8	10.5	9.8	Partenaire 2
Partner 3 Latvia, Lettonie	8.5	8.0	9.1	Finland, Finlande	11.7	11.5	9.4	Partenaire 3
Eswatini								**Eswatini**
Partner 1 South Africa, Afrique du Sud	37.5	* 50.1	* 69.4	South Africa, Afrique du Sud	80.9	* 81.2	* 77.6	Partenaire 1
Partner 2 Kenya	~0.0	* 2.5	* 5.9	China, Chine	4.0	* 1.4	* 6.6	Partenaire 2
Partner 3 Nigeria, Nigéria	...	* 2.4	* 4.7	India, Inde	~0.0	* 1.3	* 2.2	Partenaire 3
Ethiopia								**Éthiopie**
Partner 1 United States, États-Unis	4.7	4.4	* 9.8	China, Chine	12.6	24.0	* 31.9	Partenaire 1
Partner 2 Saudi Arabia, Arabie saoudite	6.3	6.3	* 9.7	United States, États-Unis	9.2	5.6	* 8.8	Partenaire 2
Partner 3 Germany, Allemagne	13.1	11.4	* 8.6	India, Inde	6.0	7.2	* 7.5	Partenaire 3
Falkland Islands (Malvinas)								**Îles Falkland (Malvinas)**
Partner 1 Spain, Espagne	* 78.1	* 79.5	* 80.9	United Kingdom, Royaume-Uni	* 73.1	* 77.7	* 54.2	Partenaire 1
Partner 2 United States, États-Unis	* 5.6	* 3.1	* 5.4	Spain, Espagne	* 0.8	* 1.2	* 29.5	Partenaire 2
Partner 3 Namibia, Namibie	...	...	* 3.1	Netherlands, Pays-Bas	* 8.2	* 9.1	* 6.1	Partenaire 3
Faroe Islands								**Îles Féroé**
Partner 1 Russian Federation, Fédération de Russie	3.6	* 4.0	* 24.8	Denmark, Danemark	26.7	* 30.4	* 56.6	Partenaire 1
Partner 2 United Kingdom, Royaume-Uni	28.4	* 17.3	* 17.4	Norway, Norvège	17.4	* 18.1	* 12.2	Partenaire 2
Partner 3 Denmark, Danemark	14.6	* 11.0	* 10.8	Germany, Allemagne	6.6	* 6.1	* 5.6	Partenaire 3
Fiji								**Fidji**
Partner 1 United States, États-Unis	15.4	11.4	17.9	Singapore, Singapour	29.9	33.1	20.8	Partenaire 1
Partner 2 Australia, Australie	20.4	21.1	12.9	China, Chine	* 3.3	6.1	16.3	Partenaire 2
Partner 3 Bunkers, Com. de soute	...	9.9	8.0	Australia, Australie	* 24.6	20.3	15.7	Partenaire 3
Finland								**Finlande**
Partner 1 Germany, Allemagne	* 10.6	* 9.5	14.8	Germany, Allemagne	* 14.9	* 13.2	15.2	Partenaire 1
Partner 2 Sweden, Suède	* 10.7	* 11.4	10.2	Russian Federation, Fédération de Russie	* 13.9	* 17.7	13.9	Partenaire 2
Partner 3 Netherlands, Pays-Bas	* 4.7	* 6.6	6.5	Sweden, Suède	* 10.6	* 10.0	10.8	Partenaire 3
France								**France**
Partner 1 Germany, Allemagne	14.5	16.2	* 14.8	Germany, Allemagne	17.2	17.3	* 15.8	Partenaire 1
Partner 2 Spain, Espagne	10.2	7.4	* 7.7	China, Chine	5.5	8.2	* 9.0	Partenaire 2
Partner 3 Italy, Italie	9.2	8.1	* 7.6	Italy, Italie	8.6	7.5	* 7.7	Partenaire 3
French Polynesia								**Polynésie française**
Partner 1 Japan, Japon	28.3	20.1	* 48.5	France	35.5	28.1	* 44.5	Partenaire 1
Partner 2 United States, États-Unis	13.8	11.6	* 25.4	New Zealand, Nouvelle-Zélande	6.9	8.1	* 8.4	Partenaire 2
Partner 3 France	13.8	13.2	* 11.8	United States, États-Unis	10.0	10.1	* 8.3	Partenaire 3
Gabon								**Gabon**
Partner 1 China, Chine	4.0	* 8.0	* 46.2	France	39.3	* 32.9	* 20.7	Partenaire 1
Partner 2 Australia, Australie	1.3	* ~0.0	* 7.9	China, Chine	1.7	* 4.9	* 19.5	Partenaire 2
Partner 3 Malaysia, Malaisie	~0.0	* 4.0	* 5.9	Lebanon, Liban	0.4	* 0.2	* 9.9	Partenaire 3
Gambia								**Gambie**
Partner 1 Viet Nam	...	~0.0	* 35.8	Côte d'Ivoire	12.6	19.4	* 29.2	Partenaire 1
Partner 2 Mali	0.1	3.4	* 27.5	Senegal, Sénégal	2.0	2.5	* 17.8	Partenaire 2
Partner 3 Guinea-Bissau, Guinée-Bissau	0.3	3.1	* 9.4	China, Chine	9.3	8.7	* 8.3	Partenaire 3

Major trading partner *(continued)*
Three largest trade partners as a percentage of total international merchandise trade in US dollars, as at 2018

Partenaire commercial principal *(suite)*
Trois principaux partenaires commerciaux en pourcentage du total de commerce international de marchandises en dollars américains, en 2018

Country or area	Major trading partner	Percentage of exports			Major trading partner	Percentage of imports			Pays ou zone
		2005	2010	2018		2005	2010	2018	
Georgia									**Géorgie**
Partner 1	Azerbaijan, Azerbaïdjan	9.6	* 15.3	15.0	Turkey, Turquie	11.5	16.9	16.1	Partenaire 1
Partner 2	Russian Federation, Fédération de Russie	17.8	* 2.7	13.0	Russian Federation, Fédération de Russie	15.4	* 4.6	10.3	Partenaire 2
Partner 3	Armenia, Arménie	4.6	9.8	8.5	China, Chine	1.9	6.4	9.1	Partenaire 3
Germany									**Allemagne**
Partner 1	United States, États-Unis	8.8	6.8	* 8.7	China, Chine	6.5	9.5	* 10.0	Partenaire 1
Partner 2	France	10.1	* 9.6	* 8.2	Netherlands, Pays-Bas	8.3	7.8	* 8.1	Partenaire 2
Partner 3	China, Chine	2.7	5.6	* 6.7	France	8.6	7.7	* 6.3	Partenaire 3
Ghana									**Ghana**
Partner 1	India, Inde	1.4	0.9	21.5	China, Chine	8.1	13.2	19.1	Partenaire 1
Partner 2	China, Chine	1.4	1.0	11.9	United States, États-Unis	7.1	13.7	8.0	Partenaire 2
Partner 3	South Africa, Afrique du Sud	* 25.1	53.5	10.2	Belgium, Belgique	5.8	5.5	5.8	Partenaire 3
Gibraltar									**Gibraltar**
Partner 1	Mauritania, Mauritanie	...	* ~0.0	* 28.8	Areas nes, Zones nsa [1]	...	* 15.0	* 59.8	Partenaire 1
Partner 2	Germany, Allemagne	* 42.3	* 2.1	* 22.3	Netherlands, Pays-Bas	* 2.7	* 9.4	* 7.6	Partenaire 2
Partner 3	Netherlands, Pays-Bas	* 0.1	* 0.1	* 12.5	United Kingdom, Royaume-Uni	* 16.7	* 14.8	* 7.0	Partenaire 3
Greece									**Grèce**
Partner 1	Italy, Italie	10.5	* 9.2	10.2	Germany, Allemagne	13.3	10.7	10.1	Partenaire 1
Partner 2	Germany, Allemagne	12.5	* 9.3	6.3	Iraq	0.1	1.3	8.2	Partenaire 2
Partner 3	Turkey, Turquie	5.4	* 6.0	6.1	Russian Federation, Fédération de Russie	7.7	9.6	7.5	Partenaire 3
Greenland									**Groenland**
Partner 1	Denmark, Danemark	86.7	88.9	* 81.3	Denmark, Danemark	71.5	* 57.6	* 72.2	Partenaire 1
Partner 2	Portugal	...	4.1	* 8.3	Sweden, Suède	16.1	* 21.6	* 9.8	Partenaire 2
Partner 3	Areas nes, Zones nsa [1]	~0.0	2.3	* 6.0	China, Chine	~0.0	1.8	* 2.6	Partenaire 3
Grenada									**Grenade**
Partner 1	United States, États-Unis	21.4	* 16.3	* 33.3	United States, États-Unis	37.5	* 31.9	* 42.0	Partenaire 1
Partner 2	Germany, Allemagne	1.6	* 6.0	* 8.6	United Kingdom, Royaume-Uni	5.8	* 4.2	* 6.9	Partenaire 2
Partner 3	Saint Lucia, Sainte-Lucie	9.3	* 11.2	* 7.4	China, Chine	3.2	* 3.4	* 4.5	Partenaire 3
Guatemala									**Guatemala**
Partner 1	United States, États-Unis	50.1	38.8	* 34.5	United States, États-Unis	33.9	37.1	* 39.9	Partenaire 1
Partner 2	El Salvador	12.1	11.7	* 11.0	China, Chine	7.2	7.1	* 10.7	Partenaire 2
Partner 3	Honduras	7.3	8.3	* 8.8	Mexico, Mexique	8.7	11.2	* 10.7	Partenaire 3
Guinea									**Guinée**
Partner 1	China, Chine	0.2	* 1.4	* 39.1	China, Chine	3.9	* 6.7	* 30.7	Partenaire 1
Partner 2	United Arab Emirates, Émirats arabes unis	~0.0	* 0.2	* 13.8	Netherlands, Pays-Bas	1.2	* 20.6	* 11.9	Partenaire 2
Partner 3	India, Inde	0.2	* 0.3	* 13.1	India, Inde	2.3	* 2.6	* 8.8	Partenaire 3
Guinea-Bissau									**Guinée-Bissau**
Partner 1	India, Inde	86.6	* 76.2	* 71.8	Portugal	37.2	* 24.2	* 30.2	Partenaire 1
Partner 2	Viet Nam	...	* 4.2	* 20.0	Senegal, Sénégal	40.9	* 21.4	* 18.2	Partenaire 2
Partner 3	Togo	...	* 8.5	* 2.4	China, Chine	2.4	* 4.0	* 10.1	Partenaire 3
Guyana									**Guyana**
Partner 1	Canada	16.0	39.6	26.9	United States, États-Unis	31.1	27.7	57.0	Partenaire 1
Partner 2	United States, États-Unis	15.5	10.2	15.4	Trinidad and Tobago, Trinité-et-Tobago	33.3	22.0	18.2	Partenaire 2
Partner 3	Panama	~0.0	0.1	10.9	China, Chine	4.1	5.8	5.5	Partenaire 3
Haiti									**Haïti**
Partner 1	United States, États-Unis	* 83.7	* 81.2	* 81.3	United States, États-Unis	* 49.3	* 35.2	* 34.8	Partenaire 1
Partner 2	Dominican Rep., République dominicaine	* 4.2	* 2.3	* 3.9	Dominican Rep., République dominicaine	* 12.0	* 23.4	* 20.2	Partenaire 2
Partner 3	Canada	* 3.8	* 3.6	* 2.8	China, Chine	* 2.2	* 7.4	* 13.6	Partenaire 3
Honduras									**Honduras**
Partner 1	United States, États-Unis	41.6	* 38.9	* 40.2	United States, États-Unis	36.8	38.5	* 34.7	Partenaire 1
Partner 2	Germany, Allemagne	8.3	7.5	* 7.9	China, Chine	2.3	7.7	* 15.0	Partenaire 2
Partner 3	Belgium, Belgique	5.2	4.3	* 7.0	Guatemala	7.8	8.9	* 8.6	Partenaire 3
Hungary									**Hongrie**
Partner 1	Germany, Allemagne	30.1	27.1	* 27.3	Germany, Allemagne	27.6	27.0	* 26.5	Partenaire 1
Partner 2	Romania, Roumanie	3.7	5.3	* 5.2	Austria, Autriche	6.6	6.0	* 6.2	Partenaire 2
Partner 3	Italy, Italie	5.5	5.3	* 5.1	Poland, Pologne	3.8	4.7	* 5.6	Partenaire 3
Iceland									**Islande**
Partner 1	Netherlands, Pays-Bas	12.5	34.0	30.2	Norway, Norvège	7.0	9.1	11.5	Partenaire 1
Partner 2	United Kingdom, Royaume-Uni	17.8	10.1	9.9	China, Chine	5.1	6.0	8.8	Partenaire 2
Partner 3	Spain, Espagne	7.4	4.7	8.2	Germany, Allemagne	13.8	7.5	8.7	Partenaire 3

21

Major trading partner *(continued)*
Three largest trade partners as a percentage of total international merchandise trade in US dollars, as at 2018

Partenaire commercial principal *(suite)*
Trois principaux partenaires commerciaux en pourcentage du total de commerce international de marchandises en dollars américains, en 2018

Country or area / Major trading partner		Percentage of exports			Major trading partner	Percentage of imports			Pays ou zone
		2005	2010	2018		2005	2010	2018	
India									**Inde**
Partner 1	United States, États-Unis	16.5	11.2	* 15.6	China, Chine	* 7.2	11.8	* 16.2	Partenaire 1
Partner 2	United Arab Emirates, Émirats arabes unis	8.4	12.3	* 9.7	United States, États-Unis	* 6.0	5.5	* 5.4	Partenaire 2
Partner 3	China, Hong Kong SAR, Chine, RAS Hong Kong	4.4	4.3	* 5.1	United Arab Emirates, Émirats arabes unis	* 3.6	8.8	* 5.2	Partenaire 3
Indonesia									**Indonésie**
Partner 1	China, Chine	7.8	9.9	15.1	China, Chine	10.1	15.1	24.1	Partenaire 1
Partner 2	Japan, Japon	21.1	16.3	10.8	Singapore, Singapour	16.4	14.9	11.4	Partenaire 2
Partner 3	United States, États-Unis	11.5	9.1	10.2	Japan, Japon	12.0	12.5	9.5	Partenaire 3
Iran (Islamic Republic of)									**Iran (Rép. islamique d')**
Partner 1	Asia nes, Asie nsa	...	...	* 42.4	China, Chine	* 6.4	10.4	* 25.4	Partenaire 1
Partner 2	Europe nes, Europe nsa [4]	23.9	18.9	* 14.0	United Arab Emirates, Émirats arabes unis	* 18.7	28.6	* 15.8	Partenaire 2
Partner 3	China, Chine	0.8	5.3	* 8.6	Rep. of Korea, République de Corée	* 5.5	6.7	* 7.1	Partenaire 3
Iraq									**Iraq**
Partner 1	Areas nes, Zones nsa [1]	...	...	* 99.8	Areas nes, Zones nsa [1]	69.0	* 94.8	* 68.4	Partenaire 1
Partner 2	Singapore, Singapour	...	...	* 0.2	Turkey, Turquie	* 7.1	* 1.0	* 7.6	Partenaire 2
Partner 3	United Arab Emirates, Émirats arabes unis	0.5	~0.0	* ~0.0	China, Chine	* 1.0	* 0.2	* 7.3	Partenaire 3
Ireland									**Irlande**
Partner 1	United States, États-Unis	18.7	* 23.8	27.8	United Kingdom, Royaume-Uni	31.2	* 28.8	21.9	Partenaire 1
Partner 2	Belgium, Belgique	* 15.1	* 14.9	13.1	United States, États-Unis	14.1	* 15.4	17.5	Partenaire 2
Partner 3	United Kingdom, Royaume-Uni	17.1	* 14.0	11.4	France	3.4	* 8.2	12.6	Partenaire 3
Israel									**Israël**
Partner 1	United States, États-Unis	* 37.8	* 33.2	27.1	China, Chine	* 4.2	* 8.0	13.7	Partenaire 1
Partner 2	China, Chine	* 1.8	* 3.5	7.7	United States, États-Unis	* 13.6	* 11.2	13.4	Partenaire 2
Partner 3	United Kingdom, Royaume-Uni	* 3.9	* 3.9	7.1	Turkey, Turquie	* 3.3	* 3.1	8.1	Partenaire 3
Italy									**Italie**
Partner 1	Germany, Allemagne	* 13.1	14.3	* 12.5	Germany, Allemagne	18.1	16.0	* 16.3	Partenaire 1
Partner 2	France	* 12.2	11.5	* 10.3	France	10.2	8.7	* 8.8	Partenaire 2
Partner 3	United States, États-Unis	* 8.0	6.1	* 9.1	China, Chine	4.6	7.8	* 7.1	Partenaire 3
Jamaica									**Jamaïque**
Partner 1	United States, États-Unis	25.6	49.6	* 45.0	United States, États-Unis	42.8	37.4	* 43.7	Partenaire 1
Partner 2	Netherlands, Pays-Bas	2.3	5.1	* 12.0	Japan, Japon	4.4	2.3	* 6.3	Partenaire 2
Partner 3	Canada	19.4	12.3	* 9.6	China, Chine	2.9	4.6	* 6.3	Partenaire 3
Japan									**Japon**
Partner 1	United States, États-Unis	22.9	15.6	* 19.3	China, Chine	21.0	22.1	* 24.5	Partenaire 1
Partner 2	China, Chine	13.5	19.4	* 19.0	United States, États-Unis	12.7	10.0	* 11.0	Partenaire 2
Partner 3	Rep. of Korea, République de Corée	7.8	8.1	* 7.6	Australia, Australie	4.8	6.5	* 5.8	Partenaire 3
Jordan									**Jordanie**
Partner 1	United States, États-Unis	* 26.1	* 13.2	* 21.5	China, Chine	9.2	10.8	* 13.5	Partenaire 1
Partner 2	Free Zones, Zones franches	5.6	7.5	* 12.5	Saudi Arabia, Arabie saoudite	23.7	* 19.8	* 13.5	Partenaire 2
Partner 3	Saudi Arabia, Arabie saoudite	* 5.9	* 9.6	* 11.3	United States, États-Unis	5.6	5.6	* 9.8	Partenaire 3
Kazakhstan									**Kazakhstan**
Partner 1	Italy, Italie	15.0	16.7	* 17.9	Russian Federation, Fédération de Russie	38.0	22.8	* 39.1	Partenaire 1
Partner 2	China, Chine	8.7	17.7	* 12.0	China, Chine	7.2	16.5	* 16.0	Partenaire 2
Partner 3	Netherlands, Pays-Bas	3.2	7.3	* 9.8	Germany, Allemagne	7.5	7.6	* 5.1	Partenaire 3
Kenya									**Kenya**
Partner 1	Pakistan	5.4	4.4	* 10.8	China, Chine	5.2	12.6	* 22.6	Partenaire 1
Partner 2	Uganda, Ouganda	16.6	12.7	* 10.4	India, Inde	5.6	10.8	* 9.9	Partenaire 2
Partner 3	United States, États-Unis	6.7	5.5	* 8.0	United Arab Emirates, Émirats arabes unis	14.2	12.1	* 8.0	Partenaire 3
Kiribati									**Kiribati**
Partner 1	Malaysia, Malaisie	...	...	* 33.2	Australia, Australie	35.6	28.1	* 21.8	Partenaire 1
Partner 2	United States, États-Unis	~0.0	...	* 21.2	Fiji, Fidji	20.9	26.8	* 21.8	Partenaire 2
Partner 3	Fiji, Fidji	15.5	2.2	* 14.9	China, Chine	2.3	5.4	* 9.6	Partenaire 3
Kuwait									**Koweït**
Partner 1	Areas nes, Zones nsa [1]	* 0.2	...	* 90.5	China, Chine	* 6.8	12.5	* 16.4	Partenaire 1
Partner 2	India, Inde	* 1.0	* 11.9	* 1.4	United States, États-Unis	* 10.8	11.4	* 10.3	Partenaire 2
Partner 3	Saudi Arabia, Arabie saoudite	* 0.7	* 0.8	* 1.2	United Arab Emirates, Émirats arabes unis	* 4.5	4.5	* 8.7	Partenaire 3
Kyrgyzstan									**Kirghizistan**
Partner 1	United Kingdom, Royaume-Uni	0.3	0.6	39.6	China, Chine	9.3	20.7	40.2	Partenaire 1
Partner 2	Russian Federation, Fédération de Russie	20.0	17.3	16.1	Russian Federation, Fédération de Russie	34.2	33.6	24.8	Partenaire 2
Partner 3	Kazakhstan	17.3	12.2	13.0	Kazakhstan	16.3	12.0	9.7	Partenaire 3

21

Major trading partner *(continued)*
Three largest trade partners as a percentage of total international merchandise trade in US dollars, as at 2018

Partenaire commercial principal *(suite)*
Trois principaux partenaires commerciaux en pourcentage du total de commerce international de marchandises en dollars américains, en 2018

Country or area / Major trading partner		Percentage of exports			Major trading partner	Percentage of imports			Pays ou zone
		2005	2010	2018		2005	2010	2018	
Lao People's Dem. Rep.									**Rép. dém. populaire lao**
Partner 1	China, Chine	* 4.2	11.7	* 36.1	Thailand, Thaïlande	* 68.4	71.8	* 61.9	Partenaire 1
Partner 2	Thailand, Thaïlande	* 37.0	53.5	* 31.3	China, Chine	* 9.2	9.8	* 18.2	Partenaire 2
Partner 3	Viet Nam	* 15.9	6.5	* 17.2	Viet Nam	* 6.2	6.6	* 10.1	Partenaire 3
Latvia									**Lettonie**
Partner 1	Lithuania, Lituanie	* 10.5	16.2	16.0	Lithuania, Lituanie	13.5	17.1	17.5	Partenaire 1
Partner 2	Estonia, Estonie	* 10.4	13.5	11.5	Germany, Allemagne	13.6	11.5	10.6	Partenaire 2
Partner 3	Russian Federation, Fédération de Russie	8.3	10.6	9.1	Poland, Pologne	6.3	7.9	8.9	Partenaire 3
Lebanon									**Liban**
Partner 1	Congo	* 0.5	* 0.9	* 51.6	Syrian Arab Rep., Rép. arabe syrienne	* 2.1	1.9	* 29.6	Partenaire 1
Partner 2	Angola	* 0.9	* 0.9	* 5.3	Austria, Autriche	0.5	0.5	* 27.1	Partenaire 2
Partner 3	United States, États-Unis	3.1	1.4	* 4.7	China, Chine	* 7.9	9.1	* 11.0	Partenaire 3
Lesotho									**Lesotho**
Partner 1	South Africa, Afrique du Sud	* 42.3	74.9	* 49.2	South Africa, Afrique du Sud	* 77.1	78.9	* 70.7	Partenaire 1
Partner 2	United States, États-Unis	* 44.5	21.4	* 45.5	China, Chine	* 3.8	2.6	* 14.8	Partenaire 2
Partner 3	Eswatini	...	0.2	* 1.7	Asia nes, Asie nsa [2]	* 5.6	5.3	* 5.3	Partenaire 3
Liberia									**Libéria**
Partner 1	Areas nes, Zones nsa [1]	20.1	...	* 30.1	Areas nes, Zones nsa [1]	...	...	* 82.2	Partenaire 1
Partner 2	Switzerland, Suisse	* 0.2	* 0.5	* 21.5	China, Chine	* 10.0	* 29.6	* 6.5	Partenaire 2
Partner 3	United Kingdom, Royaume-Uni	* 3.9	* 1.0	* 8.5	India, Inde	* 3.1	* 2.2	* 2.3	Partenaire 3
Libya									**Libye**
Partner 1	Italy, Italie	* 36.7	42.3	* 15.7	Italy, Italie	* 18.3	9.4	* 12.7	Partenaire 1
Partner 2	Germany, Allemagne	* 16.2	2.6	* 13.8	China, Chine	* 3.3	9.8	* 11.3	Partenaire 2
Partner 3	Spain, Espagne	* 9.8	9.2	* 12.6	Turkey, Turquie	* 1.8	10.6	* 9.3	Partenaire 3
Lithuania									**Lituanie**
Partner 1	Russian Federation, Fédération de Russie	11.4	15.6	14.0	Russian Federation, Fédération de Russie	27.5	32.7	14.7	Partenaire 1
Partner 2	Latvia, Lettonie	10.0	9.5	9.7	Germany, Allemagne	14.8	10.9	11.9	Partenaire 2
Partner 3	Poland, Pologne	5.3	7.7	8.2	Poland, Pologne	8.2	8.8	11.3	Partenaire 3
Luxembourg									**Luxembourg**
Partner 1	Germany, Allemagne	25.4	28.4	* 26.9	Belgium, Belgique	33.8	* 24.9	24.3	Partenaire 1
Partner 2	France	17.2	16.2	* 14.8	Germany, Allemagne	25.9	* 25.6	* 24.1	Partenaire 2
Partner 3	Belgium, Belgique	11.4	12.6	* 11.6	France	11.8	* 14.9	* 11.8	Partenaire 3
Madagascar									**Madagascar**
Partner 1	France	* 34.4	* 33.1	* 22.7	China, Chine	* 13.9	12.2	* 20.8	Partenaire 1
Partner 2	United States, États-Unis	22.0	* 4.2	* 18.7	United Arab Emirates, Émirats arabes unis	1.2	2.9	* 7.6	Partenaire 2
Partner 3	Germany, Allemagne	* 6.4	* 7.3	* 7.1	India, Inde	* 5.9	2.4	* 7.5	Partenaire 3
Malawi									**Malawi**
Partner 1	Belgium, Belgique	1.4	12.4	* 22.0	South Africa, Afrique du Sud	32.7	30.1	* 17.8	Partenaire 1
Partner 2	South Africa, Afrique du Sud	18.6	5.8	* 7.8	China, Chine	2.9	9.1	* 14.7	Partenaire 2
Partner 3	United Rep. of Tanzania, Rép.-Unie Tanzanie	0.8	0.7	* 7.7	India, Inde	4.7	7.6	* 10.9	Partenaire 3
Malaysia									**Malaisie**
Partner 1	Singapore, Singapour	15.6	13.4	* 14.3	China, Chine	11.5	12.6	* 19.6	Partenaire 1
Partner 2	China, Chine	6.6	12.6	* 13.5	Singapore, Singapour	11.7	11.4	* 11.1	Partenaire 2
Partner 3	United States, États-Unis	19.6	9.5	* 9.5	United States, États-Unis	12.9	10.7	* 8.3	Partenaire 3
Maldives									**Maldives**
Partner 1	Thailand, Thaïlande	15.3	29.9	* 48.6	United Arab Emirates, Émirats arabes unis	15.7	18.8	* 18.6	Partenaire 1
Partner 2	Germany, Allemagne	3.6	2.8	* 7.2	Singapore, Singapour	24.1	17.9	* 13.5	Partenaire 2
Partner 3	United States, États-Unis	2.9	0.7	* 7.0	India, Inde	11.3	11.5	* 12.0	Partenaire 3
Mali									**Mali**
Partner 1	South Africa, Afrique du Sud	34.9	57.1	* 41.0	Senegal, Sénégal	11.5	13.6	* 20.5	Partenaire 1
Partner 2	Switzerland, Suisse	30.3	12.1	* 21.4	China, Chine	4.9	9.9	* 15.2	Partenaire 2
Partner 3	Burkina Faso	0.2	2.2	* 6.1	Côte d'Ivoire, Côte d'Ivoire	10.2	7.9	* 9.7	Partenaire 3
Malta									**Malte**
Partner 1	United States, États-Unis	* 13.5	7.0	* 20.3	Italy, Italie	30.7	24.6	* 19.2	Partenaire 1
Partner 2	Bunkers, Com. de soute	0.1	0.1	* 10.7	Cayman Isds, Îles Caïmanes	~0.0	1.0	* 10.2	Partenaire 2
Partner 3	Germany, Allemagne	* 12.1	* 10.5	* 10.7	Canada	0.2	2.2	* 9.0	Partenaire 3
Marshall Islands									**Îles Marshall**
Partner 1	Spain, Espagne	* ~0.0	* ~0.0	* 17.2	Areas nes, Zones nsa [1]	...	...	* 95.2	Partenaire 1
Partner 2	United States, États-Unis	* 25.9	* 12.9	* 15.0	United States, États-Unis	* 21.5	* 7.6	* 1.9	Partenaire 2
Partner 3	Thailand, Thaïlande	* 35.4	* 33.6	* 14.4	China, Chine	* 11.4	* 24.3	* 1.7	Partenaire 3

21

Major trading partner *(continued)*
Three largest trade partners as a percentage of total international merchandise trade in US dollars, as at 2018

Partenaire commercial principal *(suite)*
Trois principaux partenaires commerciaux en pourcentage du total de commerce international de marchandises en dollars américains, en 2018

Country or area / Major trading partner	Percentage of exports			Major trading partner	Percentage of imports			Pays ou zone
	2005	2010	2018		2005	2010	2018	
Mauritania								**Mauritanie**
Partner 1 China, Chine	1.5	39.4	* 35.1	Rep. of Korea, République de Corée	* ~0.0	0.1	* 18.1	Partenaire 1
Partner 2 Switzerland, Suisse	...	13.1	* 15.4	United Arab Emirates, Émirats arabes unis	* 0.9	12.1	* 8.9	Partenaire 2
Partner 3 Spain, Espagne	10.7	7.2	* 11.6	Norway, Norvège	* 0.8	~0.0	* 7.8	Partenaire 3
Mauritius								**Maurice**
Partner 1 France	15.7	16.2	* 15.8	China, Chine	9.8	13.3	* 16.4	Partenaire 1
Partner 2 United Kingdom, Royaume-Uni	30.0	23.7	* 11.9	India, Inde	6.9	22.3	* 16.4	Partenaire 2
Partner 3 United States, États-Unis	9.2	10.9	* 11.2	South Africa, Afrique du Sud	8.6	8.4	* 8.5	Partenaire 3
Mexico								**Mexique**
Partner 1 United States, États-Unis	85.8	80.1	76.5	United States, États-Unis	53.6	48.2	46.6	Partenaire 1
Partner 2 Areas nes, Zones nsa [1]	~0.0	0.1	5.5	China, Chine	8.0	15.1	18.0	Partenaire 2
Partner 3 Canada	2.0	3.6	3.1	Japan, Japon	5.9	5.0	3.9	Partenaire 3
Micronesia (Fed. States of)								**Micronésie (États féd. de)**
Partner 1 Thailand, Thaïlande	* 82.0	* 30.6	* 52.5	Rep. of Korea, République de Corée	4.0	2.4	* 25.3	Partenaire 1
Partner 2 China, Chine	...	* 3.8	* 16.2	United States, États-Unis	42.9	48.7	* 22.0	Partenaire 2
Partner 3 Philippines	* 5.9	* 1.5	* 11.5	China, Chine	2.7	2.7	* 13.4	Partenaire 3
Mongolia								**Mongolie**
Partner 1 China, Chine	48.1	* 81.8	* 85.0	China, Chine	24.9	* 41.5	* 32.6	Partenaire 1
Partner 2 United Kingdom, Royaume-Uni	8.2	* 2.1	* 10.7	Russian Federation, Fédération de Russie	35.3	* 26.8	* 28.1	Partenaire 2
Partner 3 Russian Federation, Fédération de Russie	2.6	* 2.5	* 1.1	Japan, Japon	6.4	* 4.6	* 8.4	Partenaire 3
Montenegro								**Monténégro**
Partner 1 Serbia, Serbie	...	* 28.2	* 17.8	Serbia, Serbie	...	26.2	* 21.5	Partenaire 1
Partner 2 Bosnia Herzegovina, Bosnie-Herzégovine	...	7.3	* 12.7	China, Chine	...	5.4	* 9.6	Partenaire 2
Partner 3 Areas nes, Zones nsa [1]	...	0.1	* 9.4	Germany, Allemagne	...	7.1	* 8.5	Partenaire 3
Montserrat								**Montserrat**
Partner 1 Antigua and Barbuda, Antigua-et-Barbuda	29.9	2.5	* 60.8	United States, États-Unis	56.6	* 68.5	* 53.0	Partenaire 1
Partner 2 United States, États-Unis	23.6	28.5	* 9.3	United Kingdom, Royaume-Uni	7.8	* 5.6	* 11.4	Partenaire 2
Partner 3 France	1.2	25.9	* 8.1	Japan, Japon	4.8	* 5.1	* 3.3	Partenaire 3
Morocco								**Maroc**
Partner 1 Spain, Espagne	20.0	* 17.0	* 23.7	Spain, Espagne	11.6	10.6	* 16.9	Partenaire 1
Partner 2 France	30.1	22.5	* 22.9	France	18.2	15.6	* 11.9	Partenaire 2
Partner 3 Italy, Italie	5.0	4.5	* 4.6	China, Chine	5.1	8.4	* 9.0	Partenaire 3
Mozambique								**Mozambique**
Partner 1 India, Inde	* 1.8	* 1.4	27.6	South Africa, Afrique du Sud	* 40.6	34.4	26.1	Partenaire 1
Partner 2 Netherlands, Pays-Bas	* 59.7	* 52.7	21.2	China, Chine	* 2.9	3.6	11.8	Partenaire 2
Partner 3 South Africa, Afrique du Sud	* 16.5	* 20.8	17.2	United Arab Emirates, Émirats arabes unis	* 1.6	1.3	7.6	Partenaire 3
Myanmar								**Myanmar**
Partner 1 China, Chine	* 7.2	6.2	* 38.9	China, Chine	* 29.0	27.1	* 31.8	Partenaire 1
Partner 2 Thailand, Thaïlande	* 47.1	41.7	* 19.4	Singapore, Singapour	* 18.5	27.0	* 15.2	Partenaire 2
Partner 3 Japan, Japon	* 5.4	2.8	* 6.5	Thailand, Thaïlande	* 21.9	11.4	* 11.3	Partenaire 3
Namibia								**Namibie**
Partner 1 South Africa, Afrique du Sud	28.2	29.0	* 21.8	South Africa, Afrique du Sud	83.2	* 72.4	* 55.1	Partenaire 1
Partner 2 Botswana	0.4	0.7	* 12.2	Bulgaria, Bulgarie	~0.0	~0.0	* 6.5	Partenaire 2
Partner 3 Switzerland, Suisse	0.3	0.9	* 9.5	Botswana	0.2	* 0.3	* 6.1	Partenaire 3
Nepal								**Népal**
Partner 1 India, Inde	* 52.4	65.3	* 56.7	India, Inde	* 53.0	63.6	* 65.0	Partenaire 1
Partner 2 United States, États-Unis	* 29.1	6.3	* 11.2	China, Chine	* 8.4	11.0	* 12.6	Partenaire 2
Partner 3 Turkey, Turquie	* 0.2	1.0	* 6.4	Areas, nes, Zones nsa [1]	* ~0.0	...	* 2.0	Partenaire 3
Netherlands								**Pays-Bas**
Partner 1 Germany, Allemagne	23.8	22.2	* 21.9	Germany, Allemagne	19.0	20.3	* 18.5	Partenaire 1
Partner 2 Belgium, Belgique	11.7	9.9	* 10.3	Belgium, Belgique	10.8	8.9	* 10.7	Partenaire 2
Partner 3 United Kingdom, Royaume-Uni	9.2	7.4	* 8.6	China, Chine	7.6	9.3	* 9.0	Partenaire 3
New Caledonia								**Nouvelle-Calédonie**
Partner 1 China, Chine	5.6	3.5	* 49.9	France	32.3	22.3	* 40.7	Partenaire 1
Partner 2 Rep. of Korea, République de Corée	13.1	11.6	* 16.1	Australia, Australie	9.2	* 9.7	* 13.9	Partenaire 2
Partner 3 Japan, Japon	18.3	18.8	* 9.8	Singapore, Singapour	15.0	12.9	* 11.2	Partenaire 3
New Zealand								**Nouvelle-Zélande**
Partner 1 China, Chine	5.1	11.1	24.2	China, Chine	10.8	16.0	19.8	Partenaire 1
Partner 2 Australia, Australie	21.0	23.0	15.9	Australia, Australie	20.6	18.2	11.5	Partenaire 2
Partner 3 United States, États-Unis	14.9	8.6	9.6	United States, États-Unis	11.0	10.4	10.1	Partenaire 3

Major trading partner *(continued)*
Three largest trade partners as a percentage of total international merchandise trade in US dollars, as at 2018

Partenaire commercial principal *(suite)*
Trois principaux partenaires commerciaux en pourcentage du total de commerce international de marchandises en dollars américains, en 2018

Country or area	Major trading partner	Percentage of exports			Major trading partner	Percentage of imports			Pays ou zone
		2005	2010	2018		2005	2010	2018	
Nicaragua									**Nicaragua**
Partner 1	United States, États-Unis	35.4	32.8	* 58.6	United States, États-Unis	20.7	20.7	* 23.5	Partenaire 1
Partner 2	Mexico, Mexique	5.1	2.8	* 6.6	China, Chine	5.9	8.7	* 15.2	Partenaire 2
Partner 3	El Salvador	14.2	10.7	* 5.6	Mexico, Mexique	8.5	7.7	* 11.0	Partenaire 3
Niger									**Niger**
Partner 1	France	* 22.2	* 9.0	* 31.3	France	15.8	11.0	* 28.3	Partenaire 1
Partner 2	Thailand, Thaïlande	* ~0.0	1.2	* 11.6	China, Chine	5.5	43.8	* 16.2	Partenaire 2
Partner 3	Malaysia, Malaisie	...	0.7	* 11.1	United States, États-Unis	5.4	6.1	* 7.8	Partenaire 3
Nigeria									**Nigéria**
Partner 1	India, Inde	* 9.3	10.5	* 17.9	China, Chine	* 13.8	16.6	* 18.7	Partenaire 1
Partner 2	United States, États-Unis	* 45.0	34.4	* 12.8	Belgium, Belgique	* 5.1	3.9	* 12.9	Partenaire 2
Partner 3	Spain, Espagne	* 8.0	3.3	* 9.9	Netherlands, Pays-Bas	* 3.1	0.8	* 9.2	Partenaire 3
North Macedonia									**Macédoine du Nord**
Partner 1	Germany, Allemagne	17.8	21.3	47.0	Germany, Allemagne	10.4	11.2	11.6	Partenaire 1
Partner 2	Serbia, Serbie	...	21.2	7.9	United Kingdom, Royaume-Uni	1.4	5.2	9.5	Partenaire 2
Partner 3	Bulgaria, Bulgarie	3.7	8.8	5.2	Greece, Grèce	9.2	8.2	8.5	Partenaire 3
Northern Mariana Islands									**Îles Mariannes du Nord**
Partner 1	Areas nes, Zones nsa [1]	91.1	* 91.1	* 91.2	Areas nes, Zones nsa [1]	56.5	* 66.2	* 71.2	Partenaire 1
Partner 2	Rep. of Korea, République de Corée	* 0.5	* 0.6	* 4.2	China, Hong Kong SAR, Chine, RAS Hong Kong	* 12.3	* 11.4	* 12.9	Partenaire 2
Partner 3	Singapore, Singapour	* 0.1	* 0.7	* 3.3	Rep. of Korea, République de Corée	* 10.6	* 4.3	* 3.2	Partenaire 3
Norway									**Norvège**
Partner 1	United Kingdom, Royaume-Uni	25.0	27.5	* 21.1	Sweden, Suède	14.4	14.0	* 11.5	Partenaire 1
Partner 2	Germany, Allemagne	12.6	11.1	* 15.5	Germany, Allemagne	13.4	12.3	* 11.1	Partenaire 2
Partner 3	Netherlands, Pays-Bas	9.9	11.9	* 9.9	China, Chine	5.6	8.5	* 9.8	Partenaire 3
Oman									**Oman**
Partner 1	Areas nes, Zones nsa [1]	9.7	16.8	* 62.5	United Arab Emirates, Émirats arabes unis	26.1	28.4	* 38.9	Partenaire 1
Partner 2	United Arab Emirates, Émirats arabes unis	* 7.3	11.6	* 6.9	Areas nes, Zones nsa [1]	1.6	...	* 11.0	Partenaire 2
Partner 3	Qatar	* 0.4	0.5	* 4.1	China, Chine	2.4	4.8	* 5.9	Partenaire 3
Other non-specified areas									**Autres zones non-spécifiées**
Partner 1	China, Chine	21.6	28.0	* 26.3	China, Chine	* 11.0	14.3	* 19.1	Partenaire 1
Partner 2	China, Hong Kong SAR, Chine, RAS Hong Kong	16.2	13.8	* 13.7	Japan, Japon	* 25.3	20.7	* 17.6	Partenaire 2
Partner 3	United States, États-Unis	15.1	11.5	* 12.0	United States, États-Unis	* 11.6	10.2	* 12.5	Partenaire 3
Pakistan									**Pakistan**
Partner 1	United States, États-Unis	24.8	17.2	16.1	China, Chine	9.4	14.0	24.2	Partenaire 1
Partner 2	China, Chine	2.7	6.7	7.7	United Arab Emirates, Émirats arabes unis	9.9	14.0	14.4	Partenaire 2
Partner 3	United Kingdom, Royaume-Uni	5.7	5.2	7.3	Saudi Arabia, Arabie saoudite	10.6	10.2	5.4	Partenaire 3
Palau									**Palaos**
Partner 1	Areas nes, Zones nsa [1]	...	...	* 38.9	United States, États-Unis	* 31.5	34.9	* 35.8	Partenaire 1
Partner 2	Japan, Japon	* 90.8	* 82.5	* 23.4	Singapore, Singapour	...	17.9	* 15.3	Partenaire 2
Partner 3	Guam	...	* 3.1	* 14.5	Japan, Japon	* 14.2	12.3	* 12.5	Partenaire 3
Panama									**Panama**
Partner 1	United States, États-Unis	* 44.8	* 19.8	* 20.6	China, Chine	* 6.4	24.9	* 31.3	Partenaire 1
Partner 2	Colombia, Colombie	* 1.6	* 15.6	* 9.5	Singapore, Singapour	* 0.1	10.4	* 18.9	Partenaire 2
Partner 3	Areas nes, Zones nsa [1]	1.0	0.2	* 8.9	United States, États-Unis	* 26.8	20.5	* 9.5	Partenaire 3
Papua New Guinea									**Papouasie-Nvl-Guinée**
Partner 1	Japan, Japon	* 3.9	* 7.0	* 24.3	Australia, Australie	* 58.7	* 39.5	* 29.8	Partenaire 1
Partner 2	Australia, Australie	* 56.7	* 42.8	* 23.5	China, Chine	* 3.2	* 7.3	* 17.7	Partenaire 2
Partner 3	China, Chine	* 4.0	* 6.4	* 22.0	Singapore, Singapour	* 7.2	* 11.1	* 10.4	Partenaire 3
Paraguay									**Paraguay**
Partner 1	Brazil, Brésil	48.9	33.7	31.1	China, Chine	19.6	34.2	28.2	Partenaire 1
Partner 2	Argentina, Argentine	11.9	8.5	25.5	Brazil, Brésil	27.2	24.1	22.3	Partenaire 2
Partner 3	Russian Federation, Fédération de Russie	3.2	6.6	8.4	Argentina, Argentine	19.9	11.9	10.0	Partenaire 3
Peru									**Pérou**
Partner 1	China, Chine	10.9	15.2	* 26.3	China, Chine	8.5	17.2	* 22.3	Partenaire 1
Partner 2	United States, États-Unis	30.7	17.1	* 15.7	United States, États-Unis	17.8	19.4	* 20.3	Partenaire 2
Partner 3	Switzerland, Suisse	4.6	10.7	* 5.3	Brazil, Brésil	8.2	7.3	* 6.2	Partenaire 3
Philippines									**Philippines**
Partner 1	United States, États-Unis	18.0	14.7	15.6	China, Chine	6.3	8.5	19.6	Partenaire 1
Partner 2	China, Hong Kong SAR, Chine, RAS Hong Kong	8.1	8.4	14.2	Rep. of Korea, République de Corée	4.8	6.9	10.0	Partenaire 2
Partner 3	Japan, Japon	17.5	15.2	14.0	Japan, Japon	17.1	12.5	9.9	Partenaire 3

Major trading partner *(continued)*
Three largest trade partners as a percentage of total international merchandise trade in US dollars, as at 2018

Partenaire commercial principal *(suite)*
Trois principaux partenaires commerciaux en pourcentage du total de commerce international de marchandises en dollars américains, en 2018

Country or area	Major trading partner	Percentage of exports			Major trading partner	Percentage of imports			Pays ou zone
		2005	2010	2018		2005	2010	2018	
Poland									**Pologne**
Partner 1	Germany, Allemagne	28.2	26.1	* 27.2	Germany, Allemagne	24.7	21.7	* 22.7	Partenaire 1
Partner 2	United Kingdom, Royaume-Uni	5.6	6.3	* 6.4	China, Chine	5.4	9.5	* 12.1	Partenaire 2
Partner 3	Czechia, Tchéquie	4.6	5.9	* 6.3	Russian Federation, Fédération de Russie	8.8	10.5	* 6.8	Partenaire 3
Portugal									**Portugal**
Partner 1	Spain, Espagne	27.5	27.0	25.3	Spain, Espagne	30.7	32.0	31.5	Partenaire 1
Partner 2	France	13.4	12.0	12.7	Germany, Allemagne	14.3	13.9	13.9	Partenaire 2
Partner 3	Germany, Allemagne	12.3	13.0	11.5	France	8.7	7.2	7.6	Partenaire 3
Qatar									**Qatar**
Partner 1	Japan, Japon	40.0	28.7	* 19.1	United States, États-Unis	11.6	11.8	* 14.4	Partenaire 1
Partner 2	Rep. of Korea, République de Corée	15.8	16.0	* 15.6	China, Chine	5.2	9.1	* 10.4	Partenaire 2
Partner 3	India, Inde	3.5	8.6	* 12.9	Germany, Allemagne	9.2	7.2	* 9.3	Partenaire 3
Republic of Korea									**République de Corée**
Partner 1	China, Chine	21.8	25.1	* 24.8	China, Chine	14.8	16.8	* 20.5	Partenaire 1
Partner 2	United States, États-Unis	14.6	10.7	* 12.0	Japan, Japon	18.5	15.1	* 11.5	Partenaire 2
Partner 3	Viet Nam	1.2	2.1	* 8.3	United States, États-Unis	11.8	9.5	* 10.6	Partenaire 3
Republic of Moldova									**République de Moldova**
Partner 1	Romania, Roumanie	10.2	16.0	* 24.8	Romania, Roumanie	11.2	10.0	* 14.4	Partenaire 1
Partner 2	Russian Federation, Fédération de Russie	31.8	26.2	* 10.5	Russian Federation, Fédération de Russie	11.7	15.2	* 11.8	Partenaire 2
Partner 3	Italy, Italie	12.2	9.6	* 9.7	Ukraine	20.9	13.7	* 10.6	Partenaire 3
Romania									**Roumanie**
Partner 1	Germany, Allemagne	14.0	18.1	* 23.0	Germany, Allemagne	14.0	16.7	* 20.1	Partenaire 1
Partner 2	Italy, Italie	19.4	13.8	* 11.2	Italy, Italie	* 15.5	11.6	* 10.0	Partenaire 2
Partner 3	France	7.4	8.3	* 6.8	Hungary, Hongrie	3.3	8.7	* 7.5	Partenaire 3
Russian Federation									**Fédération de Russie**
Partner 1	Areas nes, Zones nsa [1]	~0.0	0.5	* 14.9	China, Chine	7.4	17.0	* 21.2	Partenaire 1
Partner 2	China, Chine	5.4	* 5.0	* 10.4	Germany, Allemagne	13.4	11.6	* 10.0	Partenaire 2
Partner 3	Netherlands, Pays-Bas	10.2	13.4	* 9.6	United States, États-Unis	4.6	4.3	* 5.5	Partenaire 3
Rwanda									**Rwanda**
Partner 1	Dem.Rep. of the Congo, Rép. Dém. du Congo	2.6	7.5	* 31.8	China, Chine	3.7	15.0	* 21.2	Partenaire 1
Partner 2	Kenya	22.0	16.3	* 16.0	Uganda, Ouganda	13.2	12.7	* 11.2	Partenaire 2
Partner 3	United Arab Emirates, Émirats arabes unis	~0.0	0.2	* 14.0	Kenya	13.5	10.1	* 7.8	Partenaire 3
Saint Helena									**Sainte-Hélène**
Partner 1	United States, États-Unis	* 22.3	* 34.2	* 35.3	United Kingdom, Royaume-Uni	* 49.4	* 45.9	* 44.6	Partenaire 1
Partner 2	Lebanon, Liban	...	~0.0	* 30.1	South Africa, Afrique du Sud	* 13.9	* 14.1	* 43.1	Partenaire 2
Partner 3	Japan, Japon	* 19.8	* 21.5	* 11.3	Greece, Grèce	* 0.1	...	* 7.8	Partenaire 3
Saint Kitts and Nevis									**Saint-Kitts-et-Nevis**
Partner 1	United States, États-Unis	91.9	* 74.2	* 68.7	United States, États-Unis	57.9	68.0	* 67.0	Partenaire 1
Partner 2	Saint Lucia, Sainte-Lucie	0.3	* 3.5	* 6.8	Trinidad and Tobago, Trinité-et-Tobago	14.1	6.5	* 4.4	Partenaire 2
Partner 3	Trinidad and Tobago, Trinité-et-Tobago	2.0	1.9	* 6.5	Canada	2.2	2.0	* 2.7	Partenaire 3
Saint Lucia									**Sainte-Lucie**
Partner 1	United States, États-Unis	14.0	57.8	* 32.2	United States, États-Unis	44.0	42.0	* 43.8	Partenaire 1
Partner 2	Trinidad and Tobago, Trinité-et-Tobago	22.5	19.1	* 7.9	Trinidad and Tobago, Trinité-et-Tobago	14.2	21.0	* 15.0	Partenaire 2
Partner 3	Areas nes, Zones nsa [1]	2.1	...	* 7.9	Areas nes, Zones nsa [1]	0.2	...	* 6.0	Partenaire 3
Saint Pierre and Miquelon									**Saint-Pierre-et-Miquelon**
Partner 1	Canada	* 0.2	* 21.4	* 36.7	France	* 49.3	* 62.5	* 57.4	Partenaire 1
Partner 2	Sudan, Soudan	...	...	* 23.7	Canada	* 31.7	* 33.1	* 34.3	Partenaire 2
Partner 3	France	* 9.1	* 14.6	* 18.4	Netherlands, Pays-Bas	* 0.9	* 0.8	* 4.0	Partenaire 3
Saint Vincent & Grenadines									**Saint-Vincent-Grenadines**
Partner 1	Barbados, Barbade	12.7	11.3	* 18.5	United States, États-Unis	33.3	33.0	* 37.9	Partenaire 1
Partner 2	Saint Lucia, Sainte-Lucie	10.9	20.6	* 16.2	Trinidad and Tobago, Trinité-et-Tobago	23.6	27.1	* 15.7	Partenaire 2
Partner 3	Dominica, Dominique	7.2	6.5	* 13.7	United Kingdom, Royaume-Uni	9.4	5.7	* 7.4	Partenaire 3
Samoa									**Samoa**
Partner 1	American Samoa, Samoa américaines	13.4	4.5	* 26.6	New Zealand, Nouvelle-Zélande	33.4	30.7	* 26.4	Partenaire 1
Partner 2	Australia, Australie	74.8	65.3	* 21.4	Singapore, Singapour	4.4	5.9	* 16.6	Partenaire 2
Partner 3	New Zealand, Nouvelle-Zélande	2.0	9.3	* 19.7	United States, États-Unis	14.0	11.5	* 11.1	Partenaire 3
Sao Tome and Principe									**Sao Tomé-et-Principe**
Partner 1	Netherlands, Pays-Bas	38.5	15.9	* 29.6	Portugal	57.0	* 62.4	* 54.5	Partenaire 1
Partner 2	Spain, Espagne	...	~0.0	* 16.6	Angola	20.4	15.6	* 19.8	Partenaire 2
Partner 3	France	1.8	0.3	* 16.1	China, Chine	0.2	2.2	* 5.0	Partenaire 3

21

Major trading partner *(continued)*
Three largest trade partners as a percentage of total international merchandise trade in US dollars, as at 2018

Partenaire commercial principal *(suite)*
Trois principaux partenaires commerciaux en pourcentage du total de commerce international de marchandises en dollars américains, en 2018

Country or area / Major trading partner		Percentage of exports			Major trading partner	Percentage of imports			Pays ou zone
		2005	2010	2018		2005	2010	2018	
Saudi Arabia									**Arabie saoudite**
Partner 1	Areas nes, Zones nsa [1]	7.8	6.2	* 74.4	China, Chine	7.5	11.9	* 14.2	Partenaire 1
Partner 2	United Arab Emirates, Émirats arabes unis	1.3	1.5	* 3.8	United States, États-Unis	15.1	13.4	* 13.2	Partenaire 2
Partner 3	China, Chine	0.7	1.4	* 2.7	Germany, Allemagne	8.3	7.9	* 6.5	Partenaire 3
Senegal									**Sénégal**
Partner 1	Mali	* 19.2	* 26.1	* 19.8	France	20.9	19.7	* 14.7	Partenaire 1
Partner 2	Switzerland, Suisse	0.2	* 7.9	* 10.1	China, Chine	3.6	8.3	* 9.7	Partenaire 2
Partner 3	Bunkers, Com. de soute	11.4	7.6	* 5.1	Nigeria, Nigéria	10.4	10.2	* 7.9	Partenaire 3
Serbia									**Serbie**
Partner 1	Italy, Italie	...	11.4	12.3	Germany, Allemagne	...	10.6	13.4	Partenaire 1
Partner 2	Germany, Allemagne	...	10.3	11.9	Italy, Italie	...	8.6	9.4	Partenaire 2
Partner 3	Bosnia Herzegovina, Bosnie-Herzégovine	...	11.1	7.9	China, Chine	...	7.2	8.4	Partenaire 3
Seychelles									**Seychelles**
Partner 1	United Arab Emirates, Émirats arabes unis	0.1	37.9	* 35.7	United Arab Emirates, Émirats arabes unis	3.8	48.0	* 25.6	Partenaire 1
Partner 2	France	14.7	19.2	* 18.1	Spain, Espagne	7.8	6.6	* 10.1	Partenaire 2
Partner 3	United Kingdom, Royaume-Uni	28.5	18.6	* 13.0	France	6.6	5.0	* 8.8	Partenaire 3
Sierra Leone									**Sierra Leone**
Partner 1	Netherlands, Pays-Bas	~0.0	* 6.3	* 23.0	China, Chine	* 5.5	* 12.2	* 16.8	Partenaire 1
Partner 2	China, Chine	~0.0	* 2.9	* 13.0	India, Inde	2.8	* 5.4	* 7.8	Partenaire 2
Partner 3	Côte d'Ivoire	~0.0	* 0.2	* 12.2	Turkey, Turquie	0.1	* 3.0	* 7.2	Partenaire 3
Singapore									**Singapour**
Partner 1	China, Chine	8.6	10.3	* 14.5	China, Chine	10.2	10.8	* 13.8	Partenaire 1
Partner 2	China, Hong Kong SAR, Chine, RAS Hong Kong	9.4	11.7	* 12.3	Malaysia, Malaisie	13.6	11.7	* 11.9	Partenaire 2
Partner 3	Malaysia, Malaisie	13.3	11.9	* 10.6	United States, États-Unis	11.7	11.5	* 10.6	Partenaire 3
Slovakia									**Slovaquie**
Partner 1	Germany, Allemagne	* 25.6	19.2	* 20.6	Germany, Allemagne	20.6	16.1	* 16.7	Partenaire 1
Partner 2	Czechia, Tchéquie	* 14.3	13.7	* 11.5	Czechia, Tchéquie	12.8	10.3	* 10.3	Partenaire 2
Partner 3	Poland, Pologne	* 6.2	7.3	* 7.6	Europe nes, Europe nsa [4]	8.4	12.1	* 8.6	Partenaire 3
Slovenia									**Slovénie**
Partner 1	Germany, Allemagne	19.9	19.6	* 20.2	Germany, Allemagne	17.2	16.2	* 17.1	Partenaire 1
Partner 2	Italy, Italie	12.7	12.1	* 11.5	Italy, Italie	17.4	15.6	* 14.5	Partenaire 2
Partner 3	Croatia, Croatie	9.1	6.7	* 8.0	Austria, Autriche	7.9	7.9	* 8.0	Partenaire 3
Solomon Islands									**Îles Salomon**
Partner 1	China, Chine	45.8	49.1	* 65.2	Australia, Australie	42.0	32.4	* 19.9	Partenaire 1
Partner 2	Italy, Italie	...	3.1	* 7.7	Singapore, Singapour	6.3	24.1	* 13.8	Partenaire 2
Partner 3	Switzerland, Suisse	...	...	* 3.9	New Zealand, Nouvelle-Zélande	6.5	5.9	* 13.2	Partenaire 3
Somalia									**Somalie**
Partner 1	Saudi Arabia, Arabie saoudite	* 3.4	* 35.7	* 51.8	China, Chine	* 3.0	* 5.7	* 18.5	Partenaire 1
Partner 2	Oman	* 3.4	* 19.0	* 24.1	India, Inde	* 6.5	* 5.6	* 17.8	Partenaire 2
Partner 3	United Arab Emirates, Émirats arabes unis	* 38.0	* 21.4	* 7.7	Oman	* 5.2	* 5.5	* 14.1	Partenaire 3
South Africa									**Afrique du Sud**
Partner 1	China, Chine	2.9	9.9	* 9.8	China, Chine	9.0	13.8	* 18.3	Partenaire 1
Partner 2	United States, États-Unis	10.4	8.7	* 7.5	Germany, Allemagne	14.0	10.9	* 11.5	Partenaire 2
Partner 3	Germany, Allemagne	7.1	6.7	* 6.6	United States, États-Unis	7.9	7.2	* 6.6	Partenaire 3
South Sudan									**Soudan du sud**
Partner 1	China, Chine	...	...	* 93.3	Uganda, Ouganda	...	...	* 46.8	Partenaire 1
Partner 2	India, Inde	...	...	* 4.8	Kenya	...	...	* 27.4	Partenaire 2
Partner 3	Pakistan	...	...	* 1.5	China, Chine	...	...	* 9.0	Partenaire 3
Spain									**Espagne**
Partner 1	France	19.2	18.2	* 14.7	Germany, Allemagne	14.7	11.7	* 12.5	Partenaire 1
Partner 2	Germany, Allemagne	11.4	11.5	* 10.9	France	14.1	10.7	* 10.7	Partenaire 2
Partner 3	Italy, Italie	8.4	8.9	* 7.8	China, Chine	5.0	7.9	* 8.3	Partenaire 3
Sri Lanka									**Sri Lanka**
Partner 1	United States, États-Unis	32.6	21.3	* 24.9	India, Inde	17.3	20.6	* 21.1	Partenaire 1
Partner 2	United Kingdom, Royaume-Uni	12.6	12.3	* 8.9	China, Chine	7.6	10.0	* 19.7	Partenaire 2
Partner 3	India, Inde	9.1	5.6	* 6.7	United Arab Emirates, Émirats arabes unis	2.7	2.7	* 7.3	Partenaire 3
State of Palestine									**État de Palestine**
Partner 1	Israel, Israël	86.6	84.9	* 83.2	Israel, Israël	70.2	72.6	* 58.2	Partenaire 1
Partner 2	Jordan, Jordanie	5.2	5.4	* 5.6	Turkey, Turquie	4.5	4.5	* 8.9	Partenaire 2
Partner 3	United Arab Emirates, Émirats arabes unis	0.4	2.0	* 2.5	China, Chine	4.2	4.6	* 7.1	Partenaire 3

21

Major trading partner *(continued)*
Three largest trade partners as a percentage of total international merchandise trade in US dollars, as at 2018

Partenaire commercial principal *(suite)*
Trois principaux partenaires commerciaux en pourcentage du total de commerce international de marchandises en dollars américains, en 2018

Country or area	Major trading partner	Percentage of exports			Major trading partner	Percentage of imports			Pays ou zone
		2005	2010	2018		2005	2010	2018	
Sudan									**Soudan**
Partner 1	United Arab Emirates, Émirats arabes unis	...	...	* 40.2	China, Chine	...	...	* 22.0	Partenaire 1
Partner 2	China, Chine	...	...	* 17.3	United Arab Emirates, Émirats arabes unis	...	...	* 10.6	Partenaire 2
Partner 3	Saudi Arabia, Arabie saoudite	...	...	* 14.2	Saudi Arabia, Arabie saoudite	...	...	* 6.9	Partenaire 3
Suriname									**Suriname**
Partner 1	Switzerland, Suisse	0.3	8.8	* 32.0	United States, États-Unis	18.9	24.6	* 31.8	Partenaire 1
Partner 2	China, Hong Kong SAR, Chine, RAS Hong Kong	0.1	~0.0	* 22.5	Netherlands, Pays-Bas	17.7	17.5	* 13.8	Partenaire 2
Partner 3	Belgium, Belgique	10.2	10.1	* 10.8	Trinidad and Tobago, Trinité-et-Tobago	19.1	23.7	* 9.7	Partenaire 3
Sweden									**Suède**
Partner 1	Germany, Allemagne	10.4	11.4	10.6	Germany, Allemagne	18.1	18.0	17.9	Partenaire 1
Partner 2	Norway, Norvège	8.7	10.0	10.4	Netherlands, Pays-Bas	6.7	6.2	9.4	Partenaire 2
Partner 3	Finland, Finlande	6.1	6.4	6.9	Norway, Norvège	8.2	8.7	8.6	Partenaire 3
Switzerland									**Suisse**
Partner 1	Germany, Allemagne	19.4	19.3	15.3	Germany, Allemagne	31.6	31.9	20.7	Partenaire 1
Partner 2	United States, États-Unis	10.9	10.1	13.2	United Kingdom, Royaume-Uni	4.4	3.9	9.5	Partenaire 2
Partner 3	China, Chine	2.1	3.7	9.7	Italy, Italie	10.5	10.2	7.6	Partenaire 3
Syrian Arab Republic									**République arabe syrienne**
Partner 1	Lebanon, Liban	2.9	3.8	* 98.1	Turkey, Turquie	4.3	9.5	* 25.3	Partenaire 1
Partner 2	Egypt, Égypte	2.3	* 3.4	* 0.4	China, Chine	* 8.1	8.8	* 21.3	Partenaire 2
Partner 3	Saudi Arabia, Arabie saoudite	5.7	4.8	* 0.3	Egypt, Égypte	* 3.5	4.2	* 4.6	Partenaire 3
Tajikistan									**Tadjikistan**
Partner 1	Kazakhstan	* 2.1	* 1.4	* 30.0	China, Chine	* 13.7	* 43.4	* 39.0	Partenaire 1
Partner 2	Switzerland, Suisse	* 1.1	~0.0	* 17.5	Russian Federation, Fédération de Russie	* 22.8	* 21.2	* 23.2	Partenaire 2
Partner 3	Turkey, Turquie	* 6.0	* 23.1	* 15.4	Kazakhstan	* 14.3	* 8.2	* 15.6	Partenaire 3
Thailand									**Thaïlande**
Partner 1	United States, États-Unis	15.5	10.4	* 11.4	China, Chine	9.4	13.3	* 21.6	Partenaire 1
Partner 2	China, Chine	8.3	11.0	* 11.0	Japan, Japon	22.0	20.8	* 15.8	Partenaire 2
Partner 3	Japan, Japon	13.6	10.5	* 9.6	United States, États-Unis	7.4	5.9	* 6.2	Partenaire 3
Timor-Leste									**Timor-Leste**
Partner 1	Indonesia, Indonésie	2.0	* 0.9	* 25.4	Indonesia, Indonésie	47.0	* 19.3	* 31.9	Partenaire 1
Partner 2	United States, États-Unis	23.9	...	* 22.3	China, Chine	1.7	* 4.7	* 15.1	Partenaire 2
Partner 3	Germany, Allemagne	3.9	* 10.8	* 13.6	Singapore, Singapour	14.6	...	* 13.1	Partenaire 3
Togo									**Togo**
Partner 1	Burkina Faso	* 18.8	* 10.5	* 17.9	China, Chine	13.2	15.1	* 19.6	Partenaire 1
Partner 2	Benin, Bénin	* 11.6	* 5.3	* 14.3	France	17.6	13.6	* 10.8	Partenaire 2
Partner 3	Ghana	* 20.3	* 5.9	* 7.6	Japan, Japon	1.8	3.0	* 5.1	Partenaire 3
Tokelau									**Tokélaou**
Partner 1	France	* 5.4	* 5.8	* 23.9	Nigeria, Nigéria	...	* ~0.0	* 81.0	Partenaire 1
Partner 2	Singapore, Singapour	...	...	* 14.1	Germany, Allemagne	* 6.0	* 18.3	* 7.0	Partenaire 2
Partner 3	United States, États-Unis	* 37.3	* 11.7	* 10.0	Samoa	* 0.8	* 0.1	* 3.6	Partenaire 3
Tonga									**Tonga**
Partner 1	United States, États-Unis	23.9	16.2	* 28.1	New Zealand, Nouvelle-Zélande	38.3	31.9	* 26.9	Partenaire 1
Partner 2	Rep. of Korea, République de Corée	0.2	0.6	* 21.2	Fiji, Fidji	22.1	10.1	* 26.0	Partenaire 2
Partner 3	Japan, Japon	51.6	10.6	* 15.6	China, Chine	3.7	5.3	* 15.6	Partenaire 3
Trinidad and Tobago									**Trinité-et-Tobago**
Partner 1	United States, États-Unis	* 58.6	48.1	* 35.6	United States, États-Unis	29.2	28.0	* 31.7	Partenaire 1
Partner 2	Guyana	* 2.9	* 2.4	* 6.9	Russian Federation, Fédération de Russie	0.2	3.4	* 14.9	Partenaire 2
Partner 3	Chile, Chili	~0.0	1.3	* 6.7	China, Chine	3.0	5.8	* 7.8	Partenaire 3
Tunisia									**Tunisie**
Partner 1	France	* 32.9	* 28.7	* 30.6	Italy, Italie	20.9	17.6	* 15.6	Partenaire 1
Partner 2	Italy, Italie	* 24.1	19.9	* 16.5	France	* 23.5	* 18.9	* 15.1	Partenaire 2
Partner 3	Germany, Allemagne	* 8.5	8.5	* 11.6	China, Chine	2.9	6.1	* 9.0	Partenaire 3
Turkey									**Turquie**
Partner 1	Germany, Allemagne	* 12.9	* 10.1	* 9.6	China, Chine	* 5.9	9.3	* 10.0	Partenaire 1
Partner 2	United Kingdom, Royaume-Uni	8.1	* 6.4	* 6.1	Germany, Allemagne	* 11.7	* 9.5	* 9.1	Partenaire 2
Partner 3	United Arab Emirates, Émirats arabes unis	* 2.3	2.9	* 5.9	Russian Federation, Fédération de Russie	11.1	11.6	* 8.3	Partenaire 3
Turkmenistan									**Turkménistan**
Partner 1	China, Chine	* 0.4	* 39.0	* 81.1	Turkey, Turquie	* 8.6	* 23.5	* 26.0	Partenaire 1
Partner 2	Afghanistan	...	* 4.4	* 4.7	Russian Federation, Fédération de Russie	* 10.6	* 14.8	* 10.1	Partenaire 2
Partner 3	Turkey, Turquie	* 3.3	* 14.4	* 3.9	Germany, Allemagne	* 6.3	* 7.0	* 10.0	Partenaire 3

21

Major trading partner *(continued)*
Three largest trade partners as a percentage of total international merchandise trade in US dollars, as at 2018

Partenaire commercial principal *(suite)*
Trois principaux partenaires commerciaux en pourcentage du total de commerce international de marchandises en dollars américains, en 2018

Country or area / Major trading partner		Percentage of exports			Major trading partner	Percentage of imports			Pays ou zone
		2005	2010	2018		2005	2010	2018	
Turks and Caicos Islands									**Îles Turques-et-Caïques**
Partner 1	United States, États-Unis	99.7	* 99.1	* 38.7	United States, États-Unis	98.3	* 98.3	* 88.1	Partenaire 1
Partner 2	Central African Rep., Rép. centrafricaine	...	...	* 10.3	United Kingdom, Royaume-Uni	...	...	* 1.5	Partenaire 2
Partner 3	Spain, Espagne	...	* 0.0	* 9.9	Dominican Rep., Rép. dominicaine	0.1	* 0.2	* 1.3	Partenaire 3
Tuvalu									**Tuvalu**
Partner 1	Thailand, Thaïlande	...	* 75.2	* 78.7	Singapore, Singapour	17.5	* 0.4	* 22.8	Partenaire 1
Partner 2	Philippines	...	...	* 8.8	Fiji, Fidji	19.7	* 23.9	* 22.0	Partenaire 2
Partner 3	Ecuador, Équateur	...	...	* 4.5	China, Chine	5.1	* 5.4	* 20.6	Partenaire 3
Uganda									**Ouganda**
Partner 1	Kenya	8.9	11.8	* 19.0	China, Chine	5.3	8.9	* 17.6	Partenaire 1
Partner 2	United Arab Emirates, Émirats arabes unis	10.4	7.5	* 15.3	India, Inde	6.4	14.7	* 13.2	Partenaire 2
Partner 3	South Sudan, Soudan du sud	...	...	* 10.3	United Arab Emirates, Émirats arabes unis	6.7	8.4	* 11.8	Partenaire 3
Ukraine									**Ukraine**
Partner 1	Russian Federation, Fédération de Russie	21.9	* 26.1	* 9.1⁵	Russian Federation, Fédération de Russie	35.6	36.5	* 14.6⁶	Partenaire 1
Partner 2	Poland, Pologne	3.0	* 3.5	* 6.3⁵	China, Chine	5.0	7.7	* 11.4⁶	Partenaire 2
Partner 3	Turkey, Turquie	5.9	5.9	* 5.8⁵	Germany, Allemagne	9.4	7.6	* 10.5⁶	Partenaire 3
United Arab Emirates									**Émirats arabes unis**
Partner 1	Areas nes, Zones nsa ¹	29.2	26.4	* 51.1	Areas nes, Zones nsa ¹	0.7	30.2	* 30.2	Partenaire 1
Partner 2	Asia nes, Asie nsa ²	...	...	* 13.8	China, Chine	8.5	* 7.3	* 8.3	Partenaire 2
Partner 3	India, Inde	4.6	* 11.0	* 3.8	United States, États-Unis	6.9	* 6.0	* 7.6	Partenaire 3
United Kingdom									**Royaume-Uni**
Partner 1	United States, États-Unis	14.4	13.9	13.4	Germany, Allemagne	13.0	12.2	13.7	Partenaire 1
Partner 2	Germany, Allemagne	10.6	10.6	9.6	China, Chine	6.8	9.8	9.5	Partenaire 2
Partner 3	Netherlands, Pays-Bas	5.8	7.6	6.8	United States, États-Unis	8.4	9.0	9.4	Partenaire 3
United Rep. of Tanzania									**Rép.-Unie de Tanzanie**
Partner 1	India, Inde	4.7	5.6	* 23.5	China, Chine	6.9	10.9	* 19.4	Partenaire 1
Partner 2	South Africa, Afrique du Sud	17.6	10.7	* 16.7	India, Inde	5.9	11.2	* 15.0	Partenaire 2
Partner 3	Viet Nam	0.2	1.1	* 7.5	United Arab Emirates, Émirats arabes unis	6.3	8.4	* 7.7	Partenaire 3
United States of America									**États-Unis d'Amérique**
Partner 1	Canada	23.4	19.5	* 18.3	China, Chine	15.0	19.5	* 21.9	Partenaire 1
Partner 2	Mexico, Mexique	13.3	12.8	* 15.7	Mexico, Mexique	10.0	11.8	* 13.2	Partenaire 2
Partner 3	China, Chine	4.6	7.2	* 8.4	Canada	16.8	14.2	* 12.7	Partenaire 3
Uruguay									**Uruguay**
Partner 1	China, Chine	* 4.5	* 10.4	* 18.8	China, Chine	6.2	13.0	* 20.0	Partenaire 1
Partner 2	Brazil, Brésil	* 13.4	* 23.4	* 16.5	Brazil, Brésil	21.3	18.3	* 19.5	Partenaire 2
Partner 3	Free Zones, Zones franches	0.9	4.1	* 16.4	Argentina, Argentine	20.3	17.0	* 12.6	Partenaire 3
Uzbekistan									**Ouzbékistan**
Partner 1	Switzerland, Suisse	* 0.1	* 0.5	* 29.1	Russian Federation, Fédération de Russie	* 26.0	* 20.0	* 24.5	Partenaire 1
Partner 2	China, Chine	* 11.5	* 19.3	* 20.8	China, Chine	* 7.0	* 14.2	* 22.8	Partenaire 2
Partner 3	Russian Federation, Fédération de Russie	* 22.0	* 22.5	* 12.6	Kazakhstan	* 7.4	* 13.3	* 11.8	Partenaire 3
Vanuatu									**Vanuatu**
Partner 1	Japan, Japon	* 4.1	4.5	* 29.6	China, Chine	* 5.2	9.9	* 19.6	Partenaire 1
Partner 2	Mauritania, Mauritanie	...	...	* 25.8	Australia, Australie	* 41.3	30.9	* 16.8	Partenaire 2
Partner 3	Thailand, Thaïlande	* 1.1	~0.0	* 7.6	Japan, Japon	* 2.2	3.7	* 9.0	Partenaire 3
Venezuela (Boliv. Rep. of)									**Venezuela (Rép. boliv. du)**
Partner 1	United States, États-Unis	45.2	* 7.6	* 39.4	United States, États-Unis	31.6	30.5	* 41.7	Partenaire 1
Partner 2	China, Chine	0.4	* 5.8	* 25.1	China, Chine	3.7	11.1	* 18.3	Partenaire 2
Partner 3	India, Inde	~0.0	* ~0.0	* 19.9	Mexico, Mexique	6.9	4.5	* 9.3	Partenaire 3
Viet Nam									**Viet Nam**
Partner 1	United States, États-Unis	18.3	19.7	* 19.3	China, Chine	16.0	23.8	* 27.5	Partenaire 1
Partner 2	China, Chine	10.0	10.7	* 16.5	Rep. of Korea, République de Corée	9.8	11.5	* 22.0	Partenaire 2
Partner 3	Japan, Japon	13.4	10.7	* 7.8	Japan, Japon	11.1	10.6	* 7.9	Partenaire 3
Wallis and Futuna Islands									**Îles Wallis-et-Futuna**
Partner 1	Singapore, Singapour	...	...	* 38.2	France	32.0	* 23.1	* 37.4	Partenaire 1
Partner 2	France	* 6.8	* 1.6	* 21.8	Fiji, Fidji	5.8	* 13.4	* 23.2	Partenaire 2
Partner 3	United Kingdom, Royaume-Uni	0.1	* 0.1	* 9.1	Areas nes, Zones nsa ¹	2.5	* 12.6	* 12.5	Partenaire 3
Yemen									**Yémen**
Partner 1	China, Chine	* 35.2	* 22.2	* 39.8	China, Chine	* 6.4	* 7.9	* 22.2	Partenaire 1
Partner 2	Oman	* 0.1	* 0.2	* 30.4	Saudi Arabia, Arabie saoudite	* 6.4	6.1	* 11.5	Partenaire 2
Partner 3	United Arab Emirates, Émirats arabes unis	* 3.3	* 5.1	* 8.3	Oman	* 0.8	0.6	* 7.9	Partenaire 3

21

Major trading partner *(continued)*
Three largest trade partners as a percentage of total international merchandise trade in US dollars, as at 2018

Partenaire commercial principal *(suite)*
Trois principaux partenaires commerciaux en pourcentage du total de commerce international de marchandises en dollars américains, en 2018

Country or area / Major trading partner	Percentage of exports			Major trading partner	Percentage of imports			Pays ou zone
	2005	2010	2018		2005	2010	2018	
Zambia								**Zambie**
Partner 1	Switzerland, Suisse	28.7	51.0	42.1	South Africa, Afrique du Sud	47.6	34.4	28.8	Partenaire 1
Partner 2	China, Chine	2.1	20.2	14.4	Dem.Rep. of the Congo, Rép. Dém. du Congo	0.9	23.8	14.7	Partenaire 2
Partner 3	Dem.Rep. of the Congo, Rép. Dém. du Congo	5.4	4.6	9.5	China, Chine	3.3	5.4	13.6	Partenaire 3
Zimbabwe								**Zimbabwe**
Partner 1	South Africa, Afrique du Sud	41.5	54.2	51.5	South Africa, Afrique du Sud	15.0	48.0	39.3	Partenaire 1
Partner 2	United Arab Emirates, Émirats arabes unis	0.7	10.3	18.1	Singapore, Singapour	0.2	0.3	21.7	Partenaire 2
Partner 3	Areas nes, Zones nsa [1]	...	...	14.7	China, Chine	2.4	5.5	5.7	Partenaire 3

Source:

United Nations Statistics Division, New York, Commodity Trade Statistics Database (UN COMTRADE), last accessed May 2019.

1   Areas not elsewhere specified.
2   Asia not elsewhere specified.
3   Undisclosed (Special categories).
4   Europe not elsewhere specified.
5   Excludes the temporarily occupied territory of the Autonomous Republic of Crimea and Sevastopol.

Source:

Organisation des Nations Unies, Division de statistique, New York, Comtrade base de données de l'ONU, dernier accès mai 2019.

1   Zones non spécifiées ailleurs.
2   Asie non spécifiées ailleurs.
3   Pays non divulgués.
4   Europe non spécifiées ailleurs.
5   Excluent le territoire temporairement occupé de la République autonome de Crimée et de Sébastopol.

Part Three

Energy, environment and infrastructure

Troisième partie

Energie, environnement et infrastructures

Production, trade and supply of energy
Petajoules and gigajoules per capita

Production, commerce et fourniture d'énergie
pétajoules et gigajoules par habitant

Region, country or area	1990	1995	2000	2005	2010	2014	2015	2016	Région, pays ou zone
Total, all countries or areas									**Total, tous pays ou zones**
Primary Energy production	360 903	380 713	412 155	476 738	530 597	567 032	570 980	568 988	Production d'énergie primaire
Net imports	-8 506	-8 833	-10 761	-13 751	-12 967	-16 188	-18 261	-21 853	Importations nettes
Changes in stocks	4 141	193	-2 969	-313	138	3 372	2 540	-4 441	Variations des stocks
Total supply	348 256	371 687	404 363	463 300	517 492	547 472	550 179	551 577	Approvisionnement total
Supply per capita	62	65	66	71	74	75	75	74	Approvisionnement par habitant
Africa									**Afrique**
Primary Energy production	28 031	32 227	37 344	45 181	47 682	45 029	45 004	44 744	Production d'énergie primaire
Net imports	-12 200	-13 010	-16 264	-20 516	-19 157	-12 806	-12 949	-11 912	Importations nettes
Changes in stocks	-11	321	-33	2	19	217	87	14	Variations des stocks
Total supply	15 842	18 896	21 113	24 661	28 507	32 006	31 968	32 819	Approvisionnement total
Supply per capita	25	26	26	27	27	27	27	27	Approvisionnement par habitant
North America									**Amérique du Nord**
Primary Energy production	89 489	93 298	96 175	97 912	100 226	114 023	114 018	109 340	Production d'énergie primaire
Net imports	7 792	9 145	15 612	20 169	12 902	1 430	1 649	2 199	Importations nettes
Changes in stocks	1 783	-923	-2 221	-153	-612	980	2 082	-1 220	Variations des stocks
Total supply	95 497	103 367	114 008	118 233	113 741	114 473	113 586	112 759	Approvisionnement total
Supply per capita	223	226	234	230	209	202	199	195	Approvisionnement par habitant
South America									**Amérique du Sud**
Primary Energy production	16 260	20 322	24 066	26 610	29 395	31 197	31 933	31 617	Production d'énergie primaire
Net imports	-3 752	-5 789	-7 316	-8 057	-7 245	-6 750	-7 668	-7 792	Importations nettes
Changes in stocks	86	-6	-13	-323	-65	165	-80	-193	Variations des stocks
Total supply	12 421	14 539	16 762	18 877	22 215	24 281	24 344	24 018	Approvisionnement total
Supply per capita	42	45	48	51	56	59	58	57	Approvisionnement par habitant
Asia									**Asie**
Primary Energy production	106 957	132 962	149 279	192 228	236 262	259 448	261 719	263 754	Production d'énergie primaire
Net imports	-11 594	-8 916	-9 719	-9 634	192	7 015	7 471	3 696	Importations nettes
Changes in stocks	1 714	603	-736	-385	1 643	1 482	163	-2 010	Variations des stocks
Total supply	93 651	123 443	140 296	182 979	234 810	264 981	269 027	269 460	Approvisionnement total
Supply per capita	30	36	38	46	56	61	61	60	Approvisionnement par habitant
Europe									**Europe**
Primary Energy production	112 829	93 292	94 693	102 594	102 548	101 103	101 163	102 064	Production d'énergie primaire
Net imports	14 000	13 520	12 290	10 806	8 049	4 653	3 791	2 855	Importations nettes
Changes in stocks	366	94	267	581	-1 128	481	221	-879	Variations des stocks
Total supply	126 463	106 718	106 716	112 819	111 724	105 274	104 734	105 798	Approvisionnement total
Supply per capita	116	147	147	154	152	142	141	143	Approvisionnement par habitant
Oceania									**Océanie**
Primary Energy production	7 337	8 612	10 598	12 213	14 484	16 233	17 142	17 470	Production d'énergie primaire
Net imports	-2 752	-3 785	-5 363	-6 518	-7 710	-9 730	-10 554	-10 900	Importations nettes
Changes in stocks	203	103	-233	-37	280	47	67	-153	Variations des stocks
Total supply	4 381	4 723	5 468	5 730	6 494	6 456	6 520	6 722	Approvisionnement total
Supply per capita	161	163	176	171	177	166	165	168	Approvisionnement par habitant
Afghanistan									**Afghanistan**
Primary Energy production	19	16	18	23	41	63	60	70	Production d'énergie primaire
Net imports	* 28	* 13	* 8	* 14	96	* 72	* 86	* 73	Importations nettes
Changes in stocks	* 0	* 0	* 0	...	...	...	...	...	Variations des stocks
Total supply	* 46	* 29	25	36	137	135	146	143	Approvisionnement total
Supply per capita	* 4	* 1	1	1	5	4	4	4	Approvisionnement par habitant
Albania									**Albanie**
Primary Energy production	99	43	34	48	69	85	88	82	Production d'énergie primaire
Net imports	* 15	4	31	43	* 22	34	8	16	Importations nettes
Changes in stocks	* 23	0	...	0	0	13	6	5	Variations des stocks
Total supply	92	47	65	91	91	104	91	92	Approvisionnement total
Supply per capita	28	15	21	29	31	36	31	31	Approvisionnement par habitant
Algeria									**Algérie**
Primary Energy production	4 380	4 748	6 556	7 534	6 200	5 900	5 883	6 283	Production d'énergie primaire
Net imports	* -3 263	* -3 485	* -5 414	-5 952	-4 551	-3 732	-3 694	-4 074	Importations nettes
Changes in stocks	* 41	-8	-27	0	9	44	-35	-3	Variations des stocks
Total supply	1 075	1 270	1 170	1 583	1 641	2 123	2 222	2 211	Approvisionnement total
Supply per capita	43	45	38	48	45	54	56	54	Approvisionnement par habitant
Andorra									**Andorre**
Primary Energy production	* 0	* 0	* 0	0	1	1	1	1	Production d'énergie primaire
Net imports	* 6	* 7	* 9	* 10	* 9	8	8	8	Importations nettes
Total supply	* 7	7	9	10	10	9	9	9	Approvisionnement total
Supply per capita	* 130	111	138	130	114	111	113	116	Approvisionnement par habitant

Region, country or area	1990	1995	2000	2005	2010	2014	2015	2016	Région, pays ou zone
Angola									**Angola**
Primary Energy production	1 198	1 585	1 803	2 934	4 085	3 942	4 172	4 101	Production d'énergie primaire
Net imports	* -960	-1 224	-1 475	-2 565	-3 547	-3 244	* -3 536	* -3 442	Importations nettes
Changes in stocks	...	17	21	5	1	-77	1	* 4	Variations des stocks
Total supply	238	343	308	363	537	774	635	655	Approvisionnement total
Supply per capita	23	28	22	22	23	29	23	23	Approvisionnement par habitant
Anguilla									**Anguilla**
Primary Energy production	* 0	* 0	* 0	* 0	* 0	* 0	* 0	* 0	Production d'énergie primaire
Net imports	* 1	* 1	* 1	* 2	* 2	* 2	* 2	* 2	Importations nettes
Total supply	* 1	* 1	* 1	* 2	* 2	* 2	* 2	* 2	Approvisionnement total
Supply per capita	* 87	* 94	* 117	* 132	* 155	* 136	* 151	* 149	Approvisionnement par habitant
Antigua and Barbuda									**Antigua-et-Barbuda**
Primary Energy production	...	...	...	...	0	...	...	...	Production d'énergie primaire
Net imports	* 5	* 4	* 5	* 7	* 8	* 8	* 8	* 9	Importations nettes
Total supply	* 4	* 4	* 5	* 6	* 8	* 8	* 8	* 8	Approvisionnement total
Supply per capita	* 68	* 60	* 65	* 75	* 79	* 77	* 78	* 79	Approvisionnement par habitant
Argentina									**Argentine**
Primary Energy production	2 064	2 722	3 404	3 609	3 343	3 065	3 100	3 181	Production d'énergie primaire
Net imports	-144	-535	-866	-683	-21	447	481	442	Importations nettes
Changes in stocks	-8	-6	-17	8	16	6	-12	2	Variations des stocks
Total supply	1 928	2 194	2 556	2 919	3 307	3 506	3 594	3 621	Approvisionnement total
Supply per capita	59	63	69	75	80	82	83	83	Approvisionnement par habitant
Armenia									**Arménie**
Primary Energy production	...	10	27	36	52	50	46	44	Production d'énergie primaire
Net imports	...	59	57	69	* 70	* 92	* 80	87	Importations nettes
Changes in stocks	...	...	...	...	* 3	...	1	0	Variations des stocks
Total supply	...	68	84	105	* 119	142	124	131	Approvisionnement total
Supply per capita	...	21	27	34	* 41	49	42	45	Approvisionnement par habitant
Aruba									**Aruba**
Primary Energy production	0	0	* 5	* 5	* 5	* 1	* 1	* 1	Production d'énergie primaire
Net imports	* 7	* 10	* 21	* 26	* 23	* 12	* 12	* 12	Importations nettes
Changes in stocks	0	...	...	...	...	...	...	...	Variations des stocks
Total supply	* 7	* 10	* 26	30	* 28	* 12	* 13	* 13	Approvisionnement total
Supply per capita	* 108	* 121	* 284	299	* 273	* 120	* 122	* 120	Approvisionnement par habitant
Australia [1]									**Australie** [1]
Primary Energy production	6 567	7 784	9 731	11 451	13 606	15 272	15 930	16 322	Production d'énergie primaire
Net imports	-2 694	-3 752	-5 412	-6 717	-7 924	-9 981	-10 595	-11 026	Importations nettes
Changes in stocks	203	104	-221	-28	264	49	81	-155	Variations des stocks
Total supply	3 670	3 928	4 540	4 762	5 417	5 242	5 254	5 451	Approvisionnement total
Supply per capita	215	217	237	233	245	223	221	226	Approvisionnement par habitant
Austria									**Autriche**
Primary Energy production	340	368	410	408	488	505	503	517	Production d'énergie primaire
Net imports	714	740	777	1 003	885	880	826	862	Importations nettes
Changes in stocks	15	-14	-10	3	-38	37	-50	-16	Variations des stocks
Total supply	1 040	1 122	1 197	1 408	1 412	1 348	1 379	1 396	Approvisionnement total
Supply per capita	136	141	150	171	168	156	159	160	Approvisionnement par habitant
Azerbaijan									**Azerbaïdjan**
Primary Energy production	...	628	803	1 155	2 759	2 475	2 472	2 427	Production d'énergie primaire
Net imports	...	-91	-319	-547	-2 239	-1 899	-1 891	-1 842	Importations nettes
Changes in stocks	...	0	-2	35	34	-9	-22	-13	Variations des stocks
Total supply	...	536	485	573	486	585	603	598	Approvisionnement total
Supply per capita	...	69	60	67	54	62	63	61	Approvisionnement par habitant
Bahamas									**Bahamas**
Primary Energy production	...	...	...	0	0	0	0	0	Production d'énergie primaire
Net imports	* 35	* 22	* 26	* 27	* 34	* 30	* 19	* 12	Importations nettes
Changes in stocks	* 9	* -1	* -1	* 0	...	* -4	* -10	* -13	Variations des stocks
Total supply	* 26	* 24	* 27	* 26	35	34	* 29	* 26	Approvisionnement total
Supply per capita	* 100	* 86	* 91	* 83	96	89	* 75	* 66	Approvisionnement par habitant
Bahrain									**Bahreïn**
Primary Energy production	294	341	706	672	849	961	957	940	Production d'énergie primaire
Net imports	* -87	* -94	-382	-353	-339	-407	-382	-378	Importations nettes
Changes in stocks	* -6	-10	-6	-28	-3	-5	-4	5	Variations des stocks
Total supply	213	257	331	348	513	559	579	557	Approvisionnement total
Supply per capita	433	459	518	480	413	418	422	391	Approvisionnement par habitant

Region, country or area	1990	1995	2000	2005	2010	2014	2015	2016	Région, pays ou zone
Bangladesh									**Bangladesh**
Primary Energy production	681	792	857	1 027	1 304	1 438	1 509	1 597	Production d'énergie primaire
Net imports	84	123	139	165	163	236	274	246	Importations nettes
Changes in stocks	-3	-4	-3	1	-26	-21	-7	-20	Variations des stocks
Total supply	769	918	998	1 191	1 493	1 695	1 790	1 864	Approvisionnement total
Supply per capita	7	8	8	8	10	11	11	11	Approvisionnement par habitant
Barbados									**Barbade**
Primary Energy production	5	5	6	4	4	2	3	3	Production d'énergie primaire
Net imports	9	8	10	* 12	* 16	* 14	* 15	* 15	Importations nettes
Changes in stocks	-1	0	-1	0	0	0	1	1	Variations des stocks
Total supply	16	12	16	17	20	17	17	17	Approvisionnement total
Supply per capita	62	47	59	64	72	58	58	59	Approvisionnement par habitant
Belarus									**Bélarus**
Primary Energy production	...	138	147	159	166	167	163	166	Production d'énergie primaire
Net imports	...	912	881	962	980	1 012	891	867	Importations nettes
Changes in stocks	...	6	-1	-4	-8	9	-13	-27	Variations des stocks
Total supply	...	1 043	1 029	1 125	1 155	1 171	1 067	1 060	Approvisionnement total
Supply per capita	...	102	102	115	122	123	112	112	Approvisionnement par habitant
Belgium									**Belgique**
Primary Energy production	544	495	570	577	646	525	445	637	Production d'énergie primaire
Net imports	1 457	1 771	1 835	1 877	1 886	1 707	1 823	1 703	Importations nettes
Changes in stocks	-4	29	-21	18	18	23	40	-18	Variations des stocks
Total supply	2 005	2 237	2 426	2 436	2 515	2 210	2 227	2 358	Approvisionnement total
Supply per capita	202	222	238	234	230	197	197	208	Approvisionnement par habitant
Belize									**Belize**
Primary Energy production	4	4	5	4	14	9	8	8	Production d'énergie primaire
Net imports	4	6	6	* 7	-2	3	5	5	Importations nettes
Changes in stocks	...	...	...	...	0	0	0	0	Variations des stocks
Total supply	8	10	11	11	13	12	14	14	Approvisionnement total
Supply per capita	44	44	44	39	40	35	38	37	Approvisionnement par habitant
Benin									**Bénin**
Primary Energy production	74	79	62	70	86	108	114	105	Production d'énergie primaire
Net imports	* 1	* 10	20	37	67	71	78	83	Importations nettes
Changes in stocks	0	0	0	2	0	2	1	1	Variations des stocks
Total supply	74	89	83	105	153	177	190	186	Approvisionnement total
Supply per capita	16	16	13	14	17	17	18	17	Approvisionnement par habitant
Bermuda									**Bermudes**
Primary Energy production	...	...	...	...	* 1	* 1	* 1	* 1	Production d'énergie primaire
Net imports	* 7	* 7	* 7	* 7	* 9	* 9	* 7	* 8	Importations nettes
Changes in stocks	...	...	...	...	...	0	0	0	Variations des stocks
Total supply	* 7	* 8	* 7	* 8	* 9	10	8	9	Approvisionnement total
Supply per capita	* 118	* 123	* 115	* 124	* 138	153	133	147	Approvisionnement par habitant
Bhutan									**Bhoutan**
Primary Energy production	41	43	46	53	73	75	77	79	Production d'énergie primaire
Net imports	* -3	* -4	* -2	-5	-16	* -10	* -13	* -13	Importations nettes
Total supply	37	39	44	48	57	64	64	66	Approvisionnement total
Supply per capita	67	76	77	73	78	83	81	83	Approvisionnement par habitant
Bolivia (Plurin. State of)									**Bolivie (État plurin. de)**
Primary Energy production	203	241	284	586	662	968	959	921	Production d'énergie primaire
Net imports	-97	-85	-78	-366	-397	-621	-608	-549	Importations nettes
Changes in stocks	0	1	-2	0	-1	0	1	-2	Variations des stocks
Total supply	106	155	208	219	266	347	351	373	Approvisionnement total
Supply per capita	16	21	25	24	27	33	33	34	Approvisionnement par habitant
Bonaire, St. Eustatius & Saba									**Bonaire, St-Eustache et Saba**
Primary Energy production	...	...	...	...	...	0	0	0	Production d'énergie primaire
Net imports	...	...	...	...	...	* 5	* 5	* 5	Importations nettes
Total supply	...	...	...	...	...	* 5	* 5	* 5	Approvisionnement total
Supply per capita	...	...	...	...	...	* 216	* 214	* 214	Approvisionnement par habitant
Bosnia and Herzegovina									**Bosnie-Herzégovine**
Primary Energy production	...	28	126	152	182	180	173	199	Production d'énergie primaire
Net imports	...	29	52	54	84	72	88	88	Importations nettes
Changes in stocks	...	...	-1	-1	-3	0	11	4	Variations des stocks
Total supply	...	56	179	206	269	252	250	282	Approvisionnement total
Supply per capita	...	17	48	54	72	71	71	80	Approvisionnement par habitant

Region, country or area	1990	1995	2000	2005	2010	2014	2015	2016	Région, pays ou zone
Botswana									**Botswana**
Primary Energy production	24	27	28	29	30	47	56	51	Production d'énergie primaire
Net imports	15	17	29	36	45	45	* 36	41	Importations nettes
Changes in stocks	0	...	...	0	0	-7	* 11	* 0	Variations des stocks
Total supply	39	44	57	65	74	98	80	92	Approvisionnement total
Supply per capita	28	28	32	35	37	45	36	41	Approvisionnement par habitant
Brazil									**Brésil**
Primary Energy production	4 490	5 038	6 308	8 344	10 050	10 965	11 842	12 183	Production d'énergie primaire
Net imports	1 555	1 918	1 713	900	859	1 638	799	45	Importations nettes
Changes in stocks	86	-106	1	-8	-8	41	-17	33	Variations des stocks
Total supply	5 960	7 062	8 020	9 252	10 916	12 562	12 658	12 194	Approvisionnement total
Supply per capita	40	44	46	50	55	62	61	59	Approvisionnement par habitant
British Virgin Islands									**Îles Vierges britanniques**
Primary Energy production	0	0	0	0	0	0	0	0	Production d'énergie primaire
Net imports	* 1	* 2	* 2	* 3	* 3	* 3	* 3	* 3	Importations nettes
Total supply	* 1	* 2	* 2	* 3	* 3	* 3	* 3	* 3	Approvisionnement total
Supply per capita	* 58	* 84	* 87	* 115	* 103	* 101	* 99	* 97	Approvisionnement par habitant
Brunei Darussalam									**Brunéi Darussalam**
Primary Energy production	668	752	813	848	775	679	673	633	Production d'énergie primaire
Net imports	* -594	-683	-744	-772	-648	-528	-560	-512	Importations nettes
Changes in stocks	* -33	-1	-4	-1	-7	3	0	-3	Variations des stocks
Total supply	107	71	73	76	136	149	114	124	Approvisionnement total
Supply per capita	424	246	224	210	349	362	273	293	Approvisionnement par habitant
Bulgaria									**Bulgarie**
Primary Energy production	407	428	410	444	442	474	505	473	Production d'énergie primaire
Net imports	730	546	358	384	291	257	275	285	Importations nettes
Changes in stocks	-44	7	-5	2	-9	-14	6	1	Variations des stocks
Total supply	1 181	966	773	826	741	744	775	757	Approvisionnement total
Supply per capita	134	116	97	107	100	103	108	106	Approvisionnement par habitant
Burkina Faso									**Burkina Faso**
Primary Energy production	85	96	69	98	118	124	126	128	Production d'énergie primaire
Net imports	* 9	10	12	16	26	40	51	42	Importations nettes
Changes in stocks	* 0	1	-1	* 0	* -2	* -2	* 4	-6	Variations des stocks
Total supply	93	104	83	114	145	165	172	176	Approvisionnement total
Supply per capita	10	10	7	8	9	9	10	9	Approvisionnement par habitant
Burundi									**Burundi**
Primary Energy production	54	62	51	79	86	56	56	56	Production d'énergie primaire
Net imports	* 4	* 4	* 5	3	5	6	* 6	7	Importations nettes
Changes in stocks	0	0	0	0	0	0	0	0	Variations des stocks
Total supply	58	66	55	81	90	61	62	63	Approvisionnement total
Supply per capita	10	11	9	11	10	6	6	6	Approvisionnement par habitant
Cabo Verde									**Cabo Verde**
Primary Energy production	1	1	1	2	1	2	* 2	* 2	Production d'énergie primaire
Net imports	* 1	* 2	* 4	* 6	7	7	* 7	* 8	Importations nettes
Changes in stocks	0	...	...	...	...	...	...	...	Variations des stocks
Total supply	* 2	* 3	* 4	8	9	9	* 9	* 9	Approvisionnement total
Supply per capita	* 7	* 7	* 10	16	18	16	* 16	* 17	Approvisionnement par habitant
Cambodia									**Cambodge**
Primary Energy production	103	98	114	105	152	178	184	191	Production d'énergie primaire
Net imports	* 18	22	28	39	72	88	111	126	Importations nettes
Total supply	121	119	142	144	223	267	295	317	Approvisionnement total
Supply per capita	13	11	11	11	16	17	19	20	Approvisionnement par habitant
Cameroon									**Cameroun**
Primary Energy production	501	457	532	442	351	398	495	500	Production d'énergie primaire
Net imports	* -326	* -219	-268	-152	-73	-83	-112	-111	Importations nettes
Changes in stocks	* 0	* 2	0	-5	-13	0	-1	0	Variations des stocks
Total supply	176	237	264	295	291	315	383	388	Approvisionnement total
Supply per capita	14	17	17	17	15	14	17	17	Approvisionnement par habitant
Canada									**Canada**
Primary Energy production	11 460	14 587	15 531	16 597	16 450	19 297	19 347	19 547	Production d'énergie primaire
Net imports	-2 538	-5 047	-5 377	-5 476	-5 955	-7 536	-7 687	-8 087	Importations nettes
Changes in stocks	170	-145	-351	-132	-307	185	75	-67	Variations des stocks
Total supply	8 752	9 684	10 504	11 253	10 802	11 576	11 585	11 527	Approvisionnement total
Supply per capita	316	331	343	349	316	325	322	318	Approvisionnement par habitant

Region, country or area	1990	1995	2000	2005	2010	2014	2015	2016	Région, pays ou zone
Cayman Islands									**Îles Caïmanes**
Net imports	4	* 6	* 7	* 7	* 8	8	8	8	Importations nettes
Total supply	4	* 5	* 7	7	8	8	8	8	Approvisionnement total
Supply per capita	138	* 159	* 165	130	144	132	132	128	Approvisionnement par habitant
Central African Republic									**République centrafricaine**
Primary Energy production	28	28	19	19	19	19	19	19	Production d'énergie primaire
Net imports	* 3	* 3	* 4	* 3	* 4	* 5	* 5	* 5	Importations nettes
Changes in stocks	0	* 0	* 0	...	...	...	...	...	Variations des stocks
Total supply	31	31	22	22	23	23	23	23	Approvisionnement total
Supply per capita	11	9	6	5	5	5	5	5	Approvisionnement par habitant
Chad									**Tchad**
Primary Energy production	43	48	55	433	324	294	375	347	Production d'énergie primaire
Net imports	* 5	* 6	* 7	* -362	* -245	* -212	* -293	* -263	Importations nettes
Changes in stocks	0	0	...	...	...	...	...	...	Variations des stocks
Total supply	48	54	62	71	80	82	83	84	Approvisionnement total
Supply per capita	8	8	7	7	7	6	6	6	Approvisionnement par habitant
Chile									**Chili**
Primary Energy production	326	344	358	390	384	540	540	525	Production d'énergie primaire
Net imports	284	437	722	791	888	927	969	1 059	Importations nettes
Changes in stocks	24	10	7	3	-6	6	4	5	Variations des stocks
Total supply	587	772	1 073	1 178	1 278	1 461	1 504	1 577	Approvisionnement total
Supply per capita	45	54	70	72	75	83	85	88	Approvisionnement par habitant
China [2]									**Chine** [2]
Primary Energy production	32 727	39 692	40 783	63 831	88 642	101 498	100 864	94 591	Production d'énergie primaire
Net imports	-1 370	* -397	* 1 426	4 251	14 225	19 634	18 874	21 563	Importations nettes
Changes in stocks	959	132	-251	-752	1 248	1 444	-187	-2 329	Variations des stocks
Total supply	30 398	39 163	42 461	68 833	101 618	119 688	119 926	118 484	Approvisionnement total
Supply per capita	27	32	33	53	75	86	86	84	Approvisionnement par habitant
China, Hong Kong SAR									**Chine, RAS de Hong Kong**
Net imports	321	382	571	578	672	587	634	643	Importations nettes
Changes in stocks	5	* -16	1	-2	129	-6	59	53	Variations des stocks
Total supply	316	398	570	579	544	593	576	590	Approvisionnement total
Supply per capita	54	65	84	85	77	82	79	81	Approvisionnement par habitant
China, Macao SAR									**Chine, RAS de Macao**
Primary Energy production	...	...	...	* 2	* 2	* 2	* 1	* 1	Production d'énergie primaire
Net imports	15	18	23	26	* 29	33	40	40	Importations nettes
Changes in stocks	0	0	0	0	0	0	1	0	Variations des stocks
Total supply	15	18	24	28	31	36	41	41	Approvisionnement total
Supply per capita	40	45	55	58	57	61	68	68	Approvisionnement par habitant
Colombia									**Colombie**
Primary Energy production	1 882	2 419	3 046	3 335	4 486	5 397	5 373	5 243	Production d'énergie primaire
Net imports	* -891	-1 267	-1 987	-2 139	* -3 081	-3 708	* -3 802	* -3 663	Importations nettes
Changes in stocks	7	48	-43	16	3	136	-58	-170	Variations des stocks
Total supply	983	1 104	1 103	1 180	1 402	1 554	1 629	1 750	Approvisionnement total
Supply per capita	30	30	28	27	31	33	34	36	Approvisionnement par habitant
Comoros									**Comores**
Primary Energy production	1	2	2	2	2	3	3	3	Production d'énergie primaire
Net imports	* 1	* 1	* 1	* 2	* 2	* 2	* 3	* 3	Importations nettes
Total supply	2	3	3	* 4	* 5	5	5	* 6	Approvisionnement total
Supply per capita	5	6	6	* 6	* 7	6	7	* 7	Approvisionnement par habitant
Congo									**Congo**
Primary Energy production	361	419	609	563	724	649	611	619	Production d'énergie primaire
Net imports	* -325	* -375	-569	-519	-649	-525	-500	-507	Importations nettes
Changes in stocks	0	0	...	0	6	14	0	0	Variations des stocks
Total supply	36	44	40	45	70	111	112	112	Approvisionnement total
Supply per capita	15	16	13	13	16	23	22	22	Approvisionnement par habitant
Cook Islands									**Îles Cook**
Primary Energy production	...	...	...	...	...	* 0	* 0	* 0	Production d'énergie primaire
Net imports	* 1	* 1	* 1	* 1	* 1	* 1	* 1	* 1	Importations nettes
Total supply	* 0	* 1	* 1	1	* 1	* 1	* 1	* 1	Approvisionnement total
Supply per capita	* 28	* 30	* 36	39	* 39	* 52	* 49	* 51	Approvisionnement par habitant
Costa Rica									**Costa Rica**
Primary Energy production	30	46	67	93	104	110	110	109	Production d'énergie primaire
Net imports	40	65	70	85	99	* 103	* 97	* 104	Importations nettes
Changes in stocks	1	0	-1	0	0	1	0	-1	Variations des stocks
Total supply	68	110	137	177	203	213	207	214	Approvisionnement total
Supply per capita	22	32	35	41	45	45	43	44	Approvisionnement par habitant

Region, country or area	1990	1995	2000	2005	2010	2014	2015	2016	Région, pays ou zone
Côte d'Ivoire									**Côte d'Ivoire**
Primary Energy production	179	178	242	451	467	540	526	561	Production d'énergie primaire
Net imports	* 26	* 68	* 28	-27	-40	38	10	-41	Importations nettes
Changes in stocks	* 1	* 0	* -8	* 5	3	-3	-6	-2	Variations des stocks
Total supply	204	245	278	418	425	580	543	522	Approvisionnement total
Supply per capita	16	17	17	23	21	26	24	22	Approvisionnement par habitant
Croatia									**Croatie**
Primary Energy production	...	209	178	199	215	182	184	185	Production d'énergie primaire
Net imports	...	115	166	212	180	146	168	169	Importations nettes
Changes in stocks	...	-2	-4	4	5	-8	2	1	Variations des stocks
Total supply	...	325	349	407	390	335	350	353	Approvisionnement total
Supply per capita	...	70	77	92	90	79	83	84	Approvisionnement par habitant
Cuba									**Cuba**
Primary Energy production	238	170	241	205	200	212	212	192	Production d'énergie primaire
Net imports	* 404	286	232	* 207	* 304	* 219	* 244	* 243	Importations nettes
Changes in stocks	-5	4	10	...	...	...	...	...	Variations des stocks
Total supply	647	452	462	412	505	431	456	435	Approvisionnement total
Supply per capita	61	41	42	37	45	38	40	38	Approvisionnement par habitant
Curaçao									**Curaçao**
Primary Energy production	...	...	...	...	...	0	0	1	Production d'énergie primaire
Net imports	...	...	...	...	...	85	93	80	Importations nettes
Total supply	...	...	...	...	...	85	93	80	Approvisionnement total
Supply per capita	...	...	...	...	...	543	589	503	Approvisionnement par habitant
Cyprus									**Chypre**
Primary Energy production	0	2	2	2	4	5	5	5	Production d'énergie primaire
Net imports	57	72	88	94	104	76	83	86	Importations nettes
Changes in stocks	-1	2	0	3	5	-2	3	1	Variations des stocks
Total supply	58	71	90	94	103	83	85	91	Approvisionnement total
Supply per capita	75	83	95	91	93	72	73	78	Approvisionnement par habitant
Czechia									**Tchéquie**
Primary Energy production	...	1 367	1 289	1 387	1 339	1 245	1 206	1 143	Production d'énergie primaire
Net imports	...	367	411	527	476	527	555	566	Importations nettes
Changes in stocks	...	-30	-49	16	-77	13	4	-34	Variations des stocks
Total supply	...	1 764	1 748	1 898	1 891	1 758	1 757	1 742	Approvisionnement total
Supply per capita	...	171	171	186	179	166	166	164	Approvisionnement par habitant
Dem. People's Rep. Korea									**Rép. pop. dém. de Corée**
Primary Energy production	1 211	838	787	923	699	773	788	891	Production d'énergie primaire
Net imports	181	83	41	-28	-77	-367	-457	-518	Importations nettes
Changes in stocks	...	...	2	...	...	...	...	...	Variations des stocks
Total supply	1 391	921	826	896	622	406	332	374	Approvisionnement total
Supply per capita	69	42	36	38	25	16	13	15	Approvisionnement par habitant
Dem. Rep. of the Congo									**Rép. dém. du Congo**
Primary Energy production	491	619	677	866	856	1 179	1 218	1 256	Production d'énergie primaire
Net imports	-11	-34	-43	-42	-24	23	-8	-17	Importations nettes
Changes in stocks	0	0	-1	0	0	...	...	...	Variations des stocks
Total supply	480	585	635	824	831	1 202	1 209	1 240	Approvisionnement total
Supply per capita	13	13	13	14	13	16	16	16	Approvisionnement par habitant
Denmark [3]									**Danemark [3]**
Primary Energy production	420	649	1 149	1 298	968	664	661	624	Production d'énergie primaire
Net imports	298	217	-384	-499	-203	20	29	38	Importations nettes
Changes in stocks	-7	57	-19	14	-45	15	21	-25	Variations des stocks
Total supply	724	810	784	785	810	669	668	687	Approvisionnement total
Supply per capita	141	155	147	145	146	118	117	120	Approvisionnement par habitant
Djibouti									**Djibouti**
Primary Energy production	2	2	3	3	3	3	4	4	Production d'énergie primaire
Net imports	* 5	* 5	* 5	* 6	* 7	* 5	* 5	* 5	Importations nettes
Changes in stocks	0	...	...	...	* 0	* -2	* -1	* -2	Variations des stocks
Total supply	* 6	* 7	8	* 9	11	11	10	11	Approvisionnement total
Supply per capita	* 12	* 11	11	* 11	13	12	11	12	Approvisionnement par habitant
Dominica									**Dominique**
Primary Energy production	0	0	0	0	0	0	0	0	Production d'énergie primaire
Net imports	* 1	* 1	* 1	* 2	* 2	* 2	* 2	* 3	Importations nettes
Changes in stocks	...	* 0	...	...	0	* 0	* 0	* 0	Variations des stocks
Total supply	* 1	1	2	* 2	3	* 3	* 3	* 3	Approvisionnement total
Supply per capita	* 14	19	24	* 31	36	* 36	* 36	* 37	Approvisionnement par habitant

Region, country or area	1990	1995	2000	2005	2010	2014	2015	2016	Région, pays ou zone
Dominican Republic									**République dominicaine**
Primary Energy production	22	24	24	28	27	16	15	18	Production d'énergie primaire
Net imports	122	212	259	* 239	271	272	303	323	Importations nettes
Changes in stocks	1	0	0	2	0	0	0	0	Variations des stocks
Total supply	143	236	283	266	298	289	318	341	Approvisionnement total
Supply per capita	20	30	33	29	30	28	30	32	Approvisionnement par habitant
Ecuador									**Équateur**
Primary Energy production	683	915	959	1 251	1 077	1 324	1 298	1 321	Production d'énergie primaire
Net imports	-428	* -577	-612	-772	-513	-648	-640	-691	Importations nettes
Changes in stocks	0	...	20	4	2	-2	4	0	Variations des stocks
Total supply	255	339	328	475	562	679	653	630	Approvisionnement total
Supply per capita	25	30	27	35	38	43	40	38	Approvisionnement par habitant
Egypt									**Égypte**
Primary Energy production	2 376	2 684	2 773	3 383	3 692	3 240	3 051	3 105	Production d'énergie primaire
Net imports	* -1 084	* -709	-449	-645	-511	262	399	645	Importations nettes
Changes in stocks	* 21	369	36	-4	-60	-1	-1	-1	Variations des stocks
Total supply	1 271	1 605	2 288	2 742	3 242	3 503	3 450	3 752	Approvisionnement total
Supply per capita	22	26	34	37	39	38	37	39	Approvisionnement par habitant
El Salvador									**El Salvador**
Primary Energy production	59	70	89	104	95	86	87	85	Production d'énergie primaire
Net imports	32	67	77	82	81	82	92	99	Importations nettes
Changes in stocks	-1	1	0	-3	-2	-1	-1	0	Variations des stocks
Total supply	92	136	166	189	178	170	180	183	Approvisionnement total
Supply per capita	17	24	28	31	29	27	29	29	Approvisionnement par habitant
Equatorial Guinea									**Guinée équatoriale**
Primary Energy production	4	18	250	869	894	846	790	810	Production d'énergie primaire
Net imports	* 1	* -12	-240	* -799	* -808	* -769	* -724	* -786	Importations nettes
Changes in stocks	...	* 1	...	1	* 6	* 4	* 9	* -19	Variations des stocks
Total supply	5	5	9	68	80	74	56	44	Approvisionnement total
Supply per capita	13	12	18	113	84	66	48	36	Approvisionnement par habitant
Eritrea									**Érythrée**
Primary Energy production	...	31	21	21	24	27	27	30	Production d'énergie primaire
Net imports	...	11	9	10	7	8	8	9	Importations nettes
Changes in stocks	...	...	0	-2	0	0	...	...	Variations des stocks
Total supply	...	42	30	32	31	34	36	39	Approvisionnement total
Supply per capita	...	13	8	7	7	7	7	8	Approvisionnement par habitant
Estonia									**Estonie**
Primary Energy production	...	139	129	163	206	233	234	196	Production d'énergie primaire
Net imports	...	74	66	57	30	16	13	10	Importations nettes
Changes in stocks	...	-3	-1	0	-2	5	15	-27	Variations des stocks
Total supply	...	217	196	220	238	245	232	234	Approvisionnement total
Supply per capita	...	151	143	164	179	186	177	178	Approvisionnement par habitant
Ethiopia									**Éthiopie**
Primary Energy production	...	885	977	1 070	1 212	1 308	1 330	1 352	Production d'énergie primaire
Net imports	...	31	43	60	82	128	136	147	Importations nettes
Changes in stocks	...	* -2	-2	-3	1	-1	0	0	Variations des stocks
Total supply	...	918	1 022	1 132	1 293	1 438	1 467	1 498	Approvisionnement total
Supply per capita	...	16	16	15	15	15	15	15	Approvisionnement par habitant
Falkland Islands (Malvinas)									**Îles Falkland (Malvinas)**
Primary Energy production	0	* 0	* 0	* 0	* 0	* 0	* 0	* 0	Production d'énergie primaire
Net imports	0	* 0	* 0	* 1	* 1	* 1	* 1	* 1	Importations nettes
Total supply	1	* 1	* 1	* 1	* 1	* 1	* 1	* 1	Approvisionnement total
Supply per capita	271	* 239	* 178	* 235	* 260	* 253	* 251	* 257	Approvisionnement par habitant
Faroe Islands									**Îles Féroé**
Primary Energy production	0	0	0	0	0	1	1	1	Production d'énergie primaire
Net imports	* 11	* 9	* 10	* 11	* 9	* 8	* 9	* 9	Importations nettes
Total supply	10	* 8	* 10	* 10	* 9	* 9	* 9	* 9	Approvisionnement total
Supply per capita	217	* 191	* 216	* 216	* 184	* 180	* 185	* 187	Approvisionnement par habitant
Fiji									**Fidji**
Primary Energy production	12	13	10	9	5	7	7	6	Production d'énergie primaire
Net imports	9	* 11	* 11	* 16	* 16	* 22	* 29	* 28	Importations nettes
Changes in stocks	-1	...	...	* 0	...	...	* 0	0	Variations des stocks
Total supply	23	* 23	22	24	21	* 30	37	33	Approvisionnement total
Supply per capita	31	* 30	27	29	25	* 33	41	37	Approvisionnement par habitant

Region, country or area	1990	1995	2000	2005	2010	2014	2015	2016	Région, pays ou zone
Finland									**Finlande**
Primary Energy production	504	549	622	699	727	759	734	738	Production d'énergie primaire
Net imports	712	636	725	761	721	681	625	622	Importations nettes
Changes in stocks	26	-27	2	27	-78	25	4	-55	Variations des stocks
Total supply	1 190	1 212	1 346	1 433	1 526	1 415	1 354	1 414	Approvisionnement total
Supply per capita	239	237	260	273	284	259	247	257	Approvisionnement par habitant
France [4]									**France** [4]
Primary Energy production	4 652	5 314	5 427	5 695	5 649	5 723	5 753	5 462	Production d'énergie primaire
Net imports	4 801	4 619	5 259	5 688	5 195	4 509	4 556	4 627	Importations nettes
Changes in stocks	71	10	148	49	-112	57	-27	-76	Variations des stocks
Total supply	9 381	9 924	10 537	11 333	10 956	10 175	10 336	10 164	Approvisionnement total
Supply per capita	165	171	178	186	174	158	160	157	Approvisionnement par habitant
French Guiana									**Guyane française**
Primary Energy production	0	1	2	2	3	3	3	3	Production d'énergie primaire
Net imports	* 9	* 8	6	* 8	* 9	* 10	10	* 11	Importations nettes
Total supply	9	9	8	10	* 12	* 13	13	* 14	Approvisionnement total
Supply per capita	79	62	47	49	* 51	* 50	47	* 50	Approvisionnement par habitant
French Polynesia									**Polynésie française**
Primary Energy production	0	0	1	1	1	* 1	* 1	* 1	Production d'énergie primaire
Net imports	* 6	* 6	* 8	* 11	* 11	* 9	* 10	* 10	Importations nettes
Total supply	* 7	7	9	12	12	11	12	12	Approvisionnement total
Supply per capita	* 34	32	37	46	46	40	42	42	Approvisionnement par habitant
Gabon									**Gabon**
Primary Energy production	609	822	609	615	590	539	562	557	Production d'énergie primaire
Net imports	-509	-765	-572	-545	-526	-426	-451	-445	Importations nettes
Changes in stocks	50	2	-25	-3	-30	...	...	...	Variations des stocks
Total supply	50	56	62	72	93	112	112	113	Approvisionnement total
Supply per capita	54	52	50	53	57	60	58	57	Approvisionnement par habitant
Gambia									**Gambie**
Primary Energy production	4	5	6	6	6	7	7	7	Production d'énergie primaire
Net imports	* 3	* 3	* 4	* 5	* 6	* 7	* 7	* 7	Importations nettes
Changes in stocks	0	...	...	...	...	...	...	...	Variations des stocks
Total supply	7	8	9	10	12	14	* 14	* 14	Approvisionnement total
Supply per capita	7	7	7	7	7	7	* 7	* 7	Approvisionnement par habitant
Georgia									**Géorgie**
Primary Energy production	...	50	55	53	58	61	58	60	Production d'énergie primaire
Net imports	...	37	65	82	82	127	141	143	Importations nettes
Changes in stocks	...	0	0	0	0	0	1	0	Variations des stocks
Total supply	...	88	120	135	140	188	198	204	Approvisionnement total
Supply per capita	...	17	25	30	33	47	50	52	Approvisionnement par habitant
Germany									**Allemagne**
Primary Energy production	...	6 050	5 645	5 706	5 377	5 004	5 007	4 833	Production d'énergie primaire
Net imports	...	7 847	8 203	8 355	8 081	7 759	7 852	8 080	Importations nettes
Changes in stocks	...	-137	-183	46	-179	-14	-16	-29	Variations des stocks
Total supply	...	14 035	14 031	14 015	13 637	12 776	12 876	12 942	Approvisionnement total
Supply per capita	...	171	170	170	169	157	158	158	Approvisionnement par habitant
Ghana									**Ghana**
Primary Energy production	138	211	192	164	148	357	372	336	Production d'énergie primaire
Net imports	* 49	* 66	79	87	120	-32	-31	2	Importations nettes
Changes in stocks	0	...	...	...	0	3	1	3	Variations des stocks
Total supply	187	277	271	251	267	321	339	335	Approvisionnement total
Supply per capita	13	16	14	12	11	12	12	12	Approvisionnement par habitant
Gibraltar									**Gibraltar**
Net imports	3	5	6	7	8	9	9	10	Importations nettes
Changes in stocks	0	...	...	...	...	...	...	...	Variations des stocks
Total supply	2	4	5	6	7	8	9	10	Approvisionnement total
Supply per capita	90	162	197	219	220	242	262	285	Approvisionnement par habitant
Greece									**Grèce**
Primary Energy production	385	391	419	432	396	368	355	281	Production d'énergie primaire
Net imports	506	581	741	831	762	613	676	680	Importations nettes
Changes in stocks	-10	10	12	-18	-11	-2	45	-2	Variations des stocks
Total supply	902	963	1 148	1 280	1 169	983	985	965	Approvisionnement total
Supply per capita	89	90	104	115	102	87	88	86	Approvisionnement par habitant

Production, trade and supply of energy *(continued)*
Petajoules and gigajoules per capita

Production, commerce et fourniture d'énergie *(suite)*
pétajoules et gigajoules par habitant

Region, country or area	1990	1995	2000	2005	2010	2014	2015	2016	Région, pays ou zone
Greenland									**Groenland**
Primary Energy production	* 0	1	1	1	1	2	2	2	Production d'énergie primaire
Net imports	* 5	* 5	* 7	9	10	7	8	* 8	Importations nettes
Changes in stocks	...	...	...	* 1	1	0	1	* 1	Variations des stocks
Total supply	5	5	7	9	11	9	9	9	Approvisionnement total
Supply per capita	90	95	127	165	186	154	157	156	Approvisionnement par habitant
Grenada									**Grenade**
Primary Energy production	0	0	0	0	0	0	0	0	Production d'énergie primaire
Net imports	* 2	* 2	* 3	3	4	4	4	4	Importations nettes
Changes in stocks	0	0	0	0	0	0	0	0	Variations des stocks
Total supply	2	2	3	3	4	4	4	4	Approvisionnement total
Supply per capita	17	23	29	33	38	35	38	38	Approvisionnement par habitant
Guadeloupe									**Guadeloupe**
Primary Energy production	1	* 2	* 2	5	* 2	5	5	6	Production d'énergie primaire
Net imports	* 16	* 19	* 24	* 28	* 30	* 29	* 29	28	Importations nettes
Total supply	18	21	26	33	* 32	34	34	33	Approvisionnement total
Supply per capita	47	52	61	75	* 72	75	76	74	Approvisionnement par habitant
Guam									**Guam**
Primary Energy production	...	...	...	...	...	...	0	0	Production d'énergie primaire
Total supply	...	...	...	...	...	...	0	0	Approvisionnement total
Supply per capita	...	...	...	...	...	...	0	1	Approvisionnement par habitant
Guatemala									**Guatemala**
Primary Energy production	143	178	229	255	279	303	289	354	Production d'énergie primaire
Net imports	52	75	75	112	110	154	186	186	Importations nettes
Changes in stocks	0	* 1	-4	6	0	13	22	9	Variations des stocks
Total supply	195	252	307	361	388	444	453	531	Approvisionnement total
Supply per capita	22	25	27	28	27	28	28	32	Approvisionnement par habitant
Guernsey									**Guernesey**
Net imports	...	...	...	1	1	1	1	1	Importations nettes
Total supply	...	...	...	1	1	1	1	1	Approvisionnement total
Supply per capita	...	...	...	17	14	9	13	17	Approvisionnement par habitant
Guinea									**Guinée**
Primary Energy production	91	110	107	109	112	113	116	117	Production d'énergie primaire
Net imports	* 14	* 16	* 21	* 26	* 36	* 33	* 37	* 40	Importations nettes
Changes in stocks	0	...	...	...	...	...	...	...	Variations des stocks
Total supply	105	126	128	135	147	146	152	156	Approvisionnement total
Supply per capita	18	17	15	15	14	12	13	13	Approvisionnement par habitant
Guinea-Bissau									**Guinée-Bissau**
Primary Energy production	17	18	20	22	24	25	25	26	Production d'énergie primaire
Net imports	* 3	* 4	* 3	* 4	* 5	* 4	* 4	* 5	Importations nettes
Total supply	20	21	23	26	28	30	30	31	Approvisionnement total
Supply per capita	20	19	19	19	18	17	17	17	Approvisionnement par habitant
Guyana									**Guyana**
Primary Energy production	9	8	9	9	8	7	7	7	Production d'énergie primaire
Net imports	* 16	* 21	22	20	24	28	27	30	Importations nettes
Changes in stocks	...	0	0	0	0	0	0	0	Variations des stocks
Total supply	25	29	32	29	32	35	35	37	Approvisionnement total
Supply per capita	34	39	43	39	43	46	45	48	Approvisionnement par habitant
Haiti									**Haïti**
Primary Energy production	52	58	65	115	131	136	139	141	Production d'énergie primaire
Net imports	13	12	20	28	28	38	40	41	Importations nettes
Changes in stocks	0	...	...	...	...	0	0	...	Variations des stocks
Total supply	65	71	84	142	159	174	179	181	Approvisionnement total
Supply per capita	9	9	10	15	16	16	17	17	Approvisionnement par habitant
Honduras									**Honduras**
Primary Energy production	91	92	64	78	93	107	118	121	Production d'énergie primaire
Net imports	32	51	65	89	98	109	96	117	Importations nettes
Changes in stocks	0	1	5	-4	-2	-10	-31	-6	Variations des stocks
Total supply	122	142	125	171	192	225	244	244	Approvisionnement total
Supply per capita	25	25	20	25	23	26	27	27	Approvisionnement par habitant
Hungary									**Hongrie**
Primary Energy production	615	583	486	434	496	462	471	479	Production d'énergie primaire
Net imports	594	521	574	728	627	592	565	597	Importations nettes
Changes in stocks	-2	11	10	8	9	55	-21	-1	Variations des stocks
Total supply	1 211	1 093	1 049	1 155	1 113	1 000	1 057	1 076	Approvisionnement total
Supply per capita	117	106	103	115	112	102	108	110	Approvisionnement par habitant

Region, country or area	1990	1995	2000	2005	2010	2014	2015	2016	Région, pays ou zone
Iceland									**Islande**
Primary Energy production	59	63	109	127	252	284	285	302	Production d'énergie primaire
Net imports	28	27	31	31	26	27	29	30	Importations nettes
Changes in stocks	0	0	2	1	-1	0	1	0	Variations des stocks
Total supply	87	90	139	158	278	311	313	331	Approvisionnement total
Supply per capita	341	338	494	534	869	946	949	996	Approvisionnement par habitant
India									**Inde**
Primary Energy production	12 283	14 212	15 763	18 212	22 888	22 557	22 818	23 301	Production d'énergie primaire
Net imports	1 196	* 2 010	3 890	4 689	6 558	* 12 120	* 13 315	* 13 371	Importations nettes
Changes in stocks	45	* -41	-155	194	252	-169	48	-214	Variations des stocks
Total supply	13 435	16 262	19 808	22 706	29 193	34 845	36 084	36 886	Approvisionnement total
Supply per capita	15	17	19	20	24	27	28	28	Approvisionnement par habitant
Indonesia									**Indonésie**
Primary Energy production	6 735[5]	8 320[5]	8 129[5]	11 351	16 854	18 664	18 075	18 885	Production d'énergie primaire
Net imports	* -2 753[5]	* -3 634[5]	* -3 577[5]	-4 243[5]	-8 530	-10 451	-8 647	-8 887	Importations nettes
Changes in stocks	223[5]	100[5]	-417[5]	21	2	282	-48	-22	Variations des stocks
Total supply	3 759[5]	4 587[5]	4 970[5]	7 087	8 322	7 931	9 476	10 021	Approvisionnement total
Supply per capita	20[5]	23[5]	23[5]	31	34	31	37	38	Approvisionnement par habitant
Iran (Islamic Republic of)									**Iran (Rép. islamique d')**
Primary Energy production	7 454	9 302	11 121	13 006	14 283	13 368	13 637	16 412	Production d'énergie primaire
Net imports	-4 634	-5 415	-5 787	* -5 682	-5 634	-3 414	-3 640	-6 166	Importations nettes
Changes in stocks	0	0	-52	103	69	-32	7	-160	Variations des stocks
Total supply	2 819	3 887	5 386	7 221	8 579	9 986	9 989	10 405	Approvisionnement total
Supply per capita	51	65	82	104	115	127	126	130	Approvisionnement par habitant
Iraq									**Iraq**
Primary Energy production	4 411	1 265	5 482	4 147	5 274	6 772	7 565	9 667	Production d'énergie primaire
Net imports	* -3 656	-193	-4 487	-2 656	-3 835	-4 629	-5 719	-7 225	Importations nettes
Changes in stocks	* 169	0	0	3	1	87	-152	133	Variations des stocks
Total supply	586	1 072	995	1 488	1 437	2 055	1 997	2 309	Approvisionnement total
Supply per capita	34	53	42	54	47	59	55	62	Approvisionnement par habitant
Ireland									**Irlande**
Primary Energy production	145	172	90	69	77	84	80	176	Production d'énergie primaire
Net imports	281	303	487	550	522	454	489	393	Importations nettes
Changes in stocks	10	28	-2	3	-8	3	14	-16	Variations des stocks
Total supply	416	446	579	615	608	534	556	584	Approvisionnement total
Supply per capita	118	124	152	148	132	114	118	124	Approvisionnement par habitant
Isle of Man									**Île de Man**
Primary Energy production	...	...	...	* 0	1	1	1	1	Production d'énergie primaire
Net imports	...	...	...	0	0	* 0	* 0	* 0	Importations nettes
Total supply	...	...	...	* 0	0	1	1	1	Approvisionnement total
Supply per capita	...	...	...	* 6	5	7	8	8	Approvisionnement par habitant
Israel									**Israël**
Primary Energy production	18	23	27	87	162	284	308	346	Production d'énergie primaire
Net imports	450	625	719	685	804	620	649	578	Importations nettes
Changes in stocks	-12	-1	-17	5	0	10	14	-29	Variations des stocks
Total supply	480	649	763	767	966	894	943	953	Approvisionnement total
Supply per capita	107	122	127	116	130	113	117	116	Approvisionnement par habitant
Italy [6]									**Italie [6]**
Primary Energy production	1 072	1 235	1 183	1 269	1 384	1 539	1 509	1 408	Production d'énergie primaire
Net imports	5 375	5 481	6 239	6 509	6 009	4 628	4 888	4 865	Importations nettes
Changes in stocks	80	3	190	-70	69	0	-5	-62	Variations des stocks
Total supply	6 366	6 714	7 230	7 847	7 324	6 168	6 402	6 334	Approvisionnement total
Supply per capita	112	118	127	134	123	103	108	107	Approvisionnement par habitant
Jamaica									**Jamaïque**
Primary Energy production	13	9	11	15	6	8	* 8	* 9	Production d'énergie primaire
Net imports	* 97	* 118	144	139	95	96	101	108	Importations nettes
Changes in stocks	-2	-3	7	1	-2	1	1	0	Variations des stocks
Total supply	113	130	148	151	103	104	108	117	Approvisionnement total
Supply per capita	48	53	57	56	37	36	38	41	Approvisionnement par habitant
Japan [7]									**Japon [7]**
Primary Energy production	3 118	4 081	4 379	4 260	4 211	1 232	1 426	1 481	Production d'énergie primaire
Net imports	15 321	16 667	17 442	17 688	16 723	17 143	16 678	16 291	Importations nettes
Changes in stocks	147	55	166	100	-6	-124	-59	-75	Variations des stocks
Total supply	18 291	20 693	21 655	21 847	20 938	18 499	18 163	17 845	Approvisionnement total
Supply per capita	150	166	172	173	163	144	142	140	Approvisionnement par habitant

Region, country or area	1990	1995	2000	2005	2010	2014	2015	2016	Région, pays ou zone
Jersey									**Jersey**
Primary Energy production	...	...	...	* 0	* 0	* 1	* 1	* 1	Production d'énergie primaire
Net imports	...	1	1	2	2	2	2	2	Importations nettes
Total supply	...	1	1	3	3	3	3	3	Approvisionnement total
Supply per capita	...	9	17	28	28	27	29	29	Approvisionnement par habitant
Jordan									**Jordanie**
Primary Energy production	6	10	10	10	9	7	8	10	Production d'énergie primaire
Net imports	136	160	190	285	300	349	359	355	Importations nettes
Changes in stocks	4	-2	-5	7	5	5	5	2	Variations des stocks
Total supply	138	172	205	289	303	352	361	362	Approvisionnement total
Supply per capita	40	39	42	54	42	40	39	38	Approvisionnement par habitant
Kazakhstan									**Kazakhstan**
Primary Energy production	...	2 663	3 367	5 131	6 770	7 092	6 791	6 737	Production d'énergie primaire
Net imports	...	-477	-1 819	-2 771	* -3 318	-3 722	* -3 575	* -3 445	Importations nettes
Changes in stocks	...	...	-12	8	88	16	-48	-43	Variations des stocks
Total supply	...	2 185	1 560	2 352	3 363	3 354	3 263	3 335	Approvisionnement total
Supply per capita	...	137	104	155	205	192	184	185	Approvisionnement par habitant
Kenya									**Kenya**
Primary Energy production	367	420	* 487	* 580	* 650	750	761	736	Production d'énergie primaire
Net imports	* 71	98	141	109	137	159	189	202	Importations nettes
Changes in stocks	0	...	...	4	-5	0	-4	0	Variations des stocks
Total supply	439	518	* 627	* 686	* 793	909	953	938	Approvisionnement total
Supply per capita	19	19	* 20	* 19	* 19	20	20	19	Approvisionnement par habitant
Kiribati									**Kiribati**
Primary Energy production	* 0	* 0	* 0	0	* 1	* 1	* 1	* 1	Production d'énergie primaire
Net imports	* 0	* 0	1	* 1	1	1	* 1	* 1	Importations nettes
Total supply	* 1	* 1	1	* 1	1	1	* 1	* 1	Approvisionnement total
Supply per capita	* 11	* 11	11	* 14	13	12	* 12	* 13	Approvisionnement par habitant
Kosovo									**Kosovo**
Primary Energy production	...	...	46	59	78	67	76	84	Production d'énergie primaire
Net imports	...	...	17	23	25	25	29	27	Importations nettes
Changes in stocks	...	...	-1	0	-2	0	-1	-2	Variations des stocks
Total supply	...	...	65	82	105	93	106	113	Approvisionnement total
Supply per capita	...	...	38	48	59	51	59	62	Approvisionnement par habitant
Kuwait [8]									**Koweït** [8]
Primary Energy production	2 799	4 802	4 748	6 080	5 557	6 943	7 004	7 284	Production d'énergie primaire
Net imports	* -2 090	-3 968	-3 941	-4 915	-4 229	-5 633	-5 634	-5 804	Importations nettes
Changes in stocks	* 142	-1	-17	31	-22	-22	-47	-30	Variations des stocks
Total supply	566	835	824	1 133	1 350	1 332	1 417	1 510	Approvisionnement total
Supply per capita	271	513	424	500	450	352	360	373	Approvisionnement par habitant
Kyrgyzstan									**Kirghizistan**
Primary Energy production	...	53	60	61	53	80	75	77	Production d'énergie primaire
Net imports	...	51	38	53	63	93	103	81	Importations nettes
Changes in stocks	...	3	-2	0	1	2	12	-4	Variations des stocks
Total supply	...	101	101	114	115	171	167	162	Approvisionnement total
Supply per capita	...	22	20	23	21	30	29	27	Approvisionnement par habitant
Lao People's Dem. Rep.									**Rép. dém. populaire lao**
Primary Energy production	54	56	57	64	98	128	162	267	Production d'énergie primaire
Net imports	* 5	* 7	* 1	* 5	* 3	* -8	* 7	* -23	Importations nettes
Total supply	60	63	58	68	100	120	169	244	Approvisionnement total
Supply per capita	14	13	11	12	16	18	25	36	Approvisionnement par habitant
Latvia									**Lettonie**
Primary Energy production	...	60	59	78	83	100	98	102	Production d'énergie primaire
Net imports	...	138	94	116	78	66	84	76	Importations nettes
Changes in stocks	...	1	-4	5	-28	-17	3	-1	Variations des stocks
Total supply	...	197	157	190	189	182	179	179	Approvisionnement total
Supply per capita	...	79	66	82	89	90	90	91	Approvisionnement par habitant
Lebanon									**Liban**
Primary Energy production	5	8	7	10	9	7	8	7	Production d'énergie primaire
Net imports	* 108	166	198	197	253	300	305	311	Importations nettes
Changes in stocks	...	...	-1	...	...	...	...	...	Variations des stocks
Total supply	* 113	174	207	206	262	306	313	317	Approvisionnement total
Supply per capita	* 38	50	55	51	60	55	53	53	Approvisionnement par habitant

Region, country or area	1990	1995	2000	2005	2010	2014	2015	2016	Région, pays ou zone
Lesotho									**Lesotho**
Primary Energy production	19	22	28	25	27	31	31	31	Production d'énergie primaire
Net imports	* 17	* 19	* 20	* 22	* 25	* 27	* 27	* 30	Importations nettes
Total supply	36	41	48	47	52	58	58	61	Approvisionnement total
Supply per capita	22	23	24	23	26	27	27	28	Approvisionnement par habitant
Liberia									**Libéria**
Primary Energy production	32	25	43	53	64	74	76	79	Production d'énergie primaire
Net imports	* 7	* 7	* 6	* 9	* 11	* 16	* 16	* 19	Importations nettes
Total supply	38	31	49	62	75	89	92	97	Approvisionnement total
Supply per capita	18	15	17	19	19	20	20	21	Approvisionnement par habitant
Libya									**Libye**
Primary Energy production	3 020	3 190	3 117	4 062	4 294	1 505	1 349	1 262	Production d'énergie primaire
Net imports	-2 676	-2 538	-2 433	-3 335	-3 365	-688	* -507	-525	Importations nettes
Changes in stocks	-124	...	...	...	69	74	* 115	* 114	Variations des stocks
Total supply	468	653	685	727	860	743	726	623	Approvisionnement total
Supply per capita	108	137	131	126	139	120	117	99	Approvisionnement par habitant
Liechtenstein									**Liechtenstein**
Primary Energy production	...	...	...	...	1	1	1	1	Production d'énergie primaire
Net imports	...	...	...	...	2	2	2	2	Importations nettes
Total supply	...	...	...	...	3	3	3	3	Approvisionnement total
Supply per capita	...	...	...	...	84	78	80	79	Approvisionnement par habitant
Lithuania									**Lituanie**
Primary Energy production	...	157	139	170	64	74	76	77	Production d'énergie primaire
Net imports	...	234	175	196	225	214	223	222	Importations nettes
Changes in stocks	...	14	8	4	3	1	4	0	Variations des stocks
Total supply	...	376	306	362	286	287	294	299	Approvisionnement total
Supply per capita	...	104	87	106	92	97	100	103	Approvisionnement par habitant
Luxembourg									**Luxembourg**
Primary Energy production	1	2	3	4	5	6	6	7	Production d'énergie primaire
Net imports	143	130	140	179	173	156	150	150	Importations nettes
Changes in stocks	0	-1	2	-1	-1	0	-1	0	Variations des stocks
Total supply	143	133	142	185	178	161	157	156	Approvisionnement total
Supply per capita	376	327	325	405	351	290	278	271	Approvisionnement par habitant
Madagascar									**Madagascar**
Primary Energy production	72	89	92	104	124	129	132	135	Production d'énergie primaire
Net imports	* 13	* 18	* 26	* 24	* 25	* 41	* 46	* 50	Importations nettes
Changes in stocks	* 0	0	0	0	-1	* 0	* 0	* 0	Variations des stocks
Total supply	85	108	118	127	150	171	179	185	Approvisionnement total
Supply per capita	8	8	8	7	7	7	7	7	Approvisionnement par habitant
Malawi									**Malawi**
Primary Energy production	56	55	56	60	64	68	68	68	Production d'énergie primaire
Net imports	* 8	* 11	* 9	* 11	* 12	* 11	* 13	* 15	Importations nettes
Total supply	64	65	65	70	76	79	80	82	Approvisionnement total
Supply per capita	7	7	6	5	5	5	5	5	Approvisionnement par habitant
Malaysia									**Malaisie**
Primary Energy production	1 794	2 791	3 082	3 770	3 450	3 738	3 748	3 787	Production d'énergie primaire
Net imports	-1 019	* -1 018	-1 115	-1 003	* -495	-240	-365	-310	Importations nettes
Changes in stocks	3	* 5	8	21	* -10	-37	-41	-50	Variations des stocks
Total supply	773	1 768	1 959	2 745	2 965	3 535	3 424	3 527	Approvisionnement total
Supply per capita	42	85	84	105	105	117	111	113	Approvisionnement par habitant
Maldives									**Maldives**
Primary Energy production	0	0	0	0	0	0	0	0	Production d'énergie primaire
Net imports	* 3	* 4	* 6	* 9	* 13	* 18	* 19	* 21	Importations nettes
Total supply	* 2	4	6	9	13	19	19	21	Approvisionnement total
Supply per capita	* 11	14	24	30	37	46	45	48	Approvisionnement par habitant
Mali									**Mali**
Primary Energy production	37	42	45	49	52	56	56	57	Production d'énergie primaire
Net imports	* 5	* 6	* 11	* 12	* 26	* 35	* 38	* 38	Importations nettes
Total supply	43	49	57	61	78	91	94	95	Approvisionnement total
Supply per capita	5	5	5	5	5	5	5	5	Approvisionnement par habitant
Malta									**Malte**
Primary Energy production	...	...	...	0	0	1	1	1	Production d'énergie primaire
Net imports	29	31	28	37	35	31	25	26	Importations nettes
Changes in stocks	0	1	0	0	-1	-2	-2	2	Variations des stocks
Total supply	29	30	29	37	35	33	27	25	Approvisionnement total
Supply per capita	79	77	72	91	85	77	63	59	Approvisionnement par habitant

Region, country or area	1990	1995	2000	2005	2010	2014	2015	2016	Région, pays ou zone
Marshall Islands									**Îles Marshall**
Primary Energy production	...	* 0	* 0	* 0	* 0	* 0	* 0	* 0	Production d'énergie primaire
Net imports	...	* 1	* 1	* 2	* 2	* 2	* 2	* 2	Importations nettes
Total supply	...	* 1	* 2	* 2	* 2	* 2	* 2	* 2	Approvisionnement total
Supply per capita	...	* 28	* 30	* 35	* 41	* 41	* 42	* 42	Approvisionnement par habitant
Martinique									**Martinique**
Primary Energy production	0	0	* 0	* 1	* 1	2	2	2	Production d'énergie primaire
Net imports	* 21	* 22	* 22	* 29	* 28	* 27	* 28	* 29	Importations nettes
Changes in stocks	0	...	...	...	...	...	...	...	Variations des stocks
Total supply	21	* 22	* 23	30	29	* 30	* 31	* 31	Approvisionnement total
Supply per capita	58	* 59	* 59	76	75	* 77	* 80	* 81	Approvisionnement par habitant
Mauritania									**Mauritanie**
Primary Energy production	11	12	13	15	34	31	30	30	Production d'énergie primaire
Net imports	* 13	* 14	16	21	7	* 23	* 24	* 23	Importations nettes
Changes in stocks	0	...	...	0	* -3	...	...	...	Variations des stocks
Total supply	* 23	* 26	29	36	45	54	* 54	* 52	Approvisionnement total
Supply per capita	* 11	* 11	11	12	12	13	* 13	* 12	Approvisionnement par habitant
Mauritius									**Maurice**
Primary Energy production	13	15	13	12	11	10	12	11	Production d'énergie primaire
Net imports	21	28	34	44	49	53	57	* 63	Importations nettes
Changes in stocks	1	2	-3	-1	-2	-2	3	6	Variations des stocks
Total supply	33	41	49	57	63	65	67	67	Approvisionnement total
Supply per capita	31	36	41	45	50	52	53	53	Approvisionnement par habitant
Mayotte									**Mayotte**
Primary Energy production	* 0	0	0	0	0	0	0	0	Production d'énergie primaire
Net imports	* 1	* 1	* 2	* 3	4	* 5	* 5	* 5	Importations nettes
Changes in stocks	...	...	...	...	0	...	...	...	Variations des stocks
Total supply	* 1	* 2	* 2	* 3	4	5	5	5	Approvisionnement total
Supply per capita	* 12	* 13	* 14	* 17	20	21	21	21	Approvisionnement par habitant
Mexico									**Mexique**
Primary Energy production	8 170	8 488	9 613	10 716	9 040	8 514	7 914	7 531	Production d'énergie primaire
Net imports	-2 983	-2 997	-3 166	-3 300	-1 621	-648	-180	269	Importations nettes
Changes in stocks	7	-7	91	-19	5	46	-48	6	Variations des stocks
Total supply	5 179	5 499	6 357	7 435	7 415	7 821	7 782	7 795	Approvisionnement total
Supply per capita	61	60	64	70	63	63	62	61	Approvisionnement par habitant
Micronesia (Fed. States of)									**Micronésie (États féd. de)**
Primary Energy production	...	* 0	0	0	0	0	0	0	Production d'énergie primaire
Net imports	...	* 2	* 2	* 2	* 2	* 2	3	* 3	Importations nettes
Total supply	...	* 2	* 2	2	2	* 2	2	* 2	Approvisionnement total
Supply per capita	...	* 15	* 17	16	15	* 20	20	* 21	Approvisionnement par habitant
Mongolia									**Mongolie**
Primary Energy production	82	72	66	138	655	677	654	959	Production d'énergie primaire
Net imports	33	* 17	21	-35	-449	-384	-365	-667	Importations nettes
Changes in stocks	...	...	...	-1	41	-50	17	-3	Variations des stocks
Total supply	116	89	87	104	164	342	272	294	Approvisionnement total
Supply per capita	53	39	36	41	61	117	91	97	Approvisionnement par habitant
Montenegro									**Monténégro**
Primary Energy production	...	...	...	25	35	29	30	28	Production d'énergie primaire
Net imports	...	...	...	16	14	11	12	14	Importations nettes
Changes in stocks	...	...	...	...	...	0	0	1	Variations des stocks
Total supply	...	...	...	42	48	40	42	41	Approvisionnement total
Supply per capita	...	...	...	67	77	64	67	65	Approvisionnement par habitant
Montserrat									**Montserrat**
Net imports	* 0	* 1	* 0	* 1	* 1	* 1	* 1	* 0	Importations nettes
Changes in stocks	...	...	...	...	0	0	0	0	Variations des stocks
Total supply	* 0	* 0	* 0	* 1	1	1	1	0	Approvisionnement total
Supply per capita	* 41	* 48	* 75	* 93	175	133	149	81	Approvisionnement par habitant
Morocco									**Maroc**
Primary Energy production	82	83	73	74	84	59	62	90	Production d'énergie primaire
Net imports	269	* 358	401	530	* 686	784	752	743	Importations nettes
Changes in stocks	-2	10	-2	0	10	64	15	3	Variations des stocks
Total supply	353	430	477	605	761	780	799	831	Approvisionnement total
Supply per capita	14	16	17	20	23	22	23	23	Approvisionnement par habitant

Region, country or area	1990	1995	2000	2005	2010	2014	2015	2016	Région, pays ou zone
Mozambique									**Mozambique**
Primary Energy production	236	248	302	429	517	776	810	745	Production d'énergie primaire
Net imports	* 12	16	-11	-65	-94	-193	* -230	* -253	Importations nettes
Changes in stocks	0	0	0	-1	0	35	* 43	* -64	Variations des stocks
Total supply	248	264	292	364	424	549	536	556	Approvisionnement total
Supply per capita	18	17	16	18	17	20	19	19	Approvisionnement par habitant
Myanmar									**Myanmar**
Primary Energy production	446	464	648	927	969	1 074	1 147	1 175	Production d'énergie primaire
Net imports	6	27	-113	-307	-305	-303	-296	-332	Importations nettes
Changes in stocks	2	-7	-3	1	2	30	30	7	Variations des stocks
Total supply	449	498	538	619	663	741	820	836	Approvisionnement total
Supply per capita	11	12	12	13	13	14	16	16	Approvisionnement par habitant
Namibia									**Namibie**
Primary Energy production	...	14	16	17	17	19	20	20	Production d'énergie primaire
Net imports	...	24	26	37	48	56	58	62	Importations nettes
Changes in stocks	...	...	...	...	0	0	0	-1	Variations des stocks
Total supply	...	38	42	54	65	75	78	83	Approvisionnement total
Supply per capita	...	23	22	26	30	32	32	33	Approvisionnement par habitant
Nauru									**Nauru**
Primary Energy production	...	...	...	...	* 0	0	* 0	0	Production d'énergie primaire
Net imports	* 2	* 2	* 2	* 1	* 1	* 1	* 1	* 1	Importations nettes
Changes in stocks	...	...	...	...	* 0	0	0	0	Variations des stocks
Total supply	* 2	* 1	* 1	* 1	1	* 1	* 1	* 1	Approvisionnement total
Supply per capita	* 188	* 148	* 119	* 84	58	* 58	* 59	* 61	Approvisionnement par habitant
Nepal									**Népal**
Primary Energy production	146	271	310	349	384	451	430	422	Production d'énergie primaire
Net imports	9	29	39	39	62	* 91	75	114	Importations nettes
Changes in stocks	-1	-1	...	...	...	* 0	0	0	Variations des stocks
Total supply	156	301	349	388	446	542	505	536	Approvisionnement total
Supply per capita	8	14	14	14	16	19	18	19	Approvisionnement par habitant
Netherlands									**Pays-Bas**
Primary Energy production	2 533	2 795	2 440	2 606	2 971	2 522	2 004	1 925	Production d'énergie primaire
Net imports	260	174	769	783	563	528	1 224	1 020	Importations nettes
Changes in stocks	5	-81	108	39	54	28	203	-115	Variations des stocks
Total supply	2 788	3 051	3 102	3 350	3 481	3 022	3 025	3 060	Approvisionnement total
Supply per capita	187	198	196	205	209	179	179	180	Approvisionnement par habitant
Netherlands Antilles [former]									**Antilles néerlandaises [anc.]**
Primary Energy production	0	0	0	0	0	...	...	...	Production d'énergie primaire
Net imports	* 71	* 94	83	84	68	...	...	...	Importations nettes
Changes in stocks	* -11	...	...	...	...	...	...	...	Variations des stocks
Total supply	82	* 95	83	84	69	...	...	...	Approvisionnement total
Supply per capita	432	* 500	464	452	344	...	...	...	Approvisionnement par habitant
New Caledonia									**Nouvelle-Calédonie**
Primary Energy production	2	1	2	1	1	1	2	1	Production d'énergie primaire
Net imports	* 20	* 26	* 28	* 36	* 47	59	61	67	Importations nettes
Changes in stocks	...	...	...	...	2	-3	1	0	Variations des stocks
Total supply	21	27	30	37	46	64	61	67	Approvisionnement total
Supply per capita	126	140	142	161	184	240	228	247	Approvisionnement par habitant
New Zealand									**Nouvelle-Zélande**
Primary Energy production	500	544	628	571	769	779	774	758	Production d'énergie primaire
Net imports	58	82	106	167	76	144	156	196	Importations nettes
Changes in stocks	1	-3	-12	-8	12	-3	-16	5	Variations des stocks
Total supply	556	629	747	746	832	926	945	949	Approvisionnement total
Supply per capita	163	171	194	181	190	203	205	204	Approvisionnement par habitant
Nicaragua									**Nicaragua**
Primary Energy production	59	66	56	62	66	91	92	90	Production d'énergie primaire
Net imports	28	37	49	57	56	61	71	72	Importations nettes
Changes in stocks	0	0	-1	0	-3	0	0	-2	Variations des stocks
Total supply	86	102	107	119	125	152	163	165	Approvisionnement total
Supply per capita	21	22	21	22	22	25	27	27	Approvisionnement par habitant
Niger									**Niger**
Primary Energy production	54	65	74	* 70	56	* 101	99	105	Production d'énergie primaire
Net imports	* 5	* 5	* 7	* 7	13	* -8	* -5	-9	Importations nettes
Changes in stocks	0	0	0	0	0	2	* 1	* 0	Variations des stocks
Total supply	60	70	81	* 77	70	* 91	94	96	Approvisionnement total
Supply per capita	8	8	7	* 6	4	* 5	5	5	Approvisionnement par habitant

Production, trade and supply of energy *(continued)*
Petajoules and gigajoules per capita

Production, commerce et fourniture d'énergie *(suite)*
pétajoules et gigajoules par habitant

Region, country or area	1990	1995	2000	2005	2010	2014	2015	2016	Région, pays ou zone
Nigeria									**Nigéria**
Primary Energy production	6 091	6 856	8 247	9 734	10 595	10 585	10 603	10 001	Production d'énergie primaire
Net imports	-3 312	-3 804	-4 595	-5 344	-5 274	-4 474	-4 622	-3 699	Importations nettes
Changes in stocks	-2	...	10	-10	-17	-18	-88	32	Variations des stocks
Total supply	2 780	3 052	3 642	4 401	5 337	6 129	6 069	6 270	Approvisionnement total
Supply per capita	29	28	29	31	34	35	33	34	Approvisionnement par habitant
Niue									**Nioué**
Primary Energy production	0	0	0	0	0	0	0	* 0	Production d'énergie primaire
Net imports	* 0	* 0	* 0	* 0	0	0	0	* 0	Importations nettes
Total supply	* 0	* 0	* 0	0	0	0	0	* 0	Approvisionnement total
Supply per capita	* 34	* 34	* 42	42	52	62	63	* 61	Approvisionnement par habitant
North Macedonia									**Macédoine du Nord**
Primary Energy production	...	112	118	108	68	61	58	51	Production d'énergie primaire
Net imports	...	43	48	52	53	59	58	66	Importations nettes
Changes in stocks	...	5	-4	-4	-1	0	0	1	Variations des stocks
Total supply	...	151	169	163	121	119	116	116	Approvisionnement total
Supply per capita	...	77	84	80	58	58	56	56	Approvisionnement par habitant
Norway [9]									**Norvège** [9]
Primary Energy production	4 977	7 543	9 340	9 372	8 736	8 243	8 632	8 718	Production d'énergie primaire
Net imports	-4 024	-6 561	-8 251	-8 242	-7 475	-7 078	-7 418	-7 570	Importations nettes
Changes in stocks	77	20	15	15	2	-36	9	12	Variations des stocks
Total supply	875	962	1 074	1 114	1 258	1 202	1 205	1 136	Approvisionnement total
Supply per capita	206	221	239	241	257	234	232	216	Approvisionnement par habitant
Oman									**Oman**
Primary Energy production	1 531	1 931	2 359	2 356	2 793	3 101	3 301	3 379	Production d'énergie primaire
Net imports	* -1 392	* -1 710	-2 079	-1 912	-2 022	-2 090	-2 202	-2 302	Importations nettes
Changes in stocks	-14	-15	-38	0	-7	-2	-2	7	Variations des stocks
Total supply	153	236	319	445	778	1 014	1 100	1 069	Approvisionnement total
Supply per capita	82	106	141	183	256	256	262	242	Approvisionnement par habitant
Other non-specified areas									**Autres zones non-spécifiées**
Primary Energy production	456	453	489	518	538	566	511	451	Production d'énergie primaire
Net imports	1 649	2 327	3 060	3 760	4 078	4 094	4 090	4 138	Importations nettes
Changes in stocks	100	117	41	42	-7	56	47	11	Variations des stocks
Total supply	2 005	2 663	3 509	4 236	4 624	4 603	4 554	4 579	Approvisionnement total
Supply per capita	98	125	158	186	200	197	194	194	Approvisionnement par habitant
Pakistan									**Pakistan**
Primary Energy production	906	1 192	1 403	2 020	2 253	2 396	2 403	2 438	Production d'énergie primaire
Net imports	385	529	680	633	843	977	* 1 025	* 1 160	Importations nettes
Changes in stocks	...	...	0	10	2	26	* 3	* 1	Variations des stocks
Total supply	1 290	1 722	2 082	2 642	3 094	3 348	3 425	3 597	Approvisionnement total
Supply per capita	12	14	14	17	18	18	18	19	Approvisionnement par habitant
Palau									**Palaos**
Net imports	...	* 2	* 3	* 3	* 3	* 3	* 3	* 3	Importations nettes
Total supply	...	* 3	* 3	* 3	3	* 3	* 3	* 3	Approvisionnement total
Supply per capita	...	* 158	* 152	* 156	141	* 146	* 144	* 144	Approvisionnement par habitant
Panama									**Panama**
Primary Energy production	24	22	28	32	26	31	36	39	Production d'énergie primaire
Net imports	42	41	75	88	98	121	113	125	Importations nettes
Changes in stocks	4	1	-1	0	-20	-15	-21	-5	Variations des stocks
Total supply	62	62	104	120	144	166	171	169	Approvisionnement total
Supply per capita	26	23	35	37	39	43	43	42	Approvisionnement par habitant
Papua New Guinea									**Papouasie-Nvl-Guinée**
Primary Energy production	251	263	220	174	95	166	422	376	Production d'énergie primaire
Net imports	* -162	* -171	* -121	* -48	* 47	* -3	* -236	* -195	Importations nettes
Changes in stocks	0	* 3	* 0	0	2	5	1	-3	Variations des stocks
Total supply	88	89	99	126	141	157	185	184	Approvisionnement total
Supply per capita	21	19	18	21	20	20	23	23	Approvisionnement par habitant
Paraguay									**Paraguay**
Primary Energy production	* 145	194	276	288	327	324	329	344	Production d'énergie primaire
Net imports	* -60	-80	-122	-109	-98	-77	-68	-76	Importations nettes
Changes in stocks	* 0	-4	2	-1	-4	1	0	3	Variations des stocks
Total supply	* 84	118	153	180	234	246	260	265	Approvisionnement total
Supply per capita	* 20	25	29	31	38	38	39	39	Approvisionnement par habitant

Region, country or area	1990	1995	2000	2005	2010	2014	2015	2016	Région, pays ou zone
Peru									**Pérou**
Primary Energy production	439	414	376	435	784	1 012	955	974	Production d'énergie primaire
Net imports	-28	60	130	108	-15	-89	-22	-25	Importations nettes
Changes in stocks	-3	23	7	-3	-13	12	-2	-63	Variations des stocks
Total supply	415	450	498	545	781	910	934	1 012	Approvisionnement total
Supply per capita	19	19	19	20	27	29	30	32	Approvisionnement par habitant
Philippines									**Philippines**
Primary Energy production	540	533	695	762	924	986	999	1 106	Production d'énergie primaire
Net imports	512	759	860	* 697	718	875	1 067	1 083	Importations nettes
Changes in stocks	13	28	4	-10	11	-11	14	63	Variations des stocks
Total supply	1 039	1 264	1 551	1 469	1 631	1 871	2 050	2 126	Approvisionnement total
Supply per capita	17	18	20	17	17	19	20	21	Approvisionnement par habitant
Poland									**Pologne**
Primary Energy production	4 350	4 161	3 318	3 281	2 808	2 831	2 840	2 791	Production d'énergie primaire
Net imports	99	58	438	686	1 351	1 168	1 196	1 282	Importations nettes
Changes in stocks	43	-36	-24	82	-93	21	31	-111	Variations des stocks
Total supply	4 406	4 256	3 780	3 886	4 251	3 977	4 004	4 185	Approvisionnement total
Supply per capita	116	111	99	102	111	104	105	109	Approvisionnement par habitant
Portugal [10]									**Portugal** [10]
Primary Energy production	142	139	161	151	242	250	224	254	Production d'énergie primaire
Net imports	596	714	864	969	717	610	692	656	Importations nettes
Changes in stocks	19	12	0	16	-15	-15	6	-6	Variations des stocks
Total supply	720	840	1 026	1 104	975	875	910	916	Approvisionnement total
Supply per capita	73	83	99	105	91	84	87	88	Approvisionnement par habitant
Puerto Rico									**Porto Rico**
Primary Energy production	* 1	0	1	0	0	1	1	1	Production d'énergie primaire
Net imports	...	...	12	24	27	55	52	59	Importations nettes
Total supply	* 1	0	13	24	27	56	53	61	Approvisionnement total
Supply per capita	* 0	0	3	6	7	15	15	17	Approvisionnement par habitant
Qatar									**Qatar**
Primary Energy production	1 009	1 364	2 449	3 718	7 428	9 166	9 316	9 519	Production d'énergie primaire
Net imports	-832	-811	-1 921	-2 991	-6 261	-7 315	-7 378	-7 638	Importations nettes
Changes in stocks	-22	0	-56	-1	3	29	110	118	Variations des stocks
Total supply	199	553	584	728	1 165	1 822	1 829	1 763	Approvisionnement total
Supply per capita	420	1 102	988	886	655	767	737	686	Approvisionnement par habitant
Republic of Korea									**République de Corée**
Primary Energy production	941	878	1 420	1 776	1 855	2 024	2 117	2 117	Production d'énergie primaire
Net imports	2 840	5 319	6 505	6 810	8 703	9 192	9 314	9 644	Importations nettes
Changes in stocks	-69	115	71	-179	117	51	67	-2	Variations des stocks
Total supply	3 851	6 083	7 854	8 764	10 441	11 165	11 364	11 762	Approvisionnement total
Supply per capita	90	136	171	186	211	222	225	232	Approvisionnement par habitant
Republic of Moldova [11]									**République de Moldova** [11]
Primary Energy production	...	4	3	4	8	31	31	33	Production d'énergie primaire
Net imports	...	* 184	* 64	* 85	69	70	69	71	Importations nettes
Changes in stocks	...	2	0	0	-2	0	0	0	Variations des stocks
Total supply	...	186	66	89	80	102	100	104	Approvisionnement total
Supply per capita	...	43	16	24	20	25	25	26	Approvisionnement par habitant
Réunion									**Réunion**
Primary Energy production	8	9	7	7	8	9	9	9	Production d'énergie primaire
Net imports	* 16	* 23	* 36	* 44	* 50	* 49	* 51	* 53	Importations nettes
Changes in stocks	0	0	1	1	0	-1	1	1	Variations des stocks
Total supply	24	31	42	49	58	58	59	60	Approvisionnement total
Supply per capita	39	47	57	61	70	68	69	69	Approvisionnement par habitant
Romania									**Roumanie**
Primary Energy production	1 695	1 335	1 194	1 173	1 155	1 109	1 116	1 045	Production d'énergie primaire
Net imports	936	591	331	446	311	214	217	287	Importations nettes
Changes in stocks	11	2	-8	-7	-7	-4	-7	-2	Variations des stocks
Total supply	2 620	1 925	1 532	1 626	1 474	1 326	1 341	1 334	Approvisionnement total
Supply per capita	113	85	69	75	72	66	67	67	Approvisionnement par habitant
Russian Federation									**Fédération de Russie**
Primary Energy production	...	40 589	41 030	50 506	53 679	55 400	56 024	57 240	Production d'énergie primaire
Net imports	...	-13 397	-14 842	-22 870	-24 601	* -24 787	* -26 097	* -26 726	Importations nettes
Changes in stocks	...	472	195	298	147	150	75	53	Variations des stocks
Total supply	...	26 720	25 994	27 338	28 932	30 464	29 852	30 461	Approvisionnement total
Supply per capita	...	180	177	190	202	212	207	212	Approvisionnement par habitant

Region, country or area	1990	1995	2000	2005	2010	2014	2015	2016	Région, pays ou zone
Rwanda									**Rwanda**
Primary Energy production	28	48	46	63	76	* 84	* 85	* 86	Production d'énergie primaire
Net imports	* 8	* 7	* 8	* 7	* 8	* 11	* 13	* 13	Importations nettes
Changes in stocks	...	...	...	0	...	...	...	...	Variations des stocks
Total supply	35	54	54	71	84	* 96	* 98	* 99	Approvisionnement total
Supply per capita	5	10	7	8	8	* 8	* 8	* 8	Approvisionnement par habitant
Saint Helena									**Sainte-Hélène**
Primary Energy production	* 0	0	0	0	0	* 0	0	0	Production d'énergie primaire
Net imports	0	* 0	0	0	0	* 0	* 0	* 0	Importations nettes
Total supply	0	* 0	0	0	0	* 0	* 0	* 0	Approvisionnement total
Supply per capita	17	* 35	36	33	38	* 38	* 37	* 37	Approvisionnement par habitant
Saint Kitts and Nevis									**Saint-Kitts-et-Nevis**
Primary Energy production	1	1	1	1	0	* 0	* 0	* 0	Production d'énergie primaire
Net imports	* 2	* 2	* 3	* 3	3	* 3	* 4	* 4	Importations nettes
Total supply	* 2	* 2	* 3	* 3	3	* 3	* 3	* 3	Approvisionnement total
Supply per capita	* 53	* 56	* 63	* 67	62	* 61	* 62	* 63	Approvisionnement par habitant
Saint Lucia									**Sainte-Lucie**
Primary Energy production	0	0	0	0	0	0	0	0	Production d'énergie primaire
Net imports	2	* 4	* 5	* 6	* 6	* 6	* 6	* 6	Importations nettes
Total supply	2	5	5	* 5	6	6	6	6	Approvisionnement total
Supply per capita	18	31	33	* 33	34	34	34	34	Approvisionnement par habitant
Saint Pierre and Miquelon									**Saint-Pierre-et-Miquelon**
Primary Energy production	...	...	* 0	0	0	0	0	0	Production d'énergie primaire
Net imports	2	1	* 1	* 1	* 1	* 1	* 1	* 1	Importations nettes
Total supply	1	1	* 1	* 1	* 1	* 1	* 1	* 1	Approvisionnement total
Supply per capita	206	164	* 125	* 149	* 160	* 174	* 174	* 174	Approvisionnement par habitant
Saint Vincent & Grenadines									**Saint-Vincent-Grenadines**
Primary Energy production	0	0	0	0	0	0	0	* 0	Production d'énergie primaire
Net imports	* 1	* 2	2	* 3	* 3	* 3	* 3	* 3	Importations nettes
Total supply	* 1	* 2	2	* 3	3	* 3	* 3	* 3	Approvisionnement total
Supply per capita	* 12	* 19	21	* 31	31	* 30	* 31	* 30	Approvisionnement par habitant
Samoa									**Samoa**
Primary Energy production	1	1	1	1	1	1	1	1	Production d'énergie primaire
Net imports	* 2	* 2	* 2	* 3	* 3	3	4	* 3	Importations nettes
Changes in stocks	...	...	...	...	0	* 0	* 1	* 0	Variations des stocks
Total supply	* 3	* 3	* 3	* 3	* 4	4	5	* 5	Approvisionnement total
Supply per capita	* 16	* 16	* 18	* 19	* 21	21	24	* 24	Approvisionnement par habitant
Sao Tome and Principe									**Sao Tomé-et-Principe**
Primary Energy production	1	1	1	1	1	1	1	1	Production d'énergie primaire
Net imports	* 1	* 1	* 1	* 1	2	* 2	* 2	* 2	Importations nettes
Total supply	* 1	1	* 2	* 2	2	* 3	* 3	* 3	Approvisionnement total
Supply per capita	* 12	12	* 12	* 13	14	* 13	* 14	* 14	Approvisionnement par habitant
Saudi Arabia [8]									**Arabie saoudite** [8]
Primary Energy production	16 769	19 932	20 284	24 162	22 115	25 904	27 184	28 132	Production d'énergie primaire
Net imports	* -13 721	-16 427	-15 797	-18 116	-14 727	-17 114	-17 294	* -19 011	Importations nettes
Changes in stocks	* 172	-12	0	0	-319	-87	161	511	Variations des stocks
Total supply	2 875	3 516	4 487	6 047	7 707	8 876	9 728	8 609	Approvisionnement total
Supply per capita	178	190	224	252	281	288	308	267	Approvisionnement par habitant
Senegal									**Sénégal**
Primary Energy production	40	44	50	52	86	76	78	66	Production d'énergie primaire
Net imports	* 41	* 43	46	65	74	88	107	108	Importations nettes
Changes in stocks	0	0	1	3	-4	-4	-4	-7	Variations des stocks
Total supply	* 81	* 87	96	114	165	169	190	180	Approvisionnement total
Supply per capita	* 11	* 10	10	11	13	12	13	12	Approvisionnement par habitant
Serbia [12]									**Serbie** [12]
Primary Energy production	...	...	...	431	440	393	449	446	Production d'énergie primaire
Net imports	...	...	...	243	212	148	164	181	Importations nettes
Changes in stocks	...	...	...	2	4	-7	1	-6	Variations des stocks
Total supply	...	...	...	672	648	550	612	633	Approvisionnement total
Supply per capita	...	...	...	82	89	78	87	90	Approvisionnement par habitant
Serbia and Monten. [former]									**Serbie-et-Monténégro [anc.]**
Primary Energy production	...	497	479	...	...	...	...	...	Production d'énergie primaire
Net imports	...	* 25	77	...	...	...	...	...	Importations nettes
Total supply	...	522	556	...	...	...	...	...	Approvisionnement total
Supply per capita	...	48	61	...	...	...	...	...	Approvisionnement par habitant

Region, country or area	1990	1995	2000	2005	2010	2014	2015	2016	Région, pays ou zone
Seychelles									**Seychelles**
Primary Energy production	0	0	0	0	0	0	0	* 0	Production d'énergie primaire
Net imports	1	* 4	* 9	* 10	6	* 7	* 6	* 8	Importations nettes
Changes in stocks	* 0	0	* 0	...	...	...	...	...	Variations des stocks
Total supply	2	* 3	8	10	6	7	7	8	Approvisionnement total
Supply per capita	31	* 39	102	115	67	73	73	90	Approvisionnement par habitant
Sierra Leone									**Sierra Leone**
Primary Energy production	43	42	49	50	52	53	54	54	Production d'énergie primaire
Net imports	* 7	* 5	* 6	* 7	* 9	* 17	* 13	* 14	Importations nettes
Changes in stocks	0	...	...	...	...	...	...	...	Variations des stocks
Total supply	50	48	55	56	60	69	67	67	Approvisionnement total
Supply per capita	13	12	13	11	9	10	9	9	Approvisionnement par habitant
Singapore									**Singapour**
Primary Energy production	...	...	...	...	25	27	28	28	Production d'énergie primaire
Net imports	493	641	783	* 774	* 1 058	* 1 123	* 1 246	876	Importations nettes
Changes in stocks	-163	2	27	-31	-25	8	41	-6	Variations des stocks
Total supply	656	640	756	805	1 109	1 142	1 233	910	Approvisionnement total
Supply per capita	218	184	193	189	219	210	223	162	Approvisionnement par habitant
Sint Maarten (Dutch part)									**St-Martin (partie néerland.)**
Net imports	...	...	...	...	...	* 11	* 12	* 12	Importations nettes
Total supply	...	...	...	...	...	* 11	* 12	* 12	Approvisionnement total
Supply per capita	...	...	...	...	...	* 303	* 305	* 302	Approvisionnement par habitant
Slovakia									**Slovaquie**
Primary Energy production	...	210	263	265	250	264	265	266	Production d'énergie primaire
Net imports	...	514	485	516	475	408	407	412	Importations nettes
Changes in stocks	...	-22	4	4	-12	15	-4	-9	Variations des stocks
Total supply	...	746	744	778	737	658	677	687	Approvisionnement total
Supply per capita	...	139	138	144	136	121	124	126	Approvisionnement par habitant
Slovenia									**Slovénie**
Primary Energy production	...	124	129	146	157	153	142	144	Production d'énergie primaire
Net imports	...	129	141	160	149	123	133	133	Importations nettes
Changes in stocks	...	-1	2	0	0	-2	-1	0	Variations des stocks
Total supply	...	254	269	306	306	279	275	278	Approvisionnement total
Supply per capita	...	129	136	153	150	135	133	134	Approvisionnement par habitant
Solomon Islands									**Îles Salomon**
Primary Energy production	* 3	* 3	* 3	* 3	* 3	* 3	* 3	* 3	Production d'énergie primaire
Net imports	* 2	* 2	* 3	* 3	* 3	* 3	* 3	* 3	Importations nettes
Total supply	* 5	* 5	* 5	* 6	* 6	* 6	* 6	* 6	Approvisionnement total
Supply per capita	* 17	* 15	* 13	* 12	* 11	* 11	* 10	* 9	Approvisionnement par habitant
Somalia									**Somalie**
Primary Energy production	58	69	85	103	124	129	129	136	Production d'énergie primaire
Net imports	* 10	* 8	* 5	* 4	* 1	* 9	* 9	* 9	Importations nettes
Changes in stocks	* 0	* 0	...	...	...	...	...	...	Variations des stocks
Total supply	68	77	90	107	126	138	138	145	Approvisionnement total
Supply per capita	10	12	12	13	10	10	10	10	Approvisionnement par habitant
South Africa									**Afrique du Sud**
Primary Energy production	4 767	5 691	6 153	6 583	6 798	6 958	6 822	6 858	Production d'énergie primaire
Net imports	* -587	-1 009	-1 171	-1 183	-586	-583	-719	-588	Importations nettes
Changes in stocks	0	-68	-41	0	59	31	-5	-5	Variations des stocks
Total supply	4 179	4 750	5 022	5 399	6 153	6 343	6 109	6 276	Approvisionnement total
Supply per capita	114	115	112	113	119	116	110	112	Approvisionnement par habitant
South Sudan									**Soudan du sud**
Primary Energy production	...	...	...	...	...	337	321	257	Production d'énergie primaire
Net imports	...	...	...	...	...	-308	-286	-225	Importations nettes
Total supply	...	...	...	...	...	30	35	32	Approvisionnement total
Supply per capita	...	...	...	...	...	3	3	3	Approvisionnement par habitant
Spain [13]									**Espagne** [13]
Primary Energy production	1 442	1 313	1 314	1 256	1 419	1 432	1 367	1 391	Production d'énergie primaire
Net imports	2 308	2 949	3 812	4 738	3 991	3 352	3 497	3 445	Importations nettes
Changes in stocks	6	69	52	78	73	52	-40	-103	Variations des stocks
Total supply	3 744	4 191	5 074	5 915	5 337	4 732	4 904	4 939	Approvisionnement total
Supply per capita	96	106	126	136	114	102	106	107	Approvisionnement par habitant

Region, country or area	1990	1995	2000	2005	2010	2014	2015	2016	Région, pays ou zone
Sri Lanka									**Sri Lanka**
Primary Energy production	135	146	156	163	184	179	181	169	Production d'énergie primaire
Net imports	54	80	144	161	170	211	217	249	Importations nettes
Changes in stocks	2	-1	4	1	-7	-18	-36	-49	Variations des stocks
Total supply	187	225	296	324	360	408	433	467	Approvisionnement total
Supply per capita	11	12	16	16	18	20	21	22	Approvisionnement par habitant
State of Palestine									**État de Palestine**
Primary Energy production	* 4	* 5	* 5	8	9	9	9	10	Production d'énergie primaire
Net imports	* 16	* 18	33	49	45	57	63	67	Importations nettes
Changes in stocks	...	...	...	0	0	-2	0	0	Variations des stocks
Total supply	20	* 22	38	58	54	69	72	77	Approvisionnement total
Supply per capita	...	* 8	12	16	13	15	16	16	Approvisionnement par habitant
Sudan									**Soudan**
Primary Energy production	...	...	...	...	...	682	658	728	Production d'énergie primaire
Net imports	...	...	...	...	...	-49	37	45	Importations nettes
Changes in stocks	...	...	...	...	...	0	0	0	Variations des stocks
Total supply	...	...	...	...	...	633	695	772	Approvisionnement total
Supply per capita	...	...	...	...	...	17	18	20	Approvisionnement par habitant
Sudan [former]									**Soudan [anc.]**
Primary Energy production	379	448	851	1 145	1 473	...	...	...	Production d'énergie primaire
Net imports	* 73	* 59	-287	-480	-762	...	...	...	Importations nettes
Changes in stocks	* 1	1	8	12	...	...	...	...	Variations des stocks
Total supply	451	506	556	654	711	...	...	...	Approvisionnement total
Supply per capita	17	17	16	17	16	...	...	...	Approvisionnement par habitant
Suriname									**Suriname**
Primary Energy production	15	17	33	32	43	40	40	39	Production d'énergie primaire
Net imports	* 15	* 16	* 1	* -4	* -4	* -4	* -11	* -10	Importations nettes
Changes in stocks	0	0	...	...	0	0	0	0	Variations des stocks
Total supply	29	34	36	26	40	36	29	29	Approvisionnement total
Supply per capita	72	78	76	53	76	67	53	52	Approvisionnement par habitant
Eswatini									**Eswatini**
Primary Energy production	* 23	* 24	34	36	33	37	36	33	Production d'énergie primaire
Net imports	* 8	* 10	* 7	* 3	* 11	* 10	* 12	10	Importations nettes
Changes in stocks	...	...	...	* 0	* 0	...	...	...	Variations des stocks
Total supply	* 32	* 34	41	40	44	48	48	43	Approvisionnement total
Supply per capita	* 37	* 35	38	37	37	37	36	32	Approvisionnement par habitant
Sweden									**Suède**
Primary Energy production	1 235	1 312	1 257	1 426	1 357	1 429	1 408	1 446	Production d'énergie primaire
Net imports	726	747	724	744	722	580	502	589	Importations nettes
Changes in stocks	-5	-29	9	32	-33	9	22	-12	Variations des stocks
Total supply	1 967	2 089	1 971	2 138	2 112	2 000	1 888	2 046	Approvisionnement total
Supply per capita	230	237	222	237	225	206	193	208	Approvisionnement par habitant
Switzerland [14]									**Suisse** [14]
Primary Energy production	428	468	500	458	526	552	509	483	Production d'énergie primaire
Net imports	584	521	524	628	564	491	499	517	Importations nettes
Changes in stocks	-5	-14	-18	6	-2	0	-15	3	Variations des stocks
Total supply	1 017	1 003	1 041	1 080	1 091	1 043	1 024	998	Approvisionnement total
Supply per capita	152	142	145	145	139	126	123	118	Approvisionnement par habitant
Syrian Arab Republic									**République arabe syrienne**
Primary Energy production	1 036	1 403	1 417	1 171	1 165	237	196	177	Production d'énergie primaire
Net imports	* -554	-813	-690	-431	-233	218	223	240	Importations nettes
Changes in stocks	6	* 5	...	1	20	0	...	...	Variations des stocks
Total supply	476	585	729	740	911	454	419	418	Approvisionnement total
Supply per capita	39	41	46	40	43	24	22	23	Approvisionnement par habitant
Tajikistan									**Tadjikistan**
Primary Energy production	...	106	103	115	115	* 126	* 131	136	Production d'énergie primaire
Net imports	...	40	38	33	29	32	32	29	Importations nettes
Total supply	...	146	141	148	143	158	163	166	Approvisionnement total
Supply per capita	...	25	23	23	19	19	19	19	Approvisionnement par habitant
Thailand									**Thaïlande**
Primary Energy production	1 089	1 322	1 700	2 144	2 952	3 348	3 133	3 283	Production d'énergie primaire
Net imports	* 699	* 1 289	* 1 308	* 1 869	* 2 027	2 300	2 509	2 537	Importations nettes
Changes in stocks	4	-25	-67	-54	33	-25	9	26	Variations des stocks
Total supply	1 784	2 635	3 075	4 067	4 945	5 673	5 634	5 794	Approvisionnement total
Supply per capita	31	44	49	61	74	83	82	84	Approvisionnement par habitant

Region, country or area	1990	1995	2000	2005	2010	2014	2015	2016	Région, pays ou zone
Timor-Leste									**Timor-Leste**
Primary Energy production	...	...	...	201	186	142	* 147	121	Production d'énergie primaire
Net imports	...	...	...	* -196	* -182	* -135	* -139	* -113	Importations nettes
Total supply	...	...	...	* 4	* 4	* 8	* 8	* 8	Approvisionnement total
Supply per capita	...	...	...	* 4	* 4	* 7	* 6	* 6	Approvisionnement par habitant
Togo									**Togo**
Primary Energy production	44	57	74	84	99	111	113	117	Production d'énergie primaire
Net imports	* 11	* 15	* 16	15	29	26	26	32	Importations nettes
Changes in stocks	0	0	0	-1	-2	-2	-3	-1	Variations des stocks
Total supply	55	71	89	99	130	139	143	150	Approvisionnement total
Supply per capita	15	17	19	18	20	19	19	20	Approvisionnement par habitant
Tonga									**Tonga**
Primary Energy production	0	0	0	0	0	0	0	0	Production d'énergie primaire
Net imports	1	1	1	* 2	* 2	* 2	* 2	* 2	Importations nettes
Changes in stocks	...	...	...	...	...	* 0	* 0	* 0	Variations des stocks
Total supply	1	1	1	* 2	2	2	2	* 2	Approvisionnement total
Supply per capita	12	14	15	* 16	16	15	16	* 17	Approvisionnement par habitant
Trinidad and Tobago									**Trinité-et-Tobago**
Primary Energy production	529	511	799	1 464	1 786	1 663	1 577	1 407	Production d'énergie primaire
Net imports	-271	-264	-378	-777	-954	-847	-753	-638	Importations nettes
Changes in stocks	6	-12	7	10	-13	-6	9	3	Variations des stocks
Total supply	251	258	414	678	845	822	816	768	Approvisionnement total
Supply per capita	206	205	321	516	636	607	600	562	Approvisionnement par habitant
Tunisia									**Tunisie**
Primary Energy production	222	205	253	274	341	274	260	252	Production d'énergie primaire
Net imports	* -27	* 6	47	71	79	162	198	210	Importations nettes
Changes in stocks	3	-9	7	-4	-7	2	7	1	Variations des stocks
Total supply	192	220	293	349	427	435	452	460	Approvisionnement total
Supply per capita	23	25	31	35	40	39	40	40	Approvisionnement par habitant
Turkey									**Turquie**
Primary Energy production	1 087	1 112	1 085	1 003	1 350	1 301	1 312	1 490	Production d'énergie primaire
Net imports	1 138	1 532	2 113	2 517	3 059	3 744	4 111	4 204	Importations nettes
Changes in stocks	34	45	-3	-28	11	-4	87	33	Variations des stocks
Total supply	2 191	2 598	3 200	3 548	4 399	5 048	5 336	5 661	Approvisionnement total
Supply per capita	40	44	50	52	61	66	68	71	Approvisionnement par habitant
Turkmenistan									**Turkménistan**
Primary Energy production	...	1 376	1 928	2 584	1 982	3 270	3 407	3 230	Production d'énergie primaire
Net imports	...	-802	-1 303	-1 779	-1 030	-2 148	-2 248	-2 073	Importations nettes
Total supply	...	574	625	805	951	1 123	1 160	1 158	Approvisionnement total
Supply per capita	...	137	139	170	187	205	208	204	Approvisionnement par habitant
Turks and Caicos Islands									**Îles Turques-et-Caïques**
Primary Energy production	0	0	0	0	0	0	0	0	Production d'énergie primaire
Net imports	* 0	* 1	* 1	* 2	* 3	* 3	* 3	* 3	Importations nettes
Total supply	* 0	* 1	* 1	* 2	* 3	* 3	* 3	* 3	Approvisionnement total
Supply per capita	* 34	* 43	* 52	* 57	* 84	* 83	* 84	* 86	Approvisionnement par habitant
Tuvalu									**Tuvalu**
Primary Energy production	...	...	...	...	...	...	0	* 0	Production d'énergie primaire
Net imports	* 0	* 0	* 0	* 0	0	* 0	* 0	* 0	Importations nettes
Total supply	* 0	* 0	* 0	* 0	0	* 0	* 0	* 0	Approvisionnement total
Supply per capita	* 8	* 9	* 10	* 13	12	* 12	* 13	* 13	Approvisionnement par habitant
Uganda									**Ouganda**
Primary Energy production	271	300	302	390	477	573	595	618	Production d'énergie primaire
Net imports	* 9	* 12	* 17	* 26	* 46	52	60	63	Importations nettes
Changes in stocks	0	...	...	...	...	...	...	...	Variations des stocks
Total supply	281	312	319	417	523	625	655	680	Approvisionnement total
Supply per capita	16	15	13	15	15	16	16	16	Approvisionnement par habitant
Ukraine									**Ukraine**
Primary Energy production	...	3 661	3 231	3 328	3 238	3 206[15]	2 552[15]	2 658[15]	Production d'énergie primaire
Net imports	...	3 411	2 343	2 458	1 762	* 1 160[15]	1 268[15]	* 1 187[15]	Importations nettes
Changes in stocks	...	0	0	-86	-490	-68[15]	66[15]	-19[15]	Variations des stocks
Total supply	...	7 073	5 574	5 872	5 491	4 434[15]	3 753[15]	3 864[15]	Approvisionnement total
Supply per capita	...	138	114	125	120	99[15]	84[15]	87[15]	Approvisionnement par habitant

Region, country or area	1990	1995	2000	2005	2010	2014	2015	2016	Région, pays ou zone
United Arab Emirates									**Émirats arabes unis**
Primary Energy production	5 177	5 661	6 571	7 293	7 496	9 342	10 233	10 542	Production d'énergie primaire
Net imports	* -4 375	* -4 533	-4 853	-5 450	* -4 860	-5 683	-6 901	* -7 115	Importations nettes
Changes in stocks	12	21	...	...	...	...	...	...	Variations des stocks
Total supply	791	1 108	1 719	1 842	2 635	3 658	3 333	3 428	Approvisionnement total
Supply per capita	437	472	567	453	319	403	364	370	Approvisionnement par habitant
United Kingdom [16]									**Royaume-Uni** [16]
Primary Energy production	8 595	10 588	11 247	8 483	6 149	4 464	4 897	4 968	Production d'énergie primaire
Net imports	-151	-1 928	-2 169	736	2 031	3 142	2 468	2 267	Importations nettes
Changes in stocks	-84	-265	-138	0	-254	141	-164	-191	Variations des stocks
Total supply	8 527	8 925	9 216	9 219	8 435	7 466	7 531	7 425	Approvisionnement total
Supply per capita	149	154	157	153	133	115	115	113	Approvisionnement par habitant
United Rep. of Tanzania									**Rép.-Unie de Tanzanie**
Primary Energy production	315	434	543	665	782	928	958	992	Production d'énergie primaire
Net imports	* 27	* 30	30	57	64	111	128	116	Importations nettes
Changes in stocks	0	...	...	...	...	...	...	...	Variations des stocks
Total supply	341	463	572	722	847	1 039	1 087	1 108	Approvisionnement total
Supply per capita	13	15	17	19	18	20	20	20	Approvisionnement par habitant
United States of America [17]									**États-Unis d'Amérique** [17]
Primary Energy production	68 588	68 963	69 339	68 124	71 893	83 426	84 051	79 672	Production d'énergie primaire
Net imports	12 528	16 273	23 218	28 307	19 907	8 875	8 593	8 916	Importations nettes
Changes in stocks	1 606	-764	-1 980	-16	-267	771	2 085	-1 145	Variations des stocks
Total supply	79 510	86 000	94 538	96 447	92 066	91 529	90 560	89 733	Approvisionnement total
Supply per capita	314	323	335	325	298	288	283	279	Approvisionnement par habitant
United States Virgin Islands									**Îles Vierges américaines**
Primary Energy production	...	...	...	...	...	* 0	* 0	* 0	Production d'énergie primaire
Total supply	...	...	...	...	...	* 0	* 0	* 0	Approvisionnement total
Supply per capita	...	...	...	...	...	* 1	* 1	* 1	Approvisionnement par habitant
Uruguay									**Uruguay**
Primary Energy production	51	45	46	45	89	113	* 126	* 126	Production d'énergie primaire
Net imports	44	66	70	75	85	85	89	88	Importations nettes
Changes in stocks	-2	4	-2	-5	1	-1	3	-2	Variations des stocks
Total supply	96	107	119	126	173	199	212	215	Approvisionnement total
Supply per capita	31	33	36	38	51	58	62	62	Approvisionnement par habitant
Uzbekistan									**Ouzbékistan**
Primary Energy production	...	2 045	2 307	2 446	2 309	2 339	2 344	2 134	Production d'énergie primaire
Net imports	...	-170	-177	-395	-499	-510	-561	-561	Importations nettes
Changes in stocks	...	88	...	...	...	...	...	...	Variations des stocks
Total supply	...	1 787	2 130	2 050	1 809	1 829	1 783	1 574	Approvisionnement total
Supply per capita	...	78	86	79	63	60	58	50	Approvisionnement par habitant
Vanuatu									**Vanuatu**
Primary Energy production	* 0	* 1	1	1	1	1	1	1	Production d'énergie primaire
Net imports	* 1	* 1	* 1	* 1	* 2	* 3	* 2	* 3	Importations nettes
Changes in stocks	...	...	...	...	* 0	* 0	0	0	Variations des stocks
Total supply	1	1	* 2	2	3	3	3	3	Approvisionnement total
Supply per capita	8	9	* 11	8	11	12	11	11	Approvisionnement par habitant
Venezuela (Boliv. Rep. of)									**Venezuela (Rép. boliv. du)**
Primary Energy production	5 953	7 962	8 965	8 283	8 139	7 437	7 361	6 751	Production d'énergie primaire
Net imports	-4 027	-5 772	-6 320	-5 883	* -4 983	-4 737	-4 891	-4 453	Importations nettes
Changes in stocks	-18	24	15	-336	-54	-33	-2	-2	Variations des stocks
Total supply	1 944	2 167	2 629	2 737	3 211	2 732	2 471	2 300	Approvisionnement total
Supply per capita	99	98	108	103	111	89	79	73	Approvisionnement par habitant
Viet Nam									**Viet Nam**
Primary Energy production	787	1 136	1 733	2 612	2 747	2 975	3 043	2 880	Production d'énergie primaire
Net imports	-3	-207	-421	-786	-422	-153	5	188	Importations nettes
Changes in stocks	-7	20	50	70	5	* 58	* 77	* 62	Variations des stocks
Total supply	791	908	1 262	1 756	2 319	2 765	2 972	3 006	Approvisionnement total
Supply per capita	12	12	16	21	26	30	32	32	Approvisionnement par habitant
Wallis and Futuna Islands									**Îles Wallis-et-Futuna**
Net imports	...	...	...	0	0	0	0	0	Importations nettes
Total supply	...	...	...	0	0	0	0	0	Approvisionnement total
Supply per capita	...	...	...	26	27	28	28	30	Approvisionnement par habitant

22

Production, trade and supply of energy *(continued)*
Petajoules and gigajoules per capita

Production, commerce et fourniture d'énergie *(suite)*
pétajoules et gigajoules par habitant

Region, country or area	1990	1995	2000	2005	2010	2014	2015	2016	Région, pays ou zone
Yemen									**Yémen**
Primary Energy production	...	713	908	844	804	678	174	65	Production d'énergie primaire
Net imports	...	-571	-712	-529	-477	-344	3	87	Importations nettes
Changes in stocks	...	0	0	40	...	...	...	9	Variations des stocks
Total supply	...	142	197	274	326	335	177	144	Approvisionnement total
Supply per capita	...	9	11	13	14	13	7	5	Approvisionnement par habitant
Zambia									**Zambie**
Primary Energy production	207	224	248	280	319	374	385	417	Production d'énergie primaire
Net imports	* 14	* 19	13	25	29	34	45	50	Importations nettes
Changes in stocks	...	-1	1	0	0	-6	...	...	Variations des stocks
Total supply	222	244	260	305	348	415	430	468	Approvisionnement total
Supply per capita	28	27	25	27	25	27	27	28	Approvisionnement par habitant
Zimbabwe									**Zimbabwe**
Primary Energy production	372	362	379	379	369	483	449	380	Production d'énergie primaire
Net imports	* 30	64	53	36	24	48	47	47	Importations nettes
Changes in stocks	0	5	-5	1	...	67	24	-39	Variations des stocks
Total supply	402	422	438	414	392	465	472	466	Approvisionnement total
Supply per capita	38	36	35	33	28	30	30	29	Approvisionnement par habitant

Source:

United Nations Statistics Division, New York, Energy Statistics Yearbook 2016, last accessed January 2019.

Source:

Organisation des Nations Unies, Division de statistique, New York, Annuaire des statistiques de l'énergie 2016, dernier accès janvier 2019.

1	Excluding overseas territories.
2	For statistical purposes, the data for China do not include those for the Hong Kong Special Administrative Region (Hong Kong SAR), Macao Special Administrative Region (Macao SAR) and Taiwan Province of China.
3	Excluding the Faroe Islands and Greenland.
4	Including Monaco.
5	Data include Timor-Leste.
6	Data include San Marino and the Holy See.
7	Data include Okinawa.
8	The data for crude oil production include 50 per cent of the output of the Neutral Zone.
9	Including Svalbard and Jan Mayen Islands.
10	Data includes the Azores and Madeira.
11	Excluding Transnistria and the municipality of Bender.
12	Excluding Kosovo.
13	Data include the Canary Islands.
14	Including Liechtenstein.
15	The Government of Ukraine has informed the United Nations that it is not in a position to provide statistical data concerning the Autonomous Republic of Crimea and the city of Sevastopol.
16	Shipments of coal and oil to Jersey, Guernsey and the isle of Man from the United Kingdom are not classed as exports. Supplies of coal and oil to these islands are, therefore, included as part of UK supply. Exports of natural gas to the Isle of Man included with the exports to Ireland.
17	Oil and coal trade statistics include overseas territories.

1 Non compris les départements d'outre-mer.
2 Pour la présentation des statistiques, les données pour la Chine ne comprennent pas la région administrative spéciale de Hong Kong (RAS de Hong Kong), la région administrative spéciale de Macao (RAS de Macao) et la province chinoise de Taïwan.
3 Non compris les Îles Féroé et le Groenland.
4 Y compris Monaco.
5 Les données comprennent Timor-Leste.
6 Les données comprennent Saint-Marin et le Saint-Siège.
7 Les données incluent Okinawa.
8 Les données relatives à la production de pétrole brut comprennent 50 pour cent de la production de la Zone Neutre.
9 Y compris les îles Svalbard-et-Jan Mayen.
10 Les données comprennent Azores et Madère.
11 Non compris la Transnistrie et la commune de Bender.
12 Non compris Kosovo.
13 Les données comprennent les îles Canaries.
14 Y compris Liechtenstein.
15 Le gouvernement Ukrainien a informé l'ONU qu'il n'est pas en mesure de fournir des donnees statistiques concernant la République autome de Crimée et la ville de Sébastopol.
16 Les livraisons de charbon et de pétrole du Royaume-Uni à Jersey, Guernesey et à l'île de Man ne sont pas considérées comme des exportations ; l'approvisionnement de charbon et pétrole à ces îles fait donc partie de l'approvisionnement du Royaume-Uni. Les exportations de gaz naturel vers l'île de Man sont inclues dans les exportations vers l'Irlande.
17 Les données sur le pétrole et le charbon incluent les territoires d'outre-mer.

Region, country or area Région, pays ou zone	Year Année	Area – Superficie ('000 hectares)				Area – Superficie (Percent of total)[&]			Sites protected for terrestrial biodiversity Sites pour la bio. terre. dans aires protég. (%)[&&]
		Total land Superficie totale	Arable land Terres arables	Permanent crops Cultures permanentes	Forest cover Superficie forestière	Arable land Terres arables	Permanent crops Cultures Permanentes	Forest cover Superficie forestière	
Total, all countries or areas	2005	13 010 426	1 405 868	148 343	4 032 743	10.8	1.1	31.0	40.10
Total, tous pays ou zones	2010	13 008 350	1 388 167	159 209	4 015 673	10.7	1.2	30.9	44.37
	2016	13 008 757	1 423 794	166 201	3 995 825	10.9	1.3	30.7	46.58
	2018	...	...	...	...	...	...	...	46.65
Africa	2005	2 964 823	216 298	30 844	654 679	7.3	1.0	22.1	...
Afrique	2010	2 964 894	226 601	33 026	638 282	7.6	1.1	21.5	...
	2016	2 964 921	234 952	33 927	621 267	7.9	1.1	21.0	...
Northern Africa	2005	838 039	41 430	5 310	36 954	4.9	0.6	4.4	21.13
Afrique septentrionale	2010	838 039	42 525	5 806	36 813	5.1	0.7	4.4	24.84
	2016	838 039	42 768	6 252	28 672	5.1	0.7	3.4	37.96
	2018	...	...	...	...	...	...	...	37.96
Sub-Saharan Africa	2005	2 126 784[1]	174 868[1]	25 534[1]	617 725[1]	8.2	1.2	29.0	34.94
Afrique subsaharienne	2010	2 126 855[1]	184 076[1]	27 221[1]	601 469[1]	8.7	1.3	28.3	40.17
	2016	2 126 882[1]	192 184[1]	27 675[1]	592 595[1]	9.0	1.3	27.9	41.65
	2018	...	...	...	...	...	...	...	41.99
Eastern Africa	2005	605 629	55 770	6 913	203 745	9.2	1.1	33.6	...
Afrique orientale	2010	605 700	62 728	7 604	196 249	10.4	1.3	32.4	...
	2016	605 727	66 405	7 907	196 088	11.0	1.3	32.4	...
Middle Africa	2005	649 682	23 346	2 762	310 491	3.6	0.4	47.8	...
Afrique centrale	2010	649 682	24 364	3 015	306 378	3.8	0.5	47.2	...
	2016	649 682	25 904	3 201	302 625	4.0	0.5	46.6	...
Southern Africa	2005	265 067	14 730	406	29 429	5.6	0.2	11.1	...
Afrique australe	2010	265 067	14 089	460	28 489	5.3	0.2	10.7	...
	2016	265 067	14 087	444	27 464	5.3	0.2	10.4	...
Western Africa	2005	606 406	81 022	15 453	74 060	13.4	2.5	12.2	...
Afrique occidentale	2010	606 406	82 895	16 142	70 353	13.7	2.7	11.6	...
	2016	606 406	85 789	16 123	66 417	14.1	2.7	11.0	...
Americas	2005	3 880 553	367 909	29 413	1 616 564	9.5	0.8	41.7	...
Amériques	2010	3 879 103	364 012	27 990	1 602 412	9.4	0.7	41.3	...
	2016	3 878 861	371 240	27 734	1 590 712	9.6	0.7	41.0	...
Northern America	2005	1 866 616	210 384	9 573	652 337	11.3	0.5	34.9	21.83
Amérique septentrionale	2010	1 865 166	199 327	7 621	656 026	10.7	0.4	35.2	25.50
	2016	1 865 166	196 031	7 244	657 396	10.5	0.4	35.2	26.23
	2018	...	...	...	...	...	...	...	26.23
Latin America & the Caribbean	2005	2 013 936[1]	157 525[1]	19 840[1]	964 227[1]	7.8	1.0	47.9	33.57
Amérique latine et Caraïbes	2010	2 013 936[1]	164 686[1]	20 369[1]	946 386[1]	8.2	1.0	47.0	36.89
	2016	2 013 694[1]	175 209[1]	20 490[1]	933 316[1]	8.7	1.0	46.3	39.13
	2018	...	...	...	...	...	...	...	39.13
Caribbean	2005	22 598	5 699	1 324	6 340	25.2	5.9	28.1	...
Caraïbes	2010	22 598	5 579	1 317	6 744	24.7	5.8	29.8	...
	2016	22 356	5 156	1 334	7 283	23.1	6.0	32.6	...
Central America	2005	245 227	29 276	4 837	89 276	11.9	2.0	36.4	...
Amérique centrale	2010	245 227	28 796	5 127	87 508	11.7	2.1	35.7	...
	2016	245 227	27 574	5 288	86 047	11.2	2.2	35.1	...
South America	2005	1 746 111	122 551	13 679	868 611	7.0	0.8	49.7	...
Amérique du Sud	2010	1 746 111	130 311	13 925	852 133	7.5	0.8	48.8	...
	2016	1 746 111	142 480	13 868	839 986	8.2	0.8	48.1	...
Asia	2005	3 102 282	492 142	70 530	580 868	15.9	2.3	18.7	...
Asie	2010	3 102 070	480 688	81 159	589 405	15.5	2.6	19.0	...
	2016	3 101 952	495 623	87 912	594 153	16.0	2.8	19.2	...
Central Asia	2005	392 679	37 043	705	12 038	9.4	0.2	3.1	12.32
Asie centrale	2010	392 679	36 998	704	11 799	9.4	0.2	3.0	15.70
	2016	392 562	37 753	771	11 686	9.6	0.2	3.0	16.48
	2018	...	...	...	...	...	...	...	16.48
Eastern Asia	2005	1 156 002	121 906	13 296	241 841	10.5	1.2	20.9	48.68
Asie orientale	2010	1 156 042	116 625	15 468	250 504	10.1	1.3	21.7	49.47
	2016	1 156 072	128 014	16 951	258 356	11.1	1.5	22.3	50.99
	2018	...	...	...	...	...	...	...	51.11

Region, country or area Région, pays ou zone	Year Année	Area – Superficie ('000 hectares)				Area – Superficie (Percent of total)[&]			Sites protected for terrestrial biodiversity Sites pour la bio. terre. dans aires protég. (%)[&&]
		Total land Superficie totale	Arable land Terres arables	Permanent crops Cultures permanentes	Forest cover Superficie forestière	Arable land Terres arables	Permanent crops Cultures Permanentes	Forest cover Superficie forestière	
South-eastern Asia	2005	434 076	65 540	36 521	217 123	15.1	8.4	50.0	31.37
Asie du Sud-Est	2010	434 067	68 117	42 500	214 594	15.7	9.8	49.4	33.66
	2016	434 050	70 174	46 303	209 992	16.2	10.7	48.4	35.21
	2018	...	...	...	...	...	...	...	35.25
Southern Asia	2005	640 034	225 413	14 631	91 519	35.2	2.3	14.3	29.18
Asie méridionale	2010	640 034	220 858	16 865	93 406	34.5	2.6	14.6	30.28
	2016	640 036	221 201	17 826	94 223	34.6	2.8	14.7	32.78
	2018	...	...	...	...	...	...	...	32.78
Western Asia	2005	479 491	42 240	5 377	18 347	8.8	1.1	3.8	11.07
Asie occidentale	2010	479 248	38 091	5 623	19 103	7.9	1.2	4.0	13.94
	2016	479 232	38 482	6 061	19 896	8.0	1.3	4.2	15.38
	2018	...	...	...	...	...	...	...	15.38
Europe	2005	2 214 115	279 192	16 138	1 004 147	12.6	0.7	45.4	57.59
Europe	2010	2 213 629	273 245	15 431	1 013 572	12.3	0.7	45.8	63.58
	2016	2 213 397	274 806	15 092	1 015 865	12.4	0.7	45.9	65.57
	2018	...	...	...	...	...	...	...	65.59
Eastern Europe	2005	1 805 641	195 108	4 505	852 968	10.8	0.2	47.2	...
Europe orientale	2010	1 805 269	190 941	4 275	859 827	10.6	0.2	47.6	...
	2016	1 805 270	194 458	4 069	860 545	10.8	0.2	47.7	...
Northern Europe	2005	170 310	18 785	135	74 437	11.0	0.1	43.7	...
Europe septentrionale	2010	170 245	19 212	111	74 570	11.3	0.1	43.8	...
	2016	169 986	18 751	107	74 768	11.0	0.1	44.0	...
Southern Europe	2005	129 659	31 212	10 045	43 296	24.1	7.7	33.4	...
Europe méridionale	2010	129 634	29 255	9 685	45 100	22.6	7.5	34.8	...
	2016	129 590	27 794	9 569	45 746	21.4	7.4	35.3	...
Western Europe	2005	108 505	34 086	1 453	33 446	31.4	1.3	30.8	...
Europe occidentale	2010	108 481	33 837	1 359	34 076	31.2	1.3	31.4	...
	2016	108 552	33 804	1 347	34 806	31.1	1.2	32.1	...
Oceania	2005	848 655	50 326	1 419	176 485	5.9	0.2	20.8	26.15
Océanie	2010	848 655	43 620	1 602	172 002	5.1	0.2	20.3	32.84
	2016	849 627	47 173	1 536	173 828	5.6	0.2	20.5	36.45
	2018	...	...	...	...	...	...	...	36.60
Australia and New Zealand	2005	794 565	49 827	403	137 824	6.3	0.1	17.3	40.00
Australie et Nouvelle-	2010	794 565	43 067	471	133 362	5.4	0.1	16.8	45.70
Zélande	2016	795 537	46 618	405	135 212	5.9	0.1	17.0	51.39
	2018	...	...	...	...	...	...	...	51.39
Melanesia	2005	52 959	453	873	38 103	0.9	1.6	71.9	...
Mélanésie	2010	52 959	511	994	38 058	1.0	1.9	71.9	...
	2016	52 959	511	994	38 037	1.0	1.9	71.8	...
Micronesia	2005	317	11	70	185	3.3	22.2	58.4	...
Micronésie	2010	317	9	69	185	2.8	21.9	58.2	...
	2016	317	9	68	184	2.8	21.4	58.0	...
Polynesia	2005	814	36	73	372	4.4	9.0	45.8	...
Polynésie	2010	814	33	68	397	4.1	8.3	48.8	...
	2016	814	35	69	396	4.2	8.5	48.7	...
Antarctica	2005	...	...	...	...	...	...	...	7.13
Antarctique	2010	...	...	...	...	...	...	...	7.13
	2018	...	...	...	...	...	...	...	10.05
Afghanistan	2005	* 65 286	7 805	105	1 350	* 12.0	* 0.2	* 2.1	0.04
Afghanistan	2010	* 65 286	7 793	118	1 350	* 11.9	* 0.2	* 2.1	6.14
	2016	* 65 286	7 729	181	* 1 350	* 11.8	* 0.3	* 2.1	6.14
	2018	...	...	...	...	...	...	...	6.14
Albania	2005	2 740	538	121	782	19.6	4.4	28.6	43.98
Albanie	2010	2 740	626	70	776	22.8	2.6	28.3	58.81
	2016	2 740	620	83	* 771	22.6	3.0	* 28.1	66.98
	2018	...	...	...	...	...	...	...	66.98
Algeria	2005	238 174	7 511	852	1 536	3.2	0.4	0.6	38.43
Algérie	2010	238 174	7 502	909	1 918	3.1	0.4	0.8	38.43
	2016	238 174	7 404	1 013	* 1 964	3.1	0.4	* 0.8	38.81
	2018	...	...	...	...	...	...	...	38.81

Region, country or area Région, pays ou zone	Year Année	Area – Superficie ('000 hectares)				Area – Superficie (Percent of total)[&]			Sites protected for terrestrial biodiversity Sites pour la bio. terre. dans aires protég. (%)[&&]
		Total land Superficie totale	Arable land Terres arables	Permanent crops Cultures permanentes	Forest cover Superficie forestière	Arable land Terres arables	Permanent crops Cultures Permanentes	Forest cover Superficie forestière	
American Samoa	2005	20	* 3	* 2	18	* 16.5	* 8.5	89.4	61.50
Samoa américaines	2010	20	* 3	* 2	18	* 15.0	* 9.5	88.6	61.50
	2016	20	* 3	* 2	* 18	* 15.0	* 9.5	* 87.5	61.50
	2018	...	...	...	...	...	...	...	61.50
Andorra	2005	47	1	...	16	1.7	...	34.0	17.90
Andorre	2010	47	1	...	16	1.6	...	34.0	17.90
	2016	47	1	...	* 16	1.7	...	* 34.0	26.08
	2018	...	...	...	...	...	...	...	26.08
Angola	2005	124 670	* 3 300	* 290	59 104	* 2.6	* 0.2	47.4	28.37
Angola	2010	124 670	* 4 100	* 290	58 480	* 3.3	* 0.2	46.9	28.37
	2016	124 670	* 4 900	* 290	* 57 731	* 3.9	* 0.2	* 46.3	28.37
	2018	...	...	...	...	...	...	...	28.37
Anguilla	2005	9	...	...	6	...	...	61.1	0.15
Anguilla	2010	9	...	...	6	...	...	61.1	0.15
	2016	9	...	...	* 6	...	...	* 61.1	0.15
	2018	...	...	...	...	...	...	...	0.15
Antigua and Barbuda	2005	44	* 4	* 1	10	* 9.1	* 2.3	22.3	18.44
Antigua-et-Barbuda	2010	44	* 4	* 1	10	* 9.1	* 2.3	22.3	18.44
	2016	44	* 4	* 1	* 10	* 9.1	* 2.3	* 22.3	18.44
	2018	...	...	...	...	...	...	...	18.44
Argentina	2005	* 273 669	* 32 898	* 1 000	30 186	* 12.0	* 0.4	* 11.0	29.69
Argentine	2010	* 273 669	* 37 981	* 1 000	28 596	* 13.9	* 0.4	* 10.4	32.00
	2016	* 273 669	* 39 200	* 1 000	* 26 815	* 14.3	* 0.4	* 9.8	33.21
	2018	...	...	...	...	...	...	...	33.21
Armenia	2005	2 847	* 455	50	332	* 16.0	1.8	11.7	24.84
Arménie	2010	2 847	449	55	331	15.8	1.9	11.6	30.54
	2016	* 2 847	446	58	* 332	* 15.7	* 2.0	* 11.7	30.54
	2018	...	...	...	...	...	...	...	30.54
Aruba	2005	18	* 2	...	~0	* 11.1	...	2.3	47.85
Aruba	2010	18	* 2	...	~0	* 11.1	...	2.3	47.85
	2016	18	* 2	...	* ~0	* 11.1	...	* 2.3	47.85
	2018	...	...	...	...	...	...	...	47.85
Australia	2005	768 230	* 49 402	* 340	127 641	* 6.4	* ~0.0	16.6	38.69
Australie	2010	768 230	* 42 568	* 400	123 211	* 5.5	* 0.1	16.0	46.22
	2016	769 202	* 46 048	* 330	* 125 059	* 6.0	* ~0.0	* 16.3	54.27
	2018	...	...	...	...	...	...	...	54.27
Austria	2005	* 8 258	1 381	66	3 851	* 16.7	* 0.8	* 46.6	63.47
Autriche	2010	8 257	1 364	65	3 860	16.5	0.8	46.7	66.09
	2016	* 8 252	1 344	67	* 3 871	* 16.3	* 0.8	* 46.9	66.35
	2018	...	...	...	...	...	...	...	66.35
Azerbaijan	2005	8 266	1 843	222	877	22.3	2.7	10.6	33.27
Azerbaïdjan	2010	8 266	1 884	227	1 008	22.8	2.8	12.2	39.42
	2016	8 267	1 999	241	* 1 166	24.2	2.9	* 14.1	39.42
	2018	...	...	...	...	...	...	...	39.42
Bahamas	2005	* 1 001	* 7	* 4	515	* 0.7	* 0.4	* 51.4	6.96
Bahamas	2010	* 1 001	* 9	* 4	515	* 0.9	* 0.4	* 51.4	7.03
	2016	* 1 001	* 8	* 4	* 515	* 0.8	* 0.4	* 51.4	24.72
	2018	...	...	...	...	...	...	...	24.72
Bahrain	2005	74	* 2	* 3	~0	* 2.0	* 4.3	0.6	19.61
Bahreïn	2010	76	* 2	* 3	1	* 2.1	* 3.9	0.7	27.46
	2016	* 78	* 2	* 3	* 1	* 2.1	* 3.9	* 0.8	27.46
	2018	...	...	...	...	...	...	...	27.46
Bangladesh	2005	13 017	* 7 911	* 800	1 455	* 60.8	* 6.1	11.2	37.92
Bangladesh	2010	* 13 017	* 7 791	* 850	1 442	* 59.9	* 6.5	* 11.1	48.00
	2016	* 13 017	* 7 764	* 830	* 1 426	* 59.6	* 6.4	* 11.0	48.02
	2018	...	...	...	...	...	...	...	48.02
Barbados	2005	43	* 13	* 1	6	* 30.2	* 2.3	14.7	2.07
Barbade	2010	43	* 12	* 1	6	* 27.9	* 2.3	14.7	2.07
	2016	43	* 7	* 1	* 6	* 16.3	* 2.3	* 14.7	2.07
	2018	...	...	...	...	...	...	...	2.07

Land (continued)
Thousand hectares and percent of total land

Terres (suite)
Milliers d'hectares et pourcentage de la superficie totale

Region, country or area Région, pays ou zone	Year Année	Area – Superficie ('000 hectares)				Area – Superficie (Percent of total)[&]			Sites protected for terrestrial biodiversity Sites pour la bio. terre. dans aires protég. (%)[&&]
		Total land Superficie totale	Arable land Terres arables	Permanent crops Cultures permanentes	Forest cover Superficie forestière	Arable land Terres arables	Permanent crops Cultures Permanentes	Forest cover Superficie forestière	
Belarus Bélarus	2005	20 283	5 542	118	8 436	27.3	0.6	41.6	34.99
	2010	20 290	5 535	122	8 534	27.3	0.6	42.1	35.40
	2016	20 299	5 684	111	* 8 653	28.0	0.5	* 42.6	49.07
	2018	...	...	...	...	...	...	...	49.07
Belgium Belgique	2005	3 028	843	21	674	27.8	0.7	22.3	80.53
	2010	3 028	834	22	681	27.5	0.7	22.5	80.58
	2016	* 3 028	849	23	* 684	* 28.1	* 0.8	* 22.6	80.77
	2018	...	...	...	...	...	...	...	80.77
Belize Belize	2005	2 281	* 70	* 32	1 417	* 3.1	* 1.4	62.1	45.75
	2010	* 2 281	* 75	* 32	1 391	* 3.3	* 1.4	* 61.0	45.77
	2016	* 2 281	* 78	* 32	* 1 361	* 3.4	* 1.4	* 59.7	45.96
	2018	...	...	...	...	...	...	...	45.96
Benin Bénin	2005	* 11 276	* 2 700	* 270	4 811	* 23.9	* 2.4	* 42.7	77.38
	2010	* 11 276	* 2 540	* 350	4 561	* 22.5	* 3.1	* 40.4	77.38
	2016	* 11 276	* 2 700	* 500	* 4 261	* 23.9	* 4.4	* 37.8	77.38
	2018	...	...	...	...	...	...	...	77.38
Bermuda Bermudes	2005	5	~0	...	1	7.4	...	18.5	16.21
	2010	5	~0	...	1	5.6	...	18.5	16.21
	2016	5	* ~0	...	* 1	* 5.6	...	* 18.5	16.21
	2018	...	...	...	...	...	...	...	16.21
Bhutan Bhoutan	2005	3 812	* 167	* 19	2 656	* 4.4	* 0.5	69.7	38.56
	2010	3 812	101	12	2 705	2.6	0.3	71.0	41.23
	2016	3 814	* 100	6	* 2 765	* 2.6	0.2	* 72.5	42.92
	2018	...	...	...	...	...	...	...	42.92
Bolivia (Plurin. State of) Bolivie (État plurin. de)	2005	108 330	3 806	199	58 734	3.5	0.2	54.2	52.77
	2010	* 108 330	* 4 297	* 219	56 209	* 4.0	* 0.2	* 51.9	54.64
	2016	* 108 330	* 4 453	* 232	* 54 475	* 4.1	* 0.2	* 50.3	56.23
	2018	...	...	...	...	...	...	...	56.23
Bonaire, St. Eustatius & Saba Bonaire, St-Eustache et Saba	2005	...	...	...	...	...	...	...	39.26
	2010	...	...	...	...	...	...	...	39.26
	2018	...	...	...	...	...	...	...	39.26
Bosnia and Herzegovina Bosnie-Herzégovine	2005	5 120	1 025	95	2 185	20.0	1.9	42.7	0.00
	2010	5 120	1 004	105	2 185	19.6	2.1	42.7	11.98
	2016	5 120	1 026	104	* 2 185	20.0	2.0	* 42.7	11.99
	2018	...	...	...	...	...	...	...	11.99
Botswana Botswana	2005	* 56 673	* 240	2	11 943	* 0.4	* ~0.0	* 21.1	47.10
	2010	* 56 673	259	* 2	11 351	* 0.5	* ~0.0	* 20.0	47.10
	2016	* 56 673	* 260	* 2	* 10 738	* 0.5	* ~0.0	* 18.9	47.10
	2018	...	...	...	...	...	...	...	47.10
Brazil Brésil	2005	* 835 814	* 69 157	* 7 276	506 734	* 8.3	* 0.9	* 60.6	42.31
	2010	* 835 814	* 70 363	* 7 100	498 458	* 8.4	* 0.8	* 59.6	47.46
	2016	* 835 814	* 80 976	* 6 570	* 492 554	* 9.7	* 0.8	* 58.9	47.58
	2018	...	...	...	...	...	...	...	47.58
British Indian Ocean Terr. Terr. brit. de l'océan Indien	2005	...	...	...	...	...	...	...	99.91
	2010	...	...	...	...	...	...	...	99.91
	2018	...	...	...	...	...	...	...	99.91
British Virgin Islands Îles Vierges britanniques	2005	15	* 1	* 1	4	* 6.7	* 6.7	24.4	9.35
	2010	15	* 1	* 1	4	* 6.7	* 6.7	24.3	9.35
	2016	15	* 1	* 1	* 4	* 6.7	* 6.7	* 24.1	9.35
	2018	...	...	...	...	...	...	...	9.35
Brunei Darussalam Brunéi Darussalam	2005	527	* 2	* 5	389	* 0.4	* 0.9	73.8	62.88
	2010	* 527	* 4	* 6	380	* 0.8	* 1.1	* 72.1	62.88
	2016	* 527	* 5	* 6	* 380	* 0.9	* 1.1	* 72.1	62.88
	2018	...	...	...	...	...	...	...	62.88
Bulgaria Bulgarie	2005	10 864	3 173	188	3 651	29.2	1.7	33.6	41.19
	2010	* 10 856	3 186	164	3 737	* 29.3	* 1.5	* 34.4	95.55
	2016	* 10 856	3 496	141	* 3 840	* 32.2	* 1.3	* 35.4	95.55
	2018	...	...	...	...	...	...	...	95.55
Burkina Faso Burkina Faso	2005	* 27 360	* 4 900	* 70	5 949	* 17.9	* 0.3	* 21.7	66.71
	2010	* 27 360	* 6 000	* 80	5 649	* 21.9	* 0.3	* 20.6	71.83
	2016	* 27 360	* 6 000	* 100	* 5 290	* 21.9	* 0.4	* 19.3	71.83
	2018	...	...	...	...	...	...	...	71.83

Land *(continued)*
Thousand hectares and percent of total land

Terres *(suite)*
Milliers d'hectares et pourcentage de la superficie totale

Region, country or area Région, pays ou zone	Year Année	Area – Superficie ('000 hectares)				Area – Superficie (Percent of total)[&]			Sites protected for terrestrial biodiversity Sites pour la bio. terre. dans aires protég. (%)[&&]
		Total land Superficie totale	Arable land Terres arables	Permanent crops Cultures permanentes	Forest cover Superficie forestière	Arable land Terres arables	Permanent crops Cultures Permanentes	Forest cover Superficie forestière	
Burundi Burundi	2005	* 2 568	* 956	* 380	181	* 37.2	* 14.8	* 7.0	51.03
	2010	* 2 568	* 950	* 400	253	* 37.0	* 15.6	* 9.9	51.03
	2016	* 2 568	* 1 200	* 350	* 281	* 46.7	* 13.6	* 10.9	51.19
	2018	...	...	...	...	...	...	...	51.19
Cabo Verde Cabo Verde	2005	403	* 48	* 2	84	* 11.9	* 0.5	20.7	14.95
	2010	403	* 50	* 3	85	* 12.4	* 0.7	21.1	14.95
	2016	403	* 50	* 4	* 91	* 12.4	* 1.0	* 22.5	15.14
	2018	...	...	...	...	...	...	...	15.14
Cambodia Cambodge	2005	17 652	* 3 700	156	10 731	* 21.0	0.9	60.8	38.12
	2010	* 17 652	* 3 800	* 155	10 094	* 21.5	* 0.9	* 57.2	39.54
	2016	* 17 652	* 3 800	* 155	* 9 330	* 21.5	* 0.9	* 52.9	39.54
	2018	...	...	...	...	...	...	...	39.54
Cameroon Cameroun	2005	47 271	5 963	* 1 250	21 016	12.6	* 2.6	44.5	25.41
	2010	* 47 271	* 6 200	* 1 500	19 916	* 13.1	* 3.2	* 42.1	28.45
	2016	* 47 271	* 6 200	* 1 550	* 18 596	* 13.1	* 3.3	* 39.3	36.31
	2018	...	...	...	...	...	...	...	36.31
Canada Canada	2005	909 351	* 45 266	* 6 873	347 576	* 5.0	* 0.8	38.2	21.18
	2010	909 351	* 43 397	* 5 021	347 302	* 4.8	* 0.6	38.2	25.43
	2016	909 351	43 766	4 644	* 347 022	4.8	0.5	* 38.2	25.66
	2018	...	...	...	...	...	...	...	25.66
Cayman Islands Îles Caïmanes	2005	24	* ~0	* 1	13	* 0.8	* 2.1	52.9	31.64
	2010	24	* ~0	* 1	13	* 0.8	* 2.1	52.9	31.67
	2016	24	* ~0	* 1	* 13	* 0.8	* 2.1	* 52.9	32.51
	2018	...	...	...	...	...	...	...	32.51
Central African Republic République centrafricaine	2005	62 298	* 1 930	* 85	22 326	* 3.1	* 0.1	35.8	74.23
	2010	62 298	* 1 800	* 80	22 248	* 2.9	* 0.1	35.7	74.37
	2016	62 298	* 1 800	* 80	* 22 154	* 2.9	* 0.1	* 35.6	74.37
	2018	...	...	...	...	...	...	...	74.37
Chad Tchad	2005	125 920	* 4 500	* 30	6 141	* 3.6	* ~0.0	4.9	70.63
	2010	125 920	* 4 500	* 35	5 508	* 3.6	* ~0.0	4.4	70.63
	2016	* 125 920	* 4 900	* 35	* 4 748	* 3.9	* ~0.0	* 3.8	70.63
	2018	...	...	...	...	...	...	...	70.63
Channel Islands Îles Anglo-Normandes	2005	20	* 4	...	1	* 19.2	...	4.0	...
	2010	20	* 4	...	1	* 21.7	...	4.0	...
	2016	20	* 4	...	* 1	* 19.7	...	* 4.0	...
Chile Chili	2005	74 353	* 1 450	* 435	16 042	* 2.0	* 0.6	21.6	33.42
	2010	74 353	* 1 271	* 457	16 231	* 1.7	* 0.6	21.8	35.19
	2016	* 74 353	* 1 270	* 457	* 18 036	* 1.7	* 0.6	* 24.3	35.66
	2018	...	...	...	...	...	...	...	35.71
China [2] Chine [2]	2005	* 938 821	* 112 250	* 12 350	* 193 044	* 12.0	* 1.3	* 20.6	46.58
	2010	* 938 821	* 107 220	* 14 500	* 200 610	* 11.4	* 1.5	* 21.4	47.10
	2016	* 938 821	* 118 900	* 16 000	* 209 864	* 12.7	* 1.7	* 22.4	47.59
	2018	...	...	...	...	...	...	...	47.59
China, Hong Kong SAR Chine, RAS de Hong Kong	2005	105	* 5	* 1	...	* 4.8	* 1.0	...	56.66
	2010	* 105	* 4	* 1	...	* 3.3	* 1.0	...	56.66
	2016	* 105	* 3	* 1	...	* 2.9	* 1.0	...	56.66
	2018	...	...	...	...	...	...	...	56.66
China, Macao SAR Chine, RAS de Macao	2005	3	...	...	...	...	...	...	0.00
	2010	3	...	...	...	...	...	...	0.00
	2016	3	...	...	...	...	...	...	0.00
	2018	...	...	...	...	...	...	...	0.00
Christmas Island Île Christmas	2005	...	...	...	...	...	...	...	60.43
	2010	...	...	...	...	...	...	...	60.43
	2018	...	...	...	...	...	...	...	60.43
Colombia Colombie	2005	110 950	* 2 026	* 1 587	60 201	* 1.8	* 1.4	54.3	24.99
	2010	110 950	* 1 763	* 1 590	58 635	* 1.6	* 1.4	52.8	30.30
	2016	110 950	* 1 689	* 1 906	* 58 475	* 1.5	* 1.7	* 52.7	37.97
	2018	...	...	...	...	...	...	...	37.97
Comoros Comores	2005	186	* 65	* 53	42	* 34.9	* 28.5	22.6	5.00
	2010	186	* 65	* 53	39	* 34.9	* 28.5	21.0	10.42
	2016	186	* 65	* 53	* 37	* 34.9	* 28.5	* 19.7	10.42
	2018	...	...	...	...	...	...	...	10.42

Land *(continued)*
Thousand hectares and percent of total land

Terres *(suite)*
Milliers d'hectares et pourcentage de la superficie totale

Region, country or area Région, pays ou zone	Year Année	Area – Superficie ('000 hectares)				Area – Superficie (Percent of total)&			Sites protected for terrestrial biodiversity Sites pour la bio. terre. dans aires protég. (%)&&
		Total land Superficie totale	Arable land Terres arables	Permanent crops Cultures permanentes	Forest cover Superficie forestière	Arable land Terres arables	Permanent crops Cultures Permanentes	Forest cover Superficie forestière	
Congo Congo	2005	* 34 150	* 490	* 57	22 471	* 1.4	* 0.2	* 65.8	51.53
	2010	* 34 150	* 510	* 66	22 411	* 1.5	* 0.2	* 65.6	61.21
	2016	* 34 150	* 550	* 77	* 22 319	* 1.6	* 0.2	* 65.4	72.12
	2018	...	...	...	...	...	...	...	72.12
Cook Islands Îles Cook	2005	24	* 1	* 1	15	* 5.2	* 6.2	62.9	7.63
	2010	24	* 1	* 1	15	* 2.9	* 2.7	62.9	7.63
	2016	24	* 1	* 1	* 15	* 4.2	* 2.1	* 62.9	7.63
	2018	...	...	...	...	...	...	...	22.45
Costa Rica Costa Rica	2005	* 5 106	* 210	* 280	2 491	* 4.1	* 5.5	* 48.8	44.76
	2010	* 5 106	* 225	* 315	2 605	* 4.4	* 6.2	* 51.0	45.33
	2016	* 5 106	* 248	* 312	* 2 786	* 4.8	* 6.1	* 54.6	45.33
	2018	...	...	...	...	...	...	...	45.33
Côte d'Ivoire Côte d'Ivoire	2005	* 31 800	* 2 800	* 4 200	10 405	* 8.8	* 13.2	* 32.7	79.13
	2010	* 31 800	* 2 900	* 4 500	10 403	* 9.1	* 14.2	* 32.7	79.13
	2016	* 31 800	* 2 900	* 4 500	* 10 401	* 9.1	* 14.2	* 32.7	79.13
	2018	...	...	...	...	...	...	...	79.13
Croatia Croatie	2005	5 596	873	73	1 903	15.6	1.3	34.0	22.75
	2010	5 596	904	84	1 920	16.2	1.5	34.3	24.41
	2016	* 5 596	872	72	* 1 922	* 15.6	* 1.3	* 34.4	72.04
	2018	...	...	...	...	...	...	...	72.04
Cuba Cuba	2005	10 644	* 3 672	425	2 697	* 34.5	4.0	25.3	42.08
	2010	* 10 644	* 3 384	* 420	2 932	* 31.8	* 3.9	* 27.5	68.33
	2016	* 10 402	* 2 989	483	* 3 254	* 28.7	* 4.6	* 31.3	73.42
	2018	...	...	...	...	...	...	...	73.42
Curaçao Curaçao	2005	...	...	...	...	...	...	...	6.07
	2010	...	...	...	...	...	...	...	6.07
	2018	...	...	...	...	...	...	...	40.41
Cyprus Chypre	2005	924	123	43	173	13.3	4.7	18.7	36.08
	2010	924	83	30	173	8.9	3.2	18.7	54.55
	2016	924	85	26	* 173	9.2	2.8	* 18.7	57.81
	2018	...	...	...	...	...	...	...	57.81
Czechia Tchéquie	2005	7 726	3 209	77	2 647	41.5	1.0	34.3	87.83
	2010	7 724	3 171	77	2 657	41.1	1.0	34.4	92.30
	2016	7 722	2 494	46	* 2 669	32.3	0.6	* 34.6	92.30
	2018	...	...	...	...	...	...	...	92.30
Dem. People's Rep. Korea Rép. pop. dém. de Corée	2005	* 12 041	* 2 350	* 200	6 299	* 19.5	* 1.7	* 52.3	10.16
	2010	* 12 041	* 2 400	* 230	5 666	* 19.9	* 1.9	* 47.1	10.16
	2016	* 12 041	* 2 350	* 230	* 4 904	* 19.5	* 1.9	* 40.7	10.16
	2018	...	...	...	...	...	...	...	10.16
Dem. Rep. of the Congo Rép. dém. du Congo	2005	* 226 705	* 6 700	* 750	155 692	* 3.0	* 0.3	* 68.7	36.63
	2010	* 226 705	* 6 800	* 765	154 135	* 3.0	* 0.3	* 68.0	38.50
	2016	* 226 705	* 7 100	* 900	* 152 267	* 3.1	* 0.4	* 67.2	38.50
	2018	...	...	...	...	...	...	...	40.10
Denmark Danemark	2005	4 243	2 332	7	558	55.0	0.2	13.1	89.16
	2010	4 243	2 421	5	587	57.1	0.1	13.8	89.63
	2016	* 4 199	* 2 375	3	* 617	* 56.6	* 0.1	* 14.7	89.65
	2018	...	...	...	...	...	...	...	89.65
Djibouti Djibouti	2005	* 2 318	* 1	...	6	* ~0.0	...	* 0.2	0.00
	2010	* 2 318	2	...	6	* 0.1	...	* 0.2	0.00
	2016	* 2 318	* 2	...	* 6	* 0.1	...	* 0.2	0.95
	2018	...	...	...	...	...	...	...	0.95
Dominica Dominique	2005	75	* 5	* 15	46	* 6.7	* 20.0	61.3	44.26
	2010	75	* 6	* 17	45	* 8.0	* 22.7	59.5	44.26
	2016	75	* 6	* 17	* 43	* 8.0	* 22.7	* 57.4	44.26
	2018	...	...	...	...	...	...	...	44.26
Dominican Republic République dominicaine	2005	4 831	* 820	* 400	1 652	* 17.0	* 8.3	34.2	72.89
	2010	4 831	* 800	* 400	1 817	* 16.6	* 8.3	37.6	72.89
	2016	* 4 831	* 800	* 355	* 2 016	* 16.6	* 7.3	* 41.7	76.23
	2018	...	...	...	...	...	...	...	76.23
Ecuador Équateur	2005	24 836	1 296	1 214	13 335	5.2	4.9	53.7	25.53
	2010	24 836	1 186	1 391	12 942	4.8	5.6	52.1	27.89
	2016	24 836	976	1 439	* 12 469	3.9	5.8	* 50.2	29.00
	2018	...	...	...	...	...	...	...	29.00

Land (continued)
Thousand hectares and percent of total land

Terres (suite)
Milliers d'hectares et pourcentage de la superficie totale

Region, country or area Région, pays ou zone	Year Année	Area – Superficie ('000 hectares)				Area – Superficie (Percent of total)&			Sites protected for terrestrial biodiversity Sites pour la bio. terre. dans aires protég. (%)&&
		Total land Superficie totale	Arable land Terres arables	Permanent crops Cultures permanentes	Forest cover Superficie forestière	Arable land Terres arables	Permanent crops Cultures Permanentes	Forest cover Superficie forestière	
Egypt Égypte	2005	99 545	* 2 563	960	67	* 2.6	1.0	0.1	37.86
	2010	* 99 545	* 2 873	798	70	* 2.9	* 0.8	* 0.1	39.64
	2016	* 99 545	2 787	947	* 74	* 2.8	* 1.0	* 0.1	39.64
	2018	...	...	...	...	...	...	...	39.64
El Salvador El Salvador	2005	* 2 072	* 702	227	309	* 33.9	* 11.0	* 14.9	9.88
	2010	* 2 072	* 673	* 225	287	* 32.5	* 10.9	* 13.9	22.39
	2016	* 2 072	* 737	* 210	* 261	* 35.6	* 10.1	* 12.6	26.58
	2018	...	...	...	...	...	...	...	26.58
Equatorial Guinea Guinée équatoriale	2005	2 805	* 130	* 90	1 685	* 4.6	* 3.2	60.1	100.00
	2010	2 805	* 120	* 70	1 626	* 4.3	* 2.5	58.0	100.00
	2016	2 805	* 120	* 60	* 1 556	* 4.3	* 2.1	* 55.5	100.00
	2018	...	...	...	...	...	...	...	100.00
Eritrea Érythrée	2005	* 10 100	* 620	* 2	1 554	* 6.1	* ~0.0	* 15.4	13.34
	2010	* 10 100	* 690	* 2	1 532	* 6.8	* ~0.0	* 15.2	13.34
	2016	* 10 100	* 690	* 2	* 1 506	* 6.8	* ~0.0	* 14.9	13.34
	2018	...	...	...	...	...	...	...	13.34
Estonia Estonie	2005	4 239	592	11	2 252	14.0	0.3	53.1	94.67
	2010	4 239	645	7	2 234	15.2	0.2	52.7	94.76
	2016	4 347	696	3	* 2 232	16.0	0.1	* 51.3	94.92
	2018	...	...	...	...	...	...	...	94.92
Ethiopia Éthiopie	2005	* 100 000	12 823	768	13 000	* 12.8	* 0.8	* 13.0	18.59
	2010	* 100 000	14 565	1 118	12 296	* 14.6	* 1.1	* 12.3	19.77
	2016	* 100 000	* 15 119	* 1 140	* 12 540	* 15.1	* 1.1	* 12.5	19.77
	2018	...	...	...	...	...	...	...	19.77
Falkland Islands (Malvinas) Îles Falkland (Malvinas)	2005	1 217	...	...	0	...	...	0.0	10.90
	2010	1 217	...	...	0	...	...	0.0	10.90
	2016	1 217	...	...	* 0	...	...	* 0.0	10.90
	2018	...	...	...	...	...	...	...	10.90
Faroe Islands Îles Féroé	2005	140	* 3	...	~0	* 2.1	...	0.1	0.00
	2010	140	* 3	...	~0	* 2.1	...	0.1	0.00
	2016	140	* 3	...	* ~0	* 2.1	...	* 0.1	6.67
	2018	...	...	...	...	...	...	...	6.67
Fiji Fidji	2005	* 1 827	* 170	* 83	997	* 9.3	* 4.5	* 54.6	3.30
	2010	* 1 827	* 165	* 85	993	* 9.0	* 4.7	* 54.3	4.89
	2016	* 1 827	* 165	* 85	* 1 022	* 9.0	* 4.7	* 55.9	4.89
	2018	...	...	...	...	...	...	...	4.89
Finland Finlande	2005	30 459	2 237	4	22 143	7.3	~0.0	72.7	72.04
	2010	30 390	2 255	4	22 218	7.4	~0.0	73.1	72.24
	2016	30 391	2 246	3	* 22 218	7.4	~0.0	* 73.1	72.65
	2018	...	...	...	...	...	...	...	72.65
France France	2005	* 54 756	18 378	1 111	15 861	* 33.6	* 2.0	* 29.0	68.81
	2010	* 54 756	18 301	1 011	16 424	* 33.4	* 1.8	* 30.0	80.13
	2016	* 54 756	18 356	992	* 17 102	* 33.5	* 1.8	* 31.2	81.17
	2018	...	...	...	...	...	...	...	81.17
French Guiana Guyane française	2005	* 8 220	12	4	8 168	* 0.1	* ~0.0	* 99.4	58.57
	2010	* 8 220	12	4	8 138	* 0.1	* ~0.0	* 99.0	67.03
	2016	* 8 220	13	5	* 8 128	* 0.2	* 0.1	* 98.9	67.39
	2018	...	...	...	...	...	...	...	67.39
French Polynesia Polynésie française	2005	* 366	* 3	* 22	130	* 0.8	* 6.0	* 35.5	3.99
	2010	* 366	* 3	* 22	155	* 0.7	* 6.0	* 42.3	5.36
	2016	* 366	* 3	* 23	* 155	* 0.7	* 6.3	* 42.3	5.36
	2018	...	...	...	...	...	...	...	5.36
French Southern Territories Terres australes françaises	2005	...	...	...	...	...	...	...	0.00
	2010	...	...	...	...	...	...	...	71.86
	2018	...	...	...	...	...	...	...	83.96
Gabon Gabon	2005	25 767	* 325	* 170	22 000	* 1.3	* 0.7	85.4	61.17
	2010	25 767	* 325	* 170	22 000	* 1.3	* 0.7	85.4	61.17
	2016	25 767	* 325	* 170	* 23 200	* 1.3	* 0.7	* 90.0	61.17
	2018	...	...	...	...	...	...	...	61.67
Gambia Gambie	2005	1 012	* 325	* 5	471	* 32.1	* 0.5	46.5	34.59
	2010	1 012	450	* 5	480	44.5	* 0.5	47.4	34.59
	2016	* 1 012	* 440	* 5	* 490	* 43.5	* 0.5	* 48.4	34.59
	2018	...	...	...	...	...	...	...	34.59

Land *(continued)*
Thousand hectares and percent of total land

Terres *(suite)*
Milliers d'hectares et pourcentage de la superficie totale

Region, country or area Région, pays ou zone	Year Année	Area – Superficie ('000 hectares)				Area – Superficie (Percent of total)&			Sites protected for terrestrial biodiversity Sites pour la bio. terre. dans aires protég. (%)&&
		Total land Superficie totale	Arable land Terres arables	Permanent crops Cultures permanentes	Forest cover Superficie forestière	Arable land Terres arables	Permanent crops Cultures Permanentes	Forest cover Superficie forestière	
Georgia	2005	6 949	* 470	* 110	2 773	* 6.8	* 1.6	39.9	19.16
Géorgie	2010	* 6 949	395	* 125	2 822	* 5.7	* 1.8	* 40.6	21.27
	2016	* 6 949	344	* 110	* 2 822	* 5.0	* 1.6	* 40.6	28.38
	2018	...	...	...	...	...	...	...	28.38
Germany	2005	34 876	11 904	198	11 384	34.1	0.6	32.6	70.71
Allemagne	2010	34 857	11 846	199	11 409	34.0	0.6	32.7	78.06
	2016	34 936	11 763	200	* 11 421	33.7	0.6	* 32.7	78.56
	2018	...	...	...	...	...	...	...	78.56
Ghana	2005	* 22 754	* 4 000	* 2 800	9 053	* 17.6	* 12.3	* 39.8	84.96
Ghana	2010	22 754	* 4 620	* 2 700	9 195	* 20.3	* 11.9	40.4	84.96
	2016	* 22 754	* 4 700	* 2 700	* 9 365	* 20.7	* 11.9	* 41.2	84.96
	2018	...	...	...	...	...	...	...	84.96
Gibraltar	2005	1	...	...	0	...	...	0.0	34.98
Gibraltar	2010	1	...	...	0	...	...	0.0	34.98
	2016	1	...	...	* 0	...	...	* 0.0	34.98
	2018	...	...	...	...	...	...	...	34.98
Greece	2005	* 12 890	2 639	1 136	3 752	* 20.5	* 8.8	* 29.1	66.10
Grèce	2010	* 12 890	2 567	1 137	3 903	* 19.9	* 8.8	* 30.3	73.17
	2016	* 12 890	2 140	1 114	* 4 084	* 16.6	* 8.6	* 31.7	73.17
	2018	...	...	...	...	...	...	...	73.17
Greenland	2005	41 045	...	...	~0	...	...	~0.0	26.11
Groenland	2010	41 045	...	...	~0	...	...	~0.0	26.37
	2016	41 045	...	...	* ~0	...	...	* ~0.0	30.26
	2018	...	...	...	...	...	...	...	30.26
Grenada	2005	34	* 2	* 4	17	* 5.9	* 11.8	50.0	30.16
Grenade	2010	34	* 3	* 4	17	* 8.8	* 11.8	50.0	30.16
	2016	34	* 3	* 4	* 17	* 8.8	* 11.8	* 50.0	42.66
	2018	...	...	...	...	...	...	...	42.66
Guadeloupe	2005	169	19	4	74	11.2	2.4	43.8	53.38
Guadeloupe	2010	* 169	21	3	73	* 12.4	* 2.0	* 43.1	80.65
	2016	* 169	23	3	* 73	* 13.7	* 1.7	* 43.0	80.75
	2018	...	...	...	...	...	...	...	80.75
Guam	2005	54	* 2	* 10	25	* 3.7	* 18.5	46.3	40.17
Guam	2010	54	* 1	* 9	25	* 1.9	* 16.7	46.3	40.17
	2016	54	* 1	* 9	* 25	* 1.9	* 16.7	* 46.3	40.17
	2018	...	...	...	...	...	...	...	40.17
Guatemala	2005	10 716	1 400	841	3 938	13.1	7.8	36.7	27.65
Guatemala	2010	* 10 716	* 1 196	* 970	3 722	* 11.2	* 9.1	* 34.7	30.75
	2016	* 10 716	* 862	* 1 183	* 3 504	* 8.0	* 11.0	* 32.7	30.75
	2018	...	...	...	...	...	...	...	30.75
Guinea	2005	* 24 572	* 2 741	* 680	6 724	* 11.2	* 2.8	* 27.4	76.38
Guinée	2010	* 24 572	* 2 900	* 700	6 544	* 11.8	* 2.8	* 26.6	76.38
	2016	* 24 572	* 3 100	* 700	* 6 328	* 12.6	* 2.8	* 25.8	76.38
	2018	...	...	...	...	...	...	...	76.38
Guinea-Bissau	2005	* 2 812	* 280	* 250	2 072	* 10.0	* 8.9	* 73.7	52.18
Guinée-Bissau	2010	* 2 812	* 300	* 250	2 022	* 10.7	* 8.9	* 71.9	52.18
	2016	* 2 812	* 300	* 250	* 1 962	* 10.7	* 8.9	* 69.8	52.60
	2018	...	...	...	...	...	...	...	52.60
Guyana	2005	* 19 685	* 420	* 28	16 602	* 2.1	* 0.1	* 84.3	...
Guyana	2010	* 19 685	* 420	* 28	16 576	* 2.1	* 0.1	* 84.2	...
	*2016	19 685	420	50	16 516	2.1	0.3	83.9	...
Haiti	2005	* 2 756	* 900	* 280	105	* 32.7	* 10.2	* 3.8	10.45
Haïti	2010	* 2 756	* 1 100	* 280	101	* 39.9	* 10.2	* 3.7	10.45
	2016	* 2 756	* 1 070	* 280	* 96	* 38.8	* 10.2	* 3.5	10.45
	2018	...	...	...	...	...	...	...	10.45
Heard Is. and McDonald Is.	2005	...	...	...	...	...	...	...	100.00
Île Heard-et-Îles MacDonald	2010	...	...	...	...	...	...	...	100.00
	2018	...	...	...	...	...	...	...	100.00
Honduras	2005	* 11 189	* 1 050	* 400	5 792	* 9.4	* 3.6	* 51.8	57.47
Honduras	2010	* 11 189	* 1 020	* 450	5 192	* 9.1	* 4.0	* 46.4	57.58
	2016	* 11 189	* 1 020	* 455	* 4 472	* 9.1	* 4.1	* 40.0	65.03
	2018	...	...	...	...	...	...	...	65.03

Land *(continued)*
Thousand hectares and percent of total land

Terres *(suite)*
Milliers d'hectares et pourcentage de la superficie totale

Region, country or area Région, pays ou zone	Year Année	Area – Superficie ('000 hectares)				Area – Superficie (Percent of total)&			Sites protected for terrestrial biodiversity Sites pour la bio. terre. dans aires protég. (%)&&
		Total land Superficie totale	Arable land Terres arables	Permanent crops Cultures permanentes	Forest cover Superficie forestière	Arable land Terres arables	Permanent crops Cultures Permanentes	Forest cover Superficie forestière	
Hungary	2005	8 961	4 601	205	1 983	51.3	2.3	22.1	81.02
Hongrie	2010	9 053	4 392	188	2 046	48.5	2.1	22.6	82.86
	2016	9 053	4 324	176	* 2 074	47.8	1.9	* 22.9	82.90
	2018	...	...	...	...	...	...	...	82.90
Iceland	2005	10 025	129	...	37	1.3	...	0.4	15.00
Islande	2010	10 025	123	...	43	1.2	...	0.4	15.65
	2016	* 10 025	121	...	* 51	* 1.2	...	* 0.5	18.02
	2018	...	...	...	...	...	...	...	18.02
India	2005	297 319	* 159 444	* 10 230	67 709	* 53.6	* 3.4	22.8	22.57
Inde	2010	* 297 319	* 157 009	* 12 225	69 790	* 52.8	* 4.1	* 23.5	22.57
	2016	* 297 319	* 156 463	* 13 000	* 70 860	* 52.6	* 4.4	* 23.8	26.10
	2018	...	...	...	...	...	...	...	26.10
Indonesia	2005	181 157	* 22 946	* 17 900	97 857	* 12.7	* 9.9	54.0	21.25
Indonésie	2010	* 181 157	* 23 600	* 21 000	94 432	* 13.0	* 11.6	* 52.1	22.81
	2016	* 181 157	* 23 500	* 22 500	* 90 326	* 13.0	* 12.4	* 49.9	23.48
	2018	...	...	...	...	...	...	...	23.48
Iran (Islamic Republic of)	2005	162 876	16 533	1 574	10 692	10.2	1.0	6.6	47.90
Iran (Rép. islamique d')	2010	162 876	15 390	1 672	10 692	9.4	1.0	6.6	48.62
	2016	162 876	14 687	1 790	* 10 692	9.0	1.1	* 6.6	48.62
	2018	...	...	...	...	...	...	...	48.62
Iraq	2005	* 43 737	* 5 200	* 190	825	* 11.9	* 0.4	* 1.9	0.00
Iraq	2010	* 43 432	* 4 000	* 220	825	* 9.2	* 0.5	* 1.9	1.34
	2016	43 413	* 5 000	* 300	* 825	* 11.5	* 0.7	* 1.9	5.10
	2018	...	...	...	...	...	...	...	5.10
Ireland	2005	6 889	1 184	3	695	17.2	~0.0	10.1	86.72
Irlande	2010	6 889	1 011	2	726	14.7	~0.0	10.5	89.30
	2016	6 889	446	1	* 760	6.5	~0.0	* 11.0	89.93
	2018	...	...	...	...	...	...	...	89.93
Isle of Man	2005	57	18	...	3	31.2	...	6.1	...
Île de Man	2010	57	25	...	3	44.5	...	6.1	...
	2016	57	24	...	* 3	41.2	...	* 6.1	...
Israel	2005	2 164	* 311	70	155	* 14.4	3.2	7.2	13.84
Israël	2010	2 164	* 294	77	154	* 13.6	3.6	7.1	15.60
	2016	2 164	* 295	97	* 167	* 13.6	4.5	* 7.7	15.66
	2018	...	...	...	...	...	...	...	15.66
Italy	2005	29 414	7 780	2 554	8 759	26.5	8.7	29.8	75.14
Italie	2010	* 29 414	7 042	2 588	9 028	* 23.9	* 8.8	* 30.7	77.95
	2016	* 29 414	6 602	2 452	* 9 351	* 22.4	* 8.3	* 31.8	77.96
	2018	...	...	...	...	...	...	...	77.96
Jamaica	2005	* 1 083	* 128	* 110	339	* 11.8	* 10.2	* 31.3	22.01
Jamaïque	2010	* 1 083	* 120	* 95	337	* 11.1	* 8.8	* 31.1	22.01
	2016	* 1 083	* 120	* 95	* 335	* 11.1	* 8.8	* 30.9	22.03
	2018	...	...	...	...	...	...	...	22.03
Japan	2005	* 36 450	4 360	332	24 935	* 12.0	* 0.9	* 68.4	64.47
Japon	2010	* 36 455	4 282	311	24 966	* 11.7	* 0.9	* 68.5	64.65
	2016	* 36 456	4 184	287	* 24 956	* 11.5	* 0.8	* 68.5	68.47
	2018	...	...	...	...	...	...	...	68.47
Jordan	2005	8 824	185	86	98	2.1	1.0	1.1	...
Jordanie	2010	8 878	178	83	98	2.0	0.9	1.1	...
	2016	8 878	237	87	* 98	2.7	1.0	* 1.1	...
Kazakhstan	2005	* 269 970	* 28 562	116	3 337	* 10.6	* ~0.0	* 1.2	9.64
Kazakhstan	2010	* 269 970	28 684	116	3 309	* 10.6	* ~0.0	* 1.2	14.75
	2016	* 269 970	* 29 395	* 132	* 3 309	* 10.9	* ~0.0	* 1.2	16.29
	2018	...	...	...	...	...	...	...	16.29
Kenya	2005	* 56 914	* 5 264	438	4 047	* 9.2	* 0.8	* 7.1	35.52
Kenya	2010	* 56 914	* 5 500	* 520	4 230	* 9.7	* 0.9	* 7.4	36.80
	2016	* 56 914	* 5 800	* 530	* 4 450	* 10.2	* 0.9	* 7.8	37.50
	2018	...	...	...	...	...	...	...	37.50
Kiribati	2005	81	* 2	* 32	12	* 2.5	* 39.5	15.0	12.54
Kiribati	2010	* 81	* 2	* 32	12	* 2.5	* 39.5	* 15.0	52.54
	2016	* 81	* 2	* 32	* 12	* 2.5	* 39.5	* 15.0	52.54
	2018	...	...	...	...	...	...	...	52.54

Region, country or area Région, pays ou zone	Year Année	Area – Superficie ('000 hectares) Total land Superficie totale	Arable land Terres arables	Permanent crops Cultures permanentes	Forest cover Superficie forestière	Area – Superficie (Percent of total)[&] Arable land Terres arables	Permanent crops Cultures Permanentes	Forest cover Superficie forestière	Sites protected for terrestrial biodiversity Sites pour la bio. terre. dans aires protég. (%)[&&]
Kuwait	2005	1 782	* 11	* 3	6	* 0.6	* 0.2	0.3	46.27
Koweït	2010	1 782	* 10	* 6	6	* 0.6	* 0.3	0.4	46.27
	2016	1 782	* 8	6	* 6	* 0.4	0.3	* 0.4	59.03
	2018	...	...	...	...	...	...	...	59.03
Kyrgyzstan	2005	* 19 180	1 284	72	869	* 6.7	* 0.4	* 4.5	22.36
Kirghizistan	2010	* 19 180	1 276	74	677	* 6.7	* 0.4	* 3.5	22.36
	2016	* 19 180	1 288	76	* 629	* 6.7	* 0.4	* 3.3	22.62
	2018	...	...	...	...	...	...	...	22.62
Lao People's Dem. Rep.	2005	23 080	' * 1 150	* 85	16 870	* 5.0	* 0.4	73.1	44.04
Rép. dém. populaire lao	2010	* 23 080	* 1 400	* 130	17 816	* 6.1	* 0.6	* 77.2	45.48
	2016	* 23 080	* 1 525	* 169	* 18 951	* 6.6	* 0.7	* 82.1	45.48
	2018	...	...	...	...	...	...	...	45.48
Latvia	2005	6 220	1 092	13	3 297	17.6	0.2	53.0	97.22
Lettonie	2010	6 224	1 173	7	3 354	18.8	0.1	* 53.9	97.26
	2016	* 6 218	1 288	8	* 3 356	20.7	0.1	* 54.0	97.26
	2018	...	...	...	...	...	...	...	97.26
Lebanon	2005	* 1 023	* 142	141	137	* 13.9	* 13.8	* 13.3	11.57
Liban	2010	* 1 023	114	126	137	* 11.1	* 12.3	* 13.4	11.57
	2016	* 1 023	* 132	* 126	* 137	* 12.9	* 12.3	* 13.4	13.08
	2018	...	...	...	...	...	...	...	13.08
Lesotho	2005	3 036	323	* 4	43	10.6	* 0.1	1.4	15.27
Lesotho	2010	3 036	322	* 4	44	10.6	* 0.1	1.4	15.27
	2016	3 036	352	* 5	* 50	11.6	* 0.2	* 1.6	15.27
	2018	...	...	...	...	...	...	...	15.27
Liberia	2005	9 632	* 400	* 215	4 479	* 4.2	* 2.2	46.5	16.36
Libéria	2010	9 632	* 480	* 180	4 329	* 5.0	* 1.9	44.9	16.36
	2016	9 632	* 500	* 200	* 4 149	* 5.2	* 2.1	* 43.1	16.36
	2018	...	...	...	...	...	...	...	16.36
Libya	2005	175 954	* 1 750	* 335	217	* 1.0	* 0.2	0.1	4.60
Libye	2010	175 954	* 1 716	* 335	217	* 1.0	* 0.2	0.1	4.60
	2016	* 175 954	* 1 720	* 330	* 217	* 1.0	* 0.2	* 0.1	4.60
	2018	...	...	...	...	...	...	...	4.60
Liechtenstein	2005	16	* 4	...	7	* 24.4	...	43.1	75.82
Liechtenstein	2010	16	* 3	...	7	* 20.6	...	43.1	75.82
	2016	16	* 2	...	* 7	* 13.5	...	* 43.1	75.82
	2018	...	...	...	...	...	...	...	75.82
Lithuania	2005	6 268	1 907	40	2 121	30.4	0.6	33.8	89.59
Lituanie	2010	6 268	2 127	31	2 170	33.9	0.5	34.6	91.56
	2016	6 264	2 143	35	* 2 182	34.2	0.6	* 34.8	91.56
	2018	...	...	...	...	...	...	...	91.56
Luxembourg	2005	243	60	2	87	24.7	0.8	35.7	62.77
Luxembourg	2010	243	62	2	87	25.5	0.6	35.7	62.77
	2016	243	62	2	* 87	25.5	0.6	* 35.7	78.68
	2018	...	...	...	...	...	...	...	78.68
Madagascar	2005	* 58 154	* 3 000	* 600	12 838	* 5.2	* 1.0	* 22.1	19.68
Madagascar	2010	* 58 154	* 3 500	* 600	12 553	* 6.0	* 1.0	* 21.6	21.74
	2016	* 58 180	* 3 500	* 620	* 12 457	* 6.0	* 1.1	* 21.4	22.11
	2018	...	...	...	...	...	...	...	24.25
Malawi	2005	9 428	* 3 200	* 130	3 402	* 33.9	* 1.4	36.1	81.64
Malawi	2010	9 428	* 3 700	* 135	3 237	* 39.2	* 1.4	34.3	81.64
	2016	* 9 428	* 3 800	* 140	* 3 129	* 40.3	* 1.5	* 33.2	81.64
	2018	...	...	...	...	...	...	...	81.64
Malaysia	2005	* 32 855	* 949	* 5 900	20 890	* 2.9	* 18.0	* 63.6	39.08
Malaisie	2010	* 32 855	* 854	* 6 250	22 124	* 2.6	* 19.0	* 67.3	39.50
	2016	* 32 855	* 882	* 7 460	* 22 209	* 2.7	* 22.7	* 67.6	39.50
	2018	...	...	...	...	...	...	...	39.50
Maldives	2005	30	* 3	* 5	1	* 10.0	* 16.7	3.3	0.00
Maldives	2010	30	* 4	* 3	1	* 13.0	* 10.0	3.3	0.00
	2016	30	* 4	* 3	* 1	* 13.0	* 10.0	* 3.3	0.00
	2018	...	...	...	...	...	...	...	0.00

Region, country or area Région, pays ou zone	Year Année	Area – Superficie ('000 hectares)				Area – Superficie (Percent of total)&			Sites protected for terrestrial biodiversity Sites pour la bio. terre. dans aires protég. (%)&&
		Total land Superficie totale	Arable land Terres arables	Permanent crops Cultures permanentes	Forest cover Superficie forestière	Arable land Terres arables	Permanent crops Cultures Permanentes	Forest cover Superficie forestière	
Mali	2005	122 019	* 5 603	* 150	5 505	* 4.6	* 0.1	4.5	33.77
Mali	2010	* 122 019	* 6 261	* 150	5 110	* 5.1	* 0.1	* 4.2	33.77
	2016	* 122 019	* 6 411	* 150	* 4 636	* 5.3	* 0.1	* 3.8	33.77
	2018	...	...	...	...	...	...	...	33.77
Malta	2005	32	8	1	~0	25.6	3.4	1.1	99.40
Malte	2010	32	9	1	~0	28.4	3.9	1.1	99.40
	2016	32	9	1	* ~0	28.3	4.1	* 1.1	99.40
	2018	...	...	...	...	...	...	...	99.40
Marshall Islands	2005	18	2	8	13	11.1	44.4	70.2	16.80
Îles Marshall	2010	18	* 2	* 8	13	* 11.1	* 44.4	70.2	23.42
	2016	18	* 2	* 7	* 13	* 11.1	* 36.1	* 70.2	25.38
	2018	...	...	...	...	...	...	...	25.38
Martinique	2005	* 106	10	8	49	* 9.4	* 7.5	* 45.8	75.08
Martinique	2010	* 106	10	7	49	* 9.6	* 7.0	* 45.8	99.12
	2016	* 106	11	7	* 49	* 10.3	* 6.1	* 45.8	99.12
	2018	...	...	...	...	...	...	...	99.12
Mauritania	2005	103 070	* 400	* 11	267	* 0.4	* ~0.0	0.3	14.62
Mauritanie	2010	103 070	* 450	* 11	242	* 0.4	* ~0.0	0.2	14.62
	2016	103 070	* 450	* 11	* 221	* 0.4	* ~0.0	* 0.2	14.62
	2018	...	...	...	...	...	...	...	14.62
Mauritius	2005	203	* 85	* 4	38	* 41.9	* 2.0	18.8	9.49
Maurice	2010	203	* 80	* 4	38	* 39.4	* 2.0	18.9	9.57
	2016	203	* 75	* 4	* 39	* 36.9	* 2.0	* 19.0	10.39
	2018	...	...	...	...	...	...	...	10.39
Mayotte	2005	37	* 10	* 10	8	* 26.7	* 26.7	20.7	15.63
Mayotte	2010	37	* 17	3	7	* 44.4	9.1	18.2	54.09
	2016	37	17	3	* 6	46.3	7.2	* 15.1	54.09
	2018	...	...	...	...	...	...	...	54.09
Mexico	2005	194 395	* 23 296	2 607	67 083	* 12.0	1.3	34.5	24.15
Mexique	2010	194 395	* 23 507	2 651	66 498	* 12.1	1.4	34.2	29.05
	2016	194 395	* 22 562	2 625	* 65 948	* 11.6	1.4	* 33.9	33.39
	2018	...	...	...	...	...	...	...	33.39
Micronesia (Fed. States of)	2005	70	* 3	* 17	64	* 3.6	* 24.3	91.4	1.29
Micronésie (États féd. de)	2010	70	* 2	* 17	64	* 2.9	* 24.3	91.6	1.29
	2016	70	* 2	* 17	* 64	* 2.9	* 24.3	* 91.9	1.29
	2018	...	...	...	...	...	...	...	1.29
Mongolia	2005	* 155 356	* 695	* 2	11 308	* 0.4	* ~0.0	* 7.3	36.45
Mongolie	2010	* 155 356	* 614	* 3	13 039	* 0.4	* ~0.0	* 8.4	39.09
	2016	* 155 356	* 567	* 5	* 12 456	* 0.4	* ~0.0	* 8.0	41.98
	2018	...	...	...	...	...	...	...	43.67
Montenegro	2005		...	...		...	...		11.86
Monténégro	2010	* 1 345	172	16	827	* 12.8	* 1.2	* 61.5	11.86
	2016	* 1 345	9	5	* 827	* 0.7	* 0.4	* 61.5	11.86
	2018	...	...	...	...	...	...	...	11.86
Montserrat	2005	10	* 2	...	3	* 20.0	...	25.0	0.00
Montserrat	2010	10	* 2	...	3	* 20.0	...	25.0	0.00
	2016	10	* 2	...	* 3	* 20.0	...	* 25.0	30.63
	2018	...	...	...	...	...	...	...	30.63
Morocco	2005	* 44 630	* 8 122	* 867	5 401	* 18.2	* 1.9	* 12.1	13.32
Maroc	2010	* 44 630	7 729	1 259	5 672	* 17.3	* 2.8	* 12.7	14.72
	2016	* 44 630	* 8 130	* 1 462	* 5 624	* 18.2	* 3.3	* 12.6	43.00
	2018	...	...	...	...	...	...	...	43.00
Mozambique	2005	78 638	* 5 000	* 250	40 079	* 6.4	* 0.3	51.0	19.02
Mozambique	2010	78 638	* 5 650	* 300	38 972	* 7.2	* 0.4	49.6	19.02
	2016	78 638	* 5 650	* 300	* 37 734	* 7.2	* 0.4	* 48.0	31.31
	2018	...	...	...	...	...	...	...	31.31
Myanmar	2005	65 336	10 059	896	33 321	15.4	1.4	51.0	22.46
Myanmar	2010	65 326	10 811	1 406	31 773	16.5	2.2	48.6	22.46
	2016	* 65 308	* 10 908	* 1 550	* 28 495	* 16.7	* 2.4	* 43.6	22.46
	2018	...	...	...	...	...	...	...	22.91

Region, country or area Région, pays ou zone	Year Année	Area – Superficie ('000 hectares)				Area – Superficie (Percent of total)[&]			Sites protected for terrestrial biodiversity Sites pour la bio. terre. dans aires protég. (%)[&&]
		Total land Superficie totale	Arable land Terres arables	Permanent crops Cultures permanentes	Forest cover Superficie forestière	Arable land Terres arables	Permanent crops Cultures Permanentes	Forest cover Superficie forestière	
Namibia	2005	* 82 329	* 814	* 6	7 661	* 1.0	* ~0.0	* 9.3	44.58
Namibie	2010	* 82 329	* 800	* 9	7 290	* 1.0	* ~0.0	* 8.9	82.37
	2016	* 82 329	* 800	* 9	* 6 845	* 1.0	* ~0.0	* 8.3	85.38
	2018	...	...	...	...	...	...	...	85.38
Nauru	2005	2	...	* ~0	0	...	* 20.0	0.0	0.00
Nauru	2010	2	...	* ~0	0	...	* 20.0	0.0	0.00
	2016	2	...	* ~0	* 0	...	* 20.0	* 0.0	0.00
	2018	...	...	...	...	...	...	...	0.00
Nepal	2005	14 335	* 2 280	* 133	3 636	* 15.9	* 0.9	25.4	50.32
Népal	2010	14 335	* 2 180	* 152	3 636	* 15.2	* 1.1	25.4	54.63
	2016	14 335	* 2 114	* 212	* 3 636	* 14.7	* 1.5	* 25.4	54.64
	2018	...	...	...	...	...	...	...	54.64
Netherlands	2005	3 376	1 111	32	365	32.9	0.9	10.8	91.32
Pays-Bas	2010	3 373	1 023	36	373	30.3	1.1	11.1	91.37
	2016	* 3 369	1 028	38	* 377	* 30.5	* 1.1	* 11.2	91.37
	2018	...	...	...	...	...	...	...	91.37
Netherlands Antilles [former]	2005	80	* 8	...	1	* 10.0		1.5	...
Antilles néerlandaises [anc.]	2010	80	* 8	...	1	* 10.0		1.5	...
	2016	80	* 8	...		* 10.0			...
New Caledonia	2005	* 1 828	* 7	* 4	839	* 0.4	* 0.2	* 45.9	15.50
Nouvelle-Calédonie	2010	1 828	* 7	* 4	839	* 0.4	* 0.2	45.9	66.12
	2016	1 828	* 6	* 4	* 839	* 0.3	* 0.2	* 45.9	66.39
	2018	...	...	...	...	...	...	...	66.39
New Zealand	2005	26 331	425	63	10 183	1.6	0.2	38.7	42.48
Nouvelle-Zélande	2010	26 331	499	71	10 151	1.9	0.3	38.6	44.00
	2016	26 331	* 570	* 75	* 10 152	* 2.2	* 0.3	* 38.6	44.27
	2018	...	...	...	...	...	...	...	44.27
Nicaragua	2005	12 034	* 2 000	* 290	3 464	* 16.6	* 2.4	28.8	73.68
Nicaragua	2010	12 034	* 1 531	* 295	3 114	* 12.7	* 2.5	25.9	73.68
	2016	12 034	* 1 504	* 286	* 3 114	* 12.5	* 2.4	* 25.9	73.68
	2018	...	...	...	...	...	...	...	73.68
Niger	2005	* 126 670	* 14 123	* 60	1 266	* 11.1	* ~0.0	* 1.0	40.66
Niger	2010	* 126 670	* 15 100	* 100	1 204	* 11.9	* 0.1	* 1.0	40.66
	2016	* 126 670	* 16 800	* 100	* 1 130	* 13.3	* 0.1	* 0.9	42.75
	2018	...	...	...	...	...	...	...	42.75
Nigeria	2005	* 91 077	* 36 000	* 6 400	11 089	* 39.5	* 7.0	* 12.2	69.18
Nigéria	2010	* 91 077	* 33 000	* 6 700	9 041	* 36.2	* 7.4	* 9.9	79.62
	2016	* 91 077	* 34 000	* 6 500	* 6 583	* 37.3	* 7.1	* 7.2	79.62
	2018	...	...	...	...	...	...	...	79.62
Niue	2005	26	* 1	* 3	19	* 3.8	* 10.8	73.5	95.28
Nioué	2010	26	* 1	* 3	19	* 3.8	* 11.5	71.5	95.28
	2016	26	* 1	* 3	* 18	* 3.8	* 11.5	* 69.2	95.28
	2018	...	...	...	...	...	...	...	95.28
Norfolk Island	2005	4	...	...	~0	...	...	11.5	44.38
Île Norfolk	2010	4	...	...	~0	...	...	11.5	44.38
	2016	4	...	...	* ~0	...	...	* 11.5	59.00
	2018	...	...	...	...	...	...		59.00
North Macedonia	2005	2 543	448	39	975	17.6	1.5	38.3	20.78
Macédoine du Nord	2010	2 522	414	35	998	16.4	1.4	39.6	21.06
	2016	2 522	416	40	* 998	16.5	1.6	* 39.6	21.06
	2018	...	...	...	...	...	...	...	21.06
Northern Mariana Islands	2005	46	* 1	* 1	31	* 2.2	* 2.2	67.7	3.84
Îles Mariannes du Nord	2010	46	* 1	* 1	30	* 2.2	* 2.2	65.9	40.59
	2016	46	* 1	* 1	* 29	* 2.2	* 2.2	* 63.8	40.59
	2018	...	...	...	...	...	...	...	40.59
Norway	2005	36 524	862	5	12 092	2.4	~0.0	33.1	51.98
Norvège	2010	36 524	826	5	12 102	2.3	~0.0	33.1	53.85
	2016	36 512	805	3	* 12 114	2.2	~0.0	* 33.2	55.91
	2018	...	...	...	...	...	...	...	55.91
Oman	2005	30 950	28	37	2	0.1	0.1	~0.0	7.82
Oman	2010	30 950	34	38	2	0.1	0.1	~0.0	7.82
	2016	30 950	56	* 29	* 2	0.2	* 0.1	* ~0.0	11.46
	2018	...	...	...	...	...	...	...	11.46

Land *(continued)*
Thousand hectares and percent of total land

Terres *(suite)*
Milliers d'hectares et pourcentage de la superficie totale

Region, country or area Région, pays ou zone	Year Année	Total land Superficie totale	Arable land Terres arables	Permanent crops Cultures permanentes	Forest cover Superficie forestière	Arable land Terres arables	Permanent crops Cultures Permanentes	Forest cover Superficie forestière	Sites protected for terrestrial biodiversity Sites pour la bio. terre. dans aires protég. (%)&&
		Area – Superficie ('000 hectares)				Area – Superficie (Percent of total)&			
Other non-specified areas	*2005	3 541	603	230	...	17.0	6.5	...	...
Autres zones non-spécifiées	*2010	3 541	598	215	...	16.9	6.1	...	...
	*2016	3 541	589	205	...	16.6	5.8	...	...
Pakistan	2005	77 088	30 170	795	1 902	39.1	1.0	2.5	36.64
Pakistan	2010	* 77 088	29 390	852	1 687	* 38.1	* 1.1	* 2.2	36.64
	2016	* 77 088	31 040	804	* 1 429	* 40.3	* 1.0	* 1.9	36.64
	2018	...	...	...	...	...	...	...	36.64
Palau	2005	* 46	* 1	* 2	40	* 2.2	* 4.3	* 87.6	17.90
Palaos	2010	* 46	* 1	* 2	40	* 2.2	* 4.3	* 87.6	17.90
	2016	* 46	* 1	* 2	* 40	* 2.2	* 4.3	* 87.6	36.55
	2018	...	...	...	...	...	...	...	36.55
Panama	2005	7 434	* 548	* 160	4 782	* 7.4	* 2.2	64.3	37.84
Panama	2010	* 7 434	569	189	4 699	* 7.7	* 2.5	* 63.2	38.84
	2016	* 7 434	* 563	* 185	* 4 601	* 7.6	* 2.5	* 61.9	38.84
	2018	...	...	...	...	...	...	...	38.84
Papua New Guinea	2005	* 45 286	* 240	* 600	33 586	* 0.5	* 1.3	* 74.2	7.32
Papouasie-Nvl-Guinée	2010	* 45 286	* 300	* 700	33 573	* 0.7	* 1.5	* 74.1	7.32
	2016	* 45 286	* 300	* 700	* 33 556	* 0.7	* 1.5	* 74.1	7.32
	2018	...	...	...	...	...	...	...	7.32
Paraguay	2005	* 39 730	* 3 460	* 100	18 475	* 8.7	* 0.3	* 46.5	23.31
Paraguay	2010	* 39 730	* 4 145	* 85	16 950	* 10.4	* 0.2	* 42.7	23.31
	2016	* 39 730	* 4 800	* 85	* 14 998	* 12.1	* 0.2	* 37.7	23.31
	2018	...	...	...	...	...	...	...	23.31
Peru	2005	* 128 000	* 3 930	* 1 090	75 528	* 3.1	* 0.9	* 59.0	...
Pérou	2010	* 128 000	* 4 085	* 1 307	74 811	* 3.2	* 1.0	* 58.4	...
	*2016	128 000	3 508	1 379	73 805	2.7	1.1	57.7	...
Philippines	2005	29 817	* 5 005	* 4 850	7 074	* 16.8	* 16.3	23.7	38.72
Philippines	2010	29 817	* 5 300	* 5 300	6 840	* 17.8	* 17.8	22.9	41.40
	2016	* 29 817	* 5 590	* 5 350	* 8 280	* 18.7	* 17.9	* 27.8	41.68
	2018	...	...	...	...	...	...	...	41.68
Pitcairn	2005	5	...	...	4	...	...	74.5	0.00
Pitcairn	2010	5	...	...	4	...	...	74.5	0.00
	2016	5	...	...	* 4	...	...	* 74.5	27.68
	2018	...	...	...	...	...	...	...	27.68
Poland	2005	30 633	12 141	378	9 200	39.6	1.2	30.0	73.43
Pologne	2010	30 628	10 829	390	9 329	35.4	1.3	30.5	87.87
	2016	30 619	10 806	393	* 9 456	35.3	1.3	* 30.9	88.10
	2018	...	...	...	...	...	...	...	88.10
Portugal	2005	* 9 147	1 305	749	3 296	* 14.3	* 8.2	* 36.0	60.46
Portugal	2010	* 9 159	1 148	714	3 239	* 12.5	* 7.8	* 35.4	70.97
	2016	* 9 161	979	760	* 3 171	* 10.7	* 8.3	* 34.6	73.90
	2018	...	...	...	...	...	...	...	73.90
Puerto Rico	2005	887	* 66	* 37	463	* 7.5	* 4.2	52.2	33.98
Porto Rico	2010	* 887	* 57	* 50	479	* 6.4	* 5.6	* 54.0	33.98
	2016	* 887	* 61	* 50	* 499	* 6.9	* 5.6	* 56.3	33.98
	2018	...	...	...	...	...	...	...	33.98
Qatar	2005	1 161	* 12	* 3	0	* 1.0	* 0.2	0.0	49.97
Qatar	2010	1 161	* 14	3	0	* 1.2	0.2	0.0	49.97
	2016	* 1 161	* 14	3	* 0	* 1.2	* 0.2	* 0.0	49.97
	2018	...	...	...	...	...	...	...	49.97
Republic of Korea	2005	9 685	1 643	181	6 255	17.0	1.9	64.6	27.31
République de Corée	2010	* 9 720	* 1 507	208	6 222	* 15.5	* 2.1	* 64.0	36.40
	2016	* 9 749	* 1 421	223	* 6 176	* 14.6	* 2.3	* 63.4	36.61
	2018	...	...	...	...	...	...	...	36.61
Republic of Moldova	2005	3 289	1 833	302	363	55.7	9.2	11.0	23.61
République de Moldova	2010	3 285	1 813	299	386	55.2	9.1	11.8	23.61
	2016	* 3 289	1 827	269	* 414	* 55.6	* 8.2	* 12.6	23.61
	2018	...	...	...	...	...	...	...	23.61
Réunion	2005	* 250	35	3	85	* 14.0	* 1.2	* 34.0	0.58
Réunion	2010	* 250	35	3	88	* 14.1	* 1.2	* 35.2	45.82
	2016	* 251	35	3	* 88	* 13.8	* 1.2	* 35.1	45.82
	2018	...	...	...	...	...	...	...	45.82

Region, country or area Région, pays ou zone	Year Année	Area – Superficie ('000 hectares)				Area – Superficie (Percent of total)&			Sites protected for terrestrial biodiversity Sites pour la bio. terre. dans aires protég. (%)&&
		Total land Superficie totale	Arable land Terres arables	Permanent crops Cultures permanentes	Forest cover Superficie forestière	Arable land Terres arables	Permanent crops Cultures Permanentes	Forest cover Superficie forestière	
Romania	2005	22 998	8 985	510	6 391	39.1	2.2	27.8	14.84
Roumanie	2010	23 005	9 146	463	6 515	39.8	2.0	28.3	64.98
	2016	23 008	8 582	418	* 6 930	37.3	1.8	* 30.1	77.29
	2018	...	...	...	...	...	...	...	77.29
Russian Federation	2005	1 638 139	121 781	1 800	808 790	7.4	0.1	49.4	26.81
Fédération de Russie		*							
	2010	1 637 687	* 119 000	* 1 650	815 136	* 7.3	* 0.1	* 49.8	26.84
		*							
	2016	1 637 687	* 123 122	* 1 600	* 814 889	* 7.5	* 0.1	* 49.8	26.84
	2018	...	...	...	...	...	...	...	26.88
Rwanda	2005	* 2 467	* 1 083	* 250	385	* 43.9	* 10.1	* 15.6	45.67
Rwanda	2010	* 2 467	* 1 124	* 250	446	* 45.6	* 10.1	* 18.1	45.67
	2016	* 2 467	* 1 152	* 250	* 487	* 46.7	* 10.1	19.7	45.67
	2018	...	...	...	...	...	...	...	45.67
Saint Barthélemy	2005	...	...	...	...	...	...	...	23.26
Saint-Barthélemy	2010	...	...	...	...	...	...	...	62.29
	2018	...	...	...	...	...	...	...	62.29
Saint Helena	2005	39	* 4	...	2	10.3	...	5.1	0.58[3]
Sainte-Hélène	2010	* 39	* 4	...	2	* 10.3	...	* 5.1	16.67[3]
	2016	* 39	* 4	...	* 2	* 10.3	...	5.1	54.85[3]
	2018[3]	...	...	...	...	...	...	...	54.85
Saint Kitts and Nevis	2005	26	4	~0	11	15.3	0.1	42.3	29.20
Saint-Kitts-et-Nevis	2010	26	5	~0	11	17.3	0.4	42.3	29.20
	2016	26	* 5	* ~0	* 11	* 19.2	* 0.4	* 42.3	29.20
	2018	...	...	...	...	...	...	...	29.20
Saint Lucia	2005	* 61	* 2	* 8	21	* 3.6	* 12.6	* 34.3	40.32
Sainte-Lucie	2010	* 61	* 3	* 7	21	* 4.9	* 11.5	* 33.8	46.05
	2016	* 61	* 3	* 7	* 20	* 4.9	* 11.5	* 33.2	46.05
	2018	...	...	...	...	...	...	...	46.05
Saint Martin (French part)	2005	...	...	...	...	...	...	...	29.21
St-Martin (partie française)	2010	...	...	...	...	...	...	...	59.34
	2018	...	...	...	...	...	...	...	59.39
Saint Pierre and Miquelon	2005	* 23	* 3	...	3	* 13.0	...	* 14.4	...
Saint-Pierre-et-Miquelon	2010	* 23	* 3	...	3	* 13.0	...	* 14.1	...
	*2016	23	2	...	3	8.7	...	13.7	...
Saint Vincent & Grenadines	2005	39	* 5	* 3	26	* 12.8	* 7.7	66.7	42.66
Saint-Vincent-Grenadines	2010	39	* 5	* 3	27	* 12.8	* 7.7	69.2	42.66
	2016	39	* 5	* 3	* 27	* 12.8	* 7.7	* 69.2	42.66
	2018	...	...	...	...	...	...	...	42.66
Samoa	2005	* 283	* 11	* 27	171	* 3.9	* 9.5	* 60.4	31.17
Samoa	2010	* 283	* 8	* 22	171	* 2.8	* 7.8	* 60.4	31.17
	2016	* 283	* 8	* 22	* 171	* 2.8	* 7.8	* 60.4	36.53
	2018	...	...	...	...	...	...	...	36.53
San Marino	2005	6	* 1	...	0	* 16.7	...	0.0	...
Saint-Marin	2010	6	* 1	...	0	* 16.7	...	0.0	...
	2016	6	* 1	...	* 0	* 16.7	...	* 0.0	...
Sao Tome and Principe	2005	* 96	* 8	* 40	56	* 8.3	* 41.7	* 58.3	0.00
Sao Tomé-et-Principe	2010	* 96	* 9	* 39	54	* 8.9	* 40.6	* 55.8	58.01
	2016	* 96	* 9	* 39	* 54	* 9.1	* 40.6	* 55.8	58.01
	2018	...	...	...	...	...	...	...	58.01
Saudi Arabia	2005	214 969	* 3 500	217	977	* 1.6	0.1	0.5	20.98
Arabie saoudite	2010	214 969	* 3 180	226	977	* 1.5	0.1	0.5	20.98
	2016	* 214 969	* 3 477	142	* 977	* 1.6	* 0.1	* 0.5	20.98
	2018	...	...	...	...	...	...	...	20.98
Senegal	2005	* 19 253	* 3 126	* 50	8 673	* 16.2	* 0.3	* 45.0	41.12
Sénégal	2010	* 19 253	* 3 800	* 58	8 473	* 19.7	* 0.3	* 44.0	41.12
	2016	* 19 253	* 3 200	* 68	* 8 233	* 16.6	* 0.4	* 42.8	41.16
	2018	...	...	...	...	...	...	...	41.16
Serbia	2005	...	...	...	...	...	...	...	24.09
Serbie	2010	* 8 746	2 654	190	2 713	* 30.3	* 2.2	* 31.0	26.35
	2016	* 8 746	2 598	188	* 2 721	* 29.7	* 2.1	* 31.1	30.23
	2018	...	...	...	...	...	...	...	30.23

Region, country or area Région, pays ou zone	Year Année	Area – Superficie ('000 hectares)				Area – Superficie (Percent of total)&			Sites protected for terrestrial biodiversity Sites pour la bio. terre. dans aires protég. (%)&&
		Total land Superficie totale	Arable land Terres arables	Permanent crops Cultures permanentes	Forest cover Superficie forestière	Arable land Terres arables	Permanent crops Cultures Permanentes	Forest cover Superficie forestière	
Serbia and Monten. [former] Serbie-et-Monténégro [anc.]	2005	* 10 200	* 3 505	* 317	3 102	* 34.4	* 3.1	* 30.4	...
Seychelles Seychelles	2005	46	* 1	* 3	41	* 2.2	* 6.5	88.4	19.46
	2010	* 46	* 1	* 2	41	* 2.0	* 3.3	* 88.4	19.71
	2016	* 46	* ~0	* 1	* 41	* 0.3	* 3.0	* 88.4	19.71
	2018	...	...	...	...	...	...	...	19.71
Sierra Leone Sierra Leone	2005	* 7 218	* 1 472	* 140	2 824	* 20.4	* 1.9	* 39.1	55.39
	2010	* 7 218	* 1 580	* 150	2 726	* 21.9	* 2.1	* 37.8	68.98
	2016	* 7 218	* 1 584	* 165	* 3 108	* 21.9	* 2.3	* 43.1	80.32
	2018	...	...	...	...	...	...	...	80.32
Singapore Singapour	2005	* 69	* 1	* ~0	16	* 1.0	* 0.1	* 23.7	21.14
	2010	* 70	* 1	* ~0	16	* 0.9	* 0.1	* 23.3	21.14
	2016	* 71	* 1	* ~0	* 16	* 0.8	* 0.1	* 23.1	21.14
	2018	...	...	...	...	...	...	...	21.14
Sint Maarten (Dutch part) St-Martin (partie néerland.)	2005	...	...	...	...	...	...	...	6.37
	2010	...	...	...	...	...	...	...	6.37
	2018	...	...	...	...	...	...	...	6.37
Slovakia Slovaquie	2005	4 810	1 391	26	1 932	28.9	0.5	40.2	73.09
	2010	4 809	1 392	25	1 939	28.9	0.5	40.3	76.30
	2016	4 808	1 347	18	* 1 940	28.0	0.4	* 40.4	83.62
	2018	...	...	...	...	...	...	...	83.62
Slovenia Slovénie	2005	2 014	176	28	1 243	8.7	1.4	61.7	86.07
	2010	2 015	185	52	1 247	9.2	2.6	61.9	86.08
	2016	2 014	184	54	* 1 248	9.1	2.7	* 62.0	88.65
	2018	...	...	...	...	...	...	...	88.65
Solomon Islands Îles Salomon	2005	* 2 799	* 16	* 65	2 241	* 0.6	* 2.3	* 80.1	7.11
	2010	* 2 799	* 19	* 80	2 213	* 0.7	* 2.9	* 79.1	9.53
	2016	* 2 799	* 20	* 80	* 2 179	* 0.7	* 2.9	* 77.9	9.53
	2018	...	...	...	...	...	...	...	9.53
Somalia Somalie	2005	* 62 734	* 1 350	* 27	7 131	* 2.2	* ~0.0	* 11.4	0.00
	2010	* 62 734	* 1 100	* 28	6 747	* 1.8	* ~0.0	* 10.8	0.00
	2016	* 62 734	* 1 100	* 25	* 6 286	* 1.8	* ~0.0	* 10.0	0.00
	2018	...	...	...	...	...	...	...	0.00
South Africa Afrique du Sud	2005	121 309	* 13 175	* 380	9 241	* 10.9	* 0.3	7.6	33.47
	2010	121 309	12 533	430	9 241	10.3	0.4	7.6	35.08
	2016	* 121 309	* 12 500	* 413	* 9 241	* 10.3	* 0.3	* 7.6	37.71
	2018	...	...	...	...	...	...	...	37.71
South Georgia & Sandwich Is. Géorgie du S.-Îles Sandwich	2005	...	...	...	...	...	...	...	0.00
	2010	...	...	...	...	...	...	...	0.00
	2018	...	...	...	...	...	...	...	100.00
South Sudan Soudan du sud	2005	...	...	...	...	...	...	...	30.26
	2010	...	...	...	...	...	...	...	33.64
	2016	...	...	...	* 7 157	...	...	...	33.64
	2018	...	...	...	...	...	...	...	33.64
Spain Espagne	2005	49 909	12 913	4 931	17 282	25.9	9.9	34.6	53.01
	2010	50 001	12 528	4 693	18 247	25.1	9.4	36.5	54.56
	2016	49 956	12 337	4 696	* 18 452	24.7	9.4	* 36.9	56.26
	2018	...	...	...	...	...	...	...	56.26
Sri Lanka Sri Lanka	2005	6 271	* 1 100	* 970	2 118	* 17.5	* 15.5	33.8	41.74
	2010	6 271	* 1 200	* 980	2 103	* 19.1	* 15.6	33.5	47.49
	2016	6 271	* 1 300	* 1 000	* 2 063	* 20.7	* 15.9	* 32.9	49.85
	2018	...	...	...	...	...	...	...	49.85
State of Palestine État de Palestine	2005	602	* 99	115	9	* 16.4	19.1	1.5	2.47
	2010	602	44	54	9	7.3	9.0	1.5	2.47
	2016	602	* 51	* 96	* 9	* 8.4	* 16.0	* 1.5	2.47
	2018	...	...	...	...	...	...	...	2.47
Sudan Soudan	2005	...	...	...	...	...	...	...	9.09
	2010	...	...	...	...	...	...	...	18.62
	2016	...	* 19 823	* 168	* 19 036	...	...	...	25.00
	2018	...	...	...	...	...	...	...	25.00
Sudan [former] Soudan [anc.]	2005	237 600	18 750	* 130	28 111	7.9	0.1	11.8	...
	2010	237 600	19 878	142	27 239	8.4	0.1	11.5	...

Region, country or area Région, pays ou zone	Year Année	Area – Superficie ('000 hectares)				Area – Superficie (Percent of total)&			Sites protected for terrestrial biodiversity Sites pour la bio. terre. dans aires protég. (%)&&
		Total land Superficie totale	Arable land Terres arables	Permanent crops Cultures permanentes	Forest cover Superficie forestière	Arable land Terres arables	Permanent crops Cultures Permanentes	Forest cover Superficie forestière	
Suriname	2005	* 15 600	49	* 6	15 371	* 0.3	* ~0.0	* 98.5	51.19
Suriname	2010	* 15 600	55	6	15 351	* 0.4	* ~0.0	* 98.4	51.19
	2016	* 15 600	65	6	* 15 328	* 0.4	* ~0.0	* 98.3	51.19
	2018	...	...	...	...	...	...	...	51.19
Svalbard and Jan Mayen Is.	2005	...	...	...	...	...	...	...	63.12
Îles Svalbard-et-Jan Mayen	2010	...	...	...	...	...	...	...	67.67
	2018	...	...	...	...	...	...	...	67.69
Eswatini	2005	* 1 720	* 178	* 14	541	* 10.3	* 0.8	* 31.5	29.98
Eswatini	2010	* 1 720	* 175	* 15	563	* 10.2	* 0.9	* 32.7	29.98
	2016	* 1 720	* 175	* 15	* 591	* 10.2	* 0.9	* 34.3	30.27
	2018	...	...	...	...	...	...	...	30.27
Sweden	2005	41 034	* 2 698	* 5	28 218	* 6.6	* ~0.0	68.8	56.65
Suède	2010	41 034	* 2 629	* 5	28 073	* 6.4	* ~0.0	68.4	57.79
	2016	40 731	* 2 575	* 5	* 28 073	* 6.3	* ~0.0	* 68.9	58.81
	2018	...	...	...	...	...	...	...	58.81
Switzerland	2005	3 952	406	23	1 217	10.3	0.6	30.8	28.51
Suisse	2010	3 952	405	24	1 235	10.2	0.6	31.3	35.22
	2016	3 952	399	25	* 1 258	10.1	0.6	* 31.8	35.23
	2018	...	...	...	...	...	...	...	35.23
Syrian Arab Republic	2005	18 357	4 675	887	461	25.5	4.8	2.5	1.12
République arabe syrienne	2010	18 363	4 687	1 009	491	25.5	5.5	2.7	1.12
	2016	* 18 363	* 4 662	* 1 071	* 491	* 25.4	* 5.8	* 2.7	1.12
	2018	...	...	...	...	...	...	...	1.12
Tajikistan	2005	13 996	* 757	117	410	* 5.4	0.8	2.9	20.46
Tadjikistan	2010	* 13 996	* 748	* 133	410	* 5.3	* 1.0	* 2.9	20.46
	2016	* 13 879	* 730	* 133	* 412	* 5.3	* 1.0	* 3.0	20.99
	2018	...	...	...	...	...	...	...	20.99
Thailand	2005	* 51 089	* 15 200	* 3 610	16 100	* 29.8	* 7.1	* 31.5	67.95
Thaïlande	2010	* 51 089	* 15 760	* 4 500	16 249	* 30.8	* 8.8	* 31.8	71.01
	2016	* 51 089	* 16 810	* 4 500	* 16 429	* 32.9	* 8.8	* 32.2	71.74
	2018	...	...	...	...	...	...	...	71.74
Timor-Leste	2005	1 487	* 170	* 65	798	* 11.4	* 4.4	53.7	14.91
Timor-Leste	2010	* 1 487	* 150	* 72	742	* 10.1	* 4.8	* 49.9	38.73
	2016	* 1 487	* 155	* 75	* 675	* 10.4	* 5.0	* 45.4	38.73
	2018	...	...	...	...	...	...	...	38.73
Togo	2005	* 5 439	* 2 100	* 150	386	* 38.6	* 2.8	* 7.1	75.00
Togo	2010	* 5 439	* 2 460	* 205	287	* 45.2	* 3.8	* 5.3	96.98
	2016	* 5 439	* 2 650	* 170	* 168	* 48.7	* 3.1	* 3.1	96.98
	2018	...	...	...	...	...	...	...	96.98
Tokelau	2005	1	...	* 1	0	...	* 0.2	0.0	2.59
Tokélaou	2010	1	...	* 1	0	...	* 0.2	0.0	2.59
	2016	1	...	* 1	* 0	...	* 0.4	* 0.0	2.59
	2018	...	...	...	...	...	...	...	2.59
Tonga	2005	* 72	* 15	* 11	9	* 20.8	* 15.3	* 12.5	9.31
Tonga	2010	72	* 17	* 11	9	* 23.6	* 15.3	12.5	9.31
	2016	72	* 18	* 11	* 9	* 25.0	* 15.3	* 12.5	9.31
	2018	...	...	...	...	...	...	...	9.31
Trinidad and Tobago	2005	513	* 25	* 22	230	* 4.9	* 4.3	44.8	40.67
Trinité-et-Tobago	2010	513	* 25	* 22	226	* 4.9	* 4.3	44.1	40.67
	2016	513	* 25	* 22	* 236	* 4.9	* 4.3	* 46.0	40.67
	2018	...	...	...	...	...	...	...	40.67
Tunisia	2005	15 536	2 730	2 166	915	17.6	13.9	5.9	15.97
Tunisie	2010	15 536	2 823	2 363	990	18.2	15.2	6.4	27.21
	2016	* 15 536	* 2 900	* 2 332	* 1 051	* 18.7	* 15.0	* 6.8	40.85
	2018	...	...	...	...	...	...	...	40.85
Turkey	2005	76 963	23 830	2 776	10 662	31.0	3.6	13.9	2.11
Turquie	2010	76 963	21 384	3 011	11 203	27.8	3.9	14.6	2.24
	2016	76 963	20 381	3 329	* 11 817	26.5	4.3	* 15.4	2.29
	2018	...	...	...	...	...	...	...	2.29
Turkmenistan	2005	* 46 993	* 2 040	* 60	4 127	* 4.3	* 0.1	* 8.8	14.41
Turkménistan	2010	* 46 993	* 1 940	* 60	4 127	* 4.1	* 0.1	* 8.8	14.60
	2016	* 46 993	* 1 940	* 60	* 4 127	* 4.1	* 0.1	* 8.8	14.60
	2018	...	...	...	...	...	...	...	14.60

Region, country or area Région, pays ou zone	Year Année	Area – Superficie ('000 hectares)				Area – Superficie (Percent of total)&			Sites protected for terrestrial biodiversity Sites pour la bio. terre. dans aires protég. (%)&&
		Total land Superficie totale	Arable land Terres arables	Permanent crops Cultures permanentes	Forest cover Superficie forestière	Arable land Terres arables	Permanent crops Cultures Permanentes	Forest cover Superficie forestière	
Turks and Caicos Islands	2005	95	* 1	...	34	* 1.1	...	36.2	27.96
Îles Turques-et-Caïques	2010	95	* 1	...	34	* 1.1	...	36.2	27.96
	2016	95	* 1	...	* 34	* 1.1	...	* 36.2	27.96
	2018	...	...	...	...	...	...	...	27.96
Tuvalu	2005	3	...	* 2	1	...	* 4.9	33.3	...
Tuvalu	2010	3	...	* 2	1	...	* 5.2	33.3	...
	2016	3	...	* 2	* 1	...	* 5.2	* 33.3	...
Uganda	2005	19 981	* 5 950	* 2 200	3 429	* 29.8	* 11.0	17.2	61.02
Ouganda	2010	20 052	* 6 750	* 2 200	2 753	* 33.7	* 11.0	13.7	72.05
	2016	20 052	* 6 900	* 2 200	* 1 942	* 34.4	* 11.0	* 9.7	72.05
	2018	...	...	...	...	...	...	...	72.05
Ukraine	2005	57 938	32 452	901	9 575	56.0	1.6	16.5	23.26
Ukraine	2010	57 932	32 477	897	9 548	56.1	1.5	16.5	23.26
	2016	57 929	32 776	897	* 9 679	56.6	1.5	* 16.7	23.66
	2018	...	...	...	...	...	...	...	23.66
United Arab Emirates	2005	7 102	* 68	189	312	* 1.0	2.7	4.4	0.00
Émirats arabes unis	2010	7 102	51	42	317	0.7	0.6	4.5	13.23
	2016	7 102	45	39	* 324	0.6	0.6	* 4.6	30.78
	2018	...	...	...	...	...	...	...	30.78
United Kingdom	2005	24 193	5 729	47	3 021	23.7	0.2	12.5	81.71
Royaume-Uni	2010	24 193	5 970	46	3 059	24.7	0.2	12.6	83.84
	2016	24 193	6 026	47	* 3 161	24.9	0.2	* 13.1	84.11
	2018	...	...	...	...	...	...	...	84.36
United Rep. of Tanzania	2005	88 580	* 9 700	* 1 660	49 920	* 11.0	* 1.9	56.4	52.55
Rép.-Unie de Tanzanie	2010	* 88 580	* 11 600	* 1 850	47 920	* 13.1	* 2.1	* 54.1	57.03
	2016	* 88 580	* 13 500	* 2 150	* 45 688	* 15.2	* 2.4	* 51.6	57.03
	2018	...	...	...	...	...	...	...	57.03
U.S. Minor Outlying islands	2005	...	...	...	...	...	...	...	75.00
Îles min. éloignées des É-U	2010	...	...	...	...	...	...	...	100.00
	2018	...	...	...	...	...	...	...	100.00
United States of America	2005	916 192	* 165 115	* 2 700	304 757	* 18.0	* 0.3	33.3	...
États-Unis d'Amérique	2010	914 742	* 155 926	* 2 600	308 720	* 17.0	* 0.3	33.7	...
	*2016	914 742	152 263	2 600	310 370	16.6	0.3	33.9	...
United States Virgin Islands	2005	35	* 2	* 1	19	* 5.7	* 2.9	53.5	33.13
Îles Vierges américaines	2010	35	* 1	* 1	18	* 2.9	* 2.9	51.9	34.01
	2016	35	* 1	* 1	* 17	* 2.9	* 2.9	* 50.0	39.38
	2018	...	...	...	...	...	...	...	39.38
Uruguay	2005	17 502	* 1 392	* 40	1 522	* 8.0	* 0.2	8.7	10.38
Uruguay	2010	17 502	* 2 033	38	1 731	* 11.6	0.2	9.9	20.72
	2016	17 502	* 2 411	* 39	* 1 868	* 13.8	* 0.2	* 10.7	20.80
	2018	...	...	...	...	...	...	...	20.80
Uzbekistan	2005	42 540	* 4 400	* 340	3 295	* 10.3	0.8	7.7	11.71
Ouzbékistan	2010	* 42 540	* 4 350	* 320	3 276	* 10.2	* 0.8	* 7.7	15.88
	2016	* 42 540	* 4 400	* 370	* 3 209	* 10.3	* 0.9	* 7.5	15.88
	2018	...	...	...	...	...	...	...	15.88
Vanuatu	2005	* 1 219	* 20	* 121	440	* 1.6	* 9.9	* 36.1	6.39
Vanuatu	2010	* 1 219	* 20	* 125	440	* 1.6	* 10.3	* 36.1	6.39
	2016	* 1 219	* 20	* 125	* 440	* 1.6	* 10.3	* 36.1	6.39
	2018	...	...	...	...	...	...	...	6.39
Venezuela (Boliv. Rep. of)	2005	* 88 205	* 2 655	* 700	47 713	* 3.0	* 0.8	* 54.1	67.37
Venezuela (Rép. boliv. du)	2010	* 88 205	* 2 700	* 700	47 505	* 3.1	* 0.8	* 53.9	67.37
	2016	* 88 205	* 2 700	* 700	* 46 519	* 3.1	* 0.8	* 52.7	67.37
	2018	...	...	...	...	...	...	...	67.37
Viet Nam	2005	* 31 007	6 358	3 054	13 077	* 20.5	* 9.8	* 42.2	27.16
Viet Nam	2010	* 31 007	6 437	3 681	14 128	* 20.8	* 11.9	* 45.6	29.97
	2016	* 31 007	6 998	4 538	* 14 902	* 22.6	* 14.6	* 48.1	40.88
	2018	...	...	...	...	...	...	...	40.88
Wallis and Futuna Islands	2005	14	* 1	* 5	6	* 7.1	* 35.7	41.5	0.00
Îles Wallis-et-Futuna	2010	14	* 1	* 5	6	* 7.1	* 35.7	41.6	0.00
	2016	14	* 1	* 5	* 6	* 7.1	* 35.7	* 41.6	0.00
	2018	...	...	...	...	...	...	...	0.00

| Region, country or area Région, pays ou zone | Year Année | Area – Superficie ('000 hectares) | | | | Area – Superficie (Percent of total)& | | | Sites protected for terrestrial biodiversity Sites pour la bio. terre. dans aires protég. (%)&& |
		Total land Superficie totale	Arable land Terres arables	Permanent crops Cultures permanentes	Forest cover Superficie forestière	Arable land Terres arables	Permanent crops Cultures Permanentes	Forest cover Superficie forestière	
Western Sahara Sahara occidental	2005	* 26 600	* 4	...	707	* ~0.0	...	* 2.7	...
	2010	* 26 600	* 4	...	707	* ~0.0	...	* 2.7	...
	*2016	26 600	4	...	707	~0.0	...	2.7	...
Yemen Yémen	2005	52 797	* 1 287	236	549	* 2.4	0.4	1.0	20.04
	2010	* 52 797	* 1 291	288	549	* 2.4	* 0.5	* 1.0	31.08
	2016	* 52 797	* 1 248	* 298	* 549	* 2.4	* 0.6	* 1.0	31.08
	2018								31.08
Zambia Zambie	2005	74 339	* 2 727	* 35	50 301	* 3.7	* ~0.0	67.7	46.29
	2010	* 74 339	* 3 400	* 36	49 468	* 4.6	* ~0.0	* 66.5	48.33
	2016	* 74 339	* 3 800	* 36	* 48 468	* 5.1	* ~0.0	* 65.2	48.33
	2018	...	...	...	...	...	...	...	48.33
Zimbabwe Zimbabwe	2005	* 38 685	* 3 900	* 100	17 259	* 10.1	* 0.3	* 44.6	80.73
	2010	* 38 685	* 4 000	* 100	15 624	* 10.3	* 0.3	* 40.4	80.73
	2016	* 38 685	* 4 000	* 100	* 13 750	* 10.3	* 0.3	* 35.5	85.88
	2018	...	...	...	...	...	...	...	85.88

Source:

Food and Agriculture Organization of the United Nations (FAO), Rome, FAOSTAT data last accessed October 2018.
United Nations Environment Programme (UNEP) World Conservation Monitoring Centre (WCWC) and World Conservation Union (IUCN) and BirdLife International, Cambridge, Sustainable Development Goals database, .

& Figures calculated by the United Nations Statistics Division.

&& Based on spatial overlap between polygons for Key Biodiversity Areas from the World Database of Key Biodiveristy Areas and polygons for protected areas from the World Database on Protected Areas.

1   Calculated by the UN Statistics Division.
2   For statistical purposes, the data for China do not include those for the Hong Kong Special Administrative Region (Hong Kong SAR), Macao Special Administrative Region (Macao SAR) and Taiwan Province of China.
3   Including Ascension and Tristan da Cunha.

Source:

Organisation des Nations Unies pour l'alimentation et l'agriculture (FAO), Rome, base de données FAOSTAT, dernier accès octobre 2018.
Le Programme des Nations Unies pour l'environnement (PNUE) Le Centre mondial de surveillance de la conservation (CMSC) et l'Union mondiale pour la nature (IUCN) et BirdLife International, Cambridge, base de données sur les Objectifs de développement durable (ODD), mai 2018.

& Chiffres calculés par la Division de statistique des Nations Unies.

&& basées sur un chevauchement spatial entre les zones clés pour la biodiversité de la base de données mondiale pour les zones clés pour la biodiversité et les polygones pour les zones protégées de la base de données mondiale sur les zones protégées.

1   Calculés par la Division de statistique des Nations Unies.
2   Pour la présentation des statistiques, les données pour la Chine ne comprennent pas la région administrative spéciale de Hong Kong (RAS de Hong Kong), la région administrative spéciale de Macao (RAS de Macao) et la province chinoise de Taïwan.
3   Y compris Ascension et Tristan da Cunha.

Threatened species
Number of species by taxonomic group

Espèces menacées
Nombre d'espèces menacées par groupe taxonomique

Country or area &	2004	2010	2015	2016	2017	2018	2019	Pays ou zone &
Afghanistan								**Afghanistan**
Vertebrates	31	31	31	35	35	34	33	Vertébrés
Invertebrates	1	1	2	2	2	2	2	Invertébrés
Plants	1	2	5	5	5	5	5	Plantes
Total	33	34	38	42	42	41	40	Total
Albania								**Albanie**
Vertebrates	33	53	54	63	62	62	61	Vertébrés
Invertebrates	4	47	58	62	68	71	71	Invertébrés
Plants	0	0	0	0	0	4	5	Plantes
Total	37	100	112	125	130	137	137	Total
Algeria								**Algérie**
Vertebrates	36	69	71	78	79	80	81	Vertébrés
Invertebrates	12	21	26	29	38	40	40	Invertébrés
Plants	2	15	17	18	18	23	24	Plantes
Total	50	105	114	125	135	143	145	Total
American Samoa								**Samoa américaines**
Vertebrates	18	21	25	27	27	27	29	Vertébrés
Invertebrates	5	57	64	64	64	64	65	Invertébrés
Plants	1	1	1	1	1	1	1	Plantes
Total	24	79	90	92	92	92	95	Total
Andorra								**Andorre**
Vertebrates	1	4	4	5	5	6	6	Vertébrés
Invertebrates	4	4	7	7	8	8	8	Invertébrés
Plants	0	0	0	0	0	0	1	Plantes
Total	5	8	11	12	13	14	15	Total
Angola								**Angola**
Vertebrates	44	77	87	99	103	108	111	Vertébrés
Invertebrates	6	7	9	9	9	11	11	Invertébrés
Plants	26	33	34	34	34	35	36	Plantes
Total	76	117	130	142	146	154	158	Total
Anguilla								**Anguilla**
Vertebrates	15	20	37	38	38	40	43	Vertébrés
Invertebrates	0	10	10	10	10	10	10	Invertébrés
Plants	3	3	4	4	4	4	4	Plantes
Total	18	33	51	52	52	54	57	Total
Antarctica								**Antarctique**
Vertebrates	8	6	6	6	6	6	6	Vertébrés
Invertebrates	0	0	0	0	0	0	0	Invertébrés
Plants	0	0	0	0	0	0	0	Plantes
Total	8	6	6	6	6	6	6	Total
Antigua and Barbuda								**Antigua-et-Barbuda**
Vertebrates	18	23	38	38	40	41	44	Vertébrés
Invertebrates	0	11	11	11	11	11	11	Invertébrés
Plants	4	4	4	4	4	4	4	Plantes
Total	22	38	53	53	55	56	59	Total
Areas n.e.s								**Zones n.s.a**
Vertebrates	1	1	1	3	3	5	7	Vertébrés
Invertebrates	0	0	1	1	1	1	1	Invertébrés
Plants	0	0	0	0	0	0	…	Plantes
Total	1	1	2	4	4	6	8	Total
Argentina								**Argentine**
Vertebrates	134	157	160	172	172	186	190	Vertébrés
Invertebrates	10	12	13	14	14	14	14	Invertébrés
Plants	42	44	70	70	70	70	75	Plantes
Total	186	213	243	256	256	270	279	Total
Armenia								**Arménie**
Vertebrates	27	29	31	34	34	33	34	Vertébrés
Invertebrates	7	6	9	9	9	9	9	Invertébrés
Plants	1	1	71	71	71	73	76	Plantes
Total	35	36	111	114	114	115	119	Total
Aruba								**Aruba**
Vertebrates	17	20	25	28	28	28	33	Vertébrés
Invertebrates	1	1	2	2	2	2	2	Invertébrés
Plants	0	1	2	2	2	2	3	Plantes
Total	18	22	29	32	32	32	38	Total

Country or area &	2004	2010	2015	2016	2017	2018	2019	Pays ou zone &
Australia								**Australie**
Vertebrates	282[1]	297[1]	304[1]	319[1]	323[1]	358[1]	363	Vertébrés
Invertebrates	283[1]	489[1]	514[1]	514[1]	531[1]	534[1]	545	Invertébrés
Plants	56[1]	67[1]	91[1]	# 93[1]	94[1]	106[1]	108	Plantes
Total	621[1]	853[1]	909[1]	926[1]	948[1]	998[1]	1 016	Total
Austria								**Autriche**
Vertebrates	20	23	24	27	26	28	28	Vertébrés
Invertebrates	44	55	69	69	71	74	74	Invertébrés
Plants	3	4	13	# 21	21	25	68	Plantes
Total	67	82	106	117	118	127	170	Total
Azerbaijan								**Azerbaïdjan**
Vertebrates	32	41	43	47	48	47	49	Vertébrés
Invertebrates	6	4	7	7	7	7	7	Invertébrés
Plants	0	0	42	42	42	43	45	Plantes
Total	38	45	92	96	97	97	101	Total
Bahamas								**Bahamas**
Vertebrates	36	44	61	65	66	71	71	Vertébrés
Invertebrates	1	11	12	12	12	12	12	Invertébrés
Plants	5	7	8	8	8	7	12	Plantes
Total	42	62	81	85	86	90	95	Total
Bahrain								**Bahreïn**
Vertebrates	18	19	19	23	23	27	33	Vertébrés
Invertebrates	0	13	13	13	13	13	13	Invertébrés
Plants	0	0	0	0	0	0	0	Plantes
Total	18	32	32	36	36	40	46	Total
Bangladesh								**Bangladesh**
Vertebrates	73	104	109	120	123	125	128	Vertébrés
Invertebrates	0	2	7	7	7	7	7	Invertébrés
Plants	12	16	21	21	21	22	23	Plantes
Total	85	122	137	148	151	154	158	Total
Barbados								**Barbade**
Vertebrates	18	24	37	39	42	43	44	Vertébrés
Invertebrates	0	10	11	11	11	11	11	Invertébrés
Plants	2	2	3	3	3	3	3	Plantes
Total	20	36	51	53	56	57	58	Total
Belarus								**Bélarus**
Vertebrates	10	10	11	14	15	15	15	Vertébrés
Invertebrates	8	6	9	9	9	10	10	Invertébrés
Plants	0	0	1	1	1	1	3	Plantes
Total	18	16	21	24	25	26	28	Total
Belgium								**Belgique**
Vertebrates	25	15	16	23	22	23	23	Vertébrés
Invertebrates	11	11	14	14	14	15	15	Invertébrés
Plants	0	1	0	# 1	1	1	17	Plantes
Total	36	27	30	38	37	39	55	Total
Belize								**Belize**
Vertebrates	36	48	70	70	69	69	73	Vertébrés
Invertebrates	1	12	12	12	12	12	12	Invertébrés
Plants	30	32	35	36	36	43	46	Plantes
Total	67	92	117	118	117	124	131	Total
Benin								**Bénin**
Vertebrates	17	47	55	66	68	70	77	Vertébrés
Invertebrates	0	1	3	3	3	3	3	Invertébrés
Plants	14	14	16	17	17	19	21	Plantes
Total	31	62	74	86	88	92	101	Total
Bermuda								**Bermudes**
Vertebrates	18	18	28	35	36	36	39	Vertébrés
Invertebrates	25	28	28	28	28	28	28	Invertébrés
Plants	4	4	8	8	8	8	8	Plantes
Total	47	50	64	71	72	72	75	Total
Bhutan								**Bhoutan**
Vertebrates	40	50	52	54	52	51	55	Vertébrés
Invertebrates	1	1	1	1	1	1	1	Invertébrés
Plants	7	8	18	18	18	43	43	Plantes
Total	48	59	71	73	71	95	99	Total

Country or area [&]	2004	2010	2015	2016	2017	2018	2019	Pays ou zone [&]
Bolivia (Plurin. State of)								**Bolivie (État plurin. de)**
Vertebrates	79	90	114	124	124	129	129	Vertébrés
Invertebrates	1	1	3	3	3	3	3	Invertébrés
Plants	70	72	99	104	104	104	112	Plantes
Total	150	163	216	231	231	236	244	Total
Bonaire, St. Eustatius & Saba								**Bonaire, St-Eustache et Saba**
Vertebrates	...	...	41	42	42	42	44	Vertébrés
Invertebrates	...	...	11	11	11	11	11	Invertébrés
Plants	...	...	3	3	3	3	3	Plantes
Total	...	...	55	56	56	56	58	Total
Bosnia and Herzegovina								**Bosnie-Herzégovine**
Vertebrates	29	44	48	51	51	50	50	Vertébrés
Invertebrates	10	22	36	36	39	42	42	Invertébrés
Plants	1	1	1	1	1	3	6	Plantes
Total	40	67	85	88	91	95	98	Total
Botswana								**Botswana**
Vertebrates	15	18	22	24	26	28	30	Vertébrés
Invertebrates	0	0	0	0	0	0	0	Invertébrés
Plants	0	0	2	2	2	2	3	Plantes
Total	15	18	24	26	28	30	33	Total
Bouvet Island								**Île Bouvet**
Vertebrates	1	2	3	3	3	3	3	Vertébrés
Invertebrates	0	0	0	0	0	0	0	Invertébrés
Plants	0	0	0	0	0	0	0	Plantes
Total	1	2	3	3	3	3	3	Total
Brazil								**Brésil**
Vertebrates	282[2]	341[2]	396	397	403	407	411	Vertébrés
Invertebrates	34	45	54	55	55	55	64	Invertébrés
Plants	381	387	516	521	532	538	582	Plantes
Total	697	773	966	973	990	1 000	1 057	Total
British Indian Ocean Terr.								**Terr. brit. de l'océan Indien**
Vertebrates	6	10	11	14	15	15	18	Vertébrés
Invertebrates	0	65	69	69	69	69	69	Invertébrés
Plants	1	1	1	1	1	1	1	Plantes
Total	7	76	81	84	85	85	88	Total
British Virgin Islands								**Îles Vierges britanniques**
Vertebrates	20	23	41	41	47	48	52	Vertébrés
Invertebrates	0	10	10	10	10	10	10	Invertébrés
Plants	10	10	10	10	10	20	20	Plantes
Total	30	43	61	61	67	78	82	Total
Brunei Darussalam								**Brunéi Darussalam**
Vertebrates	49	70	77	80	81	82	93	Vertébrés
Invertebrates	0	1	8	8	8	9	12	Invertébrés
Plants	99	99	104	104	104	116	131	Plantes
Total	148	170	189	192	193	207	236	Total
Bulgaria								**Bulgarie**
Vertebrates	35	39	42	49	50	49	49	Vertébrés
Invertebrates	9	27	37	38	48	57	57	Invertébrés
Plants	0	0	6	6	6	9	18	Plantes
Total	44	66	85	93	104	115	124	Total
Burkina Faso								**Burkina Faso**
Vertebrates	9	20	25	27	27	26	28	Vertébrés
Invertebrates	0	1	1	1	1	1	1	Invertébrés
Plants	2	3	3	3	3	3	4	Plantes
Total	11	24	29	31	31	30	33	Total
Burundi								**Burundi**
Vertebrates	22	43	45	44	46	46	46	Vertébrés
Invertebrates	4	7	7	7	7	7	6	Invertébrés
Plants	2	2	8	8	8	89	110	Plantes
Total	28	52	60	59	61	142	162	Total
Cabo Verde								**Cabo Verde**
Vertebrates	21	28	35	49	49	51	53	Vertébrés
Invertebrates	0	0	13	13	13	13	13	Invertébrés
Plants	2	3	3	3	3	51	51	Plantes
Total	23	31	51	65	65	115	117	Total

Country or area &	2004	2010	2015	2016	2017	2018	2019	Pays ou zone &
Cambodia								**Cambodge**
Vertebrates	72	107	130	137	141	145	154	Vertébrés
Invertebrates	0	67	77	79	79	79	79	Invertébrés
Plants	31	30	36	36	35	37	39	Plantes
Total	103	204	243	252	255	261	272	Total
Cameroon								**Cameroun**
Vertebrates	146	222	237	255	258	263	268	Vertébrés
Invertebrates	4	24	27	27	27	25	25	Invertébrés
Plants	334	378	433	490	490	544	559	Plantes
Total	484	624	697	772	775	832	852	Total
Canada								**Canada**
Vertebrates	62	63	68	79	81	86	93	Vertébrés
Invertebrates	11	12	22	25	27	37	38	Invertébrés
Plants	1	2	7	# 14	14	25	37	Plantes
Total	74	77	97	118	122	148	168	Total
Cayman Islands								**Îles Caïmanes**
Vertebrates	16	21	38	38	41	41	45	Vertébrés
Invertebrates	1	11	11	11	11	11	11	Invertébrés
Plants	2	2	22	22	22	22	23	Plantes
Total	19	34	71	71	74	74	79	Total
Central African Republic								**République centrafricaine**
Vertebrates	15	19	32	33	36	38	40	Vertébrés
Invertebrates	0	0	0	0	0	0	0	Invertébrés
Plants	15	17	22	24	24	25	26	Plantes
Total	30	36	54	57	60	63	66	Total
Chad								**Tchad**
Vertebrates	18	24	29	31	33	36	38	Vertébrés
Invertebrates	1	4	4	4	4	4	4	Invertébrés
Plants	2	2	5	6	6	6	6	Plantes
Total	21	30	38	41	43	46	48	Total
Chile								**Chili**
Vertebrates	83	95	98	111	112	132	135	Vertébrés
Invertebrates	0	9	12	13	13	13	13	Invertébrés
Plants	40	41	72	72	72	72	76	Plantes
Total	123	145	182	196	197	217	224	Total
China								**Chine**
Vertebrates	326[3]	374[3]	420[3]	428[3]	430[3]	431[3]	441	Vertébrés
Invertebrates	4[3]	32[3]	76[3]	76[3]	76[3]	76[3]	79	Invertébrés
Plants	443[3]	453[3]	544[3]	# 575[3]	574[3]	588[3]	604	Plantes
Total	773[3]	859[3]	1 040[3]	1 079[3]	1 080[3]	1 095[3]	1 124	Total
China, Hong Kong SAR								**Chine, RAS de Hong Kong**
Vertebrates	32	37	45	46	47	49	51	Vertébrés
Invertebrates	1	6	8	8	8	8	9	Invertébrés
Plants	6	6	7	9	9	8	10	Plantes
Total	39	49	60	63	64	65	70	Total
China, Macao SAR								**Chine, RAS de Macao**
Vertebrates	5	9	10	10	10	10	15	Vertébrés
Invertebrates	0	0	1	1	1	1	1	Invertébrés
Plants	0	0	0	0	0	0	0	Plantes
Total	5	9	11	11	11	11	16	Total
Christmas Island								**Île Christmas**
Vertebrates	12	16	18	20	20	18	22	Vertébrés
Invertebrates	0	16	18	18	18	19	19	Invertébrés
Plants	1	1	1	1	1	1	1	Plantes
Total	13	33	37	39	39	38	42	Total
Cocos (Keeling) Islands								**Îles des Cocos (Keeling)**
Vertebrates	5	11	11	12	13	13	17	Vertébrés
Invertebrates	0	17	20	20	20	20	20	Invertébrés
Plants	0	0	0	0	0	0	0	Plantes
Total	5	28	31	32	33	33	37	Total
Colombia								**Colombie**
Vertebrates	371	424	473	518	525	537	581	Vertébrés
Invertebrates	0	30	33	52	52	53	55	Invertébrés
Plants	222	227	245	257	258	261	280	Plantes
Total	593	681	751	827	835	851	916	Total

Country or area &	2004	2010	2015	2016	2017	2018	2019	Pays ou zone &
Comoros								**Comores**
Vertebrates	18	21	26	29	33	34	37	Vertébrés
Invertebrates	4	63	73	73	74	76	77	Invertébrés
Plants	5	5	7	7	7	9	9	Plantes
Total	27	89	106	109	114	119	123	Total
Congo								**Congo**
Vertebrates	29	61	71	81	82	86	86	Vertébrés
Invertebrates	1	5	7	7	7	7	7	Invertébrés
Plants	35	37	41	45	45	47	47	Plantes
Total	65	103	119	133	134	140	140	Total
Cook Islands								**Îles Cook**
Vertebrates	22	27	30	31	32	32	32	Vertébrés
Invertebrates	0	25	32	32	32	32	32	Invertébrés
Plants	1	1	11	11	11	11	11	Plantes
Total	23	53	73	74	75	75	75	Total
Costa Rica								**Costa Rica**
Vertebrates	112	142	162	166	169	171	176	Vertébrés
Invertebrates	9	27	30	31	31	31	31	Invertébrés
Plants	110	116	131	140	140	144	144	Plantes
Total	231	285	323	337	340	346	351	Total
Côte d'Ivoire								**Côte d'Ivoire**
Vertebrates	61	100	113	127	130	133	134	Vertébrés
Invertebrates	1	4	6	6	6	7	7	Invertébrés
Plants	105	106	107	112	113	117	129	Plantes
Total	167	210	226	245	249	257	270	Total
Croatia								**Croatie**
Vertebrates	46	77	84	93	94	93	93	Vertébrés
Invertebrates	11	21	67	68	73	79	79	Invertébrés
Plants	0	3	8	# 9	9	9	25	Plantes
Total	57	101	159	170	176	181	197	Total
Cuba								**Cuba**
Vertebrates	106	123	138	138	137	146	151	Vertébrés
Invertebrates	3	15	23	23	23	23	23	Invertébrés
Plants	163	166	176	179	179	179	180	Plantes
Total	272	304	337	340	339	348	354	Total
Curaçao								**Curaçao**
Vertebrates	...	...	36	36	38	38	39	Vertébrés
Invertebrates	...	...	11	11	11	11	11	Invertébrés
Plants	...	...	2	2	2	2	2	Plantes
Total	...	...	49	49	51	51	52	Total
Cyprus								**Chypre**
Vertebrates	24	31	34	41	42	42	44	Vertébrés
Invertebrates	0	4	8	12	12	15	15	Invertébrés
Plants	1	8	18	18	18	21	24	Plantes
Total	25	43	60	71	72	78	83	Total
Czechia								**Tchéquie**
Vertebrates	22	10	11	14	14	14	14	Vertébrés
Invertebrates	19	19	24	24	24	29	29	Invertébrés
Plants	4	4	10	# 15	15	31	51	Plantes
Total	45	33	45	53	53	74	94	Total
Dem. People's Rep. Korea								**Rép. pop. dém. de Corée**
Vertebrates	40	44	53	57	58	60	63	Vertébrés
Invertebrates	1	2	3	3	3	3	3	Invertébrés
Plants	3	6	8	17	17	17	17	Plantes
Total	44	52	64	77	78	80	83	Total
Dem. Rep. of the Congo								**Rép. dém. du Congo**
Vertebrates	84	162	171	183	182	187	188	Vertébrés
Invertebrates	22	51	53	53	53	55	54	Invertébrés
Plants	65	83	109	113	114	148	185	Plantes
Total	171	296	333	349	349	390	427	Total
Denmark								**Danemark**
Vertebrates	21	18	20	27	28	29	30	Vertébrés
Invertebrates	11	12	15	15	15	16	16	Invertébrés
Plants	3	3	1	# 4	4	4	21	Plantes
Total	35	33	36	46	47	49	67	Total

Country or area &	2004	2010	2015	2016	2017	2018	2019	Pays ou zone &
Djibouti								**Djibouti**
Vertebrates	19	29	34	38	38	43	49	Vertébrés
Invertebrates	0	50	57	57	57	57	57	Invertébrés
Plants	2	2	3	3	3	3	3	Plantes
Total	21	81	94	98	98	103	109	Total
Dominica								**Dominique**
Vertebrates	22	27	40	42	44	44	47	Vertébrés
Invertebrates	0	11	11	11	11	11	11	Invertébrés
Plants	11	10	11	11	11	11	12	Plantes
Total	33	48	62	64	66	66	70	Total
Dominican Republic								**République dominicaine**
Vertebrates	72	80	95	95	126	130	133	Vertébrés
Invertebrates	2	16	16	16	16	16	18	Invertébrés
Plants	30	30	42	42	42	45	49	Plantes
Total	104	126	153	153	184	191	200	Total
Ecuador								**Équateur**
Vertebrates	288	356	395	417	426	434	441	Vertébrés
Invertebrates	48	62	65	70	70	70	70	Invertébrés
Plants	1 815	1 837	1 848	# 1 866	1 862	1 864	1 882	Plantes
Total	2 151	2 255	2 308	2 353	2 358	2 368	2 393	Total
Egypt								**Égypte**
Vertebrates	43	73	83	96	97	99	105	Vertébrés
Invertebrates	1	46	55	56	56	56	56	Invertébrés
Plants	2	2	3	3	3	8	8	Plantes
Total	46	121	141	155	156	163	169	Total
El Salvador								**El Salvador**
Vertebrates	23	39	47	47	47	47	50	Vertébrés
Invertebrates	1	6	7	10	10	10	10	Invertébrés
Plants	25	27	29	29	29	30	33	Plantes
Total	49	72	83	86	86	87	93	Total
Equatorial Guinea								**Guinée équatoriale**
Vertebrates	38	60	71	85	85	86	88	Vertébrés
Invertebrates	2	2	5	5	5	4	4	Invertébrés
Plants	61	68	79	88	87	95	98	Plantes
Total	101	130	155	178	177	185	190	Total
Eritrea								**Érythrée**
Vertebrates	31	44	51	58	59	67	74	Vertébrés
Invertebrates	0	50	58	58	58	58	58	Invertébrés
Plants	3	3	4	4	5	5	6	Plantes
Total	34	97	113	120	122	130	138	Total
Estonia								**Estonie**
Vertebrates	8	8	11	14	15	15	15	Vertébrés
Invertebrates	4	3	6	6	6	7	7	Invertébrés
Plants	0	0	0	# 2	2	2	17	Plantes
Total	12	11	17	22	23	24	39	Total
Eswatini								**Eswatini**
Vertebrates	12	18	23	25	23	26	28	Vertébrés
Invertebrates	0	0	0	0	0	0	0	Invertébrés
Plants	11	11	11	11	11	12	13	Plantes
Total	23	29	34	36	34	38	41	Total
Ethiopia								**Éthiopie**
Vertebrates	65	79	89	92	90	95	99	Vertébrés
Invertebrates	6	15	15	15	15	15	15	Invertébrés
Plants	22	26	41	41	43	47	64	Plantes
Total	93	120	145	148	148	157	178	Total
Falkland Islands (Malvinas)								**Îles Falkland (Malvinas)**
Vertebrates	21	18	18	18	18	17	17	Vertébrés
Invertebrates	0	0	0	0	0	0	0	Invertébrés
Plants	5	5	5	5	5	5	6	Plantes
Total	26	23	23	23	23	22	23	Total
Faroe Islands								**Îles Féroé**
Vertebrates	11	13	14	20	20	22	23	Vertébrés
Invertebrates	0	0	0	0	0	0	0	Invertébrés
Plants	0	0	0	# 1	1	1	4	Plantes
Total	11	13	14	21	21	23	27	Total

Country or area &	2004	2010	2015	2016	2017	2018	2019	Pays ou zone &
Fiji								**Fidji**
Vertebrates	33	37	48	52	55	55	57	Vertébrés
Invertebrates	2	90	165	165	165	165	165	Invertébrés
Plants	66	65	65	65	71	78	78	Plantes
Total	101	192	278	282	291	298	300	Total
Finland								**Finlande**
Vertebrates	14	10	13	17	18	19	19	Vertébrés
Invertebrates	10	7	10	10	10	10	10	Invertébrés
Plants	1	1	2	# 8	8	8	21	Plantes
Total	25	18	25	35	36	37	50	Total
France								**France**
Vertebrates	53	62	70	80	82	84	84	Vertébrés
Invertebrates	65	91	133	137	153	160	160	Invertébrés
Plants	2	15	33	# 43	43	55	98	Plantes
Total	120	168	236	260	278	299	342	Total
French Guiana								**Guyane française**
Vertebrates	33	40	51	55	55	56	59	Vertébrés
Invertebrates	0	0	0	0	0	0	0	Invertébrés
Plants	16	16	16	18	18	18	18	Plantes
Total	49	56	67	73	73	74	77	Total
French Polynesia								**Polynésie française**
Vertebrates	46	54	63	63	66	66	67	Vertébrés
Invertebrates	29	59	65	65	62	62	62	Invertébrés
Plants	47	47	47	47	47	48	48	Plantes
Total	122	160	175	175	175	176	177	Total
French Southern Territories								**Terres australes françaises**
Vertebrates	17	21	22	24	25	25	28	Vertébrés
Invertebrates	0	0	0	0	0	0	0	Invertébrés
Plants	0	0	0	0	0	0	1	Plantes
Total	17	21	22	24	25	25	29	Total
Gabon								**Gabon**
Vertebrates	31	84	93	105	105	107	106	Vertébrés
Invertebrates	1	0	3	3	3	4	4	Invertébrés
Plants	107	120	135	162	162	172	181	Plantes
Total	139	204	231	270	270	283	291	Total
Gambia								**Gambie**
Vertebrates	17	39	48	60	60	63	68	Vertébrés
Invertebrates	0	0	2	2	2	2	2	Invertébrés
Plants	4	4	5	5	5	5	6	Plantes
Total	21	43	55	67	67	70	76	Total
Georgia								**Géorgie**
Vertebrates	33	37	38	42	43	42	42	Vertébrés
Invertebrates	10	9	15	15	15	15	15	Invertébrés
Plants	0	0	61	# 62	62	63	68	Plantes
Total	43	46	114	119	120	120	125	Total
Germany								**Allemagne**
Vertebrates	35	33	33	39	40	40	41	Vertébrés
Invertebrates	31	34	57	57	57	61	61	Invertébrés
Plants	12	12	17	# 24	19	43	83	Plantes
Total	78	79	107	120	116	144	185	Total
Ghana								**Ghana**
Vertebrates	43	83	99	112	114	118	120	Vertébrés
Invertebrates	0	1	5	5	5	5	5	Invertébrés
Plants	117	118	119	119	119	118	121	Plantes
Total	160	202	223	236	238	241	246	Total
Gibraltar								**Gibraltar**
Vertebrates	16	20	21	28	26	28	27	Vertébrés
Invertebrates	2	2	5	5	5	5	5	Invertébrés
Plants	0	0	0	0	0	1	1	Plantes
Total	18	22	26	33	31	34	33	Total
Greece								**Grèce**
Vertebrates	62	107	111	120	121	123	124	Vertébrés
Invertebrates	11	36	122	181	192	308	308	Invertébrés
Plants	2	13	58	# 60	61	71	80	Plantes
Total	75	156	291	361	374	502	512	Total

Country or area [&]	2004	2010	2015	2016	2017	2018	2019	Pays ou zone [&]
Greenland								**Groenland**
Vertebrates	11	13	16	21	22	24	24	Vertébrés
Invertebrates	0	0	0	0	0	0	0	Invertébrés
Plants	1	1	1	1	1	1	1	Plantes
Total	12	14	17	22	23	25	25	Total
Grenada								**Grenade**
Vertebrates	20	24	38	40	41	42	43	Vertébrés
Invertebrates	0	10	10	10	10	10	10	Invertébrés
Plants	3	3	3	3	3	3	3	Plantes
Total	23	37	51	53	54	55	56	Total
Guadeloupe								**Guadeloupe**
Vertebrates	25[4]	30[4]	45[4]	45[4]	48[4]	50[4]	53	Vertébrés
Invertebrates	1[4]	16[4]	16[4]	16[4]	16[4]	16[4]	16	Invertébrés
Plants	7[4]	8[4]	9[4]	9[4]	9[4]	9[4]	10	Plantes
Total	33[4]	54[4]	70[4]	70[4]	73[4]	75[4]	79	Total
Guam								**Guam**
Vertebrates	16	24	31	34	35	35	38	Vertébrés
Invertebrates	5	6	60	60	60	60	60	Invertébrés
Plants	3	4	4	4	4	4	5	Plantes
Total	24	34	95	98	99	99	103	Total
Guatemala								**Guatemala**
Vertebrates	115	140	176	176	176	175	185	Vertébrés
Invertebrates	8	8	9	13	13	13	13	Invertébrés
Plants	85	82	97	102	101	113	123	Plantes
Total	208	230	282	291	290	301	321	Total
Guernsey								**Guernesey**
Vertebrates	...	2	2	5	5	5	6	Vertébrés
Invertebrates	...	0	0	0	0	0	0	Invertébrés
Plants	...	0	0	0	0	0	0	Plantes
Total	...	2	2	5	5	5	6	Total
Guinea								**Guinée**
Vertebrates	42	107	122	132	134	138	144	Vertébrés
Invertebrates	3	5	7	7	7	8	8	Invertébrés
Plants	22	22	34	44	44	69	175	Plantes
Total	67	134	163	183	185	215	327	Total
Guinea-Bissau								**Guinée-Bissau**
Vertebrates	17	48	59	69	70	73	75	Vertébrés
Invertebrates	1	0	2	2	2	2	2	Invertébrés
Plants	4	4	5	5	5	5	10	Plantes
Total	22	52	66	76	77	80	87	Total
Guyana								**Guyana**
Vertebrates	41	46	63	65	67	73	83	Vertébrés
Invertebrates	1	1	1	1	1	1	1	Invertébrés
Plants	23	22	23	26	26	26	33	Plantes
Total	65	69	87	92	94	100	117	Total
Haiti								**Haïti**
Vertebrates	86	94	113	113	149	153	155	Vertébrés
Invertebrates	2	14	14	14	14	14	14	Invertébrés
Plants	28	29	42	42	42	80	94	Plantes
Total	116	137	169	169	205	247	263	Total
Heard Is. and McDonald Is.								**Île Heard-et-Îles MacDonald**
Vertebrates	12	12	12	12	12	12	12	Vertébrés
Invertebrates	0	0	0	0	0	0	0	Invertébrés
Plants	0	0	0	0	0	0	0	Plantes
Total	12	12	12	12	12	12	12	Total
Holy See								**Saint-Siège**
Vertebrates	...	1	1	1	1	1	1	Vertébrés
Invertebrates	...	0	0	0	0	0	0	Invertébrés
Plants	...	0	0	0	0	0	0	Plantes
Total	...	1	1	1	1	1	1	Total
Honduras								**Honduras**
Vertebrates	93	110	156	156	157	157	163	Vertébrés
Invertebrates	2	17	18	21	21	21	21	Invertébrés
Plants	111	113	120	123	123	131	134	Plantes
Total	206	240	294	300	301	309	318	Total

Country or area &	2004	2010	2015	2016	2017	2018	2019	Pays ou zone &
Hungary								**Hongrie**
Vertebrates	25	20	22	25	26	26	27	Vertébrés
Invertebrates	25	26	35	35	29	34	33	Invertébrés
Plants	1	1	10	# 12	11	45	59	Plantes
Total	51	47	67	72	66	105	119	Total
Iceland								**Islande**
Vertebrates	15	17	21	26	27	29	29	Vertébrés
Invertebrates	0	0	0	0	0	0	0	Invertébrés
Plants	0	0	0	0	0	0	2	Plantes
Total	15	17	21	26	27	29	31	Total
India								**Inde**
Vertebrates	283	390	520	528	530	540	546	Vertébrés
Invertebrates	23	113	135	135	135	135	136	Invertébrés
Plants	246	255	384	388	387	392	399	Plantes
Total	552	758	1 039	1 051	1 052	1 067	1 081	Total
Indonesia								**Indonésie**
Vertebrates	419	503	530	540	564	572	627	Vertébrés
Invertebrates	31	246	290	290	290	287	336	Invertébrés
Plants	383	393	426	427	427	436	509	Plantes
Total	833	1 142	1 246	1 257	1 281	1 295	1 472	Total
Iran (Islamic Republic of)								**Iran (Rép. islamique d')**
Vertebrates	65	82	94	105	106	111	118	Vertébrés
Invertebrates	3	19	24	24	24	24	24	Invertébrés
Plants	1	1	3	3	4	5	10	Plantes
Total	69	102	121	132	134	140	152	Total
Iraq								**Iraq**
Vertebrates	33	45	51	54	53	54	58	Vertébrés
Invertebrates	2	15	17	17	17	17	17	Invertébrés
Plants	0	0	1	1	2	2	3	Plantes
Total	35	60	69	72	72	73	78	Total
Ireland								**Irlande**
Vertebrates	18	24	32	40	41	42	44	Vertébrés
Invertebrates	3	2	6	6	6	6	6	Invertébrés
Plants	1	1	1	# 3	3	5	21	Plantes
Total	22	27	39	49	50	53	71	Total
Isle of Man								**Île de Man**
Vertebrates	...	2	3	3	3	3	2	Vertébrés
Invertebrates	...	0	0	0	0	0	0	Invertébrés
Plants	...	0	0	0	0	0	1	Plantes
Total	...	2	3	3	3	3	3	Total
Israel								**Israël**
Vertebrates	47	73	78	89	90	91	103	Vertébrés
Invertebrates	10	58	74	74	74	74	74	Invertébrés
Plants	0	0	0	9	10	23	28	Plantes
Total	57	131	152	172	174	188	205	Total
Italy								**Italie**
Vertebrates	53	70	76	85	87	89	91	Vertébrés
Invertebrates	58	77	136	141	194	222	222	Invertébrés
Plants	3	27	67	# 79	78	109	145	Plantes
Total	114	174	279	305	359	420	458	Total
Jamaica								**Jamaïque**
Vertebrates	54	58	69	71	82	87	91	Vertébrés
Invertebrates	5	15	15	15	15	15	15	Invertébrés
Plants	208	209	214	214	214	214	215	Plantes
Total	267	282	298	300	311	316	321	Total
Japan								**Japon**
Vertebrates	148	158	171	180	184	198	223	Vertébrés
Invertebrates	45	157	170	171	171	174	176	Invertébrés
Plants	12	15	23	# 46	49	50	60	Plantes
Total	205	330	364	397	404	422	459	Total
Jersey								**Jersey**
Vertebrates	...	2	2	5	5	5	6	Vertébrés
Invertebrates	...	0	1	1	1	1	1	Invertébrés
Plants	...	0	0	0	0	0	0	Plantes
Total	...	2	3	6	6	6	7	Total

Country or area &	2004	2010	2015	2016	2017	2018	2019	Pays ou zone &
Jordan								**Jordanie**
Vertebrates	27	41	40	47	47	48	55	Vertébrés
Invertebrates	3	48	61	61	61	61	61	Invertébrés
Plants	0	1	1	5	5	8	8	Plantes
Total	30	90	102	113	113	117	124	Total
Kazakhstan								**Kazakhstan**
Vertebrates	48	53	55	57	59	59	59	Vertébrés
Invertebrates	4	4	7	7	7	7	7	Invertébrés
Plants	1	16	16	16	16	14	15	Plantes
Total	53	73	78	80	82	80	81	Total
Kenya								**Kenya**
Vertebrates	99	137	157	162	162	169	176	Vertébrés
Invertebrates	27	72	84	84	86	87	92	Invertébrés
Plants	103	129	222	222	232	234	248	Plantes
Total	229	338	463	468	480	490	516	Total
Kiribati								**Kiribati**
Vertebrates	10	17	19	21	23	23	24	Vertébrés
Invertebrates	1	73	81	81	81	81	81	Invertébrés
Plants	0	0	0	0	0	0	0	Plantes
Total	11	90	100	102	104	104	105	Total
Kuwait								**Koweït**
Vertebrates	20	28	29	36	36	39	43	Vertébrés
Invertebrates	0	13	13	13	13	13	13	Invertébrés
Plants	0	0	0	0	0	0	0	Plantes
Total	20	41	42	49	49	52	56	Total
Kyrgyzstan								**Kirghizistan**
Vertebrates	12	23	23	26	26	26	26	Vertébrés
Invertebrates	3	3	4	4	4	4	4	Invertébrés
Plants	1	14	14	14	14	13	13	Plantes
Total	16	40	41	44	44	43	43	Total
Lao People's Dem. Rep.								**Rép. dém. populaire lao**
Vertebrates	72	107	148	153	147	149	164	Vertébrés
Invertebrates	0	3	21	21	21	21	21	Invertébrés
Plants	19	22	41	41	41	54	58	Plantes
Total	91	132	210	215	209	224	243	Total
Latvia								**Lettonie**
Vertebrates	15	9	13	16	17	18	18	Vertébrés
Invertebrates	8	9	12	12	12	12	12	Invertébrés
Plants	0	0	0	# 1	1	1	5	Plantes
Total	23	18	25	29	30	31	35	Total
Lebanon								**Liban**
Vertebrates	25	44	48	58	58	57	57	Vertébrés
Invertebrates	1	5	16	16	17	18	18	Invertébrés
Plants	0	1	5	10	12	24	29	Plantes
Total	26	50	69	84	87	99	104	Total
Lesotho								**Lesotho**
Vertebrates	11	10	10	11	11	13	13	Vertébrés
Invertebrates	1	2	3	3	3	3	3	Invertébrés
Plants	1	4	4	4	4	4	4	Plantes
Total	13	16	17	18	18	20	20	Total
Liberia								**Libéria**
Vertebrates	45	91	98	108	109	112	114	Vertébrés
Invertebrates	3	9	11	11	11	10	10	Invertébrés
Plants	46	47	49	52	52	53	83	Plantes
Total	94	147	158	171	172	175	207	Total
Libya								**Libye**
Vertebrates	24	42	49	55	56	56	57	Vertébrés
Invertebrates	0	0	2	4	4	4	4	Invertébrés
Plants	1	2	3	3	3	5	8	Plantes
Total	25	44	54	62	63	65	69	Total
Liechtenstein								**Liechtenstein**
Vertebrates	3	0	0	2	2	2	2	Vertébrés
Invertebrates	5	2	4	4	4	6	6	Invertébrés
Plants	0	0	0	0	0	0	4	Plantes
Total	8	2	4	6	6	8	12	Total

Country or area &	2004	2010	2015	2016	2017	2018	2019	Pays ou zone &
Lithuania								**Lituanie**
Vertebrates	12	12	14	17	17	18	18	Vertébrés
Invertebrates	5	5	7	7	7	8	8	Invertébrés
Plants	0	0	1	# 2	2	2	9	Plantes
Total	17	17	22	26	26	28	35	Total
Luxembourg								**Luxembourg**
Vertebrates	6	1	2	4	4	4	4	Vertébrés
Invertebrates	4	4	7	7	7	7	7	Invertébrés
Plants	0	0	0	0	0	0	5	Plantes
Total	10	5	9	11	11	11	16	Total
Madagascar								**Madagascar**
Vertebrates	222	283	446	527	543	551	554	Vertébrés
Invertebrates	32	100	110	110	172	194	195	Invertébrés
Plants	276	280	409	607	609	871	1 624	Plantes
Total	530	663	965	1 244	1 324	1 616	2 373	Total
Malawi								**Malawi**
Vertebrates	25	127	130	135	136	136	74	Vertébrés
Invertebrates	11	17	16	16	16	14	14	Invertébrés
Plants	14	14	25	24	24	26	37	Plantes
Total	50	158	171	175	176	176	125	Total
Malaysia								**Malaisie**
Vertebrates	190	246	269	282	288	280	343	Vertébrés
Invertebrates	19	242	262	262	264	265	282	Invertébrés
Plants	683	692	721	721	720	712	813	Plantes
Total	892	1 180	1 252	1 265	1 272	1 257	1 438	Total
Maldives								**Maldives**
Vertebrates	12	20	23	29	29	29	33	Vertébrés
Invertebrates	0	39	46	46	46	46	46	Invertébrés
Plants	0	0	0	0	0	0	0	Plantes
Total	12	59	69	75	75	75	79	Total
Mali								**Mali**
Vertebrates	19	23	31	34	34	35	37	Vertébrés
Invertebrates	0	0	0	0	0	0	0	Invertébrés
Plants	6	6	8	8	8	11	24	Plantes
Total	25	29	39	42	42	46	61	Total
Malta								**Malte**
Vertebrates	22	20	23	30	30	30	31	Vertébrés
Invertebrates	3	3	4	5	5	5	5	Invertébrés
Plants	0	3	4	4	4	4	4	Plantes
Total	25	26	31	39	39	39	40	Total
Marshall Islands								**Îles Marshall**
Vertebrates	12	17	22	25	28	28	28	Vertébrés
Invertebrates	1	67	73	73	73	73	73	Invertébrés
Plants	0	0	0	0	0	0	0	Plantes
Total	13	84	95	98	101	101	101	Total
Martinique								**Martinique**
Vertebrates	20	22	34	33	37	37	45	Vertébrés
Invertebrates	1	1	2	2	2	2	2	Invertébrés
Plants	8	8	9	9	9	9	9	Plantes
Total	29	31	45	44	48	48	56	Total
Mauritania								**Mauritanie**
Vertebrates	25	57	66	80	83	85	86	Vertébrés
Invertebrates	1	1	3	3	3	3	3	Invertébrés
Plants	0	0	0	0	0	0	0	Plantes
Total	26	58	69	83	86	88	89	Total
Mauritius								**Maurice**
Vertebrates	28	36	41	45	47	48	54	Vertébrés
Invertebrates	32	98	118	118	120	120	121	Invertébrés
Plants	87	88	90	90	90	91	91	Plantes
Total	147	222	249	253	257	259	266	Total
Mayotte								**Mayotte**
Vertebrates	6	9	15	18	18	19	22	Vertébrés
Invertebrates	1	60	69	69	70	70	72	Invertébrés
Plants	0	0	0	0	0	3	4	Plantes
Total	7	69	84	87	88	92	98	Total

Country or area &	2004	2010	2015	2016	2017	2018	2019	Pays ou zone &
Mexico								**Mexique**
Vertebrates	446	609	639	648	655	657	736	Vertébrés
Invertebrates	41	79	93	102	106	106	113	Invertébrés
Plants	261	255	377	402	401	450	529	Plantes
Total	748	943	1 109	1 152	1 162	1 213	1 378	Total
Micronesia (Fed. States of)								**Micronésie (États féd. de)**
Vertebrates	22	35	44	48	49	50	49	Vertébrés
Invertebrates	4	108	115	115	114	114	114	Invertébrés
Plants	4	5	4	4	4	4	5	Plantes
Total	30	148	163	167	167	168	168	Total
Monaco								**Monaco**
Vertebrates	9	11	13	17	18	18	19	Vertébrés
Invertebrates	0	0	3	3	3	3	3	Invertébrés
Plants	0	0	0	0	0	1	2	Plantes
Total	9	11	16	20	21	22	24	Total
Mongolia								**Mongolie**
Vertebrates	36	33	33	37	38	37	37	Vertébrés
Invertebrates	3	3	3	3	3	3	3	Invertébrés
Plants	0	0	0	0	0	0	2	Plantes
Total	39	36	36	40	41	40	42	Total
Montenegro								**Monténégro**
Vertebrates	...	44	49	57	57	56	55	Vertébrés
Invertebrates	...	28	34	35	39	42	42	Invertébrés
Plants	...	0	2	2	2	3	7	Plantes
Total	...	72	85	94	98	101	104	Total
Montserrat								**Montserrat**
Vertebrates	18	21	37	36	38	39	42	Vertébrés
Invertebrates	0	11	11	11	11	11	11	Invertébrés
Plants	3	3	6	6	6	6	6	Plantes
Total	21	35	54	53	55	56	59	Total
Morocco								**Maroc**
Vertebrates	40	86	90	101	103	105	103	Vertébrés
Invertebrates	8	40	52	60	66	69	69	Invertébrés
Plants	2	31	34	# 38	38	49	55	Plantes
Total	50	157	176	199	207	223	227	Total
Mozambique								**Mozambique**
Vertebrates	64	98	117	127	129	132	142	Vertébrés
Invertebrates	5	59	67	67	67	67	65	Invertébrés
Plants	46	52	84	84	113	122	170	Plantes
Total	115	209	268	278	309	321	377	Total
Myanmar								**Myanmar**
Vertebrates	107	143	163	178	183	187	197	Vertébrés
Invertebrates	2	64	77	77	77	77	77	Invertébrés
Plants	38	42	61	61	61	61	63	Plantes
Total	147	249	301	316	321	325	337	Total
Namibia								**Namibie**
Vertebrates	44	66	73	81	84	85	84	Vertébrés
Invertebrates	1	0	4	4	4	4	4	Invertébrés
Plants	24	26	28	28	27	27	27	Plantes
Total	69	92	105	113	115	116	115	Total
Nauru								**Nauru**
Vertebrates	5	12	12	14	14	14	15	Vertébrés
Invertebrates	0	62	68	68	68	68	68	Invertébrés
Plants	0	0	0	0	0	0	0	Plantes
Total	5	74	80	82	82	82	83	Total
Nepal								**Népal**
Vertebrates	69	83	85	87	84	84	85	Vertébrés
Invertebrates	1	3	3	3	3	3	3	Invertébrés
Plants	7	7	17	17	17	17	19	Plantes
Total	77	93	105	107	104	104	107	Total
Netherlands								**Pays-Bas**
Vertebrates	27	18	19	26	27	28	29	Vertébrés
Invertebrates	7	6	10	10	10	11	11	Invertébrés
Plants	0	0	0	# 3	3	4	19	Plantes
Total	34	24	29	39	40	43	59	Total

Country or area &	2004	2010	2015	2016	2017	2018	2019	Pays ou zone &
Netherlands Antilles [former]								**Antilles néerlandaises [anc.]**
Vertebrates	26	24	...	...	...	...	...	Vertébrés
Invertebrates	0	11	...	...	...	...	...	Invertébrés
Plants	2	3	...	...	...	...	...	Plantes
Total	28	38	...	...	...	...	...	Total
New Caledonia								**Nouvelle-Calédonie**
Vertebrates	34	61	109	114	116	117	118	Vertébrés
Invertebrates	11	97	125	125	125	125	125	Invertébrés
Plants	217	257	259	286	285	350	350	Plantes
Total	262	415	493	525	526	592	593	Total
New Zealand								**Nouvelle-Zélande**
Vertebrates	114	117	130	128	130	131	162	Vertébrés
Invertebrates	14	15	46	46	46	61	61	Invertébrés
Plants	21	21	21	# 23	23	24	24	Plantes
Total	149	153	197	197	199	216	247	Total
Nicaragua								**Nicaragua**
Vertebrates	49	61	79	78	78	79	84	Vertébrés
Invertebrates	2	17	18	20	20	20	20	Invertébrés
Plants	39	43	44	46	46	50	49	Plantes
Total	90	121	141	144	144	149	153	Total
Niger								**Niger**
Vertebrates	12	22	27	29	30	32	32	Vertébrés
Invertebrates	1	2	1	1	1	1	1	Invertébrés
Plants	2	2	3	3	3	3	4	Plantes
Total	15	26	31	33	34	36	37	Total
Nigeria								**Nigéria**
Vertebrates	61	113	127	145	148	148	151	Vertébrés
Invertebrates	1	12	17	17	17	13	13	Invertébrés
Plants	170	172	189	197	196	203	208	Plantes
Total	232	297	333	359	361	364	372	Total
Niue								**Nioué**
Vertebrates	12	20	20	22	22	22	23	Vertébrés
Invertebrates	0	23	30	30	30	30	30	Invertébrés
Plants	0	0	0	0	0	0	0	Plantes
Total	12	43	50	52	52	52	53	Total
Norfolk Island								**Île Norfolk**
Vertebrates	21	19	17	18	19	19	21	Vertébrés
Invertebrates	12	21	23	23	23	23	23	Invertébrés
Plants	1	1	1	1	2	2	2	Plantes
Total	34	41	41	42	44	44	46	Total
North Macedonia								**Macédoine du Nord**
Vertebrates	24	31	31	34	35	34	34	Vertébrés
Invertebrates	5	59	69	70	75	86	86	Invertébrés
Plants	0	0	0	0	0	5	7	Plantes
Total	29	90	100	104	110	125	127	Total
Northern Mariana Islands								**Îles Mariannes du Nord**
Vertebrates	22	29	37	39	40	40	39	Vertébrés
Invertebrates	2	51	57	57	57	...	57	Invertébrés
Plants	4	5	5	5	5	5	6	Plantes
Total	28	85	99	101	102	102	102	Total
Norway								**Norvège**
Vertebrates	22	27	30	38	40	42	43	Vertébrés
Invertebrates	9	7	10	10	10	10	10	Invertébrés
Plants	2	2	4	# 14	14	21	51	Plantes
Total	33	36	44	62	64	73	104	Total
Oman								**Oman**
Vertebrates	48	47	53	62	62	68	71	Vertébrés
Invertebrates	1	26	31	31	31	31	31	Invertébrés
Plants	6	6	6	6	6	6	6	Plantes
Total	55	79	90	99	99	105	108	Total
Other non-specified areas								**Autres zones non-spécifiées**
Vertebrates	79	104	114	123	123	129	134	Vertébrés
Invertebrates	0	122	128	128	128	128	129	Invertébrés
Plants	78	78	83	# 85	86	85	87	Plantes
Total	157	304	325	336	337	342	350	Total

Country or area &	2004	2010	2015	2016	2017	2018	2019	Pays ou zone &
Pakistan								**Pakistan**
Vertebrates	70	92	99	110	110	115	118	Vertébrés
Invertebrates	0	15	18	18	18	18	18	Invertébrés
Plants	2	2	12	12	12	12	12	Plantes
Total	72	109	129	140	140	145	148	Total
Palau								**Palaos**
Vertebrates	13	22	27	31	32	34	35	Vertébrés
Invertebrates	5	102	146	146	146	146	146	Invertébrés
Plants	3	4	4	4	4	4	5	Plantes
Total	21	128	177	181	182	184	186	Total
Panama								**Panama**
Vertebrates	113	125	148	151	153	154	161	Vertébrés
Invertebrates	2	20	22	22	22	22	22	Invertébrés
Plants	195	202	203	208	208	211	211	Plantes
Total	310	347	373	381	383	387	394	Total
Papua New Guinea								**Papouasie-Nvl-Guinée**
Vertebrates	141	139	146	155	160	161	166	Vertébrés
Invertebrates	12	171	181	181	181	180	178	Invertébrés
Plants	142	143	151	152	152	158	186	Plantes
Total	295	453	478	488	493	499	530	Total
Paraguay								**Paraguay**
Vertebrates	40	38	39	40	40	43	44	Vertébrés
Invertebrates	0	0	0	0	0	0	0	Invertébrés
Plants	10	10	19	19	19	19	20	Plantes
Total	50	48	58	59	59	62	64	Total
Peru								**Pérou**
Vertebrates	232	274	317	351	351	377	384	Vertébrés
Invertebrates	2	3	8	8	8	8	9	Invertébrés
Plants	274	274	318	334	326	328	351	Plantes
Total	508	551	643	693	685	713	744	Total
Philippines								**Philippines**
Vertebrates	225	262	291	302	306	302	284	Vertébrés
Invertebrates	19	213	237	237	238	238	240	Invertébrés
Plants	212	222	239	239	239	245	259	Plantes
Total	456	697	767	778	783	785	783	Total
Pitcairn								**Pitcairn**
Vertebrates	15	20	20	21	21	21	19	Vertébrés
Invertebrates	5	15	16	16	16	16	16	Invertébrés
Plants	7	7	7	7	7	7	7	Plantes
Total	27	42	43	44	44	44	42	Total
Poland								**Pologne**
Vertebrates	27	17	19	23	23	24	23	Vertébrés
Invertebrates	15	16	22	22	22	28	28	Invertébrés
Plants	4	4	10	# 13	13	14	32	Plantes
Total	46	37	51	58	58	66	83	Total
Portugal								**Portugal**
Vertebrates	51	71	81	92	94	98	101	Vertébrés
Invertebrates	82	79	94	97	103	197	205	Invertébrés
Plants	15	21	81	# 83	84	104	150	Plantes
Total	148	171	256	272	281	399	456	Total
Puerto Rico								**Porto Rico**
Vertebrates	44	49	70	69	69	72	76	Vertébrés
Invertebrates	1	1	0	0	0	0	0	Invertébrés
Plants	52	53	57	57	57	63	65	Plantes
Total	97	103	127	126	126	135	141	Total
Qatar								**Qatar**
Vertebrates	12	19	22	26	26	32	37	Vertébrés
Invertebrates	0	13	13	13	13	13	13	Invertébrés
Plants	0	0	0	0	0	0	0	Plantes
Total	12	32	35	39	39	45	50	Total
Republic of Korea								**République de Corée**
Vertebrates	54	58	65	72	74	78	82	Vertébrés
Invertebrates	1	3	4	5	5	8	8	Invertébrés
Plants	0	3	7	# 32	32	32	35	Plantes
Total	55	64	76	109	111	118	125	Total

24

Threatened species *(continued)*
Number of species by taxonomic group

Espèces menacées *(suite)*
Nombre d'espèces menacées par groupe taxonomique

Country or area &	2004	2010	2015	2016	2017	2018	2019	Pays ou zone &
Republic of Moldova								**République de Moldova**
Vertebrates	22	24	22	26	27	26	25	Vertébrés
Invertebrates	5	3	5	5	6	6	6	Invertébrés
Plants	0	0	2	2	2	2	2	Plantes
Total	27	27	29	33	35	34	33	Total
Réunion								**Réunion**
Vertebrates	18	16	22	24	24	24	29	Vertébrés
Invertebrates	16	73	87	87	89	89	89	Invertébrés
Plants	14	15	17	17	17	18	19	Plantes
Total	48	104	126	128	130	131	137	Total
Romania								**Roumanie**
Vertebrates	40	39	42	49	50	50	51	Vertébrés
Invertebrates	22	24	38	38	49	68	67	Invertébrés
Plants	1	1	5	5	5	7	20	Plantes
Total	63	64	85	92	104	125	138	Total
Russian Federation								**Fédération de Russie**
Vertebrates	114	93	126	134	136	139	139	Vertébrés
Invertebrates	30	25	36	36	39	39	38	Invertébrés
Plants	7	8	55	# 60	60	60	90	Plantes
Total	151	126	217	230	235	238	267	Total
Rwanda								**Rwanda**
Vertebrates	30	49	51	51	50	52	52	Vertébrés
Invertebrates	4	2	2	2	4	4	4	Invertébrés
Plants	3	4	8	8	8	41	71	Plantes
Total	37	55	61	61	62	97	127	Total
Saint Barthélemy								**Saint-Barthélemy**
Vertebrates	...	4	16	18	18	19	28	Vertébrés
Invertebrates	...	11	11	11	11	11	11	Invertébrés
Plants	...	2	2	2	2	2	2	Plantes
Total	...	17	29	31	31	32	41	Total
Saint Helena [5]								**Sainte-Hélène** [5]
Vertebrates	32	31	37	39	41	41	42	Vertébrés
Invertebrates	2	2	13	15	15	33	68	Invertébrés
Plants	26	27	30	44	44	44	45	Plantes
Total	60	60	80	98	100	118	155	Total
Tristan da Cunha								**Tristan da Cunha**
Vertebrates	...	...	...	...	...	...	42	Vertébrés
Invertebrates	...	...	...	...	...	...	69	Invertébrés
Plants	...	...	...	...	...	...	45	Plantes
Total	...	...	...	...	...	...	156	Total
Saint Kitts and Nevis								**Saint-Kitts-et-Nevis**
Vertebrates	17	24	39	39	40	40	43	Vertébrés
Invertebrates	0	10	10	10	10	10	10	Invertébrés
Plants	2	2	2	2	2	2	2	Plantes
Total	19	36	51	51	52	52	55	Total
Saint Lucia								**Sainte-Lucie**
Vertebrates	23	29	41	43	45	45	48	Vertébrés
Invertebrates	0	11	11	11	11	11	11	Invertébrés
Plants	6	6	6	6	6	6	8	Plantes
Total	29	46	58	60	62	62	67	Total
Saint Martin (French part)								**St-Martin (partie française)**
Vertebrates	...	4	38	37	39	40	43	Vertébrés
Invertebrates	...	11	10	10	10	10	10	Invertébrés
Plants	...	2	3	3	3	3	3	Plantes
Total	...	17	51	50	52	53	56	Total
Saint Pierre and Miquelon								**Saint-Pierre-et-Miquelon**
Vertebrates	2	4	7	11	12	14	16	Vertébrés
Invertebrates	0	0	0	0	0	0	0	Invertébrés
Plants	0	0	0	0	0	0	0	Plantes
Total	2	4	7	11	12	14	16	Total
Saint Vincent & Grenadines								**Saint-Vincent-Grenadines**
Vertebrates	20	24	39	41	43	44	45	Vertébrés
Invertebrates	0	10	10	10	10	10	10	Invertébrés
Plants	4	4	5	5	5	5	6	Plantes
Total	24	38	54	56	58	59	61	Total

Country or area &	2004	2010	2015	2016	2017	2018	2019	Pays ou zone &
Samoa								**Samoa**
Vertebrates	15	23	26	29	29	29	30	Vertébrés
Invertebrates	1	53	62	62	62	62	63	Invertébrés
Plants	2	2	2	2	2	2	2	Plantes
Total	18	78	90	93	93	93	95	Total
San Marino								**Saint-Marin**
Vertebrates	...	0	0	0	0	0	0	Vertébrés
Invertebrates	...	0	1	1	1	1	1	Invertébrés
Plants	...	0	0	0	0	0	0	Plantes
Total	...	0	1	1	1	1	1	Total
Sao Tome and Principe								**Sao Tomé-et-Principe**
Vertebrates	24	33	38	51	52	51	51	Vertébrés
Invertebrates	2	2	5	5	5	4	4	Invertébrés
Plants	35	35	38	38	37	49	49	Plantes
Total	61	70	81	94	94	104	104	Total
Saudi Arabia								**Arabie saoudite**
Vertebrates	37	47	57	66	68	69	77	Vertébrés
Invertebrates	1	53	59	59	59	59	60	Invertébrés
Plants	3	3	3	3	4	4	4	Plantes
Total	41	103	119	128	131	132	141	Total
Senegal								**Sénégal**
Vertebrates	40	72	82	95	98	101	106	Vertébrés
Invertebrates	0	1	13	13	13	13	13	Invertébrés
Plants	7	9	11	12	12	13	20	Plantes
Total	47	82	106	120	123	127	139	Total
Serbia								**Serbie**
Vertebrates	...	29	29	35	35	35	35	Vertébrés
Invertebrates	...	16	22	24	30	35	35	Invertébrés
Plants	...	1	5	# 6	6	7	14	Plantes
Total	...	46	56	65	71	77	84	Total
Serbia and Monten. [former]								**Serbie-et-Monténégro [anc.]**
Vertebrates	42	...	...	...	...	...	...	Vertébrés
Invertebrates	19	...	...	...	...	...	...	Invertébrés
Plants	1	...	...	...	...	...	...	Plantes
Total	62	...	...	...	...	...	...	Total
Seychelles								**Seychelles**
Vertebrates	35	45	54	55	57	58	64	Vertébrés
Invertebrates	4	100	319	319	320	320	321	Invertébrés
Plants	45	45	62	62	62	61	61	Plantes
Total	84	190	435	436	439	439	446	Total
Sierra Leone								**Sierra Leone**
Vertebrates	35	77	92	103	103	105	110	Vertébrés
Invertebrates	4	6	8	8	8	8	8	Invertébrés
Plants	47	48	58	65	66	71	111	Plantes
Total	86	131	158	176	177	184	229	Total
Singapore								**Singapour**
Vertebrates	30	58	56	63	63	67	77	Vertébrés
Invertebrates	1	162	173	173	173	173	173	Invertébrés
Plants	54	57	58	58	57	60	62	Plantes
Total	85	277	287	294	293	300	312	Total
Sint Maarten (Dutch part)								**St-Martin (partie néerland.)**
Vertebrates	...	...	37	37	39	40	43	Vertébrés
Invertebrates	...	...	10	10	10	10	10	Invertébrés
Plants	...	...	2	2	2	3	2	Plantes
Total	...	...	49	49	51	53	55	Total
Slovakia								**Slovaquie**
Vertebrates	27	15	16	19	20	21	21	Vertébrés
Invertebrates	19	17	22	22	24	32	32	Invertébrés
Plants	2	2	7	# 10	10	28	54	Plantes
Total	48	34	45	51	54	81	107	Total
Slovenia								**Slovénie**
Vertebrates	32	36	42	50	51	53	53	Vertébrés
Invertebrates	42	59	76	77	81	83	83	Invertébrés
Plants	0	0	7	# 11	11	11	26	Plantes
Total	74	95	125	138	143	147	162	Total

Country or area &	2004	2010	2015	2016	2017	2018	2019	Pays ou zone &
Solomon Islands								**Îles Salomon**
Vertebrates	52	63	70	75	77	75	77	Vertébrés
Invertebrates	6	141	151	151	151	151	150	Invertébrés
Plants	16	16	17	17	17	16	16	Plantes
Total	74	220	238	243	245	242	243	Total
Somalia								**Somalie**
Vertebrates	46	56	60	66	67	71	76	Vertébrés
Invertebrates	1	51	62	62	62	62	62	Invertébrés
Plants	17	21	43	43	46	46	49	Plantes
Total	64	128	165	171	175	179	187	Total
South Africa								**Afrique du Sud**
Vertebrates	155	185	209	219	233	248	242	Vertébrés
Invertebrates	127	159	202	202	202	208	208	Invertébrés
Plants	75	97	116	116	146	151	153	Plantes
Total	357	441	527	537	581	607	603	Total
South Georgia & Sandwich Is.								**Géorgie du S.-Îles Sandwich**
Vertebrates	12	10	9	9	9	9	9	Vertébrés
Invertebrates	0	0	0	0	0	0	0	Invertébrés
Plants	0	0	0	0	0	0	0	Plantes
Total	12	10	9	9	9	9	9	Total
South Sudan								**Soudan du sud**
Vertebrates	...	...	26	30	34	36	39	Vertébrés
Invertebrates	...	...	0	0	0	1	1	Invertébrés
Plants	...	...	16	15	15	16	17	Plantes
Total	...	...	42	45	49	53	57	Total
Spain								**Espagne**
Vertebrates	76	118	123	135	138	142	142	Vertébrés
Invertebrates	63	67	215	236	258	288	288	Invertébrés
Plants	14	55	213	# 221	221	251	306	Plantes
Total	153	240	551	592	617	681	736	Total
Sri Lanka								**Sri Lanka**
Vertebrates	112	149	159	167	167	172	175	Vertébrés
Invertebrates	2	120	130	130	130	130	129	Invertébrés
Plants	280	283	291	291	290	294	298	Plantes
Total	394	552	580	588	587	596	602	Total
State of Palestine								**État de Palestine**
Vertebrates	4	16	20	23	24	26	25	Vertébrés
Invertebrates	0	2	4	4	4	4	4	Invertébrés
Plants	0	0	0	3	3	6	10	Plantes
Total	4	18	24	30	31	36	39	Total
Sudan								**Soudan**
Vertebrates	36	49	57	63	67	73	82	Vertébrés
Invertebrates	2	45	50	50	50	50	50	Invertébrés
Plants	17	18	16	16	16	17	19	Plantes
Total	55	112	123	129	133	140	151	Total
Suriname								**Suriname**
Vertebrates	32	38	49	55	55	57	57	Vertébrés
Invertebrates	0	1	1	1	1	1	1	Invertébrés
Plants	27	26	26	27	27	27	28	Plantes
Total	59	65	76	83	83	85	86	Total
Svalbard and Jan Mayen Is.								**Îles Svalbard-et-Jan Mayen**
Vertebrates	9	3	5	7	7	9	10	Vertébrés
Invertebrates	0	0	0	0	0	0	0	Invertébrés
Plants	0	0	0	0	0	0	1	Plantes
Total	9	3	5	7	7	9	11	Total
Sweden								**Suède**
Vertebrates	20	15	16	24	25	27	28	Vertébrés
Invertebrates	13	11	15	15	15	16	16	Invertébrés
Plants	3	3	5	# 14	14	15	41	Plantes
Total	36	29	36	53	54	58	85	Total
Switzerland								**Suisse**
Vertebrates	17	14	15	18	20	22	22	Vertébrés
Invertebrates	30	28	43	43	44	47	47	Invertébrés
Plants	2	3	4	# 10	10	10	43	Plantes
Total	49	45	62	71	74	79	112	Total

Country or area &	2004	2010	2015	2016	2017	2018	2019	Pays ou zone &
Syrian Arab Republic								**République arabe syrienne**
Vertebrates	26	68	84	94	94	91	91	Vertébrés
Invertebrates	3	7	20	20	20	22	22	Invertébrés
Plants	0	3	4	13	18	26	31	Plantes
Total	29	78	108	127	132	139	144	Total
Tajikistan								**Tadjikistan**
Vertebrates	20	24	26	29	30	32	32	Vertébrés
Invertebrates	2	2	3	3	3	3	3	Invertébrés
Plants	2	14	12	12	12	12	13	Plantes
Total	24	40	41	44	45	47	48	Total
Thailand								**Thaïlande**
Vertebrates	136	201	234	245	248	255	275	Vertébrés
Invertebrates	1	185	211	211	211	211	212	Invertébrés
Plants	84	91	150	150	152	155	168	Plantes
Total	221	477	595	606	611	621	655	Total
Timor-Leste								**Timor-Leste**
Vertebrates	11	18	19	20	22	24	31	Vertébrés
Invertebrates	0	0	1	1	1	1	1	Invertébrés
Plants	0	0	1	1	1	1	3	Plantes
Total	11	18	21	22	24	26	35	Total
Togo								**Togo**
Vertebrates	22	43	51	63	65	70	74	Vertébrés
Invertebrates	0	1	3	3	3	3	3	Invertébrés
Plants	10	10	12	12	12	12	13	Plantes
Total	32	54	66	78	80	85	90	Total
Tokelau								**Tokélaou**
Vertebrates	6	10	11	14	14	14	16	Vertébrés
Invertebrates	0	31	35	35	35	35	35	Invertébrés
Plants	0	0	0	0	0	0	0	Plantes
Total	6	41	46	49	49	49	51	Total
Tonga								**Tonga**
Vertebrates	11	19	23	26	28	28	28	Vertébrés
Invertebrates	2	35	47	47	47	47	47	Invertébrés
Plants	3	4	4	4	4	5	5	Plantes
Total	16	58	74	77	79	80	80	Total
Trinidad and Tobago								**Trinité-et-Tobago**
Vertebrates	32	37	53	56	57	58	60	Vertébrés
Invertebrates	0	10	10	10	10	10	10	Invertébrés
Plants	1	1	2	2	2	50	51	Plantes
Total	33	48	65	68	69	118	121	Total
Tunisia								**Tunisie**
Vertebrates	31	57	61	70	70	71	71	Vertébrés
Invertebrates	5	11	15	17	19	20	20	Invertébrés
Plants	0	7	7	7	7	10	10	Plantes
Total	36	75	83	94	96	101	101	Total
Turkey								**Turquie**
Vertebrates	76	130	191	199	199	201	208	Vertébrés
Invertebrates	13	15	76	78	82	85	86	Invertébrés
Plants	3	5	103	# 105	107	114	132	Plantes
Total	92	150	370	382	388	400	426	Total
Turkmenistan								**Turkménistan**
Vertebrates	35	37	38	42	43	46	48	Vertébrés
Invertebrates	5	5	7	7	7	7	7	Invertébrés
Plants	0	3	4	4	4	4	4	Plantes
Total	40	45	49	53	54	57	59	Total
Turks and Caicos Islands								**Îles Turques-et-Caïques**
Vertebrates	18	22	37	37	41	42	44	Vertébrés
Invertebrates	0	10	10	10	10	10	10	Invertébrés
Plants	2	2	9	9	9	9	9	Plantes
Total	20	34	56	56	60	61	63	Total
Tuvalu								**Tuvalu**
Vertebrates	7	14	15	17	18	18	20	Vertébrés
Invertebrates	1	71	78	78	78	78	78	Invertébrés
Plants	0	0	0	0	0	0	0	Plantes
Total	8	85	93	95	96	96	98	Total

Country or area &	2004	2010	2015	2016	2017	2018	2019	Pays ou zone &
Uganda								**Ouganda**
Vertebrates	77	110	117	116	119	124	126	Vertébrés
Invertebrates	19	15	19	19	24	30	30	Invertébrés
Plants	38	41	52	52	53	64	83	Plantes
Total	134	166	188	187	196	218	239	Total
Ukraine								**Ukraine**
Vertebrates	40	45	47	52	53	53	53	Vertébrés
Invertebrates	14	15	23	23	31	38	38	Invertébrés
Plants	1	1	17	# 19	18	23	36	Plantes
Total	55	61	87	94	102	114	127	Total
United Arab Emirates								**Émirats arabes unis**
Vertebrates	23	32	33	41	41	45	49	Vertébrés
Invertebrates	0	16	15	15	15	15	15	Invertébrés
Plants	0	0	0	0	0	0	0	Plantes
Total	23	48	48	56	56	60	64	Total
United Kingdom								**Royaume-Uni**
Vertebrates	32	48	53	61	62	64	66	Vertébrés
Invertebrates	10	11	18	18	18	19	20	Invertébrés
Plants	13	14	16	# 22	22	48	78	Plantes
Total	55	73	87	101	102	131	164	Total
United Rep. of Tanzania								**Rép.-Unie de Tanzanie**
Vertebrates	144	313	346	355	355	360	366	Vertébrés
Invertebrates	33	80	129	129	125	129	147	Invertébrés
Plants	239	298	602	602	602	632	661	Plantes
Total	416	691	1 077	1 086	1 082	1 121	1 174	Total
U.S. Minor Outlying islands								**Îles min. éloignées des É-U**
Vertebrates	15	23	24	25	26	26	24	Vertébrés
Invertebrates	0	44	47	47	47	47	47	Invertébrés
Plants	0	0	0	0	0	0	0	Plantes
Total	15	67	71	72	73	73	71	Total
United States of America								**États-Unis d'Amérique**
Vertebrates	342	376	444	454	456	462	479	Vertébrés
Invertebrates	561	531	575	578	580	580	581	Invertébrés
Plants	240	245	280	# 447	477	498	556	Plantes
Total	1 143	1 152	1 299	1 479	1 513	1 540	1 616	Total
United States Virgin Islands								**Îles Vierges américaines**
Vertebrates	22	21	41	42	46	46	50	Vertébrés
Invertebrates	0	0	0	0	0	0	0	Invertébrés
Plants	9	12	12	12	12	17	17	Plantes
Total	31	33	53	54	58	63	67	Total
Uruguay								**Uruguay**
Vertebrates	48	78	79	82	82	85	86	Vertébrés
Invertebrates	1	1	2	2	2	2	2	Invertébrés
Plants	1	1	22	22	22	22	22	Plantes
Total	50	80	103	106	106	109	110	Total
Uzbekistan								**Ouzbékistan**
Vertebrates	29	34	34	39	39	43	43	Vertébrés
Invertebrates	1	1	3	3	3	3	3	Invertébrés
Plants	1	15	17	17	17	16	16	Plantes
Total	31	50	54	59	59	62	62	Total
Vanuatu								**Vanuatu**
Vertebrates	19	32	35	37	36	38	39	Vertébrés
Invertebrates	0	79	92	92	91	91	91	Invertébrés
Plants	10	10	10	10	10	10	10	Plantes
Total	29	121	137	139	137	139	140	Total
Venezuela (Boliv. Rep. of)								**Venezuela (Rép. boliv. du)**
Vertebrates	151	179	209	212	220	228	231	Vertébrés
Invertebrates	1	21	26	26	26	26	26	Invertébrés
Plants	67	70	77	82	82	81	90	Plantes
Total	219	270	312	320	328	335	347	Total
Viet Nam								**Viet Nam**
Vertebrates	144	186	239	260	260	278	310	Vertébrés
Invertebrates	0	92	127	152	152	152	154	Invertébrés
Plants	145	146	199	204	204	231	236	Plantes
Total	289	424	565	616	616	661	700	Total

Country or area &	2004	2010	2015	2016	2017	2018	2019	Pays ou zone &
Wallis and Futuna Islands								**Îles Wallis-et-Futuna**
Vertebrates	12	16	22	24	24	24	24	Vertébrés
Invertebrates	0	57	65	65	64	64	64	Invertébrés
Plants	1	1	1	1	1	1	1	Plantes
Total	13	74	88	90	89	89	89	Total
Western Sahara								**Sahara occidental**
Vertebrates	18	38	36	44	46	48	47	Vertébrés
Invertebrates	1	1	3	3	3	3	3	Invertébrés
Plants	0	0	0	0	0	0	0	Plantes
Total	19	39	39	47	49	51	50	Total
Yemen								**Yémen**
Vertebrates	34	48	57	67	68	72	78	Vertébrés
Invertebrates	2	62	68	68	68	68	68	Invertébrés
Plants	159	159	162	162	162	163	163	Plantes
Total	195	269	287	297	298	303	309	Total
Zambia								**Zambie**
Vertebrates	24	44	49	51	53	54	56	Vertébrés
Invertebrates	7	14	14	14	14	15	14	Invertébrés
Plants	8	9	20	20	21	22	28	Plantes
Total	39	67	83	85	88	91	98	Total
Zimbabwe								**Zimbabwe**
Vertebrates	24	34	38	39	41	42	43	Vertébrés
Invertebrates	2	5	5	5	5	7	8	Invertébrés
Plants	17	16	17	17	43	46	52	Plantes
Total	43	55	60	61	89	95	103	Total

Source:

World Conservation Union (IUCN), Gland and Cambridge, IUCN Red List of Threatened Species publication, last accessed July 2019.

Source:

Union internationale pour la conservation de la nature et de ses ressources (UICN), Gland et Cambridge, Liste rouge des espèces menacées publiée par l'UICN, dernier accès juillet 2019.

& Vertebrates consists of mammals, birds, reptiles, amphibians and fish. Invertebrates consists of molluscs and other invertebrates. Plants consists of plants, and since 2016, fungi and protists. Reptiles, fishes, molluscs, other invertebrates, plants, fungi & protists: please note that for these groups, there are still many species that have not yet been assessed for the IUCN Red List and therefore their status is not known (i.e. these groups have not yet been completely assessed). Therefore the figures presented below for these groups should be interpreted as the number of species known to be threatened within those species that have been assessed to date, and not as the overall total number of threatened species for each group.

& Les vertébrés se composent de mammifères, oiseaux, reptiles, amphibiens et poissons; les invertébrés se composent de mollusques et autres invertébrés. A partir de 2016, les plantes incluent aussi les champignons et les protistes. Veuillez noter que beaucoup d'espèces tels que les reptiles, les poissons, les mollusques et autres invertébrés, les plantes, les champignons et les protistes n'ont pas été encore évaluées dans le cadre de la Liste rouge de l'IUCN , donc leur statut est inconnu pour le moment (c.-à-d. ces groupes ne sont que partiellement évalués). En conséquence, les données présentées ci-dessous pour chaque groupe doivent être interprétées comme le nombre d'espèces connues et menacées parmi les espèces évaluées à ce jour, et non comme le nombre total d'espèces menacées dans chaque groupe.

1	Excluding overseas territories.
2	The figures for Amphibians displayed here are those that were agreed at the GAA Brazil workshop in April 2003; the "consistent Red List Categories" were not yet accepted by the Brazilian experts.
3	For statistical purposes, the data for China do not include those for the Hong Kong Special Administrative Region (Hong Kong SAR), Macao Special Administrative Region (Macao SAR) and Taiwan Province of China.
4	Excluding the north islands, Saint Barthélemy and Saint Martin (French part).
5	Including Ascension and Tristan da Cunha.

1	Non compris les départements d'outre-mer.
2	Les chiffres concernant les amphibiens sont ceux qui ont été convenus lors de l'atelier de l'Évaluation mondiale des amphibiens du Brésil en avril 2003 ; les "catégories conformes à la Liste rouge" n'ont pas encore été acceptées par les experts brésiliens.
3	Pour la présentation des statistiques, les données pour la Chine ne comprennent pas la région administrative spéciale de Hong Kong (RAS de Hong Kong), la région administrative spéciale de Macao (RAS de Macao) et la province chinoise de Taïwan.
4	Les îles du Nord, Saint-Barthélemy et Saint-Martin (partie française) sont exclues.
5	Y compris Ascension et Tristan da Cunha.

25

Water supply and sanitation services
Proportion of population using

Services d'alimentation en eau potable et d'assainissement
Proportion de la population utilisant des services

Country or area& Pays ou zone&	Year Année	Proportion of population using: - Proportion de la population utilisant des:					
		Safely managed drinking water services Services d'alimentation en eau potable gérés en toute sécurité			Safely managed sanitation facilities Services d'assainissement gérés en toute sécurité		
		Urban (%) Urbaine (%)	Rural (%) Rurale (%)	Total (%) Totale (%)	Urban (%) Urbaine (%)	Rural (%) Rurale (%)	Total (%) Totale (%)
Total, all countries or areas	**2005**	**86.2**	**43.0**	**64.2**	**37.0**	**26.1**	**31.5**
Total, tous pays ou zones	**2010**	**85.9**	**45.8**	**66.5**	**41.3**	**32.5**	**37.1**
	2017	**85.1**	**53.0**	**70.6**	**47.0**	**42.5**	**45.0**
Northern Africa	2005	...	...	...	32.8	...	20.1
Afrique septentrionale	2010	...	...	...	35.7	...	23.8
	2017	...	...	...	39.3	...	28.8
Sub-Saharan Africa	2005	43.7	7.4	19.6	18.4	14.9	16.1
Afrique subsaharienne	2010	46.0	8.9	22.4	19.1	16.1	17.2
	2017	50.0	11.6	26.9	19.8	17.5	18.4
Eastern Africa	2005	40.6	4.2	12.4	...	...	...
Afrique orientale	2010	45.6	5.8	15.5	...	...	...
	2017	53.2	8.9	21.1	...	...	...
Southern Africa	2005	89.3	...	...	...	...	...
Afrique australe	2010	87.2	...	...	...	...	...
	2017	81.9	...	...	...	...	...
Western Africa	2005	33.2	10.5	19.1	20.5	15.7	17.5
Afrique occidentale	2010	33.3	12.4	21.0	21.2	16.3	18.3
	2017	33.6	15.4	23.7	21.9	17.0	19.3
Northern America	2005	99.6	...	98.9	89.6	...	78.1
Amérique septentrionale	2010	99.6	...	99.0	90.1	...	79.0
	2017	99.6	...	99.0	90.2	...	79.8
Latin America & the Caribbean	2005	82.4	...	57.5	18.0	...	14.6
Amérique latine et Caraïbes	2010	82.3	39.0	73.0	25.0	...	20.7
	2017	82.3	41.7	74.3	37.0	...	31.3
Caribbean Caraïbes	2000	...	...	...	12.6	...	...
Central America	2005	...	37.3	43.8	19.5	...	15.0
Amérique centrale	2010	...	39.0	45.1	29.2	...	23.0
	2017	...	41.6	46.8	44.0	...	35.7
South America	2005	86.5	36.4	77.0	18.0	...	15.1
Amérique du Sud	2010	86.7	38.8	78.3	24.6	...	20.9
	2017	86.9	41.8	79.7	36.5	...	31.6
Asia	2005	86.1	46.8	62.9	27.3	23.7	29.8
Asie	2010	86.1	50.4	66.4	33.7	32.0	32.7
	2017	85.8	59.8	72.6	42.7	46.0	44.4
Central Asia	2005	85.2	34.4	58.2	46.6	...	...
Asie centrale	2010	87.6	41.6	63.7	49.0	...	...
	2017	90.4	52.9	71.0	49.0	...	...
Eastern Asia	2005	94.0	...	...	46.2	30.0	37.8
Asie orientale	2010	93.8	...	...	59.3	38.0	49.6
	2017	93.3	...	...	78.2	56.2	69.8
Southern Asia	2005	62.3	38.6	45.9	...	14.4	...
Asie méridionale	2010	60.7	47.1	51.5	...	24.3	...
	2017	58.5	59.9	59.4	...	38.7	...
Western Asia	2005	...	...	67.9	57.2	...	38.4
Asie occidentale	2010	...	...	71.8	60.9	...	42.4
	2017	...	...	75.8	64.0	...	45.9
Europe	2005	...	...	91.0	74.3	43.0	65.5
Europe	2010	...	...	92.4	77.9	50.1	75.6
	2017	...	...	93.4	81.1	53.3	78.9
Eastern Europe	2005	...	...	79.7	53.8	...	45.5
Europe orientale	2010	...	...	82.7	56.1	...	48.9
	2017	...	...	85.0	61.4	...	54.8
Northern Europe	2005	...	...	98.1	94.8	69.8	92.9
Europe septentrionale	2010	...	...	98.8	95.6	71.1	93.9
	2017	...	...	99.3	96.5	72.4	95.0
Southern Europe	2005	...	...	88.4	73.2	40.6	62.7
Europe méridionale	2010	...	...	91.1	82.6	63.2	76.6
	2017	...	...	94.0	85.2	65.4	79.5

Country or area&	Year	Proportion of population using: - Proportion de la population utilisant des:					
		Safely managed drinking water services Services d'alimentation en eau potable gérés en toute sécurité			Safely managed sanitation facilities Services d'assainissement gérés en toute sécurité		
Pays ou zone&	Année	Urban (%) Urbaine (%)	Rural (%) Rurale (%)	Total (%) Totale (%)	Urban (%) Urbaine (%)	Rural (%) Rurale (%)	Total (%) Totale (%)
Western Europe	2005	...	...	98.6	97.2	85.6	95.8
Europe occidentale	2010	...	...	98.7	97.8	85.7	96.4
	2017	...	...	99.0	98.4	85.9	96.9
Oceania	2005	93.4	...	...	57.9	22.1	46.4
Océanie	2010	95.3	...	...	61.6	22.8	49.2
	2017	96.1	...	...	66.7	23.5	52.9
Australia and New Zealand	2005	93.9	...	...	...	...	61.9
Australie et Nouvelle-Zélande	2010	95.7	...	...	...	...	66.1
	2017	96.5	...	...	...	...	71.9
Micronesia	2005	86.0	...	73.9	...	...	...
Micronésie	2010	87.3	...	75.9	...	...	...
	2017	89.5	...	79.2	...	...	...
Polynesia	2005	...	...	47.5	...	46.0	...
Polynésie	2010	...	...	48.6	...	46.5	...
	2017	...	...	49.4	...	46.2	...
Albania	2005	...	...	52.6	39.7	36.2	37.8
Albanie	2010	...	...	62.0	40.0	37.2	38.6
	2017	...	...	70.0	40.2	39.4	39.9
Algeria	2005	...	...	...	17.5	19.8	18.3
Algérie	2010	...	...	...	17.0	20.3	18.1
	2017	...	...	...	16.5	20.8	17.7
American Samoa	2005	...	...	12.5	...	...	...
Samoa américaines	2010	...	...	12.5	...	...	...
	2017	...	...	12.6	...	...	...
Andorra	2005	...	...	90.6	50.5	50.5	50.5
Andorre	2010	...	...	90.6	86.5	86.5	86.5
	2017	...	...	90.6	100.0	100.0	100.0
Armenia	2005	...	...	43.9	45.5	...	47.9
Arménie	2010	...	...	61.7	45.5	...	48.1
	2017	...	...	86.5	45.3	...	48.2
Australia	2005	98.3	...	...	...	...	65.1
Australie	2010	98.7	...	...	...	...	69.5
	2017	98.8	...	...	...	...	75.6
Austria	2005	...	...	98.1	100.0	92.3	96.8
Autriche	2010	...	...	98.5	100.0	92.3	96.7
	2017	...	...	98.9	100.0	92.3	96.7
Azerbaijan	2005	...	...	55.9	75.4	...	...
Azerbaïdjan	2010	...	...	68.7	84.8	...	...
	2017	...	...	73.6	92.2	...	...
Bahrain	2005	...	...	98.9	...	...	95.9
Bahreïn	2010	...	...	99.0	...	...	96.0
	2017	...	...	99.0	...	...	96.0
Bangladesh	2005	44.6	60.0	55.9	...	18.6	...
Bangladesh	2010	44.6	60.6	55.7	...	24.1	...
	2017	44.6	61.5	55.4	...	32.3	...
Belarus	2005	...	...	83.9	87.8	91.4	88.8
Bélarus	2010	...	...	90.1	85.8	84.7	85.5
	2017	...	...	94.5	81.7	76.4	80.5
Belgium	2005	...	...	99.5	...	...	86.9
Belgique	2010	...	...	99.5	...	...	90.3
	2017	...	...	99.5	...	...	97.1
Bhutan	2005	48.7	23.6	31.4	...	...	...
Bhoutan	2010	48.8	25.5	33.6	...	...	...
	2017	48.9	27.6	36.2	...	...	...
Bolivia (Plurin. State of)	2005	...	...	...	17.6	...	15.1
Bolivie (État plurin. de)	2010	...	...	...	20.2	...	18.1
	2017	...	...	...	24.7	...	22.9
Bosnia and Herzegovina	2005	...	...	88.0	7.2	...	19.1
Bosnie-Herzégovine	2010	...	...	88.5	8.6	...	19.9
	2017	...	...	88.8	11.3	...	21.6

		Proportion of population using: - Proportion de la population utilisant des:					
		Safely managed drinking water services Services d'alimentation en eau potable gérés en toute sécurité			Safely managed sanitation facilities Services d'assainissement gérés en toute sécurité		
Country or area& Pays ou zone&	Year Année	Urban (%) Urbaine (%)	Rural (%) Rurale (%)	Total (%) Totale (%)	Urban (%) Urbaine (%)	Rural (%) Rurale (%)	Total (%) Totale (%)
Botswana Botswana	2005	83.7	...	...	...	...	...
	2010	83.7	...	...	...	...	...
	2017	83.2	...	...	...	...	...
Brazil Brésil	2005	91.5	...	...	29.1	...	27.7
	2010	91.8	...	...	36.5	...	34.8
	2017	92.3	...	...	51.6	...	49.3
Bulgaria Bulgarie	2005	...	...	96.7	55.2	...	47.6
	2010	...	...	96.8	58.8	...	51.2
	2017	...	...	96.9	72.9	...	64.4
Cambodia Cambodge	2005	47.3	12.5	19.2	...	...	...
	2010	51.2	14.3	21.8	...	...	...
	2017	56.6	16.7	25.8	...	...	...
Canada Canada	2005	...	...	98.3	78.9	78.7	78.8
	2010	...	...	98.5	82.0	81.5	81.9
	2017	...	...	98.9	82.2	81.4	82.1
Channel Islands Îles Anglo-Normandes	2010	...	...	92.0	...	...	90.0
	2017	...	...	92.0	...	...	90.0
Chile Chili	2005	98.5	...	94.3	52.6	...	53.1
	2010	98.6	...	96.6	66.7	...	63.2
	2017	98.6	...	98.6	81.4	...	77.5
China [1] Chine [1]	2005	93.0	...	...	41.0	28.7	33.9
	2010	92.7	...	...	58.3	37.1	47.6
	2017	92.3	...	...	83.7	56.1	72.1
China, Hong Kong SAR Chine, RAS de Hong Kong	2005	88.2	...	88.2	92.1	...	92.1
	2010	97.2	...	97.2	91.9	...	91.9
	2017	100.0	...	100.0	91.8	...	91.8
China, Macao SAR Chine, RAS de Macao	2005	100.0	...	60.8	...	...	...
	2010	100.0	...	80.2	...	...	...
	2017	100.0	...	100.0	...	...	...
Colombia Colombie	2005	81.2	35.0	70.1	14.2	...	14.6
	2010	81.3	37.1	71.6	14.9	...	15.6
	2017	81.3	40.1	73.2	15.8	...	17.0
Congo Congo	2005	45.8	8.4	31.2	...	...	...
	2010	55.4	12.4	39.6	...	...	...
	2017	58.6	19.1	45.4	...	...	...
Costa Rica Costa Rica	2005	95.9	77.1	89.5	...	...	...
	2010	96.1	80.4	91.7	...	...	...
	2017	96.4	84.4	93.8	...	...	...
Côte d'Ivoire Côte d'Ivoire	2005	56.6	16.4	34.6	...	...	...
	2010	56.0	17.0	35.5	...	...	...
	2017	55.1	17.7	36.5	...	...	...
Croatia Croatie	2005	...	...	91.5	64.1	...	58.0
	2010	...	...	92.6	64.2	...	58.2
	2017	...	...	90.0	64.3	...	58.5
Cuba Cuba	2005	...	...	...	32.6	...	34.5
	2010	...	...	...	36.2	...	38.4
	2017	...	...	...	41.9	...	44.3
Cyprus Chypre	2005	...	...	96.3	86.4	...	76.2
	2010	...	...	98.5	86.3	...	75.9
	2017	...	...	99.6	86.3	...	75.5
Czechia Tchéquie	2005	...	...	96.8	88.0	77.3	85.2
	2010	...	...	97.4	92.4	80.8	89.3
	2017	...	...	97.9	97.8	85.1	94.5
Dem. People's Rep. Korea Rép. pop. dém. de Corée	2005	78.6	54.3	68.8	...	23.8	...
	2010	78.0	52.4	67.8	...	18.4	...
	2017	77.2	49.6	66.6	...	5.1	...
Denmark Danemark	2005	...	...	94.5	...	...	92.1
	2010	...	...	96.0	...	...	93.0
	2017	...	...	96.7	...	...	94.8

Country or area& Pays ou zone&	Year Année	Proportion of population using: - Proportion de la population utilisant des:					
		Safely managed drinking water services Services d'alimentation en eau potable gérés en toute sécurité			Safely managed sanitation facilities Services d'assainissement gérés en toute sécurité		
		Urban (%) Urbaine (%)	Rural (%) Rurale (%)	Total (%) Totale (%)	Urban (%) Urbaine (%)	Rural (%) Rurale (%)	Total (%) Totale (%)
Djibouti	2005	...	...	...	31.2	12.2	26.8
Djibouti	2010	...	...	...	35.6	15.0	30.8
	2017	...	...	...	41.5	18.9	36.4
Ecuador	2005	79.6	52.0	69.0	38.0	47.4	41.6
Équateur	2010	82.0	54.4	71.7	36.3	51.5	42.0
	2017	84.9	57.9	75.1	33.4	57.2	42.0
Egypt	2005	...	...	...	64.9	...	54.7
Égypte	2010	...	...	...	67.0	...	57.1
	2017	...	...	...	70.7	...	60.7
El Salvador	2005	81.8	...	...	...	...	...
El Salvador	2010	76.1	...	...	...	...	...
	2017	77.3	...	...	...	...	...
Estonia	2005	...	...	94.4	97.3	93.6	96.1
Estonie	2010	...	...	95.4	97.4	93.9	96.3
	2017	...	...	93.3	98.7	94.4	97.4
Eswatini	2005	75.0	...	...	...	...	...
Eswatini	2010	83.0	...	...	...	...	...
	2017	88.7	...	...	...	...	...
Ethiopia	2005	36.0	0.5	6.1	...	2.0	...
Éthiopie	2010	37.0	1.7	7.9	...	2.8	...
	2017	38.4	4.6	11.4	...	3.8	...
Finland	2005	...	...	95.4	99.0	...	99.1
Finlande	2010	...	...	98.4	99.1	...	99.1
	2017	...	...	99.6	99.3	...	99.2
France	2005	...	...	97.0	...	...	89.2
France	2010	...	...	97.3	...	...	88.8
	2017	...	...	97.9	...	...	88.4
French Guiana	2005	...	...	88.8	...	...	...
Guyane française	2010	...	...	89.6	...	...	...
	2017	...	...	90.8	...	...	...
Gambia	2005	50.1	...	...	...	...	...
Gambie	2010	59.2	...	...	...	...	...
	2017	68.3	...	...	...	...	...
Georgia	2005	...	...	76.4	7.0	...	22.9
Géorgie	2010	...	...	78.5	10.7	...	24.6
	2017	...	...	80.0	15.9	...	27.2
Germany	2005	...	...	99.8	97.5	90.5	95.8
Allemagne	2010	...	...	99.8	98.2	91.1	96.5
	2017	...	...	99.8	98.8	91.8	97.2
Ghana	2005	36.0	2.6	18.4	...	...	...
Ghana	2010	44.3	5.9	25.4	...	...	...
	2017	56.5	11.5	36.4	...	...	...
Gibraltar	2005	100.0	...	100.0	...	...	...
Gibraltar	2010	100.0	...	100.0	...	...	...
	2017	100.0	...	100.0	...	...	...
Greece	2005	...	...	99.4	86.8	...	79.9
Grèce	2010	...	...	99.8	90.8	...	84.0
	2017	...	...	100.0	96.6	...	90.4
Greenland	2005	...	...	94.5	...	...	92.1
Groenland	2010	...	...	96.0	...	...	93.0
	2017	...	...	96.7	...	...	94.8
Grenada	2005	...	...	83.2	...	...	...
Grenade	2010	...	...	87.1	...	...	...
	2017	...	...	87.1	...	...	...
Guadeloupe	2005	...	...	96.9	...	...	...
Guadeloupe	2010	...	...	97.1	...	...	...
	2017	...	...	97.4	...	...	...
Guam	2005	...	...	99.4	...	...	...
Guam	2010	...	...	99.5	...	...	...
	2017	...	...	99.5	...	...	...

Water supply and sanitation services *(continued)*
Proportion of population using

Services d'alimentation en eau potable et d'assainissement *(suite)*
Proportion de la population utilisant des services

Country or area& Pays ou zone&	Year Année	Proportion of population using: - Proportion de la population utilisant des:					
		Safely managed drinking water services Services d'alimentation en eau potable gérés en toute sécurité			Safely managed sanitation facilities Services d'assainissement gérés en toute sécurité		
		Urban (%) Urbaine (%)	Rural (%) Rurale (%)	Total (%) Totale (%)	Urban (%) Urbaine (%)	Rural (%) Rurale (%)	Total (%) Totale (%)
Guatemala Guatemala	2005	58.4	41.4	49.4	...	...	...
	2010	61.6	43.4	52.2	...	...	...
	2017	65.6	46.1	56.0	...	...	...
Honduras Honduras	2005	...	16.5	...	33.6	...	...
	2010	...	17.4	...	34.0	...	...
	2017	...	18.5	...	34.5	...	...
Hungary Hongrie	2005	...	...	56.1	95.2	98.2	96.2
	2010	...	...	70.0	95.0	98.2	96.0
	2017	...	...	89.6	94.7	98.2	95.7
Iceland Islande	2005	...	...	92.7	...	...	55.0
	2010	...	...	95.8	...	...	65.9
	2017	...	...	100.0	...	...	81.8
India Inde	2005	...	29.5	...	...	11.4	...
	2010	...	40.0	...	...	22.6	...
	2017	...	56.0	...	...	39.0	...
Iran (Islamic Republic of) Iran (Rép. islamique d')	2005	95.4	83.2	91.4	...	...	...
	2010	95.1	82.9	91.5	...	...	...
	2017	94.9	82.7	91.8	...	...	...
Iraq Iraq	2005	61.6	32.8	52.6	32.5	35.4	33.4
	2010	62.6	38.5	55.2	35.1	39.2	36.3
	2017	64.1	46.5	58.8	39.4	45.0	41.1
Ireland Irlande	2005	...	...	94.5	59.6	65.8	62.0
	2010	...	...	95.9	74.2	68.8	72.1
	2017	...	...	97.3	88.5	72.1	82.4
Isle of Man Île de Man	2010	...	...	97.2	...	...	...
	2017	...	...	97.2	...	...	...
Israel Israël	2005	99.9	100.0	99.9	83.7	82.0	83.6
	2010	99.8	99.7	99.8	87.9	86.1	87.8
	2017	99.4	99.2	99.4	93.8	91.8	93.7
Italy Italie	2005	...	...	89.2	...	...	...
	2010	...	...	91.8	96.2	96.1	96.2
	2017	...	...	95.0	96.3	96.1	96.2
Japan Japon	2005	...	...	97.9	...	...	98.2
	2010	...	...	98.1	...	...	98.7
	2017	...	...	98.5	...	...	98.8
Jordan Jordanie	2005	...	...	93.8	83.4	...	76.6
	2010	...	...	93.9	83.3	...	79.0
	2017	...	...	93.8	83.2	...	80.6
Kazakhstan Kazakhstan	2005	...	...	65.5	92.4	...	...
	2010	...	...	75.4	91.6	...	...
	2017	...	...	89.5	90.5	...	...
Kenya Kenya	2005	60.3	...	...	...	...	...
	2010	55.9	...	...	...	...	...
	2017	50.0	...	...	...	...	...
Kuwait Koweït	2005	...	...	100.0	...	...	100.0
	2010	...	...	100.0	...	...	100.0
	2017	...	...	100.0	...	...	100.0
Kyrgyzstan Kirghizistan	2005	82.1	30.5	48.7	...	...	...
	2010	87.5	40.7	57.2	...	...	...
	2017	93.5	53.9	68.2	...	...	...
Lao People's Dem. Rep. Rép. dém. populaire lao	2005	22.9	7.0	11.3	50.7	27.5	33.8
	2010	24.3	8.6	13.3	55.5	39.5	44.3
	2017	26.3	10.8	16.1	62.4	55.8	58.1
Latvia Lettonie	2005	...	...	93.0	85.6	66.9	79.6
	2010	...	...	93.8	86.9	70.9	81.8
	2017	...	...	95.2	90.2	76.5	85.8
Lebanon Liban	2005	...	...	45.2	...	...	18.1
	2010	...	...	46.3	...	...	19.6
	2017	...	...	47.7	...	...	21.8

Country or area& Pays ou zone&	Year Année	Proportion of population using: - Proportion de la population utilisant des:					
		Safely managed drinking water services Services d'alimentation en eau potable gérés en toute sécurité			Safely managed sanitation facilities Services d'assainissement gérés en toute sécurité		
		Urban (%) Urbaine (%)	Rural (%) Rurale (%)	Total (%) Totale (%)	Urban (%) Urbaine (%)	Rural (%) Rurale (%)	Total (%) Totale (%)
Libya	2005	...	...	...	...	...	28.3
Libye	2010	...	...	...	...	...	27.3
	2017	...	...	...	...	...	26.1
Liechtenstein	2005	...	...	100.0	...	...	99.7
Liechtenstein	2010	...	...	100.0	...	...	99.7
	2017	...	...	100.0	...	...	99.7
Lithuania	2005	...	...	73.1	92.3	70.5	85.0
Lituanie	2010	...	...	81.9	93.5	75.8	87.6
	2017	...	...	92.0	95.2	83.3	91.3
Luxembourg	2005	100.0	100.0	100.0	92.2	84.8	91.2
Luxembourg	2010	100.0	100.0	100.0	93.4	85.8	92.5
	2017	100.0	97.0	99.7	97.4	89.3	96.6
Malaysia	2005	...	...	93.2	...	...	78.8
Malaisie	2010	...	...	93.3	...	...	81.5
	2017	...	...	93.3	...	...	88.6
Mali	2005	...	...	...	7.7	11.7	10.4
Mali	2010	...	...	...	8.3	16.9	13.8
	2017	...	...	...	9.1	25.5	18.7
Malta	2005	...	...	100.0	93.0	93.0	93.0
Malte	2010	...	...	100.0	93.0	93.0	93.0
	2017	...	...	100.0	93.0	93.0	93.0
Martinique	2005	...	...	99.1	...	...	...
Martinique	2010	...	...	99.1	...	...	...
	2017	...	...	98.9	...	...	...
Mayotte	2010	...	...	83.7	...	...	...
Mayotte	2017	...	...	83.7	...	...	...
Mexico	2005	...	...	40.1	24.3	...	23.8
Mexique	2010	...	...	41.3	35.3	...	34.1
	2017	...	...	42.9	52.3	...	50.4
Monaco	2005	100.0	...	100.0	100.0	...	100.0
Monaco	2010	100.0	...	100.0	100.0	...	100.0
	2017	100.0	...	100.0	100.0	...	100.0
Mongolia	2005	...	...	23.5	...	...	...
Mongolie	2010	...	...	24.3	...	...	...
	2017	...	...	23.7	...	...	...
Montenegro	2010	94.6	...	89.1	30.6	...	...
Monténégro	2017	93.8	...	93.6	29.8	...	...
Morocco	2005	87.0	25.5	59.4	38.0	...	34.6
Maroc	2010	87.9	32.1	64.4	39.4	...	36.9
	2017	88.9	39.9	70.3	40.2	...	38.8
Mozambique	2005	...	...	...	...	5.6	...
Mozambique	2010	...	...	...	...	9.8	...
	2017	...	...	...	...	16.3	...
Nepal	2005	34.7	23.2	25.0	...	...	...
Népal	2010	34.5	24.2	25.9	...	...	...
	2017	34.1	25.6	27.2	...	...	...
Netherlands	2005	...	...	100.0	97.5	97.4	97.5
Pays-Bas	2010	...	...	100.0	97.5	97.4	97.5
	2017	...	...	100.0	97.5	97.4	97.5
New Caledonia	2005	...	...	88.7	...	...	...
Nouvelle-Calédonie	2010	...	...	92.8	...	...	...
	2017	...	...	96.7	...	...	...
New Zealand	2005	...	...	78.1	...	...	81.5
Nouvelle-Zélande	2010	...	...	88.7	...	...	84.5
	2017	...	...	100.0	...	...	88.7
Nicaragua	2005	66.6	30.1	50.5	...	...	...
Nicaragua	2010	67.0	29.8	51.0	...	...	...
	2017	67.4	29.5	51.6	...	...	...
Niger	2005	...	...	...	18.0	3.2	5.6
Niger	2010	...	...	...	20.3	5.0	7.5
	2017	...	...	...	23.4	6.9	9.6

		Proportion of population using: - Proportion de la population utilisant des:					
		Safely managed drinking water services Services d'alimentation en eau potable gérés en toute sécurité			Safely managed sanitation facilities Services d'assainissement gérés en toute sécurité		
Country or area& Pays ou zone&	Year Année	Urban (%) Urbaine (%)	Rural (%) Rurale (%)	Total (%) Totale (%)	Urban (%) Urbaine (%)	Rural (%) Rurale (%)	Total (%) Totale (%)
Nigeria	2005	23.8	12.6	17.0	25.7	24.9	25.2
Nigéria	2010	24.1	14.0	18.4	27.4	24.6	25.8
	2017	24.6	15.7	20.1	29.5	23.9	26.7
Niue	2005	...	...	98.1	...	...	...
Nioué	2010	...	...	97.6	...	...	...
	2017	...	...	97.2	...	...	...
Northern Mariana Islands	2005	...	...	83.7	...	...	...
Îles Mariannes du Nord	2010	...	...	86.5	...	...	...
	2017	...	...	90.2	...	...	...
Norway	2005	...	...	100.0	...	...	73.9
Norvège	2010	...	...	99.4	...	...	74.9
	2017	...	...	98.3	...	...	76.3
Oman	2005	...	...	75.1	...	...	...
Oman	2010	...	...	82.5	...	...	...
	2017	...	...	90.3	...	...	...
Pakistan	2005	49.3	31.9	37.8	...	...	...
Pakistan	2010	45.4	32.2	36.8	...	...	...
	2017	40.0	32.6	35.3	...	...	...
Paraguay	2005	69.0	33.9	54.1	50.7	45.3	48.4
Paraguay	2010	70.3	41.0	58.4	51.9	54.1	52.8
	2017	72.2	50.7	63.9	53.6	66.2	58.5
Peru	2005	57.2	16.0	46.9	23.7	...	19.6
Pérou	2010	57.9	18.0	48.5	34.9	...	28.8
	2017	58.8	20.8	50.4	51.2	...	42.8
Philippines	2005	60.3	30.7	44.2	48.9	38.7	43.4
Philippines	2010	60.8	32.3	45.2	50.7	42.9	46.4
	2017	61.5	33.7	46.7	54.0	49.6	51.6
Poland	2005	...	...	94.0	...	...	83.1
Pologne	2010	...	...	95.3	...	...	87.7
	2017	...	...	99.2	...	...	93.3
Portugal	2005	...	...	94.1	58.5	...	54.3
Portugal	2010	...	...	94.8	74.1	...	67.8
	2017	...	...	95.3	92.7	...	84.7
Puerto Rico	2005	...	...	75.0	...	...	32.5
Porto Rico	2010	...	...	80.3	...	...	32.5
	2017	...	...	94.1	...	...	32.5
Qatar	2005	...	...	96.6	...	...	86.3
Qatar	2010	...	...	96.6	...	...	88.5
	2017	...	...	96.2	...	...	96.0
Republic of Korea	2005	...	...	96.8	...	...	90.8
République de Corée	2010	...	...	97.7	...	...	95.7
	2017	...	...	98.2	...	...	99.9
Republic of Moldova	2005	...	...	50.5	74.1	...	...
République de Moldova	2010	...	...	62.2	75.2	...	...
	2017	...	...	72.9	77.9	...	...
Réunion	2005	...	...	95.8	...	...	...
Réunion	2010	...	...	96.0	...	...	...
	2017	...	...	96.2	...	...	...
Romania	2005	...	...	81.7	...	...	55.7
Roumanie	2010	...	...	81.9	...	...	63.3
	2017	...	...	81.9	...	...	76.5
Russian Federation	2005	...	...	74.9	61.4	43.6	56.7
Fédération de Russie	2010	...	...	75.3	62.2	48.4	58.6
	2017	...	...	76.0	63.4	55.2	61.3
Rwanda	2005	29.7	...	...	...	...	...
Rwanda	2010	35.2	...	...	...	...	...
	2017	43.4	...	...	...	...	...
Saint Helena	2005	...	...	88.7	...	...	...
Sainte-Hélène	2010	...	...	88.9	...	...	...
	2017	...	...	89.2	...	...	...

Country or area& Pays ou zone&	Year Année	Proportion of population using: - Proportion de la population utilisant des:					
		Safely managed drinking water services Services d'alimentation en eau potable gérés en toute sécurité			Safely managed sanitation facilities Services d'assainissement gérés en toute sécurité		
		Urban (%) Urbaine (%)	Rural (%) Rurale (%)	Total (%) Totale (%)	Urban (%) Urbaine (%)	Rural (%) Rurale (%)	Total (%) Totale (%)
Saint Pierre and Miquelon	2010	...	...	83.1	...	...	...
Saint-Pierre-et-Miquelon	2017	...	...	83.1	...	...	...
Samoa	2005	...	...	57.2	40.5	52.0	49.6
Samoa	2010	...	...	58.0	39.6	51.8	49.3
	2017	...	...	58.8	37.7	50.9	48.5
San Marino	2005	...	...	100.0	...	...	77.2
Saint-Marin	2010	...	...	100.0	...	...	77.2
	2017	...	...	100.0	...	...	77.2
Saudi Arabia	2005	...	...	...	...	...	69.8
Arabie saoudite	2010	...	...	...	...	...	73.1
	2017	...	...	...	...	...	77.8
Senegal	2005	...	...	...	16.1	15.6	15.8
Sénégal	2010	...	...	...	16.9	17.8	17.4
	2017	...	...	...	21.9	21.1	21.5
Serbia	2005	81.5	66.5	74.6	18.8	...	26.6
Serbie	2010	81.4	66.4	74.7	20.2	...	25.1
	2017	81.3	66.4	74.7	23.2	...	24.7
Sierra Leone	2005	11.0	2.9	5.9	17.5	5.6	10.0
Sierra Leone	2010	11.5	4.8	7.4	18.6	6.7	11.3
	2017	12.1	8.3	9.9	20.3	8.4	13.3
Singapore	2005	100.0	...	100.0	100.0	...	100.0
Singapour	2010	100.0	...	100.0	100.0	...	100.0
	2017	100.0	...	100.0	100.0	...	100.0
Slovakia	2005	...	...	94.7	89.5	76.5	83.7
Slovaquie	2010	...	...	97.9	89.0	76.2	83.2
	2017	...	...	99.8	88.4	75.7	82.5
Slovenia	2005	...	...	83.7	...	...	76.0
Slovénie	2010	...	...	90.1	...	...	79.4
	2017	...	...	98.1	...	...	83.0
South Africa	2005	90.4	...	...	...	...	...
Afrique du Sud	2010	87.3	...	...	...	...	...
	2017	81.9	...	...	...	...	...
Spain	2005	...	...	98.7	94.9	93.9	94.7
Espagne	2010	...	...	98.6	95.8	95.3	95.7
	2017	...	...	98.4	96.6	96.7	96.6
Sri Lanka	2005	86.2	...	...	...	...	...
Sri Lanka	2010	88.1	...	...	...	...	...
	2017	90.8	...	...	...	...	...
State of Palestine	2005	...	...	...	59.0	...	54.3
État de Palestine	2010	...	...	...	61.4	...	57.4
	2017	...	...	...	64.7	...	61.2
Sweden	2005	...	...	99.9	93.7	87.5	92.7
Suède	2010	...	...	99.9	93.9	87.7	93.0
	2017	...	...	99.9	94.2	87.8	93.4
Switzerland	2005	...	...	93.3	98.5	98.3	98.5
Suisse	2010	...	...	94.5	99.3	98.5	99.1
	2017	...	...	95.5	99.9	98.5	99.5
Tajikistan	2005	...	...	41.5	...	...	...
Tadjikistan	2010	...	...	46.0	...	...	...
	2017	...	...	47.9	...	...	...
North Macedonia	2005	97.8	95.1	96.7	11.3	...	13.5
Macédoine du Nord	2010	92.9	89.1	91.3	8.6	...	14.5
	2017	89.9	68.8	81.0	8.2	...	16.6
Tunisia	2005	...	...	63.2	77.7	...	63.9
Tunisie	2010	...	...	86.3	82.2	...	70.2
	2017	...	...	92.7	88.3	...	78.1
Turkey	2005	...	...	...	63.5	...	56.2
Turquie	2010	...	...	...	66.6	...	60.6
	2017	...	...	...	69.6	...	65.2

Country or area& Pays ou zone&	Year Année	Safely managed drinking water services Services d'alimentation en eau potable gérés en toute sécurité			Safely managed sanitation facilities Services d'assainissement gérés en toute sécurité		
		Urban (%) Urbaine (%)	Rural (%) Rurale (%)	Total (%) Totale (%)	Urban (%) Urbaine (%)	Rural (%) Rurale (%)	Total (%) Totale (%)
Turkmenistan Turkménistan	2005	85.9	61.3	72.9	...	...	...
	2010	92.2	73.5	82.6	...	...	...
	2017	96.9	90.7	93.9	...	...	...
Tuvalu Tuvalu	2005	49.2	...	...	5.2	4.3	4.8
	2010	49.5	...	...	4.7	7.8	6.1
	2017	49.8	...	...	4.2	9.7	6.3
Uganda Ouganda	2005	22.8	1.9	5.5	...	...	...
	2010	19.9	2.9	6.2	...	...	...
	2017	15.7	4.5	7.1	...	...	...
Ukraine Ukraine	2005	...	...	71.4	38.5	...	44.1
	2010	...	...	84.6	45.9	...	50.9
	2017	...	...	92.0	65.8	...	68.5
United Arab Emirates Émirats arabes unis	2005	...	...	...	...	...	91.3
	2010	...	...	...	...	...	93.4
	2017	...	...	...	...	...	96.3
United Kingdom Royaume-Uni	2005	...	...	100.0	99.0	91.8	97.5
	2010	...	...	100.0	99.0	91.8	97.6
	2017	...	...	100.0	99.0	91.8	97.8
United Rep. of Tanzania Rép.-Unie de Tanzanie	2005	10.3	...	...	16.9	8.8	10.8
	2010	28.0	...	...	24.0	15.0	17.6
	2017	35.0	...	...	31.4	22.4	25.4
United States of America États-Unis d'Amérique	2005	99.7	...	98.9	94.9	...	88.8
	2010	99.7	...	99.0	95.2	...	89.3
	2017	99.7	...	99.0	95.5	...	90.0
Uruguay Uruguay	2005	93.9	...	...	...	...	...
	2010	94.2	...	...	...	...	...
	2017	94.6	...	...	...	...	...
Uzbekistan Ouzbékistan	2005	84.8	30.9	57.1	...	...	...
	2010	85.4	30.2	58.3	...	...	...
	2017	86.1	31.1	58.9	...	...	...
Vanuatu Vanuatu	2005	...	...	40.0	...	...	...
	2010	...	...	41.8	...	...	...
	2017	...	...	44.1	...	...	...
Venezuela (Boliv. Rep. of) Venezuela (Rép. boliv. du)	2005	...	...	...	...	...	28.5
	2010	...	...	...	...	...	26.2
	2017	...	...	...	...	...	23.8
Yemen Yémen	2005	...	...	...	67.7	...	...
	2010	...	...	...	67.4	...	...
	2017	...	...	...	67.0	...	...
Zambia Zambie	2005	47.8	...	...	...	...	...
	2010	47.1	...	...	...	...	...
	2017	46.2	...	...	...	...	...
Zimbabwe Zimbabwe	2005	...	...	...	22.3	...	...
	2010	...	...	...	19.8	...	...
	2017	...	...	...	16.3	...	...

Source:

World Health Organization (WHO) and United Nations Children's Fund (UNICEF), Geneva and New York, the WHO/UNICEF Joint Monitoring Programme for the Water and Sanitation database, last accessed May 2019.

& The figures are estimated by the international agency, when corresponding country data on a specific year or set of years are not available, or when multiple sources exist, or there are issues of data quality. Estimates are based on national data, such as surveys or administrative records, or other sources but on the same variable being estimated.

Source:

Organisation mondiale de la santé (OMS) et Fonds des Nations Unies pour l'enfance (UNICEF), Genève et New York, base de données du Programme commun OMS/UNICEF de surveillance de l'eau et de l'assainissement, dernier accès mai 2019.

& Lorsque les données d'un pays sur une ou plusieurs années ne sont pas disponibles, ou lorsque plusieurs sources existent, ou s'il y a un problème de qualité des données, les chiffres sont estimés par l'organisme international. Ces estimations sont basées sur de données nationales comme les enquêtes, les registres administratifs, ou autres sources de la même variable estimée.

1   For statistical purposes, the data for China do not include those for the Hong Kong Special Administrative Region (Hong Kong SAR), Macao Special Administrative Region (Macao SAR) and Taiwan Province of China.

1   Pour la présentation des statistiques, les données pour la Chine ne comprennent pas la région administrative spéciale de Hong Kong (RAS de Hong Kong), la région administrative spéciale de Macao (RAS de Macao) et la province chinoise de Taïwan.

Country or area Pays ou zone	Year Année	Total R & D personnel Total du personnel de R - D	Researchers Chercheurs Total M & F Total H & F	Females Femmes	Technicians and equivalent staff Techniciens et personnel assimilé Total M & F Total H & F	Females Femmes	Other supporting staff Autre personnel de soutien Total M & F Total H & F	Females Femmes
Albania [1] Albanie [1]	2008	779	467	207	120	...	192	...
Algeria [1] Algérie [1]	2005	7 331	5 593	2 043	1 134	...	604	...
American Samoa [1] Samoa américaines [1]	2005	6	6	...	...	...	...	...
Angola Angola	2011	2 038	1 150	320	858	242	30	6
Argentina Argentine	2005	45 361	31 868	15 416	7 788	...	5 705	...
	2010	65 299	46 199	23 558	10 143	...	8 957	...
	2015	78 713	52 970	27 536	13 953	...	11 790	...
Armenia [2] Arménie [2]	2005[1]	6 892[3]	5 056	2 329	345	...	1 491[3]	...
	2010[1]	6 558[3]	4 981	2 261	479	...	672	...
	2016[4,5]	4 881[3]	3 682	1 917	320	168	537	283
Australia Australie	2004	116 194	81 192	...	17 600	...	17 402	...
	2008	137 489	92 649	...	24 243	...	20 597	...
	*2010	...	100 414	...	...	...	...	...
Austria [6] Autriche [6]	2004	42 891	25 955	4 740	12 067	2 901	4 869	2 471
	*2005	47 625	28 470	...	...	...	...	...
	2009	56 438	34 664	7 765	16 709	3 903	5 065	2 398
	*2010	59 923	36 581	...	...	...	...	...
	2015	71 396	43 562	10 114	22 387	4 651	5 447	2 326
	*2016	73 643	44 933	...	...	...	...	...
Azerbaijan [2] Azerbaïdjan [2]	2005	18 164[3]	11 603	6 056	1 825	...	3 086	...
	2010	17 924[3]	11 037	6 101	1 819	1 087	3 531	1 866
	2016	22 527[3]	15 548	8 871	2 019	1 060	2 574	1 468
Bahrain Bahreïn	2014	562	493	205	23	12	41	16
Belarus [2] Bélarus [2]	2005	30 222[3]	18 267	7 897	2 112	...	5 763	...
	2010	31 712[3]	19 879	8 392	2 248	...	9 585[3]	...
	2016	25 942[3]	16 879	6 686	1 618	...	7 445[3]	...
Belgium Belgique	2005	53 517	33 146	9 769	15 047	4 585[2]	5 324	2 702
	2010	60 075	40 832	12 962	14 401	5 079[2]	4 841	2 517
	2011	62 895	42 686	13 545	15 176	5 232[2]	5 033	2 575
	*2016	79 766	53 771	...	...	...	...	...
Benin [1,2] Bénin [1,2]	*2007	...	1 000	...	...	...	...	...
Bermuda [2] Bermudes [2]	2010	80	41	17	10	...	29	13
	2015	60	34	11	4	...	22	12
Bolivia (Plurin. State of) Bolivie (État plurin. de)	2002	1 090	1 040	...	...	...	50	...
	2010	2 497	1 646	...	258	...	593	...
Bosnia and Herzegovina Bosnie-Herzégovine	2005[1]	731	253	...	198	...	280	...
	2007[1]	1 554	745	...	270	...	536	...
	2016	2 109	1 422	677	216	110	188	115
Botswana [2] Botswana [2]	2005[1]	2 140	1 732	533	408	...	...	...
	2013	1 716	760	225	328	110	628	282
Brazil Brésil	#2005	174 035	96 939	...	77 096	...	...	...
	2010	260 014	136 946	...	123 068	...	...	...
	2014	347 737	183 853	...	163 884	...	...	...
Brunei Darussalam [1] Brunéi Darussalam [1]	2003	140	98	...	...	...	...	...
	#2004	...	102	...	...	...	...	...
Bulgaria Bulgarie	2005	15 853	10 053	4 673	3 778	2 256	2 022	1 349
	2010	16 574	10 979	5 506	3 704	2 189	1 891	1 172
	2011	16 986	11 902	5 940	3 263	1 970	1 821	1 139
	2015	22 492	14 236	6 818	...	...	...	...
	2016	25 060	16 001	...	...	...	...	...
Burkina Faso [2] Burkina Faso [2]	2005	942[1,7]	301[1,7]	37	225[1,7]	...	416[1,7]	...
	#2010	2 548	1 144	264	608	149	796	256
	#2014[5]	3 396	1 555	237	528	80	1 313	460

Country or area Pays ou zone	Year Année	Total R & D personnel Total du personnel de R - D	Researchers Chercheurs Total M & F Total H & F	Females Femmes	Technicians and equivalent staff Techniciens et personnel assimilé Total M & F Total H & F	Females Femmes	Other supporting staff Autre personnel de soutien Total M & F Total H & F	Females Femmes
Burundi [2]	2010	744[1]	374[1]	56	117[1]	...	253[1]	...
Burundi [2]	2011	746[1]	379[1]	55	125[1]	...	242[1]	...
Cabo Verde [1]	2002	151	60	...	15	...	76	...
Cabo Verde [1]	2011[8]	# 37	# 25	9	# 4	2	# 8	5
Cambodia	*2002[1]	494	223	50	170	...	102	...
Cambodge	2015	# 1 895	# 471	# 126	# 945	330	# 478	216
Cameroon [2]								
Cameroun [2]	2008	5 600	4 562	994	338	...	700	...
Canada	2005	218 590	136 700	...	52 825	...	29 072	...
Canada	2010	233 060	158 660	...	51 930	...	22 470	...
	2014	237 280	162 090	...	48 320	...	26 850	...
Central African Republic [2]	2005[1]	...	11	...	...	...	...	...
République centrafricaine [2]	2007[8]	...	41[1]	17	...	...	...	...
	#2009[1]	...	134	...	...	...	...	...
Chad [4,5]								
Tchad [4,5]	2016	1 097	843	43	121	17	133	18
Chile [6]	2010[9]	11 491	5 440	1 671	3 909	1 590	2 142	941
Chili [6]	*2016	16 633	8 993	2 979	5 402	2 398	2 238	829
China [10]	2005[6]	1 364 799	1 118 698	...	...	...	...	...
Chine [10]	2010	2 553 829	1 210 841	...	...	...	...	...
	2016	3 878 057	1 692 176	...	...	...	...	...
China, Hong Kong SAR	2005	22 053	18 024	...	2 346	...	1 683	...
Chine, RAS de Hong Kong	2010	24 060	20 582	...	2 159	...	1 319	...
	2016	29 047	24 865	...	2 351	...	1 831	...
China, Macao SAR [1]	#2005	413	298	77	110	...	5	...
Chine, RAS de Macao [1]	2010	676	350	116	313	158	13	9
	2016	1 749	# 1 623	# 662	# 98	# 34	28	22
Colombia	2005	...	5 264	1 808	...	...	...	...
Colombie	#2010	...	9 082	3 328	...	...	...	...
	2015	...	6 364	2 478	...	...	...	...
Congo								
Congo	2000	217[1]	102[1]	13	111[1]	22[2]	4[1]	...
Costa Rica [2]	2005	...	1 444	569	...	...	...	...
Costa Rica [2]	2010	6 156[5]	3 569[5]	1 475[5]	1 326[5]	388	1 261[5]	476
	2014[5]	6 370	4 072	1 803	1 342	416	956	292
Côte d'Ivoire [1]								
Côte d'Ivoire [1]	2005	...	1 269	210	...	...	...	...
Croatia	2005	9 270	5 727	2 710	2 633	1 196	910	584
Croatie	2010	10 859	7 104	3 485	2 601	1 280	1 154	768
	2015	10 645	6 367	3 159	3 157	1 507	1 121	720
	#2016	11 197	7 555	...	...	...	...	...
Cuba [2]	2005	33 988	5 526	2 703	...	...	28 462[11]	...
Cuba [2]	2010	16 641	4 872	2 381	...	...	11 769	...
	#2016	18 938	6 839	3 286	...	...	12 099	...
Cyprus	2005	1 157	682	239	273	98	201	105
Chypre	2010	1 302	905	337	216	89	181	101
	2015	1 246	856	328	218	92	172	89
	*2016	1 260	855	...	...	...	...	...
Czechia	#2005	43 370	24 169	6 349	13 773	5 153	5 429	2 633
Tchéquie	2010	52 290	29 228	7 429	15 971	5 141	7 092	3 369
	2015	66 433	38 081	8 923	19 350	6 102	9 002	4 391
	*2016	65 783[6]	37 338	...	...	...	...	...
Dem. Rep. of the Congo [2]	2005[3]	33 478	10 411	...	1 510	...	21 557	...
Rép. dém. du Congo [2]	2009[3]	34 820	12 470	...	1 843	...	20 507	...
	2015[1,7]	# 1 967	# 658	68	# 542	65	# 767	137
Denmark	2005	43 499	28 179	8 113	10 781	5 364	4 538	2 534
Danemark	2010	56 623	37 435	* 11 654	12 557	* 4 959	6 631	* 3 433
	2011	57 585	39 181	12 376	11 856	4 694	6 548	3 112
	*2015	59 532	42 425	13 257	...	...	...	...
	*2016	60 290	42 923	...	...	...	...	...

Population employed in research and development (R&D) (continued)
Full-time equivalent (FTE)

Population employé dans la recherche et le développement (R-D) (suite)
Equivalent temps plein (ETP)

Country or area Pays ou zone	Year Année	Total R & D personnel Total du personnel de R - D	Researchers Chercheurs Total M & F Total H & F	Females Femmes	Technicians and equivalent staff Techniciens et personnel assimilé Total M & F Total H & F	Females Femmes	Other supporting staff Autre personnel de soutien Total M & F Total H & F	Females Femmes
Ecuador	2003	...	645	...	...	...	...	...
Équateur	2010	4 769	2 110	854	1 029	300	1 630	783
	2014	8 948	6 373	2 630	1 435	714	1 140	649
Egypt	2010	86 455[1]	40 752[1,4]	16 972	20 758[1,7]	...	24 945[1,7]	...
Égypte	2016	115 641	65 097	27 871	31 795[4]	...	18 748[4]	...
El Salvador [2]	2005	...	260	81	...	...	...	...
El Salvador [2]	2010	...	516	190	...	...	...	...
	2015	1 085	# 1 001	# 404	44	15	40	21
Estonia	2005	4 362	3 331	1 317	567	274	464	305
Estonie	2010	5 277	4 077	1 688	907	404	293	211
	2015	5 636	4 187	1 831	888	428	561	392
	2016	5 771	4 338	...	...	...	...	...
Ethiopia	2005	5 112	1 608	111	779	...	2 725	...
Éthiopie	2007	6 051	1 615	125	978	...	3 458	...
	#2010	8 282	3 701	...	1 441	...	3 140	...
	2013	11 501	4 267	556	3 157	757	4 078	1 316
Faroe Islands Îles Féroé	2003	131	86	21	41	...	4	...
Finland	2005	57 471	39 582	...	...	...	...	...
Finlande	2010	55 897	41 425	...	...	...	...	...
	2016	47 429	35 908	...	...	...	...	...
France	2005	349 681	202 507	...	105 171	...	42 003	...
France	2010	# 397 756	# 243 533	* 46 001	# 118 364	...	# 35 860	...
	2015	428 643	277 631	* 74 762[9]	115 910	...	35 102	...
Gabon [1,2]	2004[7]	188	80	25	68	...	40	...
Gabon [1,2]	2009	# 839	# 531	# 118	# 142	55	# 166	66
Gambia [2]	2005[1]	84	46	4	28	...	10	...
Gambie [2]	2008	# 855	# 155	31	# 200	...	# 500	...
	2009	926	179	...	198	...	549	...
	2011	# 1 055	# 60[1]	12	# 737	...	# 233	...
Georgia [2]	2005	13 415	8 112	4 275	1 810	...	3 493	...
Géorgie [2]	2016[1,4,5]	12 475	9 103	4 757	1 595	945	1 774	919
Germany	2005	475 278	272 148	47 666	94 578	29 657	108 553	44 729
Allemagne	2009	534 975	317 307	65 258	111 660	34 277	106 008	44 018
	2010	548 723	* 327 996	...	* 113 211	...	* 107 515	...
	2015	640 516	387 982	87 756	156 202	41 497	96 332	45 205
	*2016	656 727	400 821	...	...	...	...	...
Ghana Ghana	2010	# 3 005	# 941	163	# 731	186	# 1 333	288
Greece [6]	2005	33 603	19 593	6 213	8 450	3 070	5 559	3 007
Grèce [6]	*2007	35 531	21 014	...	...	...	...	...
	#2011	36 913	24 674	9 602	6 336	2 973	5 903	2 897
	2015	49 658	34 708	12 370	...	...	...	...
	2016	41 790	29 403	...	...	...	...	...
Greenland Groenland	2004	48	40	11	8[12]	...	...	...
Guam Guam	2005	51	48	...	...	...	...	...
Guatemala [1]	2005	851	388	...	139	...	324	...
Guatemala [1]	2010	876	363	145	273	...	240	...
	2015	1 259	360	223	416	230	483	305
Guinea [1,2]	2000	3 711	2 117	122	768	...	826	...
Guinée [1,2]	2013	# 752	# 214	# 21	# 33	3	# 75	22
Honduras [2]	2003	2 280	539	143	...	...	1 741	731
Honduras [2]	2015[1,8]	# 304	# 207	# 85	91	47	# 6	# 3
Hungary	2005	23 239	15 878	...	4 591	...	2 770	...
Hongrie	2010	31 480	21 342	6 447	5 967	3 230	4 171	2 346
	2015	36 847	25 316	6 799	7 112	3 689	4 419	2 411
	2016	35 757	25 804	...	...	...	...	...

Population employed in research and development (R&D) *(continued)*
Full-time equivalent (FTE)

Population employé dans la recherche et le développement (R-D) *(suite)*
Equivalent temps plein (ETP)

Country or area Pays ou zone	Year Année	Total R & D personnel Total du personnel de R - D	Researchers Chercheurs Total M & F Total H & F	Females Femmes	Technicians and equivalent staff Techniciens et personnel assimilé Total M & F Total H & F	Females Femmes	Other supporting staff Autre personnel de soutien Total M & F Total H & F	Females Femmes
Iceland	2005	3 226	2 155	784	669	299	402	181
Islande	2009	3 397	2 505	1 000	626	279	266	96
	#2011	3 244	2 258	812	604	192	381	246
	2016	3 247	2 206	...	697	...	345	...
India	2000	318 443	115 936	11 304[9]	90 045[13]	10 363	112 462[13]	19 531
Inde	2005	391 149	154 827	19 707[9]	105 808[13]	...	130 514[13]	...
	2010	441 126	192 819	27 532	124 188[13]	...	124 119[13]	...
	2015	528 219	282 994	39 389	125 184	15 644	120 041	22 673
Indonesia	2001	51 544	42 722	...	...	...	...	...
Indonésie	* #2009[1]	...	21 349	...	...	...	...	...
Iran (Islamic Republic of)	2010[4,14]	...	54 813	14 775	...	...	...	...
Iran (Rép. islamique d')	2013	79 916	51 961	15 008	14 458	4 857	13 497	4 666
Iraq	2010[4,5]	16 857[3]	12 849[3]	4 380	1 927[3]	...	1 988[3]	...
Iraq	2016	3 741	2 371	982	952	435	418	163
Ireland	2005	16 690	11 587	3 241	3 043	797	2 060	881
Irlande	*2010	19 722	14 176	4 672	3 052	813	2 494	1 044
	2015	35 170	25 481	9 237	5 405	1 282	4 284	2 128
	*2016	36 087	26 293	...	...	...	...	...
Israel [6]	2011	70 401	55 184	11 700	9 818	2 320	5 399	2 006
Israël [6]	*2012	77 143	63 521	...	7 676	...	5 946	...
Italy	2005	175 248	82 489	26 797	...	...	...	...
Italie	2010	225 632	103 424	35 792	...	...	...	...
	2015	259 167	125 875	45 447	...	...	...	...
	*2016	258 585	126 674	...	...	...	...	...
Japan [6]	2005	896 855	680 631	...	71 726	...	144 498	...
Japon [6]	2010	877 928	656 032	...	74 857	...	147 039	...
	2016	872 340	665 566	...	64 208	...	142 566	...
Jordan	#2015[1]	3 348[15]	2 339	387	1 009	239	...	...
Jordanie	#2016[3]	...	5 660	1 189	...	...	...	...
Kazakhstan	2010	8 325	6 022	...	454	...	1 179	...
Kazakhstan	2016	16 664	12 369	...	2 661	...	1 634	...
Kenya								
Kenya	2010	# 42 566	# 9 305	1 861	# 26 384	12 024[2]	# 6 877	2 735
Kuwait	2005[1,7]	800	384	...	96	...	320	...
Koweït	2010[1,7]	829	407	152	87	23	335	145
	2015[4,5]	2 631	1 518	733[3]	210	59	862	363
Kyrgyzstan [2]	2005	3 419[3]	2 187	977	226	...	498	...
Kirghizistan [2]	2010	3 129[3]	1 974	876	261	...	428	...
	2016[4]	4 496[3]	3 454	1 707	336	161	391	239
Lao People's Dem. Rep. [1]								
Rép. dém. populaire lao [1]	2002	268	87	...	...	...	...	...
Latvia	2005	5 483	3 282	1 636	1 062	554	1 139	594
Lettonie	2010	5 563	3 896	1 823	915	401	752	439
	2011	5 432	3 947	2 045	819	387	666	440
	2015	5 570	3 613	1 809	...	...	...	...
	2016	5 120	3 152	...	...	...	...	...
Lesotho	2004	51[1]	20[1]	10[9]	21[1]	...	10[1]	...
Lesotho	2009[1]	105	46	16[9]	47	...	11	...
	2015[4,5]	72	50	20	14	7	8	2
Libya [2]	2004[1]	772	215	...	164	...	...	...
Libye [2]	2009	1 131[1]	460[1]	101	229[1]	...	268[1]	...
Lithuania	2005	11 002	7 637	3 706	1 436	939	1 929	1 280
Lituanie	2010	12 315	8 599	4 367	1 691	887	2 025	1 281
	2011	11 173	8 390	4 099	1 426	812	1 357	888
	2015	10 607	8 167	3 828	...	...	...	...
	2016	10 924	8 526	...	...	...	...	...
Luxembourg	2005	4 392	2 227	392	1 558	258	607	250
Luxembourg	2009	4 711	2 396	534	1 423	384	891	437
	2010	4 972	2 613	...	1 708	...	651	...
	2015	5 227	2 539	720	1 862	345	826	285
	*2016	5 196	2 505	...	...	...	...	...

Population employed in research and development (R&D) *(continued)*
Full-time equivalent (FTE)

Population employé dans la recherche et le développement (R-D) *(suite)*
Equivalent temps plein (ETP)

Country or area Pays ou zone	Year Année	Total R & D personnel Total du personnel de R - D Total M & F Total H & F	Researchers Chercheurs Total M & F Total H & F	Females Femmes	Technicians and equivalent staff Techniciens et personnel assimilé Total M & F Total H & F	Females Femmes	Other supporting staff Autre personnel de soutien Total M & F Total H & F	Females Femmes
Madagascar	2005	1 686[1]	879[1]	298	195[1]	...	612[1]	...
Madagascar	2010	# 1 785[1]	# 1 099[1]	371	# 326[1]	...	# 360[1]	...
	2016[4,5]	# 2 813	# 615	# 212	# 483	206	# 1 027	391
Malawi								
Malawi	2010	1 721[5]	732[5]	136	873[5]	155	116[5]	15
Malaysia	2004	17 887	12 670	4 701	1 598	...	3 619	...
Malaisie	2010	50 484	41 253	19 029	3 676	...	5 555	...
	2015	82 360	69 864	33 931	4 007	1 245	8 490	4 155
Mali	2010	856	443	62	342	44	71	34
Mali	2015[5]	1 283	538	55	322	72	423	102
Malta	2005	825	479	121	222	20[2]	124	65
Malte	2010	1 102	587	150	335	36[2]	179	87
	2015	1 422	820	218	332	34[2]	271	128
	*2016	1 430	829	...	...	...	...	...
Mauritania [2,8]								
Mauritanie [2,8]	2016	2 286[3,6]	2 263[3,6]	523[3,6]	14[1]	1[1]	9[1]	3[1]
Mauritius [5]								
Maurice [5]	2012	627	228	94	68	34	331	57
Mexico	2005	83 685	43 922	...	25 796	...	13 967	...
Mexique	2010	70 997	38 497	...	20 760	...	11 740	...
	2013	59 073	29 921	...	16 345	...	12 807	...
Monaco [1]								
Monaco [1]	2005	18	10	5	5[2]	...	3	...
Mongolia [2]	2000	2 113[1]	1 631[1]	...	294[1]	150	188[1]	...
Mongolie [2]	2005	2 283[1]	1 731[1]	819	81[1]	...	471[1]	...
	2010	2 517[1]	1 739[1]	865[1]	129[1]	48	649[1]	399
	2016[1]	2 211	1 644	807	83	27	484	298
Montenegro								
Monténégro	2015	673	523	239	81	39	68	47
Morocco	2010	28 041[1]	23 280[1]	7 744	1 697[1,7]	...	1 747[1,7]	...
Maroc	2016	40 543[1]	37 709	12 851[4,5]	1 414[1,7]	217[7]	1 420[1,7]	341[7]
Mozambique	2010	# 2 164[5]	# 912[5]	294	# 1 093[5]	...	# 159[5]	...
Mozambique	2015	2 320	1 162	336	723	217	435	144
Myanmar [1]								
Myanmar [1]	2002	7 418	837	...	6 499	...	82	...
Namibia [2]	2010	949	748	327	118	...	83	41
Namibie [2]	2014[1]	1 132	749	290	255	95	128	79
Nauru [1,2]								
Nauru [1,2]	2003	77	19	3	18	...	36	...
Nepal [2]	*2002	13 500	3 000	450	6 000	...	4 500	...
Népal [2]	2010	# 41 911[1,16]	# 5 123[1]	399	# 12 053[1]	...	# 21 167[1]	...
Netherlands	2005	93 599	47 854	...	23 265	...	22 480	...
Pays-Bas	2010	100 544	53 703	...	22 128	...	24 714	...
	#2011	117 436	61 335	15 629	34 107	7 340	21 993	8 723
	2015	129 060	79 155	21 118	...	...	...	...
	*2016	133 214	82 264	...	...	...	...	...
New Zealand	2005	18 929	12 986	...	3 200	...	2 800	...
Nouvelle-Zélande	2009	23 200	16 100	...	4 100	...	2 900	...
	2015	26 400	18 700	...	4 700	...	2 600	...
Nicaragua [2]	2002	456	256	96[9]	...	...	200	...
Nicaragua [2]	2004	371	326	...	45	15	...	...
	2012	1 225	874	...	231	...	120	...
Niger [1]								
Niger [1]	2005	595	101	...	137	...	357	...
Nigeria [1,2]	2005	66 574	28 533	4 839	10 854	...	27 187	...
Nigéria [1,2]	#2007	32 802[5]	17 624[5]	4 106	4 647[5]	1 026	10 531[5]	3 759
North Macedonia	2005	1 434	1 113	576	168	94	153	81
Macédoine du Nord	2010	1 434	1 102	620	170	104	162	106
	2016	2 107	1 778	960	177	97	152	72

26

Population employed in research and development (R&D) *(continued)*
Full-time equivalent (FTE)

Population employé dans la recherche et le développement (R-D) *(suite)*
Equivalent temps plein (ETP)

Country or area Pays ou zone	Year Année	Total R & D personnel Total du personnel de R - D	Researchers Chercheurs Total M & F Total H & F	Females Femmes	Technicians and equivalent staff Techniciens et personnel assimilé Total M & F Total H & F	Females Femmes	Other supporting staff Autre personnel de soutien Total M & F Total H & F	Females Femmes
Norway	2005	29 966	21 200	...	...	...	...	...
Norvège	2010	36 121	26 451	...	...	...	...	...
	2016	43 918	31 913	...	...	...	...	...
Oman								
Oman	2015	1 567	907	246	224	75	436	101
Pakistan	2005	53 159[4,5]	12 689[4,5]	2 053	6 471[4,5]	...	33 999[4,5]	...
Pakistan	2009	74 695[4,5]	27 602[4,5]	6 534	10 993[4,5]	...	36 100[4,5]	...
	2015[4,5]	101 519	55 611	19 097	13 450	1 259	32 458	2 504
Panama	2002	1 331[17]	297	...	...	...	1 034	...
Panama	2005	1 302[17]	344	...	...	...	...	...
	2008	1 449	463	...	377	...	609	...
	2009	531[17]	394	...	...	...	# 137	...
	2013	1 178	150	74	595	298	433	166
Papua New Guinea [5]								
Papouasie-Nvl-Guinée [5]	2016	593[1]	294[1]	85	89[1]	30	210[1]	82
Paraguay	2005	# 614	419	...	...	...	# 195	...
Paraguay	2008	667	466	...	...	...	201	...
	2011	# 496	# 317	...	79	...	# 100	...
	2015[5]	...	1 222	575	...	...	...	...
Peru [2]	2004	8 434	4 965	...	1 757	...	1 712	...
Pérou [2]	#2010	...	434	...	...	...	...	...
	2015	5 408	3 374	1 076	1 195	440	837	336
Philippines	2005	9 407[3]	6 896	3 500	897	...	1 440	...
Philippines	2009	10 366	7 505	3 882	1 116	381	1 743	708
	2013	26 577	18 481	8 872	2 765	1 041	5 140	2 086
Poland	2005	76 761	62 162	24 521	8 947	...	5 652	...
Pologne	2010	81 843	64 511	24 745	10 939	...	6 393	...
	2015	109 249	82 594	29 190	16 872	...	9 783	...
Portugal	2005	25 728	21 126	9 530	2 918	1 177	1 683	954
Portugal	2010	47 616	41 523	18 175	4 004	1 481	2 088	894
	2015	47 999	38 672	16 769	7 805	3 391	1 523	790
	*2016	50 912	40 746	...	...	...	...	...
Puerto Rico [2]	2009	5 776	2 986	...	2 790	...	...	...
Porto Rico [2]	2015	5 500	2 070	...	3 040	...	390[4,13]	...
Qatar								
Qatar	2015	3 016	1 498	451	1 002	424	516	335
Republic of Korea	2005[6]	215 345	179 812	...	26 272	...	9 261	...
République de Corée	2010	335 228	264 118	...	47 557	...	23 554	...
	2016	447 408	361 292	...	62 598	...	23 519	...
Republic of Moldova	2005	4 672[9]	2 583[9]	1 120	334[9]	...	1 755[9]	...
République de Moldova	2010	4 316	2 709	1 258	287	202	1 320	773
	2016	3 939	2 577	1 280	261	166	1 101	573
Romania	2005	33 222	22 958	10 617	4 998	2 859	5 266	2 414
Roumanie	2010	26 171	19 780	8 797	3 139	1 695	3 252	1 424
	2015	31 331	17 459	7 898	5 328	2 433	8 544	3 675
	2016	32 232	18 046	...	...	...	...	...
Russian Federation	2005	919 716	464 577	...	74 253	...	380 886	...
Fédération de Russie	2010	839 992	442 071	...	68 042	...	329 879	...
	2016	802 317	428 884	...	66 957	...	306 475	...
Rwanda [2,8]								
Rwanda [2,8]	2009	1 001[1]	564[1]	123	8[1]	...	429[1]	...
Saint Helena								
Sainte-Hélène	2000	33[1]	2[1]	...	8[1]	4	23[1]	...
Saint Vincent & Grenadines [2]								
Saint-Vincent-Grenadines [2]	2002	131	21	...	110	...	...	...
Saudi Arabia [2]	2002[1,8]	4 182	1 513	263	1 674	...	995	...
Arabie saoudite [2]	2009	2 655[1,7]	1 271[1,7]	18	658[1,7]	...	726[1,7]	...
	2013[3]	# 751 927	# 35 324	# 8 198	# 100 053	39 420	# 616 550	276 272
Senegal	2010	5 642	4 679	1 162	441	101	523	161
Sénégal	2015[5]	9 329	8 227	2 486	538	166	563	150

Country or area Pays ou zone	Year Année	Total R & D personnel Total du personnel de R-D	Researchers Chercheurs Total M & F Total H & F	Females Femmes	Technicians and equivalent staff Techniciens et personnel assimilé Total M & F Total H & F	Females Femmes	Other supporting staff Autre personnel de soutien Total M & F Total H & F	Females Femmes
Serbia	2010[18]	17 274	10 985	5 370	2 428	1 475	3 861	1 954
Serbie	2016	21 603[18]	15 015[18]	7 262	3 034[18]	1 574	3 554[18]	1 778
Seychelles [1]								
Seychelles [1]	2005	180	13	4	53	...	114	...
Singapore	2005	28 586	23 789	...	2 375	...	2 422	...
Singapour	2010	37 013	32 031	...	2 342	...	2 641	...
	2014	42 543	36 666	...	2 490	...	3 387	...
Slovakia	2005	14 404	10 921	4 484	2 245	1 218	1 238	670
Slovaquie	2010	18 188	15 183	6 376	2 087	1 046	918	589
	2015	17 591	14 406	6 029	2 116	885	1 070	599
	2016	17 768	14 149		...	...	...	
Slovenia	2005	8 994	5 253	1 777	2 820	1 067	921	501
Slovénie	2010	12 940	7 703	2 668	3 928	1 386	1 309	642
	2015	14 225	7 900	2 686	4 970	1 560	1 354	588
	*2016	14 357	8 102					
South Africa	2005	28 798	17 303	6 272	5 248	1 749	6 247	2 928
Afrique du Sud	2010	29 486	18 720	7 649	5 410	2 016	5 357	2 546
	2015	41 055	26 159	11 536	7 688	2 844	7 207	3 543
Spain	2005	174 773	109 720	41 371	39 904	13 259[2]	25 149	11 390
Espagne	2010[6]	222 022	134 653	51 831	60 697	24 052[2]	26 672	12 988
	2015[6]	200 866	122 437	47 729	55 523	22 009[2]	22 906	11 559
	2016[6]	205 873	126 633	...	...	...	...	
Sri Lanka	#2004	5 475	2 679	861	1 474	...	1 322	...
Sri Lanka	2010	5 714	2 140	842	1 851	...	1 723	...
	2014	5 106	2 057	951	1 719	621	1 330	427
State of Palestine	2007	566[1,14,18]	280[1,14,18]	94	91[14,18]	...	195[1,18]	...
État de Palestine	2010[5]	2 074	1 312	...	291	...	471	...
	2013[5]	5 161	2 492	...	772	...	# 1 483	...
Sudan [2]								
Soudan [2]	2005	23 726[3]	* 11 208[3]	* 4 483	* 5 569[3]	...	* 6 949[3]	...
Sudan [former] [2]								
Soudan [anc.] [2]	*2005	23 726	11 208	4 483	5 569	...	6 949	...
Eswatini								
Eswatini	2015	408	157	71	40	20	211	93
Sweden	* #2005	77 557	55 001	15 960[6]	...	...	...	...
Suède	*2009	77 363	47 308	14 080	19 686	4 849[2]	10 369	3 817
	*2010	77 418	49 312	...	...	...	...	
	*2011	78 445	48 702	14 721	19 194	4 860[2]	10 551	3 941
	*2015	83 551	66 734	18 195	...	...	...	
	*2016	90 690	70 372	...	...	...	...	
Switzerland	2004	52 250	25 400	...	17 130	...	9 720	...
Suisse	2008	62 066	25 142	...	21 763	...	15 161	...
	2015	81 451	43 740	...	24 353	...	13 359	...
Tajikistan [2]	2004	2 487[3]	1 548	407	247	...	692[3]	...
Tadjikistan [2]	2005	3 220[3]	1 993	...	324	...	903[3]	...
	2006	3 110[3]	1 895	735	202	...	1 013[3]	...
	2010[4,5]	2 827[3]	1 802	...	329	...	427	...
	2016[4,5]	3 894[3]	2 601	960	479	250	504	265
Thailand	2005	36 967	20 506	10 241	10 520	...	5 941	...
Thaïlande	2009	# 60 344	22 000	11 064	# 15 036	...	# 23 308	...
	2015	89 617	59 416	16 577[5]	16 539	3 950[5]	5 701	2 662[5]
Togo	#2005[8]	312	186	...	126	...	...	...
Togo	2010	# 444[5]	# 220[5]	21	# 54[5]	10	# 169[5]	14
	2016[4,5]	323[1]	242	24	18[1]	4[1]	63[1]	23[1]
Trinidad and Tobago [2]	2005	954	548	183	406	180	...	...
Trinité-et-Tobago [2]	2010	1 351	951	462	400	152	...	...
	2015	2 532	1 277	685	673	229	582	276
Tunisia	2010	15 589	14 727	7 654	499[7]	197[7]	363[7]	228[7]
Tunisie	2016	23 590	22 407	13 384	717[7]	300[7]	466[7]	284[7]

Country or area Pays ou zone	Year Année	Total R & D personnel Total du personnel de R - D	Researchers Chercheurs Total M & F Total H & F	Females Femmes	Technicians and equivalent staff Techniciens et personnel assimilé Total M & F Total H & F	Females Femmes	Other supporting staff Autre personnel de soutien Total M & F Total H & F	Females Femmes
Turkey	2005	* 49 251	39 139	13 381	* 4 753	* 988	* 5 360	* 978
Turquie	2010	* 81 792	64 341	21 056	* 10 352	* 1 741	* 7 099	* 1 551
	2015	* 122 288	95 161	31 385	* 17 318	* 3 378	* 9 810	* 2 748
Uganda [2]	2005	1 686	776	291	472	...	438	...
Ouganda [2]	2010	4 270	# 2 823	687	# 922	254	# 525	155
	2014	# 2 881	# 1 942	# 578	# 599	205	# 340	135
Ukraine	2007	132 926[9]	67 493[9]	29 620	15 045[9]	...	25 160[9]	...
Ukraine	2010[9]	116 321	60 812	...	13 053	...	21 593	...
	2016	# 71 071[18]	# 44 177[18]	# 19 386[2]	# 7 586[18]	4 204	# 19 308[18]	8 840
United Arab Emirates	2011	11 400	...	...	...	...	...	...
Émirats arabes unis	2016	...	22 308	...	...	...	...	...
United Kingdom	*2005	# 324 917	# 248 599	...	41 494	...	34 824	...
Royaume-Uni	*2010	350 766	256 585	...	59 290	...	34 891	...
	2015	413 860	284 483	...	* 88 910	...	* 40 468	...
	*2016	419 898	291 416	...	...	...	...	...
United Rep. of Tanzania	2010	2 929[1,5]	1 600[1,5]	393	472[1,5]	112	857[1,5]	310
Rép.-Unie de Tanzanie	2013[1,5]	1 967	929	228	301	62	737	277
United States of America	*2005	...	1 101 105	...	...	...	...	...
États-Unis d'Amérique	*2010	...	1 198 777	...	...	...	...	...
	*2015	...	1 379 977	...	...	...	...	...
United States Virgin Isl. [1,2]	2000	33	11	2	6	...	16	...
Îles Vierges américaines [1,2]	2005	37	6	...	12	...	11	...
	2007	42	6	...	13	...	14	...
Uruguay	2002	1 412	1 242	...	...	...	170	...
Uruguay	2010	...	1 853	...	...	...	...	...
	2016	...	2 222	1 084	...	...	...	...
Uzbekistan	2005	24 132[3]	16 723	6 663	2 206	1 099	3 113	1 547
Ouzbékistan	2010	21 555[3]	15 540	6 193	1 900	955	1 978	988
	2016	20 929[3]	15 911	6 107	1 960	944	1 742	770
Venezuela (Boliv. Rep. of) [1]	2005	...	3 248	...	...	...	...	...
Venezuela (Rép. bol. du) [1]	2009	...	5 209	2 782	...	...	...	...
	2010	...	5 803	...	...	...	...	...
	2015	...	7 488	4 615	...	...	...	...
Viet Nam	2002	...	41 117	17 585	...	...	...	...
Viet Nam	2015	167 746	131 045	58 694	11 522	4 961	16 934	9 475
Zambia [2]	2005	3 285[1]	792[1]	116[9]	1 240[1]	...	1 253[1]	...
Zambie [2]	#2008	2 219	612	188	835	270	772	360
Zimbabwe								
Zimbabwe	2012	1 741[5]	1 305[5]	332	141[5]	41	295[5]	100

Source:

United Nations Educational, Scientific and Cultural Organization (UNESCO), Montreal, the UNESCO Institute for Statistics (UIS) statistics database, last accessed September 2018.

Source:

Organisation des Nations Unies pour l'éducation, la science et la culture (UNESCO), Montréal, base de données statistiques de l'Institut de statistique (ISU) de l'UNESCO, dernier accès septembre 2018.

1	Partial data.
2	Head count instead of Full-time equivalent.
3	Overestimated or based on overestimated data.
4	Excluding private non-profit.
5	Excluding business enterprise.
6	Do not correspond exactly to Frascati Manual recommendations.
7	Government only.
8	Higher Education only.
9	Underestimated or based on underestimated data.

1	Données partielles.
2	Personnes physiques au lieu d'Equivalents temps plein.
3	Surestimé ou fondé sur des données surestimées.
4	Non compris les organisations privées à but non lucratif.
5	Ne comprend pas les entreprises commerciales.
6	Ne corresponds pas exactement aux recommandations du Manuel de Frascati.
7	Etat seulement.
8	Enseignement supérieur seulement.
9	Sous-estimé ou basé sur des données sous-estimées.

10 For statistical purposes, the data for China do not include those for the Hong Kong Special Administrative Region (Hong Kong SAR), Macao Special Administrative Region (Macao SAR) and Taiwan Province of China.	10 Pour la présentation des statistiques, les données pour la Chine ne comprennent pas la région administrative spéciale de Hong Kong (RAS de Hong Kong), la région administrative spéciale de Macao (RAS de Macao) et la province chinoise de Taïwan.
11 Including technicians and equivalent staff.	11 Y compris les techniciens y le personnel assimilé.
12 Including other supporting staff.	12 Y compris autre personnel de soutien.
13 Excluding Higher Education.	13 Non compris l'enseignement supérieur.
14 Excluding government.	14 Non compris l'état.
15 Excluding data for other supporting staff.	15 Non compris les données pour le personnel de soutien.
16 Including other classes.	16 Comprend d'autres catégories.
17 Excluding technicians and equivalent staff.	17 Non compris les techniciens y le personnel assimilé.
18 Excluding data from some regions, provinces or states.	18 Non compris les données de certaines régions, provinces ou états.

27 Gross domestic expenditure on research and development (R&D)
As a percentage of GDP and by source of funds

Dépenses intérieures brutes de recherche et développement (R-D)
En pourcentage du PIB et répartition par source de financement

Country or area Pays ou zone	Year Année	Expenditure on R&D as a % of GDP Dépenses en R&D en % du PIB	Source of funds (%) / Source de financement (%)					
			Business enterprises Entreprises	Government Etat	Higher education Enseignement supérieur	Private non-profit Institut. Privées sans but lucratif	Funds from abroad Fonds de l'étranger	Not specified/ Non précisé
Total, all countries or areas	2005	1.5	...	...	...	...	...	...
Total, tous pays ou zones	2010	1.6	...	...	...	...	...	...
	2015	1.7	...	...	...	...	...	...
Northern Africa	2005	0.3	...	...	...	...	...	...
Afrique septentrionale	2010	0.4	...	...	...	...	...	...
	2015	0.5						
Sub-Saharan Africa	2005	0.4	...	...	...	...	...	...
Afrique subsaharienne	2010	0.4	...	...	...	...	...	...
	2015	0.4						
Northern America	2005	2.5	...	...	...	...	...	...
Amérique septentrionale	2010	2.7	...	...	...	...	...	...
	2015	2.7	...	...	...	...	...	...
Latin America & the Caribbean	2005	0.6	...	...	...	...	...	...
Amérique latine et Caraïbes	2010	0.7	...	...	...	...	...	...
	2015	0.7	...	...	...	...	...	...
Central Asia	2005	0.3	...	...	...	...	...	...
Asie centrale	2010	0.2	...	...	...	...	...	...
	2015	0.2	...	...	...	...	...	...
Eastern Asia	2005	2.0	...	...	...	...	...	...
Asie orientale	2010	2.2	...	...	...	...	...	...
	2015	2.4	...	...	...	...	...	...
South-eastern Asia	2005	0.6	...	...	...	...	...	...
Asie du Sud-Est	2010	0.8	...	...	...	...	...	...
	2015	0.9	...	...	...	...	...	...
Southern Asia	2005	0.7	...	...	...	...	...	...
Asie méridionale	2010	0.7	...	...	...	...	...	...
	2015	0.6	...	...	...	...	...	...
Western Asia	2005	0.7	...	...	...	...	...	...
Asie occidentale	2010	0.7	...	...	...	...	...	...
	2015	0.8	...	...	...	...	...	...
Europe	2005	1.6	...	...	...	...	...	...
Europe	2010	1.7	...	...	...	...	...	...
	2015	1.9	...	...	...	...	...	...
Oceania	2005	1.9	...	...	...	...	...	...
Océanie	2010	2.2	...	...	...	...	...	...
	2015	1.8	...	...	...	...	...	...
Australia and New Zealand	2005	1.9	...	...	...	...	...	...
Australie et Nouvelle-Zélande	2010	2.2	...	...	...	...	...	...
	2015	1.8	...	...	...	...	...	...
Albania [1]								
Albanie [1]	2008	0.2	3.3	80.8	8.6	...	7.4	...
Algeria [1]								
Algérie [1]	2005	0.1						
American Samoa [1]	2005	0.4	...	...	...	...	...	...
Samoa américaines [1]	2006	0.4	...	...	...	...	...	...
Argentina	2005	0.4	31.0	59.6	5.7	3.0	0.7	~0.0
Argentine	2008	0.5	26.5	67.6	4.4	1.0	0.6	~0.0
	2010	0.6	...	...	...	...	...	
	2015	0.6	# 17.2	# 76.4	# 2.0	# 1.0	# 3.3	...
Armenia	2005[1]	0.3	...	77.5	...	...	4.7	17.8
Arménie	2010[1]	0.2	...	84.5	...	...	11.7	3.8
	2016[2,3]	0.2	...	72.9	...	...	1.8	25.2
Australia	2004	1.9	54.6	40.3	0.4	1.9	2.9	...
Australie	2008	2.4	61.9	34.6	0.1	1.8	1.6	...
	*2010	2.4	...	...	...	...	...	...
	*2015	1.9	...	...	...	...	...	...

Gross domestic expenditure on research and development (R&D) *(continued)*
As a percentage of GDP and by source of funds

Dépenses intérieures brutes de recherche et développement (R-D) *(suite)*
En pourcentage du PIB et répartition par source de financement

Country or area Pays ou zone	Year Année	Expenditure on R&D as a % of GDP Dépenses en R&D en % du PIB	Source of funds (%) / Source de financement (%)					
			Business enterprises Entreprises	Government Etat	Higher education Enseignement supérieur	Private non-profit Institut. Privées sans but lucratif	Funds from abroad Fonds de l'étranger	Not specified/ Non précisé
Austria Autriche	2004	2.2	47.2	32.6	0.4	0.5	19.4	...
	*2005	2.4	45.6	35.9	...	0.4	18.0	...
	2009	2.6	47.1	34.9	0.7	0.6	16.8	...
	*2010	2.7	45.1	38.3[4]	...	0.5	16.1	...
	2015	3.0	49.7	32.6	0.6	0.5	16.6	...
	*2016	3.1	# 53.4	# 30.7[5]	...	0.5	15.5	...
Azerbaijan Azerbaïdjan	2005	0.2[6]	18.7	77.5	~0.0	1.3	2.4	...
	2010	0.2	# 9.6	# 88.2	0.3	1.9	~0.0	...
	2014	0.2	30.5	67.6	0.8	0.9	0.2	...
	2016	0.2	29.9	68.5	1.4	0.2	...	...
Bahrain Bahreïn	2014	0.1	21.8	41.5	21.2	2.0	12.4	1.1
Belarus Bélarus	2005	0.7[6]	21.2	71.9	0.7	...	6.3	...
	2008	0.7[6]	36.5	57.6	0.3	0.1	5.5	...
	2010	0.7[6]	27.1	58.7	...	0.6	13.6	...
	2011	0.7[6]	45.8	45.5	...	~0.0	8.7	...
	2016	0.5	38.7	44.7	...	...	16.6	...
Belgium Belgique	2005	1.8	59.7	24.7	2.6	0.6	12.4	...
	2010	2.1	57.6	25.4	3.1	0.6	13.3	...
	2015	2.5	58.6	22.5	2.0	0.4	16.5	...
	*2016	2.5	...	...	...	...	...	...
Bermuda [7] Bermudes [7]	2010[8]	0.2	...	...	...	...	...	...
	2015	0.2	...	...	...	...	...	...
Bolivia (Plurin. State of) Bolivie (État plurin. de)	2002	0.3	16.0	20.0	31.0	19.0	14.0	...
	#2009	0.2	5.2	51.2	26.5	2.1	1.9	13.2
Bosnia and Herzegovina Bosnie-Herzégovine	2005[1]	~0.0	...	...	...	...	...	...
	2009[1]	~0.0	...	...	...	...	...	...
	2016	0.2	28.8	31.5	13.0	~0.0	26.3	0.3
Botswana Botswana	2005	0.5	...	...	...	...	...	...
	#2012	0.3	5.8	73.9	12.6	0.7	6.8	0.2
	2013	0.5	17.7	59.7	0.9	...	21.7	...
Brazil Brésil	2005	1.0	50.4	47.7	1.9	...	...	...
	2010	1.2	47.0	51.1	1.8	...	...	~0.0
	2015	1.3	47.5	50.2	2.3	...	...	~0.0
Brunei Darussalam Brunéi Darussalam	2003	~0.0[1]	6.7	86.8	...	...	6.6	...
	#2004	~0.0[1]	1.6	91.0	7.4	...	...	...
Bulgaria Bulgarie	2005	0.4	27.8	63.9	0.4	0.3	7.6	...
	2010	0.6	16.7	43.2	0.5	0.1	39.6	...
	2015	1.0	35.6	20.3	0.1	0.1	43.8	...
	2016	0.8	...	...	...	...	...	...
Burkina Faso Burkina Faso	2005	0.2[1]	...	100.0	...	...	...	...
	2009	0.2	11.9	9.1	12.2	1.3	59.6	5.9
	#2014[3]	0.2	...	98.4	~0.0	0.1	1.5	...
Burundi [1] Burundi [1]	2008	0.2	...	59.9	0.2	...	39.9	...
	2010	0.1	...	...	...	...	...	...
	2011	0.1	...	...	...	...	...	...
Cabo Verde [1,9] Cabo Verde [1,9]	2011	0.1	...	100.0	...	...	...	...
Cambodia Cambodge	2002[1]	~0.0	...	17.9	...	43.0	28.4	10.6
	#2015	0.1	19.4	23.5	0.1	22.1	34.9	...
Canada Canada	2005	2.0	49.3	* 31.8	* 7.3	2.8	8.8	...
	2010	1.8	47.2	* # 34.9	* 7.9	3.5	6.6	...
	*2016	1.6	40.6	33.1	11.8	4.2	10.4	...
Chad [2,3] Tchad [2,3]	2016	0.3	...	100.0[10]	...	...	...	...
Chile Chili	2010	0.3	25.4	40.4	12.7	1.7	19.8	...
	* #2016	0.4	35.8	46.4	14.4	1.5	1.9	...

27 Gross domestic expenditure on research and development (R&D) *(continued)*
As a percentage of GDP and by source of funds

Dépenses intérieures brutes de recherche et développement (R-D) *(suite)*
En pourcentage du PIB et répartition par source de financement

			Source of funds (%) / Source de financement (%)					
Country or area Pays ou zone	Year Année	Expenditure on R&D as a % of GDP Dépenses en R&D en % du PIB	Business enterprises Entreprises	Government Etat	Higher education Enseignement supérieur	Private non-profit Institut. Privées sans but lucratif	Funds from abroad Fonds de l'étranger	Not specified/ Non précisé
China [11] Chine [11]	2005	1.3	67.0	26.3	...	...	0.9	...
	2010	1.7	71.7	24.0	...	...	1.3	...
	2016	2.1	76.1	20.0	...	...	0.7	...
China, Hong Kong SAR Chine, RAS de Hong Kong	2005	0.8	53.0[12]	44.1	0.4	...	2.5	...
	2010	0.7	47.6[12]	47.3	0.1	...	4.9	...
	2016	0.8	48.9[12]	47.2	~0.0	...	3.9	...
China, Macao SAR Chine, RAS de Macao	2005	0.1[1]	0.2	88.0	10.0	0.4	...	1.4
	2007	# 0.1[1]	0.1	89.3	5.8	2.8	0.6	1.6
	2008	0.1[1]	0.2	91.7	6.4	1.4	...	0.3
	2010[1]	0.1	...	...	...	...	...	...
	2016[1]	# 0.2	...	61.0	6.3	0.3	...	32.5
Colombia Colombie	2005	0.1	...	...	...	...	...	...
	2010	0.2	28.8	38.7	23.2	6.0	3.3	...
	2016	0.3	50.0	29.7	15.0	2.9	2.5	...
Costa Rica Costa Rica	2004	0.4	...	...	...	...	...	...
	2009	0.5	28.7	53.0	...	2.8	1.7	13.7
	2010	0.5	...	...	...	...	...	...
	2014	0.6	1.5	56.2	...	0.5	1.4	40.4
Croatia Croatie	2005	0.9	34.3	58.1	4.9	~0.0	2.6	...
	2010	0.7	38.8	49.2	2.0	0.2	9.9	...
	2015	0.9	46.6	36.4	2.0	0.5	14.5	...
	#2016	0.9	...	...	...	...	...	...
Cuba Cuba	2005	0.5	35.0	60.0	...	...	5.0	...
	2010	0.6	15.0	75.0	...	...	10.0	...
	2016	0.3	35.0	63.0	...	...	2.0	...
Cyprus Chypre	2005	0.4	16.8	67.0	4.2	1.2	10.9	...
	2010	0.4	12.7	68.3	3.5	0.5	15.0	...
	2013	0.5	15.8	59.5	5.4	0.6	18.8	0.1
	2015	0.5	20.0	50.6	5.8	0.6	23.0	...
	*2016	0.5	...	...	...	...	...	...
Czechia Tchéquie	2005	1.2	48.2	45.2	1.2	~0.0	5.4	...
	2010	1.3	40.8	44.4	0.9	~0.0	13.9	...
	2015	1.9	34.5	32.2	0.7	0.1	32.5	...
	*2016	1.7	...	...	...	...	...	...
Dem. Rep. of the Congo Rép. dém. du Congo	2005	# 0.1[13,14]	...	100.0	...	...	...	...
	2009	0.1[13,14]	...	100.0	...	...	...	...
	2015[1,13]	# ~0.0	0.2	# 70.3	...	0.1	29.4	...
Denmark Danemark	2005	2.4	59.5	27.6	...	2.8	10.1	...
	2010	2.9	* 61.1	* 28.2[4]	...	* 3.5	* 7.2	...
	*2015	3.0	59.4	29.4	...	4.7	6.6	...
	*2016	2.9	...	...	...	...	...	...
Ecuador Équateur	2003	0.1	...	...	...	...	...	...
	2010	0.4	1.0[3]	40.2[3]	9.6[3]	0.5[3]	5.3[3]	43.4[15]
	2014	0.4	0.1[3]	42.4[3]	12.6[3]	0.1[3]	2.5[3]	42.3[15]
Egypt Égypte	2005[1,13]	0.2	...	...	...	...	...	...
	2010[2,3]	0.4	...	...	...	...	...	...
	2016	0.7	5.9	93.8	0.2	0.1	~0.0	...
El Salvador El Salvador	2010	0.1	0.6	70.1	20.8	~0.0	8.3	0.1
	#2015	0.1	41.9	29.0	21.2	1.1	6.8	~0.0
Estonia Estonie	2005	0.9	38.5	43.5	0.8	0.2	17.1	...
	2010	1.6	43.6	44.1	0.6	0.2	11.4	...
	2015	1.5	41.0	46.4	0.2	0.2	12.2	...
	2016	1.3	...	...	...	...	...	...
Ethiopia Éthiopie	2005	0.2[1]	...	69.2	...	0.1	30.8	...
	2010	# 0.2	10.8	56.0	1.1	~0.0	30.0	2.2
	2013	0.6	0.7	79.1	1.8	0.2	2.1	16.0
Faroe Islands Îles Féroé	2003	0.9	20.4	...	...	0.3	18.7	60.6[7,10,16]

Gross domestic expenditure on research and development (R&D) *(continued)*
As a percentage of GDP and by source of funds

Dépenses intérieures brutes de recherche et développement (R-D) *(suite)*
En pourcentage du PIB et répartition par source de financement

Country or area Pays ou zone	Year Année	Expenditure on R&D as a % of GDP Dépenses en R&D en % du PIB	Source of funds (%) / Source de financement (%)					
			Business enterprises Entreprises	Govern-ment Etat	Higher education Enseigne-ment supérieur	Private non-profit Institut. Privées sans but lucratif	Funds from abroad Fonds de l'étranger	Not specified/ Non précisé
Finland	2005	3.3	66.9	25.7	0.2	1.0	# 6.3	...
Finlande	2010	3.7	66.1	25.7	0.2	1.1	6.9	...
	2015	2.9	54.8	28.9	0.3	1.5	14.5	...
	2016	2.7	...	...	...	...	...	...
France	2005	2.0	51.9	38.6	1.0	0.9	7.5	...
France	#2010	2.2	53.5	37.1	1.0	0.8	7.5	...
	2015	2.3	54.0	34.8	2.6	0.9	7.6	...
	*2016	2.2	...	...	...	...	...	...
Gabon								
Gabon	2009	0.6	29.3	58.1	9.5	...	3.1	~0.0
Gambia	2009[1]	~0.0	...	...	...	...	...	...
Gambie	2011[7]	0.1	...	38.5	...	45.6	15.9	...
Georgia	2005	0.2	...	...	...	...	...	...
Géorgie	2013[1,9]	# 0.1[17]	...	46.7[18]	36.1[18]	3.1[18]	14.7[18]	0.4[18]
	2016[1,2,3]	0.3	...	...	...	...	...	...
Germany	2005	2.4	67.6	28.4	...	0.3	3.7	...
Allemagne	2010	2.7	65.5	30.4	...	0.2	3.9	...
	2015	2.9	65.6	27.9[4]	...	0.4[4]	6.2	...
	*2016	2.9	...	...	...	...	...	...
Ghana								
Ghana	2010	# 0.4	# 0.1	# 68.3	0.3	0.1	31.2	...
Greece	2005	0.6	31.1	46.8	1.7	1.5	19.0	...
Grèce	*2010	0.6	36.5	48.3	2.3	1.0	11.9	...
	2016	1.0	40.2	42.6	2.3	0.4	14.6	...
Greenland								
Groenland	2004	0.7	...	...	...	...	...	...
Guam	2001	...	...	100.0	...	...	...	...
Guam	2005	0.3	...	...	...	...	...	...
Guatemala [1]	2005	~0.0	...	42.1	57.9	...	...	...
Guatemala [1]	2010	~0.0	...	18.3	30.9	...	50.8	...
	2012	~0.0	...	23.5	27.5	...	49.0	...
	2014	~0.0	...	31.1	68.9	...	...	~0.0
	2015	~0.0	...	27.8	72.2	...	...	...
Honduras	2004	~0.0	...	...	...	...	...	...
Honduras	2015[1]	# ~0.0	...	82.5	17.5	...	...	~0.0
Hungary	2005	0.9	39.4[4]	49.4[4]	...	0.3[4]	10.7[4]	...
Hongrie	2010	1.1	47.4	39.3	...	0.9	12.4	...
	2015	1.4	49.7	34.6	...	0.7	15.0	...
	2016	1.2	...	...	...	...	...	...
Iceland	2005	2.7	48.0	40.5	...	0.3	11.2	...
Islande	2009	2.7	47.8	40.2	...	0.6	11.4	...
	2016	2.1	35.0	34.2	4.0	4.5	22.4	...
India	2005	0.8	...	...	...	...	...	...
Inde	2010	0.8	...	...	...	...	...	...
	2015	0.6	...	...	...	...	...	...
Indonesia	2001	~0.0[1]	14.7[1,12]	84.5	0.2	...	...	0.7
Indonésie	#2009[1]	0.1	...	...	...	...	...	...
	2013	0.1	...	...	...	...	...	...
Iran (Islamic Republic of)	2005	0.6	12.2	76.2	11.6	...	...	...
Iran (Rép. islamique d')	2008	0.6	30.9	61.6	7.4	...	...	...
	2010[2,19]	0.3	...	...	...	...	...	...
	2013	0.3	...	...	...	...	...	...
Iraq	2010	~0.0[2,3,17]	...	100.0[10]	...	...	...	...
Iraq	2016	~0.0	1.2	96.0	2.0	0.7	0.1	...
Ireland	2005	1.2	57.4	32.0	1.7	0.2	8.6	...
Irlande	*2010	1.6	52.2	29.4	0.9	0.5	17.0	...
	2015	1.2	48.4	25.9	1.5	0.4	23.8	...
	*2016	1.2	...	...	...	...	...	...

27 Gross domestic expenditure on research and development (R&D) *(continued)*
As a percentage of GDP and by source of funds

Dépenses intérieures brutes de recherche et développement (R-D) *(suite)*
En pourcentage du PIB et répartition par source de financement

Country or area Pays ou zone	Year Année	Expenditure on R&D as a % of GDP Dépenses en R&D en % du PIB	Source of funds (%) / Source de financement (%)					
			Business enterprises Entreprises	Government Etat	Higher education Enseignement supérieur	Private non-profit Institut. Privées sans but lucratif	Funds from abroad Fonds de l'étranger	Not specified/ Non précisé
Israel [4] Israël [4]	2005	4.1	56.2	14.5	2.8	1.8	24.7	...
	2010	3.9	36.2	14.2	1.2	1.1	47.3	...
	2015	4.3	34.3	12.8	0.4	0.9	51.6	...
	*2016	4.3	...	...	...	...	...	...
Italy Italie	2005	1.0	39.7	50.7	0.1	1.6	8.0	...
	2010	1.2	44.7	41.6	0.9	3.1	9.8	...
	2015	1.3	50.0	38.0	1.0	2.7	8.3	...
	*2016	1.3	...	...	...	...	...	...
Jamaica Jamaïque	2002	0.1	...	...	...	...	...	...
Japan Japon	2005	3.2	76.1	* 16.8	* 6.1	0.7	0.3	...
	2010	3.1	75.9	* 17.2	* 5.7	0.8	0.4	...
	2016	3.1	78.1	* 15.0	* 5.4	0.7	0.7	...
Jordan Jordanie	2002	0.3	...	...	...	...	...	...
	2008	0.4	...	...	...	...	...	...
	#2016	0.3	...	...	...	...	...	...
Kazakhstan Kazakhstan	2005	0.3	39.1	44.5	13.4	1.3	1.5	...
	2010	0.2	36.6	36.7	17.2	8.9	0.6	...
	2011	0.2	51.6	24.9	16.3	6.9	0.3	...
	2016	0.1	39.6	53.2	...	...	1.5	5.6
Kenya Kenya	#2010	0.8	4.3	26.0	19.0	3.5	47.1	...
Kuwait Koweït	2003[13]	0.1[1]	# 4.4	# 94.7	~0.0	...	0.9	...
	2004[13]	0.1[1]	6.0	93.2	...	...	0.8	...
	2005[13]	0.1[1]	7.3	92.3	...	0.4	...	...
	2009[13]	0.1[1]	2.3	96.5	...	...	1.2	...
	2010[13]	0.1[1]	5.2	94.8	...	~0.0	...	...
	2014[2,3]	0.4	1.0	90.2	5.5	1.1	...	2.3
Kyrgyzstan Kirghizistan	2003	0.2	53.7	45.1	0.1	...	1.1	...
	2005	0.2	36.4	63.6	...	...	~0.0	...
	2010	0.2	...	...	...	...	...	...
	2016[2]	0.1	4.7	88.9	0.3	...	1.9	4.2
Lao People's Dem. Rep. [1] Rép. dém. populaire lao [1]	2002	~0.0	36.0	8.0	2.0	...	54.0	...
Latvia Lettonie	2005	0.5	34.3	46.0	1.2	...	18.5	...
	2010	0.6	38.8	26.4	1.4	...	33.4	...
	2015	0.6	20.0	32.7	2.2	...	45.0	...
	2016	0.4	...	...	...	...	...	...
Lesotho Lesotho	2004[1]	0.1	...	...	...	...	...	...
	2009[1]	~0.0	3.4	15.0	2.8	...	...	78.9
	2011[1]	~0.0[9]	...	...	44.7[16]	...	3.4	51.9
	2015[2,3]	~0.0	0.8	91.1	...	0.3	7.8	...
Lithuania Lituanie	2005	0.7	20.8	62.7	5.7	0.2	10.5	...
	2010	0.8	32.4	46.0	1.5	0.2	19.9	...
	2015	1.0	28.5	35.3	1.5	0.3	34.3	...
	2016	0.8	...	...	...	...	...	...
Luxembourg Luxembourg	2005	1.6	79.7	16.6	~0.0	0.1	3.6	...
	2010	1.5	43.5	35.1	0.6	0.1	20.6	...
	2015	1.3	47.1	47.7	1.6	0.2	3.4	...
	*2016	1.2	...	...	...	...	...	...
Madagascar Madagascar	2005	0.2[1]	...	89.8[10]	...	...	10.2	...
	2009	0.1[1]	...	89.4[10]	...	...	10.6	...
	2010	0.1[1]	...	# 100.0[10]	...	...	...	...
	2011	0.1[1]	...	100.0[16]	...	...	...	...
	2016[1,13]	~0.0	...	...	...	...	...	...
Malaysia Malaisie	2004	0.6	71.2	21.5	6.9	...	0.4	...
	2010	1.0	59.6	36.4	3.5	...	0.4	0.1
	2015	1.3	# 49.6	# 35.8	7.0	...	1.7	# 6.0[5]

27 Gross domestic expenditure on research and development (R&D) *(continued)*
As a percentage of GDP and by source of funds

Dépenses intérieures brutes de recherche et développement (R-D) *(suite)*
En pourcentage du PIB et répartition par source de financement

Country or area / Pays ou zone	Year / Année	Expenditure on R&D as a % of GDP / Dépenses en R&D en % du PIB	Source of funds (%) / Source de financement (%)					
			Business enterprises / Entreprises	Government / Etat	Higher education / Enseignement supérieur	Private non-profit institut. / Privées sans but lucratif	Funds from abroad / Fonds de l'étranger	Not specified/ Non précisé
Mali / Mali	2007[1]	0.2[19]	10.1	40.9	...	...	49.0	...
	2010	0.6[3]	...	# 91.2	...	...	8.8	...
	2015[3]	0.3	0.9	43.6	0.1	0.3	32.7	22.4
Malta / Malte	2005	0.5	# 46.8	# 25.9	0.4	0.1	26.9	...
	2010	0.6	52.5	34.4	1.3	0.1	11.7	...
	2015	0.8	45.6	32.8	1.1	0.1	20.4	...
	*2016	0.6	...	...	...	...	...	...
Mauritius / Maurice	2005[7,17]	0.4	...	100.0	...	...	...	...
	2012[3]	# 0.2	0.3	72.4	20.7	0.1	6.4	...
Mexico / Mexique	2005	0.4	41.5	49.2	7.3	0.9	1.1	...
	2010	0.5	32.9	62.3	2.8	1.6	0.5	...
	*2016	0.5	20.7	67.4	5.0	6.4	0.6	...
Monaco [1] / Monaco [1]	2005	~0.0	...	98.8	...	...	...	1.2
Mongolia / Mongolie	2005	0.2[1]	10.4	77.8	0.8	...	4.4	6.5
	2010[1]	0.2	7.2	61.1	1.5	...	4.2	25.9
	2016[1]	0.2	4.9	86.3	3.7	0.8	2.1	2.1
Montenegro / Monténégro	2005	0.9	...	...	...	...	...	...
	2007	1.1	...	...	...	...	...	...
	2015	0.4	29.9	57.8	6.4	~0.0	5.9	...
Morocco / Maroc	2003	0.6	12.3	40.3	47.4	...	...	...
	2010	0.7	29.9	23.1	45.3	...	1.7	...
Mozambique / Mozambique	2002[7,14]	0.4	...	34.7	...	...	65.3	...
	2010	# 0.4[3]	...	18.8[10]	...	3.0	78.1	...
	2015	0.3	0.5[1]	43.5	13.3	...	39.9	2.8
Myanmar [1] / Myanmar [1]	2002	0.2	...	...	...	...	...	...
Namibia / Namibie	2010	0.1[1,19]	19.8	78.6	...	...	1.5	...
	2014[1]	0.3	11.1	63.2	6.0	3.9	15.8	...
Nepal [1,17] / Népal [1,17]	2010	0.3	...	...	...	...	...	...
Netherlands / Pays-Bas	2005	1.8	46.3	38.8	0.3	2.6	12.0	...
	2009	1.7	45.1	40.9	0.3	2.8	10.8	...
	2010	1.7	...	...	...	...	...	...
	2015	2.0	48.6	33.1	0.2	2.6	15.5	...
	*2016	2.0	...	...	...	...	...	...
New Zealand / Nouvelle-Zélande	2005	1.1	41.1	43.2	8.9	1.7	5.2	...
	2009	1.3	39.0	44.7	8.3	2.8	5.2	...
	2015	1.3	43.1	37.1	8.5	3.0	8.2	...
Nicaragua / Nicaragua	2002	~0.0	...	...	...	...	...	...
	2015[9]	0.1	...	...	...	...	...	...
Nigeria / Nigéria	2007	0.2[3]	0.2	96.4	0.1	1.7	1.0	0.6
North Macedonia / Macédoine du Nord	2002	0.2	7.8	76.3	7.3	~0.0	8.6	...
	2005	0.2	...	...	...	...	...	...
	2010	0.2	...	...	...	...	...	...
	2016	0.4	24.1	46.8	23.6	0.4	5.2	...
Norway / Norvège	2005	1.5	46.8	43.6	0.7	0.9	8.1	...
	2009	1.7	43.6	46.8	0.4	1.0	8.2	...
	2010	1.6	...	...	...	...	...	...
	2015	1.9	44.2	44.9	0.4	1.2	9.2	...
	2016	2.0	...	...	...	...	...	...
Oman / Oman	2013	0.2	24.5	48.6	24.4	0.1	~0.0	2.3
	2015	0.2	21.4	55.7	22.8	0.2	...	...
Pakistan / Pakistan	2005	0.4[2,3]	...	87.0	11.9	...	0.3	0.8
	2009	0.4[2,3]	...	84.0	12.1	1.7	0.9	1.3
	2015[2,3]		...	67.0	25.5	0.3	2.7	4.6

Gross domestic expenditure on research and development (R&D) *(continued)*
As a percentage of GDP and by source of funds

Dépenses intérieures brutes de recherche et développement (R-D) *(suite)*
En pourcentage du PIB et répartition par source de financement

			Source of funds (%) / Source de financement (%)					
Country or area Pays ou zone	Year Année	Expenditure on R&D as a % of GDP Dépenses en R&D en % du PIB	Business enterprises Entreprises	Government Etat	Higher education Enseignement supérieur	Private non-profit Institut. Privées sans but lucratif	Funds from abroad Fonds de l'étranger	Not specified/Non précisé
Panama Panama	2003	0.3	0.6	25.5	1.8	1.0	71.0	0.1
	2005	0.2	0.4	38.5	1.4	0.7	58.9	...
	2010	0.1	3.4	53.9	6.0	14.0	22.7	~0.0
	2011	0.2	18.9	46.7	5.0	8.7	20.7	~0.0
	2013	0.1	10.8	80.9	8.0	...	0.3	...
Papua New Guinea [3] Papouasie-Nvl-Guinée [3]	2016	~0.0[1]	4.5	38.7	7.6	0.8	39.7	8.8
Paraguay Paraguay	2001	0.1	~0.0	43.2	20.6	3.4	32.7	0.0
	2005	0.1	# 0.3	# 74.9	# 8.6	# 2.0	# 14.2	...
	2008	0.1	0.3	76.2	9.2	2.1	12.3	...
	2015[3]	0.1	0.3	73.1	2.1	4.2	10.3	10.1
Peru Pérou	2004	0.2	...	...	...	...	...	...
	2016	0.1	...	...	...	...	...	...
Philippines Philippines	2005	0.1	62.6	25.6	6.0	0.7	4.8	0.3
	2009	0.1	57.5	26.7	7.8	0.4	4.2	3.4
	2013	0.1	36.9	51.6	9.0	0.2	1.8	0.5
Poland Pologne	2005	0.6	33.4	57.7	2.9	0.3	5.7	...
	2010	0.7	24.4	60.9	2.5	0.3	11.8	...
	2015	1.0	39.0	41.8	2.2	0.2	16.7	...
	*2016	1.0	...	...	...	...	...	...
Portugal Portugal	2005	0.8	36.3	55.2	1.0	2.8	4.7	...
	2010	1.5	43.9	45.1	3.2	4.6	3.2	...
	2015	1.2	42.7	44.3	4.4	1.3	7.4	...
	*2016	1.3	...	...	...	...	...	...
Puerto Rico Porto Rico	2009	0.5	...	...	...	...	...	...
	2015	0.4	69.4	23.1	6.6	0.3	...	0.6
Qatar Qatar	2015	0.5	7.1	42.6	20.6	27.8	1.9	~0.0
Republic of Korea République de Corée	2005[4]	2.6	75.0	23.0	0.9	0.4	0.7	...
	2010	3.5	71.8	26.7	0.9	0.4	0.2	...
	2016	4.2	75.4	22.7	0.6	0.3	0.9	...
Republic of Moldova République de Moldova	2005	0.4	...	...	...	...	3.8	96.2[5]
	2010	0.4	...	...	...	...	7.4	92.6[5]
	2016	0.3	...	...	...	...	4.2	95.8[5]
Romania Roumanie	2005	0.4	37.2	53.5	4.0	~0.0	5.3	...
	2010	0.5	32.3	54.4	2.2	~0.0	11.1	...
	2015	0.5	37.3	41.7	1.7	0.1	19.2	...
	2016	0.5	...	...	...	...	...	...
Russian Federation Fédération de Russie	2005	1.1	30.0	61.9	0.4	~0.0	7.6	...
	2010	1.1	25.5	70.3	0.5	0.1	3.5	...
	2016	1.1	28.1	68.2	0.9	0.2	2.7	...
Saint Vincent & Grenadines Saint-Vincent-Grenadines	2002	0.1	...	...	...	...	...	...
Saudi Arabia [17] Arabie saoudite [17]	2005[1]	~0.0	...	...	...	...	...	...
	#2010[7]	0.9	...	...	...	...	...	...
	2013[7]	0.8	...	...	...	...	...	...
Senegal Sénégal	2010	0.5	4.1	47.6	~0.0	3.2	40.5	4.5
	2015[3]	0.8	2.1	85.4	0.1	4.5	7.9	...
Serbia Serbie	2005[4,20]	0.4	...	...	...	...	...	...
	2010	0.7[20]	8.6	59.4	28.4	~0.0	3.6	...
	2016	0.9[20]	9.2	45.6	32.3	~0.0	13.0	...
Seychelles Seychelles	2005	0.3	...	...	...	...	...	...
	2016	# 0.2	2.0[3]	56.1[3]	4.5[3]	3.2[3]	33.9[3]	0.3[3]
Singapore Singapour	2005	2.2	58.8	36.4	0.5	...	4.4	...
	2010	2.0	53.1	40.2	1.8	...	4.9	...
	2014	2.2	54.1	37.1	2.0	...	6.8	...

Gross domestic expenditure on research and development (R&D) *(continued)*
As a percentage of GDP and by source of funds

Dépenses intérieures brutes de recherche et développement (R-D) *(suite)*
En pourcentage du PIB et répartition par source de financement

Country or area Pays ou zone	Year Année	Expenditure on R&D as a % of GDP Dépenses en R&D en % du PIB	Source of funds (%) / Source de financement (%)					
			Business enterprises Entreprises	Government Etat	Higher education Enseignement supérieur	Private non-profit Institut. Privées sans but lucratif	Funds from abroad Fonds de l'étranger	Not specified/ Non précisé
Slovakia Slovaquie	2005	0.5	36.6	* 57.0	0.3	~0.0	6.0	...
	2010	0.6	35.1	* 49.6	0.4	0.3	14.7	...
	2015	1.2	25.1	31.9	3.3	0.3	39.4	...
	2016	0.8	...	...	...	...	...	...
Slovenia Slovénie	2005	1.4	54.8	37.2	0.7	~0.0	7.3	...
	2010	2.1	58.4	35.3	0.3	0.1	6.0	...
	2015	2.2	69.2	19.9	0.3	~0.0	10.6	...
	*2016	2.0	...	...	...	...	...	...
South Africa Afrique du Sud	2005	0.9	43.9	38.2	3.0	1.4	13.6	...
	2010	0.7	40.1	44.5	0.1	3.2	12.1	...
	2015	0.8	38.9	44.6	0.1	3.3	13.0	...
Spain Espagne	2005	1.1	46.3	43.0	4.1	0.9	5.7	...
	2010	1.3	43.0	46.6	3.9	0.7	5.7	...
	2015	1.2	45.8	40.9	4.3	0.9	8.0	...
	2016	1.2	...	...	...	...	...	...
Sri Lanka Sri Lanka	#2000[1]	0.1	7.7	51.7	18.5	~0.0	4.5	17.5
	#2004	0.2	0.6[12]	67.5[10]	...	...	22.6	9.3
	2010	0.1	# 40.9	55.9	0.2	~0.0	2.7	0.3
	2014	0.1	41.2	56.2	...	...	2.1	0.5
State of Palestine [3] État de Palestine [3]	2010	0.4	0.9	21.3	2.3	4.9	52.4	18.2
	2013	0.5	3.8	29.4	4.6	17.1	24.2	21.1
Sudan [7] Soudan [7]	2005	0.3	...	...	...	...	...	...
Sweden Suède	#2005	3.4	63.9	24.4	0.7	2.9	8.1	...
	2009	3.4	59.5	27.0	0.6	2.6	10.3	...
	*2010	3.2	...	...	...	...	...	...
	*2013	3.3	61.0	28.3	1.0	3.1	6.7	...
	2015	3.3	57.3	...	0.9	3.3	...	...
	*2016	3.3	...	...	...	...	...	...
Switzerland Suisse	2004	2.7	69.7	22.7	1.5	0.8	5.2	...
	2008	2.7	68.2	22.8	2.3	0.7	6.0	...
	2015	3.4	63.5	24.4	1.5	0.5	10.2	...
Tajikistan Tadjikistan	2001	0.1	0.6	97.3	...	...	0.2	1.9
	2005	0.1	2.2[18]	91.5[18]	0.3[18]	...	...	5.5[18]
	2006	0.1	0.2[18]	76.3[18]	0.2[18]	...	0.6[18]	19.9[18]
	2010	0.1[2,3]	1.9[18]	76.2[18]	0.4[18]	...	...	19.7[18]
	2011	0.1[2,3]	1.6[18]	82.1[18]	0.1[18]	...	...	15.1[18]
	2013	0.1[2,3]	...	92.5	0.2	...	0.2	7.1
	2016[2,3]	0.1	...	100.0	...	...	...	...
Thailand Thaïlande	2005	0.2	48.7	31.5	14.9	0.7	1.8	2.4
	2009	0.2	41.4	37.9	17.8	0.3	1.0	1.6
	2015	0.6	66.2	20.5	5.5	0.1	1.5	6.0
Togo Togo	2010	0.3[3]	...	88.3	...	...	11.7	...
	2012	0.2[3]	...	84.9	...	3.1	12.1	...
	2014[3]	0.3[2]	...	94.5	...	...	5.5	...
Trinidad and Tobago Trinité-et-Tobago	2005	0.1	...	...	...	...	...	...
	2010	~0.0	...	...	...	...	...	...
	2015	0.1	...	...	...	...	...	...
Tunisia Tunisie	2005	0.7	14.4	79.2	...	~0.0	6.4	...
	2010	0.7	17.1	78.1	...	...	4.8	...
	2015	0.6	18.9	77.1	...	...	3.9	...
	2016	0.6	...	...	...	...	...	...
Turkey Turquie	2005	0.6	43.3[4]	50.1[4]	...	5.8[4]	0.8	...
	2010	0.8	45.1	30.8	19.6	3.7	0.8	...
	2015	0.9	50.1	27.6	18.1	3.2	1.1	...

27 Gross domestic expenditure on research and development (R&D) *(continued)*
As a percentage of GDP and by source of funds

Dépenses intérieures brutes de recherche et développement (R-D) *(suite)*
En pourcentage du PIB et répartition par source de financement

Country or area Pays ou zone	Year Année	Expenditure on R&D as a % of GDP Dépenses en R&D en % du PIB	Source of funds (%) / Source de financement (%)					
			Business enterprises Entreprises	Govern-ment Etat	Higher education Enseigne-ment supérieur	Private non-profit Institut. Privées sans but lucratif	Funds from abroad Fonds de l'étranger	Not specified/ Non précisé
Uganda	2002	0.4	1.3	33.8	1.3	...	63.6	...
Ouganda	2005	0.2	1.7	41.5	...	...	56.9	...
	2010	0.5	13.7	21.9	1.0	6.0	57.3	...
	2014	# 0.2	# 3.4	37.9	2.3	3.3	52.4	0.7
Ukraine	2005	1.0	# 32.3	# 40.1	# 0.1	# 0.4	# 24.4	# 2.8
Ukraine	2010	0.8	26.2	46.7	0.2	0.1	25.7	1.1
	#2016	0.5[20]	36.9	39.3	0.2	~0.0	22.1	1.6
United Arab Emirates	2014	0.7	74.3[21]	25.7[13]	...	...	...	...
Émirats arabes unis	2016	1.0	...	...	...	...	...	...
United Kingdom	2005	1.6	42.1	32.7	1.2	4.7	19.3	...
Royaume-Uni	*2010	1.7	44.0	32.3	1.2	4.8	17.6	...
	2015	1.7	49.0	27.7	1.4	4.9	17.1	...
	*2016	1.7	...	...	...	...	...	...
United Rep. of Tanzania	2010	0.4[1,3]	0.1	57.5	0.3	0.1	42.0	...
Rép.-Unie de Tanzanie	2013[3]	0.5	...	...	...	...	...	...
United States of America	2005[4]	2.5	63.3	30.8	2.8	3.1	...	...
États-Unis d'Amérique	2010	2.7[4]	56.9[4]	32.6[4]	3.0[4]	3.8[4]	3.7	...
	2016	* 2.7[4]	62.3[4]	* 25.1[4]	* 3.7[4]	* 3.8[4]	* 5.2	...
United States Virgin Islands [1]	2002	0.1	...	70.8	28.0	1.2	...	...
Îles Vierges américaines [1]	2005	~0.0	...	100.0	...	...	...	...
	2007	~0.0	...	100.0	...	...	...	...
Uruguay	2000	0.2	39.3	20.3	35.7	...	4.8	~0.0
Uruguay	2002	0.2	46.7	17.1	31.4	0.1	4.7	...
	2010	0.3	47.1	22.9	26.6	0.9	1.7	0.8
	2011	0.3	8.5	30.8	45.2	0.1	6.5	8.9
	2015	0.4	4.6	28.6	59.2	0.3	7.4	...
Uzbekistan	2005	0.2	52.7	43.1[10]	...	...	0.6	3.6
Ouzbékistan	2010	0.2	35.1	57.8[10]	...	...	2.4	4.7
	2016	0.2	40.2	56.3[10]	...	...	0.8	2.7
Venezuela (Boliv. Rep. of)	2005	0.2	...	...	...	...	...	...
Venezuela (Rép. boliv. du)	2010	0.2	...	...	...	...	...	...
	2015	0.2	...	...	...	...	...	...
Viet Nam	2002	0.2	18.1	74.1	0.7[12]	...	6.3	0.8
Viet Nam	2015	0.4	58.1	33.0	0.9	...	2.9	5.0
Zambia	2005[1]	~0.0	...	...	...	...	...	...
Zambie	#2008	0.3	3.2	94.8	...	0.3	1.6	...

Source:

United Nations Educational, Scientific and Cultural Organization (UNESCO), Montreal, the UNESCO Institute for Statistics (UIS) statistics database, last accessed September 2018.

Source:

Organisation des Nations Unies pour l'éducation, la science et la culture (UNESCO), Montréal, base de données statistiques de l'Institut de statistique (ISU) de l'UNESCO, dernier accès septembre 2018.

1	Partial data.
2	Excluding private non-profit.
3	Excluding business enterprise.
4	Do not correspond exactly to Frascati Manual recommendations.
5	Including other classes.
6	Data have been converted from the former national currency using the appropriate conversion rate.
7	Overestimated or based on overestimated data.
8	Excluding most or all capital expenditures.
9	Higher Education only.
10	Including higher education.

1	Données partielles.
2	Non compris les organisations privées à but non lucratif.
3	Ne comprend pas les entreprises commerciales.
4	Ne correspond pas exactement aux recommandations du Manuel de Frascati.
5	Comprend d'autres catégories.
6	Les données ont été converties à partir de l'ancienne monnaie nationale et du taux de conversion approprié.
7	Surestimé ou fondé sur des données surestimées.
8	Exclut toutes ou presque toutes des dépenses en capital.
9	Enseignement supérieur seulement.
10	Y compris l'enseignement supérieur.

Gross domestic expenditure on research and development (R&D) *(continued)*
As a percentage of GDP and by source of funds

Dépenses intérieures brutes de recherche et développement (R-D) *(suite)*
En pourcentage du PIB et répartition par source de financement

11	For statistical purposes, the data for China do not include those for the Hong Kong Special Administrative Region (Hong Kong SAR), Macao Special Administrative Region (Macao SAR) and Taiwan Province of China.	11	Pour la présentation des statistiques, les données pour la Chine ne comprennent pas la région administrative spéciale de Hong Kong (RAS de Hong Kong), la région administrative spéciale de Macao (RAS de Macao) et la province chinoise de Taïwan.
12	Including private non-profit.	12	Y compris les fonds privés à but non lucratif.
13	Government only.	13	Etat seulement.
14	S&T budget instead of R&D expenditure.	14	Budget pour la science et technologie au lieu des dépenses de recherche et développement.
15	Including business enterprise.	15	Y compris les fonds d'entreprises.
16	Including Government.	16	Y compris l'état.
17	Based on R&D budget instead of R&D expenditure.	17	Basé sur le budget de la recherche-développement au lieu des dépenses.
18	The sum of the breakdown does not add to the total.	18	La somme de toutes les valeurs diffère du total.
19	Excluding government.	19	Non compris l'état.
20	Excluding data from some regions, provinces or states.	20	Non compris les données de certaines régions, provinces ou états.
21	Business enterprise only.	21	Les entreprises commerciales seulement.

Region, country or area	1985	1995	2005	2010	2015	2016	2017	Région, pays ou zone
Total, all countries or areas								**Total, tous pays ou zones**
Grants of patents	397 580	430 600	633 100	914 800	1 240 200	1 352 300	1 404 600	Brevets délivrés
Africa								**Afrique**
Grants of patents	...	...	4 800	9 600	8 600	7 900	9 400	Brevets délivrés
Northern America								**Amérique septentrionale**
Grants of patents	...	...	159 300	238 700	320 600	329 500	342 900	Brevets délivrés
Latin America & the Caribbean								**Amérique latine et Caraïbes**
Grants of patents	...	...	14 200	17 100	17 700	18 900	20 300	Brevets délivrés
Asia								**Asie**
Grants of patents	...	...	288 700	469 700	700 400	772 300	803 100	Brevets délivrés
Europe								**Europe**
Grants of patents	...	...	150 900	160 800	165 400	195 900	203 600	Brevets délivrés
Oceania								**Océanie**
Grants of patents	...	...	15 200	18 900	27 500	27 800	25 300	Brevets délivrés
Albania								**Albanie**
Resident filings (per mil. pop.)	...	...	...	...	5	...	...	Dem. de rés. (par mil. d'hab.)
Grants of patents	...	...	395	349	10	5	10	Brevets délivrés
Patents in force	...	...	...	349	...	1 645	4 946	Brevets en vigueur
Algeria								**Algérie**
Resident filings (per mil. pop.)	...	1	2	2	2	3	...	Dem. de rés. (par mil. d'hab.)
Grants of patents	...	118	443	1 076	353	383	...	Brevets délivrés
Patents in force	...	...	498	...	5 145	5 618	...	Brevets en vigueur
Andorra								**Andorre**
Grants of patents	...	...	...	...	...	...	4	Brevets délivrés
Patents in force	...	...	...	...	...	...	4	Brevets en vigueur
Argentina								**Argentine**
Resident filings (per mil. pop.)	...	19	27	13	13	20	9	Dem. de rés. (par mil. d'hab.)
Grants of patents	...	1 003	1 798	1 366	1 559	1 879	2 302	Brevets délivrés
Patents in force	...	...	...	...	...	...	13 115	Brevets en vigueur
Armenia								**Arménie**
Resident filings (per mil. pop.)	...	58	69	49	39	44	38	Dem. de rés. (par mil. d'hab.)
Grants of patents	...	52	126	124	81	93	74	Brevets délivrés
Patents in force	...	...	110	278	248	226	209	Brevets en vigueur
Australia								**Australie**
Resident filings (per mil. pop.)	...	99	125	109	96	108	102	Dem. de rés. (par mil. d'hab.)
Grants of patents	6 764	9 406	10 979	14 557	23 098	23 744	22 742	Brevets délivrés
Patents in force	...	...	96 403	96 293	117 906	132 994	144 555	Brevets en vigueur
Austria								**Autriche**
Resident filings (per mil. pop.)	300	217	404	497	486	471	488	Dem. de rés. (par mil. d'hab.)
Grants of patents	2 571	1 777	938	1 130	1 356	1 135	1 102	Brevets délivrés
Patents in force	...	...	95 618	102 113	121 367	142 875	146 880	Brevets en vigueur
Azerbaijan								**Azerbaïdjan**
Resident filings (per mil. pop.)	...	29	33	30	23	19	...	Dem. de rés. (par mil. d'hab.)
Grants of patents	...	9	195	126	88	131	...	Brevets délivrés
Patents in force	...	...	...	...	82	345	...	Brevets en vigueur
Bahamas								**Bahamas**
Resident filings (per mil. pop.)	13	...	...	...	5	8	10	Dem. de rés. (par mil. d'hab.)
Grants of patents	66	...	...	...	192	47	20	Brevets délivrés
Patents in force	...	...	...	...	1 132	1 077	1 082	Brevets en vigueur
Bahrain								**Bahreïn**
Resident filings (per mil. pop.)	...	...	...	...	7	6	9	Dem. de rés. (par mil. d'hab.)
Grants of patents	31	...	...	...	...	...	...	Brevets délivrés
Patents in force	...	...	...	...	...	...	245	Brevets en vigueur
Bangladesh								**Bangladesh**
Resident filings (per mil. pop.)	...	1	...	...	...	...	...	Dem. de rés. (par mil. d'hab.)
Grants of patents	118	80	182	92	101	106	144	Brevets délivrés
Barbados								**Barbade**
Grants of patents	...	...	7	...	10	26	...	Brevets délivrés
Patents in force	...	...	49	57	...	...	...	Brevets en vigueur
Belarus								**Bélarus**
Resident filings (per mil. pop.)	...	61	121	197	75	60	59	Dem. de rés. (par mil. d'hab.)
Grants of patents	...	633	955	1 222	902	949	861	Brevets délivrés
Patents in force	...	...	...	4 444	2 676	2 503	2 250	Brevets en vigueur

Region, country or area	1985	1995	2005	2010	2015	2016	2017	Région, pays ou zone
Belgium								**Belgique**
Resident filings (per mil. pop.)	78	72	208	244	265	286	278	Dem. de rés. (par mil. d'hab.)
Grants of patents	1 976	1 216	708	532	567	1 620	1 016	Brevets délivrés
Patents in force	...	...	...	89 999	90 648	97 639	102 120	Brevets en vigueur
Belize								**Belize**
Grants of patents	...	...	...	...	8	4	...	Brevets délivrés
Patents in force	...	...	...	...	128	132	...	Brevets en vigueur
Bhutan								**Bhoutan**
Resident filings (per mil. pop.)	...	...	...	...	1	5	...	Dem. de rés. (par mil. d'hab.)
Patents in force	...	...	...	...	1	1	1	Brevets en vigueur
Bolivia (Plurin. State of)								**Bolivie (État plurin. de)**
Resident filings (per mil. pop.)	1	2	...	...	...	1	5	Dem. de rés. (par mil. d'hab.)
Grants of patents	62	47	...	...	75	86	63	Brevets délivrés
Bosnia and Herzegovina								**Bosnie-Herzégovine**
Resident filings (per mil. pop.)	...	...	17	15	...	17	25	Dem. de rés. (par mil. d'hab.)
Grants of patents	...	...	46	173	...	12	4	Brevets délivrés
Patents in force	...	...	120	716	...	375	367	Brevets en vigueur
Botswana								**Botswana**
Resident filings (per mil. pop.)	...	...	...	...	1	...	1	Dem. de rés. (par mil. d'hab.)
Grants of patents	...	...	...	...	4	3	4	Brevets délivrés
Patents in force	...	...	...	...	1 514	1 999	2 035	Brevets en vigueur
Brazil								**Brésil**
Resident filings (per mil. pop.)	14	17	22	21	23	25	26	Dem. de rés. (par mil. d'hab.)
Grants of patents	3 934	2 659	2 439	3 251	3 411	4 195	5 450	Brevets délivrés
Patents in force	...	...	32 571	40 022	23 952	24 153	25 664	Brevets en vigueur
Brunei Darussalam								**Brunéi Darussalam**
Resident filings (per mil. pop.)	...	...	...	...	...	...	19	Dem. de rés. (par mil. d'hab.)
Grants of patents	...	42	26	40	...	...	41	Brevets délivrés
Patents in force	...	...	...	...	...	...	1 213	Brevets en vigueur
Bulgaria								**Bulgarie**
Resident filings (per mil. pop.)	...	44	36	34	44	35	33	Dem. de rés. (par mil. d'hab.)
Grants of patents	130	375	313	251	37	42	77	Brevets délivrés
Patents in force	...	...	2 203	6 812	10 721	11 511	12 039	Brevets en vigueur
Burundi								**Burundi**
Grants of patents	...	1	...	...	...	...	...	Brevets délivrés
Cambodia								**Cambodge**
Grants of patents	...	...	...	...	1	...	...	Brevets délivrés
Canada								**Canada**
Resident filings (per mil. pop.)	81	83	160	134	119	112	110	Dem. de rés. (par mil. d'hab.)
Grants of patents	18 697	9 139	15 516	19 120	22 201	26 424	24 099	Brevets délivrés
Patents in force	...	...	125 110	133 355	166 771	175 236	180 727	Brevets en vigueur
Chile								**Chili**
Resident filings (per mil. pop.)	10	12	22	19	25	22	24	Dem. de rés. (par mil. d'hab.)
Grants of patents	448	133	311	1 020	1 058	2 077	1 574	Brevets délivrés
Patents in force	...	...	...	8 121	11 163	12 512	12 389	Brevets en vigueur
China [1]								**Chine** [1]
Resident filings (per mil. pop.)	4	8	72	219	706	874	899	Dem. de rés. (par mil. d'hab.)
Grants of patents	44	3 393	53 305	135 110	359 316	404 208	420 144	Brevets délivrés
Patents in force	...	...	182 396	564 760	1 472 374	1 772 203	2 085 367	Brevets en vigueur
China, Hong Kong SAR								**Chine, RAS de Hong Kong**
Resident filings (per mil. pop.)	3	4	23	19	33	32	44	Dem. de rés. (par mil. d'hab.)
Grants of patents	1 030	1 960	6 518	5 353	5 963	5 698	6 671	Brevets délivrés
Patents in force	...	...	...	33 225	42 306	43 359	45 059	Brevets en vigueur
China, Macao SAR								**Chine, RAS de Macao**
Resident filings (per mil. pop.)	...	...	6	7	5	...	2	Dem. de rés. (par mil. d'hab.)
Grants of patents	...	2	5	156	36	57	21	Brevets délivrés
Patents in force	...	...	12	377	470	467	416	Brevets en vigueur
Colombia								**Colombie**
Resident filings (per mil. pop.)	2	4	2	3	7	11	12	Dem. de rés. (par mil. d'hab.)
Grants of patents	169	365	256	639	1 003	917	1 164	Brevets délivrés
Patents in force	...	...	...	...	7 858	6 623	7 024	Brevets en vigueur
Congo								**Congo**
Grants of patents	...	15	...	...	...	...	...	Brevets délivrés

Region, country or area	1985	1995	2005	2010	2015	2016	2017	Région, pays ou zone
Costa Rica								**Costa Rica**
Resident filings (per mil. pop.)	...	...	...	2	4	2	4	Dem. de rés. (par mil. d'hab.)
Grants of patents	...	...	...	45	130	67	190	Brevets délivrés
Patents in force	...	...	...	239	635	678	834	Brevets en vigueur
Croatia								**Croatie**
Resident filings (per mil. pop.)	...	57	82	62	42	45	38	Dem. de rés. (par mil. d'hab.)
Grants of patents	...	25	140	82	45	35	20	Brevets délivrés
Patents in force	...	...	1 094	2 134	5 621	6 606	7 845	Brevets en vigueur
Cuba								**Cuba**
Resident filings (per mil. pop.)	...	10	9	...	...	3	3	Dem. de rés. (par mil. d'hab.)
Grants of patents	18	77	64	...	...	93	74	Brevets délivrés
Patents in force	...	...	653	...	...	857	816	Brevets en vigueur
Cyprus								**Chypre**
Resident filings (per mil. pop.)	...	...	54	35	37	43	51	Dem. de rés. (par mil. d'hab.)
Grants of patents	43	...	68	19	...	...	...	Brevets délivrés
Patents in force	...	...	3 521	333	114	79	37	Brevets en vigueur
Czechia								**Tchéquie**
Resident filings (per mil. pop.)	...	61	65	99	104	93	94	Dem. de rés. (par mil. d'hab.)
Grants of patents	...	1 299	1 551	911	749	781	669	Brevets délivrés
Patents in force	...	...	10 165	23 415	34 837	37 889	41 606	Brevets en vigueur
Dem. People's Rep. Korea								**Rép. pop. dém. de Corée**
Resident filings (per mil. pop.)	...	...	245	326	...	...	...	Dem. de rés. (par mil. d'hab.)
Grants of patents	...	...	3 583	6 290	...	...	...	Brevets délivrés
Denmark								**Danemark**
Resident filings (per mil. pop.)	167	236	523	625	596	597	626	Dem. de rés. (par mil. d'hab.)
Grants of patents	1 054	1 120	389	155	430	409	419	Brevets délivrés
Patents in force	...	...	56 978	47 732	52 321	55 715	58 494	Brevets en vigueur
Dominican Republic								**République dominicaine**
Resident filings (per mil. pop.)	...	...	...	...	2	2	2	Dem. de rés. (par mil. d'hab.)
Grants of patents	...	...	...	...	24	21	42	Brevets délivrés
Patents in force	...	...	...	...	311	265	282	Brevets en vigueur
Ecuador								**Équateur**
Resident filings (per mil. pop.)	...	1	1	...	1	3	1	Dem. de rés. (par mil. d'hab.)
Grants of patents	...	90	38	28	14	10	17	Brevets délivrés
Patents in force	...	...	38	199	...	...	63	Brevets en vigueur
Egypt								**Égypte**
Resident filings (per mil. pop.)	3	6	6	7	8	10	...	Dem. de rés. (par mil. d'hab.)
Grants of patents	298	346	147	321	472	450	...	Brevets délivrés
Patents in force	...	...	...	3 316	3 703	3 189	...	Brevets en vigueur
El Salvador								**El Salvador**
Resident filings (per mil. pop.)	3	1	...	...	1	1	1	Dem. de rés. (par mil. d'hab.)
Grants of patents	70	61	...	...	35	40	24	Brevets délivrés
Estonia								**Estonie**
Resident filings (per mil. pop.)	...	11	19	83	47	55	69	Dem. de rés. (par mil. d'hab.)
Grants of patents	...	...	163	120	24	27	15	Brevets délivrés
Patents in force	...	...	1 395	5 317	8 356	8 924	9 710	Brevets en vigueur
Eswatini								**Eswatini**
Grants of patents	30	...	...	...	2	...	...	Brevets délivrés
Ethiopia								**Éthiopie**
Grants of patents	...	...	9	...	...	...	...	Brevets délivrés
Fiji								**Fidji**
Grants of patents	15	...	...	...	...	...	...	Brevets délivrés
Finland								**Finlande**
Resident filings (per mil. pop.)	352	403	637	628	601	560	584	Dem. de rés. (par mil. d'hab.)
Grants of patents	2 160	2 347	1 757	923	931	815	704	Brevets délivrés
Patents in force	...	...	39 450	46 622	48 242	48 588	50 764	Brevets en vigueur
France								**France**
Resident filings (per mil. pop.)	212	209	354	373	377	370	373	Dem. de rés. (par mil. d'hab.)
Grants of patents	24 195	17 918	11 473	9 899	12 699	12 374	11 865	Brevets délivrés
Patents in force	...	...	343 568	435 915	520 069	535 554	563 695	Brevets en vigueur
Gambia								**Gambie**
Grants of patents	...	...	2	...	2	2	4	Brevets délivrés
Patents in force	...	...	...	...	2	4	8	Brevets en vigueur

Region, country or area	1985	1995	2005	2010	2015	2016	2017	Région, pays ou zone
Georgia								**Géorgie**
Resident filings (per mil. pop.)	...	61	54	47	27	26	20	Dem. de rés. (par mil. d'hab.)
Grants of patents	...	133	320	258	206	177	206	Brevets délivrés
Patents in force	...	...	1 040	1 044	1 650	1 394	1 172	Brevets en vigueur
Germany								**Allemagne**
Resident filings (per mil. pop.)	415	467	875	910	884	893	887	Dem. de rés. (par mil. d'hab.)
Grants of patents	19 500	16 000	17 063	13 678	14 795	15 652	15 653	Brevets délivrés
Patents in force	...	...	434 663	514 046	602 013	617 307	657 749	Brevets en vigueur
Ghana								**Ghana**
Resident filings (per mil. pop.)	...	...	...	...	...	...	1	Dem. de rés. (par mil. d'hab.)
Grants of patents	...	...	...	...	...	25	5	Brevets délivrés
Patents in force	...	...	...	...	...	25	30	Brevets en vigueur
Greece								**Grèce**
Resident filings (per mil. pop.)	113	25	48	73	59	63	56	Dem. de rés. (par mil. d'hab.)
Grants of patents	3 294	350	320	479	262	271	261	Brevets délivrés
Patents in force	...	...	...	32 120	26 506	26 479	26 936	Brevets en vigueur
Grenada								**Grenade**
Grants of patents	...	...	...	...	9	14	...	Brevets délivrés
Guatemala								**Guatemala**
Resident filings (per mil. pop.)	9	3	1	...	...	...	...	Dem. de rés. (par mil. d'hab.)
Grants of patents	166	22	104	104	51	52	50	Brevets délivrés
Patents in force	...	...	...	590	867	883	908	Brevets en vigueur
Guyana								**Guyana**
Resident filings (per mil. pop.)	1	...	...	...	...	...	...	Dem. de rés. (par mil. d'hab.)
Grants of patents	22	...	...	...	...	57	23	Brevets délivrés
Patents in force	...	...	...	...	12	29	...	Brevets en vigueur
Haiti								**Haïti**
Resident filings (per mil. pop.)	1	...	...	...	...	...	...	Dem. de rés. (par mil. d'hab.)
Grants of patents	9	3	11	10	...	...	...	Brevets délivrés
Honduras								**Honduras**
Resident filings (per mil. pop.)	3	1	...	...	...	1	...	Dem. de rés. (par mil. d'hab.)
Grants of patents	19	...	85	81	69	53	54	Brevets délivrés
Patents in force	...	...	...	...	...	82	1 654	Brevets en vigueur
Hungary								**Hongrie**
Resident filings (per mil. pop.)	273	106	78	75	68	74	61	Dem. de rés. (par mil. d'hab.)
Grants of patents	2 095	1 910	1 126	65	365	271	155	Brevets délivrés
Patents in force	...	...	9 125	13 853	21 851	23 782	26 225	Brevets en vigueur
Iceland								**Islande**
Resident filings (per mil. pop.)	87	71	253	343	257	218	270	Dem. de rés. (par mil. d'hab.)
Grants of patents	21	11	101	139	17	22	36	Brevets délivrés
Patents in force	...	...	349	1 892	4 920	5 941	6 613	Brevets en vigueur
India								**Inde**
Resident filings (per mil. pop.)	1	2	4	7	10	10	11	Dem. de rés. (par mil. d'hab.)
Grants of patents	1 814	1 613	4 320	7 138	6 022	8 248	12 387	Brevets délivrés
Patents in force	...	...	16 419	47 224	47 113	49 575	60 777	Brevets en vigueur
Indonesia								**Indonésie**
Resident filings (per mil. pop.)	...	...	1	2	4	4	9	Dem. de rés. (par mil. d'hab.)
Grants of patents	...	...	...	...	1 911	3 005	2 309	Brevets délivrés
Iran (Islamic Republic of)								**Iran (Rép. islamique d')**
Resident filings (per mil. pop.)	4	5	58	149	...	186	188	Dem. de rés. (par mil. d'hab.)
Grants of patents	339	166	2 890	5 372	2 936	3 268	4 151	Brevets délivrés
Patents in force	...	...	...	...	43 335	46 552	42 447	Brevets en vigueur
Iraq								**Iraq**
Resident filings (per mil. pop.)	19	4	...	...	9	...	16	Dem. de rés. (par mil. d'hab.)
Grants of patents	103	32	...	...	312	...	388	Brevets délivrés
Ireland								**Irlande**
Resident filings (per mil. pop.)	205	233	264	274	178	185	164	Dem. de rés. (par mil. d'hab.)
Grants of patents	1 042	3 525	349	243	126	164	87	Brevets délivrés
Patents in force	...	...	...	79 040	118 273	147 125	169 453	Brevets en vigueur
Israel								**Israël**
Resident filings (per mil. pop.)	187	228	241	190	153	152	165	Dem. de rés. (par mil. d'hab.)
Grants of patents	1 636	2 029	2 269	2 293	4 492	4 938	...	Brevets délivrés
Patents in force	...	...	...	26 494	28 666	30 922	32 764	Brevets en vigueur

Region, country or area	1985	1995	2005	2010	2015	2016	2017	Région, pays ou zone
Italy								**Italie**
Resident filings (per mil. pop.)	35	...	...	219	...	215	215	Dem. de rés. (par mil. d'hab.)
Grants of patents	...	9 164	5 534	16 106	7 153	6 429	4 855	Brevets délivrés
Patents in force	...	...	...	229 648	279 336	287 499	297 672	Brevets en vigueur
Jamaica								**Jamaïque**
Resident filings (per mil. pop.)	...	3	4	5	2	7	4	Dem. de rés. (par mil. d'hab.)
Grants of patents	...	4	...	...	74	5	2	Brevets délivrés
Patents in force	...	...	527	...	375	328	265	Brevets en vigueur
Japan								**Japon**
Resident filings (per mil. pop.)	2 272	2 661	2 880	2 265	2 036	2 049	2 053	Dem. de rés. (par mil. d'hab.)
Grants of patents	50 100	109 100	122 944	222 693	189 358	203 087	199 577	Brevets délivrés
Patents in force	...	...	1 123 055	1 423 432	1 946 568	1 980 985	2 013 685	Brevets en vigueur
Jordan								**Jordanie**
Resident filings (per mil. pop.)	...	...	9	6	4	2	3	Dem. de rés. (par mil. d'hab.)
Grants of patents	...	...	55	64	83	121	119	Brevets délivrés
Patents in force	...	...	...	312	427	463	407	Brevets en vigueur
Kazakhstan								**Kazakhstan**
Resident filings (per mil. pop.)	...	65	101	105	75	59	63	Dem. de rés. (par mil. d'hab.)
Grants of patents	...	1 281	...	1 868	1 504	1 011	869	Brevets délivrés
Patents in force	...	...	...	581	3 934	3 218	2 625	Brevets en vigueur
Kenya								**Kenya**
Resident filings (per mil. pop.)	...	...	1	2	3	3	3	Dem. de rés. (par mil. d'hab.)
Grants of patents	98	...	48	54	24	26	43	Brevets délivrés
Kiribati								**Kiribati**
Grants of patents	1	...	...	...	...	...	...	Brevets délivrés
Kyrgyzstan								**Kirghizistan**
Resident filings (per mil. pop.)	...	26	...	26	22	15	23	Dem. de rés. (par mil. d'hab.)
Grants of patents	...	133	...	109	111	120	78	Brevets délivrés
Patents in force	...	...	...	112	347	274	256	Brevets en vigueur
Latvia								**Lettonie**
Resident filings (per mil. pop.)	...	85	53	101	83	55	54	Dem. de rés. (par mil. d'hab.)
Grants of patents	...	629	122	184	147	68	87	Brevets délivrés
Patents in force	...	...	4 012	5 680	6 938	7 419	8 808	Brevets en vigueur
Lebanon								**Liban**
Resident filings (per mil. pop.)	...	...	...	...	19	...	...	Dem. de rés. (par mil. d'hab.)
Grants of patents	...	...	...	...	279	...	...	Brevets délivrés
Lesotho								**Lesotho**
Resident filings (per mil. pop.)	...	5	...	...	...	...	...	Dem. de rés. (par mil. d'hab.)
Grants of patents	...	7	...	...	...	...	...	Brevets délivrés
Libya								**Libye**
Resident filings (per mil. pop.)	...	1	...	...	...	...	...	Dem. de rés. (par mil. d'hab.)
Liechtenstein								**Liechtenstein**
Resident filings (per mil. pop.)	...	...	4 355	8 056	9 920	10 000	10 026	Dem. de rés. (par mil. d'hab.)
Lithuania								**Lituanie**
Resident filings (per mil. pop.)	...	29	21	38	48	43	37	Dem. de rés. (par mil. d'hab.)
Grants of patents	...	494	116	84	133	103	143	Brevets délivrés
Patents in force	...	...	768	642	530	522	...	Brevets en vigueur
Luxembourg								**Luxembourg**
Resident filings (per mil. pop.)	221	86	441	990	952	1 069	1 195	Dem. de rés. (par mil. d'hab.)
Grants of patents	418	...	29	87	153	184	487	Brevets délivrés
Patents in force	...	...	...	21 346	19 040	19 960	...	Brevets en vigueur
Madagascar								**Madagascar**
Resident filings (per mil. pop.)	...	2	...	...	...	...	...	Dem. de rés. (par mil. d'hab.)
Grants of patents	...	25	32	55	23	19	23	Brevets délivrés
Patents in force	...	...	249	387	414	386	206	Brevets en vigueur
Malawi								**Malawi**
Grants of patents	43	23	...	1	1	7	...	Brevets délivrés
Malaysia								**Malaisie**
Resident filings (per mil. pop.)	1	7	20	44	41	36	37	Dem. de rés. (par mil. d'hab.)
Grants of patents	1 150	1 753	2 508	2 160	2 877	3 324	5 063	Brevets délivrés
Patents in force	...	...	...	20 908	23 538	25 117	25 313	Brevets en vigueur
Malta								**Malte**
Resident filings (per mil. pop.)	...	29	...	104	209	...	...	Dem. de rés. (par mil. d'hab.)
Grants of patents	20	19	...	4	10	6	...	Brevets délivrés
Patents in force	...	...	...	832	428	423	...	Brevets en vigueur

Patents *(continued)*
Resident filings (per million population), grants and patents in force

Brevets *(suite)*
Demandes émanant de résidents (par million d'habitants), délivrances et brevets en vigueur

Region, country or area	1985	1995	2005	2010	2015	2016	2017	Région, pays ou zone
Mauritius								**Maurice**
Resident filings (per mil. pop.)	4	3	...	...	1	2	1	Dem. de rés. (par mil. d'hab.)
Grants of patents	4	3	...	8	4	2	4	Brevets délivrés
Patents in force	...	...	...	...	...	...	46	Brevets en vigueur
Mexico								**Mexique**
Resident filings (per mil. pop.)	8	5	5	8	11	10	10	Dem. de rés. (par mil. d'hab.)
Grants of patents	977	3 538	8 098	9 399	9 338	8 652	8 510	Brevets délivrés
Patents in force	...	...	48 374	82 017	106 648	109 238	112 617	Brevets en vigueur
Monaco								**Monaco**
Resident filings (per mil. pop.)	521	423	503	539	862	1 117	1 189	Dem. de rés. (par mil. d'hab.)
Grants of patents	66	36	9	5	8	9	10	Brevets délivrés
Patents in force	...	...	37 483	53 859	63 777	85 132	88 453	Brevets en vigueur
Mongolia								**Mongolie**
Resident filings (per mil. pop.)	...	57	40	41	37	37	40	Dem. de rés. (par mil. d'hab.)
Grants of patents	5	117	197	96	234	157	105	Brevets délivrés
Patents in force	...	...	13 663	2 645	4 338	4 324	...	Brevets en vigueur
Montenegro								**Monténégro**
Resident filings (per mil. pop.)	...	...	...	37	37	16	...	Dem. de rés. (par mil. d'hab.)
Grants of patents	...	...	...	264	10	8	...	Brevets délivrés
Patents in force	...	...	...	264	2 372	...	...	Brevets en vigueur
Morocco								**Maroc**
Resident filings (per mil. pop.)	2	3	5	5	6	7	6	Dem. de rés. (par mil. d'hab.)
Grants of patents	313	354	556	808	...	352	413	Brevets délivrés
Patents in force	...	...	9 872	...	...	...	4 145	Brevets en vigueur
Mozambique								**Mozambique**
Resident filings (per mil. pop.)	...	...	...	1	1	1	...	Dem. de rés. (par mil. d'hab.)
Grants of patents	...	...	14	...	54	35	...	Brevets délivrés
Namibia								**Namibie**
Resident filings (per mil. pop.)	...	...	...	...	5	7	4	Dem. de rés. (par mil. d'hab.)
Grants of patents	...	...	...	...	23	28	16	Brevets délivrés
Patents in force	...	...	...	...	456	479	451	Brevets en vigueur
Nepal								**Népal**
Resident filings (per mil. pop.)	...	...	...	...	...	...	1	Dem. de rés. (par mil. d'hab.)
Grants of patents	1	1	3	...	2	...	...	Brevets délivrés
Netherlands								**Pays-Bas**
Resident filings (per mil. pop.)	134	137	614	511	549	536	541	Dem. de rés. (par mil. d'hab.)
Grants of patents	2 145	673	2 373	1 947	1 377	1 914	2 307	Brevets délivrés
Patents in force	...	...	135 215	135 127	160 214	164 264	165 879	Brevets en vigueur
New Zealand								**Nouvelle-Zélande**
Resident filings (per mil. pop.)	310	350	458	364	258	229	212	Dem. de rés. (par mil. d'hab.)
Grants of patents	1 732	2 641	4 189	4 347	4 259	3 910	2 430	Brevets délivrés
Patents in force	...	...	34 182	34 800	40 802	38 906	36 157	Brevets en vigueur
Nicaragua								**Nicaragua**
Resident filings (per mil. pop.)	1	...	...	...	...	...	...	Dem. de rés. (par mil. d'hab.)
Grants of patents	25	1	...	...	...	...	...	Brevets délivrés
North Macedonia								**Macédoine du Nord**
Resident filings (per mil. pop.)	...	50	26	13	...	...	...	Dem. de rés. (par mil. d'hab.)
Grants of patents	...	163	373	406	...	...	...	Brevets délivrés
Norway								**Norvège**
Resident filings (per mil. pop.)	222	259	247	334	321	335	319	Dem. de rés. (par mil. d'hab.)
Grants of patents	2 165	2 014	542	1 631	1 446	2 525	2 147	Brevets délivrés
Patents in force	...	...	...	16 534	23 087	27 930	33 150	Brevets en vigueur
Pakistan								**Pakistan**
Resident filings (per mil. pop.)	...	...	1	1	1	1	1	Dem. de rés. (par mil. d'hab.)
Grants of patents	...	474	393	238	131	214	169	Brevets délivrés
Patents in force	...	...	...	...	...	1 848	1 745	Brevets en vigueur
Panama								**Panama**
Resident filings (per mil. pop.)	6	6	...	...	4	17	8	Dem. de rés. (par mil. d'hab.)
Grants of patents	72	80	228	378	78	13	4	Brevets délivrés
Patents in force	...	...	...	378	1 684	1 734	...	Brevets en vigueur
Papua New Guinea								**Papouasie-Nvl-Guinée**
Grants of patents	...	...	...	...	70	...	...	Brevets délivrés
Patents in force	...	...	...	...	71	...	...	Brevets en vigueur
Paraguay								**Paraguay**
Resident filings (per mil. pop.)	2	...	4	3	...	...	...	Dem. de rés. (par mil. d'hab.)
Grants of patents	8	...	...	...	...	...	...	Brevets délivrés

Region, country or area	1985	1995	2005	2010	2015	2016	2017	Région, pays ou zone
Peru								**Pérou**
Resident filings (per mil. pop.)	2	...	1	1	2	2	3	Dem. de rés. (par mil. d'hab.)
Grants of patents	148	...	388	365	362	403	510	Brevets délivrés
Patents in force	...	...	2 252	2 435	2 643	2 779	2 791	Brevets en vigueur
Philippines								**Philippines**
Resident filings (per mil. pop.)	2	2	2	2	4	3	3	Dem. de rés. (par mil. d'hab.)
Grants of patents	1 281	589	1 642	1 153	2 200	4 006	1 645	Brevets délivrés
Patents in force	...	...	...	...	18 145	19 995	21 254	Brevets en vigueur
Poland								**Pologne**
Resident filings (per mil. pop.)	138	67	56	90	138	123	115	Dem. de rés. (par mil. d'hab.)
Grants of patents	4 467	2 608	2 522	3 004	2 572	3 548	2 904	Brevets délivrés
Patents in force	...	...	14 578	30 021	57 951	65 006	75 982	Brevets en vigueur
Portugal								**Portugal**
Resident filings (per mil. pop.)	8	8	19	55	103	85	77	Dem. de rés. (par mil. d'hab.)
Grants of patents	960	960	231	140	76	38	55	Brevets délivrés
Patents in force	...	...	35 871	39 076	35 080	35 649	36 821	Brevets en vigueur
Qatar								**Qatar**
Resident filings (per mil. pop.)	...	...	...	...	...	9	10	Dem. de rés. (par mil. d'hab.)
Grants of patents	...	...	...	...	...	...	37	Brevets délivrés
Republic of Korea								**République de Corée**
Resident filings (per mil. pop.)	66	1 313	2 536	2 660	3 279	3 189	3 091	Dem. de rés. (par mil. d'hab.)
Grants of patents	2 268	12 512	73 512	68 843	101 873	108 875	120 662	Brevets délivrés
Patents in force	...	...	420 906	640 412	912 442	950 526	970 889	Brevets en vigueur
Republic of Moldova								**République de Moldova**
Resident filings (per mil. pop.)	...	73	105	42	18	26	21	Dem. de rés. (par mil. d'hab.)
Grants of patents	...	227	269	132	61	70	62	Brevets délivrés
Patents in force	...	...	1 108	1 018	348	343	333	Brevets en vigueur
Romania								**Roumanie**
Resident filings (per mil. pop.)	185	80	43	69	51	53	59	Dem. de rés. (par mil. d'hab.)
Grants of patents	2 786	1 860	759	447	305	355	407	Brevets délivrés
Patents in force	...	...	8 627	2 915	17 089	18 906	20 711	Brevets en vigueur
Russian Federation								**Fédération de Russie**
Resident filings (per mil. pop.)	...	118	166	203	205	188	160	Dem. de rés. (par mil. d'hab.)
Grants of patents	...	25 633	23 390	30 322	34 706	33 536	34 254	Brevets délivrés
Patents in force	...	...	123 089	181 904	218 974	230 870	244 217	Brevets en vigueur
Rwanda								**Rwanda**
Grants of patents	1	...	3	...	...	...	176	Brevets délivrés
Patents in force	...	...	...	...	108	...	456	Brevets en vigueur
Saint Vincent & Grenadines								**Saint-Vincent-Grenadines**
Grants of patents	...	...	...	...	...	...	10	Brevets délivrés
Patents in force	...	...	...	...	...	...	10	Brevets en vigueur
Samoa								**Samoa**
Resident filings (per mil. pop.)	...	...	...	...	5	...	...	Dem. de rés. (par mil. d'hab.)
Grants of patents	4	2	...	...	64	...	...	Brevets délivrés
Patents in force	...	...	...	...	64	51	51	Brevets en vigueur
San Marino								**Saint-Marin**
Resident filings (per mil. pop.)	...	...	...	...	303	392	...	Dem. de rés. (par mil. d'hab.)
Grants of patents	...	...	...	...	290	462	...	Brevets délivrés
Saudi Arabia								**Arabie saoudite**
Resident filings (per mil. pop.)	...	1	6	12	29	41	37	Dem. de rés. (par mil. d'hab.)
Grants of patents	...	3	225	194	763	595	501	Brevets délivrés
Patents in force	...	...	...	...	2 664	3 104	3 277	Brevets en vigueur
Serbia								**Serbie**
Resident filings (per mil. pop.)	...	...	50	40	26	27	26	Dem. de rés. (par mil. d'hab.)
Grants of patents	...	...	265	427	86	68	47	Brevets délivrés
Patents in force	...	...	...	1 477	3 329	3 790	4 644	Brevets en vigueur
Seychelles								**Seychelles**
Grants of patents	2	1	...	...	...	...	...	Brevets délivrés
Sierra Leone								**Sierra Leone**
Grants of patents	...	5	...	...	...	...	...	Brevets délivrés
Singapore								**Singapour**
Resident filings (per mil. pop.)	1	41	133	176	265	286	287	Dem. de rés. (par mil. d'hab.)
Grants of patents	416	1 750	7 530	4 442	7 054	7 341	6 217	Brevets délivrés
Patents in force	...	...	43 024	43 591	46 906	48 603	49 514	Brevets en vigueur

Patents *(continued)*
Resident filings (per million population), grants and patents in force

Brevets *(suite)*
Demandes émanant de résidents (par million d'habitants), délivrances et brevets en vigueur

Region, country or area	1985	1995	2005	2010	2015	2016	2017	Région, pays ou zone
Slovakia								**Slovaquie**
Resident filings (per mil. pop.)	...	50	32	48	51	48	41	Dem. de rés. (par mil. d'hab.)
Grants of patents	...	381	560	376	82	122	82	Brevets délivrés
Patents in force	...	...	4 033	10 565	15 366	16 363	17 815	Brevets en vigueur
Slovenia								**Slovénie**
Resident filings (per mil. pop.)	...	158	215	282	...	...	...	Dem. de rés. (par mil. d'hab.)
Grants of patents	...	380	285	250	...	...	...	Brevets délivrés
Patents in force	...	...	5 201	1 485	...	...	...	Brevets en vigueur
Solomon Islands								**Îles Salomon**
Grants of patents	4	...	...	...	...	...	...	Brevets délivrés
Somalia								**Somalie**
Grants of patents	7	...	...	...	...	...	...	Brevets délivrés
South Africa								**Afrique du Sud**
Resident filings (per mil. pop.)	120	21	21	16	16	13	13	Dem. de rés. (par mil. d'hab.)
Grants of patents	6 768	5 113	1 831	5 331	4 499	4 255	5 535	Brevets délivrés
Patents in force	...	...	...	...	58 624	58 235	63 151	Brevets en vigueur
Spain								**Espagne**
Resident filings (per mil. pop.)	56	52	92	107	93	93	83	Dem. de rés. (par mil. d'hab.)
Grants of patents	9 115	686	2 769	2 773	2 561	2 308	2 011	Brevets délivrés
Patents in force	...	...	39 297	175 687	115 591	115 070	108 732	Brevets en vigueur
Sri Lanka								**Sri Lanka**
Resident filings (per mil. pop.)	2	4	8	11	10	13	13	Dem. de rés. (par mil. d'hab.)
Grants of patents	112	159	180	504	262	123	178	Brevets délivrés
Patents in force	...	...	...	...	...	710	826	Brevets en vigueur
Sudan								**Soudan**
Resident filings (per mil. pop.)	...	...	...	7	7	7	7	Dem. de rés. (par mil. d'hab.)
Grants of patents	...	...	174	125	196	164	177	Brevets délivrés
Patents in force	...	...	...	...	196	164	177	Brevets en vigueur
Sweden								**Suède**
Resident filings (per mil. pop.)	460	446	555	614	599	563	574	Dem. de rés. (par mil. d'hab.)
Grants of patents	5 681	1 541	1 911	1 380	889	866	1 031	Brevets délivrés
Patents in force	...	...	102 741	96 796	92 607	93 545	96 876	Brevets en vigueur
Switzerland								**Suisse**
Resident filings (per mil. pop.)	493	410	897	1 069	1 035	1 042	1 018	Dem. de rés. (par mil. d'hab.)
Grants of patents	6 421	1 303	...	741	687	617	771	Brevets délivrés
Patents in force	...	...	99 531	123 033	162 761	193 883	208 022	Brevets en vigueur
Syrian Arab Republic								**République arabe syrienne**
Resident filings (per mil. pop.)	...	9	6	...	11	...	7	Dem. de rés. (par mil. d'hab.)
Grants of patents	...	71	72	...	14	32	3	Brevets délivrés
Patents in force	...	...	...	...	...	...	13	Brevets en vigueur
Tajikistan								**Tadjikistan**
Resident filings (per mil. pop.)	...	6	4	1	...	...	...	Dem. de rés. (par mil. d'hab.)
Grants of patents	...	47	...	3	...	...	...	Brevets délivrés
Patents in force	...	...	...	248	237	...	...	Brevets en vigueur
Thailand								**Thaïlande**
Resident filings (per mil. pop.)	1	2	14	18	15	16	14	Dem. de rés. (par mil. d'hab.)
Grants of patents	45	470	553	772	1 364	1 838	3 080	Brevets délivrés
Patents in force	...	...	...	10 201	11 681	12 193	16 591	Brevets en vigueur
Trinidad and Tobago								**Trinité-et-Tobago**
Resident filings (per mil. pop.)	...	19	1	...	2	2	...	Dem. de rés. (par mil. d'hab.)
Grants of patents	...	87	...	...	33	60	66	Brevets délivrés
Tunisia								**Tunisie**
Resident filings (per mil. pop.)	2	3	6	11	16	21	...	Dem. de rés. (par mil. d'hab.)
Grants of patents	...	141	338	620	589	583	555	Brevets délivrés
Turkey								**Turquie**
Resident filings (per mil. pop.)	3	3	15	48	74	85	112	Dem. de rés. (par mil. d'hab.)
Grants of patents	385	763	823	...	1 723	1 764	1 900	Brevets délivrés
Patents in force	...	...	...	24 969	54 673	63 575	68 886	Brevets en vigueur
Uganda								**Ouganda**
Grants of patents	26	...	...	...	...	...	2	Brevets délivrés
Patents in force	...	...	...	...	...	19	...	Brevets en vigueur
Ukraine								**Ukraine**
Resident filings (per mil. pop.)	...	93	75	56	50	50	51	Dem. de rés. (par mil. d'hab.)
Grants of patents	...	1 350	3 719	3 874	3 014	2 813	2 590	Brevets délivrés
Patents in force	...	...	37 336	24 622	25 737	24 760	23 705	Brevets en vigueur

Region, country or area	1985	1995	2005	2010	2015	2016	2017	Région, pays ou zone
United Arab Emirates								**Émirats arabes unis**
Resident filings (per mil. pop.)	...	...	...	...	4	...	9	Dem. de rés. (par mil. d'hab.)
Grants of patents	...	...	...	...	177	222	...	Brevets délivrés
Patents in force	...	...	...	...	653	673	874	Brevets en vigueur
United Kingdom								**Royaume-Uni**
Resident filings (per mil. pop.)	348	321	372	333	306	290	282	Dem. de rés. (par mil. d'hab.)
Grants of patents	20 880	9 473	10 159	5 594	5 464	5 602	6 311	Brevets délivrés
Patents in force	...	...	...	1 231 671	1 378 617	1 346 823	1 243 678	Brevets en vigueur
United Rep. of Tanzania								**Rép.-Unie de Tanzanie**
Grants of patents	30	...	3	1	1	...	...	Brevets délivrés
United States of America								**États-Unis d'Amérique**
Resident filings (per mil. pop.)	268	466	703	782	898	913	902	Dem. de rés. (par mil. d'hab.)
Grants of patents	71 661	101 419	143 806	219 614	298 407	303 049	318 829	Brevets délivrés
Patents in force	...	...	1 683 968	2 017 318	2 644 697	2 763 055	2 984 825	Brevets en vigueur
Uruguay								**Uruguay**
Resident filings (per mil. pop.)	21	11	7	7	8	...	7	Dem. de rés. (par mil. d'hab.)
Grants of patents	196	36	...	29	19	...	27	Brevets délivrés
Patents in force	...	...	...	877	606	...	410	Brevets en vigueur
Uzbekistan								**Ouzbékistan**
Resident filings (per mil. pop.)	...	46	10	13	9	11	11	Dem. de rés. (par mil. d'hab.)
Grants of patents	...	1 233	407	192	153	166	205	Brevets délivrés
Patents in force	...	...	1 263	1 253	1 081	977	952	Brevets en vigueur
Venezuela (Boliv. Rep. of)								**Venezuela (Rép. boliv. du)**
Resident filings (per mil. pop.)	13	...	5	2	2	1	3	Dem. de rés. (par mil. d'hab.)
Grants of patents	351	...	...	...	...	...	...	Brevets délivrés
Viet Nam								**Viet Nam**
Resident filings (per mil. pop.)	...	...	2	3	6	6	6	Dem. de rés. (par mil. d'hab.)
Grants of patents	...	56	668	822	1 388	1 423	1 745	Brevets délivrés
Patents in force	...	...	...	9 103	16 149	14 398	15 226	Brevets en vigueur
Yemen								**Yémen**
Resident filings (per mil. pop.)	...	...	1	1	...	1	1	Dem. de rés. (par mil. d'hab.)
Grants of patents	...	...	...	...	15	...	28	Brevets délivrés
Zambia								**Zambie**
Resident filings (per mil. pop.)	...	...	...	...	1	1	1	Dem. de rés. (par mil. d'hab.)
Grants of patents	74	43	14	12	17	27	18	Brevets délivrés
Patents in force	...	...	2 695	3 858	6 848	7 259	7 705	Brevets en vigueur
Zimbabwe								**Zimbabwe**
Grants of patents	212	105	...	...	...	...	...	Brevets délivrés

Source:

World Intellectual Property Organization (WIPO), Geneva, WIPO statistics database, last accessed February 2019.

Source:

Organisation mondiale de la propriété intellectuelle (OMPI), Genève, la base de données statistiques de l'OMPI, dernier accès février 2019.

1   For statistical purposes, the data for China do not include those for the Hong Kong Special Administrative Region (Hong Kong SAR), Macao Special Administrative Region (Macao SAR) and Taiwan Province of China.

1   Pour la présentation des statistiques, les données pour la Chine ne comprennent pas la région administrative spéciale de Hong Kong (RAS de Hong Kong), la région administrative spéciale de Macao (RAS de Macao) et la province chinoise de Taïwan.

Country or area	2000	2005	2010	2014	2015	2016	2017	Pays ou zone
Total, all countries or areas	**6.5**	**15.7**	**28.7**	**39.7**	**42.8**	**45.5**	**48.6**	**Total, tous pays ou zones**
Northern Africa	0.6	9.6	24.6	35.3	38.9	41.7	45.5	Afrique septentrionale
Sub-Saharan Africa	0.5	2.1	6.5	14.3	17.7	19.5	21.8	Afrique subsaharienne
Eastern Africa	0.2	1.3	4.5	9.8	13.3	15.0	17.6	Afrique orientale
Middle Africa	0.1	0.7	2.1	7.0	8.7	10.5	12.2	Afrique centrale
Southern Africa	4.9	7.0	22.0	45.9	48.9	51.2	53.4	Afrique australe
Western Africa	0.1	2.5	7.7	16.7	21.1	22.9	25.2	Afrique occidentale
Northern America	40.5	68.7	75.2	78.1	79.3	80.4	80.7	Amérique septentrionale
Latin Amer. & the Caribbean	3.9	16.6	34.7	48.7	54.5	57.4	62.1	Amérique latine et Caraïbes
Caribbean	2.9	12.6	23.7	36.5	39.9	44.8	47.6	Caraïbes
Latin America	4.0	16.9	35.5	49.6	55.5	58.3	63.2	Amérique latine
Asia	...	...	22.6	35.0	38.6	41.8	45.2	Asie
Central Asia	0.5	3.3	18.4	38.7	43.8	47.3	51.0	Asie centrale
Eastern Asia	6.0	16.2	39.5	52.2	54.5	57.2	59.1	Asie orientale
South-central Asia	0.5	2.8	8.0	20.6	24.9	28.3	32.2	Asie centrale et du Sud
South-eastern Asia	2.4	8.7	18.8	30.0	35.0	39.0	44.2	Asie du Sud-Est
Southern Asia	0.5	2.8	7.6	20.0	24.2	27.6	31.5	Asie méridionale
Western Asia	3.6	11.1	32.4	47.5	50.7	54.2	62.4	Asie occidentale
Europe	13.1	35.2	57.7	71.1	71.3	73.7	75.9	Europe
Oceania	35.1	47.2	57.6	64.8	65.9	67.6	68.4	Océanie
Australia and New Zealand	46.9	63.0	76.7	84.2	85.2	86.9	87.2	Australie et Nouvelle-Zélande
Afghanistan	...	1.2	* 4.0	* 7.0	* 8.3	* 10.6	* 11.4	Afghanistan
Albania	0.1	6.0	45.0	* 60.1	* 63.3	* 66.4	* 71.8	Albanie
Algeria	0.5	5.8	12.5	* 29.5	* 38.2	* 42.9	* 47.7	Algérie
Andorra	10.5	37.6	81.0	* 95.9	* 96.9	* 97.9	* 98.9	Andorre
Angola	0.1	1.1	* 2.8	10.2[1,2]	* 12.4	* 13.0	* 14.3	Angola
Anguilla	22.4	* 29.0	* 49.6	* 70.4	* 76.0	* 81.6	* 81.6	Anguilla
Antigua and Barbuda	6.5	* 27.0	* 47.0	* 67.8	* 70.0	* 73.0	76.0	Antigua-et-Barbuda
Argentina	7.0	17.7	* 45.0	* 64.7	68.0	71.0	* 75.8	Argentine
Armenia	1.3	5.3	* 25.0	54.6	* 59.1	64.3	* 69.7	Arménie
Aruba	15.4	* 25.4	* 62.0	* 83.8	* 88.7	* 93.5	* 97.2	Aruba
Australia	46.8	63.0[3]	* 76.0	* 84.0	84.6[3]	* 86.5	86.5[4]	Australie
Austria	33.7[5]	58.0[6]	75.2[6]	81.0[6]	83.9[6]	84.3	87.9[6,7]	Autriche
Azerbaijan	0.1	8.0	46.0[8]	75.0[8]	77.0[8]	78.2	79.0	Azerbaïdjan
Bahamas	* 8.0	* 25.0	* 43.0	76.9	* 78.0	* 80.0	* 85.0	Bahamas
Bahrain	6.2	21.3	55.0	90.5[3]	93.5[3]	* 95.0	* 95.9	Bahreïn
Bangladesh	* 0.1	* 0.2	* 3.7	* 13.9	* 14.4	* 18.0	* 18.0	Bangladesh
Barbados	4.0	* 52.5	* 65.1	* 75.2	* 76.1	* 79.5	* 81.8	Barbade
Belarus	1.9	9.0	31.8[9]	59.0[10]	# 67.3[11]	71.1	74.4[2]	Bélarus
Belgium	29.4	* 55.8	75.0	85.0[6,7]	85.1[6,7]	86.5[6,7]	87.7[7]	Belgique
Belize	6.0	* 17.0	28.2[1]	* 38.7	* 41.6	* 44.6	* 47.1	Belize
Benin	0.2	1.3	3.1	* 6.0	* 11.3	* 12.0	* 14.1	Bénin
Bermuda	42.9	65.4	* 84.2	* 96.8	* 98.3	* 98.0	* 98.4	Bermudes
Bhutan	0.4	3.8	* 13.6	* 30.3	* 39.8	* 41.8	* 48.1	Bhoutan
Bolivia (Plurin. State of)	* 1.4	5.2	* 22.4	34.6[1,7]	* 35.6	* 39.7	* 43.8	Bolivie (État plurin. de)
Bosnia and Herzegovina	1.1	21.3	* 42.8	49.9	* 52.6	60.3	69.5	Bosnie-Herzégovine
Botswana	2.9	* 3.3	6.0	36.7	* 37.3	* 39.4	* 41.4	Botswana
Brazil	2.9	21.0[7,12]	40.7[7,12]	54.6[12]	58.3	60.9	67.5	Brésil
British Virgin Islands	...	18.9	37.0	37.6	37.6	37.6	...	Îles Vierges britanniques
Brunei Darussalam	9.0	36.5	* 53.0	* 68.8	* 71.2	90.0	* 94.9	Brunéi Darussalam
Bulgaria	5.4	20.0[6]	46.2[6]	55.5[6]	56.7[6]	59.8	63.4	Bulgarie
Burkina Faso	0.1	0.5	* 2.4	* 9.4	* 11.4	* 14.0	* 15.9	Burkina Faso
Burundi	0.1	0.5	* 1.0	* 1.4	* 4.9	* 5.2	* 5.6	Burundi
Cabo Verde	1.8	6.1	* 30.0	* 40.3	42.7	50.3	57.2[12]	Cabo Verde
Cambodia	~0.0	0.3	1.3	* 14.0	* 22.3	32.4	34.0	Cambodge
Cameroon	0.3	1.4	* 4.3	16.2[3]	* 20.7	* 23.2	23.2	Cameroun
Canada	51.3	71.7[9]	80.3[9]	* 87.1	* 88.5	91.2	* 92.7	Canada
Cayman Islands	...	38.0	* 66.0	* 74.1	* 77.0	* 79.0	* 81.1	Îles Caïmanes
Central African Republic	0.1	* 0.3	* 2.0	* 3.6	* 3.8	* 4.0	* 4.3	République centrafricaine
Chad	~0.0	0.4	* 1.7	* 2.9	* 3.5	* 5.0	* 6.5	Tchad
Chile	16.6[1]	* 31.2[1]	* 45.0[1]	* 61.1	76.6	* 82.3	82.3[3]	Chili

Country or area	2000	2005	2010	2014	2015	2016	2017	Pays ou zone
China [13]	1.8	8.5	34.3	* 47.9[10,14,15]	* 50.3[10,14,15]	53.2	54.3	Chine [13]
China, Hong Kong SAR	27.8[2,12]	56.9[12]	72.0[12]	79.9[12]	84.9[12]	87.5	89.4[2,12]	Chine, RAS de Hong Kong
China, Macao SAR	* 13.6	* 34.9	55.2[16]	69.8[16]	77.6[16]	81.6	83.2[7,16]	Chine, RAS de Macao
Colombia	2.2	11.0	36.5[1]	52.6[1]	55.9[1]	58.1	62.3[1]	Colombie
Comoros	0.3	* 2.0	* 5.1	* 7.0	* 7.5	* 7.9	* 8.5	Comores
Congo	~0.0	* 1.5	* 5.0	* 7.1	* 7.6	* 8.1	* 8.7	Congo
Cook Islands	* 15.7	* 26.2	35.7	* 48.0	* 51.0	* 54.0	* 54.0	Îles Cook
Costa Rica	5.8	22.1[1]	36.5[1,7]	* 53.0	59.8[1,7]	66.0	71.6	Costa Rica
Côte d'Ivoire	0.2	1.0	* 2.7	* 19.3	38.4	41.2	43.8	Côte d'Ivoire
Croatia	6.6	33.1[6]	56.6[6]	68.6[6]	69.8[6]	72.7	67.1[7]	Croatie
Cuba	0.5[17]	9.7[18]	15.9[18]	29.1[10]	37.3[10]	43.0	* 49.1	Cuba
Curaçao	...	...	...	...	...	* 61.9	* 61.9	Curaçao
Cyprus	15.3	32.8[6]	53.0[6]	69.3[6]	71.7[6]	75.9	80.7	Chypre
Czechia	9.8	35.3[6]	68.8[6]	74.2[9]	75.7[9]	76.5[9]	78.7[7]	Tchéquie
Dem. People's Rep. Korea	0.0[19]	0.0[19]	* 0.0	* 0.0	* 0.0	* 0.0	...	Rép. pop. dém. de Corée
Dem. Rep. of the Congo	* ~0.0	* 0.2	* 0.7	* 3.0	* 3.8	* 6.2	* 8.6	Rép. dém. du Congo
Denmark	39.2[20]	82.7[6]	88.7[6]	96.0[6]	96.3[6]	97.0	97.1[7]	Danemark
Djibouti	0.2	1.0	* 6.5	* 10.7	* 11.9	* 13.1	55.7	Djibouti
Dominica	8.8	* 38.5	47.5	57.5	* 65.0	* 67.0	* 69.6	Dominique
Dominican Republic	3.7	11.5	* 31.4	* 49.6	54.2[21]	63.9	* 65.0	République dominicaine
Ecuador	1.5	* 6.0	29.0[1]	45.6[1]	48.9[1]	54.1	57.3[1]	Équateur
Egypt	* 0.6	12.8	21.6[10]	33.9[10]	37.8[10]	41.2	45.0	Égypte
El Salvador	1.2	* 4.2[12]	15.9[12]	24.8[12]	26.8	* 29.0	* 31.3	El Salvador
Equatorial Guinea	0.1	1.1	6.0	* 18.9	* 21.3	* 23.8	* 26.2	Guinée équatoriale
Eritrea	0.1	0.2	* 0.6	* 1.0	* 1.1	* 1.2	* 1.3	Érythrée
Estonia	28.6	61.5[6]	74.1[6,7]	84.2[6]	* 87.2[6]	87.2	88.1	Estonie
Eswatini	0.9	* 3.7	11.0	* 26.2	* 25.6	* 28.6	* 30.3	Eswatini
Ethiopia	~0.0	0.2	* 0.8	* 7.7	13.9	15.4	* 18.6	Éthiopie
Falkland Islands (Malvinas)	58.6	* 84.0	95.8	* 97.6	* 98.3	* 99.0	* 99.0	Îles Falkland (Malvinas)
Faroe Islands	32.9	* 67.9	75.2	* 93.3	* 94.2	* 95.1	* 97.6	Îles Féroé
Fiji	1.5	8.5	* 20.0	* 37.4	* 42.5	* 46.5	* 50.0	Fidji
Finland	37.2[3,7]	74.5[6]	86.9[6]	# 86.5[22]	86.4[22]	87.7[22]	87.5	Finlande
France	14.3[2,3]	42.9[23,24]	77.3[6]	83.8[6]	# 78.0[3]	79.3[3]	80.5[3]	France
French Polynesia	6.4	21.5	49.0	* 60.7	* 64.6	* 68.4	* 72.7	Polynésie française
Gabon	1.2	4.9	* 13.0	* 38.1	* 45.8	* 48.1	* 50.3	Gabon
Gambia	0.9	* 3.8	9.2	* 15.6	* 16.5	* 18.5	* 19.8	Gambie
Georgia	0.5	* 6.1	26.9	* 44.0[2,10]	# 47.6[7,10]	59.3	60.5[7,10]	Géorgie
Germany	30.2	68.7[6]	82.0[6]	86.2[6]	* 84.4[6]	* 84.4	84.4[12]	Allemagne
Ghana	0.2	1.8	# 7.8[21]	* 25.5	* 31.4	34.7	37.9	Ghana
Gibraltar	19.1	* 39.1	65.0	* 65.0	* 65.0	* 94.4	* 94.4	Gibraltar
Greece	9.1	24.0[6]	44.4[6]	63.2[6]	66.8[6]	69.1	* 69.9	Grèce
Greenland	31.7	57.7	63.0	* 66.7	* 67.6	* 68.5	* 69.5	Groenland
Grenada	4.1	* 20.5	* 27.0	51.6	* 53.8	* 55.9	* 59.1	Grenade
Guam	16.1	38.6	* 54.0	* 69.3	* 73.1	* 77.0	* 80.5	Guam
Guatemala	0.7	5.7	* 10.5	* 23.4	* 28.8	* 34.5	* 40.7	Guatemala
Guernsey	31.9	73.6	83.6	* 83.6	* 83.6	...	...	Guernesey
Guinea	0.1	0.5	* 1.0	* 6.4	* 8.2	* 9.8	* 11.4	Guinée
Guinea-Bissau	0.2	1.9	* 2.5	* 3.3	* 3.5	* 3.8	* 3.9	Guinée-Bissau
Guyana	6.6	13.2	29.9	* 32.0	34.0	35.7	37.3	Guyana
Haiti	0.2	* 6.4	* 8.4	* 11.4	* 12.2	* 12.2	* 12.3	Haïti
Honduras	1.2	6.5[1]	11.1	* 19.1	* 27.6	* 30.0	* 32.1	Honduras
Hungary	7.0	39.0[6]	65.0[6]	75.7[6]	72.8[6]	79.3	76.8[7]	Hongrie
Iceland	44.5	87.0[6]	93.4[6,7]	98.2[6]	* 98.2	* 98.2	98.3	Islande
India	0.5	* 2.4	* 7.5	* 21.0	* 26.0	* 29.5	34.5	Inde
Indonesia	0.9	3.6	10.9	17.1[1]	22.0[1]	25.5	32.3	Indonésie
Iran (Islamic Republic of)	0.9	* 8.1	15.9[10]	* 39.4	* 45.3	53.2	* 60.4[10]	Iran (Rép. islamique d')
Iraq	...	* 0.9	2.5	13.2	* 17.2	* 21.2	49.4	Iraq
Ireland	17.9[3]	41.6[6]	69.9[6]	83.5[6,7]	83.5[6,7]	* 84.5	84.5	Irlande
Israel	20.9	25.2	67.5[25]	75.0[25]	77.4[25]	79.7	81.6	Israël
Italy	23.1	35.0[6]	53.7[6]	# 55.6[10]	58.1[10]	* 61.3	61.3	Italie
Jamaica	3.1	* 12.8	27.7[5]	40.4[5]	* 42.2	44.4	* 48.8	Jamaïque
Japan	30.0[26]	66.9[10]	78.2[10]	89.1[10]	91.1	93.2	90.9	Japon
Jersey	9.2	31.3	* 32.4	* 41.0	* 41.0	* 41.0	...	Jersey

Country or area	2000	2005	2010	2014	2015	2016	2017	Pays ou zone
Jordan	2.6	12.9	27.2[1]	46.2[1]	* 60.1	* 62.3	* 66.8	Jordanie
Kazakhstan	0.7	3.0	31.6[6]	* 66.0	70.8[27]	74.6	76.4	Kazakhstan
Kenya	0.3	3.1	7.2	* 16.5	* 16.6	16.6	* 17.8	Kenya
Kiribati	* 1.8	* 4.0	9.1	* 12.3	* 13.0	* 13.7	* 14.6	Kiribati
Kuwait	6.7	25.9	* 61.4	* 78.7	* 77.5	* 78.4	98.0[28]	Koweït
Kyrgyzstan	1.0	10.5	* 16.3	* 28.3	* 30.2	* 34.5	* 38.2	Kirghizistan
Lao People's Dem. Rep.	0.1	0.9	7.0	* 14.3	* 18.2	* 21.9	* 25.5	Rép. dém. populaire lao
Latvia	6.3	46.0[6]	68.4[6]	75.8[6]	79.2[6]	79.8	81.3[7]	Lettonie
Lebanon	8.0	10.1[10]	* 43.7[3]	* 73.0	* 74.0	* 76.1	* 78.2	Liban
Lesotho	0.2	* 2.6	* 3.9	* 22.0	* 25.0	27.4	* 29.8	Lesotho
Liberia	~0.0	* ~0.0	2.3	* 5.4	* 5.9	* 7.3	* 8.0	Libéria
Libya	0.2	* 3.9	* 14.0	* 17.8	* 19.0	* 20.3	* 21.8	Libye
Liechtenstein	36.5	63.4	* 80.0	* 95.2	* 96.6	* 98.1	* 98.1	Liechtenstein
Lithuania	6.4	36.2[2,6]	62.1[2,6]	72.1[6]	71.4[6]	74.4	77.6[6]	Lituanie
Luxembourg	22.9	70.0[6]	90.6[6]	94.7[6]	96.4	* 97.8	97.8	Luxembourg
Madagascar	0.2	* 0.6	* 1.7	* 3.7	* 4.2	* 4.7	9.8	Madagascar
Malawi	0.1	0.4	2.3	* 5.8	* 9.3	11.5	* 13.8	Malawi
Malaysia	21.4	48.6	56.3	63.7[3]	71.1[3]	78.8	80.1	Malaisie
Maldives	* 2.2[29]	* 6.9	26.5[3]	* 49.3	* 54.5	* 59.1	* 63.2	Maldives
Mali	0.1	0.5	* 2.0	* 7.0	* 10.3	11.1	* 12.7	Mali
Malta	13.1	41.2[6]	63.0[6]	73.2[6]	76.0[7]	77.3	80.1[7]	Malte
Marshall Islands	1.5	3.9	* 7.0	* 16.8	* 19.3	* 29.8	* 38.7	Îles Marshall
Mauritania	0.2	0.7	* 4.0	* 10.7	* 15.2	* 18.0	* 20.8	Mauritanie
Mauritius	7.3	* 15.2	28.3[1]	44.8[1]	50.1[1]	52.2	* 55.6	Maurice
Mayotte	1.2	...	...	...	...	...	...	Mayotte
Mexico	5.1	* 17.2	* 31.1	44.4[10]	# 57.4[10]	59.5	63.9[10]	Mexique
Micronesia (Fed. States of)	3.7	11.9	* 20.0	* 29.7	* 31.5	* 33.4	* 35.3	Micronésie (États féd. de)
Monaco	42.2	55.5	75.0	* 92.4	* 93.4	* 95.2	* 97.1	Monaco
Mongolia	1.3	2.0	10.2	19.9	* 22.3	22.3	* 23.7	Mongolie
Montenegro	...	* 27.1	* 37.5	* 61.0	68.1[6]	69.9	71.3	Monténégro
Montserrat	...	...	35.0	54.6	54.6	...	...	Montserrat
Morocco	0.7	15.1[24,30]	52.0[31]	56.8[7,32]	57.1[1,7]	58.3	61.8	Maroc
Mozambique	0.1	* 0.9	4.2	* 9.2	* 16.9	* 17.5	* 20.8	Mozambique
Myanmar	~0.0	0.1	0.3	* 11.5	* 21.7	* 25.1	* 30.7	Myanmar
Namibia	1.6	* 4.0	11.6	* 14.8	* 25.7	* 31.0	* 36.8	Namibie
Nauru	...	3.0	...	54.0[3]	54.0	...	* 57.0	Nauru
Nepal	0.2	0.8	7.9[33]	* 15.4	* 17.6	* 19.7	* 21.4	Népal
Netherlands	44.0	81.0[2,6]	90.7[2,6]	# 91.7[21]	91.7[21]	90.4[21]	93.2	Pays-Bas
Netherlands Antilles [former]	1.1	...	...	...	...	...	...	Antilles néerlandaises [anc.]
New Caledonia	13.9	32.4	* 42.0	* 70.0	* 74.0	* 74.0	* 82.0	Nouvelle-Calédonie
New Zealand	* 47.4	* 62.7	* 80.5	* 85.5	* 88.2	* 88.5	* 90.8	Nouvelle-Zélande
Nicaragua	1.0	2.6	* 10.0	* 17.6	* 19.7	* 24.6	* 27.9	Nicaragua
Niger	~0.0	* 0.2	* 0.8	1.2	* 2.5	* 4.3	10.2	Niger
Nigeria	0.1	* 3.5	* 11.5	* 21.0	* 24.5	* 25.7	* 27.7	Nigéria
Niue	26.5	51.7	* 77.0	* 79.6	* 79.6	...	...	Nioué
North Macedonia	2.5	* 26.5[6]	51.9[34]	68.1[6,7]	70.4[6]	72.2	* 76.3	Macédoine du Nord
Norway	* 52.0	82.0[6]	93.4[6]	96.3[6]	96.8[6]	97.3	96.5[7]	Norvège
Oman	* 3.5	6.7	35.8[1]	* 70.2	* 73.5	76.9	* 80.2	Oman
Other non-specified areas	28.1	58.0	71.5	78.0[21]	78.0[21]	79.7[21]	92.8[9]	Autres zones non-spécifiées
Pakistan	0.1	6.3	* 8.0	* 12.0	* 14.0	15.5	15.5	Pakistan
Palau	...	27.0	...	...	...	...	...	Palaos
Panama	6.6	11.5	40.1[35]	44.9[12]	51.2[12]	* 54.0	* 57.9	Panama
Papua New Guinea	0.8	1.7	1.3[12]	* 6.5	* 7.9	* 9.6	* 11.2	Papouasie-Nvl-Guinée
Paraguay	0.7	7.9[7,12]	19.8[7,12]	43.0[7,12]	49.7[12]	53.4	61.1	Paraguay
Peru	* 3.1	* 17.1	34.8[10]	40.2[10]	40.9[10]	45.5	48.7[24]	Pérou
Philippines	2.0	* 5.4	25.0	* 49.6	* 53.7	* 55.5	* 60.1	Philippines
Poland	7.3	38.8[6]	62.3[6]	66.6[6,7]	68.0[6,7]	73.3[6,7]	76.0[6,7]	Pologne
Portugal	* 16.4	35.0[6]	53.3[6]	64.6[6]	68.6[6]	70.4	73.8	Portugal
Puerto Rico	10.5	* 23.4	45.3[21]	69.0[36]	63.5	* 68.6	* 72.8	Porto Rico
Qatar	4.9	24.7	69.0	* 91.5	92.9[3]	* 94.3	* 95.9	Qatar
Republic of Korea	44.7[16,24]	73.5[16]	83.7[16]	87.6[6]	89.9[6]	92.8	95.1[6]	République de Corée
Republic of Moldova	1.3	14.6	* 32.3	67.0	69.0	71.0	* 76.1	République de Moldova
Réunion	13.8	28.1	* 36.3	...	...	...	...	Réunion

Country or area	2000	2005	2010	2014	2015	2016	2017	Pays ou zone
Romania	3.6	* 21.5[6]	39.9[6]	54.1[6]	55.8[6]	59.5	63.7[7]	Roumanie
Russian Federation	2.0	15.2	43.0[6]	70.5[2,4]	70.1[4,7]	73.1[2,4]	76.0[7,34]	Fédération de Russie
Rwanda	0.1	* 0.6	8.0	* 10.6	* 18.0	* 20.0	* 21.8	Rwanda
Saint Helena	5.9	15.9	24.9	* 37.6	* 37.6	* 37.6	...	Sainte-Hélène
Ascension	34.9	38.2	35.0	* 41.0	* 41.0	* 41.0	...	Ascension
Saint Kitts and Nevis	5.9	* 34.0	63.0	68.0	* 75.7	* 76.8	* 80.7	Saint-Kitts-et-Nevis
Saint Lucia	5.1	21.6	* 32.5	39.7	* 42.5	* 46.7	* 50.8	Sainte-Lucie
Saint Vincent & Grenadines	* 3.2	* 9.2	* 33.7	47.4	* 51.8	* 55.6	65.6	Saint-Vincent-Grenadines
Samoa	0.6	3.4	* 7.0	* 21.2	* 25.4	* 29.4	* 33.6	Samoa
San Marino	48.8	50.3	54.2	49.6	49.6	...	* 60.2	Saint-Marin
Sao Tome and Principe	4.6	* 13.8	18.8	* 24.4	* 25.8	* 28.0	* 29.9	Sao Tomé-et-Principe
Saudi Arabia	2.2	12.7	41.0	64.7[30]	69.6[30]	74.9	82.1	Arabie saoudite
Senegal	0.4	4.8	* 8.0[21]	* 17.7	* 21.7	* 25.7	* 29.6	Sénégal
Serbia	...	* 26.3[6]	40.9	62.1[6]	65.3[6]	67.1	70.3	Serbie
Seychelles	* 7.4	25.4	* 41.0	* 51.3	* 54.3	* 56.5	* 58.8	Seychelles
Sierra Leone	0.1	0.2	* 0.6	* 6.1	* 6.3	* 11.8	* 13.2	Sierra Leone
Singapore	36.0	61.0[3]	* 71.0[8]	79.0	79.0	84.5	84.4	Singapour
Slovakia	9.4	55.2[6]	75.7[6,7]	80.0[6,7]	77.6[6,7]	80.5[6,7]	81.6[6,7]	Slovaquie
Slovenia	15.1	46.8[7]	70.0[6]	71.6[6]	73.1[6]	75.5	78.9[6,7]	Slovénie
Solomon Islands	0.5	0.8	* 5.0	* 9.0	* 10.0	* 11.0	* 11.9	Îles Salomon
Somalia	~0.0	* 1.1	* 1.2	* 1.6	* 1.8	* 1.9	* 2.0	Somalie
South Africa	5.3	7.5	* 24.0	* 49.0	* 51.9	* 54.0	* 56.2	Afrique du Sud
South Sudan	...	...	...	* 4.5	* 5.5	* 6.7	* 8.0	Soudan du sud
Spain	13.6[5,37]	47.9[2,6]	65.8[12]	76.2[6]	78.7[6]	80.6	84.6[7]	Espagne
Sri Lanka	0.6	* 1.8	12.0	25.8	* 30.0	* 32.1	* 34.1	Sri Lanka
State of Palestine	1.1	* 16.0[12]	* 37.4	53.7[12]	* 57.4	* 61.2	* 65.2	État de Palestine
Sudan	~0.0	1.3	* 16.7	* 24.6	* 26.6	* 28.0	* 30.9	Soudan
Suriname	2.5	6.4	31.6	* 40.1	* 42.8	* 45.4	* 48.9	Suriname
Sweden	45.7	84.8[6]	90.0[38]	92.5[6]	90.6[6]	89.7	96.4	Suède
Switzerland	47.1[5,14]	70.1[5,14]	83.9[5,14]	87.4[5,14]	87.5[5,14]	89.1	93.7	Suisse
Syrian Arab Republic	0.2	* 5.6	20.7	* 28.1	* 30.0	* 31.9	* 34.3	République arabe syrienne
Tajikistan	~0.0	0.3	* 11.6	* 17.5	* 19.0	* 20.5	* 22.0	Tadjikistan
Thailand	3.7	15.0	22.4	* # 34.9[10]	39.3[10]	47.5	52.9[10]	Thaïlande
Timor-Leste	...	0.1	* 3.0	* 17.5	* 23.0	* 25.2	* 27.5	Timor-Leste
Togo	* 0.8	* 1.8	* 3.0	* 5.7	* 7.1	* 11.3	12.4	Togo
Tokelau	...	1.5	...	...	...	...	...	Tokélaou
Tonga	2.4	* 4.9	* 16.0	* 36.0	* 38.7	* 40.0	* 41.2	Tonga
Trinidad and Tobago	7.7	* 29.0	* 48.5	* 65.1	* 69.2	* 73.3	* 77.3	Trinité-et-Tobago
Tunisia	2.8	9.7	36.8	* 46.2	46.5	49.6	55.5	Tunisie
Turkey	3.8[6]	15.5[2,6]	39.8[2,6]	51.0[2,6]	53.7[6]	58.3	64.7[7]	Turquie
Turkmenistan	0.1	* 1.0	* 3.0	* 12.2	* 15.0	* 18.0	* 21.3	Turkménistan
Tuvalu	5.2	...	* 25.0	* 39.2	* 42.7	* 46.0	* 49.3	Tuvalu
Uganda	0.2	1.7	12.5	* 16.9	* 17.8	* 21.9	* 23.7	Ouganda
Ukraine	0.7	* 3.7[24,39]	23.3	46.2	48.9[40]	53.0[2,40]	* 57.1[40]	Ukraine
United Arab Emirates	23.6	* 40.0	68.0	90.4[7,34]	* 90.5	90.6[7,34]	* 94.8[7,34]	Émirats arabes unis
United Kingdom	26.8[7,9]	70.0[6]	85.0[6]	91.6[6]	92.0[6]	* 94.6	* 94.6	Royaume-Uni
United Rep. of Tanzania	0.1	* 1.1	* 2.9	* 7.0	* 10.0	* 13.0	* 16.0	Rép.-Unie de Tanzanie
United States of America	* 43.1	* 68.0	71.7[16]	* 73.0	74.6[16]	* 75.2	* 75.2	États-Unis d'Amérique
United States Virgin Islands	13.8	* 27.3	* 31.2	* 50.1	* 54.8	* 59.6	* 64.4	Îles Vierges américaines
Uruguay	10.5	20.1	46.4[10]	61.5[10]	64.6[10]	66.4	* 68.3	Uruguay
Uzbekistan	0.5	3.3	* 15.9	* 35.5	* 42.8	* 46.8	* 52.3	Ouzbékistan
Vanuatu	2.1	5.1	8.0	* 18.8	* 22.4	* 24.0	* 25.7	Vanuatu
Venezuela (Boliv. Rep. of)	3.4	12.6	* 37.4	* 57.0	* 60.0	* 60.0	* 64.3	Venezuela (Rép. boliv. du)
Viet Nam	0.3	12.7	30.7	* 41.0	* 43.5	* 46.5	* 49.6	Viet Nam
Wallis and Futuna Islands	4.8	6.7	8.2	* 9.0	* 9.0	* 9.0	...	Îles Wallis-et-Futuna
Yemen	0.1	* 1.0	12.4	* 22.6	* 24.1	* 24.6	* 26.7	Yémen
Zambia	0.2	* 2.9	10.0	* 19.0	* 21.0	* 25.5	* 27.9	Zambie
Zimbabwe	* 0.4	* 2.4	* 6.4	16.4[16]	* 22.7	* 23.1	* 27.1	Zimbabwe

Source:

International Telecommunication Union (ITU), Geneva, the ITU database, last accessed January 2019.

Source:

Union internationale des télécommunications (UIT), Genève, la base de données de l'UIT, dernier accès janvier 2019.

1	Population aged 5 years and over.	1	Population âgée de 5 ans et plus.
2	Users in the last 12 months.	2	Utilisateurs au cours des 12 derniers mois.
3	Population aged 15 years and over.	3	Population âgée de 15 ans et plus.
4	Population aged 15 to 72 years.	4	Population âgée de 15 à 72 ans.
5	Population aged 14 years and over.	5	Population âgée de 14 ans et plus.
6	Population aged 16 to 74 years.	6	Population âgée de 16 à 74 ans.
7	Users in the last 3 months.	7	Utilisateurs au cours des 3 derniers mois.
8	Population aged 7 years and over.	8	Population âgée de 7 ans et plus.
9	Population aged 16 years and over.	9	Population âgée de 16 ans et plus.
10	Population aged 6 years and over.	10	Population âgée de 6 ans et plus.
11	Population aged 6 to 72 years.	11	Population âgée de 6 à 72 ans.
12	Population aged 10 years and over.	12	Population âgée de 10 ans et plus.
13	For statistical purposes, the data for China do not include those for the Hong Kong Special Administrative Region (Hong Kong SAR), Macao Special Administrative Region (Macao SAR) and Taiwan Province of China.	13	Pour la présentation des statistiques, les données pour la Chine ne comprennent pas la région administrative spéciale de Hong Kong (RAS de Hong Kong), la région administrative spéciale de Macao (RAS de Macao) et la province chinoise de Taïwan.
14	Users in the last 6 months.	14	Utilisateurs au cours des 6 derniers mois.
15	Data refer to permanent residents.	15	Les données concernent les résidents permanents.
16	Population aged 3 years and over.	16	Population âgée de 3 ans et plus.
17	Refers only to users with access to the international network.	17	Uniquement utilisateurs ayant accès au réseau international.
18	Including users of the international network and also those having access only to the Cuban network.	18	Y compris les utilisateurs du réseau international et ceux qui n'ont accès qu'au réseau cubain.
19	Commercially not available. Local Intranet available in country.	19	Non disponible commercialement, seul l'intranet local est accessible dans le pays.
20	E-mail users.	20	Utilisateurs du courrier électronique.
21	Population aged 12 years and over.	21	Population âgée de 12 ans et plus.
22	Population aged 16 to 89 years.	22	Population âgée de 16 à 89 ans.
23	Population aged 11 years and over.	23	Population âgée de 11 ans et plus.
24	Users in the last month.	24	Utilisateurs au cours du mois passé.
25	Population aged 20 years and over.	25	Population âgée de 20 ans et plus.
26	PC-based only.	26	Sur ordinateur PC seulement.
27	Population aged 6 to 74 years.	27	Population âgée de 6 à 74 ans.
28	Population aged 12 to 75 years.	28	Population âgée de 12 à 75 ans.
29	Mobile internet users are not included.	29	Les utilisateurs de l'Internet mobile ne sont pas inclus.
30	Population aged 12 to 65 years.	30	Population âgée de 12 à 65 ans.
31	Living in electrified areas.	31	Vivant dans des zones électrifiées.
32	Population aged 5 to 75 years.	32	Population âgée de 5 à 75 ans.
33	Data as at the end of December.	33	Données à la fin de décembre.
34	Population aged 15 to 74 years.	34	Population âgée de 15 à 74 ans.
35	Multipliers were applied to residential and commercial subscriptions, taking into account the average size of households and employees per business.	35	Des multiplicateurs ont été appliqués aux abonnements résidentiels et commerciaux, en tenant compte de la taille moyenne des ménages et des employés par entreprise.
36	Population aged 18 years and over.	36	Population âgée de 18 ans et plus.
37	November.	37	Novembre.
38	Population aged 16 to 75 years.	38	Population âgée de 16 à 75 ans.
39	Population aged 15 to 59 years.	39	Population âgée de 15 à 59 ans.
40	Excludes the temporarily occupied territory of the Autonomous Republic of Crimea and Sevastopol.	40	Excluent le territoire temporairement occupé de la République autonome de Crimée et de Sébastopol.

Tourist/visitor arrivals and tourism expenditure
Thousands arrivals and millions of US dollars

Arrivées de touristes/visiteurs et dépenses touristiques
Milliers d'arrivées et millions de dollars É.-U.

Country or area of destination	Series& Série&	1995	2005	2010	2015	2016	2017	Pays ou zone de destination
Afghanistan								**Afghanistan**
Tourism expenditure		...	...	147	87	69	19	Dépenses touristiques
Albania								**Albanie**
Tourist/visitor arrivals [1]	TF	...	...	2 191	3 784	4 070	4 643	Arrivées de touristes/visiteurs [1]
Tourism expenditure		70	880	1 778	1 613	1 820	2 049	Dépenses touristiques
Algeria								**Algérie**
Tourist/visitor arrivals [2]	VF	520	1 443	2 070	1 710	2 039	2 451	Arrivées de touristes/visiteurs [2]
Tourism expenditure		...	477	324	347	246	172	Dépenses touristiques
American Samoa								**Samoa américaines**
Tourist/visitor arrivals	TF	34	25	23	20	20	20	Arrivées de touristes/visiteurs
Andorra								**Andorre**
Tourist/visitor arrivals	TF	...	2 418	# 1 808	# 2 663	# 2 819	# 3 003	Arrivées de touristes/visiteurs
Angola								**Angola**
Tourist/visitor arrivals	TF	9	210	425	592	397	261	Arrivées de touristes/visiteurs
Tourism expenditure		27	103	726	1 171	628	884	Dépenses touristiques
Anguilla								**Anguilla**
Tourist/visitor arrivals [1]	TF	39	62	62	73	79	68	Arrivées de touristes/visiteurs [1]
Tourism expenditure		50[3]	86[3]	99[3]	142	143	149	Dépenses touristiques
Antigua and Barbuda								**Antigua-et-Barbuda**
Tourist/visitor arrivals [1]	TF	220	245[4]	230[4]	250[4]	265[4]	247[4]	Arrivées de touristes/visiteurs [1]
Tourism expenditure		247[3]	309[3]	298[3]	805	804	774	Dépenses touristiques
Argentina								**Argentine**
Tourist/visitor arrivals	TF	2 289	3 823	5 325	5 736	6 655	6 720	Arrivées de touristes/visiteurs
Tourism expenditure		2 550	3 209	5 605	5 441	5 186	5 514	Dépenses touristiques
Armenia								**Arménie**
Tourist/visitor arrivals	TF	12	319	684	1 192	1 260	1 495	Arrivées de touristes/visiteurs
Tourism expenditure		14	243	694	956	988	1 140	Dépenses touristiques
Aruba								**Aruba**
Tourist/visitor arrivals [4]	TF	619	733	824	1 225	1 102	1 071	Arrivées de touristes/visiteurs [4]
Tourism expenditure		554	1 097	1 254	1 664	1 632	1 733	Dépenses touristiques
Australia								**Australie**
Tourist/visitor arrivals [5]	VF	3 726	5 499	5 790	7 450	8 269	8 815	Arrivées de touristes/visiteurs [5]
Tourism expenditure		10 370	19 719	31 064	30 872	36 786	43 982	Dépenses touristiques
Austria								**Autriche**
Tourist/visitor arrivals [6]	TCE	17 173	19 952	22 004	26 728	28 121	29 460	Arrivées de touristes/visiteurs [6]
Tourism expenditure		13 435[3]	16 243[3]	18 758[3]	20 416	20 971	22 408	Dépenses touristiques
Azerbaijan								**Azerbaïdjan**
Tourist/visitor arrivals	TF	...	693	1 280	1 922	2 044	2 454	Arrivées de touristes/visiteurs
Tourism expenditure		87	100	792	2 535	2 855	3 214	Dépenses touristiques
Bahamas								**Bahamas**
Tourist/visitor arrivals	TF	1 598	1 608	1 370	1 484	1 499	1 439	Arrivées de touristes/visiteurs
Tourism expenditure		1 356	2 081	2 159	2 554	2 608	2 598	Dépenses touristiques
Bahrain								**Bahreïn**
Tourist/visitor arrivals [1]	VF	2 311	6 313	11 952	# 9 670	# 10 158	# 11 370	Arrivées de touristes/visiteurs [1]
Tourism expenditure		593	1 603	2 163	2 372	4 021	3 836	Dépenses touristiques
Bangladesh								**Bangladesh**
Tourist/visitor arrivals	TF	156	208	303	...	...	...	Arrivées de touristes/visiteurs
Tourism expenditure		...	82	103	150	214	344	Dépenses touristiques
Barbados								**Barbade**
Tourist/visitor arrivals	TF	442	548	532	592	632	664	Arrivées de touristes/visiteurs
Tourism expenditure		630	1 081	1 074	...	...	...	Dépenses touristiques
Belarus								**Bélarus**
Tourist/visitor arrivals	TF	161[7]	91[7]	119[7]	# 4 386[7]	10 935[8]	11 060[8]	Arrivées de touristes/visiteurs
Tourism expenditure		28	346	665	1 013	1 019	1 134	Dépenses touristiques
Belgium								**Belgique**
Tourist/visitor arrivals	TCE	5 560	6 747	7 186	# 8 355	# 7 481	# 8 385	Arrivées de touristes/visiteurs
Tourism expenditure		...	10 881	...	13 073	12 697	13 750	Dépenses touristiques
Belize								**Belize**
Tourist/visitor arrivals	TF	131	237	242	341	386	427	Arrivées de touristes/visiteurs
Tourism expenditure [3]		78	214	264	372	391	427	Dépenses touristiques [3]
Benin								**Bénin**
Tourist/visitor arrivals	TF	138	176	199	255	267	281	Arrivées de touristes/visiteurs
Tourism expenditure		...	108	149	148	129	...	Dépenses touristiques

30

Tourist/visitor arrivals and tourism expenditure *(continued)*
Thousands arrivals and millions of US dollars

Arrivées de touristes/visiteurs et dépenses touristiques *(suite)*
Milliers d'arrivées et millions de dollars É.-U.

Country or area of destination	Series& Série&	1995	2005	2010	2015	2016	2017	Pays ou zone de destination
Bermuda								**Bermudes**
Tourist/visitor arrivals [1,4]	TF	387	270	232	220	244	270	Arrivées de touristes/visiteurs [1,4]
Tourism expenditure		...	...	...	370	441	513	Dépenses touristiques
Bhutan								**Bhoutan**
Tourist/visitor arrivals	TF	5	14	# 41[9]	155	210	255	Arrivées de touristes/visiteurs
Tourism expenditure		5	19	64	120	139	105	Dépenses touristiques
Bolivia (Plurin. State of)								**Bolivie (État plurin. de)**
Tourist/visitor arrivals	TF	284	524	679	882	959	1 134	Arrivées de touristes/visiteurs
Tourism expenditure		92	345	339	810	827	919	Dépenses touristiques
Bonaire								**Bonaire**
Tourist/visitor arrivals	TF	59	63	71	...	...	...	Arrivées de touristes/visiteurs
Tourism expenditure [3]		37	87	...	...	...	...	Dépenses touristiques [3]
Sint Eustatius [10]								**Saint-Eustache [10]**
Tourist/visitor arrivals	TF	9	10	11	...	...	...	Arrivées de touristes/visiteurs
Saba								**Saba**
Tourist/visitor arrivals	TF	10	12	12	...	...	...	Arrivées de touristes/visiteurs
Bosnia and Herzegovina								**Bosnie-Herzégovine**
Tourist/visitor arrivals	TCE	...	217	365	678	778	923	Arrivées de touristes/visiteurs
Tourism expenditure		...	557	662	702	773	894	Dépenses touristiques
Botswana								**Botswana**
Tourist/visitor arrivals	TF	521	1 474	1 973	1 528	1 574	...	Arrivées de touristes/visiteurs
Tourism expenditure		176	563	512	631	580	705	Dépenses touristiques
Brazil								**Brésil**
Tourist/visitor arrivals [2]	TF	1 991	5 358	5 161	6 306	6 547	6 589	Arrivées de touristes/visiteurs [2]
Tourism expenditure		1 085	4 168	5 522	6 254	6 613	6 175	Dépenses touristiques
British Virgin Islands								**Îles Vierges britanniques**
Tourist/visitor arrivals	TF	219	337	330	393	408	335	Arrivées de touristes/visiteurs
Tourism expenditure		211	412	389	484	...	...	Dépenses touristiques
Brunei Darussalam								**Brunéi Darussalam**
Tourist/visitor arrivals [4]	TF	...	126	214	218	219	259	Arrivées de touristes/visiteurs [4]
Tourism expenditure [3]		...	191	...	147	144	177	Dépenses touristiques [3]
Bulgaria								**Bulgarie**
Tourist/visitor arrivals	TF	3 466	4 837	6 047	7 099	8 252	8 883	Arrivées de touristes/visiteurs
Tourism expenditure		662	3 063	3 807	3 583	4 164	4 678	Dépenses touristiques
Burkina Faso								**Burkina Faso**
Tourist/visitor arrivals	THS	124	245	274	163	152	143	Arrivées de touristes/visiteurs
Tourism expenditure		...	46	105	152	172	...	Dépenses touristiques
Burundi								**Burundi**
Tourist/visitor arrivals [2]	TF	34	148	# 142	# 131	# 187	# 299	Arrivées de touristes/visiteurs [2]
Tourism expenditure		2	2	2	# 2	# 2	# 3	Dépenses touristiques
Cabo Verde								**Cabo Verde**
Tourist/visitor arrivals	TF	28[4]	198[11]	336[11]	520[11]	598[11]	668[11]	Arrivées de touristes/visiteurs
Tourism expenditure		29	177	387	380	401	462	Dépenses touristiques
Cambodia								**Cambodge**
Tourist/visitor arrivals	TF	220[4]	1 422[12]	2 508[12]	4 775[12]	5 012[12]	5 602[12]	Arrivées de touristes/visiteurs
Tourism expenditure		71	929	1 671	3 418	3 523	4 023	Dépenses touristiques
Cameroon								**Cameroun**
Tourist/visitor arrivals	VF	...	...	573	897	994	...	Arrivées de touristes/visiteurs
Tourism expenditure		75	229	171	476	508	543	Dépenses touristiques
Canada								**Canada**
Tourist/visitor arrivals	TF	16 932	18 771	16 219	17 971	19 971	20 798	Arrivées de touristes/visiteurs
Tourism expenditure		9 176	15 887	18 438	19 256	...	...	Dépenses touristiques
Cayman Islands								**Îles Caïmanes**
Tourist/visitor arrivals [4]	TF	361	168	288	385	385	418	Arrivées de touristes/visiteurs [4]
Tourism expenditure		394	356	465	655	657	...	Dépenses touristiques
Central African Republic								**République centrafricaine**
Tourist/visitor arrivals [13]	TF	26	12	54	121	...	...	Arrivées de touristes/visiteurs [13]
Tourism expenditure		4	7	14	...	...	...	Dépenses touristiques
Chad								**Tchad**
Tourist/visitor arrivals [4]	TF	...	...	71	120	98	87	Arrivées de touristes/visiteurs [4]
Tourism expenditure		43						Dépenses touristiques
Chile								**Chili**
Tourist/visitor arrivals	TF	1 540	2 027	2 801[2]	4 478[2]	5 641[2]	6 450[2]	Arrivées de touristes/visiteurs
Tourism expenditure		1 186	1 608	2 362	3 412	3 723	4 604	Dépenses touristiques

30

Tourist/visitor arrivals and tourism expenditure *(continued)*
Thousands arrivals and millions of US dollars

Arrivées de touristes/visiteurs et dépenses touristiques *(suite)*
Milliers d'arrivées et millions de dollars É.-U.

Country or area of destination	Series & Série &	1995	2005	2010	2015	2016	2017	Pays ou zone de destination
China [14]								**Chine** [14]
Tourist/visitor arrivals	TF	20 034	46 809	55 664	56 886	59 270	60 740	Arrivées de touristes/visiteurs
Tourism expenditure [3]		8 730	29 296	45 814	44 969	44 432	32 617	Dépenses touristiques [3]
China, Hong Kong SAR								**Chine, RAS de Hong Kong**
Tourist/visitor arrivals	TF	...	14 773	20 085	26 686	26 553	27 884	Arrivées de touristes/visiteurs
Tourism expenditure		...	13 588	27 208	42 229	37 654	38 039	Dépenses touristiques
China, Macao SAR								**Chine, RAS de Macao**
Tourist/visitor arrivals	TF	* 4 202	* 9 014	* 11 926[15]	* 14 308[15]	* 15 704[15]	* 17 255[15]	Arrivées de touristes/visiteurs
Tourism expenditure		3 233	7 181	22 688	31 500	31 030	35 726	Dépenses touristiques
Colombia								**Colombie**
Tourist/visitor arrivals	TF	1 399	933	1 405	2 978	3 317	4 113	Arrivées de touristes/visiteurs
Tourism expenditure		887	1 891	3 441	5 235	5 584	5 801	Dépenses touristiques
Comoros								**Comores**
Tourist/visitor arrivals [4]	TF	23	26	15	24	27	28	Arrivées de touristes/visiteurs [4]
Tourism expenditure		22	24	35	...	...	...	Dépenses touristiques
Congo								**Congo**
Tourist/visitor arrivals [2]	TF	...	35	194	220	211	192	Arrivées de touristes/visiteurs [2]
Tourism expenditure		15	40[3]	39	47	43	...	Dépenses touristiques
Cook Islands								**Îles Cook**
Tourist/visitor arrivals	TF	48	88	104	125	146	161	Arrivées de touristes/visiteurs
Tourism expenditure		28	91	111	154	179	183	Dépenses touristiques
Costa Rica								**Costa Rica**
Tourist/visitor arrivals	TF	785	1 679	2 100	2 660	2 925	2 960	Arrivées de touristes/visiteurs
Tourism expenditure		763	2 008	2 426	3 408	3 776	3 827	Dépenses touristiques
Côte d'Ivoire								**Côte d'Ivoire**
Tourist/visitor arrivals [16]	VF	...	...	252	# 1 441[17]	1 583	1 800	Arrivées de touristes/visiteurs [16]
Tourism expenditure		103	93	213	214	477	...	Dépenses touristiques
Croatia								**Croatie**
Tourist/visitor arrivals	TCE	1 485	# 7 743	9 111[18]	12 683[18]	13 809[18]	15 593[18]	Arrivées de touristes/visiteurs
Tourism expenditure		...	7 625	8 299	9 018	9 820	11 128	Dépenses touristiques
Cuba								**Cuba**
Tourist/visitor arrivals [4]	TF	742	2 261	2 507	3 506	3 975	4 594	Arrivées de touristes/visiteurs [4]
Tourism expenditure		1 100	2 591	2 396	2 819	3 069	3 302	Dépenses touristiques
Curaçao								**Curaçao**
Tourist/visitor arrivals [4]	TF	224	222	342	468	441	399	Arrivées de touristes/visiteurs [4]
Tourism expenditure		175	244	438	712	644	572	Dépenses touristiques
Cyprus								**Chypre**
Tourist/visitor arrivals	TF	2 100	2 470	2 173	2 659	3 187	3 652	Arrivées de touristes/visiteurs
Tourism expenditure		2 019	2 619	2 425	2 481	2 757	3 128	Dépenses touristiques
Czechia								**Tchéquie**
Tourist/visitor arrivals	TF	...	9 404	8 629	11 619	12 808	...	Arrivées de touristes/visiteurs
Tourism expenditure		...	5 772	8 068	6 766	7 041	7 693	Dépenses touristiques
Dem. Rep. of the Congo								**Rép. dém. du Congo**
Tourist/visitor arrivals	TF	35	61	81[4]	354	351	...	Arrivées de touristes/visiteurs
Tourism expenditure [3]		...	3	11	~0	4	6	Dépenses touristiques [3]
Denmark								**Danemark**
Tourist/visitor arrivals	TCE	...	# 9 587	9 425	# 10 424	10 781	# 11 743	Arrivées de touristes/visiteurs
Tourism expenditure [3]		3 691	5 293	5 704	6 685	7 046	7 969	Dépenses touristiques [3]
Djibouti								**Djibouti**
Tourist/visitor arrivals	THS	21	30	51	...	...	...	Arrivées de touristes/visiteurs
Tourism expenditure [3]		5	7	18	31	34	35	Dépenses touristiques [3]
Dominica								**Dominique**
Tourist/visitor arrivals	TF	60	79	77	75	78	72	Arrivées de touristes/visiteurs
Tourism expenditure [3]		42	57	94	202	198	182	Dépenses touristiques [3]
Dominican Republic								**République dominicaine**
Tourist/visitor arrivals [2,4]	TF	1 776[19]	3 691	4 125	5 600	5 959	6 188	Arrivées de touristes/visiteurs [2,4]
Tourism expenditure [3]		1 571	3 518	4 162	6 116	6 720	7 178	Dépenses touristiques [3]
Ecuador								**Équateur**
Tourist/visitor arrivals [1]	VF	440	860	1 047	1 544	1 418	1 608	Arrivées de touristes/visiteurs [1]
Tourism expenditure		315	488	786	1 557	1 450	1 663	Dépenses touristiques
Egypt								**Égypte**
Tourist/visitor arrivals	TF	2 871	8 244	14 051	9 139	5 258	8 157	Arrivées de touristes/visiteurs
Tourism expenditure		2 954	7 206	13 633	6 897	3 306	8 636	Dépenses touristiques

30

Tourist/visitor arrivals and tourism expenditure *(continued)*
Thousands arrivals and millions of US dollars

Arrivées de touristes/visiteurs et dépenses touristiques *(suite)*
Milliers d'arrivées et millions de dollars É.-U.

Country or area of destination	Series& Série&	1995	2005	2010	2015	2016	2017	Pays ou zone de destination
El Salvador								**El Salvador**
Tourist/visitor arrivals	TF	235	1 127	1 150	1 402	1 434	1 556	Arrivées de touristes/visiteurs
Tourism expenditure		152	656	646	1 203	1 161	1 227	Dépenses touristiques
Equatorial Guinea								**Guinée équatoriale**
Tourism expenditure		1	...	...	...	...	...	Dépenses touristiques
Eritrea								**Érythrée**
Tourist/visitor arrivals [2]	VF	315	83	84	114	142	...	Arrivées de touristes/visiteurs [2]
Tourism expenditure		58	66	...	...	48	...	Dépenses touristiques
Estonia								**Estonie**
Tourist/visitor arrivals	TF	530	1 917[20,21]	2 511[20,22]	2 961[20,22]	3 131[20,22]	3 245[20,22]	Arrivées de touristes/visiteurs
Tourism expenditure		452	1 229	...	1 885	1 942	2 144	Dépenses touristiques
Ethiopia								**Éthiopie**
Tourist/visitor arrivals	TF	103[23]	227[2,24]	468[2,24]	864[2,24]	871[2,24]	933[2,24]	Arrivées de touristes/visiteurs
Tourism expenditure		177	533	1 434	2 279	2 138	2 503	Dépenses touristiques
Fiji								**Fidji**
Tourist/visitor arrivals [1]	TF	318	545	632	755	792	843	Arrivées de touristes/visiteurs [1]
Tourism expenditure		369	722	825	1 038	1 049	1 188	Dépenses touristiques
Finland								**Finlande**
Tourist/visitor arrivals	TCE	1 779	# 2 080	2 319	2 622	2 789	3 180	Arrivées de touristes/visiteurs
Tourism expenditure		2 383	3 069	4 497	4 009	4 009	5 204	Dépenses touristiques
France								**France**
Tourist/visitor arrivals	TF	60 033[25]	74 988[26]	76 647[26]	84 452[26]	* 82 682[26]	86 861[26]	Arrivées de touristes/visiteurs
Tourism expenditure		31 295	52 139	56 187	66 419	62 965	69 894	Dépenses touristiques
French Guiana								**Guyane française**
Tourist/visitor arrivals [27]	TF	...	95	189	199	223	224	Arrivées de touristes/visiteurs [27]
Tourism expenditure		...	44	...	...	...	...	Dépenses touristiques
French Polynesia								**Polynésie française**
Tourist/visitor arrivals [1,4]	TF	172	208	154	184	192	199	Arrivées de touristes/visiteurs [1,4]
Tourism expenditure		326	759	630	758	782	...	Dépenses touristiques
Gabon								**Gabon**
Tourist/visitor arrivals [28]	TF	125	269	...	...	...	...	Arrivées de touristes/visiteurs [28]
Tourism expenditure		94	13	89	...	...	...	Dépenses touristiques
Gambia								**Gambie**
Tourist/visitor arrivals [2,29]	TF	45	108	91	135	161	162	Arrivées de touristes/visiteurs [2,29]
Tourism expenditure		...	59	80	121	120	116	Dépenses touristiques
Georgia								**Géorgie**
Tourist/visitor arrivals	TF	...	...	1 067	3 012	3 297	4 069	Arrivées de touristes/visiteurs
Tourism expenditure		...	287	737	2 049	2 315	2 971	Dépenses touristiques
Germany								**Allemagne**
Tourist/visitor arrivals	TCE	14 847	21 500	26 875	34 970	35 555	37 452	Arrivées de touristes/visiteurs
Tourism expenditure		24 052	40 531	49 126	50 652	52 175	56 173	Dépenses touristiques
Ghana								**Ghana**
Tourist/visitor arrivals [2]	TF	286	429	931	897	...	...	Arrivées de touristes/visiteurs [2]
Tourism expenditure		30	867	706	911	952	919	Dépenses touristiques
Greece								**Grèce**
Tourist/visitor arrivals	TF	10 130	14 765	15 007	23 599	24 799	27 194	Arrivées de touristes/visiteurs
Tourism expenditure		4 182	13 453	13 858	17 260	16 533	18 820	Dépenses touristiques
Grenada								**Grenade**
Tourist/visitor arrivals	TF	108	99	110	155	156	168	Arrivées de touristes/visiteurs
Tourism expenditure [3]		76	71	112	422	437	499	Dépenses touristiques [3]
Guadeloupe								**Guadeloupe**
Tourist/visitor arrivals [4,30]	TF	640[31]	372	392	512	581	650	Arrivées de touristes/visiteurs [4,30]
Tourism expenditure		458	306	510	614	...	...	Dépenses touristiques
Guam								**Guam**
Tourist/visitor arrivals	TF	1 362	1 228	1 197	1 409	1 536	1 544	Arrivées de touristes/visiteurs
Guatemala								**Guatemala**
Tourist/visitor arrivals	TF	...	...	1 119	1 473	1 585	1 660	Arrivées de touristes/visiteurs
Tourism expenditure [3]		213	791	1 378	1 580	1 550	1 566	Dépenses touristiques [3]
Guinea								**Guinée**
Tourist/visitor arrivals [32]	TF	...	45	12	35	60	...	Arrivées de touristes/visiteurs [32]
Tourism expenditure		1	...	2	27	17	17	Dépenses touristiques
Guinea-Bissau								**Guinée-Bissau**
Tourist/visitor arrivals [4]	TF	...	5	22	44	...	...	Arrivées de touristes/visiteurs [4]
Tourism expenditure		...	...	14	17[3]	12[3]	...	Dépenses touristiques

30

Tourist/visitor arrivals and tourism expenditure *(continued)*
Thousands arrivals and millions of US dollars

Arrivées de touristes/visiteurs et dépenses touristiques *(suite)*
Milliers d'arrivées et millions de dollars É.-U.

Country or area of destination	Series & Série &	1995	2005	2010	2015	2016	2017	Pays ou zone de destination
Guyana								**Guyana**
Tourist/visitor arrivals	TF	106	117	152	207	235	247	Arrivées de touristes/visiteurs
Tourism expenditure [3]		33	35	80	65	104	...	Dépenses touristiques [3]
Haiti								**Haïti**
Tourist/visitor arrivals [4]	TF	145	112	255[2]	516[2]	445[2]	467[2]	Arrivées de touristes/visiteurs [4]
Tourism expenditure [3]		90	80	383	609	511	460	Dépenses touristiques [3]
Honduras								**Honduras**
Tourist/visitor arrivals	TF	271	673	863	880	838	851	Arrivées de touristes/visiteurs
Tourism expenditure		85	465	627	671	700	722	Dépenses touristiques
Hungary								**Hongrie**
Tourist/visitor arrivals	TF	...	9 979	9 510	14 316	15 255	15 785	Arrivées de touristes/visiteurs
Tourism expenditure		2 938	4 761	6 595	6 929	7 480	8 453	Dépenses touristiques
Iceland								**Islande**
Tourist/visitor arrivals	TF	190	374	489	1 289	1 792	2 225	Arrivées de touristes/visiteurs
Tourism expenditure		309	635	562[3]	1 618[3]	2 411[3]	3 024[3]	Dépenses touristiques
India								**Inde**
Tourist/visitor arrivals	TF	2 124[1]	3 919[1]	5 776[1]	13 284[2]	14 570[2]	15 543[2]	Arrivées de touristes/visiteurs
Tourism expenditure		...	7 659	...	21 472	23 111	27 878	Dépenses touristiques
Indonesia								**Indonésie**
Tourist/visitor arrivals	VF	4 324	5 002	7 003	10 407	11 519	14 040	Arrivées de touristes/visiteurs
Tourism expenditure		...	5 094	7 618	12 054	12 566	14 117	Dépenses touristiques
Iran (Islamic Republic of)								**Iran (Rép. islamique d')**
Tourist/visitor arrivals	VF	568	...	2 938	5 237	4 942	4 867	Arrivées de touristes/visiteurs
Tourism expenditure		205	1 025	2 631	4 771	3 914	...	Dépenses touristiques
Iraq								**Iraq**
Tourist/visitor arrivals	VF	61	...	1 518	...	...	...	Arrivées de touristes/visiteurs
Tourism expenditure		...	186	1 736	4 076	2 479	...	Dépenses touristiques
Ireland								**Irlande**
Tourist/visitor arrivals [33]	TF	4 818	7 333	# 7 134	9 528	10 100	10 338	Arrivées de touristes/visiteurs [33]
Tourism expenditure		2 698	6 780	8 187	11 476	11 427	14 283	Dépenses touristiques
Israel								**Israël**
Tourist/visitor arrivals [1]	TF	2 215	1 903	2 803	2 799	2 900	3 613	Arrivées de touristes/visiteurs [1]
Tourism expenditure [34]		3 491	2 750	5 621	6 574	6 587	7 572	Dépenses touristiques [34]
Italy								**Italie**
Tourist/visitor arrivals [35]	TF	31 052	36 513	43 626	50 732	52 372	58 253	Arrivées de touristes/visiteurs [35]
Tourism expenditure		30 411	38 373	38 438[3]	39 420[3]	40 373[3]	44 548[3]	Dépenses touristiques
Jamaica								**Jamaïque**
Tourist/visitor arrivals [36,37]	TF	1 147	1 479	1 922	2 123	2 182	2 353	Arrivées de touristes/visiteurs [36,37]
Tourism expenditure		1 199	1 783	2 095	2 401[3]	2 539[3]	2 809[3]	Dépenses touristiques
Japan								**Japon**
Tourist/visitor arrivals [1]	VF	3 345	6 728	8 611	19 737	24 040	28 691	Arrivées de touristes/visiteurs [1]
Tourism expenditure		4 894	15 554	15 356	27 285	33 428	36 979	Dépenses touristiques
Jordan								**Jordanie**
Tourist/visitor arrivals [2]	TF	1 075	# 2 987	# 4 207	# 3 761	# 3 567	# 3 844	Arrivées de touristes/visiteurs [2]
Tourism expenditure		973	1 759	4 390	4 968	4 943	5 549	Dépenses touristiques
Kazakhstan								**Kazakhstan**
Tourist/visitor arrivals	TF	...	3 143	2 991	...	...	...	Arrivées de touristes/visiteurs
Tourism expenditure		155	801	1 236	1 734	1 716	1 990	Dépenses touristiques
Kenya								**Kenya**
Tourist/visitor arrivals [1]	TF	918	1 399	1 470	1 114	1 268	1 364	Arrivées de touristes/visiteurs [1]
Tourism expenditure		785	969	1 620	1 596	1 471	1 564	Dépenses touristiques
Kiribati								**Kiribati**
Tourist/visitor arrivals [38]	TF	4	4	5	4	6	6	Arrivées de touristes/visiteurs [38]
Tourism expenditure		2	3	4[3]	2[3]	3[3]	...	Dépenses touristiques
Kuwait								**Koweït**
Tourist/visitor arrivals	VF	1 443	3 474	5 208	6 941	7 055	...	Arrivées de touristes/visiteurs
Tourism expenditure		307	413	574	931	831	643	Dépenses touristiques
Kyrgyzstan								**Kirghizistan**
Tourist/visitor arrivals	VF	...	...	1 224	4 000	3 853	4 568	Arrivées de touristes/visiteurs
Tourism expenditure		...	94	212	482	477	480	Dépenses touristiques
Lao People's Dem. Rep.								**Rép. dém. populaire lao**
Tourist/visitor arrivals	TF	60	672	1 670	3 543	3 315	3 257	Arrivées de touristes/visiteurs
Tourism expenditure		52	143	385	725	717	768	Dépenses touristiques

30

Tourist/visitor arrivals and tourism expenditure *(continued)*
Thousands arrivals and millions of US dollars

Arrivées de touristes/visiteurs et dépenses touristiques *(suite)*
Milliers d'arrivées et millions de dollars É.-U.

Country or area of destination	Series& Série&	1995	2005	2010	2015	2016	2017	Pays ou zone de destination
Latvia								**Lettonie**
Tourist/visitor arrivals [39]	TF	539	1 116	1 373	2 024	1 793	1 949	Arrivées de touristes/visiteurs [39]
Tourism expenditure		37	446	...	1 279	1 282	1 082	Dépenses touristiques
Lebanon								**Liban**
Tourist/visitor arrivals [40]	TF	450	1 140	2 168	1 518	1 688	1 857	Arrivées de touristes/visiteurs [40]
Tourism expenditure		710	5 969	8 026	7 087	7 373	8 087	Dépenses touristiques
Lesotho								**Lesotho**
Tourist/visitor arrivals	VF	209	304	426	# 1 082	# 1 196	# 1 137	Arrivées de touristes/visiteurs
Tourism expenditure		29	27[3]	23[3]	34[3]	48[3]	23[3]	Dépenses touristiques
Liberia [3]								**Libéria** [3]
Tourism expenditure			67					Dépenses touristiques
Libya								**Libye**
Tourist/visitor arrivals	THS	...	81	...	...	...	...	Arrivées de touristes/visiteurs
Tourism expenditure		4	301	170	...	...	...	Dépenses touristiques
Liechtenstein								**Liechtenstein**
Tourist/visitor arrivals	TCE	...	...	64	57[41]	69[41]	79[41]	Arrivées de touristes/visiteurs
Lithuania								**Lituanie**
Tourist/visitor arrivals	TF	650	2 000	1 507	2 071	2 296	2 523	Arrivées de touristes/visiteurs
Tourism expenditure		102	920[3]	958[3]	1 153[3]	1 210[3]	1 306[3]	Dépenses touristiques
Luxembourg								**Luxembourg**
Tourist/visitor arrivals	TCE	768	913	805	1 090	1 054	1 046	Arrivées de touristes/visiteurs
Tourism expenditure		...	3 770	4 519	4 760	4 764	4 980	Dépenses touristiques
Madagascar								**Madagascar**
Tourist/visitor arrivals [37]	TF	75	277	196	244	293	255	Arrivées de touristes/visiteurs [37]
Tourism expenditure		106	275	425	696	913	849	Dépenses touristiques
Malawi								**Malawi**
Tourist/visitor arrivals [42]	TF	192	438	746	805	849	837	Arrivées de touristes/visiteurs [42]
Tourism expenditure		22	48	45	39	30	35	Dépenses touristiques
Malaysia								**Malaisie**
Tourist/visitor arrivals [43]	TF	7 469	16 431	24 577	25 721	26 757	25 948	Arrivées de touristes/visiteurs [43]
Tourism expenditure		5 044	10 389	18 152[3]	17 666[3]	18 085[3]	18 352[3]	Dépenses touristiques
Maldives								**Maldives**
Tourist/visitor arrivals [4]	TF	315	395	792	1 234	1 286	1 390	Arrivées de touristes/visiteurs [4]
Tourism expenditure		...	...	...	2 691	2 640	2 886	Dépenses touristiques
Mali								**Mali**
Tourist/visitor arrivals	TF	...	...	169	159	173	193	Arrivées de touristes/visiteurs
Tourism expenditure		26	149	208	...	...	...	Dépenses touristiques
Malta								**Malte**
Tourist/visitor arrivals	TF	1 116	1 171[44]	1 339[44]	1 783[44]	1 966[44]	2 274[44]	Arrivées de touristes/visiteurs
Tourism expenditure [3]		656	755	1 066	1 381	1 451	1 746	Dépenses touristiques [3]
Marshall Islands								**Îles Marshall**
Tourist/visitor arrivals	TF	6[4]	9[45]	5[4]	6[4]	5[4]	6[4]	Arrivées de touristes/visiteurs
Tourism expenditure		3	4	4	5	30	...	Dépenses touristiques
Martinique								**Martinique**
Tourist/visitor arrivals	TF	457	484	478	487	519	536	Arrivées de touristes/visiteurs
Tourism expenditure		384	280	472	340	365	490	Dépenses touristiques
Mauritania								**Mauritanie**
Tourism expenditure		...	...	...	31	33	24	Dépenses touristiques
Mauritius								**Maurice**
Tourist/visitor arrivals	TF	422	761	935	1 151	1 275	1 342	Arrivées de touristes/visiteurs
Tourism expenditure		616	1 189	1 585	1 680	1 824	2 005	Dépenses touristiques
Mexico								**Mexique**
Tourist/visitor arrivals [2]	TF	20 241	21 915	23 290	32 093	35 079	* 39 291	Arrivées de touristes/visiteurs [2]
Tourism expenditure		6 847	12 801	12 628	18 729	20 619	22 467	Dépenses touristiques
Micronesia (Fed. States of)								**Micronésie (États féd. de)**
Tourist/visitor arrivals [46]	TF	...	19	45	31	30	...	Arrivées de touristes/visiteurs [46]
Tourism expenditure		...	21	24[3]	25[3]	...	...	Dépenses touristiques
Monaco								**Monaco**
Tourist/visitor arrivals	THS	233	286	279	331	336	355	Arrivées de touristes/visiteurs
Mongolia								**Mongolie**
Tourist/visitor arrivals	TF	...	339	456	386	404	469	Arrivées de touristes/visiteurs
Tourism expenditure		33	203	288	279	379	462	Dépenses touristiques
Montenegro								**Monténégro**
Tourist/visitor arrivals	TCE	...	272	1 088	1 560	1 662	1 877	Arrivées de touristes/visiteurs
Tourism expenditure		...	...	765	947	978	1 109	Dépenses touristiques

30

Tourist/visitor arrivals and tourism expenditure *(continued)*
Thousands arrivals and millions of US dollars

Arrivées de touristes/visiteurs et dépenses touristiques *(suite)*
Milliers d'arrivées et millions de dollars É.-U.

Country or area of destination	Series& Série&	1995	2005	2010	2015	2016	2017	Pays ou zone de destination
Montserrat								**Montserrat**
Tourist/visitor arrivals	TF	18	10	6	9	9	...	Arrivées de touristes/visiteurs
Tourism expenditure [3]		17	9	6	9	9	9	Dépenses touristiques [3]
Morocco								**Maroc**
Tourist/visitor arrivals [2]	TF	2 602	5 843	9 288	10 177	10 332	11 349	Arrivées de touristes/visiteurs [2]
Tourism expenditure		1 469	5 426	8 176	7 765	7 921	9 086	Dépenses touristiques
Mozambique								**Mozambique**
Tourist/visitor arrivals	TF	...	578[47]	1 718[48]	1 552[48]	1 639[48]	1 447[48]	Arrivées de touristes/visiteurs
Tourism expenditure		...	138	135	202	114	164	Dépenses touristiques
Myanmar								**Myanmar**
Tourist/visitor arrivals	TF	194	660	792	4 681	# 2 907	3 443	Arrivées de touristes/visiteurs
Tourism expenditure		169	83	91	2 199	2 289	2 279	Dépenses touristiques
Namibia								**Namibie**
Tourist/visitor arrivals	TF	272	778	984	1 388	1 469	1 499	Arrivées de touristes/visiteurs
Tourism expenditure		...	363	473	540	378	393	Dépenses touristiques
Nepal								**Népal**
Tourist/visitor arrivals [49]	TF	363	375	603	539	753	940	Arrivées de touristes/visiteurs [49]
Tourism expenditure		232	160	378	509	498	712	Dépenses touristiques
Netherlands								**Pays-Bas**
Tourist/visitor arrivals	TCE	6 574	10 012	10 883	15 007	15 828	17 924	Arrivées de touristes/visiteurs
Tourism expenditure		10 611	...	...	17 558	18 306	20 352	Dépenses touristiques
New Caledonia								**Nouvelle-Calédonie**
Tourist/visitor arrivals [2]	TF	86	101	99	114	116	121	Arrivées de touristes/visiteurs [2]
Tourism expenditure		108[3]	149[3]	226	246	248	...	Dépenses touristiques
New Zealand								**Nouvelle-Zélande**
Tourist/visitor arrivals	TF	...	2 353	2 435	3 039	3 370	3 555	Arrivées de touristes/visiteurs
Tourism expenditure [3]		2 318	6 486	6 523	9 452	9 763	10 583	Dépenses touristiques [3]
Nicaragua								**Nicaragua**
Tourist/visitor arrivals	TF	281	712[2]	1 011[2]	1 386[2]	1 504[2]	1 787[2]	Arrivées de touristes/visiteurs
Tourism expenditure		51	206[3]	314[3]	528[3]	642[3]	841[3]	Dépenses touristiques
Niger								**Niger**
Tourist/visitor arrivals	TF	35	58	74	135	152	164	Arrivées de touristes/visiteurs
Tourism expenditure		...	44	106	80	84	...	Dépenses touristiques
Nigeria								**Nigéria**
Tourist/visitor arrivals	TF	656	1 010	1 555	1 255	1 889	...	Arrivées de touristes/visiteurs
Tourism expenditure		47	139	736	472	1 087	2 611	Dépenses touristiques
Niue								**Nioué**
Tourist/visitor arrivals [50]	TF	2	3	6	8	9	10	Arrivées de touristes/visiteurs [50]
Tourism expenditure		2	1	2	...	...	...	Dépenses touristiques
North Macedonia								**Macédoine du Nord**
Tourist/visitor arrivals	TCE	147	197	262	486	510	631	Arrivées de touristes/visiteurs
Tourism expenditure		...	116	199	268	283	331	Dépenses touristiques
Northern Mariana Islands								**Îles Mariannes du Nord**
Tourist/visitor arrivals [4]	TF	669	498	375	475	526	656	Arrivées de touristes/visiteurs [4]
Tourism expenditure		665	...	...	...	...	...	Dépenses touristiques
Norway								**Norvège**
Tourist/visitor arrivals	TF	2 880[51]	3 824[52]	4 767[52]	5 361[31]	5 960[31]	6 252[31]	Arrivées de touristes/visiteurs
Tourism expenditure		2 730	4 243	5 299	6 370	6 285	6 515	Dépenses touristiques
Oman								**Oman**
Tourist/visitor arrivals	TF	...	891	1 441	1 909	2 335	2 372	Arrivées de touristes/visiteurs
Tourism expenditure		...	627	1 072	2 247	2 390	2 791	Dépenses touristiques
Other non-specified areas								**Autres zones non-spécifiées**
Tourist/visitor arrivals [2]	VF	2 332	3 378	5 567	10 440	10 690	10 740	Arrivées de touristes/visiteurs [2]
Tourism expenditure		3 985	5 740	10 387	16 987	15 825	14 742	Dépenses touristiques
Pakistan								**Pakistan**
Tourist/visitor arrivals	TF	378	798	907	...	...	...	Arrivées de touristes/visiteurs
Tourism expenditure		582	828	998	915	791	875	Dépenses touristiques
Palau								**Palaos**
Tourist/visitor arrivals [53]	TF	53	81	85	162	138	123	Arrivées de touristes/visiteurs [53]
Tourism expenditure		...	63	76	156	148	...	Dépenses touristiques
Panama								**Panama**
Tourist/visitor arrivals	TF	345	702	1 324	2 110	1 921	1 843	Arrivées de touristes/visiteurs
Tourism expenditure		372	1 108	2 621	5 754	6 455	6 865	Dépenses touristiques

Tourist/visitor arrivals and tourism expenditure *(continued)*
Thousands arrivals and millions of US dollars

Arrivées de touristes/visiteurs et dépenses touristiques *(suite)*
Milliers d'arrivées et millions de dollars É.-U.

Country or area of destination	Series[&] Série[&]	1995	2005	2010	2015	2016	2017	Pays ou zone de destination
Papua New Guinea								**Papouasie-Nvl-Guinée**
Tourist/visitor arrivals	TF	42	69	140	185	179	...	Arrivées de touristes/visiteurs
Tourism expenditure		...	9	2	...	2	15	Dépenses touristiques
Paraguay								**Paraguay**
Tourist/visitor arrivals [5]	TF	438	341	465	1 215	1 308	1 584	Arrivées de touristes/visiteurs [5]
Tourism expenditure		162	96	243	348	356	399	Dépenses touristiques
Peru								**Pérou**
Tourist/visitor arrivals [2]	TF	479	1 571[54]	2 299[54]	3 456[54]	* 3 744[54]	4 032[54]	Arrivées de touristes/visiteurs [2]
Tourism expenditure		521	1 438	2 475	4 140	4 303	4 573	Dépenses touristiques
Philippines								**Philippines**
Tourist/visitor arrivals [2]	TF	1 760	2 623	3 520	5 361	5 967	6 621	Arrivées de touristes/visiteurs [2]
Tourism expenditure		1 141	2 863	3 441	6 415	6 289	8 349	Dépenses touristiques
Poland								**Pologne**
Tourist/visitor arrivals	TF	19 215[20]	15 200[20]	12 470[20]	16 728	17 471	18 258	Arrivées de touristes/visiteurs
Tourism expenditure		6 927	7 161	10 037	11 355	12 052	14 083	Dépenses touristiques
Portugal								**Portugal**
Tourist/visitor arrivals	TCE	4 572	5 769	6 756	11 723[55]	13 359[55]	15 432[55]	Arrivées de touristes/visiteurs
Tourism expenditure		5 646	9 042	12 985	15 823	17 184	21 099	Dépenses touristiques
Puerto Rico								**Porto Rico**
Tourist/visitor arrivals [37]	TF	3 131	3 686	3 186	3 542	3 736	3 797	Arrivées de touristes/visiteurs [37]
Tourism expenditure [56]		1 828	3 239	3 211	3 825	3 985	4 090	Dépenses touristiques [56]
Qatar								**Qatar**
Tourist/visitor arrivals	TF	...	...	1 700	2 941	2 938	2 257	Arrivées de touristes/visiteurs
Tourism expenditure		...	...	...	12 131	12 593	15 757	Dépenses touristiques
Republic of Korea								**République de Corée**
Tourist/visitor arrivals [57]	VF	3 753	6 023	8 798	13 232	17 242	13 336	Arrivées de touristes/visiteurs [57]
Tourism expenditure		6 670	8 290	14 367	19 055	21 174	16 999	Dépenses touristiques
Republic of Moldova								**République de Moldova**
Tourist/visitor arrivals [58]	TCE	...	67	64	94	121	145	Arrivées de touristes/visiteurs [58]
Tourism expenditure		71	138	222	300	343	439	Dépenses touristiques
Réunion								**Réunion**
Tourist/visitor arrivals [4]	TF	304	409	420	426	458	508	Arrivées de touristes/visiteurs [4]
Tourism expenditure		216	384	392	339	360	401	Dépenses touristiques
Romania								**Roumanie**
Tourist/visitor arrivals	VF	5 445	5 839	7 498	9 331	10 223	10 926	Arrivées de touristes/visiteurs
Tourism expenditure		689	1 324	1 631	2 097	2 172	2 999	Dépenses touristiques
Russian Federation								**Fédération de Russie**
Tourist/visitor arrivals	VF	10 290	22 201	22 281	33 729	24 571	24 390	Arrivées de touristes/visiteurs
Tourism expenditure		...	7 805	13 239	13 204	12 820	14 983	Dépenses touristiques
Rwanda								**Rwanda**
Tourist/visitor arrivals	TF	...	...	504	987	932	...	Arrivées de touristes/visiteurs
Tourism expenditure		4	67	224	457	470	616	Dépenses touristiques
Saint Kitts and Nevis								**Saint-Kitts-et-Nevis**
Tourist/visitor arrivals [37]	TF	79	141	98	122	...	...	Arrivées de touristes/visiteurs [37]
Tourism expenditure [3]		63	121	90	312	327	354	Dépenses touristiques [3]
Saint Lucia								**Sainte-Lucie**
Tourist/visitor arrivals [1]	TF	231	318	306	345	348	386	Arrivées de touristes/visiteurs [1]
Tourism expenditure [3]		230	382	309	810	776	801	Dépenses touristiques [3]
Saint Vincent & Grenadines								**Saint-Vincent-Grenadines**
Tourist/visitor arrivals [37]	TF	60	96	72	75	79	76	Arrivées de touristes/visiteurs [37]
Tourism expenditure		53[3]	104[3]	86[3]	211	221	217	Dépenses touristiques
Samoa								**Samoa**
Tourist/visitor arrivals	TF	68	102	122	128	134	146	Arrivées de touristes/visiteurs
Tourism expenditure		36	74	124	142	149	169	Dépenses touristiques
San Marino [59]								**Saint-Marin** [59]
Tourist/visitor arrivals	THS	28	50	120	54	60	78	Arrivées de touristes/visiteurs
Sao Tome and Principe								**Sao Tomé-et-Principe**
Tourist/visitor arrivals	TF	6	16	8	26	29	...	Arrivées de touristes/visiteurs
Tourism expenditure		...	...	...	63	69	66	Dépenses touristiques
Saudi Arabia								**Arabie saoudite**
Tourist/visitor arrivals	TF	3 325	8 037	10 850	17 994	18 044	16 109	Arrivées de touristes/visiteurs
Tourism expenditure		...	...	7 536	11 183	13 438	14 848	Dépenses touristiques
Senegal								**Sénégal**
Tourist/visitor arrivals	TF	...	769	* 900	* 1 007	* 1 210	* 1 365	Arrivées de touristes/visiteurs
Tourism expenditure		168	334	464	...	...	...	Dépenses touristiques

30

Tourist/visitor arrivals and tourism expenditure *(continued)*
Thousands arrivals and millions of US dollars

Arrivées de touristes/visiteurs et dépenses touristiques *(suite)*
Milliers d'arrivées et millions de dollars É.-U.

Country or area of destination	Series& Série&	1995	2005	2010	2015	2016	2017	Pays ou zone de destination
Serbia								**Serbie**
Tourist/visitor arrivals	TCE	...	453	683	1 132	1 281	1 497	Arrivées de touristes/visiteurs
Tourism expenditure		...	308	950	1 322	1 460	1 705	Dépenses touristiques
Seychelles								**Seychelles**
Tourist/visitor arrivals	TF	121	129	175	276	303	350	Arrivées de touristes/visiteurs
Tourism expenditure		224	269	352	483	505	585	Dépenses touristiques
Sierra Leone								**Sierra Leone**
Tourist/visitor arrivals [4]	TF	14	40	39	24	55	...	Arrivées de touristes/visiteurs [4]
Tourism expenditure [3]		57	64	26	37	41	...	Dépenses touristiques [3]
Singapore								**Singapour**
Tourist/visitor arrivals	TF	6 070	7 079	9 161	12 051	12 914	13 903	Arrivées de touristes/visiteurs
Tourism expenditure [3]		7 611	6 209	14 178	16 617	18 945	19 707	Dépenses touristiques [3]
Sint Maarten (Dutch part)								**St-Martin (partie néerland.)**
Tourist/visitor arrivals [60]	TF	460	468	443	505	528	402	Arrivées de touristes/visiteurs [60]
Tourism expenditure		...	...	681	913	871	646	Dépenses touristiques
Slovakia								**Slovaquie**
Tourist/visitor arrivals [61]	TCE	903	1 515	1 327	1 721	2 027	2 162	Arrivées de touristes/visiteurs [61]
Tourism expenditure		630	1 282	2 335	2 480	2 802	2 995	Dépenses touristiques
Slovenia								**Slovénie**
Tourist/visitor arrivals	TCE	732	1 555	1 869	2 707	3 032	3 586	Arrivées de touristes/visiteurs
Tourism expenditure		1 128	1 894	2 721	2 521	2 627	2 952	Dépenses touristiques
Solomon Islands								**Îles Salomon**
Tourist/visitor arrivals	TF	12	9[62]	21	22	23	26	Arrivées de touristes/visiteurs
Tourism expenditure		17	6	51	60	71	79	Dépenses touristiques
South Africa								**Afrique du Sud**
Tourist/visitor arrivals	TF	4 488[63]	7 369[63]	# 8 074	# 8 904[64]	# 10 044[64]	# 10 285[64]	Arrivées de touristes/visiteurs
Tourism expenditure		2 654	8 629	10 309	9 140	8 807	9 699	Dépenses touristiques
South Sudan								**Soudan du sud**
Tourism expenditure		...	...	...	22	24	26	Dépenses touristiques
Spain								**Espagne**
Tourist/visitor arrivals	TF	32 971	55 914	52 677	68 175	75 315	81 786	Arrivées de touristes/visiteurs
Tourism expenditure		27 369	49 565[3]	54 305[3]	56 532[3]	60 605[3]	68 437[3]	Dépenses touristiques
Sri Lanka								**Sri Lanka**
Tourist/visitor arrivals [1]	TF	403	549	654	1 798	2 051	2 116	Arrivées de touristes/visiteurs [1]
Tourism expenditure		367	729	1 044	3 978	4 591	5 083	Dépenses touristiques
State of Palestine								**État de Palestine**
Tourist/visitor arrivals	THS	...	88	522	432[65]	# 400[65]	# 503[65]	Arrivées de touristes/visiteurs
Tourism expenditure [3,66]		255	52	409	312	235	225	Dépenses touristiques [3,66]
Sudan								**Soudan**
Tourist/visitor arrivals	TF	29	246[2]	495[2]	741[2]	800[2]	813[2]	Arrivées de touristes/visiteurs
Tourism expenditure [3]		8	114	82	949	1 009	1 029	Dépenses touristiques [3]
Suriname								**Suriname**
Tourist/visitor arrivals	TF	43[67]	161	205	228	256	278	Arrivées de touristes/visiteurs
Tourism expenditure		52	96	69	99	74	61	Dépenses touristiques
Eswatini								**Eswatini**
Tourist/visitor arrivals	TF	300[68]	837	868	873	947	921	Arrivées de touristes/visiteurs
Tourism expenditure		54	77	51	14	13	13	Dépenses touristiques
Sweden								**Suède**
Tourism expenditure		4 390	7 628	10 674	11 307[3]	12 764[3]	14 205[3]	Dépenses touristiques
Switzerland								**Suisse**
Tourist/visitor arrivals	THS	6 946	7 229	8 628	9 305	9 205	9 889	Arrivées de touristes/visiteurs
Tourism expenditure		11 354	11 952	17 614	19 639	19 217	20 134	Dépenses touristiques
Syrian Arab Republic								**République arabe syrienne**
Tourist/visitor arrivals	TCE	815	3 571[2]	8 546[2,69]	...	...	...	Arrivées de touristes/visiteurs
Tourism expenditure		...	2 035	6 308	...	...	...	Dépenses touristiques
Tajikistan								**Tadjikistan**
Tourist/visitor arrivals	VF	...	...	160	414	344	431	Arrivées de touristes/visiteurs
Tourism expenditure		...	9	142	146	150	172	Dépenses touristiques
Thailand								**Thaïlande**
Tourist/visitor arrivals	TF	6 952[2]	11 567[2]	15 936	29 923	32 530	35 592	Arrivées de touristes/visiteurs
Tourism expenditure		9 257	12 103	23 796	48 527	52 465	62 158	Dépenses touristiques
Timor-Leste								**Timor-Leste**
Tourist/visitor arrivals [70]	TF	...	...	40	62	66	74	Arrivées de touristes/visiteurs [70]
Tourism expenditure [3]		...	...	24	51	58	73	Dépenses touristiques [3]

30

Tourist/visitor arrivals and tourism expenditure *(continued)*
Thousands arrivals and millions of US dollars

Arrivées de touristes/visiteurs et dépenses touristiques *(suite)*
Milliers d'arrivées et millions de dollars É.-U.

Country or area of destination	Series& Série&	1995	2005	2010	2015	2016	2017	Pays ou zone de destination
Togo								**Togo**
Tourist/visitor arrivals	THS	53	81	202	273	338	496	Arrivées de touristes/visiteurs
Tourism expenditure		...	27	105	212	223	...	Dépenses touristiques
Tonga								**Tonga**
Tourist/visitor arrivals [4]	TF	29	42	47	54	59	63	Arrivées de touristes/visiteurs [4]
Tourism expenditure		...	15	17	46	53	49	Dépenses touristiques
Trinidad and Tobago								**Trinité-et-Tobago**
Tourist/visitor arrivals [4]	TF	260	463	388	440	409	395	Arrivées de touristes/visiteurs [4]
Tourism expenditure		232	593	630	809	708	739	Dépenses touristiques
Tunisia								**Tunisie**
Tourist/visitor arrivals	TF	4 120[1]	6 378[1]	7 828	5 359	5 724	7 052	Arrivées de touristes/visiteurs
Tourism expenditure		1 838	2 800	3 477	1 869	1 706	1 782	Dépenses touristiques
Turkey								**Turquie**
Tourist/visitor arrivals	TF	7 083	20 273	31 364[71]	39 478[71]	30 289[71]	37 601[71]	Arrivées de touristes/visiteurs
Tourism expenditure		...	20 760	26 318	35 597	26 788	31 870	Dépenses touristiques
Turkmenistan								**Turkménistan**
Tourist/visitor arrivals	TF	218	12	...	...	...	...	Arrivées de touristes/visiteurs
Turks and Caicos Islands								**Îles Turques-et-Caïques**
Tourist/visitor arrivals	TF	79	176	281	386	454	416	Arrivées de touristes/visiteurs
Tourism expenditure		53	...	...	634	721	...	Dépenses touristiques
Tuvalu								**Tuvalu**
Tourist/visitor arrivals	TF	1	1	2	2	3	3	Arrivées de touristes/visiteurs
Tourism expenditure [3]		...	1	2	...	...	...	Dépenses touristiques [3]
Uganda								**Ouganda**
Tourist/visitor arrivals	TF	160	468	946	1 303	1 323	1 402	Arrivées de touristes/visiteurs
Tourism expenditure		...	382	802	1 046	1 069	940	Dépenses touristiques
Ukraine								**Ukraine**
Tourist/visitor arrivals	TF	3 716	17 631	21 203	12 428	13 333	14 230	Arrivées de touristes/visiteurs
Tourism expenditure		...	3 542	4 696	1 662	1 723	1 999	Dépenses touristiques
United Arab Emirates								**Émirats arabes unis**
Tourist/visitor arrivals [72]	THS	2 315	7 126	...	...	...	...	Arrivées de touristes/visiteurs [72]
Tourism expenditure		632	3 218	8 577	17 481	19 496	21 048	Dépenses touristiques
United Kingdom								**Royaume-Uni**
Tourist/visitor arrivals	TF	21 719	28 039	28 295	34 436	35 814	37 651	Arrivées de touristes/visiteurs
Tourism expenditure		27 577	41 736	40 526	65 454	61 894	...	Dépenses touristiques
United Rep. of Tanzania								**Rép.-Unie de Tanzanie**
Tourist/visitor arrivals	TF	285	590	754	1 104	1 233	1 275	Arrivées de touristes/visiteurs
Tourism expenditure		...	835	1 279	1 924	2 157	2 284	Dépenses touristiques
United States of America								**États-Unis d'Amérique**
Tourist/visitor arrivals	TF	43 318	49 206	60 010	# 77 774	# 76 407	# 76 941	Arrivées de touristes/visiteurs
Tourism expenditure		93 743	122 077	167 996	249 183	246 172	251 361	Dépenses touristiques
United States Virgin Islands								**Îles Vierges américaines**
Tourist/visitor arrivals	TF	454	594	572	642	667	...	Arrivées de touristes/visiteurs
Tourism expenditure		822	1 432	1 223	1 324	1 343	...	Dépenses touristiques
Uruguay								**Uruguay**
Tourist/visitor arrivals	TF	2 022	1 808	2 353	2 773	3 037	3 674	Arrivées de touristes/visiteurs
Tourism expenditure		725	699	1 669	2 070	2 182	2 666	Dépenses touristiques
Uzbekistan								**Ouzbékistan**
Tourist/visitor arrivals	TF	92	242	975	1 918	2 027	2 690	Arrivées de touristes/visiteurs
Tourism expenditure [3]		...	28	121	...	...	...	Dépenses touristiques [3]
Vanuatu								**Vanuatu**
Tourist/visitor arrivals	TF	44	62	97	90	95	109	Arrivées de touristes/visiteurs
Tourism expenditure		...	104	242	254	...	...	Dépenses touristiques
Venezuela (Boliv. Rep. of)								**Venezuela (Rép. boliv. du)**
Tourist/visitor arrivals	TF	700	706	526	789	601	427	Arrivées de touristes/visiteurs
Tourism expenditure		995	722	885	654	546	...	Dépenses touristiques
Viet Nam								**Viet Nam**
Tourist/visitor arrivals	VF	1 351	3 477	5 050	7 944	10 013	12 922	Arrivées de touristes/visiteurs
Tourism expenditure		...	2 300	4 450	7 350	8 500	8 890	Dépenses touristiques
Yemen								**Yémen**
Tourist/visitor arrivals	TF	61	336	1 025[2]	367[2]	...	...	Arrivées de touristes/visiteurs
Tourism expenditure		...	...	1 291	116	116	...	Dépenses touristiques
Zambia								**Zambie**
Tourist/visitor arrivals	TF	163	669	815	932	956	1 083	Arrivées de touristes/visiteurs
Tourism expenditure [3]		...	447	492	660	683	653	Dépenses touristiques [3]

30

Tourist/visitor arrivals and tourism expenditure *(continued)*
Thousands arrivals and millions of US dollars

Arrivées de touristes/visiteurs et dépenses touristiques *(suite)*
Milliers d'arrivées et millions de dollars É.-U.

Country or area of destination	Series& Série&	1995	2005	2010	2015	2016	2017	Pays ou zone de destination
Zimbabwe								**Zimbabwe**
Tourist/visitor arrivals	VF	1 416	1 559	2 239	2 057	2 168	2 423	Arrivées de touristes/visiteurs
Tourism expenditure		145	99	135	191	194	158	Dépenses touristiques

Source:

World Tourism Organization (UNWTO), Madrid, the UNWTO Statistics Database, last accessed January 2019.

The majority of the expenditure data have been provided to the WTO by the International Monetary Fund (IMF). & Series (by order of priority, see Annex II): TF: Arrivals of non-resident tourists at national borders. VF: Arrivals of non-resident visitors at national borders. TCE: Arrivals of non-resident tourists in all types of accommodation establishments. THS: Arrivals of non-resident tourists in hotels and similar establishments.

1 Excluding nationals residing abroad.
2 Including nationals residing abroad.
3 Excluding passenger transport.
4 Arrivals by air.
5 Excluding nationals residing abroad and crew members.

6 Only paid accommodation; excluding stays at friends and relatives and second homes.
7 Excludes the Belarusian-Russian border segment.
8 Includes estimation of the Belarusian-Russian border segment.
9 Including regional high end tourists.
10 Excluding Netherlands Antillean residents.
11 Non-resident tourists staying in hotels and similar establishments.
12 Arrivals by all means of transport.
13 Arrivals by air at Bangui only.
14 For statistical purposes, the data for China do not include those for the Hong Kong Special Administrative Region (Hong Kong SAR), Macao Special Administrative Region (Macao SAR) and Taiwan Province of China.
15 Does not include other non-residents namely workers, students, etc.

16 Arrivals to Félix Houphouët Boigny Airport only.
17 Figures include arrivals by land (road and railway).

18 Excluding arrivals in ports of nautical tourism.
19 Excluding the passengers at Herrera airport.
20 Border statistics are not collected any more, surveys used instead.

21 Calculated on the basis of accommodation statistics and "Foreign Visitor Survey" carried out by the Statistical Office of Estonia.

22 Based on mobile positioning data.
23 Arrivals to Bole airport only.
24 Arrivals through all ports of entry.
25 Estimated based on surveys at national borders.
26 Arrivals of non-resident visitors.
27 Survey at Cayenne-Rochambeau airport on departure.
28 Arrivals of non-resident tourists at Libreville airport.
29 Charter tourists only.
30 Excluding the north islands, Saint Barthélemy and Saint Martin (French part).
31 Non-resident tourists staying in all types of accommodation establishments.

Source:

Organisation mondiale du tourisme (OMT), Madrid, base de données statistiques de l'OMT, dernier accès janvier 2019.

La majorité des données sur les dépenses touristiques sont celles que le Fonds monétaire international (FMI) a fournies à l'Organisation mondiale du tourisme (OMT). & Série (par ordre de priorite, voir annexe II): TF: Arrivées de touristes non résidents aux frontières nationales. VF: Arrivées de visiteurs non résidents aux frontières nationales. TCE: Arrivées de touristes non résidents dans tous les types d'établissements d'hébergement touristique. THS: Arrivées de touristes non résidents dans les hôtels et établissements assimilés.

1 À l'exclusion des nationaux résidant à l'étranger.
2 Y compris les nationaux du pays résidant à l'étranger.
3 Non compris le transport de passagers.
4 Arrivées par voie aérienne.
5 À l'exclusion des nationaux du pays résidant à l'étranger et des membres des équipages.

6 Seulement logement payé; sont exclus les séjours chez des amis et membres de la famille et des résidences secondaires.
7 Exclut le segment de la frontière biélorusse-russe.
8 Comprend l'estimation du segment frontalier biélorusse-russe.
9 Y compris les touristes régionaux haut de gamme.
10 A l'exclusion des résidents des Antilles Néerlandaises.
11 Non résidents touristes dans les hôtels et établissements assimilés.
12 Arrivées par tous moyens de transport confondus.
13 Arrivées par voie aérienne à Bangui uniquement.
14 Pour la présentation des statistiques, les données pour la Chine ne comprennent pas la région administrative spéciale de Hong Kong (RAS de Hong Kong), la région administrative spéciale de Macao (RAS de Macao) et la province chinoise de Taïwan.
15 Ne comprend pas d'autres catégories de non-résidents tels que les travailleurs, les étudiants, etc.

16 Arrivées à l'aéroport Félix Houphouët Boigny seulement.
17 Les chiffres incluent les arrivées par voie terrestre (route et chemin de fer).

18 À l'exclusion des arrivées dans des ports à tourisme nautique.
19 A l'exclusion des passagers à l'aéroport de Herrera.
20 Statistiques frontaliers ne sont plus collectés, les enquêtes utilisées à la place.

21 Calculé sur la base des statistiques d'hébergement et de la " Foreign Visitor Survey" menée par la "Statistical Office of Estonia". À partir de 2004, les statistiques de frontière ne sont plus collectées.

22 Basé sur les données de positionnement mobile.
23 Arrivées à l'aéroport de Bole uniquement.
24 Arrivées à travers tous les ports d'entrée.
25 Estimations à partir d'enquêtes aux frontières.
26 Arrivées de touristes non résidents.
27 Enquête au départ de l'aéroport de Cayenne-Rochambeau.
28 Arrivées de touristes non résidents à l'aéroport de Libreville.
29 Arrivées en vols à la demande seulement.
30 Les îles du Nord, Saint-Barthélemy et Saint-Martin (partie française) sont exclues.
31 Arrivées de touristes non résidents dans tous les types d'établissements d'hébergement touristique.

30 Tourist/visitor arrivals and tourism expenditure *(continued)*
Thousands arrivals and millions of US dollars

Arrivées de touristes/visiteurs et dépenses touristiques *(suite)*
Milliers d'arrivées et millions de dollars É.-U.

32	Arrivals by air at Conakry airport.	32 Arrivées par voie aérienne à l'aéroport de Conakry.
33	Including tourists from Northern Ireland.	33 Y compris touristes à Irlande du Nord.
34	Including the expenditures of foreign workers in Israel.	34 Y compris les dépenses des travailleurs étrangers en Israël.
35	Excluding seasonal and border workers.	35 À l'exclusion des travailleurs saisonniers et frontaliers.
36	Including nationals residing abroad; E/D cards.	36 Y compris les nationaux résidant à l'étranger; cartes d'embarquement.

37 Arrivals of non-resident tourists by air.
37 Arrivées de touristes non résidents par voie aérienne.

38 Air arrivals. Tarawa and Christmas Island.
38 Arrivées par voie aérienne. Tarawa et île Christmas.

39 Non-resident departures. Survey of persons crossing the state border.
39 Départs de non-résidents. Enquête menée auprès de personnes franchissant la frontière de l'État.

40 Excluding the Lebanon, Syria and Palestine nationalities.
40 À l'exclusion des nationalités libanaise, syrienne et palestinienne.

41 Excluding long term tourists on campgrounds and in holiday flats.
41 À l'exclusion des touristes à long terme en camping ou dans des appartements de vacances.

42 Departures.
42 Départs.

43 Including Singapore residents crossing the frontier by road through Johore Causeway.
43 Y compris les résidents de Singapour traversant la frontière par voie terrestre à travers le Johore Causeway.

44 Departures by air and by sea.
44 Départs par voies aérienne et maritime.

45 Air and sea arrivals.
45 Arrivées par voie aérienne et maritime.

46 Arrivals in the States of Kosrae, Chuuk, Pohnpei and Yap; excluding FSM citizens.
46 Arrivées dans les États de Kosrae, Chuuk, Pohnpei et Yap; non compris les citoyens FSM.

47 The data correspond only to 12 border posts.
47 les données ne couvrent que 12 postes frontière.

48 The data of all the border posts of the country are used.
48 Les données de l'ensemble des postes frontières du pays sont utilisées.

49 Including arrivals from India.
49 Y compris les arrivées à Inde.

50 Including Niueans residing usually in New Zealand.
50 Y compris les nationaux de Nioué résidant habituellement en Nouvelle-Zélande.

51 Non-resident tourists staying in registered hotels.
51 Non résidents touristes dans les hôtels enregistrés.

52 Arrivals of non-resident tourists at national borders.
52 Arrivées de touristes non résidents aux frontières nationales.

53 Air arrivals (Palau International Airport).
53 Arrivées par voie aérienne (Aéroport international de Palaos).

54 Including tourists with identity document other than a passport.
54 Nouvelle série estimée comprenant les touristes avec une pièce d'identité autre qu'un passeport.

55 Include hotels, apartment hotels, "pousadas", tourist apartments, tourist villages, camping sites, recreation centres, tourism in rural areas and local accommodation.
55 Inclure les hôtels, les appart-hôtels, les pousadas, les appartements touristiques, les villages touristiques, les terrains de camping, les centres de loisirs, le tourisme dans les zones rurales et les hébergements locaux.

56 Data refer to fiscal years beginning 1 July.
56 Les données se réfèrent aux exercices budgétaires commençant le 1er juillet.

57 Including nationals residing abroad and crew members.
57 Y compris les nationaux résidant à l'étranger et membres des équipages.

58 Excluding the left side of the river Nistru and the municipality of Bender.
58 La rive gauche de la rivière Nistru et la municipalité de Bender sont exclues.

59 Including Italian tourists.
59 Y compris les touristes italiens.

60 Arrivals by air. Including arrivals to Saint Martin (French part).
60 Arrivées par voie aérienne. Y compris les arrivées à Saint-Martin (partie française).

61 Non-resident tourists staying in commercial accommodation only (representing approximately 25% of all tourists).
61 Les touristes non-résidents séjournant dans un logement commercial seulement (représentant environ 25% de tous les touristes).

62 Without first quarter.
62 Sans premier trimestre.

63 Excluding arrivals for work and contract workers.
63 À l'exclusion des arrivées par travail et les travailleurs contractuels.

64 Excluding transit.
64 À l'exclusion des personnes en transit.

65 Data on hotel activity represent the West Bank only.
65 Les données sur l'activité hôtelière ne concernent que la Cisjordanie.

66 West Bank and Gaza.
66 Cisjordanie et Gaza.

67 Arrivals at Zanderij Airport.
67 Arrivées à l'aéroport de Zanderij.

68 Arrivals in hotels only.
68 Arrivées dans les hôtels uniquement.

69 Including Iraqi nationals.
69 Y compris les ressortissants iraquiens.

70 Arrivals by air at Dili Airport.
70 Arrivées par voie aérienne à l'aéroport de Dili.

71 Turkish citizens resident abroad are included.
71 Citoyens turcs résidant à l'étranger sont inclus.

72 Arrivals in hotels only. Including domestic tourism and nationals of the country residing abroad.
72 Arrivées dans les hôtels uniquement. Y compris le tourisme interne et les nationaux résidant à l'étranger.

Net disbursements of official development assistance to recipients
Total, bilateral and multilateral aid (millions of US dollars); and as a percentage of Gross National Income (GNI)

Décaissements nets d'aide publique au développement aux bénéficiaires
Total, bilatérale et multilatérale d'aide (millions de dollars É.-U.); et en pourcentage du Revenu National Brut (RNB)

Region, country or area[&]	1975	1985	1995	2005	2010	2015	2016	2017	Région, pays ou zone[&]
Total, all countries or areas [1]									**Total, tous pays ou zones** [1]
Bilateral	14 796	25 604	46 875	81 832	92 131	111 373	118 315	123 125	Bilatérale
Multilateral	3 597	5 920	11 004	25 620	37 133	35 368	40 493	41 429	Multilatérale
Total	18 393	31 524	57 879	107 452	129 264	146 741	158 808	164 554	Total
% of GNI	1.7	1.3	1.1	1.2	0.7	0.6	0.6	0.6	% du RNB
Africa [1]									**Afrique** [1]
Bilateral	5 671	10 076	16 828	24 081	30 087	34 918	31 114	33 433	Bilatérale
Multilateral	1 105	2 247	5 015	11 740	17 732	16 137	18 794	19 455	Multilatérale
Total	6 775	12 323	21 843	35 821	47 820	51 055	49 908	52 888	Total
% of GNI	4.3	4.0	4.6	3.7	2.6	2.3	2.3	2.4	% du RNB
Northern Africa [1,2]									**Afrique septentrionale** [1,2]
Bilateral	3 062	2 849	2 703	1 705	1 844	3 712	3 585	2 282	Bilatérale
Multilateral	179	142	277	980	823	1 294	1 783	1 744	Multilatérale
Total	3 241	2 991	2 981	2 685	2 667	5 006	5 368	4 026	Total
% of GNI	8.2	2.7	1.9	0.8	0.5	0.8	0.9	0.7	% du RNB
Sub-Saharan Africa [1,3]									**Afrique subsaharienne** [1,3]
Bilateral	2 557	7 017	13 771	21 889	27 172	28 455	25 882	29 948	Bilatérale
Multilateral	926	1 968	4 594	10 532	16 425	14 268	15 880	16 616	Multilatérale
Total	3 483	8 985	18 365	32 420	43 597	42 724	41 762	46 564	Total
% of GNI	3.0	4.5	5.7	5.1	3.4	2.7	2.8	2.9	% du RNB
Americas [1]									**Amériques** [1]
Bilateral	461	2 664	5 249	4 328	6 856	8 179	8 938	6 130	Bilatérale
Multilateral	597	398	935	2 106	2 854	2 027	2 342	2 481	Multilatérale
Total	1 058	3 062	6 184	6 434	9 710	10 206	11 280	8 611	Total
% of GNI	0.3	0.5	0.3	0.2	0.2	0.2	0.3	0.2	% du RNB
North America [1]									**Amérique du Nord** [1]
Bilateral	254	1 989	2 988	2 285	4 974	3 652	5 675	...	Bilatérale
Multilateral	280	203	513	1 011	1 886	916	1 210	...	Multilatérale
Total	534	2 193	3 501	3 296	6 860	4 567	6 885	...	Total
% of GNI	0.4	0.9	0.8	0.3	0.5	0.3	0.5	...	% du RNB
South America [1]									**Amérique du Sud** [1]
Bilateral	268	743	2 186	1 962	1 726	3 393	2 789	1 841	Bilatérale
Multilateral	317	150	344	792	858	928	1 003	1 151	Multilatérale
Total	585	892	2 531	2 754	2 584	4 321	3 793	2 992	Total
% of GNI	0.2	0.2	0.2	0.2	0.1	0.1	0.1	0.1	% du RNB
Asia [1]									**Asie** [1]
Bilateral	6 319	8 655	13 082	38 172	25 914	36 018	33 192	38 311	Bilatérale
Multilateral	1 813	2 747	4 415	7 579	9 896	9 737	10 735	10 644	Multilatérale
Total	8 132	11 402	17 497	45 750	35 810	45 754	43 926	48 955	Total
% of GNI	1.5	0.8	0.6	0.9	0.3	0.3	0.3	0.3	% du RNB
Eastern and South-Eastern Asia [1,4]									**Asie orientale et du Sud-Est** [1,4]
Bilateral	1 495	2 448	7 387	6 613	5 019	3 496	2 571	...	Bilatérale
Multilateral	371	498	1 411	1 779	2 515	1 901	1 915	...	Multilatérale
Total	1 866	2 946	8 798	8 391	7 534	5 397	4 486	...	Total
% of GNI	0.7	0.5	0.4	0.3	0.1	~0.0	~0.0	...	% du RNB
South-central Asia [1,5]									**Asie centrale et du Sud** [1,5]
Bilateral	2 457	2 678	4 049	7 262	13 215	13 525	11 072	...	Bilatérale
Multilateral	1 308	1 998	2 409	4 395	5 499	6 155	6 915	...	Multilatérale
Total	3 765	4 676	6 458	11 658	18 713	19 680	17 987	...	Total
% of GNI	2.8	1.6	1.3	1.0	0.8	0.6	0.6	...	% du RNB
Western Asia [1,6]									**Asie occidentale** [1,6]
Bilateral	2 407	3 856	2 449	24 324	7 766	17 587	18 429	...	Bilatérale
Multilateral	134	181	504	1 182	1 709	1 530	1 715	...	Multilatérale
Total	2 541	4 037	2 954	25 506	9 475	19 117	20 144	...	Total
% of GNI	1.9	0.9	0.7	3.6	1.2	6.1	6.8	...	% du RNB
Europe [1,7]									**Europe** [1,7]
Bilateral	96	383	1 753	2 446	3 123	2 783	3 354	3 809	Bilatérale
Multilateral	58	28	534	1 605	2 787	4 002	4 802	4 598	Multilatérale
Total	154	410	2 288	4 051	5 910	6 784	8 155	8 407	Total
% of GNI	0.3	0.6	1.0	0.6	0.5	0.6	0.8	0.8	% du RNB
Oceania [1]									**Océanie** [1]
Bilateral	587	849	1 768	799	1 580	1 624	1 229	1 443	Bilatérale
Multilateral	24	38	62	341	269	295	454	551	Multilatérale
Total	611	887	1 829	1 141	1 849	1 919	1 683	1 994	Total
% of GNI	17.4	14.3	12.1	11.5	9.6	6.8	6.0	6.7	% du RNB

31

Net disbursements of official development assistance to recipients *(continued)*
Total, bilateral and multilateral aid (millions of US dollars); and as a percentage of Gross National Income (GNI)

Décaissements nets d'aide publique au développement aux bénéficiaires *(suite)*
Total, bilatérale et multilatérale d'aide (millions de dollars É.-U.); et en pourcentage du Revenu National Brut (RNB)

Region, country or area&	1975	1985	1995	2005	2010	2015	2016	2017	Région, pays ou zone&
Micronesia [1]									**Micronésie [1]**
Bilateral	...	...	71	102	63	77	42	82	Bilatérale
Multilateral	...	...	3	3	1	4	9	16	Multilatérale
Total	...	...	74	105	64	81	51	98	Total
% of GNI	...	...	31.4	40.5	20.8	21.7	13.2	25.1	% du RNB
Areas not specified									**Zones non spécifiées**
Bilateral	...	2 982	8 196	12 007	24 571	34 197	38 992	...	Bilatérale
Multilateral	...	462	42	2 248	3 595	3 171	3 365	...	Multilatérale
Total	1 662	3 445	8 238	14 254	28 166	37 368	42 357	...	Total
Afghanistan									**Afghanistan**
Bilateral	38	7	129	2 273	5 522	3 901	3 505	3 194	Bilatérale
Multilateral	29	9	84	542	713	366	564	610	Multilatérale
Total	67	16	213	2 815	6 235	4 267	4 069	3 804	Total
% of GNI	2.8	...	...	44.8	39.0	22.0	20.7	18.1	% du RNB
Albania									**Albanie**
Bilateral	...	...	118	192	253	232	86	70	Bilatérale
Multilateral	...	...	63	123	112	102	82	87	Multilatérale
Total	...	...	181	315	365	334	169	157	Total
% of GNI	...	...	7.3	3.8	3.1	2.9	1.4	1.2	% du RNB
Algeria									**Algérie**
Bilateral	213	161	272	252	131	36	104	123	Bilatérale
Multilateral	23	11	24	96	71	51	54	66	Multilatérale
Total	235	172	296	347	201	87	158	189	Total
% of GNI	1.5	0.3	0.8	0.4	0.1	0.1	0.1	0.1	% du RNB
Angola									**Angola**
Bilateral	4	72	304	217	146	276	62	76	Bilatérale
Multilateral	1	19	113	198	89	104	144	147	Multilatérale
Total	5	90	416	415	235	380	207	223	Total
% of GNI	...	1.4	8.7	1.7	0.3	0.4	0.2	0.2	% du RNB
Anguilla									**Anguilla**
Bilateral	2	2	3	4	-1	...	...	...	Bilatérale
Multilateral	~0	1	1	~0	9	...	...	...	Multilatérale
Total	2	3	3	4	8	...	...	...	Total
Antigua and Barbuda									**Antigua-et-Barbuda**
Bilateral	2	2	2	7	6	1	-2	-21	Bilatérale
Multilateral	1	1	~0	1	14	1	2	31	Multilatérale
Total	2	3	2	8	20	1	~0	10	Total
% of GNI	...	1.2	0.4	0.8	1.8	0.1	0.0	0.7	% du RNB
Argentina									**Argentine**
Bilateral	-11	30	131	62	100	-45	-200	-38	Bilatérale
Multilateral	23	9	17	32	30	26	203	33	Multilatérale
Total	12	39	148	94	130	-19	3	-5	Total
% of GNI	~0.0	0.1	0.1	0.1	~0.0	0.0	0.0	0.0	% du RNB
Armenia									**Arménie**
Multilateral	...	...	107	67	111	173	183	107	Multilatérale
Total	...	...	218	173	320	347	326	256	Total
% of GNI	...	...	14.9	3.4	3.3	3.2	3.0	2.1	% du RNB
Aruba									**Aruba**
Multilateral	...	...	3	...	...	...	...	...	Multilatérale
Total	...	12	26	...	...	...	...	...	Total
Azerbaijan									**Azerbaïdjan**
Multilateral	...	...	53	91	80	47	44	75	Multilatérale
Total	...	...	120	210	156	70	78	116	Total
% of GNI	...	...	3.9	1.8	0.3	0.1	0.2	0.3	% du RNB
Bahamas									**Bahamas**
Bilateral	~0	~0	3	...	...	...	...	...	Bilatérale
Multilateral	1	1	2	...	...	...	...	...	Multilatérale
Total	1	1	4	...	...	...	...	...	Total
% of GNI	0.1	~0.0	0.1	...	...	...	...	...	% du RNB
Bahrain									**Bahreïn**
Bilateral	25	73	100	...	...	...	...	...	Bilatérale
Multilateral	1	1	~0	...	...	...	...	...	Multilatérale
Total	26	74	100	...	...	...	...	...	Total
% of GNI	...	2.2	1.7	...	...	...	...	...	% du RNB

Net disbursements of official development assistance to recipients *(continued)*
Total, bilateral and multilateral aid (millions of US dollars); and as a percentage of Gross National Income (GNI)

Décaissements nets d'aide publique au développement aux bénéficiaires *(suite)*
Total, bilatérale et multilatérale d'aide (millions de dollars É.-U.); et en pourcentage du Revenu National Brut (RNB)

Region, country or area⅍	1975	1985	1995	2005	2010	2015	2016	2017	Région, pays ou zone⅍
Bangladesh									**Bangladesh**
Bilateral	760	475	658	521	505	1 606	1 372	2 575	Bilatérale
Multilateral	295	508	375	731	822	964	1 133	1 183	Multilatérale
Total	1 055	983	1 033	1 252	1 327	2 570	2 505	3 758	Total
% of GNI	5.4	4.3	2.6	1.7	1.1	1.2	1.1	1.4	% du RNB
Barbados									**Barbade**
Bilateral	2	5	~0	-3	-2	...	...	...	Bilatérale
Multilateral	3	1	1	3	18	...	...	...	Multilatérale
Total	4	6	1	-1	16	...	...	...	Total
% of GNI	...	...	~0.0	-~0.0	0.4	...	...	...	% du RNB
Belarus									**Bélarus**
Multilateral	...	...	...	18	42	34	43	46	Multilatérale
Total	...	...	...	58	136	105	-22	-253	Total
% of GNI	...	...	...	0.2	0.2	0.2	-0.1	-0.5	% du RNB
Belize									**Belize**
Bilateral	8	21	12	6	8	11	6	13	Bilatérale
Multilateral	1	1	7	6	16	17	29	21	Multilatérale
Total	9	22	19	12	24	28	35	34	Total
% of GNI	8.2	11.0	3.2	1.2	2.0	1.7	2.0	2.0	% du RNB
Benin									**Bénin**
Bilateral	36	62	229	175	388	250	244	377	Bilatérale
Multilateral	18	32	52	174	301	180	249	299	Multilatérale
Total	54	94	281	349	689	430	493	676	Total
% of GNI	8.0	9.2	13.2	7.3	10.0	5.2	5.8	7.3	% du RNB
Bermuda									**Bermudes**
Multilateral	...	~0	0	...	...	...	...	...	Multilatérale
Total	~0	1	-2	...	...	...	...	...	Total
% of GNI	~0.0	0.1	-0.1	...	...	...	...	...	% du RNB
Bhutan									**Bhoutan**
Bilateral	~0	6	60	40	53	59	32	-42	Bilatérale
Multilateral	2	14	10	38	44	38	20	161	Multilatérale
Total	2	21	69	79	97	97	52	119	Total
% of GNI	...	15.0	26.1	9.8	6.5	5.2	2.5	5.1	% du RNB
Bolivia (Plurin. State of)									**Bolivie (État plurin. de)**
Bilateral	18	129	526	386	412	589	524	787	Bilatérale
Multilateral	29	30	153	157	148	203	173	162	Multilatérale
Total	47	159	679	543	560	791	696	949	Total
% of GNI	1.9	3.2	10.5	5.9	3.0	2.5	2.1	2.6	% du RNB
Bosnia and Herzegovina									**Bosnie-Herzégovine**
Bilateral	...	...	900	309	290	119	196	85	Bilatérale
Multilateral	...	...	66	231	222	236	249	355	Multilatérale
Total	...	...	966	540	511	355	445	441	Total
% of GNI	...	...	59.4	4.6	2.9	2.2	2.6	2.4	% du RNB
Botswana									**Botswana**
Bilateral	39	71	71	8	95	41	65	63	Bilatérale
Multilateral	12	24	19	40	60	24	25	39	Multilatérale
Total	51	96	90	48	155	66	91	102	Total
% of GNI	14.4	9.4	1.9	0.5	1.3	0.5	0.6	0.6	% du RNB
Brazil									**Brésil**
Bilateral	67	54	230	113	377	719	572	-4	Bilatérale
Multilateral	66	31	34	104	88	284	103	276	Multilatérale
Total	133	85	264	217	465	1 003	675	272	Total
% of GNI	0.1	~0.0	~0.0	~0.0	~0.0	0.1	~0.0	~0.0	% du RNB
British Virgin Islands									**Îles Vierges britanniques**
Bilateral	2	2	~0	...	...	...	...	...	Bilatérale
Multilateral	~0	~0	1	...	...	...	...	...	Multilatérale
Total	2	2	1	...	...	...	...	...	Total
Brunei Darussalam									**Brunéi Darussalam**
Bilateral	~0	1	4	...	...	...	...	...	Bilatérale
Multilateral	0	~0	~0	...	...	...	...	...	Multilatérale
Total	~0	1	4	...	...	...	...	...	Total
% of GNI	...	...	0.1	...	...	...	...	...	% du RNB

Net disbursements of official development assistance to recipients *(continued)*
Total, bilateral and multilateral aid (millions of US dollars); and as a percentage of Gross National Income (GNI)

Décaissements nets d'aide publique au développement aux bénéficiaires *(suite)*
Total, bilatérale et multilatérale d'aide (millions de dollars É.-U.); et en pourcentage du Revenu National Brut (RNB)

Region, country or area&	1975	1985	1995	2005	2010	2015	2016	2017	Région, pays ou zone&
Burkina Faso									**Burkina Faso**
Bilateral	62	134	350	382	554	526	490	496	Bilatérale
Multilateral	27	54	140	316	491	471	538	394	Multilatérale
Total	89	188	490	698	1 045	997	1 027	890	Total
% of GNI	9.5	12.2	20.7	12.8	12.0	10.0	9.2	7.1	% du RNB
Burundi									**Burundi**
Bilateral	33	91	147	163	279	185	560	233	Bilatérale
Multilateral	15	46	140	202	349	181	183	195	Multilatérale
Total	47	137	287	366	628	367	742	428	Total
% of GNI	11.5	12.1	29.0	33.2	31.2	12.0	24.7	12.3	% du RNB
Cabo Verde									**Cabo Verde**
Bilateral	4	42	91	112	248	111	75	87	Bilatérale
Multilateral	5	22	25	51	79	42	38	36	Multilatérale
Total	9	64	116	163	327	153	113	123	Total
% of GNI	...	48.0	23.9	17.4	20.6	9.9	7.2	7.3	% du RNB
Cambodia									**Cambodge**
Bilateral	77	9	389	288	471	522	552	701	Bilatérale
Multilateral	4	5	117	165	210	157	177	155	Multilatérale
Total	81	14	506	453	681	679	728	856	Total
% of GNI	...	...	15.0	7.5	6.4	4.0	3.9	4.1	% du RNB
Cameroon									**Cameroun**
Bilateral	72	134	380	279	303	433	490	681	Bilatérale
Multilateral	37	18	64	138	237	230	267	531	Multilatérale
Total	110	152	444	417	540	663	757	1 213	Total
% of GNI	4.5	1.9	4.9	2.4	2.1	2.2	2.4	3.5	% du RNB
Cayman Islands									**Îles Caïmanes**
Bilateral	1	~0	-1	...	...	...	...	...	Bilatérale
Multilateral	1	~0	~0	...	...	...	...	...	Multilatérale
Total	2	~0	-1	...	...	...	...	...	Total
Central African Republic									**République centrafricaine**
Bilateral	39	73	126	37	78	295	262	256	Bilatérale
Multilateral	16	31	42	52	183	192	239	252	Multilatérale
Total	55	104	168	89	261	487	501	508	Total
% of GNI	14.5	12.1	15.3	6.7	13.1	30.6	28.5	26.0	% du RNB
Chad									**Tchad**
Bilateral	33	118	165	166	275	1	276	322	Bilatérale
Multilateral	34	61	70	221	215	606	348	326	Multilatérale
Total	67	179	235	386	490	607	624	648	Total
% of GNI	7.7	17.4	16.3	6.9	4.8	5.7	6.8	6.6	% du RNB
Chile									**Chili**
Bilateral	83	46	151	88	138	36	163	48	Bilatérale
Multilateral	31	3	9	83	44	18	16	22	Multilatérale
Total	113	49	161	171	182	54	178	70	Total
% of GNI	1.5	0.3	0.2	0.2	0.1	~0.0	0.1	~0.0	% du RNB
China [8]									**Chine** [8]
Multilateral	...	242	921	329	327	252	190	153	Multilatérale
Total	...	939	3 464	1 798	672	-332	-792	-1 045	Total
% of GNI	...	0.3	0.5	0.1	~0.0	0.0	~0.0	~0.0	% du RNB
China, Hong Kong SAR									**Chine, RAS de Hong Kong**
Bilateral	-1	18	14	...	...	...	...	...	Bilatérale
Multilateral	~0	2	4	...	...	...	...	...	Multilatérale
Total	-1	20	18	...	...	...	...	...	Total
% of GNI	~0.0	0.1	~0.0	...	...	...	...	...	% du RNB
China, Macao SAR									**Chine, RAS de Macao**
Bilateral	~0	~0	-4	...	...	...	...	...	Bilatérale
Multilateral	0	~0	0	...	...	...	...	...	Multilatérale
Total	~0	~0	-4	...	...	...	...	...	Total
% of GNI	...	~0.0	-0.1	...	...	...	...	...	% du RNB
Colombia									**Colombie**
Bilateral	39	36	170	560	575	1 275	1 003	596	Bilatérale
Multilateral	32	17	12	83	98	81	103	254	Multilatérale
Total	71	53	182	643	673	1 356	1 107	850	Total
% of GNI	0.6	0.2	0.2	0.5	0.2	0.5	0.4	0.3	% du RNB

31
Net disbursements of official development assistance to recipients *(continued)*
Total, bilateral and multilateral aid (millions of US dollars); and as a percentage of Gross National Income (GNI)

Décaissements nets d'aide publique au développement aux bénéficiaires *(suite)*
Total, bilatérale et multilatérale d'aide (millions de dollars É.-U.); et en pourcentage du Revenu National Brut (RNB)

Region, country or area&	1975	1985	1995	2005	2010	2015	2016	2017	Région, pays ou zone&
Comoros									**Comores**
Bilateral	19	32	27	5	23	30	21	29	Bilatérale
Multilateral	2	15	15	18	47	36	33	38	Multilatérale
Total	22	47	42	23	70	66	54	67	Total
% of GNI	35.9	41.7	17.9	6.1	13.2	11.5	8.6	10.2	% du RNB
Congo									**Congo**
Bilateral	43	55	117	1 350	1 048	38	35	48	Bilatérale
Multilateral	13	14	10	76	267	51	53	60	Multilatérale
Total	56	69	127	1 426	1 315	89	88	108	Total
% of GNI	7.6	3.4	10.3	35.4	14.6	1.1	1.2	1.4	% du RNB
Cook Islands									**Îles Cook**
Bilateral	5	8	10	6	13	22	-9	5	Bilatérale
Multilateral	~0	1	1	1	1	4	27	14	Multilatérale
Total	6	9	11	7	14	26	17	19	Total
Costa Rica									**Costa Rica**
Bilateral	6	237	33	19	85	87	74	66	Bilatérale
Multilateral	14	14	13	13	16	25	27	33	Multilatérale
Total	20	252	46	33	101	111	101	99	Total
% of GNI	1.1	5.6	0.4	0.2	0.3	0.2	0.2	0.2	% du RNB
Côte d'Ivoire									**Côte d'Ivoire**
Bilateral	82	110	949	16	478	302	204	347	Bilatérale
Multilateral	18	7	264	75	368	351	413	480	Multilatérale
Total	100	117	1 212	91	845	653	616	827	Total
% of GNI	2.7	1.9	12.1	0.6	3.5	2.0	1.7	2.1	% du RNB
Croatia									**Croatie**
Multilateral	...	...	5	65	121	...	...	...	Multilatérale
Total	...	...	53	123	132	...	...	...	Total
% of GNI	...	...	0.2	0.3	0.2	...	...	...	% du RNB
Cuba									**Cuba**
Bilateral	11	31	46	67	82	527	2 650	684	Bilatérale
Multilateral	9	11	17	23	51	25	28	34	Multilatérale
Total	20	42	64	90	132	553	2 678	718	Total
% of GNI	0.2	0.2	0.2	0.2	0.2	...	...	...	% du RNB
Cyprus									**Chypre**
Bilateral	18	31	15	...	...	...	...	...	Bilatérale
Multilateral	13	6	7	...	...	...	...	...	Multilatérale
Total	31	37	21	...	...	...	...	...	Total
% of GNI	6.3	1.5	0.2	...	...	...	...	...	% du RNB
Dem. People's Rep. Korea									**Rép. pop. dém. de Corée**
Multilateral	...	...	11	54	50	27	34	50	Multilatérale
Total	...	6	13	87	79	131	120	133	Total
Dem. Rep. of the Congo									**Rép. dém. du Congo**
Bilateral	219	223	136	1 094	1 042	1 663	1 058	1 394	Bilatérale
Multilateral	39	83	59	788	2 442	936	1 044	899	Multilatérale
Total	258	305	195	1 882	3 484	2 599	2 102	2 293	Total
% of GNI	2.5	4.5	4.0	16.4	16.9	7.4	6.1	6.3	% du RNB
Djibouti									**Djibouti**
Bilateral	34	71	94	46	105	137	143	93	Bilatérale
Multilateral	~0	11	12	29	27	33	44	41	Multilatérale
Total	34	81	106	74	132	170	187	134	Total
% of GNI	...	...	...	...	...	10.2	10.5	7.3	% du RNB
Dominica									**Dominique**
Bilateral	6	13	18	13	3	4	-2	-3	Bilatérale
Multilateral	2	4	7	8	30	8	11	22	Multilatérale
Total	8	17	25	21	32	12	9	19	Total
% of GNI	...	17.8	11.9	6.2	6.7	2.3	1.5	3.5	% du RNB
Dominican Republic									**République dominicaine**
Bilateral	3	155	94	28	78	241	125	75	Bilatérale
Multilateral	17	12	13	67	116	39	51	43	Multilatérale
Total	20	167	108	95	194	280	177	118	Total
% of GNI	0.6	3.5	0.7	0.3	0.4	0.4	0.3	0.2	% du RNB
Ecuador									**Équateur**
Bilateral	-10	61	161	184	119	172	126	122	Bilatérale
Multilateral	49	19	27	74	49	146	118	81	Multilatérale
Total	39	79	188	258	169	318	244	203	Total
% of GNI	0.5	0.5	0.8	0.7	0.3	0.3	0.3	0.2	% du RNB

31

Net disbursements of official development assistance to recipients *(continued)*
Total, bilateral and multilateral aid (millions of US dollars); and as a percentage of Gross National Income (GNI)

Décaissements nets d'aide publique au développement aux bénéficiaires *(suite)*
Total, bilatérale et multilatérale d'aide (millions de dollars É.-U.); et en pourcentage du Revenu National Brut (RNB)

Region, country or area&	1975	1985	1995	2005	2010	2015	2016	2017	Région, pays ou zone&
Egypt									**Égypte**
Bilateral	2 413	1 692	1 873	730	412	2 316	1 728	-499	Bilatérale
Multilateral	100	82	155	316	187	184	403	386	Multilatérale
Total	2 513	1 774	2 028	1 046	599	2 499	2 130	-113	Total
% of GNI	22.5	5.7	3.4	1.2	0.3	0.8	0.7	-0.1	% du RNB
El Salvador									**El Salvador**
Bilateral	-17	308	260	146	224	66	72	120	Bilatérale
Multilateral	34	18	19	72	78	24	57	32	Multilatérale
Total	17	325	279	218	302	90	129	152	Total
% of GNI	0.9	8.8	3.0	1.3	1.5	0.4	0.5	0.7	% du RNB
Equatorial Guinea									**Guinée équatoriale**
Bilateral	1	9	23	18	75	3	3	-1	Bilatérale
Multilateral	1	8	10	20	10	5	4	7	Multilatérale
Total	2	17	33	38	85	7	7	7	Total
% of GNI	2.1	29.5	28.3	0.9	0.9	0.1	0.1	0.1	% du RNB
Eritrea									**Érythrée**
Bilateral	...	...	119	229	49	54	16	36	Bilatérale
Multilateral	...	...	29	121	114	40	51	43	Multilatérale
Total	2	...	148	350	162	94	67	79	Total
% of GNI	...	...	25.3	32.1	7.7	...	...	...	% du RNB
Eswatini									**Eswatini**
Bilateral	5	18	49	-1	21	42	77	87	Bilatérale
Multilateral	10	6	9	47	70	51	70	60	Multilatérale
Total	14	24	58	47	91	93	147	147	Total
% of GNI	...	...	3.2	1.4	2.2	2.3	4.0	3.3	% du RNB
Ethiopia									**Éthiopie**
Bilateral	73	541	653	1 205	2 223	2 239	2 491	2 568	Bilatérale
Multilateral	59	177	224	724	1 232	996	1 582	1 553	Multilatérale
Total	132	718	877	1 929	3 455	3 235	4 074	4 121	Total
% of GNI	...	7.6	11.5	15.6	11.6	5.0	5.6	5.2	% du RNB
Fiji									**Fidji**
Bilateral	18	28	39	32	56	73	95	85	Bilatérale
Multilateral	2	3	4	34	19	30	23	61	Multilatérale
Total	19	31	43	66	76	102	117	146	Total
% of GNI	2.9	2.8	2.2	2.2	2.5	2.5	2.6	3.0	% du RNB
French Polynesia									**Polynésie française**
Bilateral	71	171	448	...	...	...	...	...	Bilatérale
Multilateral	~0	1	3	...	...	...	...	...	Multilatérale
Total	72	172	451	...	...	...	...	...	Total
% of GNI	10.4	11.4	11.3	...	...	...	...	...	% du RNB
Gabon									**Gabon**
Bilateral	58	55	140	1	82	81	22	86	Bilatérale
Multilateral	3	6	4	50	24	17	19	21	Multilatérale
Total	60	61	144	50	106	99	42	106	Total
% of GNI	3.0	2.0	3.4	0.6	0.9	0.8	0.3	0.8	% du RNB
Gambia									**Gambie**
Bilateral	4	33	25	7	52	69	7	118	Bilatérale
Multilateral	4	15	20	53	70	39	85	151	Multilatérale
Total	8	48	45	61	121	108	92	270	Total
% of GNI	7.0	19.1	5.9	10.1	13.1	12.3	9.8	27.3	% du RNB
Georgia									**Géorgie**
Bilateral	...	...	104	183	319	255	210	205	Bilatérale
Multilateral	...	...	106	110	270	194	252	241	Multilatérale
Total	...	...	209	293	589	449	463	446	Total
% of GNI	...	...	8.1	4.5	5.2	3.3	3.4	3.1	% du RNB
Ghana									**Ghana**
Bilateral	99	105	362	660	1 132	1 023	714	722	Bilatérale
Multilateral	25	89	288	493	565	746	603	541	Multilatérale
Total	124	194	650	1 153	1 697	1 769	1 316	1 263	Total
% of GNI	4.5	4.4	10.3	10.9	5.4	4.8	3.2	2.8	% du RNB
Gibraltar									**Gibraltar**
Bilateral	...	...	~0	...	...	...	...	...	Bilatérale
Multilateral	...	...	0	...	...	...	...	...	Multilatérale
Total	3	29	~0	...	...	...	...	...	Total

31

Net disbursements of official development assistance to recipients *(continued)*
Total, bilateral and multilateral aid (millions of US dollars); and as a percentage of Gross National Income (GNI)

Décaissements nets d'aide publique au développement aux bénéficiaires *(suite)*
Total, bilatérale et multilatérale d'aide (millions de dollars É.-U.); et en pourcentage du Revenu National Brut (RNB)

Region, country or area&	1975	1985	1995	2005	2010	2015	2016	2017	Région, pays ou zone&
Grenada									**Grenade**
Bilateral	2	32	8	33	10	7	-4	-8	Bilatérale
Multilateral	1	2	3	20	24	17	13	14	Multilatérale
Total	3	34	11	53	34	24	9	6	Total
% of GNI	...	21.2	3.3	7.9	4.6	2.5	0.8	0.5	% du RNB
Guatemala									**Guatemala**
Bilateral	15	64	178	204	335	331	199	282	Bilatérale
Multilateral	15	12	27	65	67	80	67	85	Multilatérale
Total	30	76	205	269	402	411	265	367	Total
% of GNI	0.8	0.8	1.4	1.0	1.0	0.7	0.4	0.5	% du RNB
Guinea									**Guinée**
Bilateral	20	74	305	89	47	246	237	245	Bilatérale
Multilateral	4	39	111	104	174	292	319	213	Multilatérale
Total	24	113	416	193	221	538	555	457	Total
% of GNI	...	...	11.5	7.3	3.4	6.4	6.4	4.4	% du RNB
Guinea-Bissau									**Guinée-Bissau**
Bilateral	17	34	95	8	-32	29	130	21	Bilatérale
Multilateral	4	22	23	59	161	66	67	93	Multilatérale
Total	21	56	118	67	129	95	197	113	Total
% of GNI	18.7	35.3	49.8	11.6	15.2	8.9	16.3	8.4	% du RNB
Guyana									**Guyana**
Bilateral	7	5	41	32	45	12	15	17	Bilatérale
Multilateral	3	6	27	70	62	20	55	34	Multilatérale
Total	10	11	68	101	106	32	70	51	Total
% of GNI	2.1	2.8	12.0	13.1	4.7	1.0	2.0	1.4	% du RNB
Haiti									**Haïti**
Bilateral	4	109	535	201	2 189	837	828	791	Bilatérale
Multilateral	38	29	120	165	700	209	244	190	Multilatérale
Total	42	138	655	367	2 890	1 046	1 072	981	Total
% of GNI	...	...	...	8.6	43.5	11.9	13.3	11.6	% du RNB
Honduras									**Honduras**
Bilateral	11	213	274	467	273	412	308	321	Bilatérale
Multilateral	26	25	101	183	198	128	105	120	Multilatérale
Total	38	238	375	649	471	541	412	441	Total
% of GNI	3.4	6.8	10.3	7.0	3.1	2.8	2.1	2.1	% du RNB
India									**Inde**
Bilateral	879	844	871	669	1 639	1 801	935	1 730	Bilatérale
Multilateral	726	743	862	1 207	1 192	1 373	1 743	1 431	Multilatérale
Total	1 605	1 587	1 733	1 876	2 831	3 174	2 679	3 161	Total
% of GNI	1.7	0.7	0.5	0.2	0.2	0.2	0.1	0.1	% du RNB
Indonesia									**Indonésie**
Bilateral	437	508	1 201	2 208	901	-167	-288	-16	Bilatérale
Multilateral	232	83	50	281	423	133	178	293	Multilatérale
Total	669	591	1 252	2 489	1 324	-33	-111	277	Total
% of GNI	2.3	0.7	0.6	0.9	0.2	0.0	~0.0	~0.0	% du RNB
Iran (Islamic Republic of)									**Iran (Rép. islamique d')**
Bilateral	-12	2	162	61	72	91	79	111	Bilatérale
Multilateral	13	9	25	40	40	19	37	29	Multilatérale
Total	2	11	187	101	112	111	116	140	Total
% of GNI	0.0	~0.0	0.2	0.1	~0.0	~0.0	~0.0	~0.0	% du RNB
Iraq									**Iraq**
Bilateral	101	19	273	21 999	2 040	1 347	2 106	2 717	Bilatérale
Multilateral	9	1	60	58	138	136	182	191	Multilatérale
Total	110	20	333	22 057	2 178	1 483	2 288	2 907	Total
% of GNI	...	~0.0	...	43.5	1.6	0.8	1.4	1.5	% du RNB
Israel									**Israël**
Bilateral	466	1 978	334	...	...	...	...	...	Bilatérale
Multilateral	2	~0	2	...	...	...	...	...	Multilatérale
Total	467	1 978	336	...	...	...	...	...	Total
% of GNI	3.2	7.8	0.3	...	...	...	...	...	% du RNB
Jamaica									**Jamaïque**
Bilateral	12	159	88	-5	-8	15	-17	26	Bilatérale
Multilateral	9	7	27	48	150	44	44	35	Multilatérale
Total	20	166	115	44	141	59	27	61	Total
% of GNI	0.7	9.1	1.8	0.4	1.1	0.4	0.2	0.4	% du RNB

31

Net disbursements of official development assistance to recipients *(continued)*
Total, bilateral and multilateral aid (millions of US dollars); and as a percentage of Gross National Income (GNI)

Décaissements nets d'aide publique au développement aux bénéficiaires *(suite)*
Total, bilatérale et multilatérale d'aide (millions de dollars É.-U.); et en pourcentage du Revenu National Brut (RNB)

Region, country or area&	1975	1985	1995	2005	2010	2015	2016	2017	Région, pays ou zone&
Jordan									**Jordanie**
Bilateral	471	598	462	593	692	1 911	2 425	2 640	Bilatérale
Multilateral	21	9	78	117	263	241	313	281	Multilatérale
Total	492	607	540	710	955	2 152	2 738	2 921	Total
% of GNI	35.0	12.4	8.4	5.5	3.6	5.8	7.1	7.3	% du RNB
Kazakhstan									**Kazakhstan**
Bilateral	...	...	48	194	140	6	30	-9	Bilatérale
Multilateral	...	...	11	31	72	77	33	68	Multilatérale
Total	...	...	59	225	212	83	64	59	Total
% of GNI	...	...	0.3	0.4	0.2	0.1	0.1	~0.0	% du RNB
Kenya									**Kenya**
Bilateral	99	366	506	475	1 163	1 655	1 378	1 626	Bilatérale
Multilateral	26	61	227	281	468	809	809	852	Multilatérale
Total	125	427	733	757	1 631	2 464	2 188	2 478	Total
% of GNI	3.9	7.2	8.4	4.0	4.1	3.9	3.1	3.3	% du RNB
Kiribati									**Kiribati**
Bilateral	6	11	13	18	22	50	49	58	Bilatérale
Multilateral	~0	1	2	8	2	15	12	19	Multilatérale
Total	6	12	15	27	24	65	61	77	Total
% of GNI	...	38.1	16.0	16.6	10.7	18.5	18.8	22.2	% du RNB
Kosovo									**Kosovo**
Bilateral	...	...	...	...	215	251	236	141	Bilatérale
Multilateral	...	...	...	0	312	186	134	251	Multilatérale
Total	...	...	...	...	528	438	370	392	Total
% of GNI	...	...	...	...	8.9	6.7	5.4	5.4	% du RNB
Kuwait									**Koweït**
Bilateral	-2	3	4	...	...	...	...	...	Bilatérale
Multilateral	2	1	~0	...	...	...	...	...	Multilatérale
Total	~0	4	4	...	...	...	...	...	Total
% of GNI	0.0	~0.0	~0.0	...	...	...	...	...	% du RNB
Kyrgyzstan									**Kirghizistan**
Bilateral	...	...	151	147	245	598	311	300	Bilatérale
Multilateral	...	...	94	91	127	172	205	161	Multilatérale
Total	...	...	245	238	372	770	516	461	Total
% of GNI	...	...	15.1	10.0	8.3	12.0	8.0	6.3	% du RNB
Lao People's Dem. Rep.									**Rép. dém. populaire lao**
Bilateral	23	15	191	105	261	394	283	348	Bilatérale
Multilateral	13	21	55	137	128	77	117	132	Multilatérale
Total	36	36	246	241	389	471	399	480	Total
% of GNI	...	1.5	14.0	9.0	5.8	3.4	2.6	3.0	% du RNB
Lebanon									**Liban**
Bilateral	7	65	147	142	319	788	970	1 085	Bilatérale
Multilateral	7	17	44	89	126	187	169	220	Multilatérale
Total	14	82	191	231	445	975	1 139	1 306	Total
% of GNI	...	...	1.6	1.1	1.2	2.0	2.3	2.5	% du RNB
Lesotho									**Lesotho**
Bilateral	12	65	81	26	92	40	50	78	Bilatérale
Multilateral	16	28	31	42	164	43	62	68	Multilatérale
Total	28	92	113	68	256	83	112	147	Total
% of GNI	11.4	18.4	8.4	3.1	8.5	3.0	4.3	5.0	% du RNB
Liberia									**Libéria**
Bilateral	8	72	51	118	959	764	566	442	Bilatérale
Multilateral	12	19	72	104	457	330	249	180	Multilatérale
Total	20	90	123	222	1 416	1 094	815	622	Total
% of GNI	3.3	11.2	...	56.4	127.2	62.4	44.8	33.5	% du RNB
Libya									**Libye**
Bilateral	-6	3	4	17	1	132	149	365	Bilatérale
Multilateral	8	2	2	6	7	26	30	66	Multilatérale
Total	2	5	6	24	8	157	179	432	Total
% of GNI	...	...	...	0.1	~0.0	0.5	0.5	0.8	% du RNB
Madagascar									**Madagascar**
Bilateral	43	118	192	517	264	400	246	360	Bilatérale
Multilateral	39	67	107	399	214	277	376	420	Multilatérale
Total	82	185	299	916	477	677	622	780	Total
% of GNI	3.6	6.7	10.0	18.5	5.5	7.2	6.5	7.0	% du RNB

Net disbursements of official development assistance to recipients *(continued)*
Total, bilateral and multilateral aid (millions of US dollars); and as a percentage of Gross National Income (GNI)

Décaissements nets d'aide publique au développement aux bénéficiaires *(suite)*
Total, bilatérale et multilatérale d'aide (millions de dollars É.-U.); et en pourcentage du Revenu National Brut (RNB)

Region, country or area&	1975	1985	1995	2005	2010	2015	2016	2017	Région, pays ou zone&
Malawi									**Malawi**
Bilateral	43	72	286	301	560	694	772	983	Bilatérale
Multilateral	20	41	149	272	456	355	469	532	Multilatérale
Total	63	112	435	574	1 017	1 049	1 241	1 515	Total
% of GNI	10.1	10.4	32.2	15.9	14.8	17.0	23.5	24.6	% du RNB
Malaysia									**Malaisie**
Bilateral	87	217	102	17	-33	-14	-64	-55	Bilatérale
Multilateral	11	10	5	12	27	13	13	26	Multilatérale
Total	98	227	107	29	-6	-1	-52	-29	Total
% of GNI	1.1	0.8	0.1	~0.0	0.0	0.0	~0.0	~0.0	% du RNB
Maldives									**Maldives**
Bilateral	2	6	45	46	49	17	14	24	Bilatérale
Multilateral	1	3	7	27	40	10	13	19	Multilatérale
Total	3	9	52	72	88	27	27	43	Total
% of GNI	...	7.5	13.9	6.4	3.9	0.7	0.7	1.0	% du RNB
Mali									**Mali**
Bilateral	67	308	401	395	770	790	728	865	Bilatérale
Multilateral	76	70	139	330	322	414	480	493	Multilatérale
Total	144	379	540	725	1 091	1 204	1 208	1 358	Total
% of GNI	17.6	27.7	20.3	12.0	10.6	9.4	8.8	9.1	% du RNB
Malta									**Malte**
Bilateral	33	18	7	...	...	...	...	...	Bilatérale
Multilateral	1	~0	2	...	...	...	...	...	Multilatérale
Total	34	18	9	...	...	...	...	...	Total
% of GNI	6.4	1.5	0.3	...	...	...	...	...	% du RNB
Marshall Islands									**Îles Marshall**
Bilateral	...	...	31	55	18	56	12	68	Bilatérale
Multilateral	...	...	2	2	7	1	1	4	Multilatérale
Total	...	...	33	56	25	57	13	73	Total
% of GNI	...	...	21.8	31.5	12.5	23.0	4.8	27.5	% du RNB
Mauritania									**Mauritanie**
Bilateral	68	179	163	91	277	240	177	163	Bilatérale
Multilateral	15	28	67	97	97	78	117	122	Multilatérale
Total	83	208	230	189	374	318	294	284	Total
% of GNI	18.7	32.9	17.2	8.4	8.7	6.8	6.4	5.7	% du RNB
Mauritius									**Maurice**
Bilateral	15	24	16	13	41	30	-31	-10	Bilatérale
Multilateral	13	3	8	22	84	48	73	22	Multilatérale
Total	28	27	24	34	125	78	42	12	Total
% of GNI	...	2.6	0.6	0.6	1.2	0.7	0.4	0.1	% du RNB
Mayotte									**Mayotte**
Bilateral	...	20	107	201	603	...	...	...	Bilatérale
Multilateral	...	~0	1	~0	1	...	...	0	Multilatérale
Total	...	21	108	201	604	...	...	...	Total
Mexico									**Mexique**
Bilateral	-41	128	386	171	398	270	643	645	Bilatérale
Multilateral	62	23	24	29	56	51	166	107	Multilatérale
Total	22	151	411	200	455	321	809	752	Total
% of GNI	~0.0	0.1	0.1	~0.0	~0.0	~0.0	0.1	0.1	% du RNB
Micronesia (Fed. States of)									**Micronésie (États féd. de)**
Bilateral	...	...	74	104	62	77	42	...	Bilatérale
Multilateral	...	...	3	3	1	4	9	...	Multilatérale
Total	...	...	77	106	63	81	51	...	Total
% of GNI	...	...	33.0	41.1	20.8	21.9	13.1	...	% du RNB
Mongolia									**Mongolie**
Bilateral	...	...	128	135	206	191	241	638	Bilatérale
Multilateral	...	...	25	61	81	45	84	127	Multilatérale
Total	...	5	153	195	287	236	326	764	Total
% of GNI	...	0.2	10.8	7.9	4.3	2.2	3.1	7.7	% du RNB
Montenegro									**Monténégro**
Bilateral	...	...	...	4	54	27	25	3	Bilatérale
Multilateral	...	...	...	0	26	73	60	115	Multilatérale
Total	...	...	...	4	80	100	86	117	Total
% of GNI	...	...	...	0.2	2.0	2.4	1.9	2.4	% du RNB

31

Net disbursements of official development assistance to recipients *(continued)*
Total, bilateral and multilateral aid (millions of US dollars); and as a percentage of Gross National Income (GNI)

Décaissements nets d'aide publique au développement aux bénéficiaires *(suite)*
Total, bilatérale et multilatérale d'aide (millions de dollars É.-U.); et en pourcentage du Revenu National Brut (RNB)

Region, country or area&	1975	1985	1995	2005	2010	2015	2016	2017	Région, pays ou zone&
Montserrat									**Montserrat**
Bilateral	4	2	9	27	16	...	39	35	Bilatérale
Multilateral	~0	~0	1	1	10	...	~0	1	Multilatérale
Total	4	2	9	28	26	52	39	36	Total
Morocco									**Maroc**
Bilateral	260	836	447	395	708	836	1 189	1 087	Bilatérale
Multilateral	10	30	54	338	278	645	803	801	Multilatérale
Total	270	866	501	733	986	1 481	1 992	1 888	Total
% of GNI	3.0	6.0	1.3	1.2	1.1	1.5	2.0	1.8	% du RNB
Mozambique									**Mozambique**
Bilateral	14	242	799	806	1 432	1 306	937	1 349	Bilatérale
Multilateral	6	54	264	483	512	509	592	449	Multilatérale
Total	20	296	1 063	1 290	1 943	1 815	1 529	1 799	Total
% of GNI	...	6.8	44.1	17.5	19.8	12.5	14.2	15.1	% du RNB
Myanmar									**Myanmar**
Bilateral	14	205	119	34	212	927	1 127	1 194	Bilatérale
Multilateral	40	107	42	111	143	242	410	348	Multilatérale
Total	55	311	160	145	355	1 169	1 537	1 543	Total
% of GNI	...	...	...	1.2	0.7	2.0	2.5	2.3	% du RNB
Namibia									**Namibie**
Bilateral	...	...	170	56	207	106	74	98	Bilatérale
Multilateral	...	...	20	58	55	37	97	88	Multilatérale
Total	...	5	190	113	261	142	170	187	Total
% of GNI	...	0.4	4.6	1.6	2.4	1.2	1.5	1.4	% du RNB
Nauru									**Nauru**
Bilateral	...	...	3	9	27	30	21	-84	Bilatérale
Multilateral	...	...	~0	~0	1	1	2	109	Multilatérale
Total	~0	~0	3	9	28	31	23	26	Total
% of GNI	...	...	...	...	48.7	25.2	17.7	17.7	% du RNB
Nepal									**Népal**
Bilateral	11	62	254	268	397	819	644	860	Bilatérale
Multilateral	29	126	126	139	370	406	419	408	Multilatérale
Total	40	188	381	407	767	1 225	1 063	1 268	Total
% of GNI	2.5	7.2	8.6	5.0	4.8	5.6	5.0	5.1	% du RNB
Netherlands Antilles [former]									**Antilles néerlandaises [anc.]**
Bilateral	28	64	97	...	...	...	...	...	Bilatérale
Multilateral	5	1	2	...	...	...	...	...	Multilatérale
Total	33	65	98	...	...	...	...	...	Total
New Caledonia									**Nouvelle-Calédonie**
Bilateral	65	145	448	...	...	...	...	...	Bilatérale
Multilateral	~0	~0	3	...	...	...	...	...	Multilatérale
Total	65	145	451	...	...	...	...	...	Total
% of GNI	7.9	17.0	12.4	...	...	...	...	...	% du RNB
Nicaragua									**Nicaragua**
Bilateral	3	84	505	486	390	341	305	442	Bilatérale
Multilateral	25	17	65	171	121	117	126	121	Multilatérale
Total	27	101	569	656	511	458	431	563	Total
% of GNI	...	...	15.1	10.6	5.8	3.6	3.3	4.2	% du RNB
Niger									**Niger**
Bilateral	106	226	211	270	402	489	490	666	Bilatérale
Multilateral	31	72	61	254	339	379	462	557	Multilatérale
Total	137	298	272	523	741	868	951	1 223	Total
% of GNI	13.2	21.3	14.9	15.4	13.1	12.2	12.8	15.4	% du RNB
Nigeria									**Nigéria**
Bilateral	65	19	88	5 954	1 072	1 492	1 362	2 194	Bilatérale
Multilateral	16	13	122	448	980	939	1 137	1 164	Multilatérale
Total	81	32	211	6 402	2 052	2 432	2 498	3 359	Total
% of GNI	0.3	0.1	0.8	6.5	0.6	0.5	0.6	0.9	% du RNB
Niue									**Nioué**
Bilateral	...	...	8	19	14	19	13	11	Bilatérale
Multilateral	...	...	~0	2	1	~0	1	4	Multilatérale
Total	2	4	8	21	15	20	14	15	Total

31

Net disbursements of official development assistance to recipients *(continued)*
Total, bilateral and multilateral aid (millions of US dollars); and as a percentage of Gross National Income (GNI)

Décaissements nets d'aide publique au développement aux bénéficiaires *(suite)*
Total, bilatérale et multilatérale d'aide (millions de dollars É.-U.); et en pourcentage du Revenu National Brut (RNB)

Region, country or area&	1975	1985	1995	2005	2010	2015	2016	2017	Région, pays ou zone&
North Macedonia									**Macédoine du Nord**
Bilateral	...	...	34	154	127	55	54	-3	Bilatérale
Multilateral	...	...	45	74	67	159	115	153	Multilatérale
Total	...	...	79	227	194	214	168	150	Total
% of GNI	...	...	1.8	3.7	2.1	2.2	1.6	1.4	% du RNB
Northern Mariana Islands									**Îles Mariannes du Nord**
Bilateral	81	158	~0	...	...	...	...	...	Bilatérale
Multilateral	~0	1	-1	...	...	...	...	...	Multilatérale
Total	81	159	-1	...	...	...	...	...	Total
Oman									**Oman**
Bilateral	138	75	74	15	-24	...	...	...	Bilatérale
Multilateral	2	2	1	4	2	...	...	...	Multilatérale
Total	140	78	75	19	-22	...	...	...	Total
% of GNI	7.8	0.8	0.6	0.1	~0.0	...	...	...	% du RNB
Other non-specified areas									**Autres zones non-spécifiées**
Bilateral	18	-10	0	...	...	...	...	...	Bilatérale
Multilateral	...	...	0	...	...	...	...	...	Multilatérale
Total	18	-10	~0	...	...	...	...	...	Total
Pakistan									**Pakistan**
Bilateral	612	305	152	746	2 093	2 308	1 788	1 407	Bilatérale
Multilateral	119	363	349	731	840	1 446	1 162	876	Multilatérale
Total	731	668	501	1 477	2 933	3 754	2 950	2 283	Total
% of GNI	6.4	2.0	0.8	1.3	1.6	1.3	1.0	0.7	% du RNB
Palau									**Palaos**
Bilateral	...	...	142	23	28	13	15	20	Bilatérale
Multilateral	...	...	0	~0	1	1	3	2	Multilatérale
Total	...	...	142	24	29	14	18	22	Total
% of GNI	...	...	...	13.1	15.8	5.1	6.1	7.9	% du RNB
Panama									**Panama**
Bilateral	7	41	39	5	116	-2	2	-37	Bilatérale
Multilateral	15	8	8	23	14	12	20	78	Multilatérale
Total	22	49	47	28	130	10	23	41	Total
% of GNI	1.0	0.8	0.5	0.2	0.5	~0.0	0.1	0.1	% du RNB
Papua New Guinea									**Papouasie-Nvl-Guinée**
Bilateral	294	237	330	214	420	484	424	440	Bilatérale
Multilateral	11	16	28	54	94	107	107	92	Multilatérale
Total	304	253	358	268	514	591	532	533	Total
% of GNI	23.7	10.8	8.2	5.9	3.9	3.0	2.8	2.6	% du RNB
Paraguay									**Paraguay**
Bilateral	-10	25	112	51	61	30	43	74	Bilatérale
Multilateral	26	8	10	13	51	30	46	69	Multilatérale
Total	17	34	121	64	112	60	89	143	Total
% of GNI	...	...	1.5	0.9	0.6	0.2	0.3	0.5	% du RNB
Peru									**Pérou**
Bilateral	40	286	356	376	-368	295	251	-138	Bilatérale
Multilateral	24	21	31	89	69	39	69	133	Multilatérale
Total	65	307	387	465	-299	335	320	-6	Total
% of GNI	0.4	2.0	0.8	0.7	-0.2	0.2	0.2	0.0	% du RNB
Philippines									**Philippines**
Bilateral	150	418	798	510	431	409	177	56	Bilatérale
Multilateral	27	37	60	77	151	106	106	104	Multilatérale
Total	176	455	858	588	582	515	284	160	Total
% of GNI	1.2	1.6	1.1	0.5	0.2	0.2	0.1	~0.0	% du RNB
Qatar									**Qatar**
Bilateral	-1	1	4	...	...	...	...	...	Bilatérale
Multilateral	1	1	~0	...	...	...	...	...	Multilatérale
Total	1	2	4	...	...	...	...	...	Total
% of GNI	~0.0	~0.0	0.1	...	...	...	...	...	% du RNB
Republic of Korea									**République de Corée**
Bilateral	207	-13	54	...	...	...	...	...	Bilatérale
Multilateral	40	4	3	...	...	...	...	...	Multilatérale
Total	247	-9	57	...	...	...	...	...	Total
% of GNI	1.2	~0.0	~0.0	...	...	...	...	...	% du RNB

Net disbursements of official development assistance to recipients *(continued)*
Total, bilateral and multilateral aid (millions of US dollars); and as a percentage of Gross National Income (GNI)

Décaissements nets d'aide publique au développement aux bénéficiaires *(suite)*
Total, bilatérale et multilatérale d'aide (millions de dollars É.-U.); et en pourcentage du Revenu National Brut (RNB)

Region, country or area&	1975	1985	1995	2005	2010	2015	2016	2017	Région, pays ou zone&
Republic of Moldova									**République de Moldova**
Bilateral	...	...	...	94	213	204	80	85	Bilatérale
Multilateral	...	...	...	75	260	108	182	156	Multilatérale
Total	...	...	...	170	473	313	262	241	Total
% of GNI	...	...	...	5.1	7.5	4.5	3.6	2.8	% du RNB
Rwanda									**Rwanda**
Bilateral	54	123	403	271	602	713	633	714	Bilatérale
Multilateral	36	54	291	302	431	373	515	512	Multilatérale
Total	90	177	695	573	1 033	1 085	1 147	1 225	Total
% of GNI	15.9	10.4	53.5	22.4	18.0	13.4	13.9	13.7	% du RNB
Saint Helena									**Sainte-Hélène**
Bilateral	...		12	22	...	82	102	65	Bilatérale
Multilateral	...	...	~0	~0	...	~0	4	1	Multilatérale
Total	3	12	13	23	54	82	106	66	Total
Saint Kitts and Nevis									**Saint-Kitts-et-Nevis**
Bilateral	1	3	2	1	-2	...	...	...	Bilatérale
Multilateral	~0	1	2	2	13	...	...	...	Multilatérale
Total	2	4	4	3	11	...	...	...	Total
% of GNI	...	4.2	1.4	0.5	1.7	...	...	...	% du RNB
Saint Lucia									**Sainte-Lucie**
Bilateral	8	4	31	4	~0	1	-7	6	Bilatérale
Multilateral	1	3	17	6	41	13	22	10	Multilatérale
Total	9	7	48	11	41	14	15	15	Total
% of GNI	...	2.9	8.0	1.2	3.1	0.9	1.0	1.0	% du RNB
Saint Vincent & Grenadines									**Saint-Vincent-Grenadines**
Bilateral	6	3	32	4	~0	3	-5	6	Bilatérale
Multilateral	~0	3	15	4	17	11	14	5	Multilatérale
Total	6	5	48	8	17	14	9	12	Total
% of GNI	18.1	3.8	15.6	1.5	2.5	1.8	1.2	1.5	% du RNB
Samoa									**Samoa**
Bilateral	2	12	34	23	75	63	-14	87	Bilatérale
Multilateral	9	6	5	20	50	31	102	45	Multilatérale
Total	12	18	38	43	124	94	89	131	Total
% of GNI	...	...	...	9.9	19.9	11.9	11.5	15.9	% du RNB
Sao Tome and Principe									**Sao Tomé-et-Principe**
Bilateral	~0	6	72	10	36	33	24	16	Bilatérale
Multilateral	1	6	12	23	14	16	24	25	Multilatérale
Total	1	12	84	33	50	49	47	40	Total
% of GNI	...	...	...	26.8	25.4	15.6	13.3	10.3	% du RNB
Saudi Arabia									**Arabie saoudite**
Bilateral	-6	16	17	23	...	...	...	...	Bilatérale
Multilateral	9	12	~0	2	...	...	...	...	Multilatérale
Total	3	27	17	25	...	...	...	...	Total
% of GNI	~0.0	~0.0	~0.0	~0.0	...	...	...	...	% du RNB
Senegal									**Sénégal**
Bilateral	103	249	489	429	654	628	433	604	Bilatérale
Multilateral	36	42	163	272	283	251	303	305	Multilatérale
Total	139	290	652	701	936	879	737	910	Total
% of GNI	6.5	10.3	13.8	8.1	7.3	6.6	5.2	5.8	% du RNB
Serbia									**Serbie**
Bilateral	...	...	92	838	300	-75	219	1 255	Bilatérale
Multilateral	...	...	3	231	361	387	414	433	Multilatérale
Total	...	...	95	1 068	661	312	633	1 688	Total
% of GNI	...	...	...	4.1	1.7	0.9	1.8	4.4	% du RNB
Seychelles									**Seychelles**
Bilateral	7	19	12	12	43	1	-7	8	Bilatérale
Multilateral	~0	3	2	6	11	6	13	11	Multilatérale
Total	7	22	13	17	54	7	6	19	Total
% of GNI	15.6	13.5	2.7	1.9	5.9	0.5	0.4	1.4	% du RNB
Sierra Leone									**Sierra Leone**
Bilateral	7	43	136	131	221	708	471	335	Bilatérale
Multilateral	10	20	76	209	237	239	223	203	Multilatérale
Total	17	64	212	340	458	946	693	538	Total
% of GNI	2.5	7.7	26.0	21.1	17.6	22.7	21.9	14.7	% du RNB

31 Net disbursements of official development assistance to recipients *(continued)*
Total, bilateral and multilateral aid (millions of US dollars); and as a percentage of Gross National Income (GNI)

Décaissements nets d'aide publique au développement aux bénéficiaires *(suite)*
Total, bilatérale et multilatérale d'aide (millions de dollars É.-U.); et en pourcentage du Revenu National Brut (RNB)

Region, country or area&	1975	1985	1995	2005	2010	2015	2016	2017	Région, pays ou zone&
Singapore									**Singapour**
Bilateral	7	21	16	...	...	...	...	...	Bilatérale
Multilateral	5	2	1	...	...	...	...	...	Multilatérale
Total	12	23	17	...	...	...	...	...	Total
% of GNI	0.2	0.1	~0.0	...	...	...	...	...	% du RNB
Slovenia									**Slovénie**
Bilateral	...	...	40	...	...	...	...	...	Bilatérale
Multilateral	...	...	12	...	...	...	...	...	Multilatérale
Total	...	...	53	...	...	...	...	...	Total
% of GNI	...	...	0.2	...	...	...	...	...	% du RNB
Solomon Islands									**Îles Salomon**
Bilateral	22	14	42	165	293	170	152	84	Bilatérale
Multilateral	1	5	6	32	40	21	23	103	Multilatérale
Total	22	19	48	197	333	190	176	187	Total
% of GNI	45.5	12.4	14.9	47.3	67.0	17.0	15.1	15.3	% du RNB
Somalia									**Somalie**
Bilateral	110	249	134	117	309	1 035	969	1 402	Bilatérale
Multilateral	55	102	54	123	197	225	215	359	Multilatérale
Total	165	351	188	240	506	1 261	1 184	1 760	Total
% of GNI	...	...	...	...	...	19.1	17.6	24.0	% du RNB
South Africa									**Afrique du Sud**
Bilateral	...	...	358	423	800	901	929	806	Bilatérale
Multilateral	...	...	28	259	236	519	251	209	Multilatérale
Total	...	...	386	681	1 036	1 420	1 180	1 014	Total
% of GNI	...	...	0.3	0.3	0.3	0.5	0.4	0.3	% du RNB
South Sudan									**Soudan du sud**
Bilateral	...	...	...	...	...	1 407	1 297	1 791	Bilatérale
Multilateral	...	...	...	...	...	267	290	392	Multilatérale
Total	...	...	...	...	...	1 675	1 587	2 183	Total
% of GNI	...	...	...	...	...	16.8	64.4	...	% du RNB
Sri Lanka									**Sri Lanka**
Bilateral	75	314	329	777	263	173	20	74	Bilatérale
Multilateral	67	125	142	263	296	254	337	223	Multilatérale
Total	141	439	471	1 040	559	427	357	297	Total
% of GNI	4.2	7.4	3.7	4.3	1.0	0.5	0.5	0.4	% du RNB
State of Palestine									**État de Palestine**
Bilateral	...	...	374	640	1 818	1 396	1 970	1 655	Bilatérale
Multilateral	...	...	140	376	695	477	432	456	Multilatérale
Total	...	...	514	1 016	2 513	1 872	2 402	2 111	Total
% of GNI	...	...	13.8	19.6	26.4	13.0	15.7	12.8	% du RNB
Sudan									**Soudan**
Bilateral	227	972	183	1 450	1 557	752	592	640	Bilatérale
Multilateral	67	153	54	376	469	148	219	200	Multilatérale
Total	294	1 125	237	1 826	2 026	900	811	840	Total
% of GNI	5.3	9.4	1.8	7.4	3.4	1.0	0.9	0.8	% du RNB
Suriname									**Suriname**
Bilateral	50	8	74	30	76	11	10	7	Bilatérale
Multilateral	3	2	3	13	25	5	6	13	Multilatérale
Total	53	10	77	43	101	16	17	20	Total
% of GNI	11.6	1.1	11.1	2.6	2.4	0.3	0.5	0.6	% du RNB
Syrian Arab Republic									**République arabe syrienne**
Bilateral	803	591	306	-3	-31	4 698	8 610	10 048	Bilatérale
Multilateral	25	19	50	74	162	222	289	313	Multilatérale
Total	827	610	356	71	131	4 920	8 900	10 361	Total
% of GNI	11.7	3.6	3.1	0.3	...	...	...	...	% du RNB
Tajikistan									**Tadjikistan**
Bilateral	...	...	49	116	210	280	197	72	Bilatérale
Multilateral	...	...	16	110	178	147	146	245	Multilatérale
Total	...	...	65	226	388	427	343	317	Total
% of GNI	...	...	5.5	10.1	5.6	4.6	4.2	3.8	% du RNB
Thailand									**Thaïlande**
Bilateral	67	392	812	-237	-132	-2	170	194	Bilatérale
Multilateral	18	55	25	72	111	61	58	56	Multilatérale
Total	85	447	836	-165	-20	59	228	250	Total
% of GNI	0.6	1.2	0.5	-0.1	~0.0	~0.0	0.1	0.1	% du RNB

31

Net disbursements of official development assistance to recipients *(continued)*
Total, bilateral and multilateral aid (millions of US dollars); and as a percentage of Gross National Income (GNI)

Décaissements nets d'aide publique au développement aux bénéficiaires *(suite)*
Total, bilatérale et multilatérale d'aide (millions de dollars É.-U.); et en pourcentage du Revenu National Brut (RNB)

Region, country or area[&]	1975	1985	1995	2005	2010	2015	2016	2017	Région, pays ou zone[&]
Timor-Leste									**Timor-Leste**
Bilateral	...	...	~0	149	250	174	178	179	Bilatérale
Multilateral	...	...	0	35	40	39	46	53	Multilatérale
Total	~0	...	~0	185	290	212	224	232	Total
% of GNI	...	...	...	21.8	8.7	7.6	9.8	8.9	% du RNB
Togo									**Togo**
Bilateral	31	74	156	42	205	110	64	130	Bilatérale
Multilateral	11	37	35	41	198	90	101	215	Multilatérale
Total	42	111	191	83	403	200	165	345	Total
% of GNI	6.8	15.3	15.1	4.0	14.6	4.7	3.6	6.9	% du RNB
Tokelau									**Tokélaou**
Bilateral	...	2	3	16	14	...	14	7	Bilatérale
Multilateral	...	~0	~0	~0	~0	...	~0	~0	Multilatérale
Total	~0	2	4	16	15	9	14	7	Total
Tonga									**Tonga**
Bilateral	3	10	30	23	55	52	63	71	Bilatérale
Multilateral	1	2	2	9	11	16	20	15	Multilatérale
Total	3	13	32	33	66	68	83	87	Total
% of GNI	...	20.2	15.6	12.6	17.4	15.5	20.5	20.1	% du RNB
Trinidad and Tobago									**Trinité-et-Tobago**
Bilateral	2	4	13	-11	2	...	...	...	Bilatérale
Multilateral	3	4	11	9	2	...	...	...	Multilatérale
Total	4	7	24	-2	4	...	...	...	Total
% of GNI	0.2	0.1	0.5	~-0.0	~-0.0	...	...	...	% du RNB
Tunisia									**Tunisie**
Bilateral	176	144	49	240	426	144	216	382	Bilatérale
Multilateral	38	17	27	128	124	331	412	394	Multilatérale
Total	214	160	75	368	550	475	627	776	Total
% of GNI	5.1	2.0	0.4	1.2	1.3	1.1	1.6	2.0	% du RNB
Turkey									**Turquie**
Bilateral	19	168	297	-57	715	139	1 028	1 075	Bilatérale
Multilateral	40	12	16	457	334	2 006	2 585	2 076	Multilatérale
Total	58	180	314	399	1 050	2 145	3 613	3 151	Total
% of GNI	0.1	0.3	0.2	0.1	0.1	0.3	0.4	0.4	% du RNB
Turkmenistan									**Turkménistan**
Bilateral	...	...	27	20	29	13	19	5	Bilatérale
Multilateral	...	...	4	10	15	11	14	24	Multilatérale
Total	...	...	31	29	44	24	33	29	Total
% of GNI	...	...	1.2	0.4	0.2	0.1	0.1	0.1	% du RNB
Turks and Caicos Islands									**Îles Turques-et-Caïques**
Bilateral	3	5	5	3	...	...	...	...	Bilatérale
Multilateral	~0	1	1	2	...	...	...	...	Multilatérale
Total	3	6	6	5	...	...	...	...	Total
Tuvalu									**Tuvalu**
Bilateral	...	3	7	5	13	42	-30	20	Bilatérale
Multilateral	...	~0	1	4	~0	8	54	7	Multilatérale
Total	~0	3	7	9	14	50	24	27	Total
% of GNI	...	...	...	24.4	27.3	88.7	44.4	44.9	% du RNB
Uganda									**Ouganda**
Bilateral	37	84	571	699	1 112	1 127	1 137	1 471	Bilatérale
Multilateral	15	96	263	497	578	502	620	537	Multilatérale
Total	52	179	834	1 195	1 690	1 628	1 757	2 008	Total
% of GNI	2.2	5.2	14.6	13.7	8.5	6.1	7.4	7.9	% du RNB
Ukraine [9]									**Ukraine** [9]
Bilateral	...	...	...	248	442	1 198	1 062	826	Bilatérale
Multilateral	...	...	...	156	214	251	461	343	Multilatérale
Total	...	...	...	404	657	1 449	1 523	1 170	Total
% of GNI	...	...	...	0.5	0.5	1.6	1.7	1.0	% du RNB
United Arab Emirates									**Émirats arabes unis**
Bilateral	3	3	6	...	...	...	...	...	Bilatérale
Multilateral	1	1	~-0	...	...	...	...	...	Multilatérale
Total	4	4	5	...	...	...	...	...	Total

31 Net disbursements of official development assistance to recipients *(continued)*
Total, bilateral and multilateral aid (millions of US dollars); and as a percentage of Gross National Income (GNI)

Décaissements nets d'aide publique au développement aux bénéficiaires *(suite)*
Total, bilatérale et multilatérale d'aide (millions de dollars É.-U.); et en pourcentage du Revenu National Brut (RNB)

Region, country or area&	1975	1985	1995	2005	2010	2015	2016	2017	Région, pays ou zone&
United Rep. of Tanzania									**Rép.-Unie de Tanzanie**
Bilateral	237	400	613	823	1 923	1 716	1 507	1 205	Bilatérale
Multilateral	57	77	258	670	1 037	866	810	1 379	Multilatérale
Total	293	477	871	1 492	2 960	2 582	2 318	2 584	Total
% of GNI	...	...	17.0	9.0	9.5	5.8	4.9	5.0	% du RNB
Uruguay									**Uruguay**
Bilateral	-8	6	62	2	29	12	4	30	Bilatérale
Multilateral	13	2	6	17	17	12	14	10	Multilatérale
Total	5	8	69	18	46	23	18	41	Total
% of GNI	0.1	0.2	0.4	0.1	0.1	0.1	~0.0	0.1	% du RNB
Uzbekistan									**Ouzbékistan**
Bilateral	...	...	76	128	117	287	288	474	Bilatérale
Multilateral	...	...	8	41	81	161	169	165	Multilatérale
Total	...	...	84	169	198	448	457	638	Total
% of GNI	...	...	0.6	1.2	0.5	0.7	0.7	1.3	% du RNB
Vanuatu									**Vanuatu**
Bilateral	12	19	42	30	106	169	81	112	Bilatérale
Multilateral	~0	2	2	11	3	18	48	20	Multilatérale
Total	12	21	45	40	109	187	129	132	Total
% of GNI	...	17.2	20.6	10.9	16.2	25.8	16.5	15.5	% du RNB
Venezuela (Boliv. Rep. of)									**Venezuela (Rép. boliv. du)**
Bilateral	-15	14	36	12	33	22	30	72	Bilatérale
Multilateral	19	2	8	36	20	15	14	14	Multilatérale
Total	4	17	45	49	53	37	43	87	Total
% of GNI	~0.0	~0.0	0.1	~0.0	~0.0	...	...	...	% du RNB
Viet Nam									**Viet Nam**
Bilateral	365	113	667	1 169	1 831	2 240	2 028	1 738	Bilatérale
Multilateral	22	38	111	525	938	918	867	654	Multilatérale
Total	387	151	778	1 693	2 770	3 157	2 895	2 392	Total
% of GNI	...	...	3.8	3.0	2.5	1.7	1.5	1.1	% du RNB
Wallis and Futuna Islands									**Îles Wallis-et-Futuna**
Bilateral	2	~0	1	72	123	106	85	89	Bilatérale
Multilateral	~0	~0	~0	~0	5	~0	~0	1	Multilatérale
Total	2	~0	1	72	127	106	85	90	Total
Yemen									**Yémen**
Bilateral	211	342	109	127	418	1 652	2 090	2 698	Bilatérale
Multilateral	40	89	63	169	249	146	211	536	Multilatérale
Total	251	431	172	296	667	1 798	2 301	3 234	Total
% of GNI	...	...	4.2	2.0	2.3	4.9	8.5	...	% du RNB
Zambia									**Zambie**
Bilateral	68	244	1 765	692	654	564	631	767	Bilatérale
Multilateral	18	75	266	478	266	234	334	270	Multilatérale
Total	86	319	2 031	1 169	919	797	964	1 036	Total
% of GNI	3.5	15.9	57.0	15.2	4.9	3.8	4.7	4.1	% du RNB
Zimbabwe									**Zimbabwe**
Bilateral	4	218	438	162	478	507	398	519	Bilatérale
Multilateral	~0	18	53	211	234	281	257	207	Multilatérale
Total	4	235	492	373	713	788	654	726	Total
% of GNI	0.1	4.3	7.2	6.8	8.2	5.5	4.4	4.6	% du RNB

Source:

Organisation for Economic Co-operation and Development (OECD), Paris, the OECD Development Assistance Committee (DAC) database, last accessed June 2019.

Source:

Organisation de coopération et de développement économiques (OCDE), Paris, base de données du Comité d'aide au développement (CAD) de l'OCDE, dernier accès juin 2019.

Official Development Assistance (ODA) is defined as those flows to developing countries and multilateral institutions provided by official agencies, including state and local governments, or by their executive agencies, each transaction of which meets the following tests: i) it is administered with the promotion of the economic development and welfare of developing countries as its main objective; and ii) it is concessional in character and conveys a grant element of at least 25 per cent.

On entend par Aide publique au développement (APD), l'ensemble des flux financiers à destination des pays en développement et des institutions multilatérales par des organismes publics (y compris les autorités étatiques et locales) ou par leurs organes exécutifs satisfaisant les critères suivants: i) elle est administrée dans le but premier de promouvoir le développement économique et social des pays en développement ; ii) elle est accordée à

31 Net disbursements of official development assistance to recipients *(continued)*
Total, bilateral and multilateral aid (millions of US dollars); and as a percentage of Gross National Income (GNI)

Décaissements nets d'aide publique au développement aux bénéficiaires *(suite)*
Total, bilatérale et multilatérale d'aide (millions de dollars É.-U.); et en pourcentage du Revenu National Brut (RNB)

des conditions de faveur et comporte une élément de subvention d'au moins 25 pour cent.

1	Including regional aid disbursements in addition to the disbursements made to individual countries and areas.	1 Y compris les versements d'aides régionales en plus des versements effectués aux aux différents pays et régions.
2	Excluding Sudan.	2 Exclut le Soudan.
3	Including Sudan.	3 Y compris le Soudan.
4	Excludes Myanmar.	4 Non compris Myanmar.
5	Includes Armenia, Azerbaijan, Georgia and Myanmar. Excludes Iran (Islamic Rep. of).	5 Y compris l'Arménie, l'Azerbaïdjan, la Géorgie et le Myanmar. Non compris la Rép. Islamique d 'Iran.
6	Excluding Armenia, Azerbaijan, Cyprus, Georgia and Turkey. Includes Iran (Islamic Rep. of).	6 Non compris l'Arménie, l'Azerbaïdjan, Chypre, la Géorgie et la Turquie. Y compris la Rép. Islamique d 'Iran.
7	Including Turkey and Cyprus.	7 Y compris la Turquie et Chypre.
8	For statistical purposes, the data for China do not include those for the Hong Kong Special Administrative Region (Hong Kong SAR), Macao Special Administrative Region (Macao SAR) and Taiwan Province of China.	8 Pour la présentation des statistiques, les données pour la Chine ne comprennent pas la région administrative spéciale de Hong Kong (RAS de Hong Kong), la région administrative spéciale de Macao (RAS de Macao) et la province chinoise de Taïwan.
9	Excludes the temporarily occupied territory of the Autonomous Republic of Crimea and Sevastopol.	9 Excluent le territoire temporairement occupé de la République autonome de Crimée et de Sébastopol.

32

Net disbursements of official development assistance from donors
Millions of US dollars and as a percentage of gross national income (GNI)

Décaissements nets d'aide publique au développement par des donateurs
Millions de dollares É.-U. et en pourcentage du revenu national brut (RNB)

Country or area	1975	1985	1995	2005	2010	2015	2016	2017	2018	Pays ou zone
Total										**Total**
$ millions	20 183	33 855	65 424	120 771	147 644	156 603	177 420	179 370	180 132	$millions
DAC total										**CAD total**
$ millions	13 315	28 858	58 896	108 397	128 484	131 563	144 921	147 160	149 323	$millions
% of GNI	0.34	0.33	0.26	0.32	0.31	0.30	0.32	0.31	...	% du RNB
Australia [1]										**Australie** [1]
$ millions	552	749	1 194	1 680	3 826	3 494	3 278	3 036	3 119	$millions
% of GNI	0.65	0.48	0.34	0.25	0.32	0.29	0.27	0.23	...	% du RNB
Austria [1]										**Autriche** [1]
$ millions	79	248	620	1 573	1 208	1 324	1 635	1 251	1 175	$millions
% of GNI	0.21	0.38	0.27	0.52	0.32	0.35	0.42	0.30	...	% du RNB
Azerbaijan										**Azerbaïdjan**
$ millions	...	...	...	...	...	13	13	19	...	$millions
Belgium [1]										**Belgique** [1]
$ millions	378	440	1 034	1 963	3 004	1 904	2 300	2 196	2 361	$millions
% of GNI	0.60	0.55	0.38	0.53	0.64	0.42	0.50	0.45	...	% du RNB
Bulgaria										**Bulgarie**
$ millions	...	...	...	...	40	41	68	62	69	$millions
% of GNI	...	...	...	...	0.09	0.09	0.13	0.11	...	% du RNB
Canada [1]										**Canada** [1]
$ millions	880	1 631	2 067	3 756	5 214	4 277	3 930	4 305	4 616	$millions
% of GNI	0.54	0.49	0.38	0.34	0.34	0.28	0.26	0.26	...	% du RNB
Croatia										**Croatie**
$ millions	...	...	...	...	...	51	41	54	...	$millions
Cyprus [2]										**Chypre** [2]
$ millions	...	...	...	15	51	18	...	...	...	$millions
% of GNI	...	...	...	0.09	0.23	0.09	...	...	...	% du RNB
Czechia [1]										**Tchéquie** [1]
$ millions	...	...	...	135	228	199	260	304	323	$millions
% of GNI	...	...	...	0.11	0.13	0.12	0.14	0.15	...	% du RNB
Denmark [1]										**Danemark** [1]
$ millions	205	440	1 623	2 109	2 871	2 566	2 369	2 448	2 568	$millions
% of GNI	0.55	0.80	0.96	0.81	0.91	0.85	0.75	0.74	...	% du RNB
Estonia										**Estonie**
$ millions	...	...	...	10	19	34	43	43	49	$millions
% of GNI	...	...	...	0.08	0.10	0.15	0.19	0.16	...	% du RNB
Finland [1]										**Finlande** [1]
$ millions	48	211	388	902	1 333	1 288	1 060	1 084	983	$millions
% of GNI	0.17	0.40	0.31	0.46	0.55	0.55	0.44	0.42	...	% du RNB
France [1]										**France** [1]
$ millions	1 493	3 134	8 443	10 026	12 915	9 039	9 622	11 331	12 504	$millions
% of GNI	0.44	0.61	0.55	0.47	0.50	0.37	0.38	0.43	...	% du RNB
Germany [1]										**Allemagne** [1]
$ millions	1 689	2 942	7 524	10 082	12 985	17 940	24 736	25 005	25 886	$millions
% of GNI	0.40	0.47	0.31	0.36	0.39	0.52	0.70	0.67	...	% du RNB
Greece [1]										**Grèce** [1]
$ millions	...	...	...	384	508	239	369	314	282	$millions
% of GNI	...	...	...	0.17	0.17	0.12	0.19	0.16	...	% du RNB
Hungary [1]										**Hongrie** [1]
$ millions	29	84	...	100	114	156	199	149	190	$millions
% of GNI	...	...	...	0.11	0.09	0.13	0.17	0.11	...	% du RNB
Iceland [1]										**Islande** [1]
$ millions	...	...	...	27	29	40	59	68	81	$millions
% of GNI	...	...	...	0.18	0.26	0.24	0.28	0.28	...	% du RNB
Ireland [1]										**Irlande** [1]
$ millions	8	39	153	719	895	718	803	838	928	$millions
% of GNI	0.09	0.24	0.29	0.42	0.52	0.32	0.32	0.32	...	% du RNB
Israel										**Israël**
$ millions	...	...	...	95	145	233	351	...	434	$millions
% of GNI	...	...	...	0.07	0.07	0.08	0.11	...	...	% du RNB
Italy [1]										**Italie** [1]
$ millions	182	1 098	1 623	5 091	2 996	4 003	5 087	5 858	4 900	$millions
% of GNI	0.10	0.26	0.15	0.29	0.15	0.22	0.27	0.30	...	% du RNB

Net disbursements of official development assistance from donors *(continued)*
Millions of US dollars and as a percentage of gross national income (GNI)

Décaissements nets d'aide publique au développement par des donateurs *(suite)*
Millions de dollares É.-U. et en pourcentage du revenu national brut (RNB)

Country or area	1975	1985	1995	2005	2010	2015	2016	2017	2018	Pays ou zone
Japan [1]										**Japon** [1]
$ millions	1 148	3 797	14 489	13 126	11 058	9 203	10 417	11 463	10 064	$millions
% of GNI	0.23	0.29	0.27	0.28	0.20	0.20	0.20	0.23	...	% du RNB
Kazakhstan										**Kazakhstan**
$ millions	...	...	...	...	...	43	31	35	...	$millions
Kuwait										**Koweït**
$ millions	859[3]	647[3]	384[3]	218[3]	232[3]	304[3]	# 1 080[4]	570[4]	...	$millions
Latvia										**Lettonie**
$ millions	...	...	...	11	16	23	30	32	34	$millions
% of GNI				0.07	0.06	0.09	0.11	0.11	...	% du RNB
Liechtenstein										**Liechtenstein**
$ millions	...	...	...	...	27	24	25	24	...	$millions
% of GNI	...	...	...		0.62	...	...	...	...	% du RNB
Lithuania										**Lituanie**
$ millions	...	...	...	16	37	48	57	59	59	$millions
% of GNI				0.06	0.10	0.12	0.14	0.13	...	% du RNB
Luxembourg [1]										**Luxembourg** [1]
$ millions	...	8	65	256	403	363	391	424	473	$millions
% of GNI	...	0.17	0.36	0.79	1.05	0.95	1.00	1.00	...	% du RNB
Malta										**Malte**
$ millions	...	...	...	...	14	17	21	25	31	$millions
% of GNI	...	...	...	...	0.18	0.17	0.20	0.21	...	% du RNB
Netherlands [1]										**Pays-Bas** [1]
$ millions	608	1 136	3 226	5 115	6 357	5 726	4 966	4 958	5 616	$millions
% of GNI	0.74	0.91	0.81	0.82	0.81	0.75	0.65	0.60	...	% du RNB
New Zealand [1]										**Nouvelle-Zélande** [1]
$ millions	66	54	123	274	342	442	447	450	556	$millions
% of GNI	0.52	0.25	0.23	0.27	0.26	0.27	0.25	0.23	...	% du RNB
Norway [1]										**Norvège** [1]
$ millions	184	574	1 244	2 794	4 372	4 278	4 380	4 125	4 257	$millions
% of GNI	0.65	1.01	0.86	0.94	1.05	1.05	1.12	0.99	...	% du RNB
Other non-specified areas										**Autres zones non-spécifiées**
$ millions	...	...	92	483	381	255	328	319	...	$millions
% of GNI			...	0.14	0.10	0.05	0.06	0.06	...	% du RNB
Poland [1]										**Pologne** [1]
$ millions	32	19	...	205	378	441	663	679	754	$millions
% of GNI	...	...	...	0.07	0.08	0.10	0.15	0.13	...	% du RNB
Portugal [1]										**Portugal** [1]
$ millions	...	10	258	377	649	308	343	381	341	$millions
% of GNI	...	0.05	0.25	0.21	0.29	0.16	0.17	0.18	...	% du RNB
Republic of Korea [1]										**République de Corée** [1]
$ millions	...	...	116	752	1 174	1 915	2 246	2 201	2 417	$millions
% of GNI	...	...	0.02	0.10	0.12	0.14	0.16	0.14	...	% du RNB
Romania										**Roumanie**
$ millions	...	...	...	...	114	158	203	220	252	$millions
% of GNI	...	...	...	...	0.07	0.09	0.11	0.11	...	% du RNB
Russian Federation										**Fédération de Russie**
$ millions	...	...	...	472	1 161[5]	1 258[5]	1 190[5]		...	$millions
% of GNI	...	...	...	0.03	0.09[5]	0.10[5]	0.08[5]		...	% du RNB
Saudi Arabia										**Arabie saoudite**
$ millions	2 569	2 443	305	1 026	3 480	579[6]	949[6]	908[6]	...	$millions
Slovakia [1]										**Slovaquie** [1]
$ millions	...	...	...	57	74	85	106	119	133	$millions
% of GNI	...	...	...		0.09	0.10	0.12	0.13	...	% du RNB
Slovenia [1]										**Slovénie** [1]
$ millions	...	...	...	35	59	63	81	76	83	$millions
% of GNI	...	...	...	0.11	0.13	0.15	0.19	0.16	...	% du RNB
Spain [1]										**Espagne** [1]
$ millions	...	169	1 348	3 018	5 949	1 397	4 224	2 560	2 581	$millions
% of GNI	...	0.10	0.24	0.27	0.43	0.12	0.34	0.19	...	% du RNB
Sweden [1]										**Suède** [1]
$ millions	566	840	1 704	3 362	4 533	7 089	4 894	5 563	5 843	$millions
% of GNI	0.78	0.86	0.77	0.94	0.97	1.40	0.94	1.02	...	% du RNB
Switzerland [1]										**Suisse** [1]
$ millions	104	303	1 084	1 772	2 300	3 529	3 582	3 138	3 091	$millions
% of GNI	0.18	0.31	0.33	0.42	0.39	0.51	0.53	0.46	...	% du RNB

32

Net disbursements of official development assistance from donors *(continued)*
Millions of US dollars and as a percentage of gross national income (GNI)

Décaissements nets d'aide publique au développement par des donateurs *(suite)*
Millions de dollars É.-U. et en pourcentage du revenu national brut (RNB)

Country or area	1975	1985	1995	2005	2010	2015	2016	2017	2018	Pays ou zone
Thailand										**Thaïlande**
$ millions	...	...	...	...	4	62	168	133	...	$millions
% of GNI	...	...	...	...	~0.00	0.02	0.05	0.03	...	% du RNB
Timor-Leste										**Timor-Leste**
$ millions	...	...	...	...	...	4	...	...	...	$millions
Turkey										**Turquie**
$ millions	...	...	107	601	967	3 919	6 488	8 121	8 562	$millions
% of GNI	...	...	0.06	0.17	0.13	0.50	0.76	0.95	...	% du RNB
United Arab Emirates [7]										**Émirats arabes unis** [7]
$ millions	1 998	366	243	510	414	4 381	4 241	3 957	4 188	$millions
% of GNI	...	...	...	...	0.14	1.18	1.21	1.03	...	% du RNB
United Kingdom [1]										**Royaume-Uni** [1]
$ millions	904	1 530	3 202	10 772	13 053	18 553	18 053	18 103	19 455	$millions
% of GNI	0.38	0.33	0.29	0.47	0.57	0.70	0.70	0.70	...	% du RNB
United States of America [1]										**États-Unis d'Amérique** [1]
$ millions	4 161	9 403	7 367	27 935	29 656	30 986	34 421	34 732	33 741	$millions
% of GNI	0.27	0.24	0.10	0.23	0.20	0.17	0.19	0.18	...	% du RNB
Areas not specified										**Zones non spécifiées**
$ millions	721	32	...	...	...	...	...	...	...	$millions
European Union (EU) [1,8]										**Union européenne (UE)** [1,8]
$ millions	722	1 510	5 398	9 390	12 747	13 670	17 106	16 440	17 131	$millions

Source:

Organisation for Economic Co-operation and Development (OECD), Paris, the OECD Development Assistance Committee (DAC) database, last accessed June 2019.

Source:

Organisation de coopération et de développement économiques (OCDE), Paris, base de données du Comité d'aide au développement (CAD) de l'OCDE, dernier accès juin 2019.

1 Development Assistance Committee member (OECD).
2 Data refer to government controlled areas.

3 Includes Kuwait Fund grants only.
4 Includes Kuwait Fund grants, State of Kuwait grants administered by Kuwait Fund as well as State of Kuwait grants.

5 Some of the debt relief reported may correspond to the credits. Statistics currently published on ODA by Russia and the estimates from the previous Chairman's reports should not be used at the same time.
6 Saudi Arabia's reporting to the OECD on its development co-operation programme consists of aggregate figures on humanitarian and development assistance by region, multilateral aid and loan disbursements and repayments by the Saudi Fund for Development.

7 Data reported at activity level, represent flows from all government agencies.
8 Refers to European Union institutions.

1 Le Comité d'aide au développement (l'OCDE).
2 Les données se rapportent aux zones contrôlées par le Gouvernement.
3 Inclut les subventions du Fonds koweïtien seulement.
4 Inclut les subventions du Fonds koweïtien, les subventions de l'État du Koweït administrées par le Kuwait Fund ainsi que les subventions de l'État du Koweït.
5 Une partie de l'allégement de la dette rapporté peut correspondre aux crédits. Les statistiques actuellement publiées sur l'APD par la Russie et les estimations des précédents rapports du Président ne devraient pas être utilisées en même temps.
6 La déclaration de l'Arabie saoudite auprès de l'OCDE relatif au programme de coopération au développement est constituée de données globales sur l'aide humanitaire, l'aide au développement par région, l'aide multilatérale, et les déboursements et les remboursements de prêts par les Fonds saoudien pour le développement.
7 Les données rapportées au niveau d'activité, ces données représentent les flux de tous les organismes gouvernementaux.
8 Se réfèrent aux institutions de l'Union Européenne.

Annex I - Country and area nomenclature, regional and other groupings

The *Statistical Yearbook* lists countries or areas based on the United Nations Standard Country Codes (Series M, No. 49), prepared by the Statistics Division of the United Nations Secretariat and first issued in 1970[1]. The list of countries or areas; the composition of geographical regions and economic, trade and other groupings used within this yearbook (as at 31 July 2018) are presented in this Annex. The names of countries or areas refer to their short form used in day-to-day operations of the United Nations and not necessarily to their official name as used in formal documents[2]. As an aid to statistical data processing, a unique standard three-digit numerical code is assigned to each country or area and to each geographical region and grouping of countries or areas. For reference, these codes, where applicable, are presented to the left of each country or area listed in this Annex. These codes range from 000 to 899, inclusive.

A. Changes in country or area names (since 31 July 2008)

The geographical extent of a country or area, or the composition of a geographical region, may change over time and users should take such changes into account in interpreting the tables in this Yearbook. A change in the name of a country or area while its geographical coverage remains the same is not usually accompanied by a change in its numerical code. Changes in numerical codes and names in the general period covered by the statistics (since 31 July 2008) in the *Yearbook*, are shown below;

Numerical code	Country or area (added or changed)	Date of change	Numerical code	Country or area (Name changes with no change in code)	Date of change
728	South Sudan	2011	748	Eswatini, *previously Swaziland*	2018
729	Sudan	2011	203	Czechia, *previously Czech Republic*	2016
531	Curaçao	2010	132	Cabo Verde, *previously Cape Verde*	2013
534	Sint Maarten (Dutch part)	2010	275	State of Palestine, *previously Occupied Palestinian Territory*	2013
535	Bonaire, Sint Eustatius and Saba	2010			
			434	Libya, *previously Libyan Arab Jamahiriya*	2011
			068	Bolivia (Plurinational State of), *previously Bolivia*	2009
			807	North Macedonia, *previously the former Yugoslav Republic of Macedonia*	2019
			498	Republic of Moldova, *previously Moldova*	2008

B. Regional groupings

The scheme of regional groupings given on the next page is based mainly on 6 continents; these continental regions, except Antarctica, are further subdivided into 22 sub-regions and 2 intermediary regions (Sub-Saharan Africa and Latin America and the Caribbean) that are drawn as to obtain greater homogeneity in sizes of population, demographic circumstances and accuracy of demographic statistics. This nomenclature is widely used in international statistics and is followed to the greatest extent possible in the present *Yearbook* in order to promote consistency and facilitate comparability and analysis. However, it is by no means universal in international statistical compilation, even at the level of continental regions, and variations in international statistical sources and methods dictate many unavoidable differences in particular fields in the present *Yearbook*. General differences are indicated in the footnotes to the classification presented below. More detailed differences are given in the footnotes and technical notes to individual tables.

Neither is there international standardization in the use of the terms "developed" and "developing" countries, areas or regions. These terms are used in the present publication to refer to regional groupings generally considered as "developed": these are Northern America (numerical code 021), Europe (150), Cyprus (196), Israel (376), Japan (392) and Australia and New Zealand (053). These designations are intended for statistical convenience and do not necessarily express a judgement about the stage reached by a particular country or area in the development process. Differences from this usage are indicated in the notes to individual tables.

---

[1] Four revisions of this document were published in 1975, 1982, 1996 and 1999. Further revisions are now published on the United Nations Statistics Division website under the M49 section.

[2] A listing in the 6 official languages of the United Nations is contained in Terminology Bulletin No. 347/Rev.1 or the UNTERM website, prepared by the Department of General Assembly Affairs and Conference Services of the United Nations Secretariat.

World

Africa

202	Sub-Saharan Africa					015	Northern Africa

014	**Eastern Africa**	834	United Republic of Tanzania note /a	**011**	**Western Africa**	012	Algeria
086	British Indian Ocean Territory	894	Zambia	204	Benin	818	Egypt
		716	Zimbabwe	854	Burkina Faso	434	Libya
108	Burundi			132	Cabo Verde	504	Morocco
174	Comoros			384	Côte d'Ivoire	729	Sudan note 736
262	Djibouti	**017**	**Middle Africa**	270	Gambia	788	Tunisia
232	Eritrea	024	Angola	288	Ghana	732	Western Sahara
231	Ethiopia	120	Cameroon	324	Guinea		
260	French Southern Territories	140	Central African Republic	624	Guinea-Bissau	**Note**	**Tables may list**
		148	Chad	430	Liberia	*736*	*Sudan [former]*
404	Kenya	178	Congo	466	Mali		
450	Madagascar	180	Democratic Republic of the Congo	478	Mauritania	/a	Includes
454	Malawi			562	Niger	---	*Zanzibar*
480	Mauritius	226	Equatorial Guinea	566	Nigeria		
175	Mayotte	266	Gabon	654	Saint Helena note /b	/b	Includes
508	Mozambique	678	Sao Tome and Principe	686	Senegal	---	*Ascension*
638	Réunion			694	Sierra Leone	---	*Tristan da Cunha*
646	Rwanda	**018**	**Southern Africa**	768	Togo		
690	Seychelles	072	Botswana				
706	Somalia	748	Eswatini				
728	South Sudan note 736	426	Lesotho				
800	Uganda	516	Namibia				
		710	South Africa				

Americas

419	Latin America and the Caribbean					021	Northern America note 003

029	**Caribbean**	659	Saint Kitts and Nevis	**005**	**South America**	060	Bermuda
660	Anguilla	662	Saint Lucia	032	Argentina	124	Canada
028	Antigua and Barbuda	663	Saint Martin (French part)	068	Bolivia (Plurinational State of)	304	Greenland
533	Aruba			074	Bouvet Island	666	Saint Pierre and Miquelon
044	Bahamas	670	Saint Vincent and the Grenadines	076	Brazil		
052	Barbados			152	Chile	840	United States of America
535	Bonaire, note 530 Sint Eustatius and Saba	534	Sint Maarten note 530 (Dutch part)	170	Colombia		
		780	Trinidad and Tobago	218	Ecuador		
092	British Virgin Islands	796	Turks and Caicos Islands	238	Falkland Islands (Malvinas)	**Note**	
136	Cayman Islands	850	United States Virgin Islands			*003*	*The continent of* **North America** *comprises Northern America, Caribbean and Central America.*
192	Cuba			254	French Guiana		
531	Curaçao note 530			328	Guyana		
212	Dominica	**013**	**Central America**	600	Paraguay		
214	Dominican Republic	084	Belize	604	Peru		
308	Grenada	188	Costa Rica	740	Suriname		
312	Guadeloupe	222	El Salvador	239	South Georgia and the South Sandwich Islands	**Tables may list**	
332	Haiti	320	Guatemala			*530*	*Netherlands Antilles [former]*
388	Jamaica	340	Honduras	858	Uruguay		
474	Martinique	484	Mexico	862	Venezuela (Bolivarian Republic of)		
500	Montserrat	558	Nicaragua				
630	Puerto Rico	591	Panama				
652	Saint Barthélemy						

Antarctica

143	**Central Asia**	496	Mongolia	034	**Southern Asia**	196	Cyprus
398	Kazakhstan	410	Republic of Korea	004	Afghanistan	268	Georgia
417	Kyrgyzstan			050	Bangladesh	368	Iraq
762	Tajikistan	035	**South-eastern Asia**	064	Bhutan	376	Israel
795	Turkmenistan	096	Brunei Darussalam	356	India	400	Jordan
860	Uzbekistan	116	Cambodia	364	Iran (Islamic	414	Kuwait
		360	Indonesia		Republic of)	422	Lebanon
030	**Eastern Asia**	418	Lao People's	462	Maldives	512	Oman
156	China		Democratic Republic	524	Nepal	634	Qatar
344	China, Hong Kong Special	458	Malaysia	586	Pakistan	682	Saudi Arabia
	Administrative Region	104	Myanmar	144	Sri Lanka	275	State of Palestine
446	China, Macao Special	608	Philippines			760	Syrian Arab Republic
	Administrative Region	702	Singapore	145	**Western Asia**	792	Turkey
408	Democratic People's	764	Thailand	051	Armenia	784	United Arab Emirates
	Republic of Korea	626	Timor-Leste	031	Azerbaijan	887	Yemen
392	Japan	704	Viet Nam	048	Bahrain		

151	**Eastern Europe**	831	Guernsey note 830	039	**Southern Europe**	155	**Western Europe**
112	Belarus	352	Iceland	008	Albania	040	Austria
100	Bulgaria	372	Ireland	020	Andorra	056	Belgium
203	Czechia	833	Isle of Man	070	Bosnia and Herzegovina	250	France
348	Hungary	832	Jersey note 830	191	Croatia	276	Germany
616	Poland	428	Latvia	292	Gibraltar	438	Liechtenstein
498	Republic of Moldova	440	Lithuania	300	Greece	442	Luxembourg
642	Romania	578	Norway	336	Holy See	492	Monaco
643	Russian Federation	744	Svalbard and Jan	380	Italy	528	Netherlands
703	Slovakia		Mayen Islands	470	Malta	756	Switzerland
804	Ukraine	752	Sweden	499	Montenegro note 891		
		826	United Kingdom of	807	North Macedonia	**Note**	**Tables may list**
154	**Northern Europe**		Great Britain and	620	Portugal	*830*	*Channel Islands*
248	Åland Islands		Northern Ireland	674	San Marino	*891*	*Serbia and*
208	Denmark			688	Serbia note 891 & /c		*Montenegro [former]*
233	Estonia			705	Slovenia	*/c*	*Kosovo*
234	Faroe Islands			724	Spain		
246	Finland						

053	**Australia and New Zealand**	057	**Micronesia**	061	**Polynesia**
036	Australia	316	Guam	016	American Samoa
162	Christmas Island	296	Kiribati	184	Cook Islands
166	Cocos (Keeling) Islands	584	Marshall Islands	258	French Polynesia
334	Heard Island and McDonald Islands	583	Micronesia (Federated States of)	570	Niue
554	New Zealand	520	Nauru	612	Pitcairn
574	Norfolk Island	580	Northern Mariana Islands	882	Samoa
		585	Palau	772	Tokelau
054	**Melanesia**	581	United States minor outlying islands	776	Tonga
242	Fiji			798	Tuvalu
540	New Caledonia			876	Wallis and Futuna Islands
598	Papua New Guinea				
090	Solomon Islands				
548	Vanuatu				

Other groupings

Following is a list of other groupings and their compositions presented in the *Yearbook*. These groupings are organized mainly around economic and trade interests in regional associations.

063   Andean Common Market (ANCOM)

068	Bolivia (Plurinational State of)	170 Colombia	218 Ecuador	604 Peru

066   Asia-Pacific Economic Cooperation (APEC)

036	Australia	344	China, Hong Kong Special	554	New Zealand	702	Singapore
096	Brunei		Administrative Region	598	Papua New Guinea	158	Taiwan Province of China
	Darussalam	360	Indonesia	604	Peru	764	Thailand
124	Canada	392	Japan	608	Philippines	840	United States of America
152	Chile	458	Malaysia	410	Republic of Korea	704	Viet Nam
156	China	484	Mexico	643	Russian Federation		

073   Association of Southeast Asian Nations (ASEAN)

096	Brunei Darussalam	360	Indonesia	458	Malaysia	608	Philippines	764	Thailand
116	Cambodia	418	Lao PDR	104	Myanmar	702	Singapore	704	Viet Nam

130   Caribbean Community and Common Market (CARICOM)

028	Antigua and Barbuda	084	Belize	332	Haiti	662	Saint Lucia
044	Bahamas (member of the	212	Dominica	388	Jamaica	670	Saint Vincent and the Grenadines
	Community only)	308	Grenada	500	Montserrat	740	Suriname
052	Barbados	328	Guyana	659	Saint Kitts and Nevis	780	Trinidad and Tobago

395   Central American Common Market (CACM)

188	Costa Rica	222	El Salvador	320	Guatemala	340	Honduras	558	Nicaragua

171   Common Market for Eastern and Southern Africa (COMESA)

108	Burundi	818	Egypt	434	Libya	690	Seychelles	894	Zambia
174	Comoros	232	Eritrea	450	Madagascar	706	Somalia	716	Zimbabwe
180	Democratic Republic	748	Eswatini	454	Malawi	729	Sudan		
	of the Congo	231	Ethiopia	480	Mauritius	788	Tunisia		
262	Djibouti	404	Kenya	646	Rwanda	800	Uganda		

172   Commonwealth of Independent States (CIS)[3]

051	Armenia	398	Kazakhstan	643	Russian Federation	804	Ukraine
031	Azerbaijan	417	Kyrgyzstan	762	Tajikistan	860	Uzbekistan
112	Belarus	498	Republic of Moldova	795	Turkmenistan		

692   Economic and Monetary Community of Central Africa (EMCCA)

120	Cameroon	140	Central African Republic	148	Chad	178	Congo	226	Equatorial Guinea	266	Gabon

892   Economic Community of West African States (ECOWAS)

204	Benin	384	Côte d'Ivoire	324	Guinea	466	Mali	686	Senegal
854	Burkina Faso	270	Gambia	624	Guinea-Bissau	562	Niger	694	Sierra Leone
132	Cabo Verde	288	Ghana	430	Liberia	566	Nigeria	768	Togo

098   Euro Area

040	Austria	246	Finland	372	Ireland	442	Luxembourg	703	Slovakia
056	Belgium	250	France	380	Italy	470	Malta	705	Slovenia
196	Cyprus	276	Germany	428	Latvia	528	Netherlands	724	Spain
233	Estonia	300	Greece	440	Lithuania	620	Portugal		

197   European Free Trade Association (EFTA)

352	Iceland	438 Liechtenstein	578 Norway	756 Switzerland

097   European Union (EU)

040	Austria	208	Denmark	348	Hungary	470	Malta	705	Slovenia
056	Belgium	233	Estonia	372	Ireland	528	Netherlands	724	Spain

---

[3] Georgia (numerical code 268) can be listed as part of this group; for example, in International Merchandise Trade statistics.

097 — European Union (EU) *(Continued)*

100	Bulgaria	246	Finland	380	Italy	616	Poland	752	Sweden
191	Croatia	250	France	428	Latvia	620	Portugal	826	United Kingdom
196	Cyprus	276	Germany	440	Lithuania	642	Romania		
203	Czechia	300	Greece	442	Luxembourg	703	Slovakia		

095 — Latin American Integration Association (LAIA)

032	Argentina	170	Colombia	591	Panama	862	Venezuela (Bolivarian
068	Bolivia (Plurinational State of)	192	Cuba	600	Paraguay		Republic of)
076	Brazil	218	Ecuador	604	Peru		
152	Chile	484	Mexico	858	Uruguay		

199 — Least developed countries (LDCs)

004	Afghanistan	262	Djibouti	454	Malawi	728	South Sudan
024	Angola	232	Eritrea	466	Mali	729	Sudan
050	Bangladesh	231	Ethiopia	478	Mauritania	626	Timor-Leste
204	Benin	270	Gambia	508	Mozambique	768	Togo
064	Bhutan	324	Guinea	104	Myanmar	798	Tuvalu
854	Burkina Faso	624	Guinea-Bissau	524	Nepal	800	Uganda
108	Burundi	332	Haiti	562	Niger	834	United Republic of Tanzania
116	Cambodia	296	Kiribati	646	Rwanda		
140	Central African Republic	418	Lao People's Democratic Republic	678	Sao Tome and Principe	548	Vanuatu
148	Chad			686	Senegal	887	Yemen
174	Comoros	426	Lesotho	694	Sierra Leone	894	Zambia
180	Democratic Republic of the Congo	430	Liberia	090	Solomon Islands		
		450	Madagascar	706	Somalia		

071 — North American Free Trade Agreement (NAFTA)

124	Canada	484	Mexico	840	United States of America

198 — Organisation for Economic Co-operation and Development (OECD)

036	Australia	250	France	428	Latvia	410	Republic of Korea
040	Austria	276	Germany	440	Lithuania	703	Slovakia
056	Belgium	300	Greece	442	Luxembourg	705	Slovenia
124	Canada	348	Hungary	484	Mexico	724	Spain
152	Chile	352	Iceland	528	Netherlands	752	Sweden
203	Czech Republic	372	Ireland	554	New Zealand	756	Switzerland
208	Denmark	376	Israel	578	Norway	792	Turkey
233	Estonia	380	Italy	616	Poland	826	United Kingdom of Great Britain and Northern Ireland
246	Finland	392	Japan	620	Portugal	840	United States of America

399 — Organization of the Petroleum Exporting Countries (OPEC)

012	Algeria	226	Equatorial Guinea	414	Kuwait	784	United Arab Emirates
024	Angola	266	Gabon	434	Libya	862	Venezuela (Bolivarian Republic of)
178	Congo	364	Iran (Islamic Republic of)	566	Nigeria		
218	Ecuador	368	Iraq	682	Saudi Arabia		

711 — Southern African Customs Union (SACU)

072	Botswana	748	Eswatini	426	Lesotho	516	Namibia	710	South Africa

069 — Southern Common Market (MERCOSUR)

032	Argentina	076	Brazil	858	Uruguay	
068	Bolivia (Plurinational State of)	600	Paraguay	862	Venezuela (Bolivarian Republic of)

Annexe I - Nomenclature des pays ou zones, groupements régionaux et autres groupements

L'Annuaire statistique répertorie de pays ou de zones sur la base de l'opuscule United Nations Standard Country Codes (Série M, n° 49) rédigée par la Division de statistique du Secrétariat de l'Organisation des Nations Unies et publiée en 1970[1]. La liste des pays ou zones; la composition des régions géographiques et économiques, commerciales et d'autres groupements utilisés dans cet annuaire (au 31 juillet 2018) sont présentées dans la présente annexe. On a eu recours à la forme brève des noms des pays et des zones usitées au cours des activités courantes des Nations Unies, et pas nécessairement aux désignations officielles utilisées dans les documents officiels[2]. Afin de faciliter le traitement des données statistiques, un code numérique unique et standard à trois chiffres est attribué à chaque pays ou zone et à chaque région géographique et groupement de pays ou de zones. Pour référence, ces codes, le cas échéant, sont présentés à la gauche de chaque pays ou zone visées dans cette annexe. Ces codes s'échelonnent entre 000 et 899.

A. Changements dans le nom des pays ou zones (depuis 31 juillet 2008)

L'étendue géographique d'un pays ou d'une zone ou la composition d'une région géographique peuvent varier au fil du temps et les utilisateurs devront tenir compte de telles modifications lorsqu'ils ont recours aux codes indiques dans la présente publication et qu'ils établissent des rapports entre les données portant sur différentes périodes. La modification du nom d'un pays ou d'une zone alors que son espace géographique demeure le même n'est pas habituellement accompagnée d'un changement de son code numérique. Changements dans les codes numériques et noms dans la période générale couverts par les statistiques (depuis le 31 juillet 2008) dans l'Annuaire, sont présentés ci-dessous;

Code numérique	Pays ou region (nouveaux codes et codes modifies)	Date de la modification	Code numérique	Pays ou region (Changements de nom sans modification du code)	Date de la modification
728	Soudan du Sud	2011	748	Eswatini, *ex-Swaziland*	2018
729	Soudan	2011	203	Tchéquie, *ex-République tchèque*	2016
531	Curaçao	2010	132	Cabo Verde, *ex-Cap-Vert*	2013
534	Saint-Martin (partie néerlandaise)	2010	434	État de Palestine, *ex-Territoire palestinien occupé*	2013
535	Bonaire, Saint-Eustache et Saba	2010	275	Libye, *ex-Jamahiriya arabe libyenne*	2011
			068	Bolivie (État plurinational de), *ex-Bolivie*	2009
				Macédoine du Nord, *Ancienne république yougoslave de Macédoine*	2019
			498	République de Moldova, *ex-Moldova*	2008

B. Groupements régionaux

Le système des groupements régionaux à la page suivante est principalement basé sur les 6 continents; ces régions continentales, à l'exception de l'Antarctique, sont subdivisées en 22 sous-régions et 2 régions intermédiaires (Afrique subsaharienne et l'Amérique latine et Caraïbes) afin d'obtenir une homogénéité accrue les effectifs de population, les situations démographiques et la précision des statistiques démographiques. Cette nomenclature est couramment utilisée aux fins des statistiques internationales et a été appliquée autant qu'il a été possible dans le présent *Annuaire* en vue de renforcer la cohérence et de faciliter la comparaison et l'analyse. Son utilisation pour l'établissement des statistiques internationales n'est cependant rien moins qu'universelle, même au niveau des régions continentales, et les variations que présentent les sources et méthodes statistiques internationales entraînent inévitablement de nombreuses différences dans certains domaines de cet *Annuaire*. Les différences d'ordre général sont indiquées dans les notes figurant au bas de la classification présentée ci-dessous. Les différences plus spécifiques sont mentionnées dans les notes techniques et notes de bas de page accompagnant les divers tableaux.

L'application des expressions "développés" et "en développement" aux pays, zones ou régions n'est pas non plus normalisée à l'échelle internationale. Ces expressions sont utilisées dans la présente publication en référence aux groupements régionaux généralement considérés comme "développés", à savoir l'Amérique septentrionale (code numérique 021), l'Europe (150), Chypre (196), Israël (376), le Japon (392) et l'Australie et la Nouvelle-Zélande (053). Ces appellations sont employées pour des raisons de commodité statistique et n'expriment pas nécessairement un jugement sur le stade de développement atteint par tel ou tel pays ou zone. Les cas différant de cet usage sont signalés dans les notes accompagnant les tableaux concernés.

---

[1] Quatre révisions de ce document ont été publiés en 1975, 1982, 1996 et 1999. D'autres révisions sont maintenant publiés sur le site internet de la Division de statistique des Nations Unies.

[2] Le Bulletin terminologique No 347/Rev.1 ou UNTERM website, intitulé "Noms de pays" établi par le Département des affaires de l'Assemblée générale et des services de conférence du Secrétariat de l'Organisation des Nations Unies, répertorie les noms des États Membres dans les six langues de l'Organisation.

001	**Monde**					
002	**Afrique**					
202	**Afrique subsaharienne**				015	**Afrique septentrionale**

014	**Afrique orientale**			426	Lesotho		012	Algérie
108	Burundi	086	Territoire britannique de l'océan Indien	516	Namibie		818	Égypte
174	Comores	894	Zambie				434	Libye
262	Djibouti	716	Zimbabwe	**011**	**Afrique occidentale**		504	Maroc
232	Érythrée			204	Bénin		732	Sahara occidental
231	Éthiopie	**017**	**Afrique centrale**	854	Burkina Faso		729	Soudan note 736
404	Kenya	024	Angola	132	Cabo Verde		788	Tunisie
450	Madagascar	120	Cameroun	384	Côte d'Ivoire			
454	Malawi	178	Congo	270	Gambie		**Note**	**Certains tableaux peuvent**
480	Maurice	266	Gabon	288	Ghana			
175	Mayotte	226	Guinée équatoriale	324	Guinée		736	*Soudan [anc.]*
508	Mozambique	140	République centrafricaine	624	Guinée-Bissau			
800	Ouganda			430	Libéria		/a	*Incluent*
834	République-Unie de Tanzanie note /a	180	République démocratique du Congo	466	Mali		---	*Zanzibar*
				478	Mauritanie			
638	Réunion	678	Sao Tomé-et-Principe	562	Niger		/b	*Incluent*
646	Rwanda	148	Tchad	566	Nigéria			
690	Seychelles			654	Sainte-Hélène note /b		---	*Ascension*
706	Somalie	**018**	**Afrique australe**	686	Sénégal		---	*Tristan da Cunha*
728	Soudan du Sud note 736	710	Afrique du Sud	694	Sierra Leone			
260	Terres australes françaises	072	Botswana	768	Togo			
		748	Eswatini					

019	**Amériques**					
419	**Amérique latine et Caraïbes**				021	**Amérique septentrionale**

029	**Caraïbes**			**005**	**Amérique du Sud**			note 003
660	Anguilla	652	Saint-Barthélemy	032	Argentine			
028	Antigua-et-Barbuda	659	Saint-Kitts-et-Nevis	068	Bolivie (État plurinational de)		060	Bermudes
533	Aruba	662	Sainte-Lucie				124	Canada
044	Bahamas	663	Saint-Martin (partie française)	076	Brésil		840	États-Unis d'Amérique
052	Barbade			152	Chili			
535	Bonaire, note 530 Saint-Eustache et Saba	534	Saint-Martin note 530 (partie néerlandaise)	170	Colombie		304	Groenland
				218	Équateur		666	Saint-Pierre-et-Miquelon
192	Cuba	670	Saint-Vincent-et-les Grenadines	239	Géorgie du Sud-et-les Îles Sandwich du Sud			
531	Curaçao note 530	780	Trinité-et-Tobago					
212	Dominique			328	Guyana		**Note**	
308	Grenade	**013**	**Amérique centrale**	254	Guyane française		003	*Le continent de l'Amérique du Nord comprend l'Amérique septentrionale, les Caraïbes et l'Amérique centrale*
312	Guadeloupe	084	Belize	074	Île Bouvet			
332	Haïti	188	Costa Rica	238	Îles Falkland (Malvinas)			
136	Îles Caïmanes	222	El Salvador					
796	Îles Turques-et-Caïques	320	Guatemala	600	Paraguay			
850	Îles Vierges américaines	340	Honduras	604	Pérou			
092	Îles Vierges britanniques	484	Mexique	740	Suriname			
388	Jamaïque	558	Nicaragua	858	Uruguay		**Certains tableaux peuvent**	
474	Martinique	591	Panama	862	Venezuela (République bolivarienne du)			
500	Montserrat						530	*Antilles néerlandaises [anc.]*
630	Porto Rico							
214	République dominicaine							

010	**Antarctique**

Monde

Asie

143 Asie centrale
- 398 Kazakhstan
- 417 Kirghizistan
- 860 Ouzbékistan
- 762 Tadjikistan
- 795 Turkménistan

030 Asie orientale
- 156 Chine
- 344 Chine, région administrative spéciale de Hong Kong
- 446 Chine, région administrative spéciale de Macao
- 392 Japon
- 496 Mongolie
- 410 République de Corée
- 408 République populaire démocratique de Corée

035 Asie du Sud-Est
- 096 Brunéi Darussalam
- 116 Cambodge
- 360 Indonésie
- 458 Malaisie
- 104 Myanmar
- 608 Philippines
- 418 République démocratique populaire lao
- 702 Singapour
- 764 Thaïlande
- 626 Timor-Leste
- 704 Viet Nam

034 Asie méridionale
- 004 Afghanistan
- 050 Bangladesh
- 064 Bhoutan
- 356 Inde
- 364 Iran (République islamique d')
- 462 Maldives
- 524 Népal
- 586 Pakistan
- 144 Sri Lanka

145 Asie occidentale
- 682 Arabie saoudite
- 051 Arménie
- 031 Azerbaïdjan
- 048 Bahreïn
- 196 Chypre
- 784 Émirats arabes unis
- 275 État de Palestine
- 268 Géorgie
- 368 Iraq
- 376 Israël
- 400 Jordanie
- 414 Koweït
- 422 Liban
- 512 Oman
- 634 Qatar
- 760 République arabe syrienne
- 792 Turquie
- 887 Yémen

Europe

151 Europe orientale
- 112 Bélarus
- 100 Bulgarie
- 643 Fédération de Russie
- 348 Hongrie
- 616 Pologne
- 498 République de Moldova
- 642 Roumanie
- 703 Slovaquie
- 203 Tchéquie
- 804 Ukraine

154 Europe septentrionale
- 208 Danemark
- 233 Estonie
- 246 Finlande
- 831 Guernesey note 830
- 833 Île de Man
- 248 Îles d'Åland
- 234 Îles Féroé
- 744 Îles Svalbard-et-Jan Mayen
- 372 Irlande
- 352 Islande
- 832 Jersey 380
- 428 Lettonie
- 440 Lituanie
- 578 Norvège
- 826 Royaume-Uni de Grande-Bretagne et d'Irlande du Nord
- 752 Suède

039 Europe méridionale
- 008 Albanie
- 020 Andorre
- 070 Bosnie-Herzégovine
- 191 Croatie
- 724 Espagne
- 292 Gibraltar
- 300 Grèce
- 380 Italie
- 807 Macédoine du Nord
- 470 Malte
- 499 Monténégro note 891
- 620 Portugal
- 674 Saint-Marin
- 336 Saint-Siège
- 688 Serbie note 891 & /c
- 705 Slovénie

155 Europe occidentale
- 276 Allemagne
- 040 Autriche
- 056 Belgique
- 250 France
- 438 Liechtenstein
- 442 Luxembourg
- 492 Monaco
- 528 Pays-Bas
- 756 Suisse

Note Certains tableaux peuvent énumérer
- 830 *Îles Anglo-Normandes*
- 891 *Serbie-et-Monténégro [anc.]*
- /c *Kosovo*

Océanie

053 Australie et Nouvelle-Zélande
- 036 Australie
- 162 Île Christmas
- 334 Île Heard-et-Îles MacDonald
- 574 Île Norfolk
- 166 Îles des Cocos (Keeling)
- 554 Nouvelle-Zélande

054 Mélanésie
- 242 Fidji
- 090 Îles Salomon
- 540 Nouvelle-Calédonie

- 598 Papouasie-Nouvelle-Guinée
- 548 Vanuatu

057 Micronésie
- 316 Guam
- 580 Îles Mariannes du Nord
- 584 Îles Marshall
- 581 Îles mineures éloignées des États-Unis
- 296 Kiribati
- 583 Micronésie (États fédérés de)
- 520 Nauru
- 585 Palaos

061 Polynésie
- 184 Îles Cook
- 876 Îles Wallis-et-Futuna
- 570 Nioué
- 612 Pitcairn
- 258 Polynésie française
- 882 Samoa
- 016 Samoa américaines
- 772 Tokélaou[corrigée]
- 776 Tonga
- 798 Tuvalu

C. Autres groupements

On trouvera ci-après une liste des autres groupements et de leur composition, présentée dans l'*Annuaire*. Ces groupements correspondent essentiellement à des intérêts économiques et commerciaux d'après les associations régionales.

071 — Accord de libre-échange nord-américain (ALENA)

124	Canada	840	États-Unis d'Amérique	484	Mexique

073 — Association des nations de l'Asie du Sud-Est (ANASE)

096	Brunéi Darussalam	360	Indonésie	104	Myanmar	418	République démocratique populaire lao	764	Thaïlande
116	Cambodge	458	Malaisie	608	Philippines	702	Singapour	704	Viet Nam

197 — Association européenne de libre-échange (AELE)

352	Islande	438	Liechtenstein	578	Norvège	756	Suisse

095 — Association latino-américaine d'intégration (ALAI)

032	Argentine	170	Colombie	591	Panama	862	Venezuela (République bolivarienne du)
068	Bolivie (État plurinational de)	192	Cuba	600	Paraguay		
076	Brésil	218	Équateur	604	Pérou		
152	Chili	484	Mexique	858	Uruguay		

130 — Communauté des Caraïbes et Marché commun des Caraïbes (CARICOM)

028	Antigua-et-Barbuda	084	Belize	332	Haïti	662	Sainte-Lucie
044	Bahamas (membre de la communauté seulement)	212	Dominique	388	Jamaïque	670	Saint-Vincent-et-les Grenadines
		308	Grenade	500	Montserrat	740	Suriname
052	Barbade	328	Guyana	659	Saint-Kitts-et-Nevis	780	Trinité-et-Tobago

172 — Communauté d'États indépendants (CEI)[3]

051	Arménie	643	Fédération de Russie	417	Kirghizistan	762	Tadjikistan
031	Azerbaïdjan	268	Géorgie	860	Ouzbékistan	795	Turkménistan
112	Bélarus	398	Kazakhstan	498	République de Moldova	804	Ukraine

892 — Communauté économique des États de l'Afrique de l'Ouest (CEDEAO)

204	Bénin	384	Côte d'Ivoire	324	Guinée	466	Mali	686	Sénégal
854	Burkina Faso	270	Gambie	624	Guinée-Bissau	562	Niger	694	Sierra Leone
132	Cabo Verde	288	Ghana	430	Libéria	566	Nigéria	768	Togo

692 — Communauté économique et monétaire des États de l'Afrique Centrale (CEMAC)

120	Cameroun	178	Congo	266	Gabon	226	Guinée équatoriale	140	République centrafricaine	148	Tchad

066 — Coopération économique Asie-Pacifique (CEAP)

036	Australie	840	États-Unis d'Amérique	598	Papouasie-Nouvelle-Guinée	704	Viet Nam
096	Brunéi Darussalam	643	Fédération de Russie	604	Pérou		
124	Canada	360	Indonésie	608	Philippines		
152	Chili	392	Japon	158	Province chinoise de Taïwan		
156	Chine	458	Malaisie	410	République de Corée		
344	Chine, région administrative spéciale de Hong Kong	484	Mexique	702	Singapour		
		554	Nouvelle-Zélande	764	Thaïlande		

063 — Marché commun andin (ANCOM)

068	Bolivie (État plurinational de)	170	Colombie	218	Équateur	604	Pérou

395 — Marché commun centraméricain (MCCA)

188	Costa Rica	222	El Salvador	320	Guatemala	340	Honduras	558	Nicaragua

171 — Marché commun de l'Afrique de l'Est et de l'Afrique australe (COMESA)

108	Burundi	748	Eswatini	454	Malawi	646	Rwanda	788	Tunisie
174	Comores	231	Éthiopie	480	Maurice	690	Seychelles	894	Zambie

---

[3] La Géorgie (code numérique 268) peut figurer dans ce groupe; par exemple, dans le cadre des statistiques du commerce international de marchandises.

262	Djibouti	404	Kenya	800	Ouganda	706	Somalie	716	Zimbabwe
818	Égypte	434	Libye	180	République	729	Soudan		
232	Érythrée	450	Madagascar		dém. du Congo				

069   Marché commun du Sud (MERCOSUR)

| 032 | Argentine | 076 | Brésil | 858 | Uruguay |
| 068 | Bolivie (État plurinational de) | 600 | Paraguay | 862 | Venezuela (République bolivarienne du) |

198   Organisation de coopération et de développement économiques (OCDE)

276	Allemagne	840	États-Unis d'Amérique	392	Japon	203	République tchèque
036	Australie	246	Finlande	442	Luxembourg	826	Royaume-Uni de
040	Autriche	250	France	484	Mexique		Grande-Bretagne et
056	Belgique	300	Grèce	578	Norvège		d'Irlande du Nord
124	Canada	348	Hongrie	554	Nouvelle-Zélande	703	Slovaquie
152	Chili	372	Irlande	528	Pays-Bas	705	Slovénie
208	Danemark	376	Israël	616	Pologne	752	Suède
724	Espagne	352	Islande	620	Portugal	756	Suisse
233	Estonie	380	Italie	410	République de Corée	792	Turquie

399   Organisation des pays exportateurs de pétrole (OPEP)

012	Algérie	218	Équateur	364	Iran (République	566	Nigéria
024	Angola	266	Gabon		Islamique d')	634	Qatar
682	Arabie saoudite	226	Guinée équatoriale	368	Iraq	862	Venezuela (République
178	Congo	360	Indonésie	434	Libye		bolivarienne du)
784	Émirats arabes unis			414	Koweït		

199   Pays les moins avancés (PMA)

004	Afghanistan	270	Gambie	508	Mozambique	694	Sierra Leone
024	Angola	324	Guinée	104	Myanmar	706	Somalie
050	Bangladesh	624	Guinée-Bissau	524	Népal	728	Soudan du Sud
204	Bénin	332	Haïti	562	Niger	729	Soudan
064	Bhoutan	090	Îles Salomon	800	Ouganda	148	Tchad
854	Burkina Faso	296	Kiribati	140	République centrafricaine	626	Timor-Leste
108	Burundi	426	Lesotho	180	République démocratique du Congo	768	Togo
116	Cambodge	430	Libéria	418	République démocratique populaire lao	798	Tuvalu
174	Comores	450	Madagascar	834	République-Unie de Tanzanie	548	Vanuatu
262	Djibouti	454	Malawi	646	Rwanda	887	Yémen
232	Érythrée	466	Mali	678	Sao Tomé-et-Principe	894	Zambie
231	Éthiopie	478	Mauritanie	686	Sénégal		

711   Union douanière d'Afrique australe

| 710 | Afrique du Sud | 072 | Botswana | 748 | Eswatini | 426 | Lesotho | 516 | Namibie |

097   Union européenne (UE)

276	Allemagne	208	Danemark	348	Hongrie	470	Malte	826	Royaume-Uni de
040	Autriche	724	Espagne	372	Irlande	528	Pays-Bas		Grande-Bretagne et
056	Belgique	233	Estonie	380	Italie	616	Pologne		d'Irlande du Nord
100	Bulgarie	246	Finlande	428	Lettonie	620	Portugal	703	Slovaquie
191	Croatie	250	France	440	Lituanie	203	République tchèque	705	Slovénie
196	Chypre	300	Grèce	442	Luxembourg	642	Roumanie	752	Suède

098   Zone euro

276	Allemagne	724	Espagne	300	Grèce	440	Lituania	620	Portugal
040	Autriche	233	Estonie	372	Irlande	442	Luxembourg	703	Slovaquie
056	Belgique	246	Finlande	380	Italie	470	Malte	705	Slovénie
196	Chypre	250	France	428	Lettonie	528	Pays-Bas		

Annex II: Technical notes

Chapter I: World summary

These world aggregates are obtained from other tables in this *Yearbook*, where available, and are compiled from statistical publications and databases of the United Nations and the specialized agencies and other institutions. The technical notes of the relevant tables in this *Yearbook* should be consulted for detailed information on definition, source, compilation and coverage.

Chapter II: Population and migration

Table 2: Population, surface area and density

The total, male and female population, sex ratio, population age distribution and population density are taken from the estimates and projections prepared by the United Nations Population Division, published in *World Population Prospects: The 2019 Revision*. Surface area are obtained from the *Demographic Yearbook*. Through this source only official national data are reported.

Total, male and female population refers to the de facto population in a country, area or region as of 1 July of the year indicated, unless otherwise stated in a footnote. Figures are presented in millions. The total population of a country may comprise either all usual residents of the country (de jure population) or all persons present in the country (de facto population) at the time of the census; for purposes of international comparisons, the de facto definition is used, unless otherwise stated in a footnote.

Population aged 0-14 years / 60 years and over refers to the percentage of the population aged 0-14 years and aged 60 years and older, respectively as of 1 July of the year indicated, unless otherwise stated in a footnote.

Population density refers to the population, as of 1 July of the year indicated, per square kilometre of surface area, unless otherwise stated in a footnote.

Sex ratio is calculated as the ratio of the population of men to that of 100 women as of 1 July of the year indicated, unless otherwise stated in a footnote.

Surface area refers to land area plus inland water, unless otherwise stated in a footnote.

Table 3: Population growth and indicators of fertility and mortality

The population rate of increase, fertility rate, infant mortality rate and life expectancy at birth are taken from the estimates and projections prepared by the United Nations Population Division, published in *World Population Prospects: The 2017 Revision*. The data are an average over five-year ranges; 2000-2005 labelled "2005", 2005-2010 labelled "2010" and 2010-2015 labelled "2015", unless otherwise stated in a footnote. Maternal mortality ratio are estimates developed by the World Health Organization, UNICEF, the United Nations Population Fund, the World Bank and United Nations Population Division and published in Trends in Maternal Mortality: 1990 to 2015.

Population rate of increase (or growth rate) is the average annual percentage change in total population size.

Fertility rate is the total fertility rate, a widely used summary indicator of fertility. It refers to the number of children that would be born per woman, assuming no female mortality at child bearing ages and the age-specific fertility rates of a specified country and reference period.

Infant mortality rate (per 1 000 live births) is the ratio of infant deaths (the deaths of children under one year of age) in a given year to the total number of live births in the same year.

Maternal mortality ratio is the ratio of the number of maternal deaths during a given time period per 100 000 live births during the same time-period. A maternal death refers to a female death from any cause related to or aggravated by pregnancy or its management (excluding accidental or incidental causes) during pregnancy and childbirth or within 42 days of termination of pregnancy, irrespective of the duration and site of the pregnancy.

Life expectancy at birth is the average number of years of life at birth (age 0) for males and females according to the expected mortality rates by age estimated for the reference year and population.

Table 4: International migrants and refugees

International migrant stock is taken from the estimates and projections prepared by the United Nations Population Division, published in *International migrant stock: The 2017 Revision.* "Refugees and others of concern to UNHCR" are obtained from the United Nations High Commissioner for Refugees, published in the Population Statistics database.

International migrant stock represents the number of persons born in a country other than that in which they live. When information on country of birth was not recorded, data on the number of persons having foreign citizenship was used instead. In the absence of any empirical data, estimates were imputed. Figures for international migrant stock as a percentage of the population are the outcome of dividing the estimated international migrant stock by the estimated total population and multiplying the result by 100.

Refugees include individuals recognised under the 1951 Convention relating to the Status of Refugees; its 1967 Protocol; the 1969 OAU Convention Governing the Specific Aspects of Refugee Problems in Africa; those recognised in accordance with the UNHCR Statute; individuals granted complementary forms of protection; or those enjoying temporary protection. Since 2007, the refugee population also includes people in a refugee-like situation.

Asylum-seekers are individuals who have sought international protection and whose claims for refugee status have not yet been determined, irrespective of when they may have been lodged.

"Other" represents the following 5 categories:

- Internally displaced persons (IDPs) are people or groups of individuals who have been forced to leave their homes or places of habitual residence, in particular as a result of, or in order to avoid the effects of armed conflict, situations of generalised violence, violations of human rights, or natural or man-made disasters, and who have not crossed an international border. For the purposes of UNHCR's statistics, this population only includes conflict-generated IDPs to whom the Office extends protection and/or assistance. Since 2007, the IDP population also includes people in an IDP-like situation. For global IDP estimates, see www.internal-displacement.org.

- Returned refugees are former refugees who have returned to their country of origin spontaneously or in an organised fashion but are yet to be fully integrated. Such return would normally only take place in conditions of safety and dignity.

- Returned IDPs refer to those IDPs who were beneficiaries of UNHCR's protection and assistance activities and who returned to their areas of origin or habitual residence during the year.

- Stateless persons are defined under international law as persons who are not considered as nationals by any State under the operation of its law. In other words, they do not possess the nationality of any State. UNHCR statistics refer to persons who fall under the agency's statelessness mandate because they are stateless according to this international definition, but data from some countries may also include persons with undetermined nationality.

- Others of concern refers to individuals who do not necessarily fall directly into any of the groups above, but to whom UNHCR extends its protection and/or assistance services, based on humanitarian or other special grounds.

Chapter III: Gender

Table 5: Proportion of seats held by women in national parliament

The table shows the percentage of seats held by women members in single or lower chambers of national parliaments as at January/ February each year (see table footnotes for specific details). National parliaments can be bicameral or unicameral. This table covers the single chamber in unicameral parliaments and the lower chamber in bicameral parliaments. It does not cover the upper chamber of bi-cameral parliaments. Seats are usually won by members in general parliamentary elections. Seats may also be filled by nomination, appointment, indirect election, rotation of members and by-election. The proportion of seats held by women in national parliament is derived by dividing the total number of seats occupied by women by the total number of seats in parliament. There is no weighting or normalising of statistics. The source for this table is the Inter-Parliamentary Union (IPU), see www.ipu.org for further information.

Table 6: Ratio of girls to boys in primary, secondary and tertiary education

The ratio of girls to boys (gender parity index) in primary, secondary and tertiary education is the ratio of the number of female students enrolled at primary, secondary and tertiary levels of education to the number of male students in each level. To standardise the effects of the population structure of the appropriate age groups, the Gender Parity Index (GPI) of the Gross Enrolment Ratio (GER) for each level of education is used. The source for this table is the UNESCO Institute for Statistics (UIS), see www.uis.unesco.org for further information.

Chapter IV: Education

Data in Tables 7 and 8 are presented using the 2011 revision of UNESCO's International Standard Classification of Education (ISCED). Data are presented in the tables based on the three main levels of educations defined as follows;

"Primary education" (ISCED level 1) programmes are typically designed to provide students with fundamental skills in reading, writing and mathematics (i.e. literacy and numeracy) and establish a solid foundation for learning and understanding core areas of knowledge, personal and social development, in preparation for lower secondary education. It focuses on learning at a basic level of complexity with little, if any, specialisation.

"Secondary education" (ISCED level 2 and 3) is divided into two different stages, i.e. lower secondary and upper secondary. Lower secondary education programmes are typically designed to build on the learning outcomes from primary. Usually, they aim to lay the foundation for lifelong learning and human development upon which education systems may then expand further educational opportunities. Upper secondary education programmes are typically designed to complete secondary education in preparation for tertiary education or provide skills relevant to employment, or both. Programmes at this level offer students more varied, specialised and in-depth instruction than programmes at lower secondary. They are more differentiated, with an increased range of options and streams available. Teachers are often highly qualified in the subjects or fields of specialisation they teach, particularly in the higher grades.

Tertiary education (ISCED levels 5-8) builds on secondary education, providing learning activities in specialised fields of education. It aims at learning at a high level of complexity and specialisation. Tertiary education includes what is commonly understood as academic education but also includes advanced vocational or professional education. It comprises ISCED levels 5, 6, 7 and 8, which are labelled as short-cycle tertiary education, Bachelor's or equivalent level, Master's or equivalent level, and doctoral or equivalent level, respectively. The content of programmes at the tertiary level is more complex and advanced than in lower ISCED levels.

For more information about the International Standard Classification of Education (ISCED) 2011 please refer to: http://www.uis.unesco.org/Education/Documents/isced-2011-en.pdf

Table 7: Enrollment in primary, secondary and tertiary education levels

The table shows the number of students enrolled as well as the gross enrolment ratio which is the number of students enrolled, regardless of age, expressed as a percentage of the eligible official school-age population corresponding to the same level of education in a given school year. Enrolment is measured at the beginning of the school or academic year. The gross enrolment ratio at each level will include all pupils whatever their ages, whereas the population is limited to the range of official school ages. Therefore, for countries with almost universal education among the school-age population, the gross enrolment ratio can exceed 100 if the actual age distribution of pupils extends beyond the official school ages.

Table 8: Teaching staff at the primary, secondary and tertiary levels

The table shows the total number of teachers at a given level of education, as well as the proportion of female teachers expressed as a percentage of the total (male and female) at the same level in a given school year. The data sources include school census or surveys and teachers' records. Teachers (or teaching staff) are defined as persons employed full-time or part-time in an official capacity to guide and direct the learning experience of pupils and students, irrespective of their qualifications or the delivery mechanism, i.e. face-to-face and/or at a distance. This definition excludes educational personnel who have no active teaching duties (e.g. headmasters, headmistresses or principals who do not teach) or who work occasionally or in a voluntary capacity in educational institutions.

Table 9: Public expenditure on education

Public expenditure on education consists of current and capital expenditures on education by local, regional and national governments, including municipalities. Household contributions are excluded. Current expenditure on education includes expenditure for goods and services consumed within the current year and which would need to be renewed if needed the following year. It includes expenditure on: staff salaries and benefits; contracted or purchased services; other resources including books and teaching materials; welfare services; and other current expenditure such as subsidies to students and households, furniture and equipment, minor repairs, fuel, telecommunications, travel, insurance and rents. Capital expenditure on education includes expenditure for assets that last longer than one year. It includes expenditure for construction, renovation and major repairs of buildings and the purchase of heavy equipment or vehicles.

Chapter V: Health

Table 10: Health personnel

The table shows four main categories of health personnel (out of 9 categories available in the source); Physicians which includes generalist medical practitioners and specialist medical practitioners; Nursing and midwifery personnel which includes nursing professionals, midwifery professionals, nursing associate professionals and midwifery associate professionals. Traditional midwives are not included here; Dentistry personnel includes dentists, dental assistants, dental technicians and related occupations; and Pharmaceutical personnel which includes pharmacists, pharmaceutical assistants, pharmaceutical technicians and related occupations.

The data are obtained from the World Health Organisation's (WHO) Global Health Workforce Statistics database which are compiled from several sources such as national population censuses, labour force and employment surveys, national statistical products and routine administrative information systems. As a result, considerable variability remains across countries in the coverage, quality and reference year of the original data. In general, the denominator data for health workforce density (i.e. national population estimates) were obtained from the United Nations Population Division's *World Population Prospects* publication. In some cases, the official report provided only workforce density indicators, from which estimates of the stock were then calculated.

The classification of health workers used is based on criteria for vocational education and training, regulation of health professions, and activities and tasks of jobs, i.e. a framework for categorizing key workforce variables according to shared characteristics. The WHO framework largely draws on the latest revisions to the internationally standardized classification systems of the International Labour Organization (International Standard Classification of Occupations), United Nations Educational, Scientific and Cultural Organization (International Standard Classification of Education), and the United Nations Statistics Division (International Standard Industrial Classification of All Economic Activities). Depending on the nature of each country's situation and the means of measurement, data are available for up to 9 categories of health workers in the aggregated set, and up to 18 categories in the disaggregated set. The latter essentially reflects attempts to better distinguish some subgroups of the workforce according to assumed differences in skill level and skill specialization.

Table 11: Expenditure on health

The series "Current expenditure" refers to all health care goods and services used or consumed during a year excluding capital spending, or rather "gross capital formation", which is the purchase of new assets used repeatedly over several years. These estimates are in line with the 2011 System of Health Accounts (SHA). Current expenditure is expressed as a proportion of Gross Domestic Product (GDP). The series Domestic General government expenditures are composed of public and private domestic sources. The Domestic public sources include domestic revenue as internal transfers and grants, transfers, subsidies to voluntary health insurance beneficiaries, Non-profit institutions serving households (NPISH) or enterprise financing schemes as well as compulsory prepayment and social health insurance contributions. All these transfers and subsidies represent public sources for health and indicate the overall governments' contribution to funding healthcare relative to other sources of funding from domestic private and external sources. Domestic General government expenditure is expressed as a proportion of general government expenditures.

Chapter VI: Crime

Table 12: Intentional homicides and other crimes

"Intentional homicides" and "other crimes" are taken from the United Nations Office on Drugs and Crime, published in their statistics database.

"Intentional Homicide" means unlawful death purposefully inflicted on a person by another person. Data on intentional homicide should also include serious assault leading to death and death as a result of a terrorist attack. It should exclude attempted homicide, manslaughter, death due to legal intervention, justifiable homicide in self-defence and death due to armed conflict.

"Assault" means physical attack against the body of another person resulting in serious bodily injury, excluding indecent/sexual assault, threats and slapping/punching. 'Assault' leading to death should also be excluded.

"Theft" means depriving a person or organisation of property without force with the intent to keep it . "Theft" excludes Burglary, housebreaking, Robbery, and Theft of a Motor Vehicle, which are recorded separately.

Chapter VII: National accounts

The National Accounts Main Aggregates Database (available at http://unstats.un.org/unsd/snaama) presents national accounts data for more than 200 countries and areas of the world. It is the basis for the publication of National Accounts Statistics: Analysis of Main Aggregates (AMA), a publication prepared by the Statistics Division of the Department for Economic and Social Affairs of the United Nations Secretariat with the generous co-operation of national statistical offices. The database is updated in December of each year with newly available national accounts data for all countries and areas.

The National Accounts Main Aggregates Database is based on the data obtained from the United Nations National Accounts Questionnaire (NAQ) introduced in October 1999, which in turn is based on the System of National Accounts 1993 (1993 SNA). The data are supplemented with estimates prepared by the Statistics Division. The updated SNA, called the System of National Accounts 2008 (2008 SNA) was finalised in September 2009. As of 2017, 83 countries and territories (European Union Member States Albania, Argentina, Armenia, Australia, Belarus, Brazil, British Virgin Islands, Brunei Darussalam, Canada, Chile, China (mainland), China, Hong Kong SAR, China, Macao SAR, Costa Rica, Dominican Republic, Ecuador, Eswatini, Fiji, Iceland, India, Indonesia, Israel, Japan, Kenya, Lao People's Democratic Republic, Lebanon, Liechtenstein, Malaysia, Mauritius, Mexico, Mongolia, Montenegro, Morocco, New Zealand, Nigeria, North Macedonia, Norway, Pakistan, Peru, Philippines, Republic of Korea, Saudi Arabia, Serbia, Singapore, Sint Maarten, South Africa, Sri Lanka, Switzerland, Thailand, Timor-Leste, Turkey, Uganda, Ukraine, the United States of America and Zambia) have started submitting data according to the 2008 SNA.

Every effort has been made to present the estimates of the various countries or areas in a form designed to facilitate international comparability. To this end, important differences in concept, scope, coverage and classification have been described in the footnotes for individual countries. Such differences should be taken into account to avoid misleading comparisons. Data contained in the tables relate to the calendar year for which they are shown, except in several cases. These special cases are posted on the National Accounts Main Aggregates Database website (http://unstats.un.org/unsd/snaama/notes.asp). The figures shown are the most recent estimates and revisions available at the time of compilation. In general, figures for the most recent year are to be regarded as provisional. The sums of the components in the tables may not necessarily add up to totals shown because of rounding.

Table 13: Gross domestic product and gross domestic product per capita

This table shows gross domestic product (GDP) and GDP per capita in US dollars at current prices, GDP at constant 2010 prices and the corresponding real rates of growth. The tables are intended to facilitate international comparisons of levels of income generated in production. Official data and estimates of total and per capita GDP at current prices have been converted to US dollars, while total GDP at constant prices are converted to 2010 prices before conversion to US dollars using the 2010 exchange rates. The conversion methodology to US dollars is described in the document on the methodology for the National Accounts Main Aggregates Database (http://unstats.un.org/unsd/snaama/methodology.pdf). For inter-country comparisons over time, it would be more appropriate to use the growth rate in the table based on constant price data, which are more indicative of inter-country and intra-grouping comparisons of trends in total GDP. The growth rate shown in the table is computed as geometric mean of annual growth rates expressed as percentages for the years.

Table 14: Gross value added by kind of economic activity

This table presents the shares of the components of gross value added at current prices by kind of economic activity.

Sector	Comprises of (in terms of ISIC 3):
Agriculture	Agriculture, hunting, forestry and fishing (ISIC A-B)
Industry	Mining and quarrying, Manufacturing, Electricity, gas and water supply (ISIC C-E) Construction (ISIC F)

Services	Wholesale and retail trade; repair of motor vehicles, motorcycles and personal and household goods, Hotels and restaurants (ISIC G-H) Transport, storage and communications (ISIC I) Other activities which includes financial intermediation, real estate, renting and business activities, public administration and defense; compulsory social security, education, health and social work, other community, social and personal service activities, private households with employed persons (ISIC J-P).

Chapter VIII: Finance

Detailed information and current figures relating to table 15 are contained in International Financial Statistics, published by the International Monetary Fund (see also http://elibrary-data.imf.org) and in the United Nations Monthly Bulletin of Statistics.

Table 15: Balance of payments summary

A balance of payments can be broadly described as the record of an economy's international economic transactions. It shows (a) transactions in goods, services and income between an economy and the rest of the world, (b) changes of ownership and other changes in that economy's monetary gold, special drawing rights (SDRs) and claims on and liabilities to the rest of the world, and (c) unrequited transfers and counterpart entries needed to balance in the accounting sense any entries for the foregoing transactions and changes which are not mutually offsetting. The balance of payments data are presented on the basis of the methodology and presentation of the sixth edition of the Balance of Payments Manual (BPM6), published by the International Monetary Fund in November 2013. The BPM6 incorporates several major changes to take account of developments in international trade and finance over the years, and to better harmonize the Fund's balance of payments methodology with the methodology of the 2008 System of National Accounts (SNA). The detailed definitions concerning the content of the basic categories of the balance of payments are given in the Balance of Payments Manual (sixth edition)

Brief explanatory notes are given below to clarify the scope of the major items.

Current account is a record of all transactions in the balance of payments covering the exports and imports of goods and services, payments of income, and current transfers between residents of a country and non-residents.

Capital account, n.i.e. refers mainly to capital transfers linked to the acquisition of a fixed asset other than transactions relating to debt forgiveness plus the disposal of nonproduced, nonfinancial assets, and to capital transfers linked to the disposal of fixed assets by the donor or to the financing of capital formation by the recipient, plus the acquisition of nonproduced, nonfinancial assets.

Financial account, n.i.e. is the net sum of the balance of direct investment, portfolio investment, and other investment transactions.

Reserves and related items is the sum of transactions in reserve assets, LCFARs, exceptional financing, and use of Fund credit and loans.

Table 16: Exchange rates

Foreign exchange rates are shown in units of national currency per US dollar. The exchange rates are classified into three broad categories, reflecting both the role of the authorities in the determination of the exchange and/or the multiplicity of exchange rates in a country. The market rate is used to describe exchange rates determined largely by market forces; the official rate is an exchange rate determined by the authorities, sometimes in a flexible manner. For countries maintaining multiple exchange arrangements, the rates are labelled principal rate, secondary rate, and tertiary rate. Unless otherwise stated, the table refers to end of period and period averages of market exchange rates or official exchange rates.

Chapter IX: Labour market

A comparable and comprehensive collection of data on labour force and related topics are available from the International Labour Organisation's (ILO) *Key Indicators of the Labour Market (KILM)* publication, which is updated every 2 years. More timely information is contained in the ILO's ILOSTAT data repository (see www.ilo.org/ilostat) which publishes data as it is received from the countries either on an annual, quarterly or monthly basis but does not include all the consistency checks nor include all the sources used by KILM. For various reasons, national definitions of employment and unemployment often differ from the recommended international standard definitions and thereby limit international comparability. Inter-country comparisons are also complicated by a variety of types of data collection systems used to obtain information on employed and unemployed persons. The ILOSTAT website provides a comprehensive description of the methodology underlying the labour series.

Table 17: Labour force participation rate and unemployment rate

Labour force participation rate is calculated by expressing the number of persons in the labour force as a percentage of the working-age population. The labour force is the sum of the number of persons employed and the number of unemployed (see ILO's current International Recommendations on Labour Statistics). The working-age population is the population above a certain age, prescribed for the measurement of economic characteristics. The data refer to the age group of 15 years and over and are based on ILO's modelled estimates, unless otherwise stated in a footnote.

Unemployment" is defined to include persons above a certain age who, during a specified period of time were:

(a)   "Without work", i.e. were not in paid employment or self-employment;

(b)   "Currently available for work", i.e. were available for paid employment or self-employment during the reference period; and

(c)   "Seeking work", i.e. had taken specific steps in a specified period to find paid employment or self-employment

Persons not considered to be unemployed include:

(a)   Persons intending to establish their own business or farm, but who had not yet arranged to do so and who were not seeking work for pay or profit;

(b)   Former unpaid family workers not at work and not seeking work for pay or profit.

The series generally represent the total number of persons wholly unemployed or temporarily laid-off. Percentage figures, where given, are calculated by comparing the number of unemployed to the total members of that group of the labour force on which the unemployment data are based.

Table 18: Employment by economic activity

The employment table presents the percentage distribution of employed persons by economic activity, according to International Standard Industry Classification (ISIC) version 4.

Chapter X: Price and production indices

Table 19: Consumer price indices

A consumer price index is usually estimated as a series of summary measures of the period-to-period proportional change in the prices of a fixed set of consumer goods and services of constant quantity and characteristics, acquired, used or paid for by the reference population. Each summary measure is constructed as a weighted average of a large number of elementary aggregate indices. Each of the elementary aggregate indices is estimated using a sample of prices for a defined set of goods and services obtained in, or by residents of, a specific region from a given set of outlets or other sources of consumption goods and services. The table presents the general consumer price index for all groups of consumption items combined, and the food index including non-alcoholic beverages only. Where alcoholic beverages and/or tobacco are included, this is indicated in footnotes.

Chapter XI: International merchandise trade

The *International Trade Statistics Yearbook* (ITSY) provides an overview of the latest trends of trade in goods and services of most countries and areas in the world, a publication prepared by the Statistics Division of the Department for Economic and Social Affairs of the United Nations Secretariat. The yearbook, see http://comtrade.un.org/pb/, is released in two volumes; Volume I is compiled earlier in the year to present an advanced overview of international merchandise trade from the previous year, Volume II, generally released six months later, contains detailed tables showing international trade for individual commodities and 11 world trade tables covering trade values and indices. Volume II also contains updated versions of world trade tables. The table in this yearbook are also updated monthly in the United Nations Monthly Bulletin of Statistics and on the trade statistics website, see http://unstats.un.org/unsd/trade/data/tables.asp#annual.

The statistics in this Yearbook have been compiled by national statistical authorities largely consistent with the United Nations recommended International Merchandise Trade Statistics, Concepts and Definitions 2010 (IMTS 2010). Depending on what parts of the economic territory are included in the statistical territory, the trade data-compilation system adopted by a country (its trade system) may be referred to as general or special.

General trade system	The statistical territory coincides with the economic territory. Consequently, it is recommended that the statistical territory of a country applying the general trade system comprises all applicable territorial elements. In this case, imports include goods entering the free circulation area, premises for inward processing, industrial free zones, premises for customs warehousing or commercial free zones and exports include goods leaving those territorial elements
Special trade system	(strict definition) The statistical territory comprises only a particular part of the economic territory, so that certain flows of goods which are in the scope of IMTS 2010 are not included in either import or export statistics of the compiling country. The strict definition of the special trade system is in use when the statistical territory comprises only the free circulation area, that is, the part within which goods "may be disposed of without customs restriction". Consequently, in such a case, imports include only goods entering the free circulation area of a compiling country and exports include only goods leaving the free circulation area of a compiling country
	(relaxed definition) (a) goods that enter a country for, or leave it after, inward processing, as well as (b) goods that enter or leave an industrial free zone, are also recorded and included in international merchandise trade statistics

Generally, all countries report their detailed merchandise trade data according to the Harmonized Commodity Description and Coding System (HS) and the data correspond and are then presented by Standard International Trade Classifications (SITC, Rev.3). Data refer to calendar years; however, for those countries which report according to some other reference year, the data are presented in the year which covers the majority of the reference year used by the country.

FOB-type values include the transaction value of the goods and the value of services performed to deliver goods to the border of the exporting country. CIF-type values include the transaction value of the goods, the value of services performed to deliver goods to the border of the exporting country and the value of the services performed to deliver the goods from the border of the exporting country to the border of the importing country. Therefore, data for the statistical value of imported goods are presented as a CIF-type value and the statistical value of exported goods as an FOB-type value.

Conversion of values from national currencies into United States dollars is done by means of currency conversion factors based on official exchange rates. Values in currencies subject to fluctuation are converted into United States dollars using weighted average exchange rates specially calculated for this purpose. The weighted average exchange rate for a given currency for a given year is the component monthly factors, furnished by the International Monetary Fund in its International Financial Statistics publication, weighted by the value of the relevant trade in each month; a monthly factor is the exchange rate (or the simple average rate) in effect during that month. These factors are applied to total imports and exports and to the trade in individual commodities with individual countries.

Table 20: Total imports, exports and balance of trade

Figures on the total imports and exports of countries (or areas) presented in this table are mainly taken from International Financial Statistics published monthly by the International Monetary Fund (IMF) but also from other sources such as national publications and websites and the United Nations *Monthly Bulletin of Statistics* Questionnaire, see the *International Trade Statistics Yearbook* for further details. Estimates for missing data are made in order to arrive to regional totals but are otherwise not shown. The estimation process is automated using quarterly year-on-year growth rates for the extrapolation of missing quarterly data (unless quarterly data can be estimated using available monthly data within the quarter). The conversion factors applied to data in this table are published quarterly in the United Nations *Monthly Bulletin of Statistics* and are also available on the United Nations trade statistics website: http://unstats.un.org/unsd/trade/data/tables.asp#annual.

Table 21: Major trading partners

Figures on major trading partners show the three largest trade partners (countries of last known destination and origin or consignment) in international merchandise trade transactions. In some cases a special partner is shown (i.e. Areas nes, bunkers, etc.) instead of a country and refers to one of the following special categories. Areas not elsewhere specified (i.e. Areas nes) is used (a) for low value trade, (b) if the partner designation was unknown to the country or if an error was made in the partner assignment and (c) for reasons of confidentiality. If a specific geographical location can be identified within Areas nes, then they are recorded accordingly (i.e. Asia nes). Bunkers are ship stores and aircraft supplies, which consists mostly of fuels and food. Free zones belong to the geographical and economic territory of a country but not to its customs territory. For the purpose of trade statistics the transactions between the customs territory and the free zones are recorded, if the reporting country uses the Special Trade System. Free zones can be commercial free zones (duty free shops) or industrial free zones. Data are expressed as percentages of total exports and of total imports of the country, area or special partner.

Data in this table consists of data as reported by UN Comtrade (at three-digit level of SITC Rev. 3 and detailed trading partners breakdown) and estimated data for missing reporters. The data are estimated either through the extrapolation of the data of the two adjacent years, or, if this is not possible, through the use of the data reported by the trading partners (so called mirror data). Mirror statistics is also used in case the partner distribution or confidential data make it necessary to adjust the reported data. In addition, modifications to the received data are made in cases where the provided data are obviously incomplete, in particular in the case of unreported petroleum oils exports in merchandise data.

Chapter XII: Energy

The Energy Statistics Yearbook (available at http://unstats.un.org/unsd/energy/yearbook) is a comprehensive collection of international energy statistics for over 220 countries and areas. The yearbook is prepared by the Statistics Division of the Department for Economic and Social Affairs of the United Nations Secretariat. The yearbook is produced every year with newly available data on energy production, trade, stock changes, bunkers and consumption for all countries and areas, and a historical series back to 1950 are available. The data are compiled primarily from the annual energy questionnaire distributed by the United Nations Statistics Division and supplemented by official national statistical publications, as well as publications from international and regional organizations. Where official data are not available or are inconsistent, estimates are made by the Statistics Division based on governmental, professional or commercial materials.

The period to which the data refer is the calendar year, with the exception of the data of the following countries which refer to the fiscal year: Afghanistan and Iran (Islamic Rep. of) – beginning 21 March of the year stated; Australia, Bangladesh, Bhutan, Egypt (for the latter two, electricity only), Nepal - ending June of the year stated; Pakistan - starting July of the year stated; India, Myanmar and New Zealand – beginning April of the year stated. Data on a per capita basis use population data from the United Nations Population Division as a denominator.

Table 22: Production, trade and supply of energy

Data are presented in petajoules (gigajoules per capita), to which the individual energy commodities are converted in the interests of international uniformity and comparability. To convert from original units to joules, the data in original units (metric tons, metric tons of oil equivalent, kilowatt hours, cubic metres) are multiplied by conversion factors. For a list of the relevant conversion factors and a detailed description of methods, see the Energy Statistics Yearbook.

Included in the production of primary energy for solids are hard coal, lignite, peat and oil shale, primary solid biofuels and wastes; liquids are comprised of crude oil, natural gas liquids, other hydrocarbons, additives and oxygenates, and liquid biofuels; gas comprises natural gas and biogas; and electricity is comprised of primary electricity generation from hydro, wind, tide, wave and solar sources. Heat comprises primary heat from nuclear, geothermal, chemical and solar sources.

Net imports (imports less exports and bunkers) and changes in stocks, refer to all primary and secondary forms of energy (including feedstocks). Within net imports; bunkers refer to bunkers of aviation gasoline, jet fuel and of hard coal, gas-diesel oil and residual fuel oil. International trade of energy commodities is based on the "general trade" system, that is, all goods entering and leaving the national boundary of a country are recorded as imports and exports.

Supply is calculated as primary energy production plus import minus exports minus international bunkers (aviation and marine) minus stock changes.

Chapter XIII: Environment

Table 23: Land

The data on land are compiled by the Food and Agriculture Organization of the United Nations (FAO). FAO's definitions of the land categories are as follows:

Land area	Total area excluding area under inland water bodies. The definition of inland water bodies generally includes major rivers and lakes
Arable land	Land under temporary crops (multiple cropped areas are counted only once); temporary meadows for mowing or pasture; land under market and kitchen gardens; and land temporarily fallow (less than five years). Abandoned land resulting from shifting cultivation is not included in this category. Data for "arable land" are not meant to indicate the amount of land that is potentially cultivable.
Permanent crops	Land cultivated with crops that occupy the land for long periods and need not be replanted after each harvest, such as cocoa, coffee and rubber. This category includes land under flowering shrubs, fruit trees, nut trees and vines, but excludes land under trees grown for wood or timber
Forest	In the Global Forest Resources Assessment 2010 the following definition is used for forest: Land spanning more than 0.5 hectares with trees higher than 5 metres and a canopy cover of more than 10 percent, or trees able to reach these thresholds in situ. It does not include land that is predominantly under agricultural or urban land use.
Sites protected for terrestrial biodiversity	Land which contributes significantly to the global persistence of biodiversity measured as a proportion of which is wholly covered by a designated protected area. Data are based on spatial overlap between polygons for Key Biodiversity Areas from the World Database of key Biodiversity Areas and polygons for protected areas from the World Database on Protected Areas. Figures for each region are calculated as the proportion of each Key Biodiversity Area covered by protected areas, averaged (i.e. calculated as the mean) across all Key Biodiversity Areas within the region.

Table 24: Threatened species

Data on the number of threatened species in each group of animals and plants are compiled by the World Conservation Union (IUCN)/ Species Survival Commission (SSC) and published in the IUCN Red List of Threatened Species. The list provides a catalogue of those species that are considered globally threatened. The number of threatened species for any particular country will change between years for a number of reasons, including:

- New information being available to refine the assessment (e.g., confirmation that the species occurs or does not occur in a particular country, confirmation that the species is or is not threatened, etc.)

- Taxonomic changes (e.g., what was previously recognised as one species is now split into several separate species or has now been merged with another species).

- Corrections (e.g., the previous assessment may have missed a particular country out of its country occurrence list or included a specific country by mistake).

- Genuine status changes (e.g., a species may have genuinely deteriorated or improved in status and therefore has moved into or out of the threatened categories).

The categories used in the Red List are as follows; extinct, extinct in the wild, critically endangered; endangered, vulnerable, near threatened and data deficient.

Table 25: Water supply and sanitation services

These data are estimated by the WHO/UNICEF Joint Monitoring Programme for Water Supply and Sanitation (JMP) based on available country sources, see https://washdata.org for further information. The proportion of the population using safely managed drinking water services is defined as the population using an improved drinking water source (the indicator used for Millennium Development Goals monitoring) which is located on premises, and available when needed, and free of faecal and priority chemical contamination. In order to meet the criteria for a safely managed drinking water service, people must use an improved source meeting three criteria:

- it should be accessible on premises,
- water should be available when needed, and
- the water supplied should be free from contamination.

If the improved source does not meet any one of these criteria but a round trip to collect water takes 30 minutes or less, then it will be classified as a basic drinking water service. If water collection from an improved source exceeds 30 minutes it will be categorised as a limited service. The JMP also differentiates populations using unimproved sources such as unprotected wells or springs, and populations drinking surface water collected directly from a river, dam, lake, stream or irrigation canal.

For the proportion of the population using "safely managed sanitation services", there are three main ways to meet the criteria for having a safely managed sanitation service. People should use improved sanitation facilities which are not shared with other households, and the excreta produced should either be:

- treated and disposed in situ,
- stored temporarily and then emptied and transported to treatment off-site, or
- transported through a sewer with wastewater and then treated off-site.

If the excreta from improved sanitation facilities are not safely managed then people using those facilities will be classed as having a basic sanitation service. People using improved facilities which are shared with other households will be classified as having a limited service.

Chapter XIV: Science and technology

Table 26: Population employed in research and development (R&D)

The data presented on population employed in research and development (R&D) are compiled by the UNESCO Institute for Statistics. Data for certain countries are provided to UNESCO by OECD, Eurostat and the Latin-American Network on Science and Technology Indicators (RICYT). The definitions and classifications applied by UNESCO in the table are based on those set out in the Frascati Manual (OECD, 2002). The three categories of personnel shown are defined as follows:

Researchers	Professionals engaged in the conception or creation of new knowledge, products, processes, methods and systems and also in the management of the projects concerned. Postgraduate students at the PhD level (ISCED level 8) engaged in R&D are considered as researchers.
Technicians and equivalent staff	Persons whose main tasks require technical knowledge and experience in one or more fields of engineering, physical and life sciences (technicians) or social sciences and humanities (equivalent staff). They participate in R&D by performing scientific and technical tasks involving the application of concepts and operational methods, normally under the supervision of researchers.
Other supporting staff	Skilled and unskilled craftsmen, secretarial and clerical staff participating in R&D projects or directly associated with (or providing services to researchers involved in) such projects.

Headcount data reflect the total number of persons employed in R&D, independently from their dedication. Full-time equivalent (FTE) may be thought of as one person-year. Thus, a person who normally spends 30% of his/her time on R&D and the rest on other activities (such as teaching, university administration and student counselling) should be considered as 0.3 FTE. Similarly, if a full-time R&D worker is employed at an R&D unit for only six months, this results in an FTE of 0.5.

Table 27: Gross domestic expenditure on research and development (R&D)

The data presented on gross domestic expenditure on research and development are compiled by the UNESCO Institute for Statistics. Data for certain countries are provided to UNESCO by OECD, EUROSTAT and the Network on Science and Technology Indicators (RICYT). Gross domestic expenditure on R&D (GERD) is total intramural expenditure on R&D performed on the national territory during a given period. It includes R&D performed within a country and funded from abroad but excludes payments made abroad for R&D. The sources of funds for GERD are classified according to the following five categories:

Business enterprise funds	Funds allocated to R&D by all firms, organizations and institutions whose primary activity is the market production of goods and services (other than the higher education sector) for sale to the general public at an economically significant price, and those private non-profit institutes mainly serving these firms, organizations and institutions.
Government funds	Funds allocated to R&D by all departments, offices and other bodies which furnish, but normally do not sell to the community, those common services, other than higher education, which cannot otherwise be conveniently and economically provided, as well as those that administer the state and the economic and social policy of the community. Public enterprises, mainly engaged in market production and sale of goods and services, funds are included in the business enterprise funds sector. Government funds also include private non-profit institutes controlled and mainly financed by government, not administered by the higher education sector.
Higher education funds	Funds allocated to R&D by institutions of higher education comprising all universities, colleges of technology, other institutions providing tertiary education (i.e. ISCED 5, 6, 7 or 8), whatever their source or finance or legal status. They also include all research institutes, experimental stations and clinics operating under the direct control of or administered by or associated with higher education institutions.
Private non-profit funds	Funds allocated to R&D by non-market, private non-profit institutions serving households (i.e. the general public), as well as by private individuals and households.
Funds from abroad	Funds allocated to R&D by all institutions and individuals located outside the political borders of a country; and all international organizations (except business enterprises), including facilities and operations within the country's borders.

The absolute figures for R&D expenditure should not be compared country by country. Such comparisons would require the conversion of national currencies into a common currency by means of special R&D exchange rates. Official exchange rates do not always reflect the real costs of R&D activities and comparisons that are based on such rates can result in misleading conclusions, although they can be used to indicate a gross order of magnitude.

Table 28: Patents

A patent is granted by a national patent office or by a regional office that does the work for a number of countries, such as the European Patent Office and the African Regional Intellectual Property Organisation. Under such regional systems, an applicant requests protection for the invention in one or more countries, and each country decides as to whether to offer patent protection within its borders. The World Intellectual Property Organisation (WIPO) administered Patent Cooperation Treaty (PCT) provides for the filling of a single international patent application which has the same effect as national applications filed in the designated countries. Data include resident intensity, patents granted and patents in force. Patent intensity is presented as the resident patent fillings per million population, where as resident Intellectual Property (IP) filling refers to an application filed by an applicant at its national IP office. IP grant (registration) data are based on the same concept. In force refers to a patent or other form of IP protection that is currently valid. Country of origin is used to categorise IP data by resident (domestic) and non-resident (foreign). The residence of the first-named applicant (or inventor) recorded in the IP document (e.g. patent or trademark application) is used to classify IP data by country of origin. The data are compiled and published by the WIPO.

Chapter XV: Communication

Table 29: Internet usage

The table shows percentage of individuals using the internet and replaces the statistics shown in previous yearbooks such as the "Number (thousands) of fixed (wired) internet subscriptions" and "fixed (wired) internet subscriptions per 100 inhabitants". Besides capturing the use of the Internet, this indicator is able to measure changes in Internet access and use. In countries where many people access the Internet at work, at school, at cybercafés or other public locations, increases in public access serve to increase the number of users despite limited numbers of Internet subscriptions and of households with Internet access. Developing countries especially tend to have many Internet users per Internet subscriptions, reflecting that home access is not the primary location of access.

Chapter XVI: International tourism and transport

The data on international tourism have been supplied by the World Tourism Organization (UNWTO) from detailed tourism information published in either the *Yearbook of Tourism Statistics* or *Compendium of Tourism Statistics*, see www.unwto.org/statistics for further information. For statistical purposes, the term "international visitor" describes "any person who travels to a country other than that in which he/she has his/her usual residence but outside his/her usual environment for a period not exceeding 12 months and whose main purpose of visit is other than the exercise of an activity remunerated from within the country visited". There are four series presented in the UNWTO *yearbook* and *compendium*, but only one series is selected to be presented in this yearbook, generally based on the following priority order to best describe an "international visitor";

Order	Series code	Series name
1	TF	*Arrivals of non-resident tourists at national borders* are visitors who stay at least one night in a collective or private accommodation in the country visited (excludes same-day visitors)
2	VF	*Arrivals of non-resident visitors at national borders* are visitors as defined in series "TF" as well as same-day visitors who do not spend the night in a collective or private accommodation in the country visited
3	TCE	*Arrivals of non-resident tourists in all types of accommodation establishments*
4	THS	*Arrivals of non-resident tourists in hotels and similar establishments*

The figures do not include immigrants, residents in a frontier zone, persons domiciled in one country or area and working in an adjoining country or area, members of the armed forces and diplomats and consular representatives when they travel from their country of origin to the country in which they are stationed and vice-versa. The figures also exclude persons in transit who do not formally enter the country through passport control, such as air transit passengers who remain for a short period in a designated area of the air terminal or ship passengers who are not permitted to disembark. This category includes passengers transferred directly between airports or other terminals. Other passengers in transit through a country are classified as visitors.

Table 30: Tourist/visitor arrivals and tourism expenditure

Data on arrivals of non-resident (or international) visitors may be obtained from different sources. In some cases data are obtained from border statistics derived from administrative records (police, immigration, traffic counts and other types of controls), border surveys and registrations at accommodation establishments. Totals correspond to the total number of arrivals from the regions indicated in the table. When a person visits the same country several times a year, an equal number of arrivals is recorded. Likewise, if a person visits several countries during the course of a single trip, his/her arrival in each country is recorded separately. Consequently, arrivals cannot be assumed to be equal to the number of persons travelling.

Expenditure associated with tourism activity of visitors has been traditionally identified with the travel item of the Balance of Payments (BOP): in the case of inbound tourism, those expenditures in the country of reference associated with non-resident visitors are registered as "credits" in the BOP and refer to "travel receipts". The new conceptual framework approved by the United Nations Statistical Commission in relation to the measurement of tourism macroeconomic activity (the so-called Tourism Satellite Account) considers that "tourism industries and products" includes transport of passengers. Consequently, a better estimate of tourism-related expenditures by resident and non-resident visitors in an international scenario would be, in terms of the BOP, the value of the travel item plus that of the passenger transport item. Nevertheless, users should be aware that BOP estimates include, in addition to expenditures associated with visitors, those related to other types of individuals. The data published should allow international comparability and therefore correspond to those published by the International Monetary Fund and provided by the Central Banks, any exceptions are listed within the *Compendium of Tourism Statistics* and the *Yearbook of Tourism Statistics*, see www.unwto.org/statistics for further information.

Chapter XVII: Development assistance

Table 31: Net disbursements of official development assistance to recipients

The table presents estimates of flows of financial resources to individual recipients either directly (bilaterally) or through multilateral institutions (multilaterally). The multilateral institutions include the World Bank Group, regional banks, financial institutions of the European Union and a number of United Nations institutions, programmes and trust funds. The source of data is the Development Assistance Committee (DAC) of OECD to which member countries reported data on their flow of resources to developing countries and territories, countries and territories in transition, and multilateral institutions. Additional information on definitions, methods and sources can be found in OECD's *Geographical Distribution of Financial Flows to Developing Countries* publication, also see http://stats.oecd.org/ for further information.

Table 32: Net disbursements of official development assistance from donors

The table presents the development assistance expenditures of donor countries. This table includes donors' contributions to multilateral agencies; therefore, the overall totals differ from those in table 31, which include disbursements by multilateral agencies.

***

Annexe II: Notes techniques

Chapitre I: Aperçu mondial

Tableau 1: Statistiques mondiales – séries principales

Ces séries d'agrégats mondiaux sont obtenues à partir d'autres tableaux figurant dans le présent *Annuaire*, lorsque c'est possible, et sont établies à partir de publications et de bases de données statistiques des Nations Unies et des organismes spécialisés ainsi que d'autres institutions. Pour davantage d'information sur les définitions, les sources, les méthodes de compilation et la couverture des données, il convient de se référer aux notes techniques du tableau correspondant dans le présent *Annuaire*.

Chapitre II: Population et migration

Tableau 2: Population, superficie et densité

Les données concernant la population totale, masculine et féminine, le rapport des sexes, la répartition de la population par âge et la densité de la population proviennent des estimations et des projections préparées par la Division de la population de l'Organisation des Nations Unies, qui sont publiées dans *Perspectives de la population mondiale : Révision de 2019*. Les données concernant la superficie sont extraites de l'*Annuaire démographique*, qui ne contient que les données nationales officielles.

La population totale, masculine et féminine correspond à la population de fait dans un pays, un territoire ou une région à compter du 1er juillet de l'année indiquée, sauf indication contraire dans une note en bas de page. Les chiffres sont présentés en millions. La population totale d'un pays peut consister de tous les résidents habituels (population de droit) ou toutes les personnes présentes dans le pays (population de fait) au moment du recensement ; pour permettre les comparaisons internationales, la population de fait est utilisée, sauf indication contraire dans une note en bas de page.

La population âgée de 0 à 14 ans/ 60 ans et plus correspond au pourcentage de la population âgée de 0 à 14 ans et 60 ans et plus, respectivement à compter du 1er juillet de l'année indiquée, sauf indication contraire dans une note en bas de page.

La densité de la population correspond à la population, à compter du 1er juillet de l'année indiquée, par kilomètre carré de superficie, sauf indication contraire dans une note en bas de page.

Le rapport des sexes est calculé en tant que le rapport de la population des hommes à celui de 100 femmes à compter du 1er juillet de l'année indiquée, sauf indication contraire dans une note en bas de page.

La superficie correspond aux territoires plus eaux intérieures, sauf indication contraire dans une note en bas de page.

Tableau 3: Sélection d'indicateurs de l'espérance de vie, de la maternité, de la dépendance et de la mortalité

L'espérance de vie à la naissance, le taux de fécondité, le taux de mortalité infantile et l'espérance de vie à la naissance proviennent des estimations et projections de la Division de la population de l'ONU, publiées dans World Population Prospects : The 2015 Révision. Les données sont une moyenne sur cinq ans ; 2000-2005 qualifié « 2005 », 2005-2010 qualifie « 2010 » et 2010-2015 qualifié « 2015 », sauf indication contraire dans une note en bas de page. Les ratios de mortalité maternelle sont des estimations de l'Organisation mondiale de la santé, de l'UNICEF, du Fonds des Nations Unies pour la Population, de la Banque mondiale et de la Division de la population de l'ONU publiées dans les Tendances du taux de mortalité maternelle: 1990 à 2015.

Le taux d'accroissement de la population (ou taux de croissance) est Le changement de la croissance annuelle moyenne dans la taille de la population totale.

Le taux de fécondité et le taux de fécondité total, un indicateur synthétique de fécondité largement utilisé. Il correspond au nombre total d'enfants que mettrait au monde une femme, en supposant aucune mortalité féminine en âge de procréation et les taux de fécondité par âge d'un pays désignée et une période de référence.

Le taux de mortalité infantile (pour 1 000 naissances vivantes) est le rapport des morts de nourrissons (les décès des enfants de moins de 1 an) dans une année donnée par le nombre total des naissances vivantes dans la même année.

Le ratio de mortalité maternelle est le ratio du nombre de morts maternelles durant une période donnée pour 100 000 naissances vivantes pendant la même période. Un décès maternel se réfère à une mortalité féminine dus à une cause liée à la grossesse ou aggravée par celle-ci ou dus à sa prise en charge (mais non pour des causes accidentelles ou fortuites) pendant sa grossesse ou son accouchement au maximum 42 jours après l'accouchement, quels que soient la durée et le lieu de la grossesse.

Tableau 4: Migrants internationaux et réfugiés

Le stock international de migrants provient d'estimations et de projections préparées par la Division de la population de l'Organisation des Nations Unies, publiées dans *International migrant stock: The 2017 Revision*. Les données sur les «réfugiés et autres personnes relevant de la compétence du HCR» ont été obtenues auprès du Haut-Commissaire des Nations Unies pour les réfugiés, et sont publiées dans la base de données de statistiques démographiques.

Le stock international de migrants représente le nombre de personnes nées dans un autre pays que celui dans lequel elles vivent. Lorsque les informations concernant le pays d'origine font défaut, on a utilisé les données sur le nombre de personnes de nationalité étrangère. Et à défaut de données empiriques, on a eu recours à des estimations. Les données font référence au milieu de l'année 2015. Le stock international de migrants en pourcentage de la population est obtenu en divisant le stock international de migrants estimé par la population totale estimée et en multipliant le résultat par 100.

Les réfugiés sont les personnes reconnues comme telles au sens de la Convention de 1951 relative au statut des réfugiés, de son protocole de 1967 ou de la Convention de l'OUA de 1969 régissant les aspects propres aux problèmes des réfugiés en Afrique; celles reconnues comme réfugiés conformément au Statut du HCR; les personnes qui bénéficient d'une forme de protection complémentaire ou jouissent d'une protection temporaire. Depuis 2007, la population des réfugiés inclut également les personnes dont la situation est assimilable à celle des réfugiés.

Les demandeurs d'asile sont des personnes qui ont déposé une demande de protection internationale et qui n'ont pas encore obtenu le statut de réfugié, quelle que soit la date à laquelle la demande a été présentée.

Les « autres personnes relevant de la compétence du HCR » se composent des cinq catégories suivantes :

Les personnes déplacées sont des personnes ou groupes de personnes qui ont été forcés ou contraints de fuir ou de quitter leurs foyers ou leur lieu de résidence habituel, notamment en raison d'un conflit armé, de situations de violence généralisée, de violations des droits de l'homme ou de catastrophes naturelles ou provoquées par l'homme, ou pour en éviter les effets, et qui n'ont pas franchi les frontières internationalement reconnues d'un État. Aux fins des statistiques du HCR, cette population ne comprend que les personnes déplacées en raison d'un conflit qui bénéficient de la protection et/ou de l'assistance du HCR. Depuis 2007, la population de personnes déplacées inclut également les personnes dont la situation est assimilable à celle des personnes déplacées. On trouvera des estimations de la population mondiale des personnes déplacées sur le site www.internal-displacement.org.

Les réfugiés de retour sont d'anciens réfugiés rentrés dans leur pays d'origine, soit spontanément, soit de façon organisée, mais qui ne sont pas encore pleinement intégrés. Ces retours ne se font normalement que lorsque leur sécurité et leur dignité peuvent être garanties.

Les déplacés de retour sont des personnes déplacées qui bénéficiaient des activités de protection et d'assistance du HCR et qui sont revenues à leur lieu d'origine ou de résidence habituel au cours de l'année.

Les apatrides sont définis par le droit international comme des personnes qu'aucun État ne considère comme ses ressortissants par application de sa législation. En d'autres termes, les apatrides ne possèdent la nationalité d'aucun État. Les statistiques du HCR incluent les personnes qui relèvent de sa compétence en vertu de cette définition, mais les données de certains pays peuvent aussi inclure des personnes de nationalité indéterminée.

Les autres personnes relevant de la compétence du HCR sont des personnes qui ne relèvent pas directement d'une des catégories ci-dessus, mais auxquelles le HCR assure protection et/ou assistance pour des raisons humanitaires ou d'autre motifs particuliers.

Chapitre III: La situation des femmes

Tableau 5: Proportion de sièges occupés par des femmes au parlement national

Ce tableau indique le pourcentage des sièges des chambres uniques ou basses des parlements nationaux occupés par des femmes, en janvier ou février de chaque année (voir les notes du tableau pour plus de détails). Les parlements nationaux peuvent être bicaméraux ou unicaméraux. Ce tableau porte sur la chambre unique des parlements unicaméraux et sur la chambre basse des parlements bicaméraux. Il ne porte pas sur la chambre haute des parlements bicaméraux. Les sièges sont habituellement attribués aux membres à l'issue d'élections parlementaires générales. Certains sièges peuvent aussi être pourvus à l'issue de nominations, de désignations, d'élections indirectes, de roulement des membres et d'élections partielles. La proportion d'élues est obtenue en divisant le nombre total de sièges occupés par des femmes par le nombre total de sièges que compte le parlement. Les statistiques ne sont ni pondérées ni normalisées. La source de ce tableau est l'Union interparlementaire, voir www.ipu.org pour plus d'informations

Tableau 6: Rapport filles/garçons dans l'enseignement primaire, secondaire et supérieur

Ce tableau indique la proportion de filles par rapport aux garçons (indice de parité des sexes) dans l'enseignement primaire, secondaire et supérieur, à savoir le rapport entre le nombre de filles inscrites dans l'enseignement primaire, secondaire et supérieur et le nombre de garçons à chaque niveau. Pour normaliser les effets de la pyramide des âges, l'indice de parité des sexes du taux brut de scolarisation pour chaque niveau d'enseignement est utilisé. La source de ce tableau est l'Institut de statistique de l'UNESCO, voir www.uis.unesco.org pour plus d'informations.

Chapitre IV: Éducation

Les données des tableaux 7 et 8 sont présentées conformément à la Classification internationale type de l'éducation de l'UNESCO (CITE, révision de 2011). Les données sont présentées dans les tableaux sur la base des trois principaux niveaux d'éducation, présentés comme suit :

L'enseignement primaire (CITE niveau 1) désigne les programmes éducatifs habituellement conçus pour apporter aux élèves les compétences fondamentales en lecture, écriture et en mathématiques (c'est-à-dire en calcul) afin d'établir une base solide pour la compréhension et l'apprentissage des principaux domaines de la connaissance et favoriser le développement personnel et social dans le but de les préparer à l'entrée dans le premier cycle de l'enseignement secondaire. Il privilégie l'enseignement à un niveau de complexité élémentaire avec peu ou pas de spécialisation.

L'enseignement secondaire (niveaux 2 et 3 de la CITE) est divisé en deux parties : le premier et le second cycles du secondaire. Les programmes du premier cycle de l'enseignement secondaire sont généralement conçus de manière à renforcer les acquis scolaires du primaire. L'objectif consiste habituellement à établir la base d'un apprentissage et d'un développement humain valables pour toute la vie et que les systèmes éducatifs pourront ensuite enrichir par de nouvelles possibilités d'éducation. Les programmes du deuxième cycle de l'enseignement secondaire visent en général à achever l'enseignement secondaire et à préparer à l'entrée dans l'enseignement supérieur et/ou à enseigner des compétences utiles à l'exercice d'un emploi. Les programmes de ce niveau offrent aux élèves un enseignement plus varié, spécialisé et approfondi que les programmes du premier cycle. Ils sont davantage différenciés et proposent un éventail plus large d'options et de filières. Les enseignants sont souvent hautement qualifiés dans les matières ou domaines spécialisés qu'ils enseignent, en particulier dans les classes supérieures.

L'enseignement supérieur (niveaux 5 à 8 de la CITE) se fonde sur les acquis de l'enseignement secondaire et offre des activités d'apprentissage dans des domaines d'éducation spécialisés. Il vise à transmettre des connaissances très spécialisées et d'un niveau de complexité élevé. L'enseignement supérieur inclut ce que l'on qualifie habituellement d'enseignement académique mais il comprend aussi l'enseignement technique ou professionnel avancé. Il comprend les niveaux 5, 6, 7 et 8 de la CITE, appelés respectivement enseignement supérieur de cycle court, enseignement du niveau de la licence ou équivalent, niveau master ou équivalent, et niveau doctorat ou équivalent. Le contenu des programmes de l'enseignement supérieur est plus complexe et plus avancé que celui des niveaux inférieurs de la CITE.

On trouvera davantage d'informations sur la Classification internationale type de l'éducation (CITE) 2011 sur le site : http://www.uis.unesco.org/Education/Documents/isced-2011-fr.pdf.

Tableau 7: Inscriptions aux niveaux primaire, secondaire et supérieur

Le tableau montre le nombre d'élèves scolarisés ainsi que le taux de scolarisation brut qui est le nombre d'étudiants inscrits, quel que soit leur âge, exprimé en pourcentage de la population d'âge scolaire officiellement admissible correspondant au même niveau d'enseignement pour une année scolaire donnée. Les inscriptions sont mesurées au début de l'année scolaire ou universitaire. Le taux de scolarisation brut pour chaque niveau comprend tous les élèves, quel que soit leur âge, tandis que la population générale considérée ne comprend que ceux dont l'âge correspond à l'âge scolaire officiel. De ce fait, pour les pays dont la population d'âge scolaire est quasi totalement scolarisée, le taux de scolarisation brut peut dépasser 100 si la répartition des âges effectifs des élèves s'étend au-delà des âges scolaires officiels.

Tableau 8: Personnel enseignant au niveau primaire, secondaire et supérieur

Le tableau montre le nombre total d'enseignants à chaque niveau ainsi que la proportion des enseignantes exprimée en pourcentage du nombre total d'enseignants (hommes et femmes) au même niveau au cours d'une année scolaire donnée. Les données proviennent de recensements ou d'enquêtes dans les écoles et des dossiers des enseignants.

Les enseignants (ou personnel enseignant) sont définis comme des personnes qui, dans l'exercice de leur métier, guident et dirigent le parcours didactique des élèves et étudiants, indépendamment de leurs qualifications et du mécanisme de transmission des connaissances (autrement dit soit face-à-face et/ou à distance). L'enseignement consiste à planifier, organiser, et mener des activités de groupe où les connaissances, aptitudes et compétences des élèves sont développés comme précisé dans le programme d'éducation. Cette définition exclut le personnel enseignant qui n'a pas de fonctions pédagogiques à la période de référence (par exemple les directeurs ou chefs d'établissements scolaires qui n'enseignent pas) et les personnes qui travaillent ponctuellement ou bénévolement dans des établissements d'enseignement.

Le personnel enseignant universitaire est le personnel employé dont la mission principale est l'enseignement et /ou la recherche. Cela comprend le personnel qui détient un grade universitaire avec des titres tels que professeur, professeur agrégé, professeur adjoint, maitre de conférences ou l'équivalent. Le personnel, comme par exemple doyen, directeur, vice-doyen, doyen adjoint, président ou chef de département, est également inclus si leur activité principale est l'enseignement ou la recherche.

Tableau 9: Dépenses publiques afférentes à l'éducation

Les dépenses publiques afférentes à l'éducation consistent en dépenses courantes et dépenses en capital engagées par l'administration aux niveaux local, régional et national, y compris les municipalités. Les contributions des ménages sont exclues. Les dépenses d'éducation courantes comprennent les dépenses en biens et en services consommés dans l'année en cours et qui devront être renouvelées au besoin l'année suivante. Elles comprennent les dépenses au titre des salaires et avantages du personnel; des services achetés ou obtenus par contrat; d'autres ressources, notamment de manuels et autres matériels d'enseignement; des services sociaux; et d'autres dépenses courantes telles que les subventions aux étudiants et aux ménages, l'ameublement et le matériel, les petites réparations, le combustible, les télécommunications, les voyages, l'assurance et les loyers. Les dépenses en capital pour l'éducation consistent en achats de biens dont la durée dépasse une année. Elles comprennent les dépenses de construction, de rénovation et de grosses réparations de bâtiments ainsi que l'achat de matériel lourd et de véhicules.

Chapitre V: Santé

Tableau 10: Le personnel de santé

Le tableau présente quatre grandes catégories de personnel de santé (sur les 9 catégories disponibles à la source) : la catégorie des médecins, qui comprend les médecins généralistes et les spécialistes; celle des infirmiers et sages-femmes comprend les infirmiers et sages-femmes qualifiés, les infirmiers auxiliaires professionnels et les sages-femmes auxiliaires professionnelles. Les accoucheuses traditionnelles ne sont pas incluses; le personnel de dentisterie comprend les dentistes, les assistants dentaires, les techniciens dentaires et les professions associées; et le personnel du secteur pharmaceutique comprend les pharmaciens, les pharmaciens assistants, les préparateurs en pharmacie et les professions associées.

Les données sont extraites des statistiques mondiales des personnels de santé de la base de données de l'Organisation mondiale de la Santé (OMS), qui sont établies à partir de plusieurs sources comme les recensements de population nationaux, les enquêtes sur la population active et l'emploi, les productions statistiques nationales et les données régulières des administrations. Il existe de ce fait d'un pays à l'autre une variabilité considérable dans la couverture, la qualité et l'année de référence des données. Généralement, les données du dénominateur pour le calcul de la densité du personnel de santé (c'est-à-dire les estimations de la population nationale) sont extraites des *Perspectives de la population mondiale* publiées par la Division de la population de l'Organisation des Nations Unies. Parfois le rapport officiel ne fournit que les indicateurs de la densité du personnel de santé, à partir desquels le stock est ensuite estimé.

La classification des personnels du secteur de la santé utilisée repose sur les critères de l'enseignement et formation techniques et professionnels, la réglementation des professions de santé et les activités et tâches des postes, c'est-à-dire sur un cadre de catégorisation des principales variables des personnels selon des caractéristiques communes. Le cadre de l'OMS repose en grande partie sur les révisions les plus récentes des systèmes de classification internationaux normalisés de l'Organisation internationale du Travail (Classification internationale type des professions), de l'Organisation des Nations Unies pour l'éducation, la science et la culture (Classification internationale type de l'éducation) et de la Division de statistique de l'ONU (Classification internationale type, par industrie, de toutes les branches d'activité économique). En fonction de la situation propre à chaque pays et des moyens de mesure, les données disponibles dans l'ensemble agrégé décrivent jusqu'à 9 catégories de personnels de santé, et jusqu'à 18 catégories dans l'ensemble désagrégé. Ce dernier reflète essentiellement une tentative de mieux distinguer certains sous-groupes des personnels du secteur de la santé en fonction de différences supposées dans les niveaux de compétence et de spécialisation.

Tableau 11: Dépenses de santé

La série « Dépenses courantes » fait référence aux biens et aux services de santé utilisés ou consommés au cours d'une année, à l'exclusion des dépenses en capital, ou plutôt de la « formation brute de capital », qui correspond à l'achat de nouveaux actifs sur plusieurs années. Ces estimations sont conformes au Système de comptes de la santé (SCS) de 2011. La dépense courante est exprimée en proportion du produit intérieur brut (PIB). Les séries des dépenses des administrations publiques générales sont composées de sources nationales publiques et privées. Les séries des dépenses des administrations publiques générales sont composées de sources nationales publiques et privées. Les sources publiques nationales comprennent les recettes intérieures sous forme de transferts et de subventions internes, les transferts, les subventions aux bénéficiaires de l'assurance maladie volontaire, les institutions sans but lucratif au service des ménages ou les régimes de financement des entreprises ainsi que les cotisations obligatoires. Tous ces transferts et subventions représentent des sources publiques de santé et indiquent la contribution globale des gouvernements au financement des soins de santé par rapport à d'autres sources de financement provenant de sources privées et extérieures nationales. Les dépenses des administrations publiques nationales sont exprimées en proportion des dépenses des administrations publiques. (Voir http://apps.who.int/nha/database/DocumentationCentre/Index/fr).

Chapitre VI: Criminalité

Tableau 12: Homicides intentionnels et autres crimes

« Les homicides intentionnels » et « autres crimes » sont extraits de l'Office des Nations Unies contre la drogue et le crime, publiés dans leur base de données statistiques.

« L'Homicide intentionnel » signifie une mort illégale infligée intentionnellement à une personne par une autre personne. Les données sur les homicides volontaires devraient également inclure les voies de fait graves entraînant la mort ou la mort à la suite d'un attentat terroriste. Il devrait exclure les tentatives d'homicide, l'homicide involontaire, les décès dus à une intervention judiciaire, les homicides légitimes commis en légitime défense et les décès dus à un conflit armé.

« L'Agression » signifie une agression physique contre le corps d'une autre personne ayant entraîné des lésions corporelles graves, à l'exclusion des agressions sexuelles ou indécentes, des menaces et des coups / coups de poing. « Les agressions » entraînant la mort devraient également être exclues.

Le vol est l'appropriation ou l'obtention illégale d'un bien dans l'intention d'en priver une personne ou une organisation de manière permanente sans son consentement et sans recours à la force. Le vol exclut le cambriolage, l'entrée avec effraction, le vol qualifié et le vol de véhicule motorisé, qui sont comptabilisés séparément.

Chapitre VII: Comptes nationaux

La base de données des principaux agrégats des comptes nationaux (consultable sur le site http://unstats.un.org/unsd/snaama) présente les données des comptes nationaux de plus de 200 pays et régions du monde. Elle constitue la base de l'analyse des principaux agrégats des statistiques de la comptabilité nationale (*National Account Statistics: Analysis of Main Aggregates*), une publication préparée par la Division de statistique du Département des affaires économiques et sociales du Secrétariat des Nations Unies avec le généreux concours des offices nationaux de la statistique. La base de données est mise à jour chaque année au mois de décembre avec les données nouvellement disponibles des comptes nationaux de tous pays et régions.

La base de données des principaux agrégats des comptes nationaux repose sur les données extraites du Questionnaire sur la comptabilité nationale des Nations Unies (NAQ) introduit en octobre 1999, qui lui-même repose sur le Système de comptes nationaux 1993 (SCN 1993). Les données sont complétées par des estimations préparées par la Division de statistique. Le SCN actualisé, appelé Système de comptes nationaux 2008 (SCN 2008) a été finalisé en septembre 2009. En 2017, 83 pays et territoires (États membres de l'Union européenne, Albanie, Arabie saoudite, Argentine, Arménie, Australie, Bélarus, Brésil, Brunéi Darussalam, Canada, Chili, Chine, Chine, RAS de Hong Kong, Chine, RAS de Macao, Costa Rica, République dominicaine, Équateur, Eswatini, Fidji, Îles Vierges britanniques, Inde, Indonésie, Islande, Israël, Japon, Kenya, Rép. dém. populaire lao, Liban, Liechtenstein, Macédoine du Nord, Malaisie, Maroc, Maurice, Mexique, Mongolie, Monténégro, Nouvelle-Zélande, Nigéria, Norvège, Pakistan, Pérou, Philippines, République de Corée, Serbie, Singapour, St-Martin, Afrique du Sud, Sri Lanka, Suisse, Thaïlande, Timor-Leste, Turquie, Ouganda, Ukraine, États-Unis d'Amérique et Zambie) ont commencé de soumettre des données conformément au SCN 2008.

Tout est mis en œuvre pour présenter les estimations des divers pays ou régions sous une forme conçue pour faciliter la comparabilité internationale. À cette fin, les différences importantes entre les concepts, la portée, la couverture et la classification sont décrites dans les notes de chaque pays. Ces différences doivent être prises en compte afin d'éviter les comparaisons fallacieuses. Les données contenues dans les tableaux se rapportent à l'année civile pour laquelle elles sont présentées, sauf exceptions. Ces exceptions sont affichées sur le site Web de la base de données des principaux agrégats des comptes nationaux (http://unstats.un.org/unsd/snaama/notes.asp). Les chiffres présentés sont les estimations et révisions les plus récentes disponibles au moment de leur établissement. En général, les chiffres de l'année la plus récente doivent être considérés comme provisoires. Les sommes des composantes des tableaux ne correspondent pas nécessairement aux totaux indiqués en raison des arrondis.

Tableau 13: Produit intérieur brut et produit intérieur brut par habitant

Ce tableau présente le produit intérieur brut (PIB) et le PIB par habitant en dollars des États-Unis aux prix courants, le PIB à prix constants de 2010 et les taux de croissance réels correspondants. Les tableaux sont destinés à faciliter les comparaisons internationales des niveaux de revenu générés par la production. Les données et les estimations officielles du PIB total et du PIB par habitant aux prix courants sont converties en dollars des États-Unis, tandis que celles du PIB total à prix constants sont converties aux prix de 2010 avant conversion en dollars aux taux de change en vigueur en 2010. La méthode de conversion en dollars des États-Unis est décrite dans le document sur la méthodologie de la base de données des principaux agrégats des comptes nationaux (http://unstats.un.org/unsd/snaama/methodology.pdf). Pour les comparaisons entre pays sur la durée, il est plus approprié d'utiliser les taux de croissance à prix constants du tableau, qui représentent mieux les tendances du PIB total dans les comparaisons entre pays et entre groupes de pays. Le taux de croissance indiqué dans le tableau est calculé comme la moyenne géométrique des taux de croissance annuelle exprimés en pourcentages pour les années.

Tableau 14: Valeur ajoutée brute par type d'activité économique

Ce tableau présente les parts des composantes de la valeur ajoutée brute aux prix courants par type d'activité économique.

Secteur	Composé de (selon la nomenclature CITI 3)
Agriculture	Agriculture, chasse, sylviculture et pêches (CITI A-B)
Industrie	Activités extractives, activités de fabrication, production et distribution d'électricité, de gaz et d'eau (CITI C-E) Construction (CITI F)
Services	Commerce de gros et de détail ; réparation de véhicules automobiles, de motocycles et de

biens personnels et domestiques, hôtels et restaurants (CITI G-H) Transports, entreposage et communications (CITI I) Autres activités, y compris intermédiation financière, immobilier, location et activités de services aux entreprises, administration publique et défense, sécurité sociale obligatoire, éducation, santé et action sociale, autres activités de services collectifs, sociaux et personnels, ménages privés employant du personnel domestique (CITI J-P).

Chapitre VIII: Finances

Des informations détaillées et les chiffres courants concernant le tableau 15 figurent dans *Statistiques financières internationales*, une publication du Fonds monétaire international (voir aussi http://elibrary-data.imf.org) et dans le *Bulletin mensuel de statistique des Nations Unies*.

Tableau 15: Résumé de la balance des paiements

La balance des paiements peut être décrite d'une façon générale comme l'enregistrement des transactions économiques internationales d'une économie. Elle présente : a) les transactions en biens, services et revenus entre une économie et le reste du monde, b) les changements de propriété et les autres changements des avoirs de cette économie en or monétaire, droits de tirage spéciaux (DTS) et en créances et engagements envers le reste du monde, et c) les transferts sans contrepartie et les écritures de contrepartie nécessaires pour équilibrer au sens comptable les écritures au titre des transactions et changements susmentionnés qui ne s'annulent pas mutuellement. Les données de la balance des paiements sont présentées sur la base de la méthodologie et de la présentation de la sixième édition du *Manuel de la balance des paiements* (MBP6), publiée par le Fonds monétaire international en novembre 2013. Le MBP6 incorpore plusieurs modifications majeures pour tenir compte des évolutions du commerce international et de la finance internationale au fil des années, et de mieux harmoniser la méthodologie de la balance des paiements du Fonds avec celle du Système de comptes nationaux 2008 (SCN 2008). Les définitions détaillées concernant le contenu des catégories fondamentales de la balance des paiements sont données dans le *Manuel de la balance des paiements* (sixième édition).

De brèves notes explicatives sont données ci-dessous pour clarifier la portée des principaux éléments.

Le compte des transactions courantes enregistre toutes les transactions de la balance des paiements couvrant les exportations et les importations de biens et de services, les revenus et les transferts courants entre les résidents d'un pays et des non-résidents.

Le compte de capital, n.i.a. porte principalement sur les transferts de capital liés à l'acquisition d'un actif fixe autres que les transactions relatives à l'annulation de la dette, plus la cession d'actifs non financiers non produits, et les transferts de capital liés à la cession d'actifs fixes par le donateur ou au financement de la formation de capital par le récipiendaire, plus l'acquisition d'actifs non financiers non produits.

Le compte d'opérations financières, n.i.a. représente le solde net de l'investissement direct, de l'investissement de portefeuille et des autres transactions d'investissement.

Les réserves sont la somme des transactions sur actifs de réserve, les engagements constituant des avoirs de réserve pour les autorités étrangères, le financement exceptionnel et l'utilisation des crédits du FMI.

Tableau 16: Cours des changes

Les taux des changes sont exprimés par le nombre d'unités de monnaie nationale pour un dollar des Etats-Unis. Les taux de change sont classés en trois catégories, qui dénotent le rôle des autorités dans l'établissement des taux de change et/ou la multiplicité des taux de change dans un pays. Par taux du marché, on entend les taux de change déterminés essentiellement par les forces du marché; le taux officiel est un taux de change établi par les autorités, parfois selon des dispositions souples. Pour les pays qui continuent à mettre en œuvre des régimes de taux de change multiples, les taux sont désignés par les appellations suivantes: "taux principal", "taux secondaire" et "taux tertiaire". Sauf indication contraire, le tableau indique des taux de fin de période et les moyennes sur la période, des taux de change du marché ou des taux de change officiels.

Chapitre IX: Marché du travail

Une collection complète de données comparables sur la population active et les sujets connexes est disponible sous la forme des *Indicateurs clé du marché du travail* (KILM) publiés par l'Organisation internationale du Travail (OIT), et mis à jour tous les deux ans. Des données plus contemporaines sont accessibles sur ILOSTAT (www.ilo.org/ilostat), le dépôt de données de l'OIT, qui publie des données annuellement, trimestriellement ou mensuellement à mesure de leur communication par les pays mais sans procéder à toutes les vérifications de leur cohérence ni inclure toutes les sources utilisées par les KILM. Pour diverses raisons, les définitions nationales de l'emploi et du chômage diffèrent souvent des définitions internationales normalisées recommandées, ce qui limite la comparabilité internationale. Les comparaisons entre pays se trouvent en outre compliquées par la diversité des systèmes de collecte de données utilisés pour recueillir des informations sur les personnes employées et les chômeurs. Le site Web d'ILOSTAT offre une description complète de la méthodologie employée pour établir les séries sur la main-d'œuvre.

Tableau 17: Taux d'activité activité et taux de chômage

Le taux de participation à la population active est calculé en exprimant le nombre de personnes de la population active sous forme de pourcentage de la population en âge de travailler. La population active est la somme du nombre de personnes employées et du nombre de personnes sans emploi (voir les Recommandations internationales en vigueur sur les statistiques du travail de l'OIT). La population en âge de travailler est la population d'âge supérieur à un certain seuil, prescrit pour la mesure des caractéristiques économiques. Les données concernent le groupe des personnes de 15 ans et plus et reposent sur les estimations modélisées de l'OIT, sauf indication contraire en note de bas de page.

La définition du chômage inclut les personnes en âge de travailler qui, au cours d'une certaine période, étaient :

a) « Sans emploi », c'est-à-dire sans emploi rémunéré ou indépendant;

b) « Disponibles », c'est-à-dire libres de contracter un emploi rémunéré ou de pratiquer un emploi indépendant au cours de la période de référence; et

c) « À la recherche d'un emploi », c'est-à-dire qui ont pris des mesures déterminées pour trouver un emploi rémunéré ou indépendant au cours de la période spécifiée

Ne sont pas considérées comme sans emploi :

a) Les personnes qui ont l'intention d'établir leur propre activité ou exploitation agricole, mais n'ont pas encore pris les dispositions nécessaires à cet effet et ne recherchent pas un emploi en vue d'une rémunération ou d'un profit;

b) Les anciens travailleurs familiaux non rémunérés qui n'ont pas d'emploi et ne sont pas à la recherche d'un emploi pour rémunération ou profit.

Les séries représentent généralement le nombre total des personnes au chômage complet ou temporairement mises à pied. Les données exprimées en pourcentages, lorsqu'elles figurent dans le tableau, sont calculées en comparant le nombre des chômeurs au total des membres du groupe de la population active sur lequel les données du chômage sont basées.

Tableau 18: Emploi par activité économique

Le tableau de l'emploi présente, exprimée en pourcentages, la répartition des personnes employées par activité économique, conformément à la Classification internationale type, par industrie, de toutes les branches d'activité économique (CITI) version 4.

Chapitre X: Indices des prix et de la production

Tableau 19 : Indices des prix à la consommation

Un indice des prix à la consommation est généralement estimé sous forme d'une série de mesures synthétiques des variations relatives, d'une période à l'autre, des prix d'un ensemble fixe de biens et de services de consommation d'une quantité et de caractéristiques constantes, acquis, utilisés ou payés par la population de référence. Chaque mesure synthétique est construite comme la moyenne pondérée d'un grand nombre d'indices d'agrégats élémentaires. L'indice de chaque agrégat élémentaire est estimé au moyen d'un échantillon de prix pour un ensemble défini de biens et de services obtenus dans une région donnée ou par ses résidents auprès d'un ensemble donné de points de vente ou d'autres sources de biens et de services de consommation. Le tableau présente les indices généraux des prix à la consommation pour tous les groupes d'articles de consommation combinés, et un indice des prix des produits alimentaires ne comprenant que les boissons non alcoolisées. Lorsque les prix des boissons alcoolisées et/ou du tabac sont inclus, cela est indiqué en note.

Chapitre XI: Commerce international des marchandises

Préparé par la Division de statistique du Département des affaires économiques et sociales du Secrétariat des Nations Unies, l'*Annuaire statistique du commerce international* (ITSY) offre un aperçu des tendances récentes du commerce de biens et de services de la plupart des pays et régions du monde. L'*Annuaire*, voir http://comtrade.un.org/pb/, est publié en deux volumes; le Volume I est établi plus tôt dans l'année pour présenter un aperçu préliminaire du commerce international de marchandises de l'année précédente; le Volume II, publié généralement six mois plus tard, contient des tableaux détaillés qui présentent le commerce international par produit et 11 tableaux du commerce mondial couvrant les valeurs commerciales et les indices. Le Volume II contient également des versions actualisées des tableaux du commerce mondial. Les tableaux de cet *Annuaire* sont également mis à jour mensuellement dans le Bulletin mensuel de statistique des Nations Unies et sur le site des statistiques du commerce, voir http://unstats.un.org/unsd/trade/data/tables.asp#annual.

Les statistiques présentées dans cet *Annuaire* sont établies par les autorités statistiques nationales de façon largement conforme aux concepts et définitions des statistiques du commerce international de marchandises recommandés par les Nations Unies en 2010 (IMTS 2010). En fonction des parties du territoire économique incluses dans le territoire statistique, le système d'établissement des données du commerce adopté par un pays (son système de commerce) sera appelé général ou spécial.

Système de commerce général	Le territoire statistique coïncide avec le territoire économique. Il est donc recommandé que le territoire statistique d'un pays qui applique le système de commerce général englobe tous les éléments territoriaux applicables. Dans ce cas, les importations comprennent les biens qui entrent dans la zone de libre circulation, les installations de perfectionnement actif, les zones franches industrielles, les entrepôts sous douane ou les zones franches commerciales, et les exportations comprennent les biens qui quittent ces éléments territoriaux.
Système de commerce spécial	(Définition stricte) Le territoire statistique ne comprend qu'une partie spécifique du territoire économique, de sorte que certains flux de marchandises auxquels les recommandations IMTS 2010 sont applicables ne sont inclus ni dans les statistiques d'importation ni dans les statistiques d'exportation du pays déclarant. La définition stricte du système de commerce spécial est utilisée lorsque le territoire statistique ne comprend que la zone de libre circulation, c'est-à-dire la partie dans laquelle les marchandises « peuvent être écoulées sans restriction douanière ». Par conséquent, dans ce cas, les importations ne comprennent que les marchandises qui entrent dans la zone de libre circulation du pays déclarant et les exportations ne comprennent que les marchandises qui quittent la zone de libre circulation du pays déclarant.
	(Définition assouplie) a) les marchandises qui entrent dans un pays aux fins du perfectionnement actif ou en ressortent après, ainsi que b) les marchandises qui entrent dans une zone franche industrielle ou en sortent, sont aussi enregistrées et incluses dans les statistiques du commerce international de marchandises.

Tous les pays communiquent en général leurs données détaillées du commerce de marchandises conformément au Système harmonisé de désignation et de codification des marchandises (SH) et les données correspondent à la Classification type pour le commerce international (CTCI, rév. 3), dans laquelle elles sont ensuite présentées. Les données se réfèrent à des années civiles; cependant, pour les pays qui communiquent leurs données selon une autre année de référence, les données sont présentées dans l'année qui couvre la plus grande partie de l'année de référence utilisée par le pays.

Les valeurs FOB comprennent la valeur transactionnelle des marchandises et la valeur des services fournis pour livrer les marchandises à la frontière du pays exportateur. Les valeurs CIF comprennent la valeur transactionnelle des marchandises, la valeur des services fournis pour livrer les marchandises à la frontière du pays exportateur et la valeur des services fournis pour livrer les marchandises depuis la frontière du pays exportateur jusqu'à la frontière du pays importateur. De ce fait, les données de la valeur statistique des marchandises importées sont présentées dans le format CIF et celles de la valeur statistique des marchandises exportées dans le format FOB.

La conversion des valeurs libellées en monnaies nationales en dollars des États-Unis s'effectue au moyen de facteurs de conversion de devises fondés sur les taux de change officiels. Les valeurs libellées en monnaies sujettes à des fluctuations sont converties en dollars des États-Unis au moyen de taux de change moyens pondérés calculés spécialement à cette fin. Le taux de change moyen pondéré d'une monnaie donnée pour une année donnée est donné par les facteurs composants mensuels, fournis par le Fonds monétaire international dans sa publication *Statistiques financières internationales*, pondérés par la valeur du commerce concerné pour chaque mois; les facteurs mensuels sont les taux de change (ou les taux moyens simples) en vigueur au cours de ce mois. Ces facteurs sont appliqués aux importations et aux exportations totales et au commerce de chaque produit avec chaque pays.

Tableau 20: Total des importations, des exportations et balance commerciale

Les données des importations totales et des exportations totales des pays (ou régions) présentées dans ce tableau proviennent principalement des *Statistiques financières internationales* publiées mensuellement par le Fonds monétaire international (FMI) mais aussi d'autres sources comme les publications et les sites web nationaux et le Questionnaire du *Bulletin mensuel de statistique* des Nations Unies, voir l'*Annuaire statistique du commerce international* pour plus de détails. Les données manquantes sont estimées afin de parvenir à des totaux régionaux mais ne sont pas présentées. La procédure d'estimation est automatisée au moyen des taux de croissance en glissement annuel trimestriels pour l'extrapolation des données trimestrielles manquantes (sauf si les données trimestrielles peuvent être estimées au moyen des données mensuelles disponibles au cours du trimestre). Les facteurs de conversion appliqués aux données de ce tableau sont publiés trimestriellement dans le *Bulletin mensuel de statistique* des Nations Unies et sont aussi disponibles sur le site Web des statistiques du commerce de l'ONU : http://unstats.un.org/unsd/trade/data/tables.asp#annual.

Table 21 : Principaux partenaires commerciaux

Les chiffres sur les principaux partenaires commerciaux montrent les trois plus grands partenaires commerciaux (les pays de dernière destination et d'origine ou de provenance) dans les transactions du commerce international de marchandises. Dans certains cas un partenaire privilégié est présenté (zones nca, abris fortifiés, etc.). Les zones ni compris ailleurs (zones nca) sont utilisées (a) pour le commerce de faible valeur, (b)si le partenaire choisi est inconnu ou si une erreur a été commise en choisissant le partenaire et (c) pour des raisons de confidentialité. Si un emplacement géographique précis peut être identifie dans zones nca, elles sont alors enregistrées en conséquence (par exemple, Asie nca). Les abris fortifiés sont des magasins de navires et d'aéronefs, qui consistent pour la plupart de combustibles et de denrées alimentaires. Les zones franches appartiennent au territoire économique et géographique d'un pays et non à leurs territoires douaniers. Aux fins des statistiques sur le commerce les opérations entre les territoires douaniers et les zones franches sont enregistrées, si le pays déclarant utilise le Système de Commerce Spécial. Les zones franches peuvent être des zones franches commerciales (boutiques hors taxes) ou des zones franches industrielles. Les données sont exprimées en pourcentage des exportations totales et des importations totales d'un pays, zone ou partenaire privilégié.

Les données dans ce tableau sont des données telles que rapportées par l'UN Comtrade (au niveau à trois chiffres de la CTCI Rév. 3 et une ventilation détaillée des partenaires commerciaux) et des données estimées pour les rapporteurs manquants. Les données sont estimées soit par extrapolation des données des deux années adjacentes, soit, si cela n'est pas possible, par l'utilisation des données déclarées par les partenaires commerciaux (données dites miroir). Les statistiques de miroir sont également utilisées dans le cas où la distribution du partenaire ou des données confidentielles rendent nécessaire l'ajustement des données rapportées. En outre, des modifications sont apportées aux données reçues dans les cas où les données fournies sont manifestement incomplètes, en particulier dans le cas d'exportations d'huiles de pétrole non déclarées dans les données sur les marchandises.

Chapitre XII: Énergie

L'*Annuaire statistique de l'énergie* (consultable sur le site http://unstats.un.org/unsd/energy/yearbook) est une collection complète de statistiques internationales de l'énergie qui couvre plus de 220 pays et régions. L'*Annuaire* est préparé par la Division de statistique du Département des affaires économiques et sociales du Secrétariat des Nations Unies. L'*Annuaire* est produit chaque année avec les nouvelles données disponibles sur la production d'énergie, le commerce, les variations de stocks, les réserves et la consommation de tous les pays et régions, et une série historique remontant à 1950 est disponible. Les données sont établies essentiellement à partir du questionnaire annuel sur l'énergie diffusé par la Division de statistique des Nations Unies et complétées par des publications statistiques officielles nationales, ainsi que des publications des organisations internationales et régionales. Lorsque les données officielles ne sont pas disponibles ou ne sont pas cohérentes, la Division de statistique établit des estimations en s'appuyant sur des éléments d'origine gouvernementale, professionnelle ou commerciale.

Les données se réfèrent à l'année civile, sauf celles des pays suivants qui se rapportent à l'exercice budgétaire : Afghanistan et Iran (République islamique d') – commençant le 21 mars de l'année indiquée; Australie, Bangladesh, Bhoutan, Égypte (électricité seulement pour ces deux derniers pays), Népal – finissant en juin de l'année indiquée; Pakistan – commençant en juillet de l'année indiquée; Inde, Myanmar et Nouvelle-Zélande – commençant en avril de l'année indiquée. Les données exprimées par habitant utilisent comme dénominateur les données démographiques de la Division de la population de l'Organisation des Nations Unies.

Tableau 22: Production, commerce et consommation d'énergie

Les données sont présentées en pétajoules (ou en gigajoules par habitant), unités auxquelles chaque produit énergétique est converti afin d'assurer l'uniformité et la comparabilité internationales des données. Pour convertir en joules les unités originelles, celles-ci (tonnes métriques, tonnes métriques d'équivalent pétrole, kilowattheures, mètres cubes) sont multipliées par des facteurs de conversion. Voir l'*Annuaire statistique de l'énergie* pour une liste des facteurs de conversion et une description détaillée des méthodes utilisées.

Les combustibles solides inclus dans la production d'énergie primaire sont l'anthracite, la lignite, la tourbe et le schiste bitumineux, biocarburants solides primaires et les déchets ; les liquides comprennent le pétrole brut, les condensats de gaz naturel, les autres hydrocarbures, additifs et oxygénats, et les biocarburants liquides; les gaz comprennent le gaz naturel et les biogaz ; et l'électricité comprend la production primaire d'électricité d'origine hydraulique, éolienne, marémotrice (vagues et courants), et solaire. Les importations nettes (importations moins exportations et bunkers) et les variations des stocks font référence à toutes les formes d'énergie primaire et secondaire (y compris les produits intermédiaires). Dans les importations nettes, les bunkers font référence aux bunkers d'essence aviation, de carburéacteur et d'anthracite, de gazole/carburant diesel et de fiouls résiduels. Le commerce international de produits énergétiques repose sur le système du « commerce général », c'est-à-dire que toutes les marchandises entrant sur le territoire national d'un pays ou en sortant sont enregistrées comme importations ou exportations.

La consommation d'énergie comprend les formes primaires des combustibles solides, les importations nettes et les variations des stocks des combustibles secondaires

L'approvisionnement en énergie est calculé comme l'énergie primaire plus les importations, moins les exportations moins les soutes internationales (aériennes et maritimes) et moins les variations des stocks.

Chapitre XIII: Environnement

Tableau 23: Terres

Les données relatives aux terres sont compilées par l'Organisation des Nations Unies pour l'alimentation et l'agriculture (FAO). Les définitions de la FAO en ce qui concerne les terres sont les suivantes:

Superficie totale des terres	Superficie totale, à l'exception des eaux intérieures. Les eaux intérieures désignent généralement les principaux fleuves et lacs.
Terres arables	Terres affectées aux cultures temporaires (les terres sur lesquelles est pratiquée la double culture ne sont comptabilisées qu'une fois); prairies temporaires à faucher ou à pâturer, jardins maraîchers ou potagers et terres en jachère temporaire (moins de cinq ans). Cette définition ne comprend pas les terres abandonnées du fait de la culture itinérante. Les données relatives aux terres arables ne peuvent être utilisées pour calculer la superficie des terres aptes à l'agriculture.
Cultures permanentes	Superficie des terres avec des cultures qui occupent la terre pour de longues périodes et qui ne nécessitent pas d'être replantées après chaque récolte, comme le cacao, le café et le caoutchouc. Cette catégorie comprend les terres plantées d'arbustes à fleurs, d'arbres fruitiers, d'arbres à noix et de vignes, mais ne comprend pas les terres plantées d'arbres destinés à la coupe.
Superficie forestière	Dans l'Évaluation des ressources forestières mondiales 2010, la FAO a défini les forêts comme suit : Terres occupant une superficie de plus de 0,5 hectares avec des arbres atteignant une hauteur supérieure à cinq mètres et un couvert arboré de plus de dix pour cent, ou avec des arbres capables d'atteindre ces seuils in situ. Sont exclues les terres à vocation agricole ou urbaine prédominante.

Sites importants pour la biodiversité terrestre dans les aires protégées	Les terres contribuant énormément à la persistance globale de la biodiversité mesurées en proportion entièrement couverte par des zones protégées désignées. Les données sont fondées sur un chevauchement entre les polygones pour les zones clés de la biodiversité provenant de la base des données mondiales sur les zones clés pour la biodiversité et les polygones pour les zones protégées provenant de la base des données mondiales sur les zones protégées. Les chiffres pour chaque région sont calculés comme la proportion de chaque zone clé pour la biodiversité couverte par des zones protégées, moyennés (c'est-à-dire, calculés comme la moyenne) à travers toutes les zones clés de la biodiversité dans la région.

Tableau 24: Espèces menacées

Les données relatives au nombre d'espèces menacées dans chaque groupe d'animaux et de plantes sont établies par l'Union internationale pour la conservation de la nature et de ses ressources (UICN)/ Commission de sauvegarde des espèces (CSE) et publiées dans la liste rouge des espèces menacées de l'UICN. Cette liste fournit le catalogue des espèces considérées comme menacées au niveau mondial. Le nombre d'espèces menacées dans un pays donné change au cours des années pour diverses raisons, entre autres :

- La disponibilité d'informations nouvelles permet de raffiner l'évaluation (de confirmer par exemple que l'espèce est ou n'est pas présente dans un pays donné, que l'espèce est ou n'est pas menacée, etc.);

- L'évolution de la taxonomie (par exemple ce qu'on reconnaissait auparavant comme une certaine espèce est à présent réparti entre plusieurs espèces distinctes, ou fusionné avec une autre espèce);

- Les corrections (par exemple l'évaluation précédente peut avoir omis d'inscrire un pays donné dans la liste appropriée ou avoir inclus un pays donné par erreur);

- Changement de statut réel (par exemple la situation d'une espèce peut s'être réellement détériorée ou améliorée et l'espèce avoir par conséquent été incorporée aux catégories menacées ou en avoir été retirée).

Les catégories utilisées dans la Liste rouge sont les suivantes : espèce éteinte, éteinte à l'état sauvage, gravement menacée d'extinction; menacée d'extinction, vulnérable, quasi menacée et données insuffisantes.

Tableau 25: Services d'approvisionnement en eau et d'assainissement

Ces données sont estimées par le Programme commun OMS/UNICEF de suivi de l'approvisionnement en eau et de l'assainissement (JMP) s'appuyant sur les sources de pays disponibles, voir www.wssinfo.org pour en savoir davantage. La proportion de la population utilisant les services d'eau potable gérés de manière sûre est définie comme la population utilisant de meilleures sources d'eau potable (l'indicateur utilise pour le suivi des objectifs du Millénaire pour le développement) qui sont situées sur les locaux, et disponibles en cas de besoin, et libre de toute contamination fécale et chimique prioritaire. Pour remplir les critères nécessaires pour un service d'eau potable gérés de manière sûre, les personnes doivent utiliser une source améliorée satisfaisant trois critères:

- Elle doit être accessible sur les locaux,

- L'eau doit être disponible en cas de besoin, et

- L'eau fournie doit être exempts de contamination.

Si la source améliorée ne répond à aucun de ces critères mais un voyage aller-retour pour chercher l'eau prend 30 minutes ou moins, elle sera alors classifiée comme un service d'eau potable de base. Si la recherche d'eau provenant d'une source améliorée dépasse 30 minutes elle sera catégorisée comme un service limite. Le JMP différencie également les populations utilisant des sources non améliorées comme les puits ou sources non protégés, et les populations qui boivent les eaux de surface recueillies directement d'une cour d'eau, d'un barrage, d'un lac, d'un ruisseau ou d'un canal d'irrigation.

Pour la proportion de la population utilisant « les services d'assainissement gérés de manière sûre », Il existe trois manières principales pour remplir les critères afin d'avoir un service d'assainissement géré de manière sûre. Les personnes devraient utiliser des installations d'assainissement améliorées qui ne sont pas partagées avec d'autres familles, et l'excréta produit doit soit être :

- Traité et évacué in situ,

- Entreposé temporairement et ensuite vidé et transporté au traitement hors site, où

- Transporté par le biais d'un égout a eaux usées et ensuite traite hors site.

Si les excréta provenant des installations d'assainissement améliorées ne sont pas gérés de manière sûre les personnes utilisant ces installations seront considérées comme ayant un service d'assainissement de base. Les personnes utilisant les installations améliorées qui sont partagées avec d'autres familles seront catégorisées comme ayant un service limite.

Chapitre XIV: Science et technologie

La recherche et le développement expérimental (R-D) englobe tous les travaux de création entrepris de façon systématique en vue d'accroître la somme des connaissances, y compris la connaissance de l'homme, de la culture et de la société, ainsi que l'utilisation de cette somme de connaissances pour de nouvelles applications. Pour tout renseignement complémentaire, voir le site Web de l'Institut de statistique de l'UNESCO www.uis.unesco.org.

Tableau 26: Population employée dans la recherche et le développement (R–D)

Les données présentées sur la population employée dans la recherche et le développement (R-D) sont compilées par l'Institut de statistique de l'UNESCO. Les données de certains pays ont été fournies à l'UNESCO par l'OCDE, EUROSTAT et "la Red de Indicadores de Ciencia y Technología (RICYT)". Les définitions et classifications appliquées par l'UNESCO sont basées sur le Manuel de Frascati (OCDE, 2002).

Les trois catégories du personnel présentées sont définies comme suivant:

Les chercheurs	Les chercheurs sont des spécialistes travaillant à la conception ou à la création de connaissances, de produits, de procédés, de méthodes et de systèmes nouveaux et à la gestion des projets concernés. Les étudiants diplômés au niveau du doctorat (CITE niveau 8) ayant des activités de R-D sont considérés comme des chercheurs.
Techniciens et personnel assimilé	Personnes dont les tâches principales requièrent des connaissances et une expérience technique dans un ou plusieurs domaines de l'ingénierie, des sciences physiques et de la vie ou des sciences sociales et humaines. Ils participent à la R-D en exécutant des tâches scientifiques et techniques faisant intervenir l'application de principes et de méthodes opérationnelles, généralement sous le contrôle de chercheurs.
Autre personnel de soutien	Les travailleurs, qualifiés ou non, et le personnel de secrétariat et de bureau participant à l'exécution des projets de R-D ou qui sont directement associés à l'exécution de tels projets.

Personnes physiques est le nombre total de personnes qui sont principalement ou partiellement affectées à la R-D. Ce dénombrement inclut les employés à 'temps plein' et les employés à 'temps partiel'. Équivalent temps plein (ETP) peut être considéré comme une année-personne. Ainsi, une personne qui consacre 30% de son temps en R&D et le reste à d'autres activités (enseignement, administration universitaire ou direction d'étudiants) compte pour 0.3 ETP en R&D. De façon analogue, si un employé travaille à temps plein dans un centre de R&D pendant six mois seulement, il compte pour 0.5 ETP.

Tableau 27: Dépenses intérieures brutes de recherche et développement (R–D)

Les données présentées sur les dépenses intérieures brutes de recherche et développement sont compilées par l'Institut de statistique de l'UNESCO. Les données de certains pays ont été fournies à l'UNESCO par l'OCDE, EUROSTAT et "la Red de Indicadores de Ciencia y Technología (RICYT)". La dépense intérieure brute de R-D (DIRD) est la dépense totale intra-muros afférente aux travaux de R-D exécutés sur le territoire national pendant une période donnée. Elle comprend la R-D exécutée sur le territoire national et financée par l'étranger mais ne tient pas compte des paiements effectués à l'étranger pour des travaux de R-D. Les sources de financement pour la DIRD sont classées selon les cinq catégories suivantes:

Les fonds des entreprises	Les fonds alloués à la R-D par toutes les firmes, organismes et institutions dont l'activité première est la production marchande de biens ou de services (autres que dans le secteur d'enseignement supérieur) en vue de leur vente au public, à un prix qui correspond à la

	réalité économique, et les institutions privées sans but lucratif principalement au service de ces entreprises, organismes et institutions.
Les fonds de l'État	Les fonds fournis à la R-D par le gouvernement central (fédéral), d'état ou par les autorités locales. Ceci inclut tous les ministères, bureaux et autres organismes qui fournissent, sans normalement les vendre, des services collectifs autres que d'enseignement supérieur, qu'il n'est pas possible d'assurer de façon pratique et économique par d'autres moyens et qui, de surcroît, administrent les affaires publiques et appliquent la politique économique et sociale de la collectivité. Les fonds des entreprises publiques sont compris dans ceux du secteur des entreprises. Les fonds de l'État incluent également les institutions privées sans but lucratif contrôlées et principalement financées par l'État.
Les fonds de l'enseignement supérieur	Les fonds fournis à la R-D par les établissements d'enseignement supérieur tels que toutes les universités, grandes écoles, instituts de technologie et autres établissements postsecondaires, ainsi que tous les instituts de recherche, les stations d'essais et les cliniques qui travaillent sous le contrôle direct des établissements d'enseignement supérieur ou qui sont administrés par ces derniers ou leur sont associés
Les fonds d'institutions privées sans but lucratif	Les fonds destinés à la R-D par les institutions privées sans but lucratif non marchandes au service du public, ainsi que par les simples particuliers ou les ménages.
Les fonds étrangers	Les fonds destinés à la R-D par les institutions et les individus se trouvant en dehors des frontières politiques d'un pays, à l'exception des véhicules, navires, avions et satellites utilisés par des institutions nationales, ainsi que des terrains d'essai acquis par ces institutions, et par toutes les organisations internationales (à l'exception des entreprises), y compris leurs installations et leurs activités à l'intérieur des frontières d'un pays

Il faut éviter de comparer les chiffres absolus concernant les dépenses de R-D d'un pays à l'autre. On ne pourrait procéder à des comparaisons détaillées qu'en convertissant en une même monnaie les sommes libellées en monnaie nationale au moyen de taux de change spécialement applicables aux activités de R-D. Les taux de change officiels ne reflètent pas toujours le coût réel des activités de R-D, et les comparaisons établies sur la base de ces taux peuvent conduire à des conclusions trompeuses; toutefois, elles peuvent être utilisées pour donner une idée de l'ordre de grandeur.

Tableau 28: Brevets

Les brevets sont accordés par un office national des brevets ou un office régional qui accomplit cette tâche pour de nombreux pays, comme l'Office européen des brevets et l'African Regional Intellectual Property Organisation. Dans le cadre de ces systèmes régionaux, le requérant demande que son invention soit protégée dans un ou plusieurs pays, et il appartient à chaque pays d'accorder ou non la protection d'un brevet sur son territoire. Le Traité de coopération en matière de brevets (PCT), administré par l'Organisation mondiale de la propriété intellectuelle (OMPI) prévoit le dépôt d'une demande de brevet international unique dotée de la même validité que les demandes nationales déposées dans les pays désignés. Les données comprennent l'intensité de l'activité des résidents, les brevets délivrés et les brevets en vigueur. L'intensité du dépôt de brevets est présentée comme le nombre de demandes de brevet déposées par des résidents par million d'habitants, tandis que le dépôt d'une demande de propriété intellectuelle (PI) par des résidents fait référence à une demande déposée par un requérant auprès de son office national de la propriété intellectuelle. Les statistiques des droits de propriété intellectuelle (enregistrement) reposent sur le même concept. L'expression « en vigueur » désigne un brevet ou une autre forme de protection de la PI en cours de validité. Le pays d'origine sert à catégoriser les données de PI en PI résidente (intérieure) et non résidente (étrangère). La résidence du premier demandeur cité (ou inventeur) enregistré dans le document de PI (par exemple une demande de brevet ou de dépôt de marque) sert à classer les données de PI par pays d'origine. Les données sont établies et publiées par l'OMPI.

Chapitre XV : Communication

Table 29: Utilisation d'Internet

Le tableau indique le pourcentage de personnes qui utilisent Internet et remplace les statistiques présentées dans les annuaires précédents comme le « Nombre (en milliers) d'abonnements à l'Internet fixe (filaire) » et le « Nombre d'abonnements à l'Internet fixe (filaire) pour 100 habitants ». Cet indicateur, outre qu'il saisit l'usage d'Internet, permet de mesurer les évolutions de l'accès à Internet et de son utilisation. Dans les pays où de nombreuses personnes accèdent à Internet au travail, à l'école, dans les cybercafés ou d'autres lieux publics, la multiplication des accès publics accroît le nombre d'utilisateurs malgré le nombre limité des abonnements et des foyers qui ont accès à Internet. Les pays en développement en particulier comptent souvent de nombreux utilisateurs par abonnement à Internet, ce qui traduit le fait que le foyer n'est pas le lieu principal d'accès.

Chapitre XVI: Tourisme et transport internationaux

Les données sur le tourisme international sont fournies par l'Organisation mondiale du tourisme (OMT) qui publie des renseignements détaillés sur le tourisme dans l'*Annuaire des statistiques du tourisme* ou le *Compendium des statistiques du tourisme*, voir www.unwto.org/statistics pour des informations plus complètes. Aux fins de l'établissement des statistiques, l'expression « visiteur international» décrit «toute personne qui se rend dans un pays autre que celui dans lequel il ou elle a son lieu de résidence habituelle, mais différent de son environnement habituel, pour une période de 12 mois au maximum, dans un but principal autre que celui d'y exercer une activité rémunérée». L'*Annuaire* et le *Compendium* de l'OMT comportent quatre séries distinctes, mais une seule est retenue pour inclusion dans le présent *Annuaire*, en fonction en général de l'ordre de priorité suivant afin de décrire au mieux le « visiteur international»;

Ordre	Code de la série	Nom de la série
1	TF	*Arrivées de touristes non-résidents aux frontières nationales* désigne les visiteurs qui passent au moins une nuit dans un logement collectif ou privé dans le pays visité (exclut les visiteurs d'un jour)
2	VF	*Arrivées de visiteurs non-résidents aux frontières nationales* désigne les visiteurs définis dans la série « TF » ainsi que les visiteurs d'un jour qui ne passent pas la nuit dans un logement collectif ou privé dans le pays visité
3	TCE	*Arrivées de touristes non-résidents dans tous les types d'établissements d'hébergement*
4	THS	*Arrivées de touristes non-résidents dans les hôtels et établissements similaires*

Ces chiffres ne comprennent pas les immigrants, les résidents frontaliers, les personnes domiciliées dans un pays ou une région et qui travaillent dans un pays ou une région limitrophe, les membres des forces armées et les diplomates et les représentants consulaires lorsqu'ils se rendent de leur pays d'origine au pays où ils sont en poste et vice-versa. Ne sont pas inclus non plus les voyageurs en transit qui n'entrent pas formellement dans le pays en faisant viser leur passeport, comme les passagers d'un vol en escale qui demeurent pendant un court laps de temps dans une zone distincte d'une aérogare ou les passagers d'un navire qui ne sont pas autorisés à débarquer. Cette catégorie inclut les passagers transférés directement d'une aérogare à une autre ou à un autre terminal. Les autres passagers en transit dans un pays sont classés comme visiteurs.

Tableau 30: Arrivées de touristes/visiteurs et dépenses touristiques

Les données relatives aux arrivées de visiteurs non-résidents (ou internationaux) peuvent être obtenues de différentes sources. Dans certains cas, elles proviennent des statistiques frontalières tirées des registres administratifs (contrôles de police, de l'immigration, comptages du trafic routier et autres types de contrôle), des enquêtes statistiques aux frontières et des enregistrements d'établissements d'hébergement. Les totaux correspondent au nombre total d'arrivées depuis les régions indiquées dans le tableau. Lorsqu'une personne visite le même pays plusieurs fois dans l'année, un même nombre d'arrivées est enregistré. De même, si une personne visite plusieurs pays au cours d'un même voyage, son arrivée dans chaque pays est enregistrée séparément. On ne peut donc pas supposer que le nombre des arrivées soit égal au nombre de personnes qui voyagent.

Les dépenses associées à l'activité touristique des visiteurs sont traditionnellement identifiées au poste « Voyages » de la balance des paiements (BDP): dans le cas du tourisme dans le pays récepteur, les dépenses dans le pays de référence associées aux visiteurs non-résidents sont enregistrées comme « crédits » dans la BDP et il s'agit de « recettes au titre des voyages ». Le nouveau cadre conceptuel approuvé par la Commission de statistique des

Nations Unies concernant la mesure de l'activité touristique à l'échelle macroéconomique (le compte satellite du tourisme) considère que la notion « industries et produits touristiques » inclut le transport de passagers. Par conséquent, une meilleure estimation des dépenses liées au tourisme par des visiteurs résidents et non-résidents dans un scénario international serait, du point de vue de la BDP, la somme des valeurs du poste « Voyages » et du poste « Transport de passagers ». Néanmoins, les utilisateurs doivent être conscients de ce que les estimations de la BDP comprennent, outre les dépenses associées aux visiteurs, celles liées à d'autres types d'individus. Les données publiées doivent permettre la comparabilité internationale et donc correspondre à celles publiées par le Fonds monétaire international et fournies par les banques centrales, les exceptions sont listées dans le *Compendium des statistiques du tourisme* et l'*Annuaire des statistiques du tourisme*, voir www.unwto.org/statistics pour des informations plus complètes.

Chapitre XVII: Aide au développement

Tableau 31: Décaissements nets d'aide publique au développement aux bénéficiaires

Le tableau présente des estimations des flux de ressources financières à destination des pays bénéficiaires soit directement (aide bilatérale) soit par l'intermédiaire d'institutions multilatérales (aide multilatérale). Les institutions multilatérales comprennent le Groupe de la Banque mondiale, des banques régionales, les institutions financières de l'Union européenne et un certain nombre d'institutions, de programmes et de fonds d'affectation spéciale des Nations Unies. Les données ont été obtenues auprès du Comité d'aide au développement (CAD) de l'OCDE, auquel les pays membres communiquent des données sur les flux de ressources qu'ils mettent à la disposition de pays et territoires en développement, de pays et territoires en transition, et des institutions multilatérales. On trouvera davantage d'informations sur les définitions, les méthodes et les sources dans la publication de l'OCDE intitulée *Répartition géographique des ressources financières allouées aux pays en développement*, ainsi que sur le site http://stats.oecd.org/.

Tableau 32: Décaissements nets d'aide publique au développement par des donateurs

Le tableau présente les dépenses d'aide au développement des pays donateurs. Ce tableau inclut les contributions des donateurs aux institutions multilatérales; les totaux diffèrent donc de ceux du tableau 31, qui incluent les décaissements des institutions multilatérales.

* * *

Annex III

Conversion coefficients and factors

The metric system of weights and measures is employed in the *Statistical Yearbook*. In this system, the relationship between units of volume and capacity is: 1 litre = 1 cubic decimetre (dm^3) exactly (as decided by the 12th International Conference of Weights and Measures, New Delhi, November 1964).

Section A shows the equivalents of the basic metric, British imperial and United States units of measurements. According to an agreement between the national standards institutions of English-speaking nations, the British and United States units of length, area and volume are now identical, and based on the yard = 0.9144 metre exactly. The weight measures in both systems are based on the pound = 0.45359237 kilogram exactly (Weights and Measures Act 1963 (London), and *Federal Register announcement of 1 July 1959: Refinement of Values for the Yard and Pound* (Washington D.C.)).

Section B shows various derived or conventional conversion coefficients and equivalents.

Section C shows other conversion coefficients or factors which have been utilized in the compilation of certain tables in the *Statistical Yearbook*. Some of these are only of an approximate character and have been employed solely to obtain a reasonable measure of international comparability in the tables.

For a comprehensive survey of international and national systems of weights and measures and of units' weights for a large number of commodities in different countries, see *World Weights and Measures*.

Annexe III

Coefficients et facteurs de conversion

L'*Annuaire statistique* utilise le système métrique pour les poids et mesures. La relation entre unités métriques de volume et de capacité est: 1 litre = 1 décimètre cube (dm^3) exactement (comme fut décidé à la Conférence internationale des poids et mesures, New Delhi, novembre 1964).

La section A fournit les principaux équivalents des systèmes de mesure métrique, britannique et américain. Suivant un accord entre les institutions de normalisation nationales des pays de langue anglaise, les mesures britanniques et américaines de longueur, superficie et volume sont désormais identiques, et sont basées sur le yard = 0.9144 mètre exactement. Les mesures de poids se rapportent, dans les deux systèmes, à la livre (pound) = 0.45359237 kilogramme exactement (*Weights and Measures Act 1963* (Londres), et *Federal Register Announcement of 1 July 1959: Refinement of Values for the Yard and Pound* (Washington, D.C.)).

La section B fournit divers coefficients et facteurs de conversion conventionnels ou dérivés.

La section C fournit d'autres coefficients ou facteurs de conversion utilisés dans l'élaboration de certains tableaux de l'*Annuaire statistique*. Certains coefficients ou facteurs de conversion ne sont que des approximations et ont été utilisés uniquement pour obtenir un degré raisonnable de comparabilité sur le plan international.

Pour une étude d'ensemble des systèmes internationaux et nationaux de poids et mesures, et d'unités de poids pour un grand nombre de produits dans différents pays, voir *World Weights and Measures*.

A. Equivalents of metric, British imperial and United States units of measure
A. Equivalents des unités métriques, britanniques et des Etats-Unis

Metric units / Unités métriques	British imperial and US equivalents / Equivalents en mesures britanniques et des Etats-Unis		British imperial and US units / Unités britanniques et des Etats-Unis	Metric equivalents / Equivalents en mesures métriques
Length — Longueur				
1 centimetre – centimètre (cm)	0.3937008	inch	1 inch	2.540 cm
1 metre – mètre (m)	3.280840	feet	1 foot	30.480 cm
	1.093613	yard	1 yard	0.9144 m
1 kilometre – kilomètre (km)	0.6213712	mile	1 mile	1609.344 m
	0.5399568	international nautical mile	1 international nautical mile	1852.000 m
Area — Superficie				
1 square centimetre – (cm^2)	0.1550003	square inch	1 square inch	6.45160 cm^2
1 square metre – (m^2)	10.763910	square feet	1 square foot	9.290304 dm^2
	1.195990	square yards	1 square yard	0.83612736 m^2
1 hectare – (ha)	2.471054	acres	1 acre	0.4046856 ha
1 square kilometre – (km^2)	0.3861022	square mile	1 square mile	2.589988 km^2
Volume				
1 cubic centimetre – (cm^3)	0.06102374	cubic inch	1 cubic inch	16.38706 cm^3
1 cubic metre – (m^3)	35.31467	cubic feet	1 cubic foot	28.316847 dm^3
	1.307951	cubic yards	1 cubic yard	0.76455486 m^3
Capacity — Capacité				
1 litre (l)	0.8798766	British imperial quart	1 British imperial quart	1.136523 l
	1.056688	U.S. liquid quart	1 U.S. liquid quart	0.9463529 l
	0.908083	U.S. dry quart	1 U.S. dry quart	1.1012208 l
1 hectolitre (hl)	21.99692	British imperial gallons	1 British imperial gallon	4.546092 l
	26.417200	U.S. gallons	1 U.S. gallon	3.785412 l
	2.749614	British imperial bushels	1 imperial bushel	36.368735 l
	2.837760	U.S. bushels	1 U.S. bushel	35.239067 l

Metric units Unités métriques	British imperial and US equivalents Equivalents en mesures britanniques et des Etats-Unis		British imperial and US units Unités britanniques et des Etats-Unis	Metric equivalents Equivalents en mesures métriques
Weight or mass — Poids				
1 kilogram (kg)	35.27396	av. ounces	1 av. ounce	28.349523 g
	32.15075	troy ounces	1 troy ounce	31.10348 g
	2.204623	av. pounds	1 av. pound	453.59237 g
			1 cental (100 lb.)	45.359237 kg
			1 hundredweight (112 lb.)	50.802345 kg
1 ton – tonne (t)	1.1023113	short tons	1 short ton (2 000 lb.)	0.9071847 t
	0.9842065	long tons	1 long ton (2 240 lb.)	1.0160469 t

B. Various conventional or derived coefficients

Air transport

1 passenger-mile = 1.609344 passenger kilometre
1 short ton-mile = 1.459972 tonne-kilometre
1 long ton-mile = 1.635169 tonne kilometre

Electric energy

1 Kilowatt (kW) = 1.34102 British horsepower (hp)
1.35962 cheval vapeur (cv)

C. Other coefficients or conversion factors employed in *Statistical Yearbook* tables

Energy

1 metric ton peat = .325 metric ton of coal oil equivalent
1 ton oil equivalent = .4186 GJ or 11.63 MWh

B. Divers coefficients conventionnels ou dérivés

Transport aérien

1 voyageur (passager) – kilomètre = 0.621371 passenger-mile
1 tonne-kilomètre = 0.684945 short ton-mile
0.611558 long ton-mile

Energie électrique

1 British horsepower (hp) = 0.7457 kW
1 cheval vapeur (cv) = 0.735499 kW

C. Autres coefficients ou facteurs de conversion utilisés dans les tableaux de l'*Annuaire statistique*

Energie

1 tonne métrique d'équivalent charbon = 3.08 tonnes métrique de tourbe
1 GJ = 2.39 tonne d'équivalent pétrol or 1 MWh = .086 tonne métrique d'équivalent pétrol

Annex IV - Tables added, omitted and discontinued

A. Tables added

The present issue of the *Statistical Yearbook* includes the following tables which were not presented in the previous issue:

Table 3	Population growth and indicators of fertility and mortality
Table 25	Water supply and sanitation services

B. Tables omitted

The following tables which were presented in previous issues are not presented in the present issue. They will be updated in future issues of the *Yearbook* when new data become available:

Table 3	Population and rates of growth in urban areas and capital cities
Table 20	Agricultural production indices
Table 21	Index of industrial production
Table 25	CO_2 emissions estimates

C. Tables discontinued

* Mobile telephone subscriptions

Annexe IV - Tableaux ajoutés, supprimés et discontinués

A. Tableaux ajoutés

Dans ce numéro de l'Annuaire statistique, les tableaux suivants n'ont pas été présentés dans le numéro antérieur, et ont été ajoutés:

Tableau 3	Croissance démographique et indicateurs de fécondité et mortalité
Tableau 25	Services d'alimentation en eau potable et d'assainissement

B. Tableaux supprimés

Les tableaux suivants qui ont été repris dans les éditions antérieures n'ont pas été repris dans la présente édition. Ils seront actualisés dans les futures livraisons de l'Annuaire à mesure que des données nouvelles deviendront disponibles :

Tableau 3	Population et taux de croissance dans les zones urbaines et capitales
Tableau 20	Indices de la production agricole
Tableau 21	Indices de la production industrielle
Tableau 25	Estimation des émissions de CO2

C. Tableaux discontinués

Les tableaux suivants ont été discontinués

- Abonnements aux services de téléphone cellulaire mobile